Latin America

Latin

FOURTH EDITION

Maps by Eileen W. James

America

by **Preston E. James**

THE ODYSSEY PRESS
The Bobbs-Merrill Company, Inc.
Indianapolis · New York

The Odyssey Press
A Division of The Bobbs-Merrill Company, Inc.
Library of Congress Catalog Card Number: 69–10222
Printed in the United States of America
Second Printing

Since World War II there has been an unprecedented increase in the number of geographers of all nations who study and write about Latin America. To these newcomers in this field of regional specialization this book is respectfully dedicated.

Preface

This book presents a geographic interpretation of what is happening in contemporary Latin America. We are dealing with economic, social, and political changes in one of the world's major culture regions, at a time when these changes are going on with unprecedented rapidity. The Latin America that many North Americans knew and loved only a few decades ago is now fast disappearing. What is causing this disappearance of the traditional ways of living, and what is the nature and pattern of the changes? In a world shrinking because of the intimacy of modern electronic communications, it is no longer possible to remain ignorant of our neighbors' problems. If government and business policy is to be wisely formulated, we must clarify the picture of the emerging societies in the other part of the American Hemisphere.

The innovations currently sweeping through Latin America are related to two worldwide systems of fundamental change in ways of living—the industrial revolution and the democratic revolution. Both revolutions began during the latter half of the eighteenth century in the countries bordering the North Sea in Europe. For some two centuries they have been spreading from the source region. As the innovations begin to penetrate preexisting cultures in different parts of the earth, the first result is conflict and confusion, perhaps resistance and reaction. The world today can be divided into culture regions in each of which a particular set of conditions and problems has developed as a result of the impact of innovation on the previous traditional societies. As both revolutions spread they have been further developed, so that the changes they bring today are not exactly the same as those that appeared originally in Europe; but the present innovations that are sweeping into Latin America can be traced back both historically and geographically. Today, however, the major source region for innovation is Anglo-America.

The specific changes that are included as parts of these revolutions are described on pages 47–48. Essentially the industrial revolution substitutes mechanical power for muscle power, and changes the individual worker from a lifter and mover of things to a puller of levers, a pusher of buttons, and a repairer of complex machines. After the industrial revolution has swept over a preindustrial society and led to the development of a mature economy, the elite made up of owners of land is replaced by an elite made up of owners of capital. In communist societies the elite is made up of the small minority who are accepted as members of the Party. The enormous increase in the production of goods and services means that all people live better than before; but it also means that there is a vast increase in the quantity and variety of necessary raw materials derived from so-called natural resources. The industrial revolution is reflected in the unprecedented growth of cities; and the relative decline in the proportion of the working force employed in farming is accompanied by a relative increase in the proportion of workers in manufacturing industry and in the service occupations. The improved techniques of medicine and hygiene result in a large drop in the death rate, and this, all over the world, is the cause of the population explosion. The problem faced by developing countries is whether the growth of the economy, including the increase in the number of jobs, can keep ahead of the growth of population. As a result of all this, the old Babylonian concept of a nation that is strong and self-sufficient and that can improve its strength by invading and conquering its neighbors' resources, must now be given up as obsolete. This must be replaced by the concept that no nation can be both strong and self-sufficient; strength is derived from the acceptance of the principle of economic interdependence, including the formation of common markets. Imagine, if you will, how such changes, sweeping over a preindustrial society, must inevitably cause conflict and confusion.

The democratic revolution, which began at the same time and in the same geographical area as the industrial revolution, has nevertheless spread in a somewhat different pattern. Reaction against the ideals of democracy has been strong in some areas, especially where dictatorships of either the right or the left are established, and where a closed society is imposed by central authority. An open society, on the contrary, is one in which it is accepted that all individuals have equal rights before the law, that people can select their own form of government, that majority rule prevails, and that issues are to be resolved by discussion and persuasion rather than by force. This involves free access to knowledge and the freedom to choose one's religion, one's form of employment, or one's place of residence. The end result of the acceptance of the democratic revolution is the formation of an open society where these principles are accepted and respected. Imagine, again, the dislocations and resistances set up in the predemocratic society when an elite finds its position undermined.

How do innovations of such a fundamental nature spread from a source region into a receiving region? Innovations do not spread in simple circular patterns, like ripples on a pond. Rather they spread rapidly in some directions, slowly in others. Where contacts between the people of a source region and those of a receiving region are closest and most frequent, innovations make their greatest impact. Generally, the contacts between two regions vary directly with the size of the populations and their economic productivity, and inversely with the distance separating them as measured in traveling time—which is only Newton's law of gravity applied to human societies. Countries with maturely developed economies have closer contacts with other maturely developed economies than with less developed economies. The two major regions in the world which are in closest contact with each other are Western Europe and Anglo-America, and this relationship is reflected in the number and variety of transportation and communication facilities and the frequency with which they are used. Whether closeness of contact results in the rapid acceptance of innovation, or in reaction and resistance, depends on a number of factors, for example on whether or not there is a strongly entrenched elite whose privileged position is threatened, or whether or not there are persuasive leaders seeking to seize power for themselves, or on other conditions that can be identified and listed.

As a result, the spread of innovation from a source region into a receiving region forms a very irregular pattern of acceptance. There are pockets of acceptance far in advance of the frontier and pockets of resistance quite close to the source region. Whether innovation spreads rapidly or slowly in any particular place depends on its point of reference with regard to all these various factors. If all the necessary observations of relevant factors could be made so that the necessary data could be gathered and fed into computers, it is not at all impossible that precise predictions could be made regarding the patterns of continued spread, the patterns of resistance, and the areas of future conflict. It is in terms such as these that geographers seek to interpret the economic, social, and political changes now going on.

Geography is also traditionally concerned with "man–land" relations, that is, with the interconnections between human societies and the natural surroundings which form the resource base. "Land," as the word is used in this book, refers to such natural features as the shape of the surface (or terrain), the climate, the water, the soil, the minerals, the cover of wild vegetation, and the animal life. Many decades ago geographers accepted the concept of "environmental determinism," which suggests that human behavior is influenced, if not determined, by the land which people occupy. There was a time when a famous student of the principles of government could say that hot climates were for dictatorships, cold climates for barbarians, and that good government could be achieved only in the temperate zone. Although such extreme positions, which were commonly accepted in the eighteenth century, would today be treated with ridicule, it is still possible for a prominent economist to suggest that the development of a mature economy would be difficult, if not impossible, in the torrid zone. Geographers abandoned such ideas many decades ago.

The general principle which guides the analysis of man–land relations today is that the significance to man of the features of his natural surroundings is a function of man's own attitudes, objectives, and technical skills. Much depends on man's perception of his environment. Clearly man's technical skills make resources out of minerals or remove minerals from the list of resources. This is not to say that the significance of the land base can be neglected: on the contrary, with every change in the attitudes, objectives, or technical skills, the land base must be reappraised. This means that a land which might be well adapted for the use of a preindustrial society may be poorly adapted for a mature economy, or vice versa. We have seen many examples of how men with hoes and machetes can grow crops on steeply sloping land, but how the use of plows and tractors radically changes the pattern of potential crop land. Modern farm technology makes the natural quality of a soil less important than the location of a soil with reference to markets for farm products. The pattern of accessibility becomes critical, and it becomes more critical as the innovations of the industrial revolution are more fully accepted.

This focus of attention on the significance of location has two results in the nature of geographic study. First, it poses great difficulties in the way of geographic writing. The words, sentences, and paragraphs provide for a communication between the author and the reader which moves through the time dimension. This is ideal for writing history, for then the subject being communicated moves through the same dimension as the medium of communication. But geography deals with things that are located with reference to each other at the same moment of time. To describe one location, and then—later in terms of the time it takes to read—to describe a different but closely interrelated location, involves a distracting shift from the time dimension to the space dimension. For this reason, history is easier to read than geography.

On the other hand, there is a language which is ideally suited to the communication of ideas about relative location. This is the language of the map. To receive the full meaning carried by the maps requires some minimum of training and experience. It is important to think of the maps in this book not just as pictures and drawings embellishing the written text but as an important part of the process of communication. There are many pieces of information and many locational concepts that can be derived from the careful study of the maps, which are not expressed in the written words. The student who is aware of the importance of the maps will not fail to refer to them frequently to clarify and extend the ideas presented in words.

This is the fourth edition of a book that was first published in 1942. A comparison of the four editions will reveal some important changes in the conditions and problems with which people were concerned. In the years leading up to World War II, many North Americans were in favor of a retreat from participation in international undertakings. Many favored a policy of isolation within the American Hemisphere. Much of the first edition deals with the reasons why a self-sufficient economy within the American Hemisphere would be an impossible goal. The second edition, published in 1950, was at a time when the attention of most North Americans was directed elsewhere than toward Latin

America. There was a complacent tendency to take Latin America for granted. The third edition in 1959 appeared just as that illusion of hemisphere unity was rudely shattered by the communist take-over of Cuba. But the greatest change in subject matter and in the problems investigated has taken place between the third and fourth editions. Today no part of the world is undergoing such fundamental change based on the varied impact of innovation.

The author is very fortunate in having the collaboration of his wife, Eileen W. James, in the compilation, design, and drawing of the maps. For this fourth edition almost all the maps have been newly prepared. Because author and cartographer could work together on this project, the maps form an integral part of the book, and not just decoration. The usual remarks about the patience and forbearance of a wife for an author-husband are irrelevant; yet any one who has had the experience of producing maps for publication will appreciate the many hours of hard concentration that were required. There were also many months of delightful travel throughout Latin America, during which time we were not only able to make many contacts with Latin-American friends and colleagues and to gather much essential data, but also to observe the varying shapes of landforms directly.

We are both greatly indebted to John C. Bartholomew and Son of Edinburgh, Scotland, who made available to us their fine, detailed maps of Latin America for use in the compilation of rivers, coastlines, boundaries, and other information. Bartholomew's maps are published in the *Times Atlas*.

There are many other people who have contributed in one way or another to this fourth edition. Among the many Latin-Americans special appreciation is extended to Nilo Bernardes and Speridião Faissol of Brazil; Maria Bacigalupo of Argentina; Manuel Concha M. of Concepción in Chile; Edmundo Viña Laborde of Uruguay; Sucre Perez B. of Guayaquil in Ecuador; Flora Jordan of Barbados; and Rafael Picó of Puerto Rico. I am indebted to many of my former and present students who assisted from time to time in the compilation of data for the maps and in the collection of references. These include Kempton E. Webb, Clarence W. Minkel, Wolfram U. Drewes, Gene Martin, Robert Layton, Robert J. Tata, Rolf Sternberg, and Stuart C. Rothwell. Charles Anderson Gauld supplied an amazing amount of data of unusual value. For the compilation of data for the statistical tables the author appreciates the assistance of Morton D. Winsberg and Justin C. Friberg.

PRESTON E. JAMES

Contents

General Introduction

Mexico and Central America

The Antilles and the Guianas

Spanish South America

Portuguese South America

General Conclusion and Appendices

Maps

General Introduction

ORGANIZATION OF AMERICAN STATES

The OAS as it will be when the "Protocol of Buenos Aires" is in effect

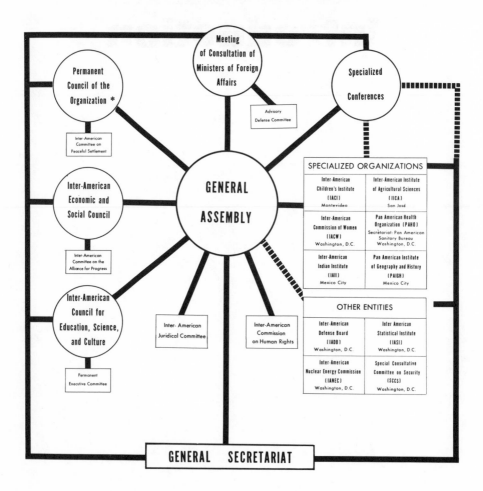

* Acts as the Preparatory Committee of the General Assembly, unless the General Assembly should decide otherwise

October 1967

Chapter 1 □ Principal

Characteristics

In no other major part of the earth are the conditions of life being so rapidly and fundamentally transformed as they are in Latin America.[1] Traditional Latin America is to be found today in only a few isolated spots. The graceful and sophisticated society of the aristocratic landowners is rapidly disappearing; disappearing also are the churchmen concerned only with men's souls, and the bemedaled army officers who back their positions of power with force. The tourists will be disappointed who expect to see that picturesque peasant dozing in the shade of a cactus with a large sombrero pulled down over his eyes. There are multitudes of formerly sick, hungry, illiterate, and hopelessly poor people who are now sensing that an improvement in the conditions of life is possible. Ignorance and apathy are no longer terms that describe the people of Latin America. Ignorance is being swept away by a flood of half-understood items of new knowledge, and apathy is being replaced by a rising chorus of vigorous protest.

Changes of so fundamental a nature cannot be neglected. In a world brought closer together than ever before by modern technology, a change in any one element of the system inevitably leads to changes in all the other elements. Yet many people in the United States who must deal with Latin-American problems are not informed about the nature of the transformations currently taking place to the south. And many people in Latin America conceive of the United States only in caricature. There is pressing need for more

[1] The name *Latin America* refers to the southern part of the American Hemisphere, but with no suggestion that its inhabitants are all of Latin origin. Similarly we refer to the northern part of the American Hemisphere as *Anglo-America*, recognizing that the population includes a great variety of people of other than British origin. Latin America, the part of America that lies south and southeast of the United States, is one of the world's major culture regions.

effective communication and more mutual understanding within the American Hemisphere.

Mutual understanding is difficult to achieve until the nature of the basic processes of change is made clear. Latin America is not an isolated island of conflict. The industrial revolution and the democratic revolution first appeared as major movements affecting the lives of vast numbers of people during the latter half of the eighteenth century around the shores of the North Sea in Europe—primarily in Great Britain, France, and the Netherlands. Both revolutions have been spreading from the area of origin, setting up conflicts and reactions wherever the new ways of living came into contact with preindustrial and predemocratic societies. Both revolutions have been further developed as they spread, especially in the culture region of Anglo-America. In Anglo-America the results of continued technological innovation have been an unprecedented increase in economic production until more than 40 percent of all the world's goods and services are produced in this one region.

The innovations associated with the industrial and democratic revolutions are sweeping over present-day Latin America. Millions of Latin-Americans are joining in a demand for better conditions of life and for an end to the social inequities of traditional Latin-American society. But these demands are not exactly like those with which we are familiar in Anglo-America. Equality in northern America refers to equality of opportunity and the right of each individual, regardless of economic status, to be treated as an equal. In Latin America the idea of equality means the equal right of every individual to be different and to be treated as a uniquely different person. When businessmen and government officials from the United States attempt to establish what they consider to be a sound process of economic development, they are baffled by the reaction they get even from educated Latin-Americans. North Americans discover that for many Latin-Americans the increase in the volume or efficiency of production is not the most important goal. Many Latin-Americans demand a change in the traditional system of inequity first.

Another problem is the lack of confidence the average Latin-American feels regarding people in power over him. This refers not only to army officers and other politically powerful people, but also to the owners of capital and the managers of businesses. In Latin America those who have gained positions of power have all too frequently misused that power for personal advantage. Dishonesty and corruption are often accepted as normal, and the exploitation of people with less power by those with more power is expected. The system in which those with power exploit those with less power has a name in Latin America—it is called capitalism. When people from the United States talk about capitalism and free enterprise, their Latin American audiences think of unregulated exploitation of those who do not own capital.

Both the people and the natural resources of Latin America have long been exploited. That this is not a new land is a fact that many North Americans find difficulty in understanding. Some of the lands that lie to the south of the United States had been exploited and abandoned by the Indians before the arrival of Columbus. In the centuries that followed Columbus the so-called "New World" was ransacked by Spaniards, Portuguese, British, French, Dutch, and other peoples of European origin. There are many parts of Latin America for which up-to-date information is lacking, for which there are not even reliable maps; but there are few parts which have not been explored and exploited first by one group and then by another. Actually Latin America is not a virgin land, awaiting the arrival of the pioneer—it is an old land, much trampled, many of its sources of accumulated treasure exploited and abandoned, many of its landscapes profoundly altered by the hand of man. Yet it is a land in which large areas remain comparatively empty of human inhabitants.

International events have made it imperative that we, in Anglo-America, become acquainted with the conditions and problems faced by these other Americans. We must understand why Latin America is in turmoil. We must gain an appreciation of the problems of economic development in very poor countries. We must have some idea what resources are available to support economic growth, and what capital requirements there are if these resources are to be put to use. We must understand why North Americans are not everywhere popular. The common tendency to regard the changes in Latin America as a result of the communist conspiracy is a dangerous oversimplification. We must know why Castro had such a following in Latin America until he proclaimed himself a Marxist-Leninist. We must know which of the Latin-American states are unified and coherent and clearly viable; and which ones are composed of uncoordinated elements. We must appreciate the states which have achieved a high degree of democracy, and know the names and locations of those which are still under autocratic rule. These are the questions we wish to ask about the people who occupy the American Hemisphere with us, and who have entered into cooperative agreements with us within the frameworks of the United Nations and of the Organization of American States.

Principal Characteristics

People and land are the basic elements of the story. A human society is not understandable unless it is considered in relation to the land it occupies; nor is the significance of the land with respect to human settlement determined without reference to the varying kinds of human societies. In Latin America four principal characteristics may serve to summarize the conditions of the people and the land. These are: (1) a relatively small population that is rapidly increasing; (2) a clustered pattern of settlement; (3) a Latin-American population that is composed of a great diversity of racial and cultural elements; and (4) a great variation from place to place in the character of the land.

A Relatively Small Population, Rapidly Increasing

The population of Latin America is still small in relation to the total land area. The eight million square miles of land in that part of the American Hemisphere that lies south and southeast of the United States represent about 15 percent of the total area of the world's inhabited continents: but the 207 million people in Latin America in 1960 made up only about 7 percent of the world's population.

The rate of population increase, however, is the highest of any major world region. Between 1920 and 1960 the population of Latin America as a whole increased more than 126 percent. During the same period the population of all the economically underdeveloped countries of the world—including those of eastern and southern Asia—increased only about 70 percent. The population of Anglo-America increased about 68 percent. In 1956 the population of Latin America and Anglo-America were about equal, with a little more than 185 million in each. It is estimated that by the year 2000, when the poulation of Anglo-America will be about 350 million, the population of Latin America will reach about 624 million.

A Clustered Pattern of Settlement

The people of Latin America are characteristically grouped together in clusters, that is in areas where settlement is concentrated. Pioneer movements out from the clusters into thinly settled territory has become common only in recent years. Even in the late 1960's the clusters of population remained for the most part distinct from each other, being separated by scantily occupied, or entirely unoccupied, territory.[2]

A population cluster is the most elementary arrangement of people on the land. Human beings generally prefer to live together in groups rather than to scatter at such intervals that contact with one another is difficult. The normal pattern of Occidental settlement in a pioneer land is one of scattered clusters, commonly strung together along a line of travel. A pattern of isolated clusters of people separated by thinly settled or unoccupied territory persisted in eastern North America until 1700. A population map of Europe in the early period of northward penetration from the Mediterranean would show a similar pattern. In the course of time the original areas of settlement of Europe

---

[2]Maps of population and other items of geographic importance are included in the chapters dealing with specific countries. They can be found most readily by consulting the index.

and of eastern North America were enlarged until they grew together, little by little filling in the scantily occupied territory which once separated them; but in Latin America this process of settlement expansion has only recently appeared except in a few places. As a result the clustered pattern of settlement persists.

Even the areas of concentrated rural settlement in Latin America have a relatively low density of population. Some of the islands of the Antilles, to be sure, rank among the more crowded portions of the earth. Barbados, with more than a thousand people per square mile, and Puerto Rico, with nearly seven hundred, approach the densities more commonly associated with such places as Java and India. Outside of the Antilles, however, only a few of the regions of concentrated settlement of Latin America have rural densities of more than 125 people per square mile. These few places are: the central area of Mexico, the highlands of Guatemala and El Salvador; the intermont basins of Costa Rica; the Antioquia region of Colombia; some of the high basins of the Peruvian Andes, and a part of the borders of Lake Titicaca; the Cochabamba Basin of Bolivia; parts of middle Chile; the oasis of Tucumán in Argentina; and parts of the northeast coast of Brazil. But most of the population clusters of Latin America have a rural density of less than 100 per square mile—and in many cases the density is less than 25.

In the midst of each of the population clusters, even the smallest, there is an urban core or nucleus, and because the areas of concentrated settlement still remain distinct from one another, there is little overlap between the territory served by one city and that served by a neighboring one. In Europe and North America, where the originally distinct areas of settlement have lost their obvious identity through expansion and the establishment of contact around the margins with other areas of settlement, the problem of separating the territory that is related to one center from the territory of another is very difficult. Commonly there is a wide zone of overlap between neighboring cities in retail trade, newspaper subscriptions, professional services, and the variety of other activities which are performed in an urban center for the people of the surrounding territory. But in Latin America this sort of overlap is rare: the economic, social, and political life of a region commonly focuses on only one large central city, and as a reflection of this the local lines of transportation and communication also converge on this one center.

Some of the cities appear to be surprisingly large when viewed in relation to the low density of the rural population in the surrounding area. Although there are many towns with a population of less than ten thousand, there are some which must be included among the world's great metropolises. In 1967 there were 11 cities in Latin America with a million or more inhabitants: Buenos Aires, Rio de Janeiro, São Paulo, Mexico City, Santiago, Bogotá, Caracas, Habana, Lima, Montevideo, and Guadalajara (Maps 1 and 2). There were about 120 cities with populations of between 100,000 and 1 million, of which 35 were in Middle America and 85 in South America. The number of cities of over 100,000 doubled during the decade between 1958 and 1968. There can be no doubt of the increasing importance of cities in Latin-American life.

There are two opposite tendencies that can be observed in and around the areas of concentrated settlement. There is a strong tendency for rural people to migrate to the cities. It is this city-ward movement throughout Latin America that is causing all the cities to grow so rapidly, out of all proportion to the urban functions that might be performed in them. Even with only partial employment, life in an urban slum is preferable to the miserable existence of a tenant farmer. Yet the opposite tendency can also be observed. There have been outward movements of pioneer settlement for many decades in certain places: in the highlands of Costa Rica; in the Antioquia region of Colombia; in the southern part of the Central Valley of Chile; and in the three southern states of Brazil. But since only about 1960, streams of pioneer settlements have moved into previously unoccupied land where new all-weather roads and motor trucks have made the land accessible to markets. However, such pioneer movements have not yet balanced the flow of people to the cities.

The clustered pattern of population bears a simple relationship to the political units. In certain countries this characteristic is remarkably well developed: only one central cluster of people marks the core of such political units as Chile, Uruguay, Paraguay, and El Salvador. In most of the countries the population clusters form the cores of the major subdivisions—states, departments, or provinces. It is less common to find two clusters in one state, or one cluster divided between two states. Notable exceptions can be observed in the central area of Mexico, in Colombia, and in the highlands of Peru.

One result of this simple relation of the population pattern to the political areas is that the political boundaries generally pass through the scantily occupied territory between the clusters. There are few parts of Latin America where the boundaries cut through the midst of areas of concentrated settlement, and national boundaries do this even more rarely than state boundaries. The fact that areas of relatively dense population are cut by national boundaries in three places in Latin America is another exceptional condition which merits special attention. These places are on the borders between Venezuela and Colombia, Colombia and Ecuador, and Peru and Bolivia.

A second result of the clustered pattern of population is the necessity for recognizing two kinds of political area. There is the *total national territory* over which a politically organized group claims jurisdiction—the whole area within the national boundaries. But only that part of the total territory which actually contributes to the economic support of the citizens of the country can be called the *effective national territory* (sometimes called the *ekumene).*

Finally, a third result of the clustered pattern of population is the nature of the transportation problems which Latin-Americans have to face. Throughout most of South and Middle America the overland routes of travel lead from the interior to the nearest or most accessible ports; the land routes which connect one region of concentrated settlement with another, even within the same country, are developed only poorly. Transportation lines across the sparsely inhabited spaces between the clusters of population can, of course, be built and maintained at government expense as a military precaution or a diplomatic gesture; but only where traffic originates in sufficient quantity along the line can it be supported on an economic basis. To be sure, automobiles and motor trucks are making these overland connections easier than before, since roads are less costly to build than railroads. But such a long inland route as the Inter-American Highway is all the more spectacular as a project and as a subject for diplomatic eloquence because such connections between the separate areas of concentrated settlements are still very rare.

The fact remains that the chief highways of approach to Latin America and the chief lines of connection between the isolated centers of population are the oceans. Even if airplanes are now changing the nature of the transportation problem for passengers and mail, the movement of commodities is still largely dependent on ships.

Whether the approach to Latin America from other parts of the world is by ship or by air, the relative remoteness of the continent must be observed. South America is literally one of the ends of the habitable earth. Its closest neighbor is the commercially unresponsive shore of Africa. Furthermore, South America is equally remote from those centers of commercial activity in the modern world which are located on either side of the North Atlantic in eastern North America and Western Europe. The fact that South America is connected by land with North America does not in reality bring it any closer to this northern part of the American Hemisphere than to Western Europe. The Isthmus of Panama, important as it may have been in providing a land bridge for the migration of the Indians, is of no importance today as a line of overland communications—in fact, it forms only a barrier to the sea routes. And South America lies almost wholly east of the easternmost part of the United States, so that the ports of such east-coast countries as Brazil, Argentina, and Uruguay are closer to Rotterdam than they are to New York.

Diverse Racial and Cultural Elements

The third of the principal characteristics of Latin America is that the population is made up of a great diversity of racial and cultural elements. In 1967 the total population of 258,642,000 was divided among 24 independent states, and numerous units with ties outside the region. There were 159 million in 18 countries descended from Spain. There were 86 million in Portuguese-speaking Brazil, 5 million in French-speaking Haiti, and 4 million in four English-speaking members of the Commonwealth. There were also 2,700,000 in the self-governing Commonwealth of Puerto Rico, associated with the United States. There were 678,000 in possessions of Great Britain, including

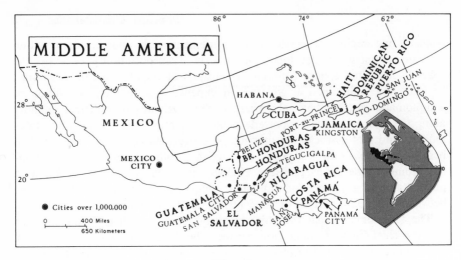

Map 1

the West Indies Associated States, 670,000 in French possessions, 544,000 in possessions of the Netherlands, and 50,000 in territories of the United States.

The diversity of race and culture in Latin America is the result of centuries of mixture. Today more than half the population is of mixed ancestry. Furthermore the ingredients are highly diverse. There are, to be sure, the three main elements—American Indians, Africans, and Europeans; but each of these elements includes a wide variety of racial mixtures.[3] The mestizo is the most common racial type, if he can be called a type, to be found in present-day Latin America. Let us consider the elements that have entered into this hybrid.

THE INDIANS

Long before the arrival of the Spanish and the Portuguese explorers, the Americas had been occupied by people from Asia. These native Americans had come into the American Hemisphere by way of the Bering Strait. Although some tribes wandered off toward the east, the main current of repeated migration led southward, some groups even pushing across Central America into South America. There is little probability that any important numbers came by boat across the Pacific Ocean, and even less probability that any came from Africa across the Atlantic.

In spite of certain general similarities among all these native peoples of America, there were wide differences both in physical character and in culture. To be sure, all the American Indians had certain common physical characteristics, such as a reddish brown or yellowish brown skin and straight black

---

[3]In Spanish America, the mixture of Indian and European is called a *mestizo;* the mixture of African and European is called a *mulatto;* and the mixture of African and Indian is called a *zambo.*

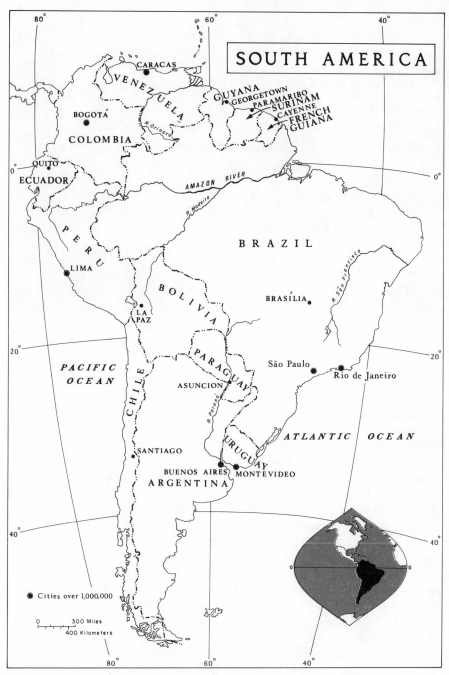

Map 2

A Mexican rural community in the mountains of Chiapas. Because of steep slopes and lack of roads, communities are very isolated. *Photo by Cia. Mexicana Aerofoto, S.A.*

hair. None of the American native cultures included knowledge of the Asian domestic animals other than the dog, and none of them included the use of the wheel. Beyond these general similarities, however, the cultures ranged widely from very primitive to highly advanced. The tribes of the southern tip of South America, in Tierra del Fuego, remain today among the most primitive people on earth. They presumably had started their migration very early and were pushed on by their more advanced successors until they had reached what is literally one of the ends of the earth. In contrast, certain of the native peoples of America were able to take a step which only a few groups in the whole history of mankind have been able to take—they had lifted themselves "from barbarism to civilization." These more elaborate cultures were developed by the *Mayas* of Guatemala and Yucatán, the *Aztecs* and certain other groups in central and northwestern Mexico, the *Chibchas* of highland Colombia, and the *Incas* of the highlands of Peru, Ecuador, Bolivia, and northern Chile. The territories occupied by these four outstanding Indian cultures are shown on Map 5, p. 14.

The cultural advance these four Indian groups were able to make was reflected in a great increase in the numbers of people who could gain a living from the land; something like three-quarters of all the native peoples in America at the time of the European conquest were located in the territories of these four advanced cultures. The obvious explanation is that a sedentary agricultural economy supports many more persons per square mile than does an economy based on shifting cultivation or on migratory hunting and fishing. Each of these cultures was based on that distinctively American food grain, maize.[4] In addition, the natives of America also made use of manioc,[5] beans, potatoes, squash, tomatoes, tobacco, and cacao. These other crops, however, were not so universally known throughout America as maize.

Both the Maya and the Inca states had reached and passed the zeniths of their development before the arrival of the Europeans. The Mayan civilization, which was the oldest of the three, was already decadent in 1492. The empires of the Aztecs and of the Incas had been formed by the conquest and assimilation of formerly separate and distinct Indian groups—a process similar to that which marked the growth of such European "nation states" as Britain, France, and Germany. The nucleus of the Aztec state was in the Basin of Mexico, and from there political control had been extended over a wide area. The Aztecs belong to the linguistic family known as *Nahua,* but their empire did not include all the Nahua-speaking tribes of Mexico. The Incas had extended their conquest from an original nucleus in the Basin of Cuzco, and had brought together in one great state the various tribes included in the two linguistic families, the *Quechuas* and the *Aymaras.* But at the time of the Spanish conquest the Inca state was already torn by civil strife.

The parts of America outside the territories of these relatively advanced Indian cultures were only very thinly occupied. The greater part of the area of the Americas was occupied by a large number of separate Indian groups, only vaguely related in certain broad linguistic families. A few of the more important Indian cultures are shown on Map 5. The tribes of tropical America ranged from semi-nomadic hunters, fishers, and primitive farmers, such as the Caribs and Arawaks of northern South America and the Antilles, to shifting cultivators whose basic food crop was manioc, such as the Tupi and the Guarani of Brazil and Paraguay. In southern South America, in addition to the very primitive peoples of southern Chile, there were semi-nomadic hunters and fishers who practiced some incidental farming, such as the Araucanians of Chile, and there were warlike nomadic hunters, such as the Abipones and the Puelche of the Argentine plains, whose chief food supply

[4]*Maize* is the word which refers specifically to the grain which we, in the United States, commonly call Indian corn, or simply corn. According to general English usage, however, *corn* refers to any common grain. In England *corn* refers to wheat, in Scotland to oats. In this book, therefore, we shall use the Indian word *maize* to designate Indian corn. It is now well established that maize was first domesticated in Mexico, a little south of Mexico City.

[5]Manioc is also known as manihot, mandioca, cassava, and yuca. The latter is not to be confused with yucca, a genus of the family *Liliaceae.* Manioc is a plant with an edible root which furnishes a starchy food now widely used throughout the tropics, but formerly known only in the Americas. It is now produced commercially as the source of *tapioca.*

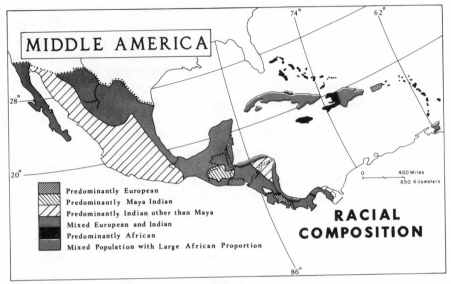

Map 3

was derived from the wild guanaco. All these varied tribes together, however, made up only about a quarter of the inhabitants of the American Hemisphere at the time of Columbus.

THE EUROPEANS

Diversity of race and culture in present-day Latin America is to be attributed not only to the native inhabitants but also to the European conquerors. There are many important contrasts to be noted between Spaniards and Portuguese; and both these groups, before they left the Old World, had already developed an extraordinary diversity of racial and cultural elements.

The Iberian Peninsula, the homeland of the Spaniards and the Portuguese, affords an easy passageway between Europe and Africa, and this was crossed repeatedly during the course of history by peoples of greatly contrasted origins. In the centuries between the struggle of Rome and Carthage and the discovery of America, the Celtic inhabitants of Iberia were mixed with other peoples from Europe and North Africa. These included the Carthaginians and the Romans, followed, after the fall of the Roman Empire, by various waves of "barbarians" from northern Europe, the last of which were the Goths. Then came the Moorish invasion from Africa which swept even across the Pyrenees into what is now southern France. Except for certain Christian Gothic states in the northwestern part of the Iberian Peninsula where the kingdoms of León and Castile were set up, and except for the border "march"

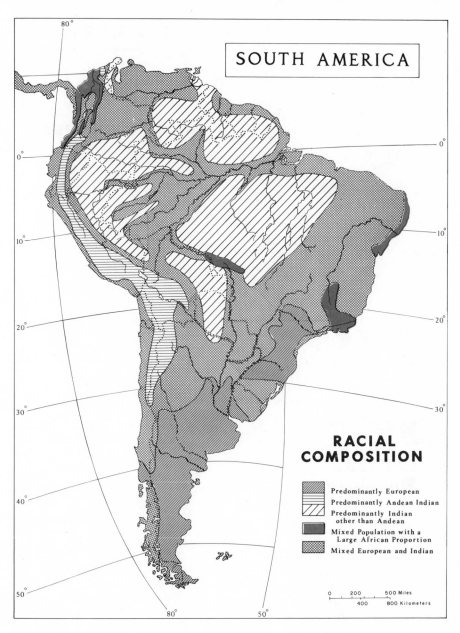

SOUTH AMERICA

RACIAL
COMPOSITION

Predominantly European
Predominantly Andean Indian
Predominantly Indian
other than Andean
Mixed Population with a
Large African Proportion
Mixed European and Indian

0   200   500 Miles

400   800 Kilometers

Map 4

Map 5

maintained by the Franks in what is now Catalonia in the northeast, the Iberian Peninsula came under Moorish rule. Little by little, however, the Christians succeeded in pushing back the Moors, and in establishing estates ruled by feudal lords and protected by *caballeros,* fighting men equipped with arms and horses. The Moors, forced to retreat step by step toward the south, were finally defeated in 1492, and their long period of rule was ended; but for eight hundred years before the discovery of America the political and economic life of Andalucía in southern Spain had been dominated by these people of Muslim faith.

Because a majority of the people who migrated to the New World during the first century of the conquest came from southern Spain and southern Portugal, the traits inherited from the Moors are of particular importance in a study of Latin America. One of the first effects of Moorish rule in Iberia was a change in agricultural practices: irrigation systems were built; fertilizer was applied to worn-out soils; and many agricultural techniques from Oriental lands were adopted. New crops were introduced, such as rice, sugarcane, and cotton. Skilled technicians from Damascus made Córdoba famous for its fine steel. From the East, also, the Moors brought the manufacture of paper to Europe. Moorish and Semitic scholars made the University of Córdoba a cultural center which was perhaps unequalled in the whole world in that period, and in the libraries of this and other cities they stored the books which preserved Greek philosophy and science for the Western World. To Iberia came also Jews fleeing from persecution in Christian Europe, and Syrians, Egyptians, and many others, including African slaves from across the Sahara. All these varied racial and cultural ingredients were mixed and fused to form a new kind of people.

One can scarcely understand the Spanish or Portuguese conquest of the New World without a consideration of the centuries of conflict between Christians and Muslims which immediately preceded the discovery of America. Spanish society was grouped in small, semi-independent units, each unit under the control of a lord. In each group society was sharply divided: on the one hand were the aristocratic landowners and the *caballeros* who supported them; on the other hand were the serfs, bound to the land, dependent on the lords and the fighting men for protection. The ownership of an estate, or service in the army or in the church were the only real roads to prestige. Commerce and industry were left to the Jews and Muslims, and in the cities whole districts were set apart for these people. But Christian intolerance of the infidel was mounting, even when the infidels were providing the chief economic support for the whole system, and in 1391 the active persecution of the non-Christian elements began in earnest. Many Jews and Moors chose to become *cristianos nuevos,* or "New Christians"; many more were massacred. Among the Christian knights there developed a fanatical zeal for the spread of the Faith; but in the process the financial stability of the country was upset.

EUROPEAN CONQUEST OF AMERICA

Two important events took place in 1492. The Moors were finally defeated in battle and forced to give up Granada to the Christians; and Columbus discovered America. It has been said that "Greed, Gold, and God" were the motivating forces which led the Spaniards into the New World. There can be no doubt that many of the conquerors were excessively greedy, especially those who, like Pizarro, conqueror of Peru, were not landowners at home, and who sought in America to achieve a coveted position in the aristocracy. There can be no doubt that there was need of gold, even among the people of highest social position, to repair the wrecked finances of Andalucía. There can be no doubt that many of the Spaniards who had been raised during the century of bitter conflict with the infidels came to the New World with a sincere, if fanatical, desire either to kill infidels or to convert them to the service of God. And there can be no doubt that both the Spaniards and the Portuguese, in common with most of the other European peoples, showed a marked reluctance to engage in that persistent hard labor which is required for the creation of a permanent society on an agricultural base.

For a people with these characteristics and attitudes, the relatively dense populations of sedentary Indians in the areas dominated by the Aztecs, the Mayas, the Chibchas, and the Incas exerted a special attraction. These peoples had already accumulated stores of what the Spaniards thought of as treasure. The Indians of these advanced states, moreover, were ready, after a brief struggle, to accept conversion to Christianity and to go to work for their new masters. To be sure, the Indians had no concept of private ownership of land, no concept of the commercial value of gold and silver, and these new ideas must have seemed as fantastic to them as men on horseback. But the great majority of the Indians had long been accustomed to work for their rulers, and the conquest was at first no more than a change of rulers.

The distribution of Indians, therefore, was the most important single factor which determined the centers and lines of the Spanish conquest. The newcomers, after landing on the shores of the Gulf of Mexico and the Caribbean, pushed their exploring parties far to the north and to the south. Within the first century most of the great sources of precious metals had been discovered and partly exploited. From the southern part of South America as far north as the present border between the United States and Canada, the Spaniards combed the new land for sources of wealth, motivated always by the hope of finding El Dorado. These Spaniards were not a soft people inclined to seek the easy way. It is quite beside the fact to insist that they sought to avoid the heat of the tropical lowlands, and that they ascended to the highlands to escape the discomforts of the lower altitudes. They were not stopped by heat, by cold, by steep slopes, by jungle swamps, or by warlike opponents. They were, however, attracted by the areas already well populated with infidels, where their form of society might be established with a laboring class already at hand. The distribution of Indians provides the clue to an understanding of the direction of the Spanish conquest (Map 6, p. 18).

Meanwhile, the Portuguese were settling Brazil. As a result of the Treaty of Tordesillas between Portugal and Spain (1494), the Portuguese had the right to all lands which might be discovered east of a line drawn north and south 370 leagues west of the Cape Verde Islands—approximately the present 50° W. longitude. The Portuguese began slowly to colonize the eastern coast of South America. By the time of the discovery of America the Portuguese in Europe had achieved a much greater degree of national unity and coherence than had the Spaniards; their interest in the New World was less in the possible spread of Christianity and less in the opportunity it offered to implant their institutions than in the discovery of new and profitable sources of wealth with which to bolster the fortunes of the homeland. In eastern South America they did not at first discover any gold or silver, and they found an Indian population which was much too small to supply the necessary labor for the production of crops. Yet the Portuguese on the coast of northeastern Brazil set up the first large plantation economy of the American Hemisphere, using slaves imported from Africa.

The idea of using African slaves to raise sugarcane was first developed by the Portuguese on the Island of Madeira off the coast of North Africa. The Portuguese expanded this new kind of economic system to other island possessions, including the Cape Verde Islands and São Tomé. The Spaniards started their own sugarcane plantations with African slaves on the Canary Islands. As early as 1505 some Africans were brought to Hispaniola to dig gold in the stream gravels; but the first establishment of a sugarcane plantation in the New World was in 1515 near the town of Santo Domingo. The first large-scale plantation economy was built by the Portuguese in Brazil after 1538, when the first slave market was set up in Salvador.

Thereafter sugar became so profitable that it attracted numerous competitors. The Spaniards imported African slaves and planted sugarcane not only in Hispaniola and Puerto Rico, but also in other areas on the mainland. During the seventeenth century the Dutch attacked and occupied the prosperous sugar colonies of Brazil's northeast coast. They remained there for some thirty years before they were finally ejected by the Portuguese. During this time they learned how to grow the cane, extract the juice, and prepare and ship the sugar to the European market. Pushed out of Brazil, they established colonies in the Antilles, where the sugarcane technology was quickly passed on to the Spaniards, the French, and the British. The British seized Jamaica from the Spaniards, and the French established themselves on the western side of the island of Hispaniola. Soon British, French, Dutch, and Danish colonies appeared in the Lesser Antilles and elsewhere—wherever Spanish

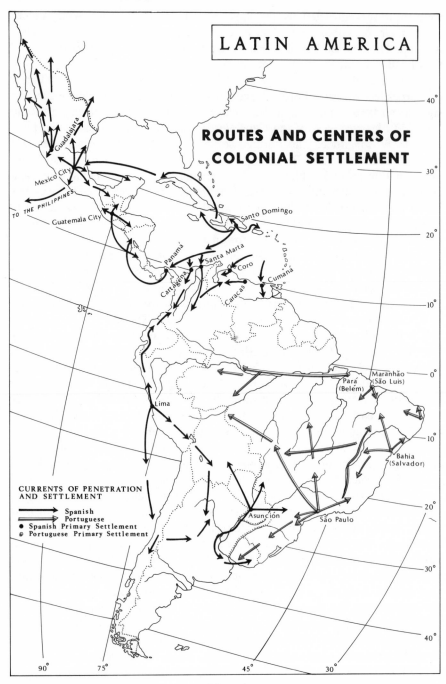

LATIN AMERICA

ROUTES AND CENTERS OF
COLONIAL SETTLEMENT

40°

30°

Guadalajara

Mexico City

TO THE PHILIPPINES

Guatemala City

Santo Domingo

20°

Panamá

Santa Marta

Coro

Cumaná

Cartagena

Caracas

10°

Maranhão
(São Luis)

Pará
(Belém)

0°

Lima

10°

Bahia
(Salvador)

CURRENTS OF PENETRATION
AND SETTLEMENT

→ Spanish
⇒ Portuguese
● Spanish Primary Settlement
◎ Portuguese Primary Settlement

20°

Asunción

São Paulo

30°

40°

90°   75°   45°   30°

Map 6

or Portuguese settlement had not been effective. At this same time the French and British began to colonize the forested eastern part of North America.

RECENT IMMIGRATION

Still more recently, another element contributing to racial and cultural diversity has been added to the population of Latin America. During the nineteenth century and the present century new immigrants from a number of European countries and from Japan have come to the New World. Although an overwhelming majority of these immigrants have entered the United States, a considerable number have gone to certain parts of Latin America, and these parts are, therefore, quite different from the rest of the continent in their racial make-up (Maps 3 and 4). In most instances this new colonization has been directed to regions which previously were of little value and were little developed. From São Paulo in Brazil, southward across the southern states, across Uruguay, and over the Humid Pampa of Argentina to the dry lands of Patagonia, there was a stretch of territory which was almost entirely devoid of signs of gold, and which was thinly populated by native peoples. Most of it would not grow sugarcane. Except for its strategic importance to the rival colonial empires of Spain and Portugal, this section of South America was of little use to the earlier conquerors. Because Spain had established a center of settlement in Paraguay, and had utilized the Plata River as a sort of "back door" to Peru, and because Portuguese colonists had threatened to establish themselves permanently on the shores of the Plata, the Spaniards paid some attention to this strategic route. But the land bordering the Plata was only a remote part of the colonial empire of Spain and was used only for the grazing of cattle and mules.

This stretch of territory, therefore, was still little developed when the new European immigration began. The considerable population of the region today is composed mostly of the descendants of people who have come to South America during the last hundred years—Italians, Spaniards, Portuguese, Germans, Poles, and lesser numbers of many other nationalities, including Japanese.

In Latin America the racial composition of the population differs notably from one region to another. Six chief areas can be identified in terms of present-day racial character (Maps 3 and 4, pp. 12 and 13): (1) areas of predominantly European population, mostly of recent origin; (2) areas of predominantly Indian population belonging to the Quechuan and Aymaran linguistic groups (Andean Indians); (3) areas of predominantly Maya Indians; (4) areas of predominantly Indian population descended from other than the Quechuan and Aymaran groups or the Mayas; (5) areas with a mixed population with a large proportion of Africans; and (6) areas with a population in which the mestizo type is predominant.

Diversity of the Land

The fourth of the principal characteristics of Latin America is the physical diversity of the land[6] itself. The natural features of South and Middle America cannot be described without the use of superlatives. The Andes of western South America, which extend almost unbroken by low passes from the Caribbean to the Strait of Magellan, form the world's longest continuous mountain barrier. The Amazon, the third longest river of the world, is the one which is navigable for ocean-going vessels the farthest upstream. In the basin of the Amazon is the world's largest area of tropical forest. In Brazil, a little north of Rio de Janeiro, is one of the world's largest and richest supplies of iron ore; in northern Chile is the world's only natural source of nitrate. Returning again to Rio de Janeiro, we find this city located on the shores of what is commonly acclaimed as one of the world's finest natural harbors. The Humid Pampa of Argentina is probably the world's best endowed area in terms of climate, water, soil, and surface for the growing of grains and alfalfa, and the feeding of high-grade domestic animals. But when all these and many other superlative features and natural advantages are considered in the light of the needs of an Occidental commercial people, many of them seem to be poorly located, or to be combined poorly with other resources. The mountain barrier stifles the commerce which might develop between the two coasts. The great river sprawls across a continent through a vast forest filled with potential commodities of commerce, but neither the river nor the forest can be effectively utilized as long as the whole area remains so sparsely populated. The enormous body of rich iron ore is located in a continent notably lacking in coal. The nitrate deposits of Chile are separated from the seacoast by the steep slopes of an escarpment, and from the world's chief markets for nitrate by great distances of ocean. The magnificent harbor of Rio de Janeiro is hemmed in by the forbidding slopes of a highland which renders access to the interior difficult and costly. The ports which serve the productive Humid Pampa have been developed in spite of a complete lack of natural harbors; and the great city of Buenos Aires, which has arisen in response to the productivity of its hinterland, is one of the most poorly endowed metropolises in the world in terms of fuel and power resources.

It is a fact of very great significance in the modern period that whereas North America possesses more than half of all the world's coal resources, South America has such meager supplies of this fuel that it can turn out only about one percent of the world's production.

---

[6]The word "land" is used throughout this book to refer to the natural surroundings of human settlement—the habitat. The natural surroundings include the surface features, the climates, the water, the wild vegetation, the soils and minerals. These features make up the resource base which forms the background of settlement.

Superlatives, yes—but superlatives that are poorly combined in terms of the needs of modern industrial society.

SURFACE FEATURES

Middle America, which includes Mexico, Central America, and the Antilles, forms a distinct break between North and South America. The geologic structures and surface forms of North America continue southward into Mexico to a little south of latitude 20° N., where they are abruptly terminated by a northwest–southeast chain of towering volcanoes. Southern Mexico, Guatemala, and Honduras belong to a structural region which extends under the Caribbean eastward to Jamaica, southeastern Cuba, Hispaniola, Puerto Rico, and the Virgin Islands—a region of folded and faulted rocks with a generally east–west trend. This "Central-American–Antillean" region is connected to South America by two chains of volcanic ridges and peaks: the Lesser Antilles and the highlands of Salvador, southwestern Nicaragua, Costa Rica, Panamá, and western Colombia.

Three chief surface divisions form the major lineaments of the strangely assorted continent of South America. These are similar to the divisions which, in happier relation to the climatic pattern and to the distribution of people, mark the surface of the continent of North America (Maps 7 and 8, pp. 22 and 23). On the west are the relatively young Andes; on the east are the Brazilian and Guiana highlands, geologically much older than the Andes, now partly covered by stratified rocks and lava flows, and in places surmounted by the massive stumps of ancient, worn-down mountains; and in the central portion of the continent lie the plains of the Orinoco, the Amazon, and the Paraguay-Paraná-Plata, filled with debris from the erosion of the highlands on either side.

For more than 4,000 miles, from the shores of the Caribbean to the end of Tierra del Fuego, the Andes stand as a barrier between eastern and western South America. Compared with the western mountains of North America, the Andes are narrower but considerably higher. Passes across the North American mountains can be found requiring a climb of only 6,000 or 7,000 feet; but most of the passes over the Andes, especially those which are located where there is need for a pass, are more than 10,000 feet above sea level. The Andes are scarcely 200 miles wide, except in Bolivia where the width is doubled. The peaks reach altitudes from 18,000 to nearly 23,000 feet. Mt. Aconcagua (22,835 ft.) is the highest mountain in the Western Hemisphere.

Geologic structures in the Andes, as in Middle America, are complex. To describe these mountains as a continuous chain is quite incorrect. Actually they are made up of several structural units more or less closely joined. In general, the mountains are formed by folded and faulted structures, but in three distinct areas there are groups of active volcanoes. These areas are in

Map 7

southern Colombia and Ecuador; in middle and southern Peru and along the border of Bolivia and Chile; and in the southern part of middle Chile.

Since the Andes cross varied climatic zones, the processes of erosion and denudation which have sculptured the surface differ widely from place to place. The southern part of the Andes was heavily glaciated during the Ice Age, and even today the border between Argentina and Chile, just north of the Strait of Magellan, crosses an extensive mantle of permanent ice. Glaciers in this region still descend into the ocean at the heads of some of the fiords, or into the lakes on the eastern side of the range. North of latitude 39° S. the glaciers never emerged from the mountains and are now confined to higher and higher altitudes as one proceeds northward. Even on the equator, however, glaciation was once active, and small remnant glaciers still exist at the higher altitudes. In Bolivia and the northern parts of Chile and Argentina a dry belt crosses the cordilleras diagonally, and here the landforms typical of mountain deserts occur. From eastern Bolivia northward the rainfall increases in the mountain zone, and stream dissection becomes more and more active. Intermont basins at various altitudes are numerous in two chief sections: in Venezuela, Colombia, and Ecuador; and in Bolivia, northern Chile, and Argentina. They are most common in areas of active volcanoes, or in the dry areas.

The pattern of surface features in South America east of the Andes, although bearing a broad similarity to the pattern of eastern North America, is quite different in its details. The greater part is made up of highlands, which extend with few interruptions from southern Colombia and Venezuela

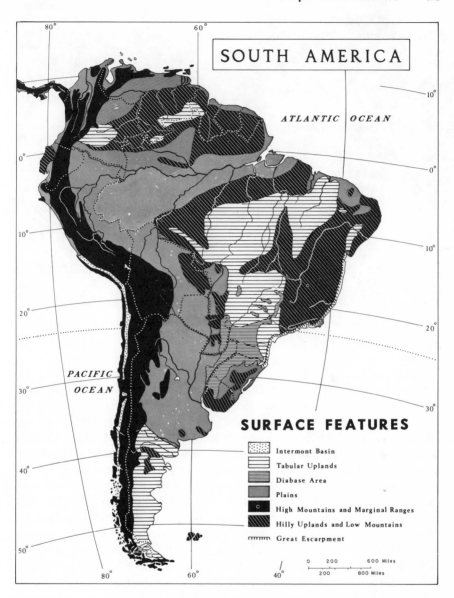

SOUTH AMERICA

ATLANTIC OCEAN

PACIFIC OCEAN

SURFACE FEATURES

Intermont Basin
Tabular Uplands
Diabase Area
Plains
High Mountains and Marginal Ranges
Hilly Uplands and Low Mountains
Great Escarpment

0   200   600 Miles
     200   800 Miles

Map 8

Cattle and sheep pasture on the Andean piedmont of Patagonia (Argentina). *Photo by Pan American Airways.*

across Brazil to the northern bank of the Plata River, and which appear again in Patagonia. Throughout this vast extent of territory three chief surface elements are associated in varying patterns of arrangement. There is a base of ancient crystalline rocks which forms a hilly upland; above this in a few places the stumps of old, worn-down mountains have produced massive, rounded forms similar to those of the Southern Appalachians in the United States; and covering the crystalline base, especially in the interior, is a mantle of stratified rock, now forming tabular plateaus with steeply scarped margins. In dry Patagonia the granites and gneisses of the crystalline base are relatively resistant to the processes of erosion and stand out prominently as hills; but in the rainy tropics such rocks are speedily decomposed and mantled with soil, forming hills of a distinctively rounded outline. The stratified formations include chiefly sandstones, which, especially in the rainy lands, are so much more resistant than the crystalline rocks that they stand generally higher than the hilly upland throughout the Brazilian and Guiana highlands. Between the sandstone strata in southern Brazil, and in small patches throughout eastern South America, are sheets of dark-colored lava known as diabase. The diabase is especially resistant, and the edges of the lava sheets stand out prominently as cuestas. Some of the great waterfalls of South America occur where the rivers plunge over the edge of the diabase formations. The Paraná Plateau of southern Brazil is one of the world's largest accumulations built by successive flows of lava—similar in origin to the Columbia Plateau of Oregon and Washington, the Ethiopian Plateau of Africa, and the Deccan Plateau of India.

The arrangement of the plains of South America is very different from that of North America. In the first place they occupy a much smaller proportion of the continent. The Orinoco Plain is separated from the Amazon Plain by a belt of highlands. The Amazon Plain, which is wide along the eastern base of the Andes, narrows to only a ribbon of floodplain along the main stream east of Manaus. Southward along the Andes the plain of the Amazon is joined with the plain of the Paraguay-Paraná-Plata system, where the alluvium brought down by the rivers from both the Andes and the Brazilian highlands has covered all but a few of the more prominent features of the underlying rock surface. Unlike North America, there is no coastal plain along the Atlantic.

There is still another very significant difference between the patterns of the two continents. Because the highlands reach their greatest elevation in southeastern Brazil, back of Rio de Janeiro, where the highest summits are just under ten thousand feet above sea level, the larger rivers flow inland away from this region. The tributaries of the Paraná rise within a few miles of the coast in São Paulo, flowing thence northwest and then south; the tributaries of the São Francisco River, and those which eventually reach the Amazon, also flow toward the north, away from the southeastern coast. This diver-

The *paramos*, or mountain grassland, in the Cordillera de Merida, Venezuela. *Courtesy of Ministerio de Fomento, Venezuela.*

gence of the major streams deprives this part of the continent of any major natural focus of routes, such as the one which carries the traffic of the Middle West of the United States through the Mohawk and Hudson valleys to New York.

South America, on the whole, is not well provided with harbors, nor with navigable rivers placed where they can benefit the currents of commerce. The Paraná-Planta is navigable for ocean ships as far as Santa Fé, but to reach the port at Buenos Aires dredges must work constantly to maintain a channel across the shallow mud banks of the Plata. On the western coast, with only a few exceptions, the ports must be protected by breakwaters.

CLIMATES

Many different climates are to be found in Latin America. As in all the continents there is a general symmetry in the arrangement of the climatic types on either side of the equator and with reference to the continental east and west coasts. The higher middle latitudes of the southern hemisphere contain a much smaller area of land than the equivalent latitudes of the northern hemisphere. South America, south of latitude 40°, projects a relatively narrow finger into the wide expanse of the southern ocean. Therefore the types of middle- and high-latitude climates associated with places distant from the moderating effect of the oceans are not found in the southern hemisphere. Compared with North America the southern part of the hemisphere has moderate climates—they are neither so cold in winter nor so hot in summer. Nowhere, even in southern South America, are the winters comparable in severity to those of Canada or the northern United States. Even in Tierra del Fuego, more than 50° south of the equator, the temperatures average above 32° in the coldest month, although in the warmest month they average below 50°.[7]

Very high temperatures are also rare in Latin America. Map 9 shows how many days with temperatures above 110° can be expected in the average year. There are no parts of Latin America, except for a small bit of Mexico along the lower Colorado River, where more than fifteen such days are experienced, as they are in eastern California and Nevada. Very hot summer days occur in a belt extending from North Dakota to Texas. and to neighboring parts of northeastern Mexico. The only part of Latin America, outside of Mexico, where temperatures over 110° occur at any time of the year is in northern Argentina.

Along the western coast of both Americas the sequence of climatic types is similar on both sides of the equator. The cool, rainy climates of the higher middle latitudes on this coast are found in southern Chile and in southern

---

[7]In this book the temperature is given in degrees Fahrenheit, the rainfall in inches.

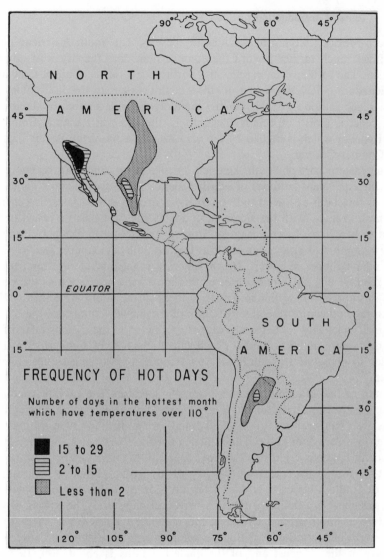

Map 9

Alaska and British Columbia. The similarity of the deeply fiorded coasts frequently swept by heavy storms which are found poleward of about latitude 45° on either continent is notable. The coast of middle Chile, like coastal California, enjoys a Mediterranean type of climate, characterized by mild, rainy winters, and cool, dry summers; but because of the greater altitude of the Central Valley of Chile its summers are also cool, quite unlike the very hot summers of the much lower central valley of California. A little equatorward of 30° on both continents, the rainfall diminishes until only drought-resistant, or *xerophytic,* types of vegetation can survive. Southern California and northwestern Mexico, like northern Chile, are deserts. The South American desert continues much farther toward the equator than does the dry west coast of Mexico. The former even reaches the northern side of the Gulf of Guayaquil in Ecuador, a few degrees from the equator, whereas the latter does not quite reach latitude 20° N. On the equatorward side of the dry lands, the west coast is moist, especially that part oi the coast in Panamá, Colombia, and Ecuador which is bathed by the very warm waters of the Pacific Equatorial Counter Current.

The eastern part of South America, on the other hand, can be compared with the equivalent latitudes of North America as regards climatic conditions only as far south as the latitude of Buenos Aires. The east coast is generally warm and rainy—with the single exception of the northeast of Brazil, where there is a region of very irregular rainfall and frequent drought. Places in eastern South America as far south as Buenos Aires are comparable to places at similar latitudes in eastern North America as regards average temperature and rainfall, but the temperatures of the South American stations are not so high in summer nor so low in winter as those of the North American stations which they otherwise resemble. Because of the higher altitudes of the interior of Brazil, relatively cool climates extend northward to the regions inland from Rio de Janeiro and São Paulo. The highland climates of southern Brazil are similar to those of the southern Appalachians of the southeastern United States.

South of the latitude of Buenos Aires, temperature and rainfall conditions differ greatly from those of the northeastern United States at equivalent latitudes. The temperatures are relatively mild, being much lower in summer and higher in winter than in the United States north of New York. Between Bahía Blanca in Argentina and the Strait of Magellan, the desert extends to the east coast—a rare characteristic in any part of the world. Although this southern part of South America is crossed by many storms, and is noted for its blustery, changeable weather, it receives very little moisture. The ranges of temperature in South America reach a maximum in the interior of Argentina a little north of the latitude of Buenos Aires, where the difference between the average of the warmest and of the coldest months is about 30°. In North America, ranges increase toward the north, because the increasing distance from the sea supplements the increasing distance from the equator; but in South America these two factors are opposed, and the ranges of temperature diminish again south of Buenos Aires.

To state that three-quarters of South America as well as most of Middle America lie within the tropics is to present a fact, but perhaps a misleading one. It is misleading because of the common tendency to assume the bad effects of a tropical climate, and also the tendency to think of all tropical climates as more or less alike. There is just as great a variety of climate within the tropical parts of the world as in the middle latitudes. An important distinction is to be made between the cool, cloudy desert of the Peruvian coast, for instance, and the hot, rainy conditions of Guiana or the hot, dry conditions along the Caribbean coast of Venezuela. The highest temperatures in South America, as in other continents, are not observed near the equator, as is popularly supposed, but rather on the border between middle and low latitudes during the summer months. The parts of South America which have temperatures averaging above 80° in the warmest month are found along the Caribbean and Guiana coasts, throughout the vast tropical area of the Amazon Basin, and also over the plains of northern Argentina, most of which lie on the poleward side of the Tropic of Capricorn. The idea that the low latitudes are characterized by intense heat is based on the effect of the humidity encountered in certain parts of these lands, and also on the high *average* temperatures and the lack of any cool season. No such extremes of hot weather are found in the equatorial regions as occur during a summer heat wave in the North American Corn Belt.

Climatic diversity is especially great in the Andes. In any mountain region the variations of exposure to the sunlight and to rain-bearing winds have the effect of producing very intricate patterns of local climate; but there are also general altitude zones based chiefly on the decrease of temperature with increasing elevation. These high-altitude climates are in no way similar to the climates of the middle latitudes, for with increasing elevation above sea level the seasonal difference of temperature becomes less and less until it practically disappears (see the statistics for Quito in Appendix A, pp. 895–903.

In the low latitudes the greatest variety of vertical zones is to be found. The snow line rises to its highest altitude between 20° and 30° north and south of the equator, sagging slightly through the low latitudes. The snow line in Colombia is about 14,500 feet above sea level. On Mt. Orizaba in Mexico, 19° N., it is about 14,600 feet in altitude. On the dry west coast of Mexico and southern Peru or northern Chile the snow line is considerably higher— in northern Chile about 20,600 feet. In western Tierra del Fuego, on the other hand, permanent snow is encountered below 2,500 feet. The upper limit of trees and the upper limits of the various crops all follow this general pattern. In general, snow lines and tree lines come closer together in wet areas, and have the widest spread where the rainfall is relatively low.

The climatic features are shown on the maps. Map 12 (p. 32) shows the average annual rainfall, and Map 13[8] (p. 33) shows the average annual water

---

[8]Map 13 was prepared by Douglas D. Carter, Southern Illinois University, for the Commission on Geography of the Pan American Institute of Geography and History. The procedure is described in C. W. Thornthwaite and J. R. Mather, "The Water Balance," *Publications in Climatology* (Laboratory of Climatology, Elmer, N.J.) Vol. 8, No. 1, 1955. This procedure takes account of the storage of water in the soil, and recognizes that as capillary soil moisture decreases the plants find greater and greater difficulty in reaching the moisture that remains in storage. The data on which this map is based came, in part, from unpublished materials in the files of the Laboratory of Climatology, and in part from "Average Climatic Water Balance Data of the Continents: Parts VI, North America (excluding the United States), and VII, South America," *Publications in Climatology*, Vol. 17, No. 2, 1964, and Vol. 18, No. 2, 1965.

deficit. The climatic types according to the Köppen system are shown on Map 11.[9]

[9] The Köppen system makes use of various letter symbols, each letter having an exact, quantitative definition. The letter combinations form climatic types. Those types which occur in Latin America are listed below, with brief qualitative characterizations:

Af, Am	Wet climate with no cool season and no really dry season
Aw, As	Wet climate with distinct dry seasons, but with no cool season
BW	Dry climates: BWh, hot deserts; BWk, cool deserts; BWk', cool deserts with no hot season
BS	Semiarid climates: h, k, and k', as above
Csb	Wet climate with mild, rainy winters and cool, dry summers
Cwa	Wet climate with mild, dry winters and hot, rainy summers
Cfa	Wet climate with mild winters, hot summers, and no dry season
Cfb	Wet climate with mild winters, cool summers, and no dry season
Cfc	Wet climate with mild winters, short, cool summers, and no dry season
Cfbi, Cwbi	High altitude climate of the tropics, characterized by extreme monotony of temperature
E	Continuously cool or cold climates, with no warm season

For exact definitions and for a discussion of the distribution of these types in the world see P. E. James, *A Geography of Man,* third edition, Boston, 1966.

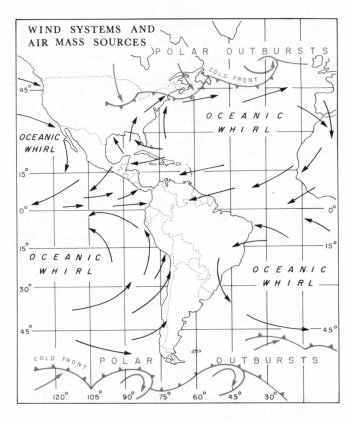

Map 10

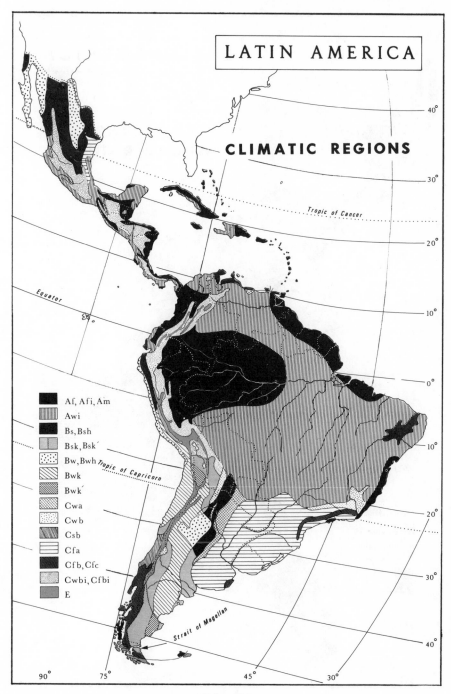

LATIN AMERICA

CLIMATIC REGIONS

Tropic of Cancer

Equator

Tropic of Capricorn

Strait of Magellan

Af, Afi, Am
Awi
Bs, Bsh
Bsk, Bsk´
Bw, Bwh
Bwk
Bwk´
Cwa
Cwb
Csb
Cfa
Cfb, Cfc
Cwbi, Cfbi
E

Map 11

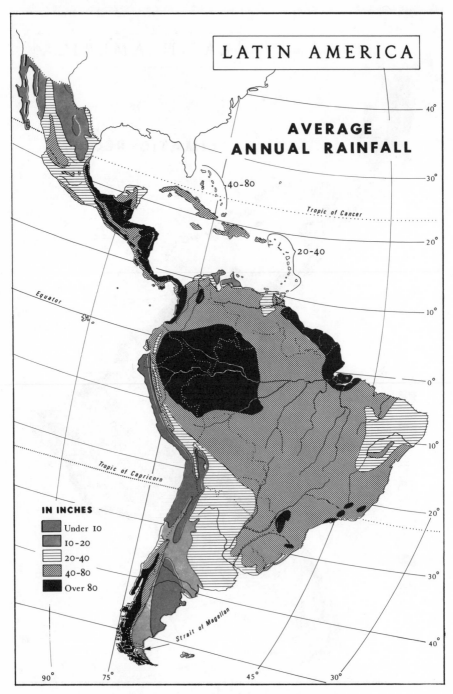

Map 12

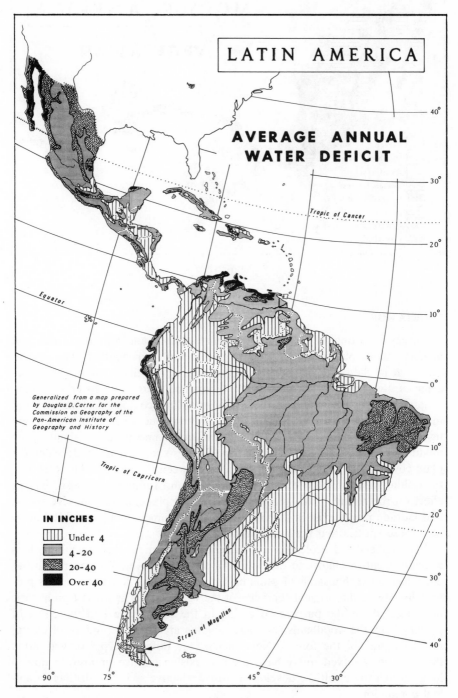

LATIN AMERICA

AVERAGE ANNUAL
WATER DEFICIT

40°

30°

Tropic of Cancer

20°

Equator

10°

0°

Generalized from a map prepared
by Douglas D. Carter for the
Commission on Geography of the
Pan-American Institute of
Geography and History

10°

Tropic of Capricorn

20°

IN INCHES

- Under 4
- 4-20
- 20-40
- Over 40

30°

Strait of Magellan

40°

90°   75°   45°   30°

Map 13

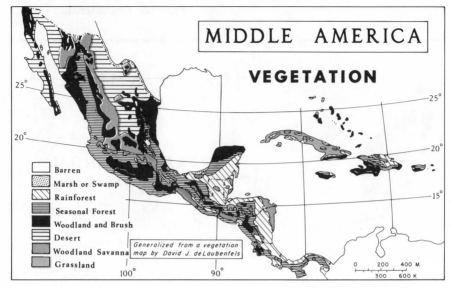

Map 14

VEGETATION

Closely reflecting the conditions of climate, water, and soil are the different associations of plants that distinguish one region from another. The vegetation, that is, the cover of noncultivated plants, is broadly related to the character of the climate. Where water is abundant there is a cover of forest. Where water is less abundant there is a woodland composed of smaller and more widely spaced trees. Also in the transition zone between abundant and insufficient water there are areas of grassland, some pure grassland, some mixtures of grassland and scrubby woodland. Where water is deficient the plant cover is less dense, with bare ground between the plants. This is the distinguishing characteristic of dry land vegetation. Temperature, also, has its effect on the nature of the plant cover: tropical plants cannot survive frosts; mid-latitude plants exist in climates where frost comes often enough to eliminate those species that are not resistant to it.

Geographers and ecologists are in general agreement that man himself is a major agent of change in the nature of the plant cover. Wherever man has been during the thousands of years he has occupied the Americas, he has profoundly altered the original character of the vegetation. The fires of prehistoric man, started for the purpose of aiding in the hunt, have had the effect of pushing back the woodlands and increasing the area of grassland, or of changing the nature of the forests. Nevertheless, the different types of vegetation that can be observed today have been in existence since prehistoric time—long enough to permit the development of distinctive soils and distinctive animal populations.

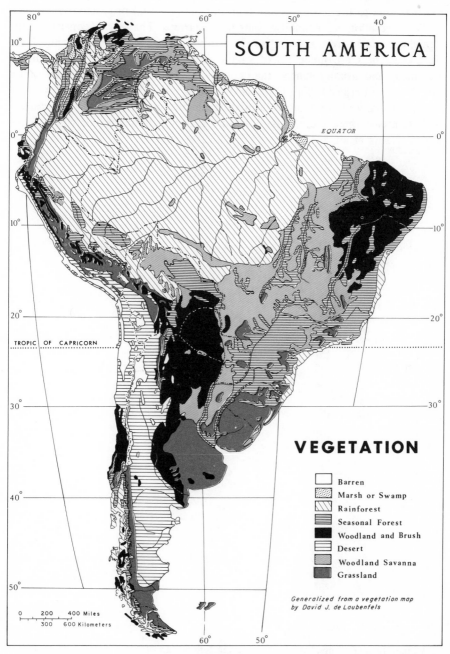

SOUTH AMERICA

EQUATOR

TROPIC OF CAPRICORN

VEGETATION

- ☐ Barren
- ▦ Marsh or Swamp
- ▨ Rainforest
- ▤ Seasonal Forest
- ■ Woodland and Brush
- ▤ Desert
- ▨ Woodland Savanna
- ▨ Grassland

*Generalized from a vegetation map
by David J. de Laubenfels*

0   200   400 Miles
300   600 Kilometers

Map 15

In a land where climatic data are insufficient and often unreliable, and where detailed soil mapping remains to be done, the cover of vegetation offers the best clue to the nature of the land and its potential productivity.

The vegetation is classified in four major groups. The *forests* consist of tall, straight-stemmed trees growing so close together that their branches interlace. The *woodlands* are made up of smaller trees, gnarled rather than straight-stemmed, and usually spaced far enough apart so that branches may touch but are not interlaced. The *grasslands* include some that are entirely without trees, but many others that are a mixture of grass and woodland. The *deserts* include areas where there is bare ground between the plants, or where there are no plants at all.[10]

---

[10]Maps 14 and 15 are based on a new vegetation map of Latin America at a scale of 1:5,000,000 by David J. deLaubenfels.

Chapter 2 □ The Appearance of Modern Latin America

These physical and biotic features of man's natural surroundings provide the stage setting on which modern Latin America has appeared. Here the traditional Spanish and Portuguese societies were established, in some cases embracing, if not digesting, a numerous population of native Indians. How did the modern states come into existence, and where are they with reference to the features of the habitat? And what are the problems of the modern period which are so deeply disturbing?

It is important to understand that the physical and biotic character of the habitat cannot control the action of the inhabitants. All too frequently we hear that people in the tropics can never work with energy and determination, or that countries not well endowed with natural resources can never be strong. Geographers have long insisted that the significance to man of the physical and biotic features of his habitat is a function of the attitudes, objectives, and technical skills of man himself. These are all elements of his traditional way of living, which we call his *culture*. Any change in the technology or other element of a culture results in a change in the meaning of the habitat. What was a barrier to people with horses or on foot may cease to be a barrier to people with automobiles. Slopes that were not unsuited to cultivation by farmers with hoes, are quite useless for farmers with plows and tractors. Mineral resources that are of great value may, with some technical improvement in a distant place, become useless overnight. The significance of the habitat must always be interpreted in terms of the attitudes, objectives, and technical skills of the people.

There is one basic requirement. Any human society that is to remain permanently in any area must learn how to form workable connections with the land resources. If the agricultural practices result in soil erosion so that the land base is destroyed, land that was once habitable may cease to be so. The problems of economic development and of the viability of states must always be examined in relation to the features of the habitat.

In modern Latin America the existence of twenty-four sovereign states is of fundamental importance in any interpretation of economic or political problems. The states differ notably in wealth, in the development and use of resources, and in the nature of political attitudes. We need to understand how these states originated, what kinds of land they include, and what changes are sweeping over them in the modern period.

The Origin of States

One of the principal characteristics of this part of the world previously described is that the boundaries between states usually pass through empty, or thinly populated territory. Some countries are built around just one central cluster of people, one area of concentrated settlement. Other countries, however, include several separate areas of concentrated settlement. How did this come about? Or we might put the question this way: why did not every separate cluster of people form the core of a separate state?

After the American and French Revolutions of the late eighteenth century, new concepts of freedom and human liberty began to spread around the world. During the first half of the nineteenth century most of the present states of Latin America established themselves as independent countries, free from European control. Among the patriots who fought for freedom there were some who were genuinely devoted to the cause of individual liberty and of equality before the law. But most of the revolutionary leaders came from small circles of politically conscious people whose concept of freedom was made up chiefly of a desire to be free from outside interference. In each separate cluster of people there were political leaders who demanded, and in some cases were able to secure, the right to local self-government. The great majority of the people were not concerned.

Whether the resulting sovereign states included only one cluster of people or several clusters depended on position with respect to the centers of colonial administration and on the strength of the local economy. At the end of the colonial period the Spanish colonies were grouped into four viceroyalties: the Viceroyalty of New Spain with its capital in Mexico City; the Viceroyalty of new Granada with its capital at Bogotá; the Viceroyalty of Peru with its capital at Lima; and the Viceroyalty of La Plata with its capital at Buenos Aires (Map 16). Near the capital cities the administrative lines were tightly held. But the difficulties of travel were such that the lines slackened progressively with increasing distance from the capital. In some places Captaincies-General, Presidencies, and other administrative units were established as semi-autonomous subdivisions of the more remote parts of the viceroyalties, as in the case of Guatemala and Chile. The northern part of the Vice-

LATIN AMERICA

ADMINISTRATIVE AREAS
ABOUT 1790

VICEROYALTY
OF
PRESIDENCY
OF
GUADALAJARA
NEW SPAIN

UNITED
STATES

Mexico

CAPTAINCY-GENERAL
OF CUBA

CAPTAINCY-GENERAL
OF SANTO DOMINGO

CAPTAINCY-GENERAL
OF GUATEMALA

San José

Caracas

TRINIDAD
(Sp.)

VICEROYALTY
OF
NEW GRANADA

Bogotá

Georgetown
DUTCH GUIANA
Paramaribo
Cayenne
FRENCH GUIANA

GALAPAGOS IS.
(Sp.)

Quito

PRESIDENCY
OF QUITO

VICEROYALTY
OF
PERU

Lima

VICEROYALTY
OF
BRAZIL

CHARCAS
La Paz
Chuquisaca

VICEROYALTY
OF
LA PLATA

Asunción

Rio de Janeiro

EUROPEAN COLONIES

New Spain	
New Granada	
Peru	SPAIN
La Plata	
Great Britain	
Netherlands	
Portugal	
France	
○ Government Seat	

Santiago

Buenos Aires

PATAGONIA

40°

20°

10°

0°

10°

20°

30°

40°

45°   30°

Map 16

royalty of La Plata was included in the Presidency of Charcas. When the wars of independence succeeded in breaking the ties with Spain, the new governments located in the old capitals of the viceroyalties were strong enough to maintain control of a number of separate clusters of people. But in more remote locations the clusters tended to break apart. Thus the separate clusters in Central America, from Guatemala southward, broke away from Mexico, and soon after broke into separate individual pieces. The clusters included in New Granada were at first held together by Bolívar, but later broke apart into three countries. Chile broke away from Peru. Bolivia and Paraguay made good their independence from Argentina.

In the case of the Portuguese colonies the situation was quite different. During the fourteen years before 1822, when Brazil became independent, the Emperor of Portugal had made his capital at Rio de Janeiro. This was the center of the whole Portuguese Empire. The declaration of independence by Dom Pedro I was supported by the political leaders of all the separate clusters of people. Only in the far south was there a separatist movement. Warfare between the Portuguese-Brazilians and the Spanish-Argentines over the border zone between them resulted in the creation of Uruguay as a buffer state.

In the Antilles, Spain succeeded in holding her colonies on Cuba and Puerto Rico until the war with the United States at the end of the century. However, the whole independence movement in Latin America was led, in 1804, by the revolt of the slaves from their French masters in Haiti. The Haitians established control over the whole of the island of Hispaniola. Only in 1844 did the surviving Spanish groups in eastern Hispaniola gain their independence from Haiti. In the 1960's the British policy of pushing the remaining British colonies as rapidly as possible toward independence resulted in the establishment of independent Jamaica, Trinidad and Tobago, Barbados, and Guyana on the South American mainland. Some of the smaller British West Indies became self-governing commonwealths associated with Great Britain.

The Struggle to Establish Order

A modern sovereign state is a politically organized area in which the people give their support to a government for the purpose of defending and fostering the development of a distinctive body of traditions and institutions. The traditions and institutions of a state are known as the *state-idea*. Unless a substantial majority of the people of a state give their support to this body of traditions and institutions, this state-idea, the state is a relatively weak one and could break apart under the pressure. If a state-idea is supported only by a minority, nothing but a strong central authority, maintained by force, can hold the state together. When independence was achieved in Latin America, the state-idea with which most of the governments started was the negative one of freedom from outside interference.

During the past century or so the states of Latin America have been engaged in a struggle to establish order among the diverse and discordant elements of which they are composed. Order, as the word is used here, implies that a sufficient proportion of the people of a state subscribe to a common state-idea; or, lacking such a proportion of supporters, that a strong central authority enforces a state-idea which is held only by a minority. In most countries the establishment of order has proved very difficult. We find, in the same region of settlement, diverse groups of people mixed but not blended, whose traditional ways of living, whose technical abilities, whose fundamental attitudes are not only different but are so inharmonious that none can really prosper in the presence of the others. For example, there are certain nations which, since their independence, have been torn by the struggle for central control between two minorities: the large landowners, anxious only to be free from government interference; and the bureaucracy whose chief interest is in politics. There are other regions where the speculative exploitation of resources competes in the same area with a group of peasant proprietors seeking to establish themselves permanently on their own small farms. There are areas where one part of the population inherits a communal tradition of land tenure and another part inherits the tradition of the private estate. These and many other discordant elements produce such divergent attitudes toward the land and its use that harmony can be achieved only through the subjugation of one element by the other.

This struggle toward order among diverse elements is a process which can be observed in any community. Order is, of course, a relative term; it suggests that a substantial majority of the people are so harmonious in their basic traditions, skills, and objectives that one form of settlement or one coordinated group of connections between man and the land can be established and maintained. Methods of reaching such order are various. Some communities are brought together through service to an ideal, great enough and universal enough to command the allegiance of diverse individuals. Other communities achieve order through the struggle with a common problem, such as the conquest of a pioneer land, or defense against a foreign enemy. Still others are given an apparent order through the lulling effects of widespread prosperity. Different methods failing, many communities in past periods, and again in modern times, have enforced order through the operation of a strong central authority. In Latin America all these methods, and many others, have been tried with varying success; but in a number of regions of settlement and in many of the independent states built around them, the establishment of a coherent society has been retarded or thwarted.

Why should the Latin-American countries find so much difficulty in reaching a solution of this problem? We do not find among these people any scarcity of able leaders, any lack of outstanding political philosophers, any dearth of poets or men of letters, or any absence of courage and resourcefulness and initiative. But we do find that Latin-American society is troubled by perhaps a greater degree of original diversity than most of the other Occidental people of the world; and we also find that these basic racial and cultural diversities have been increased through the unbalanced social and economic development of certain regions against a background which remains economically medieval. The problems that have to be faced in the establishment of order in Latin America are not simple ones.

Impact of Diverse Racial and Cultural Elements

Whether the original racial and cultural diversity of the elements which have entered into Latin-American society is to be described as an advantage or a disadvantage is a disputed question. The almost complete contrast in attitudes and objectives which exists between, for example, the descendants of the Incas and those of the Spanish conquerors is so great that even to this day the two have established only a minimum of coordination and harmony within the territory they occupy together. The impacts of pagan and Catholic, of communal farmers who use the same word for "duty to the state" as for "happiness," and the extremely individualistic Spaniards who have a strong sense of property rights—these have created internal conflicts which have yet to be resolved. Similarly in Mexico, although an attack on these fundamental diversities has been started, the lack of internal coherence in still far from solved. For these states diversity cannot yet be accounted a benefit.

In no part of the world are studies of race mixture by impartial observers more needed than in Latin America, especially in the predominantly Indian and mestizo countries and in Brazil. Many observers of race mixture insist that the mestizos do not constitute a new race of unified characteristics, but rather a mixture of ingredients so fundamentally different that they can never blend. On the other hand, there are those who see in this mixture of Indian and European the basis of a new race and a new civilization. There is a distinct movement in the Indian countries looking toward a "rediscovery" of the artistic and technical skills of the Indians, a movement tending to discredit the Spanish contribution. In Brazil the African mixture has produced every possible shade of color from very black to pure white, with all sorts of intermediate types including individuals, for instance, with blonde, kinky hair. Among many of the pure white families of Brazil there is a considerable amount of race prejudice; but not a few of the Brazilian writers extol the virtues of race mixture in producing a new fusion of racial and cultural elements—a new civilization. Among all these diversities, however, the struggle to establish order, the struggle to assimilate, to create or maintain a coherent nation, become problems of vital significance, and the changing character of these struggles conditions the relation of the people to the land.

Social Diversities within the Preindustrial Society

Racial diversity, however, is not the only source of disharmony within Latin-American society. There are social and economic cleavages which divide communities into sharply contrasted classes. Some of these class distinctions are inherent in the society of traditional Latin America; but in the modern period the arrival of the urban industrial way of living has developed a new kind of difference separating the people of the larger cities from the people of the rural districts.

In traditional Latin America the economic and social life is dominated by the large estate. We shall describe this kind of society as *preindustrial.* Prestige and security in a preindustrial society are gained first through the ownership of a large tract of land. A very minor proportion of the total population is composed of the landed aristocracy, which is enabled to live in comfort and security and with a relatively high standard because of the large area from which income is derived and because of the relatively low cost of labor. When land is no longer available, prestige, if not security, can be gained by finding a position in the government service, or by winning a commission in the army, or by entering the priesthood. But these various forms of life are open only to the fortunate minority: the vast majority of the members of preindustrial society are landless workers—peons, sharecroppers, tenants, or others. Usually they are permitted to make use of small areas for the production of their own food and for the materials necessary for clothing and shelter; they repay the owner by providing him with wage laborers, or by paying him rent for the use of land for commercial crops. This is the Latin America of the semi-independent large landowner, who wishes above all to be left alone by all government authority; it is also the Latin America of political insecurity, in which first one group and then another plots to overthrow those who are in power, rarely because of genuine differences of ideology, usually because of the desire for the rich rewards of office-holding. This is the Latin America which verges on internal chaos to such an extent that it can be held together only by the successful operation of military dictatorship. This the Latin America in which the army is the most powerful force in political life.

Impact of the Industrial Society

The history of the Occidental world during the last few centuries has been involved with the impact of the new *industrial society* and the older *preindustrial society.* This is what we call the industrial revolution. Beginning in western Europe, the new way of living, coupled with enormously increased productivity in all forms of economic activity through the use of controlled inanimate power, has gradually transformed whole sections of Europe and

America. In some instances the transformation has taken place by gradual evolution; in not a few instances it has been accompanied by violence and warfare, both civil and international. The rapid increase in the need for raw materials of all kinds has produced the present intense rivalry for the control of the productive regions, especially of the sources of power. The English-speaking peoples, who were the first to adopt the new way of living, were able to gain control of about 75 percent of the developed power resources of the world; and the challenge to this control lies behind the present international turmoil. Latin America is now experiencing the impact of industrialization upon its traditional, preindustrial society. Where the industrial way of living has become established, a new and still more profound line of cleavage has been formed across all the previous diversities of Latin-American society.

The fundamental characteristics of the industrial society should be reviewed briefly. The use of controlled inanimate power changes the emphasis from production by cheap labor to production by machines—or, in terms of economics, capital investment assumes a position of preponderant importance, and the owners of capital rather than the owners of land assume places of the highest prestige and political power. Production is enormously increased—not only total production, but also per capita production. This leads to specialization and exchange, and hence to interdependence over wide areas. Trade is transformed from a small-scale exchange of luxury goods or specialties to a large-scale exchange of staples, and as a result communities are no longer supported by the products of the territories immediately surrounding them, but from a wide variety of producing areas, most of them beyond the control of the community which absorbs the products. With life organized on such a pattern, society reaches a much higher standard of material comfort than any previous society has been able to reach; but this standard can be maintained only if a nation accepts the fact of wide geographical interdependence, turns away from provincial isolation, and cooperates with other nations in the maintenance of a stable financial structure of money and credits.

The industrial society brings profound changes in the details of human life. Prestige, we repeat, is to be gained through the ownership of capital which brings power, rather than through the ownership of land which brings security. Life becomes more speculative, less certain, but with rewards for the successful which are in a material way far beyond anything the world has offered before. There comes a notable change in the concept of time and its use. With the increased tempo of life the vague concepts of preindustrial society such as *por la mañana* or *por la tarde* must be given up for more precise concepts such as 9:45 A.M. or 3:10 P.M. Behavior of all sorts becomes more standardized. The picturesqueness of provincial costumes disappears under a uniform cover of blue denim overalls; people from Patagonia to Labrador watch the antics of Mickey Mouse; local differences in manners and customs are modified by the impact of the new patterns of life. In the big cosmopolitan centers of Latin America life follows the same routine as in

North American or European cities—this uniformity is apparent in styles of architecture, styles of dress, forms of work and recreation—in short, the whole aspect of life is changed from its variegated preindustrial base to a uniformity repeated in all the Occidental urban centers.

These changes affect the distribution of people. As long as coal remains the chief source of power, manufacturing industry is carried on at the lowest cost in large concentrated units. People gather together in great cities—cities greater than any that the world ever knew before, cities of more than a million inhabitants. Although the use of electric power may have the effect of spreading manufacturing industry over a wider area, thus transforming the life in smaller towns and villages, large concentrations of city people still perform the urban functions of commerce and administration with more efficiency. The cities are still dependent on the productivity of the land for their support, but the land base has been greatly extended; and as a result the means of transportation which tie the cities together must be greatly elaborated.

The urban-industrial way of living has come to Latin America from outside, not by slow evolution from the earlier preindustrial base. In parts of Europe and in Anglo-America, where the cities and the urban life developed out of the rural background, there is a certain normal relationship between the size of the city and the productivity of its rural hinterland. When through the artificial erection of political boundaries and barriers a city like Vienna is deprived of the hinterland which it once served, the financial and economic life of the city is disrupted. When politically independent states attempt to return to isolation and self-sufficiency, the urban-industrial society falls into chaos. All these adjustments between cities and their territories and all these disruptions of the earlier adjustments can be witnessed in Europe today. In Latin America one finds cities which have become industrial and commercial centers with an industrial way of living, but which bear little relationship in size or in function to the rural districts back of them. The contrast between the cities and the rural districts is enormous: the average tourist who journeys by boat or airplane from one city to another scarcely catches a glimpse of the Latin America which is traditional, and which is still dominant in terms of area and numbers of people.

In the early 1960's there were four metropolitan areas in Latin America in which there were more than 3 million inhabitants each. These were Buenos Aires (7,000,000), Rio de Janeiro (3,223,000), São Paulo (3,165,000), and Mexico City (3,051,000). In addition to these huge urban concentrations, which were among the 21 largest cities of the world, Latin America also had 7 cities of over 1 million, or about to reach this figure. These were Santiago (2,270,000), Bogotá (1,681,000), Caracas (1,589,000), Habana (1,463,000), Lima (1,436,000), Montevideo (1,202,000), and Guadalajara (977,000). There were 115 cities with populations over 100,000. The urban way of living had reached almost all parts of Latin America.

The arrival of the industrial revolution in any part of the world results at

In the Andean countries, much of the agricultural land is like this. A farm in southern Colombia. *Courtesy of Colombian Information Service.*

first in the creation of greater differences of wealth and poverty, greater differences of economic development, than existed before. Latin America is no exception. The gross national product per capita—that is, the total value of all goods and services divided by the number of people—shows a wide spread, ranging from Puerto Rico ($1,120 in 1966) and Venezuela ($895), to Bolivia ($149), Barbados ($140), and Haiti (with much less than $100). In terms of Walt W. Rostow's stages of economic growth,[1] five countries had entered the initial stage (the "take-off" stage). These were Argentina, Chile, Mexico, Venezuela, and Puerto Rico. Several others were about ready to enter the take-off stage. But there were several others where even the first steps toward development had not been taken. To start the process of economic growth requires the investment of between 5 and 10 percent of the gross national product each year for some twenty years in the formation of new capital. The investment must be greater in countries with high net rates of population increase, just to create new jobs fast enough to stay even with the number of new job seekers. In countries with gross national products per capita of less than $250, domestic savings do not amount to enough to start

[1]W. W. Rostow, *The Stages of Economic Development, A Non-Communist Manifesto.* Cambridge, England, 1960.

the process of growth. The cycle of poverty grows more and more difficult to break. In the decades to come these countries will slip farther and farther behind those that have made a start on the painful climb toward the construction of a mature industrial society. The contrasts of wealth and poverty will continue to sharpen.

The Democratic Revolution

Along with the industrial revolution, yet separate from it, another major change in mankind's way of living is sweeping the world. This is the democratic revolution. Like the industrial revolution, it made its start in Great Britain and in the countries around the North Sea in Europe. Although the

Teaching geography in a model school in Peru. Most children do not get this kind of education. *Courtesy of W. R. Grace.*

roots of this movement go back a long way in history, democratic principles did not become the state-ideas of politically organized areas until the latter half of the eighteenth century in Europe.[2] These revolutionary new ideas came to Latin America through contacts with the French and American Revolutions, through the writings of such men as Benjamin Franklin, and through the influence of the German geographer Alexander von Humboldt.

The democratic revolution includes at least six new concepts regarding the status of the individual citizen of a country. These are: (1) the acceptance of the principle of equal treatment before the law; (2) the guarantee of protection from the arbitrary acts of those in authority; (3) the right of the individual to be represented where laws are made or taxes levied; (4) the acceptance of the principle of majority rule and the secret ballot; (5) the right of free access to knowledge, and the right to discuss policy issues; and (6) the freedom of choice among religious faiths, or kinds of employment, or places of residence.

The democratic revolution is moving into Latin America. There are still a vast number of Latin Americans who are illiterate, who have never known such a thing as equality before the law, or protection from arbitrary police action, or the secret ballot, or even free access to news. But among the Latin-Americans there have also been a few liberal-minded persons struggling toward the ideas of democracy. The French Revolution of the late eighteenth century had a profound effect on Latin America. Although the independence movement was quickly turned away from concepts of individual equality toward the principle of freedom from outside interference, nevertheless many of those who supported the independence movement were thinking of fundamental changes in the status of the individual. Such leaders as Domingo Sarmiento (1811–88) of Argentina, Benito Juárez (1806–72) of Mexico, and many others attempted to attack the system which gave special privilege because of social or political position. Sarmiento devoted his life to the establishment in Chile, Uruguay, and Argentina of the first teacher-training institutions in Latin America, and to the development of public schools.

Such fundamental changes as those brought by the democratic revolution developed strong reactions. There were many political leaders who established strong dictatorships for the purpose of maintaining the traditional system in which power and prestige are granted on the basis of social status rather than individual achievement. In many parts of Latin America the ideas of the democratic revolution have met resistances too strong to be easily overcome. A strong central authority, supported by the power of an army, may provide a deceptive kind of order, but when pressures build up to the point of explosion, the result is armed conflict.

There are some people in the United States, and in Latin America, who label anyone who promotes a change in this traditional system as "commu-

[2]Robert R. Palmer, *The Age of the Democratic Revolution.* Princeton, N.J., 1959.

nist." This is a dangerous oversimplification, which suggests that all would be peaceful and orderly were it not for subversive activities by agents of foreign powers. There is no doubt that trained and disciplined cells of devoted communists are present in every country, ready to seize control of the government in any period of chaotic change. But most Latin-Americans subscribe wholly to the six principles of the democratic revolution. If communism means accepting the dominance of a foreign power, they are against communism: but since communism is against the United States, and since the United States does, in fact, loom as the source of the most immediate challenge to the economic independence of Latin America, many Latin-Americans join the party. Insofar as Fidel Castro falls under the domination of the Soviet Union, this example becomes the strongest anticommunist argument that could be presented. The basic objective remains to avoid domination or interference by any foreign power.

A Geographical View of the Dispersion of Innovation

The industrial and democratic revolutions have brought about the most fundamental cultural innovations that the world has seen for thousands of years. Looking at the world as a whole we see two major source regions from which these innovations are in process of being dispersed—Europe and Anglo-America. Although reaction against both revolutions has been strong in Europe, both have proceeded with a minimum of resistance in Anglo-America; and although it is clear that the democratic ideals as set forth in the United States Constitution are not yet fully applied in the field of race relations, nevertheless it is also clear that a great majority of the people of the United States do accept these ideals. In Anglo-America, therefore, the two systems of revolutionary cultural innovation have been molded into a distinctive American pattern.

Geographers are concerned with the patterns developed during the dispersion of innovations around a source region, and on the basis of theoretical studies can offer certain observations regarding the process of spread. These observations are not laws, in the popular sense of unvarying sequences of events. Rather they must be stated in terms of probability. It is probable that innovation will be transmitted most rapidly from a source region to those parts of a receiving region which are in the closest geographic proximity. Geographic proximity is not solely a matter of distance: proximity is better measured in terms of the flow of communications and the frequency of contacts. In general, the greatest volume of communications and the most frequent contacts are between the most economically active populations—between the source region and those states within the receiving region with the highest gross national products per capita. Furthermore, the volume of communications and frequency of contacts vary inversely with actual distance.

Geographers can offer another general observation regarding the process of spread. There are some kinds of innovation—especially those that undermine the power and privileged position of an elite—that produce violent reaction. This suggests that the most violent reactions against revolutionary changes in culture will appear in those parts of a receiving region that are in closest geographic proximity to the source region. This observation throws light on the conditions and problems of contemporary Europe; and it also illuminates what is happening today in Latin America.

With regard to the two source regions—Europe and Anglo-America—the cultural radiation from Europe has been felt in Latin America for a long time, but, Europe being relatively remote, innovations have appeared in only a few places, notably in Argentina and Uruguay. But cultural radiation from Anglo-America has been increasing, and has been massive since World War II. The Latin-American countries that have felt the greatest impact of innovation from Anglo-America are Mexico, Cuba, Puerto Rico, and Venezuela. Mexico, Cuba, and Puerto Rico occupy positions of the closest geographic proximity to Anglo-America both because of their actual physical situations and because of the many Mexicans and Puerto Ricans who have emigrated to the United States, and the many American tourists and businessmen who have gone to Mexico, Cuba, and Puerto Rico. Cuban sugar production was enormously increased as a result of the inflow of capital and technical assistance from the United States. Puerto Rico is a special case because its spectacular economic development has been supported by private capital and by large appropriations from the United States Treasury. Somewhat more remote is Venezuela, yet capital and technicians from the United States have produced the highest gross national product per capita of any Latin-American country by exporting oil.

Of all the Latin-American countries the most violent reactions to the outflow of innovation from Anglo-America have been in Mexico and Cuba, the countries in closest geographic proximity. Mexico was the first of the Latin-American countries to carry out a social revolution (1910–15), and to set up distinctive Mexican institutions for the purpose of perserving the Mexican national identity while at the same time adopting certain aspects of innovation. Mexico is now well advanced in the process of economic development: capital from Anglo-America is welcomed, as are technical assistance and grants of aid; but the Mexican program of transformation is guided and controlled by Mexicans. Mexico is one Latin-American country that regularly opposes accepting policies formulated in the United States in international affairs. It is the one Latin-American country that has refused to break relations with Cuba.

Cuba has long been restive under the domination of foreign interests, whether political or economic. When, as a result of the Spanish–American War, Cuba gained its independence in 1899, the United States imposed restrictions on Cuban freedom of action by retaining the right to occupy the island by force and to control certain aspects of Cuba's policies. Not until 1934 did the United States give up this special relationship with Cuba. By that time the sugar industry in Cuba was largely controlled by North American corporations, and was dependent on the special access that Cuba had been granted to reach the United States market. Cuban politics was either directly or indirectly controlled by the United States, largely for the benefit of American investors. Habana became a major tourist mecca for New Yorkers. Fidel Castro's revolt against the overwhelming influence of the United States, and against the hated dictatorship of Batista, was a characteristic reaction to this kind of cultural innovation. To escape from the close attachment to, and dependence on, the United States, Castro sought the assistance of the Soviet Union and China. Since the only organized political party in Cuba was communist, he accepted communist support. But when this placed him in peril of accepting another kind of foreign domination, he took every possible step to maintain Cuban independence of action while at the same time accepting economic and military aid.

From a geographic point of view these recent events are quite understandable. Compared with the violence of change in Cuba, the process of change in Chile proceeds with relative calm. All over the region cultural change is progressing rapidly, but because of the spotty pattern of preindustrial and predemocratic conditions, present-day Latin America shows greater contrasts of wealth and poverty, or of democratic and autocratic political systems, than existed before. It is important to understand the geographic principles that illuminate the pattern of innovation.

A Geography of Man

The struggle to establish order among these diverse elements is a basic theme which endows the present-day arrangement of people in Latin America with meaning. In each independent state, in each separate cluster of people, this struggle takes a somewhat different form and has reached somewhat different stages. As a result, the significance of the elements of the land—the potential value of the natural resources—differs from place to place and from time to time. In extreme cases we find two or more diverse groups mixed but not blended in the same area of concentrated settlement, each group motivated by different attitudes and objectives and consequently each reacting differently to the variegated background of the land. In a few instances we are encouraged by what seems to be a real advance against the forces of disunity. When we examine the map of people in detail in the light of this theme we can no longer see it only as a pattern of apparently uniform dots irregularly clustered—we see each cluster as possessing a distinct individuality, as composed of people who have made a separate and distinctive contribution, even if only a negative one, to the struggle toward the development of a coherent society.

Mexico
and
Central
America

Estados Mexicanos Unidos

Area: 761,600 square miles
Population: (1967 estimate) 45,671,000
             (last census, 1960) 34,923,129
Capital city: Mexico City; 5,000,000
Percent urban: (1960) 50.7
Birth rate per 1,000: (1966) 45.3; Death per 1,000: (1966) 9.5
Annual percent of increase: (1958–64) 3.2
Percent literate: (1960) 65.4
Percent labor force in agriculture: (1960) 53.5
Gross national product per capita: (1966) $470
Unit of currency: peso (1968: 12.49 per dollar)
Leading crops in acreage: maize, beans, cotton, wheat

COMMERCE, 1965 *(expressed in percentage of values)*
Percent of total Latin-American exports: 11.5 (1956: 10)
Percent of total Latin-American imports: 17.0

Exports (1966)

cotton 18	zinc 4
coffee 7	also sugar, frozen shrimp, lead

Exports to (1966)		**Imports from (1966)**	
United States	55 (1956: 73)	United States	64 (1956: 78)
Japan	7	West Germany	8
		France	5

Chapter 3 □ Mexico

Mexico, like Cuba, is one of the two Latin-American countries that occupy positions of the closest geographical proximity to Anglo-America, and which, therefore, have received the largest doses of cultural radiation from that source.[1] Before 1910 Mexico was an extreme example of a traditional Spanish agrarian society, ruled by a minority of wealthy landowners and kept in order by force of arms under a military dictatorship. The great majority of the people were tenant farmers whose miserable yields of maize, grown on incredibly steep mountain slopes, failed to provide enough food to keep families from hunger. But under military control Mexico had the reputation of being a safe place for the investment of capital in oil, or copper, or cattle ranches.

More than any other Latin-American country, Mexico had felt the full impact of an expanding United States. In 1836 the English-speaking settlers who had been granted land in the northern part of Mexico declared their independence and defeated Mexican troops sent to put down the revolt. Texas was an independent country from 1836 to 1845, when it became part of the United States. Between 1846 and 1848 the United States' armed forces invaded and took over the whole northern part of Mexican territory between Texas and the Pacific, and United States forces captured Mexico City in the famous battle of Chapultepec. The history books read by Mexican schoolchildren did not describe this war in the same terms as did the books read north of the Mexican border. But the Mexican government profited from close and friendly relations with the United States and from a flow of capital into mines, railroads, and other development projects.

---

[1]For a discussion of the process of cultural diffusion see pp. 43–51.

Mexico was the first country in Latin America to take vigorous and effective steps to do something about the poverty of vast numbers of people, and about the social inequity resulting from the traditional status of the landowning minority. The Mexican Revolution, which started in 1910, set the stage for the expropriation of large properties and the redistribution of land among the farmers. In 1938 the Mexican government expropriated all foreign-owned oil properties. Meanwhile, contacts with people of the United States were becoming closer as many Mexicans emigrated to the United States—some permanently, some only for a season to seek employment in farming—and as the floods of tourists from the United States brought much-needed dollars to help out the Mexican economy. Yet among the Latin-American countries, Mexico was the most likely to refuse to follow policies announced in Washington. In the 1960's Mexico continued to maintain relations with Cuba.

Let us see how the characteristics of modern Mexico have developed, and estimate the significance of its location on the margins of the Anglo-American culture region.

The Appearance of Modern Mexico

In 1821, when the Spanish colony of New Spain became the Empire of Mexico, the leaders of the independence movement were seeking to establish equal rights for those born in America and those born in Spain. The great majority of the people who lived in the new national territory were Indians or mestizos; almost all of them were illiterate farmers, for whom the question of equality with people born in Spain had no meaning. Mexico started its independent existence with a negative state-idea that was of concern to not more than 5 percent of the people. From 1821 to 1876 the country was poverty-stricken and turbulent. There were revolts and counterrevolts, as younger army officers who were not in profitable government positions sought to replace those who were in such positions. Now and then a sincere reformer made his appearance, like the Indian Benito Juárez, but reform movements aimed at improving the lot of the ordinary people were soon diverted into traditional channels. In 1876 Porfirio Díaz came into power by the usual process of army revolt.

Porfirio Díaz was one of Latin America's notably successful dictators. With a small group of trusted supporters, and with a powerful police force, he ran Mexico by decree. The government was carried on by a hierarchy of officials, all responsible to the dictator. He selected the state governors and gave them complete authority within their states. The power of the governors rested on the support of the small number of landowners. Local political bosses were picked by the governors. Anyone who felt inclined to be uncooperative was openly assassinated, or just disappeared. Only 15 percent of the total population could read or write. And not more than one or two percent were

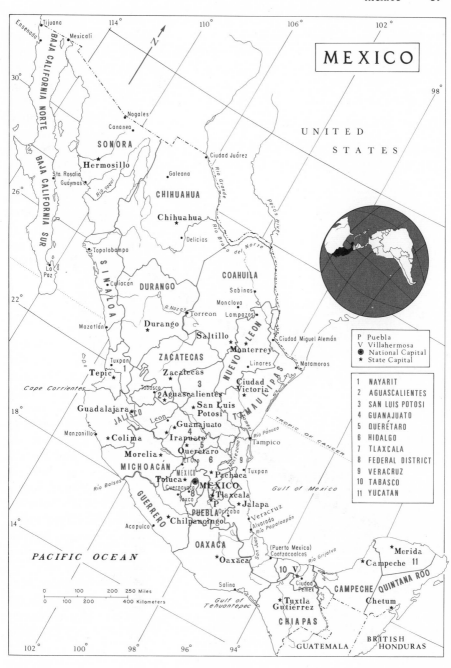

Map 17

MEXICO

UNITED STATES

SIERRA MADRE OCCIDENTAL

SIERRA MADRE ORIENTAL

SIERRA MADRE DEL SUR

Gulf of Mexico

YUCUTAN PENINSULA

ISTHMUS OF TEHUANTEPEC

SIERRA MADRE DE CHIAPAS

GUATEMALA

HONDURAS

PACIFIC OCEAN

TERRAIN

0   75   150 M
  125   250 K

30°   26°   22°

30°   26°   22°

104°   100°   96°   92°

Map 18

58

MEXICO

UNITED STATES

Gulf of Mexico

GUATEMALA

HONDURAS

30°
26°
22°

30°
26°
22°

96°
100°
104°

92°

TRANSPORTATION

— Road
+--+ Railroad
◉ Cities over 1,000,000
● Cities over 100,000
○ Other Urban Centers

0   75   150 M
    125   250 K

Map 19

59

MEXICO

Gulf of Mexico

UNITED STATES

GUATEMALA
HONDURAS

LAND USE

- ° Urban Area
- ■ Irrigated Area
  C—COTTON, F—FRUIT, M—MAIZE
  S—SUGAR CANE, V—VEGETABLES, W—WHEAT

- Coffee
- Cotton
- Cacao
- Sugar Cane
- Henequen
- Maize, Wheat, Pasture
- Uncultivated Range
- Cultivated Pasture

| 0 | 75 | 150 M |
| | 125 | 250 K |

30°
26°
22°

104°
100°
96°
92°

Map 20

60

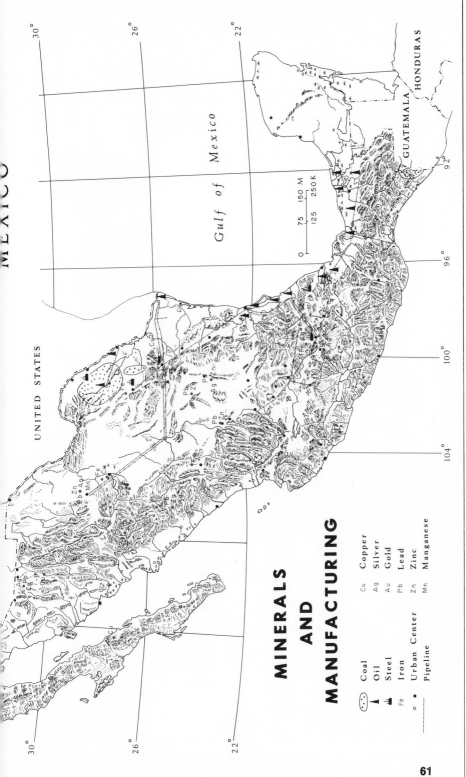

MEXICO

MINERALS
AND
MANUFACTURING

	Coal	Cu	Copper
	Oil	Ag	Silver
	Steel	Au	Gold
Fe	Iron	Pb	Lead
o •	Urban Center	Zn	Zinc
	Pipeline	Mn	Manganese

UNITED STATES

Gulf of Mexico

GUATEMALA

HONDURAS

Map 21

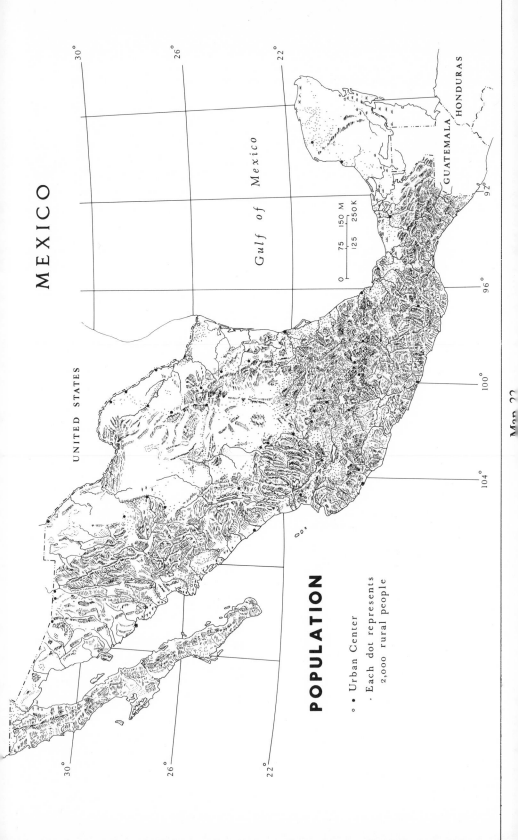

MEXICO

UNITED STATES

Gulf of Mexico

GUATEMALA
HONDURAS

30°
26°
22°

96°
100°
104°
92°

M
250 K
150
125
75
0

POPULATION

○ Urban Center
· Each dot represents
  2,000 rural people

Map 22

wealthy and enjoyed political power. In the central part of the country some 95 percent of the heads of rural families owned no land. The most striking contrast existed between the educated, gay, cosmopolitan, and very wealthy society surrounding the dictator and the great majority of the Mexicans who were illiterate, sick, and hopeless in their poverty. But under Díaz there was order and security, and foreign businessmen in the United States, Great Britain, and Germany thought of Mexico as a safe place in which to do business.

Díaz was eighty years old when he was reelected president of Mexico for the eighth time in October 1910. There was no outward sign of the impending explosion, unless it was the appearance of Halley's comet which presaged for the superstitious peasants the coming of disaster. Because by this time almost all of the wealth of Mexico was concentrated in the hands of less than 3 percent of the people, the regime was undermined largely because not enough people had a stake in it. Suddenly violence, disorder, and revolution appeared. Even the army and the police deserted the dictator, who was forced to flee for his life.

The amazing thing is that the Mexican Revolution (1910–15) was not diverted into traditional channels. After 1915 the government was captured by a succession of leaders, more or less honest, more or less able, but all devoted to the social transformation of Mexico. *La Revolución* is a word that has been used now by several generations of Mexicans and has become a common part of the national tradition and the popular vocabulary. This is a state-idea in the making, even if not every one agrees about what the revolution has been doing.

But the struggle to establish a coherent society in Mexico has been carried on in the midst of great difficulties. Diversity in the Mexican scene is not solely a matter of racial and cultural differences. Diversity is also produced by the physical land itself. Mexico has a little of everything. In addition to the spectacular snow-capped volcanoes there are rugged surfaces throughout the country where the slopes are so steep that the people who live on them think in terms of "up and down" rather than north, south, east, and west. Two-thirds of Mexico is like this. The other third is classed as level, but it includes intermont basins, narrow valley bottoms, coastal lowlands, and a wide limestone plain where solution has produced underground rivers and sinks. There are parts of Mexico so high that the air is cool, even in summer; there are also low-lying regions where the temperature, especially in summer, is very high. About half of Mexico, including the desert regions of the north and northwest, is deficient in moisture; but the other half receives an abundance of moisture.

The Mexican population is notably centralized. This is so whether we regard Mexico as a whole or look more closely at any one of the Mexican communities. The population as a whole is concentrated in one central area in the central highlands, and the outlying districts are occupied by a relatively scanty population scattered in small groups. When the distribution is examined more closely we find that even the central area is not composed of one cluster of people, but of several separate clusters, each with its own urban nucleus, each separated from neighboring clusters by thinly populated territory. The national life focuses on Mexico City; but in a similar way every smaller town and every little village is the focus of life in the community of which it is the center. The dominance of the center over the periphery appears again and again in all phases of Mexican life; and the contrast between the concentrated population of the cities, towns, and villages and that of the thinly scattered rural settlements is very great.

Is Mexico a rich land or a poor land? This question has been argued by extremists on both sides since Cortés first reported to his king that he had found a land of superlative resources. Mexico is a rich land for the mining engineer who encounters little difficulty in locating the ores where the rivers have done the work of excavation and where the coverage of vegetation is scanty. Mexico is incomparable for the tourist who seeks spectacular scenery and who can find something picturesque in poverty. Mexico could be made into a very productive meat or dairy land, for it possesses notable physical advantages for these forms of economy. But for farming, Mexico is a poor land, since so much of its area is either too steep or too dry to be classed as arable. And most of the Mexicans are farmers.

Mexico was the first of the Latin-American countries to translate the discontent of the overwhelming majority of its people into political action. In the background were many generations during which economic rewards and political power had been concentrated in the hands of a smaller and smaller minority of the people. In a land repeatedly described as containing incredible natural riches, most of the people were living in poverty. Whether we in the United States approve or disapprove of what the Mexicans have done is not the question: but it is important that we understand what has been done and that we observe the results in the establishment of a coherent state.

The Peoples and Cultures of Mexico

The varied assortment of peoples and cultures that comprise the population and the way of life in Mexico is largely the result of the mixture of Indian and Spanish ingredients. Many millions of Indians were already firmly intrenched on the land in central and southern Mexico at the time of the Spanish conquest.[2] These were the numerous Indian tribes shown on Map 5 (p. 14), including the sedentary agricultural people of the Aztec Empire. These were the Indian communities whose distribution determined, if any one factor can be said to have determined, the course and pattern of Spanish settlement. The Spanish contribution to the racial make-up of the present-day population has been relatively small. The number of registered emigrants

[2]For a discussion of Indian groups see pp. 8–13.

who left Spain during the colonial period destined to enter the territory administered from Mexico City, in New Spain, was only 300,000. Although each registration might include members of the family and servants, the total number of Spanish immigrants to New Spain must have been small compared with the number of Indians already in Mexico. Nevertheless the Spaniards possessed the advantage of technical knowledge which assured their political and economic conquest of the much more numerous native peoples. Today Mexico is a strange mixture of Indian and Spanish elements—a mixture which is not only biological, but also cultural.

Racial Composition of the Mexican People

Merely to state that in Mexico one major ingredient in the racial composition of the population is the Indian is to obscure the fact that the Indians themselves were diverse in origin and in culture. While today Spanish is the common language throughout Mexico, it is nevertheless significant that, in 1950, the taking of the census required the use of fifty different languages, and that 7 percent of the people neither spoke nor understood Spanish. More than 80 percent of the people of Mexico are Indians of one kind or another. Pure-blooded Indians, however, are estimated to make up only 30 percent, whereas Indians with some white ancestors make up at least 60 percent of the total. The people of unmixed European descent comprise about 10 percent.

These proportions have been changing gradually through the decrease in the number of the people of unmixed ancestry and the increase of the mestizo type. In 1805, the people of unmixed European descent were estimated to make up about 19 percent of the total. At that time the pure-blooded Indian group was estimated at 40 percent, and the mestizos at 41 percent. During the colonial period more than 30,000 Africans were brought in to work on the sugar plantations and in other enterprises, but by 1805 the number of pure Africans amounted to only about 21,000, or 0.2 percent of the total. The proportion of Africans is now less than one percent.

The Indian contribution to the Mexican mestizo is a relatively large one. The mestizo of Mexico has more Indian ancestors than he has white ancestors. During the whole colonial period, as we have said, a relatively small number of Europeans were listed as departing from Spain for New Spain. Few reinforcements have come from outside since Mexico became independent. Díaz, to be sure, attempted to stimulate European immigration, and about 11,000 Italians actually came to Mexico shortly after 1878, but by 1890 not more than 5,000 were left. Since then, the number of Europeans who have come to Mexico has been negligible. From a racial point of view Mexico is overwhelmingly Indian rather than Latin.

Growth of the Mexican Population

Until recently the growth of the Mexican population has not been rapid. After the decimation of the Indians by diseases introduced as a result of the Spanish conquest, the number of people in the country began slowly to increase again. It is estimated that, in 1805, Mexico had a population of about 5,800,000—probably less than the Indian population of the same territory three centuries earlier. At the same time there were approximately the same number of people in the United States. After 1824 the Mexican population required eighty years to double itself, while the United States, during the same period of time, partly because of its flood of European immigrants, made one of the largest numerical increases that history records. The Mexican population in 1956 was estimated at over 30,500,000, while that of the United States was nearly 170,000,000. Since 1950, however, the Mexican population has been growing at a faster and faster rate—chiefly as a result of the widespread application of modern hygiene and medicine. Between 1958 and 1964 the average annual rate of increase was 3.2 percent.

The Mexican birth rate is extraordinarily high. During the 1950's it was about 46 per thousand—almost twice as high as that of the United States. The birth rate has been very high as far back as the statistical data make such computations possible. Yet until the 1950's the areas of concentrated settlement in Mexico had changed little. There have been no frontiers of pioneer farming around stabilized cores of dense population. In fact the total population of the country grew only at a moderate rate.

Two chief facts account for the slow rate of population increase and for the lack of settlement expansion. First was the very high death rate which, until 1950, was among the highest in all Latin America. In 1930 it was 26.6 per thousand (compared with death rates at that same time of about 22 per thousand in Guatemala, 20 in El Salvador, 20 in Chile, 18 in Colombia, and 10 in Argentina). About a quarter of all deaths were of children under one year of age: one child out of every eight born died within the first year. The diseases were those caused by malnutrition and bad hygiene—diarrhea, enteritis, and dysentry; but respiratory diseases, also, were widespread, especially on the high plateau around Mexico City. Today all these death rates, Mexico's included, have been considerably lowered. In 1966 the Mexican death rate was down to 9.5 per thousand, and the others quoted above have been similarly lowered—which, of course, is the chief cause of the high net increase of population characteristic of Latin America as a whole.

The second reason for the slow rate of population increase in past years is that Mexico, during the whole four-and-a-half centuries of European dominance, has been a country of emigration. During the colonial period Mexico supplied most of the people of pure Spanish descent and the people of mestizo blood who occupied the Philippine Islands. From the Pacific port of

Acapulco many Mexicans set sail across the ocean to this still more distant colony of Spain. In the modern era large numbers of Mexicans have emigrated to the United States. Mexicans today form an important "minority" group in all the border states from Texas to California, and also in some of the large industrial cities of the north, such as Chicago and Detroit. Mexico, Chile, and El Salvador are alone among the countries of mainland America in having experienced persistent movements of emigration.

Poor health and emigration both betray the existence of poverty—and poverty among the great majority of the Mexican people has been the normal condition of life. Perhaps we must blame the land for its low productivity of essential foods; or perhaps the blame should be placed on the manner in which the Mexicans made use of the land. We must remember the principle, already stated, that the significance of the land base changes with the attitudes, objectives, and technical abilities of the inhabitants. Before turning to a consideration of the characteristics of the Mexican land, therefore, we must attempt to form a picture of those elements of the Mexican way of living which have contributed to a chronic condition of poverty—a traditional land problem.

Attitude toward the Land

In the central area of dense population the traditional attitude toward land was based on a mixture of Spanish and Indian ideas. To a certain extent these ideas were in strong contrast, but in other respects they ran closely parallel. The difference between the communal system of tenure and the system of private property which separates the European and the native Indian groups in many countries of Latin America was less pronounced in Mexico owing to the existence of parallel institutions among the Aztecs and the Spaniards. In at least two ways the Aztecs had developed concepts of the private ownership of land, even though a primitive agricultural communism remained the predominant form of tenure. The lands held by the *calpulli,* or the clan, included certain tracts which were owned and operated by the whole group in common, but they also included other tracts which were partitioned among the heads of families and thereafter were regarded as essentially private property which could be passed on by inheritance. The second form of private property in land formed an even closer parallel to the Spanish forms: certain of the Aztec nobles had assumed the role of feudal lords, having the right to the services of the inhabitants of specific communities. Long before the Spaniards came upon the scene a considerable proportion of the Mexican people were bending under the burden of a landed aristocracy.

Nor were the Spaniards unacquainted with the idea of communal land ownership. Although the large private estate was the common form of land tenure among the Spaniards, the typical Spanish agricultural village held title in common to three kinds of land which were definitely excluded from private ownership. There were certain areas operated in common which were devoted to the support of the village government; there were common pastures and woodlands; and there was the open tract, located just outside the village gates, used in common for a variety of activities, but not for raising crops or for grazing animals. This tract was known in Spain as the *ejido,* literally the "way out," because of its location on the way out of the village.

Yet in spite of the existence of these parallel institutions the essential contrast between the Spanish and the Indian attitude toward the land remained enormous. For the Spaniard, the sure road to prestige and economic security was the private estate. Only the very small group of Aztec nobles thought of land ownership as bringing prestige. The majority of the Indian farmers who actually used the land thought of their little plots as belonging to the community, and thought only of producing enough for their own needs. Commercial farming was unknown to the Indians. The few items taken to the local markets provided, then as now, more of an excuse for the producer to take part in the social pleasures of the market place than an element of economic support. If a few ears of maize or a piece of pottery offered for sale should actually be sold early in the day, the Mexican Indian would think of this transaction as a loss rather than as a gain. McBride estimates that the agricultural holdings were small, averaging only a few acres, hardly enough to provide even the bare necessities of food. Land was not held for profit; even among the nobles, the buying and selling of land was unknown.

The Spanish-Indian Impact

The Spanish system of the *encomienda* did not differ greatly from the Aztec system of tribute. The ruling Aztecs exploited the labor of the people they had conquered, and the Spaniards simply carried on where the Aztecs left off. In many instances the same units were taken over, a Spanish officer taking the place of an Aztec lord without further dislocation of the system. Cortés himself received from the Crown grants of *encomiendas* in various parts of Mexico, including 22 villages with a total population of about 23,000, occupying an area of roughly 25,000 square miles. By 1572 there were 827 *encomiendas* in Mexico, most of them located in the central area between Jalisco and Oaxaca, and in the Maya area of Yucatán.

The system of the *encomienda,* however, did not survive the first century of the Spanish Conquest. In its place the grant of large tracts of land by the Spanish Crown gave the owner actual title to the land, not just the right to the collection of tribute. Gradually the *encomienda* system was given up, and in the course of time more and more of the land was put into private hands. Some of the grants were small ones of less than one hundred acres; but many were much larger, consisting of many thousands of acres.

The Spaniards also brought certain parts of Mexico under their control through the establishment of missions. Especially on the remote northern frontier, the Jesuit, Franciscan, and Dominican orders founded new centers of settlement, and around each center they brought together the Indians from many small scattered communities and reestablished them on the land as farmers, teaching new agricultural techniques and importing new crops, and, incidentally, exposing the Indians to the ravages of epidemics.

The impact of the Spaniards on the Indians produced a struggle which lasted for more than four hundred years. This was the struggle for the right to own land. It involved two contrasted forms of tenure: the *ejido,* or landholding agrarian community occupied chiefly by persons of Indian descent; and the hacienda, or large privately owned, feudal estate, usually in the hands of persons of unmixed or nearly unmixed Spanish descent. By 1823 there was scarcely any good land left that was not in private hands, yet there were only about 10,000 owners of land. The Church, at that time, was the largest single landowner. By the end of the Díaz regime in 1910, a program of encouraging the shift of vast areas of public domain into private range lands had brought almost all of the country under private ownership. At this time in all but five states over 95 percent of the heads of rural families owned no land. Some eleven million rural people (out of a total population of over fifteen million) were living in small, isolated communities, raising their own subsistence crops on land they rented for that purpose, and gaining a miserable additional wage by working for the owners. The great majority of the Mexicans were living monotonously, in isolation, ignorance, and poverty, and plagued by bad diet and disease. Such was the dark picture which formed the background of the brilliant aristocratic society of the capital in the days of Porfirio Díaz. In no other Latin-American country had the concentration of land ownership in the hands of a few people gone so far.

The Mexican hacienda was more than a large land property—it was also a way of living. Ownership of a hacienda provided two things which every Mexican desired but few could hope to achieve: social prestige and economic security. Because the owner was relatively free from land and labor costs, he was able to sell his products profitably even when they were inefficiently produced and when transportation costs were high. In contrast to the almost complete self-sufficiency of the rural worker, the landowner was closely tied to the world of commerce. His standard of living was high, his diet varied and hearty; his children were educated in Europe, and the whole family had frequent opportunities to travel and develop a cosmopolitan familiarity with the outside world. Usually the hacienda owner left his estate in the hands of a manager while he and his family established their home in Mexico City or in Europe. On the occasions when the owner visited his hacienda each worker would stand, hat in hand, as this strange person from another world rode by.

Under these circumstances the establishment of an ordered society could only be accomplished through a strong central authority. Barely under the surface there was unrest and banditry. Even the revolt of 1810, which started Mexico on the road to independence, was at first an agrarian uprising. In

1857, Benito Juárez came to power with a similar movement; but like the others it was soon turned away from its basic objective—doing something about the land problem. To a considerable extent, Mexican laborers who had been in the United States and had returned were responsible for increasing the widespread discontent of the people with a system in which they participated so little. The Mexican Revolution (indicated by capital letters to distinguish it from minor revolts) which started with Madero in 1910 and ended with Carranza in 1915 was the conflict that set the stage for really fundamental reforms.

The famous Article 27 of the Constitution of 1917[3] attempts to formulate a new concept regarding private property in land. The concept is based on a functional theory of property—that the right to own property, including land, is dependent on socially harmonious use.

The Present Systems of Land Tenure

The program of land redistribution based on this article has transformed the rural life of Mexico. Between 1916 and 1934 some 25 million acres of hacienda lands were expropriated and assigned to peasant communities, in which a total of 939,000 farmers actually received land. During the presidency of Lázaro Cárdenas from 1934 to 1940, however, there was a great acceleration of the program, and in this period almost 50 million acres changed hands, and more than 7,700,000 individuals received land. By 1950 about 90 million acres had been taken from the haciendas and given to farmers in peasant communities. The hacienda as an economic unit and as a social institution was eliminated.

In Mexico, the word *ejido* refers to a farming community which has received land in accordance with the procedures set up under the constitution of 1917. The *ejido* is a rural, peasant community, a farm village. In Mexico as a whole the average number of families in each *ejido* is less than a hundred. In two areas the *ejidos* are organized as collectives; everywhere else the lands belonging to the *ejidos* have been divided into private farms. Each family works its own farm, and in most ways treats it as private property. However, the land thus parceled out cannot be sold, and if the family moves away the title to the property remains with the *ejido*. The *ejido* is organized politically, with a general assembly, an executive committee, and a vigilance committe to watch the executives. Technical assistance, education, and credit are furnished by the federal government.

The amount of land granted to each *ejidatario* (head of an *ejido* family) was supposed to be varied according to the potential productivity of the land.

[3]Based on the decree issued by Carranza on January 6, 1915, and incorporated in the constitution of February 5, 1917; now somewhat reformed in the decree of December 30, 1933. See E. N. Simpson, *The Ejido, Mexico's Way Out.* Chapel Hill, N.C., 1937; and Frank Tannenbaum, *Mexico: The Struggle for Peace and Bread.* New York, 1952.

If the land could be irrigated, the maximum was first set at 10 acres, later at 15, and then 25 acres. If the land could be cultivated but was dependent on local rainfall, the minimum area was set at 50 acres. If the land were too dry for anything but brush or agave, the minimum was 2,000 acres. Unfortunately, however, Mexico has never had much of its area surveyed on large-scale maps, adequate for the plotting of property lines; and there are few land classification studies showing the distribution of soil, slope, and water supply. As a result, some *ejidos* have found themselves with no land suited for the cultivation of crops at all; some have had no source of water available on the land given to them. Of the more than 60 million acres of *ejido* lands in 1940, only 17 million could be used to raise crops, and of this only 5 million could be irrigated. Since 1940 the expropriation of land and its redistribution to *ejidos* has slowed down because there is no more land available in the areas of concentrated settlement.

Since 1947 another kind of rural holding has made its appearance. This is the small private farm. Land suitable for agriculture in the central area was already redistributed under the *ejido* system; but outside of the central area there was still much land in private holdings, used chiefly for cattle ranching. In 1947 a new colonization law was passed by the government, permitting the expropriation of range land and the establishment of farm colonies. To make this colonization program possible, the government also undertook a major plan of irrigation and reclamation. One of the earliest and best publicized of these colonization schemes was in the valley of the Río Papaloapan, which drains from the mountains of Oaxaca southeast of Mexico City to the Gulf coast south of Veracruz. Flood control and hydroelectric development, combined with the settlement of farmers on private farms, created a whole new community in an area that was previously almost unoccupied. Where the land can be irrigated the farms can be as much as 25 acres in size. Where crops can be raised without irrigation farms can be as much as 500 acres in size.

Land cultivated under the *ejido* system still produces the greater part of Mexico's crops. *Ejidos* produce well over half of the wheat, rice, sesame, henequen, cotton, and tobacco. Yet the yields on *ejido* lands are between 20 and 25 percent lower than on private holdings, due in part to the lack of technical skills. The great cotton-producing area around Torreón, in the north of Mexico, has suffered seriously because lack of rainfall in the mountains to the west has left the great reservoir almost empty. The *ejidos,* more than the new colonies, suffer from lack of careful land surveys to determine in advance the availability of water and the distribution of soils.

These general statements concerning Mexico's revolutionary changes summarize conditions over a great variety of kinds of country. The land redistribution program cannot be properly evaluated without a consideration of the underlying qualities of the land itself, and of differences in land use that distinguish one part of Mexico from another. If it is true that the average

Mexican farmer in an *ejido* is poorer today than he was before the Revolution, as some people insist, then we need to understand the causes.

The Land

To what extent is the prevailing poverty of the Mexican farmers the result of the physical quality of the land? Was this concentration of the population in the central area due to the special agricultural productivity of that area compared with other parts of the country? When the Spaniards first arrived on the scene they were attracted by the areas which were already densely settled by sedentary agricultural Indians, and the outlying regions with their sparse populations were much less attractive. Concentration in the central area was so great that during the Díaz regime an attempt was made to promote the colonization of other parts of the national territory, but with discouraging results. Is this concentration of people in the central area, then, an inevitable result of the physical quality of the land or an evitable result of the way of living? If we assume that the Indians concentrated in Anáhuac, as they called this region, because of its relatively great adaptability to the production of maize as compared with the arid north, should we also assume that Anáhuac is still, even with European techniques, the region of highest productivity in Mexico? Or is the present concentration of people in the central area out of harmony with the potential productivity of the land? These and other problems cannot be answered until we understand more clearly the nature of the physical background of surface and climate.

The Mexican land is one of extraordinary diversity. A large part of the national territory is mountainous, and the mountains include some which have been produced by the erosion of streams in areas of contorted rock structures and some which have been produced by the explosive outburst of volcanic ash and lava. Well over half of Mexico is more than 3,000 feet above the sea; and only about a third of the country can be classed as level. Over all these surface features one finds contrasted types of climate, controlled partly by differences of altitude and partly by relation to the sources of moisture.

Surface Features

The major element of the surface configuration of Mexico is the great highland area which extends from the border of the United States southward to the Isthmus of Tehuantepec and which occupies most of the width of the country (Maps 7 and 18). Although the highland is exceedingly complex in its geologic structure and its surface form, it is convenient for our purposes to think of it as being composed of two chief parts: a *central plateau* and a *dissected border*. The surface of the central plateau is cut by few deep canyons, yet it is by no means flat, for above the moderate slopes of its bolsons and intermont basins stand block ranges and volcanoes. In the north the bolsons are mostly between 3,000 and 4,000 feet in elevation, and the block

The volcano Popocatepetl (17,887 ft.) stands high above the southeastern corner of the Basin of Mexico. In the foreground is the town of Amecameca. *Courtesy of Mexican National Tourist Council.*

ranges rise about 3,000 feet above them. South of the Bolson de Mayrán the general level of the plateau rises: the intermont basins are mostly between 7,000 and 8,000 feet, although some are as low as 5,000 feet; and above these basins great volcanoes reach elevations between 12,000 and more than 18,000 feet. The dissected borders of the highland, unlike the central plateau, have been deeply cut by streams. Furthermore, the relief of the western and eastern dissected borders is made more rugged by deep acccumulations of volcanic material, so that on these two sides the rim of the highlands is higher than the central part. On the southern dissected border, south of Mexico City, the general highland level between 6,000 and 8,000 feet is preserved, not in the basins, but on the ridge crests, and streams have cut deep valleys below what was a continuous surface.

Outside of the great highland region with its dissected borders, there are three other surface divisions of Mexico: the block mountains and basins in the northwest; the lowlands of the Gulf coast and Yucatán on the east; and the highlands of Chiapas on the border of Guatemala.

In the northwest, the surface features of southern California and Arizona continue into Mexico. The peninsula of Lower California is made up of tablelands and terraces surmounted by a few isolated block ranges with structures similar to those of the mountains east of San Diego. The Sonora desert which lies between the Gulf of California and the Sierra Madre Occidental is a mountain-and-bolson country, similar to the Mohave of southeastern California. Even the structural depression which forms the Imperial Valley of California continues southward to form the Gulf of California. Throughout the Mexican northwest rocky surfaces predominate, cut at wide intervals by the steep-sided, flat-bottomed valleys typical of arid lands.

On the eastern side of the highlands, the Gulf Coastal Plain of Texas continues southward into Mexico as far as Tampico, where it is pinched out by the outliers of the Sierra Madre Oriental and by isolated volcanic necks which stand abruptly above the general level of the plain. South of Tampico the coastal lowland is relatively narrow and in many places is broken by promontories where the highlands extend to the edge of the water. The lowlands bordering the gulf widen out again, however, at the northern end of the Isthmus of Tehuantepec, and the whole of the Yucatán Peninsula is a low-lying plain, interrupted by only a few groups of hills. Yucatán resembles Florida in that it is made up of horizontal limestone formations of relatively recent age. In the limestone, solution caverns have been opened up, and where the roofs of the caverns have collapsed there are shallow sinks, known in Mexico as *cenotes*. The drainage is underground, and there are numerous clear limestone springs.

The Isthmus of Tehuantepec separates the southern dissected border of the great highland region from the Highlands of Chiapas. This is the northwestern end of the mountainous region which extends through Central America to the lowland of Nicaragua. In Mexico it is composed of parallel ranges of block mountains, enclosing a high rift valley. Along the Pacific is the crystalline range known as the Sierra Madre de Chiapas. Inland from this, and parallel to the coast, is the rift Valley of Chiapas, drained by a tributary of the Río Grijalva. On the northeastern side of this valley there are several other ranges of block mountains, composed of folded and faulted strata and capped with volcanic materials—flows of lava and falls of ash. These mountains are much dissected by streams.

Few indeed are the places in this mountainous land where surfaces of gentle gradient are to be found. And unfortunately, where such surfaces are extensive, the climatic conditions are in one way or another unsuited to the kind of agriculture the Mexicans have wished to practice.

Climates and Natural Vegetation

In a land of such rugged surfaces and of such contrasts of altitude within short distances the climatic conditions and the cover of natural vegetation have extremely spotty and irregular patterns. As in other mountainous countries, however, there is a general vertical zoning which becomes apparent when one disregards the many irregularities of detail.

The vertical zones of Mexico result from the general decrease of average temperatures with increasing altitude. The hot country, which the Mexicans call the *tierra caliente,* reaches to about 2,100 feet above sea level on the slopes of Mt. Orizaba near the east coast. Here there are tropical forests, and the land can be used to grow crops that cannot survive frosts, such as sugarcane. The land above this altitude is called the *tierra templada,* or temperate country. Here oaks are the common trees, and the major crop is coffee. This zone rises to about 6,000 feet. Above this is the zone known as *tierra fría,* or cold country. It includes the zone of conifers, above 11,400 feet as far as the upper limit of trees at about 13,100 feet. Between the tree line and the snow line there is a zone of mountain grasslands suited for the grazing of cattle. The snow line on Mt. Orizaba is about 14,600 feet.

Many writers emphasize the "temperate" nature of the climates of tropical countries at high altitudes. Altitude, they insist, compensates for the high temperatures of the low latitudes. They point out that places near the border of Mexico and the United States have approximately the same temperatures as places in the central plateau around Mexico City. The capital, located south of latitude 20° N., has an average annual temperature of 60.1°, while El Paso, Texas, has an average of 63.0°. This comparison between average annual temperatures, however, only obscures the contrast in real temperatures between these two places. At Mexico City there is not only a much greater regularity in the daily changes of temperature, but the range between the average of the coldest and warmest months is very much less than the range at El Paso. A comparison follows:

COMPARISON OF TEMPERATURE CONDITIONS

	Mexico City	El Paso
Average of the year	60.1	63.0
Average of the warmest month	65.1 (May)	81.0 (July)
Average of the coldest month	54.3 (Jan.)	44.4 (Jan.)
Range between the monthly averages	10.8	36.6

Incidentally, El Paso, with a range between monthly averages of 36.6°, has a greater difference of temperature between summer and winter than any station in all of Latin America, including the similar latitudes of the southern hemisphere. The difference between a 10-degree range and a 36-degree range spells the difference between a middle-latitude climate and the climate of a place at a high altitude in the tropics.

Most of the Mexican territory is deficient in moisture at least for part of the year.[4] The whole northern border of Mexico from the Pacific to the

[4]An estimate of the relative areas of arid, semiarid, and rainy country in Mexico based on Thornthwaite's classification gives the following percentages of the total area:

Deficient in moisture throughout the year	49.9 percent
Deficient in moisture in the summer	1.4 percent
Deficient in moisture in the winter	35.9 percent
Deficient in moisture at no season	12.8 percent

mouth of the Rio Grande passes through arid or semiarid climates. The very dry sections are in the northwest and in the north central parts. A belt of arid country extends southward from western Texas almost to San Luis Potosí. Semiarid country includes all of the central plateau of the highlands except the southern and southwestern part—bounded by a line drawn roughly from Aguascalientes to Mexico City.

Climates with a rainy season which is not very rainy and a dry season which is really dry cover most of the rest of the country. The rainy season in Mexico generally comes in summer; but the northern part of the northwest shares with California the climatic regimen of winter rains and summer droughts. The central area receives most of its rain in summer, between June and September, during which period rain falls almost every day and the sky is generally filled with towering cumulus clouds. In fact, so cloudy is the summer season in this part of Mexico that the maximum temperatures are experienced in May rather than July (see the climatic data for Mexico City in Appendix A, p. 895).

Areas where the rainfall is adequate at all seasons of the year occur in only two sections of Mexico. There is one belt of dependable rainfall which extends southward from Tampico along the lower slopes of the Sierra Madre Oriental and crosses the Isthmus of Tehuantepec into the state of Tabasco. The other rainy section is along the Pacific coast of Chiapas, southeast of the Isthmus of Tehuantepec. These two areas together make up only about 12 percent of the Mexican territory.

In order to estimate the importance of these physical qualities of surface and climate in terms of the distribution of people in Mexico it is necessary to examine the various parts of the country in somewhat greater detail. For this purpose we shall follow the general divisions of Mexico used by the Mexican government in which the different states are put together in five groups or regions. It must be emphasized that these are not natural divisions of Mexico, but follow arbitrary state boundaries: their chief value is that they permit the use of statistics which are gathered and averaged by states. These five divisions with the states included in each of them are listed below (Maps 17–22):

1. *The North Pacific region:* Baja California Norte, Baja California Sur, Sonora, Sinaloa, Nayarit.

2. *The North:* Chihuahua, Coahuila, Nuevo León, Tamaulipas, Durango, Zacatecas, San Luis Potosí.

3. *The Gulf Coast and Yucatán:* Veracruz, Tabasco, Campeche, Yucatán, Quintana Roo.

4. *The South Pacific region:* Guerrero, Oaxaca, Chiapas, Colima.

5. *The Central region:* Aguascalientes, Jalisco, Guanajuato, Querétaro, Hidalgo, Michoacán, México, Distrito Federal, Morelos, Tlaxcala, Puebla.

The North Pacific Region

The North Pacific region extends roughly from Cape Corrientes to the border of the United States. Including 21 percent of the total area of Mexico, the North Pacific region is occupied by only about 7 percent of the Mexican people. Like the west coasts of all the continents between 20° and 30° of latitude, this is a desert, and the human settlement is closely attached to the wet spots. On its eastern side it is bounded by the exceptionally rugged Sierra Madre Occidental. This range of mountains, some 150 miles wide and 750 miles long, is crossed by only three lines of communication. The first of the three to be developed was the old colonial route from Guadalajara to Tepic. At first just a road for wagons, it later became a railroad route, and is now the route of one of the three paved motor highways that connect Mexico City with the United States. During the 1950's another road for motor trucks was built between Durango and Mazatlán. And in 1961 a railroad was completed all the way from the border of Texas, through Chihuahua, and across some of the most spectacular terrain in North America to the Pacific port of Topolobampo (Map 19).

The Sierra Madre Occidental

Except for these three routes across it, the Sierra Madre Occidental remains one of the most thinly populated parts of Mexico (Map 22). On its eastern side the mountains rise gradually from the bolsons of Chihuahua and Durango; but on the western front of the mountains there is a bold escarpment, only notched at a few places by deeply incised stream canyons. Within the mountain area the surface is extremely rugged: steep-sided longitudinal ranges with conspicuously even summits rise to elevations of about 10,000 feet; between them, deep longitudinal valleys connected by short transverse gorges have been cut along the lines of weaker rock by the torrential streams. A luxuriant cover of forest and grass offers shelter and food for a variety of game animals; and from these animals a nomadic hunting people gain a living.

Throughout the course of human history in Mexico, the Sierra Madre has played the part of a region of survival for weaker peoples. The Indians who were able to derive a meager living from the steep, forest-covered slopes, found that these same slopes and forests afforded them protection from their more aggressive neighbors. The tribes of this region not only escaped the exploitation and destruction which was the lot of their more accessible brothers during the Spanish colonial period, but even to this day they have few and only remote contacts with the centers of Mexican life.

SONORA, SINALOA, AND NAYARIT

The three states of Sonora, Sinaloa, and Nayarit, west of the western front of the Sierra Madre, descend toward the Pacific Ocean and the Gulf of California through country broken by ranges and basins. A series of terraces and flows of lava have been dissected by the streams descending from the Sierra Madre into isolated mesas and plateaus interspersed with flat valleys. Along the coast there is a lowland which varies in width from less than 10 to more than 50 miles. The summers in this area are very hot and rainy; the winters are mild and very dry. The length of the growing season, the amount of rainfall, and the number of streams bringing water down from the Sierra Madre all decrease toward the north, reaching a minimum along the border between Arizona and Sonora.

When the first Spanish explorers descended to the Pacific coast from the primary settlement center of Guadalajara, they encountered a variety of Indian cultures (Map 5, p. 14). A few of the tribes were carrying on intensive agriculture with irrigation. Especially in the south, in what is now Nayarit and Sinaloa, a sedentary farming people were raising maize, beans, and squash on the river floodplains. The Indian population, however, was neither rich enough in accumulated stores of gold and silver, nor numerous enough to attract any considerable Spanish settlement. The sedentary Indians of Nayarit and Sinaloa were divided into *encomiendas* and plundered by the explorers who first reached them (1530–31); within the first few decades of the conquest these Indians were all but wiped out by the combination of slave raids and the ravages of disease. Exploring parties which marched far to the north, seeking the fabulous cities of Cíbola, failed to discover any dense Indian populations comparable to those of the highlands between Guadalajara and Puebla, or any rich mines of precious metals. Eventually the more accessible southern part of the North Pacific region was divided into large private haciendas, and the remnants of the Indians were forced to work for their new masters.

A different form of settlement, however, was applied to the more remote country north of central Sinaloa. Northern Sinaloa, Sonora, Baja California, and California were settled by the mission system. The Jesuits were the first in the field, when, in 1590, they started the work of converting and subduing the native peoples of the territory beyond the limits of Spanish settlement. The northern outpost of settlement at that time was Culiacán. The usual practice was to establish a mission at a location carefully selected in advance, and around this mission to attempt to gather together the Indians formerly scattered over a wide extent of territory. Before the arrival of the missionaries, the native peoples lived in small groups; some were seminomadic hunters and fishers, but some practiced sedentary farming with maize, beans, and squash as their chief crops. The Fathers introduced new crops, taught methods of irrigation or adapted the Indian methods, and grouped the Indians into compact communities where they could be instructed in the Christian faith.

Unfortunately, however, the results were disastrous. The crowded settlements were exposed to the spread of contagious diseases imported from Europe: within a very brief period of time the mission settlements were decimated by epidemics of smallpox, measles, and other forms of pestilence. After an epidemic came famine: whole villages, stricken at the time of planting or harvesting, were unable to carry on the agricultural work on which they depended. When a settlement was so reduced that it could no longer exist alone, it was abandoned and its members were transferred to other mission communities. The land which was abandoned passed into the hands of a Spanish grantee, who used it for the grazing of herds of cattle, horses, and mules. Thus, step by step, the lands on which the Indians had depended for their subsistence became the private property of the conquerors.

In the centuries following the rapid destruction of the Indians which accompanied the northward advance of the frontier there was slow recuperation. Sauer estimates that the native population of what is· now roughly the territory of the three states under discussion was at the time of the conquest about 540,000. The population of the same area did not again reach this figure until about 1920—almost four hundred years later.

The hacienda system was firmly established in this part of the Northwest until it was broken up during the 1930's. Only in the remote and isolated valleys of the Sierra Madre Occidental did small Indian village communities survive with their traditional communal holdings. Almost all the good lands which were accessible were included in haciendas, on which the Indians lived and worked in increasing poverty. The land owners used the fertile irrigated valley bottoms for wheat (which the Indian workers did not eat), for cotton, oranges, and such Mediterranean crops as dates, figs, olives, and grapes. The basic food of the workers, maize, was grown mostly on the poorer lands; and on the same steep or arid farms on which the peasants grew their maize, they also raised beans, squash, and chili. When the mines in this region were active, workers were recruited from the neighboring territory; but when the mines shut down, as they did periodically for reasons wholly incomprehensible to the Indian workers, the latter drifted back to the haciendas, adding more hungry mouths to be fed. The gradual increase of population meant a gradual decline in the standard of living, for there could be no extension of the arable lands without expensive irrigation, and there could be no increase of yield per acre without a fundamental change in the farm practices.

These fundamental changes have now been made. First came the agrarian reform which eliminated the hacienda as an economic unit. In the southern part of the North Pacific region the haciendas were replaced by *ejidos* and small private farms. In the north, where irrigation is essential for the support of any agriculture, settlement since 1957 has been in government-sponsored colonies where the colonists own their own farms. Eight large dams were built

—all since World War II—on the rivers descending from the Sierra Madre Occidental. Millions of acres of new agricultural land were developed, and farms were provided for pioneer settlers mostly from the central area of Mexico.

The improvement and expansion of agriculture was the first part of the government plan for economic development in this central region. In a hot, arid climate, where sunshine is plentiful, crops grow luxuriantly if only water can be provided, and if modern techniques of drainage are used to cut down the formation of alkali (sodium salts) in places where evaporation is high. This part of Mexico is now the leading source of cotton and wheat. Vegetables such as tomatoes, melons, peas, beans, cucumbers, peppers, and garbanzos grow so rapidly that they can be exported to markets in the eastern United States a month ahead of the vegetables from California, Texas, and Florida. The pioneer farmers have been able to realize substantial profits. As a result, little towns that were sleepy and drab only a decade ago are now thriving, with new buildings to house people, offices, and retail stores. The whole economy of the region is thriving on the new activities.

The government plans for regional development did not stop with agriculture. There has been a large increase in fishing and in a variety of manufacturing industries since 1960. The Mexican government has been promoting a more varied diet, to replace the once almost exclusive use of maize. The Mexican fisheries are making an important contribution to this improvement of diet. Off the coast of Baja California there are tuna and sardines; a large shrimp bed has been found in the warm waters of the Gulf of California. Mazatlán in Sinaloa and Guaymas in Sonora now have new large freezing plants to handle the enlarged shrimp catch. This area now provides three-quarters of the Mexican shrimp. Mazatlán also has a new ship-building industry, aided by foreign investments from the Netherlands. In the late 1960's enlarged port facilities were built at Topolobampo, at the Pacific end of the railroad crossing the Sierra Madre Occidental from Chihuahua. Topolobampo is now a major shipping port for cargoes of cotton on the way to Japan.

In the state of Sonora there are also numerous small mining communities. Some of these have suffered a decline, partially a result of the Mexican policy of nationalizing all mining activities. In the late 1960's, however, new government-owned copper refineries at Cananea in Sonora and near Santa Rosalía in Baja California (Map 21) began a new effort at mining copper in these areas by rebuilding old mines and sinking new shafts. Cananea produces a large part of Mexico's copper exports.

Baja California

Isolated from the main routes of travel along the eastern side of the Gulf of California is the long narrow peninsula which forms the state of Baja California Norte (formed in 1951), and the territory of Baja California Sur

(Map 17). The surface and climate of the northern part of this peninsula are similar to those found in southern California around San Diego. At the shore of the Pacific a sea-cliff marks the first of the terraces which rise step by step toward the east. The underlying rocks are crystalline, and these appear at the surface in several places; but mostly the terraces are covered with sedimentary strata and lava flows. They are surmounted by a few ranges of block mountains, the highest of which reach about 9,000 feet. Although these ranges receive more rainfall than the very dry terrace lands, especially in the south, there is no such abundance of permanent streams as can be found in the country on the east of the Gulf of California. In Baja California there is, except for the Colorado, only one permanent stream; this is a short one near the southern end of the peninsula. The terraces, therefore, are not so much dissected as those of Sonora; there are vast areas of dry uplands, interrupted at wide intervals by steep-sided, gravel-filled valleys in which surface water appears only after a rain, but where settlement can be supported by wells. All but the southern tip of the peninsula is deficient in moisture; the northern half receives most of the small annual rainfall during the winter, as does San Diego; the southern half receives only summer rains. The winters are mild, and the summers generally cool.

Baja California was settled by the mission system. The Jesuits founded their first settlement at Loreto in 1697, and from this place new settlement spread to the southern end of the peninsula, and northward as far as latitude 30° N. After the Jesuits were expelled in 1768, the Franciscans continued the work of founding missions farther and farther toward the north; and, after an interval, the Dominicans undertook to establish mission settlements in the still unoccupied parts of Baja California. The results in each case were similar to those which followed the concentration of the Indians around the missions in Sonora and Sinaloa. Epidemics almost wiped out the native population; many of the mission communities were abandoned, and the survivors were gathered around the few remaining settlements. Most of the small clusters of people in Baja California date back to this mission period. In addition there are a few mining communities, such as Santa Rosalía, founded and maintained by a North American copper company.

But the northern part of the peninsula has enjoyed several periods of boom development. Tijuana was a favorite recreation spot for thirsty North Americans during the prohibition era. In recent times it has redeveloped the recreation business, attracting each year many millions of visitors from the United States, eager to spend dollars. The race track, the gambling houses, and other tourist attractions bring in millions of dollars to help support the Mexican economy. This concentration of recreational activities Tijuana owes to its location only a little over a hundred miles from Los Angeles.

Sixty-seven miles south of Tijuana is the new deep-water port of Ensenada. This place has become a major center of the west-coast fishing industry, where sea bass, sardines, and rock lobsters are brought ashore and canned. In addition to the fishermen and port workers, the fish-canning industry at Ensenada gives employment to nearly 5,000 people. Ensenada, too, attracts its share of tourists who come to enjoy the deep-sea fishing.

Tijuana is now connected eastward to Mexicali by a new paved automobile highway. This road climbs the terraces and ranges, where rainfall is greater than along the coast, and then descends into the desert country at the head of the Gulf. Along the road, just south of the United States border, a considerable area of new farm settlement has been made possible. Newly planted vineyards give hope that this may become one of Mexico's chief wine-producing regions.

THE COLORADO DELTA AND THE IMPERIAL VALLEY

The new state of Baja California Norte also includes the irrigated area along the lower Colorado River. In terms of both physical character and human settlement this district is distinctive. The great rift depression which forms the Gulf of California continues across the border into the United States in southeastern California. Downstream from Yuma, Arizona, the Colorado River enters this rift depression from the east and has built a huge delta of coarse alluvium in the shallow water at the head of the Gulf. The delta has completely cut off the water of the Gulf from the northern end of the depression which, today, is occupied only by a shallow salt lake. The part of the depression north of the Colorado Delta lies some two hundred feet below sea level, and water escapes from it only by evaporation. This northern end of the rift, lying partly in Mexico and partly in California, is known as the Imperial Valley.

The Imperial Valley is an oasis of great potential productivity. Its importance for the United States is especially great since it is one of the few irrigable areas where temperatures in summer are high and the winters are mild, and where, as a result, such crops as long-staple cotton, semi-tropical fruits, and winter vegetables can be raised. The part of the Imperial Valley in California produces lettuce, melons, dates, as well as cotton.

Development of the Mexican part of the Imperial Valley around the border city of Mexicali has taken place since World War II. For a long time this potentially productive area was handicapped by its isolation. There was no rail connection with the rest of Mexico that did not pass through the United States. To build a port at the mouth of the Colorado River would be very expensive because of the great tidal range at the head of the Gulf. Meanwhile the water of the Colorado was being used for the irrigation of the part of the Imperial Valley north of the border. Even the city of Los Angeles was reaching out to Lake Mead, above Hoover Dam, to add to its inadequate water supply. And at the headwaters of the Colorado, the state of Colorado was diverting water through a boring in the mountains to increase the irrigation of the plains east of the mountains. It was at this time that some settlers from the United States secured land on the Mexican side of the border and started claims for a share of the Colorado water.

Between 1936 and 1938, in the period of rapid expropriation, the land in the Mexicali district was taken from the foreign owners and distributed among Mexican peasants. An agreement was reached between Mexico and the United States regarding the use of water along the border—including not only Colorado water but also Rio Grande water, as we shall see. And a railroad was built to connect Mexicali with the main line running southward from Nogales. The Mexican farmers, however, were too poor to buy seed, or fertilizer, or agricultural machinery, or to undertake the development of irrigation. The Mexican government has now provided for the use of its share of the Colorado water to irrigate some 500,000 acres on the Mexican side of the border. And a Mexican subsidiary of Anderson, Clayton and Company has invested in ginning equipment and has provided credit for farmers. There has been an enormous increase in cotton production in this area, so that now it ranks second among the cotton-producing areas of Mexico. The city of Mexicali boasts one of the world's major concentrations of industrial equipment for the processing of cotton. The city's population, which was about 65,000 in 1950, is now almost 300,000. Here is another part of the North Pacific region that is undergoing a rapid enlargement of its economic life.

The North

The region known as the North includes 41 percent of the national territory of Mexico. Like the North Pacific region, this area also suffers from deficient rainfall, and any expansion of production or population is dependent on the construction of new irrigation works. The region is occupied by only about 20 percent of the Mexican population. With the exception of a few spots, the whole border between Mexico and the United States passes through very thinly inhabited country.

The north of Mexico is the remnant of the vast territory she once claimed but mostly did not occupy, extending to the borders of Canada. Settlement in what is now the United States did take place in the colonial period in a few places. Missions carried the frontier of Spanish settlement northward along the Rio Grande Valley, where Santa Fé was at one time an important Spanish outpost. San Antonio in Texas was established under similar circumstances. The Texas prairies north and east of San Antonio were used by the Spaniards for the grazing of cattle and the breeding of mules. The silver mines of New Spain offered a continued market for mules and meat, and the Texas prairies were the nearest wet grazing lands. Spanish claims extended much farther north than the area actually occupied.

The westward movement of pioneers from the eastern part of the United States constitutes one of the great epics of history, even if the details of the story are not always pleasant. These Anglo-American pioneers were not inclined to stop along arbitrary political boundaries, when there was empty land beyond. Instead, they moved on into territory that belonged to Mexico.

Anglo-American settlers began to pour westward first into Texas and then on to San Diego. In 1836 the Anglo-Americans in Texas declared their independence from Mexico and defeated the Mexican troops sent to put down the revolt. For nine years Texas was an independent country, joining the United States in 1845. The result was trouble with Mexico, which broke out into war in 1846. Troops from the United States captured the fort at San Diego, while another expedition invaded Mexico from Veracruz, finally occupying Mexico City. In 1848 Mexico ceded all the territory north of the Rio Grande, and from El Paso westward along the course of the Gila River. It was the Gila, flowing toward its junction with the Colorado at Yuma, that provided water for the westward journey across the dry country to California. In 1853 the strip of territory along the southern border of Arizona and New Mexico known as the Gadsden Purchase was added to the United States in order to provide the best route for the building of a railroad to the Pacific. A minor revision of the border within the city of El Paso resulting from a shift of the Rio Grande was settled in favor of Mexico in 1967.

For the Mexicans, the bitterest aspect of this great loss of territory was the discovery of gold by the Anglo-Americans near Sacramento in California in 1848.

San Luis Potosí, Zacatecas, and Durango

The first part of this great northern country which the Spanish conquerors invaded after they had established themselves in the central area between Puebla and Guadalajara was the part now included in the states of San Luis Potosí, Zacatecas, and Durango. This part of the North is composed of basins and plateaus which stand at about the same altitude as those of the central area in the state of Mexico. The basin of Zacatecas is just over 8,100 feet above sea level. The cities of San Luis Potosí and Durango are both just over 6,000 feet in altitude. The surface between them is composed of expanses of high, semiarid plateaus, with ranges of block mountains standing a few thousand feet above the general level. Most of the streams do not drain out to the sea.

As a matter of fact there is so much similarity between the physical quality of the land in the southern part of the region called the North and the Central region just south of it, that were it not for the significance attached to certain minor differences as a result of the human occupation, a division between them probably would not be made. The Central region is just a little wetter. On the map of climates (Map 11, p. 31), the boundary between the BS climates (semiarid) and the Cwbi climates (rainy summer) passes just south of the cities of Durango, Zacatecas, San Luis Potosí, Querétaro, and Pachuca; it passes just north of Aguascalientes, and Guanajuato. Mexico City is almost exactly on the border between the humid and semiarid climates as determined by the definitions of the Köppen system. That one group of cities is classified as semiarid and the other as humid should not obscure the fact that places so close together on either side of an arbitrary climatic boundary are actually very much alike. Anáhuac, the land of lakes, is only a very little wetter than the country to the north; but to a people migrating southward, Anáhuac must have seemed to be a land of plenty.

The first interest of the Spaniards in the days of the conquest was the search for wealth, especially gold and silver. The first places to be established after Mexico City and Guadalajara were mining towns. Within the first half-century the newcomers had located the chief sources of mineral wealth and started mining activities. The silver ores near Zacatecas were discovered in 1546 and active mining operations were started two years later. Guanajuato began as a mining center in 1554. The other outstanding silver-mining communities which were founded about this time were Pachuca, Querétaro and Aguascalientes in the Central region, and San Luis Potosí and Durango in the North.

These sixteenth-century mining towns became the chief political centers, dominating the territories around them. After Mexico gained its independence from Spain, they became the provincial capitals around which the new states were organized. But these old colonial towns were more than simply political centers: they were also important for smelting and refining industries, at first chiefly for the reduction of the silver ores. During the modern period other minerals have been exploited. Zacatecas today produces not only silver, but also gold and copper. Durango produces silver, gold, copper, lead, and also more than half of Mexico's small supply of iron ore.

The chief difference to be observed in the pattern of population as one passes from the Central region into the North is the decrease in the number of agricultural communities scattered throughout the country around the mining centers (Map 22). In the North the decreasing rainfall restricts agricultural settlement to the irrigable valleys. The change is not abrupt: San Luis Potosí, southern Zacatecas, and southern Durango form a transition zone between conditions characteristic of the Central region, which we shall describe later, and conditions which prevail over the vast dry country farther north.

The Sparsely Settled Mountain-and-Bolson Country

The northern parts of the states of San Luis Potosí, Zacatecas, and Durango, together with most of the states of Chihuahua and Coahuila, are included in the mountain-and-bolson country of the North. The basins, or bolsons, have typical desert landforms. The lower places are occupied by shallow, salty lakes with fluctuating shore-lines, or by salt-encrusted flats. The bolsons are bordered by the gentle slopes of alluvial fans, which only thinly mantle the rock pediments around the base of each range. The ranges themselves, with steep, rocky slopes, stand abruptly above the bolsons.

The basins of this part of the North are much lower than those of the southern border just described. The big Bolson de Mayrán is about 3,600 feet above sea level at its center; the more or less interconnected series of basins which occupy the borders of Durango, Chihuahua, and Coahuila, and which are known collectively as the Bolson de Mapimí, are only a little over 3,000 feet in elevation; in central Coahuila there is one basin which stands only 1,100 feet above sea level.

Mostly this is a land of interior drainage. The streams which rise in the scattered desert ranges lose themselves in the sandy alluvial fans almost at once when they emerge from the mountain ravines; but the larger rivers which rise in the Sierra Madre Occidental and flow eastward in Durango and Chihuahua find their way well out into the deeper depressions. The Bolson de Mayrán used to receive the drainage from two rivers, Río Aguanaval and the Río Nazas.

Only the Rio Grande and its tributaries have succeeded in capturing the drainage of certain parts of this mountain-and-bolson country. The large bolson which lies north of El Paso along the border of Texas and New Mexico is drained by the main Rio Grande. Between El Paso and the junction with the Pecos River, the Rio Grande passes through a succession of deep canyons, interrupted by only a few short stretches where the valley bottom widens out and where irrigated agriculture can be practiced. The Río Conchos, a tributary of the Grande, has cut back from the main stream through a deep gorge to the vicinity of the city of Chihuahua, where it taps the drainage coming from the Sierra Madre Occidental.

Almost all of this part of the North is semiarid or arid. Most of western Chihuahua receives between fifteen and twenty inches of rain a year, with a marked summer maximum. There is a belt of arid climate (BW) which extends southeastward from El Paso across the Bolson de Mapimí and the Bolson de Mayrán into the northern part of the state of San Luis Potosí. Near Torreón in the Bolson de Mayrán the average annual rainfall is only ten inches.

This great northern region was not attractive to the colonial Spaniards. Its scanty, nomadic, warlike Indian population could not compare with the sedentary agricutural Indians of the Central region as producers of wealth. Nor was the North so rich in precious metals as the country south of Durango. The first settlements were mining communities, but they were fewer and not so prosperous as those farther south. Effective settlement was limited to a few spots. The mission system was applied to this frontier, as in the North Pacific region, and many of the present towns owe their origin to that form of settlement.

The greater part of the vast area in this region was utilized then as now for the grazing of cattle (Map 20). Especially in western Chihuahua the summer rains support a good growth of grass on which cattle can feed. The small communities of Indians scattered throughout the region are located where water is available for irrigation, and the size of each community is roughly in proportion to the area which can be moistened. Many such communities have survived to the present time along the streams which form the headwaters of the Río Nazas.

In modern times the mining activities of the North have been more productive than those of any other part of Mexico. The state of Chihuahua with its many mining communities, small and large, usually produces more than a third of all the mineral products of Mexico, exclusive of oil. In this state there are mines of zinc, lead, and gold; but the silver mines are less important than those of the region farther south. The mining communities, like those of Sonora and Baja California, are mostly small and fluctuating in population— by no means permanent features of the map of population, as are those of the Central region. Meanwhile, commercial agriculture has also appeared in the North.

The Laguna District

The Laguna district, located about 200 miles west of Monterrey, occupies a part of the Bolson de Mayrán on the border of Coahuila and Durango. Torreón is the once-thriving urban center for an irrigation district which at one time was the show-piece of the Revolution. Visitors came to Torreón from all over the world to observe the most modern methods of land redistribution. In the mid 1950's the Laguna district produced some 60 percent of the cotton of Mexico; by the mid-1960's it was producing only 13 percent. The Laguna district had become a disaster area, from which farm families were being evacuated to other parts of the country.

It is important to know what happened in the Laguna district. First of all, before the arrival of the Spaniards, this was an area of little interest for the Indian inhabitants, for their irrigation techniques were crude, and they were more interested in hunting than in farming. The almost empty Bolson de Mayrán was given to four large landowners by the Spanish Crown. The present Laguna district, which occupies the western part of the Bolson de Mayrán, was included in a hacienda which had about 1,500 square miles of grazing land. Not until 1850 were these huge grants of land subdivided by sale and inheritance. The new owners used the parts of the Bolson where water was not too far below the surface to grow wheat. For many years the Laguna district was Mexico's chief source of wheat. Indian workers, attracted to the district by the promise of employment, were settled in little villages, around which they were permitted to use some of the land to grow their own subsistence crops, chiefly maize. Wage scales were miserably low, so that even the most industrious workers could never quite supply their families with enough to eat.

The land redistribution program was not applied to the Laguna district during the early years of the Revolution. The hacienda owners were permitted to seek their own solution for the problem of poverty. But as time went on the workers became more and more discontented with the lack of attention to their difficulties. Strikes against the hacienda owners were met by the introduction of thousands of strike breakers from other parts of Mexico. Finally, in 1936, the federal government intervened, and in a brief period of only forty-five days a vast area—over a million acres—was expropriated and redistributed. To the Indian communities went 31 percent of the whole district, and nearly 78 percent of the part of the district classified as irrigable. In the Laguna district 355 separate *ejidos* were established, with the population of about 120,000.

So hurried a division of the land could not have been carried out without error. The surveying was in some places so inaccurate that much confusion and litigation over the new boundaries developed. The lack of a careful survey of the land in advance resulted in a pattern of *ejido* properties which bears only chance relationship to the sources of water—the irrigation canals and the wells. Most serious, however, was the fact that before the land was expropriated the irrigable area was estimated to include 470,000 acres. Actually not more than 312,000 acres proved to be irrigable, which left some of the new property divisions entirely without water. In the effort to provide more water the Lázaro Cárdenas Dam on the Río Nazas was built. But by the mid-1960's ten years of drought in the headwaters of the Nazas and the Aguanaval resulted in the failure of the reservoir behind the new dam ever to fill up. Unfortunately, the lack of rainfall observations, which should have been carried out systematically before the engineering works were undertaken, makes it impossible to be certain whether a less-than-normal rainfall is really responsible for the drought.

When the *ejidos* of the Laguna district were granted lands expropriated from the haciendas, this land was to be cultivated on a communal basis. The government bank granted credit to the community for the purchase of machinery, seed, and fertilizer. It was planned that the work should be done collectively, and each head of a family would be paid according to the amount of work he had completed. But the usual difficulty with such an agricultural system appeared: because of lack of incentive, the individual farmers were not inclined to put in as much work as they might on their own properties. A change in the original collective system was made in the 1950's. The cultivation of the soil and the planting operations were still done on a collective basis. But thereafter each family was allotted a certain area of cotton. On this area the farmer and his family were responsible for bringing the crop to maturity. Harvesting was done collectively, but the individual farmer was credited with the production from his own rows of cotton. A considerable increase of production resulted.

Then came the disastrous decrease in the supply of water. On the average, in each year between 1958 and 1962 there were 235,000 acres of cotton under irrigation in this district; but by 1963 the irrigated acreage had dropped to 114,000 acres, and in subsequent years it dropped even lower. About 70 percent of the irrigated area is still used for cotton, but the total production is only a small part of Mexican cotton production. There are increasing acreages of grazing land for dairy cattle, and some areas are now even used to grow grapes.

The federal government moved thousands of farm families out of the Laguna district in the 1960's. Many have been moved to the new irrigated lands of the North Pacific region, and thousands have also been moved to colonies established in the tropical lowlands along the Gulf of Mexico in the state of Campeche. The building of manufacturing industries in Torreón is also providing employment for some 10,000 people. But there is no clear-cut reason for the disaster in the Laguna district.

Irrigation along the Río Bravo del Norte

Along the Río Bravo del Norte (the Mexican name for the Rio Grande) there are seven irrigation districts, totalling some 476,000 acres, on which the chief commercial crop is cotton. It is important to note that along the lower Rio Grande in Texas there is another irrigated area where subtropical crops can be grown. This is an area devoted to intensive use, producing citrus fruits and truck crops that are shipped all over the United States. But, unlike the lower Colorado River, where the Mexicans are dependent on water flowing out of the United States, the irrigation along the lower Rio Grande on both sides of the border is largely supplied by water flowing out of Mexico in two tributaries that join the Rio Grande northeast of Monterrey. The Río Salado provides most of the water held behind the Falcón Dam on the Rio Grande. It was this fortunate balance along the United States–Mexican border that led to the international agreement regarding water rights.

The first of the seven Mexican irrigation districts is along the Rio Grande valley, just southeast of Ciudad Juárez (37,000 acres). The second is along the valley of the Río Conchos in the state of Chihuahua, just to the east and southeast of the city of Chihuahua. La Boquilla reservoir regulates the flow of water in this area, and permits the irrigation of some 173,000 acres. Third is the small irrigated area near the Rio Grande opposite Eagle Pass (about 25,000 acres). Southwest of this, along one of the headwater tributaries of the Río Salado is a small area of some 3,000 acres that was developed by the former hacienda owner before the land was expropriated. The fifth is along the Río Salado, where the Don Martín reservoir makes enough water available to irrigate 37,000 acres. The sixth area is along the other of the two tributaries of the Rio Grande, the Río San Juan, where there are 141,000 acres under irrigation downstream from the El Azúcar reservoir. Finally, along the lower Rio Grande, opposite the much larger irrigation district in Texas, the Mexicans have some 50,000 acres supplied with water.

The Northern Sierra Madre Oriental and the Gulf Coastal Plain

The remaining part of the North includes the northern end of the Sierra Madre Oriental and the Gulf Coastal Plain north of Tampico.

The Sierra Madre Oriental is almost as great a barrier to communication as the Sierra Madre Occidental. Folded and faulted geologic structures have been eroded by torrential streams to form a bold mountain system through which routes of travel are not easy. South of Monterrey the Sierra is composed of a series of great north–south ranges, rising to elevations between six and twelve thousand feet above sea level, and separated by deep, generally flat-bottomed valleys and basins. Where these ranges are unbroken, passage over them is almost impossible; but in a few places there are breaches in the mountain ramparts. Inland from Tampico the three rivers which unite to form the Río Pánuco have cut headward into the highlands. In this section there is a confusion of very steep-sided valleys and ridges, but openings have been cut in the great ranges, and several passable routes are offered between the piedmont and the highlands. Early in the colonial period a road was built between San Luis Potosí and a port on the Río Pánuco, and now a railroad connects the mining centers of the highlands with Tampico. Farther north, communications between Linares on the piedmont and Galeana within the mountain region have been developed through a gap in the foremost Sierra range.

The most important of the pass routes, however, are in the north. Just at the city of Monterrey, the main fold axes turn from a north–south to an east–west alignment. From Monterrey northward for a short distance there are several easy passes through relatively broad valleys and basins which connect the highlands with the eastern piedmont. The ranges turn northward again in Coahuila before crossing the border into Texas. When Monterrey was founded in 1596, however, it was by no means certain whether the chief route of travel in the future would descend from Saltillo, or whether it would continue northward through Monclova to cross the Rio Grande at Eagle Pass. As a matter of fact the latter route was used more commonly than the route through Monterrey during the period of Spanish and Mexican control of Texas. The preeminence of the city of Monterrey was not assured until 1888, when the railroad from the Texas border at Laredo was built to this place with the objective of using the pass to Saltillo as the route to the highlands and to Mexico City.

Meanwhile, a small population had become established in the Sierra Madre Oriental. Here, as elsewhere, the first land grants included hundreds of square miles. During the succeeding centuries these first estates had been subdivided into somewhat smaller units. The haciendas were still large enough, however, to include good valley bottom land, steep valley sides, and the heavily forested mountains above, where charcoal was produced. On the self-sufficient estates, because the best bottom lands were used for wheat to be sold in Monterrey, the peasants had to grow their food crops—maize, beans, and chili—on slopes so steep that the soil was quickly washed away when they were cleared. The steep valley sides are still used for food crops, for when the haciendas were broken up it was found that there was not enough good bottom land to take care of more than a small proportion of the *ejidatarios*.

North of Monterrey the Sierra Madre Oriental is too dry to maintain any important communities of farming people. The small communities around Sabinas and Lampazos in northern Coahuila are supported by the mining of coal. In these districts Mexico is endowed with small but fairly good deposits of bituminous coal, a natural resource which is rare in Latin America. Coal is supplied to the Mexican railroads and to the heavy industries which have become established at Monterrey. Since 1950, also, a new oilfield has been developed in northern Tamaulipas.

The area immediately surrounding the city of Monterrey is not densely populated. The only exception is the narrow zone along the mountain piedmont which extends southward to Linares. The somewhat more adequate rainfall which reaches this zone between the front of the Sierra Madre and an outlying mountain block permits the use of this section for commercial agriculture. Sugarcane, oranges, cotton, maize, wheat, and beans are supplied mostly to the city market.

An important new cotton-growing district has been developed since 1960 in the coastal plain of southern Tamaulipas, between Tampico and Monterrey. As one goes southward along the gulf coast from the Texas border, the rainfall increases from only about 27 inches at Brownsville, at the mouth of the Rio Grande, to 44 inches at Tampico. North of Tampico, in a zone with average rainfall between 35 and 40 inches, cotton is grown without irrigation. Earlier attempts to grow cotton in this district failed because of the insect pests. But during the 1960's cotton acreage expanded rapidly, and large yields of cotton per acre were harvested as a result of the heavy application of insecticides. This became one of the major cotton-producing districts of Mexico, rivaling the irrigated cotton of the North Pacific region.

In the North as a whole, only about 5 percent of the area can be used for crops, but from this small acreage Mexico produces an important part of its exports. Most of the cotton is grown under irrigation except in the district north of Tampico. There are also large acreages of wheat and still larger areas devoted to open range for grazing animals. Along the mountain piedmonts and in a few other wetter areas, cattle are the most important animals; but there are vast areas of dry country useful only for the grazing of goats.

MONTERREY

Monterrey itself has become much more than simply a pass city: today it is one of Mexico's leading industrial centers. In 1880 Monterrey had no more than 30,000 inhabitants; its first period of rapid growth came with the construction of the railroad, as previously noted. In recent years further rapid growth has been a result of the construction of the Inter-American Highway from Laredo through Monterrey. By 1930 the city had passed 130,000 in population, and in 1963 it had grown to almost 800,000.

Today the city of Monterrey has become the hub of an extensive system of railroad lines. The main line from the United States to Mexico City passes through Monterrey, tapping the coal fields near Lampazos on the way southward from Laredo, and ascending to the highlands at Saltillo; another railroad reaches the lower Rio Grande; still another line runs southward to Tampico; and another crosses the desert country westward to Torreón. These railroads and their connections reach the most productive mineral and agricultural centers throughout the north of Mexico. In recent years the railroads have been supplemented to a greater and greater degree by paved automobile highways (Map 19).

During the 1930's another major change came to Monterrey and to the district south of it; it was in those years that the first section of the Inter-American Highway was built from the border at Laredo southward to Monterrey. Instead of climbing to Saltillo, the highway continues southward along the piedmont through Linares to a place a little south of the latitude of Tampico—the little Indian community of Tamazunchale. Thence the road makes a spectacular climb to the highland, winding with a steady grade over the extremely rugged terrain cut by the Río Moctezuma and its tributaries. It passes not far from Pachuca on its way to Mexico City. Inland from Tampico this highway passes through country formerly inhabited only by scattered tribes of Indians who supported themselves from the wild game in the forests. Now streams of automobile tourists from the United States are going and coming over the new route to Mexico City. Southward along this highway are spreading such strange things as modern air-conditioned hotels, tourist camps of the latest design with all modern conveniences, gasoline stations with electric pumps, curio shops, motels, and Indians attempting to thumb rides. The main southward stream of tourists from the United States now passes through Monterrey.

THE STEEL INDUSTRY

Monterrey and Monclova are the two chief centers of the Mexican steel industry. The manufacture of pig iron and steel started in Monterrey in 1903. At the present time modern steel mills in this city turn out about 36 percent of the total Mexican production. The plant at Monclova was started in 1944, and now produces about 32 percent of the total. A plant using scrap iron and natural gas imported from the United States is located just across the Rio Grande from Eagle Pass. This plant produces about 18 percent of the total.

The plants at Monterrey and Monclova make use of coking coal from nearby Sabinas, iron ore from Durango, limestone from local sources, and manganese from northwestern Chihuahua.[5] Both make use of adequate water supplies from nearby rivers. This part of Mexico is one of the few places in all Latin America where raw materials for steel making can be brought together at low cost, and where the steel can be transported easily to its major market. The Sabinas coal occurs in a seam a little less than five feet thick under an area about 34 miles long by 15 miles wide. With the possible exception of that of Peru, this is the best coal available in Latin America. Similarly the Durango iron mines are high in quality, and the ore is easily mined by open-pit methods. Mexican steel production was over two million metric tons in 1964.

Monterrey is also Mexico's chief center of lead smelting; and it is also a minor producer of silver, gold, copper, arsenic, bismuth, and antimony. Among the manufacturing plants in this busy city there are tile and glass factories, furniture factories, breweries, cigarette factories, and many others. The industrial growth of Monterrey has been aided since 1950 by natural gas piped from the new oilfield of the northeast.

The Gulf Coast and Yucatán

In striking contrast to all the other parts of Mexico is the Gulf region, the region including the states of Veracruz, Tabasco, Campeche, Yucatán, and Quintana Roo. This territory makes up 12 percent of the total area of the country and is occupied by 12 percent of the population. Unlike most parts of Mexico, the Gulf region is abundantly supplied with moisture—73 percent of it receives sufficient rain in all months. Also unlike most parts of Mexico, a relatively large proportion of the region is classed as level—53 percent of it fits into that category. From the point of view of the physical quality of the land, this is the best maize-growing region of Mexico; here are to be found the largest per acre yields and the fewest crop failures.

Veracruz and Tabasco

Only south of the Río Tamesí can those tropical plants survive which are unable to endure occasional spells of freezing weather. The cold air masses from North America which bring frosts to the coastal plain of Tamaulipas continue southward even as far as the Yucatán Peninsula as cool waves accompanied by heavy rains. South of Tampico, however, frosts are very rare or entirely absent. Throughout the *tierra caliente* of the Gulf Coast the hu-

[5]Robert A. Kennelly, "The Location of the Mexican Steel Industry," *Revista Geográfica,* 1954–55. See complete reference in the Appendix.

midity is high at all times of the year, averaging close to 80 percent at the port of Veracruz. The rainfall is abundant.

The vegetation of the *tierra caliente* includes both forests and grasslands. It seems probable that the original vegetation of the coastal plain as well as of the lower mountain slopes was forest, but that extensive areas of savanna have been produced as a result of repeated burnings by the Indians. The great savanna south of the port of Veracruz (Map 14, p. 34) is believed, on the basis of zoological evidence, to have once been covered with forest. Today, however, forests are found, on the plain, only along the streams and along the coast. In Veracruz the lower mountain slopes are covered with a semi-deciduous forest; southeast of the Isthmus of Tehuantepec, in the state of Tabasco, this type of forest extends across the plain to the edge of the Gulf.

The first port that Cortés established along the Gulf Coast was at a site which proved to be a poor one both because of insect pests and because of the difficulty of defense. Cortés was only interested in making a landing and starting as quickly as possible for the conquest of the great Aztec state on the highlands. Later the necessity of developing one good port on the Caribbean through which connections with the homeland could be maintained led to the selection of another site where more suitable conditions could be found. In 1609 the old port was abandoned and the new city of Veracruz was established a little farther to the south. From Veracruz a colonial road was built into the highlands by way of Jalapa, a route now closely paralleled by the modern railroad. Veracruz, now a city of nearly 170,000 people, remains the chief port of Mexico; it is equipped with breakwaters, modern docks, and other facilities for the handling of cargoes.

Except for the port city, most of the settlement of the state of Veracruz has progressed from the highlands of the interior down into the *tierra caliente*. The swampy coastal plain is still little used; but along the slopes of the mountains there is a string of plantations extending from a little south of Tampico to Orizaba. The chief concentration of people is in the zone where coffee can be grown—focusing on such towns as Jalapa, political center of the state, and Orizaba, and old center of cotton textile industries. Both Jalapa and Orizaba are between four and five thousand feet above sea level, in the *tierra templada*. Still lower, the plantations are fewer; yet there is an important production of such tropical crops as rice, sugarcane, tobacco, bananas, vanilla, rubber (Castilla), and chicle (the chief ingredient in chewing gum). From the rain forest, collectors—who go out from the plantations at certain times of the year—bring back valuable cabinet woods, gums, and a variety of other products of small bulk but of high value.

The number of plantations and of settlers decreases as one proceeds southward in Veracruz, and the southern part of the state, on the northern side of the Isthmus of Tehuantepec, is very sparsely inhabited. The Isthmus of Tehuantepec has never been of sufficient importance as a route of travel to support large cities at either side. Although only about 130 miles separate the Pacific Ocean from the Gulf of Mexico, and although the climb is no more than about 800 feet, the remoteness of the Isthmus from the centers of Mexican population and the existence of easier routes elsewhere help to explain the relatively small use of this pass. In 1907 a railroad was built from Coatzacoalcos (Puerto México) on the Gulf side to Salina Cruz on the Pacific side. The economic importance of this line is, however, very slight.

What is the reason for this neglect of the Gulf region? Here is one of the largest areas of Mexico with adequate rainfall (Map 12, p. 32) and low water deficit (Map 13, p. 33). Yet it has remained until recently very sparsely populated. The land was divided into large haciendas after the Spanish conquest, and was used as one vast cattle range. Although it was clear that maize would grow luxuriantly, the maize-growers of the highlands were less than enthusiastic about moving to the lowlands. A part of this attitude can be credited to the widespread belief that the rainy tropics are unhealthful; and indeed the Gulf region was anything but healthful until insect pests could be controlled. Malaria was once universal, and there were many other insect-borne diseases that continued unchecked because of ignorance of their causes and lack of attention to the basic rules of hygiene. Furthermore, there were no roads into this region, except for the old established highways connecting Veracruz with the highlands. The few efforts at agricultural settlement were restricted to the banks of rivers because the rivers offered the only means of shipping products to market.

In 1947 the Mexican government started a project to establish colonies in the Gulf region. The basin of the Río Papaloapan, just to the south of Veracruz was selected for the first colony. A commission was set up to plan for the economic development of the whole basin from its headwaters in the mountains of Oaxaca to its mouth on the Gulf of Mexico. Five large dams were built to control floods and to provide hydroelectric power. The lowland part of the basin—an area twice as large as Puerto Rico—was cleaned up so that malaria was practically eliminated. Farm colonies were surveyed and colonists were brought from the highlands, each family located on a 30-acre farm and provided with a house, farm equipment, and seed. Modern farm methods on productive soils produced bumper harvests of cotton, sugarcane, and maize. Ciudad Miguel Alemán, an entirely new city, grew rapidly as the chief commerical center of the lower valley. By 1960 the success of the project was proved, and other new farm colonies were being laid out all along the Gulf coast. New all-weather roads made these colonies accessible, modern health measures and modern homes made tropical living healthful and pleasant, and modern techniques of farming made possible the continued high yields from what are now recognized as among Mexico's best soils. Now farmers are coming in large numbers to get land of their own as long as land is available, and they are successful enough in making the adjustment so that most of them are remaining permanently. New agricultural colonies have been built in Tabasco, Campeche, and even on the rainy eastern side of the Yucatán Peninsula in Quintana Roo.

Like the North Pacific region, the Gulf region has become an important new source of fish for the improvement of the Mexican diet. The waters of the Gulf of Mexico yield many varieties of fish that have long been neglected by the Mexicans. These include red snapper, bass, robalo, swordfish, tuna, and sardines. In the warm, shallow waters along the coast between Veracruz and Campeche important shrimp beds have been discovered. Some 300 new shrimp trawlers built in the Netherlands are now based at Ciudad del Carmen in Campeche. Near the mouth of the Río Papaloapan, 38 miles southeast of Veracruz, is the once sleepy little fishing village of Alvarado. From this place turtles, crabs, and oysters were shipped to Mexico City by rail. Now the government has built new docks and new fish-freezing facilities in this location.

Yucatán

Yucatán was once the well-populated center of the Maya Indians. The Maya were one of the early civilizations in America, preceding the Toltecs and Aztecs, and from whom many elements of Toltec and Aztec culture were derived. But by the time of the Spanish conquest, the Maya culture had already declined. The Indians carried on a shifting cultivation, but there were no large concentrations of people to attract the attention of the conquerors. The Maya cities had been abandoned and were almost lost in the fast-growing cover of forest.

Yucatán was not entirely neglected. The town of Mérida was founded in 1542, and the few Indians were allotted to the Spanish invaders in *encomiendas*. The land was soon partitioned into large estates on which the grazing of cattle was the chief economic activity, and hides, tallow, and salt beef the chief commercial products.

There are a number of handicaps to the successful utilization of the Yucatán region. In the northwest, around Mérida, the rainfall is low; the amount of moisture increases toward the south and east until it is abundant on the borders of British Honduras and Guatemala. A scrub woodland with patches of savanna occupies the drier northwest parts of the peninsula, but as the rainfall increases toward the southeast the woodland is soon replaced by a growth of tall trees. A scanty population armed only with primitive tools finds life easier in the dry areas than where the exuberant tropical vegetation springs up rapidly to choke every clearing.

Furthermore, surface water is not easy to find in Yucatán. The peninsula is underlain by horizontal beds of limestone in which the rain water forms underground solution caverns. There are no surface streams; and only where the cavern roofs have collapsed are there pitlike cenotes in the bottoms of

Restored ruins of the Maya temples at Chichén Itzá in Yucatán. *Courtesy of Mexican Government Tourism Deparment.*

which the plentiful ground water can be reached. The native Indians, having no iron tools, were unable to dig wells and had to locate their permanent settlements close to the natural sources of surface water. This lack of water meant that there could be no great expansion of the grazing economy.

Nor were the native people of Yucatán so easy to exploit as those of the high basins of the Central region. Attempts to establish plantations of sugar-cane and indigo were not profitable. Even as late as 1847 the Indians carried out a major revolt against the landowners, which had to be put down with force.

After 1880, however, the northwestern part of Yucatán around Mérida became the world's source of henequen fiber. Long before the arrival of the Spaniards the Maya Indians had extracted the fiber from the fleshy leaves of the henequen plant and used it to make cord. During the seventeenth and eighteenth centuries the Spanish settlers used henequen fiber to make ropes for the Spanish navy. For a long time enthusiasts had written optimistic accounts of the potential utility of this product, but always there was an insufficient labor supply and no really large market.

Among the plants that are native to the drier parts of the Yucatán Peninsula are several species of agave. One of these is the *Agave fourcroydes* which is used in Mexico as the source of henequen.[6] This plant will grow on thin, stony, and dry soils and does not require irrigation. After the henequen is planted, it takes from five to seven years before the leaves can be cut. Thereafter it yields something like 250 leaves over a fifteen- or twenty-year period, at the end of which a tall flowering stalk shoots up from the center of the plant, and the plant dies. The dry limestone lands of Yucatán offer ideal conditions for the growth of henequen, and there is no other use of this land that competes with its cultivation.

Henequen production was very profitable after the world market had been developed. The major use of this coarse, strong fiber is in automatic, self-binding reapers used to harvest grains throughout the grasslands of the middle latitudes, a machine that was first marketed after 1880. At first Manila hemp from the Philippines was used in these binders, but when the Spanish-American War stopped hemp shipments in 1898, Mexican henequen was found to meet the requirements. Until 1911, Mexico was the only place in the world where henequen was produced. The large planters were the only ones who could command sufficient capital to undertake a kind of economy in which there is no income at all for the first five years or so. But in spite of efforts to maintain the monopoly, agave plants were taken out and cultivated in Cuba, Puerto Rico, the Bahamas, and Florida, as well as in parts of East Africa. In 1911 the product of these other plantations began to appear on the market. Although Mexican henequen production continued to increase to the peak year of 1916 (217,300 long tons), Mexico's share of the combined world production of sisal and henequen decreased steadily.

Efforts to rebuild the henequen industry in Yucatán followed the virtual destruction of this form of activity when the *ejido* program was undertaken. Experience in various parts of the world shows that in order to keep the processing machinery in efficient operation it is necessary to have a supply area of at least 5,000 acres. Plantations of this size exist in Kenya, Uganda, and Tanzania, but not in Yucatán. Tanzania now produces more than half of the world's supply of sisal, and also a large part of the world's henequen. The Mexican government attempted to save the industry in Yucatán by covering the cost of new plantings, and after 1953 these came into production. By 1956

---

[6]The *Agave fourcroydes* has a short trunk that looks like a pineapple. From the top sprout grayish-green, stiff, fleshy leaves. The leaves may be as much as seven feet long, with a spike at the end and thorns along the sides. The fibers are embedded in the leaf. Sisal is produced from a close relative, the *Agave sisalana,* which can be distinguished from henequen because there are no thorns on the leaves. Mexico and Cuba grow mostly henequen; but other parts of the world grow almost exclusively sisal, the fibers of which have somewhat wider utility. Another close relative of henequen, and like the sisal plant a native of Mexico, is the *Agave atrovirens,* from which the Mexicans make an alcoholic drink, *pulque;* also related is the *Agave tequilana,* source of *tequila.*

the production was almost as great as it had been before World War II. But by the mid 1960's there was a severe drop in the world price of these fibers. This was due in part to the increase of African production, but also to the increased use of synthetic fibers. In 1965 there were some 70,000 henequen planters and processers out of work in Yucatán. The promotion of Mérida as a tourist center, combining warm, sunny beaches with nearby Maya ruins, could scarcely provide employment for enough people.

The Oil Fields

The Gulf region as a whole has another resource of even greater significance to the foreign economic and political relations of Mexico—oil. We must return again to the northern part of the region, for the center of the oil industry is Tampico.

The first successful oil well in Mexico was drilled about fifty miles west of Tampico in 1901. The importance of the new fields was quickly appreciated by North American and British interests, and with the aid of foreign capital, Mexico's production was rapidly increased. In 1902 oil was discovered in the southern field on the Gulf side of the Isthmus of Tehuantepec; and in 1908 another important field was discovered inland from Tuxpan, a short distance south of Tampico. In this district three of the world's most productive oil wells were drilled. The three wells together have produced one-quarter of the total amount of oil taken out of this district, while the other three-quarters has come from more than 500 wells.

Mexican production increased rapidly to a peak in 1921. In 1904 there were 221,000 barrels shipped out, but by 1910 exports had been increased to more than 3 million barrels. Just before the beginning of World War I exports rose to 25 million barrels, and then after a slight decline continued to increase rapidly until in 1921, the peak year, Mexico exported more than 193 million barrels, 21 percent of the world's production of that year. After 1921, however, both production and export declined. In 1929 the export was a little less than 45 million barrels (compared with the 1929 production of 297 million barrels in the state of Texas). In 1932 Mexican production dropped to only 33 million barrels. In 1930 the Shell interests discovered the famous Poza Rica field, located near the southern end of the oil-producing area around Tuxpan. Production from this new field made possible the rise of total Mexican production after 1932 to 47 million barrels in 1937.

The decline in oil production after 1921 was due in large part to the changed attitude of the Mexican government and the Mexican people toward foreign oil corporations which resulted from the Revolution. The new constitution took mineral rights away from the landowners and vested them with the federal government. Increasingly, the government placed restrictions on the freedom of operation of the foreign oil companies, until in 1938 the properties of most of the companies were expropriated. The move was vastly popular in Mexico; and by 1938 the United States had renounced the traditional policy of armed interference in the affairs of other states. The North American and British companies withdrew, and after a period of negotiations were reimbursed for at least a part of what they thought the properties were worth.

Mexico's oil production and marketing was placed under the control of a government agency, *Petróleos Mexicanos,* or PEMEX. By making good use of the Poza Rica field, PEMEX was able to produce an average of about 40 million barrels a year from 1938 to 1945. After 1945 the company was able to secure technical assistance from outside, and gradually to increase Mexico's oil production through the discovery of new fields. In 1965 extended geological exploration considerably increased Mexico's known oil reserves—in fact the proved reserves in 1966 increased faster than current production. In 1965 the Mexican fields yielded 117,900,000 barrels. There were three major producing areas, all located along the Gulf coast. A new field has been developed on the Mexican side of the lower Rio Grande around Matamoros, and from this field oil and gas pipelines extend to Monterrey, Torreón, and Chihuahua. The largest production still comes from the oilfield extending from Tampico to Veracruz, and oil and gas pipelines connect this field with the major cities of the Central region. Another new field has been opened up in southern Veracruz and Tabasco, and pipelines also transport oil and gas to the Central region from this area. The new city of Ciudad Pemex in eastern Tabasco became a thriving community carved in only a few years out of uninhabited tropical forest.

The oil is associated with sulphur in southern Veracruz and Tabasco. In 1956 the existence of sulphur domes along this part of the Gulf coast—some under the water of the Gulf of Mexico—was made known by geological exploration. The sulphur is mostly exported through the port of Coatzacoalcos, but it is combined with the oil to provide the basis for a new chemical industry at Minatitlán. Here, and also in some of the cities of the Central region, Mexican resources are now being used to manufacture fertilizer, insecticides, plastics, and other new products.

The South Pacific Region

The last of the four outlying regions to be studied is the South Pacific region. This includes the states of Colima, Guerrero, Oaxaca, and Chiapas. Its area is about the same as that of the Gulf region (approximately 12 percent of the total area of Mexico), and it is inhabited by the same proportion of Mexico's population (12 percent). In contrast to the Gulf region, less than 20 percent of its area can be classed as level, for although there are no very high peaks comparable to the cones of the volcanic area, there are few parts of Mexico where the surface is more rugged.

The Southern Dissected Border of the Highlands

There are two distinct subdivisions of the South Pacific region. There is a western part and an eastern part, separated by the Isthmus of Tehuantepec. To the west of the Isthmus are the much dissected surfaces that mark the southern end of the highlands. In many respects this southern dissected border of the highlands is transitional between the surface features and geologic structures characteristic of North America and those characteristic of Central America. Many geologists insist that western North America, with its typical north–south mountain axes, ends with the volcanic area of the Central region of Mexico, and that the dominant northwest–southeast structures which appear about the latitude of Cape Corrientes belong with Central America. Yet, in terms of surface features, the country between Cape Corrientes and the Isthmus of Tehuantepec is closely related to the highland farther north. The same general upland level between six and eight thousand feet above the sea which is found in the basins of the central highland north of Mexico City is preserved also in the ridge crests of the southern dissected border. The rugged surface of the latter region is the result of stream dissection—of the formation of deep valleys cut below the general highland level. In spite of the trend of the underlying geologic structures, therefore, geographers generally place the southern limit of North America at the Isthmus of Tehuantepec.

Most of the southern dissected border of the highlands is drained by the Río Balsas and its tributaries. The main stream has opened a deep gulf well into the *tierra caliente* along the northern border of Guerrero, and the tributaries extend in dendritic fashion back into the higher country on either side. Along the eastern headwaters of the Balsas, a ridge of only slightly dissected highland connects the central part of Oaxaca with the volcanic massif of Popocatepetl and Ixtacihuatl. In the course of stream erosion, however, certain more resistant structures in the Balsas Valley were exhumed and left standing as prominent and more or less isolated blocks. An example is the small block mountain in northern Guerrero not far north of the Balsas itself, in which the old mining town and present tourist center of Taxco is situated; another example is the larger block bordering the Pacific in southern Michoacán, Guerrero, and southern Oaxaca, which is known as the *Sierra Madre del Sur*.

Flat places are remarkably few and widely scattered in this region. There are some which are situated on undissected remnants of the highland surface; there are a few narrow valley flats which develop along rivers just upstream from a gorge; and there are a few located where the valleys broaden out in small structural basins. On these flat places the people are concentrated; but the simple fact is that there are too many people in this area to be supported on a subsistence basis from the small areas of good land. Food must be raised on slopes so steep that it can be said with considerable truth that a farmer could easily slip and fall out of his farm. The patches of maize on the mountain sides are temporary, for new clearings must be made each year for this type of agriculture.

The altitude of this region determines the general nature of the vegetation cover and of the crops. No part of the South Pacific region is deficient in moisture, although most of the rain comes in summer, and the winters are dry. The vertical zones and the products corresponding to them are similar to those described for Mt. Orizaba. The *tierra caliente* is restricted to the deeper part of the Balsas Valley and to the coastal strip along the Pacific— the latter, however, being little used because of its isolation. There are a few areas high enough to get well into the *tierra fría*. But most of the land in this region lies within the *tierra templada*.

The coast west of the Isthmus of Tehuantepec is extremely forbidding. The Sierra Madre del Sur descends with very steep slopes almost to the water's edge, leaving only a narrow fringe of sandy and generally hot and dry lowland. The ports all suffer from one handicap or another: either the water is too shallow if they are situated, like Salina Cruz and Manzanillo, near the outlet of one of the silt-laden rivers; or they are isolated from the interior by steep mountain slopes, as is the case at Acapulco. The latter place, because of its excellent harbor, was selected by the Spaniards as the chief port of departure for the Philippines. But the country behind Acapulco is so difficult to cross that no railroad has ever been built to connect it with the interior, and only in 1940 was the new paved highway extended to it from Taxco. Acapulco has become, in spite of its isolation, a seaside resort of considerable popularity. The completion of the road has opened it to an increasing flood of North American tourists—a stream which has already converted Taxco, old sixteenth-century silver and tin mining center, into a still more profitable tourist center. Since a railroad connects Manzanillo, in Colima, with the interior in Jalisco, this port has become Mexico's chief inlet and outlet on the Pacific.

Chiapas

The highland of Chiapas is the second of the two subdivisions of the South Pacific region. This highland is characteristically Central American: it is composed of folded and faulted structures, partly covered with volcanic outpourings. The main structural features run parallel to the Pacific coast. Behind a narrow coastal lowland the first range of mountains, the Sierra Madre de Chiapas, rises to elevations of more than 9,000 feet within twenty miles of the ocean. Immediately northeast of this range is the rift depression known as the Valley of Chiapas. The floor of this depression is between 1,500 and 3,000 feet above sea level. It is drained by a tributary of the Río Grijalva which finds its outlet to the Gulf in the state of Tabasco. Northeast of this, again, is a succession of block mountains, each more or less level-topped but deeply dissected by streams. From altitudes of over 12,000 feet overlooking the Valley of Chiapas, these mountains drop down toward the level limestone plains of Yucatán. Most of the people in this part of Mexico live in the Valley of Chiapas, near the Pacific coast.

Here also the natural vegetation and the prevailing forms of land use are arranged by vertical zones. The *tierra caliente* of Chiapas is of greater potential value for rainy tropical crops than is the similar zone northwest of the Isthmus of Tehuantepec because of the increasing rainfall toward the southeast. On the lower slopes of the mountains in this district the Aztecs used to grow their supplies of cacao, from which they made a ceremonial drink we know as chocolate. This is perhaps the native home of the cacao tree. Cacao is still produced here, although more important today are the coffee plantations higher up on the slopes and the new cotton plantations developed at the base of the highlands along the Pacific. This district, near the Guatemalan border, had become in the mid 1960's one of Mexico's leading cotton-producing areas. The whole Pacific area has now been made accessible to the rest of Mexico by rail and all-weather motor truck highways.

The Valley of Chiapas has a population between 25 and 60 people per square mile. On parts of the valley cattle are pastured, and cattle are also pastured on the high grasslands above the tree line. From the higher parts of the valley comes wheat, and coffee is grown on the slopes on either side of the valley. The crop that occupies the largest acreage—as in Mexico as a whole—is maize.

Such are the outlying parts of Mexico. The clusters of people in these areas are highly diverse in their origin and in their present relations to the land. Yet through all the diversity there run certain prevailing themes. All parts of the country have felt the effects of the *ejido* program, in the elimination of the haciendas and the landowning class. Now there is a mixture of *ejidos* and medium-sized private farms, operated by their owners. The crop that occupies the largest acreage is maize, grown near all the villages, and on slopes that are much too steep for this kind of use and which have suffered heavily from soil erosion. But all parts of the country, too, are feeling the effects of the new program of economic development, which is resulting in improved techniques and increased yields per acre. Although the farmers on the *ejidos* are no better off than they were before the land was redistributed, for there is nowhere near enough good land to go around, some of the better private farms are operating profitably. But everywhere there is a slow but steady decrease in the number of purely subsistence farmers, and an increase in those who sell their products and use money to buy things they want from the local retail merchants.

The Central Region

The group of states which are combined to form the Central region make up 14 percent of the area of Mexico, and in these states live 49 percent of the Mexican people (Maps 23 and 24). In this region, also, are located 62 percent of Mexico's manufacturing industries. Actually, if geographic regions rather than arbitrary political divisions were considered, the area would be somewhat reduced, for most of southern Jalisco and Michoacán really belong in the South Pacific region; yet this reduction would have little effect on the proportion of the people inhabiting the central area. In this core of the Mexican state are nearly 20 percent of all the agricultural land, 45 percent of all the farmers of the country, and more than 50 percent of all the area devoted to maize. And here is the focus, also, of Mexico's twin problems—the agrarian problem and the industrial problem.

The Central region is itself a diverse land, and one which includes many areas which are only thinly populated as well as other areas which were well populated even before the arrival of the Spaniards. The land is composed of a number of well-defined basins, all drained by rivers which reach the sea, except the Basin of Mexico in which the capital city is located. Between the basins much of the land is composed of gently rounded hills through which the rivers have cut deep, narrow valleys; and the whole scene is given extraordinary beauty by the series of superb volcanic cones and by the many lesser volcanic forms scattered throughout the region from Ceboruco in the state of Nayarit on the border of the Basin of Jalisco to Orizaba which overlooks the Basin of Puebla. The Indian groups migrating from the drier north came upon this somewhat wetter country with its many lakes and its running streams fed by permanent snow fields, and saw in it a land of plenty. Anáhuac, for the Nahua peoples, was like Babylon for the Assyrians. In about 1325 the Aztecs founded their capital city of Tenochtitlán on an island in Lake Texcoco, where it could be easily defended, and from this center they extended their conquest, or at least levied tribute, over much of the territory to the south. Each of the basins of the central area, however, had its own distinct Indian culture which differed in language and customs from the cultures of other basins. The native peoples, even those who were brought under Aztec rule, were never molded into one coherent culture. Land and people remained extraordinarily diverse.

The First Spanish Settlements

The story of the conquest of Mexico by Cortés and his little band of men is one of the great epics of adventure in the New World. In 1519 Cortés arrived on the margins of the Basin of Mexico with about 350 Spaniards and more than a thousand Indian allies. But after occupying the palace of the Aztec ruler for several months, the Spaniards were forced to a disastrous retreat on the famous *noche triste*–June 30, 1520. Cortés returned the next year and destroyed Tenochtitlán: 1521 marks the date when the Spanish conquerors took over from the Aztecs the political and economic rule of the dense Indian populations of the central area. There can be no doubt regarding the objectives of this first conquest, and none regarding the reasons which led Cortés to found the city of Mexico on the site of old Tenochtitlán. Ease of living, coolness of climate, productivity of soil for plantation crops—these were definitely not the reasons for the settlement of the Spaniards in the central area. The objective was wealth—first wealth which had already been accumulated and could be carried away; then more wealth in the form of minerals ready to be mined. To furnish the necessary labor in the mines and to provide the newcomers with an adequate supply of food a large population of peaceful Indian farmers was needed; and dense Indian population also satisfied the other great purpose of Spanish conquest—the conversion of infidels to the Christian faith. Sedentary Indians and stores or mines of precious metals—these were factors which guided the course of Spanish settlement; and both were abundant in the central area.

The fifty years after the founding of Mexico City in 1521 witnessed the establishment of mining communities and the start of active mining operations at almost all the sources of precious metals in Mexico. Few new sources have been discovered since. Northeast of the capital was the silver town of Pachuca, still the richest in the world; north of the capital was the silver mine of Zumpango; northwest of Mexico City was the gold and silver center of El Oro; in the hilly country south of the Basin of Guanajuato was the silver center of Morelia, and in the mountainous country north of the Basin was another silver-mining community, Guanajuato; to the west was Guadalajara, itself a center of spreading settlement, and locally enriched by silver mines and dense Indian populations; farther to the north was Aguascalientes, and also the three prominent silver-mining towns previously described—San Luis Potosí, Zacatecas, and Durango; south of the capital was the silver mine of Taxco. The restless search for silver, gold, and dense populations of peaceful Indians led the Spaniards to the far reaches of their vast territory, far beyond the present limits of Mexico; and wherever Indians or precious metals were discovered, towns were founded and Spanish civilization was established. Where Indians and precious metals were lacking, the Spaniards either turned the area over to the missions, or they utilized it for vast cattle ranges. Meanwhile, in the Central region the Indians who escaped work in the mines and who survived the epidemics of imported diseases were able to continue to live as they had lived before the conquest—by raising basic food crops for their own use and a little surplus to pay as tribute to the lords of the land.

Pattern of Population in the Modern Period

The rural population of the Central region is still predominantly Indian,

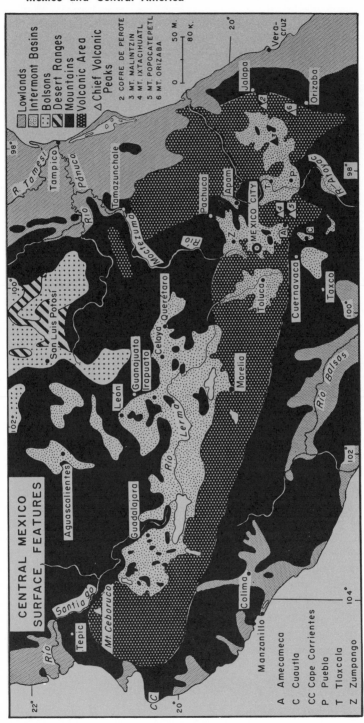

CENTRAL MEXICO
SURFACE, FEATURES

Lowlands
Intermont Basins
Bolsons
Desert Ranges
Mountains
Volcanic Area
△Chief Volcanic
   Peaks

2 COFRE DE PEROTE
3 MT. MALINTZIN
4 MT. IXTACIHUATL
5 MT. POPOCATEPETL
6 MT. ORIZABA

0   50 M.
0   80 K.

A Amecameca
C Cuautla
CC Cape Corrientes
P Puebla
T Tlaxcala
Z Zumpango

Map 23

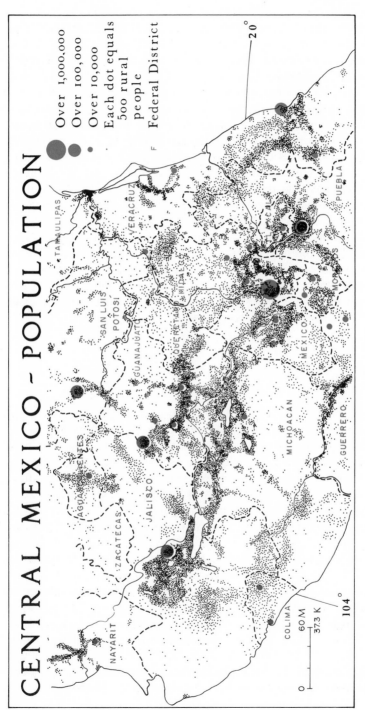

CENTRAL MEXICO ~ POPULATION

Over 1,000,000
Over 100,000
Over 10,000
Each dot equals
500 rural
people
F Federal District

Map 24

and the many forms of life adopted from the Spaniards need not obscure the fact that the great majority of these people still live in the traditional Indian manner. It is important to understand, therefore, that the concentration of the Indian grain, maize, in the Central region is a very different kind of agricultural localization from that which appears in the Corn Belt of the United States. It is a fundamental fact, basic to an understanding of Mexico's problems, that this concentration of maize in the Central region is no more than a reflection of the concentration, in that area, of the Mexican people. There is no interplay of economic forces arising from a competition among various potential uses of the land, in which certain areas come to specialize in a particular kind of crop production because of special advantages to be found there. As a matter of fact, the Central region is poorly suited to the production of maize: there are none of the steaming hot summer days and nights which, in the Middle West of the United States, are known as "corn weather"; crop failures due to cold weather, even in summer, are all too frequent, and even in good years, the yields are low. For maize farming, the land is low in productivity; but is it the land which is to blame, or is it the traditional system which fails to take advantage of those forms of production for which the land is well suited—such as stock raising? Let us examine the present patterns of people more closely.

The Seven Clusters of People in the Central Region

A closer view of this central area shows that the population is grouped in seven separate clusters (Map 24). Although the chief Spanish towns, which have since become the centers of political power, were originally located with reference to the silver and gold mines of the colonial period, the concentrations of Indian farmers were closely related to the character of the surface. The intermont basins were densely settled before the Spaniards arrived, and have remained densely populated throughout the period since the European conquest. In most cases the centers of the various basins are swampy; the people, therefore, are usually found occupying the borders of the basins and the lower slopes of the surrounding hills and mountains. At the present time, the density of the rural population in these areas of concentrated settlement is between 25 and 60 per square mile; in the vicinity of Mexico City and Puebla are certain areas with a density of from 60 to 125 per square mile.

The seven chief clusters of people can be described with reference to the basins around which they are grouped. That these clusters do not have a simple relation to the state boundaries, as is usually the case in Latin America, is a peculiarity of this area. On the facing page are listed the seven basins, and the states included in each of the areas of concentration:

An *ejidatario* cultivating maize with oxen in the Basin of Guanajuato. *Photo by J. G. Widdison.*

BASINS	STATES
1. Basin of México (Anáhuac)	Federal District, and parts of the states of México and Hidalgo
2. Basin of Puebla	Part of Puebla and Tlaxcala
3. Basin of Toluca	Part of México
4. Basin of Guanajuato	Southern Guanajuato, including bordering parts of the highlands of Guanajuato, Querétaro, and Michoacán
5. Basin of Jalisco	Part of the state of Jalisco
6. Valley of Aguascalientes	Aguascalientes, extending into nearby parts of Jalisco and Zacatecas
7. Valley of Morelos	State of Morelos, and bordering edge of Guerrero

THE BASIN OF MÉXICO

The original Anáhuac of the Aztecs was the Basin of México, an irregular-shaped depression some thirty miles east and west by fifty miles north and south. When the Aztecs knew this basin, its bottom was occupied by five separate lakes, each shallow and bordered by marshy zones. Tenochtitlán was built on an island in the midst of Lake Texcoco and was connected to the land by causeways. The Indian communities, which the Spaniards in the course of time incorporated in their haciendas, were strung along the margins of the basin and the lower and gentler slopes of the bordering hills and mountains. The irregular shape of the basin produced, therefore, a very irregular pattern of population.

The Basin of México is the only one of the seven areas of dense population which is not drained naturally to the sea. In 1607–8, however, the engineer Enrico Martinez partly drained the basin by digging a ditch and tunnel northward across a low divide to the headwaters of the Pánuco system. In the present century, further drainage operations have completed the removal of Lake Texcoco—but with results which are not altogether fortunate, for the lake-bed soils were found to contain such a high percentage of salts that not even pasture grasses would grow on them without expensive chemical treatment. Therefore, instead of acquiring a huge area of exceptionally rich farmland, as was anticipated, the city of Mexico found itself bordered by a vast expanse of empty flats, only the edges of which could be utilized. During the dry winters the bare ground gives off great clouds of dust which contribute to the unpleasant and even unhealthful conditions of the capital. And in addition, as the lake bed deposits dried out, the surface began to settle. The construction of modern tall buildings on such foundations presents a major challenge to the architects.

The population of the Basin of México, outside of the capital city, is still distributed much as in the preconquest days, in a series of small separate communities along the margins of the former lake bed. On the outskirts of the capital, the settled area has, it is true, crept well up the bordering mountain slopes, but generally only the lower slopes are occupied by villages. The cluster of people included in this area extends well beyond the immediate basin, however, both in the southeast and in the northeast. Along the western base of the great volcanoes Ixtacihuatl and Popocatepetl there are several small valleys filled with agricultural communities, the largest of which is Amecameca. Toward the northeast, along the line of the Inter-American Highway, there are stretches of gently rolling upland, utilized in scattered patches for crops. Sixty-three miles by road from the capital is the old colonial mining town of Pachuca, a closely crowded group of low buildings along narrow, irregular streets wedged against the valley head where the world's richest silver mines are located.

The crops raised in the farming communities of the Basin of México are similar to those produced in the other parts of the Central region. Maize is by far the most important in terms of acreage. On the lower hill slopes surrounding the villages are the fields of maize, commonly cultivated with oxen and wooden plows, with a technique which has shown little change since plows were first introduced by the Spaniards. The yields per acre are still notoriously small although they have been improved by government action since 1954. Sometimes in the same field with maize are beans, and nearby small plots may be devoted to the production of chili and alfalfa. The chief crop grown for sale is wheat, which is consumed largely by city people. But the maize crop, here as in other parts of Mexico, provides the basic food, eaten along with beans and chili. It is to remedy the lack of certain minerals and vitamins in this diet that the government is promoting the greater use of fish, and also of dairy products.

The Central region was formerly the chief area of *maguey* planting. The maguey is a species of agave from which a sweet liquid is derived. When fermented, this liquid becomes *pulque*.[7] The average Mexican used to consume about 15 gallons of pulque per year. This was the poor man's drink, and the *pulqueria,* where the drink was sold, was the poor man's club. Furthermore, the maguey plant can grow on thin stony soils too poor for any other use. But the general rise in the economic well-being of Mexico has resulted in a notable drop in the drinking of pulque and a corresponding rise in the drinking of beer. In the state of Hidalgo alone in 1934 there were 22 million maguey plants, but by 1960 the number was reduced to 8 million. It will not be long before this picturesque element of the traditional Mexican landscape will have all but disappeared.

The Basin of México could provide good conditions for the production of wheat and excellent conditions for the grazing of cattle. After the land redistribution program had been carried out there was, in fact, some decrease in the acreage of maize and some increase in wheat and other crops. The government undertook, also, to build up herds of dairy cattle, and to educate the city people, at least, in the benefits of drinking milk. A serious blow to this program came in 1946 when it was discovered that some of the animals imported for this purpose had developed foot and mouth disease. This is a highly contagious ailment that can be caught by any hooved animals, including wild deer. The sick animals fail to put on weight or to produce proper quantities of milk. The disease started around Veracruz and quickly spread southward beyond Tehuantepec, northward beyond Tampico, and westward into the Central region. The cattle producers of the United States were alarmed, for there seemed no reason to suppose that it would not infect herds north of the border. A vigorous program, carried out jointly by the United States and Mexico, attacked the disease. Infected animals were slaughtered, in spite of much resistance by the illiterate farmers who could not understand the reason for killing their oxen. As a result the spread of disease was halted, and since 1950 the number of cattle has again been increased.

---

[7]Pulque drinking probably originated with the Huastec Indians. The stern Aztecs, however, permitted its use only on ceremonial occasions. At one time there was much argument concerning whether pulque was beneficial or not. But it was not the reformers who have been successful in reducing the use of this drink. The fact is that to most people, beer tastes better.

THE BASIN OF PUEBLA

The second of the clusters of people of the Central region is in the Basin of Puebla. This lies on the eastern side of the volcanoes Ixtacihuatl and Popocatepetl, at an elevation of a little over 7,000 feet. The city of Puebla is 78 miles by road southeast of Mexico City, and about 200 miles west of Veracruz. The basin, which is drained by a headwater tributary of the Río Balsas, receives a much more plentiful rainfall than does Anáhuac; at Mexico City the average annual rainfall is 23 inches; at Puebla the average is nearly 35 inches. From an agricultural point of view this district is better favored than the Basin of México. But, as we have said, Cortés was not looking for farming land.

Puebla, the city, was founded by the Spaniards in 1532. The old center of the Indian communities in this basin was Cholula—the capital city of the Toltecs. Today Cholula is of little importance except for the tourist who wishes to see its many interesting churches. Similarly Tlaxcala, the center of the Tlaxcalan Indians who, from their hilly homeland on the north of the Basin of Puebla, long defied the power of the Aztecs, has today become a place of minor importance compared with the thriving Puebla. Now Puebla is a city of well over 300,000, in which a variety of manufacturing industries have been built.

The many little Indian communities which dot the floor of the Basin of Puebla and which climb the lower slopes of the surrounding hills and mountains are similar in their economy and organization to the communities of Anáhuac. The predominant crops are maize, wheat, beans, and alfalfa.

THE BASIN OF TOLUCA

West of Anáhuac is the densely populated area which centers on the city of Toluca. The Basin of Toluca, the highest in the Central region, is the first of a series of basins which are drained to the Pacific through the Río Lerma. The depression in which Toluca is located stands more than 8,600 feet above sea level, but to reach Toluca from Mexico City—a distance of only forty miles by road—it is necessary to climb above ten thousand feet over the intervening mountain range. The center of the basin is swampy, and for this reason the settlements, like those of Anáhuac, are strung along the lower slopes of the bordering hills. The crops of the basin are similar to those of the Basin of México, but with a somewhat larger proportion of the crop lands devoted to wheat as a commercial crop. Unfortunately, poor farm practices on the slopes have resulted in very serious losses by soil erosion. Few parts of Mexico show more vividly the devastating effects of misuse of land than do the western margins of the Basin of Toluca.

Included in this district of concentrated settlement is the old mining community of El Oro. The mines of this district, unlike those of Pachuca, have not remained productive; and El Oro itself was not selected as a political center, for the city of Toluca was made the capital of the state of México. As a result El Oro is no longer so important as the agricultural communities.

THE BASIN OF GUANAJUATO

The largest of the basins, and the largest area of settlement concentration in the Central region is in the southern part of the state of Guanajuato— the Basin of Guanajuato. Leaving the Toluca Basin, the Río Lerma plunges through a narrow gorge from which it emerges into the upper part of the Basin of Guanajuato only about 5,900 feet above the sea. The bottom of the basin is between 5,500 and 5,900 feet; but the Río Lerma cuts more and more deeply into it as it proceeds westward, forming a deep trench. The floor of the basin is made up of drained lake beds and soils formed on accumulations of volcanic ash which are noted for their fertility. The Basin of Guanajuato has long been considered the granary of central Mexico.

The first Spanish settlements in this general district were Guanajuato City, Querétaro, and Morelia—all in the mining sections of the bordering highlands. But as mining activities decreased in these areas, the centers of population shifted. Guanajuato, with its narrow streets and its cramped space, has declined notably. In 1880 Guanajuato had some 70,000 inhabitants, but now it has less than 20,000. Meanwhile the little towns of the agricultural areas have all grown, especially Celaya, Irapuato, and León. A variety of new manufacturing industries have been built in these towns. Near Irapuato there is a huge new oil refinery, connected by pipeline with the Poza Rica oilfield. Querétaro has laid out a new "industrial park" where many new manufacturing plants have been established just since 1960. These plants make sewing machines, baby foods, tractors, and hardware. Querétaro, which had 62,000 inhabitants in 1962, by 1966 had passed 100,000. This city is now taking advantage of its central location, close to all the major lines of transportation, to expand rapidly as an industrial and commercial center.

Although more than 75 percent of the cultivated area of the state of Guanajuato is devoted to maize, there are other crop concentrations that are more valuable. Around the town of Celaya there are fruit orchards which sell to canneries and other factories in the town. On the rolling hilly lands of northern Michoacán, wheat is the most important commercial crop.

THE BASIN OF JALISCO

Still farther to the west down the valley of the Río Lerma lies the Basin of Jalisco, second in size only to the Basin of Guanajuato. This basin stands about five thousand feet above sea level. Nestled against the base of the great volcano Ceboruco, its surface is interrupted by several small volcanic cones, now inactive, and its soils have been produced by the weathering of lava flows and ash falls. In the lowest part of the basin is the Lago de Chapala, into which the Río Lerma empties.

The Basin of Jalisco is not far from the Pacific coast, but reaching it is difficult. The Río Santiago (as the river which drains the Lago de Chapala is called) enters a gorge not far from the outlet of the lake, near the city of Guadalajara. In about 275 miles the river descends over falls and rapids 5,000 feet to the Pacific. The gorge is quite impassable for man. In spite of these difficulties the route from Guadalajara to Tepic is the main line of travel from the central area of Mexico to the whole northwest.

Guadalajara, which was one of the primary settlement centers of colonial Mexico, has maintained its importance in the modern period. Today it is second only to the capital, having a population of about 1 million. In the rural districts around Guadalajara the population of farming people is relatively dense, and a larger area is devoted to crops for local subsistence than in the other basins of the Central region. The land is used for the usual combination of maize, beans, chili, and alfalfa. Because of the greater humidity of this basin, wheat is of less importance than elsewhere in the Central region.

THE VALLEY OF AGUASCALIENTES

Two other smaller, but important, clusters of people remain to be described. One of these smaller clusters occupies the valley of the Río Verde, a tributary of the Santiago, where the mining town of Aguascalientes was founded in the sixteenth century. This place might have had a history of gradual decline similar to that of some of the other mining communities had it not been for the establishment in it of railroad shops for all the Mexican railroads. Aguascalientes is now growing, although the production of its mines is of little importance. In 1921 this town had 48,000 inhabitants, but by 1963 it had nearly 150,000.

THE VALLEY OF MORELOS

The last of the seven clusters of people commonly included in the Central region is in the Valley of Morelos, mostly in the state of that name. From the point of view of the surface features, this district should be included in the South Pacific region, since it lies within the deep gulf of the Río Balsas, south of the volcanoes of the Central Plateau. But from the point of view of population distribution and economic connections, there is much justification for including Morelos with the higher country north of it. Cuernavaca, the capital of Morelos, is thirty-six miles from Mexico City; but it is about 4,800 feet above sea level—only a little more than half as high as the national capital. Cuernavaca has long played the role of resort city, thanks to its relatively easy accessibility to the highland centers, and to its climate, which is much more comfortable than that of the places at higher altitudes. Here is a region in the tropics in which people descend, not ascend, to seek the more moderate temperatures. In the small valley lowlands, just below Cuernavaca, sugarcane was planted early in the colonial times, and Morelos became the chief source of sugar for the cities of the highlands.

The northern slopes of the valley of the Balsas are deeply dissected by the tributaries of that river. Where the surface is composed of falls of ash from the volcanoes, it is furrowed by deep, closely parallel ravines; where lava flows have been excavated by the process of river cutting, the flows stand out as prominent cliffs or detached buttes. Below Cuernavaca, the downward cutting of the rivers excavated a resistant mountain block which now stands abruptly above the valley slopes as an isolated range. In the midst of this range, explorers in the sixteenth century found a rich body of silver and tin ore: the town they founded is Taxco, now still productive as a mining center and also as a tourist paradise.

The rural population of this northern slope of the Balsas Valley is scattered in many small and mostly isolated communities—isolated not only because of the traditional system of self-sufficient agriculture, but also because of the steepness of the slopes and the difficulty of the roads. There are many little Indian villages nestled in the valley heads almost literally under the overhanging cliffs which separate them from the world above, from the communities of the highlands which are actually only a short horizontal distance away but which are very difficult to reach. Such a place is the little village of Tepoztlán, which was described in detail by the anthropologist Redfield as an example of a self-sufficient Mexican community. Other small communities, such as Cuautla, occupy miniature valley basins where the existence of flat land makes possible the cultivation of sugarcane.

During the modern period of land redistribution, the privately owned haciendas with their large stone sugar refineries have all been abandoned, their lands expropriated. Near Cuernavaca today there is one modern sugar refinery, managed by the workers, in which the cane raised by many of the *ejidos* of Morelos is ground; especially large profits are still derived, as they were in the colonial period, because this district is the nearest sugar-producing area to the big market of Mexico City. The large landowners, in pushing the cultivation of cane up the gentler slopes of the valley side, caused the destruction of those slopes by gully development. But the present *ejido* farmers, instructed in the most modern farm techniques by government experts, are making successful use of slopes which, under the hacienda system, were considered too steep for cane planting. Maize and other subsistence crops are raised by means of contour plowing and strip cropping. In this area one may observe not only the relict features of old Mexico—the abandoned stone mills, the gullied slopes—but also the features of the new Mexico, such as the co-operative mill and the lands farmed by the newest methods.

Mexico City

There are eleven cities in Latin America that have passed the million mark. Fourth among these is Mexico City. Like the chief city of most of the world's industrialized countries, Mexico City is growing at a rate much faster than that of its nearest competitor. Early in the nineteenth century Mexico City was the largest urban center in the whole American Hemisphere. It passed 300,000 in 1900 and reached a million inhabitants about 1930. By 1965 it had a population of well over 5 million.

In many ways Mexico City is a typical Spanish-American capital. Its historical nucleus is the old cathedral and the government buildings facing the *Zócalo,* as the central plaza is called. To the west of this plaza is the present commercial core, built on a pattern of narrow, right-angle streets. The Mexican capital has, also, its baroque avenue, built in the nineteenth century and patterned after the Champs Élysées of Paris. This is the Paseo de la Reforma, a wide, tree-lined avenue which was laid out to provide a long, straight approach to Chapultepec Castle from the center of the city. The castle, long the residence of the Mexican presidents, stands on the summit of a hill, some 200 feet high, which dominates the city on the west. Outside of the old central section of the capital, with its strictly rectangular pattern, the suburbs are laid out without reference to any master plan. In the modern era the lack of wide thoroughfares leading to the center of the city from the surrounding country produces almost insuperable problems of traffic congestion, but now the difficulty is being remedied by the cutting of new avenues of approach.

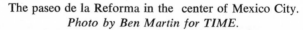

The paseo de la Reforma in the center of Mexico City.
Photo by Ben Martin for TIME.

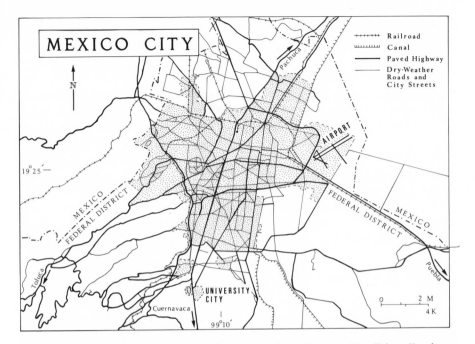

MEXICO CITY

N

Railroad
Canal
Paved Highway
Dry-Weather
Roads and
City Streets

Pachuca

AIRPORT

19°25′

MEXICO
FEDERAL DISTRICT

FEDERAL DISTRICT

MEXICO

Toluca

UNIVERSITY
CITY

Cuernavaca

Puebla

0   2 M
4 K

99°10′

Mexico City is being modernized in a number of ways. Traditionally, in a Latin-American city where automobiles are few, the most valuable residential property is located within walking distance of the central plaza, and the poorest slum districts are in the suburbs. The coming of the automobile and the construction of paved roads change this. Although the central part of Mexico City and the section which extends toward the west remain expensive residential areas, new suburban residential areas are appearing. The chief district of factories and workers' residences is toward the northwest—Tacubaya and Atzcapotzalco. The salty, dry bed of Lake Texcoco long held up the extension of the city eastward; as a happy result the city airport can now be located closer to the center of the city than would be possible if the city had grown equally in all directions.

But the bed of Lake Texcoco has also an unhappy significance for the people of the Mexican capital. The spongy lake-bed deposits offer no firm foundation for heavy buildings, and since the lake was drained the continued drying of the silt has caused a general drop in the surface level. The *Palacio de Bellas Artes,* which was started in 1900 and completed in 1935, has already settled more than five feet. The situation is further complicated by the fact that a fault line, a break in the rock crust of the earth, passes almost under Mexico City. In July 1957 a severe earthquake caused hundreds of deaths as several of the newer but poorly built structures collapsed. The architects have a solution, although an expensive one. The forty-four story "Latin-American Tower" building, which is one of the tallest buildings in Latin America, survived the earthquake without the slightest damage. It, like several of the other skyscrapers that have been built in the central area, is literally floating on huge casks.

Mexico City rivals São Paulo for leadership in manufacturing industry in Latin America. This is Mexico's largest industrial concentration. Before World War II the most important industries were textiles and food-processing plants. Since the war there has been a rapid expansion of manufacturing, in part financed by investments from the United States, and including some factories that are branches of well-known United States concerns. The factories of Mexico City now turn out a great variety of products, both consumers' goods and producers' goods. This one metropolitan center produces 56 percent of the value of all manufactures and gives employment to 60 percent of Mexico's industrial workers.

Mexico as a Political Unit

The changes in Mexico City since 1940 reflect the tremendous changes in the economy of Mexico as a whole. The Mexican Revolution had the effect of uprooting the established institutions of Mexico, such as the hacienda, of eliminating the class of large landowners, and, at first, of disrupting the economy. The internal warfare of the period from 1910 to 1915, and the constitution of 1917, set the stage for Mexico's transformation. But it was during the presidency of Lázaro Cárdenas (1934–40) that the most important changes were actually made. By 1940 much that was traditional in Mexican life had been swept aside. Since 1940 the new Mexico has been built. Mexico today is rapidly increasing its gross national product, its income per capita, so rapidly, in fact, that in the decades ahead it may well come to rival Venezuela and Argentina in economic productivity. But Mexico, as compared with either Venezuela or Argentina, has a more widely-supported state-idea, a larger degree of coherence and unity. All this is the product of Mexican leadership and bears the unmistakable stamp "Made in Mexico."

The Mexican Economy

In terms of population Mexico is the leading Spanish-American country, and is second only to Brazil in all of Latin America. Its population (42,231,000 in 1966) is far greater than that of the second Spanish-American country, Argentina. Furthermore, the Mexican population is growing at a rate of about 3.2 percent per year. The actual magnitude of this "population explosion" is not fully appreciated. It is necessary to keep in mind that it took from the time of the conquest of Mexico by the Spaniards (in 1521) to 1964 to reach the figure of 30 million people, a period of 443 years. But at present rates of growth the next 30 million will be added in only 20 years.

The changes that brought about this rapid up-turn in the rate of population increase are not unique to Mexico. As in most preindustrial parts of the world the Mexican birth rate was, and still is, very high. The net increase is due to the unprecedented decrease in the death rate, which is one of the first changes brought by the industrial revolution. Not only are professional services made available to more people, but also the increase in the proportion of the people able to read and write makes the dissemination of knowledge concerning the causes of disease more rapid. In 1944 some 53.3 percent of the Mexican people were illiterate; but by 1964 the illiteracy rate was down to 28.9 percent. More and more of the Mexican people are now informed about the greater security and material comfort that results from economic development, and they are demanding that steps be taken to provide for Mexicans the kind of life many of them have seen across the border to the north. The cultural radiation is strong in a country so close to the United States.

But how can a country move forward into the stage of economic growth where the enlargement of the economy is self-sustaining? According to W. W. Rostow, this first phase—the "take-off" stage—takes about 20 years, during which from 5 to 10 percent of the gross national product each year is used for new capital formation.[8] This means that income must be saved, not spent even for the essentials of food, clothing, and shelter. A country with a gross national product per capita of less than $200 a year has scarcely any income that can be saved. And in the presence of a rapidly growing population economic development must take place at a rate greater than that of population increase.

The money value of the new capital equipment that can provide one job in a factory varies according to the stage of development. The capital cost for one industrial job in the United States is between $50,000 and $100,000; but in Puerto Rico one new job in manufacturing industry could be provided a few years ago for only $6400. It is estimated that on the average each new job in Mexico will cost about $10,000. But consider the case of one of the new automated chemical plants, using the newest processes: the new factory required an investment of $8 million to provide jobs for 200 workers. Here one new job required a capital investment of $40,000.

The process of economic development, however, requires more than this. There must be improvements in what the economists described as "social overhead." This includes facilities that do not directly produce income, but are necessary for the developments that do produce income from goods and services. There must be roads, railroads, docks, low-income housing, electric power. In Mexico, for example, there are about 200,000 new families each year to be provided with houses; yet in the 1960's the rate of construction of new houses was only 60,000 a year. The population explosion and the movement of people from rural areas to cities have produced a major problem of

[8]W. W. Rostow, see footnote 1, p. 46.

housing shortage. In the 1960's more than half the population of Mexico lived in houses with only one room. Twenty-four million Mexicans lived in houses in which there was no running water. A new government program to hasten the construction of low-cost housing will provide 360,000 new units by 1970.

To provide employment for those who will be seeking jobs during the period up to 1980 is a huge task. It was estimated that between 1960 and 1980 the Mexican labor force would increase 67 percent, reaching 19 million. This means that each year 390,000 new jobs must be provided just to take care of the additions to the labor force. Such is the enormous challenge that must be met in any country that seeks economic development in the presence of a rapidly growing population.

The rate of Mexico's economic growth during the 1960's has been about 6.3 percent per year. In 1967 the rate of growth of the economy was 7 percent over 1966, which was between 3 percent and 3.5 percent per capita. This is well above the growth rates for most other Latin-American countries, and is well ahead of that of the United States (4.6 percent per year during the 1960's). The continued high rate of economic growth in 1967 and 1968 was supported by a large amount of domestic savings, and a strong current of direct private investment from the United States. The problem is clear: can the rate of growth be maintained over a 30-year period until continued growth becomes self-sustaining?

AGRICULTURE

Some spectacular gains have been made in Mexican agriculture since 1960. The first result of the program of land redistribution was a drop in farm production, including a decrease in the production of maize. But between 1939 and 1956 the Mexican government succeeded in changing this downward trend. By 1956 agricultural production had increased 300 percent over 1930. The area under crops was increased by about 33 percent, and there was a 50 percent gain in the area under irrigation. The increase of production was the result not only of an increase of the harvested area, but also of gains in the yields per acre of all crops. Better seeds, insecticides, fertilizers, and soil conditioners raised crop yields. For example, maize, which used to yield only 8.7 bushels per acre in the period between 1925 and 1929, now yields over 15 bushels per acre.

The increase in the yield of maize came as a result of effective teamwork between the Mexican government and a small number of agricultural experts sent to Mexico by the Rockefeller Foundation. The hybrid seed developed in the United States during the 1930's had produced very large increases in yields per acre; but when tried out in Mexico these new varieties were not successful. The farm technicians collected samples from all over the country of the highest-yielding maize that could be found. These were planted, and seeds from the best plants were selected. On some experimental farms, yields of 150 bushels per acre were produced. The next problem was to get the farmers to use the new seed. But farmers learn from demonstration; when the results of using the new seed became known the farmers began using it exclusively.

A similar story can be related for such other crops as wheat and potatoes. In 1950 Mexico had to import 427 million tons of wheat, just to feed the city dwellers who had started to eat wheat bread. By 1965 domestic wheat production had been increased so much that Mexico was able to export 465 million tons of wheat. New disease-resistant varieties of potato were developed which so greatly increased production per acre that many former subsistence farmers were now able to sell their surpluses in the national market, and then use the new income to buy consumer goods. Mexican potatoes have been sent to many parts of the world where hunger is the usual experience and starvation seems only a few decades ahead.

The increase of farm production is also the result of the use of better farm methods. Oxen and wooden plows, or men with hoes, are being replaced by modern machinery. In the rural areas storage facilities have been built, so that the farmer is not forced to sell all of his harvest at one time. New transportation facilities give wider access to markets than ever before. Between 1945 and 1950 all the Mexican railroads were rebuilt on standard gauge (4 ft. 8½ in.). Modern, all-weather highways were provided for motor trucks.

Perhaps the most important change of all, however, is the establishment of agricultural training schools for farm technicians. By 1966 Mexico had more than 700 graduate agricultural scientists. Considering that such a profession scarcely existed in Mexico in the 1930's, this corps of skilled specialists is a clear measure of the effects of the industrial revolution in the transformation of the traditional culture of Mexico.

THE GROWTH OF THE SECONDARY AND TERTIARY SECTORS

People who produce things from earth resources—such as farmers and miners and fishers—constitute the primary sector of an economy. The secondary sector includes workers in manufacturing industry. The tertiary sector is made up of people employed in providing services, such as retail storekeepers, teachers, doctors, lawyers, and other professionals. In any developing economy the improvement of agriculture inevitably results in a decrease in the proportion of the working force employed in that sector. Better farm techniques result in greater production per worker and also in the withdrawal of farming from such places as steep mountain slopes. The people who can no longer be employed in farming must find jobs in the secondary and tertiary sectors.

Mexico has expanded its manufacturing industries at a rapid rate since 1950. In 1956 the value of all manufactured products exceeded the value of agricultural products for the first time. Yet of the whole Mexican working force, more than 50 percent are still employed in agriculture. The continued development of the economy will see more and more agricultural workers move into the other two sectors. Between 1950 and 1960, for example, the value of the production of textiles in Mexico increased 177 percent; but during this same period there was a 29 percent decrease in the number of people employed in textile factories. Many of these people have moved into the tertiary sector.

All this quickening of the economic life is reflected in a rapidly expanding market for consumer goods, and for the services that sell such goods. The farmers who for the first time can raise a surplus to sell now want to buy all kinds of gadgets that they have never been able to buy before. There is a new market for household electrical appliances, so that the women will not have to work endlessly with their muscles just to prepare food. Donald Brand reports that one new gadget—the *molino de nixtamal*—will release women and young girls from the time-consuming job of mixing the dough for tortillas by hand.[9] As a result of these changes there are many new factories offering employment, and many new retail shop-keepers in the small communities that are enjoying unprecedented prosperity. Life in a Mexican community is not at all what it was even a decade ago.

EXPORTS AND IMPORTS

The nature of Mexico's foreign trade has undergone major changes since the beginning of the Revolution in 1910. Before that date the chief exports were minerals, and the chief imports were basic foods and railroad equipment. Even as late as the 1930's, the chief exports were minerals (silver, gold, lead, zinc, copper, and antimony). Oil exports, which started decreasing in the 1920's, ceased altogether after 1938, when Mexico began using all of its production for domestic purposes. Since World War II the make-up of the exports has changed radically. All agricultural exports in 1939 made up 28 percent of the total; by 1955 they made up over 55 percent. In 1964 the leading exports were agricultural products: cotton (16 percent), coffee (9 percent). Other exports included sugar, frozen shrimp, and the minerals— lead, zinc, and copper. The basic foods (maize, wheat, potatoes) are now exported, and the imports are mostly industrial goods and machinery. The leading customers for Mexico's products in 1964 were the United States (58 percent), and Japan (7 percent). Of the imports, the United States supplied 69 percent and West Germany 6 percent.

A very important part of Mexico's trade balance is derived from tourists, mostly from the United States. In 1934, tourists brought to Mexico only about $30 million; but in 1963 the income from the tourists amounted to $655 mil-

[9]Donald D. Brand, in *Focus,* Vol. 16, No. 10, 1966, published by the American Geographical Society of New York.

lion, which was larger than foreign exchange earnings from all other sources combined.

THE MEXICAN ECONOMY EVALUATED

The process of economic growth in Mexico offers an example of the importance of balanced development. The Mexicans use some 15 percent of the gross national product each year for new capital formation. This, together with a considerable investment from the United States, helps to support and modernize the economy at several different points simultaneously. This balanced approach to development is an often-overlooked essential, and Mexico demonstrates the results that can be expected when all aspects of the program are planned in advance. The purpose of decreasing the concentration of subsistence farmers in the Central region has been served by increasing the agricultural area in the North Pacific, the North, and Gulf regions. The reduction of the number of subsistence farmers everywhere has quickened the tempo of the economic life throughout the country. Notable has been the increase in small retail business in the villages and small towns. Before the *ejido* program went into effect the large landowners used to do much of their purchasing in Mexico City or in foreign countries. Now there is no part of the country where the retail stores have not felt an increase in business.

The question remains, however, whether the Mexican economy can be expanded fast enough to keep ahead of the population growth. There are many observers who believe that it cannot and that some kind of population control is essential. In the late 1960's more than half of the working force of Mexico was still employed in agriculture, and not all of these had yet emerged from the status of subsistence farmers. As agriculture is improved, larger and larger numbers of farmers must enter the secondary and tertiary sectors. The economy must expand fast enough to take care of this rearrangement of the working force together with the annual increment of new workers.

There are some observers who believe that the Mexico City metropolitan area is too large. Yet studies of the locational advantages of various parts of the Mexican territory still indicate that the greatest advantage for access to domestic markets, for the assembly of raw materials, and for the supply of workers is to be found in Mexico City itself. Nevertheless, the government is attempting to decentralize manufacturing industry. Toluca has become the automobile manufacturing center of Mexico; and many kinds of new manufactures are being developed at Querétaro, Guanajuato, and other cities of the Central region. Monterrey and Monclova still remain the centers of the steel industry.

All these developments require massive inputs of new capital. A larger part of the new capital comes from domestic sources. But Mexico is also receiving a large flow of private investment from the United States. In 1963, of all

United States investments abroad, Mexico's share was about 2 percent. The stability of Mexico was a major factor in this flow.

The Political Situation

Since the Mexican Revolution of 1910 to 1915, Mexico has gone a long way toward the solution of the basic problem of establishing order and coherence within the state. Mexico is one of the countries of Latin America that has formulated a state-idea sufficiently powerful to command the support of a great majority of the people. The system is not democratic, as we in the

University of Mexico. *Courtesy of Canadian Pacific Railway.*

United States use this term; but it is distinctively Mexican.

Ever since the adoption of the constitution of 1917 and the election of General Carranza to the presidency, Mexico has been operated by only one political party. This was called the *Partido Revolucionario Nacional.* Since 1946, in order to indicate that the purposes of the Revolution were now accepted by every one, the party was renamed the *Partido Revolucionario Institucional.* Although other political parties are not prohibited, including Communist-inspired parties, there has been no challenge to the authority of the P.R.I. When the president nears the end of his term of six years, and after consulting with other party leaders, he names his successor. The election, in which all citizens, men and women alike, express their opinions in a secret ballot, has only one slate of officers. The vote is an expression of support for the acts of the party leaders. The president has behind him the whole organization of the P.R.I. He names the governors of the states, the members who may run for posts in the congress, and the judges of the supreme court. Furthermore the party includes only civilians, and the Mexican army has become a strictly professional body.

Yet democracy of a kind is making its appearance in Mexico. The *ejidos* bring their members together in "town-meetings" for a discussion of local issues, and these issues are decided by vote of the majority. At the "grassroots" level, democratic procedures are being nurtured.

The success of the Revolution and of the party in gaining the support of the overwhelming majority of the people of Mexico has cut the ground from under both Fascists and Communists. The extreme right is represented by the *Sinarquistas,* a group organized much like the famous "Black Shirts" of Mussolini's Italy. The Communists have not failed for lack of effort, for certainly the position of Mexico on the border of the United States and the common fear of the United States entertained by many Mexicans would seem to offer the incentive and also the proper climate for Communist infiltration. But the fact is that the Mexicans have a program of change, and it is one that is strictly their own. Foreign ideas, like Communism, gain little support, and the support has declined considerably since World War II.

The P.R.I. offers the only way into politics. But it embraces all shades of political opinion, from extreme right to extreme left. A person who seeks public office has only to prove his loyalty to the program of the Revolution. The other parties do not even trouble to organize slates of opposition candidates, so certain are the P.R.I. candidates of success. In Latin America any candidate for high political office uses a newspaper to give publicity to his views. But in Mexico even the newspapers are controlled by the P.R.I.— through control of the supply of paper.

The Mexicans are a deeply religious people. This is one Latin-American country in which religion constitutes a real part of the state-idea. The Mexican Catholics focus their attention on the Virgin of Guadalupe, whose shrine is located near Mexico City. The Virgin is supposed to confer special favor on Mexicans; she is pictured as the ideal of Mexican motherhood. To a very real extent the Mexican state exists for the purpose of protecting and of supporting the ideals symbolized by the Virgin of Guadalupe.

The Mexicans are very close to the United States. Every schoolchild studies history, and in the history books he learns how the United States took the whole northern part of Mexico, and how the United States forces stormed the heights of Chapultepec and defeated the cadets of the Mexican military academy who were defending it. Along with the veneration of the Virgin of Guadalupe, the homage to the heroes of Chapultepec is also a part of the Mexican state-idea. Most of the Mexicans who can read hold an admiration for the economy of the United States; but there is also a widespread fear that the United States might again use its overwhelming power to force its weaker neighbors to adopt unwelcome policies. The Mexican is extremely conscious of his nationality, and proud of his government that can deal with other governments of the world as an equal. He is very sensitive to the suggestion of inferior status.

These attitudes are all a part of the state-idea that gives Mexico political cohesion and stability. Diverse racial groups, people of different social status, and of different income level, and people of all shades of political opinion, have become first of all Mexicans. Probably the poorest class is no better off than it was before the Revolution, and it has increased in absolute numbers. But meanwhile there has been a very great increase in the urban middle classes; and for these people the future offers hope. And all Mexicans look with pride at their writers, artists, and musicians who give expression to the deeper meanings of the changes that have swept over their country.

República de Guatemala

Area: 42,042 square miles
Population: (1967 estimate) 4,717,000
　　　　　last census (1964) 4,284,473
Capital city: Guatemala City; (1967 estimate) 652,900
Percent urban: (1950) 25
Birth rate per 1,000: (1966) 43.5; Death rate per 1,000: (1966) 16.8
Annual percent of increase: (1958–64) 3.3
Percent literate: (1950) 29.4
Percent labor force in agriculture: (1950) 67.3
Gross national product per capita: (1966) $314
Unit of currency: quetzal (1968: 1.00 per dollar)
Leading crops in acreage: maize, coffee, beans

COMMERCE, 1965 *(expressed in percentage of values)*
Percent of total Latin-American exports: 1.8 (1956: 1.0)
Percent of total Latin-American imports: 2.3

Exports (1966)
　　　　coffee 49
　　　　cotton 18　　　also bananas and chicle

Exports to (1966)		Imports from (1966)	
United States	36 (1956: 72)	United States	42 (1956: 67)
West Germany	14	West Germany	10
Japan	11	El Salvador	10
El Salvador	10	Japan	7

Chapter 4 □ Guatemala and British Honduras

GUATEMALA

Guatemala is another country that is struggling with the problems resulting from fundamental revolutionary change. The changes in attitudes, objectives, and technology are those associated with the spread of the industrial revolution and the democratic revolution. But in Guatemala these changes are taking place in an unusual setting. Traditionally Guatemala has been a country with two cultures, each occupying a distinct part of the national territory. But now the two cultures are being rapidly remade into one with one widely supported state-idea, which is giving Guatemala a distinctive national personality. The old designation—"banana republic"—is today quite irrelevant. The kind of national personality that emerges is of great concern to the United States and to the other American states.

The People

One of the two cultures of Guatemala is Indian. A little more than half of the total population is made up of descendants of the Mayas, who speak no Spanish, but rather one of several Indian dialects. The traditional Indian society is divided into small communities, occupied by groups of interrelated families, each community practicing a kind of subsistence agriculture, but with some specialization in handicrafts or farm products that support a system of Indian markets. The Indians are Catholics, but the religious rituals include interesting mixtures of Catholic and pagan forms. Each community has its own rituals for appeasing the gods and insuring good harvests. Religious practices enter into every aspect of life, ranging from the cultivation of the soil to the methods of curing the sick, or to the procedures for selecting political policy. The Indians have been traditionally separate from the rest of the Guatemalans: their land was never included in the large private estates of the people of Spanish descent, as Indian land was in Mexico. But, because their farms were not large enough to provide all the food they needed, and because they became dependent upon certain products which they themselves did not produce —such as metal hoes, machetes,[1] adzes, needles, medicines, and even certain kinds of seed—the Indians found it necessary to derive some income from this other society with which they were so closely associated geographically.

Therefore the Indians have been willing to accept temporary employment as farm laborers on the coffee or banana plantations or cattle estates. In fact, it would have been impossible to carry on these other kinds of agricultural activities without the Indian workers.

The other culture group in Guatemala is known as *Ladino*.[2] The Ladinos include all the various peoples who no longer live as Indians. If an Indian learns to speak Spanish, begins to wear shoes, gives up Indian dress, abandons the religious practices of the Indian communities, and perhaps moves away from his native community, he is classed as a Ladino. The Ladinos also include the perhaps 5 percent of the total population that is of unmixed Spanish ancestry, and the large proportion of people who are mestizos.

Guatemala has the largest population of any country in Central America. Yet only the southern third of the national territory is densely settled (Map 31, p. 175). Most of the people, both Indians and Ladinos, are concentrated in the highlands that overlook the Pacific coast. The whole northern third of the country, the part known as Petén, has almost no permanent inhabitants. This is the area that occupies the Yucatán Peninsula, on the borders of Mexico and British Honduras. There is still plenty of empty and potentially productive land into which settlement might spread.

Guatemala's population is increasing rapidly, but this rapid increase has started only recently. When Guatemala gained its independence from Spain as a part of the Empire of Mexico in 1821, the population was estimated at about 500,000. By 1865 the number had increased to 1,800,000. A census in 1921 counted just over 2 million; and another census in 1950 counted 2,788,000. But only fourteen years later the population had suddenly increased to more than 4 million. This sharp up-turn in the net rate of growth since 1950 is the result of the application of modern health measures in a country where the birth rate has always been high. In 1966 the birth rate was

[1]The *machete* is a long-bladed knife with a short wooden handle used throughout tropical America for such work as cutting brush, harvesting crops, or as a weapon. For many decades almost all the machetes sold in Latin America were manufactured at Collinsville, near Hartford, Connecticut.

[2]Whetten points out that the word *Ladino* is derived from *Latino,* and refers to persons who have adopted the way of living of the people of Latin origin. See Nathan L. Whetten, *Guatemala, the Land and the People,* New Haven, Conn., 1961.

43.5 per thousand, but the death rate had been lowered to 16.8. The average net rate of growth in the 1960's was 3.3 percent per year.

The Land

The national territory of Guatemala extends across the Isthmus of Central America from the Pacific to the Caribbean. It includes four major divisions: the Pacific coastal lowland; the highlands; the deep, wet valleys that drain out to the Caribbean between steep-sided fingers of highland; and a part of the densely forested Peninsula of Yucatán (Map 27, p. 171).

The Pacific coastal lowland is a southeastward continuation of the lowland of Chiapas. At the Mexico–Guatemala border it is about 25 miles wide, and it continues for about 150 miles across Guatemala into El Salvador, where it is pinched out by the highlands. The coast is straight, with no harbors, and until modern breakwaters were built ships had to load or unload while riding at anchor off the sandy beach. This lowland strip was covered, when the Spaniards first came upon it, by a woodland savanna. Along the base of the highlands, and on the steep slope facing toward the Pacific, the land was covered with a seasonal forest. The coastal lowland was for a long time neglected by farmers, and was used only for the grazing of cattle on the unfenced range. Only since 1960 have agricultural possibilities been realized. The whole lowland is covered by productive, porous soils of volcanic origin, developed on material washed down from the volcanic highlands. All along the Pacific coast, from Chiapas in Mexico to Costa Rica, the Pacific coastal lowland is an area of rapid new settlement.

The highlands are similar to those of Chiapas in Mexico. The underlying geologic structures run in a general west-to-east direction. On the Pacific side they are deeply mantled with volcanic ash and lava, the accumulation of which is deepest in the western part of Guatemala, where the elevation varies from about 3,500 feet to more than 10,000 feet above sea level. Standing above the upland surface are several volcanoes, some still active. The highest mountain in Central America is Mt. Tajumulco, which rises 13,816 feet above sea level. Among the volcanic cones are several basins of irregular shape, in one of which is the magnificent Lake Atitlán. The basins are between 5 and 8 thousand feet in elevation. From the prominent south-facing edge of the highlands only short, torrential streams descend to the Pacific; but the greater part of the highland area is drained to the Caribbean. The headwaters of the Caribbean drainage have cut very steep canyons into the easily eroded volcanic ash. In the high western part of the country only small patches of undissected upland surface remain as mesas sharply bordered by the walls of the canyons. Toward the east, where the volcanic cover is thinner, and where the streams have cut their valleys down close to sea level, the underlying geological structures are exposed, forming a succession of steep ridges, sharp

Lake Atitlán in highlands of Guatemala. *Photo Courtesy—Pan American Airways.*

divides, and deep valley lowlands. Some of the ridges extend all the way to the margins of the Gulf of Honduras.

The vegetation cover of the highlands exhibits the two basic characteristics of mountain geography: a general zoning by altitude, and an intricacy of detail that makes the vertical zones in some places difficult to identify. Generally, as one ascends to higher altitudes the semideciduous forest of the Pacific slope and the thick rain forest of the Caribbean slope give way to oak, cypress, and pine. Above 10,000 feet pine grows only in patches and there are wide areas of high altitude grassland.

Three deep valley lowlands converge on the narrow head of the Gulf of Honduras. In the north, on the border of British Honduras, is the valley of the Río Sarstún; in the middle is the swampy lowland in which Lake Izabal lies; near the border of Honduras is the largest lowland, the valley of the Río Motagua. Long fingers of the highlands separate these deep valley lowlands from each other.

The northern part of Guatemala includes a part of the Peninsula of Yucatán. The surface is a limestone tableland, between 5 and 7 hundred feet above sea level. The drainage is underground, except for the lakes which fill rapidly and spread over the surface during heavy rains. The whole country is densely covered with evergreen forest, in the midst of which lie the all but completely hidden ruins of the Maya cities, now visible only from the air.

The Pattern of Settlement

In Guatemala, as in Mexico, the distribution of Indians in the preconquest period has been reproduced in the modern patterns of population. The high basins of the southern highlands were occupied by a relatively dense group of sedentary agricultural people whose basic food crop was maize. The site of the present town of Quetzaltenango was the focus of this pre-Spanish settlement. Outside of the highland area, the rest of what is now Guatemala had a relatively small population of shifting cultivators or nomadic hunters and fishers.

The Spanish conquerors entered Guatemala from Mexico during the first decade after Cortés had founded Mexico City. The first expedition reached the southern highlands in 1523, and founded the first Spanish town on the site of the present Guatemala City in 1524. Antigua, founded in 1541, became the political center from which the whole Captaincy-General of Guatemala was administered (Map 16, p. 39). In 1544, Father Bartolomé de Las Casas, who led the movement to prohibit the enslavement of the Indians, founded at Cobán the first of the Spanish missions in America.

Compared with Mexico, however, Guatemala yielded little in the way of quick wealth. To be sure, there were silver mines near Huehuetenango, and these mines are still productive. But the ore bodies of this part of the Spanish domain proved disappointing. Many of the Spaniards moved on southeastward along the isthmus. The few who remained were granted large estates which they developed in the traditional Spanish manner. The greater part of each estate was used for the grazing of cattle or not used at all. On the better lands the owner tried to establish some kind of commercial agriculture that could pay the high cost of shipment to a market.

In the course of time the highland area, which was the only part of Guatemala that was settled, was divided into two sharply contrasted regions. The line of division was roughly the 5,000-foot contour, the line which in this area marks the division between *tierra templada* below and *tierra fría* above. The *tierra templada* was preferred by the Spaniards; the *tierra fría* was left for the Indians. Guatemala City, just under 5,000 feet above sea level, on the divide between the rivers draining to the Caribbean and those draining to the Pacific, was near the boundary between these two contrasted regions of settlement. The country below 5,000 feet was mostly in the southeastern part of the highlands, in the drainage basin of the Río Motagua, and along the upper parts of the escarpment where the highlands drop down to the Pacific. The country above 5,000 feet was located mostly in the southwestern part of the highlands. The third part of the country, the lowlands of the *tierra caliente* below 1,600 feet, remained almost empty until the develop-

Volcanic mountains
in highlands near
Guatemala City.

ment of the banana plantations of the twentieth century. The vast area of the Department of Petén in northern Guatemala is covered with dense forest, crisscrossed by a maze of footpaths used by the chicle gatherers in going to and from the camps where the gum is prepared for shipment. This is the world's major source of chicle for chewing gum, yet this whole area, some 33 percent of the total national territory, is occupied by less than 1 percent of the total population.

Indian Settlements of the High Country

The part of Guatemala in which more than 60 percent of the population is Indian is located in the highlands west of Guatemala City. Indian settlements are arranged around Quetzaltenango, Huehuetenango, and the shores of Lake Atitlán. Indians are also concentrated farther east around Cobán. These areas that are still predominantly Indian, except for Ladinos in the large cities and towns, were never divided into private estates by the Spanish conquerors. The Indian communities range in population from a few thousand to more than 50,000. In some, the people live in villages or towns, and each day go out to work the surrounding farms. In other districts the people live in family units on the lands they are cultivating.

The terrain in this part of Guatemala is very rugged. Each mesa-like remnant of the highland surface, isolated by thousand-foot cliffs, is occupied by one closely knit community; but to visit neighboring communities may require the ascent and descent of very steep trails passable only for people on foot or for mules. Each community has its own distinctive customs, its own religious practices, its own unique dress, and even its own dialect.

The Indians are skilled farmers. They use hoes to build ridges and deep furrows that run like contours along the slopes. As a result of this ancient practice there is very little soil erosion, even where steep mountain slopes are cultivated. Throughout the Indian area, up to an altitude of about 9,500 feet, maize is the one major crop. It occupies almost every field, often along with beans, chili, and other vegetables. Where wheat is raised, it is sold to merchants for use in the cities where people eat white bread. More than 75 percent by weight of the Indian diet is provided by maize. The yields of maize, unlike those of Mexico, are high—estimated to be as much as 40 bushels to the acre on the best lands. At the lower altitudes two crops a year can be grown on the same fields, but for every thousand feet of increased altitude, the length of the season required to ripen the crop increases by several weeks. With yields of this order it is estimated that a farm of about seven-and-a-half acres should be adequate to provide the kind of living required by an Indian family. Yet the average Indian farm is considerably less than this minimum. The available farmland in each community is too little to provide for all the inhabitants. Even with the high maize yields, many people are suffering from inadequate diet.

Why, then, is there not a pioneer movement into the many excellent but unoccupied parts of Guatemala? Why is 46 percent of the country essentially undeveloped? Why is there a chronic shortage of labor on the commercial plantations? It is simply a fact that the Indians prefer to remain at home. The small, compact communities develop a social cohesion among their members that is difficult to break, if, indeed, it were desirable to do so. When the Indian farmer finds that he must supplement the meager production from his farm from other sources he accepts temporary employment

The weekly fair at Chichicastenango, Guatemala.

picking coffee, cutting sugarcane, or working in the banana plantations; but after a time he returns again to his village. Pioneering, even in other parts of the *tierra fría* which are thinly populated today, has no appeal.

Above 9,500 feet, the upper limit of maize, the only crop which can be grown is the potato, which can be ripened up to an altitude of about 10,500 feet. The country above 10,000 feet includes the slopes of the volcanoes and certain relatively level and undissected remnants of the volcanic plateau known as the Altos Cuchumatanes, just to the north of the Indian town of Huehuetenango. Above the highest Indian villages which are supported by the potato, the land is used for the grazing of sheep. About a third of the total area is occupied by one 60,000-acre hacienda whose owner rents his land to the Indians for the pasturage of sheep and who buys the wool from the Indians.

Another interesting characteristic of the pattern of settlement in this Maya area has been described by McBride. There are many examples of towns which remain almost empty except during church festivals or fairs. Each town holds its fair on certain days of the week as determined by the ancient Maya calendar, and itinerant merchants make a practice of going from town to town to display their wares. Farmers may have city homes where they and their families come during fairs, but they actually live most of the time close to the fields they are cultivating. McBride suggests that this may have been the characteristic way of life in the cities of the Mayan empire, which seem to have been so large that one wonders how food could have been brought to them in sufficient quantities without domestic animals or wheeled vehicles.

Commercial Agriculture in the Highlands

In the most striking contrast to the Indian subsistence farms are the plantations of commercial crops on large private estates. The people of Spanish origin were not interested in subsistence; they wanted a crop of sufficient value to stand the high cost of transportation. They introduced sugarcane, wheat, and domestic animals into Guatemala, but the highly stabilized society of the Mayas has never made much of a place for these importations. The Spaniards did find two native Indian crops from which they were able to derive a profit—cacao and indigo. In the second quarter of the nineteenth century they brought in cochineal insects which were fed on a variety of cactus known as *nopal*. From the insects a kind of red dye was manufactured. Cochineal and indigo were of major importance around Antigua and Guatemala City until the manufacture of chemical dyes after 1857 put an end to the market for the more costly agricultural dyes.

After the middle of the nineteenth century the large landowners of Guatemala turned to the production of coffee, following the lead of other Central American countries. For the last eighty years, coffee has been the chief export of the country and the chief source of revenue for the treasury. The success of this form of plantation economy in Guatemala, as in other parts of Central America, is based on a combination of especially favorable climatic conditions. Coffee of the most desirable flavor is produced where the temperatures average in the 60's and 70's and where the rainfall is concentrated in one season—conditions which are met ideally in the *tierra templada* of Central America.

The large landowners who plant commercial crops have faced a chronic shortage of labor ever since the early days of settlement. One method after another has been tried to secure Indian workers: slavery, against which Las Casas waged a bitter fight in the sixteenth century; peonage or debt bondage, which was legal until recently; and other more subtle ways of forcing the Indian to seek additional wages to supplement the products of his small farm. The wages paid to the Indian are very small. But the landowner who insisted he could not continue to produce crops if it were not for the low cost of Indian labor was wrong: if the Indian were a more efficient worker he could earn higher wages, and the landowner would not need such a large number of workers.

Before World War II there were two kinds of coffee planters in Guatemala. Around Guatemala City and Antigua, and in the upper parts of the Motagua Valley, the planters were people of Spanish descent or Ladinos whose ancestors had lived in Guatemala for many generations. The landowners of this area constituted the aristocracy of the country, the class with the chief political power and social prestige. The plantations were worked by migratory hired hands.

The other class of planters were of German extraction, probably descendants of those who emigrated from Germany between 1860 and 1870, but who had retained their German citizenship. The German colonists settled as pioneers in two localities: on the Pacific slope of the southwestern part of the highlands, overlooking Ocós and Champerico; and in the rugged central highlands between Huehuetenango and Cobán. Attempts by the government of Guatemala to establish settlers in the eastern part of the country before the middle of the nineteenth century had failed; but here, as elsewhere in Latin America, the Germans demonstrated their abilities as woodland pioneers. Although foreigners made up only about 1 percent of the landowners of Guatemala in 1935, they owned over 30 percent of the cultivated area. About 48 percent of the large properties of the country before the beginning of World War II were owned by foreigners, mostly Germans, and from these properties came nearly two-thirds of the total coffee production of Guatemala.

During the early stages of World War II, the Guatemalan government accused the German planters of plotting a German invasion. They were promptly interned, or sent out of the country, and their prosperous plantations were taken over by the government. After the war the government remained in the coffee business, and has earned as much as 15 percent of the revenue of the treasury from the sale of coffee. In 1958 some of the plantations were sold to private individuals.

The finest coffee lands of Guatemala are on the upper part of the Pacific slope of the highlands, at altitudes between 1,000 and 5,000 feet. Here there is ample rainfall, but there is also a dry season from December to April during which the coffee is harvested. The deep volcanic soils are highly productive, and the coffee trees, grown under the shade of larger trees, protect the slopes from erosion. From this part of Guatemala comes some of the world's finest coffee.

Commercial Agriculture in the Lowlands

For a long time the lowlands on either side of Guatemala were avoided. People who even visited these areas contracted fever, which we now understand to be carried by mosquitoes. During the colonial period small parts of the Pacific coastal lowland were used to grow cacao and sugarcane, with the use of slave labor. Mostly these lowlands were used for cattle ranches. The animals grazed on the woodland savannas which were maintained by annual burning during the dry season. The wet lowlands on the Caribbean side remained mostly empty.

In 1899 several fruit-growing companies in the United States joined to form the United Fruit Company. The company started to make use of the lowlands of Central America for banana plantations in Costa Rica, and in 1906 began to develop banana plantations in the lower part of the Río Motagua. Puerto Barrios became a banana port, with special banana-loading docks. The workers on the plantations were mostly highland Indians who were attracted to the lowlands by the promise of higher wages, good, comfortable homes, and protection from disease. The significance of the mosquito as a carrier of disease had been discovered in Cuba, and around the plantations mosquitoes were practically eliminated. The company also built a railroad from Puerto Barrios to Guatemala City, and then on to the Pacific port of San José.

Then the company began to face the problem of banana disease. The Panama disease, which attacks the roots of the plant, and Sigatoka disease, which attacks the leaves, began first to appear in the older plantations in Costa Rica. By the 1930's the plantations in the Motagua Valley were also being attacked, and the company decided to shift its plantations to the Pacific side. In 1934 nearly 88 percent of the bananas in Guatemala were produced in the Motagua Valley, and as late as 1938 this part of Guatemala was still in the lead with 62 percent. But in 1939 the new plantations on the Pacific side came into production, and in this year they accounted for 53 percent of the total. By 1956 the Pacific side was producing 90 percent of the Guatemalan crop. The company developed a plantation at Tequisate which was equipped with an overhead spray system for the control of banana diseases. The company also gained control of large acreages of potential banana land which were held for the future expansion of the plantations. The Tequisate bananas were brought by rail to Puerto Barrios for shipment.

For a while it seemed that the overhead spray system might be the answer to the control of disease. But spray systems were expensive to install and to operate. Now the dusting of crops by airplane is found to be much less expensive and fully as effective. But the company has also developed several disease-resistant varieties of bananas. The chief areas of banana planting are once again in the lower valley of the Motagua. In 1964 the company closed its Tequisate Plantation and made it available to the government of Guatemala for farm colonization.

Since the 1950's the Pacific coastal lowland has become an area of rapid new settlement and greatly increased productivity. As in Mexico, this movement to the lowlands was made possible by the great advances in the control of insects and in other health measures. Insecticides have eliminated malaria and yellow fever, and antibiotics have greatly reduced the hazards of general ill-health. Farmers from the highlands now come in large numbers to new colonies established in the lowlands. Some of these colonies are on former United Fruit Company land, some are on the estates of former political and military leaders who have been deposed. All-weather highways and new port works make the lowlands accessible. Agricultural technologists guide the farmers in the most efficient farm practices.

Two products now come from these lowlands. The most important is cotton. In fact cotton is now being produced all along the Pacific coast of Central America, from the Tapachula district of Mexico (Map 29, p. 173) to Costa Rica. In 1950 this whole area produced less than one hundred bales: by 1963–64 it was producing over a million bales, or 2 percent of the world's cotton production. These coastal lowlands have the world's highest yields per acre for cotton that is not irrigated—some 1½ bales per acre. The crop is planted in late July, and between August and November the fields are sprayed from airplanes at least once a week, for only in this way can the insect pests be controlled. Since the cotton fields are interspersed with forests and pastures where no chemical sprays are used, useful insects are not destroyed. New cotton ginning equipment has been installed at Retalhuleu, Tequisate, and Escuintla. About 80 percent of the crop is exported to Japan, for which this whole coastal region has become a major supplier.

The other commercial product from the lowlands of Guatemala is meat. But the animals are no longer fed on the open range. Rather they are kept on planted pastures. A large packing plant has been built at Escuintla where the animals are slaughtered and the meat is processed. Heavy refrigerator trailer trucks, each holding twenty tons of meat, carry the product from even as far away as Costa Rica. The trucks cross Guatemala to the Caribbean port of Matías de Galvez, a new port near Puerto Barrios. Here the trailers are loaded on specially designed ships. Every five days one of these ships sails from Matías de Galvez for Miami, Florida. The ships also carry shrimp and vegetables. This shipment of food products to the United States has opened up a new market for the products of the Pacific lowlands of Guatemala, El Salvador, Nicaragua, Honduras, and Costa Rica.

Guatemala as a Political Unit

All these developments in different parts of Guatemala are details in a larger picture. Guatemala is feeling the impact of revolutionary change brought by both the industrial revolution and the democratic revolution. But in Guatemala this impact produces a distinctive set of problems and conditions. Guatemala is a country composed of diverse ethnic elements. Most of its people are still isolated from the international system of money and markets. Yet the Guatemalan leaders are seeking to define a national identity which will include both Indians and Ladinos.

The impact of these two revolutions in Guatemala raises a basic question of policy. In British and Anglo-American experience economic development came first, and social change followed with a minimum of dislocation. But in France social change came first. Furthermore Mexico, which is most exposed to the cultural radiation from Anglo-America, resisted the idea that economic development should come first. The Mexicans were successful in reversing the sequence. What should happen in Guatemala? There are powerful North American groups, including both private corporations such as the United Fruit Company and government agencies such as the Agency for International Development (AID), who are ready to assist in the promotion of economic development. But events in Guatemala have produced at least a consideration of the possibility of putting social change first. The Alliance for Progress calls for both social change and economic development, but does not specify which should come first.

The Economic Situation

Guatemala is still a country of very poor farmers. Some 67 percent of the workers are employed as farmers or in related activities. In this high proportion of people supported by agriculture, Guatemala is surpassed in Latin America only by Haiti. Of the total population of Guatemala, 75 percent are rural and more than 70 percent are illiterate. The great majority of the rural people are subsistence farmers who produce nothing for sale, and who are able to supply themselves with only about a third of what the experts think is a minimum diet for the maintenance of health. The gross national product per capita ($314 in 1966) is an average figure that masks the great contrast between the well-to-do minority and the very poor majority. The average income per year of the rural Guatemalans is only about $83 per person, and has been dropping slowly for many decades.

What measures would be necessary to start Guatemala on the road toward economic development? In 1966 it was estimated that in order to provide for an annual increase of 2.5 percent in the value of goods and services there would have to be an annual investment of between 50 and 60 million dollars. And since the annual population increase is 3.3 percent, the annual growth of the economy at a rate of 2.5 percent would represent a steady deterioration. Just to stay even with the population growth, maintaining the same state of poverty, would require an average annual growth of the economy by some 4.5 percent.

Yet new capital investment is not easy to arrange. In 1966 the government hoped to attract some 30 million dollars from foreign investment, and then to find 26 million dollars from domestic sources. But the well-to-do people with incomes large enough to yield some savings are often reluctant to invest these funds in Guatemala. Will the country provide stability and security, or would it be better to send savings outside for investment in the United States or in Switzerland? In 1966 the government undertook to accomplish two things: first an attempt was made to persuade the well-to-do minority that Guatemala would be a safe place for investment; and second they proposed a new—and unprecedented—tax law that would bring some revenue into the treasury. The government in 1968 was thwarted in both efforts. Armed conflict by groups from both the extreme right and the extreme left increased the insecurity of life, even in the cities; and pressure from the well-to-do people resulted in the abandonment of efforts to impose tax measures.

The economic situation since 1965 has failed to show improvement. In both 1966 and 1967 the rate of economic growth per capita was less than 1 percent. The gains in cotton and meat production on the Pacific lowlands, which brought increased revenues in 1965, slowed down in 1966 and 1967 due in part to drought and in part to the spread of cotton diseases resulting from inadequate use of insecticides. Between 1950 and 1960 exports of coffee made up between 70 and 80 percent of the value of all exports. It was an improvement, therefore, in 1964, to find that coffee made up only 46 percent of the total value of exports. In that year cotton made up 15 percent, and bananas 6 percent. But Guatemala's economic troubles were increased in 1967 by a general decrease in coffee prices.

Guatemala is no longer so largely dependent on the market in the United States for its sales abroad, or on imports from the United States, as it used to be. In 1956 the United States purchased 72 percent of Guatemala's exports and provided 67 percent of the imports; but in 1965 only 36 percent of the exports were sold in the United States, and 42 percent of the imports came from there. After 1965 there were important increases of export to West Germany, Japan, and other Central American states, and there were increases in the imports from these same countries.

THE ORGANIZATION OF CENTRAL AMERICAN STATES

A very important step toward the improvement of the economy of Guatemala, along with those of the other Central American states, was taken in 1951. Five states—Guatemala, El Salvador, Honduras, Nicaragua, and Costa Rica—formed the Organization of Central American States (*Organización de los Estados Centromericanos,* or ODECA). The idea was to reduce tariffs and promote the exchange of goods and people freely among the member states. There was to be agreement concerning the establishment of manufacturing industries, the products of which would be freely marketed in all the countries. A tire-manufacturing plant built in Guatemala City would be able to sell tires throughout the area. A paper factory in Escuintla would not find its market restricted only to Guatemala. The development of the meat, shrimp, and vegetable exports gathered from the whole Pacific lowland could not have been arranged if each state had not agreed to the unrestricted passage of goods. As in all parts of the world where common markets are established, there was a notable increase in the prosperity among all the member states, and this increase became especially noticeable after 1965. Plans were drawn up to adopt a single currency, to form a single motor vehicle registry, and for other cooperative measures. In 1967 preliminary steps were taken to include the ODECA countries in the larger Latin-American Common Market, which was to be organized by 1985, and which will be discussed in the concluding chapter of this book.

The Political Situation

These problems of economic development must be approached in the context of the political geography of Guatemala. Outsiders all too often want to isolate the economic problems, with the hope of finding solutions for them separately. But the fact is that effective planning for economic development requires an understanding of the political situation, and especially of the political differences within the national territory.

One of the basic facts about Guatemala is the existence of a sharply defined part of the national territory within which Indians make up more than 60 percent of the population. The position of this Indian part of the country on the periphery rather than in the center of the national territory presents a situation which political geographers would recognize as potentially dangerous. The disintegration of a state is made more likely when people with one state-idea are geographically separate from people with another conflicting state-idea, and when one of these areas occupies a peripheral position the danger of disintegration is magnified. But in Guatemala it is also important that the Maya Indians have not developed a group consciousness. As was said before, each community forms a miniature nationality, each with its own dialect, religious practices, distinctive dress. The Mayas, fortunately for Guatemala, do not conceive of themselves as a unified group, and until recently they remained aloof from the political life of the Ladinos. Therefore, the peripheral position of the Indian area of Guatemala has not been a factor leading to disintegration.

It did play such a role, however, during the period of the break-up of the Spanish empire. In 1821, when New Spain declared its independence from Spain, the whole of the viceroyalty was included in the short-lived Mexican Empire. But the politically powerful groups in the separate clusters of people wanted not only to be free from outside rule by Spain, but also from outside rule by Mexico. In 1823, when the Mexican Emperor Augustín de Iturbide was overthrown, the clusters of population in Central America that had been included in the Captaincy-General of Guatemala declared their independence from Mexico. It is important to note, however, that Chiapas, which was a part of the Captaincy-General of Guatemala, remained with Mexico (Map 16, p. 39). The cluster of Spanish settlers in Chiapas was in close enough touch with Mexico City so that Mexico's control of that area could be maintained. But between Chiapas and Guatemala City there was the solidly Indian area. The Indians did not take part in the political affairs of that period, but they did form an obstacle to the spread of political control from Mexico, and behind that obstacle the remaining part of the Captaincy-General of Guatemala was successful in declaring its own independence.

Each of the other Central American clusters wanted independence from Guatemala. The slow communications along miserable roads, and the difficulty of coming ashore from ships on the harborless Pacific coast, made the extension of political control more and more difficult. By 1839 the Federal Republic of Central America had broken apart. First El Salvador separated from Guatemala, thus breaking the line of land communications. Thereafter the still more remote and peripheral parts of Central America declared their own independence. Costa Rica, at the end of the line, found itself independent without asking for it.

Guatemala started its independent existence in 1839 with no positive state-idea. The large landowners and the army officers had complete control of the new country, and no powerful voice suggested that the Indians should have any rights except to work. The political leaders tended to perpetuate their hold on the higher offices, and could not be shaken loose until the younger army officers, frustrated in their ambition to gain the financial rewards of high office, could develop the power to stage a revolution or a coup d'état. When discontent stirred too dangerously, the governments in power found that they could command a kind of coherence and order by pressing claims for the territory of British Honduras, which was then, as it still is, claimed by Guatemala. The one thread tying all political groups together continued to be the resentment toward all foreign interference.

Matters were complicated when, in 1906, the United Fruit Company began operations in Guatemala. The company directed its attention to a part of the national territory until then almost unoccupied. It created economic values in areas previously outside of the effective national territory. And the revenue from taxes on banana exports provided a much-needed support for the treasury. But here was an obviously foreign enterprise, operated on entirely different principles from those common in Guatemala. Here was a part of the national territory in which even the laws were administered separately. In an economic sense it was good—but it definitely was not Guatemalan. When the company used its influence to gain advantages with the Guatemalan government, the resentment of the Guatemalans grew stronger and stronger. Nothing, not even a dispute with Great Britain over British Honduras, was as politically popular in Guatemala as an attack on the United Fruit Company. And since the company represented the United States, resentment of the United States was also strong.

Guatemala, like Mexico, was governed by a succession of military dictatorships. As in Mexico, too, some were liberal in policy, actually concerning themselves with the increasing poverty of the farm workers. All were strong when they started, and, until overthrown, maintained the country in order and quiet. The last of the Guatemalan dictators was General Jorge Ubico, who ran the country from 1931 to 1944.

Over the years an increasingly large and vocal group of students, professors, and government workers developed in Guatemala City. These people were greatly influenced by the Mexican Revolution, and many of them went to Mexico to study the changes taking place there. With the usual few interested in revolution for its own sake, there was a core of genuine liberals, concerned with establishing democracy, with ending the system of power and privilege—be it domestic or foreign. When General Ubico's dictatorship was overthrown in 1944, the liberals, who had been in exile, were able to take control of the government and demand an election. In this election the liberal-minded civilian Juan José Arévalo was named as president. A new constitution was adopted in 1945, in which numerous social reforms, patterned on the Mexican reforms, were presented. These reforms included measures to give the Indian all the rights of citizenship, to provide workers with social security and with the right to form labor unions. Minimum wage laws were enacted. For obvious political reasons, all these measures were applied strictly to the United Fruit Company, but much less strictly on the plantations of the coffee-growers. Included also was a program of land redistribution, patterned on the Mexican law. Land not in use was to be expropriated and given to the landless peasants. Again, the law was applied vigorously to the property of the United Fruit Company (which owned a considerable area of *tierra caliente* still undeveloped, awaiting the expansion of the banana plantations), and much less vigorously to the property of the other large landowners.

In 1951 Arévalo was succeeded by Jacobo Arbenz Guzmán. Arbenz has been described as an ambitious junior officer, long frustrated in his hope for advancement and in his desire for wealth. He was one of the three who plotted the revolution of 1944. When he became president in 1951, Arbenz relied heavily on the support of the communists. A small, tightly organized group of communists had been successful in identifying communism with the social revolution started by Arévalo. They were aided by the unfortunate habit of the conservative landowners of labeling all social change as communist. The communists took the credit for the new social legislation and the land reform. Under Arbenz members of the party were the ones who supervised the land expropriation and redistribution, and who were responsible for encouraging groups of peasants to seize land from the landowners. Meanwhile other party members gained control of the Guatemala radio station. The air was filled with Moscow-inspired descriptions of "Yankee imperialism" and with other propaganda directed against the United States. All this was highly popular because it took advantage of the strong sentiment of nationalism and the dislike of the United States, the most immediate focus of irritation. As Robert J. Alexander puts it, the communists "managed to divert a healthy movement for bringing democracy and social progress to Guatemala down the blind alley of international communist propaganda aimed at serving the ends of Soviet foreign policy."[3]

In 1954, a group of exiled Guatemalan army officers under Col. Carlos Castillo Armas organized a small force in neighboring Honduras. When this "army" marched across the border, the Guatemalan army refused to attack it. Soon the capital was occupied and Arbenz was forced to flee. Castillo Armas then assumed the presidency, which he held until his assassination in 1957.

The new government included many supporters who were opposed not only to the communists but also to the whole program of social reform. In many cases the land that had been expropriated was seized again by the landowners. Castillo Armas did, however, establish a new land-reform program, not under communist control. An effort was made to get the Indians to move onto government-owned land along the fertile Pacific lowland. Idle land on the large estates was expropriated, but with proper compensation to the owners, and in these places also the landless peasants were settled. On the Mexican model, government technicians were attempting to turn the Indian subsistence farmers into producers of cash crops. Under the communists the title to the land remained with the government, but the new law gives the colonist possession of the land and forbids resale for 25 years. A new tax was levied on idle land held by the large landowners in the effort to decrease the unproductive area. A part of the whole program was financed by a loan from the United States.

All this violence and turmoil gives evidence of a deep-seated unrest. It is not the Indian group that provides the unrest, but rather the new urban class in the capital and the smaller towns, and the organized workers on the coffee

[3]Robert J. Alexander, *Communism in Latin America,* New Brunswick, N.J., 1957, p. 350.

and banana plantations. The basic purposes—an end to the system of privilege, equality of treatment for the Indian, modern social legislation, opportunity to own land—are all changes in the traditional system that are being demanded throughout Latin America. Unfortunately the United States in 1945 failed to recognize the significance of Arévalo's program. Here was a clear demand for social change first rather than economic development—and for this policy the United States was not prepared. And unfortunately, also, Arbenz was not sufficiently fearful of communist support. If the underlying motive remains to free Guatemala from outside interference, the question is this: does a Guatemalan political leader fear outside interference more from the United States or from the Soviet Union? The answer is clear: until Fidel Castro provided a demonstration of the danger of accepting communist support, fear of the United States remained almost unchallenged. That the communists were serving the interests of another foreign power was not apparent at first, and when it did become apparent it was too late.

Meanwhile the successive governments since 1954 have been struggling with the problems of social and economic change. There are still powerful minorities opposed to changing the traditional system. There is serious resistance to the revolutionary idea that people with more than $5,000 annual income should be required to pay a graduated income tax. In 1968 a bill to establish a national sales tax was passed by the congress, but immediately drew such strong opposition from the liberals that the government abandoned the plan within a few weeks. It was estimated that an effective program for better housing and for an improvement of the food supply would cost something like $90 million per year over a five year period. But in 1967 the public funds devoted to these basic forms of improvement amounted to only $32 million, and in 1968 these expenditures dropped below $30 million.

The increase of unrest and violence in Guatemala was a reflection of these frustrations. There were three chief factors leading to a decrease of public security. First was the continuing health and medical programs which are not only saving people from dying but also making those who are alive less apathetic and more vigorous. Second was the program of education, which is bringing more and more young people into contact with the ideas of revolution. And third was the inability of the government to take any effective steps toward the improvement of living conditions. The use of violence by one group led to retaliation by the opposition. The students were reaching the conclusion that only the communists had the answers to Guatemala's problems; yet these same students would be vigorously opposed to the kind of autocratic control and minority rule that is also a part of communism. Guatemala's future was hanging in the balance.

BRITISH HONDURAS

The colony of British Honduras has been described as one of the world's tiny sore spots. But in a world with many sore spots, and many that are not tiny, a place in a remote location can easily be neglected. British Honduras, with its 109,000 inhabitants grouped around the town of Belize (pop. 50,000), is such a place. About 60 percent of the population is made up of the decendents of African slaves originally brought to this coast in the eighteenth and early nineteenth centuries by the British to cut wood in the forests. About 15 percent of the population is an Indian-African mixture known as "Black Caribs." These are subsistence cultivators occupying the southern part of the coastal forests. The remaining 25 percent is made up of British civil servants, Anglican missionaries, Spanish-speaking mestizos, and Mennonite colonists from Canada. In the wet forests of the backlands there are semi-independent tribes of Maya Indians who carry on a shifting cultivation of maize in temporary forest clearings.

There are two chief export products, each coming from a different part of the territory. Inland from Stann Creek there are plantations of orange and grapefruit trees, and at Stann Creek the British have built a processing plant to make canned and frozen juice. The juice is exported to Great Britain, where it enjoys the reputation of superior quality. From the valley of the Río Hondo, on the border of Mexico, comes sugar, produced by small cane plantations in this remote area. The exports vary considerably from year to year: in 1962 about 55 percent of the value of all exports was from frozen fruit juice, and sugar made up 4 percent; but in 1963 sugar made up 27 percent, timber 14 percent, gums and resins 11 percent, and fruit juice only 9 percent. A once thriving cacao plantation area has been entirely abandoned.

The forests are used to produce chicle and mahogany. Migratory workers go out into the forests to gather these products. The chicle is gathered during the rainy season, and the wood is cut during the season of somewhat less rain between November and April.

British Honduras is claimed by Guatemala. This remaining British colony on mainland Latin America is a remnant of former British holdings along the Caribbean coast of Central America, which extended as far southward as the mouth of the San Juan River in Nicaragua. The British claim to this territory was recognized by the Spanish king in 1670; but the Guatemalans insist that the British have forfeited their claim to British Honduras because of failure to build a road to the Guatemalan area of Petén. There can be no doubt that the easiest outlet to the sea from the whole northern part of Guatemala is through Belize, and if important oil sources should be discovered in this area, the need for an outlet might become pressing. But the British are reluctant to hand over the English-speaking African populations of this colony to

Guatemala. Guatemala, we may recall, is governed by people of mestizo or pure Spanish ancestry who have expressed a strong anti-African bias, and who have never accepted the importation of African workers into the banana plantations along the coast. The result is an impasse, in which the Guatemalans are denied the access to the coast which might permit the economic development of the empty northern part of their country, and in which at the same time the British taxpayers must continue to carry the burden of a dependent colony. British Honduras is being prepared for independence, but no specific date has been set for this.

República de El Salvador

Area: 8,056 square miles
Population: (1967 estimate) 3,100,000
             (last census, 1961) 2,510,984
Capital city: San Salvador; (1967 estimate) 350,000
Percent urban: (1961) 38.5
Birth rate per 1,000: (1966) 46.5; Death rate per 1,000: (1966) 10.5
Annual percent of increase: (1958–64) 3.3
Percent literate: (1961) 49.0
Percent labor force in agriculture: (1960) 59.9
Gross national product per capita: (1966) $279
Unit of currency: colón (1968, 2.50 per dollar)
Leading crops in acreage: maize, coffee

COMMERCE, 1965 *(expressed in percentage of values)*
Percent of total Latin-American exports: 1.9 (1956, 1.0)
Percent of total Latin-American imports: 2.3

Exports (1966)
coffee 46
cotton 12

Exports to (1966)		Imports from (1966)	
United States	26 (1956, 45)	United States	33 (1956, 55)
West Germany	24	Guatemala	12
Guatemala	12	West Germany	8
Japan	11	Japan	7
Honduras	9	Honduras	6

Chapter 5 □ El Salvador

Each of the five countries included in the Organization of Central American States has a distinctive personality and faces quite different problems of man–land relations. El Salvador, for example, is sharply differentiated from its large neighbor, Guatemala. In the first place, El Salvador is the smallest of the Central American countries, and it is also the one with the greatest over-all density of population. With a national territory of about 8,056 square miles, and a total population of about 3 million, there are more than 350 people per square mile. Such an over-all density figure is meaningless in most Latin-American countries because, as in Guatemala, there are large parts of the total national territory not effectively occupied. But El Salvador makes use of all of its territory. Furthermore, the population is increasing at about the same rate as that of Guatemala. With a continued high birth rate in 1966 of about 46.5 per thousand, the death rate, which was about 20 per thousand in 1950, has now been lowered to only about 10.5 per thousand.

The population of El Salvador is predominantly of Indian ancestry. During the fifteenth century, shortly before the arrival of the Spaniards, the area that is now El Salvador was invaded by the Pipil Indians, an Indian group which had picked up many culture traits from the Aztecs. The Pipil Indians settled among the more primitive tribes formerly occupying the area and intermarried with them. But the density of Indian settlement was not so great as that of the Mayas, and the attachment to the land was not so close. When the Spaniards arrived they quickly divided the land, and its Indians, into large private estates. However, not many Spaniards ever came to settle. During the colonial period only about 1,500 Spaniards remained permanently in El Salvador, in an area with an Indian population estimated at 150,000. At the beginning of the nineteenth century, when the city of San Salvador had a population of

12,000, only 624 were listed as of unmixed Spanish ancestry. Now scarcely a family can claim to be of unmixed European origin—except for some 2,000 recent immigrants. Those of unmixed Indian ancestry make up 90 percent of the population; but unlike the Maya, the people of Indian ancestry in El Salvador have abandoned Indian ways of living and the Indian language. They all speak Spanish.

The Land

El Salvador is a country with no very great elevations, but with very little flat land. Map 27, on page 171, shows that most of this little country is deeply dissected by streams. The backbone of El Salvador is the volcanic highland which continues southeastward from Guatemala. In El Salvador the elevation of this highland becomes less and less as one proceeds eastward to the Gulf of Fonseca. At the capital city, San Salvador, the elevation is only a little over 2,000 feet. Surmounting the highland there is a succession of volcanic cones, most of them inactive, which reach elevations between 7,000 and 8,000 feet above sea level. Among the volcanoes there are numerous small intermont basins, deeply filled with volcanic ash and bordered by flows of lava. As in Guatemala, the soils derived from the lava and ash are highly productive. But there are more soils derived from lava than from ash; and the lava soils are quickly eroded when the forest is cut off and the surface is allowed to become dry. Soil erosion in El Salvador, especially on the steeper slopes, is approaching a national disaster.

There is very little flat or gently sloping land. The chief such area is the Pacific lowland which continues southeastward from Guatemala as far as the port of Acajutla. Just east of this port, the coastal lowland is pinched out by flows of lava that descend from a volcano to form rocky promontories along the Pacific. From the port of La Libertad a wide lowland plain extends beyond Usulután. This plain is some 20 miles wide where it is crossed by the Río Lempa. The Gulf of Fonseca is bordered by numerous volcanic peaks.

The Río Lempa is El Salvador's largest river. It rises in the highlands of Honduras and Guatemala and flows through rugged hill country toward the Gulf of Fonseca, until, before reaching the Gulf, it turns abruptly to the south and crosses the coastal lowland to the sea. Along the Lempa there are patches of floodplain, flooded during the rainy season and dry and sandy in the dry season.

Because of the relatively low elevation of the highlands, most of El Salvador is in the *tierra caliente*. The *tierra templada* appears only in the western part of the country near the border of Guatemala, and in small circular patches on the higher slopes of the volcanoes. At San Salvador, just about the lower limit of the *tierra templada,* the temperature averages 73.6°, with a range of only about 5°. The rainfall throughout El Salvador is heavy during the season of on-shore equatorial westerlies (from the end of May to October). During the rest of the year, when the winds are chiefly from the north, there is almost no rain.

The greater part of the country was originally covered with seasonal forest. But the density of population, and the fact that the major fuel is wood or charcoal, has resulted in almost complete forest destruction. Today there is actually a serious shortage of fuel; and the removal of the forest from the steep upper slopes has greatly increased the soil erosion.

The Pattern of Settlement

The Spaniards who first entered El Salvador came from Guatemala. A road was built southeastward from the capital of the Captaincy-General to the settlements and ports of Nicaragua. This road is now followed quite closely by the paved motor highway that connects Guatemala City with San Salvador, and which continues around the Gulf of Fonseca into Honduras and Nicaragua. In the colonial period the Spanish settlers who decided to remain in this country made their homes in San Salvador. They laid out their large properties along the road which gave access to Guatemala City, and also around Sonsonate, inland from the port of Acajutla. The Pipil Indians accepted Christianity and went to work for the new owners of the land. The chief crop which the Indians raised to supply their own food was maize. The chief commercial crops, raised on the best land, were sugarcane and indigo. In the Lempa Valley cattle were pastured on the wild grasses that grew there after the forests were burned away. The cattle were driven to market in Guatemala City. In 1840 coffee was introduced from Brazil and soon became the chief commercial crop of the highlands.

Agriculture since World War II

Coffee is still the major commercial crop of El Salvador. The best coffee comes from places above 2,000 feet, and most of the plantations are located on the gentler slopes around the margins of the intermont basins. Over 80 percent of the coffee plantations are owned by fourteen wealthy families who make up the so-called coffee aristocracy of El Salvador. But now the government is making serious efforts to increase the production of other things besides coffee.

The other commercial crops that have increased rapidly in importance since 1960 are cotton, sisal, and sugarcane. The Pacific coastal lowland, similar to the lowland of Guatemala, is also enjoying a wave of new prosperity, based in part on cotton, in part on modern cattle ranches, and in part on a shrimp-fishing industry at Acajutla. Cotton is also grown on the lowland between La Libertad and the Gulf of Fonseca. Sugarcane plantations are interspersed with the cotton along this lowland. Plantations of sisal have been developed along the lower Lempa Valley and in back of the port of La Union.

This is one of the few parts of Latin America where a new food crop is being widely planted, replacing maize. The new crop is a grain sorghum, called *maicillo,* which was imported from Africa. It is more tolerant of poor, dry soils than maize and yields more food per acre on steep slopes. Maize still yields more per acre on productive lowland soils.

Industry and Power

El Salvador has made important progress since 1960 in manufacturing industries and power. In San Salvador there are several cotton-textile plants, and also a factory which makes sisal into burlap bags in which to ship coffee and sugar. The Rockefellers' Basic Economy Corporation built a plant in 1957 to manufacture soluble coffee. New textile plants have been built more recently in several small towns in the densely populated eastern part of the country near the Gulf of Fonseca. Subsistence farmers in this area have had great difficulty in providing a minimum living for their families. Each year hundreds of thousands of workers migrate to the highland coffee plantations for the harvest season from November to April. But the opening of new land for cotton planting and the construction of new manufacturing industries in this area have made a start toward reducing the rural poverty.

El Salvador has suffered from a shortage of electric power. In 1956, however, a large dam was completed on the Río Lempa, and hydroelectric power was generated for the first time in anything like adequate quantities. New generating facilities have been installed at other places along the Lempa, and the flow of the river has been regularized by a dam at the outlet of the Lago de Guija, located on the border of El Salvador and Guatemala. At Acajutla a new fertilizer plant has been put into operation. Here also there is an oil refinery and a cement plant. All these developments represent first steps in economic development.

Other Products

The unfortunate fact is that the territory of El Salvador is not only small, but it is not endowed with many resources. There is one small mining district close to the borders of Guatemala and Honduras, where gold and silver are produced, and also small quantities of mercury and lead.

El Salvador does have one other distinctive product. This is the so-called Peruvian balsam *(Myroxylon pereirae),* which, in spite of its name, has nothing to do with Peru. It is a lofty leguminous tree that grows within a small area on the slopes of the highlands north of Sonsonate. From the bark comes a reddish-brown or black viscid oil that is used in the manufacture of perfumes. The tree was taken to Ceylon where it is grown in plantations.

El Salvador as a Political Unit

El Salvador has no such problem of racial and cultural diversity as that which complicates the problem of establishing order in Guatemala. Yet few countries include a greater contrast of wealth and poverty than exists between the coffee aristocracy and the great majority of the people. The landowners have not actually controlled the politics of El Salvador since 1932, but they do resist any infringement on their privileged positions. In spite of this, El Salvador has made notable progress in economic development and in the establishment of an ordered and stable society.

The Economic Situation

Economic development in El Salvador, as in Mexico, takes place in the presence of an exploding population and contributes to an acceleration of the explosion. The net rate of population increase of 3.3 percent per year is not quite so high as that of some other Central American states; but it is taking place in a country that has no unused land for pioneer settlement, and in which the density of population is already too high to be supported by a largely agricultural economy. With no additional land for new subsistence farming, and with fewer jobs than there are potential workers, the poverty of a large proportion of the people had become critical. Out of the total population in the early 1960's only 9,000 had incomes over $1,200 per year and therefore were required to pay taxes.

Nevertheless, during the 1960's El Salvador enjoyed an unprecedented improvement of its economy. The gross national product per capita in 1955 was only $152, which placed this little country among those states requiring massive inputs of foreign aid just to get the process of development started. If all the wealth of the "fourteen families" had been confiscated, it would not have provided nearly enough money for the necessary rate of new capital formation. But in El Salvador the government recognized the need for both economic and social change in accordance with the policies set forth by the Alliance for Progress. Foreign aid was granted in large amounts, and at the same time the tax base was expanded from 9,000 to nearly 20,000—in spite of strong resistance by the wealthy minority. New capital investment went into necessary basic facilities such as new electric power plants, new all-weather highways, new docks and other port facilities at Acajutla, and also new manufacturing industries. By 1966 the gross national product per capita had risen to $279, and the rate of rise was about 4 percent per year. This means that economic development was going on at a faster rate than the rate of population growth. Although nearly 60 percent of the workers are still employed in agriculture, the proportion is being reduced by providing new kinds of employment.

El Salvador has gained enormously from the Organization of Central American States (see p. 142). The relaxation of barriers to the movement of people and goods means that products can now reach a greatly expanded market. El Salvador, also, has become another Latin-American country from which there is a steady emigration, as more and more Salvadoreans cross the border into thinly populated Honduras.

One reflection of these changes is a decreased dependence on coffee as the one major export. Not that coffee exports have declined, but rather the exports of other products have risen. In 1956 coffee exports made up 78 percent of the value of all exports, and even as late as 1961 coffee made up 59 percent. But in 1965 coffee accounted for only 51 percent. Meanwhile cotton exports contributed 20 percent and were increasing. Other products included frozen shrimp, soluble coffee, vegetable oil, and textiles. Also, part of the beef exports described in the chapter on Guatemala (p. 140) originated in El Salvador.

The dependence on the United States for foreign trade has also been decreased. In 1965 West Germany took 23 percent of the exports, and the United States took 25 percent—as compared with 80 percent in 1953. But in addition, Japan took 16 percent, Guatemala 11 percent, and Honduras 7 percent. Of the imports (of which the United States furnished 60 percent in 1953) in 1965 the United States furnished only 31 percent. In that year Guatemala sent 9 percent, West Germany 8 percent, Honduras 8 percent, Japan 9 percent, the Netherlands 5 percent, and Venezuela 5 percent. These changes are the statistical evidence of a deep-seated and much needed change in the economic structure of the region.

The Political Situation

Economic development in El Salvador is closely tied to the distinctive way in which social change is being directed. There was a time when the "fourteen families" held the veto power on matters of political policy. But since the 1930's, political power has shifted to the officers of the army. And in the modern period the army officers in El Salvador have accepted the need for social change and economic development. They are ready to cooperate without reservation with the programs of the Alliance for Progress, and they welcome private foreign investors. In the Latin-American sense, these officers are liberals, meaning that they are opposed to dictatorship of either the right or the left, and they insist on the necessity for ending the traditional privileged position of the landowners. The "fourteen families" and others who associate with them, including foreigners who have married into these families, promptly label the officers as "pink" or as communist-inspired. Yet the present political leaders of El Salvador are vigorously opposed to the Communist Party and to the policies of Fidel Castro in Cuba. They are also vigorously opposed to a continuation of the rule of the "fourteen families." The stage is set for a major political battle.

This battle has been going on since 1961. Step by step new tax laws have been passed. New opportunities for employment have been provided, and anyone, literate or not, can perceive that the level of living of large numbers of people has been raised. There is still strong resistance by the people who once held political power, but this resistance is being reduced by persuasion rather than force. Meanwhile, the great majority of the people support their government and take a new pride in being citizens of El Salvador. A state-idea, accepted by large numbers of people, is being formulated as a part of the distinctively Salvadorean struggle to establish a viable state.

República de Honduras

Area: 43,277 square miles
Population: (1967 estimate) 2,445,000
          (last census, 1961) 1,884,765
Capital city: Tegucigalpa; (1967 estimate) 195,319
Percent urban: (1961) 30.5
Birth rate per 1,000: (1966) 46–50; Death rate per 1,000: (1966) 14–17
Annual percent of increase: (1958–64) 3.3
Percent literate: (1961) 45.0
Percent of labor force in agriculture: (1961) 65.9
Gross national product per capita: (1966) $229
Unit of currency: lempira (1968, 2.00 per dollar)
Leading crops in acreage: maize, coffee, bananas

COMMERCE, 1965 *(expressed in percentage of values)*

Percent total Latin-American exports: 0.9 (1956, less than 1.0)
Percent total Lain-American imports: 1.2

Exports (1966)

bananas	50	lumber	7
coffee	14	silver	3

Exports to (1965)		Imports from (1966)	
United States	58 (1956: 63)	United States	47 (1956: 69)
West Germany	11	El Salvador	10
El Salvador	10	Guatemala	7
		West Germany	6
		Japan	5

Chapter 6 □ Honduras

Honduras suffers from certain handicaps in its struggle to achieve a national identity. Its population is grouped in several small and separate clusters, each with different economic interests, yet none of them large enough to provide a base for sound economic development. The total population of the country, which was estimated in 1966 to be about 2,363,000, is less than that of tiny El Salvador. Furthermore, a large part of northern and eastern Honduras is still not a part of the effective national territory. And in the part that is effectively occupied, the rivalry between the separate areas of concentrated settlement continues to sap the national strength.

The contrast between the dense population of what is today El Salvador and the thin population of the country to the north was a distinctive feature of the population map even before the arrival of the Spaniards. There was a great difference between the sedentary Pipil Indians and the migratory and more warlike Lencas (Map 5, p. 14). Even one small bit of Maya settlement around Copán is included in present-day Honduras. The Lencas, like the Pipil, have given up their Indian languages in favor of Spanish, and no longer cling to Indian customs as do the Maya. According to the census of 1950, some 90 percent of the people of Honduras are mestizos. There are probably less than 7 percent of people of unmixed Indian ancestry. There is only about 1 percent that could claim unmixed European ancestry. Perhaps 2 percent are Africans who work on the banana plantations of the Caribbean lowlands.

The Land

The main features of the surface described in the chapter on Guatemala continue eastward into Honduras. The volcanic region which forms the

159

southern margin of the highlands of Guatemala runs eastward into El Salvador, and only a little of the southern part of Honduras includes areas of lava and ash. The geologic structures of the Central-American–Antillean system, with their marked west-to-east or southwest-to-northeast trends, are those which underlie most of Honduras. Long, steep-sided mountain fingers point eastward toward the Caribbean, or run at a slight angle to the northern coast on the southern side of the Gulf of Honduras (Map 27, p. 171). The highest elevations are found in the westernmost part of the country, where there are peaks a little under 10,000 feet. In the vicinity of Tegucigalpa the peaks are about 6,000 feet above sea level. To the north the elevations are much less, but the slopes are even more rugged.

There is not much level land in Honduras. In the thinly populated eastern part of the country, Honduras shares with Nicaragua the extensive Miskito savannas, which we shall discuss in the chapter on Nicaragua. These plains begin east of the Río Plátano. Some of the valleys that have been cut westward into the highlands and which drain out eastward into the Caribbean from the Río Patuca southward have ribbons of floodplain along their bottoms. In central Honduras the basin of Comayagua is a level-floored surface a little over 2,000 feet above sea level. It extends for some 40 miles north and south, with a width between 5 and 15 miles. The river that drains the Comayagua basin descends to join the Río Ulúa. The lowland of the Ulúa, on which San Pedro Sula is located, is about 60 miles north and south by 25 miles east and west. Smaller valley lowlands open out to the north coast between the steep mountain ridges.

The highlands of Honduras are cut sharply across from north to south by a zone of faulted structures. The direction of these faults is readily apparent from the trend of the surface features just described. The rift valley of Honduras is occupied in the north by the lowland of the Ulúa and by the deep basin of the Lago de Yojoa. In the central part it forms the basin of Comayagua, and on the Pacific side of the isthmus it forms the Gulf of Fonseca. By following this rift, a passage across the isthmus requires a climb of only 3,100 feet above sea level.

Throughout this highland country with its steep-sided ranges, its intermont basins, its rift valley, the arrangement of the vegetation is complex in its details. Altitude zones can be observed if the details of the foreground are disregarded. Most of the country receives an abundance of rain during the rainy season from May to November, and very little rain during the rest of the year. Most of the *tierra caliente* was originally covered with a dense evergreen rain forest. The oak and pine forests, characteristic of the *tierra templada* and the *tierra fría,* may descend as low as 2,000 feet above sea level. The Miskito coast, for reasons we shall discuss later, is covered with a savanna mixed with pine and palmetto. On some of the higher basins, east of Tegucigalpa, there are also extensive savannas. No parts of the country are high enough to extend above the tree line; and no parts of the country are so dry as the middle Motagua Valley of Guatemala.

The Pattern of Settlement

The story of Spanish settlement in the parts of Central America that were thinly populated by Indians differs from that of the areas of dense Indian settlement. There were few converts to be made and few people to be put to work. In pre-Spanish times the land east of the Maya settlements and north of the Pipil settlements was thinly occupied by shifting cultivators of maize and squash and by primitive hunters and fishers. Nevertheless, in the restless search for sources of wealth and for large Indian populations to Christianize and to set to work, Spanish expeditions were sent out from Mexico and Guatemala. Cortés sent the first expedition into Honduras; but when the leader undertook to set up his colony as an independent unit, Cortés himself led a column of troops through the Gulf region of Mexico, across Yucatán, across the jungles of the lower Motagua, and into what is now Honduras. In 1525 he founded Puerto Cortés near the mouth of the Río Ulúa. The colony was brought back under the administration of Mexico, later placed under the Captaincy-General of Guatemala. San Pedro Sula was founded in 1536; Comayagua in 1537. The latter town became the administrative center of this part of the Captaincy-General of Guatemala. In 1578 silver ores were discovered in the highlands about 70 miles to the east of Comayagua, and a mining town was established in a basin near the mines at an elevation of about 3,000 feet. This was the town of Tegucigalpa. In the rivalry that ensued among these miniature concentrations of settlement, Comayagua was able to hold the leadership until, in 1880, the capital was shifted to Tegucigalpa.

The Highland Settlements

The one important cluster of people in the highlands is located around Tegucigalpa. This city had a population of over 170,000 in 1965. There are. several other small areas of concentrated settlement in the highlands, including Comayagua and Copán (not to be confused with Cobán in Guatemala).

Except for some silver mines near Tegucigalpa, the economy of the highlands is based on lumbering, stock raising, subsistence farming, and in only a few spots commercial agriculture. The extensive pine forests of the *tierra fría* offer an important resource that is actually used only where a paved road makes the lumber accessible. Along the motor highway between Tegucigalpa and Comayagua there are temporary sawmills which make use of local stands of pine. Trucks carry the lumber to El Salvador or to Caribbean ports for export. Pine logs are also used for the manufacture of paper. But the form of land use that occupies the largest area in the highlands is stock raising. The large landowners have long been accustomed to burn the forest in order to increase the growth of pasture grass. In this way a considerable part of the pine was destroyed before the lumbermen could reach it.

Where subsistence farmers occupy the land they grow maize, beans, squash, and sometimes the African grain sorghum, *maicillo.* Farmers are scattered throughout the highlands, but show a tendency to concentrate close to the towns or along the roads. A new road built from Tegucigalpa toward the east has become an axis of pioneer settlement. Not a few of the new settlers in this formerly unoccupied part of Honduras are immigrants from crowded El Salvador.

Commercial agriculture in the highlands is found in only a few small areas. The most important commercial crop is coffee, but coffee has only become important in the last few decades. Small plantations, or *fincas,* are set out among the larger trees of the forest near the upper limits of the *tierra templada.* The chief coffee plantations are around Tegucigalpa, both to the east and to the west along the highlands. There are plantations on the slopes that descend toward the Gulf of Fonseca. The latest area of new coffee planting is on the slopes on either side of Lake Yojoa. In addition to the coffee there is a very old area of tobacco-farming around Copán, and in some of the alluvial valleys in the highlands, as around Comayagua, there are newly developed farms producing cotton, maize, and beans.

The Transportation Problem

An important part of the difference between El Salvador and Honduras results from the relative isolation of the latter. The main colonial road between Guatemala City and Nicaragua went through San Salvador and skirted the Gulf of Fonseca—which route is followed today by the Inter-American Highway. The route avoided the steep climb to the highland basins of Honduras. Tegucigalpa remains to this day the only Central American capital which is not reached by any railroad (Map 28). A branch from the Inter-American highway has been built from Nacome, near the Gulf of Fonseca, up to the capital. From the capital an all-weather motor highway has now been completed through Comayagua to San Pedro Sula. In 1958 a loan from the United States was used to build a new road from Tegucigalpa northeastward to Juticalpa, which is planned to open up the almost unoccupied territory east of that town. Before the road gave access to the eastern part of the national territory, this was occupied chiefly by bands of escaped criminals who lived by raiding the isolated settlements, very much in the manner of the "wild West."

Except for these few roads, the only means of transportation over land in the highlands are rough trails, mostly not passable in wet weather for anything but mules or oxen. For many years a major problem has been to move the products of the isolated highland settlements out to a port. The string of mules and the two-wheeled ox-cart are the traditional means of transport.

Aviation suddenly lifted parts of Honduras out of the eighteenth century and dropped them into the twentieth century. In a rugged mountain country, where other means of transportation are slow and expensive, airplanes can compete successfully for the shipment even of bulky products like coffee. The company known as *Transportes Aéreos Centro-Americanos* (TACA) had its origin in Tegucigalpa, and its operations spread from this center into the international field. There is a large airport near Tegucigalpa which is a regular stop on lines which give easy connections with North and South America. Also, within a radius of 100 miles of Tegucigalpa there are more than a hundred small landing fields where passengers and freight can be picked up. Today it takes only 45 minutes to go from Copán to the capital. Most of the coffee is brought to a port in one of two ways: by plane to Tegucigalpa, thence by truck to the shores of the Gulf of Fonseca, and thence by barge to the docks at the port of Amapala, located on an island in the Gulf; or by plane to San Pedro Sula and thence by rail to Puerto Cortés. Tegucigalpa is the hub of air transportation for much of Central America, but when in 1966 San Pedro Sula opened the first landing field suitable for use by jets, the position of Tegucigalpa was again challenged.

The Caribbean Lowland Settlements

San Pedro Sula, the second city of Honduras, had almost 100,000 inhabitants in 1964. Located 38 miles up the Ulúa Valley from Puerto Cortés, this town was on the main route of travel inland to Comayagua and Tegucigalpa. It became prosperous in colonial times on the basis of sugarcane grown on the rich alluvial terraces of the valley, for which African slaves were imported in small numbers. But the lower river and the coast were avoided because of the difficulty of controlling the rivers or clearing the tangle of wet vegetation. Only in modern times has the Caribbean coast become commercially the most important part of Honduras.

Before the first-class soils and climate of coastal Honduras could be utilized, engineers had to devise methods of controlling the floods of the Ulúa and the Aguán, as well as of the nearby Motagua in Guatemala. A way was found by engineers of the fruit companies to divert the flood waters, to reduce their rate of flow enough to permit the deposition of fine silt, and then to drain off the water through dredged channels to the Caribbean. Large acreages of new land have been built up high enough so that they can be protected with levees; they are covered with from one foot to over ten feet of rich, fine silt. Banana plantations were developed along the lower river and on the fringe of plain along the Caribbean. Hundreds of miles of narrow-gauge

The "banana town" of La Lima in the valley of the Rio Ulúa, Honduras. *Courtesy of United Fruit Co.*

railroad lines bring the bananas to the ports and connect the ports with San Pedro Sula.

Two fruit companies, owned in the United States, have operated in this region: the United Fruit Company and the Standard Fruit and Steamship Company. The United Fruit Company built special banana-loading docks at Puerto Cortés and Tela. Aguán was the chief shipping port for the Standard Fruit Company. These companies cleared the jungle, drained the swamps, controlled the river floods, eliminated disease-carrying insects, laid out towns, built modern tropical houses, schools, and hospitals. A productive region was created in an area that was formerly empty and unused. The workers are mostly recruited from the highlands, and to get them to move to the lowlands the companies had to pay higher wages than those paid anywhere else in Honduras. A few African workers were brought in from Jamaica and from Costa Rica.

Shortly before 1940 the banana plantations of the Caribbean lowlands were threatened with extinction as a result of the rapid spread of Panama disease and Sigatoka. The Panama disease results from the spread of a soil fungus which infests lands where bananas are growing. Sigatoka is a leaf blight that has the effect of reducing the leaf size and the size of the fruit. After much experimentation it was found that Sigatoka could be controlled by using a copper sulfate spray, such as was used with great success on the banana plantations of the Pacific lowland in Guatemala. The only way to control Panama disease, however, was to flood the land and leave it under water for several months. Before these methods of control could be applied in Honduras, a large part of the former banana lands were abandoned. The Aguán Valley plantations are all gone. But in 1966 the plantations of the lower Ulúa Valley were being redeveloped, using spray delivered by airplane and practicing a regular flood fallow between plantings to control Panama disease. Also the United Fruit Company has developed several new varieties of banana that are resistant to disease. The company has also started to diversify the production of these lowlands by introducing oil palms from Africa, abacá (Manila hemp), coconuts, and cacao.

In the future, much of the banana production in Honduras will be derived from independent planters who buy land from United Fruit. They continue to receive technical assistance from company experts, but for the most part the company restricts its activities to buying and shipping the fruit. In this way the people of Honduras become real partners in the business, and will be less likely to want to place crippling restrictions on the company's activities. The headquarters of the United Fruit Company in Honduras have been moved from the Ulúa Valley to the port of Tela.

Meanwhile the production of other commercial crops has increased rapidly around San Pedro Sula. There are plantations of sugarcane and other food crops, which now diversify the products of an area which back in the 1930's was used almost exclusively for bananas.

Another lowland area of new pioneer settlement is along the Nicaraguan border to the east of Tegucigalpa. The extension of a new road into this frontier region has resulted in a rapid spread of settlement into formerly empty country. The movement is into an area that was under dispute between Nicaragua and Honduras until 1961.

Honduras as a Political Unit

Honduras, unlike El Salvador, is a country in which the population is relatively small in relation to the resource base. But it is a country that has been pushed toward national coherence by the pressure of its neighbors rather than by internal unity. During most of its history, Honduras has been made up of small, isolated clusters of people who had no sense of belonging together until circumstances and geography forced statehood on them. Except for the amazing development of air transportation, the modern machine age seems remote indeed; and so far there has been only a little impact from the ideas of the democratic revolution.

The Economic Situation

The population of Honduras has been increasing at the rate of 3.3 percent per year, which is about the same as the rates in neighboring countries. Yet in spite of the rapid rate of population increase, the economic growth since the mid-1960's has been going forward faster. In 1966 the gross national product per capita in Honduras was $229, but the gross products of the other countries of Central America were higher (Guatemala $314; El Salvador $279; Nicaragua $365; Costa Rica $406). In 1967, however, Honduras made no gain in its gross national product per capita.

In spite of a general slowdown throughout Central America in 1967, resulting in part from decreased coffee prices, the 1960's have witnessed a general rise in the rates of economic growth among these countries. This rise has been due to the relaxation of trade restrictions and the increased production of coffee, cotton, lumber, and food crops, as well as new investment in banana plantations. The up-turn has been helped along by the establishment of a few new manufacturing industries which will find markets throughout Central America. The new industries include a paper factory, a cigarette factory, and a plant for the manufacture of window glass, bottles, and other glass products. Power is supplied by a new hydroelectric plant built near Lake Yojoa, which sends power to Tegucigalpa and to San Pedro Sula. New highway and airport construction is also giving a substantial underpinning for continued economic growth. But there is still a long way to go. More than half the people in Honduras must still bring their products to market on their own backs or on the backs of mules.

The foreign commerce of Honduras is still dominated by the export of bananas to the United States, but the country can no longer be characterized exclusively as a "banana republic." Before World War II bananas accounted for something like 75 percent of all exports. After World War II the proportion of the total value of exports derived from bananas began to drop. In 1956, when Honduras shipped 84 percent of the world's exports of this fruit, bananas made up only 46 percent of the total value of exports from Honduras. In 1964, however, the share of bananas in the export trade was down to 36 percent. Exports that increased included coffee (18 percent) and timber (11 percent). Most of the bananas were sold in the United States, but the coffee and timber went to markets in Europe and Central America.

As in the case of the other Central American states, there has been a broadening of the foreign trade pattern. In 1964, the United States took 54 percent of the exports and furnished 49 percent of the imports. But in that year 11 percent of the exports went to El Salvador, and 12 percent went to West Germany. Imports also came from El Salvador (19 percent), West Germany (7 percent), the Netherlands Antilles (5 percent), and Guatemala (5 percent).

The Political Situation

An examination of the political geography of Honduras illuminates a fundamental problem in the establishment of a national identity. The occupied part of the national territory is sharply divided into separate clusters of people, each with somewhat different economic interests, and each jealous of advantages gained by the others. Especially important is the traditional struggle for supremacy between Tegucigalpa and San Pedro Sula. When the administrative center was transferred from Comayagua to Tegucigalpa in 1880, San Pedro Sula suffered a serious setback. But San Pedro and the whole Caribbean lowland began to climb back into a competitive position in relation to the highland settlements when the banana companies started operations along the coast. During the 1920's and 1930's the banana plantations of the Caribbean area were like a world apart, and there was little common interest between the lowlands and Tegucigalpa.

Robert J. Alexander described the situation as it had developed after World War II. "The country's whole north coast is dominated by two banana firms, . . . which command what are virtually states within a state, not only owning the land, but providing practically all the public and social services, and controlling the whole economic, social, and, until the 1950's, the political life of the region."[1] Here the foreign engineers and agronomists created what they regard as a tropical paradise. The fever-ridden coastal swamps, which come closer to meriting the description "steaming jungle" than any other part of the tropics, were transformed into a healthful, pleasant, and attractive landscape. In the modern homes and well-planned villages workers lived far better than they did in the traditional villages of the highlands. The company agricultural college, the company schools, the company recreation centers, and the company stores all combined to create a very different kind of landscape from that of the highlands.

[1] Robert J. Alexander, *Communism in Latin America,* New Brunswick, N.J., 1957, pp. 371–72.

Yet in spite of these advantages, the workers in the banana plantations went on strike against the companies. When this happened during the 1950's there were many North Americans who blamed communist agitators from Guatemala for stirring up trouble. But there were others who insisted that the workers went on strike because they harbored certain grievances which had not been adequately expressed before. It is difficult for many North Americans to understand the deep-seated Latin-American urge to escape from foreign domination. This includes the desire to escape from the benefits of foreign ideas. The desire for freedom to make one's own mistakes is a very basic urge, not only in Latin America, but throughout the underdeveloped world. In the 1960's the banana companies have recognized this point of view.

This does not mean, however, that social and political change cannot take place. Until the 1960's, Honduras had never experienced anything but a military dictatorship. Because the treasury was never very well filled, army discontent was not uncommon. But a change of party by army revolt did not mean a change of policy—only a change of the leadership which alone had access to the sources of widely enlarged income. In 1957 an "honest" election was actually held in Honduras. In this election some 30 percent of the total population were eligible to vote. Actually, only 18 percent of the total population voted, but the decision of this small politically conscious group was overwhelming support for the liberal candidates.

Unfortunately, the liberal government felt impelled to express the national image by attacking the foreign fruit companies. There was a tendency to think of business profit as a system for exploiting the workers, in accordance with ideas set forth in Europe a century before by Karl Marx. Beset by reduced yields due to banana diseases and by increased taxes and land confiscation by the government, the fruit companies reduced, or even abandoned, their plantations. In 1963, however, a new government came into power which reversed these trends. The new government expressed a willingness to cooperate with foreign-owned business and to accept the objectives set forth in the Alliance for Progress. As a result, domestic capital, which had been flowing out to Switzerland and the United States, began to flow back again. The United Fruit Company started a $15 million investment plan for rebuilding the banana plantations, but this time with independent Honduran growers selling to the company.

In 1965, another election returned to power a government that was favorable to the kinds of foreign investment needed to start the country on the road to economic development. Domestic capital was also made available. Honduras began to benefit from its membership in the Organization of Central American States, and the gross national product turned abruptly upward.

It is important also to note the position of Honduras with respect to its neighbors. In this part of Central America the countries that developed around the larger and more distinctive clusters of people were Guatemala, El Salvador, and Nicaragua. These countries have developed a strong sense of nationalism and compete aggressively with each other. Again and again Honduras has been subject to pressures from outside to throw its support to one or another of these countries. Since the others were fairly evenly balanced, Honduras has often been in a position to play the decisive role. And on many occasions outside pressures have disturbed the internal affairs of Honduras.

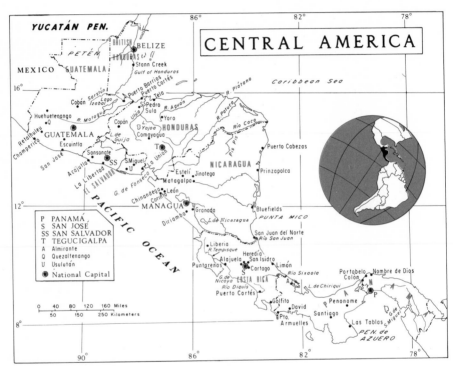

Map 26

CENTRAL AMERICA

MEXICO

BRITISH
HONDURAS

CARIBBEAN SEA

82°   78°

HONDURAS

MISKITO COAST

14°

GUATEMALA

EL
SALVADOR

NICARAGUA

10°

TERRAIN

COSTA
RICA

PANAMÁ

0   100   200 M
  100   300 K

86°   82°   78°

Map 27

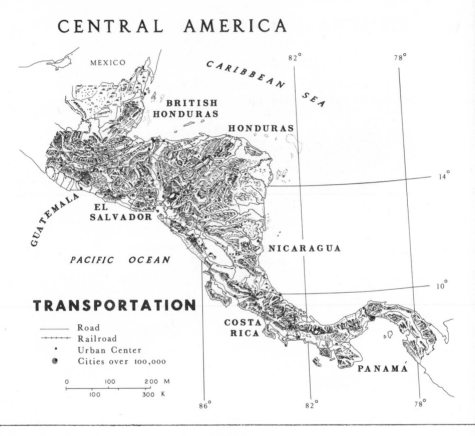

CENTRAL AMERICA

MEXICO

CARIBBEAN SEA

BRITISH
HONDURAS

HONDURAS

82°

78°

GUATEMALA

EL
SALVADOR

14°

NICARAGUA

PACIFIC OCEAN

10°

TRANSPORTATION

——— Road
+++++ Railroad
• Urban Center
● Cities over 100,000

COSTA
RICA

PANAMÁ

| 0 | 100 | 200 M |
| 100 | 300 K |

86°

82°

78°

Map 28

CENTRAL AMERICA

MEXICO

CARIBBEAN SEA

82°

78°

BRITISH
HONDURAS

HONDURAS

14°

GUATEMALA

EL
SALVADOR

LAND USE

NICARAGUA

10°

- Urban Center
- Sugar Cane
- Coffee
- Bananas
- Citrus
- Cacao, Abacá, Oil Palm
- Shifting Cultivation
- Cultivated Pasture, Cotton
- Uncultivated Range
- Chicle and Timber
- Pine Timber

COSTA
RICA

0   100   200 M

100   300 K

PANAMÁ

86°

82°

78°

Map 29

CENTRAL AMERICA

MEXICO

CARIBBEAN SEA

82°   78°

BRITISH
HONDURAS

HONDURAS

14°

GUATEMALA

EL
SALVADOR

NICARAGUA

MINERALS

10°

Au Gold
Ag Silver
Fe Iron
Cu Copper
Pb Lead
•   Urban Center

COSTA
RICA

0   100   200 M
100   300 K

PANAMÁ

86°   82°   78°

Map 30

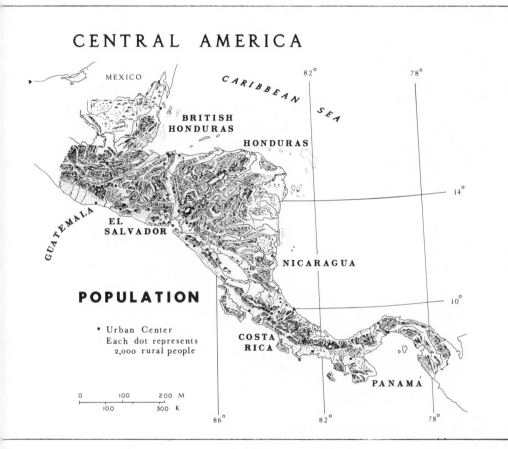

CENTRAL AMERICA

MEXICO

CARIBBEAN SEA

82°   78°

BRITISH
HONDURAS

HONDURAS

14°

GUATEMALA

EL
SALVADOR

NICARAGUA

10°

POPULATION

• Urban Center
  Each dot represents
  2,000 rural people

COSTA
RICA

PANAMÁ

0   100   200 M
100   300 K

86°   82°   78°

Map 31

República de Nicaragua

Area: 50,193 square miles
Population: (1966 estimate) 1,685,000; (last census, 1963) 1,535,588
Capital city: Managua; (1964) 248,811
Percent urban: (1957) 39.9
Birth rate per 1,000: (1966) 45–50; Death rate per 1,000: (1966) 13–16
Annual percent of increase: (1958–64) 3.1
Percent literate: (1963) 49.6
Percent of labor force in agriculture: (1963) 57.9
Gross national product per capita: (1966) $365
Unit of currency: córdoba (1968, 6.99 per dollar)
Leading crops in acreage: maize, cotton, beans

COMMERCE, 1965 *(expressed in percentage of values)*
Percent total Latin-American exports: 1.19 (1956, less than 1.0)
Percent total Latin-American imports: 1.6

Exports (1966)

cotton	44	sesame	7
coffee	18	Meat	6

Exports to (1966)		Imports from (1966)	
Japan	30	United States	46 (1956, 63)
United States	23 (1956, 38)	West Germany	7
West Germany	15	Costa Rica	6
		El Salvador	5
		Japan	5

Chapter 7 □ Nicaragua

Nicaragua, unlike Honduras, is built around one major cluster of people. Largest in area of all the Central American states, a large part of its total area remains outside of the effective national territory. The population estimated in 1966 to be a little less than 1,700,000 is smaller than that of Honduras. But in this country, also, the revolutionary cultural changes are starting to speed the process of economic development, and military dictatorships are becoming more difficult to maintain.

The core of Nicaragua, which is its largest area of concentrated settlement, is located in the Nicaraguan lowland. It was in the lowlands, not the highlands, that the Spanish explorers found Indian settlements. The Spaniards, here as elsewhere, settled where there were Indians. Today it is estimated that about 70 percent of the people are mestizos. Pure Indians make up only about 4 percent of the population, and these are found only in the more remote parts of the country. The people of unmixed Spanish ancestry make up about 17 percent. Along the eastern coast the considerable concentrations of Africans make up another 9 percent of the total.

The Land

The territory now included in Nicaragua is physically divided among four surface regions (Map 27, p. 171). The greater part of the country is made up of a triangular wedge of highland which continues southward from Honduras. To the east is the Miskito Coast, a wide belt of wet lowland extending from Punta Mico northward about as far as the Río Plátano in Honduras. The most important part of the country from the point of view of settlement is the third region—the Nicaraguan lowland. This conspicuous feature crosses the isthmus diagonally from the Gulf of Fonseca in the northwest to the valley of the Río San Juan in the southeast. Scattered over the lowland from the Gulf of Fonseca to Lake Nicaragua are numerous volcanic cones, some still active, from which the outpourings of lava and outbursts of ash and cinders have given the northern part of the lowland an unusually productive soil. The fourth region is a narrow northward extension of the highlands of Costa Rica which separates Lake Nicaragua from the Pacific.

The highlands of Nicaragua are geologically related to the highlands of Honduras. The Central-American–Antillean structures form prominent west to east ridges and valleys, but these are mantled along the southwest-facing edge by deep accumulations of volcanic materials. The highlands rise sharply from the Nicaraguan lowlands to a general elevation of between 4 and 5 thousand feet above sea level. From this southwestern edge the highlands slope gradually toward the east. Over most of the highland area the general elevation is around 2,000 feet, but there are a number of prominent peaks that stand about 7,000 feet above sea level.

Between the deeply cut valleys that drain out eastward to the Caribbean, long finger-like ridges reach toward the Miskito Coast. Just north of the lowland of the Río San Juan these ridges form cliffs on the edge of the sea; but to the north of Punta Mico the ridges end some 40 or 50 miles inland.

The whole eastern part of Nicaragua is very rainy. The Miskito Coast and the highlands back of it feel the full effect of the easterly trades which sweep in from the warm Caribbean. This is the rainiest part of Central America (Map 12, p. 32). Along the east coast the rainfall is well over 100 inches: at San Juan del Norte (Greytown) it averages over 250 inches. Very heavy rainfall is received on the highlands, especially at the heads of the valleys where the rising moist air is concentrated as in a funnel. As a result, the highlands and a part of the plain to the east are covered with a luxuriant evergreen rain forest (Map 14, p. 34). Only in the higher places is the evergreen broadleaf forest replaced by oak and pine, as in Honduras. The southern limit of pine on the highlands is just north of Jinotega. South of this the forests of the *tierra fría* are made up of oak, with no pine.

Along the lowland back of the Miskito Coast, pine also occurs. This is an area of pine savanna which extends for some 300 miles northward from Bluefields as far as the Río Plátano in Honduras. The southernmost stand of North American species of pine is a few miles to the north of Bluefields. James J. Parsons, who has studied this pine savanna in the field, points out that the pines are associated with a deeply leached soil made up at the surface of an almost pure quartz gravel or powdery quartz sand, with a hardpan underneath through which drainage is very slow.[1] It may well be that burning

[1]James J. Parsons, "The Miskito Pine Savanna of Nicaragua and Honduras," *Annals of the Association of American Geographers,* Vol. 45, 1955, 36–63.

by pre-historic Indians had the effect of eliminating a previous broadleaf woodland; but at the present time the annual burning of the savanna grasses has the effect of killing the young pine seedlings. Whatever its origin may be, this Miskito savanna is the largest pine savanna in the rainy tropics. Parsons shows that the existence of savannas of this kind in areas of very heavy rainfall makes the use of such a term as "savanna climate" highly misleading.

The Lowland

The Nicaraguan lowland is a feature of major importance in the geography of Central America. Not only does it provide a low passage across the isthmus from ocean to ocean, but it is also a major geologic and biotic boundary, for it marks the southern end of the Central-American–Antillean structures, and no North American pines are found south of it.

Within the lowland there are two large, fresh-water lakes, both draining to the Caribbean. Lake Managua is about 38 miles long by 10 to 16 miles wide. Its surface is 136 feet above sea level, and it drains southeastward through a river which is shallow even in the rainy season and which is sometimes entirely dry during the dry season. Lake Nicaragua is a little less than 100 miles long by 45 miles wide, and its surface is only 106 feet above sea level. The Río San Juan drains Lake Nicaragua to the Caribbean, running along the border between Nicaragua and Costa Rica.

The northwestern part of the Nicaraguan lowland is the scene of intense volcanic activity. Mt. Cosigüina, which stands about 3,800 feet above the sea on the peninsula to the south of the entrance to the Gulf of Fonseca, was formed in a violent explosive eruption in 1835. When it erupted the sun was completely blotted out within a radius of 35 miles, and dust from Cosigüina fell in noticeable quantities in Jamaica, 700 miles away. There are more than twenty volcanic cones between Cosigüina and Mt. Momotombo north of Lake Managua. In Lake Nicaragua there are three volcanic cones, one of which is more than 5,000 feet high. Many of these cone-shaped, explosive volcanoes are still active, and earthquakes accompanied by deep ash falls are not infrequent. In 1931 the city of Managua was devastated by an earthquake and had to be entirely rebuilt. The volcanic ash weathers into a soil of high productivity.

But the most continuously active volcano in the Nicaraguan lowland is the Masaya Caldera. This is a dome-shaped volcano, like those of the Hawaiian Islands. Instead of erupting explosively, Masaya is built up by up-welling lava, which occasionally spills over the edge of its crater in a white-hot tongue of molten material. The caldera itself is a wide basin some seven miles by four miles, with a rim which rises on the western side to an elevation of about 1,600 feet above the sea. The crater in which the molten lava is always bubbling is in the floor of this caldera. The Masaya Caldera is located just west of Granada.

The rainfall in the Nicaraguan lowland is heavy near the Caribbean, but is moderate to light in the northwestern section. The heavy rains and the tropical rain forest extend along the San Juan Valley about as far as the shore of Lake Nicaragua. Since the rain-bearing winds come from the east, the driest part of the lowland is along the base of the northern highland, where a local "rain shadow" is formed on the southwest-facing lee slope. The northeast sides of Lake Nicaragua and Lake Managua are relatively dry, and because of the high temperatures and rapid evaporation are not suitable for crops without irrigation. No large supplies of water are available for irrigation because the streams from the highlands mostly drain eastward, and the cost of pumping water up from the lakes would be prohibitive. This part of the lowland is covered only by a dry scrub woodland. The land southwest of the lakes, on the other hand, receives a moderate rainfall, most of which comes during the summer rainy season.

The Pattern of Settlement

The Nicaraguan lowland was first plundered and then settled by expeditions sent out from Panamá. As early as 1519 exploring parties were moving northward from Panamá City, seeking for sources of precious metals or gems. In the Nicaraguan lowland, along the southwestern shores of Lake Nicaragua, a moderately dense Indian population was discovered, practicing a shifting cultivation of maize and supplementing their diet with wild game and fish. These people proved to be peaceful and were quickly converted to Christianity; in gratitude they loaded the strange newcomers with gold ornaments. This display of what the Spaniards thought was only a part of a great accumulation of such gold objects led the conquerors to believe that here, indeed, was a land worthy of their more careful attention. In 1524 another expedition from Panamá founded two colonies in what is now Nicaragua: one was Granada, on the shore of Lake Nicaragua on some of the most productive land of the whole region; the other was León, on the Pacific slope at the base of one of the great volcanoes. Granada became the more prosperous, and in it dwelt some of the Spaniards whose extensive properties gave them a very adequate living. The crops of this period were indigo, cacao, and sugarcane. But the drier, poorer soils around León did not yield well enough to do more than provide subsistence crops of maize. Yet when the Nicaraguan settlements were placed under the jurisdiction of Guatemala in 1570, León was selected as the administrative center, presumably because it was more directly accessible by the road which passed through San Salvador from Guatemala City.

During the period of the California gold rush after 1849, one of the important routes of travel passed through the Nicaraguan lowland. It was the North American railroad builder Cornelius Vanderbilt who developed the Nicaraguan route. His ships brought travelers from the eastern United States and from Europe to San Juan del Norte at the mouth of the Río San Juan. The travelers were then carried up the river and across Lake Nicaragua to a landing place on its western shore. Stagecoaches carried people across the narrow ridge to the Pacific port of San Juan del Sur. Ships to transport the gold seekers to California anchored off the harborless coast.

The interest of foreigners in this route, together with the continued political rivalry of conservative Granada and liberal León, kept the country in turmoil. In an effort to bring peace between the warring factions a new capital city was founded midway between the liberal center and the conservative center. This was Managua, founded in 1858. But the warfare continued, fanned in part by the activities of Great Britain and the United States, both of which were eyeing the Nicaraguan lowland as a possible route for an inter-ocean canal. From 1912 to 1925 and from 1926 to 1933 the United States Marines enforced order within the central area, but were never able to stop the guerrilla warfare in the highlands. The rural areas, even close to the big cities, were frequently raided by bandits.

Settlements and Products of the Lowland

Most of the people of Nicaragua still live in the part of the lowland that lies between the Pacific coast and the shores of the lakes (Map 31, p. 175). Managua is now a city of nearly 250,000, and is growing rapidly. In 1966 a new twelve-story "skyscraper" rose conspicuously above the traditional low buildings of the city. But like other cities of this part of the world, the capital is surrounded by a crowded slum area into which displaced rural people come with the hope of finding paying jobs.

Nicaragua, along with Guatemala, El Salvador, and the Tapachula area of Mexico, shared the rapid development of cotton farming on the Pacific coastal lowland that began in the early 1960's. The chief cotton area in Nicaragua is between Chinandega and León, where the coastal lowland is covered with productive soils derived from volcanic ash. Here, as in Guatemala, technical assistance is provided by AID and other international agencies. The insect pests that have long made cotton-growing in Nicaragua very hazardous are now kept under control by frequent dusting of the growing crop with chemical spray delivered by airplane. Machinery is used in cultivation and harvesting. High yields, similar to those reported in Guatemala, have been achieved also in Nicaragua. Ginning facilities have been built, and the port of Corinto has been improved with a breakwater and new dock facilities. A new motor highway has been built to connect Managua with Corinto. This same coastal lowland on either side of Corinto is used to grow sugarcane.

Since 1963 a new area of intensive agriculture with irrigation has been developed between the western shore of Lake Nicaragua and the Inter-American Highway. Here farmers on small properties grow bananas, sesame, and sugarcane.

The crop which occupies more area than all other crops combined is maize. Maize, rice, and beans are the basic subsistence crop of the rural people, and are raised wherever there are settlements. Much land is also used for the grazing of cattle, and Nicaragua shares in the new export of processed beef described in the chapter on Guatemala.

The colonial cacao plantations have all disappeared because of the ravages of a tree disease which could not be controlled. More resistant cacao trees were imported and have been planted chiefly along the southern end of Lake Nicaragua.[2] A considerable part of the cacao exported from Nicaragua is actually grown across the border in neighboring parts of Costa Rica and sent to market through Nicaragua.

A number of other commercial crops are grown in this central area. Indigo has, of course, disappeared entirely. Since 1937 sesame has been cultivated, in some years with considerable success. The uncertainty of the rainfall, however, makes the cultivation of such a moisture-loving crop a somewhat hazardous venture unless it can be irrigated. In years of abundant rain, sesame can be barely profitable enough to make the farmers try it again. Acreages fluctuate greatly from year to year. Ipecac root grows wild along the eastern margin of the lowland to the east of Lake Nicaragua. Some tobacco is grown throughout the area of concentrated settlement.

Settlement in the Highlands

The highlands of Nicaragua are used, like those of the other Central American countries, for the production of coffee. Coffee was first introduced into Nicaragua in 1850, at which time large plantations were developed in the hilly belt west of the northern end of Lake Nicaragua. The coffee plantations around Diriamba, about 20 miles south of Managua, are still productive. From this area comes about half of Nicaragua's coffee.

Coffee plantations have been developed more recently in the highlands northeast of Managua. The Inter-American Highway, which has now been completed through Mexico and Guatemala and on through Central America into Costa Rica, climbs from the shores of the Gulf of Fonseca into the high country on the border of Honduras and Nicaragua (Map 28, p. 172). It passes through the Nicaraguan town of Estelí before descending to the Nicaraguan lowland east of Lake Managua. Not far from this highway, and connected to it by motor roads, are Matagalpa and Jinotega. This is the other major area of coffee production in Nicaragua, which also produces about half of the total crop. Here the plantations are all small and are worked by the owners.

[2]Cacao trees grow in very wet and humid places, protected from the wind.

Gold mining supports an entirely different kind of settlement in parts of the highlands. Nicaragua is unusual among the countries of Latin America in that none of its gold ores were discovered during the colonial period. They were discovered in 1889–90 by men who were pushing inland from the east coast, searching in the dense rain forest for sources of rubber. Gold was discovered in the valley of Río Pis Pis, a tributary of the Río Coco. The La Luz mines are a little to the south of the Pis Pis district (Map 30, p. 174). These mining districts are some 90 miles west of Puerto Cabezas, and 180 miles northeast of Managua. Daily air service now connects them with the capital and the east coast.

The gold mines of this area have been productive for a long time. They are vein mines, not placers like those of the country north of the border of Honduras. Some of the shafts have been dug to a depth of over 1,200 feet below the surface. Two mining companies, which are owned in the United States, account for the whole gold production of this part of Nicaragua and give employment to some 2,400 workers.

Settlement on the Miskito Coast

The whole rainy eastern side of Nicaragua was long neglected by the Spanish settlers of the colonial period. The sparse population of Indians, the dense forests, and the hoards of fever-carrying mosquitoes turned the Spaniards away from this region.

The whole Caribbean coast from Yucatán to Panamá, therefore, was almost unoccupied when the English pirates, seeking bases for their attacks on Spanish shipping, established the first settlements. In 1678 the governor of Jamaica set up a protectorate over the Miskito Indians, and in 1740 several colonies of Jamaica Negroes were placed in what is now eastern Nicaragua. The two most important colonies were at Bluefields and Greytown (now renamed San Juan del Norte). Eventually the British recognized Spanish sovereignty along all the Caribbean coast except only the eastern side of the Yucatán Peninsula where British Honduras still remains a British possession.

Efforts to develop the resources of this region, however, continued. The small groups of settlers along the coast have developed a succession of export products, each of which has after a time been exhausted. The list includes green turtles, sarsaparilla, mahogany, rubber, bananas, pine lumber, and the latest export—gold.

The people of the east coast are diverse in origin and speak an unusual variety of languages. Mixed with the original Miskito Indians are Negroes from Jamaica, some English settlers, and a few Spanish people. English, Spanish, and Miskito languages are used about equally, and sometimes all in the same sentence. The people of the Miskito Coast call themselves *costeños:* they call the people of the central nucleus of Nicaragua *españoles.*

Nicaragua as a Political Unit

The fact that Nicaragua is built around one single nucleus of concentrated settlement gives it a kind of unity it might not otherwise enjoy. There are no separate clusters of people in conflict with each other, as in Honduras; the core area of concentrated settlement is not divided into an Indian segment and a Ladino segment, as in Guatemala; and there is no lack of unoccupied potential cropland, as in El Salvador. The settlements of the Miskito Coast and the mining communities inland from them are remote indeed from the core area of Nicaragua, and the people in these outlying places have little influence on the political decisions or on the kind of state-idea that is eventually formulated. If banana planting had been as profitable along the Miskito Coast as it was along the Caribbean lowland of Honduras, a situation similar to that of Honduras would have developed—an essentially foreign type of settlement in a position isolated from the core of the country, yet one of great importance to the national treasury. But the very heavy rainfall and the deeply leached soils of eastern Nicaragua made banana planting especially hazardous and expensive. When the Sigatoka disease hit, the companies moved away.

The people in the core area, and especially those in the capital city, are beginning to feel the impact of revolutionary new ideas associated with the industrial and democratic revolutions. Nicaragua offers an interesting example of the process of spreading innovation. A part of the innovation is the transfer of people from subsistence farming outside of the money economy, into a new economic system of surplus production and of buying and selling; and another part of the innovation is the replacement of a military dictatorship devoted to the preservation of the special privileges of the elite, by a government devoted to the idea of relieving poverty and eliminating inequities of status and opportunity. Theoretical models of economic and social change are useful as norms against which to measure the specific conditions and problems of Nicaragua.

The Economic Situation

The population of Nicaragua is increasing at a rate of 3.1 percent per year. This is a little less than the rate of increase in El Salvador because the Nicaraguan death rate is higher than that of El Salvador. The death rate of 13 to 16 per thousand in Nicaragua suggests that the outlying parts of the country are not yet enjoying the full benefits of the new health measures. Controlling insect pests in thinly settled rural areas is not easy.

The problem of economic development in Nicaragua involves the shift of more and more people from subsistence living into the money economy. New jobs must be created at a rate faster than the growth of population, and as we have seen, this requires a large investment of savings in the formation of new capital. A large proportion of the working force (57.9 percent in 1963) is employed in agriculture, and of these the larger number are either engaged in raising their own food, or are only seasonally included in the money economy. The economic transformation of Nicaragua has started, but it has a long way to go.

The subsistence farmers of Nicaragua are in no way different from people in similar economic conditions in other parts of Latin America. The food crops they raise are maize, rice, and beans. They make use of the poorest soils and steepest slopes, for much of the better land is used for the grazing of cattle, in which the large landowners have an interest. Yields of food crops are so low on badly eroded land that these subsistence farmers are not only poor but getting poorer. Hundreds of thousands of them seek temporary seasonal employment on commercial plantations, picking cotton or coffee or cutting sugarcane. In the coffee areas the minimum wage of 85 cents a day (in 1965) is scarcely enough to bring the worker into a year-round money economy, yet it is too high for some of the marginal plantations. Why do these people not move away from the areas of concentrated settlement to form pioneer zones of new farm settlement in the unoccupied parts of the country? The fact is that few people choose to live in isolation. It is a fact —whether desirable or not—that most subsistence farmers, when they are forced to move, prefer to move into city slums than into remote uncleared patches of the forest. Yet when a road is built into potential agricultural land, pioneer farm settlement moves out along the road onto land not previously occupied. When road-building was made a part of the program of economic development, as in Honduras, new zones of pioneer expansion appeared for the first time.

Economic development also includes the use of certain parts of the country for commercial crops. In the older areas of commercial coffee-planting, the estates are large and workers are paid wages, as around Diriamba; in the newer coffee zones of the highlands, the plantations—known as *fincas*—are small and are worked by the owners. The largest development of commercial farming, however, is in the planting of cotton in back of Corinto. This is a part of the developing cotton frontier which distinguishes this whole Pacific coastal lowland of Central America, and which is making this coastal region a major source of cotton for the rapidly enlarging industries of Japan. The largest source of new employment in agriculture is in this section of the country.

Since 1957 Nicaragua has also made a start in the building of manufacturing industries. In 1958, with foreign capital, the largest meat-processing plant along the Pacific lowland of Central America was built in Managua. Processed meat from Managua is sent in refrigerator trucks over the Inter-American Highway to the Caribbean port of Matías de Galvez in Guatemala (see p. 140), where it is loaded on ships bound for the United States port of Miami. Now Managua has several other new factories, including furniture factories, metal-working plants, and textile factories. In Managua the minimum wage in 1965 was $1.12 per day. Workers who are thus employed want to buy more food and more household gadgets, more radios and more motorcycles. There is an increasing number of jobs, therefore, in retail selling and in other service occupations. The question is, can new jobs be provided fast enough to stay ahead of the population increase, thus making a continuous gain in the proportion of the workers included in the money economy?

For a few years in the 1960's Nicaragua did surprisingly well in increasing its rate of economic growth per capita. In 1955 the gross national product per capita was only $158, but between 1961 and 1965 this country achieved the highest rate of growth in Central America—8 percent per year. Then in 1966 and 1967 the rate of growth dropped to only about 3.5 percent per year, which was barely enough to stay even with the increase of population.

In 1965 two products made up 62 percent of the value of all exports. These were cotton (44 percent, up from 23 percent in 1960) and coffee (18 percent). The government was concerned about this large measure of dependence on two exports, both of which have in the past fluctuated considerably in market value. An effort was being made to diversify the exports by increasing the production of meat, tobacco, and bananas. Furthermore, geologists had identified sources of copper and bauxite, and the plan was to make them accessible through new highway construction. The highways, also, will lead to new pioneer settlement in the empty parts of the country.

Nicaragua, like other Latin-American countries, wanted to decrease its dependence on the United States, and this has been done through the increase of trade with Japan and West Germany. In 1964 Japan was Nicaragua's best market for the cotton exports. The United States continues to supply the larger part of the imports.

The Political Situation

In spite of the unity of the chief nucleus of settlement in Nicaragua, the country has yet to achieve coherence in its national life. It has been said that there are no Nicaraguans—only liberals and conservatives, *costeños* and *españoles*. When the people who lived around León and Granada asserted their independence from Guatemala in 1838 they were united in only one thing— the desire for freedom from outside control, the right to make their own mistakes. Immediately the struggle for supremacy flared up between the liberals of León and the conservatives of Granada. When political parties occupy geographically distinct areas, the situation makes internal conflict difficult to avoid.

The political situation in Nicaragua has long been complicated by the intervention of foreign interests. In 1841 Great Britain established a protectorate over the Miskito Indians on the Nicaraguan east coast, and in that same year they seized the port of San Juan del Norte. The United States started to turn its attention to the possible passageways across the isthmus only after the Mexican War had resulted in the expansion of its national territory all the way across North America to the Pacific Ocean. In 1850 the United States and Great Britain signed the Clayton-Bulwer Treaty in which both countries agreed not to occupy, fortify, colonize, or exercise dominion over any portion of Central America. Great Britain insisted that this did not include British Honduras, but it did involve the British settlements along the Miskito Coast. Nevertheless it was not until 1893 that the Nicaraguan army actually regained control of this eastern part of the country, although they had regained San Juan del Norte in 1852.

When Cornelius Vanderbilt became interested in developing the route across the isthmus for the people bound for California, he had to face constant difficulties with the warring political factions of Nicaragua. In 1855 he gave his backing to a North American adventurer named William Walker. Walker supported the forces of León, and with a band of 56 men that he brought with him he defeated the opposing troops. From 1855 to 1857 he was the president of Nicaragua, but eventually he was deposed and forced to flee the country. In 1860, involved in another bit of adventure in Honduras, he was captured and shot.

Foreign intervention continued. In 1874 the Germans blockaded the Nicaraguan coast in order to collect damages for an alleged insult to their consul. They eventually received $30,000. In 1893 the liberal General José Santos Zelaya became dictator. But when, in 1909, he signed a treaty with Great Britain giving that country the exclusive right to build a canal, the United States withdrew recognition, and Zelaya was soon deposed. When conditions seemed thoroughly out of hand, in 1912, the United States landed a force of 2,600 Marines. When order had been imposed, the force was reduced to a legation guard of only about 100 men. In 1916 Nicaragua granted to the United States the exclusive rights to build a canal, for which the United States paid a sum of $3,000,000.

By 1925 the military occupation of another country had become unpopular in the United States, and in that year the Marines were withdrawn from Nicaragua. But at once the civil war between liberals and conservatives burst out again, and in the spring of 1926 the Marines returned. Elections were carried out under the control of the United States and a liberal was elected. It was at this time that General Agusto César Sandino began his revolt against military intervention and against any government elected under foreign auspices. Sandino became the hero of all those throughout Latin America who resented the forceful interference of the "colossus of the north." When the Marines were finally withdrawn in 1933, Sandino promptly surrendered to the Nicaraguan government, after which, because of his large political following, he was shot.

The year 1932 marked the beginning of the period of Nicaraguan history during which the strong man was General Anastasio Somoza García. Somoza had been trained by the Marines and had been placed in command of the highly efficient National Guard. With this military backing he became the only real political power. In 1937 he seized the government, and thereafter he remained either as president or as the power behind the president until his assassination in 1956. During all this period he gave Nicaragua political order by prohibiting all opposition parties. He treated the country as if it were his own private estate. He took many steps to strengthen the economy of Nicaragua, usually to the advantage of the politically powerful people around him. After his death, his son, Luis Somoza Debayle, assumed the presidency, and in 1957 he was duly elected to that office.

In 1957 the long-quiet border dispute between Nicaragua and Honduras again became active. This involved the easternmost part of their common boundary, which territory had never been effectively occupied by either. In 1906 the King of Spain made an award dividing the area between the two countries, but since there were no detailed maps of the area, and only a few fishing villages along the coast, the award was never implemented. In the 1950's both Nicaragua and Honduras began to move settlers into the disputed area, and there were conflicts of jurisdiction that threatened to blow up into armed conflict. In 1957 both Honduras and Nicaragua requested the Organization of American States to seek a solution. This agency placed the matter before the International Court of Justice at The Hague, and in 1960 the court reaffirmed the award made by the King of Spain. But now the O.A.S. sent a boundary commission into the field to establish the position of the boundary and to mark it. Since the King's award had been based on a map made in 1720, there was an inevitable disagreement as to the meaning of the award, and this disagreement could only be resolved by careful mapping and by comparison of the maps with rivers and other features in the field. The boundary commission made its decision in 1961, and both countries accepted it.

Nicaragua remains a country with little experience in the orderly processes of democratic government. It has been run by a dictator, supported by a well-drilled and loyal military force. The dictator has brought material benefits to the country, and has put a stop to the political disorders which, before 1912, caused endless destruction of life and property. But Nicaragua has no state-idea to command the support of a free people. In spite of its single core of settlement, Nicaragua has a long way to go in the development of a coherent political life, or in the acceptance of the basic concepts of democracy.

República de Costa Rica

Area: 19,652 square miles
Population: (1966 estimate) 1,514,000
        (last census, 1963) 1,336,274
Capital city: San José; (1964) 330,607
Percent urban: (1950) 33.5
Birth rate per 1,000: (1966) 40.8; Death rate per 1,000: (1966) 8.8
Annual percent of increase: (1958–64) 4.3
Percent literate: (1963) 84.4
Percent of labor force in agriculture: (1963) 47.2
Gross national product per capita: (1966) $406
Unit of currency: colón (1968, 6.62 per dollar)
Leading crops in acreage: maize, coffee

COMMERCE, 1965 *(expressed in percentage of value)*
Percent total Latin-American exports: 1.1 (1956, less than 1.0)
Percent total Latin-American imports: 2.0

Exports (1966)

coffee	38	fertilizer	7
bananas	24	meat	5

Exports to (1966)			**Imports from (1966)**		
United States	54 (1956, 48)		United States	39 (1956, 54)
West Germany	18		West Germany	10
Nicaragua	7		Japan	9
Netherlands	5		United Kingdom	5
			Guatamala	5

Chapter 8 □ Costa Rica

There is no place in Latin America that is quite like Costa Rica. The contrast between Costa Rica and its neighbors in Central America is striking. In fact, Costa Rica stands out in all Latin America for the devotion of its people to the ideals and practices of democracy, for the high degree of literacy among its people, and for the incredible net rate of population increase, which is perhaps the highest in the world.

The area of concentrated settlement which forms the nucleus of Costa Rica is located in the highlands, where a small intermont basin with deep volcanic ash soils offers land of relatively gentle slope in the midst of the *tierra templada*. The densely populated core area, which occupies this intermont basin and the lower slopes of the bordering mountains, measures only about 15 miles by 40 miles. But within this area there is the densest rural population to be found anywhere in Latin America—more than 1,500 people per square mile. The people of this core area are of almost unmixed Spanish ancestry. With a high birth rate of 40.8 per thousand (1966), and an exceptionally low death rate of 8 per thousand, the population of Costa Rica as a whole is increasing at a net rate of 4.3 percent per year.

There are many other ways in which the conditions of life in this core area are distinctive. Among all the countries of Latin America, Costa Rica, along with Argentina, Uruguay, Chile, and Barbados, enjoys the prestige of a population that is more than 80 percent literate. The great majority of the farmers in the core area own and operate their own farms. The traditional large estate with tenant workers is not found in the central area; there is no small group of landed aristocracy to dominate the social life, manipulate politics with the support of an army, and collect the larger share of the benefits of the economy. In Costa Rica there is a notable feeling of equality.

Another distinctive characteristic of Costa Rica is the long-continued existence of zones of pioneer expansion. Farm settlers have been moving out from the core area for many decades, occupying previously empty land, creating new communities carved out of the forest. This kind of outward movement of pioneers has been notably lacking in Latin America until recently. But Costa Rica has had its pioneer zones for hundreds of years. Even in the modern period Costa Ricans are more attracted by the opportunities of a pioneer zone than by the presumed amenities of city life.

Yet Costa Rica, also, has its internal contrasts—its elements of diversity. In strong contrast to the homogeneous population of the central area, with its distinctive institutions and man–land relations, are the lowland areas on either side. On the Pacific side, especially in the Province of Guanacaste, nearly half of the people are mestizo in origin, racially indistinguishable from the people of Nicaragua. In this part of Costa Rica, moreover, there are many large land properties, a small landed aristocracy, and tenant workers who live in relative poverty. On the Caribbean side more than half of the people are African—mostly Jamaicans who were brought in when the banana plantations back of Puerto Limón were first being developed.

The census of 1950 counted 800,875 people in Costa Rica. In 1956 the population reached 1 million, and in 1966 it was estimated that the number had almost reached a million and a half. For the country as a whole, about 80 percent are of unmixed Spanish ancestry, 17 percent are mestizo, 2 percent are of African origin, and less than 1 percent are pure Indian.

The Land

Costa Rica is quite simple in the arrangement of its physical features (Map 27, p. 171). The backbone of the isthmus is made up of a ridge of mountains that extends from northwest to southeast. This is a continuation of the belt of hills which, in Nicaragua, separates Lake Nicaragua from the Pacific coast. The ridge slopes steeply toward the Pacific, and more gently toward the Caribbean. The highest elevations along this mountain backbone increase toward the southeast; to the southeast of San José the highest peak is 12,800 feet above sea level. The mountain ridge in this part of Costa Rica is called the Cordillera de Talamanca.

In the central part of Costa Rica, just northeast of San José and Cartago, four great volcanic cones stand in a row, their bases merged into one massive pedestal. From northwest to southeast they are named Poás (9,055 ft.), Barba (9,612 ft.), Irazú (11,417 ft.), and Turrialba (11,220 ft.). This commanding line of volcanoes stands parallel to the main crest of the mountain backbone, but about 20 miles to the northeast of it. Nestled between the steep slopes of the main cordillera on the southwest and the long gentle lower slopes of the four volcanoes on the northeast is an intermont basin, the Meseta Central, between 3,000 and 4,000 feet above sea level. This intermont basin is a structural depression, deeply filled with porous volcanic ash which remains generally level and undissected except close to the headwaters of the rivers that drain the basin. Near the rivers the surface is hilly and in many places too steep for agriculture. The southeastern part of the Meseta Central is drained by the headwaters of the Río Reventazón, which flows eastward through a deep gorge at the base of Mt. Turrialba and emerges on the Caribbean coastal lowland north of Limón. The northwestern part of the Meseta Central is drained by the headwaters of the Río Grande, which enters the Pacific a little southeast of Puntarenas.

Another important feature is the long narrow structural depression that runs parallel to the Cordillera de Talamanca in southeastern Costa Rica. This is the Valle del General, a deep lowland drained by the Río General, which runs along the southwest side of the Cordillera for some 50 miles. It is separated from the Pacific coast by another steep mountain ridge, parallel to the Cordillera but with a summit elevation of less than 5,000 feet. The drainage of the Valle del General is carried to the ocean through a narrow gorge cut by the Río Diquis. At the lowest part of the Valle, just upstream from the gorge, the elevation is only about 600 feet above sea level.

The lower country bordering the Pacific coast is made up of patches of lowland lying between the base of the highland backbone and outlying mountain blocks. The lowland of Guanacaste at the head of the Gulf of Nicoya is the largest such area of plain. It extends northward almost to the border of Nicaragua, from which it is separated only by the hilly northwestern end of the central highland. The lowland is bordered on the southwest by steep block mountains on the Nicoya Peninsula which reach a maximum elevation of a little over 3,000 feet. South of the Gulf of Nicoya the lowland is cut off as the central cordillera rises directly from the Pacific. In the southern part of Costa Rica, however, there is another lowland area where the Río Diquis comes out from the mountains. Here also a mountain block borders the ocean, and a small embayment provides a protected harbor where the new banana port, Golfito, has been built. This southernmost lowland of Costa Rica crosses the border into Panamá.

The lowlands on the Caribbean side are much simpler in their outlines. The northeastern part of Costa Rica includes the end of the Nicaraguan lowland, which extends along the base of the highlands southeastward as far as Limón. Much of this plain is poorly drained, but along the base of the volcanic mountains there is a piedmont zone of gently sloping land where drainage problems are not difficult.

The climatic conditions in Costa Rica differ notably on the Caribbean and the Pacific sides, and in the highland area are to a large extent governed by altitude. Rainfall is excessive on the Caribbean lowland and on the mountain slopes that face toward the easterly winds. A belt of more than 100 inches of average annual rainfall extends from eastern Nicaragua, across Costa Rica and Panamá into Colombia (Map 12, p. 32). On the Pacific side not only is the average annual rainfall somewhat less, but also it is distributed more unevenly during the year. In the Valle del General and all along the Pacific coastal region there is a dry season from December to April, when the prevailing wind direction is from the east. When the equatorial westerlies are on-shore from the west and southwest, rainfall is heavy. But the lowland of Guanacaste, in the lee of the Nicoya Peninsula, even at this time of the year often suffers from drought. Because of the long dry season along the Pacific coast, the vegetation on this side of the mountain backbone is a seasonal forest, whereas on the Caribbean side there is a dense evergreen rain forest. The dry Guanacaste lowland had a wild vegetation of woodland savanna when the Spaniards first reached that area.

In the highlands the pattern of climate and vegetation is complicated. None of the mountains is high enough to reach the zone of permanent snow, but on some of the higher slopes there are tall mountain-grasslands. The Meseta Central, also, lies in the rain shadow of the four volcanoes, and was covered with grass when the Spaniards first reached it. In fact, these grasslands in the vicinity of Cartago offered the first Spanish colonists the kind of open land they preferred as places on which to settle. A general vertical zoning is recognized by the inhabitants of Costa Rica. Because of the greater rainfall on the Caribbean side the zones are higher on that side than on the Pacific. Waibel gives the following limits to the vertical zones on the two sides of highland Costa Rica:

VERTICAL ZONES OF COSTA RICA*

| Zone | Altitude in feet | |
	Caribbean side	Pacific side
Tierra fría	above 5,900	above 4,900
Tierra templada	2,100–5,900	1,475–4,900
Tierra caliente	under 2,100	under 1,475

*After L. Waibel, "White Settlement in Costa Rica," *Geographical Review*, 29 (1939): 529–560.

The Pattern of Settlement

The Spaniards found no such tribes of peaceful natives in Costa Rica as they found farther north in Nicaragua. A settlement was actually attempted on the Nicoya Peninsula as early as 1522, but it was soon abandoned because of the hostility of the natives. In the highland basins there were perhaps seven or eight thousand sedentary Indians when the Spaniards first arrived, but they were soon wiped out by disease. Nor did the explorers find any gold in Costa Rica. The name was probably given to the Caribbean coast by Columbus because of the gold ornaments he found the Indians wearing. But it proved, rather, to be a *Costa Pobre*. As a result the area remained for a long time unoccupied.

Settlement of the Highlands

About 1560 this part of the isthmus was placed under the jurisdiction of Guatemala, and in 1561 the first group of settlers established themselves in the Meseta Central. In all colonial Latin America there were not many settlers like these—except for the Chileans. There were no gold mines to bring wealth, no Indians to Christianize, no native people to do the work. These settlers came to establish their own farms in pleasant surroundings, to build homes, not just to find El Dorado and return to Spain. Furthermore, in the next year Juan Vásquez de Coronado arrived from Guatemala bringing with him the wives and sweethearts of the pioneers. He also brought cattle, horses, and hogs, and in this area established what was probably one of the earliest large cattle ranches in the Americas. In this isolated spot, the people became small farmers, raising their own food and fibers, bearing children of unmixed Spanish ancestry. There was no aristocracy, no individuals who could claim special prestige because of position or status. The families that chose to come to Costa Rica were in a sense selected because of their unusual attitudes and objectives, compared with those common in colonial Spanish America.

Expansion of Settlement

The first signs of settlement expansion appeared early in the eighteenth century, while Costa Rica was still a poor country. In 1736, pioneers from Cartago moved into that part of the Meseta Central which drains to the Pacific and established there the town of San José. Still the movement did not involve any very large numbers, for in 1751 this central area was reported to include only 2,330 people, in 399 families. Nevertheless, expansion continued, and in 1790 another town (Alajuela) was founded not far from San José, and a little later a fourth town (Heredia), also in the vicinity of San José. To what extent these movements of the eighteenth century were the result of population pressure around Cartago is difficult to estimate. It is true that Cartago has a climate which is far less comfortable than that of the area around San José, for the heavy clouds and excessive rains of the eastern slopes spill over into the Meseta Central through the gap of the Reventazón Valley, while San José is to a certain extent protected by the volcanoes. Alajuela and Heredia are especially favored in terms of sunshine and mild temperatures. The movement of expansion, however, did not result in any serious or permanent decline in the density of settlement around the original nucleus of Cartago.

Costa Rica was still a poor country when the people of Mexico declared their independence, including in the new sovereign nation the whole of the area formerly administered as New Spain. But the people of isolated Costa

Rica were not greatly concerned, for in their remote location they had always been independent if only because no one was interested in them. Later, when Guatemala broke away from Mexico, this also involved Costa Rica. Finally, in 1838, when El Salvador and Nicaragua broke apart from Guatemala, Costa Rica was left to go its own way. And even at that time the highland settlements were unique in all of Latin America. In 1821 there were some 60,000 people in Costa Rica as a whole, most of them in the central area; the population density around Cartago was about 260 people per square mile—one of the greatest densities to be found at that time in all of Latin America. This was one of the very few spots where farming was being practiced by small landowners of Spanish ancestry, and where large land properties were the exception rather than the rule.

THE SPREAD OF COFFEE PLANTING

The first country in Central America to take up the cultivation of coffee was Costa Rica. The plant was introduced into this region as early as 1797, but not until 1825 was the first small shipment made to foreign countries. When Costa Rica found itself independent, its government faced the urgent need to get some kind of money crop—some kind of product to export and to tax. The Costa Ricans were the first in this part of Latin America to realize the advantages for coffee growing which are to be found in certain parts of the *tierra templada,* especially those parts which have a dry season and a porous volcanic soil. The coffee produced in such places, especially the coffee which comes from close to the upper limits, is now recognized as possessing a superior flavor. At an early date the Costa Rican government sought to stimulate this form of commercial production by offering free land to any one who would agree to set out coffee trees. The government also began the construction of cart roads both to Limón and to Puntarenas.

The result was a "coffee rush." In 1825 the first few bags were sent out, and in 1829 coffee became the chief export product of the country. Until the cart road to Puntarenas was completed in 1846, transportation had to be by muleback, and no very important volume of coffee could be moved. At first the chief market was in the west-coast countries of South America, but when the first bags were sent to Great Britain in 1845 the European market was at last opened to the Costa Rican product. Coffee exported on a large scale began about the middle of the century; after the opening of the railroad to Puerto Limón in 1891, that port became the chief outlet.

Settlement expansion after the middle of the last century went on more and more rapidly. One result of the new economic prosperity was an increase in the birth rate. With population growing at an ever increasing rate, and with the government adopting a policy of giving free land for new coffee plantations, continued pioneer expansion went on around the margins of the original settlements, yet without any accompanying decrease in the density of population in the older settled areas. Pioneers spread first down the valley of the Río Reventazón, their new settlements now extending as far as the old mission settlement of Turrialba, just under 2,000 feet in altitude. In the Turrialba region there were, in 1883, only 1,068 people; but settlement went on rapidly after 1890 when the railroad from Puerto Limón reached Turrialba. New settlement also moved up the slopes of the volcanoes—a movement which has now gone beyond the upper limits of coffee. On Irazú, at an altitude of about 9,800 feet, there are settlers who pasture dairy cattle and cultivate potatoes. Over a pass between Barba and Poás settlement has spread to the northeast slopes of the volcanoes. Another current of settlement has gone to the west of Poás, now almost completely encircling its base. Pioneers have also advanced down the railroad line which connects San José and Puntarenas; and since 1910 there has been a movement northwestward from this line along the Pacific slope of the highlands.

One of the largest pioneer movements in Costa Rica, however, has taken place since 1936 in the Valle del General. In that year a new gravel highway was completed between Cartago and San Isidro at the northwestern-most end of the Valle. This little frontier town became the jumping-off place for new settlers pouring in from the crowded Meseta Central. In 1921 the whole Valle had only a few thousand settlers, including people living in San Isidro. By 1960 there were more than 50,000 farmers, and thousands more have come since 1960. In 1962 the all-weather highway was completed down the length of the Valle del General and through the gorge of the Río Diquis to the lowlands along the Pacific. The road was extended eastward into Panamá, providing for the first time a regularly passable route of travel between the rest of Central America and Panamá. As a result settlers from Panamá have been moving into the Valle del General.

The farmers of this pioneer zone are connected to markets by all-weather roads suitable for use by motor trucks. As a result, the food products they raise in the Valle are not just for subsistence. The people in this zone now account for about half of the total Costa Rican production of maize, beans, and rice. The bottom of the Valle is too low for coffee, although some coffee is produced on the bordering mountain slopes. But as in other lowland areas in Central America and Mexico, these lands have been discovered to be highly productive for food crops.

THE PRESENT SETTLEMENT OF THE HIGHLANDS

Costa Rica is no longer isolated from the rest of Central America. Not only is the central area well supplied with paved roads, but also all-weather motor truck highways have been built to Puerto Limón and Puntarenas. The Inter-American Highway now provides an all-weather connection all the way from the United States through Mexico, Guatemala, Honduras, Nicaragua, and on across Costa Rica into Panamá. In Costa Rica the highway passes through the Guanacaste Lowland to Puntarenas, then climbs to San José and Cartago. From Cartago it descends through the Valle del General and passes through the gorge of the Río Diquis to the Pacific lowland, and on to connect with the highways of Panamá.

San José is Costa Rica's most important city and its capital. In 1964 the whole urban area, which extends beyond the limits of the political city, had a population of 330,607.

A large part of the area of this central nucleus of concentrated settlement is used for the planting of coffee. The cities of San José, Heredia, and Alajuela stand in the midst of coffee plantations. The gently sloping surface of the Meseta Central, underlain by deep, porous volcanic-ash soils, offers almost ideal conditions for this crop.

Since the early 1960's the production of coffee in this central area has been reorganized. For a long time the coffee growers of Costa Rica have been able to produce only low yields per acre. In 1956 about 56 percent of the coffee producers owned less than 1,000 trees each and had *fincas* of less than two acres. On such small holdings it was difficult to make use of modern agricultural techniques. But since 1960 many small coffee growers have sold their *fincas* and moved on to the pioneer zones. Many small *fincas* have been consolidated into larger properties which can be operated with great efficiency. As a result of this consolidation the annual per-acre coffee harvest has more than doubled since 1952. The small-farmer character of the central area has now been lost. Now only 2 percent of the coffee growers in Costa Rica produce more than half of the annual harvest. On these larger plantations the use of fertilizer and insecticides has increased many times.

In the central area coffee is grown up to about 3,200 feet above sea level. Between this and the cloud zone where there is a wet forest, most of the land is used for pasture, but in a system of rotation with crops. The crops—potatoes, maize, and vegetables—are followed by a year of pasture, then a year of fallow, then crops again. The pasture is primarily for dairy cattle. Fine herds of purebred stock are used to produce milk and butter, which are transported by truck to the city markets.

To the west of Alajuela, within the central area, is a sugarcane district. There are seven large sugar refineries. The greater part of the sugar is consumed within Costa Rica.

One reason for the continued productivity of the farms of the central area, even after four hundred years of heavy use, is the deep, well-drained soil formed on volcanic ash. Some of the finest agricultural lands in the tropical parts of the world are to be found on such volcanic soils. But every now and then volcanic regions are subject to disasters. In 1963, with no warning, Mt. Irazú began to erupt, sending forth clouds of fine volcanic ash that fell over the land to the west of it. San José itself was covered with this fine dust: people carried umbrellas and wore sunglasses to keep the irritating ash out of their eyes. The floor of the houses were covered with a gray powder that felt like sand underfoot. In the rural areas coffee plantations were ruined as the leaves became coated with ash. When the rainy season began, the thick accumulation of ash on the slopes began to slide, at one time cutting the highway between San José and Cartago. Costa Rica became a disaster area; and the only compensation was the understanding that this was the way in which the fine soils of the central area were accumulated. After 1964 the eruption ceased, and the people of the central area began to dig out.

Settlement on the Caribbean Coast

A very different kind of settlement appeared on the Caribbean lowland of Costa Rica. During the whole colonial period the Spanish communities of the Meseta Central were effectively isolated from the Caribbean by the screen of dense rain forest and by the insect-borne diseases of the lowlands. In 1871, however, the government of Costa Rica, seeking a more direct way out for the increasing shipments of coffee, contracted with a North American company for the construction of a railroad to connect San José with Puerto Limón. Since the forested coastal lands were uninhabited, the company brought in workers from Jamaica to do the job. It took nine years to build the first 70 miles; but by 1890 the line had been built up the valley of the Río Reventazón to Turrialba, and the next year it was completed to San José.

One of the North Americans in charge of the railroad project who survived the difficulties of those early years was Minor C. Keith. He appreciated the need for developing some kind of traffic on the lower part of the line in order to pay the high cost of construction. He imported rootstalks of the banana plant from the vicinity of the modern city of Colón in Panamá and planted them in Costa Rica along the new railroad. The first bananas were shipped from Costa Rica to New Orleans in 1878, and thereafter he established a regular export of bananas to both New Orleans and New York. In 1899 the United Fruit Company was formed by a consolidation of the Boston Fruit Company, which was operating in the Antilles, and several companies headed by Minor C. Keith, who was growing bananas in Costa Rica, Panamá, and the Santa Marta area of Colombia.

As skill in the solution of technological problems was developed, the planting of bananas began to increase rapidly. In 1890 some million bunches were exported rom Puerto Limón, but by 1900 exports had risen to three and a half million, and by 1907 to over ten million. By 1909, Costa Rica was the world's leading banana producer. In 1913, the peak year of production in Costa Rica, eleven million bunches were exported. By that time the United Fruit Company had developed a second banana planting district along the Río Sixaola on the border of Panamá. The bananas were moved across the border by train and exported from a small port in the Bocas del Toro area.

At first the agricultural experts of the United Fruit Company rated the Caribbean lowlands of Costa Rica as almost ideal for tropical plantation crops. The combination of heavy rainfall and hot sunshine between showers made plants grow luxuriantly. The absence of destructive hurricanes meant that one hazard of tropical agriculture did not have to be faced. The soils, derived in part from the volcanic ash washed down from the highlands, were productive and easily drained. But it soon became clear that whereas some plantings of bananas remained productive for as long as 25 years, in most places yields declined rapidly after five years or so. Furthermore, when a plantation began to decline it was better to develop a new one in a previously uncleared area than to try to replant the old one. Since there was plenty of empty land in the region the company adopted the policy of pushing the frontier of new planting northwestward along the base of the highlands.

In spite of new plantings, the peak year in the Caribbean lowland was reached in 1907. Exports from Costa Rica as a whole continued to mount until 1913, because of the new plantations along the Río Sixaola. Plantations, instead of lasting five years, began to die out in only two years. The difficulty was the spread of the Panama disease, a fungus which causes the plants to rot away at the base. Once the soil became infected bananas simply could no longer be grown, and the disease spread with alarming rapidity. At that time it was not known that the disease could be eliminated by flooding the land for several months. The company continued to work vigorously to keep new planting ahead of the spreading disease, but by 1935 production in all of Costa Rica was down to only two and a half million bunches.

Finally the struggle to maintain the plantations in eastern Costa Rica was abandoned. The company continued to purchase bananas from independent growers, but gave up its own plantations in this area, increasing its plantings in Honduras and Guatemala, as we have seen. When the second banana disease, the Sigatoka disease, appeared in 1938, the company stopped its purchases entirely. In 1942 the last banana ship was sunk at its dock in Puerto Limón by a German submarine, and all export of bananas ceased. The eastern part of Costa Rica remained a serious economic problem area. A proposal to repatriate some of the Jamaicans met an unenthusiastic response in that overcrowded island.

Since World War II, while banana planting has started again on the Pacific side of Costa Rica, the Caribbean lowlands have not been entirely neglected, either by the company or by the government of Costa Rica. As early as 1914 some of the abandoned banana lands had been planted experimentally with cacao. Now the United Fruit Company operates a cacao plantation in this area covering 23,500 acres, and small planters in the vicinity cultivate an additional 16,000 acres. The company also has some 10,000 acres of abacá (Manila hemp). The Goodyear Tire and Rubber Company has developed a small rubber plantation. In addition some of the people still plant bananas in small plots, and these are sold to independent buyers.

Nevertheless, Costa Rica has yet to accomplish as much as the Mexicans in supporting the development of this wet, tropical lowland. The success of the Papaloapan project (see p. 95) in Mexico, in country not unlike the lower Reventazón Valley of Costa Rica, suggests that similar aid to economic development in that part of the country might be accomplished. Maize, for example, which takes a whole year to mature in the highlands where most of it is grown, would mature in only three months in the wet lowlands. Two crops a year from the same land could be harvested if drainage and fertilizer problems were solved. Here is an important potential use of the land.

Settlement on the Pacific Coast

The economic development of the Pacific coast has been given greater support in Costa Rica than that of the Caribbean lowlands. The northwestern part of this area was the part first reached by the Spaniards, and in the colonial period was the part closest in touch with the administrative center of the Captaincy-General of Guatemala. To the north of the port of Puntarenas the extensive lowland plains of Guanacaste Province around the town of Liberia were divided into vast private estates and used for the grazing of cattle. This province remains even now Costa Rica's chief area of cattle production. The properties are large, combining on one estate areas of open range, forested areas in the mountains, and planted fattening pastures. The cattle are driven into the neighboring highlands on either side during the wet season, and are brought back to the lowlands during the dry season. Most of the people of the area work for wages on the large ranches. Small bits of land in the vicinity of the villages or ranch headquarters are used for the production of the basic foods, maize, rice, and beans. Since World War II there has been a considerable movement of new settlers into the southern part of the Nicoya Peninsula where maize, rice, and beans are raised for local subsistence.

The Guanacaste lowland exhibits in many places the land destruction resulting from the speculative exploitation of resources and poor techniques of pasture management. Around Liberia, near the northwestern end of the lowland, much of the land has been so severely gullied that its usefulness for pasture has been lost. Logging operations in the forest, also, have resulted in the clearing of watershed areas, thereby increasing the run-off of the rainy season and intensifying the droughts of the dry season.

In 1955, however, the government of Costa Rica undertook a development project in this area. The first step was a survey of the physical character of the land carried out on large-scale maps permitting the mapping of details. Based on a knowledge of the facts of soil, slope, drainage, and other factors, a plan for the more effective use of the land was drawn up. Because Guanacaste is sheltered on either side by mountains it remains relatively dry. The Río Tempisque, which drains the lowland into the head of the Gulf of Nicoya, carries plenty of water for irrigation. A new irrigated area was de-

Overhead spray on banana plantation near Golfito. *Courtesy of United Fruit Co.*

veloped along the western side of the river, and land was sold to pioneer farmers. This has become an important source of food for the communities of the central area.

The southeastern part of the Pacific coast is now the major area of banana planting. To the south of the end of the Peninsula of Nicoya, where the on-shore winds of the rainy season can bring an abundance of moisture between May and November, conditions are ideal for bananas. When the Sigatoka disease swept through the plantations on the Caribbean side, the United Fruit Company decided to shift its plantations to the Pacific side. In 1939 a new banana dock was built at Quepos, and plantations were laid out in the country in back of this port. As these plantations have since started to decline, the bananas have been replaced in this area with cacao, African oil palms, mahogany, and teak. The chief banana area is now in back of the modern banana port of Golfito, extending from Puerto Cortes to, and across, the border of Panamá. In these plantations spray systems have been built to deliver the copper sulfate through nozzles that spray in circular patterns like the watering systems of golf courses but much larger. The soil is treated with fertilizer and insecticides, and the bunches of bananas are dipped and washed before they are loaded on the ships. In this area banana planting has ceased to be a temporary and shifting use of the land: it has become an intensive kind of agriculture, with relatively large capital and labor investment.

Costa Rica as a Political Unit

Costa Rica is a state with a well-developed sense of national identity. Costa Ricans are conscious of being different; and because they share a clearly formulated state-idea, most Costa Ricans are less sensitive than their neighbors regarding matters of national prestige. There are five chief ways in which Costa Rica is distinctive: (1) in the absence of a landed aristocracy; (2) in the traditional support for democratic attitudes and procedures; (3) in the high rate of literacy (84.4 percent), which is exceeded in Latin America only by Argentina, Uruguay, and Barbados; (4) in the very high rate of population increase (4.3 percent per year), which is perhaps the highest rate in the world; and (5) in the fact that the movement of people to the frontiers of pioneer settlement is greater than the movement to the cities.

The Economic Situation

In terms of gross national product per capita, Costa Rica stands tenth among the independent countries of Latin America, and is better off than any of the other members of the Organization of Central American States. In 1955 Costa Rica stood sixth in Latin America, but the rapidly accelerated economic development of such countries as Mexico and Peru pushed these latter ahead in the standing. Nevertheless the value of all goods and services in Costa Rica has been gaining at a rate of about 10 percent per year.

The increase in the value of goods and services has come chiefly in the

Washing bananas before shipment. *Courtesy of United Fruit Co.*

agricultural sector. New large investments by the United Fruit Company around Golfito have increased the value of exports; but more important has been the doubling of yields of coffee per acre between 1952 and 1962. This is the result of the increased use of fertilizer and insecticide, which is also related to the consolidation of the *fincas* into larger plantations. This could not have been done if there had not been a large migration of coffee growers to the pioneer zones, especially to the Valle del General. In other countries, where the efficiency of agriculture is raised, the displaced small farmers have moved to the cities, creating there an almost insuperable unemployment problem. Costa Rica merits special attention because of the importance of the frontier as a safety valve to absorb not only the farmers displaced from the central area, but also the rapidly increasing total population. In addition to the pioneer settlements, large numbers of jobs have also been created in the service occupations.

Manufacturing has played a relatively small part in the economic development process. In this respect Costa Rica resembles Nicaragua and Honduras. In 1960 only 13 percent of the gross national product was credited to manufacturing, compared with 20 percent in Guatemala. In 1963 a much-needed fertilizer plant was built in Puntarenas attached to an oil refinery that had been built there earlier. Fertilizer is increasingly used in the coffee plantations, and in 1964 Costa Rica even exported fertilizer to other Central American countries.

Costa Rica is still heavily dependent on two export products. In 1964 coffee made up 42 percent of the value of exports, and bananas made up 25 percent. Costa Rica is more closely attached to the United States than are the other Central American states, but its trade with the other members of ODECA is increasing, and its connections reach out to West Germany, the Netherlands, Japan, and Great Britain.

The Political Situation

Costa Rica is also distinctive among the Latin-American nations in the widespread acceptance of the ideals and practices of democracy. In this little nation, as well as in Uruguay and Chile, the democratic procedures seem most firmly established.

None of these accomplishments was reached without a struggle. To be sure Costa Rica, at least in its central area, has never been burdened with the Spanish agrarian tradition. The absence of sources of gold or of an Indian population meant that the country was not very attractive to the majority of the Spaniards in the early colonial period. Instead the people who settled in the Meseta Central were a selected group whose purpose was to create a permanent community, not simply to gain quick wealth and then return to Spain. Even in the seventeenth century travelers to the Meseta Central remarked on the absence of an aristocracy and of a class that enjoyed prestige and privilege because of its status. Ideas of equality developed early, as did the tradition of the small independent farmer. To work for a living was never looked down upon in Costa Rica.

Nevertheless, experience in public administration was slight in colonial Costa Rica. In this remote and isolated part of the Captaincy-General of Guatemala, political problems generated little heat. When Guatemala broke away from Mexico, Costa Rica was included with the other countries farther to the north. Costa Rica was the end of the line, for no road reached the part of Colombia that was known as Panamá. In 1838, when the Central American countries separated, Costa Rica, without ever demanding it, found itself independent. And because of the lack of political interest, the new government fell into the hands of a dictator. But the dictator had to earn his living like anyone else, for the national treasury contained no great store of wealth, and the idea of using the printing presses to create money made little sense to the hard-working Costa Ricans.

A succession of governments, some more totalitarian than others, were all more clearly guided by public opinion than in any of the other Central American states. Costa Rica developed a reputation for freedom of speech, for liberal concepts of government, and for the avoidance of force. In 1889 the first fully free election in all Latin America was held, and the ballots were honestly counted. In spite of the existence, by that time, of opposed political parties, the results of the election were respected and the majority party took control. Since 1889, with the exception of only two brief periods, in 1917–19 and in 1948, Costa Rica has operated as a democracy. There has been freedom of access to knowledge, freedom to criticize the government, freedom to discuss public issues. There have been opposition political parties. Elections have been conducted honestly and in secret. The tradition of democracy has become an important part of the Costa Rican state-idea. Attempts to seize power by force were met, in 1948, by a popular uprising. Since 1948, Costa Rica has had no army—only a national police force.

Partly as a result of the internal cohesion and the strength of the national tradition, Costa Rica feels less limited in its freedom of action by relations with other countries. It has worked out harmonious relations with the United Fruit Company, and the company has responded by investing considerable sums of money in production for the domestic economy—as in the development of the oil palm plantations. Costa Rica has felt little need to raise the specter of outside intervention in its dealings with the United States. In 1941, on December 7, Costa Rica was the first American country to declare war on Japan, followed on December 11 by a declaration of war against Germany and Italy. In a world in conflict, there is no doubt which side Costa Rica supports.

República de Panamá

Area: 29,208 square miles
Population: (1967 estimate) 1,329,000
                (last census, 1960) 1,075,541 (excluding Canal Zone)
Capital city: Panamá; (1967 estimate) 358,200
Percent urban: (1960) 41.5
Birth rate per 1,000: (1966) 39.1; Death rate per 1,000: (1966) 9–12
Annual percent of increase: (1958–64) 2.8
Percent literate: (1960) 73.3
Percent of labor force in agriculture: (1960) 45.2
Gross national product per capita: (1966) $513
Unit of currency: balboa (1968, 1.00 per dollar)
Leading crops in acreage: rice, maize

COMMERCE, 1965 *(expressed in percentage of values)*
Percent total Latin-American exports: 0.8 (1956, less than 1.0)
Percent total Latin-American imports: 2.3

Exports (1966)

bananas	51
refined oil	30
shrimp	10

Exports to (1966)		**Imports from (1966)**	
United States	68 (1956, 96)	United States	41 (1956, 60)
Venezuela	14	Venezuela	21
Canada	8		
Japan	7		

Chapter 9 □ Panamá

The historical background of Panamá is different from that of any other Central American state. Until 1903 it was an outlying part of Colombia; its present status as an independent political unit was achieved principally as a result of the strategic importance of its position on one of the world's major pass routes. Since Balboa first revealed the geographical nature of the isthmus in 1513, the story of man in Panamá has been concerned with passage rather than with settlement. At one time or another all the great maritime nations of the world have coveted this little strip of territory, and the forces which have shaped the larger communities on either side of the isthmus are international rather than local. Panamá, the present-day state, differs from all the other Latin-American states in that it possesses no central area of concentrated settlement focusing on an urban core. The nucleus of the state is the city of Panamá. But Panamá, the city, is not a product of Panamá, the country. It came into existence, and its importance has been maintained, because it controls a pass route. Meanwhile the three small clusters of people along the Pacific coast west of Panamá City are distinctly minor ones. The greater part of the territory of Panamá remains almost unoccupied.

By 1960 the population of Panamá had passed one million. In 1966 it was estimated that there were 1,286,700 people in Panamá, including those who were living in the Canal Zone. In the whole country about 41 percent of the people live in cities, of which the largest one is Panamá City (with a population in 1965 of 331,500). Colón is the second city (with about 50,000). The outlying centers are much smaller: David (23,000) and Puerto Armuelles (10,000).

As one might expect, the racial composition of the population is highly diverse, for people from all over the world have been drawn together at the canal. It is estimated that 67 percent of the people are mestizo or mulatto. About 15 percent are of African ancestry, mostly the English-speaking descendants of people who came from Jamaica and Barbados to work on the canal construction, but also including a small number of Spanish-speaking Africans along the Pacific coast to the east of the canal who have migrated into this empty area from Colombia since 1950. About 11 percent of the Panamanians are of European ancestry. Another 6 percent are Indian, almost all of whom live along the Caribbean coast east of the canal. Another 1 percent is made up of Chinese, Indians (from India), Syrians, Turks, Lebanese, and Armenians.

The Land

Panamá occupies a narrow, curving strip of land varying in width from about 30 miles to 120 miles (Map 27, p. 171). Its mountain structures run in general from northwest to southeast. In the northwest the southern end of the Cordillera de Talamanca, which forms the backbone of Costa Rica, extends into Panamá. Near the border this range is surmounted by several inactive volcanoes, the highest and most imposing of which is Mt. Chiriquí (11,410 ft.). The range continues southeastward to the shores of the Gulf of Panamá. The volcanic peaks that rise above this range are from 4,000 to over 5,000 feet in elevation, but the general summit elevation of the backbone of western Panamá is about 3,000 feet. The separate mountain block on the Peninsula de Azuero also reaches an elevation of about 3,000 feet.

Two ranges of low mountains extend into eastern Panamá from Colombia. One is the San Blas Range, which curves along the Caribbean coast; the other is an extension of the Serranía de Baudó of Colombia which borders the Pacific. In Panamá this range is interrupted by the Bahia San Miguel, where Balboa first saw the Pacific Ocean in 1513. Both of these ranges reach elevations of about 3,000 feet. Between them is a structural depression drained by rivers which flow into the Pacific, and which is invaded in its middle portion by the Bahia San Miguel.

There are only a few small bits of lowland plain in Panamá. The largest lowland is in the far southwest around Puerto Armuelles and David. A second one is around the western side of the Gulf of Panamá, south of the main range and north of the Peninsula de Azuero. Here Penonomé and Las Tablas are the chief towns. There are also small patches of lowland around the Laguna de Chiriquí in the northwest, and around the Bahia San Miguel in the southeast.

The Isthmus of Panamá is the narrow land connection between the mountain ranges of western Panamá and the two systems of low mountains in eastern Panamá. Here the strip of land is only 42 miles wide, and a passage from the Caribbean to the Pacific requires a climb of only 285 feet. The surface, however, is made up of steep-sided, knobby hills. Because this narrow bit of land curves toward the northeast, to make the crossing from the Caribbean to the Pacific one travels toward the southeast. At Panamá City the sun rises over the Pacific.

Along the whole length of the Isthmus of Panamá there is a great contrast between the two sides. The Caribbean coast is very rainy, receiving in many places more than 150 inches a year, concentrated in a season of excessively heavy rains between May and December. At Colón the average annual rainfall is 127.9 inches. Such heavy rainfall in a land where the temperatures average nearly 80° results in the very deep decomposition of the rock and in the growth of a luxuriant cover of tropical rain forest. At the crest of the backbone ranges, however, the amount of moisture diminishes, and on the Pacific side of the isthmus it is distinctly less, although at no place is it deficient. The annual rainfall averages between 60 and 120 inches. In western Panamá there is a distinct dry season from January through March: in eastern Panamá the dry season is shorter—only February and March. As a result of the dry season the Pacific side of Panamá has a seasonal forest, interrupted in places by a woodland savanna. The Spanish settlement went chiefly to these savannas, for not only was the Spaniard a lover of open country, but also few parts of the world were so unhealthful, because of disease-carrying insects, as the Caribbean lowlands south of Yucatán.

Along both sides of the isthmus there are many deep bays providing protected anchorages. Especially important is the shallow Gulf of Panamá which forms the separation between the ranges of western Panamá and the beginning of the Serranía de Baudó of Colombia. On the Caribbean side near the opening between the ranges there are several small harbors, especially along the coast northeast of Colón. It is interesting to note that the problem of effecting a landing differs considerably on the Caribbean and on the Pacific, for the tide on the Caribbean shore amounts to no more than 27 inches, whereas the tide on the Gulf of Panamá is 21 feet.

Passage across the Isthmus

Although the Spaniards cruised along the Caribbean coast of the isthmus as early as 1501, the strategic importance of this place did not become apparent until Balboa crossed it to the shores of the Pacific in 1513. In 1519 an expedition founded the first town of Panamá (now Panamá Vieja, located some five miles to the east of modern Panamá City). On the Caribbean coast several small ports in succession were used for the landing place. At first, Nombre de Dios was the chief Caribbean port; after 1584 Portobelo, which is a little to the west of Nombre de Dios, and which has a somewhat more commodious harbor became the chief Caribbean port. Much later, when the railroad and then the canal were built, these little places were all but abandoned in favor of Colón. On the Pacific side, however, the end of the pass remained more nearly fixed.

The importance of Panamá City to the Spaniards was very great. From this place the expeditions set out to the conquest of the Pacific side of Central America as far north as Nicaragua, and to the conquest of the whole west coast of South America as far as remote Chile. Although Lima became the primary settlement center of western South America, all of the lines of connection between Lima and the mother country passed through Panamá. Here were gathered the goods sent out from Spain and the treasure collected from the rich Americas to be sent back to Spain. Then, as now, Panamá City derived its importance from the convergence of oversea interests: in its vicinity no very large area of rural settlement became established, for people came to Panamá on the way to some other destination—few of them came to stay.

With the collapse of the Spanish Empire in the New World, Panamá for a time lost some of its importance. But it was not many decades before the interests of a new maritime power began to touch the isthmus. When, as a result of the War with Mexico, the United States extended its borders to the Pacific in 1848, and almost at once the world heard of the discovery of the gold fields of California, there ensued a wild rush to this new source of riches. By all sorts of routes the people not only from the eastern United States but also from Europe made the long trip to California. All the pass routes across Middle America were tried: Veracruz to Acapulco, the Isthmus of Tehuantepec, the rift valley of Honduras, the lowland of Nicaragua, and Panamá. After 1850 more and more people arrived at the ports on the Caribbean side and made the difficult trip across to Panamá City by stagecoach or on horseback. On January 28, 1855, the first train ran from Cristobal near Colón to Ancon, near Panamá City.

But the United States was not the only maritime power which looked covetously at Panamá. The idea of providing a passage for ocean ships across the isthmus had such obvious justification in terms of time saved on many different routes leading to Europe and eastern North America that several nations gave serious consideration to canal projects. Many of the British activities in the Caribbean during the nineteenth century were motivated by the idea of controlling the strategic approaches to a canal. The French, successful in the completion of the first of the world's great canals, the Suez, were the first actually to undertake the work in Panamá. In 1878 Ferdinand de Lesseps began operations for the construction of a sea-level canal, and continued until the collapse of his company in 1889. The French had failed to consider the serious effect of the diseases carried by the tropical insects on the health and energy of the workers.

The Spanish-American War, perhaps more than anything else, made it clear to the United States that as a matter of defense alone, the construction of a canal was vital. An agreement was reached with Great Britain by which that country gave up all rights to the Panamá route in exchange for a guarantee of equal treatment in the matter of tolls for British and United States shipping. Negotiations for the right to a canal zone were being carried on with the Colombian government, when the people of Panamá, believing that the

Widening the Gaillard Cut, which runs through the backbone of the Isthmus, in November 1953. *Courtesy of the Panama Canal Co.*

negotiations had fallen through and fearing that the Nicaraguan route would be selected instead, revolted and declared their independence from Colombia The part played by the United States in encouraging the revolt is not clear; but it is certain that the United States armed forces prevented the Colombians from sending troops to put down the rebellion, and that the United States, with conspicuous haste, recognized and came to terms with the government of Panamá. The United States was granted "in perpetuity" the use, occupation, and control of a zone five miles on either side of the canal—excluding, however, the two cities at either end: Panamá City and Colón. Within the so-called Canal Zone the United States was granted "as complete authority as if it were under the sovereignty of the United States."

Work on the canal started in 1904. A widespread attack on the problem of sanitation preceded and accompanied the actual digging. The conspicuous success of this attack has had a very great influence on the methods of combating tropical disease throughout the world. Workers on the canal were recruited not only in the United States and in Europe, but also among the crowded populations of Jamaica and Barbados. A huge dam was constructed at Gatún, near Colón, impounding the water of the Río Chagres in a large lake. Access to the lake, which is 85 feet above the Caribbean, is gained through locks. The Gaillard Cut carries the impounded water of the lake across to the Pacific side, where two sets of locks permit descent to the Pacific. On August 3, 1914, the first ship passed through the completed canal.

New Canal Routes

By 1966 the canal was no longer adequate, and the existence of the Canal Zone had been challenged by the people of Panamá. The canal was not adequate because its locks—110 feet wide—could no longer accommodate the larger ships that were built. There were many cargo and passenger ships that could not use the canal, and also many of the newer aircraft carriers of the navy. Each year some 12,000 ships pass through the canal, and there are times when ships are lined up at either end waiting to start the eight-hour passage. It was estimated that by 1975 there would be well over 15,000 ships per year demanding passage. Obviously the original canal could not accommodate the expected traffic. In 1966 the United States indicated its intention to build a new sea-level canal, and a commission was appointed to study alternative routes and to make a recommendation to the Congress by June 1969. At the same time negotiations were started to formulate a new treaty with Panamá in which nothing would be granted in perpetuity, and in which the fact that the Canal Zone is a part of Panamá and not a part of the United States is recognized. The political aspects of this problem will be discussed later (pp. 218–219).

TABLE A/PERCENT OF TOTAL TONNAGE ON DIFFERENT TRADE ROUTES*

1962

East coast of Anglo-America/Asia	29.8
East coast of Anglo-America/West coast South America	13.4
Europe/West coast South America	9.0
Europe/West coast Anglo-America	8.7
Antilles and East coast South America/West coast Anglo-America	7.2
United States Intercoastal routes	8.7
Europe/Australia-New Zealand	3.2
Other trade routes	20.0

*(from David J. Fox "Prospects for the Panama Canal," *Tijdschrift voor Economische Geografie*, Vol. 55 (1964): 86–101.)

TABLE B/FORECAST OF SHIPPING DEMANDS IN 1975*

Type of Vessel	Average capacity (tons)	number of vessels
General cargo	6,500	12,716
Tankers	21,000	1,762
Ore boats	32,000	547
Colliers	30,000	334
Passenger liners	—	250

*(from David J. Fox, *op. cit.*)

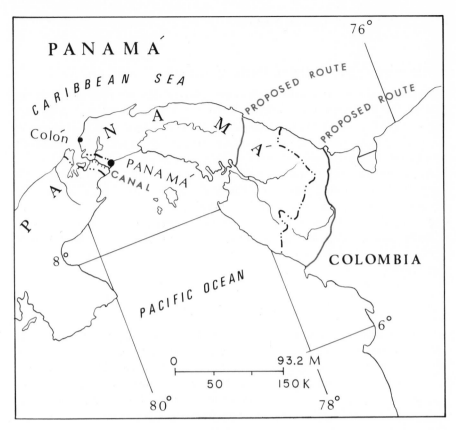

Map 32

When the study of alternative routes was started in 1966 there were three chief routes being considered. The idea of building a canal through Nicaragua had been dropped because to reach the level of Lake Nicaragua would require the use of locks. One possible solution of the problem would be to rebuild the present canal, widening it to 600 feet and providing a sea-level passage at least 60 feet deep. Because of the tidal differences on the two sides there would have to be tide regulating devices. A second solution would be to build the sea-level canal from the Bahia San Miguel, through a cut in the San Blas Range to the Caribbean (Map 32). A third solution was to cut through the Serranía de Baudó in Colombia and follow the Atrato River to the Caribbean. Because the latter two routes pass through very thinly populated country it would be possible to make use of nuclear explosives in the work of excavation, thus greatly reducing costs. It was clear that the final choice would have to be based, in part at least, on political factors.

Settlement in the Outlying Parts of Panamá

Panamá has no core area of concentrated settlement around an urban nucleus. In this respect it resembles no other Latin-American country. Its largest city, Panamá City, exists to serve the needs generated by the canal. Along the Pacific lowlands west of the canal there are three small clusters of people, but Panamá's most important city is not in any of them. One cluster is around Penonomé; another is around Las Tablas; and the third cluster is in the southwest around David and Puerto Armuelles (Map 31, p. 175). The mountainous backbone in western Panamá and the Caribbean coast are very thinly populated, except in back of Almirante. Eastern Panamá is also very thinly occupied, except for the villages of San Blas Indians on the coral islands of the Caribbean coast and for scattered forest clearings around the Bahia San Miguel.

Land Tenure and Land Use

An unusual situation exists in Panamá with respect to land tenure and land use. In the first place there are only a few areas where large private estates are to be found. Three-quarters of all the farms are less than 25 acres in size. Second, the great majority of all farmers are squatters on public land. In some cases, to be sure, families have made use of the same farms for many decades, and in their local communities their possession of the land is given some sort of recognition. But they have never gone through the formality of securing title from the government. The greater number of the farmers occupy a piece of land only temporarily and never think of claiming it as property. About 67 percent of all farmers are squatters, only 14 percent are owners, 10 percent are tenants on privately-owned land, and the remaining 9 percent have formed a variety of attachments to the estates of the private owners.

Most of Panamá is poor for farming. A tropical rainy land with many steep slopes cannot be expected to provide good agricultural prospects except where porous volcanic materials have been laid down or where large river floodplains provide fresh silt each year. In Panamá the soils, especially in the wetter areas, are deeply leached of their soluble minerals, and when the dense forest cover is removed, soil erosion goes on rapidly. Unfortunately, well-meaning people not acquainted with the problems of farming in the rainy tropics observe the thinly populated areas covered with luxuriant forest growth and assume that the movement of farmers into these areas should be promoted. The migration into the wet tropical lowlands, which is highly successful in certain areas of volcanic soil or alluvial soil, can be disastrous in other areas. In many cases the farmer who clears a patch of forest and plants his crops finds that in a year or two the clearing must be abandoned because of declining yields, and the process must be repeated in a new place. This is a wasteful form of land use, described as *shifting cultivation.*

The farmers in the area of shifting cultivation contribute little to the national economy. The chief crops are rice and maize, and, to a much smaller extent, beans. Rice is more important than maize in Panamá. It is grown on 75 percent of the farms, whereas maize is grown on only 65 percent. Along with rice and maize the shifting cultivators also grow bananas and manioc. But all these crops are consumed by the farmers themselves.

There are eight small areas where crops are raised for sale. The most important of these are the banana plantations of the Chiriquí Land Company, a subsidiary of the United Fruit Company. The first banana plantations were laid out in 1880, when banana planting spread along the Caribbean lowlands from Costa Rica. The chief port in Panamá was Almirante on the Laguna de Chiriquí. But the spread of Panama disease wiped out these plantations, and the company shifted its operations to the Pacific coast, inland from Puerto Armuelles. In the 1950's the plantations of this area produced some 60 percent of the exports of Panamá. Since 1960, however, the banana planters have learned how to control Panama disease by flood fallow—that is, by keeping the land under water for several months between banana plantings. The plantations inland from Almirante on the Caribbean coast have started to produce again. The company also purchases bananas from small independent farmers all along the coast, and even from the Indians east of the Canal Zone. Africans from western Colombia have spread as far as the shores of Bahia San Miguel, where they produce bananas for sale, in addition to maize, manioc, and plantains for their own subsistence.

In the three areas of clustered population around David, Penonomé, and Las Tablas the foods needed by the people in the cities at either end of the canal are produced. There are two intensively cultivated, irrigated, rice-producing areas, one near David, the other near Penonomé. From these areas, where the most modern kinds of agricultural technology are in use, Panamá gets such high yields that since the 1950's the country has been able to supply all its own needs for this basic food. In these same areas, and also around Las Tablas, there are sugarcane plantations. Throughout the woodland savannas of the Pacific lowlands there are large areas devoted to the grazing of cattle. The introduction of high-grade breeding stock has made these pastures far more productive of animal products than are most of the grazing areas of Latin America.

The three other areas of commercial agriculture are used for the production of coffee. These are all on the steep slopes of the mountains in western Panamá. One coffee district is on the slopes of Mt. Chiriquí, north of David, where highly productive volcanic soils can be used. Another coffee district is on the Pacific slopes of the central range of mountains north of Penonomé. The third district is on the higher slopes of the mountains of the Peninsula de Azuero, inland from Las Tablas. These coffee plantations have all been developed since World War II: only in 1958 was Panamá added to the list of countries exporting coffee.

Panamá as a Political Unit

There is no country in Latin America that is like Panamá. Settlement since the arrival of the Spaniards has been focused on the passageway across the isthmus. The economic life has been closely tied to the service of needs related to the pass route. Transportation and trade form the basic support for the economy; and the close attachment to the United States resulting from the presence of the canal is a basic fact in the political problems of the country.

The Economic Situation

There are five distinct economic groups in Panamá. At the top in terms of wealth is the relatively small number of well-to-do politicians, the handful of large landowners, the higher officers of the national guard. The country is run by these people for their own benefit. If they want to stir up anti-United States demonstrations, it is not because they are against the United States, but perhaps because such demonstrations help in their negotiations for a larger share of the canal revenues. If they do not want such demonstrations to occur they have the power to stop them. The students who do most of the demonstrating may not even be conscious of the real issues involved, and the presence of communists is incidental.

Next in order of income are a few foreign businessmen, mostly small merchants and owners of hotels and recreation facilities. Efforts by the ruling group to take these remunerative properties away from their owners and assign them to Panamanians have not been successful, partly because few Panamanians have either the skill or the interest in the operation of small retail businesses or hotels. The confiscated properties that were taken from the foreigners in 1941 were sold back to them within the next ten years. The foreigners make a good living, but have little political power and take no sides in political issues.

The third economic group is an increasing middle class of white-collar city workers. They are employed in the government offices, the retail stores, the banks, and in the Canal Zone. They do not make a good living, but if both husband and wife have jobs they can support a family. The fourth economic group includes the workers in the cities and in the Canal Zone. Many of these have part-time employment in the cities of Panamá; some 12 to 15 percent are employed in operating the canal, or in canal construction and maintenance. When the Canal Zone has a lot of work to be done, these people are well paid, but most of the time they drift from job to job, working for very low wages that permit them a bare subsistence. Finally, the fifth economic group, 50 percent of all those who are gainfully employed, is made up of farmers, most of whom are shifting cultivators on public land. Obviously the national income is very unevenly spread among the people.

The gross national product per capita of $513 in 1966 was mostly derived from activities related to the canal. These activities accounted for 50 percent of the value of all goods and services, whereas the commercial agriculture accounted for only 25 percent. The income from activities related to the canal is paid in the form of wages and salaries. The wages and salaries paid for work in the Canal Zone to only 12 to 15 percent of the labor force is about equal to the pay received by the other 85 to 88 percent for work outside of the Canal Zone. Most of the remainder of the direct income from the Canal Zone was paid to retail businesses outside of the Zone by people either living in the Canal Zone or passing through it in ships. The annual payment from the United States to the government of Panamá for the lease of the Canal Zone (formerly $430,000 a year; in 1967, when the treaty was being renegotiated, nearly $2 million) is a small fraction of the total income of Panamá. A very large part of the income is the indirect result of the presence of the Canal. The three chief sources of government revenue—the lottery, the horse races, and the taxes on liquor—are collected very largely from foreigners. In 1964, as a part of the program of the Alliance for Progress, a tax on corporate profits and capital gains was levied, and a tax on personal incomes was adopted, but revenues from these sources were still only a minor part of the total government income.

The fact is that Panamá's economy is based on selling goods and services to those maintaining, defending, or passing through the canal.

The government of Panamá, however, has been stimulated by the Alliance for Progress to broaden the base of the country's economy. This was done, in part, by introducing new agricultural technology to increase the volume and the quality of commercial crops and animals. It was also done in part by greatly increasing the shrimp-fishing activity in the shallow, muddy waters of the Gulf of Panamá, where a valuable resource had long been neglected. Now a fleet of more than 200 shrimp boats returns the catch to Panamá City where freezing plants prepare the shrimp for export. In 1958 a small steel plant was built in Panamá City, making use of scrap metal. In 1962 an oil refinery was built on the Caribbean coast, about five miles east of Colón. Venezuelan crude oil is imported in tankers, and refined petroleum products now make up a new element of the exports.

In 1964 bananas still made up 51 percent of the value of all exports. But starting in that year petroleum products appeared on the list, making up 30 percent of the total. Shrimp made up 10 percent. The United States took 60 percent of the exports, and smaller amounts went to Venezuela, Japan, and Canada. The United States and Venezuela (exporting chiefly crude oil) sent over half of the value of all imports.

The Political Situation

In Panamá there never has been any important development, economic or political, that was purely indigenous. In 1739, when the Viceroyalty of New Grenada was established with its administrative center at Bogotá, Panamá was included in it. After the success of Bolívar's effort to secure independence from Spain, Panamá was included in the new state; but in 1841, when the new state was breaking apart, Panamá also declared its independence. Troops from Colombia, however, had little difficulty in recapturing this outlying province. Panamá again seceded in 1853, but rejoined Colombia again. During the period when the British, the French, and the government of the United States were all promoting the canal idea, Panamá was administered by officials appointed in Bogotá. The situation was ripe for graft and dishonesty. From 1898 to 1903 the area was in almost constant disorder and revolt. The declaration of independence in 1903 was different from previous movements only in the presence of armed forces of the United States and in the prompt recognition afforded the new state.

The government in Panamá is controlled by the first of the economic groups previously described. These are the very few large landowners, a few businessmen, the higher officers of the national guard, and the professional politicians. There are political parties which appeal to the middle-class city people and to the students at the university for support. No party could remain in power which did not adopt a strongly nationalistic policy, and which did not follow the wishes of the politically powerful minority. In spite of the strategic importance of the canal, the communists have played only a minor role in Panamanian politics.

It cannot be said that Panamá, since 1903, has developed any very considerable degree of national coherence. The state-idea which brings support to a government in power is often the idea of reducing dependence on the United States. The students, especially, called for the seizure of the canal at the time of the Suez crisis. The formulation of a more sophisticated state-idea has yet to be accomplished. Meanwhile the economic and political dependence on the United States becomes closer and more irritating.

A very large factor in the future of Panamá depends on what the canal or the proposed new canals mean to the United States. There are many who point out that since World War II, when the United States built a two-ocean navy, the canal lost much of its strategic importance. Experts point out, also, that if the United States became involved in a nuclear war, the canal would scarcely be important enough to be worth dropping a bomb on it. But it is also clear that the use of United States armed forces in such distant places as Southeast Asia make the supply route through the canal of vital importance. The table on p. 212 shows that about 30 percent of all the traffic through the canal in 1962 was between the eastern part of Anglo-America and Asia.

If the canal were not available it would be more expensive and time-consuming to ship goods across the continent by railroad or motor truck or to send ships all the way around the southern end of South America. Both warfare in Asia and the increasing flow of commerce between Japan and the eastern United States, give the canal a considerable strategic importance to the United States—quite beyond the former need to send navy ships back and forth from one ocean to another.

On the other hand, can forecasts of shipping demands be projected with certainty, even as far as 1975? One of the spectacular new developments in the technology of ocean transport in the late 1960's has been the design and construction in Japan of super-tankers. These oil tankers are so large that they can only reach the largest ports. Even the English Channel is too shallow for them when the tide is wrong. But they carry such a large amount of oil that it is now less costly to send such ships from the Persian Gulf to Europe around the southern end of Africa than to ship oil in smaller tankers through Suez. Certainly the possibility exists that these changes in technology may change the significance of Panamá as a pass route.

The Antilles and the Guianas

POLITICAL CLASSIFICATION OF THE ANTILLES AND THE GUIANAS

Independent states, former colonies of Spain
    Cuba, Isla de Pinos
    The Dominican Republic

Independent state, former colony of France
    Haiti, Île de la Tortue, Île de la Gonâve

Independent states, former colonies of Great Britain
    Jamaica
    Trinidad and Tobago
    Barbados
    Guyana

Self-governing Commonwealth, freely associated with the United States
    Puerto Rico, Vieques

West Indies Associated States, self-governing states associated with Great Britain
    St. Kitts, Nevis, Anguilla
    Antigua
    Dominica
    St. Lucia
    St. Vincent
    Grenada and the Grenadines

Unincorporated territory of the United States
    American Virgin Islands (St. Croix, St. John, St. Thomas)

British Crown Colonies
    The Bahamas
    Caicos Islands, Turks Islands, Cayman Islands
    British Virgin Islands (Tortola, Virgin Gorda, Anegada)
    Barbuda, Redonda, Sombrero
    Montserrat

French Overseas Departments
    Guadeloupe (Basse-Terre, Grande-Terre)
        Marie Galante, Désirade, Les Saintes, St. Barthélemy, St. Martin (in part)
    Martinique
    French Guiana

Integral Parts of the Kingdom of the Netherlands
    Netherlands Antilles
        Curaçao—Bonaire, Aruba
        St. Martin (in part)
        Saba
        St. Eustatius
    Surinam

Part of Venezuela
    Margarita
    La Tortuga and outlying small islands

Chapter 10 □ The Antilles and the Guianas: Introduction

The Antilles and the Guianas make up a distinct subregion of Latin America. The Antilles includes all the islands of the Caribbean that lie between the southeastern part of northern America and the northern part of South America.[1] The Guianas, on the South American continent, are included in this part of Latin America because of their close historical connection with the islands and because of their geographical remoteness from the other South American countries.

Among the Antilles today there are six independent states, one self-governing Commonwealth associated with the United States, and six self-governing states associated with Great Britain. There are also numerous possessions of the United States, Great Britain, France, and the Netherlands. The Guianas include one independent state, a part of the Kingdom of the Netherlands, and a French overseas department. The table on the opposite page gives the political status of each of the islands and each part of the Guianas.

Physical Nature of the Islands

The islands of the Antilles are diverse in their geologic structure and their present surface features. Superficially the whole island chain might seem to be formed by the crests of one partly submerged mountain arc. Actually, however, there are several mountain systems involved, and the islands are in various stages of the process of growth and denudation.

[1]The name Antilles is derived from *Antilia,* the mythical islands that appeared on maps of the Atlantic Ocean before Columbus. Some writers prefer to call them the West Indies, an official name used by the British Colonial Office; but the French and the Dutch use the name Antilles. Sometimes the Bahamas are considered to be separate from the Antilles. In this book the Antilles includes three groups of islands: the Greater Antilles; the Lesser Antilles; and the Bahamas.

One of the main mountain systems which produce the Antilles is that which extends from Anegada Passage in the east (east of the British Virgin Islands) to the ranges of Central America in the west—the so-called Central-American–Antillean system. The main axes of mountain growth have the form of a two-pronged fork. The handle of the fork is in the east, extending in one single line of uplift from the Virgin Islands through Puerto Rico, and through the eastern part of Hispaniola[2] to the Cordillera Central of the Dominican Republic. Here the whole system reaches its greatest elevation of almost 10,000 feet. In the western part of Hispaniola the two prongs of the fork emerge, one forming the southern peninsula of the Republic of Haiti, the other the northern peninsula. The southern range continues under the Caribbean, emerging to form the Blue Mountains of Jamaica and several banks and miniature islands between Jamaica and the northeast corner of Honduras. The east–west ranges of Honduras and the central part of Guatemala form the western extremity of this system. The northern range, leaving the northern peninsula of Haiti, appears again in the Sierra Maestra in southeastern Cuba. It also is submerged under the waters of the Caribbean, appearing above the surface only in a few small islands such as the Little Cayman and Grand Cayman. It reaches the shore of Central America north of the Gulf of Honduras and crosses westward through Chiapas and Oaxaca in Mexico to the shore of the Pacific, interrupted at several places by transverse depressions.

North of the Central-American–Antillean system there are several areas which, although separated by stretches of water, are related structurally. These are the limestone platforms including the Peninsula of Yucatán, the main part of Cuba, most of the Bahama Islands, and the Peninsula of Florida.

From either end of the Central-American–Antillean system mountain chains of volcanic origin extend southeastward to connect with the continent of South America. In the west this mountain connection forms the backbone of Costa Rica and Panamá, and the chain stands high enough to make the land continuous. In the east the mountain connection consists of a string of volcanic islands, with deep passages between them, known as the Lesser Antilles. On the crest of the submerged arc which extends from the Anegada Passage in the north to the northeastern corner of Venezuela in the south, a series of volcanic cones has been built by successive eruptions until they stand, in some cases, high above the sea. Some of the cones are still in process of active growth; some have become quiet and are being worn down by the processes of stream dissection on their sides and wave cutting around their bases; some are very old and have been worn down until only the stumps of the volcanoes remain. And since these cones stand on an unstable sea floor which has a

[2]The United States Geographic Board adopted the name Hispaniola to apply to the island occupied by Haiti and the Dominican Republic. There is some historical precedent for this, although the European writers are accustomed to refer to the whole island as Santo Domingo. There is no justification for the designation of the whole island as Haiti.

tendency to subside, many of the older islands are deeply embayed and some have disappeared entirely below the water.

The Antilles lie within that portion of the tropical seas in which coral reefs can form. Coral can exist only where the ocean water is free from silt and where its temperature does not drop below 68°. The corals attach themselves to the shores of islands where these conditions exist and form fringing reefs. According to the coral-reef theory set forth by Darwin and Davis, the reefs are built higher and higher as the island sinks, with the result that they remain within the zone reached by the salt spray of the ordinary waves; but the submergence of the island reduces the area of the land and leaves the coral growth as a barrier reef, some distance off shore. In some cases the original island may be entirely submerged, leaving the coral formation as a circular atoll, with a shallow lagoon in its center. On the other hand, in those cases where the islands have been raised rather than lowered, the reefs form a sort of collar of limestone, elevated above the sea, as has occurred on Jamaica. All stages of island growth and destruction and of the development of coral reefs can be observed in the Antilles.

In spite of the existence of all these varied island forms, however, it is possible to group the Lesser Antilles into two categories. There are the islands which are relatively low, and which include considerable areas of more or less level limestone reefs. These are found chiefly on the outer or eastern side of the island arc. In contrast to these low-lying islands are the mountainous ones, some still in the process of growth. The chief islands of the Lesser Antilles, classified in this way, are presented in the following list and on Map 41, p. 302:

LOW-LYING AND MOUNTAINOUS ISLANDS OF THE LESSER ANTILLES*

(Maximum elevation in feet)

Low-lying Islands	Mountainous Islands
Anguilla (213)	Saba (2,820)
St. Martin (1,360)	St. Eustatius (1,950)
St. Bartélemy (992)	St. Kitts (4,314)
Barbuda (115)	Nevis (3,596)
Antigua (1,330)	Redonda (1,000)
Grande-Terre (eastern part of Guadeloupe—very low)	Montserrat (3,002)
	Guadeloupe (4,869)
Désirade (912)	Îles des Saintes (1,036)
Marie Galante (672)	Dominica (4,747)
Barbados (1,100)	Martinique (4,428)
	St. Lucia (3,145)
	St. Vincent (4,048)
	The Grenadines (series of rocky islands, highest one about 1,000)
	Grenada (2,749)

*After C. Schuchert, *Historical Geology of the Antillean-Caribbean Region*, ... New York, 1935.

Several of the mountainous islands are volcanic, with volcanoes that are still more or less active. Two of these volcanoes have erupted with great violence during the present century. Mt. Soufrière on St. Vincent killed more than 2,000 persons when it erupted on May 7, 1902. The eruption of Mt. Pelée on Martinique the next day covered the surrounding parts of the island with a deep layer of ash and resulted in the destruction of the city of St. Pierre with the loss of 40,000 lives. Mt. Pelée's ash is of such a mineral composition that it provides little plant food, with the result that the area covered by ash remains even today barren wasteland. Mt. Pelée itself was 4,438 feet in elevation before the eruption: after the eruption it was 4,500 feet high. The mass of material blown out through its vent is estimated to equal in bulk the whole island of Martinique.

Of still different geologic origin are the continental islands related to South America. The most easterly of these is Barbados. This island, 21 miles long by 14 miles wide, is composed of a gently rolling limestone tableland, with a maximum elevation of 1,100 feet. It is formed by an upraised portion of the continental shelf, and now stands on a wide platform only slightly submerged and bounded in places by barrier reefs.

Closer to the South American coast the islands are even more directly related to the mainland structures. The little island of Tobago is formed along a mountainous backbone, the highest elevation of which is 1,900 feet. Trinidad has a range of mountains along its northern side which reaches 3,000 feet in elevation, but the southern part of the island is made up of two hilly belts with mangrove-filled bays along the coasts between the hills. There are no corals on Trinidad, for this whole coast is bathed with silt from the Orinoco. The islands of Margarita and Tortuga off the Venezuelan north coast are part of the Caribbean coastal range. The three Dutch islands of Bonaire, Curaçao, and Aruba are formed of ancient crystalline rocks, similar in geologic structure to the Guajira Peninsula of Colombia.

Climate

In places like the Antilles one finds the truly "temperate" climates of the world. These islands are bathed by currents of warm ocean water and swept by the easterly trades of the open sea. The temperatures are moderately high, and vary little from season to season. In Habana, Cuba, for example, the average temperature is 76.9° with a range between warmest and coldest months of about 10°; San Juan in Puerto Rico has a range of less than 6°; and Bridgetown in Barbados has a range of only about 4°. From Habana to Bridgetown the average of the warmest month is about the same—between 80° and 82° (except Port-au-Prince, Haiti, which is in a lowland pocket protected from the moderating influence of the open sea). The winters, however, average a little lower in Cuba than in the islands farther east because of the exposure of that island to the cold air masses which emerge from

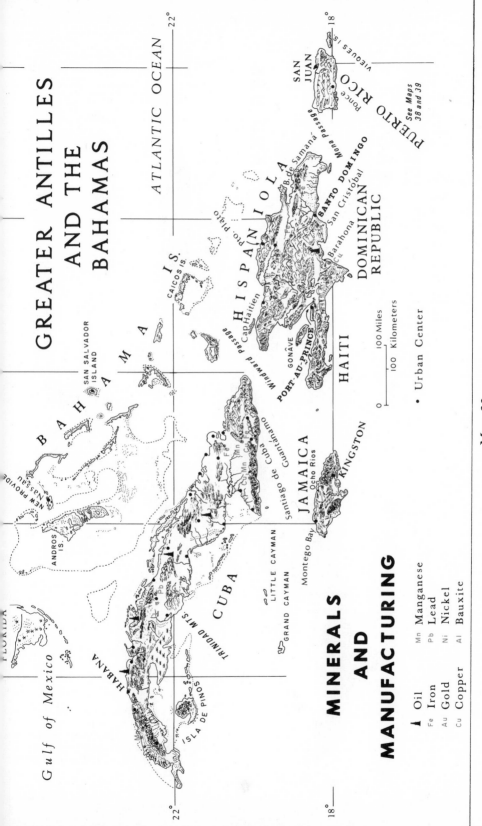

GREATER ANTILLES AND THE BAHAMAS

ATLANTIC OCEAN

22°

18°

Gulf of Mexico

FLORIDA

NEW PROVIDE

NASSAU

ANDROS IS.

B A H A M A S

SAN SALVADOR ISLAND

LITTLE CAYMAN

GRAND CAYMAN

TRINIDAD MTS.

HABANA

ISLA DE PINOS

C U B A

Montego Bay

Santiago de Cuba

Guantánamo

Ocho Rios

KINGSTON

JAMAICA

CAICOS IS.

Pto. Plata

B. de Samaná

Mona Passage

Windward Passage

Cap Haïtien

GONÂVE

PORT-AU-PRINCE

HAITI

H I S P A N I O L A

SANTO DOMINGO

San Cristóbal

Barahona

DOMINICAN REPUBLIC

SAN JUAN

Ponce

VIEQUES IS.

PUERTO RICO

See Maps 38 and 39

100 Miles

100 Kilometers

0

• Urban Center

MINERALS AND MANUFACTURING

↟ Oil   Mn Manganese
Fe Iron   Pb Lead
Au Gold   Ni Nickel
Cu Copper Al Bauxite

Map 33

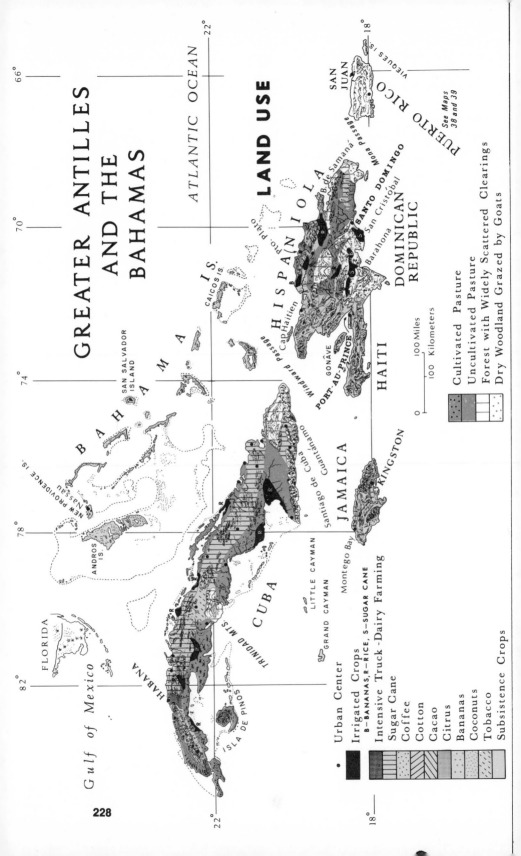

GREATER ANTILLES AND THE BAHAMAS

LAND USE

ATLANTIC OCEAN

Gulf of Mexico

FLORIDA

B A H A M A S

SAN SALVADOR ISLAND

NEW PROVIDENCE IS.
Nassau

ANDROS IS.

CAICOS IS.

HABANA

ISLA DE PINOS

C U B A

TRINIDAD MTS.

Santiago de Cuba
Guantánamo

LITTLE CAYMAN

GRAND CAYMAN

Montego Bay

JAMAICA

KINGSTON

Windward Passage

PORT-AU-PRINCE

GONÂVE

Cap Haïtien

HAITI

H I S P A N I O L A

B. de Samaná

SANTO DOMINGO

San Cristóbal

DOMINICAN REPUBLIC

Barahona

Mona Passage

PUERTO RICO

SAN JUAN

VIEQUES IS.

See Maps 38 and 39

228

Legend (left)

- ● Urban Center
- Irrigated Crops
- Intensive Truck-Dairy Farming   B=BANANAS, R=RICE, S=SUGAR CANE
- Sugar Cane
- Coffee
- Cotton
- Cacao
- Citrus
- Bananas
- Coconuts
- Tobacco
- Subsistence Crops

Legend (right)

- Cultivated Pasture
- Uncultivated Pasture
- Forest with Widely Scattered Clearings
- Dry Woodland Grazed by Goats

Scale:
0   100 Miles
0   100 Kilometers

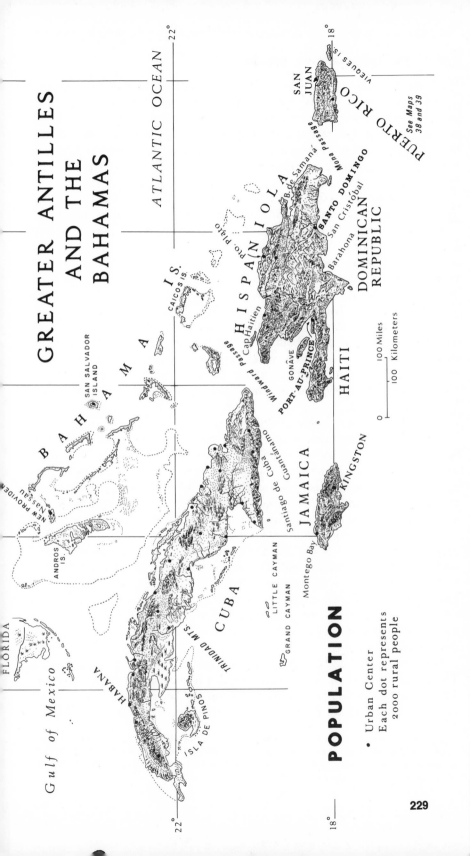

GREATER ANTILLES
AND THE
BAHAMAS

ATLANTIC OCEAN

22°

18°

SAN
JUAN

VIEQUES IS.

PUERTO RICO

See Maps
38 and 39

DOMINICAN
REPUBLIC

B. de Samana

Mona Passage

SANTO DOMINGO

San Cristóbal

Barahona

HISPANIOLA

Pto. Plata

CAICOS IS.

Cap Haitien

Windward Passage

GONÂVE

PORT-AU-PRINCE

HAITI

KINGSTON

JAMAICA

Santiago de Cuba

Guantánamo

SAN SALVADOR
ISLAND

B A H A M A

NEW PROVIDENCE

Nassau

ANDROS
IS.

LITTLE CAYMAN

GRAND CAYMAN

Montego Bay

CUBA

TRINIDAD MTS.

HABANA

ISLA DE PINOS

FLORIDA

Gulf of Mexico

0   100 Miles

0   100 Kilometers

POPULATION

• Urban Center

Each dot represents
2000 rural people

Map 35

229

North America during that season. In every month of the year the maximum temperatures are about the same; but the minimum temperatures of the winter are much lower than the minimum temperatures of summer, and this has the effect of lowering the monthly average. Excessively high temperatures, such as are experienced in the Middle West of the United States, never occur in the Antilles; but neither are the cold waves characteristic of midlatitude winters experienced.

The easterly trade winds which blow day and night throughout the year produce great differences in rainfall on the eastern and western sides of the mountainous islands. From the warm ocean water the air picks up large quantities of moisture, so that a very slight rise of the air and consequent cooling results in the formation of towering cumulus clouds and heavy downpours of rain, mostly of short duration. The rains are heaviest on the windward sides of the islands. In Jamaica, for example, the average annual rainfall at a station on the northeast side of the Blue Mountains is 222 inches; at Kingston on the south side of the island, some thirty miles distant, the average annual rainfall is only about 31 inches. The eastern sides of the islands, too, are exposed to the highest waves, so that especially for the sailing ships of the period of earliest settlement, the protected western sides offered the safest anchorages. Almost all the chief towns on the islands are now on the lee sides.[3]

Commonly throughout the Antilles there are two rainy seasons and two dry seasons. The first rainy season usually comes in May, though sometimes in June or July; the second rainy season comes in October or November. Trinidad, however, has only one rainy season; from June to December. The rain comes in the form of violent showers, followed by rapid clearing—showers which come at shorter and shorter intervals as the day progresses, followed by clear skies at night and in the early morning.

Few parts of the world offer a climate of greater comfort, especially in places exposed to the sweep of the trades, than do the Antilles. There are persons who feel the need of the stimulating effect of rapid weather change and of the low temperatures characteristic of the midlatitude winters, and who, therefore, find the Antillean climate too relaxing; but there are others who, in spite of the popular misconception regarding tropical climates, find themselves able to live in these islands with a maximum of comfort and without losing their capacity to work.

But the Antilles do not always remain undisturbed by climatic violence. This is one of the parts of the world in which tropical cyclones, or hurricanes, are frequent occurrences. The hurricane season begins in August and lasts through October. Of all the storms reported between 1887 and 1923, August

[3]In this connection it should be noted that the designation of the northern group of Lesser Antilles as "Leeward Islands" and the southern group as "Windward Islands" has no basis in terms of wind direction. The prevailing trades of this part of the world come from the northeast and the east.

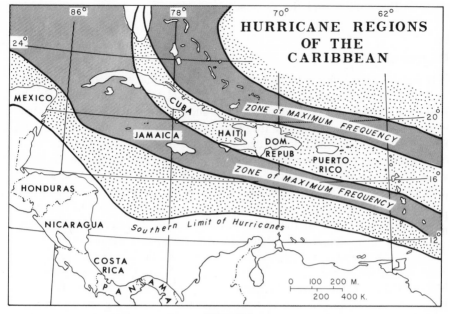

Map 36

had 16 percent, September had 33 percent, and October, 30 percent. These storms originate off the coast of Africa and sweep westward toward the Lesser Antilles, bending toward the north as they proceed. The island of Trinidad never experiences these violent storms, and the southern members of the Lesser Antilles rarely, but the northern Antilles are frequently traversed by them. The hurricanes follow two chief tracks (Map 36). One crosses the Caribbean to the Yucatán Channel, and thence proceeds across the Gulf of Mexico, where the storms either ravage the Gulf Coast of the United States, rapidly losing violence as they proceed into the interior, or curve toward the east again across Florida. The other track follows the Lesser Antilles, passing east of Puerto Rico, across the Bahamas to the east coast of the United States, after which it curves again toward the east, following the Gulf Stream. Of course there are many storms which fail to proceed along the usual tracks, and which do unexpected damage to the eastern part of the United States—all the way from southwestern Texas to New England.

A hurricane is a great whirl of air—like a dust whirl that forms over a country road on a hot summer day, only on a vastly larger scale. In the northern hemisphere it rotates always in a counterclockwise direction. Hurricanes cover hundreds of miles of territory, and even those places which do not experience the destructive violence of the storm's center are visited by high winds. Hurricanes also bring extremely heavy downpours of rain—in fact the world's heaviest rainfalls in short periods are brought by these storms. During one typhoon—which, in the western Pacific, is the equivalent of the Antillean hurricane—Baguio in the Philippines received a rainfall of 48 inches in 24 hours, the world's record.

Course of Settlement

It was to the Antilles that the Spaniards came on that momentous first voyage of Columbus in 1492. The first landing was made on an island in the Bahamas.[4] To the everlasting confusion of succeeding generations, Columbus, believing that he had reached the eastern coast of Asia, made use of the name "West Indies," and designated the native inhabitants as Indians.

Columbus and the other Spaniards who came to the Antilles in the early years of the conquest were primarily interested in finding gold. At first none of the newcomers was skilled in the geology of gold. Columbus thought that gold was the result of tropical heat, and that he would be likely to find more of it if he went closer to the equator. The Indians had never placed much value on gold, although they used gold ornaments, and when the Spaniards pressed them to reveal the places where gold could be found they could only point to places where nuggets had been picked up. There was some gold mixed in the stream gravels in the central part of Hispaniola, and nuggets were actually found—enough to lend support to stories of great wealth that spread in Spain. The result was a "gold rush." By 1513 there were fifteen towns on Hispaniola, and already the problem of providing an adequate supply of food was worrying the authorities.

The Spaniards established several settlements in the Antilles during the first two decades of the conquest. In 1496 Bartholomew Columbus, brother of the Admiral, founded Santo Domingo on the southern shore of Hispaniola. In 1502, after a disastrous hurricane had leveled the first town, Santo Domingo was reestablished on its present site, which makes it the oldest permanently occupied town in the Americas. Santo Domingo became one of the earliest of the Spanish primary settlement centers, and colonies were sent out from it to various places around the Caribbean. In 1509 a town was founded on Puerto Rico; later, because of unhealthful conditions at the first site, the colony was transferred to the present San Juan (1511). Also in 1509, a colony was established on Jamaica. The occupation of scantily inhabited Cuba began in 1511, and Santiago was its first town. Habana was founded in 1515, and thereafter this port was the usual point of departure for the voyage back to Spain. From Habana Cortés started out on his voyage of conquest to Mexico.

The Indians of the northern Antilles were, therefore, the first to feel the destructive effects of the Spanish conquest. At first friendly, they soon turned

[4]Some scholars identify the land that Columbus first reached as the island of San Salvador, and on this island there is a monument to commemorate the event. Later investigations, however, throw doubt on this identification, and suggest that his first landfall was on Caicos Island. Compare Samuel Eliot Morison, *Admiral of the Ocean Sea . . . .*, Boston, 1942, p. 227; and Robert H. Fuson, "Caicos: Site of Columbus' Landfall," *The Professional Geographer*, Vol. 13 (1961), pp. 6–9.

hostile, for in spite of the efforts of the king and queen of Spain, the natives were forced to hard and unaccustomed labor in the mines. New European diseases introduced among the Indians had a devastating effect: in 1542 Las Casas reported that the Indians in Hispaniola, Puerto Rico, Jamaica, and Cuba were almost all gone. When the Spaniards arrived in Hispaniola they had found over a million native inhabitants on that island; at that time only Cuba was thinly populated. But fifty years later there were only small remnants of the original Carib and Arawak peoples, and these were in isolated spots in the mountains.

Sugarcane

Since the Spaniards of the early days had no understanding of the origin of gold, they devoted their efforts to searching for nuggets, or to forcing the Indians to bring in their gold ornaments. Soon the sources of gold were used up, and some other basis for the economy had to be found. Early in the sixteenth century Spanish leaders attempted to import slaves from Africa and start the production of sugar, as they had been doing for many years in the Canary Islands. But the large development of the Antilles as a source of sugar did not come until a century later. By that time the main stream of Spanish settlement and the chief focus of Spanish interest had shifted to Mexico and Peru, and the older Antillean settlements were neglected.

The Portuguese in Brazil were the first to build a large-scale sugarcane plantation economy with African slaves. Before the sixteenth century sugar had long been known in Europe as an expensive luxury, sometimes even prescribed in small quantities as a medicine. But when the merchants in Amsterdam began to supply sugar to Europe from Brazil at very much lower prices than had been possible before, the sale of sugar was rapidly expanded. The Portuguese enjoyed their first period of speculative production: for nearly a century they had a virtual monopoly of the rapidly growing market. Then in 1624 the Dutch invaded and occupied parts of northeastern Brazil. Between 1624 and 1654 they held the whole coast from the Rio São Francisco to the mouth of the Amazon. During this time they learned the techniques of planting cane, extracting the juice, and preparing the raw sugar for shipment. When they were driven out, the Dutch promptly occupied parts of the Guiana coast and islands in the Lesser Antilles that had been neglected by the Portuguese and the Spaniards. From the Dutch the sugar technology was passed on to the French and the British, and along with it the importation of African slaves. Little by little during the latter part of the seventeenth century, the center of sugar production shifted from the northeast of Brazil to the Antilles.

Most of the islands changed hands several times. The chief exception was Barbados, which has been British since the first Europeans landed there in 1605. In 1640 the British colony on Barbados had in it only about 100 African slaves; but five years later there were more than 6,000 Africans on the island, and it had become one of the first places to be devoted wholly to sugarcane plantations. In 1685 the Africans numbered 46,000 and the Europeans only 20,000. In 1655 the British launched an attack on the Spanish colony of Santo Domingo, which was repulsed. In order to save the expedition from complete disgrace, the British forces made a landing on the Spanish island of Jamaica and were successful in pushing the small Spanish garrison out of most parts of the island. The Spaniards took refuge in the Blue Mountains and continued to raid the British settlements until 1660. Spain acknowledged the British ownership of Jamaica in 1670. During the century that followed, French Saint Domingue, in the western part of Hispaniola, and British Jamaica became the leading sugar producers. Trinidad remained the least developed. In 1783, just before the British seized the island from Spain, the population included 126 Europeans, 295 free Africans, and 310 slaves. When Britain seized Trinidad in 1797 the island was still largely covered with virgin rain forest.

THE END OF SLAVERY

The sugar economy of the seventeenth and eighteenth centuries was based on the institution of slavery. This meant that sugarcane planting was a rich man's business, for the establishment of a plantation, the construction of sugar mills, the purchase of slaves, all required a large capital investment. The profits for the plantation owners were in most places enormous. But life on a sugarcane island was anything but pleasant. The slaves were restless and resentful; slave labor was unwilling, wasteful, and inefficient. Not only were the slaves expensive to buy, but they also had to be fed, clothed, and housed. Many of the smaller islands became totally dependent on imported foods, such as salt cod from New England. Only in Saint Domingue and in Jamaica were the slaves permitted to use land to grow their own foods. In fact it was only on these islands that there was an abundance of hilly or mountainous land close by the cane plantations. On an island such as Barbados or Antigua, where the whole surface was suitable for cane, there was no room to waste on food crops.

But the eighteenth century was a period of history during which explosive ideas of equality before the law were being formulated. Many of the mulattoes of Saint Domingue, who were the children of French planters and African women, were sent to France for an education. In both Hispaniola and in Jamaica educated mulattoes, rejected by both pure African and pure European groups, developed an undercurrent of revolt. It was a question whether the French colony or the British colony would be most likely to suffer a slave uprising. And in the home countries there were strong anti-slavery movements. In one way or another the institution of slavery was doomed. It was in 1808 that the British parliament passed the Abolition Act which declared the slave trade to be illegal. Other countries passed similar legislation:

the United States also in 1808, the Netherlands in 1814, France in 1818, and Spain in 1820. Yet illegal trade in slaves continued. In fact it is probable that more slaves were taken out of West Africa for shipment to the Americas after 1808 than in all the years before that date.[5]

The actual end of slavery began in the British colonies after the Emancipation Act of 1833. Slaves were given their freedom in Antigua in 1834, and in the rest of the British possessions in 1836. The other parts of America followed this lead over a period of fifty years: French possessions in 1848; Dutch possessions and the United States in 1863; Puerto Rico in 1873; Danish possessions in 1876; Cuba in 1880; and Brazil in 1888.

The story in each of the islands of the Antilles was somewhat different as the plantation owners attempted to readjust the basis of the economy. If there was any one thing that the newly freed slaves wanted to avoid it was working on the sugarcane plantations, a kind of employment so clearly associated with slavery. But on the different islands the opportunities to avoid such work differed. In the former Saint Domingue, where the slaves were successful in staging a revolt against the French masters and establishing the independence of Haiti in 1804, the former slaves fled to the mountainous interior and the sugar business collapsed. In Jamaica, where there was plenty of unoccupied land suitable for peasant subsistence farming, the sugarcane plantations were also ruined. In 1842 there were nineteen plantations growing sugarcane; but by 1864 all but one plantation had gone out of business. The Africans had left the cane fields and established themselves as squatters in the interior of the island. Already experienced in raising their own foods, and with plenty of land to occupy, the Africans changed as rapidly as possible into a self-sufficient peasantry. In Barbados, however, things were entirely different. There was no place to go, no land not used for planting cane, no empty mountains in which to hide. In Barbados during the decades after the emancipation, the production of sugar actually increased, as wage workers proved to be more efficient than slaves. In Trinidad, on the other hand, although there was plenty of unoccupied land, the governor levied a tax on any person settling on crown lands. This had the effect of keeping the freed slaves at work on the cane plantations. But since there was a chronic shortage of workers on this island, the government supported the immigration of contract laborers from India. These East Indians agreed to work on the sugarcane plantations for five years, after which they could, if they wished, return to India. Many came to Trinidad between 1845 and 1916, and most of them elected to remain as free laborers.

During the nineteenth century the sugarcane planters also faced the increasing competition of sugar produced from sugar beets in middle latitude regions. Beet sugar production made its start during the time of Napoleon, when Europe was largely shut off from outside supplies. After the defeat of

[5] J. H. Parry and P. M. Sherlock, *A Short History of the West Indies,* London, 1956.

Napoleon the beet sugar growers were able to hold a part of the sugar market, aided at critical moments by tariffs and subsidies. Beet sugar was given this support for two reasons: it gave nations threatened with blockade independence from overseas sources of supply; and it increased other crop yields from lands previously used to grow beets. The table shows the gradual rise of beet sugar in relation to cane sugar during the nineteenth and twentieth centuries.

PROPORTION OF WORLD SUGAR PRODUCTION FROM CANE AND FROM BEETS*/1850–1967

Year	Proportion from cane sugar	Proportion from beet sugar
1850	86	14
1860	74	26
1870	67	33
1880	53	47
1890	41	59
1900	38	62
1910	42	58
1911–15	54	46
1916–20	74	26
1921–25	71	29
1926–30	68	32
1931–35	66	34
1936–40	65	35
1941–45	69	31
1947	74	26
1950	65	35
1957–58	60	40
1959–60	59	41
1964–65	55.5	44.5
1966–67	57	43

*Statistics through 1958: United Nations, Food and Agricultural Organization; 1959–67: Encyclopedia Americana Yearbooks for 1960, 1965, 1967.

About 1900 the technology of producing sugar from sugarcane was changed by the development of more efficient machinery for extracting the juice. The new sugar mills could produce much more sugar from the cane, but to derive the maximum of profit it was necessary to operate on a large scale. This was the beginning of the rise of Cuba to world leadership in the production of cane sugar, chiefly with the aid of capital investment from the United States. Since 1900 the proportion of the world's sugar produced from sugarcane has again risen in relation to beet sugar. For large-scale operations the island of Cuba, long a neglected Spanish colony, offered unusual advantages. After the Spanish-American War (1898), which gave Cuba its political independence, this part of the Antilles forged rapidly ahead in sugar production, leaving the Lesser Antilles far behind.

The total production of sugar in the world, during all this time, has been steadily increasing. In 1850 it was only 1,507,000 tons. During the decade 1900 to 1910 it averaged 12,600,000 tons per year. But by the crop year 1964–65 sugar production had reached the all-time high of 70 million tons. The United States established quotas to give a share of both cane and beet sugar in the American market. But after 1959, when Cuba entered the Soviet sphere, the quotas for the American markets were reassigned. Still the world total of production continued to climb. The following five chapters will show how the various islands of the Antilles shared or failed to share in this continuously expanding market.

República de Cuba

Area: 44,218 square miles
Population: (1967 estimate) 7,800,000
             (last census, 1953) 5,829,029
Capital city: Habana; (1964) 1,517,700
Percent urban: (1953) 57.0
Birth rate per 1,000: (1966) 32–37; Death rate per 1,000: (1966) 7–10
Annual percent of increase: (1958–64) 2.1
Percent literate: (1953) 77.9
Percent of labor force in agriculture: (1953) 40.9
Gross national product per capita: (1954) $556
Unit of currency: peso
Leading crops in acreage: (1950) sugarcane, maize

COMMERCE, 1964 *(expressed in percentage of values)*
Percent total Latin-American exports, 1956: 10.0

Exports (1965)
sugar   88   (1956, 74)

Exports to (1965)			Imports from (1965)		
U.S.S.R.	47	(1956, U.S. 64)	U.S.S.R.	49	(1956, U.S. 75)
China	15		China	14	
Czechoslovakia	7		United Kingdom	6	
Spain	5		Spain	5	

Chapter 11 □ Cuba

Cuba is the Latin-American country that occupies the position of closest geographic proximity to the United States. Before 1959, the cultural radiation from the Anglo-American source region fell in massive doses on little Cuba. There were many who think that the Cubans should have been grateful for the benefits of close attachment to the United States, and for the prosperity that resulted from free access to the world's greatest market for sugar. But the fact is that many Cubans followed their great nineteenth-century patriot, José Martí, in demanding freedom from outside interference from whatever source. It was Martí who exclaimed: *"Nuestro vino es agrio, pero es nuestro vino."*[1] Because of Cuba's position, the one great source of foreign interference and domination in Cuban affairs has been the United States.

The significance of this geographic position has varied with the changing attitudes, objectives, and stage of economic development of the people on the mainland. For a long time Cuba was quite neglected, the main course of Spanish conquest being directed elsewhere. Except for a few North Americans who coveted the tropical island to the south for its strategic importance, or as a potential addition to the list of slave states, Cuba remained of little interest to a people who were facing westward rather than southward. A Cuban insurrection against Spanish rule in the 1870's aroused little desire in the United States for the rescue and liberation of an oppressed people. But twenty years later, another insurrection was met with a wave of sentiment in the United States demanding military intervention for the purpose of bringing freedom to the Cubans. Without joining the ranks of those extremists who

---

[1]"Our wine is bitter, but it is our wine." Martí has many followers, including Fidel Castro, who insist on the right to make their own mistakes, even if the results are bitter.

brand all business enterprise in foreign countries as imperialistic, we must nevertheless point out that by 1896 investments by people of the United States in Cuba had mounted to between 30 and 50 million dollars. The United States was facing southward across the Caribbean as well as westward across the Pacific. Only an aroused public opinion, opposed to imperialistic expansion into territory already populated, kept the United States from extending its political area over Cuba as it did over Puerto Rico and the Philippines. Every kind of control except sovereignty, however, was applied to the newly created republic; and under the protection of the government the development of new sugarcane plantations went forward at a rapid rate.

As a result of the large capital investment in Cuban sugar production and the services of technicians, Cuba could produce sugar at lower cost than most competing parts of the world. The large preindustrial estate, with inefficient machinery and unskilled supervision, was replaced by a large-scale operation carefully managed by experts. By 1946 more than a third of all the agricultural land in Cuba was owned by about 900 large corporations, some with more than 600,000 acres. United States corporations owned 40 percent of the sugarcane lands. Of the ten largest operations, the United States owned seven, and well-to-do Cubans owned three. United States corporations also owned 90 percent of the public utilities and mines, and 50 percent of the railroads.

Yet all was not well in Cuba. Although some people in Cuba were wealthy, either as a direct or as an indirect result of sugar production, there were many who were very poor. Workers were paid good wages during the harvest season from December to June, but during the rest of the year most workers were unemployed. In Habana there were luxury hotels and beautiful homes, but there were also crude shelters made of any available material, in which there were families living in poverty and ill-health, with no incomes even for the purchase of food. In the rural areas less than 10 percent of the homes were equipped with electricity or running water; the tourists found this picturesque. Order was maintained by a dictator, backed by a well-trained army equipped with weapons from the United States. Rumblings of revolt were heard from Cubans who had been forced into exile and from students in the universities.

The changes that resulted from the revolution led by Fidel Castro which gained control of Cuba in 1959 will be discussed later. But first it is necessary to consider what Cuba was like when Castro came to power. Cuba has a population of nearly 8 million, which is increasing at the rate of 2.1 percent per year. The population density of Cuba is not nearly so great as that of some of her Antillean neighbors, but before 1959 the capital city, Habana, had passed the million mark, and in 1962 the metropolitan area had a population of one and a half million. Some 73 percent of the Cubans are of unmixed European ancestry, while 12 percent are African and 14 percent are mestizo. The other 1 percent includes Chinese, Filipinos, and other Asians.

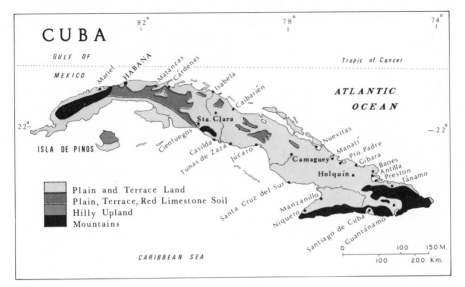

The map contains the following labels:

CUBA

GULF OF MEXICO

Tropic of Cancer

82° 78° 74°

HABANA Mariel Matanzas Cárdenas Isabela Caibarién

ATLANTIC OCEAN

Sta. Clara

22° Cienfuegos Nuevitas −22°

ISLA DE PINOS Casilda Júcaro Manatí Pto. Padre

Tunas de Zaza Camaguey Gibara

Holquín Banes Antilla Preston Tánamo

Plain and Terrace Land
Plain, Terrace, Red Limestone Soil
Hilly Upland
Mountains

Santa Cruz del Sur Manzanillo

Niquero Santiago de Cuba Guantánamo

CARIBBEAN SEA

0 100 150 M.
100 200 Km.

Map 37

The Land

More than half of the land area of the Antilles is in Cuba. The 44,000 square miles of territory extend for 785 miles in an east–west direction with a width which varies from 25 to 120 miles. At least half of the area is level enough to be suitable for machine agriculture. The soils of Cuba prove to be well adapted to a variety of crops, of which sugarcane is only one. The "temperate" tropical climate, with no frosts, only infrequent hurricanes, and with adequate and well-distributed rains, is ideal for tropical plantation agriculture. The fact that much of the island is well drained and is swept by unobstructed easterly winds reduces the problem of sanitation and the difficulties of an attack on insect-carried diseases. For the Spaniards of the colonial period these advantages were outweighed by the disadvantages of a scanty native population; for North Americans in the twentieth century, with money to risk on speculation in tropical plantations, the Cuban land had a great appeal.

Surface Features

Not more than about a quarter of the area of Cuba is mountainous. The most rugged country is to be found at the southeastern end (Maps 33 and 37). West of Guantánamo Bay, and north of the port of Santiago de Cuba, the steep slopes of the Sierra Maestra overlook the sea, rising to elevations of nearly 8,000 feet. The northern side and eastern end of the Sierra Maestra are bordered by the Guantánamo Valley (Valle Central), a gently rolling hilly country which leads out to the head of the bay. East of Guantánamo Bay stands a rough, stony highland, deeply dissected by streams, and including few patches of flat land. In these highlands are found the Cuban manganese, nickel, chromium, and iron ores formerly exploited by North American companies; but from an agricultural or a pastoral point of view the district is one of little value.

There are two other small mountainous areas. Near the middle of the island are the Trinidad Mountains, the maximum elevation of which is a little over 3,700 feet. And in western Cuba, west of Habana, there is the long, narrow Sierra de los Órganos, reaching a maximum elevation of about 2,500 feet. At the western extremity of Cuba is the rugged hill country known as the Guaniguánicos, of special interest because of its extraordinary scenery. This is a region formed late in a cycle of karst erosion, in which steep-sided limestone blocks, honeycombed with caverns, stand like great castles above irregular-shaped, flat-bottomed valleys.

Outside of these hilly or mountainous districts, the remaining three-quarters of Cuba is composed of gentle slopes. Partly on limestones, partly on other types of rock, a series of terraces has been formed, now somewhat dissected by the short streams so that in certain localities the terrain is moderately hilly. Along many sections of the coast the land is swampy, but most of Cuba is well drained. Where the terraces border the sea, the coast is cliffed; and there are many deep, pouch-shaped bays which form ideal natural harbors. Outstanding are the harbors of Habana, Santiago de Cuba, and Guantánamo.

Climate and Vegetation

Because of the generally moderate relief of Cuba, this island shows less of the contrast between windward and leeward sides than any of the other Antilles. In fact the heaviest average rainfall occurs in the western part of the island, for this section lies closest to the hurricane track (Map 36). No part of Cuba is deficient in moisture; and one of the notable features of the rainfall is its dependability during the critical agricultural season from May to November. Its two rainfall maxima correspond with the general rainfall regime of the Antilles. The temperatures are uniform, with no very great extremes. During the summers temperatures as high as 100° are sometimes recorded. The minimum winter temperatures throughout Cuba are usually in the 40's, although during the severe cold wave of February, 1958, the temperature in Camaguey dropped to 37.4°. Although they never bring freezing weather to Cuba, these cold air masses of the winter season do sometimes arrive as cool waves.

When the Spaniards first came to Cuba they found the island covered in places with semideciduous forest and in places with a patchwork of scrub woodland and grass. Waibel has reconstructed the vegetation of Cuba from the study of place names, many of which use the word *Sabana,* suggesting the existence of open patches in the midst of the woods. These grassy openings are not characteristic tropical savannas, for the grasses are not tall. Waibel describes them as a thorn-scrub steppe, in which pine and palmetto are intermingled with short grass. Rapid run-off on hard-packed soil rather than lack of rainfall accounts for the parched appearance of certain parts of the island. In 1890 forest still covered only 27 percent of the area, and scrub woodland covered 14 percent. Most of the limestone terrace lands had been cleared to expand the area of pasture.

The Pattern of Settlement

The settlements established by the Spaniards in the sixteenth century were primarily for purposes of defense. The scanty Indian population was soon almost completely wiped out by epidemics, and there was little to attract the Spaniards to the island. But the fine harbor of Habana, with the commanding heights at the entrance offered the opportunity for the construction of a strong naval base. Habana was established to guard the approaches to the Gulf of Mexico.

Inland, large cattle estates were granted by the Spanish king. Usually the properties were defined as including all the land within a league of a central point; the position of the estate headquarters was carefully noted, but the outer boundaries of the surrounding grazing land were left indefinite. As long as Cuba remained a scantily occupied pastoral country, the circular pattern of properties caused no difficulties, but much confusion was caused in the modern period of concentrated agricultural settlement.

The long period of Spanish control produced only one chief cluster of rural population. This was along the northern coast, inland from the city of Habana, and lying mostly within a radius of not over 30 or 40 miles from the capital. Outside of this one area of relatively concentrated settlement, there were several little coastal towns, each with a small zone of rural settlement around it—such as Cienfuegos and Santiago de Cuba. But the interior of the island remained almost uninhabited except at the widely spaced estate headquarters.

The people around Habana undertook the planting of sugarcane even during the eighteenth and nineteenth centuries. For this purpose African slave labor was imported. In 1850 the population of western Cuba (which included Pinar del Río, Habana, and Matanzas) totaled about 734,000 which was nearly 65 percent of the population of the whole island. Of this population centering on Habana, 325,000 were people of pure Spanish descent; and 409,000 were Africans, most of them still slaves. The chief product of the area was sugar, raised on large estates; but there was also a considerable amount of tobacco and coffee.

As long as Cuba remained a colony of Spain it was badly neglected. Roads were poor or nonexistent; methods of production were primitive and costly. The census of 1899 indicated that at that time about 47 percent of the land in crops in all of Cuba was devoted to sugarcane; smaller percentages to yams, tobacco, bananas, maize, and other food crops; 1.6 percent to coffee. At that time only 3 percent of Cuba was cultivated.

Spread of Sugarcane Planting

The treaty of 1901 between the United States and Cuba gave Cuban sugar a reduction of 20 percent on the tariff imposed on imported sugar. It also reserved to the United States the right of intervention in Cuban domestic affairs, a right which was used repeatedly until the treaty was abrogated in 1934. Because Cuban sugar paid a lower duty than sugars imported from other foreign countries, and because security was gained by the right of the United States government to intervene in Cuba, North American capital amounting to more than a billion dollars poured into the newly created republic. Roads and railroads were built; Habana was modernized; and in the rural districts new sugar mills were built to equip the sugar producers with the very latest technical devices for grinding the cane and extracting the raw sugar. In technical equipment no part of the world could compete with Cuba. The cost of production per unit was reduced three or four times as a result of this new capital investment.

The spread of sugarcane planting from the colonial nucleus around Habana took place rapidly after 1900. At that time there were 207 small mills in operation. But after 1900 most of these older mills were dismantled, and more modern, large-scale mills were built, equipped with new and more efficient sugar machinery. Most of the new mills were located in eastern Cuba, into which the planting of sugarcane had spread. In the 1950's there were 161 mills, 114 owned by Cubans, 40 owned in the United States, 6 in Spain, and 1 in France.

The first new plantations to be developed around the new mills outside of the Habana area were located along the axis of the red limestone soil known as Matanzas Clay (Map 37). This is one of the world's best sugarcane soils, located in one of the world's best sugarcane climates, in a position where the sugar could move easily to a huge nearby market. The underlying limestones weather into a deep red soil which shows no appreciable chemical or physical changes for as much as twenty feet below the surface. This is a typical low-latitude soil—deficient in silica and high in the iron and aluminum compounds. The chief element in its productivity for shallow-rooted crops is its porosity. Clay soils through which water cannot penetrate easily are generally considered poor; but this red soil of Cuba has a physical structure in which the clay particles are grouped together in floccules, leaving wide pore spaces for the downward percolation of water. As a result there is very little run-off and almost no soil erosion, and there is so little stickiness that plowing can be started within a few hours after a rain. Along the axis of this ideal soil type the sugar frontier began to swing eastward.

The red soils continue approximately to the eastern border of the province of Matanzas. Beyond this the soils are varied. There are patches of red lime-stone soils, there are deep sandy soils of fair productivity in terms of cane, and there are areas of clay which are difficult to work in wet weather. Nevertheless the sugar frontier continued its eastward spread until it reached the rugged, mountainous terrain of the southeast. The only parts of Cuba where sugarcane was not grown were the mountains, the coastal swamps, and the country to the west of Habana which is too rainy.

PRODUCTION PROBLEMS

The production of sugar in pre-Castro Cuba was an efficiently organized large-scale operation, with large capital investment and the services of highly skilled technicians. Before World War II about 60 percent of the capital came from the United States. Wealthy Cubans provided 22 percent, Spaniards 15 percent, and the remainder came from Canada and other foreign countries. By the 1950's, however, the share of the United States in the total investment in sugar production was down to 40 percent, but this included 7 of the 10 largest corporations. Most of the cane was grown by tenants who had contracts with the large mills, or *centrales*. Superintendents and inspectors from the *centrales* controlled the kinds of cane planted, the methods and standards of cultivation, the time of cutting, and the rate of delivery to the mills.

In the 1950's the large sugar corporations owned most of Cuba's best agricultural land. These sugar estates occupied 22 percent of the total area of Oriente province, 27 percent of Camaguay, 36 percent of Matanzas, and the whole of the Isla de Pinos. But not all these properties were used in any one year to grow cane. Because of the rapid decline of yields after a few years of planting, especially on the poorer soils, it was necessary to plant on new areas not previously used to grow cane. The sugar estates, therefore, included large areas reserved for future use. These reserved areas were not used to grow other crops, but they were used for the pasture of oxen which were needed as draft animals during the harvest season.

The labor requirement of sugar production, as in most cane growing areas, has always been a problem. At harvest time, from December to June, there were never enough workers. The cane was cut by hand at a rate of more than one hundred acres per day. Ox-carts carried the freshly cut cane to railroads, which then moved the cane into the *centrales* in a steady stream. The giant mills worked day and night. This rapid transportation of the cane to the mills was an essential part of the operation, because after cane is cut fermentation of the sugar sets in very quickly, and at least 2 percent per day of the sugar content of the cane is lost. It is essential, therefore, in any efficiently run sugarcane operation to move the cane to the mill and extract the juice within not more than 48 hours. Ox-carts were too slow to transport cane more than 5 miles. Motor trucks would have been better, but in pre-

Castro Cuba the rapid movement of the cane was by railroad. So many workers were needed during this period that men were recruited in nearby Haiti and Jamaica, and then returned to these places after the completion of the harvest.

The picture was very different between June and the end of November. This was what the Cubans called the *tiempo muerte,* the dead time. There were not nearly enough jobs to provide the workers with employment. Perhaps the workers were paid good wages in the harvest season, and there were fringe benefits such as health insurance and old-age retirement plans. But few people could follow family budgets to spread their incomes over the whole year. The great majority of the sugarcane workers were hopelessly in debt, and their families were on the verge of starvation. Traditionally in Cuba the period from June to November was one of social unrest.

HARBORS AND PORTS

There were still other ways in which pre-Castro Cuba was ideally suited to the development of a large-scale sugar industry. In the seventeenth and eighteenth centuries the islands of the Lesser Antilles had the advantage of small size. In those days each plantation had its own dock, to which the small sailing vessels could tie up. But in the twentieth century, when the sugar industry shifted to Cuba, the greater volume of sugar production required facilities for large ships. If all the Cuban sugar had been moved by rail to Habana and sent out through this port, the result would have been congestion and delay. But the island of Cuba is abundantly supplied with large harbors, many of them pouched-shaped bays like the harbor of Habana, all of them deep and well-protected. The fact that no *central* was more than 50 miles from a port was an important factor in reducing the cost of shipping Cuba's chief export; and the position of this many-harbored island so close to the vast sugar market of the United States was another great advantage for Cuba.

The Cuban sugar used to be sent out through 23 ports. The table opposite lists these ports running from west to east along Cuba's north coast, then from east to west along the south coast. As can be seen, Nuevitas was the port through which the largest volume of sugar moved, with Habana second, and Júcaro third. The fact that there were no ports between Nuevitas and Caibarién to serve the very productive cane area around Camaguay had the effect of concentrating shipments at Nuevitas.

In pre-Castro Cuba about 90 percent of the raw sugar was exported to be refined into white sugar in New York or elsewhere. Of the 10 percent refined in Cuba, about a third was processed in one large refinery owned by the Hershey interests, located about 50 miles east of Habana. Another 15 percent was refined near the port of Cárdenas. The remainder came from numerous small refineries attached to the large *centrales.*

EXPORTING PORTS FOR CUBAN SUGAR* (see Map 37)

Ports	Percentage of total 1948–1953
North Coast, from West to East	
Mariel	2.0
Habana	9.7
Matanzas	4.2
Cárdenas	8.2
Isabela de Sagua	6.1
Caibarién	6.0
Nuevitas	14.2
Manatí	2.3
Puerto Padre	4.5
Gibara	.6
Banes	1.2
Antilla	4.9
Preston	1.7
Tánamo (R. Sagua)	.7
South Coast, from East to West	
Guantánamo	3.7
Santiago de Cuba	4.5
Niquero	.5
Manzanillo	2.6
Santa Cruz del Sur	3.8
Júcaro	8.6
Tunas de Zaza	1.5
Casilda (port for Trinidad)	.8
Cienfuegos	7.5

*From *Annuario Azucarero de Cuba* (1948–53), Instituto Cubano de Estabilización del Azúcar; quoted in Donald R. Dyer, "Sugar Regions of Cuba," *Economic Geography*, Vol. 32)1956): pp. 177–184.

Tobacco

Since the beginning of large-scale sugar production in Cuba, this one crop has dominated Cuba's economy. Nevertheless, there is another commercial crop for which Cuba has long been famous: tobacco. It was in Cuba that the Spaniards first made the acquaintance of this plant and its use. The manufacture and smoking of cigars was taught to the Occidental world by the Indians of Cuba; Cuba was a country of tobacco and cigar production before the arrival of Columbus. Cuba is still the source of some of the world's finest tobaccos.

About half of the Cuban tobacco is still grown in the so-called *Vuelta Abajo* district, located south of the Sierra de los Órganos on the better-drained upper part of the coastal plain in Pinar del Río (Map 34, p. 228).

Here the soil is sandy and generally infertile, but possesses a physical structure which permits the maximum benefit to the plants from the use of fertilizer. The young tobacco plants are usually set out in October, and the first leaves are ready to be cut in January. The crop used to be grown on small properties which averaged only about forty acres, but the work of cultivating, harvesting, and curing the crop was so great that on each forty-acre estate the services of at least twenty men were required. Tobacco for use as cigar fillers is grown without shade, but the tobacco destined for use in cigar wrappers must be grown under cheesecloth, and must be carefully protected from insect pests, and handled in such a way that the leaf is not torn or damaged.

The Vuelta Abajo district is a relatively small area of intensive production and concentrated rural population. It forms a strip along the piedmont of the Sierra de los Órganos which is about 90 miles long, but not much more than 10 miles wide.

There are two other areas of tobacco production in Cuba. The *Partito* district, near Habana, although much smaller than the Vuelta Abajo district, produces tobacco of nearly equal quality. The *Vuelta Arriba* district, in the province of Santa Clara, also a small area, grows tobacco of inferior quality on a variety of soils.

Mining

Cuba's resource endowment also includes certain minerals. The most important of these are the manganese ores bordering the Guantánamo Valley north of Santiago de Cuba. The ore bodies are of excellent quality, but they are small and scattered. Chromite is also mined in southeastern Cuba and in other parts of the island. A large deposit of iron ore has been worked for many years in the vicinity of Santiago de Cuba. Nickel ores were mined in the highlands of eastern Cuba, and a smelter set up by the United States government during World War II at Nicaro, just east of the port of Preston, was operated until 1957. Copper is mined near Santiago de Cuba and also west of Habana. Cuba even has a small oilfield located near the north coast east of Matanzas.

Habana

All the various activities we have described come to a focus on Habana, the capital of Cuba. With a present population of about 1,500,000, Habana has spread far beyond the outlines of the original little Spanish colonial town. The fortress which long guarded the northern approach to the Spanish Gulf of Mexico still stands at the entrance to the bay. The downtown section of the city is laid out with the usual narrow streets on a rectangular plan, built around a central plaza. Along the ocean front the residential suburbs included the expensive homes of wealthy Cubans. They were also in Habana cigar and cigarette factories, luxury hotels, and gambling casinos.

Habana used to be a major tourist attraction for people in the United States, especially during the winter months. North Americans can perhaps qualify as the world's chief travelers; and to whatever country they go for rest and recreation they constitute an important source of income. The desire to escape from the unpleasant winters of the north leads a larger and larger number of people toward Florida and the Caribbean. Any increase in the general level of prosperity in the United States turns increased numbers to these southern resorts, and, before 1959, contributed a form of speculative prosperity to the urban dwellers of Habana.

Cuba as a Political Unit

After 1959 all this was changed. The revolution headed by Fidel Castro was successful in overthrowing the dictatorship, and Castro assumed power on January 1, 1959. In the years since then the Cuban economy has been rebuilt on Marxist lines, with a centrally organized and planned control of the production and distribution of goods. Large numbers of older people who disliked the rigid discipline and the loss of opportunities for personal expression emigrated from Cuba, chiefly to the United States. But the younger people were carefully indoctrinated. Children are now taken from their parents about 45 days after they are born and placed in state nurseries. Children of school age are separated from families for eleven months of the year, and are raised in boarding schools, many of which are housed in the former homes of wealthy Cubans along the coast east of Habana. Here they learn to repeat the Marxist slogans, to obey the constituted authorities, to worship Castro, and to hate the United States.

The Economic Situation

The rebuilding of an economic system is not easy. In accordance with Marxist principles the economy is now centrally planned, and the agency responsible for this planning is the *Junta Central de Planificación* (JUCE-PLAN). This agency, together with a hierarchy of subordinate agencies, allocates resources, determines production quotas, and directs the distribution of income among the workers. This is what the economists describe as a *command economy,* as opposed to a *market economy,* in which raw materials and income are distributed in terms of market demand. This is the kind of economy that many of the more advanced communist countries, including the Soviet Union, are now modifying by permitting the partial operation of a market, and by accepting personal profit as an incentive to increased production.

There are three elements in the economic policy developed by JUCEPLAN. First there is to be an effort to increase the export of sugar and other Cuban products. Second, agriculture is to be diversified, especially through the increased production of food crops and cattle. And third, more than 30 percent of the gross national product is to be invested each year in new capital—in electric power, highways, and manufacturing industries.

The first two of the three elements of Cuban economic policy concern the improvement of agriculture. This program was placed under control of the *Instituto Nacional de la Reforma Agraria* (INRA), which published its first land reform plan in May 1959. This first phase of land reform was aimed primarily at the very large properties, especially those owned by foreign interests. In October 1963 a second step was announced: all properties over 165 acres were taken over by the state; agriculture on the former sugarcane lands was diversified by the planting of cotton, yams, potatoes, and certain vegetables. Great efforts were made to mechanize the agriculture, through the spreading of fertilizer by airplane, through the replacement of oxen by tractors, and through cane-cutting machines imported from Czechoslovakia. Still, the greater part of the harvest had to be done by hand, and for this purpose work brigades including both men and women were recruited in the cities. The harvest season was extended by starting the cane-cutting in November. As rapidly as possible, the rural workers were provided with new homes and with space on which to grow basic food crops.

The results of these changes can now be assessed. In the first place the production of sugarcane dropped to a record low in 1963. There were not enough workers to harvest the crop, and the temporary migration of workers from Haiti and Jamaica had been stopped. The imported machinery was frequently idled by lack of spare parts. And in 1963 the hurricane Flora did serious damage to the central part of Cuba. By 1966, however, sugar production was up to a new high level, and in 1967 the harvest was about a million tons greater than the average of pre-Castro Cuba. Agriculture is being diversified by increased attention to food crops, fruits, cotton, oilseeds, and other crops that help to provide for year-round employment. The production of rice almost doubled between 1957 and 1960 and has continued to rise during the 1960's. The herds of beef cattle were improved through the import of high-grade stock from Canada.

An important part of the improvement of the agricultural sector was the construction of new, low-cost housing for the farm workers. There can be no doubt that these very poor people, who were the chief victims of the pre-Castro sugar economy, are now much better off. They have new, clean homes with electric power and running water and are employed the year round. For these people there has been a marked increase in purchasing power. They can now eat rice, potatoes, wheat, and vegetables; they can buy shoes which they never could afford before, and they have more simple cotton clothing available to them than they had before 1959.

The investment of more than 30 percent of the gross national product in new capital—which was accomplished by decree, not persuasion—has had

With a machete in each hand, a Cuban volunteer worker hacks down sugarcane. *United Press International Photo.*

the effect of greatly increasing the production of a variety of consumer goods. The production of manufactured goods has gone up 1.7 percent per year, and these are goods for domestic use, not for export. With aid from the Soviet Union, two large new electric power plants have been built, one at Mariel, west of Habana, one on Santiago Bay in the southeast. Around these sources of power, the government is planning to build clusters of light industries which will provide new jobs, and will turn out goods chiefly for the domestic market. The program of housing also follows a characteristic communist plan: instead of individual homes, the government is now constructing four-story apartment buildings, arranged around central plazas, with each group of buildings provided with schools, meeting halls, and central dining facilities. Machinery for prefabricating the apartment buildings and giant cranes for setting the prefabricated parts in place were provided by the Soviet Union. Numerous new urban centers are being built, one to take care of 26,000 people located at the easternmost tip of the island. The central planners are taking effective steps to stop the movement of people into Habana.

The plans, of course, are not always carried out. There is abundant evidence that a command economy cannot ever be as flexible and as efficient as an economy in which the market is at least a factor. The planners, however, are trying to lay the groundwork for economic development, with the hope that at some future date Cuba can escape from such complete dependence on the Soviet Union.

At the beginning of 1968 such escape was not in sight. The Cuban economy was being subsidized by the Soviet Union at a cost of over $400 million per year. An agreement reached in 1964 specified that Cuba would deliver 3 million tons of sugar to the Soviet Union in 1966, 4 million tons in 1967, and 5 million tons each year in 1968, 1969, and 1970. The quota has never been met. In spite of increased sugar production in 1966 and 1967, the amount fell well below the plan. In 1967 sugar made up 85 percent of the value of all exports. But the failure to meet the quotas resulted in 1967 in a reduction of the Soviet exports of oil to Cuba, so that the Cuban government was forced to ration gasoline. Year by year, Cuba's indebtedness to the Soviet Union has been increasing.

On the other hand, a start was made in 1968 on the construction of a huge fertilizer plant near Cienfuegos. By 1971 the plant should be ready to turn out some 300,000 tons of ammonium nitrate and 200,000 tons of urea per year—fertilizers which are essential if Cuba is ever to meet its planned quota of sugar export or its increase in production of fruits and beef cattle. The plant will cost about $100 million, and this capital, together with technical assistance, is being provided by Great Britain.

The Political Situation

When Cuba gained its independence from Spain in 1899 this did not bring to the island any large measure of real independence. United States and Cuban leaders worked out a new constitution. In accordance with the so-called "Platt Amendment," accepted by Cuba as part of the constitution, Cuba agreed not to incur debts its revenue would not bear, to continue the sanitary measures started by the United States army, to lease a naval base to the United States at Guantánamo Bay, and to acknowledge the right of the United States to intervene if necessary in the domestic affairs of the island. During the first thirty years of Cuba's independence the United States did, in fact, intervene many times to maintain order and to protect the increasing capital investment in the Cuban economy. Subservience to the United States, however, proved even more irritating than rule by Spain. The Platt Amendment was finally renounced by the United States in 1934.

This did not bring an end to the political conflicts, or to dishonesty and mismanagement by the persons who occupied positions of power. From 1933 to 1959 Fulgencio Batista was the one focus of political direction in Cuba. He rose from the noncommissioned grade of sergeant to become the commander in chief of the military forces. His long control over Cuban affairs was based on his ability to command the complete loyalty of the army. He saw to it that all members of the armed forces, officers and men alike, were well paid, and his treasury was well supplied with funds. For several periods Batista permitted another general to become president; and each man who has held this office has made millions of dollars. There was no such thing as political liberty, honest elections, or equality before the law.

The rumblings of revolt, as usual, were centered on the university, where the students, in accordance with Latin-American tradition, remained free from police interference. Outside, dissenters were arrested without warrants, imprisoned and tortured, or killed, or exiled. In spite of the strength of the police and the army, there were occasional guerrilla-type disorders—usually during the period of widespread unemployment between June and December. On July 26, 1953, a 26-year-old graduate of the University of Habana named Fidel Castro led a small band of men in an attack on an army barracks near Santiago. The attack was defeated and the attackers were captured. Most of them were killed, but Castro and his brother were placed in jail. When Castro was tried before a court in October of that year he acted as his own lawyer, taking the opportunity to speak for five hours on his plans for the social and political reform of Cuba. Yet Batista was so firmly in control of Cuba that in 1955 the Castro brothers were released from jail and permitted to depart for Mexico. Here Castro organized another band of men, and on December 2, 1956, he landed on the mountainous southeastern shore of Cuba. Castro had 80 men with him, but most of them were killed by Batista's army before they could get ashore. Castro, his brother Raoul, and the Argentine revolutionary Che Guevara, together with nine other survivors, managed to escape into the rugged Sierra Maestra.

From mountain hideaways Castro was able to carry on guerrilla warfare against Batista's army. Within a year he had recruited more than 2,000 followers and was strong enough to make raids on the nearby lowlands where sugar mills could be burned, or the cane set on fire. Batista's army became more and more concerned, and more and more active in rounding up suspected collaborators. In less than six years Batista's forces killed about 20,000 Cubans, some of whom were caught in overt acts of rebellion, some of whom were merely suspect. The people of Cuba, especially the large middle class of merchants and professional people, began to support Castro, as did large numbers of people in other parts of Latin America. Even the wealthy Cubans began to turn away from the brutality and oppressive acts of the dictator. Batista's 46,000-man army began to refuse to fight with Castro's guerrillas. On January 1, 1959, Fidel Castro assumed control of Cuba.

Batista had enjoyed the backing of the United States. Not only was there a United States military mission to train the Cuban army, but also the United States supplied airplanes and other military equipment. The dictator, who was becoming more and more unpopular in Cuba, was praised publicly by representatives of the United States because of his fine work in maintaining order. The Cuban people were naturally bitter about a nation that could talk about democracy and then give support and praise to the most ruthless of dictators.

Castro was able to gain control of Cuba because of the support of the Cuban middle classes. He was able to keep control of Cuba because of the support of the workers. Today he enjoys the enthusiastic support of most of the people who are still in Cuba, and those who are less than enthusiastic are at least ready to accept his rule.

At first Castro's revolt was distinctively Cuban. The person who was most quoted in support of revolution was José Martí. Castro himself is reported to have said that "communism is only another form of slavery." But in order to keep control of Cuba, especially after he started to expropriate land and seize foreign-owned property, Castro had to make use of the support of the best organized political force left in the country—the Communist Party. Furthermore, he needed help from outside to replace the former help of the United States. In 1961 he declared that his revolution was Marxist, and he proceeded to set up another tightly controlled dictatorship with himself as undisputed leader. He did this on the communist pattern, accepting the military and economic assistance of the Soviet Union. He even permitted the establishment of Soviet missile bases on Cuba. Yet Castro's chief aim remains to keep as free from outside domination as possible, and to escape from complete subservience to the Soviet Union he became a supporter of the Chinese militant brand of communism. In 1968, Castro had some forty of his lieutenants arrested because they tended to support the Soviet Union and because of their resistance to the policy of exporting revolution to other countries of Latin America.[2] Clearly all was not going well in the Marxist paradise.

Although Cuba is now the only Soviet-style autocracy in the American Hemisphere, it is nevertheless a part of the picture of revolutionary change that characterizes Latin America. Occupying the position of closest geographic proximity to the United States, Cuba's reaction against the impact of change radiating from Anglo-America has been violent. All over Latin America there are many who sympathize with the original purposes of Castro's revolution, and who admire the bearded revolutionary because he was able to defy the power of the United States and seize foreign-owned property and yet survive. Especially after the emigration of many Cubans who are opposed to Castro, the great majority of those who remain are firm supporters of the new regime. Because of Cuba's island position any attempt at military invasion would be costly; therefore Castro can survive as he might not have been able to do had he been forced to defend himself against land neighbors.

[2]For discussions of the Castro revolution and its background including the still disputed question of whether or not Castro was a communist before 1961, see Che Guevara, *Guerrilla Warfare,* New York, 1961; Herbert L. Matthews, *The Cuban Story,* New York, 1961; Theodore Draper, *Castro's Revolution, Myths and Reality,* New York, 1962; Samuel Shapiro, *Invisible Latin America,* Boston, 1963; Tad Szulc, *The Winds of Revolution,* New York, 1964; Joseph Maier and Richard W. Weatherhead (eds.), *Politics of Change in Latin America,* New York, 1964. See also additional references in Appendix B.

Although he poses less a direct threat to the security of the United States than a frustrating irritation, his influence, his training schools for subversives, and his shipments of arms and money do constitute a danger for the other countries of the hemisphere. Yet Cuba is also a clear example of what happens when a social and political revolution is allied with the Soviet Union. Castro is no more free from outside interference than was Batista. The threat of communism seems remote indeed to many Latin-Americans: but Castro has brought it much closer, and the example of regimented life under a Soviet autocracy is there for all to see. A visit to Cuba is more effective than hours of radio propaganda or pages of anti-communist argument.

République D'Haiti

Area: 10,714 square miles
Population: (1967 estimate) 4,577,000
           (last census, 1950) 3,097,304
Capital city: Port-au-Prince; (1960) 240,000
Percent urban: (1950) 12.5
Birth rate per 1,000: (1966) 45–50; Death rate per 1,000: (1966) 20–25
Annual percent of increase: (1958–64) 2.3
Percent literate: (1950) 10.5
Percent of labor force in agriculture: (1950) 83.6
Gross national product per capita: (1966) about $65
Unit of currency: gourde (1968, 5.00 per dollar)

COMMERCE, 1965 *(expressed in percentage of values)*
Percent total Latin-American exports: 0.4 (1956, less than 1.0)
Percent total Latin-American imports: 0.4

Exports
coffee   55
sugar   7
sisal   5

Exports to			**Imports from**		
United States	48	(1956, 34)	United States	56	(1956, 62)
Belgium	12		West Germany	5	
Italy	7				
Japan	6				

República Dominicana

Area: 18,703 square miles
Population: ·(1966 estimate) 3,754,000
　　　　　　(last census, 1960) 3,047,070
Capital city: Santo Domingo; (1967) 577,371
Percent urban: (1960) 30.5
Birth rate per 1,000: (1966) 47–51; Death rate per 1,000: (1966) 14–17
Annual percent of increase: (1958–64) 3.6
Percent literate: (1956) 59.9
Percent labor force in agriculture: (1950) 56.5
Gross national product per capita: (1966) $264
Unit of currency: peso (1968, 1.00 per dollar)
Leading crops in acreage: (1950) sugarcane, maize, manioc, rice, yams

COMMERCE, 1965 *(expressed in percentage of values)*
Percent total Latin-American exports: 1.8 (1956, 1.0)
Percent total Latin-American imports: 2.5

Exports

sugar	56
coffee	15
cacao	8
tobacco	5

Exports to		Imports from	
United States	88 (1956, 47)	United States	54 (1956, 65)
United Kingdom	6	West Germany	6
		Netherlands Antilles	6

Chapter 12 □ The Dominican Republic and Haiti

Two independent states of very different character are locked together within the confines of the island of Hispaniola. In the west is Haiti—Negro in race, African in many aspects of the culture in spite of a superficial French tradition and in spite of the use of the French language. In the east is the Dominican Republic—mostly mulatto, but essentially Spanish in the way of living. The western third of Hispaniola was occupied in 1967 by 4,600,000 Haitians, with a density of about 448 people per square mile. The eastern two-thirds of Hispaniola was occupied by 3,754,000 Dominicans, with a density of 200 people per square mile. On the Haitian side of the border the rugged land is marked off into a patchwork of small farms, cultivated with hoe and machete, used for the production of food crops for the people who work them; on the Dominican side of the border, behind a screen of recent agricultural colonies, there are large properties used for the grazing of cattle, large areas very thinly inhabited or entirely empty, and small areas of concentrated settlement. On one side of the border the way of living is a strange mixture of African and French customs; on the other the economic, social, and political life proceeds in accordance with the Spanish tradition, where a newly awakened population of workers and intellectuals struggles to bring about social reform and economic development against the resistance of the wealthy landowners and different factions of the army. The presence of two such contrasted peoples, politically separate, within so small an island, creates the ever-present danger of conflict.

The Land

The island of Hispaniola has the most rugged and complicated terrain of all the islands of the Greater Antilles. The story is told of the admiral who,

Port-au-Prince, Haiti, at the western end of the Cul de Sac.

being asked by the king to describe the island, crumpled up a piece of paper and replied, "There, your majesty, is Hispaniola." The story has been told of many different admirals and many different lands, but it is still a good one. Hispaniola is actually ribbed by steep-sided, narrow-crested ranges, oriented in various directions, and creased by deep valleys and pocket-like lowlands.

In the Cordillera Central the mountains of Hispaniola reach their greatest elevations. This range extends from southeast to northwest with one end on the south coast just west of Santo Domingo (formerly Ciudad Trujillo), and the other just within the territory of Haiti to the south of Cap Haitien. The summits are generally between 8,000 and 9,000 feet above sea level, but the highest peak, located in the central part of the Dominican Republic, is about 10,100 feet in elevation—Pico Duarte. The Cordillera Central is made up of a jumble of ridges and peaks threaded with rushing streams in narrow, steep-sided canyons. Most of the slopes are too steep for farming; yet, traveling over steep mountain trails one comes unexpectedly upon little flat-bottomed valleys, closely hemmed in by the precipitous slopes, on each of which a dense farming population is established in almost complete isolation from the outside world. From the northwestern end of the Cordillera Central lower but still rugged mountain ranges extend through the northern peninsula of Haiti where they point across the Windward Passage toward the Sierra Maestra of Cuba. Another extension of steep-sided ridges runs eastward to the eastern end of Hispaniola where it points across the Mona Passage to the mountains of Puerto Rico.

In the southwestern part of Hispaniola another range of mountains forms the long southern peninsula of Haiti, extending eastward into Dominican territory. This is the eastern end of the southern prong which makes up the forked system of ranges we have described in this book as the Central-American–Antillean system. In Hispaniola this range is separated from the Cordillera Central by the deep structural depression of the Cul de Sac, running from Port-au-Prince in Haiti to Barahona in the Dominican Republic.

In the northeastern part of Hispaniola there is still another distinct range of mountains, the Cordillera Septentrional, extending from the Haitian border eastward across the Dominican Republic to form the small peninsula of Samaná. The highest summits of this range are only three or four thousand feet above sea level, but the slopes are steep and the valleys deeply cut. This northeastern range is separated from the Cordillera Central by the narrow east–west lowland known in the Dominican Republic as the Cibao, and in Haiti as the Plaine du Nord.

The small lowlands and intermont basins are scattered in the midst of this confusing array of ridges and summits and in little pockets along the coast. The largest plain is in the southeast of the Dominican Republic, to the east of Santo Domingo. This is a limestone platform formed by corals and raised above the sea, similar in many ways to the limestone terraces of Cuba. The other lowland in the southern part of the island is the Cul de Sac, partly in Haiti, partly in the Dominican Republic. In the middle of the Cul de Sac are two brackish lakes, the Étang Saumâtre in Haiti and Lago Enriquillo in the Dominican Republic—the latter is some 140 feet below sea level. The Cul de Sac is a structural depression, a downfaulted block between the mountain ranges, which was at one time filled with sea water. Streams at either end of the lowland built alluvial fans which eventually sealed off the Cul de Sac from the ocean, while evaporation lowered the lake levels.

The lowland of the Cibao, on the other hand, is low and swampy only at its eastern end at the head of the Bahía de Samaná. For most of its length the floodplain of the river is bordered by terraces standing distinctly above the flood levels. The Plaine du Nord in Haiti rises gradually from the Atlantic to the base of the Cordillera Central.

In Haiti there is a wedge-like area of lowlands, the Artibonite Plain; and in the midst of the mountain ranges on the border between Haiti and the Dominican Republic is the Plaine Centrale. This is an intermont basin, standing about a thousand feet above sea level, generally level to gently rolling except where it is cut into narrow ravines by the headwaters of the Artibonite River.

In addition to these intricately arranged mountain axes and structural depressions, the surface of Hispaniola is further complicated by many small isolated mountain blocks and by many miniature valley lowlands and sea-border plains. Geologically associated with the surface features of the main island, too, are the bordering smaller islands of Gonâve off the west coast, and Tortue off the north coast.

Climate and Vegetation

A surface so complex in its pattern of slopes and basins could not fail to develop a complex pattern of climatic conditions and vegetation. The temperatures generally decrease with increasing elevation, but there are many protected pockets which are so disposed that the heating effect of the sun is especially great, and in which exceptionally high temperatures are to be observed. Port-au-Prince itself, located not only on the protected western side of Hispaniola but also in the embrace of minor spurs from the southern mountains, has one of the highest average temperatures of any major city in the Antilles. The central part of the Cul de Sac has the kind of hot-house climate, with a steamy humidity and lack of winds, which is thought by many people to be characteristic of the tropics but which is, in reality, found in only a few places.

The pattern of rainfall is also very complicated. The north- and east-facing slopes of the mountains are generally wetter than the south- and west-facing slopes, although this generalization does not apply to the southern mountains of Haiti where both north and south slopes are wet. Among the lowlands, the Cibao receives abundant moisture, especially in its eastern part, where there is a district of great agricultural productivity known as the *Vega Real*. The Plaine du Nord of Haiti receives somewhat less moisture than its eastern continuation in the Dominican Republic. The coastal plain in the southeast, on which Santo Domingo is situated, receives barely enough for crop production without irrigation, and in this area most of the sugarcane plantations are now irrigated. The Plaine Centrale of Haiti is also near the margins between humid and subhumid. But the Artibonite lowland and the Cul de Sac are both semiarid in spite of high atmospheric humidity.

The fact that moisture deficiency cannot be defined in terms of the annual amount of rainfall without reference to such other factors as rate of evaporation is well illustrated by the conditions at Port-au-Prince. At this station, 54 inches of rain are not quite sufficient to permit the growth of sugarcane without irrigation, nor does this amount of moisture support a vegetation cover more luxuriant than a deciduous thorny scrub woodland mixed with giant cacti. An average annual rainfall of less than 50 inches in the Cul de Sac produces conditions which are definitely semiarid. The evaporation which takes place where the temperatures average over 80° is very great; and where evaporation is rapid, more rain must fall in order to support luxuriant vegetation, or to make possible the practice of humid-land agriculture.

The natural vegetation of Hispaniola closely reflects these conditions of climate and surface. The wetter places were originally clothed with a dense rain forest, but the drier slopes and basins supported only a thorny scrub woodland which varied in density in accordance with the variations of the conditions of drainage. The drier northwestern part of the Plaine Centrale was covered by an open savanna, with trees only in the narrow, wet ravines; but the wetter southeastern part supported a dense scrub woodland. Only in the Cordillera Central are the elevations sufficient to reach the zone of the pines.

Such is the nature of the island of Hispaniola. This is the land now occupied by two strongly contrasted peoples, whose traditions, technical abilities, and basic attitudes are so different that the political boundary which divides Hispaniola into two parts has become a sharp culture boundary as well.

THE DOMINICAN REPUBLIC

The Spanish-speaking people of the Dominican Republic occupy the eastern two-thirds of Hispaniola. The figure of population density (200 per square mile), derived from dividing the total population by the total national territory, is entirely misleading, for actually the Dominicans are concentrated in certain areas only, and large parts of the Republic lie outside the effective national territory. About half of the population is concentrated in the eastern part of the Cibao between Santiago de los Caballeros and San Francisco de Macorís (Map 35, p. 229) and along the northern coast. A third of the population is in the capital city of Santo Domingo and in the sugarcane lands of the southern area between San Cristóbal on the west and La Romana on the east. The remainder of the population is scattered in small clusters, including the string of new agricultural colonies along the Haitian border and the small intermont valleys in the Cordillera Central. At least half of the total national territory remains almost unoccupied, which means that the Dominican Republic faces no problem of land hunger.

Of the total Dominican population, people of European ancestry make up about 28 percent, mulattoes make up 60 percent, and people of unmixed African ancestry are about 11 percent. The remaining 1 percent includes a variety of peoples, mostly Japanese and Chinese.

The Course of Settlement

The eastern part of Hispaniola was the first part of America to be occupied by the Spaniards. After two failures to establish a port on the northern coast (Navidad, now Cap Haïtien, in 1492; and Isabela, 25 miles west of Puerto Plata, in 1493), Santo Domingo was made the chief Spanish primary settlement center in 1496 (Map 6, p. 18). The newcomers led by Columbus were concerned only to find gold, and some gold they did find in the stream gravels of the Cibao. The large native population, which probably numbered more than a million, was pressed into service in the mines. The native way of living was destroyed; within fifty years most of the Indians had died from overwork and lack of food, as well as from epidemics of European diseases such as measles and smallpox. By 1550 the focus of Spanish interest had shifted elsewhere.

The Indians of Hispaniola lived in a kind of paradise, enjoying an abundant food supply and usually freedom from warfare. Their chief food crop was manioc, supplemented by sweet potatoes, peanuts, and a variety of other food crops. They grew maize, but on the islands maize was less important than the root crops. In the Cibao the Indians also grew tobacco, which they smoked in cigars or took as snuff. They also harvested a kind of tree cotton. The diet was well-balanced because the Indians also ate shellfish, fish, turtles, marine mammals and waterfowl, all of which were found in abundance around Hispaniola. But when the Spaniards arrived, obsessed with the desire for gold, the Indian agriculture was neglected. The Spanish introduction of wheat and the vine was a failure, but the cattle and pigs did very well. When Columbus first reached Hispaniola, he found the level lands mostly cleared and cultivated. Within fifty years, large areas once densely populated had been abandoned and a second growth of forest or woodland savanna had appeared. Cattle and pigs ran wild and found plenty to eat where once there had been Indian farms.[1]

With the decline of gold mining, the Spaniards who remained in Hispaniola tried other ways of making a profitable living. As early as 1515 sugarcane plantations had been developed around Santo Domingo, and African slaves were imported to do the work. Tobacco was grown in the Cibao where the Indians had been growing this crop long before Columbus. Cacao, grown in the wet eastern part of the Cibao was an important export until the disappearance of this crop after 1800. Attempts were made to grow indigo. By the end of the eighteenth century the contrast between the western part of Hispaniola and the eastern part had already appeared. By that time the French colony had been established in Haiti. In it there were 524,000 inhabitants, of whom 88 percent were African slaves; in the Spanish colony in eastern Hispaniola there were 103,000 inhabitants, of whom 30 percent were African slaves.

The last decade of the eighteenth century was one of violent disorder, leading to the utter ruin of the colonial economy. Ownership of Hispaniola passed from one country to another. In 1804 Haiti declared its independence. When

[1]For a discussion of the changes introduced by the Spaniards all around the Caribbean see Carl O. Sauer, *The Early Spanish Main*, Berkeley, Cal., 1966.

the Spanish colony declared its independence from Spain in 1821, the Haitians promptly invaded and took control of the whole island. Not until 1844 did the Dominicans succeed in pushing the Haitians back and finally gaining the status of an independent country. Ever since then the relatively small population of the eastern part of the island has lived in constant fear of the expansion of the relatively dense population of the western part, whether by infiltration across the border or by actual conquest. For a brief period, while the United States was engaged in its Civil War, Spain actually resumed control over its lost colony (1861–65). The people of the Dominican Republic voted in 1869 to ask for adoption by the United States, but the United States refused to accept the responsibility of this added territory. Loans were contracted in Europe and North America, but when funds reached Santo Domingo, the money usually disappeared and was never utilized for productive purposes. The extent to which the corruption of public officials had gone is revealed by the fact that when, in 1905, the United States undertook to collect the customs, agreeing to give 45 percent of the revenue to the government and to keep 55 percent for the repayment of debts, the 45 percent thus collected for the local treasury was greater than the whole government revenue of any preceding year.

Meanwhile, in the midst of all this confusion, certain economic advances were being made. In 1865, a colony of people from the southern United States was established on the southern side of the Peninsula of Samaná. This was similar in origin to the colonies established at about the same time elsewhere in Latin America. In Hispaniola the colonists began again to plant cacao. As a result of their example, other planters in the Vega Real also planted that crop. The Cibao during the next twenty years developed a considerable production of cacao, sugarcane, coffee, cotton, tobacco, beeswax, and honey. In 1914 sugar passed cacao as the leading export. In part, these developments were due to a small but significant immigration of Cubans, who introduced new cane-planting techniques, and also to the arrival of a group of North American Negroes who settled near the port of Sánchez on the margins of the Vega Real. Still the Dominican Republic had only two short public railroads, and its highways were all but impassable. Only trails led across the wilderness of the Cordillera Central.

The United States Marines occupied the Dominican Republic during World War I to protect the approaches to the Panama Canal, the keystone of national defense. There can be no doubt that a weak government faced with almost constant domestic troubles, and in possession of an island so strategically placed, constituted a potential menace. In 1916, therefore, the Marines landed at Santo Domingo, and soon brought the whole territory under their control. Order and security were established, roads and railroads were constructed, and a considerable gain in commercial production was effected. The rate of population increase, too, showed a marked upturn because of a rapid decrease in the death rate.

North American sentiment opposed to such foreign occupation regained enough power after the war to bring about the evacuation of the Dominican Republic in 1924. But when the Marines departed they left the country in the hands of an officer they had trained—Rafael Leónidas Trujillo Molina. General Trujillo became one of the strongest dictators in Latin America, invincible because he controlled the power of the army. He imprisoned, killed, or exiled anyone who opposed his rule. Trujillo accomplished much in building up the economy of the country, which he managed as if it were his own personal estate. He named the highest peak Pico Trujillo (now Pico Duarte), and when Santo Domingo was rebuilt following the hurricane of 1930, he named it Ciudad Trujillo. When he was assassinated in 1961, the Dominicans promptly restored the old names.

The Patterns of Settlement and Land Use

After 1930, under the dictatorship of General Trujillo, the Dominican Republic made important advances in the productivity of the economy. By 1959 about 23 percent of the total area was under cultivation. The amount of irrigated land increased from 7,500 acres in 1930 to 380,000 acres in 1959. Not only was the agricultural productivity of the areas of chief population concentration improved, but also Trujillo undertook a program of agricultural colonization to settle parts of the country previously unoccupied.

The Cibao and the North Coast

The Cibao and the north coast is the most densely populated part of the country. The lowland is well-settled for all the 150 miles between the Haitian border and Sánchez on the Bahía de Samaná, but the densest population is on the Vega Real, the plain to the east of Santiago. Here there are a little over 600 people per square mile. The region as a whole is not over-populated, however, for there are still unoccupied areas of good land, especially along the north-facing piedmont of the Cordillera Central, and along the north coast on either side of Puerto Plata.

The Vega Real is highly productive agricultural land. On fertile alluvial soil the farmers grow dry-land rice, maize, peanuts, beans, yams, and vegetables. The eastern end of the Vega is used chiefly for cacao, especially around San Francisco de Macorís. In many places bananas are grown to give shade to the cacao, or to coffee plantations on the lower slopes of the mountains to the north. Around Santiago itself there is a concentration of tobacco. West of Santiago as far as Monte Cristi the floodplain of the river is used for paddy rice. Along the northern slopes of the Cordillera Septentrional and the northern coast there are coffee plantations higher up, and cacao plantations lower down. Along the coast the crops include tobacco, bananas, manioc, and coconuts. It is in this area, just east of Puerto Plata, that a colony of displaced people from Europe was settled during the 1940's—the Sosúa Colony. These immigrant pioneers have not been so successful as the native-born Dominicans with the tropical crops which do so well in that area. At Puerto Plata there is a chocolate factory, and a match factory which makes use of wood from nearby forests.

At the westernmost end of the Cibao, there is a zone of banana plantations from which bananas have been regularly exported since 1939. These plantations, developed by the Standard Fruit Company, are irrigated and equipped with the most modern spray systems for the control of banana disease. As a result these are the most productive banana plantations in the Antilles.

The Southeast

The southeast is separated from the Cibao by a densely forested but not very high string of limestone ridges. The plains of the southeast are developed on limestone, much like the Camaguay area in central Cuba. For a long time the land has been used for the grazing of cattle, and animals have been exported from here to other parts of the Antilles both for meat and as draught animals. During the Haitian occupation, this was the one economic activity that the Spanish-speaking Dominicans could monopolize. The animals are small but hardy and well-adapted to the conditions of tropical pastures. Under Trujillo the herds were improved, and a modern dairy farm was built near the capital. Milk was sent by airplane to San Juan in Puerto Rico.

Since World War II there has been an important expansion of the sugar-cane plantations in the plains of the southeast. All along the coast between San Cristóbal and La Romana there are vast privately-owned plantations and modern mills. North of La Romana there is one plantation rented by a tenant on one of the huge cattle ranches, where cane is grown on nearly 75,000 acres in one unit. There is another concentration of sugarcane around San Pedro de Macorís, where there are now seven big mills.

The southeast of the Dominican Republic is excellent for sugarcane. It has soils that are similar to the best in Cuba. Because it is a little drier and less cloudy than Cuba, it receives more sunshine; as a result the cane cut in this area has the highest sugar content of any cane throughout the Antilles. Because of the somewhat lower rainfall, also, a large part of the new cane lands must be irrigated. The modern expansion of the sugarcane business in this area has been supported by foreign capital. The largest sugar mill in the Dominican Republic, at La Romana, is owned by the South Puerto Rico Sugar Company, which also owns the largest mill in Puerto Rico. These large-scale enterprises are making increasing use of machinery for the cultivation of the cane plantations. Tractors are replacing oxen in transporting the harvested cane to the mills. This region has depended on migrant workers to do the harvesting—workers brought in from Jamaica and Puerto Rico, and also from Haiti. But the need for extra labor is decreasing as the use of machinery increases.

Agricultural Colonies

With so much unused land, the Dominican government under Trujillo undertook to occupy the national territory more firmly by planting agricultural colonies. Most of the colonists were Dominicans. Trujillo took care of the urban slum problem by moving people away from the cities, and he also reduced the pressure on his government to provide land for landless tenant farmers by moving many of them into the new settlements. Land was given free, and colonists were to become owners of their farms after a period of about ten years. The government built houses and provided seeds, tools, machinery, and technical supervision. The colonists had to agree that until they became owners they would follow the direction of the authorities regarding the crops to be planted. In this way Trujillo not only provided the country with an adequate supply of basic foods, but also developed a surplus of vegetables for export to other parts of the Antilles. He also avoided the surplus production of crops such as sugar or cacao for which the export market fluctuates considerably from time to time. Furthermore, no colony was left in an isolated place. Each colony was accessible to an all-weather highway, and no colony was more than eight hours by motor truck from the capital.

As a result of such management, the colonial program was highly successful. There were three chief areas of colonization. One was in the lowlands in back of Barahona and in the mountains to the south along the Haitian border. In 1942 a colony of Dominicans was settled along the northern side of Lake Enriquillo on land that was supplied with water for irrigation. The chief crops were rice, coconuts, and bananas. Near Barahona, even during the 1920's, a large sugar mill was built and cane plantations were laid out. Sugarcane and rice are grown on the small delta plains at the southern end of the Cordillera Central.

The mountains south of Barahona have also been occupied. On the eastern and northeastern slopes plantations of coffee have been developed in the shade of the taller trees of the forest which remain uncut. The coffee from this area is reputed to be the best in the country.

From Trujillo's point of view the most important new colonial area was along the Haitian border in the mountainous interior. This is the area where very dense populations of Haitian farmers, making a miserable living on badly eroded lands, looked across the border at almost empty country where cattle grazed on vast private estates. In 1942 a new all-weather road was built near this border, and a string of agricultural colonies was established.

The colonists grow irrigated rice wherever irrigation is possible, and also maize and beans. On the steeper slopes they produce coffee.

The rugged Cordillera Central remains very thinly populated. On the northern slopes there are some excellent pine forests, which cover the mountains as far down as about 1,000 feet above sea level, where they are intermingled with palms. In the 1940's, however, even this empty area was invaded. An all-weather road was built up the valley south of La Vega to reach two resort towns high in the mountains.

Roads and Railroads

The Dominican Republic has few railroads. In fact, Santo Domingo shares with Tegucigalpa the distinction of being a capital city with no rail connections. The Dominican railroads were mostly built about 1875 by British investors to export cacao from the Vega Real to the port of Sánchez. There were also some railroads built about the same time in the older sugarcane plantations.

The modern Dominican Republic, however, is placing its dependence on all-weather roads and motor trucks imported from the United States. Before 1930 the easiest way to get from the Cibao to the capital city was by sea. At that time there were only 578 miles of road in the Dominican Republic. By 1950 the government road-building program had resulted in 2,044 miles of all-weather roads. This was a tremendous and costly job, much of it across steep and rainy mountains. Now there is no settled part of the Republic which is not within eight hours driving time of Santo Domingo. The all-weather truck roads have also had the effect of reducing the number of ports. Santo Domingo is now the leading port. But most of the products of the Cibao are sent out from Puerto Plata or Sánchez. The sugar, as in Cuba, is sent out from ports near the places of harvest, especially La Romana, San Pedro Macorís, and Barahona.

The Dominican Republic as a Political Unit

On May 30, 1961, General Trujillo was assassinated. The years since then have been filled with turmoil as various leaders sought to gain control of the country. As usually happens when a dictatorship is suddenly ended, all the suppressed groups that had been held in check by force could now burst forth. In the absence of any widely held state-idea there was no popular support for any program of development. The economy could only continue to function through large amounts of foreign aid.

The Economic Situation

There are many people who still think of Trujillo as a great leader and able administrator. These are people who believe that economic development must come first before there can be effective social change. There can be no doubt that Trujillo did build up the Dominican economy: on a small island not well-endowed with resources, he was able so to increase the economic production that the country enjoyed a gross national product per capita of $232 in 1955—which placed it seventh among twenty Latin-American republics at that time. To be sure, the income was not widely distributed among the people, and the largest share of a profitable economy went to the dictator and to a small group of wealthy landowners and military and government officials. Furthermore, domestic tranquillity was gained by a program of strict military rule, including the forced resettlement of slum dwellers in agricultural colonies. In spite of the relatively high productivity of the economy, most of the people remained very poor. And the high rate of population increase (3.6 percent per year, which is exceeded in Latin America only by Costa Rica) has meant that the expansion of the economy could not even stay ahead of the annual increase of job seekers. In 1966 the gross national product per capita was $264, which placed the Dominican Republic eighteenth out of twenty-four Latin-American republics.

Under Trujillo, trade was diversified. In 1961 sugar made up 42 percent of the value of all exports, followed by coffee, sorghum, tobacco, and bauxite. In 1965, however, sugar was again producing over half of the value of all exports. The dependence of the republic on the United States was increasing—in 1965 the United States took 88 percent of the exports.

The Political Situation

The other side of the picture of the Dominican Republic under Trujillo was the unrestrained use of force to maintain order and to suppress dissent. Speaking out against Trujillo was not even safe in New York; agents of the dictator abducted a Dominican citizen who was a professor at Columbia University and whose fate has never been conclusively established. The people in the Dominican Republic were never informed about issues of public policy. University students, after the death of Trujillo, noted that the only reports they ever heard from the United States were those favorable to Trujillo. Widely quoted in Santo Domingo were statements by prominent political figures in the United States that what Latin America needed was more men like Trujillo. Criticisms of the dictatorship were carefully excluded from the Dominican newspapers. The average educated Dominican, therefore, believed that the United States talked about democracy and equality of opportunity, but then gave unchallenged support to the harshest of autocratic governments. The fact that Trujillo had been trained by the United States Marines and was supported by continued military missions and by military equipment only confirmed these beliefs.

Since the assassination of Trujillo, no one strong man has appeared to take his place. An election in 1962 gave overwhelming support to a liberal government, devoted to the ideals of democracy and social change. As so often happens, a liberal regime is promptly labelled communist by those whose privileged positions are undermined or threatened. Conflicts within the army led to the exile of the liberal leaders and a return of military control. But which faction of the army should exercise this control had to be decided by force. When the country was in confusion and no one army officer could command enough support to insure control, the United States again dispatched an occupation force in 1965. This was made a part of an international occupation force, responsible to the Organization of American States, which remained in the Dominican Republic until 1966. This occupation was justified as necessary to protect the lives of foreigners in Santo Domingo, and was also recommended by representatives of the United States in the Dominican Republic who feared another communist take-over such as that of the Castro regime in Cuba. There are volumes of published reports proving beyond doubt that the communists were, in fact, responsible for the conflict and were about to seize control; and others that prove, also beyond doubt, that the whole Dominican affair had nothing to do with communism. It seems certain that tightly organized cells of trained communists exist in every country, and the time to seize control is during a period of domestic turmoil. On the other hand, the causes of political disorder in the Dominican Republic can only be understood in terms of the struggle of, on the one hand, a part of the people to rid the country of an autocratic government and to establish the principle that social change should precede economic development, and, on the other hand, the resistance of the politically powerful minority to any rapid change of the traditional system. This basic struggle, which is going on today in one form or another throughout Latin America, is complicated in the Dominican Republic by the personal ambitions of rival political leaders. This is the kind of situation to be expected when a strong dictatorship collapses.

HAITI

In Haiti, more than four-and-a-half million people are crowded into a territory approximately the size of New Jersey. Not less than 95 percent of them are pure-blooded Africans; but the 5 percent who are mulatto, inheriting the European part of their ancestry from the French planters who once owned this section of Hispaniola, now make up the Haitian aristocracy. Most of the Haitians live outside of the economic system of international trade, and even to a certain extent outside of the Haitian political system itself, which touches their lives only remotely. There is a cosmopolitan and well-educated minority of French-speaking landowners and intellectuals, set in striking contrast to the peasant farmers whose own forms of community life are dominated by the practice of religious ceremonies and other traditions inherited from Africa. Order in such a diverse society is maintained by an army under the command of a strong dictator.

Sequence of Settlement

Although five of the fifteen towns established in Hispaniola by the Spaniards early in the sixteenth century were in the western part of the island, by the end of the century none of them had survived, and this part of Hispaniola was quite neglected. In the early seventeenth century, western Hispaniola offered a fine unoccupied land base for the English and French pirates who preyed on the Spanish ships bringing silver and gold back to Spain. About 1625 the Île de la Tortue (Tortuga) became one of the chief pirate strongholds of the Antilles. Bands from this base would come over to Hispaniola to hunt the wild cattle and hogs which had escaped from the Spanish settlements in the east. Large fires were built, and over these the carcasses, laid on grills *(boucans)*, were processed for tallow. Here in the hills of Haiti, the pirates came to be known as *boucaniers,* or buccaneers. In the course of time the French drove out the English, and, supported by the French colonies on other nearby islands, they established settlements on Haiti, especially along the northern coast. In spite of repeated attempts, the Spaniards of eastern Hispaniola could not drive them out, and in 1697 Spain recognized France's claim to the western third of Hispaniola. The new French colony, now officially established, was known as *Saint Domingue.*

The French Period

The century of French ownership witnessed the rise of Saint Domingue to the status of one of the world's richest colonies—almost equal to Java as a producer of revenue for the home government. In those days, when the Antilles were producing sugar for Europe's growing markets, colonies were far from being financial liabilities. The destructive exploitation of land, together with the use of slave labor, could be made, for a time at least, to yield enormous profits to the owners. Colonies today cannot be ravaged for profit in an eighteenth- or nineteenth-century manner without the knowledge of both the home country and the rest of the world, for the television cameras and the illustrated magazines quickly spread the story, if there is a story to be spread.

The settlement of Haiti by the French sugarcane planters was concentrated on the lowlands. The first district to be developed was on the Plaine du Nord, in the territory served by Cap Haïtien, then known as Cap Français. The fertile plain was divided into a rectangular pattern of well-kept roads and large properties, all neatly bordered by hedges. The mansions of the planters were luxurious, and the prosperity of the colony became famous. Seeking more space, the French extended their plantations southward to the other two lowlands, the Artibonite and the Cul de Sac. In 1749 the town of Port-au-Prince was laid out, and in 1770 it was made the seat of government in place of Cap Français.

The shift of the center of French authority to the south was in part a result of the enormous productivity of the Cul de Sac. With the aid of their slaves the French built elaborate systems of irrigation, including long stone aqueducts, some of which are still in use. Because of the larger amount of sunshine received where the rainfall is not so heavy, these dry plains, once their moisture deficiency was remedied by irrigation, proved to be better producers of sugar than the Plaine du Nord. Soon the Cul de Sac had become the chief center of sugar planting.

As the prosperity of the colony grew, other commercial crops were added. In the lowlands, indigo was grown along with the sugarcane. Smaller areas were devoted to bananas, yams, manioc, cacao, coconuts, and cotton. Late in the French period, coffee was introduced, and several important plantations were developed, especially on the slopes of the Cordillera Central south of the Plaine du Nord.

Meanwhile the social situation in Saint Domingue was becoming explosive. The Africans greatly outnumbered the Europeans, but this condition might not have led to disastrous revolts had it not been for the mulatto class. The mulattoes, made free by a decree of the French government but not accepted on terms of equality by either the pure Africans or the pure Europeans, became more and more a source of unrest. In the meantime, Saint Domingue and the sleepy Spanish colonies of eastern Hispaniola had developed along very different lines, and the contrasts in the racial make-up of their settlers had become very great. The figures for the Spanish and the French parts of Hispaniola near the end of the eighteenth century illustrate the difference between the two:

POPULATION OF HISPANIOLA*

Colony	Year	White	Free Negroes and Mulattoes	Slaves
Spanish	1794	35,000	38,000	30,000
French	1789	30,826	27,548	465,429

*M. W. Williams, *The People and Politics of Latin America.* Boston, 1938.

Period of Independence

The liberal political doctrines of the French Revolution had a very special meaning for the mulattoes of Saint Domingue, many of whom had been sent

Heavily cropped mountain slopes of rural Haiti.

to Paris for an education. Talk of freedom and equality, together with considerable political disorder in Saint Domingue, led step by step to a revolt of the Africans, the destruction of the estates, and the hurried escape of such French landowners as were able to avoid death at the hands of their former slaves. In 1804 the Africans of Hispaniola declared their independence and adopted the Indian name of the island, Haiti. The Haitians also invaded eastern Hispaniola and in 1822 brought the whole island under their rule. The eastern part, as we have said, did not become the independent Dominican Republic until 1844.

The period of independence in Haiti resulted in a number of changes in the relation of the people to the land. The breakdown of the systems of irrigation because of the lack of strong central authority made most of the lowlands uninhabitable for an agricultural people. The result was a marked decrease in population in these areas, except in the wet Plaine du Nord and around the shores of the southern peninsula. Great numbers of the Haitians withdrew to the mountain regions, or to the southeastern part of the Plaine Centrale. The former slaves established themselves on small properties on which, with African agricultural techniques, they raised their own supplies of food. Production of sugar for export practically ceased, but the export of coffee was continued. The carefully cultivated plantations of the French were given no attention except at harvest time, and new coffee trees planted on the steep mountain slopes were allowed to grow as wild trees of the forest, entirely without care. Yet the coffee produced in this manner in Haiti proved to possess such an excellent aroma that it commanded a special place on the French market, and is to this day one of the highest-priced coffees in the world. Haitian coffee, mixed with the coffees of Brazil, together with much chicory, gives distinctive flavor to the coffee served in France.

These changes in the distribution of people and in their form of economy produced some interesting changes in the Haitian landscape which can still be observed. Today the French aqueducts, the mansions of the sugar planters, the old stone sugar mills, and many old churches remain only as ruins. The old rectangular field patterns, dear to the hearts of the Frenchmen, have also disappeared under the haphazard and irregular trails and fields of the carefree Haitians. But the old rectangular French patterns have not been entirely lost; from the ground they are no longer visible, but from the air one can still observe the faint trace of straight lines crossing at right angles. One result of the overlap of patterns is the utter confusion of land titles.

The way of living in rural Haiti today is essentially African. There are many forms of entertainment and of religious expression whose origins can be traced to the original homeland of the Africans. Voodooism is the basic religion of the masses. The markets which are held throughout rural Haiti, many of them in the open country, are attended primarily for social pleasure, not for buying and selling. The everyday life of the rural Haitian is made up of a strange mixture of African traits and French traits, with the African ones the more fundamental.

The average rural Haitian is not a person of great ambition, nor one who takes naturally to the complexities of commercial life. There is a well-known Haitian proverb that expresses the matter concisely: "If work were a good thing the rich would have grabbed it all long ago." The Haitian insists on taking pleasure in what he does, and since work does not bring him pleasure he avoids it as much as possible. Compared with the way of living on a plantation in the French period, the way of living of the rural Haitian since independence is simple indeed. Only those things necessary to satisfy the fewest wants are produced, and since the soils of the wetter parts of Haiti continue to yield abundant crops there is no need for great exertion. The attitude toward the land and toward the use of land is essentially African. Land ownership itself does not give prestige to the owner, and there is no urge to sell a surplus of things for profit. In many parts of Haiti there are cooperative agricultural societies organized to work the farms of the members collectively, and to afford the members protection or assistance in the case of accident. Although the land is cleared with the machete and cultivated with the hoe, yet the Haitians are excellent farmers, and their small gardens are made to yield an extraordinary variety of crops with the expenditure, on the part of each individual, of a minimum of labor.

Unfortunately, however, not all the people of independent Haiti are lacking in personal ambition and in the desire for power and prestige. Especially the mulattoes, who, as we have said, often had the advantage of education in Paris, take a keen interest in politics. In the course of time the government was effectively concentrated in the hands of not more than 300 mulatto families, and the majority of the former slaves found that they had new masters who also expected to be obeyed.

The political factions which developed brought chaos to Haiti. Each group in turn, as it came to power, raided the public treasury, and political corruption brought the country to financial ruin. Insecurity in the rural districts was a result not only of banditry, but also of the system of recruiting for the army—for an army had to be maintained to keep a political faction in power after it had been successful in seizing that power, and other armies had to be recruited to carry on a successful revolt. The able-bodied men were "conscripted" wherever they could be found. As a result, the men feared to venture forth on the trails, and attendance at the markets was largely restricted to the women.

From 1915 to 1934 Haiti was occupied by the United States Marines. The landings in Haiti took place a year earlier than those in the neighboring Dominican Republic. The chaotic internal conditions in Haiti during the early years of World War I were considered a threat to the defense of the Panama Canal. After the war the Marines remained to keep the peace among rival political factions. Troops from the United States were finally withdrawn in 1934 in the era of the Good Neighbor policy.

Haiti as a Political Unit

When Haiti is considered as a political unit, the most striking fact about the country is its very great poverty. Its gross national product per capita of only $78 in 1955 was one of the lowest in the world. The Haitians have no tradition of democratic processes, in spite of the influence of the French Revolution on the Haitian mulattoes. Haitian independence was gained by a revolt against slavery; when independence was gained the people were happy to be rid of their French masters, and they did not welcome new ones.

The Economic Situation

When Haiti became an independent country it had fewer than 500,000 inhabitants. From 1789 until 1950 there had been no census, nor was it thought that a census would be possible. For many years in the present century the Haitian population was regularly estimated to be about 3 million, but no one could be certain of the figure. In 1950, however, Haiti actually joined with most of the other Latin-American countries in taking a census. In that year it counted 3,097,000 people, of whom only 8 percent lived in cities and towns. Port-au-Prince, the capital and largest town, had a population in 1950 of 143,000, in 1960 of 240,000. The population is so widely spread over the whole of the

An outlying part of Port-au-Prince, Haiti.

national territory that the over-all density figure has some meaning—289 people per square mile. The rate of increase, due to the lack of past censuses, is not at all certain, but it seems to be less rapid than that of the Dominican Republic. In 1967 the population was estimated to be 4,600,000, or 488 people per square mile.

The poverty of Haiti is difficult to measure. How can a value be placed on food crops consumed by the growers? The figure for a gross national product contains too many estimates, in the making of which the Haitian peasants are not consulted. Poverty, however, can be given in terms of decreasing yields of crops, which can be observed even if not counted. The heavy and continued use of steep mountain slopes from which the forest cover has been removed results in extreme forms of soil erosion. There are large parts of Haiti in which the productivity of the land has been so reduced that the inhabitants can barely avoid starvation.

There are, of course, some exports and imports, which are of interest either to foreign corporations, to a few wealthy Haitian landowners, or to a few merchants in the cities. Of all the exports in 1965, coffee made up 48 percent, going chiefly to France. Sugar made up 7 percent, coming chiefly from one United States-owned mill, located a few miles to the east of Port-au-Prince. The western part of the Cul de Sac has again been developed for sugarcane, with workers paid wages. Sisal made up 5 percent of the exports, grown chiefly along the northern coast near the border of the Dominican Republic. There are also small areas where cacao, cotton, and bananas are produced for export. The continued cutting of logwood for timber which is exported, and the cutting of forests to make charcoal which is not exported, have both contributed to the destruction of the land through accelerated erosion. An attempt was made with foreign assistance to plant new forests on the steeper slopes, making use of such commercially valuable species as bamboo, teak, tung, and mahogany.

The Political Situation

The political situation in Haiti is chaotic. About 89 percent of the people cannot read or write and therefore are not reached directly by party political action. To be sure, Haiti has an amazing system of communication by means of drums which spread news rapidly to the most remote mountain hamlets. But there is no means for discussing issues of public policy, and no disposition on the part of the political leaders to permit such discussion. Political controversy is apt to be violent, even though limited to a small minority, mostly in Port-au-Prince.

Yet in a way there is more cohesion in Haiti the state than is to be found in most other Latin-American countries. The Haitian has one strongly held state-idea—that his government must keep Haiti free, and that the people of Haiti must be shielded from any authority. The fact that Haiti is the only French-speaking Negro republic in the Americas is a matter of national pride. Haitian delegates, who speak English or Spanish well enough, insist in Pan-American gatherings that the proceedings be translated into French. French and African traditions constitute an important part of the Haitian state-idea. Yet no government in Haiti would last long if it should attempt to use force in changing the way of living of the individual peasant.

The rural Haitian supports the idea of a Negro republic; but more than anything he supports his own personal independence. He owns a little piece of land—not large enough to give him a good living, but large enough to give him contentment. He is in no mood to join a revolution or a crusade. One party is about as bad as another in charge of the government. It doesn't much matter so long as the government attends to its business and leaves the individual alone. Here is truly a unique society in the American hemisphere, and one that adds one more element of diversity to the already diverse American scene.

Commonwealth of
Puerto Rico

Area: 3,435 square miles
Population: (1966 estimate) 2,713,000
          (last census, 1960) 2,349,544
Capital city: San Juan: (1964) 442,300
Percent urban: (1960) 44.2
Birth rate per 1,000: (1966) 30.2; Death rate per 1,000: (1966) 6.6
Annual percent of increase: (1958–64) 2.0
Percent literate: (1960) 83.0
Percent of labor force in agriculture: (1964) 21.3
Gross national product per capita: (1966) $1,120
Unit of currency: U.S. dollar

COMMERCE, 1963–1964 *(expressed in percentage of values)*

Exports

textiles 24   (1956, sugar 48, textiles 22)
sugar   14

Chapter 13 □ The Commonwealth of Puerto Rico

Something very important has happened in Puerto Rico. All over the world there are countries where a crowded population struggles hopelessly to make a bare living from antiquated agriculture. Each year the increase of people is greater than the increase of the gross national product, and each year the destruction of the resource base becomes more and more apparent. Enmeshed in a cycle of poverty, there seems no way out. Before 1940, Puerto Rico was such a country. When it became a possession of the United States as a result of the Spanish-American War it was already deep in the kind of rural poverty associated with the Spanish agrarian tradition. Then came the great sugar corporations, together with the medical services; with a high birth rate and a falling death rate, the net increase of population became alarming. In the 1930's Puerto Rico was described as "the greatest concentration of destitute people under the flag of the United States." But since 1940, Puerto Rico has provided the world with a demonstration of how such a situation can be changed, and how this can be done within the framework of the democratic system. Now thousands of visitors come to Puerto Rico from the under-developed countries of the world to see for themselves that a miracle has taken place.

The transformation of Puerto Rico, however, is no miracle. It is the result of inspired leadership and hard work. Here a Latin-American political leader, Luis Muñoz Marín, adopted a program of economic and social reform instead of seeking solutions in the traditional way through political change. Instead of demanding complete independence from the "Yankee imperialists," Muñoz laid before the Puerto Ricans an alternative. In 1952, with the approval of the Congress of the United States and with the support of more than 80 percent of the voters of Puerto Rico, this little island became the Commonwealth of Puerto Rico, voluntarily associated with the United States.[1] The more than two and a half million Puerto Ricans maintain their citizenship in the United States, travel freely back and forth to the mainland, enjoy a position within the huge area of free commercial exchange, and at the same time are granted all the rights of self-government. A program of balanced economic development has not only improved the agricultural picture, but has also led to the rapid increase of manufacturing industry, until, since 1956, the value of manufactured products has been greater than the value of agricultural products. The problems of poverty have not been solved, for Puerto Rico still has 764 people per square mile, 56 percent of them rural. But life for these people is no longer hopeless: they have a new exciting state-idea and a reason to work hard. In 1967 the Puerto Ricans again voted by a large majority to maintain their status as a self-governing Commonwealth associated with the United States.

The state-idea is made up of all the reasons why the people of Puerto Rico support their form of government. There is not just one simple reason, but a complex of ideas that make a people feel a love of country, or *patria*. As Muñoz Marín once said: "To the Puerto Rican, *patria* is the colors of the landscape, the change of the seasons, the smell of the earth wet with fresh rain, the voice of the streams, the crash of the ocean against the shore, the fruits, the songs, the habits of work and leisure, the typical dishes for special occasions and the meager ones for everyday, the flowers, the valleys, and the pathways. But even more than these things *patria* is the people: their way of life, spirit, folkways, customs, their ways of getting along with each other."[2] The Puerto Ricans can now look at the changes taking place in their land and say with feeling, *"Es bueno, y es nuestro"*—it is good, and it is ours.

The Land

Puerto Rico is a little island about 35 miles wide by 105 miles long. It is formed by a tightly folded and faulted arch, the eastern end of the Central-American–Antillean system of structures. The Cordillera Central is a continuation of the mountains of Hispaniola, from which it is separated only by the downfaulted Mona Passage. The highest peak on the backbone of Puerto Rico is just under 4,400 feet in elevation—but just north of Puerto Rico is the deepest place in the Atlantic Ocean, a fault trough which lies 30,246 feet below the surface. Puerto Rico is the much-eroded top of a great mountain system.

Very little of the island is flat, and the flat places that do exist are almost all along the coast (Map 33, p. 227). On the northern side, behind a coastal

---

[1]The relationship with the United States is expressed in Spanish: *Estado Libre Asociado.*
[2]Luis Muñoz Marín, "Development through Democracy," *The Annals of the American Academy of Political and Social Science,* Vol. 283, January 1953, pp. 1–8.

lowland, there is a zone of limestone terraces, standing not very much above the sea, but dissected to a rolling, hilly country by the numerous streams. The mountains begin abruptly south of these terraces, which are especially wide in the western part of the island. The north-facing mountain slopes are deeply dissected by the many streams which have formed narrow valleys and sharp ridges. The main crest of the Cordillera Central, which is also the divide between the streams that flow north and those that flow south, is only ten miles from the southern coast. On the rainy north side the streams are cutting vigorously, but on the drier south side many of the stream channels are filled with water only after a shower. Below the rugged belt of foothills, including a series of cuestas of tilted limestone strata, the south coast, like the north coast, is fringed by sea-border plains.

Because of the simple arrangement of these structural features the contrast between rainy northern and eastern slopes and dry southern and western slopes is sharply marked, but the variety of the contrasts is not so great as that in rugged Hispaniola. On the northeast coast, San Juan, the capital and chief city, receives a rainfall of 60 inches—which in these latitudes may be considered moderate. Ponce, on the southwest coast, receives only about 36 inches—an amount which is quite inadequate to support more than a scanty scrub woodland and which does not permit agriculture without irrigation. Ponce has somewhat higher temperatures in summer and about the same temperatures in winter as San Juan, although both enjoy the "temperate" tropical climate characteristic of the trade-wind islands. The rainfalls of the interior of the island on some of the higher slopes of the northern side are well over 100 inches.

The Course of Settlement

Puerto Rico was a paradise for the Indians, who took advantage of its productive lands to reap abundant harvests; and when the Spaniards saw a prosperous and contented Indian population, they thought they too had found a paradise. When the white men first settled on the island in 1508, there were probably between 80,000 and 100,000 native people living on it. But by 1515 the dreadful epidemics of imported diseases had reduced the Indians to not more than 4,000. As a result the plantations were abandoned and the search for precious metals given up. A few groups of colonists remained in San Juan and Ponce, and most of the interior of the island was used for the grazing of herds of cattle on large estates.

In the eighteenth century, however, Puerto Rico, along with the other Spanish possessions in the Antilles, shared moderately in the sugar prosperity. Into Puerto Rico, as into Cuba and Santo Domingo, there was some importation of African slaves, and in certain localities the cultivation of sugarcane was commercially important. About 1790 the Spanish colonies produced roughly

14,000 metric tons of sugar, while the French colonies were producing over 90,000 tons and the English colonies nearly 80,000 tons.

In Puerto Rico the new sugarcane plantations were mostly located on the lands of low relief near the coast, and in these areas the African population soon came to outnumber the Europeans. The poorer Europeans were forced out of the sugar districts, for free workers cannot compete in the same area with slaves. In the mountainous interior the "poor whites" settled as squatters on the vast, unfenced cattle range of the large landowners, and supported themselves with a shifting cultivation of maize and beans.

Between 1800 and 1825 the island colony received a considerable number of immigrants of European ancestry to balance the increase of Africans. Some of these came from Spain—from Gallegos, Asturia, and the Balearic Islands; no doubt they selected Puerto Rico because it was one of the few Spanish possessions in the New World in which the spirit of revolt from the mother country had not developed. A number of immigrants to Puerto Rico came from the other Spanish possessions in America from which they had been forced to flee because of their loyalty to the Spanish crown. Consequently, the proportion of people of European ancestry increased, and the proportion of people with African ancestry decreased. It is now estimated that 54 percent of the Puerto Ricans are of unmixed European ancestry, 40 percent are mixed European and African, and about 5 percent are African.

During the nineteenth century the colonies left to Spain in the American Hemisphere suffered from neglect and poverty. The economic collapse resulting from the decline of sugar prosperity was of course greater in those islands where the prosperity had been greater; but places like Puerto Rico also felt the effects. The Spanish government, involved with difficulties of its own in Europe, could do little to help the remnants of its colonial empire. In the nearly four centuries of Spanish rule in Puerto Rico only 166 miles of road were built, and these mostly in the sugarcane districts along the coast. The interior was all but inaccessible, and therefore was limited in its possibilities of commercial production to cattle that could be driven out to market over rough trails, or to some high-grade commodity that could command a price high enough to offset the costs of transportation by muleback. The large landowners introduced coffee and made use of the poor-white settlers of the interior as tenants and sharecroppers. So fine was the aroma of the Puerto Rican coffee that it commanded a special place on the Spanish market, much as Haitian coffee commanded a special place on the French market. The transportation costs were so high, however, that even with the high prices the Puerto Rican coffee could bring, only a small net profit was left to the landowners, very little of which was passed on to the tenants.

At the end of the nineteenth century, Puerto Rico showed all the worst aspects of the Spanish colonial system. There was the usual concentration of land ownership and wealth in the hands of a very small group, which was enabled to maintain positions of prestige and economic security through the exploitation of the much larger laboring population. In Puerto Rico these exploited rural workers were not Indians, and only in the sugar plantations along the coast were they African; in the interior the tenants were almost pure European. The majority of the people lived in isolation, illiterate and ignorant of the most elementary rules of hygiene, and producing barely enough food to maintain themselves. The political, social, and commercial life was centered in San Juan and involved the participation of only a small fraction of the total population. Such was the condition of Puerto Rico in 1898 when, largely as a result of forces and events elsewhere, this last remaining Spanish colony became a possession of the United States.

A Territorial Possession of the United States

The United States set to work right away to provide the new colony with all sorts of public works. By 1919 the mileage of all-weather roads had been increased from 166 to 739, and as a result the landowners even in the remote districts could bring products to market cheaply enough to make a substantial profit. Schools were established, and in some of them the newer techniques of agriculture and animal husbandry were taught. The proportion of people able to read and write was greatly increased. Sanitary measures were undertaken, and certain diseases, such as yellow fever, were virtually stamped out. As a result the death rate was rapidly reduced. With a high birth rate (30.2 per thousand in 1962) and a low death rate (6.6 per thousand) the population was increasing at about 2 percent per year—which is low in comparison with other Antillean countries. The average life expectancy at birth has gone up from 38 years in 1910 to 70 years in 1960. Population and growth rates from 1899 to 1966 are given in the table.

POPULATION INCREASE IN PUERTO RICO*

Year	Population	Annual Percent of Growth	Density Per Square Mile
1899	953,000		277
1910	1,118,000	1.4	325
1920	1,300,000	1.6	378
1930	1,544,000	1.7	449
1940	1,869,000	1.9	544
1950	2,211,000	1.7	642
1960	2,349,000	2.4	687
1966	2,625,000	2.0	764

*Data from 1899 to 1950 from Kingsley Davis, "Puerto Rico: A Crowded Island," *The Annals of the American Academy of Political and Social Science,* Vol. 285, 1953, p. 116; data for 1960 from U.S. Census; estimates for 1966 by the Population Reference Bureau.

Little by little it became apparent that a purely agricultural economy could not provide support for such population densities, and that all efforts to increase the gross national product were being frustrated by the increase in the net rate of growth. In the period 1950 to 1955 the birth rate was 36, and the death rate had fallen to 8—lower than that of any other political unit in Latin America. The rising net rate of increase was largely the result of better hygiene and better diet for babies.

Meanwhile, the economy of Puerto Rico had been built around the cultivation of sugarcane and the export of sugar. There are about 1 million acres of land in Puerto Rico suitable for the cultivation of crops. Of these, 300,000 acres were held by four large sugar corporations, and although the total area of sugarcane in 1940 was only 76,000 acres, the remainder was held in reserve and used to pasture the oxen needed for transporting the cane. That meant that in 1940, when the population density was 544 people per square mile of total territory, there was less than half an acre per person for commercial crops other than cane and for the basic food crops. Furthermore, much of the remainder was former cane land that had been so badly eroded as to be almost worthless without expensive reconditioning. In spite of an increasing migration of people to New York City, the poverty of those remaining grew more and more serious.

Poverty in Puerto Rico was further complicated by the nature of the sugarcane industry. As was the case in pre-Castro Cuba, the need for laborers is spread very unevenly throughout the year. There is always a certain amount of work to be done in clearing new land, plowing, planting cane, weeding, and maintaining irrigation and drainage ditches; but this off-season work adds up to only a small fraction of the labor demanded at the harvest season. For most of the people who were crowded around the sugar district there was no employment at all for several months each year, and then a period of employment and steady income during the harvest from January to June. When wages were paid they were higher in the cane plantations than elsewhere. As a result, in the period from 1900 to 1949 the coffee-growing district of the interior lost about 13 percent of its rural population; the cane areas in the same period increased 31 percent. It was estimated, about 1940, that the average annual income of a cane worker was approximately $250—all concentrated in a few months of the year.

Most of the people who worked part of the year for the sugar companies lived with their families in the poor districts of the cities, especially San Juan. They occupied shacks made from any available materials and crowded together without water, light, or streets. One of the densest slums in San Juan was *El Fanguito* (the mudhole) which covered two miles along the mud flats at the water's edge. The children of these workers saw American movies and were exposed to American advertisements. If on special occasions the daughters emerged from these districts dressed to imitate the Hollywood mode, with silk stockings and high heels, this was no indication that the family had enough to eat.

The Transformation of Puerto Rico

The transformation of Puerto Rico began in 1940. Since 1929, when the economy of the United States was shaken by the great depression, there had been little new capital investment in Puerto Rico, and production had been cut. Widespread destitution was causing considerable unrest. It was during the late 1930's that Muñoz Marín organized the Popular Democratic Party with the slogan, "Bread, Land, and Liberty." The new party was successful in 1940, and has won every election since that date. In 1947 the Organic Act was changed to permit the Puerto Ricans to elect their own governor. In 1948 Muñoz Marín became the first elected governor of the Commonwealth.

The Improvement of Agriculture

When the Popular Democratic Party came into power in the Puerto Rican Congress in 1940, reforms in the system of land tenure were immediately started. An act passed by the Congress of the United States in 1917 provided that no corporation might possess more than 500 acres of land, but this act had never been enforced. In 1940, about a third of all the arable land was owned by four sugar corporations, and there were many privately owned estates owning well over the legal limit. The Puerto Rico Land Act of 1941 gave the island government permission to acquire illegally-held land, and within the next ten years almost all of the holdings in excess of 500 acres were purchased from the corporations and from the private owners. On the land thus acquired, small cane farmers were established on what were called "Proportional Profit farms," where each worker was paid a share of the profits in proportion to the amount of work he had put in. There were also small owner-operated plantations, and a considerable increase of land where the tenants could raise food crops for their own use.

Land redistribution and the improvement of agriculture were not done blindly in Puerto Rico. The Puerto Rico Planning Board, of which the chairman was the geographer Dr. Rafael Picó, undertook to provide guidance for the more efficient use of the island's resources. A first step was an inventory and evaluation of the resource base and of the land use. This was the Puerto Rico Rural Land Classification Program under the direction of Clarence F. Jones and Rafael Picó.[3] Between September 1949 and August 1951 detailed

[3]Reported in Clarence F. Jones and others, *The Rural Land Classification Program of Puerto Rico*, Northwestern University Studies in Geography, No. 1, Evanston, Ill., 1952; and Clarence F. Jones and Rafael Picó, *Symposium on the Geography of Puerto Rico*, Río Piedras, P.R., 1955.

maps (1:10,000) of land quality and land use were made for the whole island. With the information thus made available, the planning for economic development could be carried out with the maximum effectiveness. Maps of recommended land uses were drawn up, roads were laid out, rural electrification was undertaken, and the specific sites for new residential and industrial developments were selected. The utility of such a survey goes far beyond its cost, and is reflected in improved agriculture and in an increased flow of products to markets.

Map 38 shows the areas (in solid black) that are still used to grow sugarcane. The coffee district and the tobacco district occupy the western and the eastern parts of the mountains respectively. Intermingled with sugarcane, coffee, and tobacco are many areas used to grow food crops, especially maize. Much land is also used for pasture, and there are many fields growing up in brush as a part of the cycle of land rotation. The relatively small areas used to grow coconuts and pineapples are of great economic importance. In accordance with the new land-use plan, the rainy watersheds are left with a protective cover of forest.

Great changes were introduced into the system of sugarcane production. Before 1940 the northeast coastal area was divided into a few large properties. One absentee-owned corporation operated a plantation of nearly 15,000 acres to the east of San Juan. Closer to the capital the cane plantations were owned by a few wealthy Puerto Ricans and Spaniards. By 1950, however, the sugar mills in this area east of San Juan were grinding cane produced on nearly 47,000 acres of Proportional Profit farms, each about 100 acres in size. The government had acquired the land from the private owners and had leased it to experienced individuals who would direct the planting of the cane. The workers hired by these lessees are paid at rates that are standard for sugarcane workers, and that are now higher than they were before 1940. The lessee gets from 5 to 15 percent of the profit from the sale of the cane, and the remainder is divided proportionally among the workers, depending on how much time each has given to the plantation. In addition, each plantation must leave 15 percent of its area for the free use of the workers' families for the production of basic foods, chiefly maize. Proportional Profit farms have now replaced the private properties of more than 500 acres all the way around the margins of the island. Where large cane plantations were once operated by the corporations or by private planters, now the corporations restrict their activities to the grinding of the cane, the production of raw sugar, and the export of sugar, or the sale of it to the few refineries in Puerto Rico. Because of the increased use of machinery, the land once required for the pasture of oxen can now be used for agriculture, primarily for food crops to be used in Puerto Rico. Since the export of sugar to the mainland is fixed by the system of quotas, some of the new acreage made available by the land redistribution program has been used for an expansion of other crops than

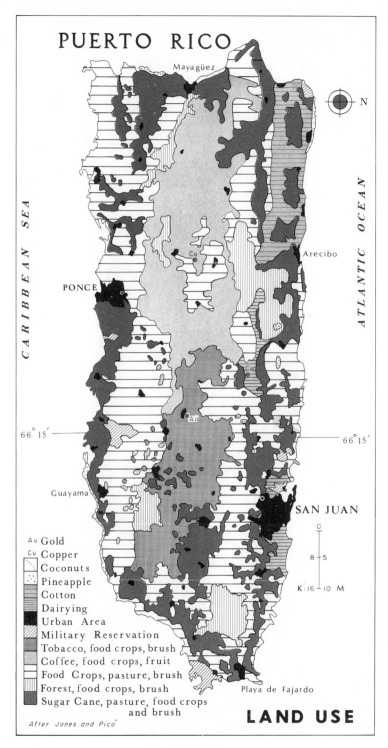

PUERTO RICO

Mayagüez

Arecibo

PONCE

Cu

N

CARIBBEAN SEA

ATLANTIC OCEAN

66° 15′   66° 15′

Guayama

SAN JUAN

Playa de Fajardo

Au Gold
Cu Copper
Coconuts
Pineapple
Cotton
Dairying
Urban Area
Military Reservation
Tobacco, food crops, brush
Coffee, food crops, fruit
Food Crops, pasture, brush
Forest, food crops, brush
Sugar Cane, pasture, food crops
        and brush

After Jones and Picó

0
8 5
K 16 10 M

LAND USE

Map 38

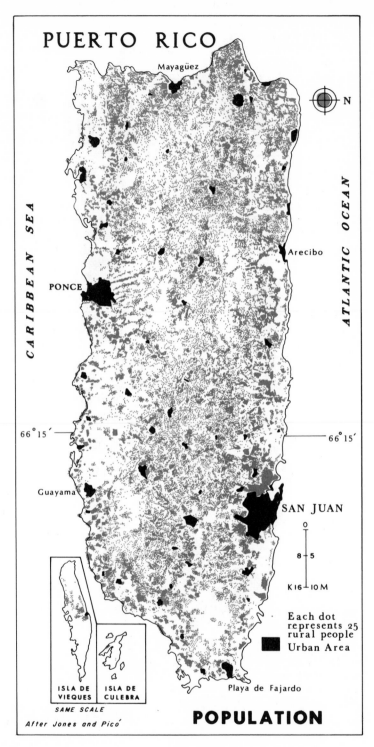

PUERTO RICO

Mayagüez

CARIBBEAN SEA

ATLANTIC OCEAN

N

Arecibo

PONCE

66°15′   66°15′

Guayama

SAN JUAN

0
8 — 5
K16 — 10 M

Each dot
represents 25
rural people
Urban Area

ISLA DE
VIEQUES

ISLA DE
CULEBRA

SAME SCALE
After Jones and Picó

Playa de Fajardo

POPULATION

Map 39

Dissected terraces in rugged country south of San Juan. *Photo by Earl Parker Hanson.*

sugarcane. The other crops in the sugarcane area include coconuts, sea-island cotton, and winter vegetables for sale in the mainland markets.

On the wet northern foothills of the mountains inland from San Juan, and in a band extending westward from San Juan, there are numerous fruit plantations. The products are chiefly pineapples and grapefruit, both of which find a ready market on the mainland. Mixed with the farms devoted to the production of fruit in this area, there are many small properties growing sugarcane, tobacco, and a great variety of food crops for the domestic market.

In the rainy east-central part of the Cordillera Central the chief commerical crop is tobacco. Because of the steep slopes of this area, machinery cannot be used, and great care must be taken to control soil erosion. Only about 20 percent of the tobacco area is used for tobacco in any one year, yet this crop is the one that brings almost the whole cash income of the farmers. The plants are started in seed beds and set out in January. It takes only three months for the crop to mature, and then a second crop can be planted in the same field. In the rotation system, tobacco is usually followed by a variety of food crops, then by pasture, then by a period of rest during which the surface is covered by a second-growth of scrubby brush. Most of

289

the farms are operated by their owners, and most of them are less than 50 acres in size.

The rainiest and most rugged part of the mountains of Puerto Rico are those in the west-central area. This is the chief coffee area, for coffee is a form of land use that offers a maximum protection for steep slopes in wet climates. Puerto Rico has been producing coffee since 1736. Although some coffee is grown on almost every farm and plantation throughout the island, the concentration in the coffee district is notable. The story of coffee production, however, involves ups and downs of prosperity. In 1897, just before Puerto Rico became a possession of the United States, coffee was the leading export of the island, with sugar only about a third as valuable. But in 1899 Puerto Rico was seriously damaged by a hurricane, which was especially destructive to tree-crops such as coffee. As a possession of the United States the Puerto Ricans found themselves cut off from their former coffee market in Spain; and they found that the people of the United States did not like the rich aroma of the Puerto Rican product. Coffee production did, however, gradually come back, until by 1915 there was almost as much production as in 1897. The chief markets were in Europe, especially in Germany. Then in 1928 the coffee plantations were again destroyed by a hurricane. The recovery this time was hampered by the great depression and by the closing of European markets by tariff restrictions. In the period just before 1940, coffee exports made up scarcely 1 percent of total exports, yet some 20 percent of all the farms and plantations listed coffee as the chief source of income. On the steep, rainy slopes of the west-central region no other crop could fit so well the physical limitations of the habitat.

The program of agricultural improvement, therefore, could not neglect the coffee problem. Six steps were taken to bring relief to planters: (1) the creation of a Coffee Insurance Corporation to insure the growers against hurricanes; (2) the organization of a fund to provide subsidy for those coffee planters who used approved plantation methods, including methods of soil conservation; (3) an overall subsidy for the coffee harvest in order to make it possible to offer coffee for sale at prices competitive with those of the Central American countries; (4) the development of a soil-conservation program in the mountainous parts of the island; (5) the establishment of agricultural experiment stations to improve the plantation methods and the variety of coffee plants; and (6) the purchase of the steeper lands from the private owners to provide for reforestation. In many places the coffee planters are using some of their properties to increase the production of limes, vanilla, plantains, bananas, and oranges.

Manufacturing Industry

To be successful, programs for the economic development of preindustrial countries must be applied to all aspects of the national economy. Where manufacturing industries are built without sufficient attention to increasing the productivity of agriculture, the result can be run-away inflation of food prices. But to try to increase agricultural production without providing employment for the people who are forced out of farming also leads to disaster. When antiquated and inefficient farm systems are improved this inevitably means that fewer people can be employed in agriculture. A part of the explanation of the success of Puerto Rico in its efforts to do something about economic underdevelopment has been the program of industrialization.

Manufacturing industry required cheap electric power. One of the first efforts of the government was the construction of new hydroelectric and steam-electric plants. By 1958 the National Planning Association study of Puerto Rico reported that here was a country in which the hydroelectric potential was fully developed.[4] A grid of transmission lines now provides electricity to all parts of the island, supplying power not only for cities and industries, but also making possible a program of rural electrification unique in Latin America.

The industrialization of Puerto Rico began with the construction by the government of a modern cement plant in 1939. This plant, and others built since that date, now provide building materials for the many new construction programs under way—for factories, highways, and low-cost housing. The government proceeded to build factories to be offered to manufacturing establishments as an inducement to move to Puerto Rico. Industries were also offered a ten-year exemption from the payment of taxes. The result was a rapid expansion of manufacturing as many companies on the mainland either moved to Puerto Rico or established branch plants there. Because the island contains no mineral resources (other than limestone, salt, and building stone) it was obviously inadvisable to insist first on the establishment of a steel industry. Instead the government planning agencies looked for a variety of light and medium industries that might either process the agricultural products of the island, or that might import raw materials and profit from the value added by manufacture. The great human resource of Puerto Rico—its dense population of willing workers, ready to be trained in special skills—was used as the basis for a sound industrial development.

In 1956 the contribution of manufacturing industry to the gross production of goods and services passed ahead of the contribution of agriculture. By this date there were some 500 new industrial plants offering 40,000 new jobs; and for each worker in a manufacturing plant there were several new job opportunities in the great variety of service occupations. The largest industry was a $2 million dollar plant built by the General Electric Company to manufacture circuit breakers. But there were all kinds of other industries: manufacturers of electric coils, rubber buckets, screen wire, synthetic textiles, neckties, frozen

[4]William H. Stead, *Fomento—The Economic Development of Puerto Rico,* National Planning Association, Planning Pamphlet 103, Washington, D.C., 1958.

foods, brassieres, ball-point pens, and hundreds of other items for the consumers' market on the mainland. As each plant was established it resulted in a transformation of the community life around it. In one little town on the south coast, long impoverished because of the seasonal unemployment of the sugarcane workers, the branch plant of a well-known mainland manufacturing concern was established. At the new plant 400 workers were hired, most of them women who had never worked before. The annual payroll amounted to $1,250,000. Almost at once a jewelry store was opened, then a furniture store, then a store selling a variety of electric appliances. A market developed for used cars. The old retail food stores could no longer handle the volume of business. This is the kind of transformation that has been going on all over Puerto Rico. By 1961 the average Puerto Rican family could buy nearly twice as many goods and services as could be purchased in 1940.

The increase in the number and size of manufacturing industries continues to accelerate. Now there are over 2,000 industries, giving employment to more than 16 percent of the working force. In the late 1960's a whole new group of industries was being attracted by capital investment in petrochemicals. On the basis of imported oil, a great variety of chemicals became available. This permitted the establishment of dozens of satellite industries, giving employment to thousands of workers, producing a great variety of things ranging from fertilizers to plastics. By the end of 1966 the investment in the production of basic chemicals had passed $250 million, and it was estimated that by 1975 the investment in factories to make things from chemicals would pass the billion mark.

Other Elements of Economic Development

There are other elements included in the program of economic development in addition to the improvement of agriculture and the development of manufacturing. Geological investigations have uncovered two important bodies of copper ore, and the mining of this ore will provide additional support for the economy. There has been a vast program of slum clearance, especially in the suburbs of San Juan. Low-cost housing provides homes for people whose shacks have been pushed out of the way by bulldozers. The road-building program has been extended all over the island. No place is now far from a paved motor highway. There is a fine new airport near San Juan, and smaller airports at all the lesser towns.

The Puerto Ricans are anxious to get their share of the growing tourist business. In San Juan, and at many outlying places along the shores, new luxury hotels have been built, attracting more than a million visitors a year. With the closing of the tourist attractions at Habana, San Juan has become popular, and has been made easily accessible by a reduction of the economy-class plane fares from New York.

Puerto Rico as a Political Unit

Puerto Rico has been transformed since 1940, and since 1952 it has been an independent commonwealth, voluntarily associated with the United States. The people of Puerto Rico have a state-idea—loyalty to their *patria* brings coherence and unity such as has been achieved in few other parts of Latin America. And while Puerto Rico has certainly benefited from its association with the United States, the leadership, the planning, and the hard work of transformation has all been strictly Puerto Rican.

The Economic Situation

Until 1960 the annual rate of population increase continued to rise. The table on page 283 shows that in 1960 the net growth was 2.4 percent. The fact is that an increase in the productivity of an economy in a country with a high birth rate has the first effect of increasing this rate. But a program of family limitation in the 1960's brought the growth rate down to 2.0 percent in 1966.

The program of economic development has been racing against the rate of population increase. The average annual rate of increase in the value of goods and services of 2.4 percent between 1940 and 1964 was about even with the rate of population growth. In 1966 the value of the gross national product per capita was more than $1,000. Although this placed Puerto Rico in the lead in Latin America, even slightly ahead of Venezuela, it was only about half of the value of economic production per capita in the poorest state of the United States—Alabama.

There are many other statistical data that demonstrate the favorable economic and demographic condition of Puerto Rico. In 1964 the proportion of the working force employed in agriculture was down to 21.3 percent. In that year 16.2 percent were employed in manufacturing industries, 8.7 percent were employed in construction, 6.4 percent in transportation and communication, and 44.5 percent in service occupations, including retail and wholesale trade. Yet the increase of jobs in manufacturing and in service occupations was not fast enough to take care of the farmers who were pushed out of farming: more than 11 percent of the potential working force was unemployed. Puerto Rico is distinctive in the proportion of the Commonwealth budget that is assigned to education—nearly 30 percent, which is the highest proportion of any national budget in the world. Some 96 percent of children between the ages of six and twelve are in school, and of the total population 83 percent is classed as literate—a rate that is exceeded in Latin America only by Argentina, Uruguay, Barbados, and Costa Rica.

The Political Situation

Since the formation of the Popular Democratic Party by Muñoz Marín and its first victory at the polls in 1940, this new party has never lost an election. The transformation of Puerto Rico has been accomplished by thoroughly democratic processes, with ample opportunity for the issues involved to be discussed publicly, and with the decision left to a plebiscite secretly recorded and honestly counted. Puerto Rico is a demonstration to the world that the problems of poverty and inequality, and of the denial of human dignity, which loom so large throughout Latin America, can be solved within the framework of democracy.

Muñoz Marín himself records the stages of his thinking about the political problem involved. At first it seemed that there were only two alternatives: to demand complete independence from the United States, or to accept inclusion within the United States as another State. Many people were inclined to think of independence as the only way to escape from the status of a dependent colony. But independence, even when granted with terms as favorable as those offered to the Philippines, meant eventual exclusion from the mainland market, and eventual restrictions on population migration. Clearly, Puerto Rico did not possess either the resources or the financial backing to support a purely domestic economic development. And in spite of the ill-effects of the period of administration by the United States between 1899 and 1948, the Puerto Ricans during that time had learned to place a higher value on economic development than did most of the other Latin-Americans. To be incorporated as a State was not at all popular in Puerto Rico, and although there are some who think that this must eventually be done, this move would not yet receive the endorsement of anything like a majority of the people. The more they develop the feeling of loyalty to *patria,* the less they are likely to accept any plan of incorporation in the United States.

The third way, developed by Muñoz Marín, seems to permit the Puerto Ricans both to have their cake and eat it. The Commonwealth elects its own governor (as it started doing in 1948); it remains essentially self-governing with regard to domestic matters; it has its own Constitution developed within the framework of the Constitution of the United States; the people enjoy all the rights of United States citizenship except that they may not vote for the president, and because they do not vote for president they pay no income tax on money earned in Puerto Rico; taxes collected in Puerto Rico remain in the Commonwealth treasury. Puerto Rico is a separate, self-governing country; yet it is an integral part of the United States. The present status of Puerto Rico was approved by the United States Congress and accepted by the people of Puerto Rico in 1952 and reaffirmed in 1967.

Puerto Rico is a better answer to the communists than all the rockets, satellites, or bombs that might be produced. That Puerto Rico has been successful in its transformation carries with it more meaning for the future of mankind than all the noisier events of the modern period on which the attention of the world's people is focused.

Jamaica

Area: 4,244 square miles
Population: (1967 estimate) 1,890,000
           (last census, 1960) 1,609,814
Capital city: Kingston; (1960) 376,520
Percent urban: (1960) 23.6
Birth rate per 1,000: (1966) 39.4; Death rate per 1,000: (1966) 7.9
Annual percent of increase: (1958–64) 1.8
Percent literate: (1960) 81.9
Percent labor force in agriculture: (1960) 42.2
Gross national product per capita: (1966) $500
Unit of currency: British pound (1968, .41 per dollar)

COMMERCE, 1966 *(expressed in percentage of values)*
Percent total Latin-American exports: (1965) 2.1
Percent total Latin-American imports: (1965) 3.4

Exports
alumina	24
bauxite	23
sugar	22
bananas	8

Exports to		Imports from	
United States	38	United States	36
United Kingdom	27	United Kingdom	22
Canada	15	Canada	11

Trinidad and Tobago

Area: 1,980 square miles
Population: (1966 estimate) 1,000,000
      (last census, 1960) 827,957
Capital city: Port of Spain; (1960) 93,954
Percent urban: (1946) 23.2
Birth rate per 1,000: (1966) 27.6; Death rate per 1,000: (1966) 6.1
Annual percent of increase: (1958–64) 3.1
Percent literate: (1946) 73.8
Percent labor force in agriculture: (1960) 19.6
Gross national product per capita: (1966) $662
Unit of currency: Trinidad and Tobago dollar (1968, 1.97 per dollar)

COMMERCE, 1965 *(expressed in percentage of values)*
Percent total Latin-American exports: 4.05
Percent total Latin-American imports: 5.65

Exports (1966)
petroleum   79   sugar   6

Exports to (1966)		Imports from (1966)	
United States	37	Venezuela	30
United Kingdom	14	United Kingdom	17
Netherlands	6	United States	14
		Saudi Arabia	13
		Canada	6
		Colombia	5

Barbados

Area: 166 square miles
Population: (1967 estimate) 248,000
           (last census, 1960) 232,327
Capital city: Bridgetown; (1960) 90,000
Percent urban: (1960) 40.3
Birth rate per 1,000: (1966) 25.9; Death rate per 1,000: (1966) 7.8
Annual percent of increase: (1958–64) 1.0
Percent literate: (1946) 91.1
Percent labor force in agriculture: (1960) 23.2
Gross national product per capita: (1964) $140
Unit of currency: East Caribbean dollar (1968, 1.97 per dollar)

COMMERCE, 1965 *(expressed in percentage of values)*
Percent total Latin-American exports: 0.3
Percent total Latin-American imports: 0.7

Exports

sugar	70
molasses	9
rum	6

Exports to		**Imports from**	
United Kingdom	42	United Kingdom	30
United States	10	United States	16
Canada	8	Canada	12
		Venezuela	7

Chapter 14 □ Jamaica and the
Lesser Antilles

Jamaica and the Lesser Antilles present a complex picture of present or recent colonial possessions of Great Britain, the United States, France, and the Netherlands. Great Britain attempted to bring most of the so-called British West Indies together under one government, but the attempt failed because of the lack of any shared state-idea. Today the British islands have been broken up into three independent states, six associated states, and several remaining colonial possessions. The United States has one unincorporated territory in the Virgin Islands. And there are several islands included in the French Antilles and in the Netherlands Antilles.

THE FEDERATION OF THE WEST INDIES

The British attempted to combine all the former British West Indies, except the British Virgin Islands and the Bahamas, under one federated government which would include a large enough population to support economic development, yet coherent enough to survive political differences. In 1958 the Federation of the West Indies was established and granted independence.

This was an unusual kind of political unit—although perhaps no more unusual than Indonesia. The national territory included scattered small islands extending in an arc from Sombrero in the Anegada Passage (Map 40, p. 300) for some 700 miles southward to Trinidad off the eastern coast of Venezuela. Also in the Federation were Barbados, 100 miles to the east of

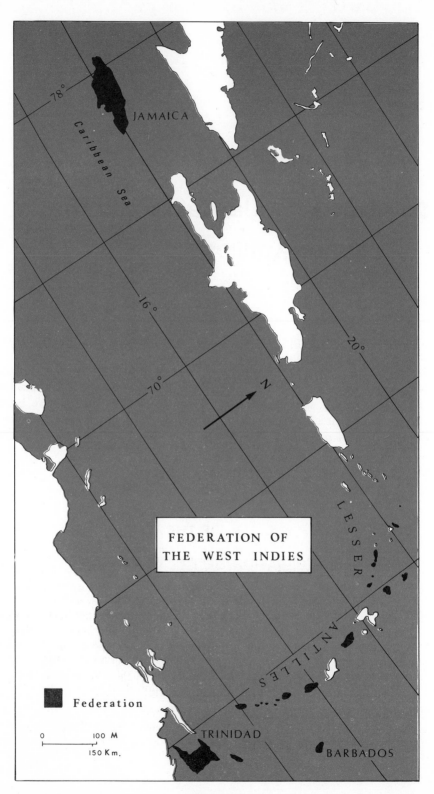

Map 40

the arc, and Jamaica, 1,000 miles to the west of it. With a total population in 1956 of about 3 million people, the density varied on the different islands from 1,378 per square mile on Barbados to only about 207 per square mile on Dominica. Jamaica, with an over-all density of 330 per square mile, and Trinidad with 360 per square mile, were near the average for the Federation as a whole. The population of these islands in 1956, just before the formation of the Federation, and in 1965, following the break-up of the Federation, is shown in the table below.

The Federation faced several problems that eventually proved impossible to solve. In the first place, Trinidad and Jamaica were relatively well-off compared with the other islands. The people of these two islands were less than enthusiastic about accepting responsibility for the economic development of their very poor neighbors. Furthermore Trinidad, where less than half of the population was of African descent, feared a flood of immigrants from over-crowded Barbados. The political leaders on the several islands could not reach an agreement about the location of the capital. The British government appointed a commission to make a recommendation regarding the site of the capital, and in 1957 this commission issued a report selecting Barbados. At this point in the negotiations, Trinidad agreed to permit the entry of immi-

POPULATION OF THE BRITISH ISLANDS IN THE ANTILLES*
1956 and 1964–1966

Political Unit	Area in Square Miles	Population 1956	Density 1956	Population 1964–66	Density 1964–66
Jamaica	4,244	1,554,000	366	1,827,000	428
Trinidad and Tobago	1,980	706,000	357	975,000	492
Barbados	166	230,000	1,378	245,000	1,476
West Indies Associated States					
St. Christopher-Nevis-Anguilla	138	55,000	397	62,000[b]	451
Antigua Barbuda, Redonda	171	53,000	308	57,000[a]	333
Dominica	305	63,000	207	67,000[a]	219
St. Lucia	238	88,000	387	100,000[a]	420
St. Vincent	150	77,000	513	85,000[b]	566
Grenada The Grenadines	133	88,000	663	96,000[a]	721
Colonies					
Montserrat	32	14,000	437	12,000[b]	375
Bahamas	4,400	96,000	22	131,000[b]	29
British Virgin Islands	59	7,760	130	7,400[b]	125
Caicos,Turks,	166			6,272[c]	37
Cayman, Sombrero and others	100			9,010[c]	90

*data from *Statistical Abstract of Latin America* and Department of State
[a]population 1965   [b]population 1964   [c]population 1966-67

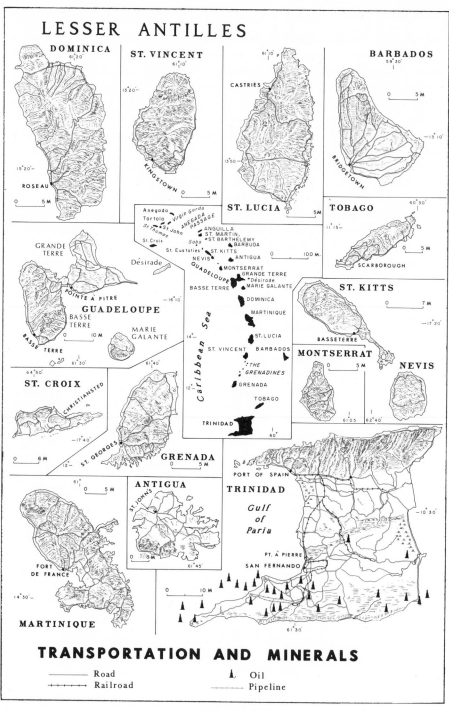

LESSER ANTILLES

DOMINICA

ROSEAU

ST. VINCENT

KINGSTOWN

CASTRIES

ST. LUCIA

BARBADOS

BRIDGETOWN

TOBAGO

SCARBOROUGH

GRANDE TERRE

Désirade

GUADELOUPE

BASSE TERRE

MARIE GALANTE

BASSE TERRE

POINTE À PITRE

Anegada
Tortola Virgin Gorda
St. John ANEGADA
St Thomas PASSAGE
St. Croix
ANGUILLA
ST. MARTIN
Saba ST. BARTHELEMY
St. Eustatius ST. KITTS BARBUDA
NEVIS ANTIGUA
MONTSERRAT
GRANDE TERRE
GUADELOUPE Désirade
BASSE TERRE MARIE GALANTE
DOMINICA
MARTINIQUE
ST. LUCIA
ST. VINCENT BARBADOS
THE GRENADINES
GRENADA
TOBAGO
TRINIDAD

Caribbean Sea

100 M.

ST. KITTS

BASSETERRE

MONTSERRAT

NEVIS

ST. CROIX

CHRISTIANSTED

ST. GEORGES

GRENADA

PORT OF SPAIN

TRINIDAD

*Gulf
of
Paria*

PT. À PIERRE
SAN FERNANDO

ANTIGUA

ST. JOHN'S

FORT DE FRANCE

MARTINIQUE

TRANSPORTATION AND MINERALS

——————— Road

+++++++ Railroad

Oil

——————— Pipeline

Map 41

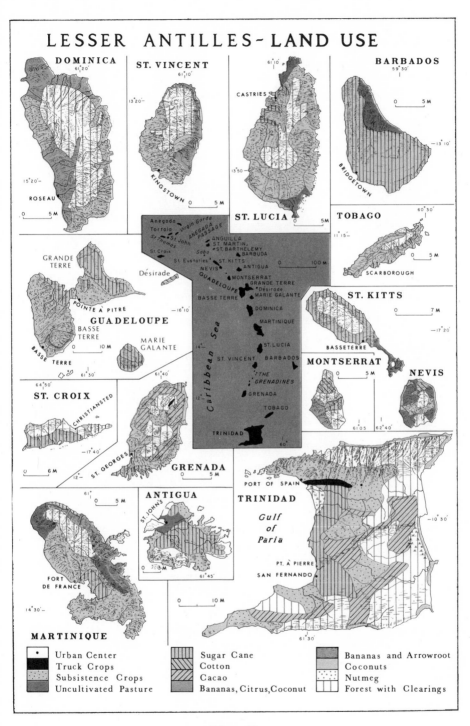

LESSER ANTILLES - LAND USE

DOMINICA
61°20'
15°20'
ROSEAU
0 5 M

ST. VINCENT
61°10'
13°20'
KINGSTOWN 0 5 M

ST. LUCIA
61°10'
CASTRIES
13°50'
0 5 M

BARBADOS
59°30'
0 5 M
13°10'
BRIDGETOWN

Anegada
Tortola   Virgin Gorda
St. Thomas   St. John ANEGADA PASSAGE
St. Croix   Saba   ANGUILLA
ST. MARTIN
ST. BARTHELEMY
St. Eustatius ST. KITTS BARBUDA
ANTIGUA
NEVIS
Désirade   MONTSERRAT
GUADELOUPE GRANDE TERRE
Désirade
BASSE TERRE MARIE GALANTE
DOMINICA
16°10'
MARTINIQUE
Caribbean Sea
14°   ST. LUCIA
ST. VINCENT   BARBADOS
THE
GRENADINES
12°   GRENADA
TOBAGO
TRINIDAD
60°
0 100 M

GUADELOUPE
GRANDE TERRE
POINTE À PITRE
BASSE TERRE
BASSE TERRE
0 10 M
MARIE GALANTE
64°50'   61°30'

TOBAGO
60°30'
11°15'
SCARBOROUGH
0 5 M

ST. KITTS
0 7 M
17°20'
BASSETERRE

MONTSERRAT
0 5 M

NEVIS
61°05' 62°40'

ST. CROIX
CHRISTIANSTED
17°40'
ST. GEORGES
0 6 M

ST. VINCENT 61°40'
12°

GRENADA
61°
0 5 M

ANTIGUA
ST. JOHNS
0 3 M
61°45'

PORT OF SPAIN

TRINIDAD
Gulf
of
Paria
10°30'
PT. À PIERRE
SAN FERNANDO
61°30'
0 10 M

MARTINIQUE
FORT
DE FRANCE
14°30'

Legend

- • Urban Center
- Truck Crops
- Subsistence Crops
- Uncultivated Pasture
- Sugar Cane
- Cotton
- Cacao
- Bananas, Citrus, Coconut
- Bananas and Arrowroot
- Coconuts
- Nutmeg
- Forest with Clearings

Map 42

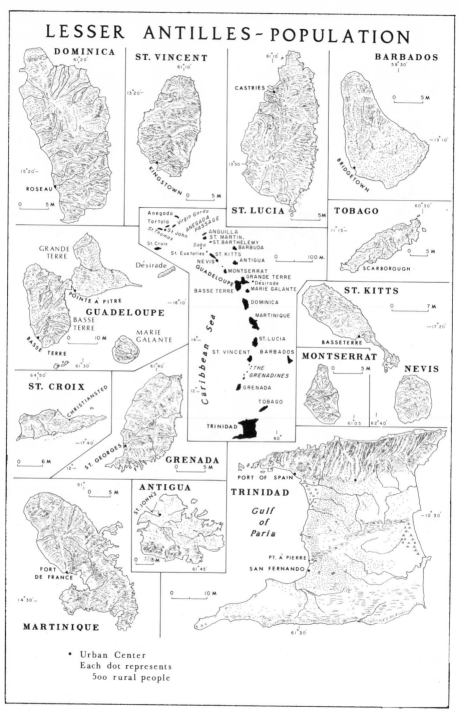

LESSER ANTILLES - POPULATION

DOMINICA

ST. VINCENT

BARBADOS

ST. LUCIA

TOBAGO

GUADELOUPE

ST. KITTS

MONTSERRAT

NEVIS

ST. CROIX

GRENADA

ANTIGUA

TRINIDAD

MARTINIQUE

• Urban Center
Each dot represents
5oo rural people

Map 43

grants from the other parts of the Federation and, in exchange, was granted the site of the capital. The United States Navy headquarters that had been set up during World War II a little to the west of Port of Spain were turned over to the new Federation for use as government buildings. In January 1958 the Federation of the West Indies became an independent state and member of the Commonwealth.

But the basic difficulty in forming a coherent state out of such widely scattered pieces was the lack of any widely held state-idea. The political leaders, who had their strong support on their own islands, were unable to find a formula to provide for national loyalties. Instead, most of the people were strongly loyal to their own islands, feeling that the Federation had been imposed on them from outside. In 1961 Jamaica withdrew. In 1962 both Jamaica and Trinidad (with Tobago) were granted independent status. Barbados became independent in 1966. In 1967 some of the smaller islands of the Windward and Leeward groups were granted self-government, leaving the conduct of foreign affairs and defense to Great Britain. The West Indies Associated States have a status similar to that of the Commonwealth of Puerto Rico.

JAMAICA

Jamaica and Trinidad, along with Puerto Rico, give support to the idea that economic growth can go forward most successfully in an atmosphere of political stability. The democratic procedures inherited from the British provide a set of institutions for the resolution of conflicting policies and interests without resort to the destructive and disruptive use of force. In spite of a population density of 428 people per square mile, and a density of 1,891 per square mile of arable land, Jamaica has been able to build up its economy until in 1964 this new state ranked eighth in all Latin America in gross national product per capita. In addition to their democratic institutions, the Jamaicans have a long record of self-reliance, and have many times demonstrated an exceptional capacity for hard work. Emigrants from Jamaica helped to dig the Panama Canal and to develop the banana plantations in Costa Rica. As migrant workers they helped to harvest the sugarcane in pre-Castro Cuba. Some 75 percent of the Jamaicans are of unmixed African ancestry, and the remainder are mostly mulatto, with a small proportion of Europeans. Yet the people of Jamaica have preserved much less of the African heritage than have the people of Haiti. A study of the reasons for the distinctive character of the Jamaicans is needed.

The Land

The island of Jamaica, which is exceeded in size among the islands of the Antilles only by Cuba and Hispaniola, is a part of the Central-American–Antillean mountain system (Map 33, p. 227). Its mountains, however, are deeply covered with upraised coral limestone, and in only a few places do the underlying geologic structures appear at the surface. The highest elevation, a little over 7,000 feet, is found in the Blue Mountains, situated in the eastern part of the island—an area of narrow ravines and sharp, knife-like ridges which descend from the central peak like the spokes of a wheel. But the Blue Mountains, and the two other much smaller mountainous areas where the underlying formations appear at the surface, are almost completely surrounded by the limestone formations which have accumulated to depths of many thousands of feet.

The limestone plateau, which at its highest point is about 3,000 feet above sea level, extends from the easternmost point to the westernmost point, a distance of 144 miles, and from the northern side of the island to the southern side, a distance of 49 miles. At many places it borders the sea with cliffs a thousand feet high, but at other places the ascent onto the plateau begins behind a narrow fringe of sea-border plain, varying in width up to 5 miles.

The surface of the limestone plateau is by no means flat. Not more than 14 percent of Jamaica can be classed as flat. Streams have cut deep valleys back from the coast, and the limestone itself is honeycombed with caverns and pitted with sinks. In the section known as the "cockpits," in northwestern Jamaica, some of the many sinks are as much as 500 feet deep. In the midst of the plateau there are several large solution basins, their bottoms deeply filled with a residual red soil which is as highly productive as the similar red soils of Cuba. The largest of these solution basins is the Vale of Clarendon, 50 miles long by 20 miles wide, which has been opened up on one side of the volcanic ridge known as the Bull's Head. These solution basins contain some of Jamaica's most productive agricultural land and are densely populated. Similiarly the coastal lowlands are generally areas of concentrated settlement, especially the large lowland which lies north and west of Kingston.

The rainfall is heaviest on the northeast side, particularly in the Blue Mountains; and it is lightest on the southern and western sides. The sea-border plains of southern Jamaica, including the one near the capital, are too dry to support agriculture without irrigation. Kingston, for example, receives an average of only about 29 inches a year. Over 100 inches are received in the plains on the northeast side. The top of the Blue Mountains, almost always deeply buried in great, billowing cumulus clouds, receives between 150 and 200 inches a year.

Although Jamaica in many ways qualifies as a tropical paradise, every now and then the tranquillity is shattered by disaster. The southern hurricane track

(Map 36, p. 231) passes over or near Jamaica. These violent storms are likely to come at least once a year between August and October, and if they do not pass directly over the island they come close enough to do damage. Occasionally, also, there are earthquakes: in 1907 Kingston was destroyed by an earthquake.

The Course of Settlement

During the seventeenth and eighteenth centuries, when Jamaica was one of Great Britain's most valuable possessions, the sugarcane plantations, from which the wealth was derived, were located on the lowland plains near the coast. The chief concentration of people was around Kingston and on the lowland that extends westward from Kingston. The interior of the island was used for the pasture of cattle or for the slaves in raising their own food crops. When slavery came to an end, however, there was an exodus of the former slaves from the sugarcane lands into the interior. The idea was to escape as completely as possible from work that was so closely associated with slavery.

Agriculture and Rural Land Tenure

The pattern of rural land tenure that resulted persisted until the 1960's. The property that was granted to the new farm settlers remained the property of all the descendants of the first settlers and could not be sold without agreement of all the heirs. By 1961 about 70 percent of all the farms on Jamaica were less than five acres in size. Yet to combine farms or sell farms would require the agreement of thousands of relatives, scattered all over the world. Furthermore, many city people in Jamaica looked on the system as a kind of social security, for if a city job were lost the individual could always move back to the farm and claim a portion of its products. Most of the people actually working the land were old folks, and the yields of the crops were low in part because of poor farm techniques, in part because of disastrous soil erosion on steep slopes. Only 15 percent of the total area of Jamaica can be considered suitable for crops, and this includes much land that should never have been cleared of its forest cover.

In 1957 a ten-year plan was drawn up for the improvement of agriculture. Steps were finally taken to cut through the legal tangle regarding land properties, and thousands of ten-acre farms were marked off. The traditional subsistence crops had been maize, yams, bananas, and other foods for sale in local markets. The agricultural improvement plan called for replacing these crops on steep slopes with such tree crops as coffee, citrus fruits, or pimento. By 1965 it was estimated that the value of crops produced on these small farms exceeded the value of crops grown on plantations for export. Once again the Jamaicans had demonstrated an ability to solve their own problems.

A large part of the interior of Jamaica is unsuited for agriculture. In places this is due to the steepness of the slope, but in large areas where solution caverns in the limestone carry water off underground the surface is too dry for crops. This is excellent pasture land, and traditionally Jamaica has been an important producer of beef for local use. The ten-year plan called for an improvement of the herds of beef and dairy cattle and also for work on the improvement of the pasture by reseeding with new varieties of grass.

COMMERCIAL AGRICULTURE

Some 40 percent of the agricultural area of Jamaica is held in a small number of large estates, operated by corporations. One of these, in the Vale of Clarendon, is about 30,000 acres in size. Eighteen large plantations are used to grow sugarcane, mostly on irrigated level land. The cane is grown not more than 5 miles away from a grinding mill or central, and these are to be found now in scattered locations on the plains. In the slave period, Jamaica was able to produce a record sugar crop of 100,000 tons, but this figure was never equalled again until the 1930's. By 1961 sugar production was up to 440,000 tons, and by the crop year of 1964–65 a record total of more than 500,000 tons was produced. Much of this sugar is exported to the Commonwealth countries, in which market Jamaica has a quota. Some sugar is made into the dark Jamaica rum in Kingston.

A traditional commercial crop in Jamaica is the banana. In 1870 an enterprising businessman from New Jersey brought a load of bananas to the United States from Jamaica, and realized a large profit from the sale of this unfamiliar fruit in New York. The company he set up to grow and ship bananas was one of those that combined in 1899 to form the United Fruit Company. Before World War II about 32 percent of the crop land of the island was used for this crop, and the annual export of bananas exceeded 25 million stems, constituting between 50 and 60 percent of the Colony's exports. The unusual fact about banana-growing in Jamaica was that most of the crop was grown by small independent farmers. There were only 30 banana plantations larger than 30 acres. The United Fruit Company had only about 800 acres before the war; in 1948 it had less than 300 acres.

The banana lends itself far better than sugarcane to small-farm production. To be sure, the banana grower is no better able to reach the market independently than is the small sugarcane planter. But the banana planter has the advantage that his crop can be harvested at any time during the year, so that he can enjoy a cash income that is not concentrated in only a few months.

During the late 1930's the Panama disease and the Sigatoka disease began to appear in Jamaica. The government took prompt measures to stop the spread of these diseases, but in spite of efforts to control the situation the banana acreage of Jamaica was, in the course of a few years, greatly reduced. Exports dropped from more than 25 million stems to less than 6 million. The island economy was shaken, and the resulting hunger and social unrest could have amounted to a major disaster had it not been for the relatively large areas devoted to subsistence crops, to the relief funds provided by Great Britain, and perhaps also to the basic qualities of self-reliance of the Jamaican people.

In the 1960's the production of bananas in Jamaica has again been greatly increased. A new variety of plant is grown which is immune to the Panama disease, and the Sigatoka disease is kept under control by the use of chemical sprays. The bananas are again produced mostly on small plantations, where they fit in easily with the production of other commercial crops. There are a few areas of large plantations, as along the rainy northeast coast, but a large part of the production comes from scattered small sources.

Other commercial crops now produced on Jamaica include high-quality coffee from the Blue Mountains, cacao from the wetter places along the coast, and also tobacco, cotton, citrus fruit, and pimento.

Bauxite

The economy of Jamaica is also supported by the mining of bauxite, the ore of aluminum. In certain parts of the world, mostly in the rainy tropics, the continued downward percolation of rainwater removes the soluble minerals from the soil, leaving a residue in which there is a concentration of insoluble iron and aluminum compounds. Where aluminum oxide (alumina) occurs in sufficient concentration to make mining worth while, the ore is called bauxite. In Jamaica in 1942, geologists discovered deep accumulations of bauxite in the bottoms of the solution basins. The bauxite has a relatively low alumina content (only 48 to 52 percent, compared with 55 to 61 percent in France and West Africa) and a relatively high ferric oxide content (15 to 22 percent), but the size of the bauxite accumulation makes large-scale mining possible, which greatly reduces the costs of production. It is estimated that Jamaica has the world's largest reserve of bauxite (some 300 million tons). The mining of bauxite in Jamaica began in 1952; in 1966 this island produced 26 percent of the world's bauxite.

Three large mining corporations are at work in Jamaica, of which two are owned in the United States: Kaiser and Reynolds Aluminum. The former has built Port Kaiser, a new port on the southern coast with an especially designed dock for loading ore ships. The bauxite is kiln-dried by both Kaiser and Reynolds to remove the water content of the ore, then transported to the Kaiser refinery at Corpus Christi, Texas, or to the Reynolds plant at Baton Rouge, Louisiana. The third corporation is the Aluminum Corporation of Canada (Alcan) which has built two refineries in Jamaica at Mandeville and Ewarton (Map 34, p. 228). Here the impurities in the bauxite are removed to produce alumina, which is then shipped to refineries in Canada where aluminum is manufactured.

Jamaican law requires that after the bauxite has been dug up by huge mechanical shovels, the land be smoothed over again and made ready for crops or pasture. The aluminum companies have returned their mined-out areas to pasture grasses and have imported high-grade beef and dairy cattle as a contribution to the island economy.

Jamaica also has a small but important source of gypsum, located near the coast about ten miles to the east of Kingston.

Jamaica as a Political Unit

Since 1960 the world has become full of independent states like Jamaica, struggling to survive in the midst of conflict and in the face of revolutionary innovation. Is every group of people with conscious feelings of nationality able to form a viable state, or is there some minimum number of people necessary for survival? Will the survival of small states depend on the organization of federations, or at least of free market areas? Puerto Rico has achieved its preeminent position in economic development in part because of the free flow of money, goods, and people back and forth with the United States. Can Jamaica count on similar support from the Commonwealth?

The Economic Situation

Jamaica has not yet solved all its economic problems. With an overall population density of 428 people per square mile, and a much higher density of population per square mile of crop land, there are still many Jamaicans living in a condition of rural poverty. There is immediate need to improve the productivity of agriculture and to reduce the necessary import of basic foods. But, as we have pointed out before, any program of agricultural improvement must bring about a reduction in the number of farmers. In 1963 about 42 percent of the working force was employed in agriculture, but already this proportion is being reduced through the change from 5-acre to 10-acre farms. And in the cities there are large numbers of displaced farmers who remain unemployed. The population is increasing at the rate of 1.8 percent per year (with a birth rate of almost 40 per thousand and a death rate of about 8 per thousand). This net increase of workers to be employed seems to make any program of development look inadequate.

Jamaica, like Puerto Rico, has for a long time supported a regular flow of emigration. Since World War II thousands of Jamaicans have emigrated each year to Great Britain where jobs are to be had in such large industrial centers as Birmingham. But when the British economy in the late 1960's failed to provide new jobs fast enough to take care of its own working force, the presence of the Jamaicans and other people from the West Indies began to cause friction. For the first time the British came face to face with problems of race relations. Because the Jamaicans are dark-skinned they are easily identified and easily become the victims of discrimination. In 1965 Great Britain began to restrict the migration of West Indians.

Since the 1950's Jamaica has been engaged in a program of industrial development, modeled on that of Puerto Rico. A period of freedom from taxation was used to attract manufacturing firms, and many companies from the United States and from the Commonwealth countries took advantage of the opportunity. There are new jobs in the bauxite refineries where alumina is produced and in the numerous sugar refineries. Factories have also been built to produce textiles and clothing, automobile tires, batteries, paint, soap, porcelain, and cement. A new oil refinery was built near Kingston by Esso West Indies, using Venezuelan crude oil. The product can be exported or used as a basis for a petrochemical industry. In 1966 a small steel mill started to operate, using imported scrap metal. But Jamaica faces the problem common to all small countries—the impossibility of taking advantage of modern large-scale technology because of the small size of the domestic market. Jamaica suffers from the disadvantage—unlike Puerto Rico—of being located at a great distance from potential customers in the countries with better developed economies.

A very important source of new jobs in Jamaica is the tourist business. In 1965 tourists provided the third largest source of income (after the export of minerals and sugar). Large luxury hotels and other kinds of tourist accommodations were built, especially at Montego Bay and Ochos Rios.

The Political Situation

Jamaica has enjoyed an enviable record of political stability. A two-party system is firmly established, with wide support among the people. Although there is a concentration of frustrated and very poor people on the outskirts of Kingston, there is no disposition among any large numbers of people to demand a change in the system. To be sure, in 1967 the leaders of both parties were old men, and there was a problem of finding new leaders. But there was no geographic separation of political groups within Jamaica to cause trouble—unless it were for the concentration of people in Kingston who could no longer tolerate the poverty of rural life. Many people recognized that the rate of industrial growth and of new jobs was not rapid enough, even to stay ahead of population growth. Most of the Jamaicans, however, looked for solutions to these problems within the political framework they have inherited from the British.

TRINIDAD AND TOBAGO

Trinidad and its small neighbor Tobago were granted independence in 1962 after the break-up of the Federation of the West Indies. Since then Trinidad has made notable gains in economic development, and, like Jamaica, has enjoyed continued political stability. With only 1,980 square miles of territory, Trinidad's 975,000 people reach an overall density of 492 per square mile, or 1,363 per square mile of crop land. Furthermore, Trindad's population is growing at a rate of 3.1 percent per year (birth rate 28 per thousand; death rate only 6.1 percent per thousand). The population is concentrated in certain parts of the island, notably on either side of Port of Spain, and there are large areas of forest reserve still unoccupied (Maps 41, 42, 43, pp. 302–304).

The Land

Trinidad does not belong geologically to the Antilles, but rather to the continent of South America. Its separation from the easternmost point of northern Venezuela is due to a fault depression in the Caribbean Coastal Range. Beyond the narrow passage which separates the island from the mainland the same mountain structures which form the coastal range of Venezuela continue across the whole northern side of Trinidad, reaching a maximum elevation of about 3,000 feet. The small island of Tobago, 22 miles northnortheast of Trinidad, is also related geologically to these continental mountains. The southern part of Trinidad is made up of two ranges of low hills, not more than 1,000 feet in elevation, crossing diagonally from northeast to southwest, and two lowland areas, now slightly uplifted and dissected by streams. Mangrove-filled swamps, separated from the sea by wide sandy bars, characterize a part of the west coast and a part of the east coast.

Trinidad lies in the path of the trade winds. At the eastern end of the northern range the rainfall is as much as 150 inches, and a belt of more than 100 inches extends southward about 5 miles inland from the east coast. Over this belt large cumulus clouds begin to form early every day, even during the drier part of the year, and drift westward across the island bringing brief but heavy downpours of rain. The rainfall decreases toward the west, dropping to between 50 and 60 inches along the west coast, and to less than 50 inches on the westernmost end of the northern range. The rainy season is between June and December, in which season, on an average, two days out of three on the western side of the island are rainy (that is, they receive at least one shower). During the season of less rain, an average of one day out of three has at least one shower. On the eastern side of the island during all months of the year there are very few days which do not have frequent showers in-

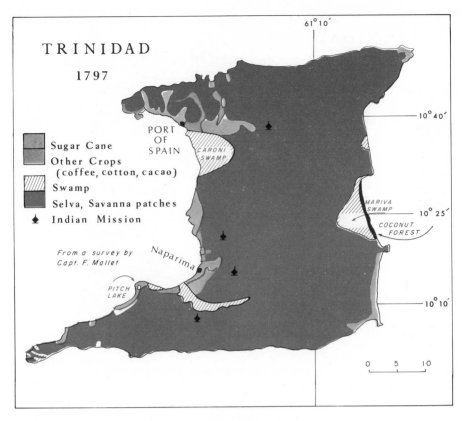

TRINIDAD

1797

Sugar Cane

Other Crops
(coffee, cotton, cacao)

Swamp

Selva, Savanna patches

Indian Mission

*From a survey by
Capt. F. Mallet*

PORT
OF
SPAIN

*CARONI
SWAMP*

*MARIVA
SWAMP*

*COCONUT
FOREST*

Naparima

*PITCH
LAKE*

61° 10′

10° 40′

10° 25′

10° 10′

0   5   10

Map 44

terspersed with periods of brilliant sunshine. In the pocket-like valleys of the northern range there are small areas, protected from the winds, which have typical hothouse climates, especially suitable for cacao.

The temperatures on Trinidad, which lies only about 10° north of the equator, are even more "temperate" than those experienced on the northern islands of the Antilles. The range between the average of the warmest and the coldest months at Port of Spain, on the western side of the island, is only about 3°, and the average for the year is about 77°. Cold air masses from North America do not reach Trinidad, nor do the hurricanes ever touch this fortunate island, for they reach the Antilles on their way across the ocean from western Africa at least two degrees of latitude farther to the north.

Trinidad was originally covered almost completely by a heavy tropical rain forest. Only the dry westernmost end of the northern range had a scanty vegetation of xerophytic character. The highest peak of the northern range, only 3,000 feet in elevation, is clothed to its summit with forest.

Settlement of Trinidad

Trinidad was for a long time a possession of Spain. Because it contained none of the resources either of land or of people that were attractive to the

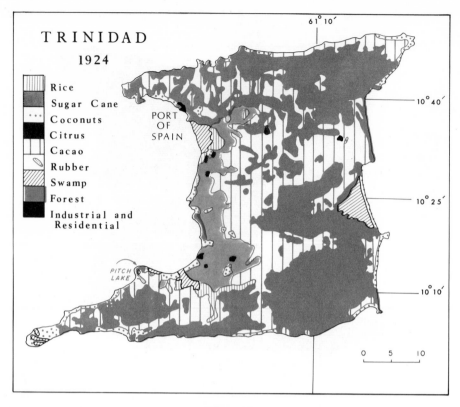

TRINIDAD
1924

- Rice
- Sugar Cane
- Coconuts
- Citrus
- Cacao
- Rubber
- Swamp
- Forest
- Industrial and Residential

PORT
OF
SPAIN

PITCH
LAKE

61° 10'

10° 40'

10° 25'

10° 10'

0   5   10

Map 45

Spaniards, it was never effectively settled by them. Port of Spain was established on the western side of the island at the southern base of the northern range, where protection from the easterly winds together with a deep anchorage and a firm landing place offered ideal conditions for a port. The island was still scantily occupied when, in 1783, the French began to appreciate the possibilities for the growth of sugarcane. Although it remained a Spanish possession, many Frenchmen came to Trinidad at that time, introducing African slaves in considerable numbers. That this late wave of settlement did little to transform the island landscape is shown by the map, prepared in 1797 by a British military engineer (Map 44). It was in this year that the British seized Trinidad, along with numerous other French and Spanish possessions in the Antilles. In 1802 most of these conquests were returned to their former owners, but Trinidad was retained and has remained British since that date. To this day, however, the population of the island reflects this background of early settlement, for there are many families of French and Spanish descent as well as those which came later from Great Britain.[1]

[1]Much of this material on the historical geography of Trinidad was first published in Preston E. James, "Changes in the Geography of Trinidad," *Scottish Geographical Magazine*, Vol. 73, 1957, pp. 158–166.

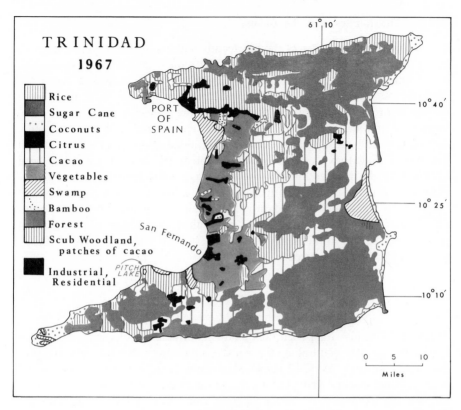

TRINIDAD
1967

Rice
Sugar Cane
Coconuts
Citrus
Cacao
Vegetables
Swamp
Bamboo
Forest
Scub Woodland,
  patches of cacao
Industrial,
Residential

PORT
OF
SPAIN

San Fernando

PITCH
LAKE

61° 10'

10° 40'

10° 25'

10° 10'

0   5   10
Miles

Map 46

The early years of British rule saw no marked change in the pattern of settlement or in the methods of land use. The acquisition of Trinidad, along with British Guiana at the same time, caused a sufficient increase in the production of sugar for the British market to bring a disastrous drop in prices. Trinidad never enjoyed such prosperity as had eighteenth-century Saint Domingue or Jamaica. At the end of the slave period Trinidad was still a poor colony with a large amount of undeveloped but potentially productive land.

Sugarcane

It was the importation of East Indian contract laborers starting in 1845 that made possible the rapid increase of sugarcane planting. In 1850 about 20,000 tons of raw sugar were produced, but by 1879 the production had increased to 67,000 tons. Sugarcane spread not only around the original plantations along the Gulf of Paria, but also to other parts of the island. All over the island the forest was cleared, the cane fields planted, and small sugar mills were set up.

The technological revolution that changed sugar production from a primitive small-scale, high-cost operation to a large-scale industry, came to Trinidad during the last quarter of the nineteenth century. At this time the planters in the Antilles were faced by serious competition from the beet-sugar growers. Failing to secure government aid in the form of subsidies and price controls, the Trinidad planters either had to go out of business or invest more capital in order to make their production more efficient. The first modern, large-scale mill was built in 1871, a short distance inland from San Fernando. This mill is still the largest producer in Trinidad. Whereas each small mill had been supplied with cane from fields immediately around it and had been operated by the planter himself, the new large mills needed at least thirty-eight square miles of cane to operate with maximum efficiency. As a result most of the small mills ceased production, and sugarcane planting concentrated again in the part of the island best suited to it (Map 45). Sugarcane is still concentrated in this same area (Map 46). In 1964–65 nearly 250,000 tons of sugar were produced.

Cacao

Trinidad has also long been famous for its production of cacao. The cacao tree grew as a wild plant along the Amazon, the lower Orinoco, and in Trinidad. Even as early as 1797 cacao plantations had been established in the steamy, pouch-shaped valleys along the southern side of the Northern Range. But the big expansion of cacao planting came after 1850, along with the increase of sugarcane planting. Whereas the expansion of sugarcane resulted in the clearing of the forest, the expansion of cacao was carried on under the shade of taller trees. By 1895 Trinidad was second only to Ecuador in the world production of cacao. The map of land use in 1924 shows how cacao planting had spread over a large part of the island to the east of the sugar district. But thereafter the increased competition of cacao production from the Gold Coast (Ghana) and from Brazil made it unprofitable to continue to grow cacao in Trinidad except in the best-favored places. As a result, by 1950 a considerable part of the cacao area had been abandoned.

Other Crops

A number of other crops were being produced in 1924. The natural coconut forest on the east-facing coast of Trinidad was being harvested if not cultivated, and Trinidad was exporting whole nuts, copra, and coconut oil. There were also smaller areas devoted to citrus fruits, rubber, coffee, and food crops, especially rice. By 1950 the coconut forests were still being harvested, but now the copra and coconut oil is sold entirely in the domestic market. The rubber plantations had disappeared, but there was an increase in the area devoted to food crops, including rice.

Oil, Asphalt, and Manufacturing Industries

The economy of Trinidad is diversified by the production of asphalt and oil, and by a considerable development of manufacturing industries. The island has long been famous for its Pitch Lake, a natural occurrence of asphalt resulting from the seepage of oil from underground into a shallow depression in the surface. The distillation of the volatile parts of the oil leaves a residue of asphalt, which continues to accumulate as fast as it is dug out. In 1595 Sir Walter Raleigh made use of the pitch to caulk his ships. In more recent times the asphalt is dug out and carried by cable line to a port on the southwestern shore of Trinidad on the Gulf of Paria. For a long time this was the world's only source of asphalt, but during the twentieth century Trinidad's product has met heavy competition from asphalt produced in oil refineries. Since World War II Trinidad asphalt has again become competitive, and large amounts have been shipped to Great Britain where it is used for street pavement.

All around the Pitch Lake in southwestern Trinidad there are oil wells. During World War II and thereafter new oil wells were drilled, even into the bottom of the Gulf of Paria. Oil and asphalt together make up the major proportion of the value of all exports. But the oil is also used in several oil refineries in Trinidad, of which the largest is the Texaco Refinery at Point-

Cutting crude asphalt at La Brea. *Courtesy of British Information Service.*

à-Pierre. Trinidad imports oil from Venezuela to feed this refinery. The oil and asphalt business gives employment to some 18,000 people.

Since World War II Trinidad has embarked on a program of industrial development. Near the Texaco Refinery there is now the largest petrochemical plant in all Latin America, producing plastics, fertilizer, synthetic rubber, and a great variety of other products. In 1966 the first automobile assembly plant in the West Indies started operation near Port of Spain, to turn out several models of British automobiles and trucks. There are also sugar refineries, flour mills, clothing manufacturers and others. Yet in spite of these developments there is still considerable unemployment among the city people.

Trinidad and Tobago as a Political Unit

Trinidad's enviable status as the possessor of one of the highest gross national products per capita in all Latin America does not mean that all the problems of creating a viable state have been met. There are still serious difficulties to be faced, and the difficulties are both economic and political.

The Economic Situation

Since Trinidad became independent in 1962 the economy has grown rapidly. Nevertheless it has not yet reached a rate of growth that stays ahead of the increase of population. Since some 40 percent of the population is under fifteen years of age, there is no likelihood that the birth rate will soon be decreased—and the death rate is already almost as low as that of Puerto Rico. The population of Trinidad is too large to be supported by an underdeveloped economy; yet it is not nearly large enough to provide the mass market that supports modern manufacturing industry. The only solution would seem to be the formation of an economic community of which Trinidad might be a part.

Trinidad was the first Latin-American country to scrap its railroads and undertake to meet its land transport needs with motor trucks and buses. All over Latin America, trucks are moving more goods, while railroads are moving the same amounts as always or less. The change was made easier in Trinidad because of its small size, and because of the short land hauls to ports on the Gulf of Paria; and also by the supplies of low-cost asphalt with which to surface all-weather highways.

The Political Situation

The potential problems that lie beneath the surface of Trinidad's political stability are related to the nature of the population. Trinidad is much less homogeneous in its population than is Jamaica. People of African ancestry make up only 43 percent of the total. In addition there are East Indians (37 percent) whose ancestors came to Trinidad between 1848 and 1916 as contract laborers, as well as smaller numbers of people of British or French ancestry, and Chinese. Some 16 percent of the population is racially mixed. Furthermore, there are important religious differences: 66 percent of the people are Christian, 23 percent are Hindu, 6 percent are Muslim, and there are smaller numbers of Buddhists and others. To get Christians, Hindus, and Muslims to work together to form a coherent national group is not easy. It is important from the point of view of political geography that in Trinidad these diverse religious and racial groups are intermingled. The problems would be much more difficult to solve if each of the religious groups occupied a separate part of the national territory. Nevertheless, the situation is potentially dangerous for the stability of Trinidad.

BARBADOS

The third of the three independent political units that were formerly parts of the Federation of the West Indies is Barbados. When British explorers in the early seventeenth century first touched at this remote island they found it unoccupied, and in 1627 a British colony was established there. Since that time Barbados has remained British. By 1640 its population consisted of 37,000 white people and 6,000 African slaves. Between 1667 and 1678 its population was reported as consisting of 20,000 white people and 40,000 slaves; but by 1786 the people of British ancestry numbered only 16,000, and Africans were more than 62,000. The steady increase of the African population in the nineteenth century brought their numbers to 180,000 in 1921–22, while the white population remained more or less steady at about 15,000. At present the population is about 79 percent African, 4 percent European, and 17 percent mixed.

The outstanding fact about Barbados is its very great density of population. With 245,000 people living on 166 square miles of area the density of population per square mile is 1,476. This is not a new condition, for even in the first century of British settlement Barbados was more densely populated than any other part of the Antilles. Barbados, like Jamaica, has been a source of emigrants who have provided an important supply of hard-working laborers wherever work was to be done around the Caribbean. Before 1965 many Barbadians emigrated to Great Britain.

In many ways Babados is ideally suited for the production of sugarcane. The island is an up-raised portion of the South American continental shelf, but continental rocks appear at the surface only in a semicircular area near the northeast coast. Most of the surface of the island is made up of terraces of coral limestone that rise, step by step, from the southwest shore until the highest terrace, 1,100 feet above sea level, forms a commanding cliff overlooking the semicircle of continental rocks (Map 41, p. 301). The terrace surfaces are gently rolling, with few slopes too steep for cultivation. The water that falls on the island mostly drains off through underground caverns in the limestone. But because of the configuration of the limestone caverns large pools of fresh water lie below the surface, from which water can easily be pumped back up again. This pumping used to be done by many windmills, but now diesel motors generate electric power to run the pumps. The average annual rainfall is between 50 and 70 inches.

Of the total area of Barbados about 85 percent is cultivated, and most of the cultivated land is in sugarcane. There are more than 200 large plantations, each equipped with a modern sugar mill. As in other sugarcane areas, there is a great seasonal difference in the demand for cane workers: work is plentiful during the harvest season from January to June, but jobs are more difficult to find during the remainder of the year. There are numerous areas where small farmers, on less than an acre of land, grow vegetables or fruit, and many of these small farmers find additional employment either as wage workers on the cane plantations, or in factories, or as employees of the numerous hotels that cater to tourists. Many of them are part-time fishermen. Only 23 percent of the labor force is employed in agriculture.

Barbados as a Political Unit

The people of Barbados enjoy a good living. To be sure the gross national product per capita of $140 in 1964 is not so high as that of either Trinidad or Jamaica, but it is much higher than that of any of the other Lesser Antilles. Furthermore, Barbados enjoys a literacy rate that is second only to that of Argentina in all of Latin America. The Barbadian schoolboy plays cricket with such enthusiasm that this island contributes more than its share of major-league players.

The economy is largely, but not exclusively, dependent on the production of sugar. Sugar contributes 32 percent of the gross national product, and raw sugar makes up some 70 percent of the value of all exports. Another 9 percent is made up of "fancy molasses," and 6 percent is high-quality rum. On the other hand, some 47 percent of the gross national product is derived from manufacturing industries, and an increasing amount comes from services performed for tourists who come to enjoy the ideal temperate climate, the delightful bathing, and the many facilities provided for recreation.

Is Barbados a viable state? When independence was granted in 1966 there were many who doubted that this little island could support the necessary economic development. But there can be no doubt of the strongly supported state-idea, the sense of loyalty to Barbados, that characterizes this politically stable and strongly coherent community.

THE WEST INDIES ASSOCIATED STATES

In 1967 six small states were created among the British islands of the Antilles. These are the West Indies Associated States, each having a status in relation to Great Britain similar to that of Puerto Rico to the United States. Each of the six states is separately associated with Great Britain; each enjoys self-government, but leaves defense and foreign affairs to the British government; each state has the right to become completely independent provided a referendum of the inhabitants favors breaking away from Great Britain by a two-thirds majority, and provided the legislature approves also by a two-thirds majority. The official name of each state is The Associated State of ———, and the group name, The West Indies Associated States, implies no form of federation. The states, listed from north to south are: St. Christopher-Nevis-Anguilla,[2] Antigua with its dependencies Barbuda and Redonda, Dominica, St. Lucia, St. Vincent, and Grenada (Maps 41, 42, and 43, pp. 302–304; and the table on p. 301).

Each of these little states suffers from over-population, poverty, and lack of economic development. St. Christopher-Nevis-Anguilla produce sugarcane and sea-island cotton, and the income fluctuates with the price that can be commanded by raw sugar, molasses, and rum. Anguilla, isolated from the other two islands, was the least developed and the most difficult to develop —in part because such low-lying islands are very dry and have no sources of water for irrigation. Antigua is better off than most of the others because it enjoys a considerable popularity as a tourist resort. On Antigua there are 33 hotels, a gambling casino, and other facilities for visitors. Dominica, St. Lucia, St. Vincent, and Grenada export chiefly bananas and other fruits such as limes, coconuts, and mangoes. St. Vincent has long been known as the world's leading producer of arrowroot, an easily digested starch used in the manufacture of cookies, puddings, and crackers for young children.

It would seem that the only hope for these small islands is to group them into some kind of federation and to give them access to a common Antillean market. But every effort of the British to establish such a federation has failed.

BRITISH COLONIES IN THE ANTILLES

There are scattered small islands in the Antilles that remain under the administration of the British Colonial Office. These include such islands as the Caicos Islands, Turks Island, the Cayman Islands, Montserrat, and Som-

---

[2]St. Christopher is popularly, but not officially, known as St. Kitts. In 1967 Anguilla attempted to withdraw from St. Christopher and Nevis, but the attempt failed.

brero. The two larger groups of such islands are the British Virgin Islands and the Bahamas.

The British Virgin Islands (Map 41, p. 302) include some 36 islands and islets, of which the largest are Tortola (20 square miles), Virgin Gorda (13 square miles), and Anegada (11 square miles). On the whole British Virgin group there are 59 square miles, and a population in 1967 of 8,650 people—a decline of several hundred since 1956. With the exception of Anegada, these islands are steep and mountainous. The highest elevation, on Tortola, stands 1,780 feet above sea level. Anegada, on the other hand, is a piece of coral reef standing no more than 30 feet above the sea.

Since the end of the seventeenth century British planters have tried to produce crops on these islands. With African slave labor they did raise sugarcane, cotton, tobacco, indigo, and other crops. But the plantations were high-cost producers, and in the nineteenth century they ceased to operate. The people, mostly Africans, who remain on the islands, now use the mountainous areas for a shifting cultivation of vegetables, followed by pasture, and then second growth scrub woodland again. The clearing of the woodland results in the production of small quantities of charcoal. On Anegada, where rainfall is scanty, there is almost no agriculture.

The British Virgin Islands are closely tied to the economy of the American Virgin Islands just west of them. The economic and social life of the remaining inhabitants has been focused on the city of Charlotte Amalie on American St. Thomas, which is the one important market for the products of the British Virgins. This little city needs supplies of food and charcoal, and these it receives in part from the nearby British Virgins. Many workers go to St. Thomas in search of employment. So close are the economic ties that on the British Virgins the dollar, rather than the pound, is the chief unit of currency.

The people of the Bahama Islands insist that they are not West Indians, and that the Bahamas are not part of the Antilles (Map 33, p. 227). There are some 3,000 pieces of land, all of them low-lying bits of coral reef. The islands are too low to receive much rainfall, and the wild vegetation on them was originally a mixture of pine and palmetto, similar to much of the vegetation of Florida. The islands were left uninhabited except for small numbers of Indians until the pirates made use of them for protected anchorages. In 1718 the British claimed the whole group, chiefly because of their strategic importance with reference to the Caribbean.

The Bahamas have a total area of 4,400 square miles and a population estimated in 1967 to be about 143,000. More than half of the population is concentrated around Nassau, on New Providence Island.

Since the beginnings of British settlement a number of economic activities have been tried. Africans, who make up 85 percent of the population, were originally brought to the islands as slaves. For a long time the Bahamas were a major source of sponges, but this product has almost disappeared since the sponge beds were attacked by disease in 1930, and since the use of sponges has greatly decreased. Today the chief exports of the islands are timber, crawfish, salt, tomatoes, cucumbers, and okra. But by far the largest source of income is from the annual flood of winter tourists from the United States. Before World War II New Providence Island was used by a relatively small group of wealthy visitors who had their own homes near Nassau. In 1949 only about 32,000 visitors went to Nassau. But as a result of the efforts of a few of the white residents of the island, new hotels and other tourist attractions were built, and an advertising campaign was undertaken. As a result the tourists now come to the Bahamas in large numbers, greatly altering the economy and the social life of the islands.

THE AMERICAN VIRGIN ISLANDS

The American Virgin Islands lie west of the British Virgins and east of Puerto Rico. These include three chief islands: St. Thomas, St. John, and St. Croix (Map 41, p. 302). The 133 square miles of land is administered by the U.S. Department of the Interior.

The United States purchased the islands from Denmark in 1917. The Danes had first visited this part of the Antilles in 1672, but their first settlement on St. John was made in 1717. They purchased St. Croix from France in 1734.

In 1967 the population of the American Virgin Islands was about 50,000. About half of the total population is concentrated around Charlotte Amalie on St. Thomas, and about half is on St. Croix. St. John has fewer than a thousand regular residents. Charlotte Amalie, with its fine protected harbor, is now the chief commercial center for the whole Virgin group, both American and British. In sailing ship days Charlotte Amalie was often the first port of call on the voyage from Europe, and when coal replaced sails, this port became a major coaling station. For modern ships there is no need to refuel so frequently, so this function is no longer important. Charlotte Amalie is a trans-shipping station for bauxite shipped by barge from the Guianas and destined to continue northward to the United States or Canada. Products are brought to Charlotte Amalie from all the islands—sugar and alcohol from St. Croix, bay leaves from St. John, vegetables and charcoal from the British Virgin Islands.

The major economic support for the islands today is tourism. Charlotte Amalie is the chief port of entry, and many remain in the city or near it. Many, however, spread out to tourist facilities all around the shores of St. Thomas and St. Croix, where they may come to spend several months in this delightful climate. In 1956, Laurance S. Rockefeller presented more than 5,000 acres on St. John to the United States government to form the nucleus of a national park. Each year hundreds of thousands of visitors come to the islands, contributing many millions of dollars to the island economy.

A major problem around Charlotte Amalie has been to provide enough water for so many people. The ground water is not nearly enough, and the small amount of rainfall on this lee side of the island provides little run-off. By law every house must be provided with a catchment area on the roof to collect rainwater, and there are cement catchment areas on the hillsides. But Charlotte Amalie was so short of water that there were occasions when water had to be shipped by tanker from Puerto Rico. Now a plant for the desalinization of sea water has been built, and as a by-product of this, a steam-electric generating station provides electric power for the city.

THE FRENCH ANTILLES

The French possessions in the Antilles were formerly more numerous than they are today. Before the downfall of Napoleon, French authority extended at one time or another over almost all the islands between Hispaniola and Tobago, except for Barbados; and on Trinidad, which never actually came under French rule, there are many people of French ancestry. Now only two chief islands remain, each of them with the status of a *département,* politically just like the divisions of the mainland of France. These are Martinique and Guadeloupe.

Martinique

The island of Martinique, between St. Lucia and Dominica, is rugged and mountainous (Map 41, p. 302). It is about 40 miles long by 16 wide, and includes along its coast several well-protected harbors, such as the one on which Fort-de-France is located. Its older volcanoes are now deeply dissected by torrential streams, but the young Mt. Pelée, near the northern end of the island, which erupted with great violence in 1902, has all the forms of a newly built volcanic cone. St. Pierre, north of Fort-de-France, was one of the major ports of the Antilles before the eruption of Mt. Pelée; this whole section of the island, however, was utterly devastated by that catastrophe. But this is not the only natural calamity which has disturbed the peace of Martinique. In 305 years there have been 33 hurricanes, 7 earthquakes, 5 serious conflagrations, 3 famines, 1 drought, 11 storms with tidal waves, and 3 volcanic eruptions. Martinique has averaged one disaster in almost every five years, which, in so densely populated an island, causes much distress and poverty.

Alcohol and rum are still the chief products of Martinique. Sugarcane was introduced from Brazil in 1654, and by the beginning of the eighteenth century this colony had become one of the most wealthy of the sugar islands. At the present time something like 80 percent of the better lands are devoted exclusively to cane. The Plain of Lamentin, bordering the Bay of Fort-de-France, is the only extensive area of level land in Martinique. It is covered with cane fields and is entirely devoid of habitations or of lands used for subsistence crops. Cane is also grown along the windward northeast coast. Almost all the cane lands are held in large estates. So specialized is the interest in sugarcane planting, that no other commercial crops have ever received much attention, although coffee, cacao, cotton, vanilla, and pineapples have all been tried at one time or another. Since World War II there has been an increase in the production and export of bananas and pineapples. The chief manufacturing plants are engaged in the refining of sugar, the distilling of exceptionally high-quality rum, or the canning of pineapples. The chief exports, most of which go to France, are bananas (35 percent), sugar (31 percent), rum (16 percent), and canned pineapples (10 percent).

Martinique is densely populated by a largely African peasantry. There is a considerable emigration to France, especially since 1946, when the colony was made an integral part of the French state and when the people of Martinique received full citizenship. In 1938 the population was estimated at 241,000; in 1967 it had reached 327,000. With only 431 square miles of area, this gives an over-all density of 719 people per square mile. The density is much higher than this around the margins of the island, especially on the edge of the Plain of Lamentin.

Guadeloupe

Guadeloupe, which lies between Dominica and Montserrat, is made up of two islands, separated by a shallow arm of the sea, the Rivière Salée, filled with mangrove. To the east is the low-lying, limestone platform of Grande-Terre, with an area of 219 square miles. To the west is Basse-Terre, with an area of 364 square miles. Basse-Terre, in spite of its name, is very rugged and mountainous. Its highest volcanic peak, Mt. Soufrière,[3] 4,869 feet in elevation, is the highest mountain in the Lesser Antilles.

The *département* of Guadeloupe includes also six small islands. Close to Grande-Terre, and, like it, formed as platforms of coral limestone, are La Désirade (11 square miles), Marie Galante (60 square miles), and Petite-Terre (two islands totalling 1.2 square miles). To the south of Basse-Terre are the Îles des Saintes (or, Les Saintes), the tops of deeply submerged peaks. Some 125 miles to the northwest, between St. Kitts and Anguilla, is

---

[3]The Mt. Soufrière on Guadeloupe is not to be confused with the mountain of the same name on St. Vincent, which erupted in 1902.

St. Barthélemy (9 square miles) and 12 miles beyond is St. Martin, of which the northern part (20 square miles) belongs to France, the southern part to the Netherlands. Both St. Barthélemy and St. Martin are made up of coral limestone on top of underlying volcanic rocks.

The population of the whole *département* of Guadeloupe in 1967 was 317,000. The population in 1938, however, was about 330,000, which means that there has been a net decrease of population, largely as a result of emigration to France since 1946. The greater part of the decrease has been on Grande-Terre, St. Barthélemy, and St. Martin. On Les Saintes, on the other hand, there has been an increase of population. Most of Guadeloupe is occupied by people of mixed African and French ancestry, but on Les Saintes the people are mostly French. The density of population on Les Saintes is over 500 per square mile, which is greater than on any of the other islands.

Guadeloupe has long been used for the planting of sugarcane. When the French first settled on the island, the chief area of cane planting was around the margins of Basse-Terre, but the chief area of production now is on Grande-Terre. There has been the usual change from small-scale to large-scale mills. In 1809 there were 411 small mills, each owned by one of the French planters of Guadeloupe and supplied with cane from his plantations. In the period since World War II there were built 13 large mills: 6 on Grande-Terre, 5 on Basse-Terre; and 2 on Marie Galante. More than 30 percent of the sugar is produced by one large mill known as Beauport, located on the northwest shore of the northern part of Grande-Terre, and supplied by cane from a large area of plantations. The change to large-scale mills has taken much of the profit away from the planters of Guadeloupe. Of the total sugar production, 60 percent comes from mills like Beauport that are owned in France, 30 percent comes from mills that are owned by wealthy people in Martinique, and only 10 percent comes from mills owned in Guadeloupe. Some of the cane is now grown by tenant farmers: for example, to supply Beauport, 14 percent is grown on corporation-owned lands, 17 percent on tenant plantations, and the remainder, some 69 percent, on small owner-operated plantations.

There is need to experiment with other kinds of crops. Sugarcane, once established as it has been in Guadeloupe, persists in part because of the large investment necessary to begin operations, and in part because of tradition and the reluctance to take a chance on other crops even when sugar gives only a meager living. At Beauport experimental plantations of sisal and other fiber crops have been started, and seem to promise good results. On Basse-Terre, where rainfall is sufficient, there has been an increase in banana planting. Because of the frequent occurrence of hurricanes, plantations that require several years to mature are risky. Only sisal can survive the big storms: sugarcane and bananas are destroyed, but can easily be replanted.

The economy of Guadeloupe is still based on sugarcane. The chief industries are sugar refineries and rum distilleries. The exports, over 70 percent of which go to France, are sugar, rum, molasses, and bananas.

There are two urban centers on the island of Guadeloupe. The capital of the *département* is the town of Basse-Terre, located on the southwestern end of Basse-Terre, the island. This place had a population in 1965 of about 16,000. The largest town and chief port is Pointe-à-Pitre, located on Grande-Terre near the southern entrance to the Rivière Salée.

The outlying islands, with the exception of Marie Galante, are either too steep or too dry for sugarcane. Production from Marie Galante is declining. La Désirade, St. Barthélemy, and St. Martin (divided between the French and the Dutch) are used chiefly for plantations of cotton, sisal, coconuts, and foods for local use. Les Saintes are too steep for much farming, and are occupied by a people whose economy is based on fishing and on making charcoal.

THE NETHERLANDS ANTILLES

The Netherlands Antilles include six islands with a total area of 371 square miles and a population estimated in 1955 as about 185,000. The six islands are in two groups. Curaçao, Aruba, and Bonaire are located between 20 and 38 miles off the coast of Venezuela (Map 51, p. 350). The other three are 500 miles away toward the northeast between St. Kitts and Anguilla (Map 41, p. 302). These are the southern part of St. Martin, Saba, and St. Eustatius.

These six islands have the status of an autonomous state in the Kingdom of the Netherlands. They are administered from the capital city of Willemstad on Curaçao (50,500 inhabitants in 1965).

POPULATION OF THE NETHERLANDS ANTILLES*

Unit	Area in Square Miles	1870	1915	1938	1955	1960
Curaçao	173	20,844	33,677	62,798	119,000	125,181
Aruba	69	3,792	9,204	28,155	56,000	58,743
Bonaire	95	3,816	6,592	5,536	6,000	5,812
St. Martin (part)	17	2,853	3,202	2,202	2,000	2,728
Saba	5	1,832	2,488	1,209	1,000	980
St. Eustatius	12	1,890	1,431	1,121	1,000	1,014

*Data from R. R. Platt, J. K. Wright, J. C. Weaver, and J. E. Fairchild, *The European Possessions in the Caribbean*, American Geographical Society, New York, 1941; and the Encyclopedia Britannica Book of the Year for 1967.

The two groups of islands differ in their economies and their problems. The one activity that gives support to the Netherlands Antilles as a whole

Entrance to the port of Willemstad, Curaçao, showing the famous pontoon bridge. *Photo Courtesy—Pan American Airways.*

is the refining of oil on Curaçao and Aruba. These two islands have increased in population while all the others were declining. None of the islands possesses resources of soil or climate to support very large populations. But when the large oil corporations built refineries to handle the crude oil shipped out from the Lake Maracaibo region of Venezuela, an entirely new kind of economic life began. For a while all the Venezuelan oil was refined here, but during and since World War II several large new refineries have been built on the mainland, such as the Creole Petroleum Corporation refinery on the Paraguaná Peninsula. In 1957 the Royal Dutch Shell undertook to enlarge and modernize the big refinery on Curaçao, and a similar job was done on the refinery on Aruba.

None of these islands is high enough to bring a very large rainfall. When Europeans first set foot on them they were covered with a scrub woodland on which even goats found it difficult to survive. But on Curaçao a distinctive kind of agriculture was developed. Dwarf orange trees could survive and produce a bitter, miniature orange. The fruit was ground up and fermented to produce the orange liqueur known as Curaçao. There were also plantations of sisal and divi-divi, which is used in tanning. But with the development of the new oil refineries, and the growth of Willemstad as one of the major trading centers of the Caribbean region, a source of fresh water had to be provided. The refineries themselves use large quantities of water, and there was a very great increase in the demand for water for domestic uses in Willemstad. During the dry season water used to be sold for one to ten dollars a ton. During 1957 distillation equipment was installed on both Aruba and Curaçao, based on models developed in the Persian Gulf oilfields. Sea water is now run through stills to make fresh water, and for the first time a plentiful supply for both domestic and industrial uses is available. The cost of the process is partially compensated by the use of the steam to generate electricity for the city.

The northern islands are of slight economic importance and have only small populations. Some little cotton is grown on St. Martin and St. Eustatius. The island of Saba, which is a simple volcanic cone rising 2,887 feet above the sea, is occupied by two contrasted population groups living inside the long-since inactive crater. The island comprises an area of only about 5 square miles. It rises abruptly from the water's edge with steeply cliffed slopes, leaving no protected anchorage around the shore. Within the crater there are several little villages, each containing a few hundred people. For a long time Saba was fairly prosperous in spite of the difficulties of access to its settlements. The population remained predominantly European, although it was served by a small group of African slaves. The chief economic activity on the island was the construction of small sailing boats to be used for com-

Oil refinery on Curaçao.

munications among the islands throughout the Antilles. The boats were built near the towns, and then lowered into the sea with ropes. The liberation of the slaves in 1863 and the gradual change to steamboats brought an end to the unique function of Saba. Now the proportion of the black population is increasing at the expense of the white.

Chapter 15 □ The Guianas

About a century after the Portuguese and the Spaniards had started the European colonial movement, the Dutch, the French, and the British also began to look for lands around the world in which to establish colonies. By this time Spain and Portugal had divided the world between them and had occupied those parts of the Americas in which there were large native populations or sources of gold and silver. The other European nations had to take what was left. In the Americas neither Spain nor Portugal claimed the forested eastern part of North America, or most of the Lesser Antilles, or the Guiana coast of South America. Columbus had sailed along the Guiana coast in 1498 but did not attempt a landing. Other Spanish explorers were discouraged from taking a closer look at the Guianas by the absence of any concentration of native peoples and by the dense cover of rain forest that made the search for gold difficult, to say the least. The Portuguese founded settlements along the Amazon, and the Spaniards had a few settlements along the Orinoco. But the stretch of low coast between these rivers remained empty and unclaimed.

Guiana is a regional name applied to that part of South America which is surrounded by water (Map 2, p. 9). The several bodies of water that surround Guiana are the Orinoco River, the Río Cassiquiare, which drains a part of the upper Orinoco southward to join a headwater tributary of the Rio Negro, the Rio Negro itself, the Amazon, and the Atlantic Ocean. The region is divided politically into five parts: Brazilian Guiana, Venezuelan Guiana, Guyana (an independent state since 1966, formerly British Guiana), Surinam (Dutch Guiana), and French Guiana. This chapter deals with the last three.

THE GUIANAS

Atlantic Ocean

TERRAIN

Map 47

Surface Features

In the Guiana region there are three different kinds of surface features (Map 47). There is a low, wet coast. In back of this is a hilly upland developed on crystalline rocks, surmounted in the remote interior by rounded low mountains which differ from the hilly area only because of greater elevation. And there are conspicuous flat-topped tabular uplands.

The low coastal lands are made up of mud, silt, and sand brought down by the Amazon River. This river carries such a huge load of alluvium that the ocean is discolored for 200 miles offshore. All this alluvium is swept northwestward along the Guiana coast by a strong ocean current moving from southeast to northwest. As a result of wave action on the margins of the alluvial plain the immediate shore is an almost continuous sandbar only a mile or so wide. The bar is broken where rivers draining from the interior keep channels open to the sea. In back of the sandbar is a belt of marshy lagoons across which the rivers meander on their way to the ocean. Because of the large tidal range along the coast, the rivers and the lagoons are flooded at high tide, and the lagoons are partially drained at low tide. This wet coastal

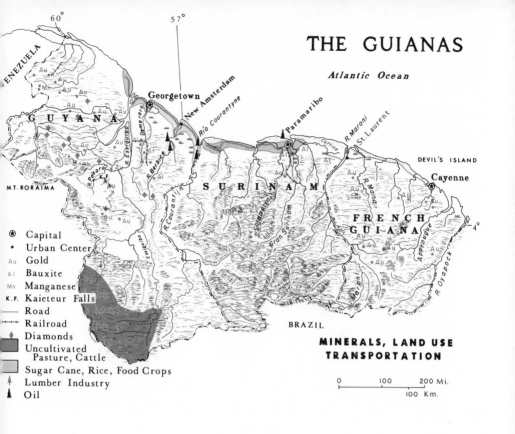

THE GUIANAS

Atlantic Ocean

Georgetown
New Amsterdam
Paramaribo
DEVIL'S ISLAND
Cayenne

GUYANA
SURINAM
FRENCH GUIANA
MT. RORAIMA
BRAZIL

⊛ Capital
• Urban Center
Au Gold
Al Bauxite
Mn Manganese
K.F. Kaieteur Falls
— Road
+++ Railroad
⧫ Diamonds
▮ Uncultivated
   Pasture, Cattle
▮ Sugar Cane, Rice, Food Crops
⧪ Lumber Industry
⧫ Oil

**MINERALS, LAND USE
TRANSPORTATION**

0   100   200 Mi.
0   100 Km.

Map 48

lowland with its bar, its lagoon, and its numerous rivers varies in width from 5 to 30 miles. In French Guiana a projection of higher ground actually extends all the way to the shore.

This lowland ends abruptly on its landward side against the margin of a hilly upland. The hills are low and rounded, and deeply mantled with soil. The underlying rocks are crystalline, and in the rainy tropics these weather to greath depths. The continuous downward percolation of rainwater through the soil dissolves the soluble minerals, leaving a deeply leached lateritic soil at the surface.

The hilly upland on crystalline rocks rises step by step toward the interior. In places the gently rolling surface is surmounted by steep-sided pinnacles of rock. In the farther interior there are irregular areas of low mountains with massive rounded outlines. The mountains reach elevations as high as 4,000 feet above sea level, but the general elevation of the hilly upland is only about 1,000 feet. The highest of the low mountains are the Tumac-Humac Mountains of Surinam.

In Guyana and Venezuela the hilly uplands are surmounted by table-like

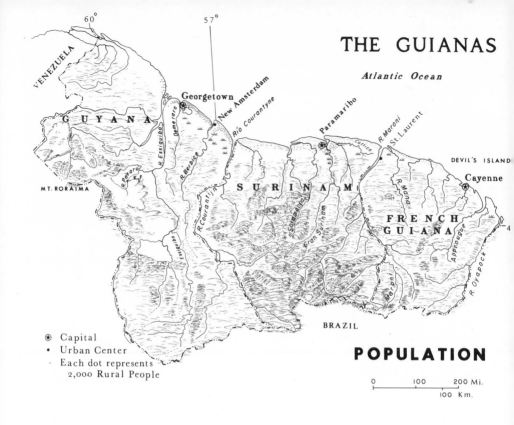

THE GUIANAS

Atlantic Ocean

Georgetown
New Amsterdam
Rio Courantyne
Paramaribo
Cayenne
DEVIL'S ISLAND

VENEZUELA
GUYANA
SURINAM
FRENCH GUIANA
BRAZIL
MT. RORAIMA

Capital
Urban Center
Each dot represents
2,000 Rural People

POPULATION

0   100   200 Mi.
100 Km.

Map 49

plateaus held up by horizontal layers of sandstone. In fact, the highest elevation in this part of South America is Mt. Roraima, located where the
borders of Guyana, Venezuela, and Brazil come together. Roraima is a
great flat-topped plateau which reaches 9,212 feet above sea level. The rivers
which rise on these sandstone plateaus drop over their cliffed sides in spectacular waterfalls. The Angel Fall in Venezuela, the highest fall in the world,
drops 3,212 feet to the surface of the hilly upland below. Kaieteur Falls in
Guyana, where the Rio Potaro, a tributary of the Essequibo, drops 741 feet,
is another such fall.

The rivers that descend from these mountains and plateaus and cross the
crystalline hilly upland toward the Atlantic are all interrupted at frequent
intervals by falls and rapids. Only short stretches of water are navigable, and
then only for shallow-draught boats and canoes. Eight of these rivers have
been of major importance; from southeast to northwest they are: the Oyapock, the Maroni, the Surinam, the Saramacca, the Courantyne, the Berbice,
the Demerara, and the Essequibo.

Climate and Vegetation

The climate of the Guiana coast is equatorial. The heat equator, which is a line drawn through the climatic stations with the highest average annual temperatures (but not the highest extreme temperatures), follows the Caribbean coast of South America, passing through Maracaibo, La Guaira, and other points in northern Venezuela. It then crosses the delta of the Orinoco and follows the coast southeastward to about latitude 5° N., where it crosses the Atlantic toward Africa. The climate of Georgetown, capital of Guyana, is representative of the climatic conditions of the whole coastal region. At Georgetown the average annual temperature is 80.6°, ranging from an average of 82.2° in the hottest month (September) to an average of 79.3° in the coolest months (January and February). As is characteristic of equatorial stations, the range between day and night, which is about 10°, is greater than the range between the coldest and warmest months. Except for the highest elevations of the interior, the altitude of the highlands is not enough to lower the temperatures significantly. In the Guianas people must adjust themselves to monotonously high temperatures—temperatures which are never excessively high, but which are never lowered by spells of cool weather.

The rainfall and humidity are also high. At Georgetown the average annual rainfall is 87.4 inches. There are two seasons of heavy rainfall and two seasons of somewhat less rain. The rainfall is heavy from April to mid-August and again from mid-November to the end of January. During the seasons of less rain there is less cloudiness and temperatures are higher. But even in the rainy seasons there are periods of very heavy downpours separated by hot sunshine. The winds throughout the year come from the northeast, bringing large amounts of moisture evaporated from the warm water of the Atlantic. The relative humidity at Georgetown averages 79 percent. Nevertheless, the constant winds which sweep across the coastal region make life quite comfortable in spite of the humidity. In modern times people have learned how to select clothing appropriate to the climate and how to build houses with air conditioning.

The vegetation cover is mostly a heavy rain forest. The wet savanna along the coast is the chief interruption of the forest; it occupies the lagoons and tidal marshes, or the river floodplains subject to more or less regular inundation. The beginning of the crystalline hills and many parts of the inner side of the lowland are covered with forest in which there are few natural openings. The forest covers the crystalline low mountains, leaving only some of the drier parts of the sandstone plateaus in dry savanna. Along the headwaters of the Essequibo and of the Rio Branco, which drains southward toward the Amazon, there is a wide belt of dry savanna, known as the Rupununi Savanna. As is common in dry savannas, the rivers are followed by fringes of galeria forest.

The European Settlements

The occupation of the Guiana region by European colonists provides a clear demonstration of an important geographic principle—that the meaning of any habitat differs for people with differing attitudes, objectives, and technical skills. The three European colonies, each developed in essentially the same natural surroundings, are today notably different in what the inhabitants have done with these surroundings.

The first Europeans to settle in Guiana were the Dutch. In 1613 they established three colonies in what later became British Guiana—on the Essequibo, the Demerara, and the Berbice. The Dutch went upstream as far as the rivers were navigable for their sailing ships, which was just about to the edge of the crystalline hilly upland. Here their African slaves made clearings in the forest and planted tobacco and sugarcane. These early settlers—like many people even today—had the idea that any soil that would grow such a luxuriant cover of forest must be incredibly fertile. Only slowly did they find out that actually the soil outside of the river floodplains was very poor for shallow-rooted crops. Deeply leached soils in the rainy tropics do not support permanent agriculture without the heavy use of fertilizers and soil conditioners. After a few years, during which the yields of crops steadily declined, the Dutch abandoned their up-river settlements and moved back down to the alluvial plain along the coast, establishing their colonies on the sandbar near the river mouths.

The alluvial soils of the coastal lowland are not leached and are potentially much more productive than those of the uplands of the interior. But to make use of the coastal lowlands much hard work had to be done to drain the marshes and keep out the ocean water at high tide. At this kind of work the Dutch were already skilled. Along the lower rivers they directed their slaves to build dikes and canals. Gates were closed at high tide to keep out the ocean water, and opened at low tide to permit the drainage of the marshes. When water was needed for growing rice, they diverted the flow of the rivers onto diked fields. All this was hard work in any climate, and in the steamy humidity of the lagoons back from the coast, infested with mosquitoes, the work could scarcely have been done without the labor of African slaves. But as a result the plantations along the Essequibo, the Demerara, and the Berbice became quite prosperous.

Dutch settlements began to spread in either direction along the coast. When the Dutch spread beyond the Essequibo toward the Orinoco, the Spaniards began to resist, and the Dutch authorities, wishing to avoid trouble, closed this part of the coast to further settlement. Settlement thereafter spread to the Courantyne and the Surinam.

Meanwhile other parts of the Guiana coast were being occupied by the French and the British. In 1643 a French colony was established on the one spot where a projection of the hilly upland extends to the edge of the ocean—at Cayenne. The colony was promptly attacked and destroyed by the Indians, but was reoccupied by the French in 1664. In 1650 the British founded a colony at the mouth of the Surinam River. These two groups of settlers, unlike the Dutch, were not familiar with the techniques of draining wet lands. The British sugarcane plantations were restricted to small bits of higher ground along the river, where soil was less productive than in the drained marshes. The Surinam plantations were not doing very well. Therefore, in 1667, the British were quite ready to give Surinam to the Dutch in exchange for the Dutch colony on Manhattan Island.

These Guianan colonies changed hands many times. The British repeatedly raided the prosperous Dutch colonies, and 1796 took possession of the Essequibo, the Demerara, and the Berbice settlements. At one time even the Portuguese captured Cayenne, which they later returned to France. Finally, in a series of treaties negotiated in Europe between 1812 and 1817, the present boundaries were fixed. French Guiana included the coast between the Oyapock and the Maroni; Dutch Guiana, or Surinam, extended from the Maroni to the Courantyne; and British Guiana ran westward from the Courantyne far beyond the Essequibo, almost as far as the delta of the Orinoco—an area that today is in dispute between Guyana and Venezuela.

Except for the brief Portuguese occupation of Cayenne, which ended in 1817, the settlements of the French, the Dutch, and the British along the coast between the Oyapock and the Essequibo were unchallenged by the Portuguese or the Spaniards. Beyond these rivers there was greater resistance: the Spaniards pushed back the British from the mouth of the Orinoco; and the Portuguese pushed back the French from the region around the mouth of the Amazon.

Since the early nineteenth century the traditions, skills, and government policies of each of the colonizing powers has brought quite different results in the Guianas. The British, in the slave period, were able to take advantage of the dikes and canals built by the Dutch to achieve a certain degree of prosperity. The Dutch in Surinam, however, had great difficulty in keeping their slaves from escaping into the forests of the interior. Escaped slaves formed independent African communities in the forests, practicing a shifting cultivation of subsistence crops. These were the Bush Negroes, who for a long time raided the Dutch settlements when they were extended back from the coast. As a result the Dutch did not build such extensive dikes and canals along the Courantyne, the Saramacca, and the Surinam as they had built earlier along the Berbice, the Demerara, and the Essequibo. When the slaves were freed (in British Guiana in 1838, in French Guiana in 1848, and in Surinam in 1863), the Africans fled from the sugarcane plantations. Some were able to escape into the forests and join the Bush Negroes. In British Guiana, where the lands that the Dutch had drained were available for agriculture, the Africans remained in rural villages to work as farmers, but not on the sugarcane plantations. In Surinam, however, where the suitable lands were all occupied by cane plantations, the Africans flocked into Paramaribo. Today in Surinam 70 percent of the people of African descent or mixed descent live in Paramaribo, whereas in Guyana only 42 percent of the Africans live in Georgetown.

Both British Guiana and Surinam attempted to solve the labor problem by bringing in workers under contract. The British first tried the Portuguese from Madeira, where sugarcane had long been grown. Then they tried Chinese and East Indians (Hindus and Muslims). The Dutch brought in East Indians and Indonesians, mostly from Java. The French tried convict labor from France. Each of these different policies had quite different results.

GUYANA

Area: 83,000 square miles
Population: (1967 estimate) 677,000
           (last census, 1960) 560,330
Capital city: Georgetown; (1960) 148,391
Percent urban: (1946) 27.6
Birth rate per 1,000: (1966) 39.9; Death rate per 1,000: (1966) 7.6
Annual percent of increase: (1958–64) 2.8
Percent literate: (1946) 75.9
Percent of labor force in agriculture: (1960) 32.3
Gross national product per capita: (1964) $281
Unit of currency: West Indian dollar (1968, 1.97 per dollar)

COMMERCE, 1965 *(expressed in percentage of values)*
Percent total Latin-American exports: 1.0
Percent total Latin-American imports: 1.0

Exports (1966)

sugar	30	alumina	17
bauxite	23	rice	13

Exports to (1966)		**Imports from (1966)**	
United Kingdom	22	United Kingdom	33
United States	22	United States	23
Canada	22	Trinidad	10
Trinidad	8	Canada	9
Norway	6		

In 1966 the former British Guiana was granted independence and adopted the name Guyana. The problems it faces today in the effort to build a sound economy and to form a viable state are directly inherited from these colonial policies.

The Population and Pattern of Settlement

Guyana's 677,000 people are of diverse ethnic origin. East Indians make up 50 percent of the total population. Although they have given up the traditional Indian costumes and have learned to speak English rather than Hindi, they tend to remain unmixed with the other elements of the population. Usually they concentrate in certain villages in which there are no other kinds of people. Africans and part-Africans make up 43 percent of the total, and 2 percent are Portuguese, Chinese, British, and North Americans. But aside from the East Indians, these other ethnic elements occupy villages where they are mixed together, as they are also in Georgetown. Another 5 percent of the population includes native Indians living in the forests of the back-country.

When the British took control of the Dutch settlements along the three rivers of what became British Guiana, they inherited the Dutch engineering works. The British promptly set their slaves to work extending the dikes and canals all along the inner side of the coastal bar. Today there is an almost continuous zone of agricultural settlement along the bar all the way from the Surinam border on the Courantyne River to and beyond the Essequibo River (Map 49, p. 334).

The pattern of settlement is distinctive. The land is divided into thousands of long, narrow strips running from the ocean back into the drained lagoons. Each strip is perhaps half a mile wide and some ten miles long. The homes of the people who work the land are built along a highway on the sandbar. Along this highway, facing the ocean, there is an almost continuous string of houses (Map 50, p. 341).

The different ethnic groups have tended to cluster in different places. The East Indians furnish most of the plantation workers where sugarcane is grown. The mixed settlements of the other ethnic groups are found where other kinds of crops are grown. The chief exception is in the area up the Berbice River inland from New Amsterdam, where an almost solid East Indian population is engaged in growing paddy rice (Map 48, p. 333).

The Economic Situation

Agriculture provides the chief support for the economy of Guyana, although only 32 percent of the workers are employed in agriculture. The chief agricultural product is sugar. Cane plantations are found all along the coast,

Natives navigating a canoe on the upper Essequibo River in Guyana. *Photo by Desmond Holdridge.*

many of them occupying the strips of farmland mixed with other kinds of plantations. In the neighborhood of Georgetown, and also around Guyana's second town, New Amsterdam, there are a few large plantations not divided into strips, and from these few large properties comes most of the sugar for export. Modern mills grind the cane and refine the sugar, and nearby are rum distilleries. Sugar and sugar products usually make up about a third of the value of all exports, mostly sold in Commonwealth countries.

Only a small part of the total national territory is used to grow crops (15 percent in 1967), and almost all of this land is along the coast. Repeatedly there are projects for spreading agriculture into the hilly lands of the interior, but each such project meets the challenge of poor soil and low productivity. The government is attempting to diversify the agriculture of the coastal zone by promoting the production of coconuts, cacao, coffee, citrus fruits, oil palms, peanuts, bananas, and vegetables—all of which grow well in the rich alluvium of the coastal lowland. A part of this program of diversification is the development of paddy rice along the Berbice, and from this area there is now enough production so that Guyana can export rice (16 percent of all exports in 1965).

The economy of Guyana is also supported by minerals, all of which come from the backlands (Map 48). The most important is bauxite. During World War II the bauxite mines around Mackenzie, some 55 miles up the Demerara River from Georgetown, were producing about 20 percent of the world's supply, and were the chief sources of this ore for the aluminum industry of the United States. In 1968 Mackenzie was connected by a paved road to

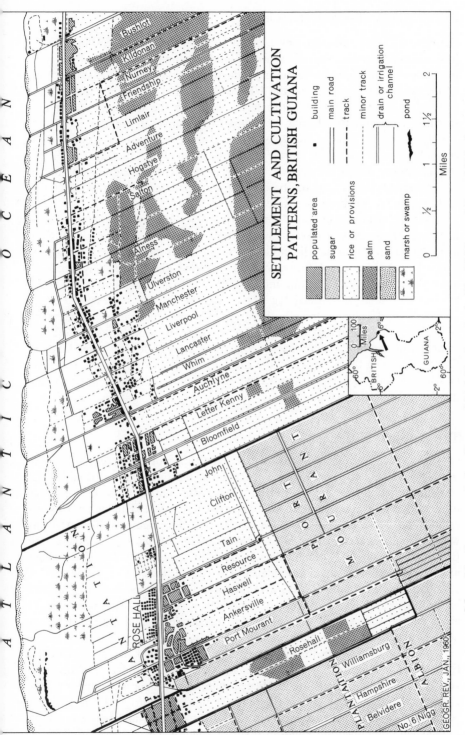

SETTLEMENT AND CULTIVATION PATTERNS, BRITISH GUIANA

- ■ building
- populated area
- ▨ sugar
- ▤ rice or provisions
- ▦ palm
- ▨ sand
- 类 marsh or swamp
- ═ main road
- ┄ track
- ┈ minor track
- ⊏ drain or irrigation channel
- pond

Miles
0   ½   1   1½   2

BRITISH GUIANA

Map 50. *Courtesy of the Geographical Review (vol. 50, 1960, p. 44), published by the American Geographical Society.*

Georgetown. The post-war development of new bauxite mines in Jamaica has reduced the proportion of the world total coming from Guyana (7 percent in 1964), but the actual volume of production remains about the same. Some of the ore continues to go to the United States, but increasing amounts are shipped to Canada. A new hydroelectric plant on the Demerara River now provides power for the refining of some of the bauxite in Guyana.

Guyana is also famous for its gold and diamonds. These are found in the crystalline rocks along the northeast-facing front of the plateau and in the stream gravels that drain away from the plateau. The chief diamond sources are in stream gravels near the base of the escarpment. It is in this same area that manganese has been discovered.

Another valuable resource of Guyana is timber and wood products. In the backlands there are vast forests covering over 80 percent of the national territory. There are the usual difficulties to be faced in cutting and transporting tropical timber—because the species of any one kind are widely scattered among other kinds of trees, and much of the most valuable wood is too heavy to float in the streams. Each log has to be brought out separately. One of Guyana's most valuable trees is the greenheart *(Ocotea rodioei)*. The heartwood of this tree is one of the most indestructible of woods, and is useful for wharf piling in places where marine organisms quickly destroy other kinds of timber. To solve the problem of the diversity of species in the forest—many of which woods have little commercial value—the government is promoting the development of tree plantations.

The Political Situation

Guyana faces serious problems in the organization of a coherent and viable state. The social and geographical separation of the East Indians from the rest of the population has already caused trouble. But not only the East Indians have tended to remain separate, identifying themselves as Hindus or Muslims rather than Guyanians; so also have the other ethnic elements. The Africans would usually describe themselves as Africans, the Chinese as Chinese, the British as British or Scottish. This is quite in contrast to Trinidad, where most people, long before independence was gained, thought of themselves as Trinidadians. But in the 1950's a remarkable change came to Guyana, and in the process of change a kind of state-idea was forged. This was brought about by the very widely held desire for independence and for the development of a self-sufficient economy.

A political leader appeared who was able to command the support of the East Indians. This was Dr. Cheddi Jagan. He took advantage of a situation very common in sugarcane areas. Here, as elsewhere, there was a great difference between the labor demand at harvest time and during the rest of the year. Most of the sugarcane workers were East Indians, and they were East Indians who had given up Hindi in favor of English. Dr. Jagan promoted the organization of the cane workers in unions, and the unions pressed demands on the plantation owners for better pay and for unemployment and health benefits. Jagan, who became the political leader of British Guiana, formulated a program of social change to be paid for by new taxes imposed on the estate owners. The estate owners retaliated by introducing machinery for the cultivation of the cane lands and for the harvesting of the cane—which greatly aggravated the unemployment problem among the East Indians. Jagan succeeded in setting the workers against the landowners and in setting the East Indians against the people of other ethnic groups. Disorder threatened the program for granting independence, as Great Britain moved in troops to control rioting. In May, 1964 serious riots broke out between the East Indians and other groups.

In late 1964 Jagan was removed from office, and a coalition government was organized. The effort was to bring some kind of coherence among the diverse ethnic groups; and such coherence was made possible by the widely supported feeling that British forces should be removed and independence granted. In 1966 independence was granted.

Is Guyana a viable state? Certainly Guyana has a more varied resource base than either Trinidad or Jamaica, yet in 1964 the gross national product per capita was much less in Guyana than in these two other newly created states. Again political stability was clearly to be correlated with economic development. If stability in Guyana is maintained, a considerable increase of the gross national product per capita can be expected; but if the increase of income goes to a small minority, and if social change does not bring greater security to the rest of the people, the East Indians, at least, are likely again to become restless and rebellious. The coalition government has undertaken measures to increase the productivity of the East Indian farms and to provide other kinds of employment to supplement work on the cane plantations. The hope remains that the feeling of nationalism, newly aroused among the Guyanians, will be strong enough to bring the diverse components of the population politically together.

SURINAM

In contrast to Guyana, there is little demand for independence among the diverse peoples of Surinam. This former Dutch colony is now one of three integral parts of the Kingdom of the Netherlands (along with the Netherlands Antilles and the Netherlands in Europe). This arrangement seems to satisfy the people of Surinam.

The Population and Pattern of Settlement

The population of Surinam is perhaps even more diverse than that of Guyana. Furthermore, the diverse ethnic groups in Surinam have not given up their traditional forms of dress, nor their languages and customs, as the different groups in Guyana have done. In Surinam about 38 percent of the total population is described as *Creole*, which here refers to people of African ancestry who are born in America.[1] In Surinam the Creole women can usually be identified by their distinctive costume, including the turbaned kerchief around the head. East Indians make up 31 percent of the total. They are known as *Hindustani*, regardless of whether they are Hindus or Muslims. These people also continue to wear their traditional Indian costumes. Some 14 percent of the population are Muslims from Java. In the back country there are the Bush Negroes who make up about 11 percent of the total. Perhaps 2 percent of the population are native Indians, known as *Amerindians* to distinguish them from Hindustani. Another 2 percent are Chinese, and still another 2 percent include Spaniards, Portuguese, Dutch, Lebanese, Syrians, English, and even some North Americans.

In Surinam there is no common language. Each ethnic group continues to use its own language. If there is any one language that almost every one can understand, it is a kind of patois made up of a mixture of African and English words, which is used nowhere else but in Surinam. The official language is Dutch, but a very large proportion of the people cannot use it. Lacking a common tongue, each ethnic group remains in separate communities, usually each one performing its own kind of work.

The pattern of settlement is one of isolated clusters. There is no continuous string of settlement tied together by a road. Rather there are scattered and isolated villages. Nor is the agricultural land continuous, for there are thriving plantations often bordered by abandoned plantations that are growing up in brush.

Each of these ethnic groups plays a different role in the economic and political life. The Hindustani are mostly small farmers who own and operate their own properties, although some are tenants on rice paddy land or on dairy farms. The small farmers raise a great variety of food crops for their own use, and for sale in Paramaribo and other urban places. The Indonesians are the plantation workers in Surinam. They work for Dutch owners growing a variety of commerical crops, such as cacao, coffee, citrus fruits, and sugarcane. Most of the Creoles are concentrated in Paramaribo, where they dominate the political life, operate small retail stores, and provide most of the

---

[1]The term *Creole* is used in the southern United States to refer to people of European (French or Spanish) ancestry born in America. But in the Guianas the term refers to people of African or mixed African and European ancestry.

professional class. The Chinese are mostly shop-keepers, restaurant proprietors, bankers, or other kinds of small businessmen.

The Economic Situation

The economy of Surinam, unlike that of Guyana, is primarily based on the mining of bauxite. Bauxite deposits were discovered along the Cottica River near Moengo in 1917, and since 1929 the mineral has been Surinam's leading export. In 1964 bauxite made up 82 percent of the value of all exports, and in that year Surinam produced 12 percent of the world's supply.

The bauxite occurs in beds some 15 to 20 feet thick, under an overburden of varying thickness. It is usually found near the edge of the hilly upland, but access to the mines is gained by navigating the meandering rivers across the lowlands, which, though very narrow, are deep enough to float ocean-going ships. The Cottica gets so narrow before the ships get to Moenga that the dense vegetation along the river banks scrapes against the ships' sides. Before World War II another bauxite mining area was opened up about 16 miles from Paramaribo on the Surinam River at Paranam. The Aluminum Company of America (ALCOA) completed construction of a refinery to produce alumina at Paranam in 1966. Electricity is furnished by a hydroelectric plant located at the big dam on the Surinam River upstream from Paranam.

There has been some development of manufacturing industries in Surinam, especially in and around Paramaribo. The St. Regis Paper Company has built a plant to make use of the abundant resource of timber in the manufacture of cardboard containers. These are sent to places around the Caribbean to use in shipping bananas. Several factories make plywood, flooring, and prefabricated houses. There is a plant for canning orange juice and pineapples, and another plant extracts coconut oil. In 1965 Surinam started to export rice (6 percent of the exports), most of which came from one modern mechanized plantation.

FRENCH GUIANA

The third of the Guianas is a *département* of France, similar to Martinique and Guadeloupe. This is French Guiana, the part of the Guianas with the smallest population and the least economic development. Most of the people on the coastal lowlands are of African ancestry, with perhaps 5 percent of the total made up of French and other Europeans. There are small numbers of native Indians living in the forests, and probably also some Bush Negroes. There are no East Indians or Indonesians to complicate the ethnic picture.

The Prison Camps

French Guiana was notorious for its prison camps to which French convicts were at one time sent. Prison camps were established after the emancipation of the slaves in 1848 as a way to solve the labor problem. The worst of the prison camps was located up the Maroni River, about 125 miles from Cayenne, at a place called St. Laurent. Health conditions here were very bad, and the lack of wind made the steamy humidity very trying. More favored prisoners were sent to Devil's Island, one of three small Îles du Salut, located about 8 miles off shore. Here there is always some wind, and the health conditions are relatively good. The policy of sending out French convicts, which was started in 1852, was terminated in 1944, and by 1946 the last of the prison camps had been abandoned. The Îles du Salut are to be developed as tourist attractions.

The Economic Situation

After the closing of the prison camps, the economy of French Guiana stagnated. The chief products came from the sawmills at St. Laurent. But in 1967 this part of France began to feel a quickening of its economic life. French businessmen from Africa were bringing new projects to French Guiana, including an increase in the manufacture of plywood. The sugarcane plantations around Cayenne and St. Laurent have been expanded, and attempts are being made to introduce cacao, pineapples, and rice. At Cayenne there is a rum distillery, a pineapple cannery, and a factory for the manufacture of ball-point pens. But the largest new industry is a shrimp-processing plant, owned in the United States, which in 1967 employed 400 workers. About 24 percent of the value of all exports are from timber and wood products, and 11 percent is from gold which is mined in small scattered localities in the back country. But the export of shrimp is providing a new and much needed diversification of the economy.

The newest development in French Guiana is the construction of a space center, to be located about 30 miles west of Cayenne along the coast. This location close to the equator will permit the launching of space satellites into orbits that cannot be reached from higher latitudes. The space center, which will be open for the use of all friendly nations, is to be devoted to such peaceful research programs as the study of weather. It is expected that the center will be opened in 1970.

Courtesy of Colombia National Tourist Service

Spanish
South
America

República de Venezuela

Area: 352,143 square miles
Population: (1967 estimate) 9,352,000
(last census, 1961) 7,523,999
Capital city: Caracas; (1966) 1,764,274
Percent urban: (1961) 67.5
Birth rate per 1,000: (1966) 47–51; Death rate per 1,000: (1966) 8–12
Annual percent of increase: (1958–64) 3.4
Percent literate: (1961) 65.8
Percent labor force in agriculture: (1961) 32.8
Gross national product per capita: (1966) $895
Unit of currency: bolívar (1968, 4.50 per dollar)
Leading crops in acreage: maize, coffee

COMMERCE, 1964 *(expressed in percentage of values)*
Percent total Latin-American exports: 27.7   (1956, 14.)
Percent total Latin-American imports: 14.8

Exports (1966)
Petroleum products   92

Exports to (1966)		Imports from (1966)		
United States	37 (1956, 38)	United States	50	(1956, 59)
Netherlands		West Germany	10	
Antilles	21	Canada	5	
Canada	8	Japan	5	
United Kingdom	7	United Kingdom	5	
		Italy	5	

Chapter 16 □ Venezuela

The winds of revolution have swept through Venezuela. As a result, a poor preindustrial and predemocratic country, long ruled by a wealthy and powerful minority, has been set on the road to modernization. Venezuela has entered the "take-off" stage of economic growth, and since 1955 it has enjoyed the largest gross national product per capita of any independent Latin-American country. Its national income, long pocketed by the dictator and a few associates, is now being more widely distributed among the people. Major steps have been taken to reduce illiteracy and to improve diet and health. In 1963, for the first time in Venezuelan history, a popularly elected government completed its term of office and was succeeded by another popularly elected government. Furthermore, the long struggle against ruthless and brutal autocratic rule has developed among the people of Venezuela a strong sense of national identity, a positive state-idea. To achieve these revolutionary changes has required a complete break with the past.

The independence movement among the Spanish colonies in America appeared early in Venezuela. Simón Bolívar, the leader in the liberation of northern South America, came from an aristocratic family in Caracas. His ideal was the freedom of American-born leaders to govern without interference from Spain. Freedom for him meant freedom from foreign authorities. Bolívar hoped to set up a "United States of South America," and for a few years he was able to hold together in Gran Colombia the territory now included in Venezuela, Colombia, and Ecuador.

Bolívar's dream of a united South America was shattered by revolt. The smaller political leaders in the several separate clusters of population, having been freed from Spanish authority, turned against authority from Bogotá where Bolívar had his capital. In 1830 Bolívar's own chief lieutenant in the

Map 51

wars against Spain declared Venezuela to be free from Gran Colombia. Bolívar, in despair, said: "Our America will fall into the hands of vulgar tyrants; only an able despotism can rule America." This was more than a hundred years ago; but the prophecy has been fulfilled quite literally during the succeeding years.

Between 1830 and 1935 Venezuela had more than a dozen rulers, but three "able despots" stand out above all the others. Páez, a mestizo peon, was the first of these, who declared the independence of Venezuela in 1830. The second was Guzmán Blanco, who first came to office in 1870. From 1909 to 1935 it was Gómez. Under each of these despots Venezuela was run like a vast private estate for the benefit of the owner, but the result was the enforcement of order among the various factions and a consequent increase of material prosperity. In the intervals between, the country was ravaged by the conflict of warring elements, no one of which was strong enough to beat the others to submission. These were periods of destruction and loss.

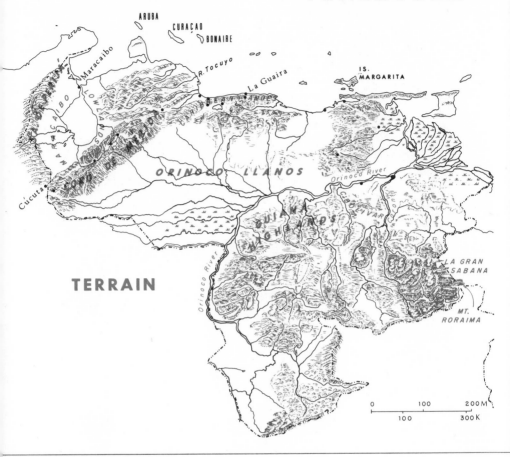

Map 52

Juan Vicente Gómez was not descended from the aristocracy. He was the son of an Indian mother and a mestizo father who lived in poverty in the high Andean country along the Colombia-Venezuela border. He was a man of tremendous ambitions, a ruthless fighter, one who ruled his country with an iron hand. His opponents were killed or exiled. But when geologists found that Venezuela possessed important oil resources, Gómez, in the years immediately after World War I, made arrangements with the large oil corporations to undertake the expensive business of producing oil. The Venezuelan treasury was suddenly filled with money. In the depression years after 1929, Gómez brought his country through without any foreign debt. When he died in 1935, mobs tore his palace to bits.

Since the death of Gómez, Venezuela has been the scene of a mighty struggle between those who favor democratic procedures, including rule by law, and those who seek to continue the traditional system of personal power. Between 1945 and 1952 political parties were given freedom to

351

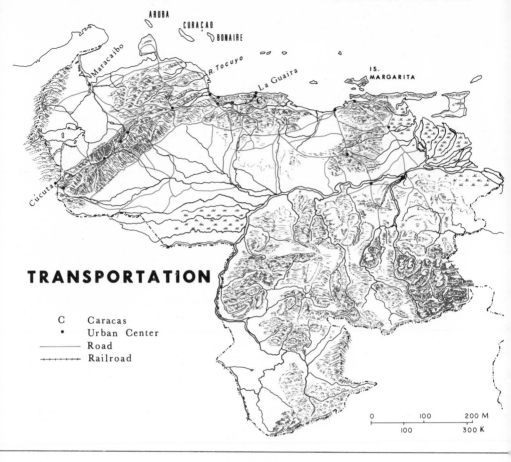

VENEZUELA

ARUBA
CURAÇAO
BONAIRE
Maracaibo
R. Tocuyo
La Guaira
IS. MARGARITA
Cúcuta

TRANSPORTATION

C   Caracas
•   Urban Center
——— Road
+++++++ Railroad

0   100   200 M
100   300 K

Map 53

organize and to discuss public policy—an unheard-of thing in Venezuela. In 1947 elections were held in which the whole adult population, literate and illiterate, took part. Some 70 percent of the voters gave their support to a liberal, civilian government. In 1948, however, the army again seized power, and until 1958 Venezuela had another period of absolute dictatorship, backed by the action of a secret police operating outside the law. In 1958 a new revolt against the dictator took place. Since 1958 the forces of democracy have successfully dealt with threats of violence from both the right and the left.

The People

Bolívar and Gómez dramatize the contrasts which exist among the people of Venezuela and some of the difficulties involved in establishing order among such diverse elements. The ingredients which have entered into the human

352

VENEZUELA

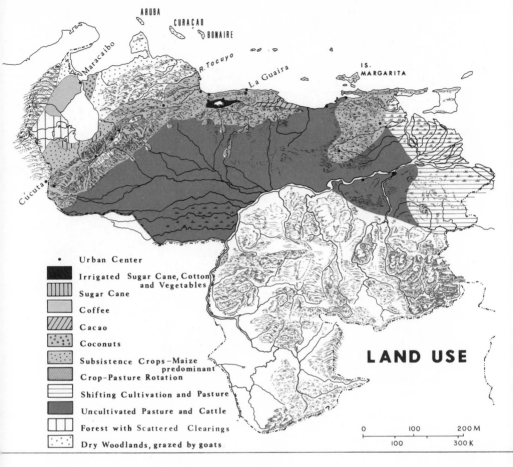

LAND USE

Urban Center
Irrigated Sugar Cane, Cotton and Vegetables
Sugar Cane
Coffee
Cacao
Coconuts
Subsistence Crops – Maize predominant
Crop-Pasture Rotation
Shifting Cultivation and Pasture
Uncultivated Pasture and Cattle
Forest with Scattered Clearings
Dry Woodlands, grazed by goats

Map 54

mixture in this country include Europeans, Indians, and Africans. In the absence of reliable census data, we may use the estimates published in the United Nations Demographic Yearbooks. These estimates indicate that 20 percent of the Venezuelans are of unmixed European ancestry, and this includes many who, like Bolívar, had only one Indian ancestor a long time back. Probably not more than 2 percent are of unmixed Indian ancestry, and another 8 percent are pure African. About 70 percent of the Venezuelans are mestizos—persons of mixed European and Indian parentage in varying ratios.

Racial percentages are not uniform throughout Venezuela. Europeans are concentrated in the larger towns and cities—in Caracas, Maracaibo, or Valencia. Pure Indians, on the other hand, survive only in the more remote places—in the Guiana Highlands south of the Orinoco River or in the forests west of Lake Maracaibo. The African mixture is greatest along the Caribbean coast, in such ports as La Guaira and Puerto Cabello. Even

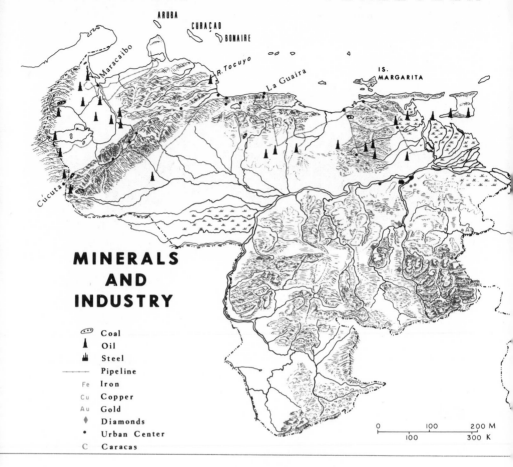

VENEZUELA

ARUBA
CURAÇAO
BONAIRE

Maracaibo

R. Tocuyo

La Guaira

IS.
MARGARITA

Cúcuta

MINERALS
AND
INDUSTRY

- Coal
- Oil
- Steel
------ Pipeline
Fe Iron
Cu Copper
Au Gold
♦ Diamonds
• Urban Center
C Caracas

| 0 | 100 | 200 M |
| 100 | 300 K |

Map 55

among the mestizos there is a notable difference between the people of the highlands and those of the lowlands. To understand these differences we must go back to the early days of the Spanish conquest.

The Indians and the European Conquest

In 1500 Venezuela was occupied by scattered tribes of Caribs and Arawaks (Map. 5, p. 14). These people lived along the northern coast of South America and on some of the islands of the Caribbean. They were primarily hunters, fishers, and migratory cultivators. Contact between the Spaniards and the Indians began along the coast during the first part of the sixteenth century. The first European settlement of the continent of South America which has survived to the present time was established at Cumaná (Map 6, p. 18), in 1523. Four years later another colony was planted at the base of the Paraguaná Peninsula at Coro. From these two bases exploring parties pushed inland. West of Coro the Spaniards entered the Maracaibo lowland

354

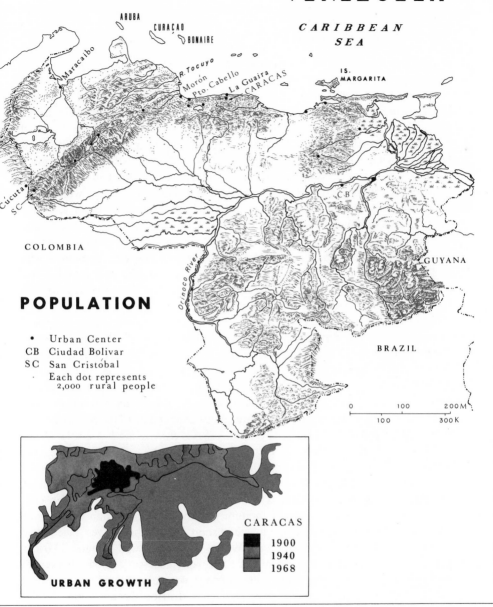

VENEZUELA

ARUBA
CURAÇAO
BONAIRE

CARIBBEAN
SEA

Maracaibo

R.Tocuyo
Morón
Pto. Cabello
La Guaira
CARACAS
CARACAS

IS.
MARGARITA

Cúcuta
SC

CB

COLOMBIA

GUYANA

POPULATION

- Urban Center
CB Ciudad Bolívar
SC San Cristóbal
· Each dot represents
    2,000 rural people

Orinoco River

BRAZIL

0   100   200M
   100   300K

CARACAS
1900
1940
1968

URBAN GROWTH

Map 56

and, coming upon Indian villages which were built on piles in the shallow
waters of the lake, they named the country "Little Venice," or Venezuela.

The territory these first Spanish explorers penetrated was less attractive
than Mexico because of the sparseness of the Indian population and the
absence of any accumulation of treasure. Nevertheless the Spaniards pressed
inland searching for gold, and in the period after 1538 they did actually discover many places where the stream gravels yielded the precious metal. The
placer mines of the valley in which Caracas was later founded, as well as
those of many scattered localities throughout the highlands, were actively
worked with gangs of Indian slaves, and for a time the Venezuelan mines
seemed to promise great wealth. But none of the sources of gold discovered

at that time proved to be better than low-grade deposits, and the gold miners were forced to turn to agriculture.

More than twenty years elapsed after the settlements at Cumaná and Coro before the first permanent town was established on the highlands, although during that period the whole highland region had been tramped over and many of the valley bottoms had been dug up in the search for gold-bearing gravels. In 1555 the town of Valencia was founded in the intermont basin which has since become the leading agricultural district of the country. The good farming land was quickly partitioned into large estates which were divided among the Spanish officers; and on these estates the Indians, Christianized and enslaved, were set to work for their new masters. Barquisimeto was also established about this time in the midst of another farming district to the west of Valencia, and in 1567 Caracas was laid out. Spaniards who had invaded the country which is now Colombia and who had founded Bogotá turned again toward the north and established San Cristóbal and Mérida in the mountains south of Lake Maracaibo.

After these first highland settlements had been made, more than a century elapsed before the Spanish occupation of other parts of Venezuela began. To be sure, some of the savanna-covered plains of the Orinoco in the neighborhood of Valencia were utilized for the grazing of cattle and even for agriculture; but the penetration of the more remote parts of the country was delayed until late in the seventeenth century. Barcelona was not founded until 1671 and Calabozo till 1695. Maturín was founded in 1710 and Angostura, now called Ciudad Bolívar, in 1764.

Meanwhile, the mixture of races proceeded rapidly. The Spaniards did not generally bring their womenfolk with them to America, but took wives from among the Indians they conquered. While great numbers of the native peoples died from the epidemics of measles and smallpox, the mestizo children showed a greater degree of immunity to these diseases than their Indian ancestors. Nevertheless, the landowners soon found themselves faced with a shortage of agricultural laborers. Where sugarcane was planted, African slaves were introduced to perform the hard work necessary for the harvesting and grinding of the cane. Since intermarriage was unrestricted either by law or by custom, the people of the sugarcane districts became considerably darker in complexion than are the inhabitants of the rest of the country.

Present Population

For a long time the population of Venezuela increased only very slowly. At the beginning of the nineteenth century Alexander von Humboldt, the famous German geographer, estimated the number of Venezuelans to be about 1 million. In 1920 another estimate based on a wide knowledge of the country but not on an actual census placed the figure at 2,400,000—not a very great increase in more than a century. After World War II, however, modern public health programs, including the control of insects, resulted in a sharp decrease of the death rate. The most recent estimates indicate that Venezuela has a birth rate between 47 and 51 per thousand, and a death rate between 8 and 12 per thousand. As a result Venezuela's net rate of increase is about 3.4 percent per year, which means that this is the fastest growing population in Latin America except for Costa Rica and the Dominican Republic. In 1967 it was estimated that the Venezuelan population was over 9 million.

Like all population data for large areas, these figures obscure important differences in density and rates of growth or decline between one area and another. There is a notable current of internal migration toward the cities. Caracas in 1967 had a population of nearly two million in its metropolitan area, and there were 6 other cities of over 100,000. An entirely new concentration of people had appeared near the junction of the Orinoco and the Caroní, in an area which only a few decades ago was an almost unoccupied wilderness. There were other smaller districts of rapid urban growth, but at the same time there were extensive rural areas from which there has been a net loss of population. To understand the significance of these population patterns we must examine, region by region, the ways in which the inhabitants have occupied the land and exploited its resources during the various periods of Venezuela's history.

The Regions of Venezuela

The territory which is now included in Venezuela is made up of four major divisions, only one of which is densely populated. The backbone of the country, not only in terms of its surface features but also in terms of population, is formed by the Venezuelan highlands, a branch of the Andes (Maps 52 and 56). A chain of high mountains crosses the border from Colombia south of Lake Maracaibo. Beyond the end of this towering range the somewhat lower but still very steep Caribbean ranges run eastward along the coast, with a gap of about a hundred miles, to the eastern tip of the Paria Peninsula. This highland backbone is so important that we shall discuss the way people have occupied it in four subdivisions: The central highlands, in which Caracas and Valencia are located; the northeastern highlands; the Segovia highlands, north of Barquisimeto, including the Paraguaná Peninsula; and the Cordillera de Mérida, south of Lake Maracaibo.

The other three major divisions of Venezuela are not so densely populated as the highlands. Within the Y formed by the high Cordillera de Mérida and the lower Sierra de Perijá on the Venezuelan–Colombian border lie the Maracaibo lowlands, in the midst of which there is an extensive lake of fresh water. This lowland constitutes the second of the major divisions of the country. The third division is a vast plain, sloping gently from the southern and southeastern base of the Andes toward the Orinoco River—a region known as the Orinoco Llanos. The Orinoco itself flows along the border between the Llanos and the Guiana highlands, a hilly upland (the fourth major division) which makes up about half of the total national territory.

The Highlands

THE CENTRAL HIGHLANDS

That part of the highland backbone which borders the Caribbean between Puerto Cabello and Cape Codera has become the core area of Venezuela. On this part of the country the political interests come to a focus, and here one finds the densest rural populations and the largest city.

The Caribbean coast which borders the central highlands is dry and hot. Some eleven inches of rain at La Guaira are not enough to support more than a scanty cover of xerophytic plants, among which the cactus is prominent. Throughout the year the prevailing wind is from the east, so that protected anchorages are to be found only on the western sides of promontories or peninsulas, yet the protection from the wind which is desirable for landing places is most undesirable for health and comfort. As far as average annual temperatures are concerned, this Caribbean coast has the highest records of the American tropics, although extreme temperatures are higher elsewhere. La Guaira, for example, has an average annual temperature of 80.8°.

The mountains of the central highlands rise abruptly from the coast to elevations of between seven and nine thousand feet. The dry conditions are restricted to the first few hundred feet of the mountain slopes. Above that an abundant rainfall supports a cover of forest which continues to the tree line between six and seven thousand feet above sea level.

The central highlands are composed of two distinct ranges, separated by the intermont basin in which Valencia is located and by the eastward continuation of this basin, the deep valley of the Río Túy. In the center of the Basin of Valencia there is a shallow body of fresh water known as the Lake of Valencia, which was visited in 1800 by Alexander von Humboldt. At that time the lake had no surface outlet, but Humboldt noted that at some previous time it had flowed out southwestward toward the Orinoco. He used this as a classic example of the unhappy effects of too much forest clearing. The level land around the lake had been plowed for the planting of indigo, and the steep mountain slopes around the margin of the basin had been cleared for the cultivation of maize. As a result the rainwater ran off in torrents instead of sinking into the ground and seeping slowly toward the lake. After torrential floods there was less water under ground, and the level of the water table dropped. Humboldt cautioned against the disasters that would follow widespread clearing of the original cover of vegetation. It happened that 25 years later another geographer visited the Lake of Valencia

Port of La Guaira, Venezuela. *Courtesy of Ministerio de Fomento, Venezuela.*

and found that it had again risen and had a surface outlet. This was during the wars of independence, when the workers had been taken into the army, the crops were neglected, and the second-growth forest had covered the slopes again. In the present century forest clearing for agriculture has gone on rapidly. Since 1900 the level of the lake has dropped sixteen feet, and again it has no surface outlet. As a result the margins of the lake are bordered by a wide belt of marshes, especially on the eastern and western sides. This basin, some 1,500 feet above sea level, is partly drained to the east by the Río Túy, which has cut back westward and captured some of the drainage that once entered the lake. The Río Túy plunges eastward through narrow gorges and over many rapids until it reaches the funnel-shaped lowland opening out eastward toward the Caribbean.

The ranges of mountains on either side of the Río Túy and of the Basin of Valencia are too narrow to include any very extensive areas of gentle slopes. A few small river basins, however, are to be found nestled in the midst of the mountain country. The most important is the Valley of Caracas. About 6 miles south of the Caribbean coast the northern range is broken by a narrow structural depression, a rift, which extends for about 15 miles east and west. In this rift valley there is a narrow strip of gently sloping land almost entirely surrounded by steep mountains.

The climatic conditions and the cover of natural vegetation in the central highlands are of an extremely complex pattern. Temperatures decrease, in general, with increasing altitude, and averages of less than 65° in the coldest month begin about 3,000 feet above sea level. The Basin of Valencia, however, is only about 1,500 feet in altitude, and the Valley of Caracas is barely 3,000 feet. Throughout the area, rainfall and humidity are high on slopes which face toward the prevailing winds. The east-facing valley of the Río Túy and also of the Río Yaracuy (west of Puerto Cabello) receive plentiful rains which support a forest cover.

The Spaniards found in the Basin of Valencia, and in other smaller basins of the central highlands, places where the slopes were gentle enough and the ground water was plentiful enough for commerical agriculture to be profitable. Failing to discover wealth in the form of precious metals, they turned to the production of commercial crops, making use of cheap land and slave labor. Soon after the conquest the highland region, as well as much of the more remote country outside of the highlands, was partitioned among a relatively small number of Spaniards. The crops which were raised included a mixture of those native to America and others introduced from the Old World. The native American food grain, maize, was widely cultivated for the needs of the workers, but only on land not suitable for the production of the crops that brought profits to the owners. Sugarcane was perhaps the most valuable of the new crops, and for a time Venezuela participated in the rapidly expanding sugar market in Europe, then being supplied chiefly from Brazil. In 1784 coffee was introduced. The landowners discovered, however, that they could tempt the foreign markets with some of the new American products, such as cacao, tobacco, and indigo. The latter crop brought such good returns during most of the colonial period that many areas of settlement were supported by the plantations not only in the central highlands but also in other less-favored parts of the country. Now that chemical dyes have taken the market away, however, indigo is no longer of any importance, and the plantations have been abandoned or put to other uses.

Although the type of agriculture has changed notably in the course of the 400 years of Spanish settlement, and Basin of Valencia has remained the chief agricultural area of the country. The well-drained lands around Valencia in the western end of the Basin were formerly used for the fattening of cattle raised on the Llanos. There were also sugarcane and cotton plantations. The workers on the plantations grew their own food crops of maize and beans on the steep hillsides bordering the basin. On the eastern side of the lake, around Maracay, there were pastures for dairy cattle, and also plantations of sugarcane and cotton. Since 1958, however, the Basin of Valencia has been transformed by the program of agrarian reform. Almost all of the privately owned estates have been confiscated. The owners received compensation, but usually much less than they thought the land to be worth. One estate, belonging to the Pimentel family, was divided in 1961 among 3,000 families. The government has provided credit, technical assistance, schools, medical centers, access roads, and rural electrification. The small farmers grow cotton for the supply of textile factories in Valencia and Caracas, and also foods such as maize, rice, and beans. There are pastures for herds of dairy cattle. The government has also removed the farmers from the bordering mountain slopes, and a program of reforestation has been started.

The density of the rural population is not very great, even in the areas of chief concentration in the central highlands. The greatest density is in the Valley of Caracas, where there are about 125 rural people per square mile. East and west of the lake in the Basin of Valencia the density of rural population is around 60 people per square mile. Even in this core area there are large empty areas.

The core area in the central highlands is also the major focus of urban and industrial growth. Caracas in 1967 had a population of 1,700,000, and it was growing faster than any other city. Unfortunately, so many rural people migrated to Caracas that it was impossible to build new housing fast enough or to provide new jobs in manufacturing industry or in service occupations to take care of the unemployed. The government took steps to increase the building of manufacturing plants in other cities, notably in Maracay and Valencia in the core area. All these cities produce textiles, leather goods, paper, cigarettes, refrigerators, and a variety of other consumer goods. A new industrial park at Valencia has attracted automobile assembly plants, firms to produce automobile parts, tires, air conditioners, and food processing plants. Thermoelectric stations using natural gas piped in from the Lake Maracaibo area provide power. Caracas is supplied with an abundance of water from the Río Túy.

The core area is also the focus of Venezuela's transportation pattern. Airlines now connect Caracas with all parts of the national territory, and journeys that used to take weeks now require only a few hours. The large airport for Caracas is located at Maiquetía, just east of La Guaira.

Railroads are less important than they once were. Most of Venezuela's railroads were built during the rule of Guzmán Blanco, between 1877 and 1893. By attracting foreign capital the dictator succeeded in equipping his country with the kind of transportation which was most desirable at that time. The railroads from La Guaira to Caracas and from Puerto Cabello to Valencia were built with British capital; and these were connected by a line between Caracas and Valencia which was built with German capital. The latter railroad was especially costly because of its 217 bridges and 86 tunnels. The very expensive nature of the construction of all these railroads, and the lack of bulky traffic, necessitated high rates for shipment, with the result that most of Venezuela's commerce continued to reach the coast or to move inland from the coast over rough trails on the backs of mules.

General Gómez was one of the earliest Latin-American rulers to appreciate the value of all-weather roads for the use of motor trucks. During the first decade of his administration a road-building program was adopted and work started on several great highways—all leading toward Caracas and the Basin of Valencia. One highway was built across the mountains south of Caracas to the edge of the Llanos. In the dry season it was possible to continue across the plains by automobile to the banks of the Orinoco opposite Ciudad Bolívar. Another road connected the Basin of Valencia with the Llanos directly to the southeast, and still another ran far to the southwest along the base of the Andes. The most important highway built by Gómez was the one which ran southwestward from Valencia along the axis of the highlands by way of Mérida to the Colombian border, a distance of 676 miles.

It was not until after 1950, however, that Venezuela's modern period of road building began. First was the problem of connecting Caracas with its seaport, La Guaira. The two are only a little more than 6 miles apart, but Caracas is about 3,000 feet above sea level, and to reach a pass over the coastal range required a climb to 3,412 feet. Furthermore the slopes were so steep that the railroad had to cover 23 miles, and the old highway 21 miles, to make the climb. In December 1953, a new super-highway was opened between La Guaira and Caracas. Bridges and tunnels carry this modern highway through the mountains rather than over them. The automobile trip from La Guaira to Caracas now takes about fifteen minutes.

Paved motor highways now connect the core area with all the other centers of population and economic activity throughout the country. A highway crosses the Llanos to Ciudad Bolívar where a bridge carries traffic to the south side of the Orinoco, and to the new industrial complex on the lower Caroní. Another highway reaches San Fernando de Apure. A branch of the Llanos highway reaches Barcelona and Cumaná. Three highways extend westward from the core area. The Inter-American Highway passes through Barquisimeto, and thence along the northern base of the Andes to the southwestern corner of the Maracaibo lowland. Here the highway climbs into the Andes to San Cristóbal, and crosses into Colombia over the Simon Bolívar International Bridge. Still another paved highway has been built around the coastal margin of the Segovia highlands all the way to Maracaibo, crossing the end of the lake on a bridge. And another paved highway runs along the southeast-facing piedmont of the Andes as far as Barinas. Gravel extensions of this highway continue farther to the southwest. An all-weather gravel road has also been built southward from the Orinoco River to reach the border of Brazil near Mt. Roraima. After 1958 there was also an important program of feeder road construction, planned so that no agricultural settlement would remain isolated from a market (see Map 53).

Superhighway carrying traffic between La Guaira and Caracas. *Courtesy of Ministerio de Fomento, Venezuela.*

THE NORTHEASTERN HIGHLANDS

While the central highlands region was being made into more and more of a focus of political, social, and economic activity, and while its chief city was growing rapidly, the northeastern part of Venezuela, beyond the Gulf of Barcelona, remained static. In this region the coastal range, which forms the two peninsulas of Paria and Araya, is only about 2,600 feet high. The central mountain core of the northeast lies south of the structural depression in which Cumaná is situated; here the summits reach 6,700 feet above the sea. Abundant rains over the whole eastern part of the region supported an original cover of selva, or tropical rain forest, in which, at present, small clearings are used for the production of cacao. The western part of the region, on the other hand, is relatively dry, and was originally covered with scrub woodland and savanna.

Most of the inhabitants of the northeastern highlands live on the drier western side. Cumaná, the oldest European settlement in South America, is now a city of more than 75,000 and Barcelona has grown to about 50,000. Near Barcelona there are some mines of lignite and semibituminous coal, which is sent out through the port of Guanta and thence by sea and by the Orinoco River to the steel plant near the mouth of the Caroní.

THE SEGOVIA HIGHLANDS

The third section into which the highlands of Venezuela may be divided is the Segovia highlands, which lie north of Barquisimeto. This is another of the poorer sections of Venezuela; it is a region of recurring droughts which have had the effect of limiting the settlement to the permanently wet spots along the river valleys. Most of the area has fewer than 10 people per square mile, although small clusters of people are located in the vicinity of Coro, around the oil refineries on the Peninsula of Paraguaná, in the valleys of the Río Tocuyo and the Río Yaracuy, and in the neighborhood of Barquisimeto.

All of this region lies north of the main axis of the highlands which, west of Puerto Cabello, trends southwestward away from the coast. North of the valley of the Yaracuy the Segovia region is composed of deeply dissected plateaus, surmounted by a few isolated ranges of low mountains and hills. The rainfall decreases and becomes less and less certain toward the north. Although the east-facing valleys of the Tocuyo and the Yaracuy receive sufficient rain to support a dense forest, the rest of the Segovia highlands are covered with patches of dry scrub woodland and savanna; excepting for the larger rivers most of the streams are intermittent.

Coro, at the base of the sandy spit which connects the Peninsula of Paraguaná to the mainland, has never prospered. The adjoining territory is sparsely inhabited by a people who produce so little for export that they can purchase

Village in the Yaracuy Valley east of Barquisimeto. *Courtesy of Standard Oil Co. (N.J.).*

little from outside. The rural people are grouped in small areas of settlement wherever water can be assured even in dry years. The Indian and mestizo inhabitants devote small patches of wet land to maize and manioc, but most of the area is used only for grazing of goats and thin scrubby cattle.

The densest populations of the Segovia highlands are in the territory between Tucacas and Barquisimeto. Near the latter city the rural population is between 25 and 60 per square mile. The greater part of the cultivated area is utilized for subsistence products, but plantations of coffee and cacao provide a small current of exports. There is one mining community in this district. The copper mines at Aroa, which were owned at one time by Bolívar, have had a history of fluctuating prosperity. Low prices in the world copper markets after World War I caused the abandonment of these mines. Today they are so badly flooded that to open them again would prove very costly.

The railroad that connects Barquisimeto to the coast at Tucacas is an extension of what was probably the first railroad to be built in South America. In 1835 Aroa and Tucacas were connected by rail, but operation of the line was given up after a few years. In 1877, at the beginning of Venezuela's chief period of railroad construction, the line was reopened and extended to Barquisimeto.

Since 1950 several changes have taken place in the Segovia region. First was the construction of a huge oil refinery by the Creole Petroleum Corporation on the western side of the Peninsula of Paraguaná. Oil from the Maracaibo area is brought to the refinery by a pipeline. More recently a wholly new center of manufacturing industry has been built at a place about 15 miles west of Puerto Cabello. The little town of Morón, with some 1200 inhabitants in 1950, was selected as the location for a huge industrial complex based on petrochemicals. Oil and gas reach Morón by pipelines. The new industries produce fertilizer, chemicals, plastics, pharmaceuticals, synthetic rubber, and many other products using oil and gas as raw materials and fuels. An oil refinery produces gasoline and other petroleum products. There are also new factories to manufacture insecticides, weed-killing chemicals, and synthetic fibers. This is all part of the Venezuelan policy of "sowing the oil," that is, of making use of income from the export of oil to create capital investments that will remain productive after the oil has been used up. The little village of Morón has been submerged in the construction of this new industrial center.

THE CORDILLERA DE MÉRIDA

The southwestern end of the Venezuelan highlands is formed by the high Cordillera de Mérida. In this region several small intermont basins are occupied by small clusters of people, predominantly mestizo; difficulty of access retarded the invasion of the region by large landowners interested in commercial production. In fact, all the more remote sections of Venezuela have suffered in comparison with the central highlands in the matter of easy access to the Caribbean ports. In the central highlands contact with outside markets has been continuous; there, the rulers of the country, wherever they may have originated, have finally established themselves. Gómez himself was born in the Cordillera de Mérida near San Cristóbal, and even spent a part of his life across the border near the Colombian city of Cúcuta; but he emerged from these remote places when he began his career as political leader. The almost complete isolation of the Cordillera de Mérida was finally ended, however, by the rise of coffee as a crop of commercial importance in the nineteenth century.

The Cordillera de Mérida is the only part of the Venezuelan highlands where permanent snow is found at higher elevations. In the vicinity of Mérida itself there are three snow-capped peaks, about 16,000 feet in altitude. The valleys and basins, however, are all at relatively low elevations, and the transverse trench through which the boundary between Venezuela and Colombia passes permits a crossing of the mountains from the Llanos to the lowlands around Lake Maracaibo with a climb to only 4,600 feet above sea level.

Farms and village in the Cordillera de Mérida, Venezuela. *Courtesy of Ministerio de Fomento, Venezuela.*

In high mountain regions of the low latitudes, such as the Cordillera de Mérida, the characteristics of the various elevations are so distinct that the local inhabitants recognize general "vertical zones." The lowest zone in Spanish America is known as the *tierra caliente,* or hot country, which may also be called the "Zone of Tropical Products." The average annual temperatures on the lower mountain slopes and in the deeper valleys are mostly between 75° and 80°, with a difference between the average of the coldest month and the average of the warmest month of not more than three or four degrees. The upper limit of this zone in Venezuela is about 3,000 feet, although of course no sharp line separates one of these general vertical zones from another. Between 3,000 and 6,000 feet in elevation is a cooler region which the people call the *tierra templada,* or temperate country, which may also be designated the "Zone of Coffee." Average annual temperatures at these altitudes vary between 65° and 75°, but the ranges between the coldest and the warmest months are a little less than those in the tierra caliente. Between approximately 6,000 and 10,000 feet in elevation is a zone which is still cooler, known as the *tierra fría,* or cold country, which we may call the "Zone of the Grains." Here, average annual temperatures are between 55° and 65°, and there is practically no difference in temperature from one month to another. The crop found at the highest altitudes is the potato, which in these mountains reaches an upper limit of a little over 10,000 feet. Above the upper limit of forests and of agriculture but below the lower limit of permanent snow, is the "Zone of Alpine Meadows" to which the people in northern South America apply the term *páramos*. In this part of Venezuela the *páramos* are found from approximately 10,000 feet to the snow line at 15,400 feet.

The intermont basins and valleys in the *tierra templada* were occupied at the time of the Spanish conquest by some of the most energetic of the native peoples of Venezuela—a people who formed a striking contrast with their less robust neighbors in the Maracaibo lowlands. The Indians, who were not interested in commerce and for whom the isolation of this mountainous country from the Caribbean was a matter of no importance, found in it far better living conditions than they did in the central highlands of Venezuela. Probably the most important reason for the high degree of habitability of the Cordillera de Mérida was that the Indians depended on maize as their basic food, and this was very productive maize country. Today this grain can be grown up to 7,500 feet above sea level; and, most important of all, up to elevations of about 6,000 feet, two harvests can be made each year. This part of Venezuela shares with the highlands of Colombia the climatic peculiarity of two distinct rainy seasons and two distinct dry seasons—the rainy seasons in Mérida come from April to June and from August to November. As a result, the Indians of this region were able to supply themselves with a greater abundance of food than the highland Indians were able to obtain in the vicinity of Caracas, where only one rainy season occurs. Better diet, probably, rather than lower temperatures, made possible the relatively dense populations of vigorous Indians; but the lower temperatures worked indirectly to improve the health conditions after the arrival of European diseases, for the fever-carrying insects are less numerous above the *tierra caliente*. The stamp of physical vigor is still on the people of this part of Venezuela.

The European settlement of the Cordillera de Mérida, however, did have to face the problem of difficult accessibility. After the first towns had been founded by the people from Bogotá, there was little further activity because of isolation and the lack of precious metals. Planters of sugarcane and indigo were unable to place their products on the market as cheaply as could the planters of sugarcane and indigo in the more accessible central highlands. Not until coffee became an important commercial crop did the people of Mérida find a product which could support the high costs of transportation development; today the Cordillera de Mérida is the chief coffee-producing region of Venezuela.

The three clusters of people in the Cordillera de Mérida are all located in the basins and valleys of the mountains at altitudes between 1,800 feet at Valera and 5,380 feet at Mérida. San Cristóbal, the urban center of the cluster that crosses the border to the area around Cúcuta in Colombia, is 2,700 feet above sea level. Because of the absence of intermont basins at higher altitudes, in the *tierra fría* and the *páramos,* these zones are very thinly populated.

The program of agrarian reform undertaken after 1958 included a major project in the western part of the state of Mérida. A gravel highway runs through the intermont basins along the axis of the high mountains, connecting Trujillo, Mérida, and San Cristóbal. Along this highway a little to the west of Mérida more than a million acres of land were made available for resettlement. More than 5,000 farm families have been settled in this area. Some 70 percent of the resettled families were formerly tenants on large privately owned estates around Trujillo, Mérida, and Táchira, and another 30 percent came from the Maracaibo lowlands. An entirely new cluster of people in an area previously less densely occupied has been created by this program. The food products they produce are partly for their own use, but partly also for shipment by truck to the large urban markets.

The Maracaibo Lowlands

Until after World War I the Maracaibo lowlands remained, along with the Segovia highlands and the northeastern highlands, among the poorer parts of Venezuela. Since this region lies midst higher land that all but surrounds it, there are no steady winds to relieve the oppressive humidity; in this area has been recorded the highest average annual temperature of any part of Latin America. The city of Maracaibo has an annual average of 82.4°, ranging from an average of 80.6° in January to an average of 84.4° in August. On the shores of the lake, after sunset, when the local winds of the daytime have died down, the steamy humidity is very trying; the southern sky is brilliantly illuminated with vivid flashes of lightning which play among the towering banks of cumulus clouds along the mountain slopes. Throughout the southern part of the lowlands and especially on the slopes of the Cordillera de Mérida, heavy rainfall supports a dense growth of selva; toward the north the decrease of rainfall produces a gradual transition from tropical rain forest, through semideciduous forest, to dry scrub woodland.

A lake, roughly 130 miles long by 75 miles wide, occupies the bottom of the Maracaibo lowlands. The southern half of the lake has fresh water, but toward the north the water becomes brackish. At its northern end the lake water passes through a strait, on which Maracaibo is located, before opening out again in the bay at the southwestern end of the Gulf of Venezuela, from which the lake waters are separated by a sandbar. The water over the bar is scarcely 7 feet deep at low tide, and only 12 feet deep at high tide. Immediately inside the bar the lake water is 30 feet deep, and the lake is navigable to its southern end.

Until 1918, however, settlement in the Maracaibo lowlands was of little importance. After coffee plantations began to send products from the Cordillera de Mérida out to the coast over the Maracaibo route, the lake became a waterway of local significance. Transportation was by sloop, and connection with ocean vessels was made at Puerto Cabello or at La Guaira. In the southern part of the Maracaibo lowlands, along the routes which led to the highlands from the lake or river ports, there were some plantations of sugar-cane and cacao, and a few patches of coconuts; but except for the population of these few settled localities and the small town of Maracaibo, the only inhabitants of the lowlands were the Indian fishermen, whose villages, built on piles out in the lake, had excited the interest of the first Spanish explorers.

The people who gained such a miserable living from the land knew nothing of the potential wealth beneath their feet, nor did the fishermen appreciate the black sticky substance that sometimes contaminated the water of the lake and fouled their fishing nets. Geologists, however, long ago reported the existence of oil and of oil-bearing formations throughout the northern part of the region and across the southern half of the Segovia highlands to the east. Not until after World War I did the petroleum companies turn their attention definitely to Maracaibo.

When the first productive oil well was drilled by the Royal Dutch Shell Company in 1917, and when the enormous potential development of the Maracaibo Basin became clear, the construction of an oil refinery near the source of oil became necessary. The Royal Dutch Shell Company, for obvious reasons, decided to build their refinery on the nearby Dutch island of Curaçao. Later, when Creole Petroleum started operations, their refinery was built on Aruba. Only small, shallow-draft tankers were able to reach the lake. But large ocean-going tankers picked up the refined oil from the Dutch islands to carry it to the United States and Europe. During World War II German submarines threatened to cut off the shipment of oil to the refineries.

Since World War II numerous oil refineries have been built on the mainland, connected with the oilfields by pipelines. The largest single oilfield in all Latin America is Lagunillas, on the eastern side of Lake Maracaibo, about 40 miles from Maracaibo. Pipelines carry the oil to the Creole refinery on the Paraguaná Peninsula, and also to large new refineries located at Cabimas, about 19 miles from Maracaibo on the eastern shore of the lake.

The government of Venezuela also undertook to make Maracaibo and the whole of the lake accessible for ocean-going ships by dredging a channel through the sandbar. In 1956 the work was completed, providing a channel 35 feet deep through the bar, which permits the passage of ships up to 28,000 tons. To protect the opening through the bar at the head of the Gulf of Venezuela, a two-mile-long stone breakwater was built a little to the east. This channel now permits ocean-going tankers to pick up oil in Lake Maracaibo, and to reach Maracaibo itself. The latter town, which had a population of 15,000 in 1918, had a population in 1966 of well over 500,000.

The Lake Maracaibo region contains large oil reserves, amounting to about 7 percent of the world's proven reserves. Maracaibo has the world's largest reserve of heavy crude, suitable for use as fuel oil. Some 40 percent of the total Venezuelan production consists of this heavy oil, used widely in the operation of ships, locomotives, and trucks, and for the generation of electricity. About 15 percent of the country's production is used for the manufacture of industrial lubricating oil, asphalt, and wax. The remaining 45 percent is light crude, similar to the oil of Texas, used for the manufacture of the more valuable light products such as gasoline. These various grades of oil will provide the resource base on which the new petrochemical industries at Morón will depend.

Most of the large oil companies have concessions in Venezuela. The largest producer is the Creole Petroleum Company (Standard Oil of New Jersey), which in 1966 accounted for 36 percent of the average daily production. The second in volume was Shell, which accounted for 28 percent. There were also sixteen other companies.

The Orinoco Llanos

The Orinoco Llanos make up the third of Venezuela's major regions. The Llanos consist of a vast, almost featureless plain lying between the Andes and the Orinoco River. This plain, covered with a mixture of savanna and scrub woodland, is approximately 600 miles long and 200 miles wide. It slopes very gradually from the base of the Andes toward the river. Even in its highest part, north and northwest of Calabozo, it is little more than 600 to 700 feet above sea level. The streams which cross it wind about in broad valleys with low gradients; and between the valleys low, mesa-like interfluves are the most conspicuous features of the landscape. If all this region were good pasture land it could support perhaps 50 million head of cattle.

But, for several reasons, it is not good pasture land. The year is divided into a rainy season and a dry season, and during these two extremes the landscape of the Llanos undergoes an extraordinary transformation. The rains begin in April, and after a period of alternating rainy and dry weather, the wettest part of the season continues from June to October. So heavy is the rainfall of these five months that the rivers are unable to carry off all the flood waters, and vast expanses of land are inundated, especially in the country near the Orinoco. At this time, animals are concentrated on the low mesas that stand as islands above the floods. After they have eaten one of these islands bare, they are driven to another, sometimes being forced to wade many miles through shallow water to reach it. Most of the herds at this time of year are driven to the higher ground between Calabozo and Valencia.

In October the rains begin to abate. After a transitional period of occasional showers in November and December, the real dry season begins in January and continues without sign of rain until the end of March. The flood waters recede; only the larger rivers continue to flow freely, and the smaller ones are gradually reduced to chains of swamps and pools along the valley bottoms. The tall rank growth of savanna grasses turns brown and hard and becomes inedible. The low bushy trees of the patches of scrub woodland lose their leaves and stand bare as if in a mid-latitude winter. The higher ground north of Calabozo with its light sandy soil becomes very dry, and the herds of cattle must be driven far to the south to the wet spots near the Orinoco. At the end of the dry season the dry grasses are regularly burned to make the young growth accessible to the hungry cattle. Only when the young green shoots of grass appear at the beginning of the rainy season or in the stagnant waters of the receding floods can cattle find satisfactory pasturage, and even then the native grasses are low in food value. Most of the year the herds barely avoid starvation.

The vegetation of the Llanos is anything but uniform. The savanna varies from tall bunch grasses which grow in the drier parts to the short grass of the wet spots. Patches of dry scrub woodland interrupt the grassy areas, and over considerable stretches there are scattered palms. Lining the courses of the permanent streams are ribbons of dense galeria forest composed of broadleaf evergreen species.

Perhaps no other kind of region is plagued by such a variety of insects as a tropical savanna. Mosquitoes and flies of many species breed in the stagnant waters or the rank grasses. They not only make life extremely uncomfortable for man and beast, but also spread a variety of diseases, some of which are deadly.

SETTLEMENT OF THE LLANOS

To the native Indians of Venezuela the Llanos were almost uninhabitable. Since these Indians lacked the technical ability to irrigate or drain the land and since they had no domestic animals to make use of the savanna grasses, they could occupy the lowlands only where there was sufficient rainfall to support their crops, or where the permanent rivers contained enough fish. Indians lived on the forested delta of the Orinoco, but they avoided the grassy plains.

Cattle were first introduced into the Llanos by the Europeans in 1548. One important advantage compensated in part for the handicaps with which these cattle had to struggle—a complete freedom from carnivorous enemies. A century later herds of wild cattle numbering perhaps 140,000 were reported as grazing on these plains. By 1812 the number had been increased, under the care of seminomadic cattlemen, or *Llaneros,* to about 4,500,000. But immediately after this the Wars of Independence reduced not only the number of cattle but also the number of Llaneros, for these hardy cattlemen were in great demand as fighters. By 1823 the number of cattle had dropped to 256,000.

During the remainder of the nineteenth century the number of animals rose or fell in accordance with the political stability of the country. Gúzman Blanco took a personal interest in the cattle business. He introduced better breeds of cattle and insisted on better methods of caring for them. As a result, by 1883 the number of animals exceeded 8 million. This was the largest count ever made: by 1920 the number was down again, this time below 3 million.

General Gómez, also, took a direct personal interest in the pastoral activities of Venezuela. He introduced the zebu cattle, crossing them with the native stock to gain a greater resistance to the insect pests. This breed of cattle, which came originally from India, has been found to provide better meat and better dairy products in the wet tropics than the common European breeds, for the rather oily hide of the zebu is more of a defense against the flies and ticks which infest the pastures.

In his later years General Gómez held a virtual monopoly of the cattle business. Large foreign-owned ranches on the Llanos which, during World War I, sent cattle to a British packing plant at Puerto Cabello, were forced out of business. This was accomplished in a very simple manner. Gómez imposed taxes on all herds of cattle driven across the state boundaries; since no clear distinction was made between his private funds and the public funds in the federal treasury, the taxes he paid on his own herds were, in reality, paid to himself. He made the taxes so high that no one could compete. He also owned the fattening pastures around the Lake of Valencia.

Cattle from the Llanos are taken to market over three chief routes. The relatively small number of animals in the eastern part of the region are mostly sold in the Antilles, either on the hoof, or as salt beef. They are shipped out by way of Ciudad Bolívar and Port of Spain, or by way of Guanta. The most important route to market, however, is through the Basin of Valencia. Whether the animals are to be slaughtered at Puerto Cabello for export, or in Maracay for the domestic market, they must first be fattened on the irrigated pastures in the Llanos.

Agricultural settlement on the Llanos has been mostly restricted to the higher ground along the Andean piedmont. During slave times large estates along this piedmont were used to grow tobacco and indigo. When slavery was ended in 1854, and when indigo was entirely eliminated by competition with the coal-tar dyes, the agricultural use of the Llanos came to an end. But since World War II, and especially since 1958, agricultural settlement of this region has gone forward rapidly. In 1956 a large resettlement project was completed in the Llanos near Calabozo. The Guárico River was impounded, a little northwest of Calabozo, by an earth dam 9 miles long and 98 feet high. Behind this dam a lake was formed, covering some 94 square miles. Downstream the land was marked off into 550 new farms, averaging about 500 acres. The reservoir permits the irrigation of about 272,000 acres during the dry season. The farms are used primarily to raise cattle. But this is done on planted and irrigated pastures, inclosed with wire fences. As a result, meat for the rapidly growing large cities of Venezuela can be supplied in sufficient quantity to make the import of meat no longer necessary.

Since 1958 the program of agrarian reform includes a number of resettlement projects, mostly located along the Andean piedmont. Much of the land which at one time was owned by General Gómez is now government property. In this part of the country the expropriation of private estates is not so important as it is in the core area. The successful establishment of a farm colony depends on the use of antibiotics and insecticides to reduce disease, as well as the reshaping of the surface by heavy machinery to provide drainage and irrigation works. The new farm settlers are encouraged to grow commercial crops of maize, rice, cotton, and sesame (for cooking oil to replace expensive imported olive oil).

There are also important sources of oil and gas under the Llanos. A large oil and gas field is located in the eastern part of the region. Pipelines have been built to Caracas, to the port of Guanta, and also southward to the new industrial concentration along the lower Caroní. Some of Venezuela's oil from the eastern Llanos is sent out to the new refinery in Trinidad.

The Guiana Highlands

About half of the national territory of Venezuela lies south of the Orinoco River in a region known as the Guiana highlands. The surface is composed of rounded hills and narrow valleys formed on ancient crystalline rocks. Standing conspicuously above the general upland level, especially in the far south along the border of Brazil and Guyana, are groups of plateaus and mesas, capped with resistant sandstone. These flat-topped tablelands reach the highest elevation in Mt. Roraima (9,219 feet above sea level). The crystalline hilly upland begins immediately south of the Orinoco River; in fact, the river in several places flows across spurs of the upland, each of which produces a narrowing of the channel and limits navigation. The first of these narrows above the mouth of the river is just upstream from Ciudad Bolívar, and suggested the original name of this town—Angostura.

The Guiana highlands are covered with intermingled savanna and semi-deciduous forest. The grassy openings are apparently extensive and very irregular in outline; the detailed mapping which would make possible the precise description of the relations of grasslands and forests in this region has yet to be done. One of the finest popular descriptions of this mixture of forest and savanna was written by W. H. Hudson in *Green Mansions.*

For several reasons the Guiana highlands are less subject to extremes of flood and drought than are the Orinoco Llanos. The year is sharply divided, as it is in the Llanos, into a rainy season and a dry season. But the hilly nature of the terrain reduces the area which is subject to floods, and the cover of forest reduces the surface run-off. Except for the factor of isolation, the Guiana highlands might be considered to be physically better suited for

Angel Falls, Venezuela, the highest falls in the world. *Courtesy of Organization of American States.*

use as grazing land than is the savanna-covered plain north of the Orinoco.

The remote Guiana highlands are still in large part outside of the effective national territory of Venezuela. Most of the spots of settlement are around the mission stations along the rivers. An estimated 30,000 "wild" Indians occupy the forests along the border between Venezuela and Brazil.

The highlands, however, are not lacking in resources. Explorers and adventurers have searched its valleys for gold and diamonds, not entirely without success. A rich vein of gold was discovered a century or so ago at El Callao. In 1885 the mine at El Callao was the largest producer of gold in the world, and it is still in operation. For a long time the only way to reach El Callao was by muleback over a miserable trail from Ciudad Bolívar. During the 1930's the first regular airlines were established, and access to El Callao became much easier. The new highway program started after 1950 has given El Callao a gravel connection, passable in all weather by motor trucks.

Now the northern margin of the Guiana highlands is being rapidly developed as an entirely new industrial area. For a long time the existence of iron ore in the rocks of the highlands has been known. In 1883 the government even granted a concession for the development of some iron mines, and ore was actually shipped out. But as long as the industrial centers of the United States were supplied with high-grade ore from Minnesota there was no urgent need to develop foreign sources of ore. During World War II the end of the rich Minnesota ore bodies came in sight. The steel manufacturers of the United States had to develop new techniques for making use of low-grade ores or to seek high-grade ores outside of the United States. Actually they did both. The search for foreign sources of high-grade ore uncovered new iron deposits in Canada, and also established the fact that the Guiana highlands contain billions of tons of ore running more than 60 percent metallic iron.

After World War II two large steel companies from the United States started operations in Venezuela. The United States Steel Corporation works on the western side of the Caroní River, taking its ore from Cerro Bolívar. The ore is dug out by huge mechanical shovels and loaded onto railroad cars to be transported to the Orinoco River. Here the ore is loaded on ocean-going ore carriers to be carried directly to the steel plant operated by the company at Morrisville, Pennsylvania, on the Delaware River, or to Mobile, Alabama, where the ore is shipped up-river to Birmingham.

The Bethlehem Steel Corporation operates on the eastern side of the Caroní River. Its ore is taken from El Pau, also dug out by mechanical shovels. The ore is shipped by rail to Palua on the Orinoco, then loaded on barges to be towed down the Orinoco to the Gulf of Paria. At Puerto de Hierro, on the southern side of the Peninsula of Paria, the ore is transferred from barges to ocean-going ore carriers which take it to the Bethlehem Steel plant at Sparrows Point, Maryland.

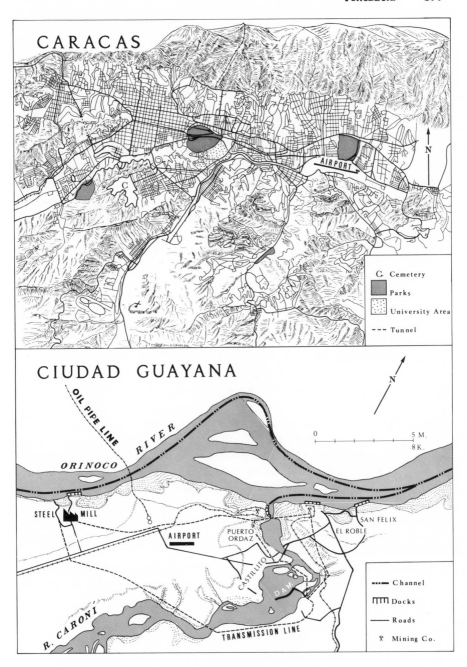

Map 57

Both companies built new communities near the mines. Modern residences, suitable for low-latitude conditions, have been provided. There are also schools, hospitals, and recreation facilities. Before ore could be shipped, a vast capital outlay went for the construction of docks, warehouses, offices, airports, water and sewage systems, and for the dredging of the Orinoco. Food had to be imported, and local sources of supply developed—all this in a region which, even as late as 1940, had been reached only by explorers.

Starting in 1955 the Venezuelan government began to invest large sums of oil income in the construction of a major center of heavy industry. At the junction of the Caroní and the Orinoco, some 60 miles downstream from Ciudad Bolívar, a new city was planned, which, it was thought, would become Venezuela's second city in ten years or so. This is Ciudad Guayana. Grouped around this city are various heavy industries. One is a huge government-owned steel plant which has nine electric furnaces, making it one of the largest such plants in the world. The Venezuelan government is supplying this plant with ore from its own mines in the Guiana highlands to the south. There are also known sources of manganese, nickel, and chromium yet to be developed. Coal is imported in the returning ore carriers. Limestone is brought from the port of Guanta near Barcelona. The steel plant started operations in 1959, and now turns out a variety of iron and steel products, such as structural steel, reinforcing rods, rails, steel sheets and tubes, seamless steel pipe for the oil and gas lines, and others.

Power to run the electric furnaces comes from the Macagua hydroelectric plant on the Caroní River 30 miles to the south. About 80 percent of the power generated at Macagua is used in the steel plant. In 1965 a huge new hydroelectric project was started at Guri, a few miles upstream from Macagua. The Caroní River probably has the largest power potential of any Latin-American river, and since the Guri Dam will produce more than can be used at present, it is planned to build the dam in three stages. When the final stage is complete the dam will be 500 feet high and will supply water to run 24 electric generators. Taking advantage of this new supply of power, the Reynolds Aluminum Company has built a refinery near Ciudad Guayana. An oil refinery has also been built, and, nearby, the first parts of a petrochemical complex.

The heavy industries that will be grouped together around Ciudad Guayana may, within a decade, form the largest such concentration in all Latin America.

Venezuela as a Political Unit

Since World War II Venezuela has become not only the leading country of Latin America in gross national product per capita, but also the country with the largest amount of capital investment from the United States, and the best customer in Latin America for United States products. As a result of the close contacts thus developed, the winds of revolution have indeed transformed both the economy and the political life. The struggle to end the traditional control of politics by a small minority of wealthy people and military men was completed in 1958, since which date Venezuela has moved a long way to establish democratic procedures and to formulate a widely supported state-idea.

The Economic Situation

Venezuela's 9 million inhabitants are very unevenly spread over the national territory, and the national income is unevenly shared. The very great prosperity of the core area attracts migrants from the remote backlands, and the largest migration is into the metropolitan area of Caracas. In fact, so rapid is the movement of country people into the city that a situation of chronic unemployment has developed there. At the same time the building of the huge new industrial complex at Ciudad Guayana has been slowed down by lack of workers. In these early stages of growth it proves difficult to get the unemployed people in Caracas to move to the more distant parts of the country, but the planners hope that as Ciudad Guayana grows and builds more of the amenities of life, it will begin to attract people away from over-crowded Caracas. About 34 percent of the Venezuelans still cannot read or write, but 13 percent of the national budget goes for education, and since 1958 the number of children in elementary school has doubled.

Economic development in Venezuela faces two basic problems. One is to increase the gross national product faster than the increase of population to be supported by the economy. The other is to provide economic opportunities outside of the chief city and to reduce the large areas of rural poverty that still exist in places remote from the cities. Since 1965 the Venezuelan gross national product has been increasing at a fast enough rate to make a gain on the population. The production of oil, which is Venezuela's chief source of income, was increased by 3 percent in 1965. In that year 694 new wells were drilled, as compared with only 498 new wells in 1963. Of the new wells, 592 produced oil. Agreements between the government and the oil companies in 1967 regarding the basis for collecting taxes meant that the companies were prepared to increase their investments in the expansion of production.

The production of oil provides Venezuela with 90 percent of its foreign earnings, and accounts for 28 percent of the national product. But the oil industry employs only 2.5 percent of the labor force. The program of "sowing the oil" calls for the investment of a considerable part of the income from oil in the formation of new capital. The government planners must resist pressures to use the income for the direct relief of poverty, hoping that the creation of new jobs will make a permanent impact on poverty in the future.

The agricultural sector of the economy has not been neglected. In 1961 only 33 percent of the labor force was employed in agriculture, which was a great change from the 51 percent in agriculture in 1955. The program of agrarian reform, which is to raise the standard of living of landless farmers and increase agricultural production, has been very successful. Just making land available for a farmer is not enough to accomplish either of these objectives. It is necessary also to set up a system of farm credit, to provide seed, farm implements, homes, water, healthful surroundings, and a means to transport the products to a market. The illiterate and landless tenant farmers also need technical advice. All these things, as well as just land redistribution, are essential parts of an effective program of agrarian reform.

To provide the conditions for an improved rural life, the government since 1960 has established 750 new farming communities where the previously landless tenants could be resettled. In each farm community there are schools and health clinics; and each community is tied into the national highway network. Machinery, technical assistance, and other necessities are provided, as they never could be to widely scattered individual landowners. Around the communities the farmers are given title to the specific pieces of land. Added together, the government since 1960 has given title to more than 8 million acres of crop and pasture land to 131,250 farm families, and the program continues. About half of the total acreage was public land, and the other half was privately owned land that was not effectively utilized by the owners. The private land was purchased, and paid for partly in cash and partly with government bonds. Furthermore, no land is given away: the new owners must pay for their farms over a period of 20 years, but never in amounts over 5 percent of the income from farming. It is estimated that in the next few years about 300,000 farmers will be eligible to take part in the program. Already the results in terms of the increase in agricultural production are spectacular. For example, the production of milk increased 59 percent between 1960 and 1965. By 1965 Venezuela was producing all its domestic needs for maize, rice, beans, meat, and other foods.

An unsolved problem has to do with the continued movement of people into the cities, and especially into Caracas. The government uses every means to keep rural people happy by raising their standard of living, and to a certain extent this effort has been successful. But still the cities grow through the arrival every month of large numbers of destitute people—more than can either be employed or provided with houses. Exciting as it may seem to people outside of Venezuela to hear about the building of a major center of heavy industry on the Orinoco, to the average illiterate country man from the Venezuelan backlands the Orinoco is still a wilderness. In Caracas there are bright lights, movies, plenty of neighbors; in the backlands there is poverty, hunger, loneliness. Somehow the existence of bright lights, jobs, and houses in these newly developing areas has to be communicated to Venezuela's increasing numbers of urban unemployed.

The Political Situation

After the death of Gómez in 1935, the army officers who succeeded him in office undertook to bring back to Venezuela a measure of political freedom and law. Political parties were permitted to organize. One result was the appearance of a strong liberal democratic movement dedicated to the promotion of those principles we associate with the democratic revolution elsewhere in the world. This movement captured the imagination and support of a great majority of the Venezuelans to such an extent that communism has remained weak and divided. In 1946 a new liberal constitution was adopted, and in 1947 an election was carried out under the provisions of the new constitution. To overcome the problem of illiteracy, ballots were printed on paper of different colors. The vote was secret and the count honest. The result was that the democratic candidate received some 70 percent of the votes.

In 1948 the army again seized control of the government. There were many people in positions of political power who regarded the compromises and delays inherent in the democratic process as intolerable, and there were others who supported the use of force to preserve the traditional system of privileges. For 9 years Venezuela was ruled by a military dictatorship, under which civil liberty was entirely eliminated. Political opponents were exiled or jailed and tortured by the secret police. The rights and dignity of the individual citizen were treated with cynical disregard, as they had been during the days of Gómez. The dictator said, "My country is not ready for the kind of democracy that brings abuses." In 1957 he had himself reelected for another term of office by a ballot on which no other candidates were offered.

In spite of the military and police force organized to support the government, a bitter revolt broke out in 1958. The revolt would have been impossible without the support of units of the army, the air force, and the navy. Younger officers, for the first time in Venezuelan history, were fighting for civil liberty, not just to remove the older colonels and generals in order to make promotion more rapid. But the military units were also supported by a civilian group in which all political parties were represented. After a period of confusion the dictator was forced to flee, and a new military-civilian government was set up, purged of all those who had supported the dictator. A new constitutional convention and a new election in 1958 returned the leadership to the forces of democracy.

The leader who emerged as the head of the new government in 1958 was Rómulo Betancourt. For many decades, ever since he was a rebellious student at the university, Betancourt had been active in the movement to bring an end to the traditional system of power and privilege for the few, with the great majority held in place by a powerful army. When he emerged as head of the new popularly elected government in Venezuela, he promptly expressed his support for other similar movements elsewhere. At a meeting in Caracas in 1958 he pledged support for Castro in his fight against Batista. But when Castro was victorious in 1959 and came to pay a visit to Venezuela, the Cuban revolutionary expressed scorn for the liberal ideas of Betancourt. He and Che Guevara began to organize guerrilla forces to fight against Betancourt. His plan was to make the Andes of western Venezuela into a kind of Sierra Maestra from which to wage war throughout northern South America. Betancourt, however, was as much opposed to a dictatorship of the left as he was to a dictatorship of the right. In 1961 Venezuela broke relations with Cuba.

The Betancourt government undertook a fundamental program of social change as well as of economic development. The idea was not only to raise the level of living of the Venezuelan people, and to use the income from oil to create many new jobs, but also to see to it that the income was more widely distributed among the people. Of course there were many whose positions of privilege were threatened who believed sincerely that Betancourt was a communist; and this idea might have gained more followers had it not been for Castro's efforts to organize anti-government guerrillas in Venezuela and to supply them with arms from Cuba. Ever since the days of Bolívar one idea to which every one could subscribe was the desire to be free from outside interference. Castro ran blindly against one of the most fundamental Latin-American political principles. But Betancourt had to defend his country from threats of force from both the communists and from the extreme right.

On March 11, 1964 a very important event took place in Caracas. Betancourt completed the term of office to which he had been elected—the first such completion of an elective office in Venezuelan history. He turned over the presidential sash to his duly elected successor. The election had been carried out in the face of communist threats to attack the polls. By a large majority, the liberal noncommunist party was returned to power.

All these struggles against the use of force and against the traditional autocratic system have helped to create in the Venezuelans a strong sense of pride in their nation. A widely held state-idea gave Venezuela the kind of coherence and order that is so much needed in this period of fundamental change. In spite of Castro's efforts there is no part of the national territory in which any opposition group is in control. Once again the basic principle has been demonstrated: that the best defense against communist attack is a strong liberal democratic movement, in which social change and economic development are skillfullly blended.

República de Colombia

Area: 439,734 square miles
Population: (1967 estimate) 19,215,000
            (last census, 1964) 17,482,420
Capital city: Bogotá; (1964) 1,680,758
Percent urban: (1951) 38.0
Birth rate per 1,000: (1966) 42–46; Death rate per 1,000: (1966) 13–17
Annual percent of increase: (1958–1964) 3.2
Percent literate: (1951) 62.3
Percent labor force in agriculture: (1957) 66
Gross national product per capita: (1966) $292
Leading crops in acreage: maize, wheat, rice
Unit of currency: peso (1968, 16.1 per dollar)

COMMERCE, 1965 *(expressed in percentage of values)*
Percent total Latin-American exports: 5.6 (1956, 5.0)
Percent total Latin-American imports: 5.3

Exports (1966)
coffee   59
petroleum   13

Exports to (1966)		**Imports from (1966)**	
United States	47 (1956, 71)	United States	48 (1956, 62)
West Germany	12	West Germany	11
Spain	5	United Kingdom	5

Chapter 17 □ Colombia

Colombia is the country which occupies the northwest corner of South America, where the great mountain system of the Andes as it approaches the Caribbean is frayed into parallel cordilleras separated by deep longitudinal depressions. Only the western third of the Colombian national territory lies within the region of mountains and valleys; but within this third there are more different kinds of land than are to be found in any comparable area in Latin America, perhaps in the world. There are giant peaks and ranges so high that their summits are permanently white with snow; there are high basins where the air is always chilly; there are forest-clad slopes where tropical showers feed torrential rivers; and there are lowlands, alternately baked in the tropical sun and drenched with violent rains, where the air is always warm and humid. This western third of Colombia is the part in which almost all the Colombians live. The eastern two-thirds, which is mostly outside of the effective national territory, is composed of a portion of the Guiana highlands, a portion of the Orinoco Plains, and even a small bit of theAmazon Plain (Map 59). Such is the variety of terrain, of cordilleras and intermont basins, of lowland plains, of towering heights and swampy lowlands, into which this country is divided.

The diversity of western highland Colombia is not solely a matter of mountainous terrain and varied climates. It is also a matter of diverse people. There are six distinct regions of concentrated settlement which differ from one another not only because of differences of the land, but also because of differences between the people and their forms of economy. There are districts occupied by a mestizo people, not unlike the inhabitants of the highlands of Venezuela; there is one district where most of the inhabitants are pure or nearly pure Indian, not unlike the people of highland Ecuador; and there

385

Map 58

COLOMBIA

75°

69°

CARIBBEAN SEA

Barranquilla

Cartagena

PANAMA

Caribbean Lowlands

Sa. Nevada de Sta. Maria

Sa. de Perija

TERRAIN

0   100   200
    100   300

VENEZUELA

PACIFIC OCEAN

Río San Juan

Buenaventura

Río Atrato

CORDILLERA CHOCÓ

CORDILLERA OCCIDENTAL

CORDILLERA CENTRAL

CORDILLERA ORIENTAL

BOGOTÁ

ORINOCO LLANOS

Tulcán

Río Caquetá

BRAZIL

AMAZON BASIN

PERU

Amazon River

Map 59

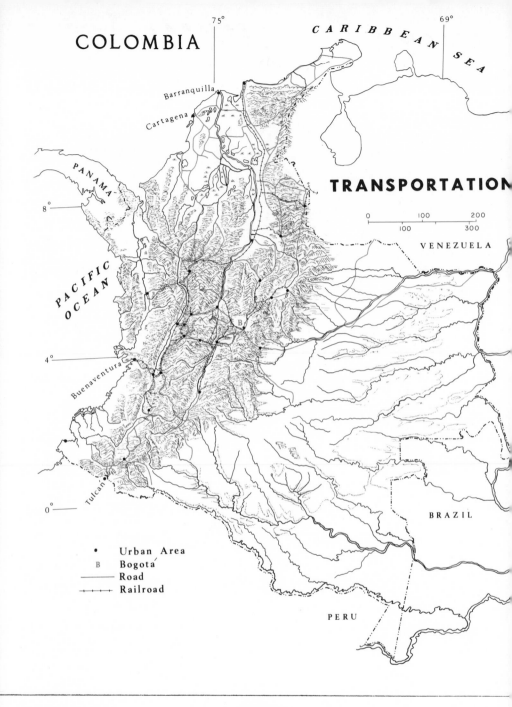

COLOMBIA

75°

CARIBBEAN SEA

69°

Barranquilla
Cartagena

PANAMA

8°

TRANSPORTATION

0   100   200
   100   300

VENEZUELA

PACIFIC
OCEAN

B

4°

Buenaventura

0°

Tulcán

BRAZIL

• Urban Area
B Bogotá
—— Road
+++ Railroad

PERU

Map 60

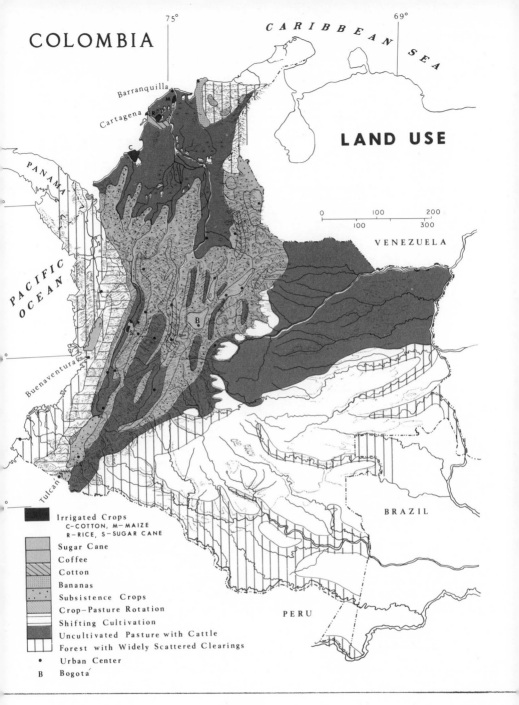

COLOMBIA

75°

69°

C A R I B B E A N   S E A

Barranquilla

Cartagena

C

M

LAND USE

PANAMA

PACIFIC OCEAN

0   100   200
   100   300

VENEZUELA

B

Buenaventura

BRAZIL

Tulcán

PERU

Irrigated Crops
C–COTTON, M–MAIZE
R–RICE, S–SUGAR CANE
Sugar Cane
Coffee
Cotton
Bananas
Subsistence Crops
Crop–Pasture Rotation
Shifting Cultivation
Uncultivated Pasture with Cattle
Forest with Widely Scattered Clearings
• Urban Center
B Bogotá

Map 61

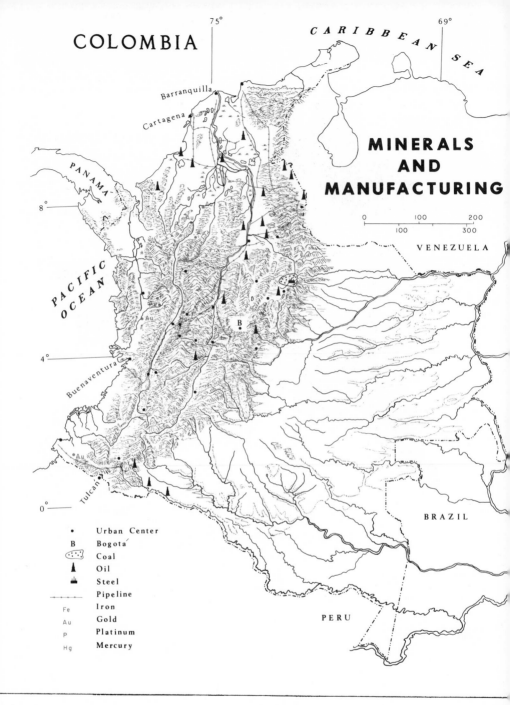

COLOMBIA

CARIBBEAN SEA

75°   69°

Barranquilla
Cartagena

PANAMA

8°

PACIFIC
OCEAN

MINERALS
AND
MANUFACTURING

0   100   200
    100   300

VENEZUELA

Au

B

4°

Buenaventura

Au

0°

Tulcán

BRAZIL

- • Urban Center
- B Bogotá
- Coal
- Oil
- Steel
- Pipeline
- Fe Iron
- Au Gold
- P Platinum
- Hg Mercury

PERU

Map 62

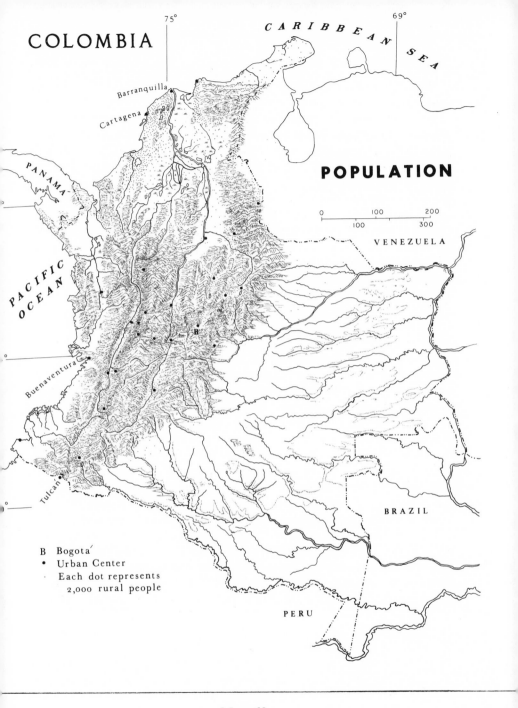

COLOMBIA

75°

69°

C A R I B B E A N   S E A

Barranquilla

Cartagena

PANAMA

PACIFIC
OCEAN

Buenaventura

Tulcan

POPULATION

0   100   200
   100   300

VENEZUELA

B

BRAZIL

B   Bogotá
•   Urban Center
    Each dot represents
    2,000 rural people

PERU

Map 63

391

are districts where a large proportion of the people are of African ancestry. The long course of Colombia's history of settlement provides many opportunities to illustrate the importance of people and culture in determining the habitability of different kinds of land.

The major features of western Colombia are boldly marked (Map 8, p. 23). Four great ranges of mountains, separated by deep longitudinal valleys, run north and south. Along the Pacific coast between Panamá and Buenaventura lies the Serranía de Baudó, a range which belongs geologically to Central America. On the east this range is bordered by a broad lowland extending from the Caribbean to the Pacific, drained in the north by the Río Atrato and in the south by the Río San Juan. East of this lowland, and bordering the Pacific south of Buenaventura, is the Cordillera Occidental, or western cordillera. Still farther to the east is the highest of the Colombian ranges, the Cordillera Central. From the border of Ecuador as far as Cartago the Cordillera Occidental and the Cordillera Central are separated by a wide structural depression, a rift valley, drained in the south by the Río Patía and in the north by the Río Cauca. From the northern end of this trench, downstream from Cartago, the Cauca makes its way toward the Caribbean through a series of profound gorges cut through the very rugged but not very high country where the Cordillera Central and the Cordillera Occidental are joined. The Cordillera Central is the easternmost of the Colombian ranges between the border of Ecuador and approximately latitude 2° N. Here the eastern cordillera, or Cordillera Oriental, has its beginning. This wide cordillera continues northward and northeastward into Venezuela. About latitude 7° N. it separates into two branches, one forming the western rim of the Maracaibo lowland, the other the southern rim. Between the Cordillera Oriental and the Cordillera Central, and drained by the Río Magdalena, is a deep structural valley—a lowland which merges at its northern end with the lowlands along the coast of the Caribbean. Another individual mountain group, the Sierra Nevada de Santa Marta, stands prominently on the eastern edge of the Caribbean lowlands and towers above the Caribbean itself. This mountain group is separated from the end of the Cordillera Oriental by the structural depression drained by the Río César.

The People

The people who occupy this exceptionally diverse terrain are of European, Indian, and African ancestry. Estimates as to the proportions of these racial ingredients are little more than informed guesses. The sociologist T. Lynn Smith arrived at the following estimate: people of European ancestry, 25 percent; people of African ancestry, 8 percent; people of unmixed Indian ancestry, 5 percent; mestizo, 42 percent; mulatto, 20 percent.[1] But even these

[1] T. Lynn Smith, "The Racial Composition of the People of Colombia," *Journal of Inter-American Studies,* Vol. 8 (1966), pp. 210–35.

informed estimates can be quite misleading, for within the three chief racial groups there are many strongly contrasted varieties, and the racial proportions differ widely from one part of the country to another.

The Native Indians

Before the European discovery of America the territory which is now Colombia was occupied by Indians of many different cultures. There were tribes whose way of living can be described as primitive, since it included very little choice in the manner of making a living and included little knowledge of the arts. But there was one group of tribes with a culture almost as advanced as that of the great Indian civilizations of Peru and Mexico. These were the Chibchas, a sedentary agricultural people who occupied the high basins of the Cordillera Oriental (Map 5, p. 14). In this remote mountain region the Chibchas had been brought together politically under the leadership of two chiefs–the *Zipa*, whose capital was near the present city of Bogotá, and the *Zaque*, whose capital was on the site of the modern city of Tunja. The political ability of the Chibchas of this region of high basins was far superior to that of any of the other tribes in Colombia. The Chibchas of the highlands were superior to other Colombian tribes whose languages were so closely related to theirs that anthropologists commonly group them together. Like most of the highland Indians of America, all the Chibcha tribes were dependent on the basic food staples: maize and potatoes. They also derived part of their food from the guinea pig which they had domesticated. Like the other highland Indians from Mexico to Chile, the Chibchas had no concept of private property in land. These Indians had established fixed settlements, and in places favorable to their form of agriculture the density of population was comparable to that of highland Mexico and Peru.

The Indians who occupied the Cordillera Central and the Cauca Valley are included in the general Chibcha group; yet in many ways they were distinct from the highland Chibchas of the Cordillera Oriental. Politically they were much less advanced: in the vicinity of Cartago, for example, the Spaniards found the Indians living under the rule of more than sixty petty chieftains. On the other hand, the Indians of this part of Colombia were more advanced than the highland Chibchas in their technique of pottery-making and their knowledge of metallurgy. Since gold was plentiful in the territory they occupied, they were especially skilled in the use of this metal and of alloys of gold with silver and with copper. The tribes of the Cauca Region fed themselves chiefly by hunting and fishing, but they supplemented their diet with maize, manioc, and yams. They also planted cotton and made cotton textiles.

As anthropological studies progress, a greater and greater variety of Indian cultures is described. Indians with an agriculturally advanced technology lived in the Sinú valley and along the shores of the Gulf of Urabá. Ridged fields along parts of the lower Magdalena bear witness to the presence in this lowland area of a relatively dense population of sedentary Indian farmers. But by the time of the arrival of the Spaniards the lowland areas had been abandoned and the fields were overgrown with wild vegetation.

The European Conquest

A result of the Spanish conquest of Colombia was a great increase both in the area that could be used for human habitation and in the variety of land use. The Spaniards brought with them cattle, horses, and sheep; they introduced wheat, barley, and sugarcane and a number of farm practices previously unknown to the natives. These importations increased the agricultural productivity of the high basins, because the European grains gave better yields at these altitudes than did the Indian maize, and domestic animals made possible the spread of settlement above the upper limit of the potato into the lands which had previously been considered uninhabitable.

The first Spanish settlements in Colombia were along the Caribbean coast (Map 6, p. 18). Balboa founded a colony on the western side of the Gulf of Urabá which was perhaps the first European settlement on the continent, though the place was abandoned after a few years. The oldest surviving Spanish colonies are Santa Marta (founded in 1525), and Cartagena (founded in 1533). The first expeditions to enter the highland country to the south were organized to search for the mineral wealth which the stories of El Dorado had magnified. When the Spaniards discovered in the eastern highlands the relatively dense populations of peaceful, sedentary Indians, they were surprised and delighted, for here, they soon realized, was the chief wealth of the country—Indians to work on the land or in the mines, Indians to be converted to Christianity.

Many writers assert that the Spaniards climbed into the mountains in order to escape from the heat of lowlands: but the real incentives seem rather to have been gold and dense Indian populations. There is little to suggest that the Spaniards were the kind of people to place comfort or ease of living before the attainment of these objectives. Where gold was to be found, there the Spaniards settled; but such settlements were in many cases temporary, as all gold-mining settlements are apt to be. Where sedentary Indians were found, there also the Spaniards settled; and these settlements were likely to be permanent because they were based on the exploitation of a stable supply of Indian labor. Bogotá was founded in 1538. It was located in the Basin of Cundinamarca in the remote fastness of the Cordillera Oriental, accessible only with great difficulty from the coast, but easily accessible to the largest single area of densely populated native peoples. Bogotá, center of economic life in the colonial period, became, and still remains, the political center of Colombia.

The Spaniards entered from three directions: (1) From Santa Marta expeditions ascended to the high basins of the Cordillera Oriental, and after the founding of Bogotá, other expeditions went northward along the Cordillera Oriental, and even pushed into the Cordillera de Mérida in what is now Venezuela. (2) From Cartagena many Spaniards advanced southward into the Cauca Valley, where, between 1536 and 1540, they founded numerous small mining towns in localities where the stream gravels contained rich stores of gold. (3) Meanwhile, a third group of Spaniards came northward from Peru by way of Quito, founding Pasto and Popayán in southern Colombia, and meeting the Spaniards from Cartagena in the latitude of Cali.

The Spanish conquest produced great changes in Colombia. The sedentary Chibchas soon learned to care for the European domestic animals and to cultivate the European grains. The Indians in the high basins became serfs attached to the large estates, owned by the officers of the conquering army; and new Indian communities were established in the *páramos*—the high country above the upper limit of agriculture but below the limit of permanent snow. In these higher regions the Indians remained predominant in numbers, but the wealth in terms of the European economy was accumulated by the new land-owning aristocracy.

Meanwhile, the more primitive Indians of other parts of Colombia were proving to be quite inadequate to meet the labor demands of the conquerors, whether in the placer mines or on the plantations where the new commercial crops, sugarcane and indigo, were cultivated. The native peoples were ravaged by imported diseases against which they had no immunity and were unable to adapt themselves easily to the hard work demanded by the Spaniards. By the end of the first century after the conquest, the more primitive tribes of Colombia had either been wiped out by epidemics or had withdrawn to the remote selvas of the Pacific slope. The Spaniards, therefore, resorted to African slaves, who came, in the course of time, greatly to outnumber the Europeans in certain parts of the lowlands.

Development of Colombia since the Conquest

By 1770 Colombia had a population of about 800,000. A century later the population had grown, chiefly by natural increase, to about 3 million. Well into the nineteenth century gold remained the chief economic interest of the ruling group, and even today Colombia is the leading gold-producing country of Latin America. In the twentieth century oil and platinum were added to the list of mineral products. Yet during all this time most of the people of Colombia were engaged in agriculture rather than in mining. Maize was by far the leading crop, but commercial crops of sugarcane, tobacco, indigo, and cacao were also cultivated. During the second half of the nineteenth century, cinchona bark, the source of quinine, was gathered in the forests. These various economic activities suffered, before the Wars of Independence, from excessive taxation and trade restrictions imposed by the mother country, and, after independence, from the recurring internal conflicts which plagued the country.

The cultivation of coffee added an important factor to the economic life of Colombia. Not until after 1880 did the mild, high-grade coffee produced in the highlands begin to find a preferred place in the markets of Europe and North America. Little by little coffee came to be even more important than it was in Venezuela, and Colombia today is the world's second largest producer of this commodity. The spread of coffee planting in the *tierra templada,* on slopes too steep for most other forms of agricultural use, brought increased productivity and a rapid growth of new settlement to parts of Colombia which had previously been of little economic importance.

All these various economic activities served to mark off the Colombian territory into strongly contrasted regions. But during and since World War II even more striking diversification has been produced by the rapid development of manufacturing industries. At first the leading industrial center was Medellín in the department of Antioquia, but in the 1960's the rapid development of Cali in the Cauca Valley pushed that city ahead of Medellín. Manufacturing industries are now scattered throughout the country, supporting a rapid increase in the urban population. In 1964 not only was the population of Bogotá well over a million, but there were also 16 cities of over 100,000 inhabitants. As long as manufacturing industry was concentrated in just one region, the establishment of a coherent society was made more difficult: the spread of manufacturing to other cities greatly aids in stabilizing Colombian politics.

The Land

Fundamental to the diversity which characterizes Colombia is the rugged surface of the western third of the country, in which most of the people live. The spotty patterns of distribution of all the elements of the physical land come not only from differences of soil and degree of slope, but also from differences in the orientation of the slopes with relation to the sun and to the rain-bearing winds. Furthermore, the mountains are high enough to include all the various vertical zones from sea level to the zone of permanent snow.

Surface Features

The four ranges of the Colombian mountains include a variety of geologic structures and surface forms. The westernmost range, the Serranía de Baudó, is by far the lowest and the narrowest. The highest summit is less than 6,000 feet above sea level, but the intense erosion produced by the very heavy rainfall on sharply tilted layers of stratified rocks has resulted in a surface composed of steep slopes and sharply crested ridges. In spite of the low altitude, therefore, some of the most rugged country in all of Colombia is to be found along the coast north of Buenaventura. Nevertheless, the Serranía de Baudó is so narrow at one place, at the head of the Río Truando, a tributary of the Atrato, that this has been studied as a possible canal route.

The next two ranges to the east, the Cordillera Occidental and the Cordillera Central, are alike in their geologic structure, being composed of massive crystalline rocks. Together they form the western and eastern flanks of a great arch which extends south from the Caribbean coastal lowlands almost to the southern border of Ecuador. In Colombia both cordilleras have crests which remain unbroken by stream valleys except in the places where the Río Cauca has cut a way out to the north and the Río Patía one to the west. Otherwise the crests of the two ranges are the divides between the streams that rise on either side. Both these cordilleras lack large intermont basins. There are, however, narrow, ribbon-like valley lowlands along some of the streams—for example, the lowland of the Río Cauca north of Cartago, on which is the city of Antioquia. In these mountains the steepness of the slopes varies considerably, but there are few patches of level land.

The Cordillera Central is the highest of all the Colombian ranges. It extends like a wall for more than 500 miles, forming a massive pedestal of crystalline rocks 30 to 40 miles wide, above which rise several volcanic cones, with their snow-clad summits more than 18,000 feet above the sea. The Cordillera Occidental, on the other hand, is relatively low. Its summits are only about 10,000 feet in altitude, not high enough to reach the snow line, and between Cali and Buenaventura there is a pass which requires an ascent of only a little over 5,000 feet.

The Cordillera Occidental and the Cordillera Central are separated, south of Cartago, by a deep rift valley. Along the crest of the arch of crystalline rocks, the keystone, as it were, has broken into blocks and fallen, forming a depression which continues either as a valley lowland or as a series of high basins from Cartago in Colombia to Cuenca in Ecuador (Map 66, p. 432). Between Cartago and Cali the rift valley is deepest—the valley floor is only about 2,300 feet above sea level. South of Cali, however, the valley is filled to great depths with ash dropped into it from the bordering volcanoes. In the southern part of the rift valley in Colombia, in the drainage area of the Río Patía, the floor is at an elevation of more than 8,000 feet.

East of the Cordillera Central lies the deep Magdalena Valley, and beyond it the Cordillera Oriental. This range of mountains has a much more intricate surface pattern than the other ranges because of the nature of its geologic structure. It is composed of folded stratified rocks over a crystalline core. The eastern border of this cordillera and the ridges, valleys, and basins within the cordillera all show a marked alignment from northeast to southwest, parallel to the axes of the folds. The western margin of the Cordillera Oriental, on the other hand, borders the Magdalena Valley along a north–

south line, formed by a series of faults which cut diagonally across the folds.

Within the Cordillera Oriental there are three chief groups of surface features. The highest crests, which form the first group, are not continuous as in the Cordillera Central: there are many short ridges, arranged in echelon following the axes of the folds in a general northeast–southwest direction. Many of these crests are high enough to reach the zone of permanent snow, and some of them still have small glaciers, remnants of much larger ones which sculptured the high surfaces during the glacial period. The rivers rise in the snowfields and *páramos* and descend into the bordering high valleys and basins as mountain torrents.

The second group of surface features in the Cordillera Oriental is composed of the high basins of the central area around Bogotá. The streams, cutting headward into the heart of the range, have not yet extended their deep valleys into this central area. At an elevation of between eight and nine thousand feet above sea level there is a surface of gentle gradient, forming three large intermont basins and a number of smaller basins and valleys. The margins of these basins are bordered by alluvial fans, where the mountain torrents descend from the snowfields and *páramos;* but after crossing the fans, the streams meander with sluggish currents through broad valleys, forming swamps and even lakes in the centers of the basins.

The deeply dissected lower slopes below the high basins make up the third group of surface features. As the streams reach the border between the basins and the dissected lower slopes they plunge over spectacular falls; in the well-known Falls of Tequendama, the Río Bogotá drops more than 400 feet. The valleys in this part of the cordillera are narrow and steep-sided; in only a few places do terrace remnants or small valley flats provide patches of level land.

The Magdalena Valley separates the folded Cordillera Oriental from the crystalline Cordillera Central. Its structural similarity to the Rhône Valley of France is striking, since both are the result of faulting along the margin between young folded mountains and older crystalline *massifs.* The Río Magdalena is barely navigable for shallow-draught boats as far as Neiva; with an interruption midway in its course, however, at the rapids at Honda. The valley is very deep, for even at the latitude of Girardot, some 460 miles from the Caribbean, it is scarcely 1,000 feet above sea level. Upstream from Girardot the slope of the valley bottom becomes greater; beyond Neiva the river is frequently interrupted by rapids.

The Caribbean coastal lowlands, formed in part by the alluvial deposits of the Magdalena and the Cauca, lie nestled in a rough triangle between the sea, the western base of the Sierra Nevada de Santa Marta, and the long descending spurs of the Cordillera Central and the Cordillera Occidental. Rows of low hills half buried in alluvium extend northward to the shores of the Caribbean.

The Falls of Tequendama, near Bogotá. *Courtesy of Colombian Information Service.*

The rest of Colombia is mostly outside the effective national territory. The very high Sierra Nevada de Santa Marta, the summits of which reach 19,000 feet, stands as an isolated block of mountains on the margin of the Caribbean. Beyond it is the Guajira Peninsula, composed of a platform of crystalline rocks with a few knobby hills standing above it. East of the Cordillera Oriental the northeastern part of Colombia includes a continuation of the Llanos of the Orinoco. Between the Llanos and the Plains of the Amazon, a westward projection of the Guiana highlands reaches the base of the Andes south of Villavicencio. All these regions are thinly populated, in some cases by Indian tribes which are independent of any political control by the Colombians.

Vertical Arrangement of the Climates

In such a mountainous country as highland Colombia the climatic conditions and the natural vegetation which reflects these conditions present a most intricate pattern. Variations in exposure to the sun, variations in hours of sunlight, and sharp differences in rainfall within small areas are characteristic. In general, however, all this intricacy of detail resolves itself into broad vertical zones which are especially discernible when one of the mountain ranges is viewed from a distance.

Vertical zoning has more meaning in terms of human settlement in Colombia than in any other part of Latin America. Three principal facts account for this. In the first place, the Colombian Andes are near the equator and are high enough to reach the snow line. This permits the maximum possible amount of vertical differentiation, for as the snow line descends in higher latitudes so also do the other altitude limits. The second principal fact is that in Colombia areas of relatively gentle slope are to be found at various elevations from sea level up to the snow line. Finally, the Colombian Andes are occupied by a European people whose many different ways of gaining a living make possible the use of lands at all altitudes.

The vertical zones are similar to those of the Cordillera de Mérida in Venezuela. The *tierra caliente* has a general upper limit of about 3,000 feet. The *tierra templada,* or zone of coffee, lies between 3,000 and 6,500 feet. The *tierra fría* extends from 6,500 to a little over 10,000 feet. Above the *tierra fría* are the treeless *páramos,* which extend to the snow line at about 15,000 feet above the sea.

A very common and often repeated error is to think of the high-altitude climates of the tropics as similar to the climates with the same average temperatures which are found at sea level in the middle latitudes. Many writers on Colombia have stated that by ascending to the *tierra fría* one reaches temperatures comparable to those of climates much farther from the equator. This is true if we consider average annual temperatures only; but it is far from true if we consider seasonal variation of temperature or variety of weather. In the tropical regions, even at sea level, the range of temperature between the average of the warmest month and the average of the coldest month is only about three or four degrees. As one ascends the mountains the ranges of temperature become less. At Bogotá, 8,660 feet above sea level, the average annual temperature is 58.1°—exactly the same as the average annual temperature of Knoxville, Tennessee; but in Bogotá the difference between the averages of the warmest and the coldest months is only 1.8°, while the difference at Knoxville is 38.1°. To describe Bogotá as having a "perpetual spring climate," as is so frequently done, is to create a very false impression, for there is none of the weather variety characteristic of a mid-latitude spring.

The Regions of Settlement

The different kinds of people who occupy these different kinds of land are grouped in six major regions of concentrated settlement (Maps 58 and 63). With only a few exceptions, each of the departments into which the Colombian national territory is divided has a core of concentrated settlement, and the department boundaries generally pass through areas that are thinly populated. The six regions of settlement may be outlined as follows:

1. The High Basins of the Cordillera Oriental
    Cundinamarca, Distrito Especial
    Boyacá
2. The Valleys at Lower Altitudes in the Cordillera Oriental
    Santander, Norte de Santander
    Cundinamarca
    Huila
3. The Antioquia Region
    Antioquia, Caldas, Quindío
    Tolima
4. The Cauca Valley
    Riseralda
    Valle del Cauca
    Cauca
5. The Pasto Region
    Nariño
6.   The Caribbean Coastal Lowlands
    Bolívar, Córdoba, Sucre, Antioquia
    Magdalena, César
    Atlántico

The High Basins of the Cordillera Oriental

The high basins of the central, headwater area in the Cordillera Oriental are among the most densely populated parts of Colombia. The largest of the basins is in Cundinamarca. The city of Bogotá, capital of Colombia, is located near the southeastern margin of this basin. Bogotá is now much more than the urban core of this one cluster of people; it is the political, social, and artistic focus of the whole country. But it is no longer the economic focus. Farther north, in Boyacá, there are several smaller basins, each densely populated, in which the urban centers are Chiquinquirá, Tunja, and Sogamoso. The rural population of this whole central region of the Cordillera Oriental is between 25 and 60 per square mile, with a few areas of more than 60. Bogotá, now much larger than the economic activities of Cundinamarca would justify, has more than a million and a half inhabitants.

When the Spaniards first invaded the Cordillera Oriental they found the high intermont basins occupied by a relatively dense population of Chibchas. The different tribes in the Basin of Cundinamarca had been united under the leadership of the *Zipa*. But the *páramos* between Cundinamarca and the neighboring basins were quite uninhabitable so far as the Indians were concerned, and political authority had not been extended across to the territory of the *Zaque*. The Chibchas were sedentary agricultural Indians who offered the conquerors a source of abundant and inexpensive labor. In 1538 the Spaniards founded the town of Bogotá on the slopes of the alluvial fan overlooking the Basin of Cundinamarca. The basin itself, together with much of the surrounding high country, was promptly divided into large estates on which the Indian communities remained as chief source of wealth for the owners.

The economic activity of most of the people of the high basins is still the production of food. Emerald mines, located a little southwest of Chiquinquirá, and various localities (Zipaquirá, Nemocón, and Sesquile) where salt was mined before the arrival of the Spaniards remained active after the conquest. Gold was not found in any abundance in the Cordillera Oriental. In the present century the emerald mines have been worked only periodically. The Europeans, however, extended the area of habitable land and increased the food-producing capacity of the land already inhabited by the introduction of wheat, barley, and cattle. Maize, the grain used by the Indians, can be cultivated up to an elevation of 8,850 feet; and, as in the Cordillera de Mérida in Venezuela, it can be harvested twice a year—the first and largest harvest coming in August, and the second and less certain harvest in December. Wheat is now grown up to 9,800 feet, and barley and potatoes up to about 10,500 feet. The *páramos* are utilized for pasture.

The high basins of Cundinamarca and Boyacá are now more densely populated than in the period before the conquest. Green pastures and fields of ripening crops are bordered by rows of willows and eucalyptus trees following the property lines and the roads; small villages are scattered widely over the basin floors and the bordering alluvial fans. The mestizos and Indians who make up the majority of the rural people are still primarily subsistence farmers. They grow their own food crops on lands too poor for other uses, and, in addition, earn a miserable wage by working on the estates of the landowners.

In striking contrast to this traditional rural scene is the new steel plant at Belencito near Sogamoso in Boyacá (Map 62). This is the Paz del Río steel plant, completed in 1954. This location has one great advantage over any other place in Colombia—it is supplied with the basic raw materials within a radius of only a little over 20 miles. The iron ore comes from a low-grade ore body near the little town of Paz del Río, 21 miles north of Belencito. Less than 20 miles away there are some of the best coal measures in this part of South America, from which good quality coking coal can be mined. Half a mile from the steel plant there is a large outcrop of limestone. The large quantity of water needed in a steel plant comes through an 18-mile pipeline from Lake Tota, south of Sogamoso. But the only connection with the rest of Colombia is by rail to Bogotá, 160 miles to the south, or by motor truck over steep and winding mountain roads. Nevertheless by 1966 steel production had reached 216,012 tons. In 1968 the plant was being expanded to bring the capacity up to 500,000 tons per year by 1975.

Another striking feature, which contrasts with the poverty of the rural background in the high basins, is Bogotá itself. In spite of the difficulty of reaching it from other parts of the country, in Bogotá are gathered many elements of the national life which come from far beyond the borders of the department; to it come not only political leaders from all parts of the country, but also writers, artists, social leaders, and students. It is with justice that Bogotá is frequently called the "Athens of America." Its cosmopolitan atmosphere, its large proportion of people of European origin, as well as its beautiful buildings, combine to set it off sharply from rural Cundinamarca.

The Valleys at Lower Altitudes in the Cordillera Oriental

The second of the six regions of settlement in Colombia is located in the valleys of the Cordillera Oriental at elevations below 7,000 feet. This part of Colombia, together with the Magdalena Valley to the west, was thinly populated by relatively primitive Indians before the arrival of the Spaniards. Although the intermediate altitudes were more comfortable than the continuously cool high basins, there was little to attract settlement. The main course of conquest was directed to the Chibcha areas higher up, and here a pattern of large estates with tenant workers has persisted to the present time. Only after the highlands had been occupied did some of the poorer Spaniards

Steel plant of Paz del Río at Belencito, 160 miles north of Bogota in the Cordillera Oriental. *Courtesy of Acerias Paz del Río, S.A.*

and their mestizo sons move down to the steeply-sloping valleys below. The chief concentrations of small-farmer settlements developed at four places at intermediate altitudes: around Bucaramanga in Santander; around Cúcuta and Ocaña in Norte de Santander; along the west-facing lower slopes of the Cordillera Oriental in Cundinamarca; and around Neiva in the Department of Huila.

THE SETTLEMENTS OF SANTANDER

The big movement of European population into the northern part of the Cordillera Oriental took place in the nineteenth century. Since this region contained little gold, and since the wealth-producing crops—sugar, cacao, indigo, and cotton—could scarcely compete with the products of better favored areas near by, Santander and Norte de Santander remained of small importance during most of the colonial period. Between 1860 and 1885, however, a resource was found in the forests of this region which could at last break down the barriers of isolation—this was the bark of the cinchona tree, a source of quinine. For a time Bucaramanga became one of chief collecting and shipping points for cinchona bark, and the population already in the region was re-enforced by a small number of Europeans and mestizos from other parts of the country. However, when the Javanese plantations of cinchona captured the market, there was neither enough capital nor enough labor available for the establishment of competing plantations in the Andes, the native habitat of cinchona.

A new commercial product, however, began to enter the export trade of Colombia soon after 1850. This was coffee—a crop which we have already seen occupying the steep mountain slopes in areas of sparse population in Venezuela. Coffee, which came at least indirectly from Java, more than compensated for the loss of the cinchona trade to Java. Today, coffee is grown on many of the mountain slopes around Bucaramanga (Map 61), where there are many small owner-operated *fincas*. The present population of this district includes a higher proportion of Europeans or near-Europeans than does the population of the high basins where the Chibchas were already occupying the land effectively before the arrival of the Spaniards.

Production in the Bucaramanga district has been diversified by the establishment of plantations of cacao, tobacco, and cotton below the zone of coffee. In the town of Bucaramanga there are textile factories and establishments for the manufacture of straw hats—industries which are based on small but dependable supplies of local raw materials. The markets for these products are found throughout Colombia; goods are shipped in and out between Bucaramanga and the Magdalena Valley by motor truck.

THE SETTLEMENTS OF NORTE DE SANTANDER

The story of the settlement of the valleys of Norte de Santander around Cúcuta and Ocaña is similar to that of the European occupation of Santander, except that the isolation of the northern department is even greater than that of the southern one. The deep dissection of this part of the Cordillera Oriental has produced a surface so rugged that transportation between Bucaramanga, Ocaña, and Cúcuta has been carried on with great difficulty. Cúcuta found its easiest outlet northeastward across the Maracaibo lowlands in Venezuelan territory. A railroad line was built from Cúcuta to a navigable river which flows into Lake Maracaibo. In both Ocaña and Cúcuta the products which have paid for the first connections with the rest of the world were cinchona and coffee.

In recent years, however, an oil field in Norte de Santander, located in the southwestern corner of the Maracaibo lowlands, has been opened up by a North American company. Machinery for the drilling of wells and for other construction was brought in by airplane. In 1939 a road, passable for automobiles, was built from the Magdalena Valley across this rugged terrain to the Maracaibo lowlands north of Cúcuta, and a pipe line 263 miles long brings the oil to a small port on the Caribbean Coast south of Cartagena.

THE SETTLEMENTS BORDERING THE MAGDALENA VALLEY

Since the introduction of coffee after 1850, other areas of concentrated settlement developed at intermediate altitudes bordering the deep valley of the Magdalena. In Cundinamarca, overlooking that part of the valley between Honda and Girardot, there are coffee plantations on the slopes; coffee plantations are also found around Neiva, farther to the south.

In more recent times, with the invention and use of insecticides, settlers have moved down onto the valley bottom. Between Honda and a little upstream from Girardot, on either side of the river, there are small farmers who grow food crops and cotton. This has become Colombia's leading area of cotton production, accounting for 57 percent of the national production since 1960.

The Antioquia Region

During the 1920's the Antioquia region went through a process of rapid economic development and expansion which made Medellín and the area of settlement that focuses on this city the economic heart of Colombia. Antioquia maintained this position until after 1960, when economic growth began to catch up in other parts in Colombia—in Cali, for example. The story of the rise of Antioquia to economic preeminence is an important part in the analysis of modern Colombia.

The Antioquia region includes the clusters of people in the departments of Antioquia and Caldas on either side of the Cauca Valley, and on the eastern side of the Cordillera Central in Tolima. The central nucleus of this area of concentrated settlement is the city of Medellín, located in a small valley lowland about 5,000 feet in altitude in the Cordillera Central. The colonial gold-mining town of Antioquia located in the lowland along the Río Cauca is today a place of small importance and should not be confused with the department of the same name. The people in the departments of Antioquia, Caldas, Quindío, and Tolima—which make up the Antioquia region— not only assumed leadership in the economic life of Colombia, but also, as a result of their high birth rate, were able to expand the frontiers of their original settlement around Medellín and to send out new colonies without decreasing the density of the original nucleus. The Antioquia region merits close attention not only as one of the diverse elements in the Colombian scene, but also as one of the four places in the whole of mainland Latin America where expansion took place before World War II without a decline of the older settlements behind the frontier.[2]

THE LAND

The Cordillera Central, in which these four departments are situated, is very different in its surface character from the Cordillera Oriental. There are no intermont basins at higher altitudes. At lower altitudes, however, there are a number of places where the valleys widen to enclose small ribbons of flat land along the streams. The largest area of this sort borders the Río

[2]James J. Parsons, *Antioqueño Colonization in Western Colombia*, Ibero-Americana 32, Berkeley, Cal., 1949.

Cauca where the town of Antioquia was established; but there are many other smaller bits of valley lowland along the tributaries of the Cauca. Medellín was built in a valley basin which extends for only about 12 miles along a tributary of the Río Porce. Most of these small but important pieces of flat land are at elevations of between two and six thousand feet; and all of them are so isolated by steep valley sides and by narrow gorges upstream and downstream that access to them is not at all easy. Otherwise this is a region of steep slopes and very narrow valleys.

The Cordillera Central to the south of Medellín, east of Manizales, Pereira, Cartago, and Armenia, is surmounted by a cluster of volcanoes, some of which have been active in historic times. The highest is Mt. Tolima (18,438 ft.) which erupted in 1829, causing a heavy fall of ash over the country to the west of it. This part of the Cordillera Central is deeply mantled with volcanic ash, which provides a soil of exceptional productivity. Along the eastern side of the Cauca Valley there are terraces of ash, now cut by streams draining from the high mountains. On these mountains the tree line is about 11,500 feet above sea level, and the snow line is about 15,000 feet. The dissected ash terraces which form the foothills east of the Cauca Valley are in the *tierra templada,* between 4,000 and 5,000 feet above sea level. This ash-covered western slope of the Cordillera Central is known by the regional name of El Quindío.

THE SETTLEMENT OF ANTIOQUIA

The first penetration of this rugged mountain country by Europeans was made by people from Cartagena. They advanced over steep slopes and through dense forests seeking for the gold which was believed to be plentiful in the stream gravels. They did discover a wealth of precious metals, and in 1541 they founded the town of Antioquia near the Río Cauca in the midst of placer mines. But for permanent settlement the region was handicapped, as far as the Spaniards of the colonial period were concerned, by a lack of Indian workers. By the end of the colonial period Antioquia was a poor region. In spite of its gold there was little prosperity because of the high cost of food.

It was in the late colonial period that events took place in this region which led to its transformation. A Spanish administrative officer, Juan Antonio Mon y Velarde, sought to increase the local production of food and so to decrease the cost of living. In 1788 he ordered everyone not engaged full time in mining to plant maize, and he appointed enforcement officers to see that the order was carried out. With the increase of maize he urged the farmers to increase the number of hogs and poultry and to sell them to the miners. In 1789 he received permission to establish four new agricultural colonies. Each family received from the Crown a town lot and a rural *finca,* the size of the latter being determined by the number of persons in the family. The average *finca* thus granted was between fifty and sixty acres. These new colonies were located in the *tierra templada* of the Cordillera Central in the vicinity of the town of Medellín, which had been established in 1675. Medellín became the chief market for the area, where the farmers and miners met to exchange their products.

Medellín and the settlements around it remained isolated from the rest of Colombia. Between Medellín and Cartagena there is a rugged and deeply dissected country, so difficult to cross that not until 1955 was an automobile highway completed all the way to the Caribbean. A trail, used mostly by mules, connected Medellín with Cartago at the northern end of the broad Cauca Valley, from which communications with the Pacific port of Buenaventura by way of Cali were relatively easy. But the most common route used for the very small trade in or out of Medellín was an ox-cart road, 120 miles long, to Puerto Berrío on the Magdalena, crossing the Cordillera Central by a pass only 5,800 feet above sea level. Although Medellín soon replaced the older town of Antioquia as the chief center of the region, the people remained in isolation, largely self-sufficient. They exported only a little gold and silver, which were still taken from the stream gravels throughout the area.

THE ANTIOQUEÑOS

From these beginnings there emerged in the modern period a distinctive and cohesive group of people. The Antioqueños, the people of Antioquia, are known throughout Colombia for their peculiar qualities, for their shrewd business sense, their willingness to work hard, their aggressiveness, their ability to colonize new lands. Racially they are no different from the mixed populations of other parts of Colombia, yet they insist on speaking with pride of *la raza antioqueña.* So cohesive have they become that they think of themselves first as Antioqueños and only second as Colombians. The Antioqueños have long performed their own manual labor and have operated their own businesses. Visitors who penetrated this part of the country in the nineteenth century described the inhabitants as an alert, virile, efficient people quite different from the light-hearted, more artistic, but certainly less businesslike people of Bogotá. "To these energetic and efficient people," wrote a German traveler in 1880, "belongs the future of Colombia." This same writer reported that the retail business in this region, unlike that of all other parts of Colombia, had not fallen into the hands of Germans and Syrians, but was being carried on almost exclusively by Antioqueños. During the turbulent period which lasted from the collapse of Bolívar's Gran Colombia to the beginning of World War I, the people of Antioquia remained isolated and relatively free from the warfare that devastated other parts of Colombia. In their protected valleys the Antioqueños developed a strong sense of unity. They were, and still are, devoutly Catholic and politically conservative.

Without their extraordinary birth rate, however, this small group of isolated settlers might never have achieved more than local significance. Large families have long been the rule. Even today families of 15 or 20 children are not uncommon. Since the period of original settlement in the sixteenth and seventeenth centuries, the Antioquia region has not received any important number of new immigrants, yet the settlements have been expanding at a faster and faster rate since Mon y Velarde set the pattern in the late eighteenth century.

The tendency to send out new colonies outside of the original nucleus first appeared about 1800. This was long before coffee had entered the economic life of Colombia; it was at a time when the only exports from the region were gold and silver, and when the agriculture of the Antioqueños consisted in the shifting cultivation of maize, sugarcane, bananas, and beans for local subsistence. Expansion took place chiefly to the south of Medellín, following the forested intermediate slopes on the western side of the Cordillera Central. As soon as the highly productive soils derived from volcanic ash were uncovered, the movement of settlers southward went on more rapidly. Manizales, about 75 miles south of Medellín, was founded in 1848, and in the second half of the nineteenth century many new towns to the south of Manizales were settled.

The increase of population in the Antioquia region is extraordinary when we remember that it has not been supported by immigration. In 1778 there were 46,000 people in Antioquia. By 1808 the number had increased to 110,000, and by 1883 it was over 500,000. In 1918 the two departments of Antioquia and Caldas, into which the original political unit had been divided, numbered 1,200,000, and there were more than 170,000 Antioqueños in the neighboring departments of Tolima and Valle. In 1954 the two departments had passed 2,800,000. Medellín, which had 88,000 people in 1924, by 1964 had reached 777,000. Manizales, only a little over 120 years old, is now a city of 187,000. But the fastest growing city in Colombia during the 1960's was Pereira, which in 1964 had reached 223,000.

TRANSFORMATION OF ANTIOQUIA

The first step in the transformation of Antioquia came with the introduction of coffee. Although the new crop appeared in Santander soon after 1850, it was slow to reach remote Antioquia. Even as late as 1880, the Antioqueños were still carrying on a shifting cultivation of food crops for local consumption. But during World War I and the decade that followed, the Antioqueños suddenly embraced a new economic life. In the short span of two decades the small farmers began to plant coffee on their *fincas*. The small patches devoted to the new crop were shaded under the cover of taller trees, forming a thick cover of vegetation over the steep slopes. The whole Antioquia area took up coffee planting, and the frontier of new settlement continued southward all the more rapidly. Three long fingers of pioneer settlement now extend southward on either side of the Cauca Valley, and in Tolima on the eastern side of the Cordillera Central, overlooking the Magdalena Valley.

These changes in the economic activities have involved an elaboration of the routes of circulation. Formerly Antioquia could only be reached from Puerto Berrío and from Cartago. Except for the ox-cart road from Puerto Berrío to Medellín the only route over the high Cordillera Central was a trail from Ibagué to Armenia over the Paso del Quindío (11,434 ft.). But when the people of Antioquia began to produce coffee for export, the facilities for transportation had to be provided. One of the earliest of these was a cable line built over the mountains from Manizales to a point on the railroad near Honda. The next step was to extend railroads into the region from the Cauca Valley and from the Magdalena Valley. The railroad from the Pacific port of Buenaventura to Cali was extended to Cartago, and then to Manizales. Medellín was reached for many years by a single-track narrow gauge line that climbed to the pass from Puerto Berrío and that almost, but not quite, joined up with another line from Medellín to the western side of the pass. The gap was covered by ox-cart. Today there is a tunnel through this pass and the railroad connects Puerto Berrío and Medellín. The little locomotive that used to pull the cars from Medellín up to the pass has now been set on a pedestal in the city as a very unusual kind of monument. Since World War II, as elsewhere in Latin America, the motor truck and the all-weather highway have provided better facilities for transportation than the railroads.

MANUFACTURING INDUSTRY

The Antioquia region was further transformed by the development of manufacturing industries. During the 1930's Medellín became Colombia's leading industrial city. Since World War II new, modern plants have been built in Medellín, and industrial development has also spread to the other urban centers of the region—Manizales, Pereira, and Armenia.

The Cauca Valley

The Cauca Valley region is the part of the structural depression drained by the Cauca River between Popayán in the south and Cartago in the north. The cluster of population that forms this region remains distinct from that of the Antioquia region, which occupies the slopes on either side of the Cauca Valley but does not descend into it. The Cauca Valley area of concentrated settlement is in Riseralda, Valle del Cauca, and Cauca.

THE LAND

The deep rift valley that separates the Cordillera Occidental and the Cordillera Central southward from Cartago is a major surface feature of both Colombia and Ecuador. As we have pointed out, this structural valley is

Hydroelectric project in the mountains north of Medellin. *Courtesy of Colombian Information Service.*

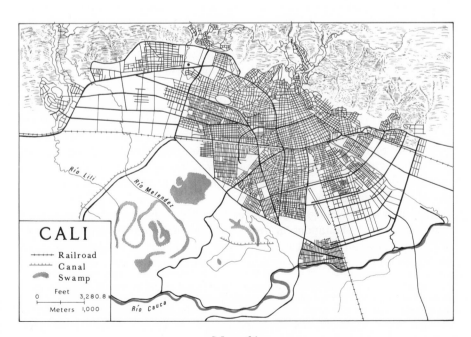

Map 64

deeply filled with ash in the southern part of Colombia. The rivers that drain it have cut deeply into the ash, leaving the original surface as high terraces on either side.[3] Popayán is located on such a terrace, 5,500 feet above sea level and about 1,000 feet above the Cauca River which here emerges from the Cordillera Central. From Popayán to a short distance upstream from Cali the Cauca flows through a narrow gorge, deeply cut into the valley floor. But just upstream from Cali it emerges onto a floodplain some 15 miles wide which extends northward for about 125 miles to Cartago. Below Cartago the Cauca again enters a narrow gorge. At Cali the floodplain of the Cauca is in the *tierra caliente,* about 2,300 feet above sea level. The city of Cali is built on a low terrace on the western side of the floodplain at an elevation of 3,140 feet (Map 64). Palmira occupies a similar site on a terrace to the east of the floodplain at an elevation of 3,500 feet.

When the Spaniards first entered the Cauca Valley they found it covered mostly with a woodland savanna. Along the floodplain the swamps were filled with bamboo interspersed with patches of dense evergreen broadleaf forests. Back from the floodplain, however, the terraces and alluvial fans were covered with tall, rank grass and scattered low trees. The rainfall which supports this vegetation is abundant, coming in two seasons—from March to May and from September to November.

SETTLEMENT IN THE CAUCA VALLEY

The Spanish invaders who entered the Cauca Valley both from the north and from the south found little gold; but they did find a land suitable for the production of that new wealth-bringing commercial crop, sugarcane. The Indians, however, proved quite inadequate as a supply of labor. Diseases introduced by the white men killed great numbers of the natives. Nor were these tribes of the Cauca region so ready to engage in agricultural work as the Chibchas of the central basins in Cundinamarca. Therefore the Spaniards soon brought in African slaves. The land was divided into large estates, some containing more than 2,500 acres; on the terraces and fans of the eastern side of the valley large areas of sugarcane were cultivated, and the African slaves were grouped in small villages scattered throughout the plantations.

Cali and Popayán have played contrasting roles in the social and economic life of the Cauca region. Here we discover a relationship similar to that developed between Valencia and Caracas, where the Spanish landowners, after establishing their plantations in areas warm enough and wet enough for the production of sugar, then selected for their own places of residence locations on higher ground where the air is cooler and where disease-carrying insects

---

[3]The part of the Cauca Valley between Cartago and Popayán was at one time filled with a lake into which the volcanic ash was dropped. The lake bed deposits have been deeply dissected by the main stream and by the tributaries. The terraces on which Popayán, Armenia, Pereira, and Manizales are built are remnants of the old lake floor.

are fewer. Popayán became an aristocratic town, occupied very largely by people of unmixed European ancestry. Even the owners of the placer gold mines of Antioquia came to live in Popayán, leaving their mines, as the sugarcane planters left their estates, in the care of overseers. But Popayán is not a national capital like Caracas. It is still a predominantly European place, the home of many of Colombia's aristocratic families, a town rich with colonial tradition, but not a place of great economic significance in the modern era.

RURAL LAND USE IN THE MODERN PERIOD

When slavery came to an end, the old sugarcane plantation economy fell to pieces, as it did in so many places when the former slaves sought other kinds of employment. Sugarcane plantations were reestablished in parts of the Cauca Valley during the latter part of the nineteenth century by a North American planter. The cane is grown on the low terraces along the eastern side of the valley. Around Cartago there are also plantations of cacao; and the district around Palmira is known for its plantations of tobacco.

But even as late as 1959 most of the area of the Cauca Valley was used for the pasture of beef cattle. Some 8 percent of the owners of land in the valley owned more than two-thirds of the area, most of it divided into ranches of more than 125 acres. The pastures were not cultivated. The animals fed on the wild grasses, moving onto the river floodplain at low water and moving to the higher land on either side when the floods spread over the low places. The result was a relatively small production of food per acre from the potentially most productive part of the area. Meanwhile most of the subsistence farmers of the region raised their own food crops on the bordering mountain slopes. The contrast between the well-to-do landowners and the very poor, illiterate peasants was striking. Most of the peasants suffered from malnutrition and disease and from a complete lack of confidence in any government-sponsored program to relieve their poverty.

The Cauca Valley became one of the parts of Colombia seriously disturbed by sporadic and uncoordinated peasant revolt. In Colombia this is known as *la violencia*. Bands of armed men would rob and kill, or occupy unused private land and defy the authorities to remove them. We shall discuss the causes and patterns of *la violencia* later in Colombia as a whole, but clearly in the Cauca Valley the stage was set for an explosion. Yet the landowners continued to resist any real redistribution of land, and the landowners held the political power.

In 1961 the Colombian government established the *Instituto Colombiano de la Reforma Agraria* (INCORA) which was charged with the development and the administration of a program of agricultural improvement. In the Cauca Valley INCORA undertook to build an irrigation system along the floodplain just upstream from Cartago, involving about 50,000 acres. Parts of the large properties in this area were expropriated and divided among peasant families. Other parts were left to the original owners and were also supplied with water for irrigation. An attempt was made to increase the production of rice and maize and other food crops. The large owners used the land left to them to plant sugarcane. The project stimulated some movement of peasants down from the mountain sides into the valley, but by the late 1960's little had yet been done to improve the productivity of agricultural land use in the valley as a whole.

CALI

The town of Cali became the chief commercial center of the valley. Located at the eastern end of the pass over the Cordillera Occidental to the Pacific port of Buenaventura, Cali became the focus of the lines of travel for the whole Cauca region. In 1912 Cali had a population of 27,000; by 1918, after the opening of the Panama Canal had provided a nearby market along the Pacific coast, it had grown to 45,000. By 1950 Cali had passed 200,000. But the rapid modern growth of Cali only began in 1958, since which time this urban center has become a modern metropolis with a population in 1964 of over 800,000. Cali had passed Medellín to become the second city of Colombia. What caused this sudden increase in the rate of growth?

Industrial growth in Cali had started before 1958. By that time there were more than 40 manufacturing plants, nearly half of them founded and owned by people of Antioquia who foresaw a boom development in this Cauca Valley city. At that time only 9 plants were owned by foreigners. But since 1958 there has been a sudden increase in the number of large manufacturing plants owned by foreign firms, mostly North American. Most of them are branches of well-known North American companies, such as Colgate-Palmolive, Gillette, Goodyear, Grace, Home Products, Quaker Oats, and Squibb. There are also factories owned by French, Germans, Swiss, Swedes, Lebanese. In all, nearly half of the manufacturing plants in Cali are foreign-owned. There are textile factories, food processing plants, manufacturers of metals and pharmaceuticals as well as of a great variety of consumer goods.

The Alliance for Progress has also undertaken, with financial help and technical assistance from AID, to bring other improvements into the Cauca Valley. Dams built on several of the tributary streams on either side of the Cauca Valley now generate electric power which is carried to the whole valley in an interconnected grid of power lines. The industries at Cali are major users of this electric power. Also a large number of new schools have been built and staffed with teachers. In March, 1964, nineteen new elementary schools were inaugurated, and since then many more have been completed. A new university was built at Cali, and with help from the Rockefeller Foundation and from the Ford Foundation professors from the United States were made available.

Cali at night. The bright lights of the city are in stark contrast to the darkness of the rural areas. *Photo by W. R. Grace & Co.*

Yet in spite of all these developments in the Cauca Valley almost half of the population was still illiterate, unemployed, and desperately poor. Not very many of the peasants could find jobs in the new industries until they had learned to read and write. The Jesuit Fathers established the *Universidad Campesina* at a small town about 35 miles northeast of Cali, where peasants could be trained in the basic skills of leadership. The hope was that little by little the unskilled and illiterate rural people could be brought into the developing modern economy.

Large numbers of peasants, seeing the bright lights of Cali, have moved to the city and now occupy shantytowns around the outskirts. There are not enough new houses each year to take care of an annual increase of over 8 percent. The sanitary facilities, the public transportation, and the schools are still not adequate to take care of this rapid rate of growth.

The Pasto Region

Another and entirely different area of concentrated settlement is found in the southern part of Colombia, partly in the Cordillera Central, partly in the structural depression drained by the Río Patía. This cluster of people forms the center of the Department of Nariño and is focused around the town of Pasto. Here the population is composed almost entirely of Indians and mestizos, the properties are small, and there is little commercial production.

The southern part of Colombia is made up of two ranges of mountains, the Cordillera Central and the Cordillera Occidental. Where the folded Cordillera Oriental comes to an end, about 2° north of the equator, the Cordillera

Central becomes the easternmost of the Colombian Andes. Between the Cordillera Central and the Cordillera Occidental lies the southward continuation of the great rift valley, drained, in this region, by the Río Patía. This part of the rift valley resembles the upper part of the Cauca Valley around Popayán, for its ash fill is deeply dissected by the streams and the initial surface is represented only by isolated terrace remnants. The elevation of these terraces is considerably higher than that of the terraces around Popayán—8,510 feet at Pasto. The Río Patía escapes from the rift valley through a gorge which crosses the Cordillera Occidental to the Pacific coast, and which is so narrow and deep that it is quite useless as a line of travel. The whole region is one of abundant moisture, with two rainy and two dry seasons.

THE SETTLEMENT

There is no commercial focus on Pasto such as has been developed in the Cauca region on Cali. The Indian subsistence farmers occupy the small valley flats in the cordillera or the small terrace remnants and basins in the rift valley, wherever the slopes are gentle enough to permit the growth of crops. They cultivate chiefly grain and potatoes, and utilize the high *páramos* for the grazing of cattle. Commercial exchange is still largely by barter at the more or less regular fairs held in the numerous small towns and villages. Exchange with the outside world, however, is small.

At one time Pasto was a more important commercial center than it is today. Rubber and cinchona bark were gathered in the forests of the eastern mountain slopes, in the valleys of the Río Caquetá and the Putumayo. From these very remote districts the easiest routes of export were up the rough mountain trails to Pasto. Transportation was partly on muleback, partly on the backs of Indian porters. From Pasto a trail crossed the Cordillera Occidental and descended by way of Barbacoas to the Pacific port of Tumaco. Since the decline of rubber and cinchona, Pasto has lost this activity, and the trails to the east have been largely obliterated by the growth of luxuriant vegetation. A small trade in food products today descends from Pasto to supply the communities of African-descended gold miners in the coastal zone.

There is one INCORA project in Nariña. To the west of Pasto, some 1,500 families have been resettled on 100-acre farms, formed by combining some of the traditionally small farms of this region and extending the farmed area. A road has been built eastward to the eastern slopes of the mountains, and along the road some 150,000 farmers have been moved into a new pioneer zone. These projects were designed to relieve the pressure of too many people on too small an area of settlement around Pasto.

The Caribbean Coastal Lowlands

The sixth group of settlements is on the Caribbean coastal lowlands. Three clusters of people occupy this region: one centers on the port of Cartagena,

INCORA resettlement project in Nariño. *Courtesy of Colombian Information Service.*

in the departments of Bolívar, Córdoba, Sucre and Antioquia; another centers on Santa Marta, in the departments of Magdalena and César; and the third centers on Barranquilla, in the department of Atlántico.

Where the Río Magdalena emerges from its structural valley between the Cordillera Oriental and the Cordillera Central it enters a lowland plain built by deposits of river alluvium. This is a land subject to frequent inundations, much of it swampy even at low water; a land marked off in a crescentic pattern of meandering rivers and abandoned channels, with little strips of habitable ground on the natural levees bordering the channels. The maze of swamps, oxbow lakes, and rivers is fed by the waters of four streams: the Magdalena, the Cauca, the San Jorge, and the César. Most of the surface east of the Magdalena is permanently covered with water—there are vast shallow lakes or reed-filled marshes with fluctuating outlines, known as *ciénagas*. West of the Magdalena large areas disappear under water during the season of floods, but dry out during the single dry season from October to March, at which time cattle may be pastured on them. At present the main outlet for all this water is through the mouth of the Magdalena, and this mouth, discharging into the virtually tideless Caribbean, was, until recently, so clogged with sandbars that ocean ships could not enter, nor river boats leave. The whole area is covered with dry scrub woodland and wet savanna.

From the beginning of the colonial period to the present day the story of the settlement of the Caribbean coastal lowlands is one of continued rivalry among three ports for the commerce moving in and out of the interior of Colombia. The Río Magdalena, difficult and unsatisfactory as it is for navigation, has remained until recently the chief route between the coast and the centers of population in the highlands. At the northern end of the Magdalena route, however, Cartagena, Barranquilla, and Santa Marta have competed for the traffic, and as the fortunes of each of them has risen and fallen the clusters of people in the districts around them have increased or decreased.

CARTAGENA

During most of the colonial period Cartagena was able to maintain a lead over the other competing ports. Cartagena was founded in 1533 on the shores of a protected harbor, near a fortress which commanded the entrance to the bay. Just south of Cartagena a natural side channel of the Magdalena provided a connection with the main river navigable for the shallow-draught boats and canoes of that period. Cartagena became one of the chief ports of colonial Spanish America, and its fortress was a key unit in the system of defense. During the Wars of Independence, however, neglect permitted the side channel to fill with silt until it was no longer navigable; whether as a cause or as a result of this neglect, Cartagena lost its preeminence and declined in population.

During the present century Cartagena has regained some of its importance. The construction of a railroad to Calamar on the Magdalena served to divert some of the river trade. Along the railroad line there is a district of dense rural settlement where sugar and cotton are raised on both large and small plantations. There is one modern sugar mill in this district. The country between Cartagena and Barranquilla is also utilized, beyond the zone of plantations, for the grazing of cattle. The rural population is predominantly of African descent.

Also included in the hinterland of Cartagena are three INCORA projects. One is southeast of the port, where an irrigation system has made an area of nearly 70,000 acres available for the resettlement of 2,500 families, and for the production of a variety of food crops, including rice and maize. A second project is along the lower Sinú, including its delta, where land once used for the grazing of cattle has been divided up into farms for 400 settlers who grow food crops and cotton. The third project is along the eastern side of the Gulf of Urabá, where a new pioneer zone has been made available through the construction of motor truck highways. The newest zone of banana plantations is along the highway from Medellín to Turbo. The bananas are moved by barge from the plantations to ships at anchor in the Gulf of Urabá.

Cartagena is the chief outlet for the products of the Atrato Valley. Connection with this remote part of Colombia is by river boat and airplane. The chief products that are brought to Cartagena for export are gold and platinum, for this is the most productive gold area of South America. For many years Colombia has been among the two or three leading producers of platinum in the world. Both gold and platinum are taken from the stream gravels near the headwaters of the Atrato and San Juan rivers. But placer mining requires few workers, and when modern mechanical dredges are used the number of jobs in mining is greatly decreased. As a result there has been a steady current of migration of African miners southward into the forests of the west coast south of Buenaventura, where they have proved better able to maintain themselves than the Indian inhabitants of the forests. Some have also moved north along the Pacific coast into Panamá. The Atrato region has a small nucleus of population around Quibdó, but otherwise is occupied by only a few widely scattered settlements. Quibdó enjoys the dubious distinction of having an average annual rainfall of 415 inches, which makes it one of the rainiest places on earth.

The coast of the Caribbean south of Cartagena has been selected for the ends of two oil pipelines. One from the Barrancabermeja field in the Magdalena Valley ends at Mamonal, just south of Cartagena, where a new oil refinery has been built; the other from the Colombian part of the Maracaibo lowland runs westward to the Caribbean at Coveñas. The figures for oil exports are included in export data for Cartagena, although these terminals add little to the economic importance of the city.

The economic importance of Cartagena, however, has changed very greatly since World War II. The completion of the all-weather highway from Medellín to Cartagena has given this port a tremendous advantage over its rivals in handling the commerce of the Antioquia region. Much of the coffee that used to go to the Magdalena and thence to Barranquilla now moves by truck directly to Cartagena. The coffee exports are now about equally divided between these two places. Furthermore El Dique, the old silted up channel of the Magdalena, has now been dredged deep enough to permit the largest river steamers to reach Cartagena. The railroad to Calamar has been abandoned. As a result of all these changes, Cartagena, which still had only about 75,000 inhabitants after World War II, in 1964 had almost reached 200,000.

SANTA MARTA

On the eastern side of the Caribbean coastal lowlands is the Santa Marta district, centering on the old colonial port of Santa Marta. This place, like Cartagena, enjoys the advantages of a good harbor; and through the *ciénagas* on the eastern side of the Río Magdalena, shallow-draught boats and canoes could reach Santa Marta with fully as much ease as they could reach Cartagena. When Cartagena's connection with the main river was no longer navigable, Santa Marta took its place for a time as the chief commercial center of the region. Both of these rivals, however, were placed at a disadvantage when steamboats began to operate on the Magdalena, for neither Santa Marta nor Cartagena could be reached by these much larger vessels until the dredging of El Dique had been carried out.

Santa Marta has long been known as a banana port. The United Fruit Company established one of its earliest plantations along the west-facing

The Barrancabermejo oil refinery on the Río Magdalena. *Courtesy of Colombian Information Service.*

piedmont of the Sierra Nevada de Santa Marta and built special banana-loading docks at Santa Marta. Around the company plantations before World War II there had been a considerable expansion of planting by small owners, mostly of African descent, who sold their bananas to the company for shipment. In 1940, however, the whole region was hard hit by a banana disease that all but wiped out the plantations. Production dropped from over 7 million bunches a year to less than 1 million. Then a new spray system was devised to control the disease, and production in the protected areas was greatly increased. Now the company leaves the production of bananas to independent growers, giving them technical assistance, including spraying service. The company buys the bananas from the growers and ships them out through the special banana docks at Santa Marta.

In 1961 the railroad from Bogotá by way of Honda was extended along the eastern side of the Magdalena Valley to Santa Marta, giving this city a renewed volume of trade. Imports destined for all the cities of the Cordillera Oriental and for the Magdalena Valley can now go either by way of Santa Marta or by way of Barranquilla. Santa Marta is also in process of being developed as a seaside resort area for the people of Bogotá. Special excursion trains on the railroad carry passengers overnight to the warm tropical sunshine along the Caribbean—which has a strong appeal to people whose homes are in the *tierra fría.*

BARRANQUILLA

The third commercial center of the Caribbean coastal lowland, and the one which for nearly a century controlled the trade of the Magdalena Valley, is Barranquilla. This town was brought quickly to a leading position about the middle of the nineteenth century, when steamboats began to navigate the river as far as the Honda rapids. For a long time Barranquilla was only a river port, since the sandbars at the mouth of the river prohibited the entrance of ocean steamers. In 1862 a short railroad line was built from Barranquilla to a place just west of the river mouth, where a pier was constructed far enough into the shallow waters of the Caribbean to be reached by ocean ships. Later this first port was abandoned because of rapid silting, and Puerto Colombia, the present port, was built. This place is now connected with Barranquilla by both railroad and automobile highway. Before World War II the mouth of the Magdalena had been dredged deep enough to permit the entrance of ocean steamers of 10,000 tons.

Other transportation changes, however, have started to divert some of Barranquilla's commerce to Cartagena, and in the next ten years it is expected that most of the commerce moving in and out of the Magdalena Valley will pass through either Cartagena or Santa Marta. To compensate for this loss the government is stimulating the increased industrial development of Barranquilla. Already this city has a considerable number of new factories which make use of imported raw materials to manufacture goods for the domestic market. The planners, looking at Colombia's economy as a whole, think that a steel industry in Barranquilla, using imported raw materials, could supply steel products to the domestic market more cheaply than could be done from Belencito. The population, which was about 275,000 in 1951, in 1964 was over 500,000.

The new highway cut through forested mountains from Medellín to Turbo, near the Gulf of Urabá. *Courtesy of Colombian Information Service.*

The cluster of people in the Department of Atlántico also includes some agricultural settlers. West of the Magdalena there is a small but densely populated area devoted to the production of cotton and sugar—an area of small properties and of predominantly African population. Negro farmers, also, are strung along the natural levees on either side of the Magdalena, raising vegetables and fruit which they bring to the Barranquilla market in canoes. There is an INCORA irrigation and resettlement project in this area which affects about 25,000 acres.

Colombia's Transportation Problem

The rugged terrain in which these six regions of concentrated settlement are embedded has greatly complicated the problem of communication and transportation. The physical barriers that separate one region from another are greater than those that separate Colombia as a whole from its neighbors. Difficulty of communication has long aggravated the problem of establishing order among these diverse clusters of people.

A first glance at the map (Map 59, p. 387) suggests that the Magdalena Valley ought to offer a fine natural route of access to the highlands. In fact this has been the chief route of access since the earliest days of Spanish settlement. Each of the areas of concentrated settlement, except that in Nariño, has been connected with the river.

Actually, however, the Magdalena route has never been satisfactory. Obstacles to navigation on the Magdalena begin at its mouth, where sandbars long prevented the entrance of the deep-draught ocean vessels. Even shallow-draught river boats have difficulty with the river, for above Calamar the channel frequently shifts because of changes in the position of sandbars. The river is subject to sudden, short floods produced by local storms on its mountain tributaries. The annual fluctuation of the water-level is also large, with the lowest water coming in November. Slowly and painfully the stern-wheel river steamers feel their way upstream—until further navigation, even at high water, is stopped by the rapids at Honda, 615 miles up the river from the Caribbean. Upstream from Honda the river is again navigable for shallow-draught boats as far as Neiva.

In spite of these difficulties, the several highland centers have all established their outlets through river ports. Ocaña and Bucaramanga have their own small river ports. The thriving communities of Antioquia around Medellín are connected with Puerto Berrío. Manizales is connected by a cable line over the Cordillera Central to a station on the railroad near Honda. The settlements of Boyacá and Cundinamarca are reached by several roads which descend to the river banks between Honda and Girardot. The construction of a railroad between Girardot and the capital was begun in 1880 and completed in 1909. But the high cost of building and operating this line necessitated such high freight rates that a large proportion of the goods shipped between Bogotá and the Magdalena continued to move by muleback or ox-cart. In recent years motor trucks have been more effective than the railroad in competing with these more primitive forms of transportation.

Honda was at one time a commercial center of major importance. Because of its location at the head of navigation on the lower river, Honda was the point where goods destined for the coast were gathered from all the surrounding country—not only from Cundinamarca, but also from the Cauca Valley on the western side of the Cordillera Central. A road from Honda was built over the high Paso del Quindío from Ibagué to Armenia. The road continued by way of Cali, Popayán, and Pasto to Quito in Ecuador. Honda became a major focus of colonial routes, and for a time was one of the leading commercial centers of South America. But the importance of Honda was undermined by the construction, in 1884, of a railroad which tapped the traffic of the lower river about 25 miles below the town and provided transportation around the rapids. This railroad was eventually extended upriver to Girardot and Neiva. A second railroad was built directly from Bogotá to navigable water below Honda, which resulted in bypassing both Girardot and Honda. In 1961 this line was extended all the way (418 miles) to Santa Marta, giving Bogotá an all-rail connection with the Caribbean for the first time.

The trip upstream from the Caribbean ports to Bogotá used to take from eight days to a month. Now, passengers and mail are flown from Barranquilla to Bogotá, a distance of about 450 miles, in about an hour. Colombia, in fact, had the first commercial airline to be placed in regular operation in the American Hemisphere—a German line which was started in 1920, flying along the Magdalena between Barranquilla and Girardot. The airlines are now nationally owned and operated; regular flights reach all of the chief centers of the country in a few hours from Bogotá; places which once required months of hard travel to visit are now easily accessible from the capital. But airlines do not solve the problem of transporting such things as wheat, coffee, or manufactured articles.[4]

Since World War II the all-weather highway and the motor truck are at last beginning to provide low-cost transportation for the highland settlements. From Bogotá paved roads now extend in four directions along the relatively smooth surface of the high basins. Beyond these basins gravel roads have now been extended through mountainous terrain to provide connections between the capital and all the other regions of settlement. One road runs northeastward to Cúcuta and to the Venezuelan border where it connects with the new paved highway to Caracas. Another highway crosses the moun-

---

[4]Ross N. Pearson shows that the river will continue to carry bulky industrial products in competition with other forms of transportation for a long time. Ross N. Pearson, "An Analysis of Trade on the Río Magdalena," *Papers of the Michigan Academy of Science, Arts and Letters,* Vol. 46, 1961 (1960 meeting), pp. 435–49.

tains east of Bogotá and descends steeply to Villavicencio, thence continuing almost 90 miles eastward across the plains to navigable water on the Río Meta. The first of the all-weather highways to Bogotá connects the capital with Honda; and this road has now been extended over the Cordillera Central to Medellín. Motor trucks now can go from Bogotá to Medellín in 24 hours, but the road they use is one of the steepest and most winding mountain roads in the world. The airplane makes the trip in less than an hour. Another highway now has been built westward down to the Magdalena River at Girardot; thence it climbs by way of Ibagué to a pass over the Cordillera Central which is a little lower than the old Quindío road—only 10,760 feet.[5] Another road connects Cartago with Medellín, thus finally giving this city an easy outlet to the Pacific. The road over the Cordillera Central is a part of the Inter-American Highway system. It continues southward by way of Palmira, Cali, Popayán, and Pasto to join with the central highway of Ecuador.

Colombia as a Political Unit

No other political unit in Latin America contains so many diverse elements within a comparable area as does Colombia. The total national territory includes a vast extent of land east of the Andes in which settlement by Colombians is either very scanty or entirely lacking. No land communication exists between the effective national territory of Colombia and its remote outpost of Leticia on the Amazon. To be sure, some of the Colombian Llanos of the Orinoco are utilized for cattle, as they are across the border in Venezuela. But within the western third of the national territory, where most of the Colombians live, there is an extraordinary diversity of physical conditions. This diversity comes in part from the rugged surface, but in part, also, from the existence at these latitudes of the maximum variety of vertical zones. The effect of these altitude differences is permitted full expression in terms of settlement because of the existence of intermont basins and valleys all the way from sea level to the snow line, and because of the importation of cattle, European grains, sugarcane, and coffee, which made possible the extension of productive land use to all the different altitude zones.

The diversity of the Colombian scene, however, is more than a matter of physical setting alone. As we have seen, there are six regions of concentrated settlement. Among the separate clusters of people, we have observed contrasts in racial composition, contrasts in the economic life and the level of living, contrasts in political attitudes. If the genius of Bolívar was unable to hold Gran Colombia together we need not be surprised; rather, we can marvel that he was able to hold together in one country the six regions of settlement that were closest to Bogotá.

[5]James J. Parsons points out that there is another still lower pass over the Cordillera at the place where the Departments of Caldas, Tolima, and Valle come together. This route has never been developed, yet it requires a climb of only 9,776 feet above sea level.

The Economic Situation

The census of 1964 showed that the population of Colombia had reached 17,482,000, and by 1967 it had passed 19 million. The population was increasing at a rate of 3.2 percent per year. Major shifts of population within the country were taking place as large numbers of rural peasants were moving into all the big cities, partly to seek employment opportunities, partly to escape from the social disorder and the disruption of community life resulting from *la violencia*. Some of the urban areas were increasing at such fantastic rates as 8 percent per year, as in the case of Cali. In 1964, 38 percent of the population lived in cities, yet agriculture was contributing over 40 percent of the gross national product. Large numbers of city people were unemployed. The gross national product per capita was $292, which placed Colombia fourteenth among the 24 independent Latin-American countries. To start the process of economic development with such a low rate of production requires a large amount of foreign financial aid, and this has been granted through the Alliance for Progress and other international agencies. A growth rate of over 4 percent for the economy means that there is a small margin of gain over the increasing population.

The fact remains that large numbers of Colombians, perhaps over half of them, are poor, illiterate, and not even aware of what the words "economic growth" might mean. These are the people who, in desperation, turn to raiding and killing, and whose activities made large parts of rural Colombia unsafe. The programs of INCORA, the building of schools, the technical assistance for the improvement of agriculture and for the more efficient use of resources, are all intended to attack *la violencia* at its source.

Meanwhile the increase of manufacturing industry in certain cities, notably in Cali, has started to provide employment, but not yet in sufficient amount. A middle class of white-collar workers is emerging, and on these people rests the hope for the establishment of order on which economic growth must be based.

Agriculture continues to provide the chief support for the economy. Of the exports in 1966, coffee made up 59 percent and oil 13 percent. But INCORA and other agencies are seeking to diversify the agriculture and to make the farms more productive. Already Colombia has become self-sufficient in producing cotton for its textile factories. The oil companies are seeking new oilfields, and in 1965 a new field was, in fact, discovered in the Putamayo Valley, along the eastern base of the Andes in southern Colombia. A pipeline was built across the mountains to the port of Tumaco on the Pacific.

The United States plays a relatively important role in the economic life. The spectacular developments at Cali are the result of a large amount of private investment from the United States. It was estimated in 1964 that at least a thousand citizens of the United States were living in Cali. The Cauca

Valley Corporation—a private agency for planning the more effective use of water and the generation of electric power—was headed by experienced North American planners who gained much of their experience in the administration of the TVA. The United States takes over half of the exports and furnishes over half of the imports. Colombia also trades with West Germany, Great Britain, and the Netherlands.

But clearly the improvement of the economy, and any important attack on the large proportion of very poor people, will depend on the improvement of the political situation, on the development of a coherent and stable population.

The Political Situation

It would be difficult to conceive of a geographic pattern of internal arrangement that would appear to make the achievement of political unity and coherence more difficult than in Colombia. Yet the fact is that the ideas and ideals of liberal democracy have gained considerable support, and in spite of long continued internal conflicts there is hope that the individual citizen may before long enjoy a greater measure of equality before the law and may participate in political decisions more effectively than he has in the recent past.

For a long time after Bolívar was forced to give up his efforts, Colombia was torn by civil war. The economy of the country suffered severely from the devastation. Only the Antioqueños were spared from the most serious effects of the disorders because of the isolation of their settlements. Then for a time it seemed as if a political balance had been achieved and democratic procedures could be developed. This came about in part because the six regions of settlement were more or less balanced, and no one of them was powerful enough to subdue all the others.

The rise of Antioquia after World War I changed all this. When Antioquia turned to the commercial production of coffee, and especially when Medellín developed as Colombia's leading industrial center, this one region gained the economic advantage over all the others. The Antioqueños did what the economists recommend: they saved their money and invested it in new capital, new factories, new means of production. The Antioqueños were the business people of Colombia, and as they played a larger and larger part in the economy, they also began to play a larger part in the political life. Yet the Antioqueños continued to think of themselves as Antioqueños first and Colombians second. A military dictatorship gained control of the country, as the conservatives of Antioquia sought to keep the liberals of Bogotá from recapturing the government. Civil liberties disappeared, newspapers were tightly controlled; in short, political order was imposed by force.

No small part of *la violencia* was politically inspired by the bitter rivalry of these two political parties, each occupying a separate part of the national territory. Nor was this something new in Colombian experience, but only a return to the violence of much of the nineteenth century. Now outlaw bands could act in the name of one or another political party and could make life in a rural village dominated by the other party very risky. There can be no doubt that communists joined these bands and even provided some arms and some leadership. But they did not create the bands. And when it became clear that communism in Cuba was bringing subservience to another foreign power, communist influence dropped rapidly in Colombia. When some of these guerrilla bands declared their independence of the central government and set up their own local administration, this was not a result of communist subversion, but only the act of desperate men who had lost hope in the normal processes of government.

In 1957 a new effort to find a compromise between the extremes of political opinion was made. The conservative and the liberal parties agreed to a coalition in which liberal and conservative leaders would assume the presidency alternately and in which the various government offices would be staffed equally by people of both parties. Yet throughout all these political changes the agricultural, industrial, and financial interests have maintained their control of government policy. The large landowners, even now, resist the substance of land redistribution. When they support measures to expropriate large unused private properties, they then resist carrying out these measures. When the large numbers of landless peasants become sufficiently disillusioned concerning the intentions of the government to carry through measures for the relief of hunger and poverty, they turn to banditry.

Between 1958 and 1965 three presidents were elected and held office, in accordance with the requirements of the coalition. The army has regained control of the rural areas in most parts of the country. Slowly—very slowly— the processes of economic development move forward; but the social change that would strip political power from the traditional holders of such power— the large landowners—has yet to take place. The greatest hope that such change will take place step by step, rather than by violent revolt, rests with the growing middle class in the cities. Furthermore, the rise of the Cauca Valley and Cali to preeminence in the national economy provides a much-needed balance against the predominant position of Antioquia.

The problem remains: can a state-idea be formulated that will command the support of a great majority of the people, Antioqueños as well as the people of Pasto, or Cali, or Barranquilla, or Bogotá? Can modern leaders, with much better means of getting about in this mountainous country, and with more effective ways of communicating with distant parts of the country than Bolívar possessed, be able to bring political order and coherence to such a diverse country, and to make diversity itself a source of strength rather than weakness?

República del Ecuador

Area: 109,483 square miles
Population: (1967 estimate) 5,508,000
          (last census, 1962) 4,649,648
Capital city: Quito; (1966) 421,700
Largest city: Guayaquil; (1966) 625,600
Percent urban: (1950) 34.6
Birth rate per 1,000: (1966) 46–51; Death rate per 1,000: (1966) 15–18
Annual percent of increase: (1958–64) 3.1
Percent literate: (1962) 67.5
Percent labor force in agriculture: (1962) 56.5
Gross national product per capita: (1966) $224
Unit of currency: sucre (1968, 17.77 per dollar)
Leading crops in acreage: maize, rice, potatoes

COMMERCE, 1964 *(expressed in percentage of values)*
Percent total Latin-American exports: 1.5 (1956, 1.0)
Percent total Latin-American imports: 2.0

Exports (1966)

bananas 47	coffee 22	cacao 14

Exports to (1966)

United States	51 (1956, 60)
West Germany	16
Belgium	6
Italy	5

Imports from (1966)

United States	39 (1956, 52)
West Germany	16
United Kingdom	7
Japan	7

Chapter 18 □ Ecuador

In Ecuador the problem of establishing order and coherence in the national life stubbornly resists solution. The problem is vastly complicated in this country by one simple geographic fact: that the population includes two very different groups of people, each concentrated in a different part of the national territory. One group is made up largely of Indians, who live in small rural communities in the high Andes, work as self-sufficient farmers, and are little interested in sentiments of nationality or in programs of economic development. The other group is Spanish and mestizo. These people live in the highland cities, but are mostly concentrated in the coastal lowlands in back of Ecuador's chief city, Guayaquil. They are very much concerned with the production of things for export, with programs of economic development, and with the idea of Ecuador as a nation. Communication between these two groups is minimal.

Compared with Colombia, Ecuador is much simpler in its geographic arrangement. The backbone of the country is formed by the high ranges of the Andes. There are two high cordilleras, surmounted by towering volcanoes and separated by a series of ten intermont basins, all of them lying within the *tierra fría*. To the west of the Andes is the coastal region, composed partly of swampy lowlands, partly of low hills. The coastal region is covered in the north by a dense rain forest, but toward the south, as the rainfall becomes less, the vegetation changes from wet forest to dry scrub woodland and savanna. The third part of Ecuador lies east of the Andes. This is the Oriente, the rainy forested eastern slopes and piedmont of the Andes which descend toward the Amazon plains beyond.

The size of the national territory of Ecuador is uncertain because of a boundary dispute with Peru and because of the lack of accurate maps. At one time Ecuador claimed, but did not effectively occupy, large areas east of the Andes which are now accepted as Brazilian or Colombian territory. In 1942 a treaty was accepted by Ecuador and Peru which gave Peru owner-ship of the left-bank tributaries of the Río Marañón as far upstream as they were navigable by launches. A commission was appointed to fix the position of the boundary on accurate maps. But in the late 1950's, when it became clear that the arrangement of surface features and drainage lines was not at all what was expected, the Ecuadorians claimed that the treaty was void. The Peruvians point out that 900 out of 947 miles of the boundary have been mapped and accepted, and that the completion of the survey requires only a revision of the language of the treaty. Furthermore, Peruvians occupy and administer the whole area that constitutes the hinterland of Iquitos (Map 71).

If a boundary approximately like that shown on Map 65 is accepted, Ec-uador would have a total area of a little over 109,000 square miles (including 3,075 square miles in the Galápagos Islands). But most of the Oriente re-mains outside of Ecuador's effective national territory.

Population and Settlement

Until 1950 there never had been a census of the population of Ecuador. In that year the official count registered a little over 3 million people. In 1968 it was estimated that the population had reached 5,650,000. This sug-gests a growth rate of about 3.1 percent per year. Estimates of the proportion of people of different ethnic origins vary widely. Whether Indians make up 60 percent of the population, as one anthropologist estimates, or only 39 per-cent, as is officially estimated, cannot be answered with certainty, partly be-cause the census takers usually decide such questions in terms of social status. The official estimates say that people of unmixed European (mostly Span-ish) ancestry make up about 10 percent, and that 41 percent of the popu-lation is mestizo. There are also enough Africans and mulattoes to make up another 10 percent. The pure Indians make up about 100 percent of the rural people of the highlands. The people of European origin are concentrated in the cities, along with mestizos who have learned to live like the people of Spanish ancestry. The people of African origin are concentrated mostly in the northern part of the coastal lowland.

Course of Settlement

The high basins of Ecuador were already occupied by a dense population of sedentary Indians before the Spanish conquest. Shortly before the Euro-peans arrived on the scene, the Incas had extended the boundaries of their Empire northward to include Quito. But the distance which separated this northernmost region from the capital at Cuzco was so great that communica-tions were difficult to maintain and the power of the central authority was

Map 65

established only because the Inca himself spent much of his time in Quito. The Inca Empire was threatened with division and internal discord at the time when the Spaniards reached the shores of Peru.

Except for temporary landings along the coast made by Pizarro and his men as they worked their way southward, Ecuador was not entered by the Spaniards until after the conquest of Peru. In 1534 an expedition advanced northward from Peru and occupied the Indian town of Quito. From Quito the Spaniards continued northward into the Cauca Valley of Colombia, founding the towns of Pasto and Popayán (Map 6, p. 18). In 1538 a settlement was established where the hilly ground borders the Guayas River—a settlement which has now grown into the city of Guayaquil (Maps 65 and 66).

Spanish explorations, however, did not bring to light any important sources of gold in this part of South America. The search of the stream gravels in the southern part of the coastal lowland—south of the dense rain forest of

Map 66

northern Ecuador—did not find much gold. The Spaniards pushed their search down the eastern slopes, always supposing that gold must be more plentiful close to the equator. In 1542 the Spaniard Orellana sailed the length of the Amazon to its mouth, but without discovering what the Spaniards most desired—gold and large concentrations of Indians. Ecuador remained isolated and poor.

Isolation and poverty, rather than any strong sentiment of nationality, gave Ecuador its political independence. During the colonial period Quito had been administered first from Lima and later from Bogotá (Map 16, p. 39). When the Wars of Independence freed the colonies from Spain, Quito was included with Colombia and Venezuela in Gran Colombia which Bolívar

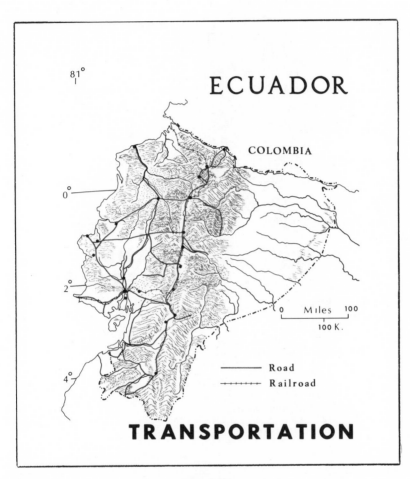

Map 67

attempted to form and administer from Bogotá. But the demand in Ecuador, as in Venezuela, was freedom from outside interference, and "outside" did not necessarily mean only outside of America—it meant also an attempt to govern from another cluster of population within the same continent.

Formation of the Northern Boundary

These historical events have left certain curious features in the present-day political geography of this part of South America. One of these features is the position of the northern boundary of Ecuador with reference to the areas of concentrated settlement (Maps 65 and 69). This is one of the

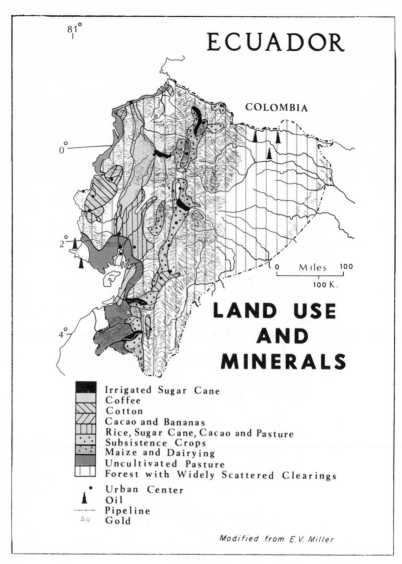

ECUADOR

COLOMBIA

LAND USE
AND
MINERALS

Irrigated Sugar Cane
Coffee
Cotton
Cacao and Bananas
Rice, Sugar Cane, Cacao and Pasture
Subsistence Crops
Maize and Dairying
Uncultivated Pasture
Forest with Widely Scattered Clearings
• Urban Center
⚓ Oil
——— Pipeline
Au Gold

Modified from E.V. Miller

Map 68

three places in Latin America where an international boundary cuts through
the center of a cluster of people. The manner in which the boundary between Ecuador and Colombia was established through the Basin of Tulcán
offers an illustration of one of the main themes of this study of Latin America—namely, the existence within the same territories of peoples of strongly
contrasted ways of living, of diverse groups which have mixed but never blended.

The development of national sentiment which made the drawing of a
boundary necessary took place among the Spaniards and the mestizos who
had adopted Spanish attitudes and objectives. The desire for independence
was strongest in the political centers—in Bogotá and Quito; and the position of the dividing line which separated the territory adhering to one of

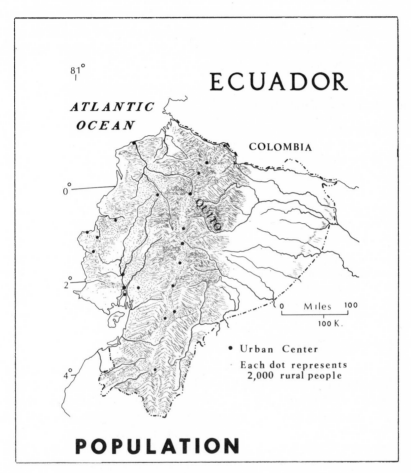

Map 69

these centers from the territory adhering to the other was determined more by conditions in the capitals than by local arrangements along the border. The people actually separated by the boundary are mostly pure-blooded Indians, to whom the distinctions of nationality even to this day seem unimportant.

The actual position of the line was the result of historical events at the time of the separation of Colombia and Ecuador. The territory around Pasto in Colombia, which had originally been settled from Quito, might well have become a part of Ecuador had not a revolt in the Ecuadorian capital given the armies of Bogotá the advantage at a critical moment, which they accepted by pushing southward into territory formerly administered from the rival center. Since the Spaniards lacked detailed information regarding the arrangement of intermont basins and of the Indian communities, the clear separation of the Basin of Tulcán from the Basin of Ibarra by the Páramo de Boliche was ignored. The boundary was established on an obvious natural feature—the Río Tulcán, which cuts through the middle of the intermont basin.

The Regions of Settlement

Unfortunately for the establishment of order among such diverse elements as exist together in Ecuador, the political center of the country is located in the midst of the Indian communities of the Andes whereas the economic center of the country is located on the coast. Quito, the capital, a city of 422,000 inhabitants, is situated where the problems of foreign commercial and political relations seem remote indeed. Guayaquil, the chief commercial city, with a population of 626,000, is located on a navigable river on the low plains west of the Andes. This geographical separation of the political and the commercial centers and the fact that the contacts between the highland Indian communities and the lowland settlements are not intimate are major factors in the interpretation of Ecuador's internal difficulties. Let us consider each of the regions in turn.

The Highland Region

From the northern border of Ecuador for about 250 miles southward to the Basin of Cuenca (Map 66), the Andes are similar in geologic structure to the Cordillera Occidental and the Cordillera Central of Colombia. Together these two cordilleras form an arch of crystalline rocks, with a section along the axis which has collapsed to form a continuous north–south rift. But in Ecuador the volcanic activity which borders this rift is much greater than it is in Colombia. Standing on either side of the structural depression in Ecuador are some 30 volcanoes, some of them among the largest in the world. The highest of these peaks is Mt. Chimborazo (20,577 feet), which lifts its majestic cone far into the zone of permanent snow. Many of these volcanoes are still active. The clouds which gather around the summits of Cotopaxi and its neighbors are lighted at night by the reflection of the molten lava in their craters. Because these volcanoes are of the acidic and explosive type, it is impossible to say whether any one of them is or is not dangerous; like Vesuvius in Italy, each cone may remain quiet for centuries, only to return to violent activity with little warning. The beautifully symmetrical cones have been built of successive flows of lava and falls of ash and dust. Because the prevailing winds are from the east the ash falls are deep over the structural depression and the western slopes.

Stream dissection in this loose volcanic ash is enormous. The slopes of the inactive volcanoes are cut into very rugged "badlands." Where streams have extended their headwaters back into the ash-filled intermont basins, deep canyons have been excavated. Only beyond the reach of these streams have the gentle slopes of the initial basin floors been left uncut.

The natural vegetation of highland Ecuador is a product not only of the climate, but also of the peculiarities of the soil material. Although the rainfall, which is concentrated in one rainy season from November to May, is enough to support forests where temperatures permit, so porous is the unconsolidated ash that the moisture is speedily absorbed. Forests actually do cover the slopes of the mountains to about 10,000 feet above sea level. But the intermont basins, even though they lie between 7,000 and 10,000 feet, were originally covered with only a dense growth of brush. During the long history of human settlement much of the brush has been cut to make charcoal, or burned to provide more room for pasture, so that today grassy *páramos* cover about half the total area of the highlands. Altitude limits define the distribution of crops, with potatoes reaching an average upper limit at about 10,500 feet and an extreme limit at 11,800 feet.

THE INTERMONT BASINS

The people of highland Ecuador are concentrated in distinct clusters, each occupying one of the several intermont basins. Within the zone between the two cordilleras there are ten large basins, arranged in a line from north to south—most of them forming parts of the same rift valley which we have already noted in Colombia as extending southward from Cartago. Each basin is occupied by a dense population which is mostly Indian and mestizo, and which makes use of the land for the cultivation of subsistence crops or for the grazing of cattle.

The three northernmost basins in Ecuador are drained by streams which descend westward to the Pacific. The Basin of Tulcán, which is cut in the middle by the boundary between Ecuador and Colombia, lies at an elevation of 9,500 feet and is, therefore, too high for any crops except the potato. The Páramo de Boliche, just south of the Basin of Tulcán, is used as common pasture by the nearby Indian communities, but contains few fixed settlements. Just south of this *páramo* lies the Basin of Ibarra, formed as a sort of amphitheater of high terrace remnants around the head of the deeply incised valley of the river which drains it. On the remnants of the basin floor, some seven or eight thousand feet above sea level, there are numerous small Indian villages, and around them the farmers raise grains and potatoes. Far down in the bottom of the valley, only 2,500 feet above sea level, there are small plantations of sugarcane and cotton, owned by the people of Ibarra.

The basin of Quito is next, going south. Here again there is a kind of rim around the edge of the basin which represents the surface of the original ash-fill. Quito is built on this rim at an elevation of about 9,350 feet above

A suburb of Quito, 9,350 feet above sea leavel. Indian farms on the slopes in background. *Photo Courtesy—Pan American Airways.*

sea level. The Río Guaillabamba which drains westward to join the Río Esmeraldas has cut its gorge back through the Cordillera Occidental. When it reached the loose ash deposits in the Basin of Quito the river excavated the central part of the basin, forming an inner basin with a generally level floor at about 7,500 feet above sea level. The Embassy of the United States in Quito is located on the very edge of the sharp drop that separates the outer rim from the inner basin—a drop of nearly 2,000 feet. The city of Quito, which was built on the site of an old Inca city, occupies a piece of the high rim overlooking the inner basin, and climbs the lower slopes of the volcano Pichincha. The land use differs in the two parts of the basin. The lower inner basin is divided into large estates owned by well-to-do people who live in Quito. Indian tenants on these properties raise maize and pasture dairy cattle. On the higher outer rim and on the bordering mountain slopes the population is almost entirely Indian. They are subsistence farmers raising wheat, barley, and potatoes, and pasturing sheep. From Quito, it seems as if the whole slope of Pichincha is marked off in a patchwork of little Indian fields as far up as the limit of the potato.

South of the Basin of Quito the high *páramos* form a narrow connection between the eastern and western cordilleras. South of this, again, lies the Basin of Latacunga, in which are found the small towns of Latacunga and

Ambato, which were almost entirely destroyed by an earthquake in 1949 but have been rebuilt on the same sites. This is a dry and relatively poor area, deeply dissected by the headwaters of the east-flowing rivers. The Basin of Latacunga and the Basin of Riobamba, next going south, are all but completely separated by the massive pedestal of Mt. Chimborazo. The area around Riobamba, like the area around Ambato and Latacunga, is made up of such porous material that only small parts of the district are capable of raising crops. Over this difficult terrain, avoiding the deeply dissected valleys, and winding around the lower slopes of Chimborazo, passes the railroad, which has been built at great cost to connect Quito with Guayaquil (Map 67).

South of the Basin of Riobamba is the Basin of Alausí. This is not a structural basin, like the others, but a widening along the valley of a river which drains westward to the coastal region. The railroad to Quito takes advantage of this valley flat in its difficult ascent from the lowlands. The Basin of Alausí, lying below 8,000 feet and having an alluvial soil, is intensively utilized for subsistence crops of wheat, barley, and potatoes.

The southernmost of the structural basins of Ecuador is the large one in which the town of Cuenca is located. Cuenca, with a population of less than 100,000, is the only town in the highlands besides Quito which could be said to have a dominantly urban function. The Basin of Cuenca and the Basin of Quito are the two most productive areas of the highland region. Around Cuenca gentle slopes at an elevation between eight and nine thousand feet above sea level, a soil which is less porous than that of most of the highland basins, and a plentiful rainfall combine to provide good conditions for the growth of maize and the pasture of dairy cattle. A larger proportion of the floor of the basin is devoted to the production of food for the human

The marketplace in Ambato, Ecuador. *Courtesy of Braniff International.*

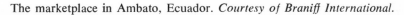

inhabitants, instead of feed for the animals, than is the case in any of the other high basins. Cuenca is also one of the centers for the weaving of Panama hats, the straw being brought to the highlands from the coastal region. Since World War II several other manufacturing industries have located in Cuenca to take advantage of the supply of low-cost workers. A Chilean businessman has built a ceramic factory to produce bathroom fixtures and tile. A branch plant of a Japanese firm makes sewing machines. There are television sets manufactured, and also watches and radios. There is even a factory to make springs for automobiles.

Three other intermont basins, developed along stream valleys, lie to the south of Cuenca. These are Oña, Loja, and Zaruma. The people concentrated in these districts cultivate subsistence crops and raise cattle. Loja and Zaruma are the only highland settlements which do not send their few products to Guayaquil exclusively; they supply small numbers of cattle to the oases of the Peruvian coast to the southwest of them.

Throughout the highland region of Ecuador the forms of Spanish and Indian life are strangely mixed. Only in Quito and Cuenca are there any important numbers of people with Spanish ancestors, and these are either officeholders in the government or landowners who have large private properties in the vicinity. On the private estates there are many villages of Indian tenants who pay rent to the owners. But the land is not all divided into private holdings: there are numerous Indian landowning communities, practicing their traditional communal form of tenure. The economic life is for the most part the production of foods for local subsistence, but from both the private estates and the Indian communities cattle are sold regularly, though in small numbers, outside the region. The animals descend on the hoof over the mountain trails and must be fattened in the lowland pastures before they are marketed.

The highland region suffers from too great a density of rural people to be supported by farming. For a long time there has been a steady current of

The waterfront at Guayaquil on the Río Guayas. *Courtesy of Sucre Pérez B.*

emigrants from the highlands to the coastal lowlands. In 1870 more than 90 percent of the population of Ecuador was in the highlands. By 1941 the proportion of the total population in the highlands had dropped to 60 percent. In the late 1960's about half of the total population was in the highlands and half was in the coastal lowlands on the west.

The Coastal Region

The people of the coastal region, unlike those of the highlands, are engaged most of the time in the production of goods for export. The population is largely mestizo, with a concentration of people of Spanish ancestry in Guayaquil. In the north, including Esmeraldas, there is a considerable mixture of African and mulatto; and south of this along the coast there are communities that are almost pure Indian.

THE LAND

One of the narrowest zones of climatic transition in all South America is to be found in the coastal region of Ecuador. Within a few degrees of latitude one passes from tropical rain forest in the north to desert in the south. In the northern part of the coastal region, Ecuador shares with Colombia the double maximum of rainfall, with enough annual rainfall to support a selva. Not far south of the border of Colombia, however, the double rainy season gives way to a single rainy season from December to June. As one goes farther south the rains begin later and end sooner. At Guayaquil they come between January and May. At the tip end of the Santa Elena Peninsula, west of Guayaquil, there is very little rainfall, and the arid conditions reach the shore south of the Gulf of Guayaquil at about the border between Ecuador and Peru. The Santa Elena Peninsula is the northern end of the great dry belt which stretches southward, first on the western side of the Andes and then on the eastern side, almost to the Strait of Magellan (Map 11, p. 31).

A distinctive feature of the coastal lowland is the huge size of the alluvial fans along the western base of the Andes. The streams that are cutting into the ash-fill in the highland basins bring a heavy load of alluvial material which they drop on emerging from the mountains onto the lowlands. Huge fans slope gently westward from the ends of the mountain valleys across the plains for some 30 or 40 miles. At the apex of the fan the elevation is 1,500 to 2,000 feet above sea level. The fans are largest in the north where the volcanic ash accumulation in the highlands is greatest.

Beyond the fans the rest of the coastal lowland is relatively flat, crossed by sluggish, meandering streams. Only west of Guayaquil is there a belt of low hills, some 2,500 feet high, that rise above the plains. In the north the Río Esmeraldas collects the drainage from several rivers pouring down from the mountains. South of this the drainage is collected in the Río Guayas. Upstream from Guayaquil the Guayas and its tributaries cross a wide area of floodplain; but at Guayaquil the drainage is constricted where the river cuts through the easternmost end of the hilly belt. Guayaquil itself is located on the high ground where the hilly belt reaches the banks of the river. Upstream and downstream from Guayaquil the river banks are low and swampy.

There are two observations to record concerning the surface features and the related soils. As we have noted in the discussion of Central America, the most productive soils in the rainy tropics are found where fresh, porous soil material covers the surface. Such soil may be derived from volcanic ash, as along the coastal lowland of Central America or the coastal lowland of Ecuador; or it may be derived from river alluvium, as in the Papaloapan Valley of Mexico; or it may be derived from underlying limestones, as in Cuba and parts of the Antilles. Where the soil material has been exposed to the continued percolation of rain water over long periods of time, it is deeply leached of its soluble minerals. Such soils are often used only for shifting cultivation. The second observation regarding coastal Ecuador is that rice grows best in a hot, humid climate where there is an abundance of water. It would be difficult to find a more potentially productive rice paddy area than the Guayas lowland, upstream from Guayaquil.

SETTLEMENT ALONG THE COAST

Population and land use in coastal Ecuador change as one travels southward from the Colombian border. In the tropical rain forests, African subsistence farmers have long carried on a shifting cultivation in temporary forest clearings. As they migrated southward along the Pacific coast of Colombia, the Africans have been more successful at occupying the rain forests than the Indians. Only in isolated places have Indians survived in the forests. The African communities raise maize, manioc, and other food crops, and from time to time they pan for gold in the stream gravels. They were able to find gold where the Spanish settlers missed it. They also cut balsa wood and send it for export through the port of Esmeraldas. After World War II, when a new all-weather highway was built into the forests southeast of Esmeraldas, African farmers spread away from the coast along this road, and the new crop they started to plant was the banana. Esmeraldas became a banana-shipping port. The bananas are brought by truck to Esmeraldas, and then carried by barge from the city about a mile downstream to the river mouth where the ocean-going banana ships ride at anchor.

As the climate becomes drier and the forest cover thinner on the southern side of the equator in the Province of Manabí, the Indians are able to hold their own against the African subsistence farmers. The northernmost of the Indian communities is Chone. Sedentary subsistence farming rather than shifting agriculture becomes the rule. There are small plantations of cacao and bananas, and cotton becomes a major commercial crop. From the wood-lands come the tagua nut, used in the manufacture of imitation ivory for buttons. This district is also the chief center for the manufacture of Panama hats. Straw from a native tree is used to weave these hats. Annual hat fairs are held in Chone, Jipipjapa, and Montecristi.

The port of Manta has had a new surge of economic activity since 1950. This is now Ecuador's chief fishing port. A fleet of small boats is based here. In the months from April to August, and again from October to January, the fishing boats put out to sea to catch tuna, bonito, and other species. They also bring back shrimp. At Manta there are fish canneries and a plant for making fish meal.

SETTLEMENT ALONG THE BASE OF THE MOUNTAINS

A separate pattern of settlement has appeared on the inner side of the coastal lowlands, along the western base of the mountains. The earliest such settlement took place along the railroad from the Guayas River, opposite Guayaquil, that climbs toward the base of the Andes and then continues on the long journey to Quito. Here plantations were laid out to grow rice, cacao, bananas, and sugarcane. Much of the land was—and still is—used to pasture cattle.

The large alluvial fan farther to the north along the divide between the Esmeraldas drainage and the Guayas drainage was for a long time isolated and very difficult to reach. This area was occupied by the Colorado Indians—who were the only Indians to survive in the rain forests and who were able to hold onto their lands because of their isolation from the African communities nearer the coast. But in 1947 their isolation was ended by the completion of a truck road from Quito down the western slopes to the apex of the allu-vial fan at Santo Domingo de los Colorados (Map 67).

Santo Domingo became a boom town almost overnight, as pioneer settlers moved down from Quito. Later the road was extended to Esmeraldas, and then southward to Guayaquil. As the roads were extended, new pioneers occupied additional lands on the productive slopes of the fan. Pioneers came from Quito, from Guayaquil, from foreign countries—even some from the United States. The chief crop they raised was the banana, which at first found its best market in Quito. Cacao was also raised, and again the market was in the candy factories in Quito. When the road was built all the way to Esmeraldas, some of the bananas went out in that direction; later they went southward to Guayaquil. But still a large proportion of the products of the Santo Domingo area continued to reach Quito.

THE GUAYAS LOWLAND

The part of the coastal region of greatest commercial importance is the lowland to the north and east of Guayaquil, and its extension along the eastern shore of the Gulf of Guayaquil. Although this lowland is the most productive part of Ecuador in terms of export products, its population is not nearly so dense as that of the highland basins. There are a few spots of more than 25 persons per square mile, but most of the region has between 10 and 25. For an Occidental people interested in the cultivation of tropical commercial crops, the most productive parts of the region are to be found on the alluvial fans, or on the natural levees of the floodplain zone. It is interesting to speculate regarding the differences in the density and pattern of settlement which might have resulted if the inhabitants had been rice-growing Orientals —for in the inundated area with its abundant water much more paddy rice could be raised. To the people of Ecuador, however, the wet lands are less attractive than the well-drained fans.

The Guayas lowland has long been the chief source of Ecuador's exports. In the early years of the present century, Ecuador was famous as the world's leading producer of cacao and until 1941 this was the chief export. During World War II there were a few years when rice was more valuable than cacao as an export. Since 1951 Ecuador has become the world's leading producer of bananas.

Cacao. For many years the crop that brought big financial rewards to the large landowners of lowland Ecuador was cacao. In some years cacao made up as much as 75 percent of the value of all exports, and Ecuador was famous for this product. Big profits were made on the crop—in some cases as much as 25 percent on the investment. The landowners could live in luxury in Guayaquil or travel for long periods in Europe. The paid managers and tenants were only expected to provide income, not to care for the trees or the land.

After 1916 however, Ecuador's cacao plantations were progressively ruined by a succession of plant diseases. Cacao plantations, some of them abandoned, still occupy a large acreage in the Guayas lowland. Most of these plantations are along the river banks where climatic and drainage conditions are almost ideal. The high rainfall and humidity, and the absence of winds, offer great natural advantages for this crop. In the 1960's Ecuador began to make a come-back in its cacao production, partly as a result of the use of disease-resistant varieties, partly as a result of the better technology, including sprays for the control of disease. Cacao is again an important Ecuadorian export.

Rice and Coffee. The Guayas lowland and the mountain foothills are also ideal for the production of rice and coffee. During World War II, when rice shipments from southeast Asia were cut off, Ecuador rapidly expanded its acreage of this basic food crop. Production is concentrated on a relatively small area, but each year there are two harvests. During the dry season (April and May) rice is planted on the floodplains of the rivers, and harvested during December and January. Another crop is planted on the lower fan slopes during December and January, at the beginning of the rainy season, and this rice is harvested from May to July.

The agricultural practices are haphazard—not at all like the careful farming of the Oriental rice lands. Production is at a low cost per unit only because of the use of virgin soils. On the large Ecuadorian estates, tenant workers first clear the virgin forests on previously unused land. The planted crop is given almost no care; harvesting is by hand, with the machete. After the shocks are dried in the sun, the rice is threshed by beating it on the ground. After the harvest the land is permitted to grow up again in forest and new rice fields are cleared on other parts of the estates. The system is still speculative, and brings speculative profits.

The third commercial crop of Ecuador is coffee. This crop is grown mostly on small, owner-operated farms on the lower western slopes of the Andes, and in the coastal hilly belt. Most of it is grown at altitudes of less than 3,000 feet, for which reason its flavor is not so good as is that of the Venezuelan or Colombian coffees. Expansion has been slow, for coffee cannot compete with bananas, rice, and cacao in bringing speculative returns.

Bananas. The speculative development of banana-planting in Ecuador began right after World War II. The banana was not a new crop in the Guayas lowland, for scattered small plantations had long been used for the supply of the local market and the United Fruit Company had established a plantation in 1933 at Tenguel. This plantation is still operated as a demonstration of the good results to be obtained from intensive land use, with large investment in spray and other cultivation methods. Meanwhile, the decrease in banana production in the Caribbean area after 1940 was largely made up by a great increase of planting in Ecuador. Most of the crop is raised by small planters. The banana buyers visit the plantations to make purchases and the fruit is then sent by motor truck to a port.

Banana planting by small farmers has developed in five chief areas. The first to appear was the country inland from Esmeraldas, previously described.

As other highways have been built, new pioneer settlement based on bananas has appeared. The main highway from Guayaquil to Quito passes through the hilly country on the headwaters of the Río Guayas, and here the land is devoted almost exclusively to bananas. Quevedo has become a major market center. Similarly, along the highway that runs westward from the Río Guayas into the mountains, there are many new banana plantations. Farther south along the mountain piedmont is the fourth major area, developed to the north of the plantation at Tenguel. In the far south an important new area of bananas has been established in what was formerly a mangrove swamp along the coast. This is the only commercial banana area in Ecuador that is irrigated. Banana-planting might have proved to be just as speculative and temporary as the cacao-planting, especially when banana diseases began to appear. But by 1967 a new variety of disease-resistant banana had largely replaced the former varieties. This is the high-yielding Cavendish banana.

A major problem in Ecuador has always been the high cost of transporting the bananas to the refrigerator ships. There are no specialized banana-loading docks, such as are found in most of the Caribbean ports or in Golfito, and there are no railroads to transport the stems from the plantations to the ports. Generally speaking, bananas cannot be grown profitably more than a mile and a half from a highway. The stems are carried to the highway on muleback or by porters, and here they are loaded on motor trucks. From the river banks the stems must be loaded on barges to reach the ocean-going ships. For these and other reasons, Ecuador remains a high-cost producer.

The Galápagos Islands

About 650 miles to the west of Ecuador the isolated Galápagos Islands rise some 5,000 feet above the surface of the Pacific Ocean. There are 12 large islands and many smaller ones, volcanic in origin, which belong to Ecuador. Since they are bathed by the cool Peru Current, temperatures on the Galápagos Islands are never very high, and along the shores there is little rainfall. Clouds and rainfall are more abundant over the volcanic craters.

The census of 1950 counted only 1,346 people on the islands. When Charles Darwin visited them in the 1830's they had been uninhabited by man for so long that the native animals showed little fear of the members of his party. With the opening of the Panama Canal, however, the islands took on a strategic importance for its defense. Offers by the United States to purchase the islands from Ecuador met with vigorous opposition. During World War II Ecuador permitted the United States to establish an air base on one of the islands which was returned to Ecuador in 1946. Since 1967 the use of the islands for a satellite tracking station has disturbed the giant turtles that are a distinctive element of the island fauna. Biologists and wildlife protectors have met in Ecuador and in the United States to urge the protection of these turtles.

Ecuador as a Political Unit

The problem of establishing order and coherence in the national life of Ecuador still remains to be solved. The contrast between the stolid subsistence farmers of the Andes and the speculative planters of the lowlands makes almost impossible the formulation of a nationally acceptable state-idea. As a result, governments are insecure, policies uncertain.

The national economy of Ecuador is supported very largely by the export of bananas, and to a lesser extent by the export of coffee and cacao. Yet Ecuador is faced by the possible loss of its preeminent position as the world's leading producer of bananas. The replacement of the Gros Michel variety by the new Cavendish banana has helped to maintain production, because the Cavendish is resistant to the usual banana diseases. But the large North American fruit companies find that the shipment of bananas through the Panama Canal is so expensive that bananas produced on the Pacific side of Latin America must find their market on the Pacific coast of the United States. The banana plantations on the Pacific coast of Guatemala have been closed, and the market in the western United States is supplied chiefly from Golfito in Costa Rica. New banana plantations on the Gulf of Urabá in Colombia and on the Caribbean side of Central America supply the markets in the eastern United States.

Several steps were taken to save the banana exports in Ecuador. First a Swedish firm began to buy bananas from Ecuadorian growers and ship them to markets in Europe and along the western side of South America. Then, Japan is building a fleet of 10 or 12 banana ships to be operated by Ecuador, to carry bananas to the rapidly increasing market in prosperous Japan. Nevertheless, the share of Ecuador in the world production of bananas has been dropping since 1961, when it supplied 24 percent of the world total.

Ecuador has attempted to solve the shipping problem by building a new ocean port. Before 1963 the banana ships anchored in the Gulf of Guayaquil or off Esmeraldas, and the bananas were brought to them by barge. In 1963 a new deep-water port—Puerto Nuevo—was opened. It is located on a deep side-channel about 5 miles south of Guayaquil. A canal has been cut from the Río Guayas to this side-channel, so that barges carrying bananas can reach the new port. Here the ships can tie up at wharves. As a result, since 1964 some 70 percent of the banana shipments have moved through Puerto Nuevo and about 10 percent through Esmeraldas (Map 70).

Ecuador is trying to do something about the low gross national product per capita ($224 in 1966, placing Ecuador twentieth among the independent Latin-American countries). With foreign assistance, plans were drawn up to diversify the economy and to reduce the dependence on bananas. The *Instituto Ecuatoreano de Reforma Agraria y Colonización* attempted to increase the production of wheat, oilseeds, and beef cattle by introducing technical

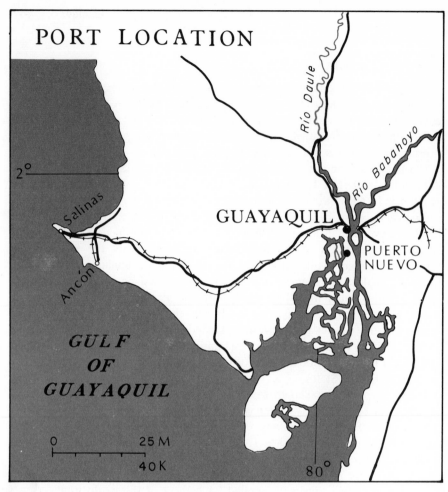

PORT LOCATION

Río Daule

Río Babahoyo

GUAYAQUIL

PUERTO
NUEVO

Salinas

2°

Ancón

GULF
OF
GUAYAQUIL

0   25 M

40 K

80°

Map 70

improvements among the subsistence farmers. Some 1800 farm families were resettled and provided with housing, water, machinery, seeds, and credits. An attack was made on the relatively high proportion of illiterates by building new schools and training teachers.

The economy was also diversified by increased attention to fishing and manufacturing. The port of Manta has become Ecuador's chief base for the fishing fleet. The new cannery at Manta prepares tuna for export and also for use in the domestic market. Another plant at Manta prepares fish meal for use as poultry feed. In Guayaquil since 1960 several new manufacturing plants have been built. There is a plant to make cardboard boxes for use in shipping bananas. A North American tobacco company is experimenting with the growing of tobacco to be used in the manufacture of cigarettes at Guayaquil. There is a new plant for the manufacture of automobile tires. In

Puerto Nuevo: Guayaquil is in the distance. *Courtesy of Sucre Pérez B.*

Quito there are new textile factories, shoe factories, breweries, and other manufacturers of consumer goods. The new industrial plants in Cuenca have been mentioned. But these are only a start toward the process of economic development; the gross national product is still low, and the income is not widely distributed among the people, many of whom remain outside of the money economy.

Ecuador remains a country that is politically divided into two quite different parts. Again and again during the period since Ecuador became an independent country the government has been unable to establish effective control over the more remote parts of the national territory. At the beginning of the period of independence, internal strife in Quito resulted in the loss of what has become southern Colombia. More recently, Ecuador's claims to the Oriente have been in conflict with those of Peru. But while the Ecuadorians have done little to penetrate these eastern lowlands, the Peruvians, from their port of Iquitos, have established trading connections along all the rivers. The still unsettled boundary dispute remains a source of potential trouble.

Meanwhile, Ecuador has been granting North American oil companies the right to explore for oil along the eastern base of the Andes, in the part of the Oriente that remains Ecuadorian. A new oilfield has been discovered along the Río Putumayo, and it is now known that this field is partly in Colombia, partly in Ecuador. An agreement has been reached between Ecuador and Colombia for the joint development of this field, and for the shipment of the oil in the Colombian pipeline to the port of Tumaco. Perhaps the search for El Dorado in the form of productive oil wells will some day provide Ecuador with the income necessary to make effective progress toward the development of the economy.

República del Perú

Area: 496,222 square miles
Population: (1967 estimate) 12,012,000
           (last census, 1961) 10,420,357
Capital city: Lima; (1961) 1,436,231
Percent urban: (1961) 47.1
Birth rate per 1,000: (1966) 42–46; Death rate per 1,000: (1966) 13–15
Annual percent of increase: (1958–64) 3.0
Percent literate: (1961) 60.1
Percent labor force in agriculture: (1961) 49.1
Gross national product per capita: (1966) $378
Unit of currency: sol (1968, 40 per dollar)

COMMERCE, 1965 *(expressed in percentage of values)*
Percent total Latin-American exports: 6.6 (1956, 5)
Percent total Latin-American imports: 8.4

Exports (1966)

fish meal	27	iron ore	7
copper	24	sugar	6
cotton	11		

Exports to (1966)		Imports from (1966)	
United States	43 (1956, 41)	United States	39 (1956, 50)
West Germany	11	West Germany	13
Japan	10	Japan	7
Netherlands	6	Argentina	6
Belgium	5	United Kingdom	5

Chapter 19 □ Peru

For more than four hundred years Peru, like Ecuador, struggled with the problems resulting from the existence of two incompatible cultures within the same area. In Peru the Indians had built one of the great pre-Columbian civilizations in the American Hemisphere—the empire ruled over by the Incas. To Peru was directed one of the main currents of Spanish colonial conquest, and Lima, like Mexico City, became a major primary settlement center. The Indians and the Spaniards met and mixed, but they never were amalgamated into a coherent society. The patterns developed by the Spaniards were superimposed upon those developed by the Indians, with little blending between the two. But now, in the last two decades, the first steps toward finding some kind of workable solution of the problem are being taken.

Nor are these racial and cultural contrasts the only elements of diversity in Peru. The national territory is divided into desert coast, mighty ranges of mountains, rainy and densely forested eastern slopes, and wet tropical plains. Furthermore, the significance of these contrasted parts in terms of human settlement has changed very greatly in the course of history. And additional diversity has come to Peru in modern times through the growth of an industrial society which contrasts strangely with the traditional Spanish society in the smaller towns and the rural districts.

Peru is still as much Indian as it is Spanish. To understand the way of living of more than half of the people one must go far back to a study of the Inca civilization in the pre-Columbian period. For, always in the background of the growing industrial cities is the still unsolved discordance between Spaniards and Indians, a discordance which has marked the Peruvian landscape and colored Peruvian problems since the two civilizations first came into contact with each other.

451

The Empire of the Incas

The rise of the civilization of the Incas was, in itself, an extraordinary thing—an event overlooked by most North Americans because, unlike the history of the civilizations of Mesopotamia or Egypt, Inca history is not essential to an understanding of the main stream of Occidental culture. Only for some of the Andean peoples of South America—for the peoples of Ecuador, Peru, and Bolivia—is a knowledge of this Indian culture of compelling importance because of the numerous present conditions of life which can be traced back to Indian origins. The ancient civilizations of Mesopotamia, Egypt, India, and China all began in the highly productive valleys of great rivers, where closely knit and coherent societies originated partly through the necessity for the cooperative use of water. But the Incas built their civilization in a territory which would seem to be as unsuited to economic prosperity and political unity as any that could be imagined. From a center in a small intermont basin high in the Andes the lines of authority were extended far to the north and to the south over a land creased by profound canyons and separated into compartments by gigantic, snow-capped ranges. In the land of the Incas, as one writer puts it, everything was inferior except man. The achievement, considered in this light, assumes all the greater importance.

The Growth of the Empire

The Andes of Peru, Bolivia, and Ecuador had been occupied by well-developed cultures for many thousands of years before the appearance of any unifying political structure to tie them together. Along the Peruvian coast there were expert weavers of textiles as early as 8500 B.C. In fact, these Indians had discovered every known way of weaving textiles before the Europeans reached Peru. Around Lake Titicaca an ancient civilization, much older than the Inca, had domesticated the potato and other wild plants of the area.[1]

The extension of political control over the territory from northern Ecuador to middle Chile and the successful administration of this area were accomplished by a relatively small ruling group. Actually, the name "Inca" was applied only to this ruling group which formed the hierarchy of administrators and which surrounded the emperor himself, the Sapa Inca. The origin of these people, who formed the nucleus of the state, is shrouded in mystery and legend. Only during the reigns of the last nine emperors can the story

[1] E. P. Lanning, "Early Man in Peru," *Scientific American,* Vol. 213 (1965), pp. 68–76; David R. Harris, "New Light on Plant Domestication and the Origins of Agriculture; A Review," *Geographical Review,* Vol. 57 (1967), pp. 90–107.

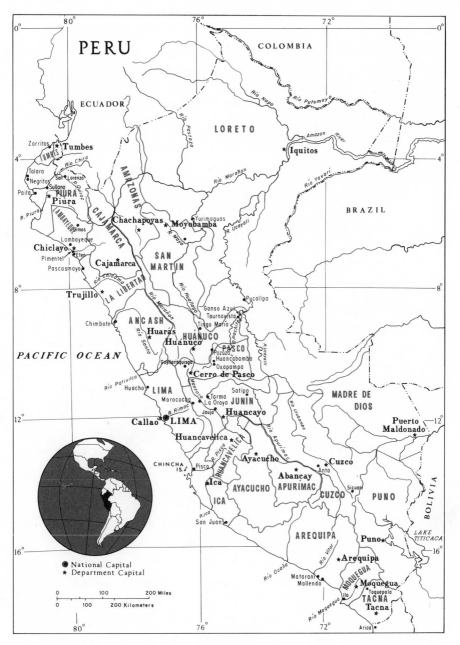

Map 71

Map 72

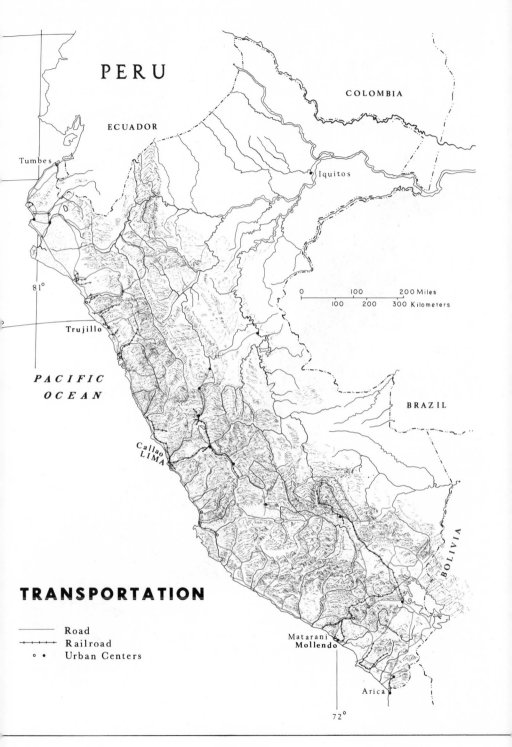

PERU

COLOMBIA

ECUADOR

Tumbes

Iquitos

81°

Trujillo

PACIFIC
OCEAN

BRAZIL

Callao
LIMA

BOLIVIA

TRANSPORTATION

——— Road
+++++ Railroad
∘ • Urban Centers

Matarani
Mollendo

Arica

72°

Map 73

455

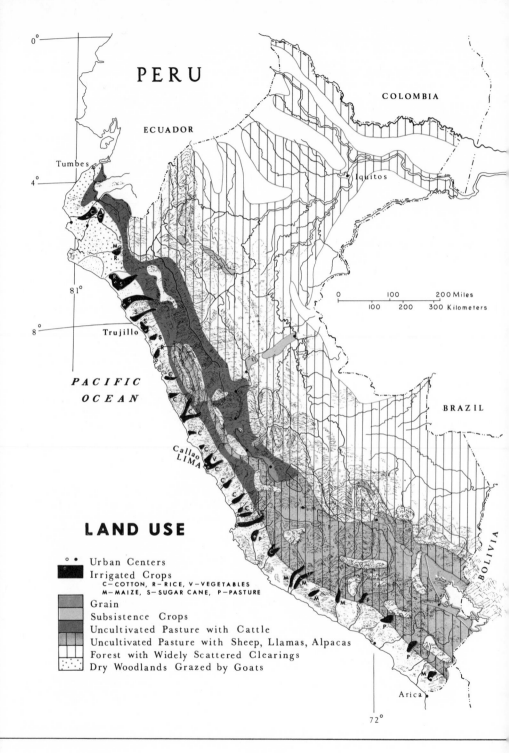

PERU

COLOMBIA

ECUADOR

Tumbes

Iquitos

PACIFIC
OCEAN

BRAZIL

Trujillo

Callao
LIMA

BOLIVIA

LAND USE

Urban Centers
Irrigated Crops
C—COTTON, R—RICE, V—VEGETABLES
M—MAIZE, S—SUGAR CANE, P—PASTURE
Grain
Subsistence Crops
Uncultivated Pasture with Cattle
Uncultivated Pasture with Sheep, Llamas, Alpacas
Forest with Widely Scattered Clearings
Dry Woodlands Grazed by Goats

Arica

0°

4°

81°

8°

72°

0   100   200 Miles
   100   200   300 Kilometers

Map 74

456

PERU

COLOMBIA

ECUADOR

Tumbes

Iquitos

81°

Trujillo

PACIFIC
OCEAN

BRAZIL

Zn Cu
Pb
Au

Callao
LIMA

MINERALS
AND
MANUFACTURING

BOLIVIA

Coal	
Oil	
Steel	
Fe	Iron
Au	Gold
Cu	Copper
Pb	Lead
Zn	Zinc
V	Vanadium
Hg	Mercury
	Pipeline
∘ •	Urban Center
▲	Fishmeal Plants

Fe

Cu

Matarani
Mollendo

Cu

Arica

72°

Map 75

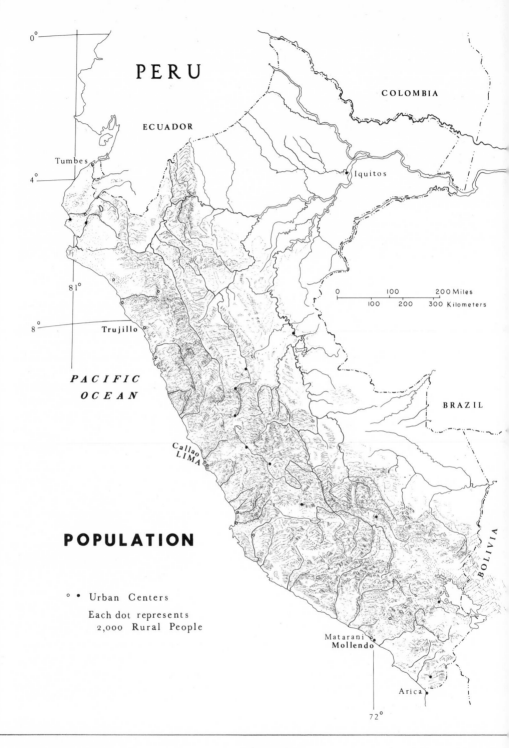

PERU

COLOMBIA

ECUADOR

Tumbes

Iquitos

PACIFIC
OCEAN

BRAZIL

Trujillo

Callao
LIMA

BOLIVIA

POPULATION

○ • Urban Centers

Each dot represents
2,000 Rural People

Matarani
Mollendo

Arica

Map 76

of the gradual extension of power from the Cuzco[2] Basin be established with clarity—and this period lasted from about the end of the twelfth century to the third decade of the sixteenth century, when the Spaniards entered upon the scene. The first of the Inca conquests was the densely peopled Basin of Titicaca, where the earlier Indian civilization had already flourished and declined. The conquest of the peoples of the Peruvian coast was not a very difficult military feat, since these communities, being dependent on water for irrigation, were easily subject to attack from the highlands. The borders of the empire were extended southward to middle Chile, southeastward to the edge of the Argentine plains near the present site of Tucumán, and northward to what is now Southern Colombia (Map 5, p. 14). The Incas never were successful in penetrating the forests of the eastern slopes or in conquering the forest tribes in the plains east of the Andes. The last Sapa Inca to rule the empire as a unit found great difficulty in carrying on his administration over so vast an extent of territory; in fact, he spent much of his time in the newly conquered northern part, making his secondary capital at Quito. Just before his death in 1523 or 1524 he divided the empire into a northern and a southern part, to be ruled over by two of his sons. Civil strife between these two broke out shortly before the arrival of the Spaniards in 1531.

To estimate the population of the Inca Empire is not easy, and anthropologists differ widely in their opinions on the matter. A leading authority places the figure between 16 and 32 million. The most recent estimates place the present population of Ecuador, Peru, and Bolivia just over 20 million. In other words, accepting medium estimates of pre-Columbian population, it has taken more than 400 years for the population of this mountainous area to return to densities comparable to those of the Inca period. How did so many people support themselves in this difficult land?

Culture of the Incas

Whatever may have been the earlier diversity of people and ways of living in the territory conquered by the Incas, the benevolent and paternalistic rule from Cuzco minimized the chief differences and set a uniform stamp over all but the most recently invaded communities. The whole empire was divided into four parts, each served by one of the great Inca roads which focused on the capital city: with reference to Cuzco these parts lay to the north, the northwest, the southeast, and the south. Within each of these four parts the subjects of the Sapa Inca were systematically arranged in groups of standard sizes. Before the Inca conquest, the largest political unit was the *ayllu*, a village community of variable size which held its lands in common. The Inca

---

[2]The word *Cuzco* is the Quechuan word for navel, referring to the outline and sharply defined borders of the intermont basin.

recognized the family rather than the individual as the basic unit of the empire. Groups of families were administered as communities by appointed officials: groups of 10, 50, 100, 500, 1,000, 10,000, and 40,000 families. The groups were kept at these approximate sizes by the resettlement of families in new colonies. This whole logical and systematic organization was responsible to and derived its authority from the Sapa Inca, who held complete power over the lives of every one of his subjects and in whom was vested the ownership of land.

In the state organized by the Incas the individual existed only as a part of a household; and the household existed only for the service of the state. Inca administration had as its chief function the maintenance of production and the distribution of surplus commodities. The state had no important contacts with people beyond the borders of the empire—there were no problems of foreign relations, but only problems of domestic production and supply. The Inca engineers increased the arable area by control of the water supply and by the construction of terraces (or *andenes*) on the valley sides. Just as wheat, barley, and rice formed the food bases of the ancient civilizations of Asia and Africa, maize was the basic food of the Incas. But it was supplemented by other foods. At the higher altitudes the hardy grain *quinoa* and potatoes were important. The former, combined with peppers, was used in a kind of soup; potatoes were used to produce *chuñu,* a potato meal which is still one of the chief foods of the Andean Indians. The dried meat of llamas was also included in the diet of the ordinary people—fresh meat was generally restricted to the Inca and his family. In addition to these foods, the ordinary people had an alcoholic beverage made of maize—a kind of beer known as *chicha;* and they were addicted to the chewing of coca leaves mixed with clay. Both chicha and coca[3] are still consumed by the highland Indians from Ecuador to northern Chile.

The products of each community were divided at the discretion of the Inca administrators into three parts. One part went to the priests of the sun; one part was used for the support of the Inca and his family; and one part was left for the support of the community. There was usually a surplus above the immediate needs of the Inca. This surplus was stored in warehouses and was available for distribution in any part of the empire where crops had failed.

The lives of individuals were closely and benevolently regulated under this system. There was no need for imagination, no need for ambition and initiative, no need to depart from the standard routine, no need to worry about poverty and hunger. Work was assigned by age groups, beginning with coca picking and other light work for people between 16 and 20, culminating in a period of maximum labor between 25 and 50, and decreasing beyond 50.

---

[3]Not to be confused with cacao, the source of chocolate. Coca is a small shrub from which cocaine is extracted.

Marriages were arranged by the authorities, leaving the individual only a slight range of choice. The Incas carefully preserved certain recreations; they set aside three days in every month for fairs at which each family could exchange its products for the products of other families. At these fairs no set standards of value were imposed, but each transaction was the result of a specially arranged barter. As in the case of most of the Indian fairs of both South America and Middle America, going to market was fully as much a social function as a commercial one.

The problem of communications within the empire was a major one. The roads which led in four directions out of Cuzco were paved, or in places cut out of solid rock. Suspension bridges spanned some of the deep canyons. Since there were no wheeled vehicles and no domestic animals that men could ride, travel was entirely on foot, and the roads were designed accordingly. Communications were maintained by relays of runners—men specially trained from boyhood for this particular service.

The domestication of some of the native Andean animals was also a major achievement. The Indians of the Inca Empire had no poultry, no horses, no cattle, no sheep, no hogs, and no cats; they used the dog only as a pet, or in some cases for hunting purposes; and they used the guinea pig for food. But they did domesticate two native Andean animals: the llama and the alpaca.

The llama remains even now one of the most important beasts of burden in the highlands of Peru and Bolivia. As a carrier he is by no means as efficient as the mule. Although gentle and easily handled, the llama has a remarkably stubborn disposition, for when he is tired or feels overloaded he will promptly lie down and resist all efforts to move him, even resorting to the unpleasant habit of spitting, camel-like, at those who come within range. He can carry no more than about 100 pounds; and he must be driven at a leisurely pace, in a herd, grazing as he goes. A llama herd can cover little more than 10 miles a day.

The smaller and less sturdy alpaca, a relative of the llama, is still used for its wool. Fine alpaca wool was the basis of the Inca textiles.

The artistic and technical achievements of the Incas were of a high order. The designing and weaving of textiles from alpaca wool and from cotton was one of their most notable skills. Their pottery was colorful and finely modeled, yet it was made without the use of a wheel. Like all other native American cultures, the Inca culture included no practical application of the circle—a geometric figure of which, however, they were not ignorant. The Inca engineers never made use of wheels, they never built towers, or columns, or keystone arches. Yet they were able to build suspension bridges, to construct long irrigation ditches over rugged surfaces, to terrace the mountain slopes, and to build massive walls with stones so closely fitted together that, without mortar, they have resisted the forces of destruction to the present day. The Incas were skilled workers in metals, and although they had no knowledge of iron, they did know how to make bronze from copper and tin. They had no written language, but they kept accounts in the form of knotted strings known as *quipus*. Their decimal system of figuring was much less cumbersome than the Roman system used by the Spaniards. And their peculiar plaintive music is only just now being "discovered."

The Inca state may be described as a form of benevolent paternalism. To make use of other terms, such as "socialist" or "communist," with meanings derived from modern European forms is only to obscure the truly indigenous quality of the Inca way of living. In one fundamental way the Inca concepts differed essentially from the concepts of the Spanish conquerors. The Incas had only an elementary understanding of the idea of private property. To be sure, the family dwelling and its contents, together with the land on which it stood, was regarded as belonging to its occupants as long as they, themselves, desired to use it. But the native Peruvians had no understanding of the ownership of land for prestige or profit. Land, as such, had no value—its value was only in terms of what it could produce; the ownership of land being vested in the Sapa Inca, and earlier in the *ayllu* as a community, such ownership did not constitute a means to prestige. Nor did the Incas understand the concept of the exploitation of natural resources for personal gain. In all these basic ideas they differed radically from the people who conquered them; and in the years since the conquest the descendants of both groups have yet to find a common ground of understanding on these questions.

The European Impact

The amazing story of the conquest of Peru by Francisco Pizarro and his little band of fewer than 200 men equipped with 27 horses is well known. Taking advantage of dissension among the rulers of the Empire, the Spaniards were able to complete the overthrow of the Incas in the comparatively brief period between January, 1531, and November, 1533, in which month the conquerors made their victorious entry into Cuzco. Once the leadership of the ruling group had been removed, the majority of the inhabitants, long accustomed to unquestioning obedience to central authority, easily accepted the new rulers.

Immediately after the conquest, profound differences began to appear between the Spanish way of living and that of the Indians. These differences were reflected in the complete reorientation of the economic life which took place within a few years. The Spaniards were interested in their overseas connections, and as a result the coastal region was abruptly changed from a place remote from the center of political and economic activity to the place on which these activities focused. The longitudinal roads of the Incas were abandoned in favor of short transverse roads leading from various parts of the highlands to the nearest ports on the coast. Lima was founded in 1535, and, with its port Callao, assumed preeminence as the primary settlement center from which the Spanish culture was spread over almost all of western

South America. Lima became the center of political power, the center of social life, the center of commerce—a city of fabulous wealth.

Contrasts in Land Tenure and Agricultural Systems

One of the first methods used by the Spaniards to collect wealth from the Indian communities was the system known as the *encomienda.* This system was based on the theory that conquered peoples should pay tribute to the conquerors. The Spanish crown delegated the right to receive this tribute from a specific group of Indian communities to certain of the officers of the army and to others who could establish their right to such a claim.

The *encomienda,* which carried with it no right to the ownership of the land, was scarcely enough for the conquerors of Peru. Few of the men under Pizarro, few even of the officers, were in any way members of the Spanish aristocracy: Pizarro himself had been a swineherd on one of the large feudal estates of Spain. Such adventurers passionately desired the opportunity to acquire land and so to gain a position of prestige. Grants of land by the Spanish crown, therefore, soon led to the creation of vast private estates and to the formation of a new aristocracy. But the ownership of land which brought prestige did not also bring economic security to the owner unless that land included a supply of Indian workers, for under the Spanish system production of any sort, whether in the mines or in the fields, was dependent on the labor of the native peoples.

On estates, or *haciendas,* which measured thousands of square miles in area, the more remote districts could not be brought under the effective supervision of the owner or his managers. In the more accessible parts of the haciendas the owners made use of the Indian workers to raise commercial crops; but in the more distant places the Indian communities continued to use the land in the traditional way, only paying a kind of rent to the new owner. When the properties changed hands the Indian communities were transferred as a part of the land; in fact, it was the presence of the Indians which gave the land its value. In this way the two contrasted systems of land tenure—the traditional communal system of the Indians and the system of private property introduced by the Spaniards—continued to exist together in the same area.

The European conquest also resulted in a serious decrease in the food supply. To be sure, the introduction of cattle and sheep made habitable large areas of high mountain grassland which had remained without permanent settlement in Inca times. But great numbers of Indians were removed from the coastal oases or from the highland agricultural centers for work in the mines, and since most of the latter were at very high altitudes this work proved very exhausting and many of the workers never returned to their homes. The irrigation systems which the Inca engineers had built and the Indian communities had maintained were permitted to break down through neglect. The increased habitability of the highlands through the introduction of cattle and sheep did not compensate for this loss of agricultural productivity at the lower altitudes, for the use of land for pasture does not produce as much food per square mile as does the cultivation of crops, especially with the intensive methods which the Incas had developed.

Population Changes

The decrease in the food supply was accompanied by an enormous decline in the Indian population. Great numbers of the Indians died from overwork in the mines and from epidemics of smallpox and measles. By 1580, about fifty years after the arrival of the Spaniards, the number of Indian inhabitants in the territory of the Inca Empire had been reduced by about a third.

The present Peruvian population is still predominantly Indian. Some 46 percent of the inhabitants are of unmixed Indian ancestry, and 38 percent are mestizo. Perhaps 15 percent are of pure European descent, and 1 percent is Oriental (Japanese and Chinese). It is significant that the proportion of pure Indian is being gradually reduced: in 1876 pure Indians made up 58 percent of the population. In terms of language, there is still a large proportion of people who speak no Spanish—only Quechua or Aymara, the two Indian languages (35 percent). The number of people speaking only Spanish is also high (46 percent). Most of the Peruvians still live in the highlands (62 percent), where the clusters of people are predominantly Indian. About 25 percent occupy the coastal region, and 13 percent are in the forested eastern part of Peru.

The Highlands

In all the highland provinces of southern Peru the Indians make up more than 70 percent of the total population. There are minorities of white or mestizo landowners, storekeepers, government and army officials, and priests. In the highlands there are some communities, however, which are supported by mining activities and which have a larger proportion of Europeans; and there are others which are given over chiefly to commercial agriculture, and there the proportion of pure Indian drops to perhaps 60 percent.

Surface Features

Throughout most of highland Peru three fundamental surface elements combine to make up the mountain scene. These three elements are in some ways similar to the elements which form the Cordillera Oriental of Colombia —a range which, like the ranges of highland Peru, is composed of folded and faulted geologic structures. The first of these elements is a high-level surface of gentle slopes. Above this surface stands the second element—towering groups and ranges of high peaks. And below the high-level surface is the third element—profound canyons with sides so steep that to climb up or down is extremely difficult. The westernmost rim of high ranges which overlooks the Pacific coast forms the continental divide; the tributaries of the Amazon rise in the highest areas, cross the high-level surface through broad valleys with low gradients, and descend turbulently through the canyons as they follow devious routes through the body of the highlands toward the eastern plains.

The high-level surface is one of the distinctive features of the Peruvian Andes. In the Cordillera Oriental of Columbia only a few basins of the central area in Cundinamarca and Boyacá are preserved from the active headward cutting of the streams—and the surface in this region is only between 8,000 and 9,000 feet above the sea. In Peru the high-level surface is much more extensive, and it lies between 10,000 and 15,000 feet in altitude. The valleys of this area are broad, the streams sluggish and meandering. Long-continued denudation has stripped the cover of loose material even from the gentle hillsides, so that much of the highland surface is composed of naked rock, or rock only thinly veneered with waste material. Many of the valley basins are filled to their rock rims with smooth sheets of gravel washed down from the bordering slopes. Because of the great elevation, most of this high-level surface is beyond the range of agricultural settlement, except in the deeper valley basins which lie somewhat below the general upland level but above the heads of the canyons.

The groups and ranges of high peaks which form the second element of the Peruvian landscape stand on the high-level surface as on a platform. These are the only parts of the Peruvian mountains that exhibit truly alpine forms. The highest of the summits are between 18,000 and 20,000 feet above sea level. At the latitude of Lima, the snow line is about 16,500 feet in elevation; in southern Peru the snow line is between 17,000 and 19,000 feet. On some of the ranges above the snow line small remnant glaciers exist even today, but during the glacial period ice action was much more vigorous than now and resulted in the creation, at the higher altitudes, of typical alpine forms—cols, horns, cirques, and troughlike valleys, with strings of little clear mountain lakes and knobby moraines. Most of the ranges run in a northwest–southeast direction, but they are not continuous, and there are many ranges which depart from the normal trend to cross diagonally from southwest to northeast.

The classical description of these ranges, frequently repeated, has unduly simplified the pattern of arrangement. It is definitely incorrect to describe the Peruvian Andes as composed of three or four parallel cordilleras, like the Andes of Colombia. On many maps the stream divides are shown as mountain ranges, and places where many streams rise are represented as mountain "knots." The facts are quite different. Actually, the several ranges are not continuous and are generally arranged in echelon with no connection between the separate rows of peaks. The idea of the mountain knot should be dropped entirely from the descriptions of the Andes.

The canyons which have been cut below the high-level surface are tremendous. Some of them are nearly twice as deep as the Grand Canyon of the Colorado in southwestern United States. In many places the rivers pass through narrow gorges with vertical rock walls; in a few spots along the canyon bottoms there are narrow ribbons of terrace land, or small alluvial cones where tributary streams reach the main valley. But because of the impossibility of following the rivers either upstream or downstream and because of the difficulty of climbing the canyon walls to the high-level surface far above, these little valley flats on the canyon bottoms are among the most isolated spots in the country.

Except for the deep canyons and the alpine forms of a few of the highest peaks, the roughest surfaces in the Peruvian Andes are to be found on the wet eastern slopes. Here the heavy rains support many streams, and as a result these eastern slopes have been cut into a maze of narrow ridges and ravines. From the standpoint of difficulty of travel, it is these eastern slopes rather than the main body of the highlands that form the chief barrier.

The zone of the much dissected eastern slopes extends farthest westward into the highlands along the Ecuadorean border, close to the main channel of the Amazon (or its headwater—the Marañón). In one place in southern Ecuador the continental divide has been pushed within 30 miles of the Pacific Ocean. Along the border of Ecuador and Peru it is possible to cross from the Pacific to the Amazon lowlands with a climb of only a little over 7,000 feet. In southern Peru the zone of dissected eastern slopes is much narrower. From the crest of the giant range which stands northeast of Lake Titicaca to the eastern base of the highlands there is one very steep drop from over 20,000 feet to less than 1,000 feet.

Volcanic activity in present-day Peru is limited to the southern part of the highlands. Here a fourth element is added to the complex of surface forms. South of latitude 14° S. great cone-shaped volcanoes appear and continue southward along the western side of Lake Titicaca and along the border of Chile and Bolivia. The best known of these great volcanoes is El Misti, which overlooks the city of Arequipa. In this southern part of the Peruvian highlands the high-level surface is deeply covered with falls of ash and flows of lava.

Climate and Vegetation

The climatic conditions of the highlands of Peru are as varied as the surface features. With increasing distance from the equator the various altitude limits, including the snow line, rise gradually to a maximum elevation at about latitude 20° S. The upper limits of the various zones, therefore, are higher in southern Peru than they are in Ecuador and Colombia. The upper limit of crops, for instance, is about 14,000 feet above sea level between Cuzco and Arequipa about latitude 16° S.; and in this same region the snow line is between 17,000 and 19,000 feet. The annual range of temperature is somewhat greater than it is nearer the equator; Cuzco, for example, has a range of about seven degrees, as compared with three-tenths of a degree at Quito in Ecuador. The range between day and night is still greater than the annual range—at the higher altitudes freezing temperatures may be expected in every month of the year. Also, during the day there is a very great difference between shade temperatures and temperatures in places exposed to the sun. Anyone who experiences the penetrating cold of an Andean night can easily comprehend the primitive instinct to worship the sun.

High altitude exerts a limiting effect on human energy. Whether because of decreased pressure, lack of oxygen, or other factors, physical labor at altitudes over 12,000 feet is not easy. Mountain sickness, known in Peru as *soroche*, produces a feeling of nausea and dizziness and may lead to serious results, especially for persons with weak hearts. Respiratory diseases at these altitudes are fatal. Since so much of Peru lies near or above 15,000 feet, altitude is of definite importance in the understanding of human distribution.

Unlike the Andes of Ecuador and Colombia, which receive abundant rain over most of their area, the Peruvian Andes include conditions ranging all the way from very wet to very dry (Map 13, p. 33). Throughout the Peruvian highlands the rains come from October to April. But the amount received is adequate for agriculture without irrigation only on the northern and eastern sides; the western side bordering the coast is very dry, as are also many of the deeper canyons. Within the highland region there are vertical zones based on temperature differences; but these zones are diversified by variations of the rainfall factor. For example, the relative positions of the snow line and the tree line vary with the rainfall: snow lines are generally higher in dry regions whereas tree lines are lower; the zone of high grasslands is, therefore, widest in dry areas and narrowest in wet areas. In certain parts of the wet eastern slopes the forest ascends almost to the snow line; but in most parts of highland Peru the grasses and shrubs above the tree line are the most widespread and characteristic of the vegetation forms.

The categories of vegetation shown on Map 15 (p. 35) reflect not only the vertical zoning, but also the increasing width of the dry zone as one moves from north to south. The forested eastern slopes and the plains beyond are called the montaña. In Peru forests occur only in the east and north. The selva climbs the lower east-facing slopes of the Andes; but higher up it gives way to a "mountain forest," composed of a dense growth of smaller trees— a formation which the Peruvians and Bolivians call the *ceja de la montaña*, or "eyebrow of the forest." The upper limit of trees on these slopes in most places is about 11,000 feet above sea level (Map 77). North of Cajamarca the area occupied by mountain forest widens to cover most of the highlands along the Ecuadorian border. In drier spots the desert vegetation known as "xerophytic shrub" makes its appearance. The grasses and shrubs of the highlands become more and more xerophytic toward the south. The "mountain grassland" of northern Peru is similar to the vegetation type called *páramos* in Colombia, being composed of bunch grasses mixed with taller plants. The vegetation known as *puna* appears first on the western side of the highlands a little north of Huarás, but extends over most of the width of the highlands in the south. In this formation the bunch grasses are more widely spaced than in the mountain grassland of the north, and other plants associated with the grasses are low, without stalks, and with hairy leaves. The *puna* becomes even more xerophytic in the zone of volcanic activity in the south, where the tola bush, a hardy, resinous plant, is able to maintain itself on a land which suffers from low rainfall, porous ash soil, and continuously low temperatures.

Population and Settlement

The highlands of Peru, like those of Ecuador, have long been occupied by Indian communities. The Quechua-speaking tribes were clustered in spots of dense population before the days of the Inca conquest, and the same population pattern has survived the centuries of both Inca and Spanish rule. Here in the Peruvian mountains the concentrations of people have remained relatively permanent.

The agricultural practices that are traditional in these highland Indian communities are inefficient. Crops are planted and harvested somewhat less effectively than they were in the days when agricultural activities were supervised by the Inca administrators. Furthermore, since the Indian communities are located on lands owned by people of Spanish ancestry, the Indians never know when they may be required to move. There has never been much incentive to improve either the land or the methods of using it. Land in most places is still prepared for planting with a small foot-plow, which requires more human effort for the same results than is necessary where such implements as the hoe or the forked stick drawn by oxen have been adopted from the Europeans. Grain is winnowed, too, by tossing it in the wind, or threshed by driving animals over a threshing floor. Any program which has as its objective the raising of the economic status of the highland Indians faces the problem of overcoming resistance to the introduction of more efficient agricultural and pastoral techniques.

The kinds of crops which are produced depend mostly on altitude. Because all the altitude zones are higher in Peru than they are nearer the equator, the upper limits of the various crops are found at greater elevations than in Ecuador and Colombia. The crop which reaches the upper limit of all agriculture is the potato, grown to approximately 14,000 feet in Peru. The zone of grains lies between 10,000 and 13,000 feet, with approximate upper limits for maize at 11,000, for wheat at 12,000, and for

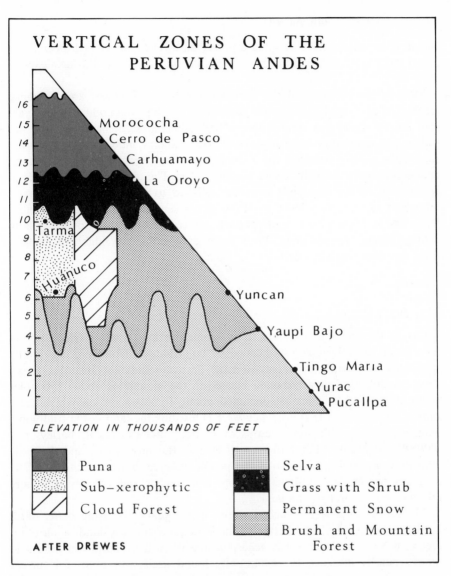

VERTICAL ZONES OF THE PERUVIAN ANDES

Morococha
Cerro de Pasco
Carhuamayo
La Oroyo
Tarma
Huánuco
Yuncan
Yaupi Bajo
Tingo María
Yurac
Pucallpa

ELEVATION IN THOUSANDS OF FEET

Puna
Sub-xerophytic
Cloud Forest

Selva
Grass with Shrub
Permanent Snow
Brush and Mountain Forest

AFTER DREWES

Map 77 (from Wolfram U. Drewes)

barley at 13,000. Sugarcane is grown at altitudes up to 8,000 feet, and bananas and oranges occur up to 6,000 feet.

Above the upper limit of agriculture is the *puna*. Unlike the *páramos* of Colombia, the Peruvian *puna* was habitable for the native peoples because they possessed llamas and alpacas. Unlike the *páramos,* also, the *puna* is too poor a grazing land to support cattle, but after the Spanish conquest, sheep were introduced into this part of the Andes. In southern Peru, the high

Indian communities have adopted a purely pastoral economy and have established remote commerical contacts with the outside world through exports of wool.

Most of the products of the Peruvian highlands, however, are consumed locally. Mines supply the larger proportion of the commodities which are sent out of the region, and a few of the highland settlements are the unstable and temporary kind associated with mineral industries. Where railroad lines have penetrated the mountains, a few agricultural and pastoral commodities are brought down to the coast. The wool of southern Peru is sent out of the highlands over the railroad to Arequipa and Matarani; the wheat of the valley basin of Huancayo is sent to Lima over the Central Railroad. In some places food products are transported over rough trails to nearby mining communities. With these exceptions, the highland populations are commercially inert.

The Vicos Project

One of the first effective steps to overcome this inertia was started in 1952 by a group of anthropologists headed by Dr. Allan R. Holmberg and jointly sponsored by Cornell University and the Peruvian Indianist Institute. It became possible to rent a hacienda located in the mountains about 250 miles north of Lima. The hacienda included about 40,000 acres on which there were 1,700 Quechua Indians. They were cultivating the land in the traditional manner, growing subsistence crops of maize, potatoes, wheat, barley, rye, quinoa, and beans. They had some livestock. But crop yields and domestic animals were poor, and most of the people suffered from malnutrition. The idea was to get these Indians to adopt better seeds and animals and more effective agricultural techniques.

These objectives were reached within a few years. By using better seed, fertilizer, insecticides, and better methods of preparing the land, a large increase of food production was achieved, and when these surpluses were sold on the nearby markets, the community found itself with funds for further capital improvement. Furthermore, the Indians were brought together for discussions of policy issues, and before the conclusion of the project they had learned how to elect representatives and how to share in the decision-making process. In 1962 the Indian community was able to purchase the hacienda with the help of a loan from the Peruvian government and to become an independent land-owning community—the first successful effort to incorporate an Indian population into the economic and political system of the Europeans.[4]

[4] Allan R. Holmberg et al. "The Vicos Case: Peasant Society in Transition," *The American Behavioral Scientist*, Vol. 8 (1965): 3–33.

Mining Centers of the Central Andes

There is a large concentration of mining settlements in the central Andes inland from Lima. The oldest and best-known of these mining communities is Cerro de Pasco, located about 110 miles northeast of Lima and just about on the drainage divide between the Río Huallaga and the Río Mantaro, both head-waters of the Amazon. Cerro de Pasco is at an elevation of 14,200 feet above sea level. The silver ores near Cerro de Pasco were first discovered in 1630, and about 30 years thereafter Peru took the lead among the world's silver produc-ers. Although the mines of Cerro de Pasco continued to yield well, Peru was able to maintain this lead only from 1661 to 1680, when it was surpassed by Mexico. For hundreds of years the silver ores were reduced in crude smelters near the mines, and silver bars were carried, over a steep trail, 200 miles to the city of Lima. Late in the nineteenth century, when the silver ores were near-ing exhaustion, Cerro de Pasco began to decline in population, for at this altitude no other support for so large a concentration of people could be found.

The railroad which now climbs up the valley of the Río Rimac from Lima and taps this great mining region around Cerro de Pasco, as well as nearby agricultural areas, is one of the most remarkable examples of moun-tain railroad-building in the world. This line, surveyed by Henry Meiggs, a North American engineer, is of standard gauge (4 ft., 8½ in.) and maintains a 4 percent grade without use of rack or cable. It clings to the sides of almost vertical walls, passing through many tunnels and over many bridges on the way to Oroya. In places the canyon of the Rimac is too narrow to allow the maintenance of the grade by ordinary means; spiral tunnels within the mountain or a series of switchbacks over which the trains move alternately forward and back are among the devices used to gain altitude. In one place the road is built in the bed of the stream, which is diverted through a boring to one side. The highest point on the main line is reached in a tun-nel through the divide at an elevation of 15,665 feet. A branch line to con-nect with the copper mines at Morococha reaches the highest elevation attained by any standard-gauge railroad in the world—15,865 feet. Con-struction on the main line was started in 1870, but it did not reach Oroya until 1893. Since then it has been extended northward to Cerro de Pasco, and beyond to the coal mines at Goyllarisquisga. The line has also been ex-tended southward from Oroya to Jauja and Huancayo.

In 1902 a mining corporation was organized to take over 941 mineral claims in the vicinity of Cerro de Pasco. The venture was a highly speculative one, especially as the installation of modern machinery, the construction of the railroad from Oroya, and other necessary developments cost about $25 million. Yet the corporation has prospered because it can exploit a variety of ores, some of them never before of much value. Cerro de Pasco was reborn and has again become the center of Peru's chief mining area. The Indian laboring population has been trained to carry on the skilled work demanded in the mines and smelters. The most important mineral is copper, but in addition the corporation has also developed the production of silver, gold, lead, zinc, and bismuth. Peru has become the leading exporter of bismuth, a mineral which is now recovered from the flue dust of the Cerro de Pasco copper smelter.

The ores in the richly mineralized rocks at Cerro de Pasco have been mined by the open-pit method. The city of Cerro de Pasco was perched on the edge of the world's largest open-pit lead and zinc mine, and the geologists found that these ores continued under the city. In 1966 a project was started to move the city of Cerro de Pasco to a new site about 2 miles to the north. A wholly new, planned city has been built to take care of the 30,000 people who are supported by the mining activities.

Other mining companies in this part of Peru produce smaller quantities of various minerals. From the mines at Mina Ragra, located more than 16,500 feet above sea level near Cerro de Pasco, comes an important part of the world's supply of vanadium. Among the other enterprises, the old quicksilver mines at Huancavelica should be mentioned. During the colonial period these mines were of very great importance, but since 1850 they have been closed and the community has declined in population.

Settlement in the Southern Andes

The old Inca capital of Cuzco has long been the center of one of the most densely populated parts of the Peruvian Andes. Cuzco, a city of a little less than 100,000 inhabitants, occupies the extremity of a small basin some 9 miles south of the Urubamba Valley and separated from that valley by a gorge; the level to gently sloping floor of the Cuzco Basin, approximately 11,000 feet above sea level, is occupied by a dense farming population. West of Cuzco and included in the same district of cencentrated settlement is the partly isolated basin of Anta, an old lake plain with exceptionally productive soils. Also included in this same district is the Urubamba Valley, which is densely populated between Sicuani (about 13,000 ft. in altitude) and the beginning of the Gorge of Torontoy northwest of Cuzco (about 11,000 ft.). These three basins, Cuzco, Anta, and the Urubamba, have been occupied since the earliest times of which there is any record by a relatively dense population of sedentary Indian farmers. Today most of the Indians are tenants on large estates and produce grains for local consumption.

Still another major concentration of people is located around the shores of Lake Titicaca, extending without interruption across the international boundary into Bolivia. Here, as in the Tulcán Basin on the border of Colombia and Ecuador, the international boundary was drawn without reference to the cluster of Indian populations already on the land. The Indians who live around Titicaca speak Aymara, not Quechua, and are the descendants of

Llamas on trail leading out of the old Inca capital of Cuzco. *Courtesy of Standard Oil Co. (N.J.).*

those who formed the early pre-Inca civilization, and also of the people who first grew the potato as a crop. Today the Indian farmers grow potatoes, barley, quinoa, and maize.

Outside of the areas of concentrated settlement, the southern highlands of Peru are occupied by a widely scattered population of Indian shepherds. The utilization of the high country for pasture demands a wider spacing of the villages than is the case in predominantly agricultural areas. Wherever the presence of a small basin or valley offers protection from the ceaseless winds of the *puna,* there an Indian community is usually to be found, varying in size from a single family to several hundred people. Most of these communities are located at very high altitudes, and from this region

Bowman reported what is believed to be the world's highest permanent human habitation. The stone-walled and thatch-roofed shepherd's hut that has this distinction was found at an elevation of 17,100 feet, only a few hundred feet below the snow line.[5]

At these altitudes domestic animals provide the basis of existence, both for the large landowners and for the Indian tenant shepherds. The owners of the haciendas are interested only in the export of wool from the alpaca. These rather delicate animals can be clipped only at intervals of two to five years; yet good profits are made from the shipments of the wool, which is produced at very low cost and which is becoming more and more popular for fine textiles in the distant markets. Alpaca wool, with some low-grade sheep's wool, is gathered from the whole highland region of southern Peru at the wool market of Arequipa and shipped out through the port of Matarani.

The Indian shepherds themselves make small profit from this trade. They are essentially subsistence pastoralists who manage to support themselves from their herds. They use the wool of both sheep and llamas to spin thread and to make their own clothing; they derive most of their food supply from the meat of these animals; they use the dried dung of the llamas as a fuel; and they make use of the llama to transport the products demanded by the landlords.

The Eastern Border Valleys and the Eastern Plains

Quite different from the relatively stable and unchanging Indian communities of the highlands are the small settlements in the eastern border valleys of the Andes and on the eastern plains, both of which are included in the forested region known as the *montaña*. Few of these eastern clusters of people have proved stable; although the land is described as a paradise in terms of its climate and the productivity of its soils, the difficulty of access to it had defeated efforts to bring it into effective use until the day of the airplane and the highway for motor trucks.

The Land

The region we are considering is one which contains so many difficulties of travel that it, rather than the higher country to the southwest, forms the chief barrier to trans-Andean communication. The half of Peru's total national territory that lies east of the mountains is effectively utilized in only a few scattered places. In 1968, however, highways across the mountains and a highway running along the eastern side of the mountains to connect with highways in Bolivia and Brazil were under construction.

---

[5]A mining camp at 17,500 feet has also been reported from Peru.

This eastern part of Peru is a land of heavy rainfall and dense forests. In the lowlands the forest makes travel very difficult except on the rivers. Ocean steamers drawing less than 14 feet of water can sail up the Amazon all the way to the Peruvian port of Iquitos, about 2,300 miles from the Atlantic Ocean. Above Iquitos the rivers are navigated by shallow-draught launches and canoes. Beyond the heads of launch navigation, travel over the wet eastern mountain slopes in even more difficult than in the selva of the lowlands.

The eastern Andean slopes are much dissected by the rivers draining from the mountains. The valleys are narrow with steep sides; the divides between the streams are sharply crested. The slopes merge with the plains through a zone of cuestas with trellis drainage; beyond the outermost cuesta only a few low hills interrupt the prevailing flatness of the country. The great rivers which drain the highlands emerge from the mountains through impressive water gaps. The Huallaga and the Urubamba are navigable at high water for shallow-draught boats and canoes within the mountain region; but the Marañón is not navigable above the Pongo de Manseriche, the gap through which it emerges from the Andes, for in the last hundred miles before it reaches the plains it drops over many rapids from about 1,500 feet to only about 500 feet above sea level.

Settlements of the Eastern Border Valleys

So difficult has been the penetration of these eastern border valleys that settlements have been established in only three districts. The most important is the central district, connected with the highland towns of Cerro de Pasco, Oroya, and Jauja. Settlers have also gone into this eastern country from Cuzco in the south and from Cajamarca in the north.

THE CENTRAL DISTRICT

There are four pioneer settlements in the eastern border valleys of the central district which illustrate the vital importance of transportation in such projects. The four settlements are Huánuco, Tarma, Pozuzo, and Tingo Maria-Pucallpa. Huánuco, located about a hundred miles north of Cerro de Pasco, was founded in 1539 in a small valley basin along the Río Huallaga, about 6,300 feet above sea level. Its settlers were enthusiastic about the delightfully mild climate and the productivity of the soils. But the colony languished because of the enormous cost of transportation. Tarma, only 45 miles northeast of Oroya, was another colonial settlement in a delightful and productive spot, yet so isolated that only products of great value per unit of weight could be sent out to market. The chief exports of these two places were coca leaves and *aguardiente* (sugar brandy).

In 1858 the Peruvian government undertook to bring in immigrant colonists

Intermont Valley in the Andes near Huánuco. *Courtesy of C. A. Gauld.*

from Germany to start a movement into these eastern border valleys. There were 50 families, 174 people, from Bavaria—all experienced farmers and all Catholics. Unfortunately, by the time the immigrants reached Peru the government had been changed and support for the venture had evaporated. Nevertheless the Germans were determined to reach the lands that had been promised to them. It took two years for the group to cross the Andes and reach the middle Huancabamba valley where they established the town of Pozuzo. Each colonist had his own farm and did his own work. Visitors to Pozuzo in the early twentieth century brought back reports of the neatness of the European-style homes, the attractiveness of the people, and the efficiency of their methods of farming. Yet there was no prosperity. For a time coca leaves were used for the production of cocaine, which was valuable enough to stand the high costs of shipment. When this was prohibited, the settlers had to fall back on unprocessed coca leaves and brandy. Unlike the settlement in Antioquia, the Pozuzo Colony has expanded but little beyond its original area. Its population is still only about 2,000. The colonists must send out their products by a three- or four-day muleback journey to the end of the new highway near Oxapampa.

In 1943 the first road across the Andes to navigable water in the *montaña* was opened. This highway starts up the valley of the Río Rimac from Lima, climbing in 87 miles to the Anticona Pass, 15,889 feet above sea level. From Oroya the road climbs again to Cerro de Pasco, 14,000 feet above sea level. Then it descends to Huánuco, at an elevation of 6,273 feet.

When the road reached Huánuco that sleepy colonial town suddenly burst into new activity. But the boom town of eastern Peru in the 1950's was Tingo María, 135 miles to the northeast of Huánuco, at an elevation of 2,204 feet. From Tingo María the highway climbs over the last range of the Andes and crosses the eastern plains 288 miles to Pucallpa, a river port on the Río Ucayali. As a result of this new connection to a market (842 miles from Pucallpa to Lima), settlement is going on rapidly around Tingo María, and east of the mountains all the way to Pucallpa. The chief product sent to Lima by truck is lumber; other products that now reach the market are maize, bananas, tea, coffee, as well as the traditional coca leaves.

Another new highway leaves from Oroya and descends to Tarma. This road has now opened up the valleys below Tarma as far as Oxapampa, and may some day be extended to Pozuzo. Around Oxapampa there has been no such rush of new settlement as at Tingo María because most of the land is in large private properties owned by people who live in Lima. The land-owners have profited from the easier access to markets to a greater degree than have the tenants who work on their lands.

Still another highway was built from Oroya southeastward through Huan-cayo, Ayacucho, and Abancay to Cuzco, for the first time giving these high-land communities easy access to markets. From a place on the road near Jauja, a road was built to Satipo on the way to navigable water on the Río Apurimac. But in 1947 this road was destroyed by an earthquake, and Satipo was left once more in isolation. The community remained economically stagnant as the settlers waited for the government to solve their problems of transport.

A new and somewhat experimental form of settlement is being attempted at Tournavista on the Río Pachitea, a tributary of the Ucayali south of Pucallpa. In 1954 the government granted about a million acres to Le Tourneau, manufacturers of heavy earth-moving machinery in the United States. Starting in that year a road was cleared through the forests from a place on the highway near Pucallpa. The clearing of the road and of lands to be used for farming was done for the first time by machinery. In addition to large bulldozers and scrapers, Le Tourneau developed a huge "tree roller," 110 tons in weight, which pushes over all but the largest trees and grinds up the branches and trunks into a pulp. This, scattered on the cleared land, makes an efficient organic fertilizer. Estimates indicate that in spite of the success of the tree roller in chewing up the forest, it still costs more to clear the land by machinery than it does by local labor. Near Tournavista, the headquarters of the Le Tourneau colony, oil has been dis-covered. From Ganso Azul, oil is sent to a refinery at Iquitos, and thence sent out by way of the Amazon. If the region proves to be as rich in oil as is hoped, pipelines will be built to carry the oil to a Peruvian port on the Pacific.

THE SOUTHERN DISTRICT

The settlements of the eastern border valleys in southern Peru are almost entirely restricted to the lower Urubamba. The upper part of the Urubamba Valley ends abruptly a short distance northwest of Cuzco at the beginning of the Gorge of Torontoy. In the next twenty miles the river drops 3,000 feet, from over 11,000 to about 8,000 feet. Then, at elevations between 1,000 and 8,000 feet, a series of small basins along the lower river are occupied by settlers. A railroad was built from Cuzco toward the isolated settlements below the Gorge of Torontoy; but of the proposed 112 miles of line between Cuzco and Santa Ana, only 50 were completed before the collapse of rubber production stopped all such costly projects. For a great many years the settlers of the lower Urubamba remained in economic stagnation, unable to send their products over the steep narrow trails to market. After World War II another of the Peruvian highways was built, finally giving access to the lower valley.

THE NORTHERN DISTRICT AND THE MARGINAL HIGHWAY

The northern district became the newest zone of pioneer settlement after it was made accessible to the Pacific coast in 1968. A highway starts at Olmos, 50 miles north of Lambayeque on the edge of the coastal desert, and climbs over the mountains, down into the deep valley of Río Marañón, and up again over the range on the eastern side of the valley. Then the highway descends through the potentially productive middle valley of the Río Mayo, a tributary of the lower Huallaga. It passes close to the old colonial town of

Iquitos, river port in eastern Peru.

The rivers provide the only routes of travel in eastern Peru.

Moyobamba to the new vigorously growing pioneer center of Tarapoto. The road has been built from Tarapoto to Yurimaguas, a river town east of the mountains.

Moyobamba and Yurimaguas have long been among the more isolated spots in the interior of South America. Moyobamba was founded in 1539 on a mesa-like elevation overlooking the Río Mayo valley. From its productive soils a variety of food crops and fibers have been grown, so that the town, in spite of its isolation, could support itself. Yet it lost population. During the period of the rubber boom in the Amazon, between 1880 and 1910, Moyobamba decreased in population from 12,000 to 5,000. Now it has increased again to about 12,000. Until it was reached by the highway its few products, such as tobacco, coffee, and cacao, were sent over narrow trails to Yurimaguas, and thence downriver in launches to Iquitos.

Iquitos itself is the chief commercial center of the montaña of eastern Peru. Founded in 1863 by the Peruvians, it assumed considerable importance during the rubber period; but in common with most of the other towns of the Amazon it has since declined. The products which come to its warehouses include small amounts of many different commodities gathered from scattered sources over the vast extent of territory in eastern Peru. Traders in Iquitos send their small launches up all the navigable rivers. Ocean steamers come 2,300 miles up the Amazon from the Atlantic to pick up the products of this rapidly developing area. Iquitos is now a town of about 44,000 people and has definitely established its position as commercial center for a large, if thinly populated, part of the upper Amazon region.

Tarapoto has become the chief focus of settlement in this part of eastern Peru. The highway across the mountains to the Pacific coast will give it one all-weather motor truck outlet; and another highway is projected to climb the Huallaga valley to Tingo María, and thence to Lima. In 1966 Tarapoto had 20,000 inhabitants, but it could easily double in population within a few years after the completion of its highway connections

From Tarapoto, also, a new highway is being built southeastward along the base of the mountains. This is the *Carretera Marginal,* projected eventually to connect with the highways of Bolivia and Brazil. When the montaña is thus made accessible for motor trucks a considerable movement of pioneer settlers is anticipated.

These various communities provide an opportunity to observe the relative costs of different means of transportation.[6] Since World War II all of them have been provided with airports, and airplanes bring them within a few hours, even minutes, of major markets. Journeys that once required weeks of hard travel on muleback can now be made by air or by motor bus. The motor truck provides the cheapest form of transportation. Air transport, which is, of course, much faster, costs ten times as much as truck transport. The most costly form of transport is by mule, which is about twenty times as expensive as by truck.

The West Coast

The third of the great natural divisions of Peru is the west coast. Here the political and economic heart of the country has become established in a setting of strong individuality. To be sure, between 20° and 30° of latitude on the west coasts of all the continents there is a combination of cold ocean water and dry land; but in no other continent does this desert condition extend so far toward the equator as in South America along the coast of Peru.

One comes upon this remarkable region with dramatic suddenness. Proceeding southward from Panamá through the warm waters off Colombia, the ship has scarcely reached the equator before the balmy softness of tropical air is replaced by a chill reminiscent of the coast of southwestern Spain or of southern California. On the land the first signs of increasing aridity are noted on the coast of Ecuador, only about a degree south of the equator. The transition from tropical rain forest to desert is unusually rapid: in about four degrees of latitude one passes through scrub woodland, woodland savanna, scattered xerophytic shrub, to barren desert. In Peru, between Tumbes and Chiclayo, where the surface is not covered with live dunes, there is a scattering of desert plants, but south of Chiclayo most of the land is bare.

---

[6]Wolfram Drewes, *The Economic Development of the Western Montaña of Central Peru as Related to Transportation,* Ph.D. dissertation, Syracuse University, 1957.

Surface Features

Along the coast of Peru the areas of flat land are small and disconnected. In the north, although the western base of the Andes continues in its southeast–northwest direction, the coast bends in a broad arc toward the west, leaving, between Piura and Chiclayo, a wide belt of lowland. The greater part of this area, however, is covered with moving sand dunes. Between Chiclayo and a point just north of the mouth of the Río Santa the coastline and the base of the mountains come gradually together, and the coastal lowland is pinched out. From the Río Santa as far as Pativilca the precipitous rocky slopes of the Andes rise directly from the Pacific. Along this stretch of coast there are protected harbors for small ships in the tiny rock-encircled bays, such as the one on which Chimbote is located. South of Pativilca as far as Pisco the alluvial fans built by the rivers are so large that they have almost grown together along the coast, producing a narrow lowland of irregular width, interrupted here and there by rocky spurs from the Andes. From Pisco southward the coast is bordered by a range of low mountains which, back of Mollendo, reaches an altitude of 3,000 feet. Behind the coastal range, separating it from the base of the Andes, is a bleak, rocky surface, deeply and intricately dissected by streams which mostly remain dry throughout the year—a surface which begins only a little below the crest of the coastal range and rises to over 5,000 feet at the base of the Andes. The places where man can establish agricultural settlements on this coast are limited not only by aridity but also by the ruggedness of the surface.

Climate and Fauna

The basic cause of both the dryness and the coolness which are characteristics of the west coast is the presence of cold water offshore, the so-called Peru Current.[7] Along all the continental west coasts with the exception of that of Australia there are equatorward-moving currents of cold water, accompanied along the immediate shore by upwelling water from below with especially low temperature. But in no other part of the world are these phenomena so strongly developed as off the west coast of Peru and northern Chile. This cold-water current in made up of two distinct parts with contrasting characteristics. The *Peru Oceanic Current* is found at an irregular distance offshore: it is cold, but not so cold as the water nearer the land; it is poor in marine organisms, and is of a deep indigo color. This oceanic current, under the influence of the earth's rotation, tends to swing to the west away

[7]This current was formerly called the Humboldt Current by some writers because the great German geographer, Alexander von Humboldt, was the first to measure its temperature. Oceanographers have adopted the policy of using geographic names for all major currents. Hence the agreement to use the name Peru Current.

from the land. The other division of the coastal waters is the *Peru Coastal Current* which is some 50 to 100 miles in width and is fed by the upwelling water. It moves northward faster than the oceanic current; its water is colder, and is remarkably uniform in temperature all the way from Chile to northern Peru—having an average temperature between 58°and 64° along the shore. This current contains a tremendous quantity of marine organisms and is of a greenish color.

As a result of the cold water, the air temperatures all the way from northern Chile almost to the equator are lower than the averages for each latitude. For example, the average annual temperature at Lima is 66.7°, which may be compared with the average 76.6° at Salvador in Bahia on the east coast of Brazil at the same latitude.

Most of the time this coast receives very little rain. The average precipitation at Lima is only 1.9 inches per year, but for many years at a time *no* rain falls. In the north, at Piura (about 6° S.) there is a little rain each year, but at the latitude of Chiclayo (about 7° S.) one has to climb the slopes of the Andes to an elevation of more than 3,000 feet to reach the zone of annual rains. At Lima (about 12° S.) this zone is over 5,000 feet up, and south of Pisco (about 14° S.) it is over 7,000 feet above the sea. The coastal zone below receives rain only at intervals of many years, although it is frequently foggy and cloudy.

The reasons for this peculiarity of the climate are easy to understand. The south and southwest winds which prevail along the Peruvian coast[8] cross water which is progressively cooler and cooler toward the land. Crossing cold water, air is cooled below near the earth's surface. With cool, heavy air below and lighter air above the atmosphere remains stable and there is little or no rain. Nevertheless, because the temperature of the air is continuously

[8]According to the classical descriptions of the world's wind systems this part of the Southern Hemisphere should lie in the zone of the southeast trades. On a rotating earth, however, all moving bodies tend to advance along curving lines, not straight lines: in the Northern Hemisphere deflection is to the right, in the Southern Hemisphere to the left. A more realistic generalization of the world's wind systems, therefore, recognizes the existence of great whirls of air. These are centered around the permanent areas of high pressure located over the eastern parts of the ocean basins about latitude 30° north and south. Clockwise whirls in the Northern Hemisphere and counterclockwise whirls in the Southern Hemisphere produce, in the low latitudes, generally easterly winds; in the middle latitudes, westerly winds; but along the continental west coasts the winds are more nearly from a poleward direction, and along the east coasts from an equatorward direction. As a matter of fact the winds on the coast of Brazil south of latitude 8° S. are predominantly from the northeast, and those on the west coast are from the south and southwest between middle Chile and the equator. These facts are more fully presented in P. E. James, *A Geography of Man*, 3rd edition, Boston, 1967, pp. 471–75, 518–19; and in G. T. Trewartha, A. H. Robinson, and E. H. Hammond, *Elements of Geography*, 5th edition, New York, 1967 pp. 72–75. (See Map 10, p. 30.)

lowered, it may be brought to the point of condensation and sea fogs may be formed along certain parts of the coast. Whether or not these fogs appear, the air on reaching the land is forced to rise against the front of the coastal range or the Andes, and the rise causes adiabatic cooling of the already cool air. Because of the stability of the air, however, this rise along the mountain front is sluggish. During the winter of the southern hemisphere, when the winds are strongest, the rise is sufficient to lower the temperature to the condensation point and to produce a heavy sheet of stratus clouds. From the bend of the continent at Arica northward to about 11° south of the equator this coastal cloud is thick and persistent from June to October; north of that latitude the cloud is thinner and more irregular. In spite of gray skies, more than a few drops of rain seldom fall, and the land below remains parched and barren. Where, on the other hand, the cloud rests against the slopes of the coastal range or the lower foothills of the Andes, the heavy mist, known as *garúa,* supplies a soaking moisture to the land. The dense growth of quick-flowering plants and grasses which appears with the garúa is described in Peru as *loma.* In the neighborhood of Lima the zone of the *lomas* begins about 2,600 feet above sea level and extends to approximately 4,600 feet; toward the south the lower limit descends somewhat and the upper limit rises. The *lomas* supply pasturage for animals during the cloudy season, from June to October; at just the opposite season from the rainy period in the highlands, which comes in the summer, from October to April.

The climatic peculiarities of the coastal region are matched by other elements of strong individuality. In contrast both to the barren waters of the Peru Oceanic Current and to the barren surface of the land is the water of the Peru Coastal Current. Here there is an exceptional richness of microscopic marine organisms or diatoms. The chemical composition of this water together with the protection from too much sunlight under the coastal cloud provides the necessary environment for a rich organic life. These microscopic organisms, in turn, provide the necessary food for a most amazing number of fish. Immense schools of small fish are preyed upon from below by larger fish, and from above by a bird population that is one of the most extraordinary spectacles the world has to offer. There are long lines of pelicans flying close to the water; there are clouds of cormorants that hover above the schools of fish; and there are places where the water is broken into spray by flights of gannets diving for their food. The excrement of these birds, deposited in part on the islands and promontories where they nest, and preserved in the arid climate, forms one of Peru's most notable resources—*guano,* a fertilizer containing from 14 to 17 percent of nitrogen.

The bird colonies on the islands and promontories of the coast occur in almost unbelievable numbers. A study of one of the Chincha Islands, off Pisco, led to some interesting estimates. On one relatively small area there were some 5,600,000 birds. To feed such a colony would require not less than a thousand tons of fish each day. A million birds provide about 10,000 tons of guano per year. Here, indeed, is one of the most remarkable examples of an intricately balanced complex of the organic and the inorganic: at the base, cold water exceptionally rich in microscopic organisms; supported by these organisms, a vast numbers of birds, whose guano is preserved in the rainless climate, in turn produced by the cold water; and on the land men enabled to raise irrigated crops year after year on the same soil with the aid of this fertilizer.

But every now and then this whole harmony of interrelated parts is utterly destroyed. Every year in the north, as far south as Chimbote, winds from across the equator bring southward a back eddy of warm water, which spreads over the surface of the cold water. Because this back eddy appears about Christmastime or during January, February, and March, it is called El Niño, the Christ Child. In normal years it forms only a thin surface covering over the cold water and is soon dissipated. But at somewhat irregular intervals, for reasons not yet fully understood, the north wind is stronger, the invasion of El Niño is more vigorous, and warm water covers the cold water all the way to northern Chile. On one of these occasions, in 1925, the temperature of the water in Callao harbor, which is normally in the low 60's, rose to 80°. Invasions of El Niño have been recorded in 1891, 1925, 1941, 1953, 1957, and 1965.

The disasters which accompany this change surpass the traditional seven plagues of Egypt! First, the warm water greatly increases the humidity in the air. Then the warm, moist air bounces when it strikes the land, instead of rising sluggishly; its vigorous rise results in the formation of towering cumulus clouds from which come deluges of rain. At Trujillo, between 1918 and 1925, the total rainfall was only 1.4 inches; but during the month of March, 1925, a total of 15.5 inches fell, and, on the three days from the 7th to the 9th the rainfall was 8.9 inches. But this is not all. The fish depart from the coast, following the colder water with its supply of food; the birds, whose characteristically high rate of metabolism requires that they feed at frequent intervals, starve to death by the millions. Floods of water destroy irrigation systems and cover the fields with coarse gravel; the houses, built for a dry climate, crumble and collapse; roads and bridges are washed out; insects of great variety fill the air, bringing discomfort and disease to the harassed inhabitants. Only slowly is the balance of nature restored; as the next long period of aridity begins, men start the work of rebuilding.

Disasters of this sort are too widely spaced to demand that the Peruvians adopt costly protective measures. Along the northern part of the coast the greatest amount of destruction occurs; in the middle section the heavy rains do less damage; along the coast of northern Chile these years bring only showers. Records indicate that such events took place even during the Inca period; in more recent times the last year of major disaster was 1925.

Agriculture

Such is the physical character of this unusual region. Life in it must be adapted not to the rare floods, but to the prevailing aridity—to the decades which may pass with no more than a few drops of rain. Life, in such a land, is given by water. But of the 52 streams which descend from the western slopes of the Andes to the coastal region of Peru, only 10 have sufficient volume to continue across the desert and discharge throughout the year into the ocean. These are the streams which rise far back in the mountains among the snowfields of the highest cordilleras. All the rivers lose volume downstream, and those which rise lower down among the lesser summits dry up completely during the dry part of the year. The first trickle of moisture from the highlands appears in the river channels in October or November. From December to March the streams are in flood, but by June or July the amount of water begins to decrease rapidly. From August to October most of the channels are dry.

The Incas practiced agriculture in this region before the arrival of the Spaniards. Their irrigation works and the terraces on the lower slopes, with which they increased the arable area, were carefully built and maintained. The ruins of their cities in the vicinity of Lima and Trujillo are still visible. The first result of the Spanish conquest, however, was the shift of labor from the production of food to the search for gold: the irrigation systems and the terraces were neglected and eventually abandoned.

During the whole colonial period, and, in fact, during most of the nineteenth century, agriculture in Peru was solely for local subsistence or for the production of food crops for the highland mining communities. Where the rivers descending from the mountains created little strips of green along the desert coast, these usually supported small farming communities, isolated from each other and from the capital at Lima. But about 1884 several foreign-owned corporations began to improve the irrigation systems in the better oases and to plant crops for export, especially long-staple cotton and sugarcane. By the time of World War II there were a little more than a million acres of irrigated land along the coast, mostly used for cotton, sugarcane, rice, vineyards, or vegetables. Most of these oases were in the northern part of the coast where sunshine is more abundant. South of the oasis of Ica and its port Pisco, oases used for commercial crops were few. In the period of the 1950's, however, many new irrigation projects were started, and especially in the 1960's there has been a rapid increase in irrigated area, and even the creation of new irrigated areas.

The Northern Oases

PIURA, SULLANA, AND THE SAN LORENZO GROUP

The northernmost of the major irrigated areas of the Peruvian coast includes the group of oases around Piura, Sullana, and San Lorenzo. This group is served by the port of Paita. Water is brought by two rivers: the Río Chira and the Río Piura. The Chira carries the largest annual flow of water of all the Peruvian west coast rivers (p. 487). The Piura carries much less water and is less dependable. In 1532, when Pizarro started his march southward toward Cuzco, he founded the town of Piura near its present site—which makes it the oldest Spanish settlement in Peru. Irrigation used to be carried out with a minimum of river control. At high water the river used to spread out among the sand dunes south and west of the town, and the area thus moistened was used to grow food crops and cotton. The water was more dependable along the Chira, and when Peru began growing cotton for export early in the twentieth century, the irrigated area around Sullana was used for Egyptian cotton. In modern times, however, both Piura and Sullana grow mostly an extra-long staple variety known as Pima, which was introduced to this area from the United States.

The largest new irrigation project in Peru was completed in 1967, adding more than 160,000 acres of irrigated land to the Piura-Sullana oasis. Work was started in 1953 when water was diverted from the upper Río Quiroz and carried in tunnels bored through the mountains to the plains north of Piura. In 1959 a dam was completed impounding a large reservoir from which more than 35,000 acres of previous desert could be made available for settlement. Between 1965 and 1967, 44,000 acres of irrigated land were added through the construction of canals, and an additional 83,000 acres were developed around the old Piura oasis. This new irrigation development is known as the San Lorenzo Project.

The San Lorenzo Project is not only the largest in Peru, but also it makes use of the most advanced irrigation technology and the newest ideas of community planning. Studies of the rate of salt accumulation were made, and where necessary drainage tiling was installed. Heavy earth-moving machinery is used to keep the canals in good working order, to level and dike the fields to be irrigated, and to build and maintain access roads. Landing fields were prepared for the use of small planes engaged in crop-dusting operations. The irrigated area was divided into seven communities, each supplied with houses equipped with electricity and running water. Schools, recreation centers, and public buildings were provided. The engineers in charge of the project also established centers in each community to train the colonists in irrigation techniques, and experimental farms to try out and demonstrate new methods and new crops. A new town was built—known as San Lorenzo—which is the

AVERAGE ANNUAL FLOW OF WATER IN SELECTED
RIVERS OF THE PERUVIAN WEST COAST*

Rivers, north to south	Flow in millions of cubic meters
Chira	5587
Quiroz	2184
Piura	670
Chicama	762
Santa	5056
Pativilca	1337
Rimac	958
Pisco	892
Ica	331
Chili-Vitor	445
Moquegua	50
Caplina	34

*Gonzalo de Reparaz, *El Programa de Estudios de la Zona Arida Peruana,* A UNESCO Report, 1958.

urban focus of the whole project. It is anticipated that before very long San Lorenzo will grow larger than both Piura and Sullana together. The reservoir has been developed as a recreation center, attracting visitors from other parts of Peru, and even from foreign countries, who are seeking water sports and sunshine.

As the San Lorenzo Project was being built, friction developed between the administrators in charge of the project and the people who occupied the older oases along the Río Chira and the Río Piura. The project, these people claimed, was taking water from the upper parts of the streams on which they, too, were dependent. To avoid conflict it was agreed to reduce the planned acreage of new crop land and to provide water for a considerable enlargement of the irrigated area around the older centers. It is almost always a problem to divide a scarce resource—water—with justice for all interested parties, and sometimes this problem leads to conflict. But in the San Lorenzo Project a solution was found that was satisfactory to all concerned.

The agriculture developed on the irrigated lands is diversified so that the demand for water can be spread as evenly as possible throughout the year. There has been a large increase in the acreage of Pima cotton, which brings a good price on foreign markets; and there has also been an increase of maize, rice, vegetables, fruits, and feed for cattle. The settlers on the new farms were not familiar with the care of fruit crops, and much effort was given to persuading them to try raising avocados, mangoes, citrus fruits, and bananas. To market the fruit, plants were built at San Lorenzo to can or dehydrate fruit and vegetables. San Lorenzo also has a meat-processing factory.

San Lorenzo is important for five chief reasons. First, it provides for the settlement of landless tenant farmers, many of them from the highlands. Second, it increases the production of foods for domestic consumption. Third, it takes a first step toward providing the Peruvians with a better diet. Fourth, it demonstrates how the newest irrigation technology can be successfully applied in Peru. And fifth, it demonstrates how the quality of life in planned communities can be improved and how people of Indian ancestry can be made a part of a coherent national society.

THE OLMOS OASIS

Another entirely new irrigated area has been created out of desert land that formerly was used only by nomadic goatherders. This is at Olmos. The Olmos Project was started in 1962, and when completed will provide for the irrigation of about 190,000 acres. The water is being brought to Olmos via a tunnel drilled through the continental divide to divert some of the water that used to flow to the Amazon. Olmos, which is connected both north and south by the Inter-American Highway, is also the Pacific end of the trans-Andean highway to Yurimaguas, discussed above. The Olmos Oasis will also greatly increase the supply and diversity of basic foods.

THE CHICLAYO OASES

About fifty miles to the south of Olmos is one of the older irrigated areas of the Peruvian coast. Three distinct irrigated areas are served by the ports of Pimentel, Eten, and Pacasmayo. In the oases of the Chiclayo district the higher parts of the alluvial fans, where water is most abundant, are used by a few large sugarcane estates. If there is enough water, the small farmers downstream can use it to raise rice and other food crops. In fact, the Chiclayo Oases produce a large proportion of Peru's rice crop, but this proportion may be reduced when the Olmos district gets into full production. Even in the Chiclayo Oases, projects for an increase of the water supply have been undertaken. A considerable expansion of the irrigated area has been gained along the northern border of the district, where additional water is provided by tapping some of the Amazon drainage.

THE TRUJILLO OASES

South of the Chiclayo Oases are the irrigated lands around Trujillo and its port, Salaverry. This district is occupied by large sugarcane plantations on which more than half of the sugar produced in Peru is grown. The tendency here is to consolidate smaller plantations into a few larger ones. In 1922 there were 33 sugar *centrales;* the number now is less than 15. One large corporation in the valley of the Río Chicama, north of Trujillo, owns

Modern sugarcane refinery near Trujillo. *Photo by W. R. Grace & Co.*

the land that was once divided among about 60 independent planters. The corporation grows about 37,000 acres of sugarcane and 12,000 acres of other food crops. The total area of this property is some 220 square miles, but most of it remains uncultivated because it cannot be irrigated. The corporations of the Trujillo Oases are owned in the United States (W. R. Grace and Company) and in Great Britain and Germany.

The Trujillo Oases are among the most productive of the coastal region. The latest agricultural techniques are used, and the *centrales* are equipped with the most modern machinery. Among all the world's sugarcane areas, the yield per acre of sugar in the Trujillo Oases is second only to the yields of cane plantations in Hawaii. As a reflection of the large capital investment in this district, Trujillo has grown rapidly until in 1961 it passed the 100,000 mark. The port of Salaverry has been improved by the construction of a breakwater and two docks, one of them especially devised for the loading of bags of sugar onto ocean vessels. A pipeline along the breakwater permits ships to load molasses without coming in to the docks.

CHIMBOTE AND THE RIO SANTA

South of Trujillo the slopes of the Andes reach the edge of the water, and although the Río Santa has an annual flow which is exceeded among the west coast rivers only by the Río Chira, there is no flat land on which to develop a large oasis. Nevertheless, Chimbote has become one of the most important cities along the coast, and the water of the Río Santa has not been allowed to flow unused into the sea.

This water is used to generate electric power and is sent by long canals northward along the coast to enlarge the Trujillo Oases, even as far north as the valley of the Río Chicama. The Santa rises in the high country north of Cerro de Pasco, and after crossing stretches of the high-level surface plunges abruptly into a deep valley on the Pacific side of the continental divide. Some of the highest mountains in Peru, the Cordillera Blanca, overlook the Santa Valley from the northeast. Tributaries bring to the Santa a large volume of water throughout the year from the glaciers and snowfields of the high mountains. In a distance of 100 miles, the Río Santa descends from nearly 14,000 to about 7,000 feet. In the middle part of the valley, on either side of the town of Huarás, there are Indian communities in which the farmers are engaged in raising subsistence crops on land they do not own.

The hydroelectric installations are downstream from these Indian communities. In the Cañon de Pato the river drops 1,400 feet in 6 miles. Four hydroelectric generating stations have been built inside the canyon walls, and the water pours through them in sequence. A large amount of power is generated and is connected to Chimbote by transmission lines.

At Chimbote is Peru's largest steel plant. The iron ore is made into pig iron and steel by a process using electricity. Carbon is provided by pulverized anthracite coal from the Ancos-Galgada coal mines, a short distance inland. The pulverized anthracite is mixed with pitch. Limestone is quarried along the same railroad line that reaches the coal mines. Iron ore comes from the Marcona mines, inland from the port of San Juan, 500 miles to the south.

Chimbote is also Peru's chief fishing port and has the largest concentration of fish meal manufacturing plants. We shall discuss this most recent of Peru's economic activities later.

The Middle Oases

The middle oases include those developed along the rivers to the south of the Río Santa as far as, and including, the Río Ica. This is the part of the Peruvian coast where the spurs of the Andes reach the sea, and where there are few large level areas on which irrigation can be developed even where water is available. The Río Pativilca, for example, brings down a relatively large volume of water, but the oasis it supports is restricted by the size of the valley. The largest of the middle oases is that supported by the Río Rimac, on which Lima and Callao are built.

In the oases of this middle group cotton is more important than sugarcane. The increasing thickness of the coastal cloud as one travels southward means that the amount of sunshine is cut down. To grow sugarcane with a high sugar content, plenty of sunshine is required. In this middle group not enough sugar can be produced per acre to permit sugarcane to compete with cotton. The cotton grown in these oases is a long-staple Peruvian variety (known as Tanguis), which is hardier than the Pima variety grown in the northern oases. The greater part of the cotton grown in Peru is Tanguis.

In addition to cotton and small amounts of sugarcane, a number of other crops are grown in these oases. Around Lima a large part of the irrigated area is devoted to truck crops to supply the cities. The oases south of Lima, especially Pisco and Ica, specialize in the cultivation of vineyards. The port of Pisco gives its name to a brandy which is sold along the whole west coast of the Americas from Chile to California.

The Southern Oases

South of Ica most of the oases are used only for the production of sub-sistence foods. The area which might be devoted to irrigation is limited not only by the increasing aridity of the highlands as one proceeds southward, but also by the rugged nature of the coastal region itself. Most of the inhabitants of these oases are Indians, and the density of population within the oases is much less than where there is commercial production. Ribbons of cultivated land follow the narrow valley bottoms from the mountains to the sea, but in most years it is only the upper parts of these oases that can actually be irrigated. According to the system in Peru, the property owners upstream have the first right to the water, and in dry years—which are more frequent than wet years—there may not be sufficient volume to provide for the properties downstream.

Two of the oases south of Ica are commercially important. The largest of these is the oasis of Arequipa, located in a valley just within the mountains at the base of the volcano El Misti. Water is brought from several small streams, including the Río Chili. In 1958 a dam was completed on the Río Blanco, a tributary of the Chili, and a reservoir was formed to increase the water available for irrigation. The irrigated land is used for an intensive culti-vation of food and feed, all of which are consumed locally. Animals fattened on alfalfa are exported. Arequipa is of chief importance as a wool market, serving the whole southern part of the highlands. A railroad and road extend inland to Cuzco and also to Puno on the shores of Lake Titicaca. Arequipa in 1961 had a population of over 135,000.

The port which has served Arequipa since colonial days is Mollendo. This place, however, has long been recognized as one of the spots along this harborless coast where landing operations are most difficult. Mollendo faces toward the south and lies quite open to the unobstructed sweep of waves driven by the prevailing winds. The Peruvian government built an entirely new port about 7 miles northwest of Mollendo. At the new location a small promontory gives some protection from the south, and the natural conditions of the site were improved by the construction of two breakwaters. Inside the harbor thus created, ships tie up at a dock which has been equipped with the newest loading devices. The railroad from Arequipa has been extended along the coast from Mollendo. This new port, which is known as Matarani, was completed early in 1941.

The other commercial oasis of the southern group lies south of Arequipa. The farmers in the valley of Moquegua, served by the port of Ilo, specialize in vineyards and plantations of olives. Tacna, the southernmost of the Peruvian oases, is of prominence only for historical reasons, for it, like most of the other spots of settlement in the south, grows crops primarily for the local food supply.

Mineral Production on the West Coast

The west coast is also important for its mineral production. Oil was first discovered along the coast in northern Peru in 1864. The northernmost field is at Zorritos, just south of Tumbes. The peak of oil production in this area was between 1872 and 1898, during which time 29 wells were drilled. But now most of Peru's oil comes from the Lobitos and Negritos fields, located in a belt about 80 miles long on either side of Talara. An oil refinery has been built at Talara, and from this port comes most of the exported oil. The oilfields and refinery, formerly the properties of British and American oil companies, are now owned and operated by the Peruvian government.

The existence of good quality coal has been known for a long time, but the development of coal mining has been held up by the difficulties of providing transportation. The coal mines at Goyllarisquisga, 16 miles from Cerro de Pasco, were the first to be opened up to provide the fuel to generate power for the smelters. But Peru did not become a major exporter of coal until after the railroad had been built up the Río Santa Valley and the docks had been built at Chimbote. There are other known coalfields in Peru, but the use of the coal must await further transportation development.

In 1956 work started on a new mining area in Peru. At Toquepala in southern Peru there are about a billion tons of low-grade copper ore (about 1 percent copper). Enough reserve is known to be located here to make large-scale operations profitable in spite of the low proportion of copper. First it was necessary to strip off an overburden of 120 million tons of rock. This was done with heavy machinery, including a fleet of huge trucks, some that can carry 85 tons of rock or ore at a load. A water supply for the mines, homes for the workers, and a railroad and highway to the port of Ilo had to be built. Then at Ilo a breakwater and dock were provided. About 10 miles north of Ilo, on the coast, a huge ore smelter has been built. Electricity is provided by a thermoelectric plant at the smelter. All this preliminary investment is based on the presence at Toquepala of what is estimated as one of the world's largest bodies of copper ore.

There are also important bodies of iron ore along the Peruvian coast. The mines at Marcona, inland from the port of San Juan, were developed during the 1950's. Iron ore from Marcona supplies the steel industry at Chimbote as well as a smaller iron and steel plant at Lima. In 1967 a new pelletizing plant was placed in operation at San Juan, thus greatly reducing the cost of shipping the iron. Iron pellets are now shipped to Chimbote and also are exported to the United States, to Europe, and to Japan. A subsidiary of the Marcona Corporation, the San Juan Carriers, Ltd., operates one of the world's largest fleets of modern bulk ore carriers.

Lima and Callao

The political, social, and economic focus of all these separate clusters of people and their diverse activities is on Lima and its port, Callao. During the colonial period most of western South America came under the dominance of Lima, and the influence of this center was felt even as far as the mouth of the Plata in Argentina. Now Lima has been shorn of its control over this wide hinterland. Lima is a city of ancient traditions; but as the center of modern Peru, it is becoming industrialized and is growing rapidly in population (Map 78).

In 1535 Pizarro selected this site for the foundation of his capital because it combined two special advantages which were important to the Spaniards. In the first place, they found here one of the larger irrigable areas of the coastal region, for the Río Rimac brings down a dependable supply of water to an alluvial plain of broad dimensions. The other advantage was the presence of an offshore island, and a long gravelly promontory which points toward the island from the mainland. Island and promontory together provided a protection from the waves brought in from the open Pacific by the prevailing southwest winds. In Callao harbor it was possible to anchor in calm water. To be sure, they could have found other large irrigable areas along the coast, and other places where small harbors offered protection to the small ships of the sixteenth century—for example, in the bay of Chimbote. It was the combination of a large irrigable area and nearby protected anchorage which was unique: for the first time this combination became significant when the seafaring Spaniards wrested the control of the country from the landlocked Indians.

The city of Lima, 8 miles inland from Callao, was laid out in the characteristic Spanish manner on a strictly rectangular pattern around a central plaza. In most of the Spanish colonial cities the dimensions of the blocks, the width of the streets, and even the arrangement of the government buildings

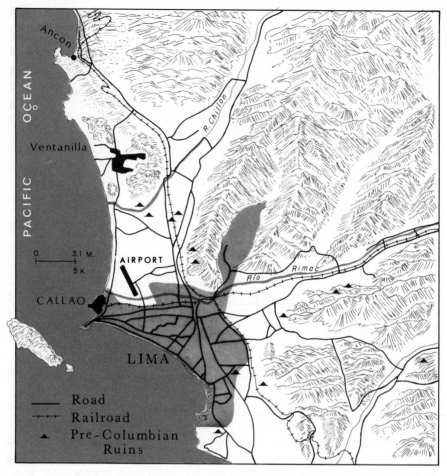

Map 78

and the church around the plaza were all standardized. Lima incorporated all these features which characterize Spanish cities from California to the Strait of Magellan—although this city was laid out before the plan had been prescribed by law.

Lima, now a city well over a million, performs a variety of functions. As the capital it has attracted and given support to an army of government workers, representative of all the different parts of Peru. As chief commercial center of Peru, it receives most of the country's imports, and most of the business enterprises of the country have offices there. As center of art and education, Lima has drawn to itself many artists, literary people, and teachers; the University of San Marcos, the oldest university in South America, attracts students not only from Peru but also from beyond its borders. Because Lima is the capital of a Latin country it is also a social center, and in it are concentrated many of the aristocratic landowning families. Their high standard of living is possible for only a very small proportion of the whole population in a land where poverty is so widespread; this small group, through the exploitation of large areas of the Peruvian soil, has created in Lima the flower of the older Spanish civilization.

Disturbing changes began to appear in the urban scene during World War I. New political ideologies taken up by the relatively small but powerful student population resulted in a more realistic study of the "Indian problem." But of even more profound significance is the new industrialization and the changing attitudes engendered by it. In addition to the big mineral smelters in the Andes and the petroleum and sugar refineries of the northern part of the coastal region manufacturing industries have now made their appearance in Lima and Arequipa. Factories produce foodstuffs, cotton and woolen textiles, cigarettes, matches, beverages, leather, soap, and various kinds of clothing. A steel fabricating plant to manufacture mining machinery was built to the south of the city in 1964. The Peruvians stand third in Latin America in their use of electric power, partly as a result of the Río Santa developments. In 1965 a huge dam and hydroelectric station was completed on the Río Mantaro, downstream from Huancayo. Electric power is supplied by transmission lines to Lima-Callao and to the mines and processing plants at Marcona and San Juan.

In the midst of Lima's historic buildings and narrow streets, new styles of architecture are bringing changes which tend to make this place look more and more like all other modern cities. Industrial slums, and all the social problems which accompany them, have been added to the rural poverty of the older Peru. In modern Lima are to be found the same problems and the same new attitudes toward life which characterize the larger urban centers of all the Occidental world. Modern Lima exhibits the latest ideas imported from other continents, now strangely in contrast to the traditional ideas of the country, just as colonial Lima used to display, for the wondering eyes of the Indians, the strange ideas and materials brought to the new land from Spain.

Peru as a Political Unit

Peru is a good example of the rapidity of the economic and social changes currently sweeping over Latin America. In 1959, when the third edition of this book was published, Peru was described as still seeking a solution to the presence of two incompatible cultures within the national territory. The traditional political elite—the large landowners and the army—were still in control, although the beginnings of a split could be seen. Economic development was directed chiefly to the production of a few export products—minerals, cotton, and sugar. The great majority of the people remained poor and without hope for bettering their status. Peru was a strange and fascinating land for the tourist; Peru was an opportunity to make large speculative profits for the person interested in commercial production; Peru was something quite different for the Indian farmer, who saw all these other activities going on in his country, but who played only a small part in them.

Within less than five years these remarks were no longer valid. With the election of a liberal government in 1963 there were several fundamental changes of policy. With the increase of technical and financial assistance from such international agencies as the Alliance for Progress and the United Nations, certain unprecedented steps have been taken to attack the problem of poverty and inadequate food supply. Peru is moving into the revolutionary orbit that began in Mexico in 1910.

The Economic Situation

In 1967 the population of Peru was estimated at a little over 12 million. Peru had a census in 1961 in which about 10 million were counted, representing an increase of 4 million over the last previous census in 1940. But censuses in Peru have never been very reliable. In fact, when the Peruvian Naval Air Service took air photographs of parts of Peru during the years between 1928 and 1930, whole communities of Indians were "discovered" in isolated Andean valleys that had never been visited even by the tax collectors.[9] Even today such lost communities continue to exist. It was figured in 1960 that Peru's population had been underestimated by at least 7 percent. Therefore estimates of the net rates of growth (3 percent per year) are not reliable. It was clear, however, that the gross national product per capita in 1960 was very low.

For the first three and a half centuries of European rule in Peru, the commercial part of the economy was focused on mineral exports. Silver and gold were the commodities for which the Spaniards prized their colony. It was not until late in the nineteenth century that sugarcane and cotton began to rival the mineral exports. In 1900, sugarcane made up 32 percent of the value of all exports. Since 1925, when the sugar plantations suffered much damage, cotton has usually been ahead of sugar as an export. During World War II, oil exports rose to first place in the list, and for a year or so cotton dropped far down. Generally, however, the agricultural exports have shown a steady gain, whereas the mineral exports have shown great fluctuations from year to year. Copper exports dropped after 1940, but with the development of the new mines at Toquepala this commodity again occupies a larger place in the Peruvian economy. The rapid development of iron ore production and the concentration of this ore in pellet form is another new develop-

[9]George R. Johnson, *Peru from the Air,* (New York: American Geographical Society, Special Publication No. 12), 1930.

A fish meal plant on the desert coast of Peru. *Photo by W. R. Grace & Co.*

ment, along with the opening up of some of Peru's coal resources for sale abroad.

The most spectacular change in the economic sector, however, has been the sudden rise of Peru to the status of the world's leading exporter of fish products. Strangely, the incredible wealth of fish in the Peru Coastal Current remained for centuries untouched. Fish entered to only a very minor degree

Anchovies being loaded into fish-processing plant. *Photo by W. R. Grace & Co.*

into the diet of a people suffering from malnutrition. Now the Peruvians catch more fish than any other country in the world.

The use of the fish resource actually started during World War II, when the United States encouraged the export of salt fish to help out with the world's food problem. By 1950 there were some 3,000 small wooden boats and some 8,000 fishermen bringing in tuna to canning factories along the coast. In that same year an imaginative Peruvian businessman decided to risk some capital in purchasing trawlers and building a plant to convert fish into fish meal. Just at this time there was a program in Europe to increase the production of chickens, and there was a rising demand for poultry feed. It was found that the anchovies in the Peru Coastal Current could be processed into a powdery meal richer in protein than any other available feed. In 1951 the United States, without consulting the Peruvians, raised the tariff on imported canned tuna high enough to exclude the Peruvian product from the American market. But the export of fish meal opened up a new source of speculative profits.

Several things followed these events. First the Peruvians reacted to the increase of the United States tariff by claiming sovereignty over the sea for 200 miles offshore, instead of the traditional 12 miles. This excluded from the Peru Coastal Current waters fishing vessels from California that had been catching tuna and other fish for the North American market. Peru encouraged Ecuador and Chile to make the same claim. The argument about the extent of territorial waters was even carried to the United Nations; but by the time the necessary studies could be carried out, the United States began to shift toward an acceptance of the 200-mile limit as a result of the activities of the Soviet trawlers off Alaska. And in Peru there was a rush of investors, large and small, to buy fishing boats and set up fish-processing plants. Thousands of Indians from the highlands migrated with their families to the coastal ports where they were employed either in the trawlers or on land. To the amazement of many people, the illiterate Indians proved to be very efficient workers who could learn skills quickly from just observing how jobs were done. By 1959 the export of fish meal had climbed to 109,000 tons, and in addition the Peruvian fishermen were exporting to the United States over a million tons of canned bonito and large quantities of frozen tuna, skipjack, swordfish, and shrimp. The fishing industry was providing jobs, directly or indirectly, for half a million people.

The first fish-processing plants were located at Callao, and the fishing fleet was based at this port. But it happens that the production of fish meal causes a very unpleasant odor. The city of Lima decreed that no new fish-processing plants could be built there. So the industry shifted to Chimbote, and this already industrialized center has now become the major fishing port for Peru. One large corporation accounts for a major part of the total production, but there are hundreds of smaller plants. During the early 1960's something like 600 new fish-processing plants were built all along the Peruvian coast, but with the chief concentration around the bay of Chimbote. The unpleasant odor seemed like perfume when the profits began to come in.

The fishing industry supports a variety of related activities. There is a new ship-building industry located at Chimbote where steel is available at relatively low cost. There are new manufacturing plants that produce nets and other gear.

Nevertheless the people who now make a living from fishing find new problems to worry about. In 1965, El Niño made one of its periodic invasions, covering the cold water of the coastal current farther to the south than usual. The anchovies followed the cold water away from the shore, and the birds died by the thousands. The fish meal producers were faced with ruin, and the Peruvian government had to provide funds to cushion the shock. The question was raised whether too many trawlers were catching too many anchovies. Fortunately in 1966 and 1967 the normal pattern of currents was restored, and the anchovies again appeared along the coast. A special research project, staffed by Peruvian and North American oceanographers, began to look for the causes of the shifts of El Niño and to examine the food supply and breeding habits of the anchovies.

As a result the investments of new capital in various aspects of the Peruvian economy, there were notable gains in the value of goods and services. In 1966 Peru had a gross national product per capita of $378, which moved this country up to eleventh place among the independent countries of Latin

Engineers at a fish meal plant at Chimbote study sonar chart showing location of schools of anchovies in the coastal waters. *Photo by W. R. Grace & Co.*

America. The economy was growing at more than 5 percent per year, which was well ahead of the 3 percent estimated growth of population. Expansion was taking place in manufacturing, in the volume of exports, in construction, and in the value of domestic retail trade. A larger and larger proportion of the Peruvians were beginning to experience rising standards of living. The country seemed to be almost ready to enter the "take-off" stage of economic development.

The Political Situation

Meanwhile, a fundamental change had taken place in Peru's political situation. Until 1963 the political control of Peru had remained firmly in the hands of the traditional elite—the large landowners and the officers of the army. To be sure, Peru had its liberal movement demanding an end to special privileges for the ruling minority and a greater share in the national economy for the Indians. In 1924 a political party known as the *Alianza Popular Revolutionaria Americana,* or APRA, was formed. The Apristas, or members of APRA, urged a land reform program that would return the land to the Indian communities, a system of universal education that would reduce the illiteracy rate, and an economic program that would include the Indians in the national system of production and consumption. The Apristas were ready to stir up revolutionary change on the Mexican pattern. They were resisted by the traditional authorities, and the leaders were forced to seek asylum in foreign embassies. But the APRA program gained the enthusiastic support of a majority of the literate people of Peru, and was only prevented from being accepted as national policy by the authority of a dictator backed by the power of the army. Nevertheless, because of the presence of this movement, communism in Peru remained relatively weak.

In 1962 Peru held an election in which people who could qualify as literate were permitted to vote. In this election the conservatives formed an alliance with the Apristas, which had the effect of shocking the officers of the army into a break with the conservatives for the first time in Peruvian history. The army remained solid in its refusal to permit APRA to come to power, even when the latter received more votes than any other party. The elections of 1962 were annulled and a new election called. In 1963 many people realized that APRA would never be permitted to take office, and that a vote for this party would be wasted. An alternative was presented by a Popular Action Party led by Fernando Belaúnde Terry. Belaúnde received a clear majority of the votes and was permitted to take office.

Belaúnde is a member of a wealthy, landowning family, a professional architect, a political liberal. During the years from 1963 to 1968 he gained the support of an overwhelming majority of the Peruvians, so that it became more and more difficult for the army to interfere. In 1964 the government enacted a program of agrarian reform that drew protests from the landowners. Many of the traditional elite, whose privileges are now threatened, have insisted that Belaúnde is indeed a communist. When the Vicos Project resulted in the transfer of land ownership to an Indian community, the whole undertaking was challenged as communist inspired. Yet an objective view of what was happening in Peru makes clear that Belaúnde was leading a peaceful revolution toward the same ends that Mexico reached by years of internal conflict. However, in 1968 the army again seized control and Belaúnde was exiled. The forces of resistance were still strong.

República de Bolivia

Area: 424,162 square miles
Population: (1967 estimate) 3,801,000
       (last census, 1950) 3,019,031
Capital city: La Paz; (1966) 362,298; legal capital: Sucre; (1966) 59,701
Percent urban: (1950) 33.9
Birth rate per 1,000: (1966) 42–46; Death rate per 1,000: (1966) 20–23
Annual percent of increase: (1958–64) 1.4
Percent literate: (1950) 32.1
Percent labor force in agriculture: (1957) 85
Gross national product per capita: (1966) $149
Unit of currency: boliviano (1968, 11.75 per dollar)

COMMERCE, 1964 *(expressed in percentage of values)*
Percent total Latin-American exports: 0.9 (1956, 1.0)
Percent total Latin-American imports: 1.1

Exports (1966)
tin 67
silver 5
lead 5

Exports to (1966)		**Imports from (1966)**	
United Kingdom	45	United States	44 (1956, 38)
United States	43 (1956, 61)	Japan	13
West Germany	5	West Germany	11
		Argentina	5

Chapter 20 □ Bolivia

The establishment of a coherent state with a stable government has proved especially difficult in Bolivia. In 1952 a social revolution wiped out the traditional large-landowning class and resulted in the nationalization of the chief source of wealth—the tin mines. Great hopes were expressed that something could be done about the status of the Indian and that steps could be taken to attack the widespread poverty. But in the years that followed, a mixture of social idealism and political opportunism diverted the revolution from its aims. Why should the formulation of an effective state-idea be so very difficult in Bolivia?

The Bolivian problem can be clarified by examining it in the context of its geographic setting, for the internal arrangement of lands and people within the Bolivian national territory is perhaps even more important than the separation of Bolivia from the sea. To a greater extent than in any other Latin-American country, the Bolivian population is arranged in scattered small areas of settlement, isolated from one another, and from the outside world, by empty areas. Before the War of the Pacific (1879–83) Bolivian territory extended to the Pacific around the port of Antofagasta. Bolivia lost its seacoast to Chile not only because the Chilean military forces were stronger, but also because Chileans rather than Bolivians were carrying on the effective exploitation of the nitrate resources of the Atacama. From 1932 to 1935 Bolivia was engaged in another war, this time with Paraguay. As a result it lost a large part of the Chaco which it had claimed but had not been able effectively to occupy.

The physical character of the habitat in which the Bolivians are struggling to establish a coherent state is marked by extremes of altitude and aridity. The Bolivian people are located mostly on the high Altiplano south of

Lake Titicaca, and in the valleys of the Eastern Cordillera. Separating these clusters of people from the west coast are high, bleak, wind-swept plateaus, towering ranges of volcanic peaks with passes above 13,000 feet, a desert which is one of the driest in the world, and an escarpment more than 2,000 feet in height which drops steeply to a harborless coast. In western and southern Bolivia the great dry belt of South America which extends from southern Ecuador almost to the Strait of Magellan crosses the Andes diagonally from northwest to southeast. Between latitudes 20° S. and 30° S., within that zone which is dry on the western sides of all the continents, South America is so deficient in moisture that the land is almost entirely barren of vegetation. Even in the high Western Cordillera of the Andes there is so little rainfall that few streams emerge from the mountains. Unlike coastal Peru, where numerous streams flow across the desert into the ocean, in what is now northern Chile only one river rises in the Andes and flows all the way across the desert to the Pacific. East of the Western Cordillera, over the whole southwestern part of the present Bolivian territory the rainfall is so scanty and so uncertain that only a few spots can be found where drinkable water is available.

The internal force by which a state might be enabled to expand across such physical barriers is lacking in Bolivia. Like Ecuador and Peru, this state is made up of people of very different cultural traditions—the Indian and the Spaniard. But in Bolivia the problems of cultural diversity are further complicated by the arrangement of the population in small and more or less isolated clusters and ribbons of settlement. Furthermore, the Indians of the Titicaca Basin and of the Altiplano between Lake Titicaca and Lake Poopó are Aymaras (Map 5, p. 14). They are the descendants of a people whose civilization flourished in this region a century before the time of Christ. Conquered first by the Incas, then by the Spaniards, they have nevertheless maintained their language and their customs with little change and have been able to cling stubbornly to their ancestral lands. Among all these diverse elements the Bolivian state has never been able to develop any strong sense of political coherence.

The weakness of the Bolivian state constitutes a threat to the peace and security of the hemisphere. Weakness in any state invites aggressive action, with or without force, by more powerful neighbors. Weakness in Ecuador invited armed invasion from Peru, as it did earlier from Colombia. But the danger of weakness in Bolivia is rendered much more serious than that of Ecuador for two chief reasons; first, the Bolivian territory contains important stores of tin and other metals and of oil; and second, Bolivia's still undeveloped oil fields lie easily accessible to the two chief rival powers of South America, Brazil and Argentina.

The People

Bolivia, like Peru, Ecuador, and the southern part of Colombia, is occupied by a population which is more than half pure Indian. Much of Bolivia

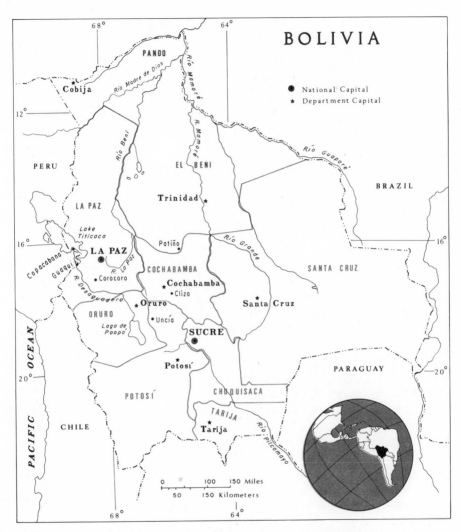

Map 79

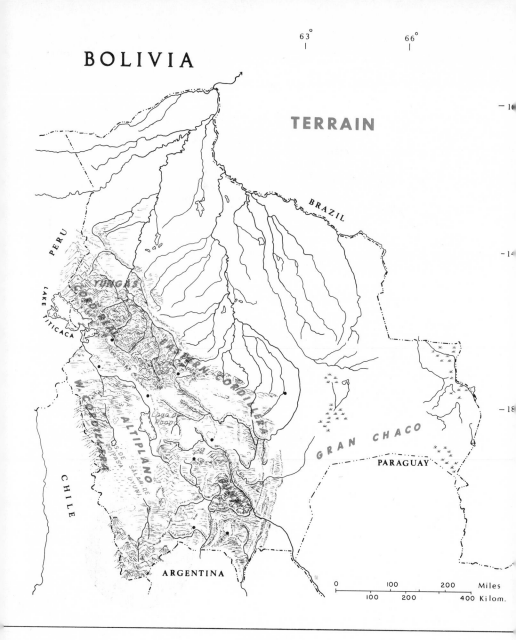

BOLIVIA

TERRAIN

63° 66°

PERU

BRAZIL

LAKE TITICACA

YUNGAS

CORDILLERA

W. CORDILLERA

ALTIPLANO

EASTERN CORDILLERA

Lago de Poopó

SO. DE COIPASA   SALAR DE UYUNI

GRAN CHACO

PARAGUAY

CHILE

ARGENTINA

0	100	200	Miles
100	200	400	Kilom.

Map 80

506

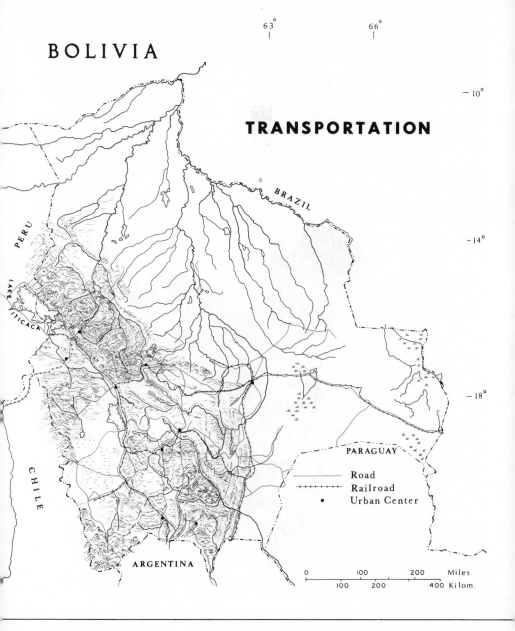

BOLIVIA

TRANSPORTATION

PERU

BRAZIL

LAKE TITICACA

CHILE

PARAGUAY

——— Road
+++++ Railroad
• Urban Center

ARGENTINA

0   100   200   Miles

100   200   400 Kilom.

Map 81

507

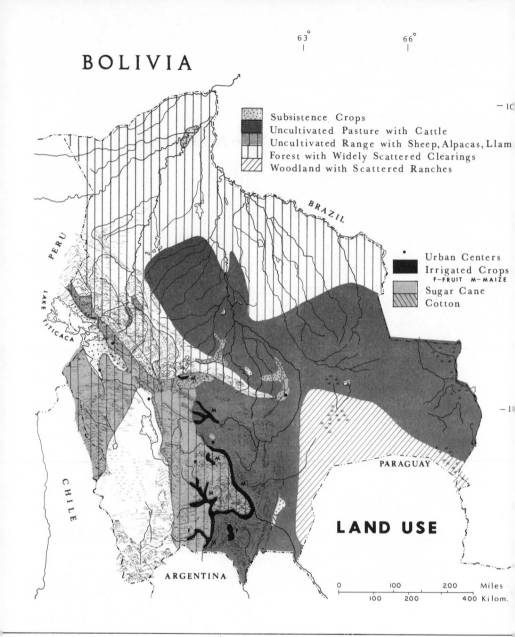

BOLIVIA

63° 66°

Legend

- Subsistence Crops
- Uncultivated Pasture with Cattle
- Uncultivated Range with Sheep, Alpacas, Llam
- Forest with Widely Scattered Clearings
- Woodland with Scattered Ranches

PERU

BRAZIL

LAKE TITICACA

- Urban Centers
- Irrigated Crops
  F–FRUIT M–MAIZE
- Sugar Cane
- Cotton

CHILE

PARAGUAY

LAND USE

ARGENTINA

| 0 | 100 | 200 | Miles |

| 100 | 200 | 400 | Kilom. |

Map 82

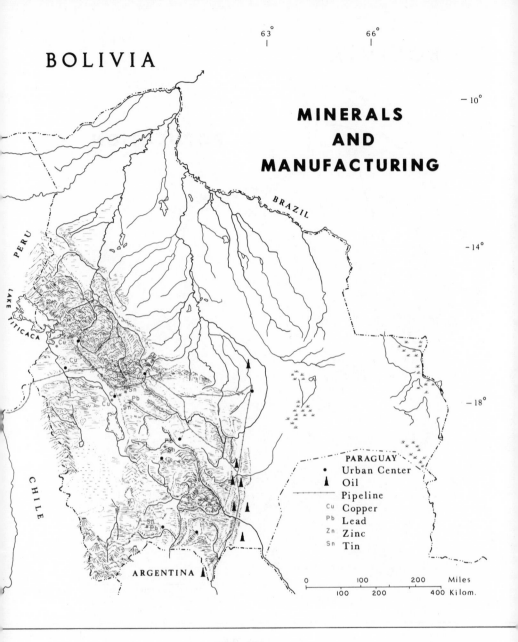

BOLIVIA

MINERALS
AND
MANUFACTURING

63°   66°

−10°

BRAZIL

PERU

LAKE TITICACA

−14°

−18°

Cu

Cu

Cu   Sn
Cu   Pb
Sn   Sn

CHILE

Sn
Pb

ARGENTINA

PARAGUAY
•   Urban Center
▲   Oil
—— Pipeline
Cu Copper
Pb Lead
Zn Zinc
Sn Tin

0   100   200   Miles
100   200   400 Kilom.

Map 83

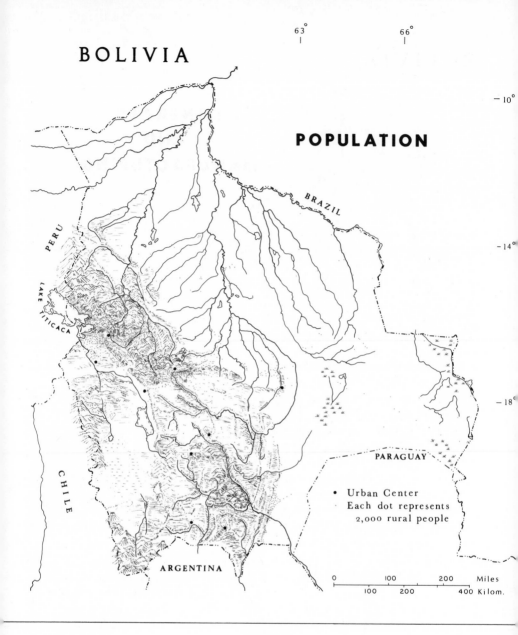

BOLIVIA

POPULATION

−10°

BRAZIL

−14°

PERU

LAKE TITICACA

−18°

PARAGUAY

CHILE

• Urban Center
· Each dot represents
  2,000 rural people

ARGENTINA

63° 66°

0   100   200   Miles
   100   200   400 Kilom.

Map 84

510

was included within the limits of the Inca Empire, and Quechua is still a common language of many Bolivians. In the northern part of the Altiplano, around Lake Titicaca and Lake Poopó, are the descendants of the pre-Inca civilization whose language is Aymara. In Bolivia as a whole, people of unmixed Indian ancestry make up about 53 percent and mestizos form another 32 percent. People of unmixed European ancestry are only about 15 percent.

The various clusters of people in Bolivia, however, are quite diverse in their racial composition. In the highland regions the clusters located at the higher altitudes have the largest proportion of Indians. Around the shores of Lake Titicaca, where the density of population in certain areas exceeds 125 per square mile, the people are almost exclusively Indians. Even in the city of La Paz, the actual capital (although Sucre is the legal capital), the Indians form the majority of the inhabitants. In the department of La Paz, Indians make up about 75 percent of the total. Lower down in the valleys and basins of the Eastern Cordillera there are more mestizos and Europeans: in the Basin of Cochabamba, for example, which has a density of population of over 325 people per square mile, 70 percent is made up of mestizos and Europeans. With such differences of racial composition added to the contrasted economic outlook found among the various groups, the formation of a strong national unity is extremely difficult.

The Aymaras form a distinct and important part of the Bolivian population. The anthropologist Weston La Barre reported that "while the Quechua is docile, submissive, and obedient, the Aymara is hard, vindictive, bellicose, rebellious, egotistical, cruel, and jealous of his liberty."[1] But if these people are hostile in their dealings with people of Spanish origin, this attitude is not without cause. The Aymaras have been defending their lands and their way of living for centuries. Conquered first by the Incas, then by the Spaniards, they have been treated with cruelty and forced to accommodate themselves to the wishes of outsiders. Although the Aymaras, being mostly illiterate and unable to speak Spanish, have had little or nothing to say about the political and economic policies of Bolivia until recently, they nevertheless make up the overwhelming majority of the farmers, the herders, and the miners of the country. Again and again their traditional communal system of land tenure has been officially abolished, yet the Indian village, or *ayllu,* continues to operate on a communal basis as it has for thousands of years. The Aymara is fiercely attached to his land and nothing but force or absolute economic necessity can separate him from it.

The Physical Diversity of Bolivia

Bolivia, like Colombia, is about one-third mountainous and about two-thirds lowland; and most of the lowland two-thirds lies outside of the effective

[1]Weston La Barre, "The Aymara Indians of the Lake Titicaca Plateau, Bolivia," *The American Anthropologist,* Vol. 50 (1948): 1–250.

national territory. Part of the plains of eastern Bolivia are drained by the headwaters of the Amazon and part by the Paraguay and its tributaries. The plains in the southeast, south of Santa Cruz, are part of the great lowland region known as the Gran Chaco. But most of the Bolivians live in the one-third of the national territory which is mountainous.

It is in Bolivia that the highlands of the Andes reach their greatest width: about latitude 18° S., between Arica on the Pacific coast and Santa Cruz on the eastern plains, the mountain zone is approximately 400 miles wide. The highlands of Bolivia are made up of three distinct parts: the Western Cordillera; a string of high intermont basins known collectively as the Altiplano; and the Eastern Cordillera.

The Western Cordillera is a southward continuation of the volcanic region which begins north of Arequipa in Peru. Along its crest are numerous active volcanoes, some of which, in the symmetry of their cones, rival the famous El Misti in Peru. East of the Western Cordillera are the basins of the Altiplano, the northernmost of which is occupied by Lake Titicaca. Spurs extending eastward from the Western Cordillera all but separate these high basins, but on the eastern side of the Altiplano, along the west-facing front of the Eastern Cordillera, there is a continuous passageway of gentle gradient which extends from the shores of Lake Titicaca southward across Bolivia.

The northern part of the Eastern Cordillera is a southeastward continuation of the high ranges of Peru. The mountains which stand northeast of the Titicaca Basin and of the city of La Paz are very high, some of them more than 21,000 feet above sea level; and the descent from these great elevations to the eastern plains is remarkably abrupt. This rainy and heavily forested northeastern slope of the Eastern Cordillera, which is the equivalent of the eastern border valleys region of Peru, is known in Bolivia as the Yungas.

A notable change in the character of the Eastern Cordillera takes place about latitude 17° S., where the predominant direction of the slope turns from northeast to east. A line drawn a little north of due west from Santa Cruz to the edge of the Altiplano, passing just north of Cochabamba, marks the approximate southern end of the Yungas. South of this line the Eastern Cordillera is composed of a great block of the earth's crust which has been tilted eastward, its upper surface sloping gently toward the eastern plains, its western edge forming a sharply defined escarpment overlooking the basins of the Altiplano. The top of this block, like the highlands of Peru, is composed of a high-level surface of slight local relief, standing, near the western border, between 12,000 and 14,000 feet above sea level. Above this surface there are irregularly placed and discontinuous ranges of high peaks, and below it are deeply excavated valleys and basins. This high-level surface in the Eastern Cordillera of Bolivia is known as the Puna.[2] Streams which drain

---

[2]The word *Puna,* designating a region, should not be confused with the same word used to designate a vegetation type.

eastward to the lowlands of eastern Bolivia have extended their headwaters back into the Puna, a few of the larger ones even reaching the margin of the Altiplano. Generally, however, the Eastern Cordillera south of latitude 17° S. can be divided into a western high part where the Puna surface is only slightly dissected, and an eastern lower part where the streams have cut the Puna into long fingerlike remnants standing high between the valleys.

The northwest–southeast and the north–south surface features of highland Bolivia just described are crossed diagonally by the zone of aridity. From about latitude 20° S. almost to the Strait of Magellan, the eastern base of the Andes is dry. As a result of this climatic arrangement, each of the major surface divisions of Bolivia can be subdivided into a northern wetter part and a southern drier part. Most of the people occupy the northern basins of the Altiplano and the basins and valleys of the Eastern Cordillera along the line of transition between the very wet Yungas and the very dry south.

The Western Cordillera and the Altiplano

For an agricultural or a pastoral people, the habitability of the western part of Bolivia decreases from northeast to southwest as aridity increases. The Western Cordillera has the smallest population of the highland regions, for here aridity and altitude are combined. In the northern part, north of latitude 20° S., several small rivers rise among the volcanic peaks, some draining westward toward the Atacama of northern Chile, some eastward toward the Altiplano of Bolivia. In little valleys between 11,500 and 15,000 feet above sea level there are narrow ribbons of irrigated land on which meager crops of potatoes and hay are raised. Toward the south, where only rare sources of water are to be found, the land remains almost uninhabited except by occasional seminomadic shepherds.

THE TITICACA BASIN

In the Titicaca Basin the conditions of life are not so extreme as in the Western Cordillera. The boundary of the zone of deficient moisture crosses the Altiplano south of Lake Titicaca, and north of this line the rainfall is adequate for the cultivation of crops without irrigation. Around the shores of the lake extremes of temperature are moderated by the presence of the open water. Because the lake is very deep—918 feet at the maximum depth—the temperature of Lake Titicaca remains nearly constant throughout the year, at about 51°. As a result, the air temperatures around the margins of the lake do not drop so low at night or in winter as they do at similar altitudes farther from the water. The surface of Titicaca is 12,507 feet above sea level; but maize and wheat can be ripened in the Titicaca Basin to an elevation of 12,800 feet.

These physical advantages for an agricultural people have been reflected since the earliest times of which there is any record by the presence of a relatively dense population around the shores of Lake Titicaca. This area of concentrated settlement formed the core of the ancient civilization whose ruined temples may still be seen on the promontories and islands of the lake. Along the railroad not far east of Guaqui are the ruins of the city of Tiahuanaco, once the chief market city of the highlands. It was in this region that the potato was probably first cultivated, and the potato is still the staple food of the Aymaras. They also grow the Andean grain, quinoa; and they supplement these foods with dried meat of the llama and with fish. The only items regularly brought to the region from elsewhere are the coca leaves from the Yungas, which the Indians chew to deaden the pangs of hunger, and the maize from which the Indians make an alcoholic drink known as *chicha*.

The Aymaras have preserved their ancient customs and their language in spite of conquests. The first step in the development of the Inca Empire around its capital, Cuzco, was the conquest of the Titicaca Basin. Yet this was the only area in which the Incas were unable to implant the Quechua language. After the Spanish conquest the Aymaras were forced to labor in the silver mines of Potosí and other places. Whatever hard work there was to be done, the Aymaras were the ones who did it. Yet the conquerors were never successful in separating them from their lands. To be sure, the Titicaca Basin was divided into large private estates owned by people of Spanish descent, but the Indian villages continued to occupy their own lands on a communal basis, paying the landowners a rent. The owners lived elsewhere, some in Cochabamba, some in La Paz, some even in Europe, leaving overseers to collect the rents.

The fact that the dense cluster of people in the Titicaca Basin is cut by the boundary between Peru and Bolivia is an eloquent illustration of the extent to which the culture of the Spaniard has been superimposed on that of the Indian. Political boundaries and all they stand for are Spanish importations, and until the Indian can see a difference between being a Peruvian and being a Bolivian, the boundary has little meaning. Twice every year, on February 2 and August 6, a great fair is held at Copacabana, located on the peninsula which almost cuts the lake in two and almost on the boundary between the two nations. Indians travel on foot, or by balsa rafts, from all around the Titicaca Basin. They come also from as far away as Cuzco, and from Tucumán in Argentina. There is an amazing amount of travel among these sedentary and essentially self-sufficient Andean communities, not only to Copacabana but also to several other regular fairs in different parts of the highlands.

INDIAN SETTLEMENTS SOUTH OF LAKE TITICACA

The number of agricultural Indian communities decreases south of the Titicaca Basin. Indian settlement, with a population density of between 10 and 25 per square mile, extends southward along the valley of the Río Desaguadero about as far as the margin of sufficient moisture. As the aridity increases the Desaguadero takes on the braided, shifting channel of a typical dry-land river, and the settlements along its banks are spaced at wider and wider intervals.

The Desaguadero drains into Lake Poopó. This lake is salty, for, although the waters of Lake Titicaca are only slightly brackish, the Río Desaguadero on its way south crosses saline beds from which a certain amount of salt is carried away in solution; but the saltiness of Poopó is also the result of the fact that the water escapes from it mostly by evaporation. Lake Poopó averages 12,120 feet above sea level, but in times of flood it rises rapidly and may overflow into the Salar de Coipasa, a salt flat located to the southwest. Still farther to the south the Salar de Uyuni is a great wind-swept salt flat, now totally arid. Since Lake Poopó is only about 10 feet deep at the deepest part its waters change temperature rapidly and so exert little influence on the temperature of the air in its vicinity.

East of Lake Poopó there is a more or less continuous band of Indian settlements along the west-facing piedmont of the Eastern Cordillera. Each stream which emerges from the mountains has built an alluvial fan, and on these fans the Indian communities have become established. The pattern of settlement differs from that of the Titicaca Basin, however, in that the villages are located high on the fan slopes where water is available, rather than close to the lake. The cultivated fields are located on the upper parts of the fans; the lower slopes where water is less certain are used for pasture. The marshy and salty shores of Lake Poopó are uninhabited.

MINING COMMUNITIES OF THE ALTIPLANO

In addition to the agricultural Indian communities of the Altiplano there are two clusters of population in this region which originated as mining centers. One of the oldest mining communities in this part of South America is located not far east of the Río Desaguadero and a short distance south of the main railroad line between La Paz and Arica. This is Corocoro. Since the earliest period for which evidence is available, there has been a mining population located here, for this is one of the two sources of native copper in the Americas (the other source being on the shore of Lake Superior in northern Michigan). Because copper was present here in pure form, not as an ore which had to be smelted, it was used by the native peoples long before knowledge of metallurgy made possible the utilization of other sources of copper. Corocoro is still exclusively a mining community, with only a small population; from the group of mines in the vicinity comes about 90 percent of the copper production of Bolivia.

The city of Oruro is the center of the other important mining community of the Altiplano. A range of low hills, about 4 square miles in area and rising some 1,200 feet above the general level of the Altiplano, contains ores of both silver and tin. During the colonial period this district was one of the chief sources of silver, and Oruro, located at the eastern base of the hills, became a town of considerable importance. But mining communities, with few exceptions, are subject to major fluctuations of prosperity and of population as a result of the speculative character of the business of seeking and selling the ores, especially in a land which is too high and too dry for the inhabitants to find other means of livelihood. With the decline of silver production during the nineteenth century the Indian workers moved away and the community was largely abandoned; but with the rise of tin mining in more recent years, the community has once again regained its position of importance. Now Bolivia's first tin smelter is being built in Oruro.

The status of Oruro at the present time as the third largest city of Bolivia, with a population of nearly 80,000, is a result of other activities than those related to mining. In the first place Oruro enjoys a position on what has been, since the conquest of this territory by the Incas, a major route of travel. The Altiplano, as described above, is not composed of one level and uninterrupted surface, as it is frequently shown to be on generalized maps. The spurs and outliers from the Western Cordillera divide it into a number of more or less separate basins. Each basin is deeply filled with sands and clays deposited in the bottoms of the extensive lakes which occupied much of this territory during the glacial period. But along the eastern border of the Altiplano the several basins are connected, and a level route of travel is available from the southern end of the Titicaca Basin far to the south. This route is now followed by one of Bolivia's main railroad lines. Two major branches join this main line in the vicinity of Oruro: one serves the tin-mining district around Uncía in the Eastern Cordillera; the other reaches the important agricultural basin of Cochabamba, lower down on the eastern slopes. Oruro, as the focus of these routes, has become a supply center, connecting Bolivia's most productive agricultural district with the most productive mining district.

LA PAZ

La Paz, political center and chief commercial city of Bolivia, is the world's highest big city. Located 12,000 feet above sea level, the 362,000 people of La Paz are wedged into a narrow valley in the Altiplano, where a tolerable compromise can be worked out between comfort and accessibility (Map 85).

La Paz is quite literally in the Altiplano rather than on it. The traveler approaching the city from the port of Guaqui at the southern end of Lake Titicaca does not become aware of the presence of a large urban center. The smooth surface of the Altiplano rises gradually toward the steep face of the Eastern Cordillera, known in this section as the Cordillera Real—a majestic mountain wall which is topped by the enormous snowcapped peaks of

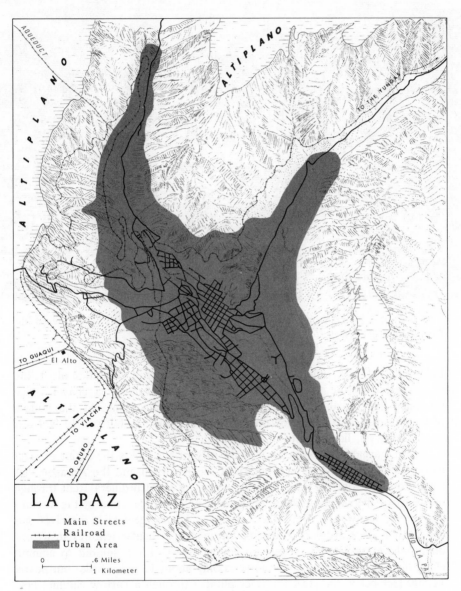

Map 85

The city of La Paz from the edge of the Altiplano, looking east toward the Cordillera Real. *Photo by Ronald McDonald.*

Illampú (21,275 ft.) and Illimani (21,185 ft.). Not until the station of El Alto is reached does the traveler find himself at the brink of a chasm which separates him by about 3 miles from the mountain front. At the bottom of the chasm, 1,400 feet below the rim of the Altiplano, but still 11,909 feet above sea level, lies the city of La Paz.

This remarkable site occupied by the city of La Paz is the result of river cutting. The Río La Paz, a tributary of the Río Beni and the Amazon, has cut headward from the rainy eastern slopes of the Cordillera Real through the heart of the range until its headwaters now include some of the streams descending westward toward the Altiplano. The gorge which the river has cut through the Cordillera is one of the most spectacular features in a continent where spectacular gorges are commonplace. From summit to summit along the crest of the range the gorge is only about 12 miles wide; but nearly 11,500 feet below the crest the river plunges through a narrow channel bordered by almost vertical cliffs, through an opening impassable for human beings. Where the headwaters of the Río La Paz have reached the loose lake-bed deposits of the Altiplano a deep chasm has been excavated parallel to the mountain front, and through this trench are diverted not a few of the streams which once fed Lake Titicaca. A less promising place for a large city would be difficult to imagine.

The Spaniards, not the Indians, chose this site for La Paz. The native people regarded the deep trench along the front of the mountains as un-inhabitable; likewise two other similar trenches, one east of the middle of Lake Titicaca, and the other far to the south, east of Uyuni, also remained unoccupied. But for the Spaniards this site combined accessibility to the chief colonial route of travel with a measure of protection from the cold winds of the Altiplano. The main colonial road from Lima to the silver mines of highland Bolivia passed Lake Titicaca on the southwest side, where the spurs which reach the edge of the water are fewer and less rugged than those on the northeast side. Emerging from the Titicaca Basin, the road led over to the eastern side of the Altiplano where the way to the south was open. This brought the main line of travel to the very edge of the chasm. No other site could so readily combine accessibility to the road with shelter from the winds. Once established, this city controlled the passage of goods to and from Lima; and later, when railroads were built, they were all brought to a focus on La Paz.

But the site has proved anything but favorable for the growth of a large city. The cramped space in which the buildings are wedged, necessitating a departure from the strictly rectangular pattern usual in Spanish American cities, has handicapped growth. Nor is the climate, even in this protected spot, easily to be endured: the rapid changes of temperature together with the rarefied atmosphere make respiratory diseases not only common but extremely dangerous. Only the most phlegmatic persons can long remain at these altitudes without showing evidences of nervous strain. In almost every respect La Paz is unsuited for the role of chief city, and its continued pre-eminence is indeed a measure of the difficulties of reaching the comfortable valley communities of the eastern slopes.

The Eastern Cordillera

La Paz, then, was established along one of the major trade routes of colonial South America—a route which connected the primary settlement center on the west coast with the rich mines of the Bolivian highlands, and led on southeastward to the plains of Argentina. At one end of the road was Lima, the center of Spanish colonial life. The major objective of the road in what is now Bolivia was the silver-mining community of Potosí.

MINING COMMUNITIES

In 1544 the Spanish conquerors of Peru in their restless search for El Dorado discovered the Cerro Rico, a conical mountain which stands above the Puna surface of the Eastern Cordillera. The top of this mountain reaches 15,680 feet above sea level, and the altitude of its base, where the city of Potosí was founded, is 13,780 feet. The bulk of the mountain is made up of one of the richest ore bodies known anywhere in the world—an ore containing not only silver, but also tin, bismuth, and tungsten. In 1554, however, the Spaniards wanted silver, for tin was then much more cheaply supplied to Europe from European sources, and bismuth and tungsten had no uses. Out of this one mountain, between its discovery and the beginning of the seventeenth century, came about half of all the silver produced in the world during those fifty-six years. The "royal fifth" which was poured into the Spanish treasury played a vital role in shaping the course of European history.

The desire for wealth can lead some men to endure the most severe hardships and, at least temporarily, to overcome the most severe handicaps. The mining town of Potosí at one time had 160,000 people in it despite the fact that the climatic conditions at this place were such that La Paz must have seemed blissfully comfortable by comparison. The average winter day, according to recent figures, ranges in temperature from about 3° to 45°, and snows are not uncommon. Moreover the colonial engineers faced a difficult problem in providing power for the mines and the ore crushers. Fuel on the highlands is scanty; even today the mines are forced to depend for fuel on such resinous plants as *yareta,* gathered from great distances at what would be enormous cost were it not for the cheapness of Indian labor, and on equally scanty supplies of *taquia,* the dried dung of llamas. These fuels were useless to the sixteenth-century colonists, however, for at that time there was no knowledge of steam power. Instead, the engineers of Potosí devised a water-power system by building more than thirty small reservoirs in the neighborhood, which provided enough water to turn the wheels of more than a hundred mills.

Potosí, after its dazzling rise to wealth, suffered the fate of most mining communities. Exhaustion of the more immediately available ores, advances in technology that made possible the use of other poorer ores in more accessible locations, combined with a series of natural disasters at Potosí—including the flood of 1626 when one of the dams above the city broke—combined to put an end to the preeminence of this one place. First Peru and then Mexico took the lead in the production of silver; Potosí began to decline in population since no other means of support could be found in such a locality. For more than two centuries Potosí remained a ghost town, occupied by no more than a few hundred people in the midst of the ruins.

Shortly before the beginning of the present century the exploitation of Bolivia's tin ores began. Increasing demand resulting from new industrial uses, together with the exhaustion of the more accessible European sources, led to a rise in the market price of tin. The average price for the period from 1924 to 1933, for example, was more than double the average of the decade from 1894 to 1903. The result was a reawakening of mining activity around the ancient silver town of Potosí. Today this place has a population of about 43,000.

Other mining communities in the Eastern Cordillera of Bolivia are now

The mining community of Pulacayo, ten miles northeast of Uyuni on the western slopes of the Cordillera. The mines produce silver, tin, and other metals. *Courtesy of Grace Line.*

more important than Potosí. The rich tin ores between Oruro and Uncía were discovered at the end of the nineteenth century. By the beginning of World War II three big mining corporations controlled some 80 percent of the Bolivian tin production. These were Patiño, Hochschild, and Aramayo. The Bolivian Simón Patiño (1860–1947) was the owner of the mines at Uncía, from which he built one of the world's largest fortunes. From his home in France, Patiño for many years virtually dictated Bolivian political policy. The three big corporations were not interested in investing their profits in Bolivia. There were no tin smelters in Bolivia, but all the ore was exported to Great Britain or the United States for processing. The largest volume of production was, in 1929, with 47,070 metric tons; since that time Bolivia has produced between 25,000 and 35,000 tons each year. From these exports the Bolivian treasury derived 70 percent of its income. Patiño, whose mines produced more than half of the total Bolivian production of tin, was also Bolivia's leading banker and for much of his life was the Bolivian ambassador to France or Spain. After 1920 he never returned to his native country.

Frequent armed conflicts developed in the mining communities. The workers were Aymara Indians, recruited from the Indian communities of the Altiplano. They were paid such low wages that all suffered from inadequate diet.

When the deep resentment of the Indians was expressed in strikes, order was restored by armed force. One of the first steps of the revolutionary government that came into power in 1952 was to nationalize the properties of the three mining interests, which, since that date, have been operated by the government.

Tin mining is not the only mining activity in the Eastern Cordillera. Bolivia has about 14 percent of the world's reserves of antimony, and about 2 percent of the world's reserves of tungsten. It also mines lead, zinc, silver, copper, and gold. The chief mining centers are shown on Map 83.

AGRICULTURAL COMMUNITIES

The densest clusters of rural people in Bolivia are found in the intermont basins and valleys at lower altitudes in the Eastern Cordillera. The population in these valleys, moreover, includes a larger proportion of Europeans or strongly Europeanized mestizos than is to be found in the other population clusters of Bolivia. The communities in the larger basins of Cochabamba, Sucre, and Tarija, together with many smaller communities in this general region, form the heart of the Bolivian state, for here are to be found the majority of the people for whom the sentiment of nationality has much real meaning. If some of these people reside temporarily in La Paz, their homes are nevertheless in the communities of the eastern slopes.

The valleys of the Eastern Cordillera south of the Yungas have been cut into the Puna surface by two chief river systems: one is the Río Grande, a tributary of the Río Mamoré, the Madeira, and the Amazon; the other is the Río Pilcomayo, a tributary of the Paraguay, the Paraná, and the Plata. The valleys in the Eastern Cordillera are of irregular width. There are places where they are narrowly constricted as the streams pass over stretches of resistant rocks; upstream from such places, however, the valleys generally broaden out to form long ribbons of flat land, or, in a few instances, relatively wide valley basins. For the most part the streams follow very winding courses, even where they are deeply intrenched in the Puna surface—a feature which the physiographers describe as "intrenched meanders." The valleys and basins have been excavated several thousand feet below the Puna surface. They form irregularly shaped belts where the temperature is considerably higher than that of the Puna country on either side. Since the streams carry an abundant supply of water, especially during the rainy summers, irrigation is possible even where the local rainfall is low.

COCHABAMBA, SUCRE, AND TARIJA

The largest concentration of settlement in Bolivia is in the Cochabamba Basin. There can be no doubt that living in this basin is much more comfortable than living in the towns of the Altiplano. Cochabamba is only 8,389 feet above sea level, and the average temperature of the coldest month is 57°, as compared with 43° at La Paz. The basin itself is about 15 miles long by 6 miles wide. In this restricted area, surrounded by high and almost uninhabited Puna, there is a population density of more than 325 people per square mile. The city of Cochabamba, with a population of just a little less than 100,000, is Bolivia's second city. The good agricultural land in the basin is used to grow maize, barley, alfalfa, and fruit.

The other basins and valleys of the Eastern Cordillera are similar in general character. The town of Sucre, long designated hopefully as the legal capital of the country, occupies a basin which, although smaller than that of Cochabamba, is also crowded with a dense agricultural population. The Basin of Tarija, still lower down on the eastern slopes, is famous for its fine vineyards and orchards of olives, pears, peaches, and apples. Both Cochabamba and Sucre have been able to market grain and cattle in the high mining communities, with which they were long connected only by trails, but Tarija found great difficulty in sending its products outside the immediate locality until the era of all-weather highways and motor trucks after 1950. The narrower valleys, not wide enough to be called basins, yet still wide enough for cultivation, are followed by many miles of ribbon-like farms. Here indeed are the garden spots of Bolivia.

PROBLEM OF ACCESSIBILITY

Settlements by people who practice the European way of living, however, do not prosper in isolation. Comfortable and productive as these eastern valleys undoubtedly are, to provide them with transportation was very costly. Such products as coca, cacao, and coffee, which can stand high transportation costs because they have a high value per unit of weight, cannot be grown in the country south of the Yungas because of the increasing aridity. For such bulky products as grain, or such perishable products as fruit, a cheap means of transportation is essential.

The chief difficulties which stand in the way of transportation development are not only the rugged terrain and the steep grades necessary to reach the Altiplano, but also the geographical arrangement of the settlements themselves. The focus of economic and political power is not sharp, because the people of this core of the Bolivian state are scattered in numerous relatively small communities, each anxious for government support of local projects, but each ready to block the projects which bring advantages only to other communities. The largest cluster of people is in the Cochabamba Basin, and although the density is high in this basin the area is not great. The other communities are still smaller, many of them strung in narrow bands along the winding valley bottoms. The physical difficulty of providing these scattered communities with a common political and economic focus, of gathering enough of the products of the Eastern Cordillera together in one place to pay for the

Tin mine in the Yungas, east of La Paz. *Photo by W. R. Grace & Co.*

expensive construction of railroads or roads constitutes a problem that is not easily solved, even with financial aid from outside.

The story of the attempt to provide Cochabamba with a rail connection with the highland mining centers illustrates the difficulties involved. Between 1913 and 1917 work on a railroad was in progress. In anticipation of the final solution of the problem of access to a market, there was a land boom in the Cochabamba Basin. Despite the reluctance of landowners to sell even parts of their estates, certain pieces of land actually were sold, but for prices ranging as high as $2,000 an acre. But the railroad, which cost more than $154,000 per mile, had either to tap a large volume of traffic or charge very high rates. The area served could not provide enough traffic to make low rates economically possible, and high rates prevailed. Thus as a result of costly transportation, heavy mortgages, and high land valuations, only losses came to the landowners. The general depression which followed cast a gloom over the community from which it was unable to recover until the 1950's. Later, when the railroad was extended eastward to Cliza, there was no land boom in that district.

All-weather highways and motor trucks, as elsewhere, provide a better solution to the problem of accessibility than do the railroads. Since the 1950's truck roads have been built to connect with the Peruvian highways on either side of Lake Titicaca. From near La Paz a main highway has been built along the old colonial road through Oruro to Potosí, and on through Tarija to connect with the Argentine highways along the eastern piedmont of the Andes. A road has been built from La Paz over a high pass in the Cordillera Real and down through the Yungas to a river port on the Río Beni. Another road connects Oruro with Cochabamba, and this has now been extended to Santa Cruz on the eastern plains. Both Oruro and Cochabamba are connected with Sucre, and from Sucre a road descends to the eastern piedmont on the edge of the Chaco. These truck roads for the first time provide the eastern valleys and basins with access to the highland urban centers and eastward with the plains. The opportunity is given to develop an enlarged domestic market for the agricultural products of the various parts of Bolivia. At the same time the airplane makes these once isolated and remote areas of settlement accessible for passengers and mail.

THE SETTLEMENT OF THE EASTERN PLAINS

The highway program has also resulted in making the eastern plains accessible to the highland centers. Santa Cruz is the chief transportation focus, and a beginning has been made in the construction of a marginal highway along the front of the mountains to connect Santa Cruz with the proposed Peruvian highway and southward with the Argentine highways at Yacuiba.

The part of Bolivia that lies east of La Paz, Cochabamba, and Tarija can be divided roughly into a northeastern region that is rainy and a southeastern region that is relatively dry. In both divisions new pioneer settlements within the mountains and along the mountain piedmont appear as soon as the highway provides access. But much of the land that extends far to the east to the borders of Brazil and Paraguay still lies outside of Bolivia's effective national territory.

The Bolivian Yungas forms a very distinct natural division of the country. The region includes the northeastern slopes of the Cordillera Real northeast of La Paz and north of Cochabamba. As a matter of fact, the Yungas forms the southern extremity of a region which extends unbroken along the eastern Andes from Colombia, across Ecuador and Peru, as far as Santa Cruz. In Peru this rainy and densely forested region is known as the eastern border valleys, and in Ecuador as the Oriente. The much narrower fringe of woodland which continues south of Santa Cruz along the mountains well into Argentina is composed of a lighter type of forest.

At the top of the Yungas stands the narrow but towering Cordillera Real. The pass by which access to the Yungas is gained from La Paz requires a climb to an elevation of over 15,000 feet. Then, on the eastern side, the drop to the lowlands of the Río Beni is amazingly steep. The railroad descends 14,250 feet in 50 miles and has the longest stretch of 6 percent grade of any railroad in the world. The motor truck road winds about through the rugged terrain as it descends toward the Beni.

A belt of sandstone ridges through which the Río Beni and its tributaries pass in a series of water gaps marks the foothills zone of the Andes. Beyond lie the eastern plains, covered partly with selva, partly with wet savanna. These plains of northeastern Bolivia, together with the neighboring part of southeastern Peru, suffer from extreme isolation, not only because of the steepness of the mountain barrier to the west, but also because the Río Madeira, which gathers the water of the Madre de Dios, the Beni, and the Mamoré, is interrupted by a long stretch of rapids as it flows northeast toward the Amazon. The Madeira-Mamoré Railroad, built in 1913, failed to reach the lower end of navigable water on the Beni at Riberalta.

These wet lowlands have not always been thinly populated. Recent studies by archeologists have revealed evidence that they were once occupied by a fairly dense population of agricultural people, who protected themselves against flooding by extensive dikes and terraces. By the time the Spaniards reached this region, however, the former population was gone.

Since the arrival of the Spaniards, three different kinds of products have attracted settlers to the Yungas and to the plains beyond. Among the earliest sources of wealth in this region was gold. The gravels of the Río Tipuani, located about 60 miles east of La Paz, within the zone of the Front Ranges, proved to contain large quantities of this metal; up to 1800, while Bolivia was producing about 10 percent of the total gold production of South America, the Yungas was the chief Bolivian source; even today placer works along the Río Tipuani are still active. All of the workers must be recruited in the Indian communities of the highlands.

Settlers have also been attracted to the valleys of the Yungas at intermediate altitudes, roughly from two to six thousand feet, by the possibilities of producing coca, coffee, and sugar. These products, like gold, have less difficulty in supporting the high costs of transportation than do the bulky products of the Eastern Cordillera south of the Yungas. Coca leaves have continued to find a steady demand among the highland Indians, as they did in the period before the arrival of the Spaniards; sugar, converted into sugar brandy, also finds a market steady enough to permit shipment from the Yungas. As in the eastern border valleys of Peru, however, the system by which relatively few landowners were enabled to make a profit was based on the exploitation of Indian labor—on production from which the costs of land and labor were all but eliminated.

Cinchona bark and rubber were also sources of wealth for settlers in the northeastern part of Bolivia. Highland Indians were called upon to collect these wild products from the selva; and many of the communities at the intermediate altitudes in the Yungas were all but abandoned in the rush for new profits. But first cinchona and then rubber were virtually eliminated as South American products by the cheaper plantation methods of Malaya, Sumatra, and Java. Before 1912, when South American production began rapidly to decline, rubber was so valuable that expensive railroad projects were undertaken, such as the line from La Paz. The Brazilians, as part of the payment for Acre Territory, agreed to build a railroad around the Madeira Rapids to give eastern Bolivia access to ocean shipping. The collapse of the rubber business in the Amazon came before this line had been completed to Riberalta, which is at the lower end of navigation on the Río Beni.

The scattered settlements along the rivers of the northeast were for a long time all but lost in the wilderness. Small quantities of rubber were collected and sent out. The wet savannas are still used for the grazing of cattle. Along the lower Beni are small communities of self-sufficient Japanese colonists who were settled there before World War II. Now, since the 1950's, the extension of roads and new facilities for river transportation are beginning to tie even these isolated places to the highland centers.

The Bolivian Chaco

The southeast of Bolivia differs from the northeast in that it is relatively dry and becomes drier as one approaches the Argentine border. The line of division between the northeast and the southeast can be drawn approximately along the latitude of Santa Cruz. Along the lower eastern mountain slopes, south of Santa Cruz, the wet forest occupies only a narrow band which continues southward well into Argentina. Most of the piedmont zone of the Andes, like the plains which stretch eastward to the Río Paraguay, is covered with dry scrub woodland and patches of dry savanna. The Front Ranges are composed of parallel ridges or cuestas of brilliant red sandstone, with broad longitudinal valleys from 2 to 15 miles in width. A trellis pattern of rivers is developed, with the main streams crossing the ridges in water gaps so narrow that access to the neighboring valleys must be gained by climbing over the intervening ridges rather than by following the rivers. The eastern plains form a part of that large area, shared by Bolivia, Paraguay, Brazil, and Argentina, which is known as the Gran Chaco.

The town of Santa Cruz is the focus of settlement in this region. It was founded in 1560 by settlers from Asunción. Santa Cruz is located about 20 miles east of the front of the mountains, in the midst of a well-watered area of gently sloping land, at an elevation of 1,575 feet. Its climate is humid, but not excessively so, and its temperatures are mild. In this isolated spot a few of the Spanish settlers received large grants of land. In spite of the comfort of the climate and the productivity of the land, the estates were so isolated from the rest of the world that they had to remain essentially self-sufficient. The road back to the Río Paraguay was long, and raids by unfriendly Chaco Indians frequent. But the climb to Cochabamba over steep, winding trails was also difficult. The only products that could pay the high cost of transportation were hides and *aguardiente*. Most of the Chaco area around Santa Cruz was used for cattle grazing.

The first break in the isolation of the Santa Cruz area came after World War I. In 1920 a concession was granted to a North American oil company to explore for oil along the Andean piedmont. Several oil fields were discovered along the front of the mountains south of Santa Cruz, near the Argentine border. It seemed certain that much larger oil sources would be discovered eventually. But Bolivia was not enthusiastic about permitting the development of these fields by foreign-owned corporations or about marketing the oil in oil-poor Argentina and Brazil.

From 1932 to 1935 Bolivia was engaged in a war with Paraguay. Settlers from Asunción had moved into the disputed southeastern part of the Chaco where both countries claimed sovereignty. The Paraguayans, brilliantly led and more accustomed to conditions in this lowland area than were the soldiers brought down from the highlands, were victorious. When the war came to an end in 1935 the new boundary was drawn along the line reached by the Paraguayans. Bolivia lost a large part of the Chaco which it had claimed but never effectively occupied; but the Paraguayans failed to advance far enough to reach the Andean piedmont with its potential oil fields.

The war had the effect of jarring the Bolivians into action. The concessions of the North American corporation, which had been held in reserve and had not been further explored, were expropriated in 1937. A government-owned corporation—the *Yacimientos Petroliferios Fiscales Bolivianos* (YPFB)—was formed to undertake responsibility for developing the oil fields. The actual work of exploration, the drilling of wells, the building of refineries and pipelines, was done by foreign-owned corporations under contract with YPFB. As a result, a considerable development of oil production from the fields south of Santa Cruz took place. In 1965 about 75 percent of the total Bolivian oil production came from these fields; but by this time new and very promising oil fields had been opened up north of Santa Cruz. Southeast of Santa Cruz a large gas field was discovered. To get all this oil and gas to a market, pipelines were built. The first pipeline connected southward to Argentina and then up into the mountains to Sucre, Cochabamba and La Paz. In 1966 this line was extended to Arica, and the first shipment of Bolivian crude oil went out from that port in northern Chile. Oil refineries were built in Cochabamba, Sucre, Santa Cruz, and in the oil fields of southern Bolivia. In 1967 a gas pipeline was planned to carry gas all the way eastward to the city of São Paulo in Brazil.

Meanwhile the Santa Cruz area had also become a major center of new pioneer farm settlement. The government made great efforts to convince the highland Indian farmers that life in the eastern lowlands was really not bad. A small movement of new colonists started after the road to Santa Cruz was completed in 1953, and by 1967 the number of migrants had greatly increased. Land was available in the lowlands for the overcrowded communities of Cochabamba and the Titicaca Basin. Sugarcane, maize, rice, and various fruits were produced and transported to the city markets in the highlands by motor truck.

Bolivia as a Political Unit

A few decades ago the continued possession of the Chaco by Bolivia would have seemed most unlikely. The isolation of the Chaco from the rest of Bolivia was a matter of grave danger for international peace when it became clear that the Chaco would some day emerge as an important source of oil. The Chaco was easily accessible to Brazil and Argentina, both of which lack sufficient oil; the stage was set for conflict. Even if actual armed invasion is made difficult as a result of the agreements of the Organization of American States, nevertheless acts short of war can also disturb the peace. The secession of the colonists around Santa Cruz from the rest of Bolivia was unsuccessfully attempted in 1959.

If Bolivia is to survive as a political entity two compelling needs must be met. First, the various diverse sections of the country must be brought together by better facilities for transportation and by the organization of a national market accessible to all the previously isolated parts. And second, the political leaders must formulate a state-idea powerful enough to unite a majority of the people against the forces of disintegration. In 1967, with foreign aid, both needs had been recognized and steps to do something about them had been taken.

The Economic Situation

Bolivia held a census in 1950 which counted a little over 3 million people. In 1967 the population was estimated at 3,801,000—a rate of growth of about 1.4 percent per year. Some 63 percent of the working force was engaged in agriculture. Bolivia stood twenty-second out of 24 in Latin America in terms of gross national product per capita, which means that most of the people are hopelessly poor.

No program of economic development can get underway until certain preconditions are met. In the first place, nearly 70 percent of the people are illiterate. Until skills can be taught there is no hope of improving the productivity of the farmers, and no hope of establishing modern manufacturing industries. People must be taught to read and write before they can develop a desire for economic development, as well as a capacity to play the essential roles of both producer and consumer in an integrated national economy.

Before 1952 the minority of wealthy landowners and mine owners, along with the higher officers of the army, lived in a world apart. The great majority of the inhabitants of Bolivia were Indian farmers who remained essentially outside of the economic system of buying and selling. Since 1952 an effort has been made to improve the living conditions of these people and to bring them into a national economy. There is still a long way to go.

The Bolivian government is attempting to improve the productivity of mining. When the mines were expropriated in 1952, production dropped. In the late 1960's production was somewhat improved, but production per miner was still very low—partly because of the policy of giving employment to all the workers who had been engaged in mining. In 1966, on the other hand, Bolivia's increase in the production of oil over 1965 was more than 60 percent—the largest rate of increase in all Latin America.

Minerals make up some 98 percent of Bolivia's exports. Of these, tin in 1964 accounted for 72 percent, silver 5 percent, and lead 4 percent. Whereas Bolivia in 1955 was exporting 20 percent of the world's tin, by 1966 it exported only 11 percent. Most of the world's tin comes from Malaysia and Indonesia, where the ore is dredged from stream gravels. In Bolivia the ore of tin must be dug out of solid rock in mines located at very high altitudes. The ore must be smelted, and until 1968, when a tin smelter was built in Oruro, all the smelting was done in England and the United States.

ROUTES OF ACCESS TO THE HIGHLANDS

Ever since the discovery of the silver at Potosí a major problem in the high Andes has been the development of routes of access to the coast. Four chief routes have been utilized since the early colonial period. Three of them connect Bolivia with the Pacific ports of Mollendo (Matarani), Arica, and Antofagasta; the fourth route follows the old colonial highway into Argentina. Along all four of these routes railroads and truck roads have now been built.

The flow of traffic between the settlements which form the center of the Bolivian state and the coast has shifted from time to time as the various railroads have been completed. The first railroad to be built, in 1874, was the line from Mollendo to the port of Puno on Lake Titicaca. Shortly after this, steamer service was inaugurated on the lake between Puno and Guaqui. By 1902, railroad and steamer provided a relatively fast connection between La Paz and the sea, and for a time the copper from Corocoro was sent out by this route instead of over the old mule and llama trail to Arica.

Meanwhile, in 1889, a railroad was built from Antofagasta to Uyuni, and was extended in 1892 to Oruro and in 1910 to La Paz. The opening of this line drained off all the mineral production of southern Bolivia, in spite of the fact that in 1884 Bolivia had lost to Chile its seaport, Antofagasta. The third railroad to reach the highlands was built from Arica to La Paz in 1913, with a short spur to Corocoro. This railroad, which makes use of a long section of rack and cog, is by far the shortest of the three routes to the Pacific. Arica is now constituted as an international port with a Bolivian customs house. In spite of the fact that it remains outside of the Bolivian national territory, this port is once again becoming the chief outlet on the Pacific, regaining a position it held during the colonial period when it was reached by mule trails not only from La Paz but also directly from Oruro. Arica is the terminus of the oil pipeline from the eastern plains.

The railroad which extends southeastward to Argentina by way of La Quiaca, Jujuy, and Tucumán, was completed in 1925. This is now competing, but not with great success, for a share of the exports which originate south of Potosí.

In the modern period, as in Peru, highway construction is proving less costly. A truck road climbs to Puno from Arequipa and continues along the southwestern shore of Lake Titicaca into Bolivia. This new highway now closely parallels the old colonial mule trail, running near La Paz, southward to Potosí, and thence on into Argentina. Now, also, a railroad is projected to complete the gap between Puno and the Bolivian railroads. When completed, this might again permit the Peruvian route to compete with the line to Arica. Since 1960 numerous feeder roads connect with this main route. Important steps have been taken to meet the first of the two needs in the formation of a viable state—the transportation facilities to tie the separate areas of concentrated settlement together.

The Political Situation

Steps have also been taken to formulate a state-idea to which people of Spanish ancestry as well as those of Indian ancestry can give their support. To take such steps required a fundamental change in the established political and social institutions, and such change in a country where a majority of the people are illiterate Indians requires a revolutionary movement.

Government in Bolivia had long been based on military power. The three large tin-mining corporations—Patiño, Hochschild, and Aramayo—held the political power, and decisions of policy were made in Paris or New York, not in La Paz. The army kept order in Bolivia and did not hesitate to use force in maintaining that order. But the war with Paraguay dealt the army a humiliating defeat. The soldiers recruited among the Indians for service in the war not only experienced the shock of losing a war, but also for the first time had an opportunity to look beyond the limited horizons of their ancestral communities. After the war, many drifted to the cities or to the mines, where they became second-class citizens. The national election of 1951 revealed the nature of the problem: out of a population of three and a half million, less than 200,000 were permitted to vote. The Quechuas could endure such a situation stolidly; but the Aymaras were inclined to resort to violence.

In 1952 a revolutionary party seized control of the government. The leader was Víctor Paz Estenssoro, a member of the landowning class, an intellectual, a man of strong social idealism and sense of nationalism. The party was the *Movimiento Nacionalista Revolucionario,* or MNR, which set forth a statement of objectives similar to those formulated by APRA in Peru. The MNR had the support of a majority of the people—the intellectuals, the students, the city workers, and the miners. Opposed were the landowners, the army officers, and some of the illiterate tenant farmers who had only a hazy idea of what issues were involved.

The first step was the expropriation of the tin mines, in December 1952. The decree was enormously popular because educated Bolivians felt that the corporations were bigger than the state and that they were exploiting the resources of the state without investing very much in the economic development of Bolivia. The Patiño interests were producing 60 to 65 percent of the value of all tin exports, and the other two together 10 or 15 percent. Patiño's heirs were living in luxury in Paris and New York, while the miners in Bolivia were suffering starvation and disease. The housing and medical services provided by the mine owners could not outweigh the well-known fact that almost everyone employed in the mines was in debt to the company stores. So the expropriation of the mines was inevitable. The compensation that was eventually paid was not considered adequate by the owners.

The second step, in August 1953, was the agrarian reform law. The little parcels of land that the landlords had given to their tenant workers to use for their own subsistence immediately became the properties of those who worked them. A plan was announced whereby farm families could be granted additional land expropriated from the large holdings and which the tenant farmers had formerly cultivated for the benefit of the owners. In the Cochabamba Basin some groups of farmers seized the large properties by force, but generally this redistribution of land was accomplished by legal steps. No property was expropriated if it was being cultivated by machinery and by modern technology. Furthermore, the owners of expropriated land were compensated.

During this period the communists presented a plan for the immediate expropriation of land without compensation and for the formation of collectives. The MNR had to defend its policies against assaults both from the left and the right. To guard against military interference from the right, the army was completely reorganized in 1953. To guard against interference from the left the peasants were armed and organized into a militia.

During this period of agrarian reform certain difficulties appeared. In the first place no adequate surveys of land quality were made. The advisors from Mexico had made no such survey and did not recommend it to the Bolivians. Furthermore it proved impossible even to make maps of properties due to the lack of trained surveyors. In 1953 there were not more than 300 trained map-makers in all of Bolivia; and with great effort this number was raised to 642 in 1956—still quite inadequate for the task of a national land redistribution program. And in the second place, there was not nearly enough arable land to provide farms for all the people who wanted farms. Each farmer was to be given land ranging from 25 to 2,000 acres, depending on the potential productivity. But with no maps of potential productivity the actual land distribution resulted in many inequities. Very soon it became apparent that very few of the farmers could be given farms large enough for the support of a family. This was the underlying situation that stimulated the migration of colonists to the eastern plains.

Important results have come from Bolivia's revolution. It can be said that *"Ya no hay indios en Bolivia"*—now there are no Indians in Bolivia. The former tenant farmers are know officially as *campesinos,* or peasants. They are granted equal treatment before the law and the right to discuss issues of public policy and to express their wishes through the ballot. The vast majority of the people who have benefited from the revolution have found a state-idea for supporting their form of government. But unfortunately in such a period of rapid change there are ample opportunities for personal gain, and some of those in positions of power have taken full advantage of these opportunities. The revolutionary government would have collapsed quite soon had it not been for the financial assistance of the United States, where the responsible officials in charge of Latin-American policy were convinced that the failure of the revolutionary program would have offered an open invitation for a communist take-over.

In 1964 opposition political parties threatened the continued rule of the MNR. In a general election—with only MNR candidates on the ballot—the MNR received the endorsement of 69 percent of the electorate, in spite of efforts by the opposition to boycott the election. Strikes declared by the miners' unions against the government were a reaction to the declared policy of holding back on wage increases. When the public order seemed again to be threatened, the army, air force, and national police joined forces to seize the government and send Paz Estenssoro into exile.

After fifteen years of rule by the MNR, certain steps have been taken that cannot be retraced. There can be no return to the traditional agrarian system of large landowners and tenant farmers. The *campesinos* are not likely to accept again the position of subservience they occupied as Indians. The majority of the people of Bolivia who felt that for a time Bolivia had a system of government worthy of their support are not likely to accept a return to military dictatorship of the traditional kind. Furthermore, the new facilities for transporting people and goods among Bolivia's separated areas of concentrated settlement, can, if they are properly maintained, continue to knit the state more closely into a coherent unity. But the problems of political stability and of economic development have yet to be solved. It would seem that the Bolivians are still beset by so many critical problems that the struggle to establish order and to create a coherent state have become even more difficult than they were before the revolution.

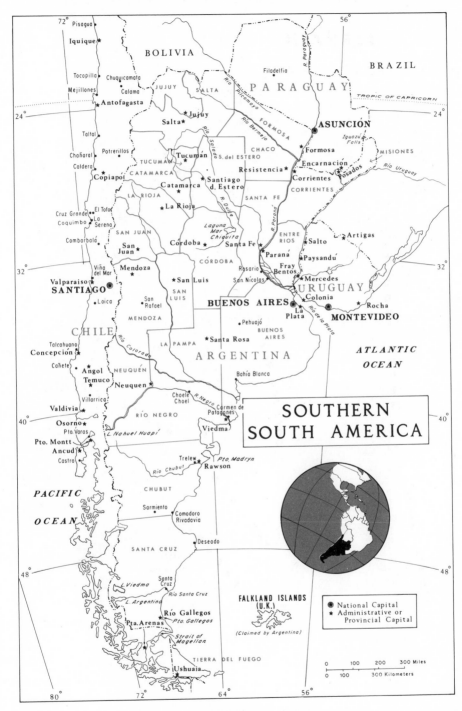

SOUTHERN SOUTH AMERICA

BOLIVIA

BRAZIL

PARAGUAY

TROPIC OF CAPRICORN

72° Pisagua
Iquique★
Tocopilla · Chuquicamata
Mejillones · Calama
▪Antofagasta
24°
Taltal
Chañaral · Potrerillos
Caldera
▪Copiapó
Cruz Grande · El Tofo
Coquimbo · La Serena
Combarbalá
Viña del Mar
Valparaiso★
SANTIAGO◉
· Loica · San Rafael
CHILE
Talcahuano
Concepción★
Cañete
▪Angol
Temuco★
Villarrica·
Valdivia★
40°
Osorno★
Pto. Varas
Pto. Montt★
Ancud★
Castro·

PACIFIC

OCEAN

48°

80°

JUJUY · SALTA
★Jujuy
Salta★
TUCUMÁN ★Tucumán
CATAMARCA
Copiapó · Catamarca★ · Santiago d. Estero
LA RIOJA · ★La Rioja
SAN JUAN
San★ Juan · Córdoba★
Mendoza★
SAN LUIS
MENDOZA
★San Luis
LA PAMPA
★Santa Rosa
NEUQUÉN
Neuquen★
Choele Choel
RÍO NEGRO
Viedma★
L. Nahuel Huapí
Trelew★ · Pto. Madryn
Río Chubut · Rawson★
CHUBUT
Sarmiento· · Comodoro Rivadavia
· Deseado
SANTA CRUZ
L. Viedma · Santa Cruz
L. Argentino · Río Santa Cruz
Río Gallegos
Pta.Arenas★ · Pto. Gallegos
Strait of Magellan
TIERRA DEL FUEGO
Ushuaia▪

Filadelfia·
R. Pilcomayo
Río Bermejo
FORMOSA
CHACO
S. del ESTERO
Resistencia★
SANTA FE
R. Dulce
Laguna Mar Chiquita
Santa Fe★
CÓRDOBA
Rosario·
San Nicolás·
Pehuajó·
BUENOS AIRES
ARGENTINA
Bahía Blanca·
Carmen de Patagones·

56°
R. Paraguay
ASUNCIÓN◉
Iguazú Falls
Formosa·
Encarnación★ · MISIONES
Corrientes★ · Posadas★
CORRIENTES · Río Uruguay
ENTRE RIOS · Salto★ · ★Artigas
Paraná★ · ·Paysandú
Fray Bentos · ·Mercedes
BUENOS AIRES◉ · Colonia★
La Plata · ·Rocha
URUGUAY · **MONTEVIDEO**◉

ATLANTIC

OCEAN

FALKLAND ISLANDS (U.K.)

(Claimed by Argentina)

◉ National Capital
★ Administrative or Provincial Capital

| 0 | 100 | 200 | 300 Miles |
| 0 | 100 | | 300 Kilometers |

24°
32°
40°
48°

72° · 64° · 56°

Map 86

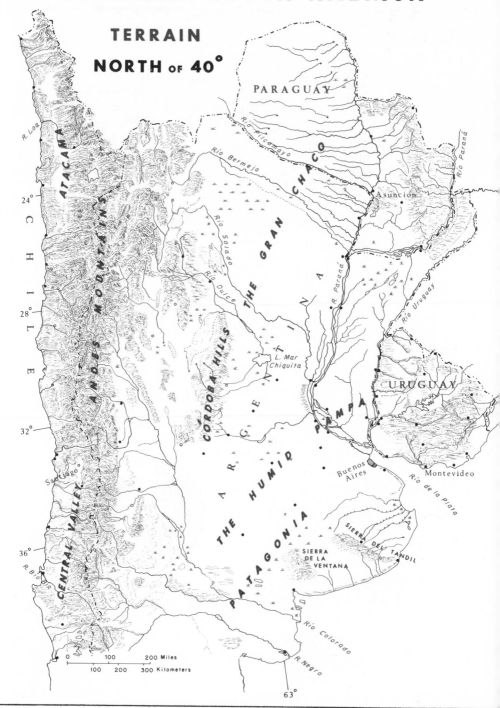

SOUTHERN SOUTH AMERICA

TERRAIN
NORTH OF 40°

PARAGUAY

R. Loa

ATACAMA

C H I L E

ANDES MOUNTAINS

CORDOBA HILLS

THE GRAN CHACO

Río Pilcomayo

Río Bermejo

Río Salado

Río Dulce

Asunción

A R G E N T I N A

R. Paraná

Río Paraná

L. Mar
Chiquita

Río Uruguay

URUGUAY

THE HUMID PAMPA

Buenos
Aires

Santiago

CENTRAL VALLEY

R. Bío-Bío

Montevideo

Río de la Plata

P A T A G O N I A

SIERRA
DE LA
VENTANA

SIERRA DEL TANDIL

Río Colorado

R. Negro

24°

28°

32°

36°

63°

0   100   200 Miles

100   200   300 Kilometers

Map 87

SOUTHERN SOUTH AMERICA

SOUTH OF 40°

ARGENTINA

Río Negro

TERRAIN

ISLA
DE
CHILOÉ

R.Chubut

Golfo de
San Jorge

R.Deseado

ATLANTIC

OCEAN

PACIFIC

R.Chico

OCEAN

Strait of Magellan

ISLA GRANDE

40°
44°
48°
52°

40°
44°
48°
52°

72°
63°
57°

0   100   200 Miles
10   200   300 Kilometers

Map 88

24°

28°

32°

36°

○   •   Urban Centers
────────   Roads
┼┼┼┼┼┼   Railroad
╷╷╷╷╷╷╷╷   Canal

0   100   200 Miles
   100   200   300 Kilometers

63°

Map 89

538

SOUTHERN SOUTH AMERICA

SOUTH OF 40°

ARGENTINA

ATLANTIC

OCEAN

CHILE

TRANSPORTATION

+++++++++ Railroad

————— All Weather Road

∘ • Urban Center

40°

44°

48°

52°

40°

44°

48°

52°

0   100   200 Miles

10   200   300 Kilometers

72°   63°   57°

Map 90

539

SOUTHERN SOUTH AMERICA

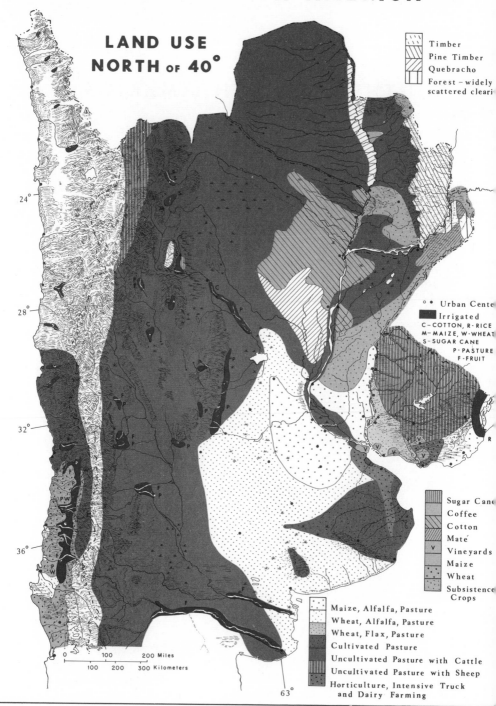

LAND USE
NORTH OF 40°

Timber
Pine Timber
Quebracho
Forest – widely
scattered cleari

° • Urban Cente
■ Irrigated
C – COTTON, R – RICE
M – MAIZE, W – WHEAT
S – SUGAR CANE
P – PASTURE
F – FRUIT

Sugar Cane
Coffee
Cotton
Maté
V Vineyards
Maize
Wheat
Subsistence
    Crops

Maize, Alfalfa, Pasture
Wheat, Alfalfa, Pasture
Wheat, Flax, Pasture
Cultivated Pasture
Uncultivated Pasture with Cattle
Uncultivated Pasture with Sheep
Horticulture, Intensive Truck
    and Dairy Farming

24°
28°
32°
36°

0   100   200 Miles
  100   200   300 Kilometers

63°

Map 91

SOUTHERN SOUTH AMERICA

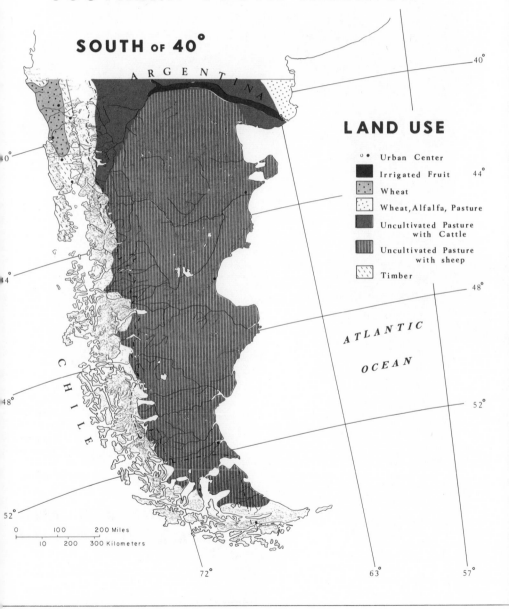

SOUTH of 40°

ARGENTINA

CHILE

40°

40°

44°

48°

52°

LAND USE

∘ •	Urban Center
■	Irrigated Fruit
▨	Wheat
⋰	Wheat, Alfalfa, Pasture
▦	Uncultivated Pasture with Cattle
▥	Uncultivated Pasture with sheep
⋱	Timber

44°

48°

ATLANTIC

OCEAN

52°

0   100   200 Miles

10   200   300 Kilometers

72°

63°

57°

Map 92

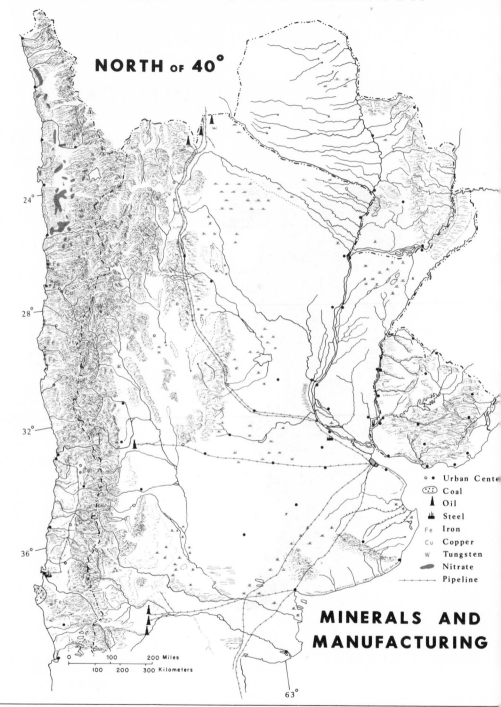

NORTH OF 40°

	Urban Center
	Coal
	Oil
	Steel
Fe	Iron
Cu	Copper
W	Tungsten
	Nitrate
	Pipeline

MINERALS AND MANUFACTURING

100   200 Miles

100   200   300 Kilometers

Map 93

SOUTHERN SOUTH AMERICA

SOUTH OF 40°

ARGENTINA

ATLANTIC

OCEAN

CHILE

MINERALS
AND
MANUFACTURING

```
···  Coal
▲    Oil
──── Pipeline
∘•   Urban Center
```

40°

44°

48°

52°

0   100   200 Miles
  10   200   300 Kilometers

40°

0°

4°

48°

52°

72°   63°   57°

Map 94

543

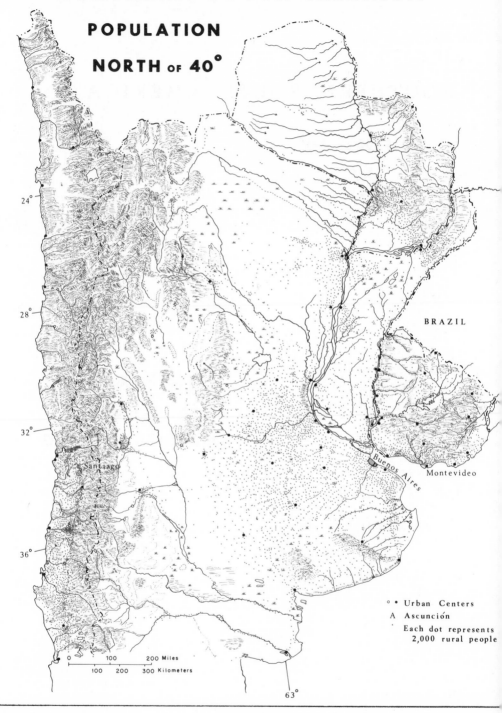

SOUTHERN SOUTH AMERICA

POPULATION

NORTH OF 40°

24°

28°

BRAZIL

32°

Santiago

Buenos Aires

Montevideo

36°

○ • Urban Centers

A Ascunción

Each dot represents
2,000 rural people

0   100   200 Miles

100   200   300 Kilometers

63°

Map 95

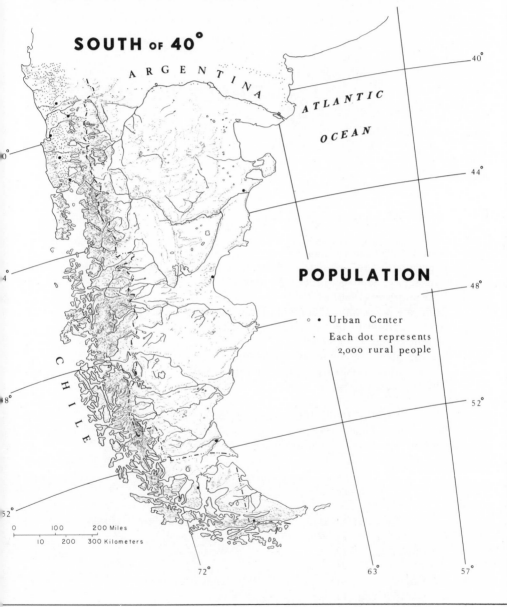

SOUTHERN SOUTH AMERICA

SOUTH OF 40°

ARGENTINA

ATLANTIC

OCEAN

CHILE

POPULATION

○ • Urban Center

Each dot represents
2,000 rural people

40°

44°

48°

52°

72°   63°   57°

0   100   200 Miles

10   200   300 Kilometers

Map 96

República de Chile

Area: 292,257 square miles
Population: (1967 estimate) 9,000,000; (last census, 1960) 7,374,115
Capital city: Santiago; (1966) 2,270,000
Percent urban: (1960) 67.2
Birth rate per 1,000: (1966) 32.8; Death rate per 1,000: (1966) 11.2
Annual percent of increase: (1958–64) 2.3
Percent literate: (1960) 83.6
Percent labor force in agriculture: (1960) 27.5
Gross national product per capita: (1966) $501
Unit of currency: escudo (1968, 5.70 per dollar)

COMMERCE, 1964 *(expressed in percentage of values)*
Percent total Latin-American exports: 6.3 (1956,7)
Percent total Latin-American imports: 7.1

Exports (1965)

copper 59	iron ore 11	nitrate 5

Exports to (1965)		**Imports from (1965)**	
United States	31 (1956, 51)	United States	39 (1956, 45)
West Germany	13	West Germany	11
Japan	11	Argentina	8
Netherlands	11	United Kingdom	6
United Kingdom	11		

Chapter 21 □ Chile

The core of the Chilean state is made up of one area of concentrated settlement. But the whole of the national territory stretches for 2,630 miles from Arica, at latitude 18°28′ S., to Cape Horn, at latitude 55°59′ S.; and at no place is the eastern border of the country as much as 250 miles from the sea.[1] Southern Chile is one of the rainiest parts of South America, where glaciers descend from snow-covered mountains to a deeply fiorded coast. Northern Chile is one of the driest places on earth; in it is one of the few weather stations where no rain has ever been recorded. Yet these two ends are Chilean only in the sense of possession. The real Chile is the beautiful land between: a land which forms a narrow strip between high mountains and the sea; a land covered with fields of growing crops and green pastures, bordered by graceful rows of Lombardy poplars, eucalyptus, or weeping willows; a land of dense population.

The geographical unity of Chile's one central cluster of people gave this country a distinct advantage in the development of a coherent society. This advantage, moreover, was supported by a racial homogeneity which is greater

---

[1]The shape of this national territory raises certain difficulties in cartography. In this book the whole of southern South America, including Chile, Paraguay, Argentina, and Uruguay, is shown on Map 86. Maps 87 to 96 inclusive are enlargements of the part of southern South America that lies north of 40°S. and the part that lies south of 40°S. Still larger-scale maps of middle Chile are Maps 97 and 98, the Atacama is on Map 99, and the Chilean lake district is on Map 100.

In addition to the parts of Chile shown on these maps, Chile also owns several small islands far out in the Pacific Ocean: Rapa Nui (Easter Island), Sala y Gomez, San Felix, San Ambrosio, and Juan Fernandez. Chile also claims a pie-shaped sector of the Antarctic continent between 50° and 90° west longitude.

than that of any other country on the west coast of South America. To be sure, the usual social distinction appeared between the small minority of landowning aristocrats and the large majority of landless tenants, but this social gap was bridged in Chile by the strongly paternalistic character of the system. More than elsewhere on the west coast, the landowners lived on their estates and took a very definite part in the life of the rural communities. In this respect the development of Chile has been notably different from that of the countries to the north where the landowners usually reside in the cities.

The traditional preindustrial society has now been challenged. Large private estates with tenant workers are still to be found in rural Chile, but if current programs are carried out, by 1972 they will be broken up and the land redistributed through sale. The primitive agricultural methods and inefficient forms of land use are in process of rapid change. Meanwhile, there has been a considerable development of manufacturing in the cities. A modern steel plant has been built near Concepción. In Concepción, Santiago, Valparaiso, and Validivia there are many new factories producing consumer goods. The industrial society brings new diversity to the Chilean scene; people who work for wages and people whose prestige is based on financial success in the operation or ownership of businesses have developed attitudes and objectives which are utterly foreign to those of the people of traditional agrarian society. So far the transformation in Chile has been going forward with much controversy but with a minimum of conflict.

The People

Chile is a mestizo country. Its population includes none of the profound racial diversities found in the lands farther north. Only about 5 percent are pure-blooded Indians. The number of people of Spanish descent whose ancestry remains unmixed is approximately 30 percent. The remaining 65 percent are mixtures of Indian and Spanish in various degrees. This mestizo group is more Spanish than are the mestizo groups of Peru, Bolivia, and Ecuador. It is said that in the more prominent families of Chile there have been no Indian ancestors for eight or nine generations.

The Indians

The Chilean Indians were not at all like the Quechua and the Aymara groups which had been dominated by Inca rule. It has been estimated that at the time of the Spanish conquest there were some 500,000 natives in the middle part of Chile, roughly between the modern Valparaiso and Puerto Montt. In the forests south of the Río Bío-Bío, the warlike Araucanians had held the Incas at bay, using the woods to good advantage in fighting armies whose previous experience had been in open country. The Araucanians had achieved a culture level not unlike that of the Iroquois of North America:

they were hunters and fishers, but they derived a large part of their food supply from a shifting cultivation of maize.

The Araucanian tribes inhabiting the more open country north of the Río Bío-Bío were brought under the influence of the Incas. The latter succeeded in pushing their conquest south to the Río Maule (Map 5, p. 14), but since the road to Cuzco was long and difficult, the hold on this remote frontier was weak. Just inland from Valparaiso lies a basin watered by the Río Aconcagua to which the Incas gave the name "Vale of Chile," and in which they established their southernmost settlement. South of the Vale of Chile, in the vicinity of the present city of Santiago, the Araucanian tribes had either been taught or had discovered how to build simple irrigation ditches and how to raise crops year after year on the same land. Thus fixed in position, they formed a kind of "march" to protect the Inca settlements farther north from the attacks of the still warlike and seminomadic tribes from the southern forests. These sedentary Araucanians, rather than the more primitive tribes farther south, made the largest contribution to the racial composition of the Chilean mestizo. But Inca rule, even in the Vale of Chile, was not able to wipe out the strong sense of independence and individual initiative which still distinguishes the descendants of the Araucanian tribes from the descendants of the Andean Indians.

The Spanish Conquest and Race Mixture

The first Spanish explorers to penetrate the really formidable barriers that isolated middle Chile were moved by the same desires as those which led Pizarro to his conquest of Peru. But Chile had little to offer. Its stream gravels contained little gold, and its Indians were much less docile than those of Peru. When Pedro de Valdivia tried to organize an expedition he found few volunteers ready to face the hardships of the overland march to a land of reported poverty. Nevertheless, with a small army, he reached middle Chile and founded the city of Santiago in 1541 and the city of Concepción in 1550. Almost at once the newcomers were involved in war with the Araucanians—a war which continued with few interruptions until the second half of the nineteenth century. In spite of the absence of precious metals and the warlike character of the Indians, the Spaniards were drawn to middle Chile because of the productivity of its soils and because of its attractive climate. In many respects this new land reminded the Spaniards of Andalucía, the province of southern Spain from which most of them had come. The surface of middle Chile was soon marked off in big agricultural or pastoral estates, the ownership of which created a new aristocracy. Those who desired wealth in the form of gold went elsewhere.

The Spaniards who first came to Chile seem, like the Indians, to have been different from those who established themselves in other parts of Spanish America. During the first two centuries most of the invaders came from the south of Spain, from those provinces in which the Moorish influence had been present longest and was most penetrating. After the beginning of the eighteenth century, however, Chile began to attract more and more people from the northern part of Spain, and these, according to the Chilean writer Luis Thayer Ojeda, were a very different type from the restless, adventure-loving southerners.

Race mixture was as free and as little accompanied by prejudice in middle Chile as in other parts of Latin America. There were few white women in Chile during the early years of the Spanish conquest, and each soldier was soon attended by several native women. It is said that there were four women to every man in the frontier posts established to protect the settlements against Araucanian raids; in one week during the year 1580, 60 children were born at a post where 160 men were stationed. The territory was soon swarming with mestizo children produced by the mating of two exceedingly virile and warlike racial types—the best of the Spanish soldiers, selected for bravery and endurance because of the difficulty of reaching Chile and the women they had captured from the indomitable natives.

Social differences soon began to appear in this new society. The contrast between the owners of land and those who did not own land was becoming greater and greater, in spite of the fact that no racial differences separated these two classes. Among the mestizo children, the girls had the better chance to marry well; the boys usually were less fortunate. Indian and Spanish blood, however, mixed freely whether among the landowning aristocracy or among the tenants who were becoming more and more closely attached to the big estates.

Out of this mixture has come a new racial type, the Chilean mestizo, who is a far more virile and energetic person than the mestizo produced by the mating of Spanish and Quechua. The Chilean laborer, whether in the city or the country, is noted for physical strength, endurance, bravery, loyalty, and a spirit of independence. To what extent these qualities are the result of a more invigorating climate, or of a better diet, or of superior racial inheritance contributed both by the Indian and Spanish elements, cannot be estimated. It is more than likely that all these things have contributed to the peculiar qualities of the Chilean people.

Concentration of People in Middle Chile

The result of four centuries of Spanish control in Chile has been the notable concentration of people of this type in the region which may be termed the "cradle of Chilean nationality." In the original Vale of Chile, and in the Central Valley between Santiago and Concepción, a relatively dense population has been built up. In the rural areas around Santiago the density is well over 250 per square mile. Santiago itself is a city of over 2 million; Valparaiso, together with Viña del Mar, has a population of over 400,000;

and Concepción's metropolitan area includes some 270,000. Antofagasta is also over 100,000.

The Chilean nation is formed around just one nucleus of concentrated settlement. About 72 percent of the total population is in middle Chile, the area between Coquimbo and the Río Bío-Bío near Concepción. If to this core area is added the northernmost part of southern Chile, between the Río Bío-Bío and Puerto Montt, this includes 90 percent of all the people in Chile. In middle Chile are concentrated all the activities of Chilean life; the political, economic, social, and artistic center of the nation is Santiago. As far as politics are concerned, there is no subdivision of the national territory into provinces or departments: there are no provincial legislatures, no state governors, no separate police forces. The provinces of Chile are used chiefly for census purposes.

Middle Chile

The core of the Chilean nation in middle Chile is by no means simple in its internal arrangement. Although this small ribbon of territory has a degree of natural unity because of its climate, the surface features divide it into smaller units (Map 97).

Surface Features

In the first place, from one-third to one-half of the width of middle Chile is occupied by the high ranges of the Andes. South of about latitude 27° S. the Andes narrow down to one dominant cordillera on the crest of which stand some of the highest peaks of the continent. At the head of the Río Aconcagua in Argentina, Mt. Aconcagua reaches an elevation of 22,835 feet —the highest peak in the American Hemisphere. As far as latitude 33° S. the passes over the cordillera are all above 10,000 feet. South of Talca a string of active volcanoes stands out prominently to the west of the main range. The summits of the higher mountains are snow-covered; the lower slopes are densely forested; and between the trees and the permanent snow the zone of alpine pastures becomes narrower and narrower toward the south, until it disappears entirely south of about 40° S. The snow line at latitude 33° S., near Santiago, is at an elevation of between 13,100 and 14,700 feet; but it drops rapidly toward the south, reaching only about 11,500 feet at latitude 35° S.

Another third of the width of middle Chile is occupied by a zone of coastal plateaus and terraces. The highest elevations are reached in the north, where the flat-topped surfaces stand some 7,000 feet above sea level. In the south, around Concepción, the highest elevations are between 1,000 and 2,000 feet. The plateaus are deeply dissected by small streams which have cut steep-sided, V-shaped ravines, and are interrupted by larger valleys where the

MIDDLE CHILE

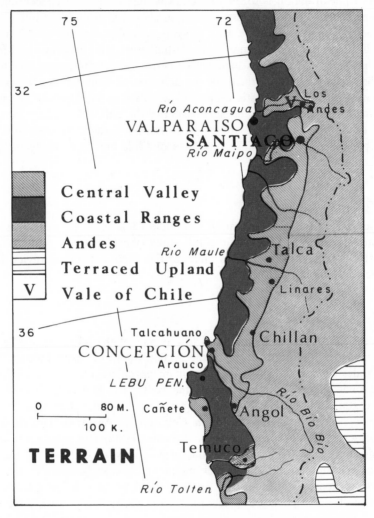

Map 97

Andean streams flow through to the ocean. Along most of the coast the cliffs rise from the edge of the water, and there are no harbors except where promontories give partial protection from the prevailing southerly winds, as at Valparaiso, Talcahuano (the port for Concepción), and Arauco.

Between the Andes and the coastal plateaus there is a structural depression of varying width known as the Central Valley. The streams which descend from the Andes cross this depression more or less at right angles and plunge through canyons in the plateaus to reach the sea. Only along the southernmost of the rivers, the Río Bío-Bío, does a broad, flat-floored valley extend all the way to the Pacific. The Central Valley is divided by spurs of the Andes into separate basins, in some cases completely separated from the basins to the north and the south. Between Santiago and Concepción, these basins are continuous; along the Bío-Bío the Central Valley is between 30 and 50 miles wide. The Vale of Chile, along the Río Aconcagua, is isolated by a mountain spur from the valley of the Río Mapocho, in which Santiago is located, and this spur requires a climb to about 2,600 feet in crossing from one basin to the other. Between the Vale of Chile and the beginning of the desert at Coquimbo the spurs of the Andes extend so far westward that the basins of the Central Valley are pinched out.

The floors of the basins which form the Central Valley are not level. The Andean streams have built great alluvial fans sloping from east to west. The elevation of the Central Valley near Santiago varies from 2,300 feet along the mountain front to 1,100 feet where the Río Maipo enters the zone of coastal plateaus. Santiago itself is at an elevation of 1,700 feet above the sea. The Central Valley along the Río Bío-Bío is much lower, sloping from about 900 feet to about 300 feet.

Climate and Vegetation

The most distinctive feature of middle Chile is the climate. Between Coquimbo at latitude 30° S. and Concepción south of latitude 36° S. there is a transition between the desert of the north and the continuously rainy lands to the south. This is a climate of mild, wet winters and cool, dry summers, to which the name "mediterranean" is commonly applied. A similar type of climate is found on the west coasts of all the continents between 30° and 40° of latitude.

The temperatures are never extreme. At Valparaiso the coldest months (June and July) average 52.3°, whereas the warmest month (January) averages 63.7°—temperatures which are a little lower than those of San Diego in California. In the Central Valley, where protection from the chilling effect of the cool sea is just about compensated by increased elevation, the averages are similar to those of the coast, although the extremes are somewhat greater. Temperatures at Santiago average 45.7° in the coldest month and 68.7° in

The city of Santiago. *Courtesy of Braniff International.*

the warmest month. Freezing weather is sometimes experienced in the Central Valley, but snow is a rare occurrence.

Rainfall increases steadily from the desert margin toward the south. The length of the summer dry season becomes shorter and shorter until, south of the latitude of Concepción, there is no season which is essentially rainless.[2] Throughout middle Chile, however, the summer is either entirely dry, or receives an average of less than half an inch in the driest month. The total annual rainfall is only 4.5 inches at Coquimbo; it is 9.0 inches at Los Andes in the Vale of Chile; it is 13.8 inches at Santiago; and it is 30.1 inches near Concepción. South of Concepción the rainfall increases rapidly (Map 12, p. 32).

The winter rains of this region are produced, as in other mediterranean regions of the world, by the interaction of cold and warm air masses, known to meteorologists as cyclonic storms.[3] The normal air movement over middle Chile in both summer and winter is from the southwest; it is produced by air circulating around the permanent center of high pressure at about latitude 30° S. in the South Pacific. Throughout the year this stream of relatively warm, humid, and light air is penetrated at intervals by masses of heavy,

[2]On Map 11, p. 31, the Csb climate is the "mediterranean" type, with mild wet winters and dry cool summers; the Cfbs climate has no dry season, although more rain falls in winter than in summer; the B climates are arid or semiarid.

[3]The term *cyclone* should not be confused with the popular word cyclone which refers to a tornado. A meteorologist uses this word to refer to any whirling storm. In most parts of the middle latitudes of the world the alternation of warm and cold air masses is associated with the passage of cyclones (see Map 10, p. 30).

cold air from the Antarctic. As a cold air mass advances northward, the lighter oceanic air forms along its front a whirl which circulates in a clockwise direction. The cold air masses and the whirls they set up pass at close intervals throughout the year across southern Chile; but in winter some of the cold masses are strong enough to move northward along the Chilean coast beyond Concepción. The whirl along one of these advancing fronts brings strong winds from the northwest and north; and these are replaced by a sudden shift to southerly winds as the cold front passes by. The advancing cold air, being relatively heavy, forces the whirling air ahead of it to rise, and this rise brings rain. The approach of a cold air mass, therefore, is heralded by a shift of the wind from the usual southwesterly direction to the northwest and north. Since the cyclonic whirls sometimes, in winter, develop considerable velocities, and since the storm winds come from a northerly direction, the Chilean harbors, protected from the south but open to the north, were peculiarly dangerous for ships caught in them at such times, before breakwaters were built to protect them. Because these cold air masses never push beyond Concepción in summer, this season in middle Chile remains very dry; and because only the strongest winter storms push far into the region north of Concepción, the rainfall brought at this season decreases toward the north.

The intermediate zone between the land which is seldom rainy and the land which is seldom dry was at one time covered by a distinctive type of vegetation—mediterranean evergreen broadleaf woodland consisting of a scattered growth of scrubby trees which retain their leaves throughout the year. The first patches of this type of forest appear on the slopes of the coastal plateaus a little south of Coquimbo, and the forest becomes denser and more extensive toward the south. Throughout the region, however, there are many areas where the forest is replaced by a growth of low evergreen bushes of a type remarkably similar in appearance to the *maquis* of southern Europe and to the *chaparral* of California. This typical mediterranean vegetation ends abruptly along the Río Bío-Bío (Map 15, p. 35).

The Chilean Hacienda

Such, then, are the distinctive qualities of both land and people which set this core of the Chilean state apart as unique in all Latin America. But unique as are the setting and the actors, the process of settlement and the impact of changes in the modern period are only variations on the common Latin-American theme.

The institution around which the process of settlement took place was the hacienda. As elsewhere in lands newly conquered by Spain, the Spanish crown divided the area into private holdings which were granted to members of the army. The size of the grants varied according to the position of the person to whom the grant was made. There were town lots for those who wished to live in the urban centers; there were small farms for the soldiers of lower rank;

and there were vast estates, measured in square leagues, for the officers of higher rank. The large landowners and their descendants assumed their places, in accordance with the Spanish agrarian tradition, as members of the aristocracy, as leaders of the political, economic, and social life.

The census of 1925 revealed statistically the results of four centuries of settlement. In that year middle Chile, outside of the cities, was divided into 82,084 rural properties. Of these properties, 76,588 were classed as "small," since they were less than 200 hectares in size.[4] Only 5,396 properties, about 7 percent of the total number, were classified as haciendas. But this relatively small number of all rural properties included 89 percent of all farmland in middle Chile. In the Vale of Chile, 98 percent of all farmland was included in 3 percent of the properties. There were 375 haciendas of more than 5,000 hectares each—that is larger than 12,350 acres. This group was less than 1 percent of all rural properties, yet it included 52 percent of the privately owned land of middle Chile. These are figures that remind one of the concentration of land ownership in Mexico before 1910.

The large landowners of Chile, like those in other Spanish-American countries, were primarily interested in raising high-grade animals, mostly cattle and horses. As a result, they made use of the small area of good land in middle Chile to raise feed crops under irrigation—chiefly alfalfa, oats, clover, and vetch. The animals were driven into the high mountain pastures above the tree line in summer, and the irrigated feed crops in the Central Valley were used to keep the animals fat during the winter—a characteristic form of *transhumance,* which was traditionally developed in Spain and other Mediterranean countries. In the Central Valley only about one field in ten in any one year was used to grow food crops. And the chief food was, and still is, wheat. Chile is the only country in Latin America in which wheat occupies more area than maize. In Chile, bread made from wheat rather than from maize is eaten by all classes. To supplement their diet, the workers on the haciendas were permitted to use small additional bits of land to raise potatoes, beans, peas, lentils, onions, artichokes, and peppers.

There were certain small areas, also, that were used for vineyards. Vineyards were to be found in Chile from Arica in the north as far south as the Río Bío-Bío. Throughout middle Chile vineyards occupied at least part of the land on each hacienda; but the major concentration of this kind of land use was in the Vale of Chile and around Talca. Less than half of the area in vineyards was irrigated—usually the vines were planted on bordering slopes too steep for other uses.

---

[4]One hectare equals 2.47 acres; 200 hectares equal 494 acres. There are 640 acres in a square mile. These "small farms" of about 500 acres are much larger than those spoken of as small farms in the United States or in the Old World mediterranean regions.

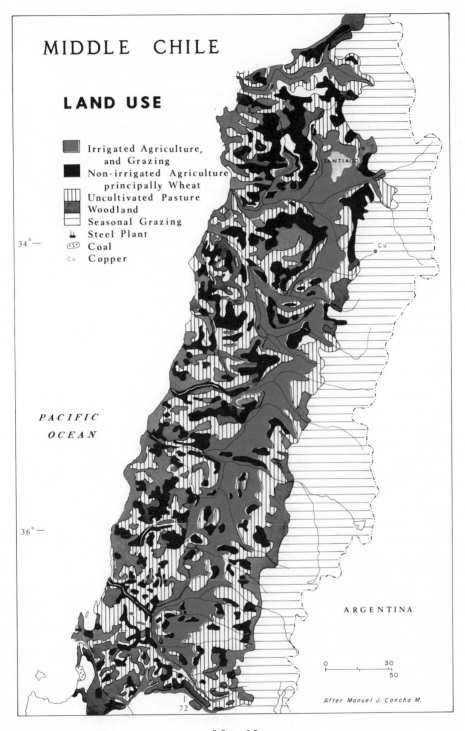

MIDDLE CHILE

LAND USE

Irrigated Agriculture, and Grazing
Non-irrigated Agriculture principally Wheat
Uncultivated Pasture
Woodland
Seasonal Grazing
Steel Plant
Coal
Cu Copper

PACIFIC
OCEAN

SANTIAGO

Cu

ARGENTINA

0   30
        50

After Manuel J. Concha M.

Map 98

THE INQUILINOS

The *inquilino,* or tenant worker, was the traditional victim of this agricultural system. The tenant workers were not racially different from the landowners, as was the case in Mexico and Peru. But their status in the system was quite different. The same families occupied the same haciendas for centuries, and the hacienda owner, the *patrón,* was accepted as the hereditary master. The owner would not think of letting his *inquilinos* starve, or go without legal advice, or without the services of the midwives; but no pressure of opinion among the aristocracy could force the owners to do anything about the miserable standards of living that tradition accorded to the tenants. The *inquilino* family was provided with a house with a mud floor and thatch roof. There was no provision for cooking, which was done outside even in winter. The houses were not heated. There were no toilet facilities inside or outside, and the water supply came from contaminated irrigation ditches. It is little wonder that for every thousand children born in Chile, 248 used to die within the first year. If, on Saturday nights, the Chilean *inquilino* sought the solace of the local vintages to excess, he could scarcely be blamed.

POPULATION PRESSURE

Population pressure began to appear in middle Chile as early as 1870. The number of rural people in the area between Coquimbo and Concepción was about 1,425,000 according to the census of 1885; in 1925 the same area counted a rural population of 1,497,000. Meanwhile the total population of Chile nearly doubled, and after 1925 the number of rural people in middle Chile began to increase rapidly. In this situation something had to change.

How was this over-all increase of the Chilean population absorbed? Before World War II the increasing numbers of people were absorbed in six different ways. First, the recruiting of the army for the war with Peru and Bolivia (1879–83) jarred many of the *inquilinos* out of their traditional attachment to the haciendas. Second, the rise of the nitrate industry in northern Chile attracted workers, who came in a steady stream from middle Chile. Third, the rise of other mining industries, chiefly copper and coal, absorbed additional numbers of workers from middle Chile. Fourth, a steady current of emigration carried some of the excess population of middle Chile across the Andes into the Argentine oases on the eastern side. Fifth, a large number of people from the rural districts of middle Chile became the pioneers who pushed the frontier of settlement southward into the forests of southern Chile. And sixth—and of greatest importance—within middle Chile itself, the large manufacturing cities, whose rise began during World War I, absorbed a very large part of the excess population of the rural districts. In these various ways, partly by expansion, partly by emigration, and partly by internal re-

The port of Valparaiso. *Courtesy of Braniff International.*

arrangement, Chile took care of its increasing numbers without increasing the rural population density of the nucleus.

Land Redistribution

By 1950, however, the pressure of people on the traditional economy was becoming explosive. To be sure, the Chilean economy was expanding more rapidly than the economies of most other Latin-American countries. Already the consumption of electric power per capita was the largest in Latin America. Furthermore, the Chilean landowners—unlike the landowning classes of other Spanish-American countries—were not unwilling to invest money in business. The members of the aristocracy did not lose prestige when they undertook to manage industries or commercial firms. After 1950 an increasing number of landowners actually divided their properties into small lots and sold them, investing the proceeds in manufacturing industries. Where the land was redistributed in this way there was a decrease in feed crops and an increase of the area planted with orchards—oranges, apples, pears, peaches, and lemons. But most of the purchasers of these small country estates were white-collar workers in the cities.

The proportion of very poor people in Chile was increasing in spite of these changes. There were still large rural areas operated as traditional haciendas, with many families living as *inquilinos*. Furthermore, the *inquilinos* who had left the estates to find jobs in the mines or in industries were also being paid wages that were too low to provide families with adequate food and shelter. What was considered adequate was no longer the traditional mud-floored, comfortless hut, because in the cities the workers could see that there was a better way to live, but that better way required a larger income. Labor unions, many communist controlled, called strikes and staged disorders that threatened the stability of this traditionally stable country.

On July 16, 1967, a new agrarian reform law was passed by the government of Chile. The political problems involved in this law will be discussed later. The impact of these agrarian reforms on middle Chile will be drastic. By 1972 some 15 million acres of privately owned land will be expropriated by the government and will be made available in small farms to more than a million landless farm workers. For many decades, Chile has had to import such basic foods as wheat, butter, potatoes, and vegetables because of the failure of its agricultural system to produce these items. Therefore, aside from ending the institution of tenantry, the basic purpose of the new law is to increase the production of these necessary foods. Yet in every Latin-American country where land redistribution programs have been put into effect, the first result has been a decrease in food production—as was the case in Mexico. The question is—can the Chilean farmers do better than their Latin-American colleagues? In any case, the Chilean hacienda as an institution will cease to exist.

Northern Chile

Before returning to a discussion of what these economic and political changes mean in Chile as a whole, we must examine the outlying parts of the country—the northern and southern regions. Northern Chile, which includes the part north of latitude 30° S. at Coquimbo, is the dry region, known as the Atacama (Map 99).

The Atacama is one of the most distinct natural divisions of the South American continent. Here is to be found one of the very few spots on the face of the earth where no rain has ever been recorded and where the surface of the land remains barren over vast areas. Here the two chief groups of people who have occupied the desert have done so in strongly contrasted ways. The Indian settlements, closely attached to the sources of water, have remained isolated, static, unchanging; the Europeans, after neglecting the region for centuries, suddenly acquired a strong interest in the desert because of the discovery of its unique resource, sodium nitrate. But while the Indian villages survived the passage of the centuries almost unchanged, the Europeans, during the last century, "conquered" the desert in a spectacular wave of settlement and exploitation, only to find that their occupation of the region was precarious. Disputes and conflicts over questions of ownership led to actual warfare in which Chile was victorious over Peru and Bolivia; and more recently the Europeans in the Atacama have had to face the problem of markets, a problem which arises largely from economic and political conditions outside of the region and beyond the control of the Chileans.

The Coast

No part of the west coast of South America is more forbidding, more utterly desert-like in aspect, than the stretch of about six hundred miles be-

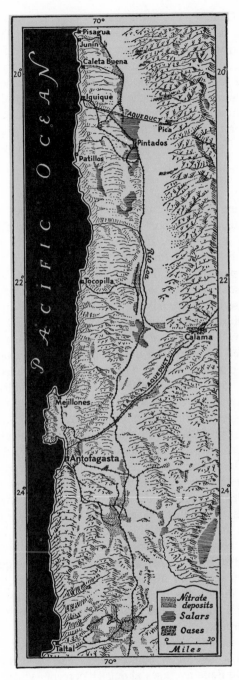

Map 99

tween Arica and Caldera. From the water's edge the cliffed escarpment of
the coastal plateau rises like an unbroken wall 2,000 to 3,000 feet above the
sea. Only one river, the Río Loa, makes its way across the desert and through
the coastal plateau to empty into the sea. There are no harbors, no protected
anchorages. Along the lower slopes of the coastal escarpment there are narrow wave-cut terraces, now lifted above the sea by the gradual emergence of
the land; and on these narrow shelves, clinging with an insecurity that is more
than apparent—for there are earthquakes in this region—are such towns as
Pisagua, Iquique, Tocopilla, Mejillones, Antofagasta, Taltal, and Caldera.

The Desert

The wealth of the Atacama, for a people of European culture, lies back
of the coastal plateau. Each port is dependent on its connections with the
mining districts of the interior, and these connections are maintained either
by railroad or cable line. The railroads zigzag up the steep escarpment which
faces the Pacific, passing over the crest through shallow, dry ravines about
2,000 feet above sea level. East of the plateau a very different kind of landscape is found. A series of dry basins, or *bolsons,* some 50 miles in width and
approximately 2,000 feet in elevation, separate the coastal plateau from the
base of the Western Cordillera of the Andes. The plateaus consist only of a
rim of low, rounded hills between the smooth-floored bolsons of the interior
and the sharp drop to the Pacific. The bolsons are invaded on the east by
enormous alluvial fans which spread out from the mouths of the Andean
valleys and extend into the basins for as much as 40 miles west of the mountain front. The lowest parts of the bolsons, therefore, are near their western
sides, close to the rim of hills at the crest of the coastal escarpment. Many
signs indicate that at one time these basins were filled with lakes, which have
since completely dried up, leaving deposits of salts. A series of layers are
recognized, one of them containing the valuable *caliche* which is composed
of sodium chloride, sodium nitrate, and a variety of other substances including iodine salts. The caliche layer varies in thickness from a few inches
to many feet, with an average of perhaps one foot.

The Atacama is now one of the driest places on earth. For years at a time
no rain falls, so that the average figures of rainfall are quite meaningless.
Over a period of 20 years, for instance, 14 years passed at Iquique without a
drop of rain, and during the 6 years in which some rain did fall the total
amount was only 1.1 inches. Back of the coastal plateau, at Calama, no rain
has ever been recorded.

Although the coast and the interior are alike in having this rainless condition, in other ways they differ considerably. The coast has a much higher
relative humidity. Iquique averages about 81 percent, while Calama averages
only 48 percent. The cloudiness on the coast is high, while the interior remains almost cloudless. The temperatures on the coast are more uniform

than those of the interior; the latter show a greater range, not only between seasons, but also between day and night. Under the clear skies in the interior the rapid loss of heat at night and in winter often brings the temperature close to the freezing point; at such times low fog banks hang over the desert, soaking the surface with dew. Both the coast and the interior are entirely barren of vegetation.

Permanent settlement in a desert is dependent on water, and supplies of surface water in the Atacama are meager. Tacna is the southernmost of the Peruvian oases, and just across the border in northern Chile is its twin— Arica. Between Arica and Copiapó only one river gathers sufficient volume in its headwaters to persist in its flow across the desert—this is the Río Loa; where the Loa emerges from the Western Cordillera the only large oasis settlement between Arica and Copiapó is established, the oasis of Calama. Immediately downstream from Calama the Río Loa enters a deep and narrow canyon from which it emerges to enter the Pacific. In this canyon the water is not available for the support of oasis settlement. Even the mouth of the Loa is not used as the site of a port, for the gap through the coastal plateau is too narrow to serve as a route to the interior. The first surface water to reach the ocean south of the Loa is the Río Copiapó; and the oasis of Copiapó, a ribbon of cultivation almost 90 miles long, is generally regarded as marking the southern limit of the Atacama.

Except for the Río Loa, therefore, the Atacama is without surface streams. The valleys descending from the Western Cordillera have surface water at irregular intervals, although many of them remain permanently dry. A sheet of water, however, is constantly seeping down through the gravel fill in these Andean ravines and out into the alluvial fans. Wells in the gravel within the mountain valleys can tap a small but fairly dependable supply of water; but the alluvial fans beyond the mountain front act like sponges permitting the water to sink to such depths that it is beyond the reach of ordinary wells. There are parts of the bolsons far to the west where the water table lies not far from the surface again—in one or two spots even close enough to be within reach of plant roots.

The Atacama as a Region of Transit

During the long history of Indian and Spanish settlement in this region, and down to the second quarter of the nineteenth century, the Atacama remained an area of sparse population, playing the part of a barrier with no intrinsic value. The Indians of the Inca Empire wished to cross it from north to south because it separated the centers of settlement in the highland basins of Cuzco and Titicaca from the frontier region of middle Chile. The Spaniards wished to cross it from east to west because it lay between the mines of high Bolivia and the nearest navigable water. Each arrived at a workable arrangement of routes of travel which made possible the crossing of this inhospitable region with a minimum of hardship.

The Indians established a road leading from north to south through Calama and Copiapó and on into middle Chile. To cross the desert region between the main oases, however, required numerous smaller supply stations where food, water, and shelter could be provided. The little valley oases of the Western Cordillera served this function. The small communities supported by the oases varied in size from only one family to several hundred persons, according to the amount of water available. In their mountain valleys they were sheltered from the winds and dust of the desert—minute habitable spots in a barren land which were so well hidden that in some cases lighthouses were built on near-by ridges to guide travelers to them.

The Spanish conquest shifted the emphasis from north–south communications along the Andean front to east–west lines of travel. The Spaniards soon recognized the importance of the Indian settlement of Calama, and made it a major focus of communications—like Tacna and Arequipa to the north. Whereas Arequipa found its one outlet through Mollendo, and Tacna its outlet through Arica, Calama established its connections with the Pacific at several places in turn. At first the chief port was Cobija; later Mejillones and Antofagasta shared the trade of Calama. But none of these ports was easily reached; no one of them possessed outstanding advantages over the others. When travel from the interior passed through Calama and down to the little ports on the Pacific, the old piedmont oasis settlements of the Indians lost their function as supply stations and, supporting their small populations in complete isolation, they were forgotten by the world outside.

When the Wars of Independence established the national existence af Peru, Bolivia, and Chile, the political boundaries in this region were not carefully defined. The important oases came definitely under one or the other of these countries, but the exact marking of the boundaries in the uninhabited country between was not a matter of concern. Tacna was definitely Peruvian; Calama belonged to Bolivia; and the oasis of Copiapó was in Chile.

Rise of the Nitrate Industry

While the main problem in the Atacama until early in the nineteenth century was the maintenance of a route of travel across it, there were some attempts to explore the desert for minerals. Prospectors entered the region from Tacna and from Copiapó, and the first discoveries were of sources of silver and copper. Between 1832 and 1845 silver mining in the vicinity of Copiapó resulted in the concentration of so many people in that oasis that they could not all be fed—a situation which was noted by Charles Darwin when he visited the place on his voyage around the world. Even as late as 1880, the development of silver mines in the country back of Taltal led to the establishment of that port. Copper, too, was found and mined, especially in the Western Cordillera, but copper mining was of little importance except during the years between 1850 and 1875. The two large copper mines which have survived to the modern period are Chuquicamata, near Calama, and Potrerillos, 75 miles inland from Chañaral.

The prospectors who found silver and copper in the mountains bordering the desert also learned of the presence of layers of sodium nitrate under the sands and gravels of the desert floor. But sodium nitrate was only a curiosity until someone found a use for it. According to the story, a German who was living in Chile in 1809 threw some handfuls of sodium nitrate on his garden and was amazed at the luxuriant growth of his plants. For the world's leached or heavily overworked soils, one of the pressing needs was for a fertilizer that would replace the nitrogen. The sodium nitrate of the Atacama began to find markets in the Cotton Belt of the United States, in the soils of low natural fertility of parts of Europe, and in the heavily overworked soils of Egypt. In 1831 a shipment of 110 tons of nitrate was sent to England, where it quickly found favor. By 1860 a thriving mining industry had been established in the Atacama. With an abundance of nitrate available not too far below the desert surface, and with no competing sources of natural nitrate anywhere in the world, an almost unlimited future in the fertilizer market seemed to be assured. Exports by 1860 had passed 50,000 tons a year.

However, the big scramble for quick profits in the Atacama began when a way was found to use sodium nitrate in the manufacture of smokeless powder. As long as black powder was in use, sodium nitrate was of no value, because this salt has the property of absorbing moisture from the air and going into solution. About 1860 smokeless powder came into use in explosives, and sodium nitrate found a new and rapidly expanding market. By 1895 exports from Chile had gone well beyond the million mark.

But the nitrate industry of northern Chile was established under adverse natural conditions. The nitrate fields lie in the bolsons east of the coastal plateau in five distinct areas between Pisagua in the north and Taltal in the south. The labor of digging up the caliche from the desert floor, moving it to the refineries, carrying through the refining process, and transporting the nitrate and its by-product, iodine, to the coast required the services of many workers. And these workers had to be brought to an area where there was no water, no vegetation, no means of building or maintaining settlements other than by importing supplies from outside. Even water had to be piped for hundreds of miles from the Western Cordillera, or brought to the mining communities in tank cars. Profitable production under such conditions could last only as long as the nitrate exports continued to pay the costs of maintaining the workers in the desert. When, early in 1914, speculative overproduction of nitrate brought such financial difficulties that the whole economic structure of the industry was threatened, thousands of people had to flee this region, which offered no other means of supporting life. Then came World War I, and exports rose to peaks of more than 3,000,000 tons a year; workers streamed back into the Atacama, and the conquest was carried on with renewed confidence. At this time about 65,000 workers were employed in the nitrate operations; the whole region, including its ports, had a population of 270,000.

Political Changes in the Atacama

Meanwhile the political control of this region had been rearranged. Even before 1860 the vague boundaries in the Atacama had caused disputes over questions of jurisdiction, and temporary definitions of the boundaries were from time to time worked out. The development of the industry was being carried forward chiefly by Peruvians and Chileans. In 1879 about 59 percent of the capital invested in nitrate was Peruvian, about 19 percent was Chilean, 14 percent was British, and 8 percent was German. Although some of the richest fields were in Bolivian territory, the Bolivians had invested little capital in the new industry and had sent few laborers to this remote part of their country. They did, however, wish to tax the new source of wealth; and quite naturally the Chilean companies operating in Bolivian territory felt that the taxation was excessive. Then the Peruvian government, in 1876, finding itself in serious financial difficulties, sought to reestablish its finances by expropriating the privately owned nitrate plants within Peruvian territory and attempting to run the industry as a government monopoly. In the midst of growing confusion the Chileans landed troops at Antofagasta, declaring war on both Bolivia and Peru.

The War of the Pacific lasted from 1879 to 1883. Chile was victorious, and its military forces even occupied Lima. The Treaty of Ancon (1884) resulted in the permanent transfer of ownership of the Peruvian section of the Atacama to Chile, reserving for later decision the fate of the oasis of Tacna and its port Arica. Bolivia was also deprived of its part of the Atacama and shut off from the sea. Chile, in complete control of the nitrate country, continued the development of the industry and collected the growing revenues, thereby offering the world the rare example in modern times of a war which paid for itself.

From 1884 to 1929 the question of the final disposal of Tacna and Arica remained unsolved. Tacna and Arica lie beyond the northernmost of the nitrate fields, and possession of them was in no direct way related to the exploitation of minerals. Chile perhaps desired to protect the fields from this nearest base of possible attack; Bolivia, shut off at Antofagasta, pressed claims for an outlet at Arica; and Peru, through much propaganda, claimed Tacna and Arica as sacred territory which had been occupied by a conqueror. After many attempts at settlement the territory was finally divided between Peru and Chile. Tacna was awarded to Peru, Arica to Chile, and Bolivia was given the right of free entry through Arica and the use of the railroad from that port to La Paz.

Decline of the Nitrate Industry

During this period of controversy, the exports of nitrate were bringing wealth to Chile. About a third of the selling price—which Chile could dictate since the Atacama was then the only important source of this mineral—was made up of the export tax. Into the Chilean treasury was pouring a golden stream, amounting to between 30 and 35 million dollars a year. Foreign capital was invested in the area in increasing amounts: by 1901 the British investments represented 55 percent of the total; 15 percent was Chilean; 14 percent was German; and 10 percent was Spanish. Most of the workers, however, were Chileans.

Chile lost its monopoly of the world's nitrate and its speculative profits after World War I. Before 1914 German engineers had developed a process for extracting nitrogen from the air, using a large amount of electric power. During World War I, when Germany was cut off from nitrate shipments from Chile, the atmospheric process was perfected, and after the war nitrate-producing plants were built in Norway and on the Tennessee River in Alabama. In 1928 there was a sudden collapse of the world nitrate market, as the product of these new plants became available. Since that time a world conference of nitrate producers established quotas, and Chile has continued to export about 2 million tons a year, about 40 percent of which is sent to the United States for use as fertilizer. Chile also extracts iodine as a by-product.

The mining of copper is much more important to Chile than the nitrate works. At Antofagasta a large copper refinery has been built. We shall discuss copper and other minerals later.

The "Conquest" of the Atacama

During all these chaotic developments which involved war, transfer of national territory, a spectacular rise of prosperity and an equally spectacular collapse, the Indian villages along the Andean piedmont remained undisturbed. Each community, nestled in its little valley, is essentially an independent unit, producing little for export and buying little from the outside. Water is still the primary need, and the population of each oasis is closely adjusted to the amount available. Some of the larger oases, perhaps with 500 inhabitants, have built reservoirs and aqueducts to increase the supply and insure the regularity of water, but many smaller oases depend solely on wells sunk in the gravel of the valley bottoms. Near the villages the valley sides are terraced and irrigated, and on these fields maize is raised for human consumption, and alfalfa for the sheep, llamas, and goats. The food supply consists of maize, meat, goat's milk, and cheese. The women make pottery and spin and weave the wool for clothing. Rarely, an itinerant trader with his goods loaded in a motor truck comes to town to sell the products of the outside world.

The inhabitants of the piedmont towns have other means of support in a few activities outside the immediate village locality. They own herds of sheep, llamas, and goats, which they pasture during a part of the year on the scanty grasses of the higher Andes. In years of unusually heavy rainfall in the high mountains the pasturage may be so abundant that animals are actually imported from a distance—in one case driven over the mountains from the plains of Argentina. But such periods come only once or twice in a lifetime.

Which one of these contrasted kinds of settlement represents a conquest of the desert? Surely not the nitrate settlements. Only the unchanging "out-of-the-world" communities of Indians have formed a permanently workable connection with the resources of the land. The copper mines, based as they are on a very large supply of ore, will continue productive for a long time. But all such mining activities face two ultimate dangers: that the supply of ore is used up, or that a technological innovation makes the ore no longer useful. To provide economic support for the nitrate workers who are no longer needed in such numbers, the Chilean government has built a copper refinery, a fish meal plant at Iquique, and several smaller industrial plants at Arica. A hydroelectric power plant located high in the Andes near the border of Bolivia sends power to the mines and to these port cities.

Southern Chile

In the opposite direction lies southern Chile. The traveler crossing the Río Bío-Bío southward leaves behind him the open landscapes of middle Chile and abruptly enters a land which was once forested. Instead of irrigated fields on sloping alluvial fans, here are farms created on cleared land, still bristling with stumps and littered with the wreckage that accompanies forest-clearing the world over; here, instead of the mud fences and the white-washed mud buildings with thatch or red-tile roofs characteristic of the north, are frame houses roofed with shingles; here the long stately rows of Lombardy poplars and the graceful weeping willows are entirely lacking; here, instead of the large estates of a landed aristocracy, there are medium-sized farms, few more pretentious than the others—for rural democracy is a system which flourishes best under pioneer conditions. The contrast between the region north of the Bío-Bío and that south of it is one of more than superficial aspect—it is a contrast of social systems, a contrast of attitudes of mind. For a forest-bred people this region is potentially as rich as the desert of the north was for a people who understood best the exploitation of mineral wealth.

Surface Features

The fundamental elements of the land in middle Chile are continued southward (Map 88, p. 537). On the east the Andes dominate the scene; on the west the coastal plateaus and terraces border the sea, extending the length of the island of Chiloé; and between the Andes and the plateaus is the Central Valley.

The Andes are not so high in southern Chile as they are to the north, and the passes through them are much lower. During the Ice Ages the work of the glaciers, which was limited to the higher parts of the Cordillera at the latitude of Santiago, was extended to lower and lower altitudes with the increase in distance south of the equator. At latitude 39° S., just a little south of Temuco, the valley glaciers at one time emerged from the mountains into the Central Valley in great tongues of ice. The glaciers scraped and broadened the mountain valleys into U-shaped troughs, and around their lower ends they piled the coarse gravel they had torn from the heart of the Cordillera, forming a horseshoe pattern of knobby morainic hills. Behind each moraine, south of latitude 39° S., there is a valley lake—similar in origin to the famous lakes of the Alpine piedmont in Italy. Above these lakes the mountains take on more and more of the features of a range heavily sculptured by the ice—sharp horns, high cirques, deep valley troughs. At present only a few small relict glaciers are to be found high in the mountains in sheltered spots facing to the south, but the limit of permanent snow is lower than it is near Santiago: at the head of the Bío-Bío it is between 6,500 and 8,000 feet (depending on the exposure); inland from Valdivia, about latitude 40° S., it is

The dairy region around Puerto Varas on Lake Llanquihue. In the background is the volcano, Mt. Osorno (8,725 ft.).

approximately 5,000 feet above sea level. In this region, where the rocky slopes permit, the dense forest reaches the snow line, leaving no intermediate zone of alpine pastures for the summer grazing of cattle and sheep.

In addition to the glacial features, the landforms of the Cordillera are varied by the appearance, south of latitude 35° S., of a row of enormous cone-shaped volcanoes, snow-covered at their summits. These volcanoes stand to the west of the main Cordillera, adding a touch of scenery to the Chilean lake district which places this region among the most spectacular of the world. Their appearance is remarkably similar to that of the great volcanoes of the Pacific Northwest of the United States, like Mt. Hood or Mt. Rainier—except that the Chilean volcanoes are still active. Major earthquake disasters have hit this part of Chile frequently. During the present century there were earthquake disasters in 1906, 1928, 1939, and 1960.

The coastal plateaus border the Pacific as they do in middle Chile. After the gap at Concepción, the range again appears in typical form—the form of a dissected plateau—in the peninsula of Lebú. In elevation it is about the same as the region north of Concepción, reaching a maximum, south of Valdivia, of about 5,000 feet. Along the backbone of the island of Chiloé the range is approximately 2,600 feet in altitude. Drowned river mouths at Talcahuano and Valdivia provide protected harbors.

The Central Valley also continues into southern Chile. Its eastern margin, however, is no longer smoothed by the broad alluvial fans: instead its Andean border is festooned with moraines and dotted with marginal lakes. The rivers cross it at right angles, and between these rivers spurs of the mountains separate the valley into a series of compartments. The valley floor continues southward from the Bío-Bío at approximately three to four hundred feet above sea level. It ends abruptly at Puerto Montt, descending to sea level in a series of terraces which remind one strongly of the northern end of the Puget Valley at Tacoma in the state of Washington.

Climate and Forest

There is a very close similarity, also, between the climates of Chile and those of the Pacific coast of the United States. Traveling southward in Chile, or northward in California, one leaves a climate of mild, wet winters and dry summers for a climate of stormy winters and cool summers which, although not so rainy as the winters, are nevertheless not dry. Many days with gray skies, many violent storms, very heavy rainfall—these are the characteristics which distinguish the west-coast climates of all the continents poleward of approximately 40°. Valdivia has about the same average temperature in its warmest month as Tacoma, Washington (Valdivia, 61.9°; Tacoma, 62.2°); but its coldest month is milder than that of Tacoma (Valdivia, 45.5°; Tacoma, 38.3°). Valdivia, however, receives almost three times as much rainfall as does Tacoma (Valdivia, 104.8 in.; Tacoma, 40.4 in.). Storminess in-

THE CHILEAN LAKE DISTRICT

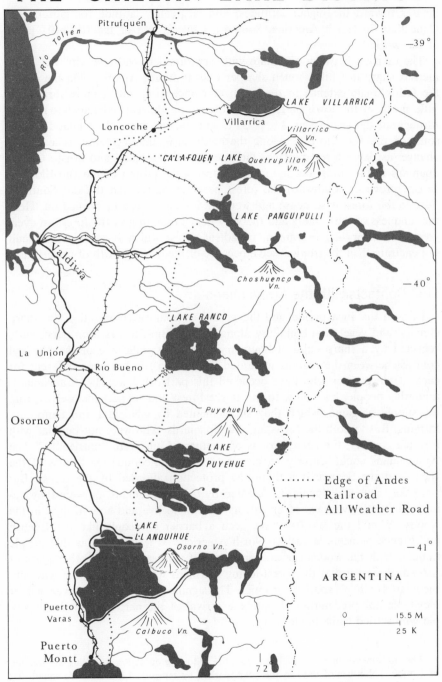

Map 100

creases toward the higher latitudes, and is greater, latitude for latitude, in Chile than in North America. Southern Chile is one of the stormiest parts of the world.[5]

The division between a climate with dry summers and one with wet summers is sharp in Chile—much sharper than in North America. On the coast, the Csb climate extends to the south of Concepción; but it ends abruptly a little north of the town of Lebú. To the south, the Cfb climate has rainfall throughout the year (Map 11, p. 31). The change takes place inland a little south of the Río Bío-Bío. Along the coast, also, the vegetation reflects this change, as dense forest replaces the open scrub woodland and brush. Grassy openings in the forest occur in the Central Valley south of the Bío-Bío, but as one proceeds southward the forest becomes wetter and thicker. South of Osorno the forest is so dense and wet that it cannot even be burned off. Here the mildness of the winters and the very heavy rainfall give the forest an evergreen character—an evergreen, broadleaf forest which is far more difficult to penetrate than the tropical selva because of the dense growth of underbrush.

First Contacts with the Araucanians

In both the Inca period and the period of Spanish colonization the sharp climatic and vegetation boundary along the Río Bío-Bío has been persistently reflected by a sharp cultural boundary. Yet the significance of the physical contrast between the regions separated by the Bío-Bío has been different for each of the peoples who have occupied this part of Chile. The Araucanians, a hunting people, knew how to live in the forest and support themselves from the supply of game, which they supplemented by incidental and temporary farming. But to both the Incas and the Spaniards, who were not familiar with forested country, the heavy woods of southern Chile were "unfriendly." The Araucanians could scarcely have withstood the all-conquering armies of the Incas and the Spaniards without the protection afforded by the forest. But were the Incas and Spaniards defeated by the Araucanians, or were they defeated by their own lack of knowledge of how to live and how to fight in the woods? Would the Bío-Bío have been a barrier to people like the English and French pioneers of eastern North America? At least we know that people familiar with the woods carved homes out of similar forests in other parts of the world; and it was the forest-loving Germans who finally led the way into the heart of Chile's southern frontier. The significance of the forest was neither inevitable nor predetermined until the arrival of the particular kinds of people who settled Chile made it seem so.

---

[5]The storminess can be appreciated from the following quotation regarding the weather of Chiloé: "Number of days in the year marked by tempest, 17; storm, 25; squall, 93; rain, 108; cloudy weather, 20; variable weather, 93; sun, 51." Quoted from Alfredo Weber by G. M. McBride, *Chile, Land and Society,* New York, 1936, p. 317.

As a matter of fact, the Spaniards who conquered the Inca Empire and who marched across deserts and high plateaus to seek wealth and position in Chile were not the kind of people to stop on the borders of unfamiliar country. Under the leadership of Pedro de Valdivia these fearless adventurers plunged southward into the heart of Araucanian country. Before 1560 they had placed settlements on navigable waters at Arauco, Imperial, Valdivia, and on the island of Chiloé at Castro; and they had even placed settlements inland wherever meadow lands offered them the opportunity—at Cañete, Angol, Villarica, and Osorno. The Araucanians were divided into groups, according to the *encomienda* system and allotted to the favorites among the officers of the army. But the Araucanians were not like the Quechuas, nor were they as powerless as the tribes farther north who had no woods in which to fight. Almost constant Indian attacks, with the Indians invisible behind the trees, finally culminated in a great uprising which, between 1600 and 1602, resulted in the almost complete elimination of the Spaniards from the region. The only settlements that survived were those at Arauco, Valdivia, and Castro. The others were all destroyed, and the Spaniards, without much regret, abandoned the region.

For more than two hundred years after the arrival of the Spanish, southern Chile remained Indian country. The seminomadic Araucanians established fixed settlements as, little by little, they adopted ideas which crossed the frontier. Their communities were not clustered in the Spanish manner, but it was customary for each family to remain as a separate unit of settlement. They practiced a shifting cultivation of maize and potatoes, chiefly in the meadows and glades where the heavy labor of clearing the forest was not necessary. From the Spaniards they adopted cattle and poultry. Along the frontier, and around the isolated Spanish settlements of the coast, the warfare and the raiding never ceased. Only Castro, on its island, was safe. Not until 1885 did Valdivia form a land connection with the rest of Chile.

Settlement of "Araucania"

The Araucanians, with the Seminoles of Florida, have the distinction among all the Indian tribes of the Americas, of never having been conquered by force of arms. They were conquered, little by little, by contacts with the white man's civilization. Even today, however, this sturdy group of Indians, now incorporated in the Chilean nation, persists in its occupation of a part of the southern region. There are more than 70,000 Araucanians concentrated in the valley of the Río Tolten, south of Temuco, and more than 100,000 in southern Chile as a whole; and their number is slowly increasing. The Chilean government has attempted to have the communal holdings of the Indians converted into private farms. But in spite of continued efforts to persuade the Indians to take this step they have mostly resisted it, and the Indian communities continue to hold and farm their lands in common.

Puerto Montt in southern Chile.

The first serious steps leading to the establishment of settlements in the interior were taken by foreign immigrants in the decades which followed 1850. Small groups of Germans, each group containing only a few hundred people, were established between 1850 and 1854 near Valdivia, at Puerto Montt and at Puerto Varas on the shores of Lake Llanquihue. Pioneering was not easy in this wet country where travel through the forest was almost impossible during the winter months, but the German colonists showed what could be done. Up to 1864, when the arrival of new settlers from Germany practically ceased, the total number who had entered this part of Chile was only 3,367. Even today they form an insignificant proportion of the total population—not more than about 30,000 in all of Chile including Chilean-born descendants of the immigrants. But these Germans were great pioneers: they were willing to work very hard to produce the material comforts which they were not content to be without; their homes were substantial and permanent; they built good roads; their agricultural techniques were carefully maintained even in the face of obstacles. By industry and persistence these few colonists exerted great influence on the settlement of Chile's frontier. The census of 1930 showed 9,808 foreign-born people in the southern region, of whom some 3,000 were German. There were, also, nearly 2,000 Spaniards, and smaller numbers of French, Italians, Swiss, and other European peoples. The Germans, here as elsewhere in the Americas, soon gave up political allegiance to the fatherland, in spite of recurring rumors to the contrary; but they did implant a distinctly German civilization in the new land—distinctly German in the architecture of the buildings, the agricultural methods, the cleanliness, the emphasis on schooling, and in the social manners and customs of even the second and third generations.

While these foreigners led the way, and still play a part in the economic life of the region out of all proportion to their numbers, the great flood of pioneer settlers came from middle Chile, recruited largely from the *inquilino* class. After the conclusion of the war with Bolivia and Peru in 1883, the returning army was sent to the southern frontier to establish finally the Chilean control of the Araucanians. Chile might have pursued the policy of settling its soldiers on this frontier, but the opposition of the ruling class to this procedure was considerable, arising from the desire for an abundance of labor in the older parts of Chile. Nevertheless about 6,000 new colonists were settled in the south, and probably many more became squatters on Indian communal lands and escaped the official census. The number of settlers was no doubt greater than it would have been if war had not broken the strong traditional ties of the Chilean *inquilino* with his hacienda. At any rate, the number of settlers in the years after 1883 was large. The population of the province of Valdivia, for instance, which had only 8,860 inhabitants in 1835, increased to 53,090 in 1875, and to 133,443 in 1907. The population of the provinces carved out of the old frontier was, in 1960, nearly 2 million. While relatively few upper-class Chileans were involved in this movement—and for this reason Chilean literature, which is almost exclusively the product of the upper classes, has shown little of the effect of the frontier—the migration of people from middle Chile accounts for about one in every five persons; continued over the decades it has been one of the most potent forces in the transformation of Chilean life.

Today the frontier region in southern Chile is largely occupied. Only in the wet evergreen forests southwest of Osorno are arable lands still available for pioneer settlement. The great earthquake of 1939, which destroyed Chillán and did severe damage to Concepción, resulted in a considerable movement of people to this last bit of southern frontier. The earthquake of 1960, which centered on the Lebú Peninsula, did not result in any large movement of people southward.

The farms of southern Chile are devoted chiefly to the raising of livestock, and to a lesser degree to the production of food crops. About 40 percent of the cattle in Chile are raised on the rich green pastures south of the Bío-Bío. Most of these animals are used for meat rather than for dairy products, although the cool, moist climate with mild winters is ideally suited to a dairy economy. Because of the absence of pastures in the Andes, transhumance is not practiced in southern Chile, but there is a more or less regular movement of herds and herders through the relatively low passes to the oases of northern Patagonia in Argentina, especially Neuquén. At one time a considerable number of Chileans emigrated permanently to that oasis, and there is still a small current of emigration across the Andes to Argentina.

Less than 20 percent of the total area of southern Chile is devoted to food crops. On this area, however, is produced an important share of Chile's wheat crop—mostly soft wheat which is adapted to the rainy conditions of the climate. Most of the wheat lands are in the territory just north of Temuco. In addition to wheat, the crops include potatoes, oats, apples, and hay. In spite of the abundance of trees, some of which could be used for lumber, Chile does not have a large lumber industry. Lumber is still imported, while the forests of the south are burned to make room for pastures or crops. The woods of the forests are utilized at only a few places where nearby markets create a demand: around Valdivia, for instance, where there are furniture factories; or on the island of Chiloé where there is a boat-building industry. Otherwise the wood is used only for fuel.

Settlement of Chiloe

The island of Chiloé, which occupies a geographical position very similar to that of Vancouver Island in North America, must be included in the frontier region of southern Chile. But the settlement of Chiloé presented even greater difficulties than that of the mainland. The rainfall is so heavy that the extraordinarily dense evergreen forests cannot be burned. Apparently the cost of cutting the trees and pulling the stumps is so great that agriculture is not profitable. The colony of Castro, and others established later, such as Ancud, have never been very successful. A scanty population, grouped in isolated patches along the east coast, especially around Castro, and on some of the islands east of Chiloé, is able barely to maintain itself against the forest.

The Far South

The remainder of southern Chile, extending southward from the island of Chiloé, makes up a third of the total national territory, yet it is occupied by a scant 1 percent of the total population of Chile.

This "Far South" of Chile is a region of high winds and heavy rains, a region of steep rocky slopes and storm-tossed waters. Glacial activity in the Andes, during the Ice Age, was increasingly vigorous toward the south. The glacial troughs of the Andes inland from Valdivia are small compared with the deep excavations made by the ice farther to the south—excavations which completely cross the range, so that the streams draining to the Pacific in many instances have their headwaters on the eastern side of the mountains. The glacial troughs are drowned along the coast, forming an amazingly intricate pattern of channels and islands. Between Puerto Montt and about latitude 44° S., structural conditions similar to those in middle Chile continue southward, partly under the water. But south of 44° S. the Central Valley disappears—there is only a labyrinth of fiords with steep rocky margins, with

Southern Chile is a land of violent winds, driving clouds, and rain. *Courtesy of Chilean Consulate General.*

a dense tangle of soggy forest wherever trees can fix their roots; a landscape almost constantly shrouded in cloud and driving rain; the outermost islands shaken by the pounding surf where the world's stormiest ocean dashes against a continent.

The snow line descends rapidly toward the south. On the volcano Osorno, northeast of Puerto Montt, it is about 5,000 feet above sea level. In Tierra del Fuego the zone of permanent snow is only 2,300 feet above the sea. The tops of many of the mountains are covered with ice caps; at several places glaciers still discharge icebergs into the coastal fiords.

It would be difficult to find a more unpleasant climate. There are few hours of sunshine, few hours when the wind is not blowing. Rainfall reaches more than 200 inches per year in certain places. At Evangelist's Island, opposite the western end of the Strait of Magellan, the temperature of the warmest month averages 46.8°, and of the coldest month 39.0°. Snow and sleet are common throughout the winter. Only protected places offer somewhat better conditions—for example, Punta Arenas near the eastern border of the mountains on the Strait of Magellan. At Punta Arenas the average temperature of the warmest month is 52.5°; and this place, being in the lee of the mountains, receives only 19.4 inches of rain. The section of the border between Chile and Argentina which runs east of the mountains, and even gives Chile a small stretch of east coast at the eastern end of the strait, includes the only part of the far south where any important numbers of settlers are to be found.

THE INHABITANTS

Some of the world's most primitive tribes occupy this southern coastland of Chile. Apparently the weakest of them occupy the poorest place at the very extremity of the continent, having been pushed there, no doubt, by the movement of stronger peoples from the north. The various tribes of this part of South America (Map 5, p. 14), all of whom speak distinct languages and have quite different culture traits, can muster all together not more than a thousand people. The sections of the coast they occupy are mostly shut off from other sections by barriers of one kind or another. With their canoes these people are able to travel along the inland fiords, living chiefly on fish. Peninsulas, such as that of Taitao, or of Brecknock at the western end of Tierra del Fuego, make it necessary for mariners to face the waves of the open ocean if a passage is to be made by boat; they are major barriers and dividing lines between the culture areas.

PASTURES AND OILFIELDS

Until the middle of the nineteenth century the southernmost part of South America was largely neglected. As long as ships were moved by sails, the Strait of Magellan was not very useful; but when steamships were developed it became possible to navigate the narrow waters and to sail against the wind to the west. Punta Arenas was founded in 1847 because Chile wanted to maintain its claim to the Strait. A short distance inland a small coalfield was discovered, and Punta Arenas became an important coaling station on a major shipping route. But after the opening of the Panama Canal, the Strait of Magellan was visited only by local coasting ships, or tourist ships; and when these were converted to oil, Punta Arenas became only a kind of curiosity.

Meanwhile, however, attention was called to the advantages of this climate for the production of wool and mutton. Sheep were brought in through Punta Arenas in 1878 and were pastured on the unfenced short-grass steppe along the eastern front of the Andes to the north (Map 15, p. 35). The sheep did very well in this area, producing good quality wool and mutton. Punta Arenas became a port of call for ships exporting these products. In addition to people of Spanish ancestry, some of whom came directly from Spain, there were also Scots, Welsh, Germans, Yugoslavs, and other Europeans.

The changes resulting from the adoption of technological innovations which are sweeping over Latin America today have arrived even in this remote part of the world. For a long time the owners of the sheep pastures resisted attempts to improve the grazing by plowing up the wild vegetation and planting better grass. If the wild vegetation cover were removed, they said, heavy wind erosion would destroy the resource base entirely. But after World War II, a group of agricultural engineers carried out certain highly successful experiments. In 1959 one large sheep-and-cattle corporation adopted the new technology. With machinery they plowed the native steppe and planted grass on some 300,000 acres, with spectacular results. It cost about $3.00 an acre to clean off the wild vegetation, and another $3.00 to plant and bring the new pastures to full growth. But this expenditure of money was more than compensated for by increased productivity. Whereas the unimproved steppe could carry about 0.25 sheep per acre, the improved pasture could carry 1.4. The yield of wool per sheep increased about 10 percent. The sheep now give 12 to 15 pounds of wool per animal per year—compared with 1 pound per sheep in the Bolivian Altiplano. Furthermore, the mutton sheep put on weight faster and produced higher quality meat, thus commanding a better price. And now cattle can also be grazed in the same area—about 1 head of cattle per 100 acres of pasture.

Punta Arenas has had a new burst of life. A mutton-freezing plant prepares the meat for shipment to Great Britain. About half of the wool goes to foreign markets, and the other half is sent to the textile factories in middle Chile. Punta Arenas in 1966 was a city of more than 50,000 people, with modern buildings and a booming economy.

In 1945 oil and gas were discovered on Tierra del Fuego across the Strait of Magellan from Punta Arenas. Continued exploration has enlarged the known reserves, and pipelines were built to bring both oil and gas to ports. Oil and gas were also discovered north of the Strait to the east of Punta Arenas, and this area now produces about half of the oil and gas of southern Chile. Oil in Argentine territory north of the border has also been found, and this is sent to Chilean ports by extensions of the pipelines. The oil is sent in tankers to refineries in middle Chile. The gas is liquified and sent north to supply the cities between Santiago and Concepción. In 1967 work was started on a petrochemical plant located in Tierra del Fuego on the Strait of Magellan, which will produce chemical fertilizer for export.

In the past two decades the formerly empty, wind-swept land has been occupied and developed. The new settlements in the oilfields and at the oil-shipping ports are thoroughly modern—with modern style buildings, centrally heated, with theaters, shops, recreation facilities, and other evidences of the arrival of a new way of living. On Tierra del Fuego in 1967 the world's southernmost swimming pool was opened. More than half the people in this new area of settlement own their own automobiles—something which is not at all possible even for upper middle class urban people in middle Chile.

There are still problems and uncertainties. Unless risk capital is invested in continued exploration for more oil sources, the time may come when the present known reserves are used up. Some other economic support would then have to be found. The investment of $6.00 per acre required to convert the wild steppe into highly productive pastures, as well as the period of three or four years when there is no income from the land, makes the adoption of improved technology impossible for the small ranchers, who are therefore likely to be forced out of business—unless the Chilean government, with foreign aid, undertakes the improvement of the pastures for the benefit of the ranchers. In any case, the far south of Chile is not likely to be abandoned. Around Punta Arenas experiments have proved that vegetables such as lettuce, cabbage, cauliflower, artichokes, beets, turnips, carrots, potatoes, and garlic grow very well. Someone has to teach farmers how to grow these things, someone has to build the necessary processing plants and the shipping facilities, and someone has to sell the idea of eating such things to the people of middle Chile. And as for timorous souls who fear the devastation of much of the world in a nuclear war, it appears that these settlements along the Strait of Magellan might be a source from which the world would be repopulated by mankind.

The Mines of Copper, Iron, and Coal

Punta Arenas is 1,200 miles by ship from middle Chile. Even its rapid development in recent years does not mean that any large numbers of people could emigrate from Chile's core area to the far south. Neither the north of Chile nor the south can provide an outlet for pioneer settlement, or do more than provide some additional support for the national economy through the production of oil, copper and nitrate. But in addition to these mineral products, there are also mines of copper, iron, and coal located in various other parts of the national territory.

The Copper Mines

The Andes of Chile contain a vast amount of low-grade copper ore. In the nineteenth century, when copper mining started, only high-grade ores could be used; but improvements of technology made during the first decades of the twentieth century made possible the use of the low-grade ores—which are in such enormous quantity that the considerable investment needed to exploit them is amply justified.

The northernmost of the Chilean ore bodies is at and around Chuquicamata, where mining started in 1915 by the Anaconda Copper Company. For many years it was believed that at Chuquicamata was the world's largest low-grade ore body, but since World War II an even larger body of such ore has been opened up at Toquepala in southern Peru (see pp. 492–493.). In recent times the Chuquicamata ores have been extended to vast new ore bodies both to the north (Sagasca), and to the south (Exotica). Chuquicamata and these other neighboring ore bodies are mined by open-pit methods. At Chuquicamata the pit is already more than two miles long by half a mile wide. Hundreds of thousands of tons of ore are taken out by gigantic mechanical shovels each day and moved to the smelters. The copper ingots are then moved into the new electrolytic refinery at Antofagasta, which is supplied with electric power from the generating plant in the Andes to the east (p. 568).

Farther south, some 75 miles east of the port of Chañaral, are the copper mines at Potrerillos and, a few miles to the north, El Salvador. Here the ore body cannot be reached by open-pit mining. In 1967 another new electrolytic refinery was placed in operation next to the copper smelter.

A third cluster of ore bodies is in the Andes both to the north and south of Santiago. The world's largest underground copper mine is at El Teniente, about 100 miles southeast of Santiago, a mine formerly owned by the Braden Copper Company, a subsidiary of the Kennecott Copper Company. A little northeast of Santiago, and just south of the Trans-Andean Railroad, is the newly developed Río Blanco copper mine. Still farther north—about 150 miles north of Santiago, and east of Combarbalá—is a new ore body at Loica which will be developed during the next decade. A considerable amount of molybdenum is found associated with these copper ores, which in the future will provide Chile with still another mineral export.

Iron Ore, Coal, Steel, and Sulphur

Chile also possesses the raw materials needed for a steel industry. The mining of iron started in 1908, when a French company undertook to make use of an ore body at El Tofo, 5 miles inland from Cruz Grande in northern Chile. From 1922 to 1952 the Bethlehem Steel Company, which then owned El Tofo, took out some 50 million tons of ore. Chile, before World War II, was the leading iron-ore exporter of Latin America. The El Tofo ore body is now almost exhausted; but since 1956 iron mining has moved to newly discovered ores. Iron ore has been found in three parts of Chile: (1) a body of high-quality ore in the mountains east of Antofagasta near the Argentine border—the high elevation (over 15,000 feet) and the distance from the coast will make the exploitation of these ores costly, but the ore body is large enough to support a large-scale operation; (2) a belt running parallel to the coast from southeast of La Serena to just north of Chañaral—this belt is about 300 miles long and less than 20 miles wide, located not more than 50 miles from the coast (El Tofo was the first discovery of ore in this area, but now there are some dozen known ore bodies); (3) in southern Chile south of Concepción there is a large amount of low-grade (30 percent iron) ore.

Over 90 percent of Chile's iron production is exported, mostly to Japan and the United States; and to reduce the costs of shipment, pelletizing plants have been built. The ore-shipping ports are being improved to accommodate the new super-ore carriers of over 100,000 tons.

In the Lebú Peninsula, just south of Concepción, Chile has some low-grade coal (subbituminous and lignite). The coal measures slope westward under the sea, and mining is already being carried on several miles out under the water.

In 1947, with financial aid and technical assistance from the United States, Chile built a modern steel plant at Huachipato, an industrial suburb of Concepción. Iron ore is brought by ship from Cruz Grande and other ports in northern Chile, 500 miles north of Huachipato. Coal comes by rail from Lota, the northernmost of the mining centers on the Lebú Peninsula. Limestone is shipped from a quarry in southern Chile, 900 miles to the south. The capacity of the Huachipato steel plant has been increased step by step until in 1968 it could produce over a million tons of steel per year.

Sulphur is another of Chile's mineral products. This mineral is found in the craters of the towering volcanoes of the Western Cordillera along the boundary between Chile and Bolivia. Although the deposits are of excellent quality and are very large, they occur at such high altitudes (17,000 to 20,000 feet above sea level) and in such remote places that to develop sulphur mining on a large scale would be very difficult. Most of the sulphur actually mined is used in Chile, but some of it is exported.

The Growth of the Industrial Cities

The transformation of Chilean life, which has been going on at a faster and faster rate since 1920, is reflected in the growth of industrial cities. When the *inquilino* is jarred loose from the estate on which his ancestors worked, he becomes a *roto,* one who is unattached. As we have seen, many of the *rotos* take jobs in the mining communities. Now that land for pioneer settlement in the south is no longer abundant, the cities offer the chief opportunities for employment. In the cities there is a growing middle class of shopkeepers, small-businessmen, government workers, and workers in an increasing number of service occupations. And in the cities there is an increasing number of jobs for wage workers in manufacturing industries. By the mid 1960's, Chile had tied Venezuela for the lead in the proportion of the population living in cities—67 percent. Argentina was second with 62 percent.

Although Chile has many small cities and towns, four conurbations have passed 100,000 each. The most important of these is Santiago, the capital. Santiago was laid out in 1541 on the typical rectangular plan which the Spaniards used almost everywhere in that period. As the focus of the political life of the thriving new colony, Santiago soon established its position as the largest and most beautiful of the Chilean cities. By 1865 the national capital had a population of 115,000. The rate of growth turned up sharply during World War I, and by 1920 Santiago had passed 500,000. The census of 1952 counted 1,750,000 in the metropolitan area, and by 1966 the number had reached 2,347,000. The original rectangular nucleus is now the hub of a wide zone of industrial suburbs and slums where the growing city has invaded the surrounding countryside.

Chile's second city is the port of Valparaiso, located near the mouth of the Río Aconcagua at the outlet of the productive Vale of Chile. A railroad descends to the coast through a narrow valley cut through the coastal plateau, and reaches the sea at the beautiful residential and resort town of Viña del Mar, only a short distance north of the port. Valparaiso itself is built on a

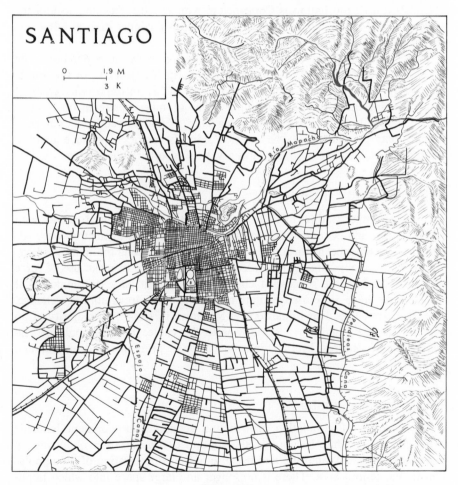

Map 101

north-facing bay which provides shelter from the southerly winds. The steepness of the slopes at the water's edge made the use of a rectangular pattern impossible: the streets at successively higher levels follow the semicircular contours of the bay; so steep are the connections between different levels that elevators have been installed to carry passengers from one level to another. The business district is built on a narrow terrace near the edge of the water; above it are residential areas; and, higher up, hilltop slums overlook the whole scene. A breakwater now gives the bay protection from the storm winds from the north, and makes it possible for ships to tie up at docks. In 1964 Valparaiso itself had a population of 280,000, and Viña del Mar, which is really a part of the same urban center, had 136,000—a total for the Valparaiso conurbation of 416,000.

Chile's third conurbation is Concepción, with its port Talcahuano and the adjoining steel city of Huachipato. The Concepción conurbation in 1964 had a total population of 270,000.

There were also several other cities rapidly growing in population. The other city over 100,000 in 1964 was Antofagasta (105,000). In the south, the city of Valdivia was a little less than this, but is an important center of manufacturing industry. Valdivia, built some 11 miles upstream on a small river that used to be navigable for sailing ships, is now served by an out-port, Corral, near the mouth of the river. Valdivia's factories produce textiles, wood products, leather products, and a variety of other consumer goods.

Chile as a Political Unit

Chile is another Latin-American country that is going forward rapidly with social change and economic development, but in its own distinctive way. Although there have been disruptive strikes, especially among the mine workers, and there are groups among the citizens who would like to make use of force either to speed up the process of change or to hold it back, the majority of the Chileans have supported evolutionary rather than revolutionary change. The election of President Eduardo Frei Montalva in 1964 by a majority of 56 percent was the Chilean voters' answer to the choice between violence and democratic procedures. Frei has introduced major programs of economic and social reform.

The Economic Situation

The problem of population growth and economic development is made more difficult in Chile because of the continued concentration of income in the hands of a small minority, and because of the concentration of the population in one central area. There is no longer any large space into which population could expand, and therefore the problems of growth must be faced where they are most threatening.

The problem of economic development in Chile can be summarized in figures. In 1967 the population was estimated to be almost exactly 9 million and was growing at the rate of 2.3 percent per year. An increase in the rate of growth is likely because of the progressive lowering of the death rate. Since no large pioneer zone exists, it is necessary to create jobs in the core area faster than the number of people looking for jobs increases. The gross national product per capita in 1963 was not much higher than it had been in 1953, but since the elections of 1964 there has been an acceleration of the rate of economic growth. In 1966 the gross national product per capita of $501 places Chile seventh among the independent Latin-American countries. But the concentration of the national income in the hands of a small minority is still a serious problem: in 1967 about 2.5 percent of the owners of land still owned 75 percent of the land, and about 25 percent of the total population was still living on a subsistence basis, essentially outside of the money economy. But the high proportion of literate people (83.6 percent), the large proportion of urban people, and the relatively small proportion of the working force employed in agriculture (27.5 percent) were favorable to continued economic growth.

Chile has been the world's second largest producer of copper for a long time. In 1965 Chile produced about 11 percent of the world's copper (as compared with the 24 percent produced by the United States). Copper accounted for nearly 60 percent of the value of all exports from Chile; yet it produced less than 10 percent of the gross national product. The copper mining represented an investment of about $750 million, chiefly by corporations owned in the United States—the Braden Copper Company (a subsidiary of Kennecott Copper), the Cerro Corporation, and Anaconda. To many people in Chile—and not only to the illiterate—it seemed like a perfect example of the removal of the national wealth of Chile by foreign interests. The presence of American-owned and managed mining operations was a source of irritation, and an easy target for communist propagandists. Frei's opponents in the election of 1964 proposed, if elected, to nationalize the copper mines.

Frei's policy was to cooperate with the foreign corporations and to create the kind of political climate that would lead to increased foreign investment. The Braden Copper Company was renamed *Sociedad Minera El Teniente,* and Chile purchased 51 percent of the stock, leaving Kennecott with the other 49 percent. With Chilean ownership, and the unpopular foreign name removed, there seemed some prospect that the mine workers would refrain from strikes and other forms of work stoppage. With the Cerro Corporation (Cerro de Pasco Copper Company), the arrangement was for Chile to own 25 percent of the stock, and for the company to invest a large sum of new capital in the development of the ores at Río Blanco. A similar arrangement was made with Anaconda to invest more money in Chuquicamata, and also in El Salvador and Exotica, with Chile owning a 25 percent interest. It was further agreed, that in the development of any new ore bodies (such as the one at Sagasca), Anaconda would hold 51 percent and Chile 49 percent. In each case, Chile's share was provided by loans from international agencies.

The United Nations started a "Chilean Mining Project" in the 1960's to use expensive modern technology in the search for new ore bodies. The Loica copper ores were discovered in this way. Also the United Nations group discovered the large body of high-grade iron ore near Vallenar. Continued exploration will certainly bring to light additional ore bodies.

LAND REFORM

Frei's program also calls for an acceleration of the process of land reform. As in the Mexican constitution of 1917 (see p. 70), land ownership must now fulfill a social function, and land that fails to produce the kinds of crops for which it is suited will be expropriated, with compensation to the owners. In 1967 the new reform law decreed fundamental changes which, as was pointed out, will end the existence of the Chilean hacienda as an institution. But the law continues to be attacked from the left because it does not go far enough and from the right because it is too drastic. The plan is to make Chile self-sufficient in basic foods by 1972.

Frei's program also calls for a diversification of the exports. Chile still depends too heavily on mineral exports (copper in 1965, 70 percent; iron ore 11 percent; and nitrate 4 percent). Plans call for the export of some 300,000 tons of steel by 1970. Chile is one of the leading supporters of the Latin-American Free Trade Association, from which it would stand to gain much. If Chilean industries can sell only to the Chilean market, this would scarcely pay for the high cost of modernization. But with Chilean resources, and Chilean skills, the economy would gain very greatly from access to a wider market.

The Political Situation

Before 1920, Chile's record of political stability had been almost unbroken. Its political life had been disturbed by few conflicts, and successive governments had all been dependable in meeting foreign obligations. It was stable, however, because its preindustrial and predemocratic society was undisturbed by change. The army and the landlords were in full control. Although most of the people were very poor, the paternalistic nature of the hacienda did not make poverty so burdensome as to cause a popular revolution. Furthermore, the War of the Pacific provided excitement; and after the War, pressures in middle Chile were relieved by the existence of the southern frontier of pioneer settlement.

Since 1920, however, Chilean politics have ceased to be calm. The movement of the *inquilinos* into the cities and the rise of the urban-industrial group have brought new pressures on the preindustrial political institutions that have inevitably led to unsettled conditions. There has been a series of military coups, dictatorships, and a popular revolution. In 1931 and 1932 Chile faced financial disaster because of the great decrease of its exports during the depression years. Exports dropped to less than a sixth of their 1929 value, and government revenues dropped to less than a third. Political instability, then, is the reflection of deep-seated changes in Chile's way of life. A struggle is now going on between the new urban workers and the conservative landowners, the traditional rulers of Chile. Underneath this struggle is population pressure—land hunger and the resultant demand for a more equitable distribution of the arable lands.

There is a large volume of popular discontent. The wages of the mine workers and the factory workers are still low. For a time the *rotos* were contented because they seemed to be better off than they were as *inquilinos*. But as more city people began to buy food at the markets, in the face of inadequate supply, prices have risen dangerously, so that now wages are not enough to provide for the needs of a family. There is strong popular support, therefore, for Frei's program of land reform.

As in so many other countries of Latin America in process of fundamental change, Frei's Christian Democratic Party must defend itself from attacks from both left and right. The Christian Democrats are opposed to communism because it is antireligious and antidemocratic, because it is clearly subservient to the Soviet Union, and because of its program of command economy. Frei's program is to develop in Chile a pluralistic, democratic, and welfare-oriented regime. Economic planning, and government participation in the mining enterprises, would, according to Frei, moderate the abuses of unrestricted capitalism, and avoid the dangerous concentration of power which is a part of the communist system. But the Christian Democrats are also under fire from the right, from those who prefer the traditional system with its special privileges for the fortunate few.

Between these extremes, democracy hangs by a slender thread. But because of the geographic arrangement of the Chilean nation, all these issues must be fought out within one compact central area. The problem would be infinitely more complex if all the opposition came from people located in one segment of the national territory, especially if this segment were in a peripheral position. But in the political geography of this country, the outlying parts of Chile are of no importance. The contestants in the central area are closely intermingled where escape from the necessity of finding solutions is not possible.

 República del Paraguay

Area: 157,047 square miles
Population: (1967 estimate) 2,161,000
          (last census, 1962) 1,851,890
Capital city: Asunción; (1964) 321,187
Percent urban: (1950) 34.6
Birthrate per 1,000: (1966) 42–46; Death rate per 1,000: (1966) 12–17
Annual percent of increase: (1958–64) 2.6
Percent literate: (1962) 74.3
Percent labor force in agriculture: (1950) 53.4
Gross national product per capita: (1966) $224
Unit of currency: guaraní (1968, 123.5 per dollar)

COMMERCE, 1965 *(expressed in percentage of values)*
Percent total Latin-American exports: 0.6 (1956, less than 1.0)
Percent total Latin-American imports: 0.6

Exports (1966)

meat	28	oilseeds	9	tobacco	5
lumber	22	quebracho	6	hides	5

Exports to (1966)		**Imports from (1966)**	
Argentina	32	United States	21 (1956, 29)
United States	23 (1956, 35)	Argentina	21
United Kingdom	8	West Germany	19
Uruguay	6	United Kingdom	6
Netherlands	5		

Chapter 22 □ Paraguay

Paraguay is a little country that somehow missed being a paradise. With a climate which is mild but not too mild and rainy but not too rainy, and with a soil which might yield abundant harvests of such subtropical crops as maize or rice, the central district in which the Paraguayans are concentrated possesses the physical qualities to permit an agricultural people to live in comfort if not in luxury. But it takes more than a comfortable climate or a satisfactory soil to lift people out of poverty.

The Paraguayan state is geographically simple. It is composed of one nucleus of clustered population (Map 95, p. 544), and its boundaries are drawn through the scantily occupied territory which surrounds this single nucleus. The one cluster of people, moreover, is racially homogeneous. Yet Paraguay, like the other states we have discussed, does not fail to illustrate in its own peculiar way the dominant theme of diversity. Not only are the Paraguayan people quite different in physical appearance and in racial composition from all the other population groups of the continent, but also, within the country, there are major contrasts of class and caste. There are profound differences between the minority of landowners, army officers, and government officials on the one hand, and the great majority of landless workers on the other. The Paraguayans are a gentle people who seem anything but warlike and belligerent; nevertheless the destiny of this inland state has been warped by two disastrous wars within a century. What Paraguay might have been is no longer important.

The People

The Paraguayans are mostly mestizo. Some 97 percent of them have at least one Spanish ancestor; but the predominant racial strain is Guarani Indian.

Perhaps 3 percent are pure Indian, but the number of people of pure European ancestry is very small. Some of those who are unmixed with Indian are the descendants of Germans and other Europeans who settled in Paraguay after 1870. There are almost no Africans and very few Orientals.

The Indians of Paraguay belong to the linguistic family known as Tupi-Guarani (Map 5, p. 14). This linguistic family was at one time concentrated in the basin of the Río Paraguay, and spread from that center over a large part of South America east of the Andes. The Guarani had even invaded the Quechua country in the Front Ranges of eastern Bolivia and established themselves there before the arrival of the Spaniards. They make up most of the coastal people of Brazil, and tribes which speak this same language are found even far in the interior of the Amazon. Before the arrival of the white men the Tupi-Guarani tribes practiced a shifting cultivation of maize and manioc, supplementing their diet with fish and game. Generally they were a friendly people, quite in contrast to their pugnacious brothers, the Abipones and the Puelche of Argentina or the Araucanians of Chile, or even the various other Indian groups of the Brazilian interior.

The Spanish Conquest

The establishment of a Spanish primary settlement center on the eastern side of South America had very different results from those which followed the founding of Lima (Map 6, p. 18). In Peru the Spaniards thought for a time that they had discovered El Dorado; but no such wealth awaited the colonists who came to South America from the east. In 1536 an expedition under Pedro de Mendoza landed on the shore of the Plata and established a settlement which was called Buenos Aires. But the boundless grassy plains contained no wealth of gold and silver, and the nomadic, warlike Indians were not disposed to be friendly. Nor could the Spaniards practice the kind of agriculture which, in the modern era, has turned this region into one of the world's leading sources of food. To the sixteenth-century Spaniards the Argentine grassy plains were low in potential productivity. In spite of its strategic location near the mouth of the Plata, Buenos Aires lacked the qualifications in terms of mines or large native populations which might have permitted it to become a primary settlement center. Shortly after its foundation, the colony was abandoned.

Meanwhile the Spaniards had pushed on up the Paraná, hoping to find a short route to Peru. In 1537 they had advanced far enough upstream to get beyond the savage Pampa tribes; and on the first bit of high ground which bordered the river within Guarani country, they founded the town of Asunción. As a route to Peru, however, the Paraguay-Paraná-Plata proved to be anything but satisfactory. Even to reach Asunción was such a difficult journey through the maze of shifting and shallow channels that a later Spanish expedition was brought overland directly from the east coast of what is now

Brazil. Asunción was isolated; but in the territory which has since become the nucleus of Paraguay, the productivity of the land and the numerous native population of friendly and adaptable Guarani offered the conditions necessary for the establishment of a Spanish feudal society.

Asunción became a primary settlement center. Lacking any source of wealth comparable with that which made Lima one of the wonders of the sixteenth-century world, this inland town nevertheless played the part of a nucleus of Spanish settlement from which the Spanish occupation of south-eastern South America radiated. Colonists advanced northwestward across the Chaco to found the town of Santa Cruz not far from the eastern base of the Andes. Settlements were spread also toward the east; and the final successful establishment of Spanish colonies on the margins of the Argentine grassy plains was accomplished by people who descended the Paraguay-Paraná-Plata from Asunción. Santa Fé was one of these colonies, founded in 1573; in 1580 the site of Buenos Aires was reoccupied.

Present Population

Few Spanish reenforcements came to Paraguay after the early expeditions of the sixteenth century. As a result, the Guarani contribution to the Paraguayan mixture is a relatively large one—not only of blood, but also of language and ways of living. To the European eye, however, the Paraguayan mestizo is by no means displeasing; for his complexion is lighter than that of the mestizo produced by the mixing of Spaniards and the highland Indians of the Andes, and his features are not so harsh. The Guarani language is still the popular language of Paraguay, and many of the place names throughout this part of South America, including the southern part of Brazil, are Tupi or Guarani words.

A third element of the Paraguayan population of today is made up of European immigrants who entered the country after 1870. The number is small, for most of the Europeans who came to South America during this period settled in Argentina or Brazil. But a few families of Italians, French, Spaniards, English, and Germans found their way to Asunción and settled there, intermarrying with the Paraguayans. At the present time the influence of this group in the economic, political, and social life of the country is of much greater importance than their numbers would suggest. In 1936 an experimental pioneer colony of Japanese farmers was settled some 80 miles southeast of Asunción. After World War II several other Japanese colonies were established, most of these a short distance north of Encarnación. Until recently the Japanese have mixed but little with their Paraguayan or European neighbors.

The Land

The Paraguayans live in a natural paradise. They enjoy the comfort of a mild climate, yet one which is not lacking in the stimulating effects of moderate weather change. They have an adequate supply of good soil for agricultural use. They possess forests and grasslands. Their country is neither monotonously flat nor sharply separated into contrasting extremes of mountain and plain. To be sure, the Paraguayans lack minerals; but perhaps mineral resources are not to be considered essential to a paradise.

The eastern third of Paraguay is an elevated plateau varying from one to two thousand feet in altitude (Map 87, p. 536). This is the western part of the great Paraná Plateau, a land composed of successive flows of dark-colored lava interbedded with layers of red sandstone (Map 8, p. 23). From the central part of the state of Rio Grande do Sul in southern Brazil, the southern and western edge of the plateau forms a commanding scarp or cuesta, cliffed at the top. The Río Paraná crosses it near Posadas and Encarnación. The scarp continues far northward across Paraguay and the Brazilian state of Mato Grosso. The Paraná, which flows southward through the center of the plateau, drops over the great Guaira Falls located where the northern border of Paraguay reaches the river. From the Guaira Falls to the place where the Paraná emerges from the plateau near Posadas and Encarnación the river flows in a deep valley cut through the lava flows. This valley forms the eastern border of Paraguay.

Between the cliffed edge of the Paraná Plateau and the Río Paraguay there are low, flat plains, generally inundated at high water, interrupted in two places by "peninsulas" of crystalline hills. The ancient crystalline rocks which form the basement complex of the Brazilian highlands are deeply buried beneath the lava flows of the Paraná Plateau, but they emerge to the west to produce a country strikingly different from the plateau. Granites and gneisses in warm, wet climates are much more rapidly decomposed than are lava flows or sandstones. Instead of the sharp features of the plateau, with its notably tabular profiles and its steep-sided canyons, the crystalline hilly uplands to the west are gently rounded in profile and of relatively slight relief. One of the peninsulas of crystalline hills extends northwestward to the Río Paraguay north of Concepción, even forming a few isolated mounds west of the river; the other peninsula reaches the left bank of the Paraguay at the site of Asunción. The central area of concentrated settlement in Paraguay is located on the belt of crystalline hills between Encarnación and Asunción.

The remainder of the territory east of the Río Paraguay is composed of a lowland plain, much of it subject to annual floods. Between the two peninsulas of crystalline hills two great bays of lowland bend far to the east of the river. One of these lies south of Concepción; the other forms a triangle of low country in the southwest, bordered along the northeast side by the hilly country of central Paraguay, and on the other two sides by the Paraguay and Paraná rivers. Along the immediate riverbanks there are natural levees sufficiently elevated to stand above all but the highest floods; but back of these narrow strips the back marshes are filled with stagnant water during the rainy season, and drain out only during the dry part of the year.

West of the Río Paraguay lies that vast alluvial plain known as the Gran Chaco—a region composed of unconsolidated sands and clays brought from the wasting Andes by the great rivers. The Río Pilcomayo, which forms the northern border of Argentina, and the Río Bermejo cross this plain with winding, shifting courses. Their braided channels change in pattern after each flood season, leaving additional complications in the already intricate pattern of crescent-shaped swamps and abandoned levees. The remainder of the Chaco is an almost featureless plain sloping gently from the base of the Andes to the Río Paraguay.

Vegetation and Climate

The natural cover of vegetation in Paraguay, as in other parts of the world, shows a general correspondence to the pattern of the climatic conditions, but conforms with the pattern of the surface and soil. Since the rainfall is highest on the Paraná Plateau and diminishes toward the west, the vegetation cover is densest in the east and thins out westward. Asunción has an average annual rainfall of a little over 50 inches, which, in these latitudes, is moderate (Map 12, p. 32, and Map 15, p. 35).

Semideciduous forests, reflecting this abundance of rain, cover the eastern part of Paraguay. They are composed of tall broadleaf trees; some of the species are evergreen and some deciduous. The forest is densest in the moist valleys of the plateau and thins out on the red sandy soils of the crystalline hilly belts. The lava soils, too, support a relatively dense tree growth, but sandy soils on the plateau, where the red sandstones come to the surface, are marked by patches of scrub woodland and palm.

Between the semideciduous forest and the Río Paraguay the vegetation is mostly savanna. In the wet spots there are some treeless areas covered with tall, coarse grass, but for the most part the savannas are mixed with scattered palms. Each tributary stream is followed by a dense screen of galeria forest.

Very different is the vegetation of the Gran Chaco. There are a few spots of palm savanna along the western banks of the river, but along most of its course the Paraguay is a major vegetation boundary. To the west are the deciduous scrub woodlands. In a zone along the river these woodlands grow luxuriantly, and among the species of scrubby trees is the quebracho (*Quebrachia lorentzii*), a tree valuable as a source of tannin (see p. 621). But as the rainfall decreases toward the west, the woodland becomes more and more xerophytic. There are thickets of thorny, deciduous trees and brush. Interrupting the woodlands in places where the soil is sandy are irregular openings covered with coarse savanna grasses. Over much of the Chaco there are no surface streams, but the water table is only a few feet below the surface. During the long dry season many patches of alkali make their appearance, and in many places the ground water is salty.

These features of surface, soil, drainage, and vegetation are combined in a land which is located near the margins of the low latitudes. During the winter (April to September), temperatures are in the 60's and 70's; during the summers (October to March), the temperatures range from the high 70's to the 90's. Maximum temperatures of 110° and over occur during this period (Map 9, p. 27). On the other hand temperatures in both summer and winter vary with the passing weather. Cold air masses from the south alternate with warm air from the north. During the passage of a cold front it is not uncommon for temperatures to drop as much as 30° in a half hour.

The Course of Settlement

At first it looked as if the settlers of Paraguay might succeed in creating a paradise. After the establishment of the nucleus of Spanish colonization around Asunción, the first penetration of the southern and eastern part of the country began in 1608 with the arrival of the Jesuit missionaries. The scattered and shifting tribes of Guarani Indians were gathered together around the missions and were taught to adopt a sedentary way of living. Thirty-two Jesuit missions were established in Paraguay east of the Río Paraguay. For the Indians, the new way of living based on farming, cattle raising, and the collection of forest products meant a more adequate and varied diet and greater security from famine. Unfortunately, however, the Jesuits could not maintain their isolation. Little by little they began to produce goods for sale outside of their small communities, eventually even trading their wines and tobaccos in the distant settlements along the eastern front of the Andes. This economic expansion brought the Jesuits into conflict with the large landowners who wanted both the profits of commerical enterprise and the assistance of the Indian workers. In 1767 the Jesuits were expelled and, for the Indians, paradise was lost. The mission communities fell apart. Those in the outlying sections of the country were entirely abandoned as the Indians drifted toward the central area around Asunción. The natives, unwilling to return to their former way of living, were speedily attached to the large estates through a system of debt bondage —in other words, they were reduced to a state of peonage. The result was the depopulation of the outlying districts and the increase of population in the center.

Independence and War

When the first independent Argentine government was set up in Buenos Aires in 1810, a claim was made for jurisdiction over the whole area then included in the viceroyalty of La Plata (Map. 16, p. 39). The Paraguayans, however, had no desire to be ruled from Buenos Aires. The political leaders at Asunción were successful in resisting Argentine efforts to expel the Spanish authorities, but since the only connection with Spain was downstream by way of Buenos Aires, the Paraguayans soon had to set up their own independent government. Without conflict, Spanish authority was passed to the dictator J. G. R. Francia. In 1840 Francia was succeeded by Carlos Antonio López, and he was succeeded by his son Francisco Solano López in 1862. During all this time the country was ruled by a powerful clique of army officers with the support of the few landowners. Always afraid of being forced to become a part of Argentina, the dictators built a strong army.

A major concern of the rulers of Paraguay was to gain an outlet to the sea that would free them from Argentine control. They were negotiating with Uruguay for such an outlet in 1864 when Brazil intervened to protect its southern boundary. The Paraguyans then resorted to force. Crossing the arm of Argentine territory east and south of the Río Paraná (Map 86, p. 535), they attempted to invade southern Brazil. This brought Brazil, Uruguay, and Argentina into an alliance against them and started a war that lasted from 1865 to 1870. It took five years for the armies of the triple alliance to defeat the Paraguayans, but at the end of the war Paraguay was devastated. Before the war Paraguay had a population of about 1,300,000; at the conclusion, the population had been reduced, according to some estimates, to less than 250,000, of whom only 28,746 were males.

From this crushing disaster Paraguay struggled slowly back, aided not a little by the European immigrants who brought new hope to a tired people. By 1912 the population was estimated to be about a million, and the ratio between the sexes was nearly normal again. But the economic development of Paraguay progressed slowly in the face of high transportation costs. In 1913 a railroad was completed all the way from Buenos Aires to Asunción, using ferries across the Paraná near Buenos Aires, and again near Posadas. But the volume of traffic was so low that high freight rates had to be charged. Before World War II, the cost of shipping a cargo from Buenos Aires to Asunción was about the same as the cost of shipping the same cargo to Yokohama.

The river has never offered an easy solution to the problem. Its braided channel is subject to frequent shifts of position and winds about to such a degree that many miles of sailing are required to cover only a short direct distance. Settlements located on the banks of the main channel are left with no access to the river when the channel shifts to another part of the floodplain; or sandbars are formed which make the river too shallow for navigation at the landing places. The main channel touches the base of higher ground not subject to flood at only a few spots—notably at Rosario and Santa Fé in Argentina, and at Asunción. Modern, ocean-going steamers can ascend the river only as far as Santa Fé and encounter much difficulty above Rosario. Yet in spite of the fact that the Paraguay-Paraná-Plata is such a poor river for navigation, it provided, until the present century, the only connection between Asunción and the outside world.

The Chaco

Most of the Paraguayan people are concentrated on the eastern side of the Paraguay-Paraná-Plata. The Chaco, which lies west of the river, is a world apart. As far as physical conditions are concerned, this great alluvial plain between the river and the base of the Andes bears a striking resemblance to the Ganges Valley of northern India. The climate of the two regions is similar; the scrub forest of both can be placed in the same general category of natural vegetation; and the similarity is increased by the presence in both regions of great sprawling rivers, subject to annual floods and frequent shifts of channel. Only in detail do the two pictures differ. But while the Ganges Valley is densely populated—more than a thousand rice- and wheat-growing farmers per square mile—the Chaco is one of the larger areas of very sparse population in Latin America. The Chaco is divided among four states— Argentina, Paraguay, Bolivia, and Brazil; yet only a small proportion of it can be included in the effective national territory of any of them.

This is the wilderness over which the Paraguayans and the Bolivians fought a war starting in 1932. Bolivia and Paraguay have each set forth abundantly documented legal arguments to support their claims to the territory north of the Argentine border and west of the Brazilian border. Between 1926 and 1931 the Paraguayans established about 35 villages of Canadian Mennonites some 125 miles west of the Río Paraguay on land which the Bolivians also claimed. Meanwhile the Bolivians placed army detachments far to the east in territory which the Paraguayans claimed. Although the whole area remained largely a wilderness, with few trails and few places where boundaries were clearly marked, the Paraguayans and Bolivians both pushed forward their outposts. The Bolivians were being led to believe, incredible as it may seem, that the extension of political territory to the banks of the Paraguay would in some miraculous fashion solve their problem of isolation. The Paraguayans were no doubt motivated to a certain degree by the strong hope that oil would prove to be available not only along the Andean front, but also in the plains east of the mountains. From 1932 to 1935 the two countries were locked in a death struggle: each of them, already burdened with debt, contracted new debts to pay the huge cost of armaments. The war was ended in 1935 when both sides were literally exhausted. A new boundary was drawn approximately along the line of battle as it was at the time of the armistice. It represented a considerable gain of new territory for Paraguay but left the known oil fields in the hands of the Bolivians.

Paraguay as a Political Unit

Paraguay is often used as an example of a successful dictatorship by those who believe that most underdeveloped countries are not ready for democracy.

General Alfredo Stroessner, who came to power in 1954, runs a "police state" with a firm hand. Every now and then Paraguay goes through the motions of an election, and Stroessner is returned to a new term as president. The dictatorship is not an oppressive one, and it is certain that the president has the support of a large majority of the politically powerful people. It is clear, also, that Stroessner has taken several important first steps toward economic development.

The Economic Situation

In 1967 it was estimated that Paraguay had a population of over 2 million, chiefly concentrated on the hilly belt between Asunción and Encarnación. About 65 percent of the people are rural, and 53 percent of the working force is employed in agriculture. The estimated rate of growth is 2.6 percent per year; but Paraguay's two wars have had the effect of reducing the population drastically. Not more than 2.5 percent of the Paraguayans own land, and almost all the farmers are squatters on the public domain, or on privately owned estates. But since land has always been abundant in Paraguay in relation to the total population, little prestige is attached to land ownership, and the squatter type of land occupancy is accepted as normal.

Most of the farmers raise subsistence crops of maize and manioc, with lesser acreages of rice, beans, oranges, and vegetables. There are numerous small plantings of bitter orange. The largest crop grown for sale is cotton.

Paraguay has taken some preliminary steps toward raising the level of the economy. In 1954 the only Latin-American country with a lower gross national product per capita than Paraguay was Haiti; but in 1965 the gross national product capita of $224 placed Paraguay in a tie with Ecuador for twentieth place.

One preliminary step toward improving the economy has been the construction of all-weather highways passable for motor trucks. By 1968 it was possible to travel by automobile at all times of the year to the Brazilian border near Iguaçu Falls, where an international bridge connects with the Brazilian highways; to Encarnación, where a ferry connects with the Argentine city of Posadas; and from the right bank of the Paraguay River all the way across the Chaco to the border of Bolivia. Additional roads were under construction to make the whole northeastern part of Paraguay accessible.

These highways have made possible the improvement of the economy of outlying farm colonies and also the resettlement of landless farm families from the crowded central area. The Mennonite colonies in the Chaco have been enlarged and increased in number, and other colonies have been established in eastern Paraguay. The most productive of the Mennonite colonies centers on Filadelfia, a town 270 miles northwest of Asunción, which was connected to the central area only in 1961. Since that date the farmers can market eggs, butter, cheese, and poultry in Asunción. There are now about

15,000 people in these Mennonite communities, operating farms that cover more than 2 million acres. In addition to foods for the Asunción market, the Mennonites also produce oilseeds, cotton, and beef cattle.

Under Stroessner's direction, also, Paraguay has for the first time enjoyed electric power in sufficient amount, and also gasoline at reasonable cost. A new hydroelectric power plant was completed in 1968 on the Río Acaray near its junction with the Paraná, and transmission lines make this electricity available throughout the central area. In 1966 an agreement was reached with Brazil for the joint development of the power potential of the Guaira Falls. In 1966, furthermore, a new oil refinery started operation in Asunción, and a start had been made for the construction of a pipeline to the Bolivian oil field at Camiri.

The city of Asunción, now with over 300,000 inhabitants, has also been improved. Electricity is now available in a large number of poorer homes that never had any before. In 1963 the city was served by a new water system that for the first time made drinkable water available in bathroom taps. Now towering above the older and lower buildings of the city, there is a new fourteen-story hotel. Near the city there are new factories, including a meat-packing plant which for the first time permits the export of Paraguayan beef.

In fact, frozen meat now makes up some 28 percent of the value of all exports. Timber from the forests of eastern Paraguay in 1966 made up 22 percent of all exports. Other exports were oilseeds, quebracho extract, tobacco, and hides. The quebracho extract is a major source of tannin for tanning leather; it is produced in tannin factories along the Paraguay River, to which the quebracho logs are brought to be processed. Also exported in small quantities is petigrain oil distilled from the unripe fruit of bitter orange trees, which is used in the manufacture of perfume.

The Political Situation

Neither the industrial revolution nor the democratic revolution have yet reached Paraguay. But Paraguay has developed more of a sense of national unity than most of its neighbors. Perhaps this can be explained in part by Paraguay's inland position and by the geographic unity of its one nucleus of concentrated settlement. Ever since 1810 Paraguay has sought freedom from outside interference, but the search had been largely frustrated. Although Paraguay emerged from the Chaco War as the victor over Bolivia, the military effort left the country even more impoverished than before. Also, the returning soldiers were less ready to accept economic misery and the lack of opportunity for political expression than they had been before the war.

In 1954, when the government in power planned to nationalize some of the few industries, General Stroessner, with the backing of the conservatives, took over the presidency. Since that time no opposition press has been tolerated, and in the elections there is only one candidate. On the other hand, Stroessner has not felt the need to resort to excessive police action. The great majority of the people are outside the range of political affairs, and most of those in political power give their support to the dictator. There is widespread support for Stroessner's policy of building for the future improvement of the economy. If goals are not set too high, it could be that Paraguay might some day become a kind of paradise.

República Argentina

Area: 1,072,067 square miles
Population: (1966 estimate) 22,691,000; (last census, 1960) 20,005,691
Capital city: Buenos Aires; (1960) 6,763,000
Percent urban: (1947) 62.5
Birth rate per 1,000: (1966) 21.8; Death rate per 1,000; (1966) 8.3
Annual percent of increase: (1958–64) 1.6
Percent literate: (1960) 91.4
Percent labor force in agriculture: (1965) 19.3
Gross national product per capita: (1966) $700
Unit of currency: peso (1968, 345 per dollar)

COMMERCE, 1965 *(expressed in percentage of values)*
Percent total Latin-American exports: 15.0 (1956, 12)
Percent total Latin-American imports: 13.9

Exports (1966)			
wheat, maize, and other grains	33	wool	8
meat and meat products	33	hides	5
oilseeds, vegetables	8		

Exports to (1966)		**Imports from (1966)**	
Italy	16	United States	23 (1956, 20)
Netherlands	10	Brazil	14
United Kingdom	10 (1956, 23)	West Germany	9
Brazil	8	Italy	7
West Germany	6	United Kingdom	6
China	5		
Spain	5		
United States	4 (1956, 12)		

Chapter 23 □ Argentina

Argentina was the first Latin-American state to start the process of economic growth and development. By 1930 this country was preeminent in Latin America: it had the highest gross national product per capita, the highest value of foreign trade, the highest percentage of literacy, the largest proportion of the population living in cities, the largest area of farmland per person, and the smallest proportion of the working force employed in agriculture. Furthermore, by 1930 it had enjoyed almost seventy years of uninterrupted constitutional government. Its internationally famous newspaper, *La Prensa,* had long stood for equality before the law, for widespread public education, for free access to knowledge, and for the open discussion of political issues. But then, since the 1930's, Argentina's economic growth came to a standstill, it suffered a succession of military interventions and one disastrous dictatorship. Its people are sharply divided on basic issues of public policy. What happened to Argentina?

Argentina's rapid economic growth before 1930 was in large part the result of investments of British capital and the export of such primary products as meat, wheat, maize, and linseed. But when the great depression led to the collapse of the system of international trade, Argentina was one of the major victims. The dominance of primary exports resulted in the creation of an almost exclusive focus of Argentine life on the great port city of Buenos Aires. The Argentine territory was composed of contrasted regions, each of which made its distinctive contribution to the social, economic, and political life of the nation. But each region was more closely attached to Buenos Aires than to its neighbors. The problem now is to rebuild the economy by developing an internal integration among the regions, and to provide a larger measure of coherence among the different social and political groups.

The People

Against a diverse background ranging from lofty mountains to vast plains, from regions of extreme drought to regions of abundant moisture, and from continuously cold and stormy lands to lands which, like Paraguay, border on the tropics, the Argentine people have distributed themselves in a pattern which is notably uneven and diverse in character (Maps 95 and 96). Two chief population zones can be described: there is the string of oasis settlements along the eastern piedmont of the Andes, focusing chiefly on Tucumán, Mendoza, and Córdoba; and there is the larger and entirely different concentration on the Humid Pampa, focusing on Buenos Aires.

The degree to which the Argentine national life is concentrated in the immediate hinterland of Buenos Aires is extraordinary, especially when we understand that this concentration is a product of the last century. Buenos Aires itself is not only the largest city of Argentina and the largest city in Latin America, but also it is the largest urban center of the Southern Hemisphere, and second only to Paris among the Latin cities of the world. The Humid Pampa makes up about 22 percent of the total area of Argentina; yet in this one region there are some 14 million people, about 66 percent of the entire Argentine population. In this region are nearly 70 percent of all the railroads, 84 percent of all the automobiles, 86 percent of all the territory used for the production of cereal and flax, 63 percent of all the cattle, and 85 percent of all the industrial production. Argentine economists figure that in this one region is concentrated 82 percent of the productive capacity of Argentina.

In proportion to the concentration of economic activity in this region, the density of the rural population is surprisingly low. There are only a few spots near Buenos Aires where the population exceeds 100 per square mile. The zone with densities between 25 and 60 per square mile extends westward from the capital city for only about 200 miles. Most of the Humid Pampa has a rural density of between 10 and 25 people per square mile. On the other hand, more than 70 percent of the people in this region live in towns and cities. In the metropolitan area of Buenos Aires there were more than 7 million people in 1967, or 34 percent of the nation's populace. Outside of Buenos Aires, but within the area of the Humid Pampa, there were eight cities of more than 100,000 in population.

The other clusters of people in Argentina are quite different from the great cluster around Buenos Aires: the oasis settlements of the Andean piedmont represent a much older colonization, and a colonization which came from the north and west, from across the mountains, rather than from the east across the plains (Map 6, p. 18).

Outside of the piedmont oases and certain smaller concentrations in the North, the rest of Argentina is very sparsely settled. Nearly half of the national territory, in fact, is occupied by less than 8 percent of the people: over vast areas there is a population density of scarcely 2 people per square mile.

Racial Character and Origins

The Argentine people are different from any Latin-Americans we have discussed hitherto. The overwhelming majority are of unmixed European descent. In 1930 it was estimated that 74 percent were Argentine-born of European parents, and 24 percent were recent immigrants born in Europe. Since 1930, the current of immigration has greatly decreased, so that the proportion of European-born Argentines is now less than 24 percent. The official Argentine estimates place the proportion of people of unmixed European ancestry at 97 percent; but this figure certainly conceals the presence of considerable numbers of mestizos in the outlying parts of the country on the borders of Chile, Bolivia, and Paraguay. In the Humid Pampa the population is exclusively European, and made up mostly of families that have arrived in Argentina since 1853. Only about 3 percent of the whole population is pure Indian; and the proportion of Africans is negligible.

The Argentine territory was originally settled by people who came from Peru, Paraguay, or Chile. We have already noted that the first attempt to establish a settlement on the Plata shore in 1536 ended in failure. Asunción became the primary settlement center from which the Spaniards spread over much of the surrounding territory. Corrientes, Santa Fé, and Buenos Aires (1580) were established by people from Ascunción.

Meanwhile, however, the northwest of Argentina was being occupied by people who came either directly or indirectly from the other great Spanish culture center, Lima. The chief route of settlement followed the old Inca road to the southeastern outpost of the Inca Empire, near Tucumán. Since the early route to Chile avoided the Atacama and the high Puna country by making a long circuit to the east and then crossing the single range of the Andes south of latitude 28° S., this eastern piedmont of the highlands was intimately connected with the settlement of Chile during the sixteenth century. The first Spanish stronghold, and the center from which other colonies in this region were established, was Santiago del Estero, founded by people who returned from middle Chile in 1551 and 1553. From this center other settlements were made at Tucumán (1565), Córdoba (1573), Salta (1582), La Rioja (1591), and Jujuy (1593). The eastern piedmont settlements farther to the south were settled also by people who came across the mountains from Chile: Mendoza (1561–62); San Juan (1562); and San Luis (1596). A strong current of immigrants from Chile in more recent times has supplemented the population of the Argentine oases from Mendoza to Neuquén, and people of Chilean origin are the chief settlers of the eastern Andean border in southern Patagonia. The reasons for this outward movement of Chileans during the latter part of the nineteenth century have already been discussed: its result was the development in this part of Argentina of a population of mestizo character, with a background of tradition quite different from that of the inhabitants of modern Buenos Aires.

The people of all the early settlements had trouble with the nomadic Indians of the Argentine plains (Map 5, p. 14). The Abipones, the Puelche, and other tribes of the Pampas and Patagonia, although not numerous, were independent and warlike. They resisted the invasion of the Spaniards as they had that of the Incas. These migratory hunters of the guanaco and the rhea never could be tamed for agricultural labor as the Guarani had been tamed. If they lacked the shelter of the forests that their brothers, the Araucanians, enjoyed, they nevertheless were more than a match for the Spaniards on the arid or semiarid plains and plateaus where knowledge of the water sources was of primary importance. The adoption of horses and firearms by these Indians had much the same effect as on the Indians of the Great Plains of North America. Greatly increased mobility and capacity to kill the wild game was a temporary advantage; but the decreasing numbers of the animals made the Indians even more warlike in their struggle for wider hunting grounds. Until the last quarter of the nineteenth century a line of forts across the Humid Pampa barely held the weak barrier of the Río Salado; they provided a quite inadequate protection for the settlements along the Paraná-Plata shores and the route to Córdoba. As late as 1876 it was estimated that something like 40,000 head of cattle were stolen every year in Indian raids—many of them being sold in Chile. With the campaign of 1879–83, however, the Indians were pushed back and the line of forts was extended to include more and more of the grassy plains. Not until the year 1880 was the settlement of Bahía Blanca, at the southern margin of the Humid Pampa, connected by land with the towns to the north and west. But the Indian days are now gone, and only on reservations in the more remote and unattractive regions can pure Indian peoples be seen today.

During the colonial period the piedmont settlements of the northwest and west belonged to a different world. They were connected economically with the west coast. At Salta a fair was held each year at which mules and cattle from the grassy plains were sold to the mining peoples of the Andes. But the seminomadic *gauchos* of the plains or the inhabitants of the small Plata ports had little real contact with the inhabitants of the piedmont oases.

The story of the rapid increase of European immigration after the middle of the nineteenth century, the spread of railroads and agriculture, the growth of Buenos Aires, is a story which belongs properly to the discussion of the settlements of the Humid Pampa. Its effect has been to create a new and quite different kind of population, moved by different purposes, and achieving a very different way of living from that of the older piedmont settlements. But the latter have not been left untouched. They have been reoriented economically, and now come definitely within the influence of Buenos Aires; they maintain no more than a mere trickle of commerce with the countries on the other side of the mountains. Tucumán and Mendoza, too, have received a considerable current of immigration, in part composed of people from other Argentine provinces. Today the long struggle between these contrasted portions of Argentina for economic domination is at an end. Buenos Aires is at the present time the focus of everything Argentine.

The Land

The Argentine national territory includes a wide variety of kinds of land (Maps 87 and 88). The Argentine geographers recognize four major physical divisions, each with numerous subdivisions. Except in the far south, the border with Chile runs through rugged, mountainous country. The first major division, the Andes, runs from the cordilleras of the dry north to the heavily glaciated and ice-covered mountains of Patagonia. It includes also the very dry southern part of the Bolivian Altiplano, and the lower but also very dry basin and range desert west of Córdoba and south of Tucumán. The eastern piedmont of the Andes with its succession of oasis settlements may be included in this first major division of the country.

The second major division is the North—a region which comprises the three chief kinds of land already described for Paraguay. There is the vast alluvial plain of the Chaco, with its tropical scrub-woodland cover. On the east and south of the Río Paraná there is Argentine Mesopotamia, the land between the rivers (the Paraná and the Uruguay), composed partly of floodplain, partly of gently rolling and well-drained interfluves. In the far northeast there is an arm of Argentine territory which extends onto the Paraná Plateau.

The third major division of the country is the Pampas—the great plains which lie south of the Chaco and east of the Andean piedmont. Most of these plains were originally covered with a growth of low scrubby trees and grasses, a vegetation type known as *monte;* but toward the southeast of the Pampas, where the rainfall is heavier and the summers remain cool, tall prairie grasses were once probably more important than the *monte*. It is customary to divide the Pampas into a wetter eastern part and a drier western part—designated respectively as the Humid Pampa and the Dry Pampa. When the Argentines refer to *La Pampa,* they are referring to the territory of that name which lies mostly within the Dry Pampa.

Finally, the fourth major physical division of Argentina is Patagonia, the region south of the Río Colorado. This is a land of arid, wind-swept plateaus, crossed at wide intervals by strips of green vegetation along the valley bottoms. In the far south of Patagonia Argentina shares with Chile the land of continuously cool and stormy weather, where winters are never severe, but where there is never any summer.

The various currents of settlement, which brought not only changes in the character of the population, but also changes in the relationships between

The Iguazú Falls on the border between Argentina and Brazil. The river, some 2.5 miles wide, drops over hundreds of separate falls with wooded islands between them. *Courtesy of Brazilian Government Trade Bureau.*

the people and the land, have also had the effect of developing and diversifying the regions of Argentina. Some of the most distinctive divisions of the country, and some which are commonly described as "natural" regions, have in reality been given their marked individuality by the selective process of human settlement. The Humid Pampa, for example, was not a region of definite personality to the Indian whose wild game made little distinction between what we call "humid" and "semiarid." Nor did the herders of the scrub cattle and mules of the colonial period find any sharply defined line between the *monte* and the tall bunch grasses. The western margin of the Humid Pampa was not a conspicuous feature until grain farming made it so. In fact our concept of the terms "humid" and "semiarid" is based fundamentally on the needs of occidental wheat farming under the economic system of the late nineteenth century. The Humid Pampa has been "developed" as a result of the last hundred years of settlement.

The popular consciousness of regions is the product of many generations of experience. In pioneer lands the settlers seldom are aware of the regional divisions that the geographer describes to them. Because pioneer settlement by occidental peoples is so closely tied to the lines of transportation, the divisions of a frontier territory commonly recognized by the settlers themselves are the areas served by the different routes of access. The people living in the Argentine Humid Pampa still think of themselves as in the zone of this or that railroad line; to this day popular consciousness of the unity of the Humid Pampa has not proceeded far enough to bring into common use any proper name for it.

The regions of Argentina as they have been developed by the activities of the inhabitants are all focused on that nucleus of the country, the Humid Pampa, and its great urban center, Buenos Aires. Until after 1853, however, the Humid Pampa played a subordinate role, and the outlying portions of the country—the Northwest, Mesopotamia, the Chaco, and Patagonia—all had most of their connections with foreign countries. Little by little the domination of Buenos Aires has been extended to more and more remote places. Contact with this growing urban center meant the possibilty of selling in an expanding market; but, in each case, recent years have revealed that such contact also leads inevitably to economic vulnerability in time of financial depression. Before turning to the central region itself, let us consider the parts of Argentina that surround it.

The Northwest

No physical change distinguishes Bolivia from the Northwest of Argentina. The same natural divisions of the land are found on either side of the border; from west to east one proceeds from the Altiplano with its dry intermont basins, across the undissected Puna, across the eastern margin of the Puna where the east-flowing streams have cut deep valleys, across the zone of the

Front Ranges, and finally to the Chaco. Puna and Altiplano together in northern Argentina are approximately 250 miles wide, standing between 11,000 and 13,000 feet above sea level. Above the Puna surface there are isolated ranges, some of which reach elevations of more than 19,000 feet; and especially along the eastern margin, the Puna surface has been cut by streams; here the commanding east-facing front of the Puna is breached at several places by broad valleys, or *quebradas,* which offer relatively easy routes of access to the high country beyond. Between the eastern front of the Puna and the western margin of the Chaco there is a zone of Front Ranges, composed of parallel cuestas and hogback ridges, separated by roughly north–south structural depressions, or *valles.* About the latitude of Tucumán this country comes to a southern ending: south of Tucumán the mountain landscape and the landscape of the eastern piedmont are quite different from the landscapes farther north.

The natural vegetation, also, is a southward continuation of the types already described in Bolivia. The high Puna is covered with a scanty growth of widely spaced xerophytic shrubs. On the east-facing edge of the Puna and on the tops of some of the more prominent Front Ranges there is a narrow belt of mountain forest—a *ceja de montaña*—composed of a dense growth of broadleaf trees. A deciduous scrub woodland covers the Chaco and invades the *valles* of the Front Range zone. All these types reach a southern ending at approximately the latitude of Tucumán.

The decreasing supply of moisture along the eastern piedmont is reflected not only in the increasingly xerophytic character of the natural vegetation, but also in the type of agriculture. South of Tucumán no crops can be raised along the piedmont without irrigation. From Tucumán northward irrigated and unirrigated crops are mixed: some of the sugarcane at Tucumán is unirrigated as are also some of the fields of maize in the *valles* around Salta and Jujuy. But in this zone there are also many irrigated spots, especially where the alluvial soils are very porous. Generally there is no permanent surface water in the *valles,* and irrigation is limited to the heads of the alluvial fans that emerge from the *quebradas.* Tucumán, however, is abundantly supplied with water from the several streams which descend from the Sierra de Aconquija, a commanding range more than 17,000 feet high, which here forms the eastern border of the mountain zone.

South of about latitude 27° S., the territory lying between Tucumán, Mendoza, and Córdoba is dry land, composed of elongated and roughly north–south ranges and broad depressions with salt flats or salt lakes along their bottoms. This is a typical basin and range landscape, similar to the Great Basin region of the United States—a region mostly without exterior drainage.

Colonial Settlement in the Northwest

Even before the arrival of the Spaniards, the permanent settlements in this part of South America were made by people who came from the highlands.

The Incas established a fortress in the vicinity of Tucumán, and maintained their control of the Indians inhabiting the *valles* of the Front Range zone. The Incas, however, were unable to do more than hold in check the raids of the nomadic Indians of the plains. Proceeding along the Inca road, the Spaniards, on the way to Chile, passed through what is now the Argentine Northwest. All the important towns, as we have said, were established between 1551 and the end of the sixteenth century.

During the whole colonial period these settlements were attached economically to the highlands and to the west coast. The restriction of Spanish colonial trade to the Panamá route kept Buenos Aires in the category of a smuggling port; but the Argentine plains produced one item of such importance to the highland centers that the whole economic life of the region was oriented toward the Northwest. If there is any one creature to which credit should be given for the conquest of the South American continent it is the mule, for this animal alone made possible the transportation of goods over the rugged mountain trails at very high altitudes. And the Argentine plains became the chief source of this patient, sturdy, but sterile, offspring of a mare and a jackass. Because mares could not be kept at the high altitudes and on the scanty feed available in the mining regions of Peru and Bolivia, it was necessary to breed the mules elsewhere and maintain a constant stream of reinforcements on the way toward the highlands.

The mule trade developed distinct currents of movement and centers of commerce. The breeding went on mostly on the grassy basins between Córdoba, Rosario, and Sante Fé. In this district there were seminomadic herders of cattle and mules, who, like the *llaneros* of Venezuela, established no permanently fixed settlements. These were the picturesque *gauchos*. The cattle were of value chiefly for their hides, but the demand for young mules was apparently unlimited. The young animals were first concentrated on irrigated pastures around Córdoba, Santiago del Estero, and Tucumán. Each year, in the latter part of April, herds of two-year-old mules were started northward, reaching Salta before the end of June. From June until February they were fed on irrigated pastures in the *valles* around Salta. In February and March an annual fair was held at which three-year-old mules were traded for silver from Peru and Bolivia or for expensive products imported through Lima and Panamá from Spain. By the end of March, when the summer rains had subsided enough to make the trails passable, the new owners started northward with their mules, and the plainsmen started on the return journey southward. During the colonial period Salta, through its annual fair, was the main commercial center of this whole region. There, during the latter part of the eighteenth century and the early part of the nineteenth, as many as 60,000 mules were traded annually.

Salta and Jujuy in the Modern Era

Salta today is a place of small importance. No longer the focus of the economic life of the chief area of settlement in Argentina, Salta is now a remote outpost, with only a vestige of its former commerce in livestock. A narrow-gauge, single-track railroad has been built westward across the high, arid, and very thinly populated Andes to the nitrate-mining communities of the Atacama, following a route over which cattle used to be driven on the hoof. Very little traffic, however, is carried on this costly line. Only very minor commercial contacts are maintained between the communities of the *valles,* which produce wheat and maize, and the communities of the highlands, which produce wool and salt. The large estates of the *valles,* which include many square leagues of mountain pasture, are still used primarily for the production of low-grade beef animals. In the winter, when the lowlands are dry, the cattle are driven into the highlands; in the summer they return to the pastures lower down. The croplands of the lowlands, irrigated or unirrigated, are used mostly for the production of the food crop maize and the feed crop alfalfa, on which the animals are fattened for local markets.

The problems of settlement in the modern era in the *valles* of northwestern Argentina are similar to those previously described for Bolivia. The difficulty is primarily the result of remoteness and small area. From the point of view of climate and soil these districts could be made very productive; but each *valle* is too small to support a community large enough to pay the high costs of building roads to outside markets. Scattered, isolated communities of small size, like those of highland Bolivia, are the result.

Tucumán

Tucumán, on the other hand, has been able to solve the problem of access to a market. The growth of this city to a population of about 290,000, and the concentration in the Tucumán district of more than 300 people per square mile, is the result of an interesting combination of factors, among which the factor of location is of fundamental significance.

During the colonial period Tucumán enjoyed a strategic position on the main route of travel between the Argentine plains and Salta. The roads from Rosario, Córdoba, and Santa Fé converged on Tucumán rather than on Salta because here the crossing of the dry belt was relatively easy. Two rivers, the Salado and the Dulce, provide an ample supply of surface water along this route: north of the Salado no road crossed the Chaco from the Paraná to the Andean piedmont. Tucumán was the center through which almost all the colonial trade of Argentina passed. This town was an important outfitting point not only for people starting northward toward Salta, but also for those who wished to enter the grassy plains to the southeast. Wagon manufacturing and harness making were undertaken, and in the course of more than two centuries a considerable amount of wealth was accumulated by the people of this active community. When the colonial period came to an end and Argentina reoriented its economic life, Tucumán remained a city of wealth and historic tradition.

The rise of modern Tucumán as a sugarcane district came late in the nineteenth century. Physical and economic conditions were favorably combined at just this one spot for the successful planting of sugarcane for the supply of the Buenos Aires market: Tucumán was barely within range of the big metropolis, transportation costs until recently having been too high for the shipment of sugar from places farther north; and Tucumán also lies barely within the range of sugarcane, for the frosts are too severe for this crop farther south and east. In just this district, moreover, an alert and active people possessed the necessary capital, aided by some additional capital from British investors, to start the new plantations and set up the sugar mills. The rapid development of sugarcane planting started during the last quarter of the nineteenth century and had reached full development by the beginning of World War I.

The Tucamán district possesses several physical advantages for the cultivation of sugarcane which are not to be duplicated elsewhere in the northwest of Argentina. The zone of Front Ranges comes to an end just north of Tucumán, and the eastern border of the Puna is surmounted, just west of Tucumán, by the high Sierra de Aconquija. No obstruction stands between this range and the warm, moist winds from the east. The result is a zone of abundant rainfall on the slopes of the Aconquija, supporting there, at intermediate altitudes, the southernmost end of the dense tropical semideciduous forest. From this belt of abundant rain and from the snowfields higher up, several permanent streams descend to the piedmont, crossing the alluvial fans to join the Río Sali—a headwater of the Río Dulce, which flows by the site of Tucumán itself. As a matter of fact, the rainfall at Tucumán is about 37 inches a year, and between the Río Sali and the base of Aconquija there is not only an abundance of water in the streams, but also enough rainfall in the average year to render irrigation unnecessary. The rainfall, however, is subject to irregularities, and irrigation is actually practiced to guard against drought. On the eastern side of the Sali there are no tributary streams to provide water for irrigation, and the rainfall decreases rapidly as one proceeds away from the mountains.

This island of abundant rainfall produced by the slopes of the Sierra de Aconquija is also an island of relatively mild winter temperatures. The cloud banks have the effect of cutting down night radiation so that the minimum winter temperatures do not drop so low as they do under clear skies even somewhat farther north. Close to the base of the mountains the Tucumán area is frost-free, for this zone is given additional protection by the rapid air drainage near the tops of the alluvial fans. As one proceeds eastward the decrease of the fanslopes and of the protecting blanket of cloud results in an increase in the frequency of frosts. Near the mountain, frosts are limited to pockets where the cold air accumulates, but farther out, killing frost nearly every winter makes sugar production costly and speculative. Frost-free areas are found for about 35 miles east of the mountain front.

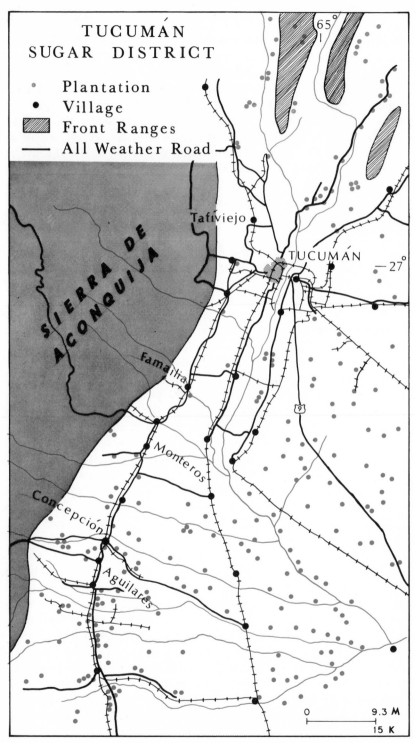

TUCUMÁN SUGAR DISTRICT

- Plantation
- Village
- Front Ranges
- All Weather Road

SIERRA DE ACONQUIJA

Tafíviejo

TUCUMÁN

Famaillá

Monteros

Concepción

Aguilares

65°

—27°

9

0   9.3 M

15 K

Map 102

SUGARCANE PLANTATIONS

All these facts, however, were not known to the first cane planters of Tucumán. They have been discovered chiefly by the wasteful process of trial and error; and the wreckage is still visible of plantations developed too far to the east where frosts are too severe. Of much greater importance in determining the location of the first plantations were the roads and railroads. Sugarcane growing started near the city of Tucumán, and one line of estates was extended southeastward along the east side of the Río Sali, where the land was easier to clear than it was nearer the mountains. In 1874 a railroad was built southward from Tucumán on the west side of the Río Sali to connect with Córdoba, and this became a second axis of new sugarcane planting; and between 1888 and 1890 a branch railroad was built in the form of a loop to open up the country closer to the mountain front. New plantations were set out at once along this line. Most of the plantations which have since filled in the space between these railroads are supplied with systems of irrigation.

Meanwhile the sugar planters have actually invaded the mountain region, climbing the lower slopes of the Sierra de Aconquija. In this section irrigation is not practiced, for the abundant rainfall and the rich forest soil bring high cane yields. Although the sugar content of the cane of the mountain slopes is less because of the decreased amount of sunshine, up to a certain point this decrease is not serious. Through the whole area sugarcane occupies more than 60 percent of the land devoted to crops, and the sugar area is more than twice as great as that used for maize—which is a very different agricultural picture from that of Jujuy and Salta where maize occupies the larger acreage.

The cane lands of the Tucumán District are owned and operated in a variety of ways. There are large estates on which the work is performed by hired laborers; there are estates worked by tenants who pay rent to the owners; and there are many independent growers working on their own small properties. The refineries, or *ingenios,* are not owned by the individual planters but by independent companies; the network of railroad lines necessary to bring the cane promptly to the mills at harvest time is also owned and operated by independent companies. The competition that develops each year among the mill owners for the purchase of cane from the planters has the effect of raising the price which the planters receive.

Sugarcane planting is a form of agriculture which requires the services of a large number of people. As the new industry developed it was necessary to recruit gangs of laborers in neighboring communities such as Santiago del Estero, Catamarca, and even Córdoba. As time went on, the population of the Tucumán area was increased by the arrival of many people from other parts of northern Argentina who settled permanently on the cane plantations or in the vicinity of *ingenios*. Relatively few came directly from foreign countries, and for this reason Tucumán still retains a character distinct from that of the other big cities of Argentina. At present the Tucumán District has a population of nearly 800,000 people, and a much higher rural density than that of any other part of Argentina. Nevertheless, the labor demands of the harvest season are so great that during the period from June to October many additional workers come to the sugar district from small communities scattered throughout the North and Northwest.

Mendoza and the Other Vineyard Oases

Agriculture changes notably south of Tucumán. North of that city maize and sugarcane in varying proportions are the chief crops. Although the rainy season both to the north and to the south of Tucumán is in summer, the annual rainfall diminishes so rapidly toward the south that no crops can be raised nor animals pastured without the aid of irrigation. South of Tucumán, alfalfa rather than maize is the crop which covers the largest area, and vineyards assume first place in the commercial life. The so-called vineyard oases include three large ones: Mendoza in the middle, San Juan about 100 miles to the north of Mendoza, and San Rafael about the same distance south of Mendoza. In addition to the three large oases, there are the smaller irrigated areas of La Rioja and Catamarca, which lie between San Juan and Tucumán.

In this part of Argentina the great dry belt of South America spreads its full width across the plains to the east of the Andes. Between Córdoba and Mendoza the rainfall is very slight. At Mendoza itself the average is only 7.6 inches, and at San Juan, 3.5 inches. This is also the zone of transition between the hot deserts of the north and the cool deserts of Patagonia.

Water for irrigation is essential for permanent settlement in this desert land. Wherever streams which tap the snowfields of the high Andes emerge from the mountains onto the eastern piedmont, oases are established. The oasis of San Juan is supported by the Río San Juan. For many miles south of San Juan no permanent streams break through the eastern rampart of the Andes; then two important rivers, the Río Mendoza and the Río Tunuyán, emerge within a short distance of each other. The water of these two streams is used to form the large irrigated tract around Mendoza. Still farther south two other rivers, the Diamante and the Atuel, support the oasis of San Rafael.

The region as a whole is one of interior drainage. The streams descend from the mountains over broad alluvial fans which stretch out eastward with gradually decreasing slopes. Only the larger streams persist in their flow across these fans. All unite their waters in a zone of sloughs or playas, which, on some maps, are indicated with a river symbol, although a current of surface water is in reality only developed in time of flood. Occasionally water makes its way through these sloughs to the Río Colorado, but most of the time it escapes only by evaporation.

The rural landscape of the vineyard oases is distinctive. Always in the background are the naked, rocky slopes of the easternmost ranges which shut out the view of the higher peaks, such as Aconcagua. In the foreground on irrigated land are straight rows of vines, some festooned on trellises, some pruned low on wires, but all threaded with the little irrigation ditches. There is a large area devoted to fields of rich green alfalfa, which is used for the fattening of range cattle—the traditional activity of the whole northwest piedmont. Between the fields and along the sides of the dusty roads there are long rows of tall, slender poplars; and here and there groups of houses are to be seen, low, one-story structures with whitewashed adobe walls and red-tiled roofs.

Mendoza preserves much less of the atmosphere and tradition of colonial Argentina than does Tucumán. A disastrous earthquake in 1861 destroyed the colonial city, and modern Mendoza dates from that catastrophe. Furthermore, when the population of the Mendoza oasis made a very rapid growth during the early years of the present century, much of the increase was the result of the arrival of immigrants direct from Italy. In 1914 the population of Mendoza included 31 percent who were foreign born. Today, with a population of about 110,000, Mendoza has a much larger proportion of people of Italian descent than is the case in Tucumán.

CROPS AND PRODUCTS OF THE VINEYARD OASES

Vineyards and alfalfa, as we have said, are of predominant importance in the oases south of Tucumán. Of the 840,000 acres of irrigated land included in the oases of Catamarca, La Rioja, San Juan, Mendoza, and San Rafael, more than half is devoted to vineyards and the rest to alfalfa. The chief concentration of wine manufacture is in the Mendoza oasis.

Two different groups of people carry on the two processes of growing the grapes and making the wines. In Mendoza the making of wine is an expensive process which, because of the high temperatures which prevail at the harvest time, requires a considerable capital investment in special equipment. Big wineries, or *bodegas,* purchase the grapes from the owners of the vineyards and manufacture the wine in large quantities. The wineries control the whole grape-growing process by specifying the type of grapes to be grown on each piece of land, by selecting the date for the harvest, and by setting the price to be paid for the juice. There are a few large properties owned by the wineries, but a very large number of the vineyards are less than 125 acres in size. Over half of them are owner-operated.

MENDOZA AS A PASS CITY

In addition to its functions as the commercial and manufacturing center of an oasis community and as the political center of a state, Mendoza also plays the role of a pass city. Its importance as a pass city dates back to the first century of Spanish settlement. At that time the most important colony on the

Argentine piedmont of the Andes was Tucumán, and the most important colonies on the Chilean side were in the Vale of Chile, inland from Valparaiso, and in the Central Valley around Santiago. Passes over the Andes near Tucumán are very high and require a long, difficult journey across desert country. But the most direct route to the Vale of Chile is the route over the Uspallata Pass, just west of Mendoza. To be sure, this pass requires a climb of 12,650 feet above sea level, but the approaches on both sides are direct. South of Uspallata there are passes which are much lower: the route from the head of the valley of the Bío-Bío to Neuquén on the Argentine side requires a climb of only 4,518 feet, and still further south there are passes below 1,000 feet. But these lower passes south of Uspallata were not used during the colonial period because, first, they were far off the direct line between Tucumán and Santiago, and second, travelers south of Mendoza or south of the Bío-Bío were constantly exposed to Indian attacks. Consequently the Uspallata Pass became the chief line of travel between the Argentine piedmont and middle Chile, and Mendoza was the point of departure on the eastern side.

The volume of travel over the Uspallata was never so great as that which flowed from the Argentine plains through Tucumán and Salta northward into the highlands. Because of the similarity of the products of middle Chile and of the Argentine piedmont oases, there was no pressing demand for exchange between the two regions. Since independence, the economic interests of Argentina and Chile have developed along very different lines, and lines which are not at all complementary to each other. When the construction of a railroad was undertaken in 1889, this traditional route was followed because it was still the most direct one between Buenos Aires and Santiago. The railroad was not completed until 1910, when a long tunnel was opened through the main cordillera. But operation of the line proved difficult and the revenue small. The grades were steep, requiring the use of many miles of rack and cog; almost every winter heavy snows blocked the line in spite of the construction of snowsheds.

Passengers and mail between Chile and Argentina are now largely carried by air. Since 1940 an automobile road has connected the two sides of the mountains, and the railroad is still in operation. But during the summer months many tourists prefer the roundabout but very beautiful route through the Chilean and Argentine lake districts which leads to Neuquén.

Mining Communities of the Northwest

In addition to the agricultural communities of the Northwest there are a few clusters of people engaged in the exploitation of minerals. Mining activities are not of great significance in Argentina; yet the relatively small mineral production includes some products that are of international importance. Argentina supplies the whole of the United States' imports of asbestos, and 8 percent of the United States' imports of beryllium. In addition to these items there are mines of lead, zinc, copper, silver, tungsten, mica, fluorspar, asphalt, and sulphur. There are some low-grade lignite deposits being used near Mendoza. Around Mendoza, along the front of the Andes, is also one of Argentina's important oil fields. Another oil field is near the border of Bolivia, north of Salta.

Argentine Mesopotamia

The Northwest is a land of mountains and piedmont oases, a land which was settled from Lima and for centuries was intimately linked with Chile and Peru. The northeastern part of Argentina, the region known as Mesopotamia, is, on the other hand, a land of abundant rains, of forests and rolling grassy plains, a land which has its closest foreign connections with Paraguay and Uruguay. Not only does it differ physically from the Northwest, but it also differs greatly in the traditions and viewpoints of its inhabitants.

Mesopotamia, or the country between the Paraná and Uruguay rivers, is composed of gently rounded, grass-covered interfluves, or *cuchillas,* and swampy, forest-filled valleys. It is a region of hot, rainy summers and mild winters, not unlike the wetter portions of Oklahoma and Texas. The arm of Argentina that is bent around the southern and eastern part of Paraguay, known as Misiones, includes a portion of the Paraná plateau, a region of abundant rains and dense mixed forests of pine *(Araucaria)* and broadleaf species. Here the Paraná and its tributaries have cut deep canyons in the flat-topped plateau; and where these rivers drop over the edges of the lava formations there are spectacular falls—the Guaira Falls of the Paraná and the Iguazú Falls on the Río Iguazú.

Settlement of Lowland Mesopotamia

The first settlements in Mesopotamia were made along the Río Paraná by people returning southward from Asunción. Corrientes was founded in 1588, and Paraná (opposite Santa Fé) at about the same time. Both of these places were located where high ground not subject to inundation stands close to the main channel of the river.

The Río Paraná, however, has played the part of a barrier, isolating the people on either side of it, rather than the part of a great artery of travel, on which the interests of the people on either side are focused. Even the wild vegetation is different on the two sides of the river. With its winding and shifting course, its annual floods that cover a very wide area, its shallow channel frequently clogged with sandbars, the Paraguay-Paraná-Plata is a very poor route of travel.

The little town of Corrientes offers an interesting illustration of the small importance of the river as a line of travel. At first glance Corrientes would seem to occupy a position of extraordinary strategic importance, for just upstream the two great branches, the Alto Paraná and the Paraguay, join. The fact is, however, that Corrientes, far from being a focus point of the routes of travel, occupies only a remote and isolated corner of Mesopotamia. It is reached by road and railroad from the main line of transportation to Posadas. The district around Corrientes has remained chiefly pastoral in its economic activities, although tobacco from this area was of some importance in the colonial period. The town and the district it serves have suffered for their dependence on the river.

The settlement of the interior of Mesopotamia has never been pushed with so much vigor as the settlement of the Pampa shore, south of Santa Fé. The pastures of Mesopotamia might have been just as good for the raising of mules as those of the Rosario–Santa Fé district, but the mules on the north and east side of the wide belt of floodplain could have been brought to the western side only with very great difficulty. Mesopotamia is still used primarily for the grazing of cattle on large estates. Its southeastern part has become one of Argentina's leading sheep districts, and one of the major sources of the wool which enters into Argentine exports. During the 1930's maize and flax crossed the Paraná and invaded the southern part of Mesopotamia, which is now the leading flax-producing area of Argentina. The northern part of the region, however, remains purely pastoral.

Settlement of Misiones

The settlement of Misiones has been supported since colonial times chiefly from the production of *yerba maté*. *Maté,* or Paraguay tea, is a beverage made from the leaves of a tree native in the Paraná pine forests of this part of South America, the *Ilex paraguayensis*. The first European settlements in this area were established by the Jesuit Fathers, who built missions and brought the native Indian inhabitants together in fixed agricultural communities; the planting of *yerba maté* was first attempted around these missions. When the Jesuits were expelled (from Brazil in 1759, and from the Spanish colonies in 1767), the plantations were abandoned, and the *maté* production was derived wholly from the collection of leaves from trees growing wild in the forests.

After World War I the plantation system was again introduced, this time concentrated in the area just east of Posadas. Small clusters of people are grouped permanently on these plantations, but since the labor requirements are heavy only at the harvest time, the groups of permanent workers are small. *Maté* pickers are in such great demand at harvest time that they must be recruited from a wide area, some of them coming even from Paraguay and Brazil.

Maté is little used outside of Argentina, Paraguay, Uruguay, and southern Brazil. The Argentine planters sell most of their product in the domestic market, although since World War II there has been an attempt to export *maté* to North America and Europe.

Meanwhile, it has been found that the Misiones area is well-suited to the growth of tea *(Thea sinensis).* After World War II, Argentina became the chief producer of tea in the American hemisphere. Plantations have been developed chiefly along the high ground in the south central part of Misiones, midway between the Paraná and Uruguay Rivers. Access to the plantations is by motor truck along an all-weather highway.

The Chaco

Between the Río Paraguay-Paraná and the piedmont settlements of the Northwest lies another of the larger divisions of the Argentine North. This is the Gran Chaco, the Argentine part of the great lowland region which extends northward from about latitude 30° S. into Paraguay, eastern Bolivia, and western Brazil. The Argentine Chaco, like the country farther to the north, is a region of deciduous scrub woodland interspersed with patches of grassy savanna. There are places where the thorny, deciduous trees grow close together in veritable thickets, difficult to penetrate. There are places, especially near the rivers, where taller trees form bands of dense semi-deciduous forest. There are places where the scrub trees are widely spaced, like apple trees in an old orchard, and where the forest floor itself is grass-covered. And there are also places where the forest is interrupted by extensive savannas—perhaps the result of repeated burnings, perhaps the result of conditions of the soil or ground water.

Some of the highest temperatures recorded in any part of South America occur in the Chaco. This region is located on the margins of the tropics, in a climatic position more or less similar to that of the Ganges plain of India and of the Gulf Coast of Texas and Louisiana. The summers in these latitudes are very hot: although none of the Chaco stations record temperatures so high as those of northern India, they are similar to those of the Gulf Region of North America; month by month the temperatures of Santiago del Estero are within a few degrees of the temperatures of New Orleans. Occasionally even in summer, and frequently in winter, there are cool spells, introduced by thundershowers, as cold air masses of polar origin push northward through this lowland against the stream of hot and humid equatorial air from the north. The winters are mild and relatively dry, with occasional frosts in the southern part of the region.

The rainfall is heaviest in the east and decreases toward the west. Corrientes receives an average of 48.5 inches a year, but Santiago del Estero, about 75 miles east of Tucumán, receives an average of only 20.4 inches. With the high rate of evaporation which exists in a region of such high temperatures, 20 inches is not sufficient to permit agriculture without irrigation. The boundary between sufficient moisture and deficient moisture runs north and south through the Chaco about midway between the Paraná and the piedmont of the Andes (the line between BSh and Cwa on Map 11, p. 31).

The whole Chaco is a great lowland plain, interrupted in few places by prominent surface features. It is composed mostly of the alluvium brought by the rivers from the erosion of the Andes. During the summer rainy season, vast areas near the streams are inundated. Along the eastern side of the Chaco, near the Paraná, the summer floods are sometimes not more than a foot or so in depth, leaving the railroad embankments and the permanent settlements standing above the sheet of water like islands and peninsulas. The drier western side of the Chaco is flooded only along the courses of the few streams—the Pilcomayo, the Bermejo, the Salado, and the Dulce. These rivers follow braided and shifting courses, changing position each year during the period of high water, in some years changing the pattern of their channels radically. As a political boundary, therefore, the Pilcomayo is anything but satisfactory, and may become a source of trouble as the region is developed.

Settlement of the Chaco—the Southern Border

Most of the Chaco region remains scantily inhabited. The chief areas of permanent settlement are to be found along its southern and eastern margins, focusing on Santiago del Estero, Santa Fé, Resistencia, and Formosa.

The oldest of the settlements on the margins of the Chaco is the string of agricultural communities along the courses of the Río Salado and the Río Dulce. Long before the arrival of the Spaniards, the Indians had made sporadic use of the floodplains of these rivers, for after the annual floods there was enough moisture to support good crops of maize. From Tucumán to Santiago del Estero, the Dulce is closely confined between high banks. At Santiago, however, the floodplain widens, and the river channel is split into numerous distributaries in a typical braided pattern. In the shallow depressions of the floodplain, after the floods recede, good yields can be had from the planting of maize, wheat, flax, and cotton. Croplands irrigated in this manner by the annual floods are known in Argentina as *bañados*.

The pattern of these *bañados* along the courses of the Salado and the Dulce is neither continuous nor permanent. Not all of the floodplains can be utilized in this way, for where coarse gravel has been deposited, or where the surface is so low that it remains covered with stagnant water after the flood season is over, *bañados* cannot be developed. Moreover, the distribution of these arable spots along the rivers is not fixed; not only does the channel shift from year to year, but also each flood changes the pattern of fine and coarse alluvium, and of low places which do not dry out sufficiently. As a result this district has witnessed notable changes in the areas devoted to crops, and some of the early communities have been entirely abandoned and new ones have sprung up. Santiago del Estero, located at the lower end of the narrow channel on the Dulce, enjoys greater stability than the other towns of this district.

The agricultural population of the Santiago area is not closely attached to the land. The private estates, into which the whole area is divided, include not only stretches of floodplain along the rivers, but also large areas of grazing land in the scrub woodland to the north. When some of the land on an estate is found to possess the necessary qualities for the development of a *bañado,* tenant farmers are introduced and crops are planted. When the conditions change and crops can no longer be raised, the tenants depart. In the meantime the pastoral activities of the estate go on without interruption. During the period of rapid growth in the sugarcane district around Tucumán, the population of the Santiago district declined rapidly; at present there is a movement back from Tucumán toward the cotton fields of Santiago del Estero.

The Quebracho Forests

The penetration of the Chaco forest has taken place both northward from Santiago del Estero and westward from a number of places along the Río Paraguay-Paraná. The first groups to enter were interested primarily in exploiting the forest itself, not in the development of agriculture. Among the scrub trees of the Chaco there is the species known as quebracho (literally "break-ax," because of its very hard wood)—a tree which contains a high percentage of tannin, used in the tanning of leather. In no other part of the world is there a similar forest from which this valuable substance can so easily be extracted.

The true quebracho, known botanically as *Quebrachia lorentzii,* grows under very peculiar conditions. It is found chiefly in the eastern part of the Chaco on the west side of the Paraguay-Paraná, and apparently occurs in dense growth only in those places where the ground water is strongly impregnated with salt. The presence of salty streaks in the ground water of the Chaco is a phenomenon which has never been adequately explained, but one which seems to be responsible for the presence of this valuable source of tannin.

In the western part of the Chaco there is another species of quebracho which has a dark red wood, and which contains much less tannin. The *Quebracho Santiagueño* or *colorado*—the red quebracho—contains only about 10 percent of this substance, but the true quebracho, known in Argentina as the *Quebracho Chaqueño,* contains as much as 30 percent. The red quebracho, which is the chief type exploited along the railroad running northward a little east of Santiago del Estero, is used mainly for its wood: for telephone poles, fence posts, railroad ties, firewood, and for the manufacture of charcoal. In the treeless plains of Argentina the red quebracho has a wide variety of uses.

The exploitation of quebracho for tannin led to the first movement of settlers into the eastern Chaco. In 1850, woodcutters from Corrientes crossed the river to Resistencia and from there began the exploitation of an area especially rich in this forest resource. It is estimated that an average of something like 500,000 acres are cut over every year, and that at the present rates of cutting there will be enough trees to last for about 150 years.

One of the major problems of the quebracho industry is the shipment of the logs to the mills where the wood is processed for the extraction of tannin. Because this process requires a large amount of water, the mills must all be located near the Paraná itself, or in a zone some 30 to 60 miles wide in which there are tributaries to the Paraná. Inland from this zone of tributaries only the four large rivers previously mentioned cross the Chaco, and only in their floodplains can surface water be found with any certainty. The railroads which have been built northward from Santa Fé, with numerous branches extending westward into the forest, are used to ship the logs to the mills. Oxen drag the logs to the railroads, and forest cutting is restricted to a zone less than 10 miles wide on either side of the tracks. Beyond this zone of cutting, the Chaco remains a wilderness.

Agricultural Settlement in the Eastern Chaco

The people who cut and haul the quebracho or work in the mills are not the ones who have settled on the land as farmers. At first, most of those who did attempt permanent settlement were cattle ranchers, who grazed their animals on the grassy savannas, and who sold a small but steady supply for meat to the forest workers.

The big agricultural development in the eastern Chaco, however, came during the 1930's and was associated with the rapid increase of cotton production in Argentina. There are two chief axes of pioneer settlement. One is along the railroad which runs northwestward from Resistencia, and the other is along another railroad running in a similar direction inland from Formosa. Cotton can be grown without irrigation as far west as the 32-inch rainfall line—which is about 160 miles west of the Paraguay-Paraná. Resistencia is the chief nucleus of this new zone of pioneer settlement, which has now extended northwestward about as far as climatic conditions are satisfactory for cotton without irrigation.

The location of these zones of specialized cotton production in the northern part of the Chaco rather than in the south, near Santa Fé, is the result of the distribution of private properties. Wherever the quebracho cutters left clearings in the Chaco forest, the land is available for agricultural or pastoral use, but in the southern part of the region the land is already divided into large private estates, used chiefly for the grazing of beef cattle. Only in the north are there large tracts of public domain—one of the few areas left in Argentina where the public domain is physically suitable for agricultural settlement.

The majority of the colonists are people of European origin who have come from the Humid Pampa. Many nationalities are represented: Czech, Spanish, Russian, Yugoslav, Bulgarian, and Austrian. Italians, who are very numerous in the central part of Argentina, are almost entirely absent from this frontier. On units of land ranging from 60 to 250 acres the colonists have cleared the forest, where it is was not already cleared, and, without previous experience, have undertaken the planting, cultivating, and harvesting of cotton.

The cotton grown in these Chaco settlements is mostly marketed in Argentina. Cotton gins are spread throughout the cotton-producing zones; and the cotton bales are transported by rail to Resistencia and Formosa. The bales are then shipped by river boat to Buenos Aires where there are numerous textile factories.

Patagonia

The hot, humid forests of northern Argentina present a most complete contrast to the cool, dry, wind-swept plateaus of the south. South of the Río Colorado lies that part of Argentina which is given the general regional name of Patagonia. In this vast area which makes up more than 25 percent of the national territory there are found only about 2.5 percent of the Argentine people. Over most of the area the population density is less than 1 per square mile.

Patagonia is a land of strong individuality. The roar of the wind seldom ceases, and in the winter men and beasts seek the shelter of canyons and cliffs. It is not a steady, strong breeze like the trade winds of the low latitudes, but a boisterous stormy wind that carries rolls of cloud with it and that frequently changes its direction as different air masses sweep by. The haze of dust makes objects in the typical Patagonian landscape indistinct even at short distances. In the west are some of the world's most spectacular mountains, carved by glaciers, and even now mantled in certain parts with glacial ice which is the nearest approach to an inland icecap that is to be found outside of the Polar regions. Along the piedmont of the Andes there is a succession of marginal lakes, their upper ends deep in the mountain canyons where the water laps against the ice cliffs of the descending glaciers. The lower ends of these lakes are held in by knobby moraines, dumped by the formerly more extensive ice tongues of the glacial period. Here the green lake waters, churned into whitecaps by the violent winds, dash noisily on shingle beaches.

The Climate

In spite of its relatively high latitude, Patagonia is not a land of extreme temperatures. Most of this part of South America lies between 38° and 55° of south latitude—latitudes which are the equivalent of the territory in North America between Chesapeake Bay and Labrador. But very low winter temperatures, like very high summer temperatures, are the result not only of latitude but also of protection from the moderating influence of the open oceans. The range of temperature, in general, increases with increasing latitude and distance from the sea: the world's greatest ranges between summer and winter are found in the higher middle latitudes of northern Siberia. But in South America the tapering of the land toward the south means that increasing latitude brings decreasing distance from the sea. The greatest ranges of temperature, therefore, in the whole of South America are found in the territory between Córdoba, Santiago del Estero, and Mendoza. Farther south the ranges decrease. The result in Tierra del Fuego is a marine type of polar climate (E on Map 11, p. 31), in which the warmest month averages a little below 50°, but the coldest month averages above 32°.

As one proceeds southward, the last of the hot summers is to be found in the valleys of the Río Colorado and the Río Negro. At Choele-Choel, on the Río Negro, the average of January is 75.4°. At Colonia Sarmiento, however, the warmest month averages 64.6°; and at Santa Cruz the average is only 58.6°.

No part of Argentine Patagonia receives much rainfall except the mountainous country along the western border (Map 12, p. 32). Furthermore, a great contrast exists between the summer maximum of rainfall at Mendoza, and the winter maximum from Neuquén southward. In Patagonia, as far south as the Strait of Magellan the moisture is brought chiefly by the winter storms. The total amount of precipitation is very small: only 5.3 inches at Santa Cruz and 4.9 inches at Colonia Sarmiento. A deficiency of moisture persists along the east coast from near the mouth of the Río Negro to a short distance north of the Strait of Magellan. Most of the eastern piedmont of the Andes, also, is subhumid, with short steppe grasses forming a continuous sod cover only in a narrow zone along the mountain front. In a few places, however, where valleys cross the cordillera and permit the penetration of the moisture-laden winds from the Pacific all the way to the eastern piedmont, there are little islands on the Argentine side where the rainfall is heavy enough to support a forest.

The desert of Patagonia is the only example in the world of an arid east coast in latitudes poleward of 40°. This aridity is only partly due to the rain barrier of the Andes. As cold air masses cross the southern part of the continent, cyclonic whirls precede the cold fronts as in the northern hemisphere, but with a clockwise, instead of a counterclockwise, rotation. This brings air onshore from the Atlantic. Moisture would be precipitated by these cyclonic storms if the air from the east had not crossed a wide zone of cold water—the Falkland Island Current, which bathes eastern South America as far north as the southeastern edge of the Humid Pampa. This cold water is fully as important as the Andes in accounting for the aridity of Patagonia. Heavy sea fogs, like the *garúas* of Peru, are common, especially in the far south.

Surface Features and Water Supply

Landing on the desert coast of Patagonia is not easy. Cliffs at the water's edge mark the beginning of the plateaus. In the southern part of the country there are a few embayments of the river mouths, such as those on which Santa Cruz and Puerto Gallegos are situated; but even here the building of port facilities is made difficult by the very great tidal range. The water rushes in and out of the Río Santa Cruz, for instance, with a range in the spring tide of as much as 48 feet.

Back of the coast the main part of the Patagonian highland is made up of two surface elements. There are vast areas of level-topped plateaus, rising like a series of gigantic steps toward the west, where the highest tablelands are well over 5,000 feet above sea level. These great plateaus are formed of horizontal strata, some of sedimentary origin, some composed of flows of dark-colored lava. The second surface element stands above the plateaus—areas of hilly land, composed of resistant crystalline rocks.

A number of deep canyons cross the Patagonian plateaus from west to east. Most of them contain no surface water at any time of the year, but a few carry some water all of the time, and a few have surface water intermittently. Along the canyon bottoms, even those which are permanently dry, common wells sunk in the gravel fill can tap a good supply of ground water. These canyons, with their water supply and with their cliffed sides, shelter most of the ranches of the country and offer the only safe routes of travel across the desert.

Outside of the canyons, the plateaus offer little to support settlement. In the higher crystalline hills or the higher plateaus the winter precipitation not infrequently comes in the form of snow, which, melting slowly, supports a fairly good growth of short grass, suitable in the spring for the grazing of sheep. During the summer, the plateaus are too dry even for sheep.

Plateaus and crystalline hills come abruptly to an end where the Andean structures begin. In many places the westernmost of the plateaus stand with cliffed sides facing toward the Andes, but separated from the steep mountain slopes by a narrow belt of lowland. This lowland forms a discontinuous series of basins between 1,000 and 2,000 feet above sea level, which, taken together, can be called the Pre-Andean Depression. On the bottom of the Depression are the markings of glacial moraines and the beds of the formerly more extensive glacial lakes. From Punta Arenas on the Strait of Magellan, the Depression offers a continuous passage northward as far as Lake Argentino, the southernmost of the marginal lakes. North of this the Depression is interrupted at intervals by spurs of the Andes. The northernmost basin which forms a part of the Pre-Andean Depression lies north of Lake Nahuel Huapí.

The physiographic history of the southern Andes is a remarkably interesting one, and one of considerable human importance. Even before the glacial period the rivers on the western side of the mountains had cut headward across the cordillera until they had shifted the continental divide all the way to the western rim of the plateaus. The Pre-Andean Depression was mostly drained to the Pacific by rivers which plunged westward through narrow canyons. The ice of the glacial period invaded these canyons and gouged them out into broad U-shaped troughs with hanging tributary valleys, characteristic of country sculptured by mountain glaciers. During the ice age, the glaciers not only invaded the Pre-Andean Depression, but, south of latitude 49° S., crossed the entire width of Patagonia and reached to the Atlantic. During the late stages of the last glacial period, however, while the ice still blocked the valleys across the Andes, the marginal lakes on the eastern piedmont were ponded and forced to drain eastward. As the ice continued to melt away and the mountain canyons were again opened, the lakes returned once more to the Pacific drainage. Today the cover of ice in the mountains remains only between latitudes 46° S. and 51° S., with a break at latitude 48° S. All the lakes except Viedma and Argentino now drain westward; these two still find an outlet across the desert plateaus through the Río Santa Cruz.

The relation between the drainage divides and the crest of the Cordillera gave rise to what might have become a serious boundary dispute between Chile and Argentina. The Chileans claimed the drainage divide as the boundary while the Argentines claimed the crestline of the mountains—a conflict made possible by the vague wording of the boundary description in the Treaty of 1881. Instead of settling the dispute by battle the two countries requested Great Britain to make an award. After a map of the country had been drawn, and the distribution of people had been studied, an award was made which granted to Argentina much of the lake country in the north, but gave Chile a wide stretch of country east of the mountains in the south, including both sides of the Strait of Magellan. A small section of the boundary in southern Patagonia was found to be incorrectly mapped, and this, also, was settled by arbitration in 1967.

European Colonization

European colonization in Patagonia is a recent development. Before the nineteenth century the only settlement along the east coast was at Carmen de Patagones (on the Río Negro opposite the town of Viedma). Since this district was a source of salt, which was shipped by boat to Buenos Aires, Carmen de Patagones enjoyed a certain degree of permanence. The rest of the country was left to the nomadic tribes of Puelche and Tehuelche who hunted the fleet-footed guanaco and the rhea (a kind of ostrich) with their characteristic implement, the *bola*.[1] When the tribes adopted horses and firearms from the white men, the hunting range was greatly increased, but the increased capacity to kill the wild game soon destroyed the food supply, and the region would have become uninhabitable had it not been for the white men's cattle, stolen from the ranches along the Plata shore. The sparse population of treacherous natives was finally all but wiped out in a series of vigorous military campaigns between 1879 and 1883.

After the Indian wars came the chief period of colonization in Patagonia. When the period began, the only established settlements were Carmen de Patagones, Punta Arenas, and Trelew. As soon as the menace of Indian attack had been eliminated, however, new colonists began to move into the region. The pioneers included people of many European nationalities, especially Welsh, Scottish, and English. Settlement spread into Patagonia along three chief routes. From the Humid Pampa at Bahía Blanca one stream of settlement spread southward along the coast, and inland up the canyons. By 1890 the coast as far south as Puerto Deseado had been occupied. Meanwhile another stream of colonization was advancing north from the Chilean port of Punta Arenas. Sheep were brought to the Pre-Andean Depression through Punta Arenas in 1878, and the development of sheep-raising in this district was especially rapid between 1885 and 1892. Settlers from Punta Arenas also pushed eastward along the Strait and into Tierra del Fuego. Some turned north along the coast, meeting the settlers from the north in the vicinity of Santa Cruz shortly before the beginning of the twentieth century. A third route of colonization led southward from Neuquén into the northern part of the Pre-Andean Depression, past Lake Nahuel Huapí, a movement which was supported in part by people who came from Chile. In addition, the Welsh settlement at Trelew, established in 1865, sent out, in 1888, new colonies to Colonia Sarmiento and Diez y Seis de Octubre. The discovery of oil in 1907 led to the development of a small settlement at Comodoro Rivadavia, which is still Argentina's chief oil field. Many different European nationalities, as well as Argentines and Chileans, are now represented in the population of Patagonia.

Stock Raising

Most of Patagonia is devoted to sheep-raising; and sheep-raising is a way of life which supports only a very sparse population. The land is divided into

---

[1]There are two kinds of *bolas*. For catching the rhea two round stones are tied together by a rawhide thong some eight feet in length. The more elaborate *bolas* consist of three stones tied to a common center. The hunter holds the smallest of the stones in his hand and whirls the other two around his head; then, taking aim, he throws them. When the *bola* strikes the legs of an animal it winds about them.

Bariloche on Lake Nahuel Huapí in Northern Patagonia. *Photo Courtesy—Pan American Airways.*

ranches which are measured by thousands of squares miles. On these ranches the few people are clustered about the ranch headquarters which are usually located in the shelter of a canyon where water is available. Very little irrigation is practiced in these places, and when small bits of land are irrigated, it is usually to provide feed for the horses. The concentration of sheep around the headquarters during the shearing and dipping periods creates a serious problem of overgrazing. The population density in the range country is very low, for on a ranch of some 10,000 square miles there is employment for not more than 100 men.

The little ports along the coast are used for the shipment of wool. Most of the time there is little activity at these places and little traffic on the railroads which connect them with the interior. But after the shearing period, when the wool begins moving to the coast, there are a few months when the shipping facilities are kept busy. From the ranch headquarters the wool is carried by wagon or motor truck to the nearest railroad. As rapidly as possible the wool is moved to the ports, where small coasting steamers carry the product to the big wool depot at Buenos Aires.

Very little of Patagonia is used for the grazing of animals other than sheep. Where the rainfall is somewhat heavier along the Andean piedmont and where there is a narrow belt of steppe grass, physical conditions are not unsatisfactory for cattle. Yet sheep are more important than cattle in the steppe-country inland from Punta Arenas and also in Tierra del Fuego around Ushuaia, the world's southernmost town. Only in the northern part of the Pre-Andean Depression between Neuquén and Diez y Seis de Octubre is cattle ranching of major importance.

The River Oases

The only cropland in Patagonia of any importance is to be found along the exotic rivers—the Colorado, the Negro, and the lower Chubut. The valley of the Santa Cruz is too cool for crops. Simple irrigation works make possible the cultivation of crops on the valley floors, which, being some 100 to 300 feet below the plateaus, are sufficiently protected from violent winds. Alfalfa is the chief crop, and along the Río Negro between Neuquén and Viedma, and in the district between Rawson and Puerto Madryn there are small concentrations of cattle. In terms of animal units (seven sheep being the equivalent of one head of cattle) cattle are actually more numerous in these districts than sheep. The animals are fattened on the irrigated alfalfa before being shipped to the Humid Pampa.

Meanwhile a new activity has appeared in the Río Negro oasis. Between 1910 and 1921 the Argentine government and a private railroad company joined to finance the construction of modern irrigation works including dams, reservoirs, and canals on the Río Negro and its tributaries. About 148,000 acres were thus made available for crops, and were laid out in small properties of 250 acres each. Alfalfa is still the chief crop of this area in terms of acreage, but vineyards and fruit orchards have been added, creating an oasis district very similar to Mendoza. In fact the wine grapes of the Neuquén district are said to be superior to those from the older oases farther north. The Río Negro valley is now Argentina's chief pear-producing district.

In the course of some ninety years, then, Patagonia has gone through a sequence that resembles the history of settlement in other outlying parts of Argentina. Today the destiny of Patagonia is as closely tied to Buenos Aires as is that of the North and Northwest. But the mineral resources of Patagonia are beginning to play a more and more important part in the national economy. Argentina's largest source of oil and gas is around Comodoro Rivadavia, and two pipelines carry the gas to Buenos Aires. Another major source of oil and gas is around Neuquén, and this field has also been connected with Buenos Aires by pipelines. In the 1960's geologists discovered a large body of good quality iron ore at Sierra Grande, located near the coast in the southern part of the province of Río Negro. Other smaller bodies of ore have been identified, and there is some poor-quality coal in southern Patagonia, near the Chilean border.

The Humid Pampa

A vast grass-covered plain can, in its own way, be as spectacular as snow-capped mountains or wind-ruffled lakes. No European experience prepared the early Spanish colonists for the boundless monotony of billowing grasses which greeted them on the Paraná-Plata shore. For days they could travel without encountering features distinctive enough to vary the scene: repeated endlessly were the views of tall, plumed grasses, or of coarse rushes in the marshy spots, whispering and rustling in the shifting winds which were almost never still. And through the haze of wind-borne dust the sunset colors were splashed brilliantly across the skies, or reflected, blood-red, in the tawny waters of the Plata.

Although the Spaniards found this region covered with tall prairie grass, it is not improbable that the landscape had already at that time suffered an important modification of its natural condition. Schmieder arrived at the conclusion that the prairie had replaced an earlier scrub-woodland cover as a result of fires lighted by the Indians. To the west the land was covered with the *monte,* an impoverished continuation of the tropical scrub wood-lands of the Chaco. The *monte* is composed of deciduous broadleaf scrub trees and bushes with a marked xerophytic character. The Argentines distinguish between a *monte alto,* which grows in the wetter places and which includes trees 25 to 30 feet in height, and *monte bajo,* in which the plants are more widely spaced and seldom more than 10 or 12 feet in height. Essentially the formation is a tree-steppe, for between the trees there is a cover of short grass. According to Schmieder, the *monte* was formerly much more widespread, perhaps covering the whole of the Humid Pampa. The tall bunch grasses of the prairie could survive the fires set by the Indians, which seem to have had the effect, before the arrival of the Europeans, of pushing back the *monte* border farther and farther toward the dry west.

The Climate

The rainfall on much of the area of the Humid Pampa is sufficient for the support of trees—indeed the many trees which have been planted around the *estancia* headquarters since the agricultural conquest have survived without difficulty. At Buenos Aires the average annual rainfall is about 37 inches, and over the whole northeastern section of the region the average is only a little below 40 inches. In this zone, also, the amount is very evenly distributed throughout all months of the year. The amount of rain decreases toward the southwest, dropping to 21.5 inches at Bahía Blanca, and to about 16 inches along the dry margin of the Humid Pampa. The seasonal distribution shows more and more of a concentration in the summer (December, January, and February) as one proceeds westward. At Córdoba the driest month (June, 0.1 in.) has very much less than the rainiest month (February, 5.4 in.).

The dependability of rain is a factor which has become critical since the spread of agriculture. The country around Rosario and Pergamino suffers very rarely from drought. This seems to be an "island" of dependable rainfall, however, for dry years come more frequently as one proceeds away from Rosario in any direction. At Pergamino, for instance, located a short distance south of Rosario, an examination of the rainfall over a 25-year period shows that the two summer months of December and January together received at least 6 inches in all but 3 of the years. At Rufino, on the other hand, only 125 miles southwest of Pergamino, this amount failed to come in 10 years out of 25; and during the same period Buenos Aires received less than this amount of summer rain in 9 of the years. The dependability of the summer rain, which has become a matter of critical importance because of the necessities of the maize crop, decreases also toward the north. The greatest rainfall uncertainty is found in the dry lands to the west.

The Humid Pampa may be described in general as a region of mild winters and hot summers. The growing season between killing frosts varies from about 300 days along the Paraná-Plata shore to about 140 days south of Bahía Blanca. Despite the annual frosts—which, incidentally, greatly reduce the number of insect pests as compared with the regions farther north—the winters are mild, and the absence of deep or long-continued snow cover makes agricultural and pastoral operations possible in the open throughout the year. The summers are especially hot in the northwest, but toward the southeast they are cooler. The southeastern part of the region around Mar del Plata and Tandil are distinctly cool—so cool, in fact, that grains do not thrive in this section. Such climates are due to the presence of the cool Falkland Island Current.[2]

A comparison of the average temperatures of Buenos Aires and of cities in the eastern part of the United States is instructive. Buenos Aires has about the same temperature in January (73.6°) as does New York in July (73.5°). During the winter the average temperature of the coldest month at Buenos Aires (July, 48.9°) is about the same as that of the coldest month at Charleston, South Carolina (January, 49.8°).

Buenos Aires and the Humid Pampa also share with eastern North America the characteristic of variable weather. Cold air masses from the south cross the Argentine plains toward the northeast or north, bringing cool or cold weather and clear skies. Along their fronts they meet and force upward

[2]In the Köppen system most of the Humid Pampa is classified as Cfa. From Tandil to the southeast coast around Mar del Plata, the symbol is Cfb. Córdoba is Cwa. The BSk climate borders the Cfa on the dry margin, extending in a half circle from the southern part of the Córdoba Hills to the coast south of Bahía Blanca (Map 11, p. 31).

the warm, humid, and relatively light air of tropical origin, thereby producing clouds and rain. This interaction of air masses is similar to that which takes place in North America where cold air from Canada moves southeastward toward the Gulf of Mexico or the warm Atlantic Ocean, meeting as it advances the more buoyant air which originates at lower latitudes. Along the front of advancing cold air masses the light tropical air forms whirls or eddies which appear on the weather maps as "lows" or cyclones, rotating in North America in a counterclockwise direction, in South America in a clockwise direction. Along the immediate cold front especially violent local up-currents of warm, moist air produce thunderstorms. The territory around Buenos Aires is noted for the violence of its thunderstorms and the magnificence of its displays of lightning. During the passage of these various kinds of air masses the weather changes from cloudy, warm, muggy, and depressing, to clear, cool, dry, and bracing. Occasionally in winter, severe cold spells do reach Buenos Aires—as in June 1967, when the temperature fell to 22°. The people of the Humid Pampa distinguish between the *norte,* or sultry north wind, and the *pampero,* or invigorating wind which comes to them across the Pampa.

Soil and Surface

The wind is a very important element in the physical character of the Humid Pampa. Although less violent and blustering than the wind of Patagonia, there are times when the *pampero* may blow with considerable force, and when the air is filled with dust whirled aloft from the dry surfaces to the west and south. In fact, this burden of fine rock particles carried by the wind, picked up in the arid west and dropped in the more humid east, is responsible in large measure for the character of the soil and the surface of the Humid Pampa.

The Argentine plains are actually composed of a deep accumulation of loose material resting on top of a hilly surface of granite and other ancient crystalline rock. This buried surface is a southward continuation of the rocky hill country of Uruguay. Rock outcrops are common throughout Uruguay as far as the northern shore of the Plata. South of the Plata, on the other hand, the hilly surface is deeply buried. At Buenos Aires, for example, the bedrock lies beneath 985 feet of river alluvium and wind-blown dust. A few of the more prominent features of the buried surface still protrude above the cover; the Sierra del Tandil (1,600 ft.) and the Sierra de la Ventana (4,200 ft.) form conspicuous hills rising above the general level of the plains. Around the base of each of these Pampa sierras there is a gently sloping apron of alluvial material. A similar, but larger, apron of alluvial material spreads out around the base of the easternmost of the marginal ranges, the Sierra de Córdoba, sometimes called the Córdoba Hills. The city of Córdoba which is located near the base of this range, near the top of the alluvial apron, is about 1,300 feet above sea level. Except for these aprons, however, the surface of the Humid Pampa is so nearly level that only the presence of marshy spots, or the use of surveyor's instruments, reveals the slight irregularities that do exist. Except near the Pampa sierras and the Sierra de Córdoba, the soil is entirely free from stones or pebbles. Here is a land where gravel is unknown.

Examined more closely, however, the surface and soil of the Humid Pampa are found to differ from place to place (Map 103, p. 634). The shallow mud flats along the Plata shore are bordered by a steep bank, the *barranca,* which rises abruptly about 100 feet above the river level. The *barranca* is especially steep where the Río Paraná washes against its base between Rosario and the eastern end of the delta, where the Paraná becomes the Plata. Above the *barranca* is the Northeast Pampa Rim, a surface which slopes almost imperceptibly southwestward from the crest of the *barranca.* Along the Paraná-Plata the *barranca* is fretted by narrow, flat-bottomed ravines which have been cut back from the river into the plain. Beyond the heads of these short ravines, however, there is remarkably little relief. The Northeast Pampa Rim stands high enough above the water table so that its fine-grained, dark-colored soils are well-drained.

The Northeast Pampa Rim merges very gradually with a zone of marshes southwest of Rosario and Buenos Aires. This part of the Humid Pampa may be called the Salado Slough. During wet periods the rise of the water table converts a large proportion of the surface into shallow, reed-filled lakes, inhabited by innumerable water birds. For much of the year, however, the Salado Slough is composed of only a line of marshes with the water table at, or slightly below, the surface, and the sluggish current of the Río Salado[3] is lost among the coarse grasses. Because of the abundant rainfall the marshes are not salty.

South and southwest of the Salado Slough, and extending to the southern limit of the Humid Pampa, is an area that has been called the Southern Pampa. This surface, also, is bordered along the sea by a *barranca* which is especially prominent along the southern shore, east of Bahía Blanca. The surface, except for the alluvial aprons around the Pampa sierras, is composed of almost imperceptible swells of higher ground, interspersed irregularly with shallow, marshy depressions. In a few places sand dunes stand conspicuously above the surface of the plain; but for the most part the soil is developed on a powdery, yellowish, wind-blown material known as *loess.* Under much of the Southern Pampa there is a layer of carbonate of lime known as the *tosca.*

---

[3]The reader should particularly note the presence of at least three rivers in Argentina named *Salado.* There is the Río Salado which crosses the southern part of the Chaco from the neighborhood of Tucumán to Santa Fé; there is the Río Salado which drains the zone of playas east of Mendoza, and which in time of high water enters the Río Colorado; and there is the Río Salado on the Humid Pampa, to which reference is made here.

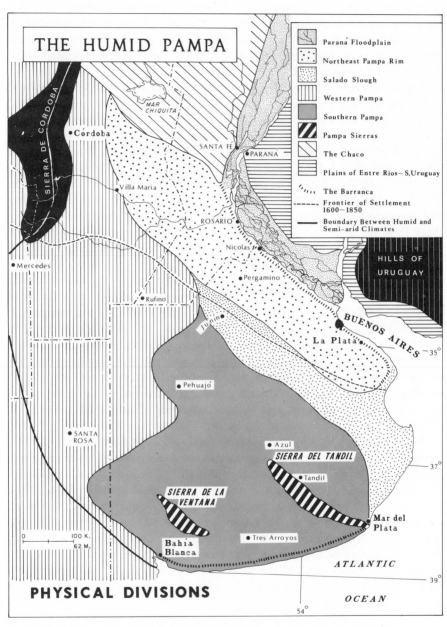

THE HUMID PAMPA

Paraná Floodplain
Northeast Pampa Rim
Salado Slough
Western Pampa
Southern Pampa
Pampa Sierras
The Chaco
Plains of Entre Rios–S,Uruguay
The Barranca
Frontier of Settlement 1600–1850
Boundary Between Humid and Semi-arid Climates

SIERRA DE CORDOBA

MAR CHIQUITA

•Córdoba

SANTA FE

•PARANA

Villa Maria

ROSARIO

Nicolas

HILLS OF URUGUAY

•Mercedes

•Pergamino

Rufino

Junin

BUENOS AIRES

La Plata

35°

Pehuajó

SANTA ROSA

•Azul

SIERRA DEL TANDIL

37°

•Tandil

SIERRA DE LA VENTANA

0   100 K.
     62 M.

Bahia Blanca

•Tres Arroyos

Mar del Plata

ATLANTIC

PHYSICAL DIVISIONS

OCEAN

39°

54°

Map 103

This seems to be the result of the solution of lime in the upper layers of the soil and the redeposition of the lime lower down by percolating rain water. In the wetter parts of the Humid Pampa the lime is carried away through the ground water, but with increasing aridity toward the southwest the percolating water does not regularly penetrate to the ground water table, and the burden of salt is redeposited below. The origin seems to be similar to that of the calcareous accumulations of the semiarid grassland soils of North America and Russia. Where the *barranca* east of Bahía Blanca has been cut by ravines, the *tosca* layer is exposed along their sides.

The whole western part of the Humid Pampa has been invaded by relatively coarse, wind-blown material from the Dry Pampa to the west. This area can be called the Western Pampa. Here the soil material is sandy rather than powdery, and in places there are strings of live sand dunes. This is the dry margin of the Humid Pampa, where soils similar to those of the North American Great Plains would develop if it were not for the continued deposition of new soil material blown in from the arid lands by the prevailing westerly and southwesterly winds. Throughout the Western Pampa the water table remains close enough to the surface so that it is easily reached by the roots of the alfalfa plant.

These various subdivisions of the Humid Pampa, however, were not apparent to the early Spanish colonists. People became aware of regional differences in terms of the uses they wish to make of the land. The individuality of the Humid Pampa has been brought out in the course of the agricultural settlement: for a nonagricultural people with scrubby, half-wild cattle, the latent contrasts within the area which have been made prominent only in terms of alfalfa, wheat, and maize, could scarcely have been noticed. Even the tall bunch grasses of the prairie could not have seemed radically different from the grassy and tree-scattered *monte* to the west, for the animals did about as well on one as on the other.

Settlement before 1853

When the Spanish colonists reestablished themselves along the Paraná-Plata shore they had come downstream from Asunción. Santa Fé was founded in 1573; and the site of Buenos Aires was reoccupied in 1580. The first colony at Buenos Aires had failed largely because of the jealousy of the people of Asunción who refused to permit sufficient support to reach it. When the site was reoccupied by people from Asunción, the chief purpose was to provide a place where ships, after the long voyage from Spain, could find fresh provisions and water before starting on the long and difficult trip upriver to Paraguay. Buenos Aires, moreover, could stand guard over Spanish interests at the mouth of the Plata. A century later, in 1680, when the Portuguese founded Colonia on the opposite shore of the Plata, the settlement at Buenos Aires became an important outpost in the Spanish and Portuguese struggle for the control of the Plata estuary.

The Paraná-Plata shore, however, was not a very attractive place for the Spaniards of that period. In the district which is called the Northeast Pampa Rim, the land was divided into huge *estancias,* and herds of horses, mules, and cattle were pastured on the unfenced range with a minimum of attention from the owners. A line of forts was placed along the Salado Slough to guard the scattered *estancias* and the few towns from the raids of Indians. The forts, however, were only partly effective, for even after the middle of the nineteenth century the Indians on certain occasions penetrated the country that was settled northeast of the Salado and raided the outskirts of the towns.

Within the district of the Northeast Pampa Rim where the pastoral settlement was concentrated, the Humid Pampa underwent an important and rapid transformation. For the native guanaco and rhea the Europeans substituted herds of domestic animals; and with these animals they introduced, perhaps without intention, the seeds of European grasses. The new species of grass spread rapidly throughout the area of the settlements. In an amazingly short time the native tall bunch grass, the *pasto duro,* was replaced by a dense lawn-like growth of European grasses which formed a thick sod, the *pasto tierno.* A notably sharp vegetation boundary was developed along the Salado where no such boundary had existed before. Travelers of the early nineteenth century commented on the great difference to be observed between the tall bunch grasses of the Indians' hunting ground southwest of the Salado, and the rich green carpet of well-cropped grasses in the pastoral zone.

The people who owned the *estancias* and the hired *gauchos* who performed the necessary work on the estates were not an agricultural people. When wheat farming made its belated appearance near the end of the eighteenth century it was carried on by tenants, and was scorned by the vast majority of the settlers. Wheat was raised in the flat bottoms of the ravines which drain to the Paraná and the Plata, and on the Pampa in a semicircle some 25 miles in width around Buenos Aires. Late in the eighteenth century, flour was actually exported to the purely pastoral region of Mesopotamia.

Meanwhile the Salado Slough remained a sharply defined cultural boundary separating the Europeans from the Indians, and the *pasto tierno* from the unchanged *pasto duro.* Convoys of wagons crossed the Humid Pampa to the southwest in search of salt, but there was little interest in laying out *estancias* in the vast territory between the Salado and Bahía Blanca. This lack of attention to what has been described as one of the world's most favorable natural pasture lands cannot be laid to the hostility of the Indians, for the *gauchos* were not the kind of men to be stopped by the attacks of scattered tribes of savages. The fact is that the owners of the cattle estates could place little value on this Indian country: there was no opportunity to develop the latent agricultural possibilities, for the world was not ready for such development; and from the point of view of the pastoralist whose mules were to be driven inland by way of Tucumán to the market at Salta, there was plenty of good grazing land west of Rosario, and the country south of the Salado Slough was too remote to be interesting.

In the period between the establishment of independence from Spain (1810–16) and the drafting of the federal constitution (1853) the minds of men in Argentina were for the most part focused on problems other than those of settling the land. Aside from some attempts to plant colonies on the coast of Patagonia, and some southward expansion of the cattlemen along the eastern side of the Humid Pampa, the frontiers of occupied country remained little changed while the great issue of the day—centralism versus federalism—was being fought out. During the long domination of the dictator Rosas (1829–52), the strong central authority of Buenos Aires was imposed on the outlying parts of the country with an iron hand. Rosas was overthrown in 1852, and in 1853 a federal system was adopted. Until 1861 the Province of Buenos Aires tried to remain separate from the federation, and during this time Paraná was the Argentine capital. When, in 1862, Argentina was united under President Bartolomé Mitre, and Buenos Aires again became the capital city, the stage was set for those profound changes which have produced modern Argentina. But the essential features inherited from the period before 1853 which have colored the period since that date must not be overlooked. Argentina advanced toward the modern period with four fundamental characteristics: first, a scanty population—only about 900,000 in 1800 and 1,200,000 in 1852; second, a people almost exclusively interested in horses, cattle, and sheep and not at all in agriculture; third, an abundance of free land of first-rate quality for grazing and grain farming; and fourth, the tradition of the large private estate.

The Beginning of the Modern Period

There was no precedent for the transformation which followed. The Argentine grasslands, together with the other mid-latitude grasslands of the world, passed through a spectacular and unique period of development. The advance of the frontier of settlement across first-class agricultural lands accompanied by the widespread prosperity brought by expanding markets and increasing land values, was a phenomenon characteristic of one period of economic history, and chiefly, too, of one kind of place. Most of the world's humid grasslands were scantily occupied and little used except for pasture before the middle of the nineteenth century. The various techniques developed during the last century not only made possible the agricultural use of the grasslands, but also the connection of these remote places with the city markets by much cheaper forms of transportation than had hitherto been available. Agricultural machinery for the first time in history made possible the cultivation of large areas from which yield per acre was small; on the open grasslands the new wire fences[4] made possible the separation of the agricultural land from pastures, and also one pasture from another so that the breeding of animals could be controlled; well-drilling machines and inexpensive windmills made it possible to get water where water was difficult to find at the surface; and railroads and steamships made it possible to transport the products of the farms to the expanding city markets. All these technological innovations became available only in the nineteenth century.

A fundamental characteristic of this period of human history was the rapid increase in the rate of population growth in the world as a whole. This population increase formed the basic support for the expanding markets, which, in turn, made possible the system of credits and investments. And credits and investments led to continuously expanding production, which provided support for more and more people. It is difficult, sometimes, to realize how unprecedented were the changes introduced during this period of human history and how unprepared mankind was to adjust human institutions to an economy of plenty.

THE NEW MEANS OF TRANSPORTATION

The transformation of the Argentine Humid Pampa began with the development of the means of transportation, with the construction of roads and railroads. Roads were remarkably difficult to maintain. As long as travel was free in any direction—as it was in the period before fences were built—the problem was not serious; for when the ruts were worn too deep into the loose soil the carts or horses could follow a new route to one side of the old one. But when fences were placed along the property lines and the roads could not be shifted, wagon wheels soon cut through the grass cover and exposed the fine Pampa soil. During and after each rain the fine material was turned into a quagmire, and when the mud dried out, the wind picked up the powdery dust and whirled it away, with the result that, in time, the roads were several feet below the general level of the plain. Even now the unpaved rural roads are impassable for motor vehicles except in dry weather; in a country so free from stones, even gravel for road surfacing must be imported from a distance.

The construction of railroads, on the other hand, has been very simple. On the nearly level surface there is no need for cuts, fills, bridges, tunnels, or even for curves. In few parts of the world are construction costs lower.

---

[4]Experiments were made with different kinds of wire fences, but until the 1860's the steel was of such poor quality that wires could not be pulled taut, and fences frequently broke. Smooth wire fences were preferred because they did not injure the livestock, and when strong steel was finally manufactured, the wire fences came into common use— five strands of wire for cattle, seven for sheep. Barbed wire was tried as early as 1844, but was not manufactured at low cost until after 1878. In Argentina, unlike other open grasslands in the world, smooth wire was preferred over barbed wire, even after the latter became available at low cost. The Argentine *estancieros* could afford the relatively high cost of smooth wire. (From an unpublished paper by Rolf Sternberg.)

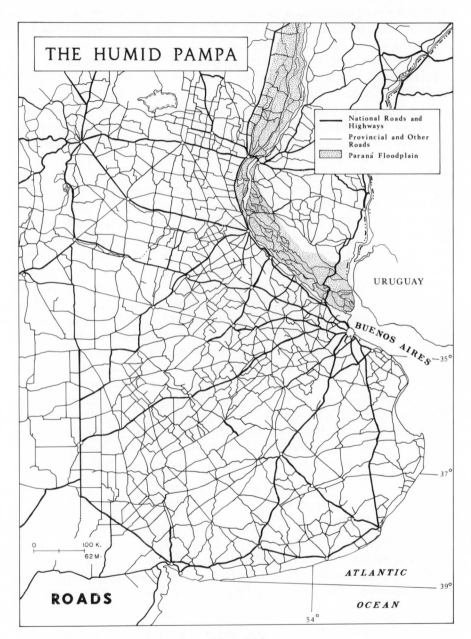

THE HUMID PAMPA

National Roads and
Highways
Provincial and Other
Roads
Paraná Floodplain

URUGUAY

BUENOS AIRES
—35°

37°

ATLANTIC
—39°

OCEAN

ROADS

0   100 K.
    62 M.

54°

Map 104

The first railroad started operations in 1857. It ran for 6 miles in a straight line southwestward from Buenos Aires. Shortly thereafter a railroad was built along the old colonial mule route from Rosario to Córdoba and Tucumán. During the next few decades railroads were built out of all the leading ports of the Humid Pampa, usually running in straight lines toward indefinite—or impossibly distant—objectives. A few of these lines have actually been extended beyond the borders of the Humid Pampa, but most of them have not. By 1910 Argentina's central region was crisscrossed by a series of overlapping fans, converging on Buenos Aires, Rosario, Santa Fé and Bahía Blanca[5] (Map 89, p. 538).

The Argentines generally think of the Humid Pampa as being divided into four major zones, each zone served by the main line and branches of one of the large railroads. The whole southeastern part of the region constitutes the zone of the Ferrocarril del Sud, the main line of which runs southward from Buenos Aires, and which connects with La Plata, Mar del Plata, and Bahía Blanca. A second zone is formed by the main line and branches of the Ferrocarril Oeste, which runs southwestward from Buenos Aires. The third zone is a narrow one, served by the main line of the Ferrocarril de Buenos Aires al Pacífico, which runs westward from the capital through Junín to Mendoza. The fourth zone is that served by the Ferrocarril Central Argentino, which runs from Buenos Aires northwestward to Rosario, Córdoba, and Santa Fé.

These various railroad lines were not financed by the Argentines. Wealth among the *estancieros* was in the form of herds and land, not money or bank credits. After 1853, when foreign capital felt secure in Argentina, many investors in Europe saw opportunity for profit in this rapidly expanding region. Between 1880 and 1886 the flow of British capital into Argentina was especially strong; most of the railroads were built by British companies, they made use of British rolling stock, and they burned British coal. The meter-gauge line to Tucumán and the northwest, however, was built by a French company.

THE NEW ESTANCIAS

The railroads paid good dividends to their stockholders; and to the people of Argentina they brought unheard-of prosperity in the form of booming land values. But the whole process of land settlement and of property division was fundamentally different from the process of settlement in the grasslands

---

[5]The first railroad and many of those which followed were built on a broad gauge (5 ft. 6 in.)—a gauge adopted originally to fit rolling stock which the British had built for use in India but had sent to Russia for use in the Crimean War. There is no uniformity of gauge, however. Some of the lines are built on the so-called standard gauge (4 ft. 8½ in.), and some are built on narrow gauge. The line which runs from Buenos Aires through Córdoba and Tucumán northward to Bolivia was built on a 1-meter gauge.

of the United States which was going on at the same time. In North America after 1862 the small homesteader was able to get a farm of 160 acres practically free of cost. In Argentina, the land, even before the coming of the railroads, was already partitioned in large units and given to a favored few in government grants.

The spread of the large estates over the Pampa was rapid after 1853. The first advance across the Salado was made in the east. As early as 1875 the line of forts protecting the occupied part of the Pampa from the Indians had been pushed forward to the southern coast, east of the Sierra de la Ventana. The next year, in 1876, the line of forts had been pushed still farther to the west, and by 1879 the forts were along the Río Negro. The Indians were finally eliminated as a menace to the settled parts of the country in a military campaign which lasted from 1879 to 1883.

The line of sloughs along the Río Salado suddenly lost its significance as a major culture boundary. After three centuries when this natural feature formed the limit of European settlement, and was also a major vegetation boundary, one generation saw the established limits overrun. The previously occupied parts of the Pampa were divided up into vast private estates, 100,000 acres or so in area.

The Pastoral Base

Life on the new *estancias* was still not agricultural. The owners were mostly Argentine creoles, men raised in the pastoral tradition, men whose chief occupation was the handling of herds of cattle, sheep, and horses, men for whom the surest road to prestige rested in the ownership of land. Foreign markets, as far as the landowners were concerned, meant markets for cattle. At first the herds were made up of the Argentine cattle, descendants of the scrub animals of the colonial period. They were permitted to run at will on the vast, unfenced range, and to breed without care and without thought of quality. Such animals were good for the production of hides, tallow, and salt beef; but the meat was lean and had a strong taste. In 1877 the first refrigerator ship made it possible to send frozen meat to Great Britain, but British taste would not accept Argentine meat. The result was the importation of high-grade beef cattle from Britain, and the careful breeding of these animals on fenced-in pastures. This important shift from scrub cattle to carefully selected animals took place between 1880 and 1900.

The change in the pastoral technique created many other changes in the relation of the people to the land and in the productivity of the land. The scrub cattle could get along well enough on the poor grasses of the *monte,* and they could thrive on the *pasto duro* of the untamed prairie. They could endure the insect pests of the Chaco, or the long overland marches with little feed and water. But not so the big clumsy beef animals bred from British stock. Because the new cattle could not survive the ravages of Texas fever, for the first time the southern limit of the country infested with ticks, or *garrapatas,* became a significant geographic boundary. But in addition to requiring tick-free pastures, the new animals required a better source of feed than the uncultivated pastures, even the *pasto tierno,* could supply. Rapidly after 1890, the *estancieros* came to realize the necessity of shifting from a grazing industry based on uncultivated pastures to one based on a cultivated crop. Alfalfa was the feed crop they adopted, and on the Humid Pampa alfalfa did exceptionally well. But alfalfa had to be planted on plowed land, and then cut and fed to the animals. These practices required the services of many more workers than had ever been needed to care for the wild scrub animals of the earlier period. At last the *estancieros* wanted immigrants.

IMMIGRANTS

Other people in Argentina had felt the need for more settlers long before the *estancieros* did. Juan Bautista Alberdi (1810–84), one of the foremost political philosophers of Latin America, was engaged in writing his famous treatise on a proposed basis of political organization for the Argentine Republic while the country itself was in the grip of the tyrant Rosas. "The enemy of union," wrote Alberdi, "is not Rosas, but distance." He was one of the first to recognize that to govern a land it is necessary to populate it, a principle which, in this book, forms the basis for the contrast between total and effective national territory. Alberdi and many of the other important men of his time never ceased to emphasize the necessity for stimulating the immigration of Europeans. That Europeans actually came in large numbers to the Argentine Humid Pampa distinguishes this region as well as the nation of which it is the economic center from the other nations and regions we have discussed up to this point.

In 1856 the first group of agricultural immigrants was brought from Europe. This group consisted of 208 families of German- and French-speaking Swiss. Since the land in the more accessible parts of the Humid Pampa was already in private hands, this colony was established on land granted by the province of Santa Fé and located a short distance northwest of the city of that name. The first colony, known as Esperanza, was developed largely through the initiative of a private citizen, Aaron Castellanos, and was soon bordered by a number of other similar colonies of European immigrants. After 1882 the district around Santa Fé became one of the first important sources of wheat.

The tide of immigration began to rise more and more rapidly. The total population of the country, which had been 1,200,000 in 1852, increased to 2,500,000 in 1880, and of these 173,000 were people born in Europe. The first peak year of immigration was reached in 1889, when 218,744 second- and third-class passengers came to Buenos Aires. In every year, however, there was a considerable return current of emigrants who were either discouraged and homesick, or successful and ready to return to the homeland to settle down in higher social positions. The immigration figures for 1889 must be balanced against 40,649 emigrants. The depression and panic of 1890–91 resulted in a net loss of population in Argentina, but thereafter the tide swelled rapidly again, to advance with few setbacks to the peak year of 1913, when 302,047 entered and 156,829 left. Between 1857 and 1900 approximately 2,000,000 immigrants arrived in Buenos Aires and 800,000 departed —giving a net increase of 1,200,000. After World War I immigration picked up again, reaching another peak in 1929, when there were 427,455 arrivals and 348,234 departures. During the 73 years between 1858 and 1930 the total immigration amounted to 6,300,000 people. After 1930 the immigration was reduced to a mere trickle.

Meanwhile the racial character of the Argentine population was being profoundly altered by this stream of new Europeans. The composition of the population in 1914 and again in 1935 is presented in the following table:

RACIAL CHARACTER OF THE POPULATION OF ARGENTINA*

	1914	1935
Born in Argentina of pure European stock	5,185,000	9,480,000
Born in Argentina with traces of Indian or African stock	400,000	300,000
Born in Europe	2,300,000	2,500,000
Total population	7,885,000	12,280,000

*From A. E. Bunge, "Present Economic Situation of the Argentine," *Revista de Economia Argentina.* 34:286.

The European immigrants whose arrival changed so radically the character of the Argentine people were largely of Italian and Spanish nationality. These two groups together made up almost 80 percent of the newcomers. Between 1857 and 1924, of those who remained in the country, 1,300,000 were Italians and 1,025,000 were Spaniards. Represented also in the stream of immigration by substantial numbers were French, Germans, Austrians, Russians, British, and Swiss. After 1930 most of the immigrants came from eastern Europe, especially Poland.

TENANTS AND THE RISE OF AGRICULTURE

The immigrants were desired by the landowners, we have said, because they were needed to plant and cut alfalfa for the high-grade beef animals. The native Argentines themselves were still interested, primarily, in breeding fine cattle and horses and in providing these animals with adequate feed. The immigrants brought agriculture to Argentina, and agriculture was encouraged by the landlords as a by-product of the expansion and improvement of the grazing facilities. The most effective way to prepare the land for the planting of alfalfa was to rent it for a period of four or five years to tenants and to permit them, for a share of the crop, to raise wheat. The *estancieros* and their hired hands were neither numerous enough to undertake this work of cultivation, nor were they willing to do so. They were, however, anxious to secure tenants for their estates, and soon found that in addition to increasing their alfalfa acreage they could derive considerable profit from a share of the crops. The contracts obliged the tenants to plant the land with alfalfa and to move away after a specified number of years. The alfalfa fields then yielded well, giving as many as three cuttings a year, for five or ten years, after which new tenants would be secured, and the cycle repeated. Naturally the tenant homes were rude, temporary shelters, and the attachment of the agricultural workers to the land was lose and easily broken. Yet it was the tenant group that made the Humid Pampa one of the world's leading surplus grain and meat regions.

With the rise of wheat farming to a place of major importance, the demand for more workers to take care of the peak load of the harvest season began to exceed even the supply of tenants. In November and December there was an insistent demand for field hands to work for wages on a temporary basis. In response, there developed a regular seasonal migration of laborers who would come from Italy to Argentina in the spring and early summer of the Southern Hemisphere, and who would return to Italy during the months from March to June to harvest the Italian wheat crop. Many of these *golondrinos,* or swallows, as they were called, made the trip between Italy and Argentina again and again. After 1914, this form of seasonal migration practically ceased.

Only with the development of commercial agriculture, between 1880 and 1900, did the present outlines of the Humid Pampa come sharply into focus. As the new alfalfa-fed beef animals of the fenced pastures replaced the half-wild animals, and as cultivated grains and alfalfa replaced the *pasto duro* and the *monte,* a new regional boundary began to appear. Grain-farming and alfalfa pushed westward as long as yields were sufficient to make this system profitable. Yields of wheat and alfalfa were high enough within what we now call the Humid Pampa; farther to the west there was not enough moisture to support adequate crop yields. Wheat and alfalfa were cultivated approximately as far as the 16-inch rainfall line west of Bahía Blanca, and as far as the 23-inch rainfall line west of Santa Fé. Less rainfall is needed to produce adequate crop yields in the south where temperatures are lower and evaporation is less. These particular values of rainfall became significant natural features because of the farm technology and the balance of costs and prices during this part of the nineteenth century. The Humid Pampa, as distinct from the Dry Pampa, made its appearance. The development of the Humid Pampa is reflected in the statistics of exports: in 1894 the three chief pastoral products together (wool, meat, and hides) made up 63 percent of the total value of exports; but in 1903, for the first time, the value of the combined agricultural products (maize, wheat, and linseed) exceeded the value of the animal products. The immigrant farmers supplied the necessary manpower to reshape the economic destiny of the region and to redraw its geographic bounds; but the Argentine landowners were the ones who profited most from the spectacular increase of land values.

The acreage and production of wheat, maize, and alfalfa continued to increase until 1930. In 1875 the food grains and alfalfa together occupied some 840,000 acres; but by 1900 these crops covered 14,800,000 acres; and by 1929 the acreage was 61,500,000. Then came the worldwide collapse of international trade and a great reduction in the value of the traditional Argentine exports. Acreages decreased as more and more of the land was planted with grass and used as uncultivated pastures. By 1960 the food grains and feed crops covered 24,500,000 acres. In that year the grains and alfalfa occupied 39 percent of the area of Buenos Aires Province, and 52 percent of the area was used for grass pasture. The production of wheat in 1961–62 was only about 5,500,000 tons, compared with an annual average of 6,600,000 tons between 1934 and 1938. In 1964–65 a bumper crop of over 10,000,000 tons was produced, but in 1965–66 production dropped back again to 5,600,000 tons. Maize, which averaged 7,800,000 tons a year between 1934 and 1938, was only about 5,000,000 tons in the period 1961 to 1965; but in 1965–66 it was up to 7,200,000 tons.

LAND-USE DISTRICTS

The process of transformation that changed the Humid Pampa from an open range country of low productivity to a highly productive grazing and farming region, resulted also in the development of a new pattern of land-use districts. These subdivisions of the Humid Pampa, which had appeared before 1930, are still the chief contrasted parts of the whole area. There are four districts (Map 91, p. 540). The first is the pastoral district, located in the southeast between Mar del Plata and Tandil. In this area more than 80 percent of the productive area is used for livestock pasture without agriculture. The second is the alfalfa-wheat district, in which alfalfa is the chief cultivated crop in terms of acreage. This is the chief area of wheat cultivation. The third division of the Humid Pampa is the maize district, located around Rosario, where maize is more important than wheat. The fourth division is the zone of intensive farming and dairying—the truck, dairy, and fruit district, located around the margins of Buenos Aires.

The Pastoral District. The pastoral district is that part of the Humid Pampa where more than 80 percent of the productive area is used for the grazing of animals. Alfalfa and wheat cannot be grown in this part of the Humid Pampa, except at high cost, for two reasons. First, this is a part of the Salado Slough, where a large proportion of the surface is so wet that to use it for crops would require drainage. And second, the moist, cool summers (Cfb) are not beneficial for such crops as maize, but they are ideal for the

Cattle roundup on an *estancia* in the Humid Pampa. *Photo by W. R. Grace Co.*

rich growth of pasture grass. In this district, therefore, livestock ranching without agriculture has survived as the predominant form of land use.

The grazing activities of this area, however, are not at all the same as those which once characterized the whole of the Humid Pampa. The pastoral district is now a zone of concentration of high-grade mutton and wool sheep; it is a zone of increasing importance in the production of butter; and it has become the chief breeding ground for beef cattle. Because of the ticks, the Northwest of Argentina has been unable to play the role of breeding ground for animals later to be fattened on the feed crops of the agricultural region. Northern Patagonia, which is free from ticks, might play this part. At present, however, the chief source of yearling steers is this pastoral district of southeastern Buenos Aires Province. The existence within the Humid Pampa itself of good range lands in the southeast, unsuited to alfalfa and wheat is, indeed, one of the most serious limitations on the rapid development of the pastoral possibilities of northwestern Patagonia.

Because agriculture is so little developed in the pastoral district, this area has received few immigrant tenants. Few people are needed to care for herds of sheep or cattle, although the spread of dairying may lead to a demand for the services of more workers. At present, however, this district has the lowest density of rural population of any part of the Humid Pampa—a density ranging from 10 to 25 people per square mile.

The Alfalfa-Wheat District. The greater part of the Humid Pampa is included in the alfalfa-wheat district. In a broad crescent, extending for 600 miles along the western side of the Humid Pampa from Santa Fé in the north to Bahía Blanca in the south, the chief commercial crop is wheat. Wheat acreage reached nearly 23 million in 1928–29. In the 1930's it dropped to only about 14 million acres, but climbed again to over 20 million just before the beginning of World War II. During and after the war the acreage dropped again to about 14 million, where it remained, except for a slight rise in 1964–65.

The steady underlying base of the rural economy of the alfalfa-wheat district is still pastoral. The owners of the *estancias* are more interested in producing high-grade animals than in farming. The wheat and alfalfa are grown by tenants as an incidental by-product desirable in order to maintain the productivity of the pastures. As a result of the temporary nature of the relation of the tenants to the lands they cultivate, the region can register sharp differences in the acreage of crops and pastures from year to year, yet without severe economic dislocations. When the prices of grains are down, the landowners dismiss their tenants. On the former cultivated land the tenants plant pasture grass before moving away—and the pastures can be maintained by not over-grazing them for many years until a new cycle of alfalfa and wheat is needed. As we shall see later, the departure of large numbers of tenants from the rural areas, where their votes could be controlled by the landlords, to the cities, where they could vote as they pleased, had a major impact on Argentine politics during World War II.

Several forces are leading to a decrease in the number of large estates. The change is taking place slowly: there are still at least 50 families in Buenos Aires Province with holdings of more than 75,000 acres each. There is still a steady resistance to the temptation to turn the increased land valuation into money through actual sale, as in Chile. Much of this resistance is explained by the traditional attitude of the Argentine landowner toward money income. He does not invest surplus income as people do in North America or in parts of Europe; he spends it—for better living, for the construction of golf courses, polo fields, and swimming pools on the estate, or for a residence in Buenos Aires, or for travel and a European education for his children. He does not achieve prestige in society through the possession of money income, but rather through the ownership of land, the production of high-grade animals, and by the establishment of his family in a town house in the capital. Increasing land values, therefore, have not led to the sale or mortgaging of estates to the same extent as in North America. There are no colonies of retired farmers expecting to live on income from investments. Nevertheless, there has been a trend toward the reduction in the size of the large holdings.

The movement to subdivide the large estates comes chiefly from three sources. In the first place, the inheritance law in Argentina, as in all countries whose legal systems are based on Roman law, provides that all the children of a family must share equally in the estate left by the parents; thus, an *estancia* of 100,000 acres inherited by four children is converted into four *estancias* of 25,000 acres each. In the second place, some of the landowners have been less successful than others in managing their estates; they have run into debt through extravagant living and have been forced to sell their lands piece by piece. As a result, the map of 1967 shows a greater variation in the

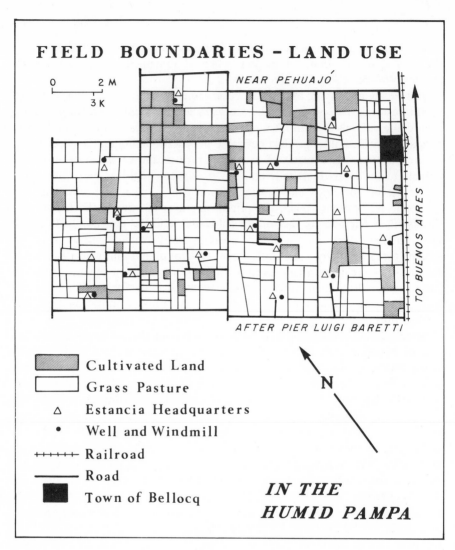

FIELD BOUNDARIES – LAND USE

0   2 M

3 K

NEAR PEHUAJÓ

TO BUENOS AIRES

AFTER PIER LUIGI BARETTI

N

IN THE
HUMID PAMPA

▨ Cultivated Land
☐ Grass Pasture
△ Estancia Headquarters
• Well and Windmill
+++++ Railroad
——— Road
■ Town of Bellocq

Map 105

size of properties than does the map of 1930. The *estancia* is still the chief form of land tenure; but there are also small farms, or *chacras,* where small landowners raise vegetables or pasture dairy cattle. The map of field boundaries and land use in the central part of the alfalfa-wheat district near Pehuajó (Map 105) shows some of the results of this break-up of the *estancias.* The cultivated areas are where tenants are raising alfalfa or wheat; the pastures are planted with grass and are used for the grazing of cattle. Each *estancia*

A tenant farmer harvests his crop on a huge field in the Argentine Humid Pampa. *Photo by W. R. Grace & Co.*

has its central group of buildings, usually surrounded by planted trees; and near each *estancia* headquarters there is a well and a windmill.[6]

In the alfalfa-wheat district, tenant farms range from 370 acres in the north to over 1,000 acres in the south; there is a distinct tendency toward increase of size with the increased use of machinery. About 25 percent of the wheat crop is now raised on owner-operated mixed grain and livestock farms, on which the workers, being hired for wages, are somewhat more permanently attached to the land than in the case of the renters. Perhaps this last type of property is the one toward which the agricultural system is tending; but the trend will be slow because it must advance against the basic adverse attitude of the Argentine landlord toward agriculture as an occupation.

Wheat was the first grain crop to achieve a place for itself against the pastoral tradition of the Argentine Humid Pampa. It was grown first along the Northeast Pampa Rim, especially in the vicinity of Buenos Aires. Its great spread was coincident with the settlement of the country south of the Salado Slough after 1880. Wheat, also, first brought prosperity to the colonies of European immigrants established northwest of Santa Fé. In the course of time

[6]From Pier Luigi Beretta, "Analisi delle sedi rurali nella Regione Platense," *Bolletino della Società Geografica Italiana,* Vol. 7 (1966): 538–62.

wheat was planted in almost all parts of the Humid Pampa and proved successful in all but the southeastern part.

The yield of wheat, however, has been found to vary considerably within the Humid Pampa (Map 106). The best yields are in an area southwest of Rosario, where an average of from 17 to 20 bushels to the acre is reported. Yields between 13 and 17 bushels are to be had on the average through the central part of Buenos Aires Province and southward to the southern shore. Yields decline rapidly, however, to the southwest, dropping to between 6 and 9 bushels along the dry margin west of Bahía Blanca. At present most of the wheat comes from the zone yielding less than 17 bushels to the acre, and almost none from the area of highest yields.

The Maize District. The explanation of this exclusion of wheat from the area of highest yields is to be found in the competition of other grains. Since 1895, wheat has been challenged more and more successfully by maize, which, also, has its highest yields in the central district around Rosario. In this district an average of between 30 and 40 bushels to the acre is to be expected (Map 107). By 1912 there were approximately 9,500,000 acres of maize in Argentina, and most of it was in this central district newly developed out of the previous wheat area around Rosario. Maize held its precedence over wheat in this zone because its yield amounted to nearly twice that of wheat, and both crops used to bring about the same returns to the growers per bushel of grain. Beyond the limits of the Rosario district, there is a decline in the yield of maize indicating the relatively small area in which a favorable combination of fertile, well-drained soil, moderate temperatures, and dependable rainfall is found. Maize, especially, declines rapidly in its yield per acre as one moves into areas more frequently subject to drought. At Pergamino, in the center of the Rosario district, where the years of drought have been only 3 out of 25, the average yields of maize are about 38 bushels to the acre. Ninety miles to the southwest, where the years of drought came 10 times in a period of 25 years, the maize yields are only 17 bushels to the acre. This decrease is also partly due to the sandy nature of the soil and perhaps to other conditions of drainage or temperature. In the maize district, where maize yields are twice those of wheat, maize occupies as much as 75 percent of the land devoted to crops. Farther out toward the south and west, wheat soon equals maize and then exceeds it in acreage. In most of the area devoted chiefly to wheat the yield is nearly double that of maize, and in the territory west of Bahía Blanca it is even greater.

Flax entered the agricultural scene on the Humid Pampa about 1900, and was extensively planted in the maize area. At first it was a favorite crop in the preparation of new land for other crops or for pasture. It, too, yields better in the Rosario district than elsewhere; but because of its greater resis-

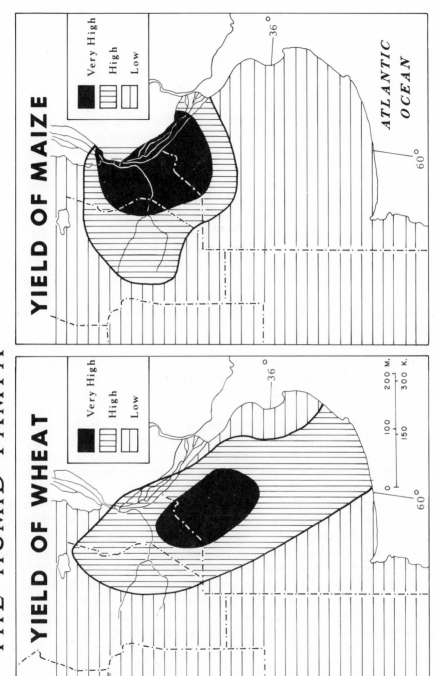

THE HUMID PAMPA

YIELD OF WHEAT

Very High
High
Low

36°

60°

0   100   200 M.

150   300 K.

Map 106

YIELD OF MAIZE

Very High
High
Low

36°

60°

ATLANTIC
OCEAN

Map 107

tance to heat and drought its yields do not drop off so fast as those of maize, especially to the north and east. In the maize district, maize yields three times as much as flax per acre, but in Mesopotamia, north of the Paraná, it yields less than twice as much as flax. Entre Ríos, at present, is the chief flax-growing province of Argentina.

The third of the major agricultural divisions of the Humid Pampa, therefore, was developed after 1895 when maize had proved to be more profitable than wheat in the central district of high grain yields. Today the maize district centers on the river port of Rosario. The area in which maize is predominant remained fairly steady from 1918 to 1928, but after 1928, when maize prices increased in relation to wheat prices, the maize district began to expand. In 1935–36 more land was planted to maize than to wheat in the Humid Pampa. The increase of the area planted to maize was made by extending the boundary of the maize district westward into territory where the yield per acre is less than it is in the area around Rosario. With the start of World War II, when the acreage of all grains dropped rapidly, maize dropped more than the others, and since the war this shrinkage has continued. Maize now occupies only five or six million acres, which is considerably less than the figure for 1912.

The Argentine maize district has produced maize very largely for export, not for the fattening of hogs and cattle as in the United States. Most of the maize is of the "flint" variety, characterized by small, hard grains, low in water content—a type which is easily shipped and which for a long time held a preeminent position in Europe as a poultry feed. The "dent" varieties used in North America chiefly to fatten animals are not popular in Argentina, and even in the maize district the local herds of animals are fattened on alfalfa. The decrease of the maize district in Argentina is related to the rise in the export of Peruvian fish meal, which the European poultry producers consider a better poultry feed than maize.

Even in the maize district a sharp distinction still persists between the landowners whose interest is primarily in the grazing industries, and the tenants who raise the crops. About 66 percent of the landed properties are large ones, still partly used for alfalfa pastures, and partly subdivided into tenant farms. Livestock and maize production still are two separate enterprises, involving the labor of two distinct groups of people. There are too few workers on the *estancias* to permit the cultivation of crops; and the tenure of the tenants is too insecure and their capital too small to permit their making a heavy investment in animals for fattening. Nevertheless there are more small farms and more large estates which have been devoted entirely to tenant farms under the supervision of a manager in the maize district than elsewhere on the Humid Pampa.

Most of the crop is raised by tenants. Italian immigrants are settled on tracts of land of between 175 and 250 acres. In many instances the same tenant families have been planting maize with little rotation on the same pieces of land for 30 or 40 years; and frequently, also, one finds that these people have saved a considerable amount of money. Many of the more thrifty tenants have been able to buy small properties elsewhere, which they in turn rent to other tenants. The striking contrast in attitude toward money between these Italian tenants and the Argentine landlords is nowhere more clearly exhibited than in the use of money income. The desire to increase their wealth is to a much greater degree the dominant motive of the Italians than of the Argentines. Money saved is put to work to make more income while the family continues to live in what seems like a comfortless adobe house, built to provide shelter and with no consideration for permanence. There is no feeling for land ownership as such, no pride in property, no desire to remain on the land if, for any reason, it should fail to provide a substantial income. Unless this fundamental contrast in psychological attitude toward money and land is recognized, there can be no real understanding of the relation of people to the land in the Pampa.

The maize district is the part of the Humid Pampa which, except for the surroundings of the city of Buenos Aires, has the greatest density of rural people. The maize district as a whole falls into the category of areas having between 60 and 125 people per square mile. But this general figure gives, perhaps, a wrong impression. For on nearly half the area of the maize district the densities are much less than this, and in the areas occupied by the Italian tenants, the rural densities are well above the average figure.

The Intensive Truck, Dairy, and Fruit District. The maize district is bordered on the east by a zone of intensive farming, devoted to supplying the market of the great metropolis of Buenos Aires. Small vegetable gardens even invade the outer fringes of the city. In this district around Buenos Aires there are two chief advantages for intensive farming: there is the easy access to the urban market, and there is the land which is ideally suited to the production of garden crops. The soil is fine-grained, deep, and well drained; the rainfall is abundant and evenly distributed throughout the year; the winters are so mild that there is no season when fresh vegetables cannot be provided. This is the land from which the Spanish settlers of the sixteenth century could derive only a meager living.

Not until World War I, in fact, did the zone of intensive farming begin its important development. Before 1914 the people of Argentina had to depend on foreign supplies of dairy products. European canned milk and butter provided for the needs of the Buenos Aires market. Only when international trade was cut off did the Argentines turn to the production of their own food supplies.

Dairying is now concentrated in the zone to the southeast of Buenos Aires, extending southward into the eastern part of the Humid Pampa. Because of the large proportion of swampy land in this section, and because of the cool summers and abundant rains, rich pastures of grass furnish good grazing for herds of high-grade dairy animals. Alfalfa and maize do not prosper. The population, therefore, is largely composed of pastoral specialists rather than farmers. Most of the land is divided into large estates, subdivided and rented to tenant dairymen.

Vegetables for the Buenos Aires market are produced close to the city. The small farms range from a few acres to 25 or 30. The truck farms are clustered along the railroad lines and on land within the urban limits not otherwise used. As the Argentine diet changes to include more and more fresh vegetables, the prosperity of this fringe of intensive truck farming increases.

Similarly the increase in the demand for fresh fruit among the people of Buenos Aires is reflected in a concentration of orchards located within easy range of the market. The delta of the Río Paraná provides a remarkably favorable site for fruit-growing. Along the floodplain of this river, the presence of the warm water from the north permits a long southward extension of tropical or subtropical kinds of vegetation. It has been found that such fruits as apples, pears, plums, peaches, and many others, yield excellently on the islands near the junction of the Paraná and the Uruguay. The suburb of Buenos Aires known as Tigre is not only a recreation center but is also the nucleus of a new fruit-orchard district. Much of the land on the islands is owned by large fruit companies and worked by hired laborers. In addition to the orchards, there are plantations of willow and poplar which supply materials for the construction of the baskets and boxes in which the fruit is sent to market.

Within the relatively small area of this general district of intensive dairying, truck farming, and fruit raising, the density of the rural population is much higher than anywhere else in the Humid Pampa. In the immediate vicinity of the city, densities mount to well over 125 persons per square mile.

Buenos Aires

The city of Buenos Aires itself constitutes another division of the Humid Pampa, but one in which several million people are concentrated, and on which the interests and activities of the whole Argentine state come to a focus. Greater Buenos Aires is a thoroughly cosmopolitan center. It is the product not of Argentina alone, but of the Occidental world; it constitutes an expression of that heroic age of economic expansion which led to the creation of metropolises in many parts of the world and to the flowering of urban society.

Like all the great cities of the Occidental world, Buenos Aires preserves in its patterns and forms the record of its long history. The marks still remain of the contrasted functions it has performed during its advance from a frontier post in a remote part of the Spanish colonial empire, to one of the world's great commercial and industrial metropolises. Most of the city growth, however, took place under the influence of the period of urban architecture and planning which produced such great urban avenues lined with buildings of uniform front as the Champs Elysées of Paris, the Avenida Rio Branco of Rio de Janeiro, the Paseo de la Reforma of Mexico City, or Commonwealth Avenue of Boston. The central avenue of Buenos Aires is the famous Avenida de Mayo. The so-called modern period of urban architecture is also finding expression in Buenos Aires, in the changed appearance of store fronts and in the numerous skyscrapers which now diversify the skyline. Only by looking behind the façade can we find the elements which are more strictly local in origin, the elements which give distinctive personality to this great city.

FOUNDING AND GROWTH

The place first selected for the establishment of a colony in 1536, and again in 1580 when the Spaniards came downstream from Asunción, possessed one important advantage. It was the only spot along this stretch of the Plata shore where the water was deep enough to permit boats to reach a dry landing place at the base of the *barranca*. Mostly, the southern shore of the Plata is low and marshy, with wide mud flats exposed when the wind blows from the south; but at one place the small tributary stream known as the Riachuelo provided an anchorage for the shallow-draught boats of the sixteenth century close to the higher ground of the Pampa. Otherwise this site had little to recommend it.

From 1580 to 1853 Buenos Aires was a place of very minor importance. Until 1778 oversea commerce was not permitted, for Spain wished to limit trade with the colonies to the Panamá route. Buenos Aires, which did a small business in smuggled goods, had the main function of sealing this back door to the Spanish domain. After 1680, when the Portuguese established a fort on the opposite shore of the Plata at Colonia, Buenos Aires played the part of a defense post, occupying a place of great importance in the struggle for the control of the Paraná-Plata. When the British attempted to occupy Buenos Aires in 1806 and 1807, the fact that this little town held the key to the control of a wide and potentially rich hinterland was beginning to be understood.

The development of the agricultural possibilities of the Humid Pampa was accompanied by the spectacular growth of the urban nucleus on which all these developments focused. In 1778, when Buenos Aires was opened as a port, the population was only 24,203. In 1855, at the beginning of the modern period, the future Argentine capital had 90,000 inhabitants. By 1870, however, it had increased to 270,000; and by 1890, it had reached 668,000. Buenos Aires passed the million mark in 1909, and at the time of the census of 1914, it had 1,500,000 people. After World War I the growth of the city continued, reaching 2,197,000 in 1932. At present its population is estimated at well over 7 million. Associated with this rapid growth have come all those social and economic phenomena which are characteristic of modern Occidental cities: the rapid rise of land values in the center; the development of "blighted areas" in the old residential zone near the center, and in the suburbs; the rapid expansion of the city along the lines of travel, including the establishment of detached suburbs and satellite towns; and the over-rapid subdivision of land into small residence lots in the scramble for profits by land speculators.

THE URBAN PATTERN

The urban pattern of Buenos Aires has developed around the original rectangular nucleus just north of the Riachuelo. The center of the plan is the Plaza de Mayo, out of which the Avenida de Mayo extends westward as far as the capitol building. The main artery which continues to the west and southwest is the Avenida Rivadavia. As the city has been extended in this direction the various subdivisions one after another have been built along the Avenida Rivadavia, their right-angle streets conforming to the orientation of the central thoroughfare. The extensions of the city to the northeast have been attached similarly to the main avenue which leads through San Isidro and San Fernando to Tigre

In the center of Buenos Aires, traffic congestion has led to the modification of the original rectangular plan. From the Plaza de Mayo diagonal avenues have been cut both to the northwest and to the southwest. The northern diagonal, the Avenida Saenz Pena, has become the axis of the commercial core. Buenos Aires also has built two systems of underground electric railways which converge on the Plaza de Mayo from the west and the northwest.

Buenos Aires has spread far beyond the original political city—which became the Argentine Federal District. Figures for the population of the political city have little meaning: all the people in communities that are functionally related to the central city and which form an almost uninterrupted built-up area must be included in the Buenos Aires conurbation. In the census of 1960 there were 6,763,000 people in the whole conurbation: by 1967 the total number had passed 7 million. Outside of the Federal District in 1960 there were eighteen separately administered units[7] (Map 108).

[7]Greater Buenos Aires in 1960 included:

Districto Federal	2,967,000	*Merlo	100,000
*Almirante Brown	135,000	*Moreno	59,000
Avellaneda	330,000	Morón	344,000
*E. Echeverria	69,000	Quilmes	318,000
*F. Varela	42,000	San Fernando	92,000
Gen. San Martin	279,000	San Isidro	196,000
*Gen. Sarmiento	168,000	*Tigre	92,000
*La Matanza	403,000	*Tres de Febrero	262,000
Lanús	382,000	*Vicente Lopez	250,000
Lomas de Zamora	275,000	Total	6,763,000
		(*added since 1947)	

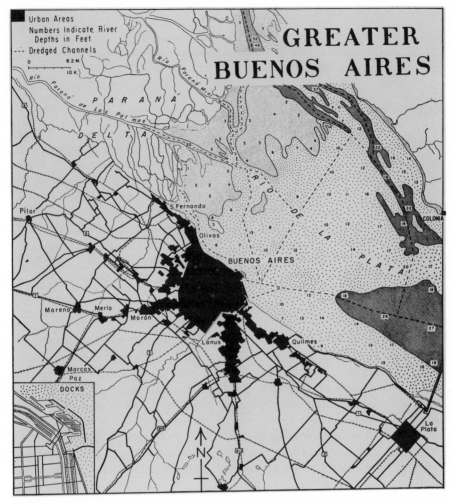

Map 108

THE PORT

With the development of the Humid Pampa in the late nineteenth century Buenos Aires was faced with the necessity of building an artificial port. The original Riachuelo, where the small sailing ships of the sixteenth century had been able to reach dry ground along the *barranca,* was totally inadequate for steamships. Map 108 shows that the main channel of the Río de la Plata is along the Uruguayan shore, and that the fresh water from the Paraná spreads over relatively shallow mud flats along the Pampa shore. A deep channel had to be dredged to Buenos Aires, and to keep the channel open dredging operations had to be continuous. Along the shore immediately east of the eastern end of the Avenida de Mayo, four connected basins were built where ships could tie up at docks. But even by the time of World War I it was clear that these docks were wholly inadequate. Many of Argentina's exports were diverted to the outport of La Plata, located 35 miles to the southeast. Entirely new port works were built immediately to the north of the old port. This new port was completed in 1935.

Argentina as a Political Unit

What happened to Argentina? Here is a state that started along the road to economic development earlier than any other Latin-American country, and had entered the "take-off" stage as early as World War I.[8] By 1930 Argentina led all the other Latin-American states in gross national product per capita, in the adequacy of the national diet, in the proportion of people living in cities, in the percentage of literacy, and in the stability of constitutional government. Then the development ceased, and constitutional processes were abandoned. Many Argentines found themselves confused, with no clear course of action or common purpose.[9] After so promising a start, how could these difficulties have arisen?

The Economic Situation

Argentina took its place among the chief commercial nations of the world during the latter part of the nineteenth century. The North American Civil War, following soon after the fall of Rosas, offered Argentina an unexpected opportunity to gain a foothold in the European markets, especially those of Great Britain. Argentina supplied meat and wheat; and in exchange, Great Britain supplied coal and manufactured articles of all kinds. British investments in railroads and packing plants, British purchases of Argentine foods, British sales of manufactured products in the expanding Argentine market, British coal shipments which formed the bulk cargoes to support the British steamship lines—these were the links which connected Argentina with Great Britain. The prosperity of the one was closely reflected in the prosperity of the other. Argentina could supply food at relatively low cost to the urban people of Great Britain, and the urban people of Great Britain were kept busy manufacturing the many things which the Argentines needed to buy. For the owners of capital and the owners of land, the system was a highly satisfactory one. Even the tenants who were doing most of the work were, for a time, satisfied with the arrangements, since they were living much better than in Spain or Italy. But the system contained the seeds of its own destruction, for there was a very great inequality in the distribution of the income. The landowners in Argentina were, as a group, among the world's wealthiest people.

[8]W. W. Rostow, *The Stages of Economic Growth* . . . . Cambridge, England, 1960, p. 38.
[9]Aldo Ferrer, *The Argentine Economy,* Berkeley, Cal., 1967, p. 209.

Even before the outbreak of World War I, however, small but significant changes in these relationships with Great Britain were appearing in Argentina. In 1880, Argentina imported some two and a half million pounds of flour and produced almost none. But in 1913, newly constructed flour mills in Buenos Aires were producing two million pounds a year and were being expanded. It was, however, the dislocations of 1914 that brought the first important challenge to the theory that such remote countries as Argentina should produce only raw materials and that the industrial centers of Europe and North America should supply the necessary manufactured articles to these places.

When Argentina was cut off from the usual sources of manufactured goods, she turned to the development of domestic manufacturing industries. Machinery was imported. Factories were built, and tariffs were set up to protect the infant enterprises. By 1920, shoes made from the local supplies of leather and cut for the Argentine trade could compete, for the ordinary market, with expensive imported shoes. Similarly, the woolen textiles made in Buenos Aires could meet the competition of all but the highest-grade textiles from Great Britain. The value of Argentina's exports made possible the purchase of industrial machinery and fuels.

The world-wide economic depression of the 1930's was a major disaster to Argentina. The prices on the international markets for agricultural and livestock products fell sharply, while the prices of manufactured goods remained high. Foreign private investment of new capital in Argentina almost entirely ceased. Argentina's capacity to pay for imports dropped in 1930–34 to only 46 percent of what it had been in 1925–29. This stimulated the building of factories to produce consumer goods, and it also stimulated a frantic search for fuel.

For its vital coal supplies Argentina was dependent on Great Britain. British coal was high in quality and low in cost. Because it formed a bulk cargo on ships sailing out from Britain destined to bring wheat back, the shipping costs were low. But when World War I suddenly reduced the coal shipments, Argentina faced a serious crisis in its fuel supply. In World War II this happened again. To keep the railroads running, wood was used as a fuel, and even maize and other grains soaked in linseed oil. By the end of World War II British coal had become more expensive, partly because the British mines were nearing exhaustion.

Argentina began to search frantically for domestic sources of coal. Small coal seams of poor quality were found along the Andean piedmont between San Juan, Mendoza, and San Rafael. The largest domestic source, however, was found at Río Turbio, near the Chilean border in southern Patagonia. The coal has a high sulphur content and cannot be made into coke. On the other hand, modern technology is providing a way to use such low-grade coal in industry. Río Turbio coal can be used near the mines more cheaply than imported coal.

Argentina has also been searching for oil and gas. In 1907 oil was discovered at Comodoro Rivadavia, and since then this field has accounted for the largest share of Argentine oil production. Now two pipelines carry gas from Comodoro Rivadavia to Buenos Aires. Oil and gas were also found along the Andean piedmont in three places. In the far north, Argentina shares a southward continuation of the Bolivian fields. A pipeline carries oil and gas from the Bolivian field and from northern Argentina to Buenos Aires. Oil and gas have also been discovered around Mendoza and around Neuquén. More recently it has been found that Chile's oil and gas along the Strait of Magellan and in Tierra del Fuego extend across the border into Argentina.

We have pointed out previously the important role played by the large oil corporations in discovering and developing oil and gas production. The process of exploration requires a large supply of risk capital as well as technical skill. But when an oil field has been developed there are many people who become resentful of the profits that flow out of the country and who advocate government ownership of national resources. As early as 1936, even before Mexico took the step of nationalizing its oil, the Argentine government placed all its oil and gas under the exclusive control of a government agency— *Yacimientos Petrolíferos Fiscales,* or Y.P.F. But for various reasons oil production dropped, and Argentina had to import some 60 percent of its needs. When the private companies were again permitted to operate for a time in the 1960's, a large expansion of the oil and gas production took place, and for a time it seemed that Argentina would become self-sufficient in these fuels. Then political pressure on the government to draw up new contracts with the companies again had the effect of reducing the rate of new discovery. The problem of how to secure an adequate supply of oil and gas without giving the private companies too much freedom has yet to be worked out to everyone's satisfaction; but in 1967 the foreign oil companies were again invited to seek concessions in Argentina.

The situation regarding hydroelectric power is also frustrating. At the Iguazú Falls, located on the northern border of the Argentine province of Misiones, 800 miles from Buenos Aires, there is a potential horse power of some 325,000 kw. There is also an abundant waterpower potential in the southern Andes, where optimists have long envisioned the establishment of industries. What is frustrating is that although the total power potential is large, none of it is located where population and industries make an enlarged supply of power necessary. Today, steam-electric power stations around Buenos Aires are supplied with fuel by the gas pipelines.

THE ECONOMY SINCE 1930

The world never returned to the economic patterns of the pre-1930 era. Since World War II no country can accept the role of supplier of raw materials in exchange for manufactured products from industrialized societies. The policy now is to build an integrated industrial structure, based on such fundamental necessities as steel. It has been abundantly demonstrated that modern economies are vastly strengthened, and the general material levels of living are raised, when countries with diversified, modern manufacturing industries, nationally integrated, are free to exchange products over a wide international market.

In Argentina there are several obstacles to renewed development. First is the lack of a clearly defined economic policy: there are many who want to return to the export of primary products of the type that brought prosperity before 1930; there are others who seek to establish a nationally self-sufficient corporate state on the fascist model; and few are those who support the policies of international cooperation and interdependence. And second, the geographic patterns of interchange were built to facilitate an export economy: each region has close ties to Buenos Aires; but the interregional connections are poorly developed.

THE ECONOMIC POLICIES OF PERÓN

The dictator Juan Domingo Perón, who ruled Argentina from 1946 to 1955, established a fascist-type state. The government assumed complete control of the national economy. The central bank was nationalized, thus assuring Perón of a source of credit to finance his undertakings. All foreign trade was placed under the control of a government agency. The producers of meat and grain sold their products to this agency, and the agency sold the products abroad at the best possible prices. The income derived in this way was not returned to the agricultural interests. The government paid off its foreign debt by purchasing the railroads owned by British and French stockholders, and by purchasing also such foreign-owned utilities as gas, electricity, and telephones. The British railroads were sold largely to pay for essential imports of beef into Great Britain in the immediate post-war years.

In 1947 the Perón government announced its first "Five-Year Plan" (1947–51). The plan included large public works and industrialization aimed at making Argentina economically independent of the rest of the world. As a result slums were cleared, roads were built, irrigation systems were improved, and cities were given a modern look. The number of factories jumped from about 40,000 in 1935 to more than twice that number in 1950; and the number of workers employed in manufacturing industry increased from 577,000 in 1935 to 1,108,000 in 1950. In addition to the food industries already in existence, there was a considerable increase in leather goods and textiles, in metal and machinery, and in petrochemicals, paper, and plastics. Foreign capital was welcomed, but only under strict government control. Argentina remained dependent on imported coal, but to reduce this dependence a pipeline was built to carry gas to Buenos Aires from Comodoro Rivadavia.

Perón started plans to build a steel plant on a site at San Nícolas on the

Paraná River below Rosario. A United Nations study published in 1954 estimated that steel could be produced at San Nícolas at low enough cost to be competitive with imported steel.

All these steps in economic development speedily used up the capital available to Argentina, at the same time undermining the productivity of the meat and grain producers, on whose efforts the previous economic position of the country was based. The large landowners were being called on by Perón to finance the nation's economic development. The results were the decrease of the acreage of the grains, and eventually even a shortage of beef for domestic uses. Perón did succeed in attracting private investors from the United States, and secured a loan from the Export-Import Bank to finance the proposed steel plant at San Nícolas. But when he drew up a contract with the Standard Oil Company of California for oil exploration which was submitted to the Argentine congress for approval in 1955, the result was a revolt of the armed services and the forced resignation of the dictator.

THE ECONOMY SINCE 1955

Since 1955 Argentina has faced the unpleasant task of rebuilding its shattered economy. Not only did Perón flee the country with a substantial proportion of the national treasury, but also he left a mountain of debts. Perhaps the most serious problem was the large number of workers who had never "had it so good," and who were ready to express their wish in the ballot for a return of Perón's policies, if not of Perón himself.

By 1950 the process of economic growth had ceased. Between 1950 and 1955 the gross national product increased 3.2 percent per year, but the population was increasing at almost the same rate, which meant that there was no upward movement of the economy. Between 1961 and 1963 there was actually a decrease in gross national product of more than 5 percent per year. The Argentines, who were accustomed to a high level of living, found themselves in trouble—and trouble was made clear to individual families through the discovery that there was an insufficient supply of meat in the retail stores.

Then in 1964 there was an upturn in the economy. Unemployment was reduced, there was an increase of industrial production and an increase in the supply of agricultural products. The gross national product per capita rose 8 percent in 1964. In 1966 Argentina had a gross national product per capita of $700, second only to that of Venezuela.

There were several gains in basic heavy industry. In 1960 the San Nícolas steel plant (*Sociedad Mixta Siderurgica Argentina,* or SOMISA) started turning out steel. In 1967, with an annual capacity of 750,000 tons, it employs 7,900 workers. The iron ore comes from Brazil, Chile, and Peru, although it is planned to secure about a quarter of the iron ore needs from Sierra Grande by 1970. Coal comes from the United States. Gas comes by pipeline from Bolivia and northern Argentina. Enlargement of SOMISA was planned so that it could produce over 2 million tons annually by 1972. A second and smaller steel plant was built at Rosario. Meanwhile, starting in 1961, a huge complex of petrochemical industries was started at San Lorenzo, 15 miles upstream from Rosario. The chemical industries will use oil from Bolivia and northern Argentina, and will manufacture gasoline, synthetic rubber, fertilizer and other industrial chemicals. The beginnings of a nationally integrated industrial system were appearing.

Much yet remains to be done. In 1967 a major problem was the virtual collapse of the railroads. Owned and operated by the government, they were losing a million dollars a day, and contributed about half of the total budget deficit. Of the 173,000 railroad workers, it was estimated that some 50,000 were superfluous; but the powerful railroad unions resisted all efforts to reorganize the working force. Of the 3,570 steam locomotives that the railroads owned in 1966, about 2,500 were more than 50 years old, and only 170 were less than 20 years old. There were about 1,000 new diesel engines, but already 400 of these were out of service. As a result only about 8 percent of the freight was being moved by rail; most of it went by motor trucks or by boat. The lack of rail transportation was a disaster to the wheat growers in 1964–65—when the farmers produced an abundant 10 million tons—because thousands of tons rotted on sidings along the railroads before freight cars became available. A first step toward national economic integration will be a complete renovation of the railroads, the construction of many miles of new all-weather highways, and the further extension of pipelines.

FOREIGN TRADE

Argentina is not yet an exporter of manufactured goods, as it must eventually become. In 1965 about 38 percent of the value of all exports was made up of wheat and maize, and another 38 percent was made up of animal products, chiefly meat and wool. Argentina is still Latin America's largest exporter of wool. Vegetable oils and oilseeds made up 11 percent.

The traditional close integration of Argentine trade with Great Britain has now been completely broken. The table shows the proportion of Argentine exports going to certain countries in 1938, 1945, 1954, and 1965.

EXPORTS OF ARGENTINA GOING TO CERTAIN COUNTRIES*
Percentage of the value of all exports

Country	1938	1945	1954	1965
Italy	2	—	3	16
The Netherlands	7	2	6	11
Great Britain	33	25	18	10
Brazil	7	9	9	7
West Germany	12	—	9	7
United States	8	22	14	6
China	—	—	—	6
Soviet Union	—	—	—	5
Belgium	7	3	3	—
Others	19	36	33	32

*For 1938 and 1945: the Pan American Union; for 1954: the Committee on Latin-American Studies, University of California at Los Angeles; for 1965: the Encyclopaedia Britannica Book of the Year (1967).

Of the imports in 1965 the United States sent 23 percent, Brazil sent 14 percent, West Germany sent 9 percent, Italy sent 7 percent, and only 6 percent came from Great Britain.

THE GROWTH OF THE TERTIARY SECTOR

In mature economies that continue to expand there is an increasing demand for a great variety of services. Employment in service occupations—the tertiary sector—becomes greater than in either primary or secondary sectors. The services that are normally demanded include education, entertainment, sales, and a great variety of professional services. In Argentina since 1950 there has been a rapid increase of employment in the tertiary sector; but a closer look at this employment shows how very different it is from the tertiary sector of a mature economy. The jobs are mostly in public service. As employment in agriculture dropped, reaching 25 percent of the labor force in 1963, and employment in industry also dropped to under 20 percent, there was a corresponding increase of the proportion of jobs in service occupations. But in Argentina it was not demand for such service that produced the jobs: it was the stagnation of growth in the other sectors that left workers with no alternative but to accept government jobs. The national budget had to provide for these jobs, which meant that there was less to spend on highways, railroads, ports, electric power, or other elements of social overhead.

This movement into the tertiary sector was reflected in the rapid expansion of urban population, and the concentration of some 34 percent of the total Argentine population in Buenos Aires. This growth of the chief city, out of all proportion to the other cities of Argentina, is another aspect of the imbalance in the economy and the lack of internal integration among the parts of the country.

The Political Situation

One of the first great Argentine political leaders was Domingo Faustino Sarmiento, born in San Juan in 1811, a child of poor parents. At the age of sixteen he came upon a biography of Benjamin Franklin. From Franklin he learned that a democracy could thrive only if it gave every child an equal chance to become an informed, literate citizen. During the rule of General Rosas, Sarmiento was exiled to Chile, where he became well-known as a liberal writer. In 1845 he visited the United States and Europe, and became a disciple of Horace Mann. Returning to Chile, he established the first teacher-training school in Latin America, and Chile's school system became the best in all the Latin-American countries. After the fall of Rosas, Sarmiento returned to Buenos Aires where he helped to set up the new government. He was Argentina's second president, and during his presidency (1868–74) he established schools, museums, libraries, and art collections. Democracy in Argentina was well launched. After the death of Sarmiento in 1888, the liberal tradition was carried on by the universities and by the great newspapers of Buenos Aires.

What happened to democracy in Argentina? In the first place it is clear that Sarmiento's educational reforms were only preliminary. Politics after 1853 remained under the tight control of the small minority of landowners. To be sure, the governments were progressive and stable, but they were not democratically selected, nor were policies opened to public discussion. No government could be elected, and no policy could be adopted without the approval of the landowners.

By the early decades of the twentieth century political conditions began to change in Argentina. The flood of immigrants had changed the traditions of the people. And as more and more immigrants left their tenant farms in the rural areas to become city wage workers, they escaped from the political control of the ruling groups. Especially when World War I made industrial development in Buenos Aires necessary, a new class of urban workers and a new middle class of shopkeepers and government employees began to appear. The long rule of the Conservative Party was broken in 1916 with the election of Hipólito Irigoyen, the candidate of the *Union Cívica Radical*. The Radical Party was firmly based on the city voters.

The long practice of constitutional government ended in 1930 when the Radical Party was tumbled from power by a military coup. From 1930 to 1958 the government of Argentina remained in the hands of army officers. The graft and corrupt practices that had become commonplace sadly discredited democracy, and the army officers, most of whom had been educated in German military schools, were inclined to take Italy or Germany as a model. Argentina proposed to become a third force in the world—neither communist nor capitalist, and sought to lead the Latin-American countries away from the dominance of the United States and Great Britain. During World War II the government was strongly in favor of Germany and Italy. In 1943, when it seemed that Argentina was about to yield to pressure to break relations with Germany and Italy, another army coup kept Argentina neutral.

Meanwhile a very important shift of population was taking place. When the acreages of grain were reduced, the tenants planted their farms with alfalfa and moved away. Having no places to go in the rural areas, they moved in large numbers into the cities, especially Buenos Aires. But there was no un-employment problem, for Argentina was rapidly building new industries and was undertaking programs of slum clearance in the city itself. To a much greater degree than in 1916, here was a worker group free from political control in the cities. Moreover the workers were not at all indoctrinated with the traditional ideas of democracy, for their background was Italian and Spanish. It was at this point that Juan Domingo Perón, an obscure army colonel with tremendous personal ambitions, made his appearance as Secretary of Labor in the military government. He promoted a whole series of social and economic benefits for the workers, among whom he became a popular hero. He called the workers his *descamisados,* his "shirtless ones." For the first time in Argentine history there was a political leader working for the poor people. He brought them together as a class, opposed to the rule of the landowners and to the "Yankee imperialists." Aided by his glamorous and equally ambitious wife Eva Duarte Perón, he rose quickly in power, until in 1945 he assumed the presidency. By that time the army was concerned about the rise of this new political leader, and they tried to remove him from office and place him in confinement. But so great was the popular uprising in Buenos Aires that the army had to give in.

In 1946 Perón held an election. It was probably Argentina's first uncontrolled and entirely honest election. Perón, the hero of the *descamisados,* received 1,478,372 votes, compared with 1,211,666 received by his rival.

Perón's policies were calculated to gain and keep the support of the workers. In addition to his economic policies, which we have discussed above, he decreed a variety of social changes, including higher minimum wages, paid vacations, various social security and health measures. He aroused the workers against the traditional rulers of Argentina, leading even to the burning of the famous Jockey Club, center of the social life of the aristocracy. He took a stand at meetings of the American states in favor of isolationism, and opposed everything that looked like "Yankee imperialism." He drew Argentina closer to the Soviet Union, while strictly controlling communist activity in Argentina. He painted a picture to his devoted followers that showed Argentina assuming a new position of dignity in the world, midway between the Soviets and the nations of the free world.

As we have seen, Perón led his country into bankruptcy. After the death of the people's darling Evita, he took desperate measures to keep his followers in line, for many were already disillusioned when his economic promises were not fulfilled. He even went so far as to arrest certain priests of the Catholic Church who were charged with efforts to undermine his government. But finally, when he planned to permit the entrance of a North American oil company (Standard Oil of California) to undertake the development of Argentina's presumed oil reserves, the army officers felt the time had come to revolt. After a short period of bitter fighting, Perón was forced to flee and a military government assumed control.

Since the departure of Perón, Argentina has had a succession of elected civilian presidents, interrupted by repeated military coups. In 1962, when it seemed clear that the pro-Perón candidates for public office would be elected, the army again stepped in to stop his return from exile in Spain. By the late 1960's Perón's once loyal supporters had split into a number of separate parties, and it was estimated that about 65 percent of the voters were actually against him. But all the other political parties were also fragmented, and only the army seemed to provide any effective organized power. It is part of the Spanish-American attitude described as *machismo* that causes a political leader to lose face if he is forced to compromise. Yet compromise is the essence of the democratic process, and when the failure to compromise results in the formation of innumerable small splinter parties, only a military dictatorship can provide the necessary cohesion.

One of Argentina's major problems is rebuilding a sense of national purpose, a widely supported state-idea. Is this country to return again to the ways of constitutional government with democratic institutions, or is it to accept an authoritarian government? Will it seek economic isolation from the rest of the world, including the rest of Latin America, or will it give support to the establishment of a Latin-American Free Trade Area?

These are the problems with which the leaders of the once prosperous and stable Argentina must wrestle.

República Oriental del Uruguay

Area: 68,536 square miles
Population: (1966 estimate) 2,749,000; (last census, 1963) 2,592,563
Capital city: Montevideo; (1963) 1,154,465
Percent urban: (1955) 33
Birth rate per 1,000: (1966) 24–27; Death rate per 1,000: (1966) 7–9
Annual percent of increase: 1958–64, 1.4
Percent literate: (1963) 90.3
Percent labor force in agriculture: (1963) 7.6
Gross national product per capita: (1966) $569
Unit of currency: peso (1968, 7.4 per dollar)

COMMERCE, 1965 *(expressed in percentage of values)*
Percent total Latin-American exports: 1.9 (1956, 3)
Percent total Latin-American imports: 1.8

Exports (1966)   wool   45   meat   24   hides   9

Exports to (1966)			Imports from (1966)		
United Kingdom	14		Brazil	14	
United States	12	(1956, 12)	United States	12	(1956, 16)
Netherlands	9		West Germany	11	
West Germany	8		Kuwait	10	
Italy	7		Venezuela	7	
Brazil	6		Argentina	7	
Spain	5		United Kingdom	5	
France	5				

Chapter 24 □ Uruguay

Uruguay is the most coherent and the most democratic state in Latin America. Yet these conditions were not achieved without a struggle. For a long time the territory along the northern shore of the Plata River—which the settlers in Buenos Aires called the *Banda Oriental,* or eastern shore (of the Uruguay River)—was a no-man's-land between the Portuguese and the Spaniards. It was invaded again and again from both sides, as each sought to occupy and hold the strategic position at the mouth of the Plata. Uruguay gained its independence because of the intervention of Great Britain and the agreement between Argentina and Brazil to recognize the existence of an independent buffer state between them. Uruguay, like Argentina, has been largely populated by immigrants from Europe who came after the middle of the nineteenth century. Since the beginning of the twentieth century the Uruguayans have been able to establish order and coherence through democratic procedures. Since World War II they have made the transition from a feudal society to the democratic socialism of a welfare state—the only one of its kind in Latin America. But they did this without going through any of the intermediate stages of economic growth, with the result that the welfare state now suffers from economic insecurity.

The People

Uruguay, like Paraguay and Chile, is composed of only one area of concentrated settlement; but unlike either Paraguay or Chile, this one area includes the whole of the national territory. Uruguay is one of the few states where the effective national territory and the total national territory are the same. The one cluster of people is centered around Montevideo, a city of

669

about 1,200,000 in a total population of about 2,750,000. This means that some 47 percent of the people of Uruguay live in the metropolitan area of their chief city. Next in size are Salto and Paysandú, each a little over 60,000. The densest rural population is in the south and west, between Paysandú and Montevideo; the remainder of the country has a scattered population with a density of less than 25 people per square mile.

The composition of the Uruguayan population is similar to that of Argentina. The great majority—over 90 percent—are of unmixed European ancestry, mostly from Spain and Italy, but with many other European nationalities represented in small numbers. There are no Indians and only 1 percent of Africans.

The Land

In many different ways Uruguay is a transitional land between the Humid Pampa and the hilly uplands and plateaus of Brazil. There is a southern fringe of alluvial land, bordering the lower Uruguay and the Plata Rivers (Map 87, p. 536); but most of the country is hilly, with soils derived from the decomposition of the underlying crystalline rocks. In contrast to the monotonous stretches of tall grass which greeted the Spaniards when they first entered what is now Argentina, the Uruguayan landscape was composed of wooded valleys in which rushing streams of clear water could be found, and of long, gentle, grass-covered slopes rising to distant hills. Uruguay has been called "The Purple Land," because of the faint purplish tinge given to the scene by the vistas of tall prairie grasses on smooth slopes.[1]

The Uruguayan geographers divide their country into several regions, basing their divisions on the character of the surface. Along the eastern coast there is a zone of lowland, composed of sandy beaches, lagoons, and wind-tossed dunes. Inland from this is a belt of hills, running from the southern part of Brazil southwestward to the southern coast of Uruguay in the vicinity of Montevideo. This belt of hills is arranged along the divide between the shorter streams flowing directly to the Atlantic, and the longer streams which flow westward to join the Río Uruguay. The summits along the *Cuchilla Grande,* as the divide is called, reach elevations of about 1,500 feet above sea level. (The highest elevation in Uruguay is only 1,650 feet.) Westward from the Cuchilla Grande the land slopes gently toward the Río Uruguay; along the divide the valleys are narrow and the streams turbulent: but lower down, the valleys broaden out, and in a few places the streams have developed small floodplains. The Río Uruguay itself, however, is interrupted at several points by falls and rapids, notably at Salto. The head of navigation for ocean steamers is at Fray Bentos.

[1] See W. H. Hudson's description of Uruguay in the early nineteenth century in his book *The Purple Land.*

In three parts of Uruguay the granites are covered with more recent formations. (1) Along the east coast, as we have said, the sandy shore deposits obscure the underlying rocks. (2) Along the Uruguay-Plata shore there is a fringe of level country where the crystallines are buried under typical Pampa deposits—river alluvium and loess. (3) In the central and northwestern part of the country there is an extensive cover of rock formations of later age than the granites. In the valley of the Río Negro these later formations are relatively weak and do not produce landscape features strikingly different from those of the crystalline area except for the absence of granite blocks along the hill crests. In the northwest, Uruguayan territory includes the southernmost portion of the Paraná Plateau. Flows of dark-colored lava now remain as flat-lying and very resistant formations bounded by sharp cliffs or cuestas. The profiles of the hills are tabular rather than rounded, and the valley sides are angular rather than smoothly curved.

Vegetation and Climate

Vegetation and climate are also transitional between the Argentine Humid Pampa and southern Brazil. Most of Uruguay was originally covered with a tall-grass prairie similar to the *pasto duro* of the Pampa. At one time the stream valleys were followed by ribbons of forest, and scattered palms were, and still are, mixed with the tall grass in the southeast. Today less than 4 percent of the area of Uruguay is forested.

The climatic conditions, too, are of a transitional character. The climate of Uruguay, perhaps more than that of any other part of the middle latitudes, can be described as "temperate." Throughout the country, the average temperatures of the coldest month are not far from 50°—similar to the winter averages in Georgia and South Carolina. The summers, however, are cooler than in the corresponding part of North America; at Montevideo the average of the warmest month is 72°, approximately the same as the average of the warmest month in Boston, and a little lower than that of Buenos Aires. The rainfall is evenly distributed throughout the year, with no regular season of excessive rain or of drought. On the average the rainfall varies from about 38 inches at Montevideo to nearly 50 inches in the north. Although there is a considerable irregularity in the total fall from year to year, periods of prolonged drought are rare. This irregularity, however, might have a more serious effect on such crops as maize than it has on the pasture grasses.

Settlement

Enthusiasts have described Uruguay—with its freedom from climatic extremes, its prevailing gentle slopes, and its abundance of clear water and nourishing grasses—as the world's finest grazing land. Yet Uruguay offered the enthusiasts the opportunity to observe this happy combination of elements only after the Plata region had been occupied by Europeans for more than 250 years. The physical qualities which make Uruguay such a fine grazing land could not operate to bring prosperity to the inhabitants until the large international markets had developed in Europe and North America, and until the local people were ready to undertake the production of surpluses for export.

During the colonial period, Uruguay was remote from the centers of both Portuguese and Spanish settlement. Remoteness in the case of the Portuguese was chiefly the result of the great distance between Uruguay and the primary settlement center at São Paulo. Yet by 1680, the Portuguese had pushed southward all the way to the Plata shore and had established a fortress at Colonia, opposite Buenos Aires (Map 6, p. 18). Remoteness from the Spanish settlements on the Humid Pampa was primarily the result of the river barrier. The Paraná-Plata is so wide, and is bordered by such a labyrinth of swamps and shifting channels, that to cross it, or even to use it as a line of travel, has always been difficult. The Spaniards were interested in their connections through Tucumán and Salta with Peru; for the trade in mules, even the grassy Pampas on the southern shore of the Plata east of Buenos Aires were considered too remote to be valuable as breeding and grazing grounds. The *Banda Oriental* was even more isolated with respect to the routes to Peru.

The Beginnings of Settlement

For nearly 200 years after the Spaniards first reached the Plata region, they made no fixed settlement in what is now Uruguay. The Banda Oriental was occupied chiefly by nomadic cattle herders, or *gauchos*. Cattle were introduced between 1611 and 1617, and were permitted to run wild and to multiply. Gangs of *gauchos* followed the herds, rounding up a few animals here and there for slaughter. Only the hides were of value unless the animals were killed near the shore, where the carcasses might be used in the making of tallow or salt beef. There was no attempt to claim ownership of the land, no attempt even to establish ranch headquarters. The bands of *gauchos* fought as readily for Portugal as for Spain, and when no profitable fighting was to be had, they would battle among themselves.

The idea of land ownership came slowly to Uruguay. The first Uruguayan contacts with the commercial world were with the Brazilian traders who came to buy hides. Later the Argentine cattle buyers crossed the river from Buenos Aires to deal with the *gauchos*. In the course of time these buyers found it easier to establish fixed headquarters and to employ herders to keep the cattle nearby than to follow the half-wild herds over the vast interior of the country. At first, only the ranch headquarters were definitely established, and the boundaries with neighboring ranches were left undefined; but as more and more of the land was occupied, boundaries became important. As the zone of ranches, or *estancias,* moved northward from the Plata shore, the nomadic *gauchos* were pushed to the more distant parts of the country. The landowners replaced the *gauchos* with hired workers and peons—men who were attached to the estates by some form of debt bondage. Even then the interior of Uruguay remained a land of men, for unmarried males rather than men with families were preferred as workers.

The Towns

As this type of rural settlement we have just described spread northward across Uruguay, small villages and towns began to appear. Generally these settlements were located at road junctions, and since the easiest lines of travel followed the water partings, or *cuchillas,* and avoided the wooded valleys, a few of the small villages were established on the ridge-tops. At the smaller road junctions perhaps only one or two retail stores would appear, surrounded by a cluster of dwellings; but at the larger junctions, small towns with a considerable population of merchants would be established. Uruguay became a land of small scattered trading villages and of widely spaced ranches.

Montevideo was not founded until 1726, when Portuguese advances finally forced the Spaniards to build a permanent fortress on the Uruguayan shore. They selected an excellent site where the hilly belt of the Cuchilla Grande reaches the southern shore, providing a small sheltered harbor dominated by a low conical hill on which the fortress could be built. Almost at once Montevideo became the chief urban center of the Banda Oriental, and most of the roads of the interior were redirected to lead to this new port. There was not then, and there never has been since, any competitor to challenge the supremacy of Montevideo as chief center of the economic, political, and social life of the country.

Uruguay as a Buffer State

National independence came to Uruguay as a result of influences beyond its borders. For centuries the conflict between the Spaniards and the Portuguese continued without decisive action. When Brazil declared its independence in 1822, Uruguay was included as a part of the Brazilian national territory. In 1825 the Uruguayans, with Argentine assistance, organized a resistance to the Brazilians, and defeated a Brazilian force in 1827. But by this time it was clear that neither Argentina nor Brazil could gain complete control of this border area. Meanwhile the British had occupied Buenos Aires in 1806 and 1807, and Montevideo in 1807. If Britain had not been involved in difficulties in Europe at this time, the whole Plata region might have become a British dominion. In 1828 the British, whose interest in this part of South America had not been diminished by the failure to hold the port cities, succeeded in getting both Argentina and Brazil to agree on the recognition of an independent Uruguay as a buffer state.

The Pastoral Economy

As in Argentina, it was the investment of British capital that started Uruguay on the road to economic development. The British were the first to appreciate the potential commercial value of the grasslands of the Humid Pampa and of Uruguay for the grazing of animals. At the time of independence, Uruguay was already grazed by millions of cattle, but the only products that could be exported were hides, tallow, and some salt beef. Uruguay was also used for the breeding of mules, and the mules were sent northward to mining communities in Brazil. In 1840 high-grade Merino sheep were brought in from Britain and the grazing of wool sheep spread rapidly. By the middle of the century it was estimated that there were about two million sheep and about three and a half million cattle feeding on the still unfenced range.

The second British investment was made in 1864. The Liebig Meat Extract Company of London opened a plant at Fray Bentos on the Río Uruguay, and for the first time the ranchers could sell their cattle for meat rather than hides alone. In 1868 a British company started to build a railroad to connect Montevideo with the back country.

Two inventions opened the way for major changes in the pastoral economy. One was the introduction of barbed wire that made possible the fencing of pastures and the control of animal breeding. The other was the development of the refrigerator ship that made possible the shipment of frozen meat across the equator. Both these inventions came to Uruguay in the 1870's. In 1880 the first Hereford beef animals arrived from Britain, and within two decades Herefords and Shorthorns had replaced the rangy creole cattle. Meanwhile the export of wool continued to be highly profitable. By 1900 it is estimated that there were 18,500,000 head of sheep and 7 million head of cattle. The animal census of 1961 counted 21,480,000 sheep and 8,670,000 cattle. This means that Uruguay leads all other countries in the world in the ratio of animals to people.

The first modern large-scale packing plant or *frigorífico,* was built in 1902 at Fray Bentos with British capital. Subsequently three other large-scale *frigoríficos* were located at Fray Bentos, two owned by packing firms in the United States, one owned by the Uruguayan government. The meat exports came largely from the foreign-owned plants, and the Uruguayan-owned plant was used to supply the domestic market. The Uruguayans are accustomed to eating more meat even than the Argentines—almost a pound per person per day.

Land Use in Rural Uruguay

There are two major divisions of rural Uruguay. The greater part of the national territory is used for the grazing of sheep on uncultivated pastures (Map 91, p. 540). The land is divided into large private *estancias,* on which

A large cattle range in the southern part of Uruguay. *Courtesy of Moore-McCormack Lines.*

the various pastures are separated by barbed wire fences. Some 81 percent of Uruguay is used exclusively for pasture.

Agriculture is concentrated in the southwestern part of the country, but with scattered crop areas invading the pastoral region. Along the Uruguay River from Paysandú southward, and along the Plata shore as far as Montevido, where the loess soils are similar to those of the Humid Pampa, the land is used for crop-pasture rotation. Along the Uruguay River the chief crop is wheat, but farther east maize becomes more important than wheat. Crops also include flax, peanuts, and sunflowers. The pastures of this area are used almost exclusively for cattle. Throughout this same agricultural area there are small concentrations of grapes. Uruguay is only exceeded in Latin America by Chile and Argentina as an exporter of wine.

During and since World War II the government has followed the policy of encouraging the expansion of agriculture. An area of concentrated rice paddies has been developed in the northeast, slightly back from the salty shores of the Laguna Merin (Portuguese, Lagôa Mirim). Uruguay has now become almost self-sufficient in rice production. As in Argentina, imports of olive oil were cut off by the war, and to provide a domestic supply of cooking oil the cultivation of peanuts was promoted. During the 1950's sunflowers were widely cultivated for the oil they provide. Peanuts and sunflowers vary in acreage from year to year, and land used for these crops is now found scattered even within the pastoral zone. The government also supported the cultivation of sugar beets in the southern part of the country, but after 1955 it began also to support the planting of sugarcane in the far northwest. A district of concentrated dairy production has made its appearance around Montevideo.

The expansion of agriculture has invaded some of the best cattle pastures. As a result, since World War II there has been a decline in the volume and quality of meat production. In 1952 one of the North American frigoríficos was closed. Meat exports have declined while wool exports continue to rise.

Transportation

Uruguay's railroad system, like that of Argentina, was built chiefly with British capital, made use of British rolling stock, and burned British coal. The first line was built out of Montevideo in 1868, and by 1911 the present rail system was essentially complete. Connections were made with Brazil at three places on the border. All of the Uruguayan railroads are built on one uniform gauge (4 ft., 8½ in.). After World War II, the government used some of its sterling credits to purchase the British interests, and now the whole system is government-owned.

Since the war, the government has also undertaken an important program of highway construction. Highways have been extended parallel to all the rail lines, and into many parts of the country between the rail lines. Except for a few paved highways near Montevideo, all the roads are gravel-surfaced. Unlike Argentina, where gravel is difficult to find, Uruguay is abundantly supplied with this road-surfacing material, and the extension of all-weather roads has not been such a difficult task as it proved to be south of the Plata. Motor trucks and passenger buses now provide most of Uruguay's transportation.

Montevideo

Montevideo, now a city of over a million, has grown out of proportion to the rest of the country. It performs the functions of government, of commerce, and of manufacturing. It is also a major resort center, attracting a large number of tourists from Argentina who enjoy the fine beaches nearby and the hotels and gambling casinos. Montevideo is also the major land base of the South Atlantic fishing fleet, to which the fleet returns in winter to repair and resupply the ships. Montevideo is the one focus of Uruguayan life—a focus which is even sharper than that of Argentina on Buenos Aires.

Uruguay as a Political Unit

Uruguay is distinctive among all the countries of Latin America for the efforts it has made to do something about the inequities of the economic system and the injustices of the political life. To a large extent these efforts resulted from the influence of Uruguay's great leader, José Batlle[2] y Ordóñez

[2]Pronounced *Báje*.

(1856–1929). Uruguay became Latin America's one example of a "welfare state," but unlike other welfare states of the modern world, Uruguay took a single leap from a feudal, agrarian society to a society in which every individual is guaranteed security and equity. Now some of the economic problems that were originally bypassed must be solved.

The Economic Situation

Out of the total population of Uruguay—about 2,750,000 in 1966—it is estimated that the labor force is about 1 million. The rate of population increase is about 1.4 percent per year, which is the lowest in all Latin America. But the welfare system includes family allowances, workmen's compensation, unemployment insurance, free compulsory education, subsidized housing, and unusually liberal retirement benefits and pensions. After 30 years of work a man is eligible for a pension for the rest of his life; and a woman is eligible for a pension after working 25 years, or after reaching the age of 47. Furthermore, no one who earns less than $1400 a year is called upon to pay an income tax—which means that 97 percent of the people are exempt. Payroll taxes on businesses sometimes amount to 80 percent of the labor costs. It is the labor force of 1 million that must support this expensive welfare system.

Wool is Uruguay's chief export. Here the clip is sorted and graded before being bagged for shipment. *Courtesy of Moore-McCormack Lines.*

Meanwhile the Uruguayan gross national product per capita has risen but little since 1955. The national economy is in difficulties because of the relatively slow rise of the value of the exports and the rapid increase of the cost of imports. The government attempted to subsidize the increase of manufacturing industry to replace expensive imports. In 1950 some 22 percent of the gross national product came from agricultural and pastoral activities. But in 1964 only 15 percent came from the traditional products, and 23 percent came from manufactures. Trade and tourists together made up nearly 30 percent.

The development of manufacturing industries faces two chief problems. First is the lack of raw materials, except for wool, meat, and hides. There are no fuels, no minerals of importance. And second, the economies of a large-scale manufacturing operation cannot be secured because of the small size of the domestic market. The Uruguayans are relatively well off compared with many Latin-Americans; but they are not numerous enough to support modern industry. For Uruguay, the development of a common market becomes a matter of the greatest importance. In the 1960's Uruguayan industries produced almost all the consumer goods sold on the domestic market, but at high cost.

Electric power for the cities and industries comes from a steam-electric station in Montevideo, and from two hydroelectric plants on the Río Negro, 150 miles away.

The Political Situation

Uruguay is generally rated by Latin American specialists as the most thoroughly democratic country in Latin America. It owes this status to two things: first, to the existence of a small, compact, and homogeneous population; and second, to the appearance of Batlle.

Batlle became president for the first time in 1903. According to the consitution then in force, the presidential term was four years, after which the president could not be a candidate for reelection. But in most parts of Latin America, leaders who have once tasted political power are loath to relinquish it. With a constitution or without one, a leader who can command sufficient military power not infrequently establishes a dictatorship and denies the citizen their right to vote, or even to discuss political questions. But in 1907 Batlle refused to continue in office, in spite of the fact that he had by that time gained a very large public following. Uruguay has long had two major political parties— the *colorados* and the *blancos*. Batlle was a *colorado,* a progressive, a man who was vigorously opposed to dictatorships. After his term in office he went to Switzerland to study first-hand the methods of democratic government.

In his second term as president (1911–15) Batlle introduced the reforms for which he is famous. He made an accurate diagnosis of the causes for the chronic disorders of his country and he set himself to find a political solution.

He recognized that one major cause of disorder was the gap, so common throughout Latin America, between the wealthy landowners and the workers. "It is not necessary," said Batlle, "that the rich should be made poorer, but only that the poor should be made less poor." In his effort to find legislation that would make the poor less poor, he was aided by the fact that the gap between rich and poor was by no means so great in Uruguay as it was in Argentina. Furthermore, the large landowners were much less opposed to entering into business than were the landowners across the Plata. The reforms proposed by Batlle gained many supporters not only among the members of his own party, but also among the *blancos*.

The constitution under which Uruguay was governed had been adopted in 1830, modeled on that of the United States. In it the president assumed broad powers. This was a situation which worried Batlle. He recognized that the traditional Spanish-American demand for freedom consisted in reality of the demand by political leaders to govern their own communities without interference from outside. The tradition of the strong man, the *caudillo,* the political boss, was deeply implanted. Batlle thought that a remedy for this tendency would be to reduce the power of the president by making him simply the presiding officer over a governing council. The idea was derided by the *blancos,* and even many of the *colorados* were not ready to support it wholeheartedly. A new constitution adopted in 1917, which went into force in 1919, represented a compromise in which the president still had large powers.

But the influence of Batlle did not come to an end with his death in 1929. Pressure to reduce the power of the presidency became especially strong after an elected president actually did sieze control of the country between 1933 and 1938. Finally in 1951 the *blancos* agreed to the reform originally proposed by Batlle, and in 1952 Uruguay ceased to have a president. The executive branch of the government was placed in the hands of a governing council.

The change, however, did not provide the hoped-for solution. With the costs of the welfare program rapidly mounting, the dominant *colorado* party, with its strength concentrated in the large industrial cities, found itself under increasing pressure from the *blancos,* a party which represents the majorities in the rural areas and smaller towns of the interior (Map 109). In 1958 the *blancos* won the election for the first time in more than 90 years. Still inflation and mismanagement of certain government-owned industries continued to arouse widespread discontent. The election in November 1966 resulted in a return of the *colorados* to office. In this election, also, there was a referendum regarding the form of government, as a result of which the unwieldy governing council was abandoned and Uruguay went back to a presidential system. In March 1967 a single president again took office.

Nevertheless, democratic procedures have become traditional. There is complete freedom of news and knowledge, and freedom to discuss political issues. All adults have the right to vote, and the vote is by secret ballot,

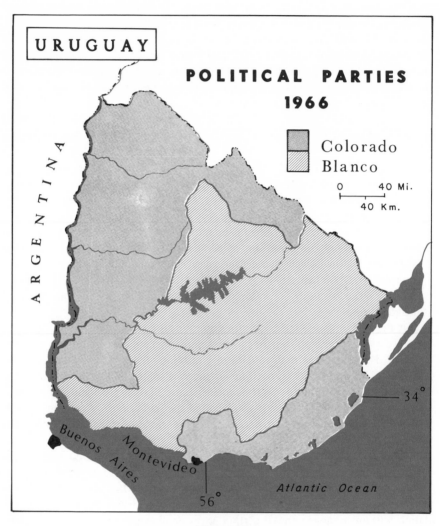

Map 109

honestly counted. Of course, when measures leading to the development of a full welfare state were proposed, they were promptly endorsed by a majority of the voters; nevertheless, criticism of the inefficiency of the government bureaucracy has been unrestricted. It is not likely that the citizens would vote to give up so comfortable a system.

The problem remains whether any government can solve the economic dilemma posed by the high cost of the welfare state. A program of strict economic planning has been adopted which includes increases in the supply of electric power, rebuilding of the ports, and extension of the highways. A United Nations team of agricultural experts made a survey of Uruguay's pastures and soils, and recommended a number of basic changes in the pastoral system. Among other things, a large amount of fertilizer was recommended to increase the carrying capacity of the hitherto-uncultivated pastures. The major support for the economy, however, must come from a large increase in the productivity of manufacturing industry through new capital investment in large-scale operations. The fact remains that the Uruguayan domestic market is too small to absorb the kind of increase in manufacturing production that is required. No country in Latin America is more desperately in need of the kind of solution offered by the clearing away of trade barriers and by the development of the Latin-American Common Market.

Portuguese
South
America

República Federativa do Brasil

Area: 3,286,470 square miles
Population: (1967 estimate) 85,655,000; (last census, 1960) 70,967,185
Capital city: Brasília (1967) 400,000
Largest cities: São Paulo (1967) 5,383,000
              Rio de Janeiro (1967) 4,031,000
Percent urban: (1960) 45.1
Birth rate per 1,000: (1966) 40–44; Death rate per 1,000: (1966) 10–13
Annual percent of increase: (1958–64) 3.1
Percent literate: (1950) 49.4
Percent labor force in agriculture: (1950) 59.1
Gross national product per capita: (1966) $307, (1967 est.) $313
Unit of currency: cruzeiro (1968, 2.7 per dollar)

COMMERCE, 1965 *(expressed in percentage of values)*
Percent total Latin-American exports: 16.2 (1956, 20)
Percent total Latin-American imports: 12.5

Exports (1965)

coffee	44	iron ore	6	sugar	4
manufactured goods	7	cotton	6	lumber	3

Exports to (1966)		Imports from (1966)	
United States	33 (1956, 50)	United States	39 (1956, 29)
West Germany	8	West Germany	9
Argentina	6	Argentina	8
Italy	6	Venezuela	5
Netherlands	5		

Chapter 25 □ Brazil: Introduction

The United States of Brazil is the Portuguese-speaking country that occupies almost half of the total area of the South American continent, and is inhabited by almost half of the population of South America. With 3,286,478 square miles of territory, Brazil is exceeded only by the Soviet Union, China, Canada, and the United States. But with the exception of Canada, the populations of these countries are all much larger than Brazil's 86 million. Nevertheless, Brazil's population is increasing at a rate of 3.1 percent per year. There are still large areas of the Brazilian backlands that are very thinly inhabited and large areas that remain outside of the effective national territory.

At first glance it would seem that Brazil offers great possibilities for population expansion and for a rapid westward movement of the frontier of settlement. Although the United Nations Food and Agriculture Organization estimates that only about 2 percent of the total national territory is at present actually used for crops, the estimates of the potential crop land are usually highly optimistic. But not always. There are some students of Brazil who insist that the limits of better quality agricultural lands have already been reached, and that the empty backlands are not actually of much potential value. The major problem of Brazilian geography—and a problem of the utmost practical importance—is how the resource base of this vast territory should be evaluated. Unfortunately the detailed field surveys on which such an evaluation must eventually be based have not yet been made.

A part of the answer can be found by viewing the Brazilian land in the perspective of historical geography. What has been the experience of people who have tried to make use of the backlands? And what has been the story of settlement in the areas already densely populated? What factors have supported the growth of two large conurbations, only a little more than 200

Map 110

Map 111

miles apart, competing with each other for recognition as Brazil's primate city? The reader who has followed the story of settlement in Latin America thus far will appreciate that there are no simple answers to these questions. The interplay of forces which has produced the present distribution of people in Brazil involves an understanding of the changes that have taken place through time, and also of the differences from place to place. It involves an analysis of the changing significance of the physical features of the land as the attitudes, objectives, and technical skills of the people have changed. All too often efforts to interpret the course of events in Brazil and to project meaningful forecasts into the future have failed through too much reliance on overall averages and generalizations regarding the country as a whole. The fact is that Brazil is highly diverse, not only in the characteristics of the land, but also in the characteristics of the people. No real understanding of Brazilian problems can be gained without an examination of the separate parts of the country.

The treatment of Brazil starts with an introductory chapter to provide a general frame of reference. This is followed by chapters on each of Brazil's six major regions of settlement: (1) the Northeast; (2) the East; (3) São Paulo; (4) the South; (5) the Central-West; and (6) the North.[1] In the concluding chapter Brazil is treated as a political unit.

---

[1]The states and territories of Brazil are shown on Map 110, and the grouping of the states in six regions, as used in this book, is on Map 111. The following table lists the states, and gives the proportion of the total area and total population in each region:

The Northeast: 18 percent of the area; 32 percent of the people. Includes Maranhão, Piauí, Ceará, Rio Grande do Norte, Paraíba, Pernambuco, Alagôas, Sergipe, Bahia.

The East: 8 percent of the area; 25 percent of the people. Includes Minas Gerais, Espírito Santo, Rio de Janeiro, Guanabara.

São Paulo: 3 percent of the area; 18 percent of the people. Includes São Paulo State.

The South: 7 percent of the area; 17 percent of the people. Includes Paraná, Santa Catarina, Rio Grande do Sul.

The Central-West: 22 percent of the area; 4 percent of the people. Includes Mato Grosso, Goiás, Distrito Federal.

The North: 42 percent of the area; 4 percent of the people. Includes Acre, Rondônia, Amazonas, Pará, Roraima, Amapá.

The islands of Fernando de Noronha in the Atlantic Ocean, about 225 miles northeast of Cabo São Roque, are not shown on the maps.

The *Fundação Instituto Brasileiro de Geografia e Estatística,* which is the Brazilian government agency charged with taking the census, and with preparing the maps of the enumeration areas, uses a somewhat different grouping of states in major regions. The Brazilians include Bahia and Sergipe in the East; and they do not separate São Paulo from the South. Otherwise the groupings used in the book and those used officially by the Brazilian government are the same.

SOUTHERN BRAZIL

TERRAIN

ATLANTIC OCEAN

300 M.
250 K.

Map 112

SOUTHERN BRAZIL

TRANSPORTATION

Railroad
Road

BOLIVIA

PARAGUAY

ARGENTINA

ATLANTIC OCEAN

0   300 M.
     250 K.

48°

Map 113

SOUTHERN BRAZIL

BOLIVIA

18°

22°

Rio de Janeiro

LAND USE

- Urban Center
- Irrigated Rice
- Horticulture, Truck and Dairy Farming
- Sugar Cane
- Coffee
- Cotton
- Cacao
- Sisal
- Oranges
- Bananas
- Vineyards

- Maize
- Wheat
- Maize, Wheat, Pasture
- Shifting Cultivation and Pasture
- Cultivated Pasture
- Uncultivated Pasture with Cattle
- Maté and Pine
- Quebracho
- Forest with Widely Scattered Clearings

0   300 M.
250 K.

48°

Map 114

SOUTHERN BRAZIL

BRASÍLIA

BOLIVIA

PARAGUAY

Vitória

PORT LOCATION

AIRPORT

VITÓRIA   TUBARAO

ATLANTIC OCEAN

3.1 M.
5 K.

S.P.

Rio de Janeiro

Piaçaguera

MINERALS
AND
MANUFACTURING

ARGENTINA

URUGUAY

W

•	Urban Center		
⚒	Steel Mill		
S.P.	São Paulo		
▬	Coal	W	Tungsten
Fe	Iron	Al	Bauxite
Mn	Manganese	Au	Gold
Sn	Tin	Ni	Nickel
◆	Diamonds	----	Pipeline

0   300 M.
250 K.

48°

Map 115

SOUTHERN BRAZIL

BRASÍLIA

BOLIVIA

18°

PARAGUAY

22°

Rio de Janeiro

• Urban Center

· Each dot represents
  2,000 rural people

POPULATION

ARGENTINA

ATLANTIC OCEAN

URUGUAY

0   300 M.
      250 K.

48°

Map 116

Map 117

NORTHERN BRAZIL

GUYANA (SURINAM) FRENCH GUIANA

ATLANTIC OCEAN

0 _____ 300 Miles
200 Kilometers

BOLIVIA

−14°

42°

TRANSPORTATION

——— Road
+++++ Railroad

Map 118

NORTHERN BRAZIL

LAND USE

Sugar Cane
Cotton
Coffee
Cacao
Sisal
Tobacco
Rubber
Jute
Pepper

Urban Center
Irrigated Agriculture: R–Rice, V–Vegetables
Horticulture, Truck and Dairy Farming
Cultivated Pasture
Uncultivated Pasture with Cattle
Forest with Widely Scattered Clearings
Shifting Cultivation and Pasture

Map 119

Map 12

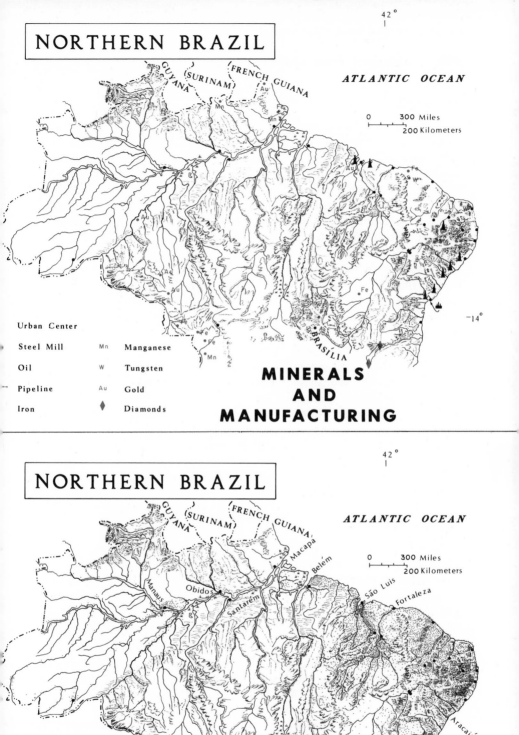

NORTHERN BRAZIL

ATLANTIC OCEAN

GUYANA (SURINAM) FRENCH GUIANA

Au

Mn

Mn

0   300 Miles
  200 Kilometers

Fe

W

Au

Au

Fe

Fe

BRASÍLIA

Mn

−14°

Urban Center		
Steel Mill	Mn	Manganese
Oil	W	Tungsten
Pipeline	Au	Gold
Iron	♦	Diamonds

MINERALS AND MANUFACTURING

NORTHERN BRAZIL

ATLANTIC OCEAN

GUYANA (SURINAM) FRENCH GUIANA

Macapa

Belém

Manaus

Obidos

Santarém

São Luis

Fortaleza

Aracajú

Salvador

Ilhéus

−14°

0   300 Miles
  200 Kilometers

POPULATION

• Urban Center

Each dot represents
2,000 rural people

The Land

What can be said of the Brazilian land? Is it, or is it not, endowed with superlative resources? Many writers on Brazil have pointed out that only a very small part of the vast national territory is too wet, or too dry, or too steep to permit some kind of economic use. If slopes up to 35° are considered useful for agriculture, as they are today in Brazil, then not more than 20 percent of the national territory can be considered beyond the limits of potential use. A much larger proportion of the Soviet Union and Canada are unproductive because of cold, and a much larger proportion of China is unproductive because it is too dry. Furthermore, Brazil is known to contain a vast store of iron ore and manganese. But there is another side to the picture. Perhaps more than any other large country in the world, and certainly much more than the United States, Brazil faces problems resulting from the unfavorable geographic arrangement of its features. Resources are not combined in area in a way to favor low-cost development. Along the greater part of the eastern coast the land faces the sea with a steep escarpment across which there are few easy routes of travel. The passage to the interior is especially difficult back of the superlative natural harbor on which Rio de Janeiro is situated. Meanwhile the world's longest navigable river winds endlessly through empty forests. Very little of the Brazilian territory is mountainous: yet the mountains are all located in Brazil's core area back of Rio de Janeiro and São Paulo. From the mountains the rivers radiate inland, runing thousands of miles southward to the Plata or northward to the Amazon to find a way out to the sea. The absence of a clear natural focus of routes scatters and isolates the clusters of people.

Surface Features

Only a very little of Brazil's vast territory can be described as a plain (Maps 112 and 117). Along the western border of the country, in the south, Brazil does include a portion, but a very small portion, of the lowlands of the upper Paraguay. The largest area of plain, however, is in the upper Amazon Basin, where level lands stretch eastward into Brazil from the base of the Andes in Bolivia, Peru, Ecuador, and Colombia (Map 8, p. 23). The Amazon lowland, unlike most river lowlands, becomes narrower downstream: in the eastern part of the basin only a ribbon of floodplain carries the river through the highlands.The Atlantic coast, especially in those areas which are densely populated, is bordered by only small, discontinuous bits of lowland; there is no real coastal plain like that of eastern North America.

The greater part of the Brazilian territory is made up of highlands. The Brazilian highlands, south of the Amazon, and the Guiana highlands north of it, are both constructed of a basement of geologically ancient crystalline rocks, covered, in part, by stratified sandstones and limestones, and by sheets of diabase. Throughout the highland regions both north and south of the Amazon, three chief kinds of surface features occur together in a complex pattern. Where the crystalline rocks are exposed, the surface is made up of gently rounded hills, deeply mantled with a fine, reddish, clay soil. Above this surface, bodies of especially resistant crystalline rocks stand out boldly as low mountains. Where the covering of sandstone strata or diabase remains over the basement crystallines, the surface is tabular in form, with large flattish areas along the stream divides or between the deeply cut stream valleys. In the south, extending into Paraguay and Uruguay, are the diabase flows that make up the Paraná Plateau.

In only a few places do mountain ranges rise above the general highland surface. These occur especially in southeastern Brazil, where there are several such ranges, composed also of crystalline rocks, but of types which are more resistant to erosion than the granites and gneisses. These stand above the crystalline hilly uplands with rounded outlines, strongly reminiscent of the outlines of the Great Smoky Mountains of the Southern Appalachians in North America. The highest elevation in Brazil, the Pico da Bandeira, a little northeast of Rio de Janeiro, is only 9,462 feet above sea level. In the Guiana highlands, Mount Roraima, which is really not a mountain but a plateau held up by an unusually resistant portion of the sandstone cover, is almost as high as the Pico da Bandeira, reaching 9,219 feet above the sea.

The Brazilian highlands, for the most part, drop off sharply toward the Atlantic. In the northeastern part of the country, north of the city of Salvador in Bahia, there is a gradual rise from coast to interior; but from Salvador southward to Pôrto Alegre in Rio Grande do Sul, the coast is backed by a steep, wall-like slope—the Great Escarpment—which, from the ocean, so much resembles a range of mountains that one part of it is called the Serra do Mar. Back of Rio de Janeiro and Santos, the Great Escarpment rises to an elevation of 2,600 feet, and in certain places in this part of Brazil it is surmounted by ranges which reach elevations between 7,000 and 8,000 feet above sea level. In Bahia the Great Escarpment is cut by three major rivers, but between latitudes 18° S. and 30° S. it is crossed by only two deeply cut valleys—those of the Rio Doce and the Rio Paraíba; otherwise it remains scarcely notched along its crest. In only two places—between Santos and São Paulo, and between Paranaguá and Curitiba—is this escarpment concentrated in one sea-facing slope. Along most of its course it is broken into a series of steps, forming parallel escarpments.

The rivers which drain the Brazilian highlands all descend over the steep margins in falls and rapids. Most of these rivers have their sources in the central and southeastern part of the highlands—some on the very crest of the Great Escarpment. The Paraná system is fed by several tributaries in São Paulo, Paraná, and Santa Catarina which rise within sight of the Atlantic Ocean, flow westward into the interior, and join the Paraná along the western borders of these states. Similarly, the headwaters of the Rio Uruguay flow westward before turning to the south on the Argentine border. The Paraná drops over the resistant diabase formations near the northeastern border of Paraguay, forming the Guaíra Falls (known in Brazil as the *Salto das Sete Quedas*); from these falls downstream as far as Posadas in Argentina, the Paraná passes through a valley cut deeply into the plateau. The Uruguay is interrupted by rapids all the way to Salto in Uruguay. The whole southern part of the Brazilian highland is drained through these circuitous channels southward to the Plata.

Similar features are exhibited by the rivers which drain northward. The São Francisco rises north of Rio de Janeiro and flows parallel to the coast for more than a thousand miles before it turns eastward in the northern part of Bahia and descends over the Paulo Afonso Falls to the Atlantic. The great tributaries of the Amazon, the Tocantins-Araguaia, the Xingú, and the Tapajóz, all rise in the central area, flow northward, and descend over falls and rapids as they approach the Amazon. Only the Amazon itself is navigable far into the interior. Even the Madeira is interrupted by hundreds of miles of rapids where it crosses the westernmost edge of the Brazilian highlands.

The fact that the Brazilian highlands face the Atlantic with a steep escarpment or a series of escarpments, and that the rivers drain inland away from the southeast coast, means that there is no natural focus of routes on this part of the country. That the lines of travel actually do come to a focus on Rio de Janeiro and São Paulo is a result of human effort, overcoming the lack of any large natural convergence of routes on these places.

The Climates

In that large portion of the continent of South America which belongs to Brazil there are many varieties of climate (Map 11, p. 31). Brazilian climates contain few extremes, either of temperature or of moisture; yet they are by no means so monotonously uniform, or so unbearably hot and damp, that the human spirit is deadened. If the Brazilian people in certain regions appear to be lacking in energy, this cannot be interpreted as the inevitable result of the climate until such other elements as diet and disease have been evaluated.

A considerable amount of misinformation exists regarding the temperatures of tropical countries like Brazil. The world's highest temperatures are not found near the equator, but in the deserts some 25° or 30° of latitude from it. Average annual temperatures increase as one approaches the heat equator—which, in South America, passes along the Caribbean and Guiana coasts through such places as Maracaibo and Georgetown. The ranges of temperature between coldest and warmest months, however, decrease as one comes closer to the heat equator. In the equatorial regions temperatures are moderately high throughout the year, but they never are so high in those regions as they are in summer in the lower middle latitudes. In South

America the only place where temperatures of 110° are experienced at any time of the year is in the northern part of Argentina (Map 9, p. 27). Along the Amazon the highest temperatures are usually in the 90's (Manaus once recorded a high of 101.5°), and the lowest temperatures are in the 60's (Manaus once recorded 53°). The averages for the year are around 80°. In the dry region of northeast Brazil, the highest temperature recorded by any station was 106.7°; but as one proceeds southward along the coast where rainfall and cloudiness are greater than in the Northeast, the maximum temperatures are much lower. At Rio de Janeiro the average temperature of the warmest month is 79.0°—about the same as the average of the warmest month at Raleigh, North Carolina. The average of the coldest month at Rio de Janeiro is 68.7°—which is similar to that of the coldest month at Miami, Florida. In the highlands of Brazil, temperatures are lower than at the same latitudes on the coast; in the highlands of southern Brazil temperatures are similar to those of the Southern Appalachians. The northern limit of frosts is found in the northern part of the state of Paraná and the southern part of São Paulo.

Human comfort, however, is not a matter of temperature alone, but of humidity and wind as well. Relative humidity, especially along the Brazilian coast, is considerably higher than at the places mentioned in southeastern North America. At Raleigh the average relative humidity is 60 percent whereas at Rio de Janeiro it is 78 percent. In places exposed to the open sweep of the wind, the high humidity may be compensated, but in protected places, or in places where the winds are not steady, the humidity may become uncomfortable. It is because of the irregularity of the winds at Rio de Janeiro that so many Europeans and North Americans who live there complain of the heat during the summer months.

The rainfall is another climatic element which is neither excessive nor deficient in more than a few small parts of the Brazilian territory (Maps 12 and 13, pp. 32 and 33). More than 80 inches a year are received in four sections of the country—in the upper Amazon lowlands, along the coast from Belém northward, in scattered spots along the Great Escarpment and on the mountain summits of the southeast, and in a small area in the western part of the state of Paraná. On the slopes of the Serra do Mar between Santos and São Paulo there is a belt of very heavy rainfall, concentrated in a narrow band along the Escarpment.

Moisture deficiency is limited to a small part of the Northeast. There are spots in this region which receive less than 10 inches a year; but most of the area receives between 20 and 25 inches. The problem of the Northeast is one of rainfall irregularity—variations between excessive rains and droughts. In certain parts of this region, floods or droughts were recorded more than 50 times between 1835 and 1935. As settlement begins to penetrate to the Brazilian interior, areas of climatic risk unknown now may be discovered.

In most parts of Brazil the rain is heaviest in the summer, and a winter dry season is a regular occurrence. The southern states, however, from the southern part of São Paulo State southward, have no real dry season, but only a season of somewhat less rain in winter. In the Amazon Basin, the rains come mostly from January to June; the other half of the year is less rainy.

Weather

Brazilian weather is produced by the interaction of air masses from three different source regions. Along the east coast, air from the South Atlantic Oceanic Whirl approaches the coast of Brazil from an easterly and northeasterly direction. In the southern-hemisphere summer (January) air also reaches the Brazilian interior from the North Atlantic Oceanic Whirl. Especially in the southern-hemisphere winter (July) cold air masses of Antarctic origin move northward not only along the east coast but also through the continental interior. The position of Brazil with respect to these source regions is indicated on Map 10, p. 30. The prevailing movements of air in January and July over Brazil are shown on Maps 122 and 123. The air from

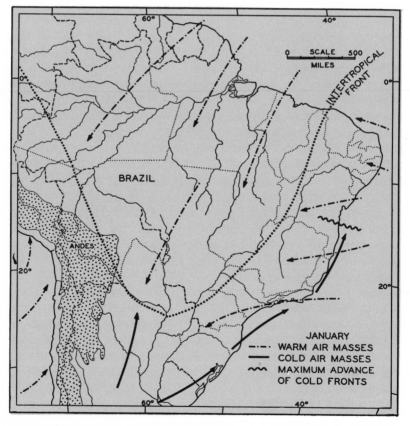

Map 122

the South Atlantic Oceanic Whirl is relatively dry and stable; when air masses of this origin are present in any area the weather is usually clear. The air from the North Atlantic Oceanic Whirl, being heated below by contact with the warm land, is less stable, so that its presence is marked by the many puffy cumulus clouds and by showery weather. The cold air masses, being heavy compared with the relatively warm, light air of tropical origin, push under the warm air causing the latter to rise. Along the advancing cold fronts there are often violent thunderstorms and heavy rains. After the front has passed the air of polar origin is apt to be unstable since it is warming close to the earth's surface and still cold aloft. This results in a descent of the colder air from above, pushing up the warm air from below. Air masses of this particular nature always produce cloudy weather with frequent showers.

The sequence of events during the advance of a cold air mass from the south is shown on the series of maps (Maps 124a, b, c, d, e, and f). The cold air mass first appears as an outburst of cold air from the Antarctic Continent.

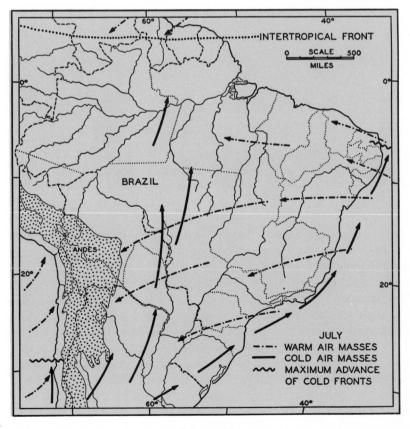

Map 123

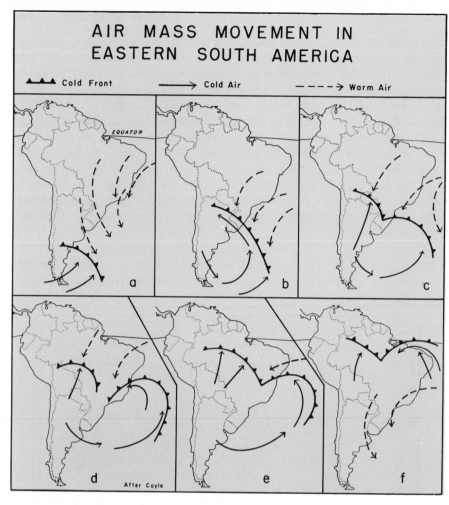

AIR MASS MOVEMENT IN
EASTERN SOUTH AMERICA

▲▲▲ Cold Front   ────→ Cold Air   ─ ─ ─→ Warm Air

EQUATOR

a   b   c

d   e   f

After Coyle

Map 124

It approaches southernmost South America from the south or southwest. Map 124a shows the front passing across Patagonia and approaching the Humid Pampa. Behind the front the Pampero will carry dust from the desert areas eastward to the Humid Pampa. As the front passes there will be violent thunderstorms at Buenos Aires, with a sharp drop of temperature as the cold air replaces the warm air from the north. Map 124b shows the front moving northward across Uruguay to southern Brazil. If the air mass is large enough it may bring snow and freezing weather to that area. Map 124c shows the air mass in the process of being split by the Brazilian highlands. The cold air, being heavy, stays close to the earth's surface, and tends to be deflected by prominent terrain features, especially the Andes, but also the Brazilian highlands. One part of the air mass moves northward through Paraguay on into the interior of Brazil; the other part moves northward along the coast, bringing stormy weather to Rio de Janeiro. Map 124d shows the air masses continuing northward through the interior and along the coast, now bringing rainy weather to the coast of Bahia and to the headwaters of the Paraguay River. On Map 124e the air masses have continued northward all the way to the Amazon and into the coastal area of the Northeast of Brazil. Actually only the strongest winter outbursts of cold air go as far as this. Others die out and are picked up in the main streams of the Oceanic Whirls before they travel so far north. Map 124f shows one of the rare winter air masses that pushes all the way to the equator and across it. Air masses have been followed all the way into the Caribbean, but this happens only rarely. When the cold air masses penetrate the Amazon region the result is cool, showery weather, with temperatures in the low 60's, a type of weather known in Brazil as a *friagem*.

The part of the Northeast of Brazil which is subject to recurring floods and droughts lies between Natal and São Luís and extends southwestward along the valley of the Rio São Francisco about as far as the border between the states of Minas Gerais and Bahia. It is best shown by the area of scrub woodland (Map 15, p. 35). Along the east coast south of Natal there are more or less regular rains resulting from the passage of cold air masses from the South (as on Map 124e). At São Luís, also, there are fairly regular rains during the period when the intertropical front is pushed southward into the Brazilian interior. The intertropical front each year moves to the east of São Luís (Map 122). In some years the intertropical front moves eastward all the way to the east coast, in which case the whole Northeast receives abundant rains. In other years it fails to move much beyond São Luís, and then the Northeast suffers from drought.

Natural Vegetation

The various conditions of climate together with those of the underlying surfaces and soils are expressed in the cover of natural vegetation (Map 15, p. 35). The heavy rainfall of the Amazon Basin and of the coast south of Salvador is reflected in the tropical rain forest, or selva. The Amazon region contains the world's largest area of such forest. The selva is composed of evergreen, broadleaf trees, some of great size mixed with others of lesser size. In places where the selva has been carefully studied, as many as three thousand different species of trees per square mile have been identified. The branches are interlaced overhead in such a dense canopy of foliage that not much light can reach the forest floor, and as a result these forests contain little underbrush except along the banks of rivers, or in places where, for some reason or other, the foliage has been thinned. The soils under such forests, where they are not covered at frequent intervals by newly deposited material, are generally very poor in plant foods and in humus, for the heavy rains percolating through the upper layers of the soil dissolve the soluble minerals, and the vigorous bacterial action under conditions of high temperature and humidity quickly destroys any organic matter that falls to the ground.

In places that are not quite so rainy or so continuously warm as those which are covered with selva, the forest which appears is described as seasonal, or semideciduous. This category of forest, however, covers a considerable variety: where rainfall is heavy and ground water conditions favorable, this forest is almost evergreen, for only a few species of trees drop their leaves in the dry season; at the other extreme, where water is not so readily available at least during the dry season, the forest is mostly deciduous and only a few species of trees retain their leaves throughout the year. The more luxuriant type of semideciduous forest is known in Brazil as *mata da primeira classe* (first class forest); the poorer type of deciduous forest is known as *mata seca* (dry forest). The extensive forests of the East and São Paulo, which extend southward along the valley of the Paraná, are first class forests: in this part of Brazil they are denser and composed of taller trees than the evergreen forests of the wet coastal zone.

The interior of Brazil, south of the evergreen forests of the Amazon, is covered with a mixture of forest and grassland *(mata* and *campo)*. The exact patterns of these vegetation types have yet to be mapped with accuracy, although in certain small areas their relations to soil, surface, and drainage have been studied. It is clear that the wetter areas are marked by luxuriant stands of semideciduous forest *(mata da primeira classe)*. Such forests occur as galerias along all the larger streams and in patches on the interstream areas, usually where the underlying rock is diabase. The relatively high water table under these forests seems to be a result of soil conditions rather than a reflection of greater rainfall. Where the soils are less retentive of moisture— and this includes a very large proportion of the total area—the land is covered with a mixture of scrubby deciduous woodland and grass. In places the scrub woodland is predominant, forming, according to Waibel, a vegetation type which is neither true forest nor true grassland, and which should be identified as a new category, known as *campo cerrado* (literally a "closed grassland"). In other places there are vast expanses of savanna with scattered trees or patches of forest (*campo sujo,* literally "dirty grassland"). In other places, especially in the South, there are open grasslands with no trees except in the valley bottoms *(campo limpo,* literally "clean grassland"). In the interior of the northeast, where droughts occur frequently, there is a kind of thorny, deciduous, drought-resistant woodland which the Brazilians call *caatinga*.

In the southern part of São Paulo State two types of vegetation appear which belong to the middle latitudes rather than the tropics. These are the Araucaria forests and the prairies. The Araucaria or Paraná Pine forest is composed of a mixture of pines and smaller broadleaf species, and is found in places where frosts come at more or less regular intervals. The line between the semideciduous forests, which cannot survive frosts, and the Araucaria forests is sharp. At about the same latitude, also, the woodland savannas give way to pure tall-grass prairies, with dense ribbons of forest along the deeper river valleys—a vegetation type which continues southward into Uruguay.

To what extent the large areas of campo cerrado and the smaller areas of prairie can be credited to the use of fire by the Indians is still disputed. There are some who insist that the practice, still continued, of burning the grass at the end of each dry season to provide better pasture or to aid in hunting has had the effect of creating the grasslands by pushing back the woody plants, as in the Humid Pampa. Others point out, however, that the prairies and the campos occur on certain kinds of land. Like all the major kinds of vegetation, they are fairly good indicators of the underlying characteristics of slope, soil, and drainage and so of potential uses of land. There can be no doubt of the importance of fire in the creation of grasslands; but it seems also to be true that grasslands have been created only in certain kinds of settings. Unlike the midlatitude grasslands, the soil and water conditions under the tropical grasslands are poor for the growth of shallow-rooted crops.

Mineral Resources

Brazil possesses superlative but poorly matched mineral resources. When the French geologist Gorceix, in a poetic moment, exclaimed that Brazil's state of Minas Gerais had a "breast of iron and a heart of gold," he neglected to point out that there was in that state a deficiency of fuels which could be used to produce the high temperatures necessary for smelting. The gold and diamonds of this region did form the basis of the prosperity of Brazil during the eighteenth century—in fact, during that period Brazil produced 44 percent of all the gold of the world. But the iron and manganese, and the many other industrial metals available in Brazil, have only recently been mined on more than a small scale. Manganese has been exported for many years, but not on a scale which would be justified by the size and quality of the ores. Iron smelting with charcoal has been going on for a long time—until the problem of providing a steady supply of charcoal has become acute because of the almost complete destruction of the nearby forests. A very good grade of steel is produced. During World War II a new steel plant was built at Volta Redonda in the Paraíba Valley—the largest steel plant now in operation in all Latin America. Ore comes from Minas Gerais, and some of the coal from the South. But Brazil's coal contains such a high proportion of ash and sulphur that it must be processed before it can be used to make coke. At Volta Redonda it is mixed with coal imported from West Virginia. Brazil also possesses important quantities of copper, lead, zinc, nickel, chromium, quartz crystals (for use in radios), industrial diamonds and gem stones. Its chief zone of minerals is the prominent range of mountains running roughly north and south through central Minas Gerais (Maps 115 and 120). Important manganese deposits also occur on the Bolivian border, near Corumbá and in the Territory of Amapá, just north of the mouth of the Amazon.

A lack of fuels has long retarded economic development in Brazil. One result has been the continued use of charcoal until large areas that were once forested are now completely denuded of tree cover. There are some coal deposits in Rio Grande do Sul and Santa Catarina, but the coal is of poor quality and expensive to use. In spite of much costly exploratory work, the only important oil fields that have been discovered are in the Northeast—in Bahia and Sergipe. Brazil gets most of its domestic supply of oil from this area.

One potential natural resource that Brazil does have in abundance is water power. The Brazilian highlands, which create so many transportation problems, provide opportunities for hydroelectric development. The rivers that rise in the high country to the north of Rio de Janeiro descend over many rapids as they flow inland on their roundabout courses to the sea, and they pour over the margins of the highlands in spectacular falls. But until recently, the major power sites were too far inland for the electricity to be transmitted to the coastal cities. In fact the earliest major engineering work that provided São Paulo with electric power was built at the headwaters of the river draining to the Paraná on the very crest of the Great Escarpment. The Rio Paraíba was also used to send power to Rio de Janeiro. But in the late 1960's major hydroelectric installations had been built or were being built on rivers that had formerly been too far away. Generators at the Paulo Afonso Falls on the São Francisco (Map 117) were sending power to all the major cities of the Northeast, and a start had been made to use the whole long course of the São Francisco for a series of power stations. The tributaries of the Paraná and the east-flowing Rio Doce were being developed. But the largest projects of all were on the Paraná itself.[2]

The People

None of the many advantages and disadvantages inherent in the physical make-up of Brazil have real significance for us in terms of human settlement until we know about the people and their way of living. Perhaps nowhere on earth is there a greater mixture of different kinds of people than in Brazil. The primary ingredients are Portuguese, Indian, and African, but during the past century the population has been much altered by the arrival of millions of immigrants from Europe and Asia. All these elements have mixed freely, for one of the important traits brought by the Portuguese was the absence of any taboo against race mixture, except among the aristocracy. Each ingredient, therefore, has given certain easily observable physical characteristics to the new race of Brazilians, and has contributed numerous culture traits to the Brazilian civilization.

[2]In the late 1960's major hydroelectric installations were being enlarged or newly constructed at Paulo Afonso and Tres Marías on the São Francisco, at Mascarenhas on the Rio Doce, at Furnas on the Rio Grande, and on the Paraná at Urubupungá, Jupiá, and Ilha Solteira. Agreement had been reached with Paraguay for the development of the enormous power potential at Sete Quedas.

Early Racial Ingredients

The Indians who inhabited Brazil in 1500 were chiefly of Tupi-Guarani stock—a linguistic group to which the Indians of Paraguay also belong (Map 5, p. 14). In almost every respect these Indians of eastern South America were a contrast to the Quechuas of the Andes. The Tupi-Guarani tribes were hunters, fishers, collectors, and shifting cultivators. They lived in small, scattered groups with no form of intertribal political organization. Their basic food crop was manioc rather than maize. It is estimated that the Indian population of 1500 in all of Brazil was only about 800,000.

As a source of labor, the Tupi-Guarani proved quite inadequate. In the first place, great numbers of them died of European diseases in the early years of the conquest. Those who survived were handicapped by the traditional Indian attitude toward work. Agriculture was left to the women; the men devoted themselves to hunting, fishing, and fighting. The men could not adjust themselves to the agricultural work demanded by the Europeans. Free intermarriage, however, between the Portuguese men and the Indian women introduced many of the physical and psychological traits of the Indians into the resulting population.

Africans, also, made an important contribution to the composition and character of the Brazilian people. Beginning in 1538, slaves from Africa were brought across the ocean, especially to the Brazilian Northeast, where there was a demand for field hands in the new sugar industry. The African was not only a good worker, but he also possessed a knowledge of technological processes which has often been overlooked. The Sudanese, it should be remembered, were the inventors of the process of iron smelting. This technological ability they brought with them to Brazil, along with their rhythmic music and their superstitions. The African foremen on the plantations, or later in the gold mines, knew more about the technological processes than did many of the Portuguese owners. From the seventeenth to the nineteenth century, agricultural and mining enterprise in Brazil owed a large debt to the African laborers and technicians.

From the Portuguese, however, came the main characteristics of the Brazilians. Even before their departure from Europe, the Portuguese were already made up of a most remarkable variety of racial and cultural elements, inherited from the various peoples who had successively conquered the Iberian Peninsula. Like the Spaniards, they included ingredients of Celtic, Nordic, and Mediterranean origin; and especially in the south of Portugal, around Lisbon, there was a large mixture of Moorish blood and of Moorish and Semitic culture traits. Moreover, the Portuguese from Lisbon were familiar with the use of African labor, for slaves had been brought to this part of Portugal in considerable numbers during the period when Prince Henry's ships were exploring the African west coast. Like the Spaniards too, the Portuguese had the traditions of feudalism and of large private estates—traditions which profoundly influenced the relations of people to the land throughout Latin America.

The Portuguese had long been accustomed to commerce and to adventuring in distant places when they came to America in search of quick wealth. Like most of the Europeans who came to the New World—including the English—the foremost objective was to loot the rich resources of a virgin land. The Portuguese were much less interested than the Spaniards in implanting their institutions in America; they had little of the fanatical zeal for the spread of Christianity that their Spanish brothers possessed. They were attracted less by the prospects of earning a living by persistent toil than by the opportunities for speculative profit. As one Brazilian writer puts it, the idea was "to collect the fruit without planting the tree." Whereas some of the peoples of America have been led by force of circumstances to be content with less spectacular returns for more intensive forms of economy, the Brazilians, with their huge land area, and their small numbers, are still seeking new ways for the speculative exploitation of the treasures stored up in nature. This is the Brazilian variation of the theme of El Dorado.

Course of Settlement

History and geography have both contributed to the settlement of Brazil and to the development of the present patterns of population. In the history of settlement in the 400 years since the Portuguese first planted successful colonies on the coast of South America, three products, in turn, have dominated a period. Each period has been characterized by the spectacular rise of a commercial product, by the sale of this product in an expanding market and the collection of promoter's profits, and by the eventual decline of prosperity owing to increasing competition from areas of production outside Brazil, where people were willing to invest in "the planting of the trees." Each of Brazil's great products has led to the development of one specific region, and has given rise to an area of concentrated settlement around an urban nucleus. As one product after another has passed its zenith and begun its decline, the population has moved on to new frontiers, or remained decadent. The chief products which have thus punctuated Brazilian history and have colored the Brazilian map are sugar, gold, and coffee. In addition there have been minor interludes neatly set off in time and space—dominated by rubber, cacao, oranges and other products.

The early decades of Portuguese colonization, however, were not associated with any of these commercial developments. For several decades after it was announced that South America extended far enough to the east to lie within the Portuguese hemisphere (see p. 17), the Portuguese took no steps to establish possession. Exploring parties found no sources of gold and gems comparable to those of India, and no rich native civilizations which invited pillage. At the beginning of the sixteenth century Portugal was a poor country with a population which probably did not number more than 1 million. As a result of the voyages of exploration, sent out at first by Prince Henry, the route to southern Asia had been discovered, and Portugal was attempting to establish control of this new-found source of wealth. Brazil was neglected until the encroachments of the French and the Spaniards made it imperative for the Portuguese either to establish colonies on the American coast or to relinquish her claims. In the 1530's the whole coast of Brazil from Belém near the mouth of the Amazon to Florianópolis in what is now Santa Catarina was divided into some fifteen *capitanias,* each granted as the hereditary property of one of Portugal's prominent families. This system led to a very uneven distribution of settlements, for those *capitanias* which came under the direction of capable organizers and administrators flourished, while others which came under the direction the men of lesser ability were often not settled at all. The earliest successful colony was established at São Vicente, near the present port of Santos, in 1532. A settlement was also made at Ilheus in southern Bahia in that same year. Another successful settlement was made in 1537 at Olinda, near the site of Recife in the state of Pernambuco. Recife itself was not founded until 1561. A settlement at Salvador in 1534 was wiped out by Indians, but was rebuilt permanently in 1549. Meanwhile a mission was established on the present site of São Paulo in 1554—the first of the Brazilian settlements on the highlands.

The three chief primary settlement centers from which the Portuguese carried forward their conquest of Brazil were São Paulo, Salvador, and Recife (Map 6, p. 18). These are the places which correspond to Mexico City, Cartagena,, Lima, and Asunción in Spanish America. Rio de Janeiro. founded on its present site in 1567, was at first only a fortress and naval base for the protection of the coast, and not at all a primary settlement center.

Sugar Colonies

The first Europeans to make successful use of the soil for the cultivation of commercial crops in America were the Portuguese. The Spanish colonists were too much involved in the search for precious metals to do more than experiment with commercial agriculture. But for several decades before the Portuguese settled in Brazil they had been using their island possessions in the Atlantic, such as Madeira, for the cultivation of sugarcane. By 1470 they had broken the Venetian monopoly of the sale of sugar to Europe (the sugar came to Venice from southern Asia by way of the Arab traders). When permanent colonies were established on the coast of Brazil, and when the lack of gold made some other source of wealth important to find, the Portuguese began to expand their sugarcane plantations on the mainland. The first plantations were developed at São Vicente in 1532, using Indian workers. But the *capitanias* in the Northeast were much closer to the European markets, and distance in the days of sailing ships was more important than it is today.

Furthermore, the Indians proved to be poor as agricultural workers, except in the cultivation of tobacco. Meanwhile, the owners of the *capitanias* of the Northeast, who had been accustomed to the management of large estates in Portugal, began to appreciate the possibility of developing a profitable plantation economy based on sugarcane and African slaves. The problem was twofold: how to finance the purchase of slaves and sugar machinery, and how to reach a large enough market to make the investment pay.

These problems were solved by the Dutch. The merchants of Flanders and the Low Countries had access to a potentially enormous market for sugar, provided that a steady supply could be guaranteed at a reasonable price. The Dutch merchants financed the purchase of slaves and machinery, furnished the transportation, and collected the profits from refining the sugar in Antwerp and Amsterdam and then selling it throughout Europe. Portugal benefited from the manufacture and sale of sugar-mill equipment, and from collecting royalties. In the seventeenth century the Northeast of Brazil was the world's chief source of sugar.

After 1621 the Dutch control of the European sugar trade was menaced by Spain. From 1580 to 1640 a single king ruled over both Spain and Portugal. When Philip IV started his rule in 1621, he interfered with shipments of sugar to the Dutch refineries. In 1624 the Dutch seized the city of Salvador, but were soon driven out by the Portuguese colonists. From 1630 to 1654, however, the Dutch occupied the whole coastal area of the Northeast from the Rio São Francisco to the Amazon. Without any help from Portugal, which was involved in a struggle to gain freedom from Spain, the Portuguese in Brazil resisted the Dutch invasion, and finally in 1654 recaptured Recife. This was a very important episode in Brazilian history, for the cooperative effort necessary to push out the Dutch built certain loyalties and traditions among the people of the Northeast. Today this region is notable for its political solidarity.

Gold

While sugar production was bringing wealth to the people of the Northeast, especially in the states of Bahia, Pernambuco, and Paraíba, the settlers in southern Brazil were enjoying no such prosperity. The people of São Paulo were poor; they had discovered no source of wealth within their means to exploit; yet they were not at all content to accept this situation. From São Paulo a series of semimilitary expeditions went forth into the interior of the country. These expeditions were called *bandeiras* and the members of the expeditions were called *bandeirantes*. The first objective was to find gold—which had already been discovered in many of the stream gravels of the country south of São Paulo. But gold in the South proved to exist only in small quantities, and the *bandeirantes* had to seek other forms of wealth to exploit. They found Indians; large numbers of the native peoples, having first been brought together around the mission stations, were carried into slavery. Intermarriage with the Indian women became common, and the area occupied by the explorers from São Paulo soon had a considerable proportion of half-breeds —a racial type which in Spanish America is called mestizo, but which in Brazil is called *mameluco*.[3] The *bandeirantes* traveled slowly over the vast interior of the continent, pushing the borders of Brazil far to the west and to the south, as far as they could go without entering dense forests. Searching restlessly for slaves, gold, or any other sources of wealth, they grazed their animals on the savannas and even stopped to plant and harvest crops on the way. These hardy adventurers established the colony of Colonia on the shores of the Plata opposite Buenos Aires in 1680; they pushed westward to the Paraguay north of Asunción; they even roamed into the Northeast, into the scrub woodland country inland from the sugar colonies. Finally, in 1698, they discovered rich gold-bearing gravels in the central part of Minas Gerais, on the headwaters of the Rio São Francisco. Shortly thereafter, other gold discoveries were made: at Cuiabá in Mato Grosso in 1719; and near the former capital of Goiás in 1725. In Minas Gerais, in the country a little to the north of the gold fields, diamonds were discovered in 1729.

The discovery of gold and gems, especially the discoveries in central Minas Gerais, came at a time when the prosperity of the sugarcane planters of the Northeast had passed its zenith. Declining yields on soils which had been cultivated for many years and increasing competition from other areas were decreasing profits in the Brazilian region. It is not in the Brazilian tradition, under such circumstances, to aim at reducing the costs of production through the use of better agricultural practices. Income in the Northeast was spent to raise the standard of living of the aristocracy, not for investments which might lower the cost of production per unit. That would be "planting the trees." Brazil suffered, moreover, from the curse of great area; virtually limitless area meant the ever-present possibility of moving on to new lands and of exploiting new resources; it meant the lack of any compelling reason for the intensification and stabilization of economic life in any one region. When the discovery of gold was announced in Minas Gerais, the result was a gold rush, in which not only Paulistas (as the people from São Paulo are called) and Portuguese from the home country participated, but also many former sugarcane planters of the Northeast who came bringing their slaves.

The gold period started early in the eighteenth century, reached its peak of development between 1752 and 1787, and was definitely over by the beginning of the nineteenth century. During this time southern and central Minas Gerais was transformed from a wilderness into a well-populated agricultural, pastoral, and mining region, dotted with many small towns, and with its rural districts partitioned among a relatively small number of landlords. The settlement of this part of Brazil led to the development of Rio de Janeiro as a port, for this place came to be the chief outlet for the gold, and the chief

[3]The word *mestiço* in Portuguese refers to any person of mixed blood, often mixed Caucasian and Negro.

urban nucleus of the new region of settlement. Great quantities of gold were sent back to Portugal, greatly to the profit of the king and of the mine owners in Brazil. But little of this prosperity was shared by the workers of Minas Gerais. By the beginning of the nineteenth century the best sources of gold and diamonds had been exhausted, and Brazil was ready for a new form of speculative development.

Coffee

Recent Brazilian history has been dominated by the commercial production of coffee, and this activity is concentrated in the state of São Paulo, inland from the city of that name. Like the sugarcane planters, the people of São Paulo found themselves providing a very large proportion of the world's supply of a new commodity which was rising rapidly in popular favor. Coffee planting started around Rio de Janeiro and at other places on the coast from Santos to the Amazon; but by the end of the first quarter of the nineteenth century there was a definite concentration of coffee in the Paraíba Valley, inland from Rio de Janeiro. From this district, coffee planting spread westward into São Paulo State—a movement which was increasingly rapid after 1850. Most of the European immigrants who came to Brazil after 1850 went to the new coffee lands of São Paulo, with the result that the new region of concentrated settlement was occupied by a very different kind of people from those of the older sections of Brazil. Coffee supported the rise of the great city of São Paulo. Now, in the modern era, São Paulo has become the leading center of manufacturing industries in all of Latin America.

Other Commercial Products

Meanwhile, other agricultural or forest products were leading to the rapid development, followed by the equally rapid decline, of other parts of Brazil. Rubber created havoc in the Amazon Valley. The rubber-producers of this area reached a mighty crescendo of speculation and wild spending in 1910; but thereafter rubber ceased to be one of the exports of Brazil. Cotton, cacao, various wild fruits, nuts, dyes, and other substances led to minor and local flurries of speculation at various times and places. The collection of *maté* leaves in the Araucaria forests of southern Brazil is one of these. In each case Brazil, after a period of feverish growth, was forced to yield to other sources of supply, where more intensive methods of production were applied. The result, in Brazil, has been a lack of stability of settlement.

Subsistence Agriculture

But during the four and a half centuries of Brazilian settlement, commercial agriculture has been less important in terms of area than has been subsistence farming and the grazing of cattle. While contrasted regions were being developed by commercial agriculture, the basic use of the land has been remarkably uniform throughout the history of Brazil and throughout the settled area.

The system is one of land rotation carried on in a seemingly limitless area. First a landowner comes into possession of a large tract of forest, perhaps on the margins of one of the areas of speculative development. With few exceptions the large landowners, like those of Argentina, have been more interested in raising cattle than in agriculture; but to create pastures in lands covered with semideciduous forest it is first necessary to clear the forest. For this hard work the landowner makes a contract with a tenant. The latter stakes out an area of some ten acres and starts clearing it. He cuts down all but the largest trees, and at the end of the dry season (September in many parts of the country) he sets fire to the debris. After the burning he plants crops in whatever space he can find among the charred logs and stumps. On soil enriched by wood ash he secures good yields of maize, rice, beans, and manioc. After sharing some of the crop with the landowner, the tenant has a small surplus above the needs of his own family with which he can buy salt beef *(xarque)* or *rapadura* (a sugar candy) or *caxaça* (a brandy made from sugar), or perhaps some cotton cloth for his wife. But after a few years, usually not more than three, the poverty of the soil begins to show up in decreased yields. The tenant then plants pasture grass and moves to a new part of the forest. The landowner has some new pasture for his cattle, but he takes no care of the pasture and little by little a second growth of trees chokes out the grass. After a few years he moves his cattle to another pasture, leaving the old clearing to the forest. In the course of four centuries vast areas of Brazil have been cleared and abandoned, not once but again and again.

THE DESTRUCTION OF THE FOREST

The kind of agriculture we have described has been applied very largely to one kind of country—the land covered by the semideciduous forest. For more than four centuries the relatively small area of this forest type has supported Brazil's commercial agriculture and also the production of food for the Brazilian people. Agriculture has not been successful in the grasslands because the soils are so poor that harvests do not repay the effort of planting. Nor has agriculture been successful in the rain forests, for in these regions also the soil yields too little. Map 125 shows in general outline the gradual progress of the destruction of the semideciduous forest. In 1700 only the forests of the Northeast and a few spots around São Vicente and Rio de Janeiro had been cleared. Between 1700 and 1800 large areas in the vicinity of Rio de Janeiro, in the Paraíba Valley, and in southern Minas Gerais were cleared to provide food for the gold and diamond miners. By 1930 the clearing of the forest had swept over São Paulo and southward into the southern

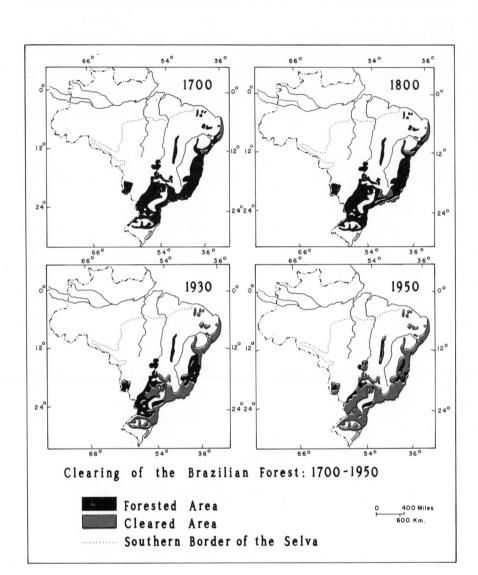

Clearing of the Brazilian Forest: 1700-1950

Forested Area
Cleared Area
Southern Border of the Selva

0   400 Miles
600 Km.

Map 125

states. It had also progressed in the Northeast. By 1950 only a very little of the virgin forest remained. Near Rio de Janeiro and São Paulo, and in the Paraíba Valley the second growth had been cleared so often, and at such brief intervals that now even second growth brush will not come back on the bare land. On steep slopes soil erosion goes on at a terrifying rate. Before most Brazilians were aware of the situation, the resource base on which the country had depended had been destroyed. Instead of unlimited area, now there was land hunger as pioneers hacked away at the last remnants of forest a thousand miles inland.

Contrasts in Social Organization of Rural Brazil

As a result of these contrasted uses of the land different kinds of social organization have been formed. In the areas where commercial agriculture is predominant, the rural workers are only loosely and temporarily attached to the land belonging to any one owner. But in those parts of the backlands where subsistence farming and cattle-raising are the basis of the economy, there is a very close attachment of the tenant farmer to the owner of the fazenda, the *fazendeiro*. The landowner is named as the godparent, the *compadre,* of the tenant's children. This is a binding social relationship in which the *compadre* assumes responsibility for the children in case the father is killed or becomes unable to work. It is a form of social security that depends on the strength of custom rather than law. But not uncommonly the children of deceased parents are taken into the owner's home and raised along with his own children. In return for this protection, the tenant agrees to accept the owner's direction in voting. The *fazendeiro* then has a marketable commodity, much desired by people running for political office. For a price he can deliver a specified number of votes. The system is not one that generates demand for reform: the rural workers find in this system a real security in an otherwise insecure society; the landowners find in it an additional source of income; and the politicians find in it a dependable support in the competition for public office.

Immigration

During the nineteenth century, the population and the social organization of certain parts of Brazil were transformed by a new kind of immigration. Until the late nineteenth century the rate of population increase was slow. Birth rates were relatively low, and infant mortality was very high because of bad hygiene and the lack of nourishing foods. The arrival of Africans in the Northeast built up there the densest population of any part of Brazil. Even as late as 1870 half of all the people in Brazil lived in this region. Early in the nineteenth century the German geographer Alexander von Humboldt estimated that the population of Brazil was composed of about 920,000 people of European origin, about 1,960,000 people of African origin, and about 1,120,000 Indians and *mamelucos*—a total of only 4 million by the end of nearly 3 centuries of settlement.

A rapid increase in the population of Brazil took place during the period of new European immigration after 1850. Between 1822, when Brazil became an independent country, and World War II, about 5 million immigrants arrived, most of them after 1900. But not all of Brazil was equally affected by this stream of new arrivals: over half of them went to São Paulo State, where coffee was demanding the services of an army of workers.

This stream of immigrants was made up mostly of Europeans. About 34 percent were Italians, 30 percent were Portuguese, 12 percent were Spaniards, 3 percent were Germans, and the remaining 21 percent included many different nationalities. There are today a little under 200,000 Japanese in Brazil—also mostly in São Paulo State. After 1918 the number of Italian immigrants dropped to almost nothing, while Poles, other eastern Europeans, and Japanese increased rapidly.

The first people to penetrate the southern part of Brazil, the part south of the São Paulo coffee region, were the *bandeirantes* who made use of the prairies for the grazing of cattle and mules. Later, in 1824 in Rio Grande do Sul, and in 1850 in Santa Catarina, colonies of German farmers were established. In these states, however, the immigrants were not tenants or wage workers on large estates, but small landowners, occupying and cultivating their own properties. In the course of time, these colonies were added to by new groups of Italians and Poles.

The Cities and the Sertão

Does Brazil have a great capacity for further population expansion? Is it true that a new, vigorous movement into the thinly peopled backlands might be developed, creating the kind of wealth that supported the economy of the United States during the decades following the Civil War? Brazil's population has been growing at a faster and faster rate. In 1872 there were about 10 million Brazilians; in 1920 there were well over 30 million; in 1950 more than 50 million; and in 1960 more than 70 million. It was estimated in 1967 that the population had passed 85 million. The rate of growth—3.1 percent per year—is above the Latin-American average. Meanwhile the cities of Brazil are growing at phenomenal rates, as a result of the increasing movement of people from the rural areas. There is a swelling volume of internal movement from the thinly peopled backlands into the areas already well-populated. Brazil's cities, therefore, have grown much faster than the urban facilities such as water, light, housing, or even food, could be expanded.

Brazilian cities are ultra-modern in appearance. Brazil's architects lead the world in creating new forms. The people who live in these cities are learning rapidly to abandon some of the traditional ways of living of Brazil. Some Brazilian writers now insist that the "real Brazil" is not to be found in the cities at all. The real Brazil, they say, is only to be found in the back country —in the thinly peopled wilderness beyond the frontiers of concentrated settlement; in the land which the Brazilians call the *sertão*[4].

The *sertão* is not a wilderness in the sense that it is made up of unexplored territory. Actually it has been tramped over, lived in, its resources exploited, and its landscapes modified in many ways over the course of more than four centuries. The *sertão* forms a sort of penumbra around the margins of the effective national territory: a transition zone of shifting population, but one in which a way of living has become established which has withstood the forces of change over hundreds of years. Aside from groups of people temporarily engaged in seeking for gold, the economy of the *sertão* is essentially pastoral—the grazing of herds of cattle on the open range. Scattered throughout the vast area of the *sertões* there are small groups of people clustered more or less permanently around ranch headquarters or in small towns. Contact with the regions of concentrated agricultural settlement is made through annual fairs held in border towns. Beyond the frontier of close settlement the pastoral *sertão* extends indefinitely inland; its area can be roughly, but not exactly delimited as the zone with a population density between 2 and 10 per square mile.

The pastoral inhabitants of the *sertão* are not like the Brazilians in the cities or even those in the agricultural areas. They are almost pure Portuguese with a mixture of Indian. They are essentially democratic, knowing no rigid class distinctions, for the ranch owners look, act, dress, and live like their workers. They are a fiercely independent people, courageous, resourceful, and superstitious; but they are so widely scattered or gathered in such small groups that they cannot support the cost of those numerous things which bring a society forward from a pioneer life to one which can be described as modern. It was remarked not so long ago that here the pioneer way of life had become permanently established.

To the Brazilian who lives in the great cities, the *sertão* has always exerted a strange fascination. For centuries people have believed that a vast wealth of resources was lying dormant in the interior, awaiting only the arrival of people brave enough, resourceful enough, and persistent enough to find ways to make use of this wealth. Yet the only people who seemed to have formed workable connections with the land were the widely scattered herders. These settlers were not to be thought of as a fringe of pioneers engaged in the occupation of new lands in advance of a moving frontier: rather they were the fragments of population left from the many groups which have attempted to exploit the supposed wealth of the backlands. They represent a very old, stabilized society in a land long occupied.

---

[4]Pronounced sair-tong'. The plural is *sertões,* pronounced sair-tó-aish.

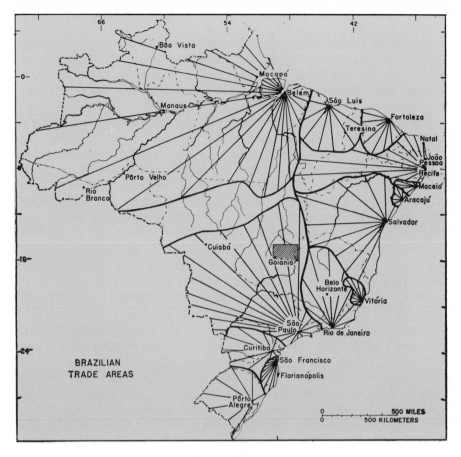

Map 126

Since 1960, however, the Brazilians have taken major steps to do something about the emptiness of the backlands. First they built a new capital city —Brasília—located in the midst of the *campo cerrado,* almost at the headwaters of three of Brazil's great rivers. Highways have been built for thousands of miles through almost empty country to connect Brasília with the still more remote interior. From all over the backlands, people are being attracted to the capital, while thousands of others have made clearings along the highways to grow mostly subsistence crops. The great question today is whether this effort to rearrange the Brazilian population will be permanently successful, and what the settlement of the *campo cerrado* will mean in the broader terms of national economic development.

Chapter 26 □ Brazil:

The Northeast

The Northeast plays a part in Brazilian national life which resembles that played by New England in the national structure of the United States. Salvador in Bahia, Recife in Pernambuco, and São Luis in Maranhão were three of the four primary settlement centers of the Portuguese in America (Map 6, p. 18). Along the coast, the first of Brazil's major economic cycles passed through the stages of rapid growth, spectacular flowering, and long, slow decadence. Here the African contribution to the Brazilian way of living was first mingled with the contributions from Portugal. Here a European people, with the help of the Africans, first built a civilization in the tropics. And here was the first area of Brazil where people experienced the stark contrast between the wealth and prosperity of the coastal settlements and the poverty and misery of a seemingly endless backland—the interior of the Northeast was the traditional Brazilian *sertão*. The region has supplied more than its share of Brazil's intellectual, artistic, and political leaders. For centuries, too, the chief product of the Northeast has been people—people who have migrated to other parts of the country where economic opportunity seemed to beckon. Workers from the Northeast panned gold in Minas Gerais, planted coffee in São Paulo, tapped rubber in the Amazon, harvested cacao in southern Bahia. People from the Northeast built the great cities of Rio de Janeiro and São Paulo, and molded the fantastic shapes dreamed by the Brazilian architects for Brasília.

The Northeast has long been described as one of the major poverty spots of Latin America. In a country of such vast size it seemed more profitable to start new economic ventures elsewhere, rather than to try to remedy the plight of an old region of settlement. Furthermore the backlands have been plagued by a series of natural disasters, which were rendered all the more disastrous because of the numbers of people dependent on the land for a bare subsistence. Efforts to do something about the impact of the droughts only aggravated the problem by speeding the rate of population increase. A German geographer in the 1930's concluded that the best way to relieve the distress of the people of the backlands was to promote a major emigration to other parts of Brazil. But now, in the late 1960's, something effective has at last been started. Now the Northeast is experiencing a rate of economic growth faster than that of any other part of Brazil, and faster, also, than most other parts of Latin America. This is now a region that is not only spectacular for the poverty and hopelessness of its people, but it is also spectacular for the measures being taken to relieve poverty and to bring new hope to the inhabitants.

The Northeast as defined in this book[1] includes 18 percent of the area of Brazil and 27 percent of the population. It includes, also, 9 of the 26 states and territories into which the national territory is divided.

The Land

The Northeast is made up of two strongly contrasted parts. First there is the zone of the *Mata,* the forested area. This is in the belt of dependable rainfall (mostly over 40 inches annual average) along the coast south of Natal. Although the forest has been almost entirely removed, the area it once covered is marked by reddish clay soils. In contrast to this coastal zone is the zone of the *Caatingas,* the land of recurring droughts and disastrous floods, a land covered with drought-resistant scrubby trees and brush. The soil is hard, sandy, and light-colored. Throughout the zone of the *Caatingas* there are little islands of wetter land on hilltops which were once forest-covered like the zone of the *Mata.*

Surface Features

Five major kinds of surface features are of chief importance among the landscapes of the Northeast region (Map 117). The first category is described as "broad plains with erosion remnants." Formed on massive and geologically ancient crystalline rocks the plains rise gradually from sea level on the coast of Ceará southward to some 1,500 feet above sea level in northern Bahia. The surface is strikingly uniform over vast areas; yet irregularly scattered over the surface are low knobs and sharply pointed rocky fingers *(inselberge)* that are remnants of erosion, standing above the general level because of superior resistance to the destructive action of air and water.

The second category includes the hilly uplands and low mountains which are also formed where the crystalline rocks are especially resistant. These features are massive and rounded in outline. Several such uplands are to be

[1]See Maps 110 and 111, pp. 686 and 687; and footnote 1, p. 688.

seen rising above the broad plains in Ceará, but the largest such area is in Pernambuco and Paraíba. This is the Borborema, the rounded summits of which stand between 2,500 and over 3,000 feet above sea level.

The third category of surface is the cover of sandstone strata which still remains lying over the crystallines in Piauí and Maranhão, and in small outliers farther to the east in Ceará, Rio Grande do Norte, and Paraíba. The eastern edge of the continuous sandstone cover forms a conspicuous cuesta facing toward the east on the border between Ceará and Piauí. A detached outlier is the flat-topped Chapada de Araripe on the southern border of Ceará, the top of which is about 2,000 feet above sea level.

The fourth category includes the coastal *taboleiros*. These are flat-topped mesa-like forms held up by a cover of relatively recent sedimentary strata in a narrow belt running from Rio Grande do Norte southward—southward, in fact, almost as far as Rio de Janeiro. In the Northeast the *taboleiros* rise sharply back of the beaches and bars of glistening white sand along the shore. The flat tops stand between 150 and almost 500 feet above sea level. The rivers that cross the zone of *taboleiros* have cut through the sedimentary strata and have uncovered the crystallines below. On the inland side, the *taboleiros* and the hilly lands developed on the crystallines are at about the same elevation. The distinction is visible in the landscape because of the change from tabular to rounded forms. But the most important change is in the fertility of the soil. The *taboleiros* carry a sandy, deeply leached and very infertile soil; the crystalline hills are covered with a reddish clay soil which has furnished the chief agricultural support for more than four centuries.

The fifth category includes the sedimentary basin of Bahia. Here sedimentary strata occupy a canoe-shaped hollow in the crystallines. The strata, which are up-turned along the margins, form conspicuous cuestas facing out away from the sedimentary basin. The northern end of the sedimentary basin is north of the São Francisco in Pernambuco; toward the south, the sedimentary strata underlie the bay (Baía de Todos os Santos) which gave Bahia its name. The lowland around the bay is known as the Recôncavo. Here the sedimentary strata have been dropped down between two up-standing blocks of crystalline rock. One such block is on the east where the city of Salvador is situated. The other is on the west where the lowland of the Recôncavo stops abruptly at the base of the east-facing scarp. This sedimentary basin is of great importance to Brazil, for not only did its clay soils support sugarcane plantations for some four centuries, but also in modern times oil has been found there.

The Rio São Francisco

Brazilians, especially those of the Northeast, have a sentimental, almost mystical attachment to the Rio São Francisco. This great river rises in the central part of Minas Gerais and flows for thousands of miles northward through the backlands, the *sertões*. Minas Gerais, Bahia, and Pernambuco are states which enjoy much political power in Brazil; and they share a common feature of their *sertões*—the São Francisco.

Yet the São Francisco has been stubbornly uncooperative. To be sure, it is navigable for shallow-draft river steamers from Juazeiro in Bahia to Pirapora in Minas Gerais. But downstream from Juazeiro the river is slightly intrenched in the surface of the broad plains and its current increases as it approaches the Paulo Afonso Falls. Below the falls the river flows for the remaining hundred miles to the ocean through a deep canyon with only a few, disconnected bits of floodplain near the mouth. The river has been likened to the Nile: yet it is no Nile, for the use of its water to irrigate a richly productive floodplain is not possible. Even in its mid course, upstream from Juazeiro, the floodplain is not very wide. Throughout most of the dry part of the Northeast, where the water of the São Francisco would be most valuable, the lay of the land is such that irrigation would be costly and could be applied only to small areas.

The Paulo Afonso Falls are located near the western border of Alagôas. The crystalline rocks in this area are broken by two systems of faults (cracks in the bedrock), one running from southwest to northeast, the other from northwest to southeast. Along the resulting lines of weakness the river has cut an angular course. The falls are produced where the water has excavated a deep trench running from southwest to northeast, at right angles to the course of the river at this point. Into this trench the water descends about 275 feet in a series of tremendous cascades. The resemblance to the Victoria Falls of the Zambesi in Africa is striking.

Climate and Vegetation

The fundamental contrast between the two parts of the Northeast is a result of climatic differences and of resulting differences in the natural vegetation and soil. The coast south of Cape São Roque receives regular rains, brought by the cold air masses as they push far to the north in the southern-hemisphere winter. Recife, for example, receives an average annual rainfall of about 65 inches, most of which occurs between April and July. This coastal zone of abundant rains extends inland for only about 40 or 50 miles in Pernambuco, but becomes narrower in the state of Sergipe. On the coast northwest of Cape São Roque, São Luis de Maranhão receives an average annual rainfall of about 85 inches, most of which occurs between January and June, as in the eastern part of the Amazon Basin. These rains, we may recall, are brought by the indraft of warm, moist air from the equatorial North Atlantic. Between eastern Maranhão on the west and the coast of Pernambuco on the east lies a triangular-shaped zone of irregular rainfall, subject to intervals of floods and droughts.

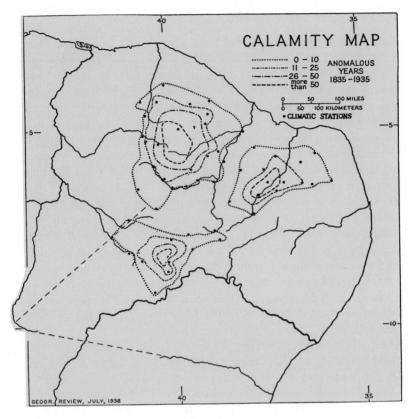

Map 127

During the 1930's a German geographer, Friedrich Freise, examined the records of climatic stations in the Northeast.[2] He prepared what he called a map of "Calamities" (Map 127). He outlines three areas where, during the period from 1835 to 1935, there were more than 50 years of either flood or drought. Other parts of the Northeast show varying tendencies toward recurring calamities. He found that in so-called good years about 90 percent of the rain in the backlands falls between December and April or early May. Generally the rains start in October—the first showers being known as *cajú* rains, because the tree which produces edible *cajú* nuts buds forth with new leaves and flowers at this time. In the rainy season the moisture is brought in violent showers of brief duration and small areal extent. The whole rainfall of a month may fall during four or five showers, all occurring within a few days of each other.

In bad years several irregularities may appear. Sometimes a whole year may pass in certain localities without any rain at all. Sometimes there are

[2]Friedrich Freise, "The Drought Region of Northeastern Brazil," *Geographical Review*, Vol. 28 (1938): 363–78.

rains in December and January, but none after that. In other years there may be no rain from January to the end of March, followed by excessive downpours in April and May. Any of these departures from the normal results in disaster for the farmers, and if several abnormal years come in succession, there may be a widespread failure of the pasturage on which herders must depend. It should be noted, however, that even within the area of uncertain rainfall there are "islands" of heavier rainfall located on the tops of the higher elevations, such as the Borborema or the Chapada de Araripe. Even in dry years these summits are well watered, and in wet years the rainfall in these places is very heavy.

The vegetation of the Northeast reflects these climatic contrasts. The zone of dependable rainfall along the east coast was marked originally by a belt of semideciduous forest, becoming a rain forest in southern Bahia. On the higher summits of the dry area there were also patches of semideciduous forest. Very little of these forests remain. Where the forest has been cleared from the higher slopes the result has been to increase the contrast between flood and drought, for when the rains come the run-off is rapid and the valleys below are flooded. In between the rains the water in the valleys of the dry area disappears.

The broad plains of the interior are covered with *caatinga,* a tropical scrub woodland consisting of low, thorny, deciduous trees. In the wetter areas the *caatinga* is dense and the trees stand as much as 30 feet in height. In the drier areas, however, the *caatinga* is low and the trees are widely spaced. After the first rains the *caatinga* is colorful, with green leaves and brilliant flowers. During the dry season, or the years of drought, the leaves drop from the trees, which stand bare and brown in the intense sunshine. In the *caatinga* there are many valuable plants: there is the *caroá,* from which fiber can be produced; there is the Mamona plant which gives castor oil. Among the trees is the Oiticica palm, from which an oil is produced useful as a possible substitute for tung oil in the manufacture of paint; and there is the Carnauba palm from which a wax is extracted, valuable as a coating or polishing material. There are also many trees, like the *cajú,* which produce tasty fruits scarcely known today outside of the Northeast. Large areas of the *caatinga* have been cleared for firewood and charcoal, or simply burned to make room for pasture grasses or for the forage crop, *palma,* a variety of spineless cactus which, because of its high water content, makes especially good feed for cattle, goats, and donkeys during the long dry periods.

Settlement

In the first decades of the sixteenth century the only product of the Northeast was dyewood from the semideciduous forest. The dyewood was taken to Lisbon where it was found to be similar to Brazil wood, which was commonly in use for dyeing in the Middle Ages. The name "Brazil" had already been applied to some islands which were supposed to lie in the Atlantic, and it was easily extended to the new land after dyewood was discovered there.

During the first few decades of Portuguese settlement in Bahia, the colonists learned from the Indians how to grow tobacco and how to smoke it in the form of cigars. The earliest agricultural development in the Northeast was located on the high country to the west of the Recôncavo. The Indians were set to work growing tobacco, with which they were already familiar. As we shall see later, this area has been used continuously for the production of tobacco for more than four centuries.

Sugar Plantations

After a few decades, however, the Portuguese began to sense the possibilities of profit from the commercial production of sugarcane. This Moorish crop, already familiar to the Portuguese through their experience with cane plantations in the Madeira Islands, gave excellent yields in the rainy, forested parts of the Northeast. The sandy *taboleiros* of the immediate coast proved to be of little agricultural value because of the rapid percolation of the rain water; but the reddish clay soils on the crystallines and on the low-lying sedimentary formations were extraordinarily productive when first put to use. Forest clearing and cane planting spread rapidly in two chief areas: one in parts of the Recôncavo of Bahia, near Salvador; the other at the base and lower foothills of the Borborema in Pernambuco, near Recife.

After 1538 in Bahia and after 1574 in Recife, African slaves were imported in large numbers. From then on, the population of the sugar region of the Northeast comprised four classes: the Indians, who survived in considerable numbers only in Bahia; the African workers on the plantations; the Portuguese landowners who drew a sharp color line against intermarriage with the Africans; and the poorer people of Portuguese descent who were not landowners, many of whom took Indian or African wives, and most of whom settled in the towns and cities as small traders or fishermen. On the plantations, or *fazendas,* the wealthy landowners built themselves substantial homes of stone and cement, erected churches, and set up the *engenhos,* or sugar mills. In contrast to the *casa grande,* or the home of the plantation owner, were the miserable *senzalas,* or slave quarters, built of mud and thatch. Yet from the *senzalas* came the African foremen who actually supervised the preparation of the land, the planting and harvesting of the cane, the extraction of the juice, the boiling of the juice to form brown sugar, and the packing of raw sugar in bags for shipment. The African foremen became the masters of the sugar-producing technology.

The sugar lands were soon occupied by a relatively dense population. As the children of the first plantation owners grew up and married, they were established on new plantations, with new *engenhos,* often utilizing virgin land in the same valley as the parental estate. Little by little the plantation area was extended until it covered all the good soils, and perhaps even pushed for short distances into the bordering *caatinga*. Nevertheless, the striking contrast in vegetation and rainfall dependability led to the development of a sharply defined frontier, and to the growth of compact settlement in the agricultural area. Had this first zone of settlement been located in a position where the semideciduous forests and good soils extended indefinitely inland, it is quite possible that the population density necessary to support the cost of a civilized way of living for the aristocracy could not have been built up.

The Dutch played an important part in this development of the sugar economy of the Northeast. The Dutch merchants were the ones who financed the purchase of slaves and of sugar machinery (p. 112). They transported the sugar to Antwerp and Amsterdam where the raw sugar was refined; and then they sold the sugar throughout Europe. As has been stated earlier, when Spain threatened to stop this profitable arrangement, the Dutch reacted by occupying parts of the Northeast. In 1624 they seized Salvador, but the following year the Portuguese colonists recaptured their city. In 1630 the Dutch occupied Recife and Olinda, and from this base they extended their control to the whole coastal area from the Rio São Francisco to the Amazon. The Dutch were pushed out of Maranhão in 1644, but they remained in Pernambuco until 1654. During their stay in Brazil they learned how to make use of African slaves in the various processes of sugar production. Many of the landowning Portuguese families intermarried with the Dutch, and even now Dutch names and physical traits are to be found among the well-to-do families of the region.

Decadence of the Sugarcane Plantations

When the Dutch were driven out of the Northeast of Brazil they turned their attention to the Guianas and to the Lesser Antilles. Here they passed on their knowledge of sugarcane planting to the Spanish, the French, and the British. By the end of the seventeenth century the sugar producers of Brazil began to face increasing competition in the markets of Europe. The new plantations were equipped with better machinery and were located closer to Europe. Only by investing capital in more intensive methods and more efficient machinery could the Brazilians hope to compete, but this did not appeal to the plantation owners.

When gold was discovered in Minas Gerais, and diamonds shortly afterward, this new speculative opportunity for quick profits had an immediate appeal. Between 1710 and 1720 there was a strong movement out of the Northeast, especially out of Bahia. Many plantation owners moved southward with their slaves, following the valley of the Rio São Francisco to its headwaters in the mining regions of Minas. From 1729 to 1745 the movement was revived, leading to the newly opened diamond fields of northern Minas Gerais and southern Bahia. It is estimated that 500,000 people left the sugar lands of the Northeast before the middle of the eighteenth century. Between 1780 and 1790, there was another big exodus of owners with their slaves, involving some 150,000 people, according to Freise, this time to the state of Maranhão, where a new coffee frontier was being established. Early in the nineteenth century some 100,000 people left the Northeast for the new coffee frontier in the Paraíba Valley, inland from Rio de Janeiro.

These emigrations, however, did not permanently reduce the population of the Northeast. As sugarcane plantations were offered for sale, often in small pieces, they were bought by people who had not succeeded in getting land earlier, but who had been able to put aside some funds. The new owners continued to produce sugar by the traditional wasteful and inefficient methods. After the emancipation of the slaves in 1888, sugar production continued with the use of tenant workers.

Sugarcane in the Modern Period

Sugarcane is still grown in the Northeast, and in about the same areas that have been used for this purpose for four centuries. Yields per acre are among the lowest to be found in any of the sugar-producing regions of the world. In the Northeast the yield is about 15 tons of cane per acre, compared with nearly 19 tons per acre in São Paulo State and 27 tons per acre in Puerto Rico. In fact, the Northeast has been able to continue selling sugar on the domestic market in competition with São Paulo only because of the government policy of providing protection through tax measures.

In the 1960's there were two kinds of cane plantations in the Northeast. There are some relatively modern, large-scale *usinas,* most of them located in the Recôncavo of Bahia, or in the cane area west and south of Recife on the lower slopes of the Borborema (Map 119). *Usinas* have been built, also, in some of the valleys near the coast that cut through the *taboleiros* in Sergipe, Alagôas, and Paraíba. Around the *usinas* there are extensive cane plantations, in many cases enlarged through the purchase of numerous smaller plantations. The *usinas* are owned in some cases by corporations, in other cases by recent immigrants who bring with them up-to-date ideas about sugar technology. But only a few of the *usinas* can produce sugar at low enough cost to compete on an open market with the plantations of São Paulo.

The second type of sugarcane plantation in the Northeast is even less efficient. These are the *engenhos* where small-scale operators plant cane on some of the poorest cane land of the region—on the steeper slopes, the tops of hills in the interior, the badly eroded lands where the yields per acre of cane are much less than the regional average. The syrup is still boiled in large iron pans over wood fires. The product of the *engenhos* is made into a kind of brown sugar cake, known as *rapadura,* which is eaten by the poorer people throughout the Northeast.

In 1967, however, the program of economic development for the Northeast included a reconstruction of the sugar industry.[3] New and modern sugar-mill machinery was to be installed over a 5- to 7-year period. Modern agricultural practices were to be introduced, including the use of machinery, fertilizer, insecticides, and better varieties of cane. It was estimated that one result of modernizing the sugar industry would be that 180,000 of the 360,000 cane cutters would be out of work. Here, as elsewhere wherever agriculture is modernized, agricultural workers are eliminated and must be provided with other kinds of employment. We shall see later what is planned to meet this situation.

Tobacco in Bahia

Another small area in the Northeast has been used continuously for one kind of crop for more than four centuries. This is the district of Bahia, located on the highlands just west of the Recôncavo, where the Portuguese colonists made use of Indian slaves to grow the Indian crop, tobacco. This part of the Northeast receives abundant rainfall; the soil is sandy and porous, permitting rapid drainage; and the surface is nearly flat, which means that soil erosion is not important.

The cane planters started growing tobacco in this district as a kind of by-product, a source of additional income. The first clearing and planting was done by Indians, and it was the sale of the tobacco that paid for the first imports of slaves from Africa. After African labor replaced the Indians, the planters found that growing tobacco was a good way to keep the slaves employed when they were not needed for the cane harvest. The tobacco was exported to Portugal, and from there was sent all over Europe. Bahia tobacco became famous during the sixteenth century, and in the Netherlands and Germany it still enjoys the reputation of being especially fine for the manufacture of cigars.

When the slaves were freed in 1888, many of them left the sugarcane plantations. Because tobacco could be raised with little or no capital, many African farmers moved into the tobacco district where they rented small pieces of land from the large landowners. Most of the tobacco is raised by very poor tenant farmers on miniature farms, every square foot of which is used, if possible, for tobacco. Since there are no storage or curing facilities available in the tobacco district, the crop must be sold as soon as it is harvested. The tobacco companies are able to buy the leaves at very low prices.

There is one unique feature of this tobacco district which makes it distinctly different from any other agricultural district in Brazil excepting certain of the German colonies in the South. These are the only such districts

[3]The program of economic development for the Northeast was under the direction of a government agency known as the *Superintendência do Desenvolvimento do Nordeste*—SUDENE.

where fertilizer is regularly used. Without fertilizer the porous, sandy soil of the Bahia tobacco district could scarcely have continued to support this one crop for such a long time. Actually the nature of the soil aids in the effective use of manure, mixed with straw and waste from the tobacco warehouses. There is never enough fertilizer available: the amount of fertilizer is the chief factor in determining the acreage of tobacco, for physical conditions suitable for this crop occur in a much larger area than that actually used. The tenant farmers are too poor to use more than the bare minimum of fertilizer, and as a result the yields per acre are low and the condition of poverty persists. The few large landowners who grow tobacco are able to use a larger amount of fertilizer per acre, obtaining much larger yields. The landowners, however, prefer to keep cattle and sell the manure rather than undertake large-scale planting themselves.

Some of the tobacco is sent by small sailing ships across the bay to Salvador for export to Europe; but a large part of the harvest is manufactured into cigars in the small towns along the western side of the bay. There are several cigar manufacturing plants here, employing mostly women. The cigars are hand-rolled by skilled workers.

Other Specialized Crop Areas in the Zone of the Mata

In the zone of the *Mata* along the east coast between Salvador and Natal, and in small humid spots in the hilly parts of the interior, there are a number of small areas in each of which just one crop is produced (Map 119). Coffee is planted in two chief places: in Pernambuco on the wet, east-facing slopes of the Borborema, above the sugarcane plantations; and in some of the hilly areas of Ceará. In the state of Paraíba, around Campina Grande, there is a small district within which the land is used to grow agave, the plant with long, spiked leaves from which sisal fiber is extracted. Sisal production started during World War II and for a time thereafter commanded good prices on the world market wherever there were manufacturers of coarse twine and rope. But increasing competition with East African countries, and with parts of the Antilles, reduced the profits for the Brazilian product. The agave plant grows on steep slopes with poor thin soils; but since it requires clean clearing and fails to provide any protection itself, wherever agave is grown on sloping land the result is disastrous soil erosion. Also among the specialized agricultural districts in the zone of the *Mata* are the strips of land along the coast used for plantations of coconuts, and the miniature bits of floodplain along the lower São Francisco used for paddy rice.

The Pastoral Settlement

Even during the height of the sugar period, when Brazil was the world's first example of an enormously profitable plantation system based on slave labor, most of the area of the Northeast was devoted to pastoral use. The owners of the vast cattle ranges shared in wealth and prestige with the cane planters. The enormous grants of land included both the zone of the *Mata* and the zone of the *Caatinga*. One large estate included what is now the state of Sergipe together with a large part of northern Bahia. Associated with the raising of cattle there developed a system of shifting cultivation which we have described as land rotation. Tenant farmers cleared the forest or the *caatinga* to produce pasture; after a few years of cropping the newly cleared land they moved on to new parts of the region. In the course of 400 years, the Northeast has been cleared, cropped, grazed, and abandoned many times.

Land Rotation and the Pastoral Base

Most parts of the Northeast are used for the grazing of cattle or goats. The poorer areas, where water is most difficult to find, are used for unimproved pasture, and here the chief product is goatskin, for which the owners receive premium prices on the world market because of the high quality of the product. Areas not quite so poor are used for a combination of cattle-grazing and agriculture with the characteristic system of land rotation.

Neither the zone of the *Mata* nor the zone of the *Caatingas* is suited for the grazing of cattle under natural conditions. Where the *mata* has been cleared grass pastures can be planted and in some places maintained. On the deeply leached soils of the *taboleiros* of the zone of the *Mata* the grass is so poor in calcium that cattle grazing on it develop bone deformities; but elsewhere in the zone of the *Mata* pastures can be developed with a higher animal capacity than in most other parts of the region. There is no grass in the zone of the *Caatingas,* but grass can be planted and used for a few years after the *caatinga* has been cleared. So it is that agriculture is an essential part of the pastoral system.

The tenant farmer lives in extreme poverty and uncertainty. His occupation of any piece of land is temporary, his home simple, his possessions few. Movement to a new location presents no problem, nor does it involve new experiences, for he has never known a home that was permanent. He and his numerous sons and daughters travel freely over the vast expanse of the region, and without reluctance seek reported sources of economic gain in distant parts of Brazil. From Ceará came most of the workers who gathered rubber in the Amazon before 1910; from all parts of the Northeast come the unskilled workers who harvest cacao in southern Bahia, or who plant cotton and coffee in parts of São Paulo State, or who build the modern edifices of São Paulo, Rio de Janeiro, and Brasília.

In the Northeast, the pastoral landlord welcomes the tenant farmer. In the zone of the *Caatingas,* the tenant clears away the scrubby trees and at the end of the dry season he burns the tangle of branches and dead leaves. On the completely cleared opening, protected from grazing animals by a brush fence, he plants his crops all mixed together on the same land, seeking, in his own way, to secure maximum return for his efforts in a short time. He plants maize, beans, manioc, and cotton. He expects to have a small surplus, especially cotton, that he can sell in exchange for *rapadura* and rice. He plants his crops on any area he can find; he cannot use bare rock, or places mantled with coarse, bouldery gravel; but where his crops can take root, no place is too steep or too dry. In better places, where he can expect better yields, he must share half-and-half with the owner; where the land is so poor that only very low yields can be expected, the tenant takes all he can harvest. If in years of drought he harvests nothing, the landlord is not the loser. After a few years, usually not more than two or three, yields begin to decline; the tenant then plants grass in the better places, or *palma*[4] in the drier places. He moves away and the landowner moves in his cattle or goats. The newly created pasture is heavily grazed for a few years as the scrubby trees again invade and reclaim the land.

In 400 years, no part of the Northeast has been spared. The original vegetation has been cleared, perhaps several times. Under the intense tropical sunshine, clean clearing has the effect of killing the bacteria which have the normal function of creating humus. The result is that the soil now contains little or no organic matter. In those places where population is relatively dense, the interval between clearing becomes shorter and shorter, and the soil on which the whole system rests is gradually destroyed. The poverty of the tenant farmers and also of the smaller landlords becomes greater, but at a rate which is imperceptible.

Commercial Crops in the System of Land Rotation

During the periods of the system of land rotation when the land is used to grow crops, the tenant must first of all provide himself with food. He grows maize, beans, and manioc for this purpose, and in some places on newly cleared land he may grow enough so that he has a small surplus to sell. But he also grows certain crops which he does not use himself. For many years now the Northeast has produced castor oil from castor beans; and also oiticica oil, valuable as a substitute for tung oil in paint manufacture.

But in the state of Rio Grande do Norte, in western Paraíba, in central and southern Ceará, and in eastern Maranhão, the most important commercial crop of the zone of the *Caatingas* is cotton. Although tree cotton was one of the wild products of the *caatinga* before the arrival of the Portuguese, the kind that is now grown by the tenant farmers is a short-staple variety, similar to American Upland cotton. It was first introduced into Brazil in 1750. The first period of rapid expansion of cotton production took place during the North American Civil War, when Great Britain had to look to other countries

---

[4]Palma was introduced from South Africa in 1934, and, since it is 93 percent water, it provides important feed to mix with cotton-seed cake for the cattle in the dry season.

for the raw materials to keep her textile factories operating. In 1871–72 the Northeast accounted for about 85 percent of the Brazilian cotton exports. Although in the modern period more than two-thirds of Brazil's cotton is grown in São Paulo State, cotton in the Northeast is still an important part of the system of rotation. Fiber is now less important than cotton-seed cake which has become a major source of feed for the cattle. Without the income from the sale of the cake, cotton might well disappear from this region.

Droughts

The curse of the *sertão,* for both pastoralists and farmers, is the repeated calamity of flood and drought (Map 127). During the early centuries of settlement, there were so few inhabitants that the herders could escape the worst effects of these disasters. During the eighteenth century the shifting of settlers from the *sertão* into the outer margins of the agricultural region repeatedly reduced the population pressure of the interior. Not until the nineteenth century were so many people living in the *sertão* that the problem of surviving the calamities became critical. Since then floods and droughts have commonly been followed by a vast influx of refugees into such coastal cities as Fortaleza, where they remain until conditions in the interior improve.

Between 1877 and 1879 the interior of Ceará was visited by one of the most prolonged droughts in its history. The economic life of the whole interior was disrupted, and great numbers of refugees came to the cities. Fortaleza grew in a short time from a town of 30,000 people to one of 125,000, and the problem of feeding so large a number became critical. It was at this time that the rubber boom was getting started in the Amazon forests, and the demand for rubber gatherers far exceeded the possible supply of workers in that region. In 1878 about 54,000 people left Ceará to gather rubber along the far stretches of the Amazon and its tributaries. Most of these people never' returned; today the old rubber sections of the Amazon are largely occupied by the scattered descendants of people who came originally from Ceará.

Similar but less spectacular emigrations occurred during other years of drought, especially in 1915, 1932, 1939, and 1958. So high is the birthrate in this region, and so frequent are the years of poverty, that it is possible to say that one of the most important export products of the Northeast is people.

The first steps by the Brazilian government to attack the problem of the droughts were taken between 1880 and 1889 by the Emperor Dom Pedro II. During the last decade of the empire he had a number of earth dams, lined with stones, constructed along the water-courses of the area with the intention of conserving the water and protecting the valleys against flood. But the plans were faulty; the dams were soon washed out or the reservoirs filled up with silt.

In the drought-stricken *caatinga* zone of western Paraíba, a hungry animal searches ruined cotton field in vain for something to eat. *Paulo Muniz, Life Magazine* © *Time Inc.*

The attention of the federal government was again directed to the Northeast when, in 1910, a special commission began the study of the causes and effects of the droughts. The *Inspetoria Federal de Obras contra as Secas* was made responsible for the supervision and coordination of practical measures designed to shield the people of the Northeast from these calamities.

The *Inspetoria* undertook to build large reservoirs, or *açudes,* and to promote the use of water for irrigation. Since the reservoirs are all located where the rainfall is sufficient to permit the accumulation of some surface water, that is in hilly areas, there is little or no flat land near these reservoirs that can be used for irrigation. Where flat land does lie downstream from a reservoir, as in one place in the western part of Paraíba, failure to provide adequate drainage has resulted in a thick accumulation of salt.

Intensive Agriculture

Nevertheless, there are many miniature spots of intensive agriculture in the zone of the *Caatingas*. These spots are found along the banks of rivers and reservoirs in places that are alternately flooded and exposed by the uncontrolled rise and fall of the water. Such periodically flooded strips are called *vazantes,* and the intensive agriculture practiced on them is called *vazante agriculture.* The most important areas of this sort are along the north-flowing rivers of Piauí, Ceará, and Rio Grande do Norte. These valleys have very low gradients, and only along the natural levees close to the winding streams are there lands suited to agriculture. The drainage of the back marshes, considering the very low gradient of the rivers, presents insuperable problems. Furthermore, along these rivers the land properties have been subdivided by inheritance into long narrow bands at right angles to the rivers. An individual property may be several miles long and only a few yards wide. Only the part near the river is used for *vazante* agriculture: the part back from the river is used for pasture.

Vazante agriculture is also practiced around the margins of the numerous reservoirs. Because there is so little flat land at or near the water level, there are only narrow strips available for this kind of use. Around the public reservoirs the land has been divided into small lots and made available for farmers.

Along the banks of the Rio São Francisco there are some miniature strips of *vazante* agriculture. From Juazeiro to the sea there are only a few places where low water exposes any important areas of potential crop land. Some of these places are sandbars in the river channel. Others are isolated bits of floodplain, like those used for rice along the lower river in the zone of the *Mata*. Elsewhere the steep river bank itself is used for vegetables and fruit for local subsistence. The spots of agriculture are close to the little towns that have grown up where there are ferries across the river—such as Cabrobó, Jatinã, and Petrolandia. The fact is that the São Francisco below Juazeiro flows through thinly peopled country and constitutes a barrier rather than an axis of settlement.

Products from Wild Plants

The economy of the Northeast is also supplemented by the collection of a variety of products from wild plants. Even before the arrival of the Europeans, the Indians would collect tree cotton and use it to weave textiles. Some tree cotton is still collected. It has a long, silky fiber that makes it valuable for the manufacture of strong cord. Also in the *caatinga* there is a small, drought-resistant plant known as *caroá,* from the bayonet-like leaves of which it is possible to remove the fibers. Places in the scrub woodland where the *caroá* plants are growing in abundance are marked off, and arrangements are made with the landowner to permit the entrance of gatherers. Temporarily employed workers collect the leaves and bring them to a little portable mill where the fibers are removed. After the plants are all collected the mill is moved to a new location. *Caroá* fiber is used in the small towns and villages of the Northeast to weave hammocks and for other household purposes.

Carnauba wax is another product collected from wild trees in the *caatinga*. In places where the ground water is close to the surface, especially along the lower courses of the rivers of Rio Grande do Norte, Ceará, and Piauí, there are fairly dense stands of carnauba palms. The wax adheres to the outer surfaces of the leaves. Government regulations now limit the number of

Carnáuba palm plantation in Ceará. *Courtesy of Brazilian Government Trade Bureau.*

leaves that can be cut from any one tree and the frequency of cuttings. The wax is a white, powdery substance, used in the manufacture of self-polishing floor waxes, shoe polish, lipstick, phonograph records, carbon paper, and protective coatings for metal. For the landowners the carnauba palms are a most valuable resource, for with a little care they remain productive for as long as two centuries. Under the shade of the palms pasture grasses thrive in the moist soil. Where the palms are present in large numbers, a stable and profitable kind of economy can be developed, with a form of land use that is the least destructive of the resource base of any practiced in the Northeast.

Another valuable tree found only is this part of Brazil is the Babaçu palm, from which an oil is extracted. Babaçu palms are especially numerous in the states of Piauí and Maranhão, inland from São Luís, where the vegetation is a mixture of savanna and palms. Though there were once at least a billion trees in this area, wasteful and destructive methods of collecting the palm nuts have already destroyed a large proportion of them. From those trees that are still productive, two bunches of nuts each year can be harvested. If plantations of babaçu palms could be developed, where the use of the trees and the extraction of the oil could be properly supervised, it is estimated that production might reach 300,000 tons of oil each year. But no such plantations have been developed, and the wasteful, speculative system continues.

Cacao and Rubber in Southern Bahia

The whole southern part of the state of Bahia, south of Salvador, receives enough rainfall to support a tropical rain forest vegetation. This part of the state is not at all like the rest of the Northeast: its conditions and problems are more like those of the region known as the East. During the present century, plantations of cacao have been developed in this once thinly inhabited part of Bahia. The chief cacao-shipping port is Ilheus.

Ilheus was settled by the Portuguese colonists in 1532. At this site the *taboleiros* are interrupted, and the crystalline rocks reach the shore. A steep hill, standing close by a small protected harbor, provided a landing place that could be defended from the attacks of Indians. Ilheus, and a few other forts, were occupied early in the sixteenth century chiefly to keep other European powers away.

Not for two centuries was there any real penetration of the dense forests. In 1746 cacao trees were brought to Ilheus from Maranhão and planted in clearings inland from that port. It was found that the trees did very well. But is was not until 1907 that high-yielding cacao trees were imported from Ceylon. The earliest plantations, inland from Ilheus, were developed on land that had been completely cleared of the selva. The trees were shaded with bananas, and in this older part of the cacao district they still are shaded in this way. But all the new plantings made since the introduction of the trees from Ceylon have been under the protection of the taller trees of the original forest. From a production of only about 10,000 metric tons in 1900, production was increased to almost 130,000 metric tons in 1940, and to more than 150,000 tons per year in the 1960's.

The cacao district has been developed on the red clay soils, known as *massapê,* which form on crystalline rocks under forest cover. The soils of the *taboleiros* proved to be so infertile that it did not pay to clear them. Cacao is grown in a belt some 50 to 100 miles wide between the inner margin of the *taboleiros* and the base of the Great Escarpment. As soon as one starts to climb onto the highlands, cacao is replaced by the traditional system of land rotation in which the chief crops are maize, rice, beans, and manioc, and the chief use of the land is for pasture.

Within the cacao district the plantation methods have been destructive and speculative. Excepting for a few model plantations which have remained productive for more than a century, most of the area is poorly cultivated. The plantation owners are businessmen who carry on the commercial and financial transactions and who collect most of the profits. The plantations are left to managers who reside in the cacao district. A major problem, each year, is to recruit enough workers to do the work of harvesting, scraping the seeds from inside the pods, placing them in bags and transporting them to the plantation headquarters. Here the cacao seeds must be fermented and dried on platforms or trays, and quickly covered when it starts to rain. The cacao harvest starts in April, but the chief harvest season is from September to December. Workers from the backlands of Bahia and even farther north move into the cacao district for these months and are immediately hired by the plantation managers. After the harvest they disappear, mostly on foot, either to return to little isolated clearings in the *sertão*, or to seek other kinds of employment in the cities. This regular, and now long-established, seasonal migration of workers links the cacao district more than any of the other agricultural areas of this part of Brazil to the people of the *sertão*.

In spite of the destructive methods, and in spite of the violence which has on occasion broken out in this region as a result of conflicts in property claims, it nevertheless is Brazil's leading cacao-producing area. From this one district almost 20 percent of the world's cacao used to come as recently as 1955–60. For many years Brazil was second only to Ghana. But in the late 1960's Brazil's share of world production dropped to only 10 percent, due chiefly to the rapid increase of production in other African states.

Just to the north of the cacao district, at a place called Ituberá, the Firestone Tire and Rubber Company has developed a rubber plantation. This part of Bahia has climatic conditions that are just as good as the Amazon region for growing rubber; and it has the added advantage of being much more accessible to the manufacturing plants in São Paulo.

A Program of Economic Development

Here, then, are the two contrasted parts of the Northeast: one with more or less dependable rains, with agricultural and pastoral areas carved out of the original forest; the other a *sertão* with unstable, shifting patterns of people. Here the peculiarly Brazilian relationship of an area of concentrated settlement and a bordering *sertão* had its first and perhaps most typical development. No small part of the intense nationalism and the almost mystical attitude toward the possibilities of economic development in the backlands is due to the presence of large numbers of people from the Northeast in the other parts of Brazil, and to the numerous political, literary, and artistic leaders who were brought up in the Northeast.

The first part of the Brazilian backlands to be made accessible by the construction of all-weather roads was the interior of the Northeast. During World War II, when some feared a German invasion of the Americas starting with this easternmost part of the South American continent, a network of motor-truck roads was built. Two major north–south roads connected Salvador with Recife and João Pessoa, and with Fortaleza. Ferries provided for crossings of the São Francisco at Petrolandia and Jatinã. East–west highways were built inland from each state capital. In 1950 this whole network was connected by road with Rio de Janeiro and São Paulo.

The first result of this program of road-building was a rapid increase in the use of motor-trucks, and the development of a regional economy to replace the isolated subsistence economies of each locality. Owner-operated trucks went from one market town to another, buying and selling the products of these small communities and linking them together in a new pattern of trade.

But from this kind of development the typical tenant farmer benefited little. As a result of new medical services and new efforts to control disease-carrying insects the death rate was cut down: the continued high birth rate resulted in a rapid increase of the net rate of population growth. All this spelled deepening poverty and hopeless misery for the *sertanejos,* the inhabitants of the *sertão.* No longer sick, however, these people began to band together to demand, sometimes with force, that something be done to provide them with a better living.

In 1959 the Brazilian government established SUDENE (see p. 730). Its purpose was to speed up the process of development in the Northeast, to diminish the great gap between the levels of living in this region and those of the country in and around Rio de Janeiro and São Paulo. SUDENE represents Brazil's effort to do something about the poverty of its own people in what was generally conceded to be the major poverty spot in the hemisphere.

The first step is one that must set the stage for programs of economic development anywhere in the world—to persuade the people that economic development is desirable, and that the essential changes in the traditional system are acceptable. With a social system of the kind described on page 717, who is likely to advocate change? The major obstacle to programs of development is likely to be the traditional way of living which is not easily abandoned. In the Northeast it was traditional to blame the poverty of the people on the recurrence of natural disasters and difficult to demonstrate that the disasters were largely man-made. SUDENE undertook to change the attitude of the influential people toward development programs by holding a number of public discussions of the problems of regional development, and by involving the community leaders in the planning process.

Another first step was the construction of schools. In 1967 alone some

850,000 new pupils were enrolled in schools. The start of an attack on the widespread illiteracy of the people was made.

The improvement of agriculture is a major part of the program. Modern technology is being introduced not only among the sugarcane plantations, but also in the cacao district and among the poor tenant farmers and stockmen. New and more productive varieties of crops were made available. The steep and badly eroded hilly lands were designated for reforestation. More than forty centers were established for the improved breeding of hogs and cattle.

A new search for mineral resources was undertaken. New oil wells were drilled in the Recôncavo Basin, and in the bay to the south of it. New sources of oil were discovered in Sergipe and Alagôas, and Piauí and Maranhão. Important new sources of gypsum, tungsten, and iron were found.

A program for the increased use of the fish resource was drawn up. Traditionally, what little fishing was carried on was by fishermen from coastal villages who went out to sea in small sailboats called *jangadas*. These consisted of some logs tied together like a raft, and moved by a triangular sail. But the market for the fish was small, mostly restricted to the immediate shore. Yet the ocean waters are rich in edible species of fish. In 1966 there were 24 foreign companies operating out of Recife and Fortaleza to catch lobsters and send them by airplane to European markets. The coastal waters of Maranhão abound with shrimp. But the problems to be overcome included replacing the *jangadas* with modern fishing boats, building modern fish-processing plants at the ports, and persuading the people that fish are good to eat.

The improvement of agriculture, as we have seen, reduces the number of jobs in farming. Alternative kinds of employment must be offered—perhaps in mining, or fishing, or in the construction of roads and ports, or in the tourist industry. But at the start, the most important new kind of employment must be in manufacturing industries.

In 1967 a new way to find speculative profits had been offered to the Brazilians in Rio de Janeiro and São Paulo. A notable flow of new capital into the Northeast was set off by an announcement that any corporation in Brazil would be permitted to deduct 50 percent of its income tax liability each year, provided that the equivalent amount of money be invested in the Northeast for approved industrial development. In 1968 a steel plant was being built on a site near Salvador, where it could be fueled with natural gas. The oil and salt of Sergipe and Alagôas are to be made the basis for a petrochemical industry. At Salvador, Recife, and the smaller towns, many thousands of new jobs are being made available in factories producing textiles, assembling automobiles, processing foods, making machine tools or ceramics or a variety of consumer goods.

These developments require a great increase in the supply of electrical energy. A hydroelectric plant at the Paulo Afonso Falls, which started to supply electricity in 1954, has now been enlarged to generate some 455,000

The water front at Salvador. The sailing boats bring goods across the bay. The upper city is reached by elevators.

kilowatts. From Paulo Afonso electricity is transmitted to all the coastal cities. By 1971 it is planned to boost the power from this source to 1,220,000 kilowatts and to build new power lines to reach more communities. Smaller places not near power lines are to be given electricity for the first time from generators powered by Diesel engines. A power dam was being built on the Río Parnaíba to supply some 50,000 kilowatts for use in Piauí and Maranhão.

In the late 1960's the part of Brazil enjoying the fastest rate of economic growth was the Northeast. About half of the new capital was coming from

the Brazilian government, which was receiving financial aid from the United States as a part of the program of the Alliance for Progress. Brazil was also increasing its collection of domestic taxes. In addition, some 35 percent of the new capital was coming from private Brazilian investors, and about 15 percent was coming from foreign countries. Still, the question remained: was the rate of growth fast enough to provide jobs for workers no longer needed in agriculture, as well as for the vast number of young people soon to enter the job market?

Chapter 27 □ Brazil: The East

On the shore of Guanabara Bay midway between the North and the South of Brazil, there is a city which started as a defense post to guard a thinly populated sector of the Portuguese realm, but which has grown in size and in the extent of its influence until today it has become the focus of everything Brazilian. The breath-taking beauty of the site on which this city has been built places it among the scenic wonders of the world. But it is not until the visitor stops to look beyond his first impressions that the full significance of this place is revealed. For the city is not an exotic growth which, like something cast up by the sea, has taken root on the shore: it is a product of all the vast extent of territory and all the varied activities of the people who occupy nearly half of the South American continent. There is a reflection, for those who understand, of every part of Brazilian life—the irresponsible optimism of those seeking speculative wealth; the deep hopelessness of those who live in poverty in the areas of decadence; the gay sunshine of tropical coasts and the somber mysterious shadows of great forests; the lost settlers of the *sertão,* those scattered, isolated victims of vast area; and the great cities where the newest concepts of crowded urban living have come to Brazil from across the water. All these facets of Brazil are reflected in the city on Guanabara Bay—Rio de Janeiro.

Rio de Janeiro is more than just the urban nucleus of one of the zones of concentrated settlement. Today the city is far bigger than the productivity of its immediate hinterland would justify. Yet the settlement of the East gave Rio de Janeiro its start, and the roads of this region, and of the *sertão* beyond it, still lead to the shores of Guanabara Bay.

The zone of concentrated settlement, which we call the East, is not a unit in the minds of the inhabitants. No such regional consciousness is found in

this part of Brazil as is found in the Northeast. The people think of themselves as belonging to one of the states: Guanabara, Rio de Janeiro State,
Minas Gerais, or Espírito Santo (Map 110). Yet the states do not coincide
exactly with the outlines of the areas of settlement (Map 116). The whole
northern half of Minas Gerais lies in the *sertão*. The western part of Minas
Gerais—the part known as the Triangulo—belongs to the area focusing on
São Paulo City, and the eastern part of Sao Paulo State—the part known
to the Brazilians as the Norte—lies within the hinterland of Rio de Janeiro
(Map 126).

Within the states or parts of states which are thus combined in a region
of settlement, the variety of local contrasts is greater than in the Northeast. One of the outstanding characteristics of the East is the intricate
arrangement of its surface features, and the absence of any wide natural
focus of lines of travel.

The population of the East is scattered in small, isolated units, and
is loosely attached to the land. The settlers who came to the region first in
search of gold remained to gain a living from agricultural and pastoral
activities. But the story of the long process of readjustment since the decline
of gold mining is a complex one. Again and again new speculative forms
of land use have been introduced. Each time this has happened there has
followed a period of hectic expansion accompanied by rapidly rising values
and an influx of population, and then a period of sudden collapse, decadence, and abandonment. Always, at the end of each speculative cycle,
the land has been returned to pastoral uses. The present pattern of scattered settlement, the multiplicity of small towns, the grass-covered terrain
which was once forested, the spots of new and thriving development—none
of these features in the East can be understood without a knowledge of
the cross-currents of settlement and resettlement which have moved back
and forth across a stage so ill adapted for the play.

The Land

The physical background of the land is itself one of great diversity. The
East is made up of many little natural areas each more or less distinct
from the others. The intricacy is due chiefly to the surface configuration;
the climatic conditions and the cover of vegetation, compared with those
of the Northeast, exhibit wider zones of transition and fewer striking contrasts.

Surface Features

The surface features of the East consist chiefly of a complex arrangement of crystalline hilly uplands and low mountains (Map 112). There are

almost no large level areas except on the two deltas along the eastern coast —those of the Rio Doce and of the Rio Paraíba—and along the floodplain of the middle Paraíba. Small valley flats, terrace remnants, and isolated bits of high-level surfaces otherwise deeply dissected are scattered throughout the area. Only far in the interior are any remnants of the nearly level cover of sandstone strata to be found.

The mountains of the East stand above the general surface of the crystalline hilly uplands. Most of these mountains are massive and rounded, owing their existence to beds of resistant quartzite or other types of crystalline rock which are less easily decomposed than the granites and gneisses. The highest peak in Brazil is the Pico da Bandeira (9,462 ft.), located on the border between the states of Minas Gerais and Espírito Santo. Another relatively high range is the Serra dos Orgãos, just northeast of Guanabara Bay. There is also the massive Serra da Mantiqueira, on the southwestern border of Minas Gerais, just north of the Paraíba Valley. Only in these three places, however, do mountains rise above the upper limit of trees, which in this part of Brazil is found between 6,200 and 6,500 feet above sea level. In the central part of Minas Gerais, south and east of Belo Horizonte, is the southern end of the Serra do Espinhaço, the northern end of which is near Juazeiro in Bahia (Map 117). The Serra do Espinhaço forms the divide between the tributaries of the Rio São Francisco and the rivers that drain directly eastward to the Atlantic (ten of them, from the Rio Doce that reaches the ocean north of Vitória, to the river that flows into the Recôncavo near Salvador).

The story of the origin of the landforms included in the area classified as crystalline hilly upland constitutes an important lesson in geomorphology. From the east coast traveling toward the west one crosses a succession of steps in the zone of the Escarpment, reaching the surface of the upland between 2,600 and 2,800 feet above sea level. Toward the west is still another step to the top of the Serra do Espinhaço at about 3,600 to 5,200 feet above sea level. Viewed from a distance, the landforms look like an unfinished relief model on which the several layers have been put together, but on which the sharp edges of the layers have not yet been smoothed over. These landforms are the result of successive uplifts of the highlands, each starting a new erosion cycle. The oldest and highest erosion surface is preserved today in the uniform summit elevations of the Serra do Espinhaço, and this same surface is found over wide areas in the Central-West in the state of Goiás. A second and lower surface is represented by the uniform height of the hilltops of the hilly upland. And successive uplifts have resulted in still lower erosion surfaces, each in process of eating back into the one just above it.[1]

The Serra do Espinhaço is important not only for its landforms, but also, in a very practical sense, for the rich endowment of minerals that it con-

[1]Lester C. King, "A Geomorfologia do Brasil Oriental," *Revista Brasileira de Geografia*, Vol. 18 (1956): 147–265.

tains. The southern part of this range contains the gold and diamonds that supported settlement in the eighteenth century, and the iron and manganese that are of such great importance today. Access to the Serra do Espinhaço from the coast has long been a major Brazilian problem. The Rio Doce does in fact offer a good route of travel from the coast to the eastern base of the Serra do Espinhaço; but for the eighteenth-century Portuguese, slope was less of a barrier than dense forests, and the Rio Doce valley for them was anything but easy.

The next river south of the Rio Doce is the Rio Paraíba. But this river actually does not provide a route of access to central Minas Gerais, for its valley runs parallel to the part of the coast on which Rio de Janeiro is situated. Furthermore, although there is a broad floodplain in the middle part of the valley (from the big bend of the Paraíba a short distance east of São Paulo City [Map 129, p. 772] to Volta Redonda northwest of Rio de Janeiro), between Entre Rios and the beginning of the delta above Campos the Paraíba descends turbulently for about a thousand feet through a narrow, rocky gorge.

We can understand the difficulty of travel in the East more clearly if we consider the profile of a route from the coast near Rio de Janeiro northward to the crystalline hilly upland of central Minas Gerais. Along the immediate coast there is an outlying block mountain, separated from the front of the Great Escarpment by a zone of low country. A break in this mountain block permits the sea to come in through a narrow opening. This is the famous entrance to the bay on which Rio de Janeiro is located— an opening guarded by the Sugar-Loaf, a typical knobby peak formed wherever in the rainy tropics crystalline mountains are exposed to the wash of waves at their base. Guanabara Bay, however, is bordered by mountains only at its entrance: most of the shores of the bay are low, swampy, and fringed with mangrove. The lowland, known as the Baixada Fluminense,[2] is not flat—it is best described as a "hilly lowland," with a surface composed of low rounded hills shaped like half oranges.

The northern edge of the Baixada Fluminense is sharply terminated by the base of the Great Escarpment. East of Petrópolis this escarpment is surmounted by the Serra dos Orgãos, and passes in this section are much higher than those farther to the west. In the vicinity of Petrópolis the passes are between 2,000 and 3,000 feet above the sea. In the northwest corner of the Baixada Fluminense, however, there is one pass which requires a climb of only 1,463 feet. From the crest of the Great Escarpment the descent to the Paraíba Valley—here a little over 1,000 feet above sea level—is not difficult.

The Paraíba Valley offers an easy route of travel from the pass westward toward São Paulo; but for one who wishes to reach the upland of Minas Gerais the valley can only be considered a barrier. Beyond it, to the north,

---

[2] *Baixada* is pronounced by-sháh-dah

the ascent to the hilly upland, even if one travels to the east of the Serra da Mantiqueira, requires a steep climb through winding valleys to the general ridge-top level of about 2,600 feet.[3]

Climate and Vegetation

The climatic features of the East have a rather surprising simplicity. The effects of altitude, to be sure, are reflected in the lower temperatures, and in a vertical change in the character of the vegetation on the higher mountains. The narrow coastal fringe has temperatures characteristic of most tropical east coasts. They are not excessively high at any time of the year, and, especially in winter, are often surprisingly low owing to the passage of cold air masses. High humidity, however, does increase the unpleasantness of the hotter part of the year, especially in places which are sheltered from the compensating effect of the wind. During the summer months the wealthier people of Rio de Janeiro seek the lower temperatures (9° lower) and the more active social life of the community at Petrópolis, on the crest of the Great Escarpment. The temperatures of the interior are lower than those of the coast. Belo Horizonte, on the northwestern side of Serra do Espinhaço, averages a little over 72° in its warmest month and about 62° in its coldest month.

The rainfall, too, has a relatively simple distribution over eastern Brazil. On the slopes of the Great Escarpment, and on the sides of the mountains near the coast, rainfall of more than 80 inches is recorded in a number of scattered localities. Over most of the area, however, the amount remains with little variation between 40 and 60 inches. Throughout this area, also, the rainfall maximum comes during the summer months, and the cool season is relatively dry. Not until one reaches the northern and western side of the Serra do Espinhaço does he encounter a dry season of real moisture deficiency, for nearer the coast even the winter season has a considerable number of rainy days.

These climatic characteristics are reflected in the natural vegetation of the East (Map 15, p. 35). To reconstruct the actual details of the distribution is not always easy, for over much of the region the original cover has been

---

[3]The details of the surface features are even more intricate than the broader pattern. Throughout the zone of the Escarpment the details of ridges and valleys are controlled by two major fault trends. The faults are not recent, for this is not a region of frequent earthquakes. But they have become zones of weakness which are quickly excavated by the rivers. One system of faults runs from north-northeast to south-southwest; the other crosses the first, running from east-northeast to west-southwest. The excavation of valleys and scarps along these faults result in the formation of an exceedingly complex pattern of angular block mountains of rhombic shape. These two dominant trends appear not only in the minor landforms, but also in such major surface features as the Paraíba Valley, the Serra da Mantiqueira, the trend of the Great Escarpment, and even the trend of the coast on either side of Cabo Frio.

entirely changed during the period of European settlement. The coastal zone, the front of the Great Escarpment, and no doubt some of the very rainy spots on the mountains farther inland were covered originally by a dense rain forest which proved to be a very considerable barrier to Portuguese penetration. The southern and eastern parts of the highlands were covered with a semideciduous forest which extended inland as far as the Serra do Espinhaço; and even today this forest covers large areas of the Rio Doce Valley and of the mountains of Espírito Santo. The Serra do Espinhaço itself as well as the São Francisco Basin to the west of it was covered, and still is, largely with scrub woodland, except in the south where the use of wood for charcoal has practically destroyed the last vestiges of the original forest. The line between the scrub woodland and the savanna is not at all sharp, but the line in southern and western Minas Gerais, between semideciduous forest and savanna, was apparently a very distinct boundary—perhaps sharpened as a result of the common practice of burning the savanna. The savanna, covered with scattered thickets of scrub woodland *(campo cerrado)* and threaded by galerias along the streams, extends westward from the São Francisco Valley into the interior region known as the Central-West.

Settlement

Such is the nature of the East, a land in which a very important part of the story of Brazil has been enacted. This is the land with the heart of gold and the breast of iron; but it is a land not easy to penetrate, and not easy to move about in, for its surface and its forests are barriers to easy travel, and there is no natural focus of routes.

At first the highlands of the East remained less well known than many more remote parts of Brazil. When Rio de Janeiro was finally established on its present site after the French had been dislodged in 1567, its function was that of a defense point, not that of a nucleus from which colonization of the interior was contemplated. In fact, the site on the shores of Guanabara Bay was deliberately selected for its inaccessibility from the interior, in order that the fortress might have additional protection from possible attacks.

The first exploring party to reach the highlands ascended by the easiest possible route—not from Rio de Janeiro, but through the valley of the Rio Doce from Vitória. This great natural highway to the interior might have played a very different role in the course of settlement had it not been occupied by a group of exceptionally warlike Indians—the Botocudos (Map 5, p. 14). These savage tribes resisted the white men, and, like the Araucanians of Chile, took advantage of the white man's lack of knowledge of the forest to retard the advance of the Portuguese. Although the coast of Espírito Santo and southern Bahia was colonized very early, the only settlements which survived the attacks of Indians were places like Vitória, on an island, and Ilheus, on a site which could easily be defended from the interior. Most of the coast between Campos and Salvador was abandoned, and even today this section of Brazil remains a great empty space on the population map, and the Rio Doce Valley is only in the late 1960's being developed as a major line of travel to the interior.

It was not until 1698 that Minas Gerais became important. In that year *bandeirantes* from São Paulo discovered gold in the stream gravels of the southern part of the Serra do Espinhaço. Until that time, however, they, like the rest of the Portuguese, generally neglected Minas. The chief routes into the interior ran northward from Itu and then southward from Sorocaba (Map 130, p. 773). People from São Paulo had also pushed northeastward into the middle part of the Paraíba Valley, where Taubaté became the chief town.

The Gold Period

The gold which was the chief cause of the rapid settlement of the East after 1698 was found at many scattered localities throughout Minas Gerais, but chiefly in the central area around the southern part of the Serra do Espinhaço. Although there are veins of precious metal in the rocks of this range, the mining of the eighteenth century was entirely in the stream gravels. Many towns were established near the places where mining proved to be especially profitable. One of the most important of these towns—the place which soon became the political center of this part of Brazil—was Villa Rica (now known as Ouro Preto). There were several other mining towns near Ouro Preto in the Serra do Espinhaço or along its margins. After the discovery of diamonds in 1729 near Tijuco (now known as Diamantina) there was a rush of new settlers still farther toward the north.

The people who poured into Minas Gerais came chiefly from three places. A large number were new immigrants from Portugal, mostly not men of means but adventurers seeking a quick road to wealth. Many Paulistas entered Minas also, and during the early years of the eighteenth century they even fought for the political control of the territory. The Paulistas were defeated, but their numbers continued to swell the ranks of the gold seekers. There were also considerable numbers of former plantation owners from the Northeast, especially Bahia, who, with their slaves, moved into the new zone of exploitation. Villa Rica supplanted Salvador as a place of great wealth; gold supplanted sugar.

To estimate the amount of gold produced in this region is difficult, owing to the lack of records. The "royal fifth," which was returned to the crown of Portugal, gives some clue. The total amount was probably considerably less than that which has been taken from California in the years since 1849. But it was sufficient, during the period from 1700 to 1800, to make Brazil the leading gold producer of the world, accounting for about 44 percent of the gold produced during that century.

COLONIAL ROADS

With the discovery of gold and diamonds and the beginning of the settlement of Minas Gerais, the question of an outlet for the region became important. The desire of the Portuguese government to maintain its control of gold exports, and also, perhaps, the fear of raiders, led to the selection of one port of shipment and the prohibition of shipment from any other port. Several possible routes to the coast from central Minas Gerais were available. The most direct way, and by far the easiest one in terms of grades, would have followed the Rio Doce eastward to Vitória; but as we have said, the presence of warlike Indians in that territory made it one to be avoided. The way northward to the Brazilian capital at Salvador required not only a long river trip on the São Francisco, but also a difficult overland journey from Juazeiro to the coast. The obvious advantage of attaching this newly discovered gold district to the established political center of Brazil had to be given up.

The selection of Rio de Janeiro as the port of shipment for the gold was by no means inevitable. Perhaps if the Paulistas had been able to establish their claim to the political control of Minas Gerais, the main roads to the coast would have been built to São Paulo and Santos. At first, much of the gold was carried by mules over the route to Taubaté, and thence directly southeastward to a little port on the coast. The most direct route from Villa Rica to a place on the coast south of Cabo Frio led a little over three hundred miles to the shores of Guanabara Bay, and this easily defended naval base had the additional advantage of protection from pirates. When the seat of government was moved to Rio de Janeiro in 1763, this town had already gained preeminence as the chief port of Brazil.

DECADENCE

The gold fever lasted for about a century. All through the interior, stream gravels and hillsides which were found to contain gold were worked over by placer methods. Even today there are many spots which remain desolate wastes—miniature, man-made badlands, where the earth was torn and furrowed in the frantic search for the precious metal and then abandoned. But between 1800 and 1830 there was a rapid decline in the search for gold. The richer placer deposits had been worked over, and other parts of the world were producing gold at lower cost. Except for certain vein-mining enterprises, to be described later, and except for sporadic attempts to rework the old deposits, gold mining in southern Minas Gerais was at an end.

The people, whose sole means of support had been mining, were forced to find another basis for existence, or to move away. They did both. During

The small town of Guarará, east of Juiz de Fora in Minas Gerais. On the hill is old coffee land, now used for pasture. The ditch on the hillside marks a property line, and animals do not cross it.

the first third of the nineteenth century, there was a large emigration from Minas Gerais. It is impossible to estimate the number of people actually involved, but the results of this movement may be observed in the present character and distribution of people throughout the neighboring regions. A great many Mineiros (people of Minas Gerais) returned to the Paraíba Valley in São Paulo State, where, at that time, the planting of coffee was just entering the period of speculative expansion. Many of the planters who established themselves, in the middle of the nineteenth century, around Ribeirão Preto were formerly proprietors of gold mines in Minas. Most of those who went to São Paulo carried with them a considerable capital won from the gold fields. The poorer people who possessed a sufficient love of the unknown headed northward and northwestward into the *sertões*. People from the mining districts were chiefly responsible for the thinly scattered pastoral settlement of the whole southern part of the São Francisco Basin, and for the movement of pastoralists on westward into Goiás.

During the past century the story of settlement in the East has been punctuated by repeated attempts to reestablish some basis for speculative profit. Most of these endeavors were successful for short periods of time and in different geographic locations. But the stabilized and permanent support for the people of rural Minas Gerais remains the grazing of cattle for meat or dairying.

Belo Horizonte and Ouro Preto

Meanwhile, certain major changes in the pattern of settlement took place. One of these was the transfer of the state capital of Minas Gerais from the old colonial mining town of Ouro Preto to the entirely new city of Belo Horizonte. Ouro Preto occupied a mountainous site in the Serra do Espinhaço where there was no room for expansion. In 1896 the political center of the state was moved to a place where an entirely new city plan could be laid out. The new site was literally on the edge of the *sertão* on the northern and western side of the Serra do Espinhaço, where a large area of gently sloping land was available. New government buildings, new residences, amazingly wide streets, and a street pattern similar to that of Washington, D.C., give Belo Horizonte an atmosphere entirely different from that of the older cities. The new capital has grown rapidly: in 1920 there were some 55,000 inhabitants; in 1950 it had a population of about 350,000; by 1970 it will have passed 1 million. Ouro Preto, with fewer than 10,000 people surrounded by homes once occupied by 60,000 people, and with some 14 fine examples of colonial churches, has been made a national monument.

Ouro Prêto, the old capital of Minas Gerais, in the midst of the Serra do Espinhaço. *Courtesy of Brazilian Government Trade Bureau.*

Land Use in the East

The present patterns of land use in the East (Map 114, p. 691), like those of population and of the lines of circulation, are the result of a complex record of historical geography. There have been several cycles of speculative growth in certain restricted areas, and of subsequent collapse. The basic form of rural land use is pastoral, and this has provided the support for the kind of social and economic system previously described (p. 717). Among the agricultural cycles that have left their imprint on the landscape of the rural East are the sugar, coffee, rice, and orange cycles. In addition, there are considerable parts of the East not touched by any of these; and now the signs of rapid and fundamental agricultural change have appeared.

The Sugar Cycle

The earliest of the speculative cycles to develop in the East was the cultivation of sugarcane. Sugarcane was not a new crop in this part of Brazil, for it had been grown since early colonial times in the lower areas along the coast. Wealthy sugarcane growers owned plantations around the outskirts of colonial Rio de Janeiro, and the word *engenho* is preserved in the names of many of the sections of the city—for example, Engenho Novo, one of the northern suburbs. By the end of the sugar period there was a considerable amount of production coming from large plantations around Rio de Janeiro and Campos. According to figures given by João Antonil in 1711, the state of Rio de Janeiro in that year produced almost as much sugar as the state of Pernambuco.

For a time the new gold fever retarded the expansion of cane plantations. With the decline of gold mining many of the owners of large estates in the interior turned to the production of sugarcane. Especially in southeastern Minas Gerais, sugarcane became a crop of major importance. The higher parts of the upland which were too cool did not share in this cycle, but most of the lower valleys, even in the mountainous sections, were utilized for cane.

Several factors contributed to the decline of sugarcane planting in the East. One was perhaps the large and growing market for beef in Rio de Janeiro, which, with the scanty transportation facilities available, had to be supplied from nearby sources in order to satisfy the Brazilian preference for freshly killed meat. It became almost as profitable to fatten beef for the city market as to grow sugarcane. Another was the impoverishment of the soils, after years of hard use, especially the light soils of the Paraíba Delta. Still another reason, according to Deffontaines, was the almost complete deforestation, for the production of sugar or alcohol requires a plentiful supply of cheap fuel. At the present time, sugar production in the East has been greatly reduced in the face of the booming sugar district of São Paulo State. The landowners have turned their cane fields back into cattle pastures; a large number of people formerly employed in the cane fields have emigrated to other parts of Brazil. Only in a few spots are small areas still devoted to sugarcane.

The Coffee Cycle

Coffee was the second crop to achieve such importance in the East that it attracted new settlement and drew people away from the other parts of the country. The coffee tree had been grown around Rio de Janeiro and in the Paraíba Valley since about 1774, but its value as a commercial crop came only with the rise of a market for coffee in the cities of Europe and North America in the early nineteenth century. The first area of rapid expansion of coffee planting was in the Paraíba Valley, especially on the higher terraces and lower mountain slopes of the southern side of the valley whence the product could easily be sent out over the road to Rio de Janeiro. People came from various parts of Brazil to swell the current of migration to this new region of prosperity, and many were those who moved into the Paraíba Valley from the decadent gold-mining towns of interior Minas Gerais. The peak of production in the Paraíba Valley was reached soon after the middle of the century. From about 1860 down to the present, the coffee plantations of the Paraíba Valley have continued to decline, and are now almost entirely gone. There never had been much care of the trees or the land, and the wasteful method of planting coffee in vertical rows only on the slopes— which agricultural specialists do not advise—resulted in a gradual decline of yields. The competition with better favored areas in São Paulo State sealed the doom of the coffee *fazendas* of the Paraíba Valley. More and more of the area was utilized for pasture.

Coffee was planted widely over the southern part of Minas Gerais, especially the southeastern part, as well as in the Paraíba Valley. After the freeing of the slaves in 1888, for a decade the state government attempted to bring in agricultural immigrants by offering subsidies of various kinds, as was being done with much success in neighboring São Paulo. But the conditions of life on the *fazendas* of Minas, especially the low wages and the fact that the tenants were located in scattered and isolated homes, did not appeal to the prospective immigrants. In spite of the effort, therefore, the main current of European immigration never affected Minas Gerais significantly. The coffee plantings, whether because of inadequate care, or because of poor soils, or both, little by little declined in yield and were abandoned. The life of the plantations was extended perhaps longer than might otherwise have been the case by various schemes introduced by the growers of São Paulo to maintain the price of coffee. Today a small amount of coffee still filters out from eastern Minas Gerais and from the bordering mountain districts of Espírito Santo and Rio de Janeiro. The greater part of the land, however, has been returned to grass pasture for the grazing of herds of cattle.

It was the need to provide an inexpensive means of shipping the bags of coffee to the ports that started the first large expansion of railroad-building. The first railroad in Brazil had been built in 1854 to connect one of the small landing places on the northern shore of Guanabara Bay with the base of the Great Escarpment. Soon after, another railroad was built from Rio de Janeiro to the base of the escarpment near the only low pass. This became the *Central do Brasil*. In 1873 the tracks of the Central were laid across the Great Escarpment to the Paraíba Valley. By 1875 the main line had been extended to Juiz de Fora in southern Minas Gerais, and by 1877 a branch of the main line had been built along the Paraíba Valley to São Paulo City. But by that time it was too late; the coffee plantations of the Paraíba Valley were already on the decline, and coffee planting was moving elsewhere.

The Rice Cycle

The development of a specialized rice district in the middle Paraíba Valley marks the appearance of still another agricultural cycle. Rice is one of the major items of diet of the Brazilian people, and is widely grown as a subsistence crop for local use. It would have been strange indeed if a district of specialized rice production had not appeared to supply the large and growing urban populations of Rio de Janeiro and São Paulo. As it happens, there is a section of the Paraíba Valley which is physically well suited to this crop and which borders the branch of the Central running between the two metropolises.

The middle part of the Paraíba Valley, from the big bend of the river not far from São Paulo City to the beginning of its gorge east of Entre Rios, remains broad and open between the bordering ranges of mountains. Its bottom, however, is not entirely flat. On either side it is lined with a series of terraces, somewhat dissected by tributaries to the Paraíba which in places have cut the loose terrace gravels into very rough and hilly terrain. At intervals the terraces, which stand some 50 to 100 feet above the river, advance toward the center of the valley, carried on the shoulders of buried ridges of solid rock. In these places the river flows over small rapids, bordered by high terraces on either side. Upstream from each of these narrows, the terraces retreat, leaving a wide zone of swampy floodplain through which the river meanders. The floodplain at these wide points is between 5 and 10 miles across.

The first settlement of the Paraíba Valley avoided the floodplain and even the flatter parts of the terraces. Brazilians have always preferred the hilly locations on which to plant tree crops. The coffee plantations, therefore, were mostly back from the center of the valley. But the little towns which were strung along the road between Rio de Janeiro and São Paulo were commonly located near the narrow places, where the valley could be crossed without entering the floodplain swamps. Three of the larger towns were connected directly southward by mule trails to little ports along the coast, and actually found these outlets cheaper than the longer route to Rio de Janeiro. With the decline of coffee, the Paraíba Valley also declined in population; and the coming of the railroad cut off the little remaining activity at the ports.

The use of the floodplain for the cultivation of rice on a commercial scale began in the period between 1918 and 1920. Much earlier a bit of swampy land near Taubaté had been cleared and used for rice with excellent results, but the product was consumed only locally. In 1918, however, high prices for rice in São Paulo and in Rio de Janeiro, together with the enterprise of some immigrants who came to the valley through São Paulo, resulted in a boom period of speculative development. Land values began to soar as more and more of the floodplain area was cleared and planted. The fortunate owners became wealthy; in a few years most of them had departed to share in the delights of life in São Paulo or Rio de Janeiro, leaving their estates in the hands of tenants, who also for a time were able to make good incomes both for themselves and for the owners.

Several features of this district of concentrated rice production serve to illustrate the fundamentally exploitive character of Brazilian land use. In the first place, the most important factor governing the selection of land on which to grow rice has been accessibility to the railroad. In a zone along the southern side of the floodplain, the rice fields are almost continuous, and, here, are close to the line of the Central which follows the edge of the southern terrace. Varying physical qualities of the floodplain soil or of the supply of water are disregarded—in other words, there is no sign of close adjustment of the patterns of land use to the varying character of the land. Then, too, there is no attempt to control the supply of water beyond a minimum of drainage ditches. The somewhat irregular natural floods of the Paraíba are used to cover the growing rice; if the flood fails, the rice is not covered; if the flood is too high, the rice cannot be harvested. There is no reservoir upstream, no public diversion canal, none of the hydraulic works one expects to find in a district specializing in the production of rice. We have heard so much of the intensive methods of the Oriental rice growers that we forget that rice can be grown also with very much less work. Of course the yields per acre are low. In the rice district there are fewer than 100 rural people per square mile; and there is no reason to suppose that they are more permanently established than were the coffee growers before them. In fact, a new boom crop has now made its appearance. This new crop is the orange.

The Orange Cycle

The orange cycle had its beginnings during the 1930's. Plantations of orange trees were set out in the Baixada Fluminense on the steep slopes of the hills, always with the trees arranged in vertical rows. Orange planting spread rapidly along the line of the Central through the Paraíba Valley and continued, as we shall see, into the state of São Paulo. Production increased so rapidly that by 1937 oranges ranked fifth among the Brazilian exports. About a quarter of them went to Argentina, but the remainder were sold in Europe, mostly in Great Britain, where the exceptional sweetness of the Brazilian product found much favor.

World War II put a temporary halt to the progress of the orange cycle. The plantations were for a time almost abandoned. Most of the trees on the higher parts of the slopes have died, while those at the base of the hills where water is abundant continued to thrive. There was even some increase in the domestic market for oranges, especially in São Paulo where street vendors now sell oranges to eager customers, one orange at a time. But the traditional Brazilian diet does not include much fruit. After the war the export of oranges to Europe again increased, with the major supply coming from São Paulo. The annual Brazilian production is usually between twenty and thirty million boxes.

Use of Land for Pasture

Always in the background of any speculative agricultural development is the possibility of a return to the use of the land for pasture. Through the centuries cattle have provided the one steady source of income, although, of course, it is a moderate income, and in the grazing areas there are no rapidly rising land values. Yet a surprisingly large proportion of southern Minas Gerais and the neighboring parts of Rio de Janeiro State is devoted exclusively to pasture. The traditional system of land rotation includes scattered, temporary fields devoted to the food crops: maize, rice, beans, manioc, and bananas. At the end of the period of cropping, the tenant plants grass and moves to a new place. But close to the large cities, as in the Baixada Fluminense and the Paraíba Valley, the pressure on the land to produce not only food but also charcoal has permitted a shorter and shorter period of rest under second-growth forest. As a result the soil has been so eroded and leached that now even the forest cannot come back on it. The landscape of these areas is completely denuded of trees, and resembles some of the hillier parts of western Texas. The carrying capacity of the land for cattle has been steadily declining. Close to the big cities the land is now so unproductive that it remains mostly empty—often described by the Brazilians as the *"sertão* Fluminense."

Still the demand of the city people for food—basically for rice and meat— is steadily increasing, and food prices are steadily rising. Cattle are brought from the open ranges of the distant backlands to fattening pastures in the once-forested regions. They are then sent by rail to slaughterhouses in the cities. Because of the demand for freshly killed meat rather than refrigerated meat, the supply must be regularly maintained. There is also an increasing demand for dairy products. Most of the pastures which can send milk to the cities within eight hours are used for dairy. This is a zone with a radius of not much more than 125 miles. Beyond this zone there are several communities where Swiss immigrants have concentrated on the production of cheese.

Colonies of Small Landowners

There are many Brazilians who see clearly the danger of permitting the traditional form of agricultural and pastoral land use to continue. The extent of soil destruction and the impoverishment of the natural plant cover have been described in many professional papers, and the agricultural schools have taught better agricultural methods for many generations. For a long time political leaders in Brazil have cherished the hope that more efficient farm methods might be demonstrated and spread among Brazilian farmers through the establishment of colonies of European immigrants, each farmer operating his own small property. Attempts of this sort date back to the early nineteenth century. In 1818, for example, a group of Swiss were given lands near Nova Friburgo in the Serra dos Orgãos. Unfortunately this colony never prospered, chiefly because of its isolation from any possible market for its surplus products. From a maximum of some 1,600 persons, the number dwindled to not more than a dozen families. Nevertheless, these Swiss immigrants are responsible for the start of cheese production in many of the communities of Rio de Janeiro and southern Minas Gerais, and for many of the delicious brands of cheese sent regularly now to the city markets.

Another group of colonists established since 1900 in the Serra da Mantiqueira has not been any more successful. Germans, Italians, and French were brought to Brazil with government aid and given lands in this mountain region north of the Paraíba Valley. Most of the original settlers have drifted away, and some of their settlements are now completely deserted. Isolation is chiefly responsible for this failure also; for isolation imposed the necessity for self-sufficiency, and self-sufficiency made impossible the kind of prosperity and material gain which the immigrants desired.

A more important current of pioneer, small-farmer settlement was directed to the mountains of Espírito Santo. The coast of this state was one of the earliest parts of Brazil to be occupied by the Portuguese; but the settlements were so continuously subjected to the attack of warlike Indians that the Portuguese were forced to abandon all but a few defensible spots. In the nineteenth century a considerable part of the forest lands of western Espírito Santo was cleared and planted with coffee by the large landowners moving in from Minas Gerais. But the zone in between these two areas of Brazilian settlement—between the coastal towns and the coffee *fazendas* of the western border—remained unoccupied.

As the Indians were little by little subdued through contact with the Brazilians, this mountainous and heavily forested country in central Espírito Santo was opened for European colonization. At first, from about 1840 to 1850, the colonists were chiefly Austrian and German; from 1877 to 1899 was the period of Italian colonization, which accounted for some 65,000 persons, a little less than double the estimated number of Germans; in the 1920's the immigrants included many Poles. In each case the land was divided into small properties of about 125 acres each; and the newcomers built substantial homes and did their own work. They planted maize, rice, manioc, and coffee, depending on the latter crop for a cash return. Where the mountain settlements were too high to produce coffee, they have for the most part been abandoned; but coffee, until about 1930, brought considerable profit to the colonies at lower altitudes.

Prosperity from coffee, however, did not mean stability. Contrary to the hopes of the government, the immigrants failed to continue their own efficient farm methods. Instead they adopted the system of land rotation. After a few years, when the coffee yields of the plantations in Espírito Santo began to decline, the colonists planted pasture grass, rented their farms to the cattle owners, and moved on northward to virgin land. As a result, a frontier of pioneer settlement crept steadily northward toward the Rio Doce. But it was a frontier that left behind it devastated lands, used now for temporary pasture. The earlier settled lands declined in the value of production and in the density of population. This is what we have called a "hollow frontier" because of the declining population back of the pioneer zone.

In 1926 a new bridge was built across the Rio Doce at Collatina. This immediately opened the virgin forests north of the river to settlement. A wave of new pioneer settlement went forward into this zone, again with coffee as the chief commercial crop, with patches of the basic food crops, and with pasture as the end result. So the colonies of small farmers, yielding to the lure of speculative profits from the use of virgin lands, have broken up, many of the original settlers having drifted into the cities, many of the sons and daughters having adopted the speculative system of land rotation which they learned from their Brazilian neighbors.

There is another area of small-farmer settlement in the East where the story runs along somewhat different lines. The Baixada Fluminense around Guanabara Bay, with its hilly surface and its tidal swamps, was never an important area of settlement. It was a matter of comment among the travelers to Brazil during the nineteenth century that most of the food supply for Rio de Janeiro City came from a great distance: from Campos, from São Paulo, from Minas Gerais. There were only a few sugarcane plantations on the more favorable sites, and a few coffee plantations which were later used for cattle. The demand for charcoal for use in cooking in the city resulted in the rapid destruction of the forest; but the lowland was occupied by few permanent settlers.

In 1935 the federal government began work on a project to drain and clear the swamps on the northern side of Guanabara Bay. Dikes and gates were built so that water from the rivers could escape at low tide, but the sea water could not return at high tide. The mangrove was cleared away and a considerable area of productive soil was reclaimed. On this new land farmers were settled on small properties; some were selected from among applicants from Brazil, some from foreign countries, including Japan. In this mixed colony a high degree of stability has been achieved for two reasons: first, there is no vast area of virgin land in the vicinity; and second, the colony is located close to a large market. The farmers grow vegetables and bananas which they sell in nearby Rio de Janeiro.

Signs of Agricultural Change

The traditional system of land rotation was never effectively challenged by the settlement of immigrant colonists in the East. With only a few exceptions the colonists have themselves adopted the Brazilian system. Yet, as we have seen in the introductory discussion of Brazilian agriculture, the kind of land on which the system of land rotation has been practiced for four centuries is now almost used up. And the destruction of the resource base has been most complete in those areas that are near the large urban centers.

About 1950, however, an entirely new development began to appear in Brazil. With technical assistance from the International Basic Economy Corporation (IBEC), an agency privately established by Nelson Rockefeller, some of the *fazendeiros* of the Paraíba Valley were encouraged to try out modern farm technology. The lands they owned were among the poorest of the valley. But by applying methods of rebuilding the soil through the use of soil conditioners and fertilizers, and by using machinery to plow horizontal furrows along the contours instead of vertically up and down the slopes, these worn-out lands have been made highly productive. A more spectacular example of how modern technology can rescue thoroughly destroyed land could not have been devised. From this original undertaking, near São José dos Campos, the use of modern technology is now rapidly spreading— but chiefly into progressive São Paulo State.

It is important to note what this kind of agricultural improvement has meant. On the *fazenda* that first attempted to make use of the new technology (owned by Sr. Olivo Gomez) there were some 800 tenants, enjoying the usual kind of close attachment to the owner, but living in great poverty. When the new methods were adopted, this meant that only about 300 tenants would be needed. Sr. Gomez, anticipating the need to remove some 500 tenants from the land and yet feeling responsible for their welfare, invested capital in a new textile plant in São José dos Campos, which provided employment for the workers displaced from farming. For Brazil as a whole, the much-needed improvement of agriculture must be accompanied by a large investment of new capital in other kinds of employment.

Minerals and Industries in the East

The East of Brazil possesses other resources than those of soil and vegetation. This region is also endowed with a remarkable store of minerals, of which gold is by no means potentially the most important. Although the decline of the placer gold workings left many of the earlier settlements of Minas Gerais stranded, this decline was not the result of the exhaustion of the minerals but only the playing out of the more obvious and accessible deposits. There is still a wealth of gold and diamonds, and in addition there are many other minerals of vital importance in terms of modern large-scale industries. Perhaps these mineral resources may lead to the development of a stabilized pattern of settlement where farming and stock-raising failed.

One of the sources of gold, indeed, has continued to support a stabilized mining community for more than a century. This is the famous Morro Velho mine, which was opened up by a British company in 1834 and has been continuously in operation ever since. It is located in the Serra do Espinhaço, a short distance south of Belo Horizonte, at a place where a most unusual ore body was discovered. Morro Velho has the distinction of having one of the two deepest mines in the world: its shafts have followed a rich gold-bearing vein to a depth of more than 8,000 feet. At a depth of 6,726 feet, the rock in the shaft had a temperature of 121°, and it was necessary to build an air-cooling plant to permit operations at lower levels. Yet the richness of the ore has provided a steady income in spite of increasing costs.

Iron and Steel

Brazil's outstanding mineral reserve, however, is its extraordinary supply of high-grade iron ore. Iron and maganese have been found at many places in the crystalline rocks of the Brazilian highlands, but the largest ore bodies are in and around the southern end of the Serra do Espinhaço. These ore bodies have an iron content of 50 to 68 percent, with very few impurities (phosphorus, for example, only .02 percent). Furthermore, these ores are so disposed that they can be mined by simple quarrying without expensive tunnels and shafts.

The Brazilians were aware of their endowment of iron ore as early as 1590, a century before gold was discovered in Minas Gerais, but no special value could be placed on so large a body of ore until modern methods of large-scale mining and the modern demand for things made of steel were developed. In 1817 a French engineer named Monlevade built a blast furnace in Caeté in the Serra do Espinhaço, east of the site of Belo Horizonte. The furnace was fired with charcoal to smelt the iron. In 1825, French capital was used to form the *Companhia Siderúrgica Belgo-Mineira,* located at Sabará near Caeté. In 1921 the plants of Belgo-Mineira were expanded and a new one was built at Monlevade, near Sabará, where that company now operates the largest steel plant in the world that is wholly dependent on charcoal. So great was the demand for fuel that large areas of Minas Gerais were completely denuded of forest and the Belgo-Mineira and other charcoal-using plants were faced with a crisis. Now extensive plantations of fast-growing Eucalyptus provide the charcoal.

Still, after World War I the Brazilian ore bodies lay almost untouched. When the quantity and quality of these ores was first described scientifically in 1910 by the North American geologist Orville Derby, then head of the Brazilian Geological Survey, there was a scramble for mining concessions. The ore bodies were quickly divided up among British, North American, French, German, and Brazilian owners. The largest ore body was found to be located at Itabira, on the eastern side of the Serra do Espinhaço in the valley of the Rio Doce. Another large ore body was identified at Lafaiete, near the main line of the Central on the southern flank of the mountains (Map 115). In 1919 a British–North American syndicate, headed by the veteran North American business builder, Percival Farquhar,[4] laid plans for the large-scale mining and export of iron ore from Itabira. The chief problem was the development of a modern railroad to connect Itabira with the coast, and the construction of a modern ore dock. Farquhar employed the best engineers to draw up the plans. He had command of enough capital to finance the project, and he had the assurance of a large market for the ore in the Ruhr of Germany. But in Brazil he met stubborn opposition. There were some who feared the economic dislocations that would inevitably follow the building of a large-scale industrial enterprise, in which costs per unit would be much less than in the old small-scale operations. There were some who were genuinely disturbed by the idea that a foreign-owned corporation might gain too large a measure of control over a part of the national territory. The great majority of those Brazilians in positions of political power subscribed then, as they do now, to the principle that Brazilian resources should be used to enrich Brazil, or at least Brazilians. As a result the first large-scale mining and export of iron ore in Latin America took place in Venezuela, not in Brazil.

During World War II, however, Brazil started to build a modern steel plant. As a part of a program of wartime cooperation between Brazil and the United States, a loan was granted to purchase steel-making equipment. North American technicians were assigned to the task of building the plant and

---

[4]See the masterful study of this important person by Charles A. Gauld, *The Last Titan, Percival Farquhar: American Entrepreneur in Latin America,* Hispanic American Reports, Special Issue, Stanford University, 1964.

The Gilherme Guinle steel plant in the Paraíba Valley, formerly Volta Redonda. *Courtesy of Brazilian National Steel.*

training the workers. Construction started in 1942, and the first steel was produced in 1946. The first unit had a capacity of 300,000 tons annually. The capacity has now been expanded to more than a million tons, and plans are drawn up to provide a capacity of 3,500,000 tons—which means that Brazil's steel plant is the largest in Latin America. It is owned by the government and operated by the *Companhia Siderúrgica Nacional.*

The Gilherme Guinle Steel Plant, as the plant is now called, was built at Volta Redonda in the Paraíba Valley, near the western border of the state of Rio de Janeiro. There are a number of advantages to this site. In the first place, railroad and motor highway give access to the two largest markets for steel in Brazil—Rio de Janeiro and São Paulo, which together account for 75 percent of the total steel consumption of the country. In the second place, Volta Redonda is a good place at which to assemble raw materials. The iron ore comes from Lafaiete in Minas Gerais, the manganese from Congonhas, the limestone from quarries in western Minas Gerais. The Rio Paraíba provides a sufficient supply of water, which is needed in large quantities in steel manufacture. Coal has to be lifted over the Great Escarpment from a seaport. A part of the supply comes from coal mines in Santa Catarina in the South of Brazil. But this coal must be pulverized, washed, and made into briquettes before it can be used. Brazilian coal supplies about 30 percent of the needs at Volta Redonda. The remainder is imported from West Virginia and from Poland. In order to insure the uninterrupted movement of coal, the railroad was entirely rebuilt: tunnels were enlarged, heavier rails were installed, and the line was electrified. Much of the coal now comes through the port of Angra dos Reis.

In addition to the Gilherme Guinle plant, two other large-scale steel operations have been built in Brazil, making use of imported coal. One is the Brazilian owned *Companhia Siderúrgica Piaçaguera* (COSIPA), located on the bay near Santos in the state of São Paulo. The other is the *Usinas Siderúrgicas Minas Gerais* (USIMINAS), located on the Rio Doce in the state of Minas Gerais. This one is owned by private investors in Brazil (60 percent) and Japan (40 percent). Two new charcoal-steel plants have been built in Minas Gerais: one is the Mannesmann plant at Belo Horizonte, which is a German and Brazilian company; and the other is a Brazilian company—the *Companhia Aços Especiais Itabira* (ACESITA)—which makes high-quality steel for special uses. In 1964 there were 131 smaller plants producing pig iron and steel, about half of the total production being made with charcoal and half with coal. As a result of the completion of the large-scale plants, the export of iron and steel products, which was 16,500,000 metric tons in 1964, rose to 30 million tons in 1965.

Within the states that make up the East, there were many new factories built since 1960 to make use of this supply of domestic steel. Consumer goods of great variety are manufactured, mostly for sale in Brazil. In 1965 there were five shipbuilding firms with yards located around Guanabara Bay. The largest was a Japanese company known as Ishikawajima, in the state of Guanabara. It was equipped to manufacture marine engines and ships up to 100,000 tons.

In 1962 the Brazilians and ten Japanese firms drew up what was then the largest contract for the export of iron ore ever negotiated. Over a fifteen-year period, Brazil is to send some 50 million tons of ore to Japan. At last the development which Percival Farquhar foresaw during the 1920's is being realized. The ore comes largely from Itabira and is carried down the Rio

The new iron-ore shipping port of Tubarão, north of Vitória. *Courtesy of Brazilian Government Trade Bureau.*

Doce valley by a newly-built railroad. The ore-shipping docks at Vitória were totally inadequate for such a huge volume of shipping, and therefore new facilties were built at Tubarão,[5] a few miles north of Vitória (inset on Map 115). Long piers protected by breakwaters can accommodate the new 100,000-ton ore carriers, loading 6,000 tons of ore each hour. It is planned to build another steel plant at Tubarão, using coal brought in by ship. And since the process of converting iron ore into pellets, from which water has been largely eliminated, has greatly reduced the cost of shipping ore, a pel-letizing plant is being built, also at Tubarão. The huge new ore-shipping port includes automatic car-dumping machinery, repair shops, and a great variety of other pieces of equipment needed to guarantee the handling of a huge vol-ume of ore without expensive delays.

In 1966 the Brazilian government issued a decree permitting the construc-tion of other ore-shipping ports by private firms, provided that they "do not constitute a public burden, or endanger national security." As a result, an-other iron-ore mining company, the Antunes-Hanna combine, is investing a large amount of money in opening up new iron mines, building transporta-tion, and establishing another ore-shipping port similar to Tubarão. The Antunes interests are made up of private Brazilian investors, and the Hanna interests are owned in the United States. Within a few years the Antunes-Hanna combine will become the world's largest iron-ore mining and exporting company. Pelletizing plants and the latest and most efficient machinery will be available for the low-cost production and shipment of ore. The Antunes-Hanna port will be built on Sepitiba Bay to the west of Rio de Janeiro.

The Sertões of the East

In back of these spectacular new developments of the industrial East, are the *sertões*—the thinly peopled backlands. From these remote areas come small but important supplies of such minerals as zirconium, chromium, molybdenum, nickel, tungsten, titanium, industrial diamonds, beryl, mica, and quartz crystals for electrical use. Brazil is famous for its semiprecious gem stones, such as aquamarine, amethyst, tourmaline, and topaz. But the major product of the backlands is cattle. The important fact is that for not only the people of Pernambuco and Bahia, but also those of Minas Gerais and Rio de Janeiro, the great valley of the Rio São Francisco is *the sertão*.

The Rio São Francisco rises in Minas Gerais, only a short distance north-west of Rio de Janeiro. More than a thousand miles to the north it turns sharply to the east to plunge in numerous falls and rapids to the sea. From Juazeiro and its twin town Petrolina on the opposite bank of the river, the São Francisco is navigable for small river steamers as far upstream as Pirapora, at the end of the railroad from Belo Horizonte. The lower part of the valley, in Bahia, is more subject to droughts than is the part farther south

[5]Not to be confused with the port for shipping coal in Santa Catarina.

in Minas Gerais. Its inhabitants are clustered in small villages and towns, closely attached to the sources of water where land is irrigated. The wetter upper part seems to have greater agricultural possibilities, yet today it is more thinly inhabited. The completion of the railroad to Pirapora resulted in a depopulation of the rural districts of this area as people sought the greater economic opportunities at the railhead.

The whole valley is a region of poverty. The chief use of the land is for the grazing of cattle, and these are driven on the hoof to cattle fairs on the margins of the *sertão,* notably at Tres Coraçoes and Campo Belo in Minas Gerais. All over the vast expanse of country there are small villages and towns lost in leagues of empty land. Between them trails, passable for jeeps in the dry season, are traveled at all times by mule trains and oxcarts. Small areas are used for raising cotton, rice, manioc, maize, and sugarcane, but the agricultural products that are sent out of the region are very few. Salt from springs near Juazeiro is shipped upstream for the cattle of Minas Gerais. From the little port of Januária, salt is carried by pack train all over the *sertões* of Goiás.

Most of the land is divided into large private estates, but not even the estate owners are prosperous. Life in the *sertão,* which seems so mysterious to the city-dwellers of Brazil who have never visited such regions, has actually resulted in a kind of democracy in which no one enjoys sufficient income to make him the object of envy or to give him much economic or political power over his fellows. The poor hygiene and inadequate diet create a patient resignation or apathy in the face of difficulties. For the inhabitant of the *sertão* there is no mystery about the process of living in the "backlands"; any move toward a solution of the problems of bettering the economic life, he feels, must come from what to him is indeed a mystical power—the federal government.

Rio de Janeiro

Perhaps nowhere in South America is the contrast between city and country sharper and more vivid than between the hinterland of the Brazilian East and Brazil's magnificent city, Rio de Janeiro.[6] In contrast to the emptiness and poverty of much of the interior of the East, Rio de Janeiro is one of the most

[6]The whole urban area of Rio de Janerio in 1960 was made up as follows:

Rio de Janeiro	3,233,000
Nova Iguaçu	258,000
São Gonçalo	196,000
São João de Meriti	192,000
Duque de Caxias	176,000
Níteroi	229,000
Total in urban area:	4,284,000

The entrance to Guanabara Bay and the Sugar Loaf, Rio de Janeiro. *Courtesy of Brazilian Government Trade Bureau.*

strikingly beautiful cities in the world. Established originally where the knobby ribs of the coastal mountains border the western side of Guanabara Bay (Map 128), the city now occupies several narrow lowlands between projecting rocky ridges. It has extended both northward into the lowland back of the coastal mountains and southward to the crescentic beaches of white sand which are festooned from headland to headland along the Atlantic. During the period since the beginning of this century, the old, unhealthful, unimproved Portuguese city, which reminded one of an overgrown rural village, has been transformed into a metropolis. Fine new docks border the bay; the mangrove swamps, once infested with fever-carrying mosquitoes, have been cleaned away; and along the margin of the water a stone seawall has been built, with a wide tree-lined avenue between it and the first row of buildings. In the downtown section, at one end of the famous Avenida Rio Branco, a group of new office buildings, constructed on modern lines, has made its appearance; and along the nearest of the Atlantic beaches, in the Copacabana district, modern-style apartment buildings and hotels face the open ocean. Against the background of green, forest-clad mountains, bare rocky cliffs, and blue water, the city presents an unforgettable picture in a frame of unparalleled design.

Not all of the city is beautiful, however. Rio de Janeiro has its slums, the *favellas,* some of them located on the slopes of the rocky ridges which overlook the throbbing business district or the gay beach at Copacabana. The nearly 5 million people who live in the urban area include many who are crowded into miserable homes and who have little opportunity to appreciate the magnificence of the picture of which they are a part.

The modern-style skyscrapers strung along the bay or along the Atlantic give the impression that this growth is not something that has sprung from the land, but rather something which has come from across the sea. Investigation confirms the impression. Rio de Janeiro made its start, to be sure, during the great gold period of Minas Gerais, when it was selected as the outlet for the wealth of the East. But when the capital of Brazil was transferred from Salvador to Rio de Janeiro in 1763, and especially when, in 1808, the Portuguese king, fleeing from Europe, made Rio de Janeiro the capital of the whole Portuguese world, the little town with its muddy or dusty streets, and its bad record for fevers, began to extend its influence far beyond the limits of its immediate hinterland.

In the modern period, Rio de Janeiro has actually left its immediate hinterland far behind. Its hinterland today is all of Brazil. Located midway between the clusters of people grouped along the coasts of the Northeast and of the southern part of Brazil, (Maps 116 and 121), and located also close by the economically most productive state of São Paulo, Rio de Janeiro has become the hub of commercial exchange for all these widely scattered communities. But its connections are *by sea;* coasting steamers, in fact, carry by far the greater proportion of Brazil's whole domestic trade. Of all the imports to Brazil from foreign countries, nearly half come to Rio de Janeiro. Some of the imported goods are then shipped by coasting steamer to other ports of Brazil, both north and south. Steel and other manufactured products originating in the East are sent by steamer to other areas of concentrated settlement along

The beach at Copacabana, Rio de Janeiro. *Photo Courtesy—Pan American Airways.*

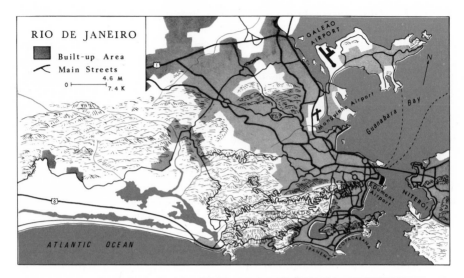

Map 128

the coast. No small part of the continued growth of this city is due to the fact that most of Brazil's 86 million inhabitants live near the coast, not inland: any important movement of people inland would reduce the importance of Rio de Janeiro.

Because Rio de Janeiro was chosen as the capital, as well as because it is preeminent in economic advantages, much of the wealth of Brazil has been concentrated there. The interests of the nation focused on the capital, and to the capital came the leaders of business, politics, and art. Like the picture in a crystal ball, Rio de Janeiro mirrors the complete Brazilian scene, from the throbbing activities of the cities to the utter desolation of the *sertão*. When Brazil's capital was moved to Brasília in 1960, and when efforts were made to move people into the backlands, it seemed that Rio de Janeiro might decline in importance. When and if this happens, it will be because Brazil has adopted the policy of looking inward. As long as Brazil plays its part in the modern world, Rio de Janeiro will continue to grow.

Chapter 28 □ Brazil: São Paulo

Only a little more than 200 miles southwest of Rio de Janeiro is another city of over 5 million inhabitants—São Paulo. We can understand how Rio de Janeiro might have attained its great size, for, as we have said, in it are focused the interests of the people scattered over the whole of Brazil— not only the political interests of the nation but also the commercial, intellectual, and artistic. On first thought São Paulo might seem to be just another example of the trend toward a multiplicity of urban centers. Yet cities of over a million are not created simply by decree; they achieve such numbers only as the result of the operation of social and economic forces. The processes that led to the rise of this other great metropolis, today the largest center of manufacturing industry in Latin America, must be examined in order to understand why Brazil is one of the few countries of the world with no primate city.

The cluster of people of which São Paulo City is the urban nucleus is of recent origin, and only since the middle of the last century has it wielded a predominant influence in Brazilian economic affairs. In the historical background is that great trilogy of wealth-bringing products—sugar, gold, and coffee. The story of São Paulo is the story of the sweep of coffee across the state, and of the consequences of that wave of speculative exploitation. The beginnings date back to the early decades of the nineteenth century, to a period when "coffee shoppes" had become a fad in England and when coffee was being advertised as the cure for a long list of diseases. The new beverage gained swiftly in popularity. As in the case of the spread of the sugar market three centuries earlier, Brazil began to produce at the very beginning of a rising market, and went on to capture the larger share of the international trade. This is a commercial situation in which a maximum of profits are to be made by the producers with a minimum of investment in

771

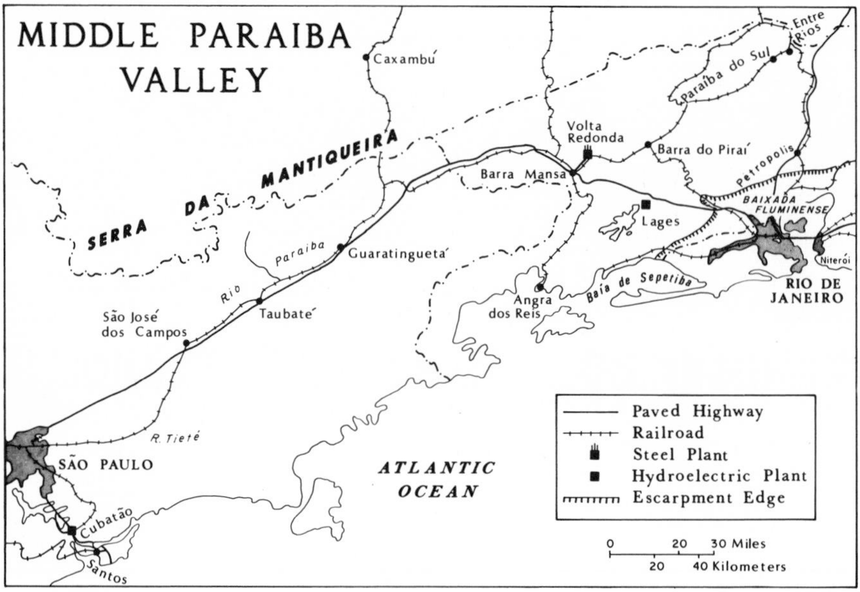
MIDDLE PARAIBA VALLEY
Caxambú
Entre Rios
Paraiba do Sul
Volta Redonda
Barra do Piraí
Petropolis
SERRA DA MANTIQUEIRA
Barra Mansa
BAIXADA FLUMINENSE
Lages
Rio Paraiba
Guaratinguetá
Niterói
Baía de Sepetiba
RIO DE JANEIRO
Angra dos Reis
São José dos Campos
Taubaté
R. Tieté
SÃO PAULO
ATLANTIC OCEAN
Cubatão
Santos
Paved Highway
Railroad
Steel Plant
Hydroelectric Plant
Escarpment Edge
0 20 30 Miles
20 40 Kilometers

Map 129

production. In the decade between 1870 and 1880 Brazil was furnishing about half of the world's supply of coffee. Brazil still provides nearly 40 percent of the world's exported coffee, in spite of greatly increased production in Colombia, Middle America, and some African countries.

Since early in the present century Brazil has been plagued by the overproduction of coffee. In the year ending in September 1966 Brazil's total coffee production amounted to 37,600,000 bags (46 percent of the total world production). But the International Coffee Agreement now sets quotas for the coffee-producing countries of the world, and Brazil's quota for 1966 was 17,300,000 bags. Brazil had enough coffee in storage to supply the whole world market for more than a year. Only in 1966 did the Brazilian government start to take effective steps to reduce coffee production by uprooting millions of coffee trees.

In the development of coffee as Brazil's principal product, the state of São Paulo has played the leading role. This one state has produced between 65 and 75 percent of all the coffee in Brazil. After the end of the coffee period in 1930, São Paulo took the lead in developing other commercial crops, including sugarcane, cotton, oranges, and bananas. Furthermore, the spectacular development of manufacturing industries, especially since World War II, was concentrated in and around the city of São Paulo. As a result São Paulo has achieved a level of economic production unequalled in any other part of the country. This one state has been furnishing from 30 to 40 percent of the revenue of the federal treasury. Today in the rural areas of São Paulo we find the largest measure of acceptance of the new technologies

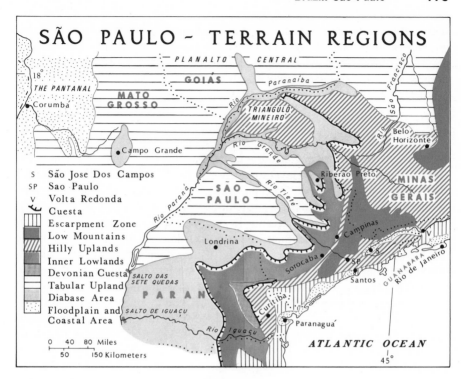

Map 130

of agriculture; and in urban São Paulo we find the kind of businesslike atmosphere and hustle that characterizes the other great metropolitan centers of the western world. The contrast between São Paulo and most other parts of Brazil is striking (see Maps 112, 113, 114, 115, and 116).

The Land

The land on which these events are taking place is arranged in a pattern somewhat more convenient for the needs of the inhabitants than is the case in the East. There is the familiar combination of crystalline uplands, low mountains, and tablelands of stratified rock as in other parts of the Brazilian highlands, but the design of all these elements is much simpler than that of the East. Along the low coast the climatic conditions are those of the rainy tropics, but in the highlands distinctly lower temperatures are experienced. In the southern part of the state, the beginning of the zone of transition appears between areas suited to tropical plants and areas from which such plants are excluded because of low temperatures and frosts. São Paulo also has the *terra roxa.*[1]

Surface Features

Immediately back of a narrow zone of wet lowland along the coast, the Great Escarpment rises to elevations between 2,600 and 2,900 feet. Generally the Atlantic margin of the Brazilian highlands is composed of a wide zone of block mountains and narrow structural valleys, descending by a series of steps from the unbroken upland to below sea level (Map 112). This is the situation in Espírito Santo and in Rio de Janeiro; and it is also the situation in the southwestern part of São Paulo State, where the angular valleys of the zone of the Escarpment are threaded by the tributaries of the Rio Iguapé. But from a point somewhat southwest of Santos northeastward approximately to the border between the states of São Paulo and Rio de Janeiro, the Great Escarpment forms one unbroken slope from the edge of the upland to the sea. This is the section to which the name Serra do Mar was originally applied. Where the Iguapé brings down to the coast a heavy load of waste material worn from the eroded edge of the highlands, the foot of the Escarpment is bordered by a narrow alluvial lowland, rearranged by the waves and shore currents into long curving beaches of white sand backed by mangrove-filled lagoons. Santos is built at the easternmost end of this lowland fringe. Where the single slope of the Great Escarpment descends directly to the water's edge and is drained only by short torrents, so little alluvium is brought down that the bays and promontories are largely unmodified by bars and spits, and the island of São Sebastião remains separated from the mainland. The Baía de Sepitiba, on the border between São Paulo and Rio de Janeiro, is open to the Atlantic, with only the beginning of a sandbar forming on its eastern side.

Above the Great Escarpment the upland, which is drained by the tributaries of the Rio Paraná, has a conspicuously even skyline, especially striking as one reaches the crest of the Serra do Mar above Santos and enters the gently sloping hill country of the São Paulo Basin. The valleys on the upland are broad and generally swampy along their bottoms; the interfluves rise in broad sweeping curves to the uniform summit elevation of about 2,600 feet above the sea. A few ranges of low mountains, or strings of mountain knobs, stand above this general level, and one such range separates the basin of São Paulo from the interior of São Paulo State. Between the São Paulo Basin and the Paraíba Valley there is a sharp drop: the Central Railroad which

[1] *Roxa,* in Portuguese, means "purple"; it is pronounced ró-shah.

The Great Escarpment between Santos and São Paulo consists of one steep slope, about 2,600 feet high. This air view shows the reservoir on the crest of the escarpment. In the background is the lowland around Santos. *Courtesy of São Paulo Tramway, Light, and Power Co.*

connects São Paulo with Rio de Janeiro by way of the Paraíba Valley descends about 550 feet in 15 miles at it leaves the São Paulo Basin.[2]

Only the eastern and southern parts of São Paulo State lie within the area of crystalline rocks. On the inland side of the range of mountains which separates the São Paulo Basin from the rest of the state there is

[2]Persons interested in the physiography of Brazil should note the river capture which has taken place east of São Paulo City. The São Paulo Basin is drained by the Rio Tietê, which crosses through a gap in the mountains northwestward toward the Paraná. In recent geologic times, the streams which now form the headwaters of the Paraíba were tributaries of the Tietê. The big bend of the Paraíba is the result of the capture of these headwaters by the stream which flows eastward to reach the Atlantic near Campos (Map 129, p. 772). The eastern part of São Paulo State which was thus transferred to the Paraíba drainage is now a conspicuously even-topped upland, with its summit level about the same as that of the São Paulo Basin; the valleys have been deeply incised in intrenched meanders below the upland surface.

only a narrow band of crystalline upland. Beyond this the granites and gneisses disappear beneath a covering of stratified rocks, the layers of which dip gently toward the west and north. Map 130 shows the northern end of the great Paraná Plateau. Geologically this plateau is a structural basin of sedimentary rocks with layers of diabase (see also Map 8, p. 23, and Map 112, p. 689). The oldest sedimentary layers, which rest on the crystallines, are easily eroded by the streams. As a result, where these layers outcrop they have been excavated to produce an *inner lowland,* and the streams which descend into this inner lowland from the edge of the crystalline upland do so over falls and rapids. Along the margin of the crystallines in São Paulo there is a string of towns, such as Sorocaba, Itú, Campinas, and Mogi-Mirím, where the relationships are similar to those of the "fall-line" towns of the southeastern United States, except that the rivers are flowing inland rather than toward the ocean.

Among the various layers of rock which cover the granites and gneisses in the Paraná Plateau, some are more resistant than others. In the midst of the inner lowland, for instance, there are certain strata which are enough stronger than the formations on either side of them to hold up a belt of low hills along their outcrop. But the inner lowland is sharply terminated in the north and west by the steep face of a cuesta, capped by almost vertical cliffs of diabase. This rock, which is of volcanic origin, was originally laid down in molten sheets either on the surface or squeezed between layers of rock near the surface. Being so much more resistant than the sedimentary rocks around it, the outcrop of diabase, throughout this part of Brazil, is marked by steep cliffs; and because the diabase layer dips toward the north and west, like the other rocks in the western part of São Paulo, the steep face of the cuesta is always toward the south and east athwart the lines of traffic. In southern São Paulo the general level of the inner lowland is between 1,900 and 2,200 feet above the sea; but the top of the diabase cuesta, like the top of the crystalline upland, rises some 600 feet higher. The cuesta is sharp and continuous where it enters São Paulo from Paraná, and is interrupted only in its northward swing where the northwest-flowing rivers have cut water gaps through it. In northern São Paulo, the diabase cuesta cuts across the inner lowland and borders the crystallines, here standing above the general level of the hilly upland to the east. Since the diabase in the north is much broken by faults, the cuesta appears in detached pieces.

From the crest of the diabase cuesta the land slopes gently westward toward the Rio Paraná. Although the southern part of the Paraná Plateau is mostly composed of diabase at the surface, in São Paulo this rock appears only in a narrow band where its outcrop forms the cuesta. Most of the Paraná Plateau in western São Paulo is made up of sandstones resting on the diabase, with the latter exposed only in the valley bottoms. Wherever the rivers encounter diabase in their channels they form rapids, as is the case along much of the course of the Rio Paraná.

Soils

The soils of São Paulo State are closely related to the underlying rock. On the crystalline upland the reddish clay soil, known as *massapê,* is formed similar to that found throughout eastern Brazil where the crystallines are exposed under a semideciduous forest cover. Among the soils of the Paraná Plateau, the *terra roxa,* formed on the outcrops of the diabase, is the best known. This is a deep, porous soil containing considerable humus, which can be easily recognized by its dark reddish-purple color. When it is wet it becomes so slippery and sticky that travel over it is very difficult, and in dry weather it gives off a powdery red dust which stains everything it touches. On the outcrops of sandstone, a light-colored, sandy soil is formed, known as *terra arenosa.* These popularly recognized soil types have been described and mapped by the state soil survey.

Soils cannot properly be described in such general terms as good or bad, fertile or infertile. Fertility is always in relation to the use intended for the soil. The *terra roxa,* for example, is excellent for coffee trees, especially as its porosity allows the roots to penetrate far into the ground. Its chemical composition, however, is such that, for cotton, it is an inferior soil, for the plant tends to form branches and leaves instead of fiber. Detailed technical studies by soil specialists and agronomists are needed in any agricultural region to determine which soils and which techniques are best suited to bring desired results. One important point regarding many of the soils of São Paulo has been made clear by the experience of the past half-century: that is their tendency to erode rapidly, especially when they are used without fertilizer for the production of cotton. When, through bad agricultural practices, the *terra roxa* is allowed to dry out at the surface, it is especially liable to erode during the next heavy rain.

Climate and Vegetation

São Paulo as a whole is a region of abundant moisture (Maps 11, 12, 13, pp. 31, 32, 33). Along the coast the amount of cloudiness and rainfall is great. One of the rainiest places in Brazil is found on the slopes of the Great Escarpment and of the zone of the Escarpment. An average of nearly 150 inches is recorded on the Serra do Mar between Santos and São Paulo. The zone of heavy rains, however, is narrow; São Paulo City, less than 35 miles from Santos, receives an average annual rainfall of only 56 inches. Most of the state receives between 50 and 60 inches, and only the Great Escarpment and the zone of the Escarpment are likely to remain sparsely inhabited because of excessive moisture.

A very important change occurs in the regimen of the rainfall along the southern boundary of São Paulo. In the south there is no winter dry season such as is found generally throughout the highlands of tropical Brazil. A little south of Sorocaba a rather sharp line separates the area of winter drought from the area of year-round rain.

Temperatures show marked differences between the coast and the interior of São Paulo. At coastal stations like Santos the temperature is moderately high, ranging from 66° in winter to 78° in summer. On the higher parts of the plateau average temperatures are some ten degrees lower. At São Paulo City the coldest and warmest months average 58° and 69° respectively. Toward the west and north in the interior of the state the temperatures increase; in the valley of the Paraná the average of the coldest month is above 65°.

There is an important temperature boundary as well as an important rainfall boundary in southern São Paulo and northern Paraná, where the northern limit of frosts appears. Frosts occur at times in the higher mountains of the East, in Minas Gerais, but south of the latitude of Sorocaba they come frequently enough to make the planting of tropical crops somewhat hazardous. In the boundary area, frosts occur only in the higher valleys and on south-facing slopes. In northern Paraná, frosts come almost every year, but they are distributed in patches or frost pockets, interspersed with many frost-free spots. In middle Paraná there are no frost-free spots on the plateau, and freezing temperatures are experienced every winter. Frosts do not occur along the coast, nor in the Paraná Valley and its deeper tributaries.

The various climatic features which have been described are nicely reflected in the pattern of the natural vegetation (Map 15, p. 35). Along the coast and on the rainy slopes of the Escarpment there is a dense tropical rain forest composed of broadleaf evergreen species with many epiphytes and lianes. In the cloud zone of the upper part of the Escarpment the trees are moss-covered and the ground is almost constantly soaked with moisture. On the highlands, however, forests and grasslands are intermingled. Semideciduous forests once grew luxuriantly on the slopes of the mountains and over most parts of the crystalline upland; dense forests marked the outcrops of diabase to such a degree that some of the early travelers in that region said that a map of forests was a map of the geology. Semideciduous forests, becoming denser toward the west, covered the whole of western São Paulo down to the Rio Paraná. This river formed and still forms an amazingly sharp vegetation boundary, for immediately west of it are the woodland savannas which the Brazilians call *campo cerrado*.

Within the forested areas of São Paulo State there were numerous grassy openings. The São Paulo Basin itself was originally grass-covered, with trees only in the rainy zone near the crest of the Escarpment and on the surrounding mountains. The inner lowland was occupied by savanna with scattered scrubby trees and with galeria forest along the streams. South of Sorocaba, however, where there is no longer a dry season, the savannas were transformed by degrees into pure grass prairies, which the Brazilians call *campo limpo*. These prairies continue southward into Paraná.

The tropical semideciduous forest mixes with the midlatitude forest of Paraná in a wide zone of transition in northern Paraná and southern São Paulo. The forests to the south are composed of Araucaria pine with an undergrowth of broadleaf species not unlike the pine-oak forests of the southern Appalachians. Pines grow in places where frosts occur once in every ten years or so; the semideciduous forest is evidence that the place is frost-free.

Settlement before the Coffee Period

The first permanent settlement on the highlands of Brazil was a mission founded in 1554 on the site of the city of São Paulo. Many settlements had already been made along the coast, and in the Northeast the coastal zone was beginning to witness the rise of the sugarcane planting. No route from the coast to the highlands anywhere south of Salvador offered greater ease of penetration for the colonial Portuguese than the one from São Vicente (near Santos) to São Paulo. Not only was this part of Brazil inhabited by fewer and less hostile Indians than the region between Cabo Frio and Salvador, but the physical barriers to penetration of the interior were narrower here than they were anywhere else. A single ascent led from the coast to the upland, but, what was more important, the forest belt in this section was narrowest. To be sure, this ascent offered no advantages like those of the broad valley of the Rio Doce; but the Portuguese were less interested in an easy climb than they were in avoiding heavy woods. When a road was built over the Great Escarpment to São Paulo it made the ascent not by the easier grades now followed by the railroads, but over the very nose of a steep spur where the forest was a little less dense than in the ravines on either side. At no other point along the coast between Salvador and southern Brazil could the barrier of rain forest be crossed in so short a distance. Less than 30 miles inland the settlers came upon the open campos of the São Paulo Basin. Unlike the North American pioneers who built their homes in the woods and shrank from the open prairies, these Portuguese settlers felt secure only when they had emerged from the forests. The São Paulo mission was founded on the lower terraces overlooking the swampy valley of the Tieté in the midst of country covered with tall grass and scattered thickets of scrub trees.

The people who came to São Vicente and São Paulo were not wealthy. Anyone in Portugal with private means or with any standing at court went to Salvador or Recife; the less important came to São Paulo. They were a vigorous, energetic, adventurous people, and, coming mostly from the south of Portugal, they inherited no small amount of Moorish restlessness and lack of stability. They could not afford African slaves and the Indians were poor workers; nor was the land in the São Paulo Basin productive of wealth-bringing crops. So they began to look for other sources of wealth.

The Bandeirantes

For more than a century expeditions from São Paulo pushed into the interior of the continent, searching restlessly for sources of profit. A glance at the map (Map 6, p. 18) will indicate the enormous extent of territory they covered. From the shores of the Plata to the southern limit of the Amazon selva, the *bandeirantes* tramped through the endless *sertões* pasturing their herds of cattle. They stopped here and there to pan the stream gravels for gold or to plant temporary fields of maize. They mated with the Indian women and increased their numbers by hordes of *mameluco* children. They were not gentle people, these *bandeirantes*. Wherever they found Indians grouped together around one of the Jesuit missions they carried them away to be sold into slavery. When there were battles to be fought, or dangers to be encountered, the *bandeirantes* were ready and eager. Their expeditions were more than simply exploring parties: they constituted a way of living for a restless people in a land which, for them, contained few resources they could turn into wealth. They pushed the boundaries of Brazil far to the west of the original line of demarcation between Spanish and Portuguese territory as defined by the Treaty of Tordesillas (about 50° W.). Few are the parts of this vast domain which have not been lived in, picked over—in a sense, ransacked; many little communities now lost in the great interior of Brazil had their origin in expeditions which remained in the wilderness instead of returning eventually to São Paulo. Not until gold was discovered in Minas Gerais in 1698 and in Mato Grosso in 1719, did the wealth for which the *bandeirantes* had been searching at last come to some of them.

Sorocaba

The rise of the gold-mining communities of Minas Gerais, however, did not bring great prosperity to São Paulo, although many of the Paulistas were attracted to the new source of wealth. The large and growing population of the East did offer a market for cattle and mules. In the *sertões* of the west and south cattle were permitted to graze and breed almost without care, and mules were raised especially in Rio Grande do Sul and the Banda Oriental. It is interesting that on the two sides of the continent there should have developed the same sort of mule and cattle trade, with trails leading northward to the centers of settlement from the remote prairies east and west of the Paraná-Plata. On each side, one town achieved major importance as the scene of the annual livestock market: Sorocaba, a little west of São Paulo, played the same role for eastern South America that Salta played for the western part (p. 609).

Every year during June and July Sorocaba was crowded with people. Herders brought mules and cattle from the far south or from Mato Grosso;

buyers came not only from Rio de Janeiro and Minas Gerais, but also from distant Bahia and Pernambuco. During most of the period from the early seventeenth century until the railroads appeared in the late nineteenth century, Sorocaba remained the outstanding example in all of Brazil of a market town located on the border between the *sertões* and the regions of denser population along the coast. A town which performed this function of handling the trade and other contacts between the settled areas and the empty backlands is described in Portuguese as a *boca do sertão,* a mouth of the *sertão.*

At the close of the gold period, about 1800, the area of concentrated settlement was still in the hinterland of Rio de Janeiro, and what is today the state of São Paulo was on the fringe of settlement. The little towns of São Paulo, Campinas, and Sorocaba were *bocas dos sertões.* Around Sorocaba and Campinas the owners of *fazendas* cultivated small areas of maize or sugarcane, but derived most of their incomes from the sale of beef cattle. There was little then to differentiate this region from the other sections of the East, of which it was essentially a part. When, in the nineteenth century, coffee began to be grown in the Paraíba Valley, some of the planters around Campinas and Sorocaba added this crop to their small plots of maize and sugarcane. In the São Paulo Basin itself temperatures were too low for coffee.

The Spread of Coffee over São Paulo

In 1847 a forward-looking landowner from the vicinity of Limeira took a radical step. He had been cultivating the usual crops with African slaves, but realizing that slavery as an institution was doomed, he undertook, with government aid, to bring to his estate some eighty families of German peasants—four hundred persons in all—who were established as tenants, or *colonos.*

At first the change was slow, but the fifteen years between 1885 and 1900 witnessed the sudden transformation of the São Paulo region from an outlying part of the East to a new and independent region of settlement focusing on the city of São Paulo and the port of Santos. This sudden transformation was the result of three developments which were so closely linked that to separate cause from effect is almost impossible. The three developments were the increase of the European and North American market for coffee; the spread of coffee over São Paulo State; and the rapid immigration into São Paulo State of millions of Europeans. The result of these three developments was the profound alteration of both the Paulista landscape and the Paulista way of living.

Immigration

The figures of the population of the state tell the story. In 1872 there were about 837,000 inhabitants, located chiefly in the Paraíba Valley, and

A coffee *fazenda* in São Paulo State. Unshaded coffee covers the hill slopes. Coffee is drying on the platforms in the valley.

in the mountains and hilly uplands of the territory around Campinas, Sorocaba, and São Paulo. In 1890 there were 1,384,000 people, and the frontier of new coffee planting was beginning to roll north and west. By 1900 the population of the state had nearly doubled, reaching 2,280,000. The census of 1960 gave São Paulo a population of nearly 13 million, or more than 18 percent of the population of Brazil.

The rapid increase of population was the result of immigration which both caused and was caused by the increasing prosperity of the region. During the fifty years between 1886 and 1936 São Paulo received 2,847,687 new arrivals, or an average annual immigration of 57,000.[3]

In each of the years 1891, 1895, 1912, 1913, and 1929 the number of immigrants exceeded 100,000; but in 1903, after the first small financial crisis of the coffee region, and in 1918, after World War I, the number dropped below 20,000. Only in one year, 1915, did the departures outnumber the arrivals, but during the whole period about 48 percent eventually left Brazil. During all this time Brazil as a whole received about 4,600,000 immigrants, a somewhat smaller number than entered Argentina. São Paulo's share of this immigration was about 60 percent. There was another drop after 1936; but in the decade after World War II another 400,000 immigrants came to Brazil.

Many nationalities and races were involved in this migration. As in Argentina in the same period, Italians were the most numerous, coming in maxi-

[3]Figures from Estado de São Paulo, "Movimento migratorio no Estado de São Paulo," *Bol. da Directoria de Terras, Colonias e Immigração,* Vol. 1, 1937: 31–158, and "Cincoento anos de Immigração," *Bol. do Ministerio de Trabalho, Industria e Commercio* (Rio de Janeiro), April 1937: 301–14.

mum numbers from 1890 to 1900, and again just before 1914. After 1918 the number of Italian immigrants dropped greatly. After Italians, in total numbers, came Portuguese, Spaniards, Japanese, Germans, Russians, Poles, Austrians, Turks, Lithuanians, and others.

Most of the Japanese and many of the Germans went to the state of São Paulo, which also received immigrants from other parts of Brazil. The rise of São Paulo as a region of speculative agriculture led to much emigration from other parts of Brazil. The number of Brazilians living in São Paulo at the time of the 1950 census but born in other states was more than a million. The state of Bahia contributed the largest number of Brazilian immigrants to São Paulo State, with Minas Gerais second.

Compared with the migration of Europeans into North America during this same period, those who went to Brazil and to Argentina were only a trickle. The question can still be asked, "Why did so few people go to Brazil?" A part of the answer to this question is offered by the conditions of life on the *fazenda paulista* and also by the objectives of the Europeans who were led to migrate in such numbers to the New World. It is probably a mistake to believe that the majority of the immigrants came because they desired religious liberty or freedom from oppression. Most of them came because they had heard that in America one could become rich.[4] In North America some did become rich, but in South America, in Argentina and in Brazil, the immigrant worker found himself face to face with the long-established tradition of the aristocratic landowner and the tenant, of "master and man." Most of the profits derived from the spread of wheat cultivation in Argentina went to the landowners; in Brazil this same story was repeated, for the *fazendeiros* pocketed not only most of the income from the sale of coffee, but also the profits from the increase of land values. The wages paid to the *colonos* were only for subsistence, not a real share of the profits. Failing to gain a part of the "unearned increment" of land values, the immigrants to South America sent back discouraging reports which must have compared poorly with stories of the quick wealth to be made in North America.

The Fazenda Paulista

Nevertheless, opportunities to become wealthy were much better on the *fazenda paulista* than in other parts of Brazil. Although in São Paulo State there are longer hours of work than in Minas, and the laborers are expected to work harder than in the easy-going East, the wages are higher. Those who are diligent, thrifty, and perhaps lucky, have been able to purchase some land of their own or to move to the city and find employment in the factories.

---

[4] See the treatment of this subject in R. F. Foerster, *The Italian Emigration of Our Times* (Harvard Economic Studies, Vol. 20), Cambridge, Mass., 1919.

Coffee production requires a considerable amount of labor. As a first step in the development of a new plantation, the landowner draws up a contract with a tenant obligating him to clear a tract of virgin forest and plant coffee. While the young trees are growing to bearing age, which takes from four to six years, the *colono* family is permitted to grow its own food crops, such as maize, rice, and beans, between the rows of coffee. At the end of that period, however, the *colono* must turn the plantation over to the owner and move elsewhere.

When the new coffee *fazendas* come into production, a large number of rural people are settled on the land. Unlike the tenants in most other parts of Brazil, those on the *fazenda paulista* are not scattered in individual homes, but are grouped together in villages. The owner himself commonly moves to his new estate, together with managers and overseers. The *fazendeiros* of São Paulo as a group are closely in touch with the business of producing coffee; they are not, like the ranchers of Argentina or even of other parts of Brazil, interested primarily in pastoral life and willing to leave farming to tenants.

Except for the *fazendas* of the Paraíba Valley, which resemble those of the East, the typical *fazenda paulista* is by no means a social unit comparable to the sugarcane plantations of the Northeast or to the typical *fazenda* of the East. There is no *compadre* system to attach the tenants to the landowners. The *fazenda paulista* is essentially a business enterprise which brings a group of people together for a brief period for the sake of profit. Contracts with tenants generally run for only one or two years, after which the tenant family usually moves elsewhere. Not only is the tenant loosely attached to the land on which he works, but even the owner fails to develop any sentimental attachment to his property, and is ready at the first sign of decreasing profits to move on to the virgin lands of the frontier. The objective of both *fazendeiro* and tenant is more wealth; there is no intention of remaining permanently in the rural districts. The dream of every Paulista is a home in the city. This attitude of mind colors the whole relationship between the people and the land.

LAYOUT OF THE FAZENDA PAULISTA

The layout of the typical *fazenda* of São Paulo State resembles that of other parts of Brazil in the relation of its boundaries to the terrain. Estates are divided from each other along the ridge tops or drainage divides. The coffee trees are planted almost exclusively on the ridges and slopes, and almost exclusively also in vertical rows. The accompanying map of land use in an area near Taquaritinga (Map 131) shows what is typical of the central area of coffee production. The land devoted to coffee occupies the tops and sides of the ridges, less than half of the total area. The valleys are used for pasture or for food crops or they are left in brush. Standing on the ridge tops

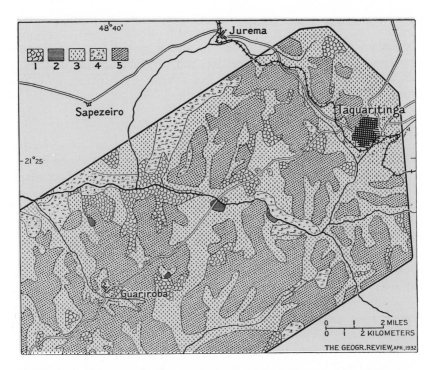

Map 131. Land use in São Paulo: *1 Forest; 2 Truck crops; 3 Pasture; 4 Brush; 5 Coffee.*

one can see little but coffee—long straight rows of coffee as far as the eye can reach. The people, the estate headquarters, and buildings and drying platforms of the *fazendas* are all grouped in the valley.

The *fazenda paulista* usually contains certain standard buildings and other equipment needed for the harvesting, drying, and shipment of coffee. The harvest, which begins sometime in May and lasts till August, consists in stripping the "cherries" from the branches of the trees and transporting them to a central part of the *fazenda* where the coffee seeds are to be extracted. First the cherries are dumped into large tanks of water in which the ripe and green ones are separated and the sticks and stones eliminated. The cherries are then carried to drying platforms, which are usually made of black tile to absorb the sun's heat. On many *fazendas* the transportation is by small canals, in which the cherries are floated. On the drying platforms the cherries have to be raked over frequently and in case of rain must be quickly gathered into small piles and covered with tarpaulins. When the cherries are thoroughly dry they are put through a machine which removes the husks and then through other machines which grade the seeds according to shape, weight, and size. The coffee is then put in bags (of 60 kilos each) and is ready for shipment or storage. All these processes require not only

an abundant supply of cheap labor, but also a special set of structures—
tanks, canals, drying platforms, husking and sorting machines, and storage
sheds, as well as a home for the owner and homes for the tenants; all of these
are found on the *fazenda.*

DISTRIBUTION OF THE COFFEE FAZENDAS

The first advance of the coffee plantations into São Paulo State followed
the preexisting roads, but as the qualities of the soil and surface best adapted
to coffee were discovered, a pattern was gradually evolved which came more
and more closely to resemble that of the underlying land. Outside of the
Paraíba Valley, the first part of São Paulo State to become a center of
coffee planting was the district around Campinas, where, between 1860 and
1885, the new plantations supplanted the older Paraíba *fazendas* as the chief
sources of coffee. From Campinas two roads led into the interior, and along
these roads coffee made its advances. One extended northward along the
edge of the crystallines through Mogi-Mirím to Uberaba in Minas Gerais;
the other went toward the northwest, through Limeira to Araraquara. For
a time Campinas, at the focus of these two routes through the coffee plantations, grew more rapidly than São Paulo City.

Certain parts of the region soon appeared to be better suited to coffee than
others. The open savannas were avoided in favor of the heavily wooded
ridges. Already in the neighborhood of Campinas the planters had discovered
the advantages of the *terra roxa* which had developed on the narrow dike of
diabase that cuts through the basement crystallines near that town. It is on
this dike, in fact, that the *Instituto Agronómico de São Paulo,* with its big experimental plantations, is now located. The *fazendeiros* soon discovered the
terra roxa around Ribeirão Preto to the north and São Carlos to the northwest, and they concentrated their attention on these districts.

The great wave of coffee planting in the period between 1885 and 1900
followed not only the routes out of Campinas, but also moved westward from
Sorocaba, encountering the diabase cuesta near Botucatú. Where the map of
the forests once vaguely reflected the distribution of the *terra roxa,* the map
of coffee began more and more to do the same thing, but with greater preci-
sion. So well have coffee trees planted on the *terra roxa* maintained their
yields that the areas of diabase still appear on the coffee map as zones of
concentration.

The spread of the coffee plantations, however, did not stop at the western
edge of the *terra roxa.* In spite of the sustained yields, no tendency to in-
tensify the methods of production on the *terra roxa* appeared until after 1950.
The lure of virgin lands beyond was too strong. On the interfluves between
the various streams draining to the Paraná the coffee plantations were pushed
rapidly westward and northwestward, occupying the poorer sandy lands, which,
however, gave very high yields when they were first cleared. Fingers of settle-

ment were extended along the railroad lines to Barretos, Rio Preto, far out along the line to Mato Grosso beyond Araçatuba, to Marília, and in the south as far as the Paraná. Coffee had also crossed the border into the northwestern part of the state of Paraná before 1930.

Other Uses of Land in the Coffee Region

Within the coffee region itself a relatively small proportion of the land has been used for the chief crop. Before 1875 most of the *fazendas* grew coffee on only a part of the cultivated land and used the rest for the traditional Brazilian combination of food crops—maize, rice, and beans—and sometimes for a little sugarcane and cotton. During the period of coffee speculation new plantations had almost all their cultivated lands in coffee; but the cultivated lands were only on the ridges, and on every *fazenda* a large proportion of the land was in valleys. The valley land was used only incidentally for pasture or small temporary gardens cultivated by the tenants for their own needs. Certain districts in the state specialized in other crops. In the lowland around Sorocaba, for instance, a small area was devoted to cotton. Fruit orchards of various kinds appeared around Limeira and on the railroad between Sorocaba and São Paulo. Around the outskirts of the city of São Paulo there was a considerable development of truck gardening. Throughout the state the area devoted to pasture has regularly exceeded that used for all crops.

Lines of Transportation

During the settlement of São Paulo State certain dominant lines of circulation were established, first by the old colonial cattle and mule roads and later by the railroads. Today the zones of the several railroads are the divisions of the state which are known to the average citizen—rather than the natural divisions suggested by the geographers (Map 132).

The first stem of the railroad system appeared when a British company built a line from Santos to São Paulo in 1867. The trains were lifted or lowered over the Serra do Mar by means of cables and stationary steam engines, burning British coal. The broad-gauge (5 ft. 3 in.) tracks of the São Paulo Railway passed through the city of São Paulo, and across the mountains which separate the capital from the interior, to the terminus of the line at Jundiaí. The contract under which the São Paulo Railway had the exclusive right to connect the interior with the docks at Santos ended in 1946. Since that date the railroad has come under Brazilian ownership and has been renamed the *Estrado de Ferro Santos–Jundiaí.* The Sorocabana Railway has completed a second connection (meter gauge) with Santos which does not go through São Paulo City.

The interior of São Paulo, however, has three chief railroad zones. The first is the zone where the Paulista, which is owned and operated by Bra-

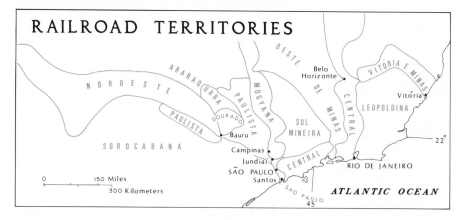

RAILROAD TERRITORIES

Map 132

zilians, extends with the same broad gauge from the end of the E. F. Santos–Jundiaí at Jundiaí through Campinas, Limeria, and São Carlos to the northern border of the state. A branch line reaches the town of Marília. Aided by the revenue from the richest part of the state, the Paulista is one of the better railroads in Brazil—in fact, in all South America.

The second railroad zone of São Paulo covers the northeastern part of the state which includes the rich coffee district around Ribeirão Preto. This zone is served by the narrow-gauge Mogyana which connects with the Paulista at Campinas. The Mogyana extends to Araguarí in the Triangulo of Minas Gerais, whence another company has built a line to Anápolis in southern Goiás. Anápolis is still the closest rail connection between the cities of the East and of São Paulo and the new federal capital at Brasília.

The whole southern part of São Paulo and most of the western part is covered by the zone of the Sorocabana. A narrow-gauge line goes westward from the city of São Paulo through Sorocaba. The main line continues westward to the Rio Paraná, but two important branches lead to the north and the south of it. The first branch connects at Baurú with the Noroeste, a railroad which has been built across the Rio Paraná and the state of Mato Grosso by way of Tres Lagôas and Campo Grande to the Bolivian border near Corumbá. This line has been extended across the Bolivian Chaco to Santa Cruz. From a junction near Sorocaba the second branch extends, through connections with other lines, across the southern states all the way to the border of Uruguay where the railroads of that country offer regular serviçe to Montevideo.

These various railroad lines extending far into the interior of the country are creating a larger and larger focus of transportation on the city of São Paulo. Many small branch railroads attached to the main trunk lines throughout São Paulo State give the coffee region a density of railroads exceeded in South America only by that in the Humid Pampa of Argentina. Also in the coffee region all-weather roads for automobiles and motor trucks are being built. Generally the zone which is accessible to a railroad is limited to a band not more than 15 or 20 miles wide on either side of the tracks. Good gravel roads, however, greatly extend this area. Although the development of roads and railroads has gone far beyond anything to be found in other parts of Brazil, there are still districts of considerable size in which one of the major problems is that of securing sufficiently inexpensive transportation to make commercial activities profitable.

The Decline of Coffee

The spread of coffee over São Paulo State and into other parts of tropical Brazil created a vast amount of speculative wealth, and supported the railroad development we have just described. This wealth also supported the rise of São Paulo City and gave São Paulo State a commanding position in Brazilian politics. But the speculative development of an area inevitably leads to crisis and collapse. Early in the twentieth century the signs of unhealthy growth appeared and led, step by step, to serious financial difficulties. In 1930 these difficulties were among the chief causes of the revolution which swept Getúlio Vargas into the presidency. By this revolution São Paulo lost its control of Brazilian politics. Brazil entered a period of totalitarian government, and the coffee cycle came to an end. Let us look at the process that ended the coffee cycle.

THE COFFEE CRISES

The *fazendeiros* were well off in the period from 1885 to 1896. Land was cheap, the market for coffee was active, and profits were fabulous. Apparently the only problem was to secure enough labor. Coffee production crept ominously upward. In 1899 Brazil produced 9 million bags, but in the next year the big plantings of the early 90's brought the production up to 11 million bags. In 1901 it went up to 16 million. In 1902 the state of São Paulo had about 530 million trees of bearing age, and 135 million more trees which had been planted since 1899 were about to come into production. The stage was set for disaster.

The first major crisis was postponed by two things. In 1902 the government prohibited new plantings for a period of five years, and there were severe frosts in the zone of Sorocabana. But the relief was only temporary; in 1906, at a time when the whole world was consuming 12 million bags of coffee a year, the Brazilian crop was 20 million bags.

This same year the government adopted a system of *valorization* providing that coffee should be purchased by the state or federal government and stored till the market was ready to absorb it. Since the coffee market is a relatively inelastic one, and coffee can be stored for many years without deterioration, there probably would have been no good effect from the government's policy were it not for the fact that years of big coffee harvests are almost always followed by years of small ones. Moreover, the government extended the prohibition of planting to 1912. As a result of small harvests between 1909 and 1912, and the prohibition of planting, the government was able to sell the stored coffee and thus to liquidate its investment.

In 1917, however, another huge harvest made a second valorization scheme necessary. In 1918 severe cold greatly reduced the coffee harvest—and even killed banana plants as far north as Limeira. The government again was able to sell the coffee it had bought, and succeeding years of low yields even made it possible for the government to realize a profit.

In 1924, however, a policy of permanent coffee defense was adopted, but it was not accompanied by any real effort to control the rate of new coffee planting. Merrily the planters pushed forward, aided by the big immigration of the decade after 1918. In 1928 Brazil had a crop of 26 million bags, and in 1930 of 28,200,000 bags. The resources of the government were at an end and the world had already plunged into depression. In March 1929, the price of coffee was 24.8 cents a pound, but by October 1931 it had dropped to 7.6 cents. The collapse of the financial structure brought with it political revolution. In October 1930, a successful revolution brought Getúlio Vargas into power, and the era of the first Brazilian republic (1889–1930), which was associated with the rise of coffee in São Paulo State, came to an end.

São Paulo State is still the largest producer of coffee in Brazil. In 1966 this state accounted for 37 percent of the Brazilian total; but in 1954 São Paulo had produced nearly half of the total. Since 1966 the coffee produced in São Paulo has come from smaller and smaller acreages, as the planters have adopted improved agricultural technology. Between 1966 and 1967 the area of São Paulo used to grow coffee trees was cut nearly in half—from 4 million acres to about 2 million acres. In 1966 the Brazilian government started a program to reduce the number of coffee trees. The goal was to uproot some 700 million trees, or about 20 percent of the total number of trees in Brazil. The difficulty was that in 1966 Brazil had 62 million bags of coffee in storage, or more than enough to satisfy the whole world market for coffee in a year (50 million bags). Yet Brazil's quota for the export of coffee, set by the International Coffee Agreement, amounted in 1966 to only 17,300,000 bags. We shall return to these national problems later.

Changes in Settlement and Land Use

The pioneer movement, which started when coffee planters began clearing the forest around Campinas and which swept like a wave over São Paulo State, did not come to an end with the collapse of the coffee boom in 1930. Since that date the frontier of agricultural settlement has advanced still farther to the west, supported, however, by many small farm settlers who occupied their own small farms. Some of these pioneers moved into the northern part of Paraná; others moved out along the railroad lines into western São Paulo, or

northward into Minas Gerais and Goiás. Furthermore there was a large concentration of Japanese farmers both around São Paulo City and also in the
western part of the state. The most recent changes have come from the policy
of breaking up the large land properties and encouraging small-farmer settlement in the former coffee zones.

Settlement in Northern Paraná

The Rio Paranapanema marks the boundary between São Paulo and Paraná.
Just south of this river, around the city of Londrina, is a zone of pioneer settlement that was rapidly developed during the 1930's. In many ways Paraná
differs from São Paulo. The surface features are similar to those of western
São Paulo—including long, narrow valleys cut back eastward by the tributaries of the Paraná, separated by gently rolling interfluves that stand high
above the valleys. But there are two other peculiarities in the physical character of northern Paraná that distinguish this area from the country north of
the Rio Paranapanema. In the first place, a much larger area in western
Paraná is covered with *terra roxa* soil than in western São Paulo. And in the
second place, the northern part of Paraná is in the transition zone between
land with frost every year and land that never has frost. The original forest
consisted mostly of broadleaf, semideciduous trees, with a mixture of Araucaria
pine in areas subject to frosts.

Shortly before 1930 the coffee frontier was just beginning to cross the
Paranapanema into northern Paraná. The uncleared woodland in advance
of the zone of settlement, as in São Paulo State, was divided in large properties, although the only inhabitants of the land were scattered groups of Indians and half-breeds, chiefly near the Rio Paraná. A British land company
combined several large properties by purchase, and proceeded to make a survey of the land. The *Companhia de Terras Norte do Paraná* planned the settlement of this area in 1931, before the first clearing was made in the virgin
forest. The railroad and the main and secondary roads were laid out along
the ridges and the towns were located at intervals suitable to the proposed
economy. Rural lots were given narrow frontages along the ridge-top roads,
and were extended in strips down to the streams on both sides. When the
settlers purchased their lots, they agreed, according to the law of Paraná, to
leave at least 10 percent of their land in forest—a very important regulation
both for conserving valuable timber and for protecting the steeper slopes from
soil erosion. Instead of the haphazard and irregular pattern of settlement
characteristic of the frontier in São Paulo State, the Paraná colonies show all
the effects of careful planning. In 1944 the British company was sold to a
Brazilian syndicate and renamed *Companhia de Melhoramentos Norte de
Paraná*. This company continued the sale of land to new colonists, but relaxed the control of land use to permit larger acreages of coffee. The result
was a rapid increase in coffee planting, much of which spread into areas sub-

ject at intervals to frost. Tremendous profits were made in the early 1950's when the new coffee plantations came into bearing age. But in 1953 widespread frosts wiped out a large part of the Paraná plantations. Since that time another wave of coffee planting has taken place, and by 1966, when São Paulo was producing 37 percent of Brazil's coffee, the northern part of Paraná was producing 30 percent.

In spite of the differences which set off the Paraná colonies from the pioneer zone of São Paulo State, the district is essentially a part of the São Paulo region. The main source of its colonists is São Paulo; its chief connections are with the city of São Paulo by way of the Sorocabana; its closest contacts, as indicated by business offices and newspaper circulation, are with São Paulo rather than Curitiba, the capital of Paraná.

The Japanese Colonists

Between 1884 and 1962 some 235,000 Japanese settled in Brazil, 70 percent of them in São Paulo State. Compared with the other immigrants of this period, more of the Japanese have tended to remain in Brazil. Whereas 13 percent of the Italians, 42 percent of the Portuguese, and 50 percent of the Spaniards have remained in São Paulo, 93 percent of the Japanese immigrants have remained. Japanese are in all the businesses and professions, and they have the largest proportion of college graduates of the ethnic groups in the Brazilian population.

Some of the earliest Japanese settlements were around the outskirts of São Paulo City. On small farm properties these hard-working people supply a large part of the truck crops for the urban population. There is one Japanese cooperative near São Paulo with 7,000 members, which owns 1,500 tractors and other pieces of farm machinery, and which maintains its own experimental farm for the improvement of the crops.

Many Japanese farm settlers moved to the western part of São Paulo State during the 1930's. The largest concentration of Japanese farmers is around the city of Marília, which is a major area of cotton production. Most of the Japanese are still farmers, although many, too, have gone into urban pursuits. Some of the truck farmers around the city make larger incomes in a year than do the workers employed in manufacturing industry.

Recent Changes in Paulista Agriculture

Several important changes have come to the agriculture of São Paulo since 1960. In the first place, the program of reducing the area in coffee, started in 1966, has resulted in a rapid increase of other kinds of crops. Much land is used for the typical Brazilian food crops—maize, rice, and beans. There has also been an increase of acreage in soybeans, peanuts, sunflowers, oranges, and cotton. Some of the coffee area has been made into planted pasture for beef cattle.

The most significant change to be observed today in Brazilian agriculture is the appearance in São Paulo State of modern scientific land use. The industrial revolution has come to the farm in other parts of the world, notably in the United States, where it has been demonstrated that lands low in natural productivity or lands worn out by improper farm practices can be made highly productive through the use of chemical and organic fertilizers, new soil conditioners, and new machinery. Terraces and other soil conserving structures can stop soil erosion and permit the rebuilding of soils. New breeds of animals can be fattened on less feed, and new varieties of plants can vastly increase the yields per acre. Notable among these crops is the so-called "hybrid corn," which has doubled the yield of this grain during the past two decades. These things have been done, with the result that farm productivity has been vastly increased in the United States since World War II. And at the same time modern agriculture results in a large decrease in the number of farmers.

The new agricultural technology, initiated by Olivo Gomez in the Paraíba Valley after World War II (p. 761), has now spread over the whole interior of São Paulo State, with spectacular results in terms of increased crop production. A major problem in Brazil has been the lack of any storage facilities, such as silos or grain elevators, where farmers can store their harvests until market prices are good. Hitherto a farmer had to sell at once after the harvest, usually to middlemen whose profits have been enormous. Now crop storage facilities have been built throughout the state.

The state government has also levied a tax on all large properties that are neither used to grow crops nor planted with trees. It is proving profitable for the former large coffee growers to sell their lands in parcels of 125 acres. The government undertakes, also, to provide machinery, loans, and technical assistance to the small farmers, thereby not only increasing the flow of farm products to the cities, but also providing the farmers with notably increased incomes.

São Paulo City

The growth of the city of São Paulo has reflected the economic development of its hinterland. In 1883 the city had a population of only 35,000. There was little to distinguish it from many of the other small towns in the vicinity which had also been founded in the colonial period; its streets were narrow, irregular, and mostly unpaved; little had been done to modify the natural conditions of its site. In fact, Campinas had been growing more rapidly in the period before 1883 because it, rather than São Paulo, was the focus of the two chief routes of early coffee expansion.

Two important factors seem to have led to the sudden rise of São Paulo. In the first place, the spread of coffee cultivation between 1885 and 1900 opened up for the first time the zone of the Sorocabana, and the major focus of routes was shifted from Campinas to São Paulo. In the second place, São

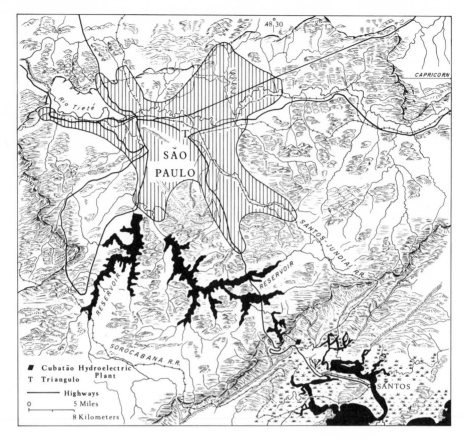

Map 133

Paulo, being a little higher and cooler, was not subject to such serious epidemics of fever as Campinas. At any rate, it was in this period that modern São Paulo made its beginning. Several new manufacturing industries were started, including textile plants, shoe factories, and other industries utilizing local raw materials. In 1905 Brazil was reported to have 110 cotton textile plants employing 39,000 workers, and most of these were located in São Paulo and Sorocaba.

The population of São Paulo increased from 35,000 in 1883 to 239,000 in 1900. It passed the million mark about 1930, at which time it was still much smaller than Rio de Janeiro. In 1967 São Paulo was a little over 5 million, and Rio de Janeiro was a little smaller.[5]

[5]The metropolitan area of São Paulo includes the following politically independent cities according to the census of 1960:

Santo André	232,000
São Caetano	114,000
Guarulhos	78,000
São Bernardo	65,000
São Paulo	3,300,000

Manufacturing Industries

São Paulo started its growth by performing three chief functions. It was the one commercial center for the coffee region. The hinterland that the city serves extends far to the north of São Paulo State, and includes the most productive territory of Brazil (Map 126, p. 720). And São Paulo is the political center of Brazil's richest state. Because of the wealth of this state, its influence in the federal government has been far greater than that of any other state and also that of most groups of states. But the extraordinarily rapid growth in recent decades has been based on the expansion of manufacturing industry. São Paulo is now the leading manufacturing city of all Latin America.

The new industries of São Paulo were given many advantages by the federal government because of the strong political influence of the Paulistas. One of these advantages was a high protective tariff. Another was a tax of 2 percent on the value of all goods handled at all the ports of Brazil except Manaus on the Amazon, and Santos, the port of São Paulo. In those industries for which the raw materials as well as the finished products have to be sent to and from other parts of the country by ship, this tax had the effect of compensating the cost of hauling goods over the steep escarpment.

The concentration of modern, large-scale manufacturing industries in São Paulo is notable. In the metropolitan area there are some 27,000 factories, employing over a million industrial workers. São Paulo alone accounts for 53 percent of the total industrial production of Brazil. The Paulista industries are varied. They include foods and beverages, cotton and rayon textiles, clothing, shoes, chemical products, electrical goods, tires and other rubber manufactures, metal products, machinery, and many others. São Paulo is the leading center in Latin America in the manufacture of automobiles. Nearby is the Piaçaguera steel plant (near Santos); and at Mogi das Cruzes a new plant for the manufacture of ball bearings has been built by a Swedish firm. At Santos a new petrochemical industrial complex has been started, using oil imported from Kuwait, which manufactures a great variety of chemicals and fertilizers. Bottled gas is distributed from here all over Brazil.

São Paulo enjoys the largest flow of investment into new capital formation of any part of Latin America. Much of this comes from the United States. In 1966 there were some $800 million of direct private investment, the largest North American investment in manufacturing industries in Latin America. But a large part of the flow of new capital is from domestic sources, in part from the sale of land by former coffee planters. Because of the high ratio of profits to investment, which frequently runs between 25 and 50 percent, domestic capital is attracted to this booming city. In fact, this movement from agriculture into manufacturing industry constitutes the latest of Brazil's speculative cycles.

The people who live in São Paulo enjoy incomes far above the average levels of other parts of Brazil. As a result, some 250,000 Brazilians migrate there each year from other parts of the country. They come by trucks all the way from the backlands of the Northeast, or from the rural areas of Minas Gerais. The slum areas of the city are filled again as rapidly as slum-dwellers are offered jobs.

São Paulo generates and consumes almost half of all the electric power of Brazil. One large Canadian-owned corporation, the Brazilian Traction, Light and Power Company (known in Brazil as the "Light") was producing about 60 percent of the total power produced in Brazil in the period after World War II. This company serves both Rio de Janeiro and São Paulo. One of its earliest installations was on the Rio Tieté, downstream from São Paulo; another was on the Rio Paraíba, downstream from Entre Rios. But the most spectacular of the power installations was developed on the very crest of the Serra do Mar, overlooking Santos (Map 133). Here a reservoir was built, supplied in part by the heavy rainfall, in part by water pumped up from the swampy valley of the Rio Tieté at São Paulo. From the reservoir water is dropped 2,378 feet to a power plant near Cubatão at the base of the Serra.[6]

In 1966 construction started on the huge Urubupungá hydroelectric power complex, located on the Paraná River at the junction of the Rio Tieté. The first power station at Jupiá started generating 1,400,000 kilowatts in 1968. The second unit, 55 miles upstream at Ilha Solteira, will begin to generate 3,200,000 kilowatts, probably by 1973. Together the whole Urubupungá complex will increase Brazil's electric power supply by some 50 percent. The power will be fed into a transmission network covering all of São Paulo, much of Minas Gerais and Paraná, the southern half of Mato Grosso, and even reaching to northern Rio Grande do Sul.

Urban Pattern

São Paulo City itself is a very different sort of place from Rio de Janeiro. In it we find a pattern of arrangement similar to that of most large American metropolises. The central business district is the famous Triangulo, developed on a triangular piece of flat-topped terrace along the southern side of the Tieté Valley. Tributary streams have cut back into the terrace in deep ravines, leaving this isolated bit of undissected surface on which the original mission station was placed. In the Triangulo as late as 1949 there were only three skyscrapers. Now the whole center of the city has been transformed by the construction of new tall buildings. São Paulo is like New York in the almost continuous work of tearing down "old" buildings and replacing them with modern steel and glass structures. Around the margin of the Triangulo there

---

[6]A North American engineer, A. W. K. Billings, is responsible for this development. To him the people of São Paulo owe a considerable debt of gratitude for the works which made possible the beginning of urban development.

São Paulo, a growing metropolis. *Courtesy of Brazilian Government Trade Bureau.*

developed the usual "blighted area" of what were once elegant residences; and in the bottoms of the ravines that bounded the Triangulo there were slum districts similar in appearance (but very different in location) to the hillside *favellas* of Rio de Janeiro. These slum districts have now been cleared out, and the areas they once occupied have been made into avenues and parks. Meanwhile, low-cost urban housing has been provided for people displaced from the former slums. For many miles around the outside of São Paulo City there are residential suburbs. Along the railroads, both within the city limits and outside, there are compact industrial districts; and farther out from the urban nucleus there are satellite industrial towns. Still-unoccupied residential subdivisions have been laid out around the periphery of the metropolitan area, invading the zone of truck farms.

São Paulo City is as modern as Detroit or Chicago. Its life is a mixture of much the same vitality and optimism combined with the same frustrating social and engineering problems caused by rapid and unplanned urban growth. Here the industrial revolution has established itself. When the people of São Paulo refer to Brazil as a freight train with a locomotive pulling 21 empty cars, they are thinking of their own state as the locomotive, and the other Brazilian states as a load to be moved by this one great concentration of productive capacity.

Chapter 29 ☐ Brazil: The South

The region known as the South possesses certain characteristics which set it off sharply from the São Paulo region and from the older regions of settlement in the East and the Northeast. It includes three states: Rio Grande do Sul, Santa Catarina, and Paraná (Map 111, p. 687).[1] Each of these states has a distinct core of concentrated settlement. Each of the cores was originally a colony of small farmers, including many who were immigrants from Germany, Italy, Poland, and other European countries. The three states make up 7 percent of the total national territory of Brazil, and are occupied by 17 percent of the total Brazilian population (Maps 112, 113, 114, 115, and 116).

The pioneer zones we have discovered in Brazil are of three chief kinds. The most widespread kind is associated with shifting cultivation, or land rotation, by which system a relatively small number of people destroys large areas of forest by clearing, burning, cultivating crops for a few years, and then moving on to new areas. This is the kind found in the transition zones between the settled areas and the *sertões*. The second kind is the so-called "hollow frontier," where a wave of pioneer settlement is followed by a wave of land abandonment, or by a shift of the prevailing land use from crops to pasture. This kind was characteristic of São Paulo before 1930. The third kind of pioneer zone is one in which an outward movement of new settlement expands around an original nucleus without reducing the population density of the nucleus, and without any important continued current of immigration. This third kind characterized the three areas of concentrated settle-

[1]The new zone of pioneer settlement in northwestern Paraná belongs geographically, if not politically, to the São Paulo region. However, since the regions used in this book are defined by groups of states or single states for statistical convenience, the whole of the state of Paraná is included in the South.

ment in the South before World War II. This third kind of pioneer settlement —before World War II—was found in only four parts of mainland Latin America: in Costa Rica, in the Antioquia region of Colombia, in southern Chile, and in the South of Brazil.

Important changes have appeared since World War II. Now there are many zones of solid pioneer settlement in Latin America, based in each case on the construction of an all-weather highway to connect the rural settlements with urban markets. In the South of Brazil, however, where pioneer settlers have moved out along a new road, they have adopted the traditional Brazilian system of shifting cultivation. Starting even back in the 1930's, but continuing most strongly since 1950, people have moved out from the older cores of concentrated settlement into the almost empty forests of western Santa Catarina and southwestern Paraná. In the absence of established nuclei such as that provided around Londrina in northwestern Paraná, the settlers have made temporary clearings by the techniques of slash and burn, and have cultivated maize, rice, beans, potatoes, and manioc, and fed hogs for sale. Then after a few years they have abandoned the clearings and moved on to new parts of the forest. The destruction of this remaining part of Brazil's forests is now proceeding rapidly (Map 125, p. 716).

The Land

To what extent is the character of the land itself responsible for the contrast between the South and the other regions of concentrated settlement in Brazil? In any attempt by mankind to occupy any part of the earth for a long period of time, it is a prime necessity that a workable connection be made between the methods of gaining a living and the resources of the land. A connection cannot be said to be permanently workable if it is a destructive one, and if it leads, therefore, to the decline of population or to the impoverishment of the people. Any attempt to interpret the arrangement of people without reference to the character of the land on which they live is incomplete. Let us, therefore, see what significant changes take place in the physical quality of the region south of the border of São Paulo as compared with the lands to the north of it.

Surface Features

As far as surface features are concerned we find very similar country north and south of the border of São Paulo. The same fundamental elements are to be found. There are the coastal zone and the Great Escarpment. Inland, the crystalline hilly uplands appear, surmounted in a few places by low mountains. Farther on are the inner lowlands, the east-facing cuestas, and the tablelands of the Paraná Plateau sloping gently westward toward the Rio Paraná.

The Great Escarpment is a commanding feature of the region as far south as Pôrto Alegre. In Paraná between the port of Paranaguá and the highland city of Curitiba, the Escarpment forms one single slope, as it does in back of Santos in São Paulo State. In Santa Catarina, on the other hand, the Escarpment is broken into a wide zone of blocks broken by faults and threaded by torrential streams draining to the ocean. Here the landforms are similar to those of the Iguapé Valley in southern São Paulo State.

The zones of the crystallines, the inner lowland, and the east-facing cuesta that marks the edge of the diabase continue from São Paulo into Paraná and Santa Catarina. These zones bend inland in Paraná, so that Curitiba is located in the midst of a wide zone of crystalline hilly land. But in Santa Catarina the eastern edge of the diabase swings all the way eastward until the cuesta stands on the very crest of the Great Escarpment. This is the sharply marked surface feature which the Brazilians call the Serra Geral.

The surface features of the southern half of Rio Grande do Sul are quite different (Map 8, p. 23). The Great Escarpment, which has its northern end in Bahia west of the Recôncavo, reaches its southern end just to the north of Pôrto Alegre. The diabase cuesta turns sharply toward the west, crossing the state of Rio Grande do Sul in an east–west direction. The cuesta overlooks the valley of the Rio Jacuí which drains eastward to the Lagôa dos Patos. South of the Rio Jacuí there are crystalline rocks and gently rolling hilly country that extends into Uruguay all the way to Montevideo. These hilly lands, however, are only about 1,000 to 1,500 feet above sea level. There are also flat-topped mesas covered with diabase to the south of the diabase cuesta, and these forms also extend southward into the northwestern corner of Uruguay.

The coast of this southern part of Brazil is rocky and precipitous only between São Francisco and Tubarão. The alluvial lowland of southern São Paulo continues southward to form the swampy, flat country around Paranaguá and São Francisco. Itajaí and Florianópolis, on the contrary, are located in the midst of hilly country, Florianópolis on the western side of an island which is essentially a part of the zone of the Escarpment but which has been separated from the mainland by the sinking of the coast. South of Tubarão, and extending into Uruguay almost to Montevideo, the hilly land of the interior is fringed by a wide coastal zone of alternating sandbars and lagoons, with many sand dunes. The largest of the lagoons are the Lagôa dos Patos, into which drains the Rio Jacuí, and the Lagôa Mirím. All this water passes out to the ocean through an opening in the sandbar near the port of Rio Grande do Sul.

The most important difference in the surface features of the South as compared with those of São Paulo is the much greater area of diabase and of the resulting *terra roxa*. The diabase underlies much of western São Paulo, but only along the crest of the cuesta or in the deeper valleys is it not covered by layers of sandstone. In Paraná, Santa Catarina, and northern Rio Grande do Sul the diabase is exposed at the surface over all the territory west of the cuesta, even extending across the border into Argentina and Paraguay. This is one of the world's largest lava plateaus. The Rio Paraná and its tributaries have cut deep canyons back into the resistant diabase, and at the heads of these canyons are some of the world's most spectacular waterfalls. The Guaíra Falls on the Paraná, known in Brazil as the *Salto das Sete Quedas,* are located at the northeast corner of Paraguay. Better known are the Iguaçu Falls, produced where the Rio Iguaçu, on the border of Brazil and Argentina, tumbles over the edge of the diabase into the deep valley of the Paraná. The falls on the Rio Uruguai are smaller, and are scattered along the course of the river downstream to the Uruguayan town of Salto.

The varied geological structure of the South of Brazil permits the existence of many different kinds of mineral resources. In the crystalline area of Rio Grande do Sul, for instance, there is copper; in Santa Catarina and Paraná there are small sources of high-quality iron ores; and among the sedimentary strata which lie between the crystallines and the diabase there are seams of coal. The coal is thick enough to be mined at two places—at São Jerônimo in Rio Grande do Sul and inland from Tubarão in southern Santa Catarina[2] (Map 115, p. 692).

Climate and Vegetation

Some of the climatic and vegetation contrasts along the southern border of São Paulo on the highlands have already been described. The northern limit of frosts, revealed by the arrangement of the pine forests, is a line of great significance. Frosts, however, are limited to the highlands and are never experienced either in the deep valley of the Paraná or along the coast. Frosts occur rarely in the valley of the Jacuí in Rio Grande do Sul. Of similar importance is the change in southern São Paulo from the tropical rainfall regimen marked by dry winters to the regimen of abundant rains in all months, characteristic of the South (Map 11, p. 31).

From Sorocaba southward on the highlands, the vegetation cover undergoes a gradual change from tropical semideciduous forest to pure grass prairie. The semideciduous forest extends far southward in the deep valley of the Paraná, but is replaced at higher elevations by the frost-resistant pine forests. The prairies which occur in patches throughout southern São Paulo, Paraná, and Santa Catarina become more extensive than the forests in Rio Grande do Sul south of the Uruguai Valley. This is a region of plentiful rainfall in which the prevalence of grass instead of forest has never been adequately explained.

The details of forest–grassland distribution in this broad zone of transition are closely related to the underlying rock formations. Much of the inner lowland is grass-covered. The diabase and the crystallines become less and less forested as one proceeds southward. "Predominant grasslands with ravine-

---

[2]Not to be confused with the iron-ore shipping port of Tubarão in Espírito Santo.

head forest patches" describes the vegetation of the diabase plateau in northern Rio Grande do Sul.

Contrasts of climate and vegetation along the coast are not so abrupt as on the highlands. The climatic conditions in summer show only minor differences between Santos and Rio Grande do Sul. There are the same gray skies, the same heavy rainfall, the same high temperatures. The average temperature of the warmest month at Santos is 77.9°, at Blumenau, 75.9°, at Pôrto Alegre, 76.5°, and at Santa Maria, near the head of the Jacuí Valley, 76.8°. But the winters are definitely cooler in the South. The coldest month at Santos averages 66.0°, at Blumenau, 58.3°; and at Pôrto Alegre, 56.3°.

The cooler winters are reflected in the vegetation cover by the gradual elimination of the tropical rain forest, and by the descent of the semideciduous forest from the higher part of the Escarpment almost to sea level. The rain forest, which forms a continuous screen of dense growth all the way southward from Bahia, reaches its southern end a little north of latitude 30° S. It is replaced by the lighter semideciduous forest; and this forest also extends in a band along the south-facing slope of the highland far across Rio Grande do Sul.

Relation of the Population Clusters to the Physical Features

The relation of the clusters of people to these features of the surface, the climate, and the natural-cover vegetation needs to be observed carefully. In Paraná, as in São Paulo, the chief area of settlement is on the upland, in an area of crystalline hills; in each the coastal zone is well settled only in the vicinity of the port; and in each the chief urban center, the nucleus of the highland population cluster, is located above a place where the Great Escarpment forms a single slope. Farther south, in Santa Catarina and Rio Grande do Sul, the population clusters occupy the lowlands and valleys, and the highlands are sparsely settled. It should be noted that the winters of the South are cooler, although the possible effect of this on the activities of the inhabitants must be balanced by the fact that most of the agricultural work is done in summer under conditions of temperature and humidity which are scarcely to be distinguished from those of the coastal region farther north. The cooler winters reduce the activity of disease-carrying insects, although no part of Brazil is far enough south to extend beyond the limits of these insects. Frosts prohibit the planting of coffee except in northern Paraná, as previously described, but on the lowlands sugarcane can be raised, even in the Jacuí Valley of Rio Grande do Sul. These are the chief contrasts between São Paulo and the South which are inherent in the land itself.

Settlement before 1822

Not until a historical study of settlement shows an actual causal connection between the facts concerning the land and the distribution of people can such a connection be asserted. To point out the relation between the lowland settlements and the cooler winters, or between the highland settlements and the places where the Great Escarpment forms one slope rather than a zone is not to establish any proof that this relationship was actually a motivating force in the minds of the settlers. For involved in this question are also the physical qualities, the psychological attitudes, the inherited traditions and taboos of the people, and all the countless accidents which play such an important part in the irrational course of human events.

Currents of Penetration

During the colonial period two groups of people entered the southern part of Brazil. One of these came southward along the highlands from São Paulo. The *bandeirantes*, ill at ease in the heavily forested country, soon discovered the grassy prairies in the inner lowland south of Sorocaba, and followed them southward into Paraná. As early as 1680 an expedition had followed the grassland belt to the Banda Oriental and had founded, on the shores of the Plata opposite Buenos Aires, the town of Colonia, which the Portuguese called Sacramento. Before the middle of the seventeenth century the grasslands of Paraná had been divided into large cattle estates, and animals from this *sertão* were being sent back to the markets of the East. By the middle of the eighteenth century the open *campos* of Santa Catarina had been similarly occupied.

Meanwhile the *bandeirantes* had also been successful in the discovery of gold in this southern *sertão*. In 1654 a small source of precious metal was discovered in the stream gravels of the crystalline upland of Paraná and the little town of Curitiba was founded in the midst of the mining country by people who came overland from São Paulo.

The second group of people entering the south came from São Vicente near Santos and pushed southward along the coast. There were two chief objectives: the discovery of gold and the protection of this southern part of Brazil from the Spaniards and the French. Small quantities of gold were found in the stream gravels of the coastal zone between Iguapé and Paranaguá; and to connect the new mining centers with São Vicente—a connection which was maintained by ship—the little ports of Iguapé and Paranaguá were established, the latter in 1654.

Both Paranaguá and Curitiba, therefore, were originally founded to serve small mining communities. One had its connections with São Paulo, the other with São Vicente; for more than a decade there was no connection between them. Contact was finally made in 1668, when the Portuguese crown granted a *capitanía* of all the lands "around Paranaguá." The new governor promptly extended his control over the highland mining community of Curitiba, and thereafter the two places were closely united. Not until railroads were built late in the nineteenth century did people discover that, from the point of view of easy grades, by far the best route from the coast to the plateau was from São Francisco and Joinvile to Rio Negro in southern Paraná.

Meanwhile, southward penetration along the coast continued. Wherever the nature of the terrain seemed to offer special advantages for defense, forts and garrison towns were established, such as São Francisco and Florianópolis. Island sites were especially advantageous owing to the danger of attacks by the Indians who lurked in the dense forests of the mainland. Pôrto Alegre, on a ridge of high ground near the head of the Lagôa dos Patos, faced the unobstructed prairie lands of the south for which Spaniard and Portuguese were already competing.

Colonial Cattle Road

For the most part the two currents of settlement remained separate and distinct. The forest of the zone of the Escarpment proved to be as much of a barrier to the people of the South as it had to those of São Paulo. The coastal fortresses made few connections with the land back of them; but the grasslands of the interior and of the south were quickly occupied by the cattlemen.

The chief connection of the southern *sertões* with the centers of Brazilian colonial life was an overland trail. The annual fair at Sorocaba attracted convoys of mules and cattle that traveled all the way from the Banda Oriental. Towns were established as supply stations along the way. The concentration of grazing animals in the grasslands of Paraná and southern São Paulo must have rivaled that in the Triangulo of Minas Gerais around Uberaba.

Parts of this old colonial cattle road are still visible in the region. Over most of the route no evidences remain of the exact course of the road, if indeed there ever was a well-defined road through the grassy prairies. But wherever the cattle had to pass through heavily wooded valleys to cross a stream, they were forced to follow a narrow way. Over the centuries that this route was followed, the feet of countless animals have cut paths on the valley slopes which have led to the formation of gullies. Where the old road crosses each valley today the slopes are carved into miniature "badlands" with narrow ravines and knife-edge ridges. The present automobile road and the railroad follow approximately the line of this old trail, and from them the signs of the cattle days can still be seen.

On the whole the great southland remained a *sertão,* occupied at a few points by military garrisons, and oriented economically toward Sorocaba. The people of São Paulo were much too poor to become sugarcane planters, even where climatic conditions permitted. Furthermore, although gold formed the basis of the original settlements in the crystalline area of Paraná and along the coast next to it, no such rich gold-bearing gravels were found here as in Minas Gerais. It was not a very valuable country in the colonial period, and the Portuguese hold on it was not very strong.

Principally with the idea of establishing a firmer grip on the southern border where wars with the Spaniards were very troublesome, the government of Portugal decided to populate the area with people who could be depended on to hold their lands, if necessary, by force of arms. A number of settlers from the Azores were introduced into the grasslands south of Pôrto Alegre. They were primarily soldiers and pastoral people, not agricultural colonists; they were selected for their ability to fight, not for any ability to labor. In the course of time most of the grassland area of Rio Grande do Sul was thinly occupied by a mixture of Portuguese of this type and of Spaniards.

Population Cluster of Rio Grande do Sul

The creation of the present three distinct clusters of population in the South has been largely accomplished since the independence of Brazil. Of the three, Rio Grande do Sul is the largest. It is therefore appropriate to discuss this state first and then to proceed in order northward to São Paulo with discussions of Santa Catarina and Paraná.

In 1822 the new Brazilian emperor Dom Pedro I recognized the necessity of getting a stronger hold on the South to guard against the threatened northward expansion of the Spaniards. In 1824, consequently, a group of German peasants, laborers, and craftsmen were brought over and settled in the new colony of São Leopoldo, located in the previously neglected forest lands a little north of Pôrto Alegre. Between 1824 and 1859 more than 20,000 Germans were brought to Brazil with government aid and placed on small farms in this region. Most of the German colonies were arranged in a kind of festoon along the terraces of the northern side of the Jacuí Valley and on the lower slopes of the cuesta where red sandstones form the underlying rock. They all began as clearings in the semideciduous forest, where such typical German crops as rye and potatoes were planted. Somewhat later maize was planted to be fed to hogs.

At first the conditions in the new colonies were bad. Only recently in Brazilian history has the construction of good all-weather roads to connect a zone of settlement with a market been widely recognized as a necessity, and even today in too many instances this necessity is overlooked. The establishment of colonies which are promptly lost in the *sertão* without a chance to market their products and to buy such things as salt, oil, or clothing, can only result in instability of settlement and in the continued migration of the settlers to more accessible places. In the South those colonies which were able to solve the problem of transportation were successful. The sad plight of the isolated pioneers of Rio Grande do Sul was reported in Germany in 1859, and for a time further emigration to the region was prohibited. Little by little, however, the problem was solved, in part by connections with river ports along the Rio Taquarí or other tributaries of the Jacuí which gave access to Pôrto Alegre, and in part by the construction of the railroad westward from that city. Land values were, and still are, determined more by the proximity of a piece of land to a line of transportation than by the quality of the land itself. Fortunately, Pôrto Alegre stands at the focus of what is perhaps the finest system of inland waterways in Brazil outside the Amazon.

Between 1870 and 1890, a new group of pioneers arrived in Rio Grande do Sul. These were the Italians, who came chiefly from the provinces of northern Italy. They settled on lands along the crest of the diabase cuesta, above the German settlements, but still in the belt of the semideciduous forest. Alfredo Chaves and Caxias are the centers of the Italian colonization as São Leopoldo is the German center. Like the Germans, the Italians occupied small farms and built substantial homes, creating a landscape strikingly different from that of the Northeast, the East, or São Paulo, where the habitations of the rural workers are only temporary, camplike structures. The houses of the European colonists are built of wood and made in the architectural styles familiar in the homeland. As the Germans concentrated their attention on rye, maize, and hogs, so the Italian settlements could always be distinguished by the presence of vineyards.

Expansion of the Colonies

The most extraordinary feature of this zone of pioneer colonization, however, was the development of a zone of new pioneer settlement in the forested area around the margins of the original nucleus. By 1859 a census indicated the presence in Rio Grande do Sul of 20,493 Germans. Two generations later, about 1909, there were no fewer than 200,000 people of German descent. During the whole period from 1824 to 1934, somewhat fewer than 85,000 immigrants from Germany came to Rio Grande do Sul; yet the population of German descent just before World War II numbered about 600,000, out of a total population of 3,500,000.

The process of expansion reminds one of Antioquia in Colombia. Here was no hollow frontier; yet the very individuals who were found clearing the forests at the edge of settlement were again and again the same. As in the United States the people with the pioneer spirit, the unquenchable optimism of the frontier, could not endure the civilization they worked so hard to establish. They sold their properties, often with an increase of forty or fifty times the original value, and moved on, leaving the settlements to their less adventuresome sons and daughters. From São Leopoldo settlers advanced westward along the lower slopes of the diabase cuesta and on the terraces above the northern bank of the Jacuí, founding one after another the string of German settlements which reach now beyond Santa Maria. After the belt of woodland along the cuesta had been occupied, the German pioneers, together with other Europeans, entered the forests along the Rio Uruguai in the northwestern part of the state.

Although the forested parts of Rio Grande do Sul had originally been partitioned among a few landowners, the landowners were only too glad to sell their land in small lots at reasonable prices, for they had been unable themselves to get such wealth from this region as the *fazendeiros* of São Paulo were getting from their properties. By 1909 there was scarcely a large estate left in the zone of the European settlements. As a result, the small farmers of the South, unlike those elsewhere in Brazil, were not forced to adapt themselves to a society already established; they were free to create their own society, which was essentially a rural democracy.

The Italian pioneers shared with the Germans an extraordinary biological vitality. Among the people who live today on the large pastoral estates of the South, the net growth of population is 6.9 per thousand; but among the colonists living on their own small properties, the net growth is 23.9 per thousand. This applies not only to the Germans but also to the Italians, and, in the regions farther north, to the Poles. The Italians, however, did not expand over as much territory as the Germans. There is a spirit of attachment to the family among these people that keeps several generations together, if not in the same home, at least nearby. The young men have provided an important source of temporary laborers on the job of railroad construction and in the *maté* forests, but they always return home to add their wages to the family income. The result is an increasing density of population around the original colonial nuclei.

Present Region of Settlement

The European colonists are credited in this part of Brazil with the creation of the vital spark of energy which, in the course of time, has produced a civilization out of the wilderness. The influence of these people in the whole life of this zone of settlement can scarcely be measured, for it goes far beyond mere numbers of citizens of European descent. Although the dominant theme of the region is Brazilian, it is a new kind of Brazil set off from the rest of the country by the presence of a considerable number of people who know how to engage in the hard physical work of pioneering in the forests and who are content with the relatively modest profits of an economy which is not speculative.

In the rural area back of Pôrto Alegre, five chief zones of settlements can now be discerned—zones which are highly contrasted in their populations and their forms of economic life, but zones which have now been brought to a distinct focus on Pôrto Alegre. The first of these zones is the oldest—the pastoral zone—which lies south of the Rio Jacuí and extends almost unbroken to the borders of both Uruguay and Argentina. In a few scattered spots in the forest just west of the Lagôa dos Patos there are small settlements of farmers producing maize, rice, and beans. But the open prairies have long been divided into vast cattle ranches and used exclusively for pasture like those of Uruguay to the south. This is the domain of the *gauchos,* the herdsmen whose cattle and sheep roam the pastures of the large estates with a minimum of care. The products of the pastoral economy are chiefly hides, wool, and *carne seca,* or dried beef (also known as *xarque*), which is a

An important product of Rio Grande do Sul is *carne seca,* or dried beef, which is eaten by the poorer people throughout Brazil.

widely used food among the poorer people throughout Brazil. The small town of Bagé is the trade center for this pastoral zone. Pelotas, located on the river draining Lagôa Mirim into the Lagôa dos Patos, and accessible for ocean vessels, is the chief processing and exporting center. Pelotas has the largest factories for the production of *carne seca* in the whole country.

The second zone in the rural background of Pôrto Alegre is the floodplain of the Rio Jacuí—especially of its northern tributary, the Rio Taquarí. Of the four zones, this is the most densely populated, and almost entirely by the so-called Luso-Brazilians, that is Brazilians of Portuguese origin. Its one big product is rice, and the system of production is characteristically Brazilian. There are no public works controlling the water—no reservoirs, canals, drains, or other works built and maintained at public expence. Each owner must develop these things for himself. Unfortunately, unlike the rice district of the Paraíba Valley, the natural floods of the Jacuí system come at the wrong time of the year for rice, for the heaviest rains in this part of the South come in winter. Some of the estates have small reservoirs for storing the flood water until summer; others have small pumps to provide the necessary water for irrigation. Most of them depend on such moisture as is left over from the winter floods, like the *vazante* farmers of the Northeast. The system of land tenure, too, is the large estate with tenant workers. Yet this one district, which represents about 12 percent of the total area used to grow rice in Brazil, produces about 19 percent of the Brazilian supply of this basic food.

No contrast of settlement could be sharper than that drawn between the Luso-Brazilian rice area and the German settlements on the terraces and cuesta slopes to the north which constitute the third zone. Not only are the villages strikingly different in their architecture, and the rural habitations obviously intended to be permanent homes, but also the care taken in the cultivation of the land and in the embellishment of the natural landscape informs one that here, at last, is a district in which people intend to live permanently. Maize and hogs predominate among the farm products, but there are also rye and potatoes. Around Santa Cruz, too, has appeared one of Brazil's chief tobacco-growing districts. Rio Grande do Sul, since 1950, has produced more tobacco than Bahia (38 percent of the whole Brazilian production in 1960, compared with 20 percent for Bahia).

Still higher above the valley of the Jacuí is the fourth zone—the zone of the Italian colonies. Here again the character of the rural homes and of the villages is different, but if there is perhaps less of the German neatness, there is none the less an air of stability. From the many vineyards draped over the rounded hills of the front of the cuesta come more than 60 percent of the grapes produced in Brazil, and a large part of the wines. These products do not enter into foreign markets, but they are able to compete with imported wines throughout Brazil, especially for the use of the poorer people.

The fifth zone is the one most recently developed. It is located on the Paraná Plateau in the northern part of the state. The headwaters of the Rio Taquarí, draining southward, and those of the Rio Uruguai draining northward, have cut back into the diabase, creating a rolling hilly surface with a vegetation cover partly of prairie (on the ridges between the valleys) and partly of semideciduous forest (in the valleys). Into this area has come the latest movement of pioneer farmers, derived in part from the German colonists in zone three, and in part from more distant regions. The occupation of this area by farmers has taken place largely since 1940 and has been supported by generous government subsidies. Wheat is the crop that the government planners wanted to introduce here as part of the program to relieve Brazil from dependence on foreign sources. In 1960 Brazil produced more than 700,000 tons of wheat, which was less than half of the country's requirements. Almost 75 percent was grown in this part of Rio Grande do Sul.

Pôrto Alegre

Industrial development during the last twenty years has made big advances throughout Rio Grande do Sul, especially in the city of Pôrto Alegre. After São Paulo and Rio de Janeiro, Pôrto Alegre now has the largest industrial equipment. Its industries make use of the products of the agricultural and pastoral hinterland. Leather tanning is one of the oldest of the industries, for the German settlers long ago made a home occupation of the preparation of the hides they purchased from their neighbors, the *gauchos*. There are many textile factories manufacturing woolen yarn, and woolen cloth and garments. The sheep of the southwestern part of the state provide the raw material. In addition there are many breweries, wineries, and other food-processing establishments scattered throughout the small towns of the farming area, or concentrated in larger units in Pôrto Alegre and Pelotas. Electricity is generated in a steam-electric plant which makes use of local sources of coal.

Today Pôrto Alegre, which is the capital of Rio Grande do Sul, has a population of almost 800,000. Built on a ridge of hills which reaches the left bank of the river, it is situated near the junction of five waterways—the Lagôa dos Patos and four tributaries of the Jacuí which converge on the site from the northeast, north, and northwest. Many of the connections between Pôrto Alegre and its hinterland are by water. In addition, railroads now connect Pôrto Alegre with the Argentine lines at Uruguaiana and with the Uruguayan lines at Sant'Anna do Livramento. The railroad center where these lines cross, and where the long overland connection northward to São Paulo begins its ascent of the diabase cuesta, is the growing town of Santa Maria.

The city of Pôrto Alegre is an inland center. It cannot be reached by ocean steamers loaded with full cargoes because the Lagôa dos Patos is too shallow. The entrance to the lake across the bar at the southern end of Lagôa dos Patos has been dredged to permit the entrance of large vessels to the port of Rio Grande do Sul and medium-sized vessels to Pelotas. Rio Grande is the chief port for Pôrto Alegre with which it is connected by lake barges.

Coal

The industrial establishments of Pôrto Alegre, and to a certain extent those of the smaller communities of Rio Grande do Sul, derive most of their power from local supplies of coal. The smaller plants use coal to supplement wood, which is the prevailing fuel. But the coal mines are chiefly supported by the demand for coal in the capital city, both for power and for the production of gas.

There are two chief coal-mining districts in the South. The one which is of greatest importance in the supply of Pôrto Alegre is the district around São Jerônimo, located in the open *campos* a short distance south of the Rio Jacuí. There are three mines in this district. The mine workers are settled in a model community which would put to shame some of the mining villages of North America. The cost of transportation is low, for the haul by rail from São Jerônimo to the banks of the river is a short one, and the rest of the haul to the wharves of Pôrto Alegre is by river barge—one of the cheapest means of transportation.

The coal itself, however, is of distinctly low grade. It occurs in seams which vary greatly in thickness and contain narrow lenses of clay and much pyrite.

As it comes from the mines, this coal contains as much as 40 percent ash, though when it is put through a washing process at the mine, the ash content can be lowered to between 20 and 30 percent. Nevertheless, the impurities are so great that special types of equipment are required when the coal is used for heat or gas. Only in an inland city like Pôrto Alegre could such coal compete, without government aid, with imported coals; but the high cost of transshipment of foreign coals from ocean steamers to lake boats has the same effect as a protective tariff in insuring a market for the product of the local mines.

The second coal-mining district is in Santa Catarina, inland from Tubarão not far from the southern border of the state. There are several mines in this district, all requiring a forty-mile rail haul to the nearest port, near Tubarão. The coal of Santa Catarina, however, is of somewhat better quality than that of Rio Grande do Sul. Although the ash content is still very high, certain of the coals from Tubarão can actually be made into coke; and it is coal from this source which is being shipped to Rio de Janeiro for use at Volta Redonda.

Population Cluster of Santa Catarina

The next population cluster north of Rio Grande do Sul is that of Santa Catarina, which contains only about a third as many people as its neighbor on the south. Both in its origin and its present condition it differs greatly from the district just described.

European Colonies

When Dom Pedro I decided to establish colonies of Europeans in the South, his attention was focused chiefly on Rio Grande do Sul. Only one such attempt seems to have been made farther north. A group of German mercenaries who had revolted from the Brazilian army in Rio de Janeiro were placed in a colony not far from Lages, above the crest of the Serra Geral. This was not long after 1822. But almost at once this locality was found to be impossible for the colonists owing to the attacks of the Indians who lived in the forests of the zone of the Escarpment. The new settlers abandoned their homes on the upland, and fled to the coastal settlements around Florianópolis. As the Indian menace was gradually eliminated, the forested country between the pastoral *sertões* of the highlands and the not very prosperous Luso-Brazilian towns clinging to the coast was left virtually unoccupied.

In 1848 a German surgeon named Dr. Herman Blumenau recognized the possibilities of settlement in this district. He saw in the valleys of the zone of the Escarpment similarities to the Rhine, and pictured a day when these valleys might form important highways to the interior. His immediate concern was the settlement of a number of Germans from Pomerania who came "seeking liberty, happiness, and eternal tranquillity, through close attachment to this new land." The 17 original colonists who arrived in 1850 were supplemented by more than 6,000 before 1870. There were two chief colonial centers. In 1850 the town of Blumenau was established in the valley inland from the port of Itajaí; in 1851 the town of Joinvile was settled in the lowland behind the port of São Francisco. Among the people who settled in Santa Catarina were representatives of many different parts of Germany, although the Pomeranian group was the largest. Today the Pomeranian style of house, made of brick with outside beams, is a characteristic feature of the landscape, as is also the presence of good all-weather roads.

This new pioneer zone did not remain purely German. A number of Austrians and Swiss joined the group, and also a large contingent of Italians. In 1882 the German-speaking people made up 71 percent of the total, the Italians 18 percent, and the Portuguese only about 11 percent.

A rapid increase of population took place also in this region, and expansion from the original nuclei has been notable. Pioneer settlers moved on up the narrow valleys above Blumenau and pushed inland from Joinvile. Then, as the route from Joinvile over the zone of the Escarpment was found to be in reality the easiest one along this whole stretch of coast, the German frontiersmen advanced up and over the crest of the Serra Geral and began to expand over the highlands. Rio Negro was settled in 1887. Today Germans from Santa Catarina, who can trace their origin back to the settlements at Blumenau and Joinvile, are found all over the interior of Santa Catarina and Paraná, and, as merchants and businessmen, in the city of Curitiba. A small but important development of manufacturing industry has appeared in the towns of the coastal zone.

Present Region of Settlement

A close inspection of the present condition of this zone of concentrated settlement in Santa Catarina throws additional light on the process of settlement in Brazil as a whole. There are some districts where the agricultural methods are excellent and where population has been stabilized. But there are other districts where the pioneers have adopted the Brazilian system of land rotation, and where shifting and temporary forms of settlement have appeared.

STABILIZED AGRICULTURE

In the original centers of settlement in the Itajaí Valley and around Joinvile stabilized agriculture has brought prosperity to the farmers. The farm buildings are substantial and well-kept. The fields are carefully cultivated and show the results of good farming methods. Cattle are kept in barns where the manure can be accumulated, and the fields are regularly fertilized to maintain the productivity of the soils. The same fields are used for crops in rotation year after year. The chief crops are maize, manioc, potatoes, barley, rice, and hay. In the Italian colonies, paddy rice is more important than maize. There are a number of places where tobacco is raised as a money crop. But the chief products sold by the German farmers are pork and lard (from hogs fed with maize) and milk and butter from fine herds of dairy cattle. Here, indeed, is a highly successful form of land use, and one which has given the farmers a moderate degree of prosperity if not speculative wealth.

LAND ROTATION

Why, then, have some of the pioneers who have moved out from this stabilized zone adopted the wasteful system of land rotation? There seem to be two conditions leading to the practice of land rotation. One is the attempt to raise crops on excessively steep slopes. Stabilized agriculture can never appear on slopes so steep that soil erosion destroys the resource base. Only by the laborious construction of terraces and retaining walls could such steep slopes be permanently used for crops. But farmers working with hoes can produce good yields on newly cleared lands with slopes up to 35°. The fact that such lands deteriorate rapidly after the first harvest means that the farmer must move on to new clearings, leaving the old fields to grow up again in second-growth forest for a period of regeneration. Land rotation, on steeply sloping land, has appeared along the headwaters of the zone of the Escarpment. Instead of leaving these headwaters covered with forest, as proper land management would dictate, pioneers have been permitted to strip away the original forest. In most parts of Brazil where this system of land use is followed, there is a large enough area to permit the second-growth forest to remain untouched for a period of 30 years or more. But in this part of Santa Catarina the land holdings, owned by individual farmers, are only about 85 acres in size—quite different from the vast holdings where the system of landowners and tenant farmers is in force. Small farms of this size are ill-adapted to the system of land rotation, for the farmer cannot leave a field in second-growth forest for a sufficiently long period. As a result, soil does not recuperate, yields gradually decline in successive periods of cropping, and a kind of creeping poverty settles over the rural area.

The other condition leading to the use of the system of land rotation is difficulty of access to a market. In many other parts of Latin America, we have shown how the success of settlement is related directly to the costs of transportation. The isolated, self-sufficient peasant, maintaining himself on his own products, is still all too common in Latin America; but in the course of time he is being eliminated by the spread of better forms of economy and by his own destruction of the resource base.

MANUFACTURING INDUSTRIES

Better material standards of living are achieved when agriculture and industry are combined in a community. The stabilized agriculture of the settlers in Santa Catarina has brought prosperity because food-processing plants and other manufacturing enterprises were built in the towns to provide a nearby market for the farm products. The first processing plants to be established in Blumenau, Joinvile, and other towns in this area, prepared the pork products and dairy products for shipment to outside markets, chiefly in Rio de Janeiro. Santa Catarina butter regularly reaches the large urban markets of the East and São Paulo. There were also numerous small breweries producing an excellent quality of beer until they were put out of business by the large-scale breweries of São Paulo. In the modern period, textile factories produce more than half of the value of all manufactures. But there are many other diversified industries. There is a paper factory, and, in one small town, the most modern porcelain factory in Brazil. All these industries are relatively small; yet they are of the greatest importance in providing employment to the increasing number of people for whom there is no more space left on the farms.

Population Cluster and Colonies of Paraná

The settlement of Paraná is different, again, in its origin and its composition from that of the other southern states. Paraná includes fewer Germans, for one thing; and most of the Germans who are widely scattered over the state came originally from the expanding colonies of Santa Catarina. Among the European pioneers the first to be established in Paraná were the Italians. Today, however, most of the people there are of Slavic origin—Poles, Russians, Ruthenians, and Ukrainians. The characteristic covered wagons of these people represent a peculiar importation from Europe into this part of the Latin-American landscape.

European Colonies

Colonization by European immigrants has taken place much more recently in Paraná than farther south. Between 1876 and 1879 the state government conceived and carried through a plan to colonize the rural territory around Curitiba with small farmers whose products would help supply the needs of the city. The land available for settlement of this kind was limited on the east by the increasing rainfall near the crest of the Great Escarpment and on the west by the bold front of a cuesta that here separates the crystalline hilly upland from the inner lowland. The elevation of some 3,000 feet restricted crops to those that could be produced in places where there were annual frosts. All the land had long before been included in large estates; but since these estates had never brought their owners much wealth, there was no objection when the state government offered to purchase them from the *fazendeiros*. After securing title to the land, the government proceeded to mark off small lots, and, displaying most unusual foresight, to build good roads radiating from Curitiba throughout the new pioneer area. Italians

and Poles, brought to Brazil with the aid of the state government, were settled on the land; and since the area was readily accessible to a large and
growing urban market where these colonists could sell their eggs, milk, vegetables, and meat, the whole scheme was successful and profitable. By 1885
there was no room for new colonists in this area; the Germans who began to
come into Paraná from Joinvile in Santa Catarina about this time, after establishing a group of farms around Rio Negro, had either to proceed into the
inner lowland to the west or to remain in Curitiba as merchants.

The establishment of pioneer colonies, however, did not stop after the
completion of the Curitiba scheme. Since 1890 many new colonies have
been planned and settled, some by private land companies, and others under
government auspices—for the state government has maintained its intelligent
interest in pioneering. Some of these colonies have prospered; others have
failed. In almost every case the determining factor has been the degree of
accessibility to a market.

One of the earlier colonial ventures was a marked failure because of
isolation. Between 1889 and 1896 about 51,000 Poles entered Paraná, and
were sent to a new pioneer zone then being established on the northern
slopes of the Iguaçu Valley, west of União da Vitória. The rich *terra roxa* of
this region gave the new settlers amazingly good crops, but only those colonists who had been established within ten miles of the railroad could get their
products to a market easily enough to make a profit. Those who went hopefully to more distant regions were literally lost in the *sertão*. After a few years
of trial they found that the only product they could get to a market was hogs
driven over trails impassable for wheeled vehicles. Soon these remote settlers
followed the example of the mixed breeds of the western forests (known in
this part of Brazil as *caboclos*): they adopted the system of land rotation,
making clearings in the forests, planting maize, permitting the hogs to do their
own harvesting, and then abandoning the openings for new land. A considerable area of the forests of western Paraná has thus been destroyed by a very
small number of people.

Other colonial settlements, however, were more fortunate. The Polish
colonies within reach of transportation facilities became stabilized. Around
Ponta Grossa a settlement of Russians, Poles, and Germans was established
about 1898 and proved to be as successful as the earlier colonies around
Curitiba; Ponta Grossa, a supply town on the old colonial cattle road, has had
a new lease on life in recent years, since it has become an important rail junction and a focus of the new state automobile roads now being built into the
western *sertão*. A little north of Ponta Grossa, along the railroad line, a Dutch
colony has been successful; and during the 1930's a new German colony was
established, partly on the open grasslands, partly in the forest, but within a
comparatively short distance from the town of Castro.

The newest frontier in Paraná lies to the west of the diabase cuesta, on
the good *terra roxa* of western Paraná. We have already described the re-

markable Paraná colonies of the northwestern part of the state—colonies which belong geographically to the São Paulo region. Farther south there are other new pioneer areas, occupied by Poles and Germans, such as Mundo Novo, Terezina, and Guarapuava. New automobile highways are being built to these places, and even before they are surfaced with gravel, motor trucks are at work bringing the products of the frontier farms back to the thriving cities. The lesson has been well learned in Paraná: that pioneering involves both colonists placed on the land and urban markets in which they can sell their produce.

Forests of Western Paraná and Santa Catarina

The forests of western Paraná and Santa Catarina offer today Brazil's chief area for new colonization. This is the part of Brazil where there is the largest area of good land, free from tropical insects, and not so remote as to make the costs of road building excessive. Perhaps this is the largest area with these qualities left in the world, where European colonization can still be carried on and where land can still be made available to settlers at low cost.

The forests of western Paraná are themselves of considerable value. They are an important source not only of lumber for construction, (giving rise to such thriving lumber centers as Piraí, north of Castro), but also of charcoal, which is Brazil's most widely used fuel. The problem of charcoal and firewood is becoming more pressing as the more accessible forests are cut for these purposes; fully half of the freight carried by the railroads of Paraná consists of these forest products.

Maté

The forests of western Paraná and Santa Catarina also include important stands of *Ilex paraguayensis,* the tree whose leaves are used for *maté.* Between March and September each year a small army of *maté* collectors goes into the forests—collectors recruited now from many of the pioneer colonies, especially from among Italians and Poles. The leaves are stripped from the trees and dried over small fires before being shipped by mule to the nearest railroad. Curitiba has become Brazil's chief *maté* center, where the leaves are further dried and pulverized before being packed for shipment.

Maté is widely used throughout southern Brazil, Uruguay, and Argentina, but outside of this part of South America, it is little known. Because no very large market has ever been built up, it has never brought such speculative prosperity to Curitiba as other wild products have brought to some other Brazilian cities. Before World War II Brazil was producing about half of the total world production of *maté,* and Argentina was accounting for about half of the world consumption of this beverage. But Argentina developed plantations of *maté* trees in Misiones, and the costs of production were greatly reduced. Argentina became the world's leading *maté* producer, although there is still some export of the Brazilian product, and there is a large domestic market for it in the southern states.

Characteristics of the South

There are, then, certain important differences between the South and the other parts of Brazil. One peculiarity of the country south of the Paulista border is the absence of any source of speculative wealth. To be sure, certain parts of the South can and do grow sugarcane; but in the sugar period of the sixteenth and seventeenth centuries, the people of São Paulo who were settling the southern *sertão* were not wealthy enough to pay the heavy cost of setting up *engenhos* and buying slaves, and in those days sugarcane was excluded from the South for reasons of tradition and economic background. Later, although gold was discovered, and even led to the foundation of some of the chief towns, no such wealth of precious metals and gems was ever gained from any part of the South as led to the boom settlements of Minas Gerais. Because of frosts, coffee can only penetrate the northern fringe of Paraná, and so, during the last half century, the South could not share in this great speculative product. Finally, the collection of *maté* failed to bring in such wealth as rubber brought to the Amazon.

As a result of all these things, the system of the large rural estate, with its feudal society and its many tenant workers, could never become well established in the South except on the grazing lands of the *campos*. The forests, although partitioned like most Brazilian lands among a few owners, were never effectively occupied by the Luso-Brazilians. When colonists arrived in Brazil who were familiar with the techniques of forest living, these lands were mostly empty and ready for settlement. The pioneers who established themselves in the South were able to create their own society of small farmers, unhampered by the presence of any other social organization. There can be no doubt of the great contribution made by the German pioneers, who, as in southern Chile, led the way into the forests; but one may doubt whether the settlers of Blumenau would have been able to perserve their "eternal tranquillity" any more effectively than did the German settlers in Espírito Santo if big speculative profits from the planting of coffee had been within their reach.

Chapter 30 □ Brazil:
The Central-West

We have discussed the area occupied by 92 percent of the Brazilians. The four regions of settlement—the Northeast, the East, São Paulo, and the South—include 36 percent of the area of the country. The remaining 64 percent of the area of Brazil is occupied by only 8 percent of the people. This concentration of settlement on or near the Atlantic coast is one of the basic facts of Brazilian geography; and it constitutes a problem which many Brazilians believe requires prompt remedial action.

In each of the regions of settlement bordering the Atlantic we have described a *sertão,* a thinly peopled backland on the border of the area of concentrated settlement. The first, and traditional, Brazilian *sertão* was the zone of the *Caatingas* of the Northeast. The great valley of the Rio São Francisco, partly covered with *caatinga,* partly with that mixture of savanna and scrub woodland known as *campo cerrado,* is the common *sertão* of Minas Gerais, Bahia, and Pernambuco. Back of São Paulo are the *sertões* of southern Mato Grosso and southern Goiás. These are the areas included in what the Brazilians call "The Central-West." In terms of states, this region comprises Mato Grosso and Goiás; in terms of the habitat the Central-West is the high country of the Brazilian interior that is mostly covered with *campo cerrado.* It is toward this great, empty interior of Brazil that many Brazilian leaders would like to direct a mass migration—*a marcha para oeste.* It is in the very center of this vast expanse of land that the Brazilian government has established its new city Brasília, which in April, 1960, became the capital of Brazil (Maps 112, 113, 114, 115, and 116).

The Land

The Brazilian backlands of the Central-West are not very well known in detail. Enough is known about them to permit a good general description of their characteristics; but the kind of detailed mapping on which planned settlement should be based is entirely lacking. This is not to say that the region has never been occupied by man, nor to say that it has never been explored by people of European origin. Scarcely any remote valley or ridge remains that has not been tramped over by the *bandeirantes* and their successors. Many are the places dug into miniature badlands in the frantic search for gold or diamonds. Many are the scattered miniature settlements lost in the wilderness. Very few are the spots not privately owned. Yet in terms of an understanding of the potential utility of the land there is much still to be found out.

Surface Features

The vast level surfaces of the Brazilian Planalto Central stand along the major stream divides. These surfaces are at about the same altitude as the top of the Serra do Espinhaço—between 3,600 and 5,200 feet above sea level, surmounted by a few peaks about 6,000 feet above sea level. The wide distribution of surfaces of low relief standing at about this altitude is a remarkable feature of the geomorphology of South America east of the Andes. This vast, nearly level surface has been exposed to the leveling action of running water during millions of years of geologic time, and constitutes one of the oldest such surfaces yet identified.[1] The surface bevels underlying rocks of varying degrees of resistance. Farther to the east the resistant quartzites stand out as low mountains, because the weaker rocks around them have been excavated by stream action. But the streams have not yet had time enough to cut back into the central part of the highlands. The headwaters of the Paraná, the São Francisco, and the Tocantins-Araguaia reach back toward the still undissected remnants of this very ancient erosion surface (Maps 112 and 117, pp. 689 and 694).

On top of this ancient erosion surface the mantle of soil has been exposed to the action of percolating water for a very long period of geologic time. It has lost most of the soluble minerals, and the finer rock particles have been carried down by percolating water, leaving at the surface a coarse, porous soil, low in fertility for shallow-rooted plants. Under the coarse surface soil there is a layer of cemented iron oxide, ten feet or more in thickness. This lateritic formation is known as *cangá*. To break it up requires dynamite and bulldozers.

Farther to the south in southern Mato Grosso, in the drainage basin of the Paraná-Paraguay, the high surface grades almost imperceptibly onto the tabular upland which continues westward from São Paulo State. Far to the west, along the eastern side of the Paraguay Valley, the diabase and sandstone

[1]L. C. King, "A Geomorphologia do Brasil oriental," *Revista Brasileira de Geografia,* Vol. 18 (1956): 147–265; see also P. E. James "The Geomorphology of Eastern Brazil, as Interpreted by Lester C. King," *Geographical Review,* Vol. 49 (1959): 240–46.

layers hold up a steep, west-facing scarp, similar to the diabase cuesta in São Paulo. From beneath this scarp crystalline rocks emerge, as in Paraguay, extending westward into the Chaco as fingers of hilly upland. The Paraguay River is bordered by these crystalline hills at Corumbá.

Climate and Vegetation

In a country for which detailed scientific data are largely lacking, the cover of vegetation offers the most reliable guide to land quality. The few stations where weather data are gathered indicate that the Brazilian interior is characterized by hot, rainy summers, and cool, dry winters. The passage of cold air masses from the south brings heavy frontal rains, especially when these masses of polar air push northward against the moist indraft of air from the tropical North Atlantic. In the southern-hemisphere winter, however, the air over the interior is generally stable and there is a long dry season. The vegetation reflects these general climatic conditions, but in detail reflects the underlying conditions of soil and water.

Specialists disagree regarding the origin of the *campo cerrado*. There are some who insist that the original vegetation was a scrub woodland and that the savanna openings here, as elsewhere, have resulted from long-continued burnings by the Indian inhabitants. There are others, however, who insist that the intricate intermingling of savanna and scrub woodland may have been modified in detail by fire, but that the vegetation as a whole reflects the moisture and temperature conditions of a tropical wet and dry climate. Monica Cole points out that the *campo cerrado* is associated with the remnants of the ancient erosion surface, and that where this surface is cut by streams the valleys are filled with semideciduous forest or selva.

Important light has been thrown on the nature of this habitat by Leo Waibel.[2] He agrees that the vegetation has been affected in detail by fire; but he points to many ways in which the nature of the plant cover reflects underlying conditions, especially the occurrence of water. There are at least five categories of vegetation that are of significance in forecasting the value of an area for agricultural settlement. The first of these is the dense semi-deciduous forest consisting of trees that reach 100 feet in height, and of which only 10 percent lose their leaves in the dry season. This is the *mata da primeira classe* (first-class forest), which reflects an abundance of water. These forests occur in the valleys of the rivers that are cut below the general upland surface. In many places they reflect the existence of layers of diabase exposed in the valleys. The second category is the *mata da segunda classe* (second-class forest), in which the trees are seldom more than 50 or 60 feet tall, and of which 30 percent lose their leaves in the dry season. The third vegetation type is the *cerradão,* a dense growth of scrub woodland, with trees only 30 to

[2]Leo Waibel, "Vegetation and Land Use in the Planalto Central of Brazil," *Geographical Review,* Vol. 38 (1948): 529–54.

FOREST AND SAVANNA
IN THE PLANALTO CENTRAL

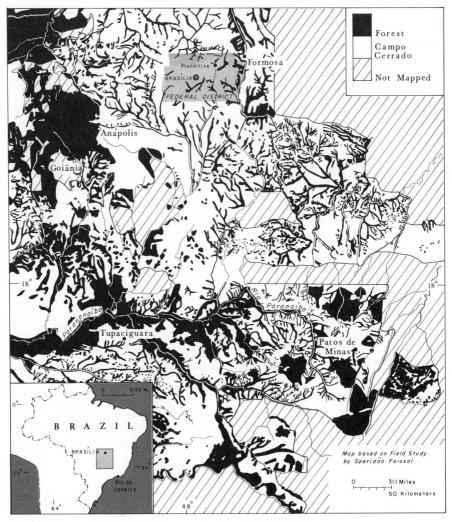

Map 134

50 feet in height, but close enough together to form a complete cover over the ground. The fourth category is the *campo cerrado,* which Waibel regards as transitional between woodland and savanna. In the dry season only about 5 percent of the ground under the *cerradão* receives direct sunlight, but under the *campo cerrado* 80 to 90 percent receives direct sunlight. The *campo cerrado* covers about 75 percent of the total area of the upland surface. The areas of this surface where the soil is especially porous and where the water sinks too far below the reach of the plant roots are covered by grasslands

which Waibel divides into *campo sujo* (savanna with scattered individual scrub trees) and *campo limpo* (savanna with no trees). The *campo limpo* in central Brazil is a short-grass steppe rather than a tall-grass prairie as in the South of Brazil.

On the wet lowland of the Paraguay Valley the vegetation is a savanna with scattered palms, which the Brazilians call *pantanal*. Much of these lands are flooded at high water.

The general map of vegetation (Map 15, p. 35) does not show all the details described by Waibel. It does show the manner in which semideciduous forest grows in the valleys. It shows also that the western limit of the semideciduous forest of São Paulo is drawn in a striking fashion along the Paraná. Why should this river form such a sharp vegetation boundary? The question has not yet been adequately answered. The map also shows an "island" of semideciduous forest surrounded by *campo cerrado* in the southern part of Goiás—this is the Mato Grosso de Goiás, located to the west of Anápolis and north of Goiânia. The details of forest and *campo cerrado* distribution are shown for a small area northeast of Goiânia mapped by the Brazilian geographer Speridião Faissol (Map 134).

The First Penetration of the Sertões

The *sertões* beyond the São Paulo frontier were first penetrated more than three centuries ago by *bandeirantes*. Restlessly searching for sources of wealth, the explorers pushed far to the north and west. They followed the Tieté Valley through the belt of forest in western São Paulo and crossed the highlands of southern Mato Grosso to the Rio Paraguay. In 1682 they found gold at Goiás. In 1719, shortly after the discovery of gold in Minas Gerais, they found gold-bearing gravels in the vicinity of Cuiabá, on one of the headwater tributaries of the Paraguay. In many scattered places between Cuiabá and Goiás, gold and diamonds were both found in small quantities. To Cuiabá came many gold seekers with African slaves whose descendants today form a large portion of the population of the *sertões* of that district (Map 4, p. 13). The chief use which the *bandeirantes* and their descendants made of the *sertões,* however, was for the grazing of cattle. In the course of time the better areas were divided into huge estates with vague boundaries, over which cattle ranged with a minimum of care required.

The roads to the *sertão,* like all the roads developed by the Portuguese, seldom were turned aside from the most direct routes by steep slopes, but they were turned aside by dense forest. The semideciduous forest along the eastern side of the Rio Paraná proved to be so great a barrier to roads between the *sertões* of southern Mato Grosso and the town of São Paulo that long detours around the northern end of the forested area were necessary (Map 15, p. 35). Convoys of cattle, and mule and oxcart loads of mineral products returned to São Paulo by way of western Minas Gerais. The lines of travel not only from southern Mato Grosso, but also from distant Cuiabá, skirted the northern end of the forests on the way to that part of the state of Minas Gerais which is known as the Triangulo. Into this part of Minas, too, came the road from Goiás. The routes from all the *sertões* of the north and west came to a focus on the town of Uberaba, whence a well-traveled course could be followed southward to Campinas and São Paulo. It was over this same course that the coffee frontier moved northward into the interior.

The development of railways and highways has brought a rearrangement of routes and of the means of transportation by which São Paulo is connected with its farther hinterland. Between 1910 and 1940, railroads were extended far to the west and south. From the end of the Mogyana system, the railroad was built to Anápolis in the southern part of Goiás. From Baurú the Noroeste Railroad was built through the forest to the Paraná, and thence by way of Tres Lagôas and Campo Grande to the Paraguay River and across it to Corumbá. Later, this line was extended across Bolivia to Santa Cruz (Maps 81, p. 507, and 113, p. 690). Transportation on these new railroads was much faster than by oxcarts, but long single-track lines, passing through sparsely populated country, are very difficult and costly to operate. Goods are reported to have taken three weeks in transit from the end of the railroad in Goías to São Paulo. Now the railroad has an uncompromising competitor in the motor trucks for which passable roads now extend far into the interior beyond the railroads. From Goiás a motor truck can make the trip all the way to São Paulo in from four to six days. Airplanes, too, have reduced to hours many of the journeys which not so long ago were measured in weeks or months.

Settlement in Southern Mato Grosso

Most of the area of southern Mato Grosso is used for the grazing of cattle on unfenced ranges. The estates average as much as 5,000 acres each, employing only a small number of herders to carry on the necessary work. A string of ranch headquarters runs north and south along the base of the scarp facing the pantanal. The animals make use of the pantanal during the dry part of the year and ascend to the high pastures above the scarp in the rainy season. Permanent rural settlements are found only at these ranch headquarters. For the whole district, Campo Grande has become the leading commercial town, a position it achieved first when the Noroeste Railroad gave it rail connection to the east.

In the southern part of Mato Grosso, near the border of Paraguay, the semideciduous forest crosses the Rio Paraná. Since World War II this bit of forest land has been rapidly occupied by pioneer farmers. The forests have been cleared, and in the new clearings coffee trees were planted. Among the young trees the farmers planted maize, rice, beans, and manioc. As the coffee trees reached bearing age, the area was given access to a market by an extension of the railroad southward from near Campo Grande to Ponta Porã on the border of Paraguay. Brazilians have also planted coffee across the border in Paraguay.

Only recently has the Paraguay lowland been made directly accessible to the rest of Brazil. During the first three-quarters of the nineteenth century the use of the Paraguay for navigation was discouraged by the unfriendly policies of the dictators of Paraguay. After the Paraguayan War, however, the river was opened to international commerce, and small river boats began to make regular trips to this remote western part of Brazil. Corumbá was established originally as a defense post where the crystalline hills offer a site for strong fortifications. When the river was opened to international traffic, Corumbá's importance was increased because it was the head of navigation for the river boats which ascend from Buenos Aires and Asunción. In addition to the products which originate farther upstream, Corumbá now sends out both iron ore and manganese from important mines developed during World War II at nearby Urucum.

Settlement on the Planalto Central

The most vigorous new pioneer zone in the period since World War II has been located in the last patches of semideciduous forest around the margins of the Triangulo in western Minas Gerais, and in the Mato Grosso de Goiás northwest of the boom town of Anápolis. Between 1940 and 1950 some 50,000 settlers moved into Goiás. Some came from São Paulo State, some from Minas Gerais, some even from the states of the Northeast. The lure was the rumor of quick profits from virgin lands. A part of the Mato Grosso de Goiás was developed as a federal colony, but all around the federal colony there are farming areas in process of development by private land companies. The farmers in either case occupy their own small properties, clearing the forest and planting maize, rice, beans, manioc, sugarcane, and coffee. The land is hilly, since it is located in the valley of the Rio Tocantins; when the forests are cleared and the land cultivated with the hoe, soil erosion is rapid, and the streams change from clear water to a chocolate brown color. After a few years crop yields decline here, as elsewhere, and the farmers plant pasture grass and rent their lands to cattle-owners, which is a modification of the usual system in which the farmer pays rent, or a share of the crop, for the right to use the new clearings for agriculture. In either case, the end result is the creation of pasture and the departure of the farmers. Only now there is no new area of virgin forest left.

It is in this area in Goiás, along one of the tributaries to the Tocantins, that a group of people from the United States bought land and started what was intended to be an isolated and self-sufficient refuge from a world in conflict. Virginia Prewett tells the story of optimism followed by frustration and discouragement, which has come to most of these pioneers.[3]

[3]Virginia Prewett, *Beyond the Great Forest*, New York, 1953.

One of the rare fences and cattle-guards marking property lines in the *campo cerrado* of Goiás.

But the greater part of the Central-West is *campo cerrado*. The westward movement was strongly supported as long as there were virgin forests to clear, and as long as the traditional system of land rotation could be practiced. But the important question now is what can be done with the *campo cerrado*?

There have been a few attempts to make use of *cerrado* lands. Several colonies of displaced people from Europe were brought to southern Goiás and settled in this kind of country. In spite of help in the form of machinery and seeds, these colonies have not prospered, and some have been abandoned. On one area of especially good alluvial soil, a Brazilian landowner has planted rice, using Japanese laborers, and has shipped the rice to Rio de Janeiro by airplane. This project has been profitable. But another effort to grow cotton with machinery on a large level area of *campo cerrado* was a complete failure. It is clear that there are differences within the *campo cerrado*, differences in soil quality and in the availability of water, which can only be revealed either by the wasteful process of trial and error or by a modern detailed land-classification survey.

There can be no doubt that modern technology, largely developed in the United States since 1950, can make naturally poor soils highly productive. The new technology involves a variety of achievements in the fields of science and agricultural engineering. There are new soil conditioners, new chemical fertilizers, new machines that do the work of hundreds of laborers with hoes, new varieties of crops that yield more per acre than was ever possible before, and new breeds of animals that get fat faster on less feed. It has been amply demonstrated that these new methods of farming and stock raising can be applied successfully to soils formerly considered too poor in minerals to be useful. Almost any soil can now be made productive by proper management. But the new technology requires a number of other changes. First, the land must be level enough so that machines can be used, or it must be land that can be made level by bulldozers. Hilly land, of the kind hitherto preferred in Brazil for agricultural use, can no longer be used with the new technology. Second, if the land is to be used to provide more food for urban people without an increase in food prices, it must be easily accessible to market. Third, there must be a considerable increase in the amount of new capital devoted to the improvement of agriculture. And fourth, there must be a major decrease in the number of farm workers.

In the Central-West of Brazil, since 1960, these changes have actually been introduced. There are parts of the *campo cerrado* lands that have been used to grow rice with notable success. Huge acreages are involved, but the number of farm workers is minimal. There can be no doubt that the new technology can be applied to these lands, and that they could be made highly productive for food crops and pasture. Such a development would help to solve Brazil's food problem, but it would only aggravate the political problem arising from the demand of poor subsistence farmers for small pieces of land of their own. Such farmers would be high-cost producers, and without modern technology would be foredoomed to disaster on many parts of the Brazilian interior. We shall return to this problem in the concluding chapter on Brazil.

Goiânia

There have been three occasions when the Brazilians have shifted their state capitals, creating new cities where no city existed before. The earliest was when Teresina became the capital of Piauí in 1852. The second was the shift of the capital of Minas Gerais from Ouro Preto to Belo Horizonte in 1898. Another was the shift of the capital of Goiás from the old gold-mining town of Goiás to Goiânia in 1937. Goiás was established in 1682 when gold was discovered in the stream gravels along one of the headwaters of the Rio Araguaia, at an elevation of only 1,900 feet. Goiânia, 75 miles to the southeast of Goiás, was high enough to escape the malarial mosquitoes. It now competes with Anápolis for the service of a wide area in southern Goiás, since both places are reached by rail and by all-weather highways. From Anápolis the highway has been extended northeastward to Brasília.

Brasília

In 1823, just after Brazil had declared its independence from Portugal, José Bonifácio suggested that a new capital should be established on the Planalto Central near the geographical center of the national territory, and that it should be named Brasília. In every constitution that Brazil has adopted since the end of the Empire in 1889, there has been a section authorizing the

Map 135

establishment of a new federal district and a new capital city in the interior. Maps used to show a rectangle labeled "future Federal District," located near the center of the country, and near the headwaters of all the major rivers. Few Brazilians doubted that someday this plan would become reality: this was a part of the mystique of the *sertão*. Still, the magnitude of the costs involved and the lack of facilities of travel even to visit these backlands delayed the project. It was the determination of President Juscelino Kubitschek to do something about moving the capital that finally translated words into action.

In 1957 the Brazilian Congress approved the actual construction of a new capital. The government was officially transferred to Brasília on April 21, 1960. On that date the former Federal District became the State of Guanabara. Brasília has become one of the most spectacular accomplishments in Brazilian history, and a source of deep pride for most Brazilians, even those who are most critical of the whole undertaking.

The selection of the site reflects the realities of Brazilian political geography. Two separate commissions, one staffed by professional geographers, examined the Brazilian backlands and prepared recommendations regarding the location. For the site it was necessary to have proper terrain and climate, adequate supplies of water, a forested area nearby where vegetables could be grown and dairy cattle pastured, and where charcoal could be produced, and a number of other needs such as building materials, good subsoil suitable for foundations, and attractive landscapes and recreation areas. The geographers selected a place near Tupaciguara in the Triangulo of western Minas Gerais (Map 134). Here, it was felt, the various requirements would be met most adequately. But the second commission, composed of representatives of each of the states, would not consider a location so close to São Paulo. A majority of the state representatives agreed on a location almost on the divide between three major rivers: the Paraná, the Tocantins, and the São Francisco. The selection of this site reflects the fact that the Northeast has nine states, each with a vote, whereas the South and São Paulo, even if they work together, have only four votes. After the position of the federal district was established, the Belcher Associates of Ithaca, New York, were given the contract to carry out an air survey of the area and to select the actual site of the city.

The site selected for the new capital was in the midst of *campo cerrado* some 80 miles northeast of Anápolis. The headwaters of one of the tributaries of the Paraná has here excavated a dale—a broad, gently sloping amphitheater—slightly below the general level of the Planalto. The elevation of the amphitheater is about 3,500 feet above sea level. Only a short distance to the north is a headwater tributary of the Rio Tocantins; and only a short distance to the east is a headwater tributary of the São Francisco. All these headwaters are within the rectangular area (2,245 square miles) defined as the Federal District.

The idea of building a new city to rise in spectacular fashion above the Planalto in the midst of the *sertão* appealed to the imagination of the Brazilians. A contest was held for the design of the new city, and the winner was an engineer named Lúcio Costa. The plan he developed resembles a bird in flight, with a residential axis extending more or less north and south, and a monumental axis running east and west (Map 135). The monumental axis starts in the east at the Praça dos Três Poderes (the Plaza of the Three Powers, i.e., legislative, executive, and judicial). Grouped around the plaza are the Palácio do Planalto, which houses the administrative offices of the

The Senate and Chamber of Deputies and office buildings for members of Congress in Brasília. *Photo Courtesy—Pan American Airways.*

President, the two 28-story office buildings for the legislators, the two modernistic structures in which the Houses of Congress meet, and the Supreme Court building. Nearby are the buildings to house the various ministries. Also along the monumental axis are the new cathedral, built mostly underground, and a museum to house important government documents. The modernistic designs of these public buildings were drawn by Brazil's famous architect, Oscar Niemeyer, one of the designers of the United Nations Building in New York. Along the residental axes there are separate groups of apartment buildings, each group arranged around its own recreation area containing a school, a theater, a shopping center, and other facilities. Each group is occupied by the workers in one of the ministries. Along the side of the northern residential axis are the spacious grounds of the new Universidade do Brasília.

The city is bordered on its eastern side by an artificial lake. Behind a dam, the waters of the small streams draining the city site are backed up toward the southwest and toward the northwest. At the easternmost point of land, almost surrounded by water, is the Palácio da Alvorada (the Palace of Dawn), which is the home of the President. Around the shores of the lake are lots reserved for private homes, clubs, hotels, restaurants, and the embassies of foreign nations. It seems probable that the part of the lake shore reserved for embassies will become one of the world's most spectacular exhibitions of modern architecture, as the larger nations employ some of the world's leading architects to design their buildings.

The planners of Brasília wanted to prevent the formation of shantytowns, or *favellas*. They have been successful in keeping such slum areas from developing within the city, but about five miles to the southeast a *favella* did appear. This was originally known as the *cidade livre,* but since 1961 it has been officially named the *Núcleo Bandeirante.* In spite of a program of government-built housing for the use of unskilled workers with very small and uncertain incomes, such people continue to move to Brasília faster than houses can be built. The *favella,* therefore, cannot be eliminated. People are attracted to the new capital from all the thinly peopled backlands, thereby reducing the already small populations of these areas. At the same time, around the outskirts of the city a zone of market gardens has been developed, where small farmers—mostly people of Japanese ancestry who have migrated from São Paulo—are engaged in supplying the city with fresh fruit and vegetables.

Brasília is planned to serve only one function—that of federal capital. There are to be no manufacturing industries producing goods for export, nor are there to be any commercial establishments excepting those needed to serve the needs of the people of the city. The planners designed a city for some 500,000 inhabitants, and by 1967 about 400,000 were already in residence.

BRASÍLIA'S CONNECTIONS

The best way to reach Brasília is still by airplane. The flight from Rio de Janeiro by jet takes two hours and a half, and there are five flights each day back and forth. From Brasília there are also less frequent flights to the other parts of the country, including the hitherto remote parts of the North.

Brasília is still not reached by a railroad. The nearest rail head is at Anápolis, 80 miles to the southwest. Anápolis, which was a small frontier town of 18,000 in 1950, had grown to 80,000 by 1965. The extension of the railroad to Brasília is planned.

The main overland connections, however, are by motor vehicle over all-weather roads. A paved road runs diagonally across the Federal District north-eastward to Formosa, southwestward through Anápolis to Goiânia, and thence southeastward to São Paulo. Another paved road has been completed south-eastward from the Federal District to Belo Horizonte, and thence to Rio de Janeiro. These roads now carry a heavy traffic of motor trucks.

Among the more spectacular developments of the 1960's are the two high-ways, completed and eventually to be paved, running northwestward from Goiânia to Cuiabá and then on through the selva through Rondônia and Acre, to connect with the Marginal Highway of Peru, and northward from Anápolis all the way to Belém at the mouth of the Amazon (Map 118, p. 695). The effect of these roads will be discussed in the next chapter. The road to Belém is followed by an almost continuous stream of heavily laden trucks, and has given rise to a large amount of new pioneer settlement in a previously unoccupied part of Brazil.

Chapter 31 □ Brazil: The North

The North includes the great Amazon Basin with its vast, thinly populated stretches of tropical rain forest and its complex pattern of rivers. This is another part of Brazil, like the Central-West and the Northeast, in which the government is seeking to promote economic development and to provide for new settlement. The North, like the Northeast, the East, and São Paulo, has had its period of speculative development when it was the one major source of rubber for the world, but the subsequent collapse, when rubber production moved to Southeast Asia, was far more complete than anything experienced in the other regions of Brazil. Now, after three-and-a-half centuries of Portuguese settlement, the Amazon remains one of the world's larger areas with a population density of less than one person per square mile. The North includes the states of Pará, Amazonas, and Acre, and the federal territories of Amapá, Roraima, and Rondônia (Maps 110 and 111, pp. 686 and 687).

Much too simple is the answer commonly given to the problem of sparse population in the Amazon—that the climate is unsuited to settlement by Europeans. Contained in the thick forests of the area there is a wealth of resources, some already exploited, some awaiting use. Many well-informed persons who have traveled in this region have been impressed with its possibilities. Why, indeed, should this part of Brazil be occupied by so few people, when the value of the exports, measured on a per capita basis, places the Amazon among the world's richest regions?

The Land

Popular misinformation seems to be more widespread regarding the North of Brazil than it is regarding any other region of South America. This is the result in part of the deep-seated preconceptions concerning the effect of tropical rainy climates on people of European origin, in part of the exaggerated stories of the rubber days, and in part, no doubt, of the well-known Hollywood version of life in the tropical forests. The Amazon region is, actually, the world's largest area of tropical rain forest; it does lie almost exactly along the equator; it is true, as Roy Nash puts it, that the problem here is "whether man can be happy in the rain"; yet we may not assume that the mechanical ingenuity of European people cannot lead to a solution of tropical living as it has led to the solution of living in the severe winter climates of the higher middle latitudes, long relegated to barbarians by the writers of the past.

Surface Features

Only a small proportion of the Amazon region can be described as a plain. Above the junction with the Rio Negro and the Rio Madeira (Map 8, p. 23, and Map 117, p. 694), the plain widens out like a spatula, until a distance of some 800 miles separates the highlands to the north and to the south. This is the part of the basin lying just east of the Andes, drained by the Purús, the Juruá, the Javary, and the main stream.[1] Most of the surface of this large area is underlain by unconsolidated gravels, sands, clays, and silt. About 90 percent of this surface is above the level of the highest floods. The floodplain of the main stream is mostly less than 50 miles wide.

East of the junction of the Amazon with the Rio Negro and with the Rio Madeira, the bordering highlands come closer and closer together, until only the immediate floodplain of the river is left as a band of lowland between them. East of the junction of the Xingú, however, the plain again widens out, leaving a broad area of low country on either side of the mouth. This lowland extends along the coast northward into the European colonies of Guiana and southeastward to Maranhão. Because of the gradual submergence of the land where the Amazon empties into the sea, its mouth is embayed; there is no delta, although the yellow, silt-laden waters discolor the ocean for as much as 200 miles offshore.

The floodplain of the Amazon is similar in its pattern and its dimensions to the lowlands bordering other great rivers, such as the lower Mississippi. The area covered by water in time of flood is only 20 miles wide at Obidos and Santarém, but for most of the course below the Rio Negro it is 50 or 60 miles wide. The floodplain is bordered by sharp valley bluffs which stand at least 150 to 200 feet above the swamps along the river. The river meanders

[1]The main course of the Amazon is given different names in different sections: The Peruvians call it the Río Marañón; from the Brazilian border eastward as far as the junction of the Rio Negro, the Brazilians call the main stream the Solimões; and from the Rio Negro to the sea they call it the Amazonas. We use the English name, Amazon, to refer to the whole course of the main stream as far as the Pongo de Manseriche in Peru where the Río Marañón emerges from the Andes (Map 72, p. 454).

across this lowland between the valley bluffs, swinging at intervals against the margins of the floodplain; frequently its channel is shifted, leaving oxbow lakes and swamps; along its banks, and also along the sides of the abandoned channels, there are natural levees which stand a little higher than the rest of the floodplain; and all these features between the bluffs are arranged in the characteristic crescentic patterns of all river-built plains.

The Guiana and Brazilian highlands, which all but join near the mouth of the Amazon, are built of the same fundamental elements. There are the crystalline hilly uplands, surmounted by a few massive mountain ranges, or by conical-shaped mountain remnants, and surmounted also by the sandstone-capped tabular uplands or plateaus. The Amazon itself follows the axis of a huge structural basin, a portion of the earth's crust which is in the process of sinking very slowly. Immediately bordering the river in its lower course are the tabular remnants of relatively young sedimentary rocks which cover the deeply buried crystallines, as along the coast of the Northeast. On the northern side of the floodplain northeast of Santarém, the edge of these younger strata forms a *taboleiro,* the top of which stands as much as 1,150 feet above sea level, a major landmark along the river.

The Amazon River System

More water drains through the Amazon River system into the ocean than is drained through any other river system in the world. From a drainage area of 2,368,000 square miles, the average discharge of water at the river mouth is 3,400,000,000 gallons per minute, or about 11 percent of all the water drained from the continents into the oceans of the whole world. If there is any one natural resource which the Amazon Basin offers in superlative abundance it is water. Furthermore, the Amazon water is amazingly pure. The chemical purity of water in the Rio Negro, the major Amazon tributary from the north, is the equivalent of distilled water. The water of the Rio Tapajós is so clear that an object on the bottom is clearly visible 20 feet below the surface. Only in time of flood does the river carry large quantities of alluvium.

The channel through which all this water flows was measured for the first time in 1963 by a group of Brazilian and North American hydrologists.[2] They found that the channel varies in width from only 1 mile in the narrower places to as much as 5 or 6 miles, with an average width of perhaps 2 or 3 miles. In the narrower places the water is as much as 300 feet deep, but the average is closer to 20 to 40 feet. The channel has a very low gradient: at Manaus, some 900 miles upstream, the elevation is only about 100 feet above sea level. When the tide comes in from the Atlantic, a tidal bore some

[2] R. E. Oltman, H. O'R. Sternberg, F. C. Ames, and L. C. Davis, Jr., *Amazon River Investigations, Reconnaissance Measurements of July 1963,* U.S. Geological Survey Circular 486, prepared in cooperation with the University of Brazil and the Brazilian Navy, Washington, D.C., 1964.

3 to 15 feet high rushes upriver at about 10 to 15 miles per hour and is even felt at Óbidos, 500 miles from the sea.

Measurements of the rate of flow at high and low water stages were made at Óbidos, where the channel is very narrow. At high water stage in July the flow was 7,640,000 cubic feet per second; at low water stage in November the flow was 2,560,000 cubic feet per second. At high water stage the water spreads out over the floodplain, covering all of it to depths of between a few inches and several feet. The floodplain is marked off in a maze of side channels, abandoned meanders, or oxbow lakes and swamps. The tributaries, especially those along the southern side, are blocked where they join the main river by the natural levees consisting of mud, silt, sand, and gravel dropped by the river as the floods subside. Most of these tributaries form lakes at their mouths, some 5 to 10 miles in width and extending upstream for 50 to 100 miles.

Because of the great depth of the water ocean-going ships can sail far into the interior of South America. Ships drawing 20 feet can reach Manaus, and those drawing about 14 feet can reach Iquitos in eastern Peru.

The Amazon tributaries, however, are all interrupted by falls and rapids where they cross areas of crystalline rock. The falls of the Madeira, above Pôrto Velho, which may be reached by shallow-draught ocean vessels, are situated where the river cuts through the westernmost projection of the Brazilian highland. The tributaries west of the Madeira are all navigable for river boats far upstream into Acre. East of the Madeira, on the other hand, the Amazon tributaries are all interrupted by rapids within 200 miles of the main stream. The Tapajós is navigable for 175 miles, the Xingú for 120 miles, and the Tocantins for about the same distance. In the highlands these streams are so frequently interrupted by falls and rapids that they are quite useless for navigation except by canoes or shallow-draught riverboats. On the northern side, the Rio Negro is navigable for riverboats even through the narrows above Manaus; and the Rio Branco is navigable for small boats far upstream.

Soils

The myth of the fertility of tropical soils has long been subject to attack, yet it remains strangely persistent. The forests of the rainy tropics are luxuriant because of the warm, moist climate. On tropical plains where the soil is exposed throughout the year to the percolation of water under conditions of high temperature the soluble minerals are leached out, leaving only the relatively insoluble iron and aluminum compounds at the surface. Also, the finer soil particles are carried down, leaving the surface horizon coarser than it was originally. Add to these things the fact that organic matter falling on the ground is quickly destroyed so that relatively little of it gets mixed with the mineral soil to form humus, and the essential poverty of the soils may be appreciated. Only on the river floodplains, where new layers of silt are deposited with each flood, are there any fertile soils.

Fertility, however, is not a quality inherent in soil alone: it can only be measured in terms of specific soil uses. The tropical lowland soils, outside of the floodplains, are infertile for shallow-rooted crops; ordinary food crops growing in soils which are so deficient in mineral properties do not provide the mineral salts necessary for good diet. Tree crops adapted to the climatic conditions, on the other hand, are more dependent on favorable ground-water conditions than on the quality of the surface soil.

Climate

One of the commonest items of misinformation concerning the Amazon region is the belief that its temperatures are unbearably high. As a matter of fact, they are not so high as those of summer in the Mississippi Valley. The highest temperatures in South America occur in the Gran Chaco of Argentina (Map 9, p. 27). Temperatures in the Amazon region are high, but not excessive; the most disagreeable effect of the temperature is its monotony—disagreeable, that is, to people accustomed to the nervous strain of the rapid and extreme temperature changes characteristic of mid-latitude cyclonic climates. At Manaus, for example, the highest temperature ever recorded is 101.5° and the lowest is 69.4°; the highest temperature recorded in New York is 106°. In Manaus the average for the year is 81.0°, and the range between the average of the warmest and coldest months is only 3.1°.

The humidity, on the other hand, may be high enough to be very uncomfortable, especially in places protected from the wind. In the rainy tropics the steady movement of the easterly trade wind over the oceans brings great quantities of moisture onto the land, but it also makes living quite comfortable in spite of the humidity. As one proceeds inland the relative humidity decreases—at Manaus it averages 78 percent—but the wind also decreases in strength and becomes variable. Day and night throughout the year, the winds blow strongly on the eastern coasts; but inland there are times when the wind dies down. The difference between daytime temperature and night temperature may be as much as 15°; such a drop results, in some protected places, in low banks of fog.

The rainfall of the whole Amazon area is abundant. Only in the upper part of the basin and along the coast are the averages more than 80 inches a year (Map 12, p. 32); but no part of the area can be considered dry. The rains come during the period from January to June when the warm, moisture-laden equatorial air masses from the North Atlantic sweep far southwestward into the interior of South America (Map 122, p. 702). The drier part of the year, from July to December, is in reality only a season of less rain. In both rainy and dry seasons precipitation comes in the form of violent showers followed by sudden clearing. Great rolls of cumulus cloud, the swish of rain on the leaves of the forest, and the smell of the warm earth suddenly moistened are common experiences in this region. The nights are almost always brilliantly clear.

The Forest

It is with the forest, more than with any other feature of this region, that man must contend. In the forest are the riches of the region; on the control of the forest the settlers must expend the greater part of their energies, and when this work is relaxed the deep, mysterious cover of growing things creeps back again to hide from view all traces of man's destructive presence.

The forest looks monotonous, but in reality it is as diversified as the land itself. It is composed of many different species of trees and shrubs, thousands of species in a square mile; and there are few places where many plants of one kind are concentrated. In the absence of a rhythm of life imposed by cold or drought, each species of tree burgeons forth with flowers, ripens its fruits, and drops its leaves, each in its own period. Birds of the most extraordinary variety, drawn to feed on the ripened fruit of a forest giant, will move to a new locality as other trees are ready to tempt their appetites. But all this life, this exuberant vitality of growth, is concentrated high overhead in the foliage of interlaced branches. Underneath, on the floor of the forest, where man must move about, all is dark, silent, deathlike. Only where light can penetrate to the ground, as along the banks of a stream, or in a clearing which has been abandoned, does that thicket of underbrush appear which is popularly termed "jungle."

On the higher surfaces of the crystalline uplands there are numerous interruptions to the thick cover of forest (Map 15, p. 35). Grassy savannas, with scattered trees come even to the edge of the valley bluff north of Óbidos. In many places the forest is patchy with grassy openings. On stretches of the floodplain, too, there are marshy areas filled only with coarse grasses—areas of wet savanna on which scrawny cattle graze, knee-deep in water.

The Amazon forests differ remarkably from those of Africa in that they do not harbor a population of large animals. Monkeys, snakes, insects, and birds live in the treetops; sometimes tapirs can be found coming to the water to drink; and in the rivers are many kinds of fish and turtles. But on the whole, the Amazon region is deficient in large land animals.

Settlement before the Rubber Period

The two centers of Portuguese wealth in Brazil during the first part of the colonial period were Salvador and Recife. Although the mouth of the Amazon was included in Portuguese territory by the Treaty of Tordesillas, the dense forests and the widespread annual floods along the great river discouraged settlement. Belém was founded in 1615 on the Pará River, 86 miles from the Atlantic, by an expedition sent out from São Luis de Maranhão, the purpose of which was to secure this northernmost bit of Portuguese territory from the invasions of the Dutch and the English.

Penetration of the Amazon

The penetration of the Amazon was accomplished by the missionaries. In 1616 a Jesuit mission was established at Belém, and from this place the Fathers moved inland along the rivers. Upstream, wherever the river in its meandering course swept against the base of the valley bluff and so provided high ground next to the navigable river channel, mission stations were built. Although all but the mouth of the Amazon was originally assigned to Spain by the Treaty of Tordesillas, and the river was first explored by the Spaniard Orellana in 1541, the Spaniards were too much involved with the occupation of the Andean country and the Pacific coast to pay much attention to this vast domain, so difficult to reach from their side of the continent.

The missionaries, unintentionally, brought disaster to the native peoples. Epidemics decimated the Indians who were crowded together around the mission stations, and those who survived disease were carried away by the slave raiders. Today scarcely 10,000 Indians inhabit the great empty forests. Small tribes are found chiefly in remote places, for the surviving natives have learned to fear and avoid white men. The Indians still practice a shifting cultivation of manioc and maize, supplementing their starchy diet with fish and eggs, rarely with a little meat, but sometimes with the fruits and nuts they find in the forest. They make little permanent impression on the forest, for their abandoned clearings are soon obliterated by new growth—made visible only from the air by the multicolored foliage.

Agricultural and pastoral activities in the North are concentrated in only a few spots. Marajó Island opposite Belém was used for the grazing of cattle —cattle pastured on the wet savannas, forced to swim for their lives during periods of high water, cattle hardy enough to survive the insect pests of this lowland area. Belém prospered for a time during the eighteenth century on the production of coffee, cotton, and rice, until other parts of Brazil produced these things more cheaply. Small areas of shifting agriculture appeared around the mission stations at Santarém, Óbidos, and Manaus. Around each of these places there were miniature plantations of cacao, sugarcane, and other tropical specialties, but remarkably little area was devoted to subsistence food crops. Back of Óbidos, and in places along the floodplain, the savannas were used for cattle. Far up the Rio Branco, north of Manaus, cattle still are pastured on the dry savannas.

Nevertheless, further attempts to establish agricultural colonies in the region were actually made. Shortly after the end of the North American Civil War a group of people from the Southern states of the United States, desiring to continue under a regime of slavery, established a settlement not far from Santarém, bringing their slaves and tools with them. In the 1870's this group was visited by a North American traveler who found it filled with pioneer zeal, enthusiastically engaged in clearing the forest and planting cotton and sugarcane. But the place selected for the colony was too remote. Although steamboats sailed the Amazon after 1866, making Santarém a regular port of call, the cost of transporting the small volume of cotton or sugar to distant markets, and of importing essential articles, was so great that the North American colony near Santarém was almost entirely cut off from the outside world. No occidental pioneer colony which remains in isolation has been successful in the modern period, whether in the Amazon or elsewhere. Today only a few impoverished families remain, and these have lost the optimism which is the chief strength of the successful pioneer.

The Rubber Period

When the world was ready for rubber, the Amazon region began the spectacular period of forest exploitation which resulted in scattered settlement in widely separated places. In the tropical rain forest south of the main stream, and in the headwater areas of eastern Bolivia, Peru, Ecuador, and Colombia, there are two chief species of tree from which rubber can be produced. The better of these species is *Hevea brasiliensis,* from which latex, a milklike substance, can be extracted from cuts in the bark. The other is the *Castilla ulei,* from which rubber can be extracted only by cutting down the tree. Like all the other species in the tropical rain forest, both Hevea and Castilla trees are widely scattered, seldom with many individuals standing close together. No source of rubber comparable to the Hevea tree has been found in any other part of the world, although most of the world's natural rubber now comes from a variety of Hevea which is much more productive than the native wild trees of the Amazon.

Exploitation of Rubber

Rubber was not a product of major importance until two things happened. The first was the discovery of the vulcanizing process in 1839 by Charles Goodyear—a process which makes it possible to keep rubber from becoming sticky in hot weather or brittle in cold weather. The second was the manufacture of various mechanical and electrical devices in which rubber is an essential element, such as automobile tires and electric insulation. In 1827 Belém exported 69,174 pounds of rubber; in 1853 the exports jumped suddenly to 5,214,560 pounds.

Here was a situation characteristically Brazilian. A new world market of unlimited possibilities suddenly makes its appearance; Brazil finds itself in possession of a monopoly of the raw material needed to supply this market; the chief factor limiting the increase of production is the scarcity of labor. The immediate result: a frantic rush to the rubber forests and a mad scramble to share in this new source of speculative wealth. Land was purchased in Belém or Manaus without any preliminary survey, much as one would draw

The opera house at Manaus with its green and orange dome stands above the city as a monument to the wealth of the rubber period. *Photo by Francisco Silva, Jr.*

a hand in a poker game. Later, the purchaser would find out whether he was wealthy beyond his dreams or had completely lost the purchase price—all depending on the number of rubber trees that could be found in his forest. Who in that region and in that atmosphere of speculative profit could have thought of undertaking the hard work of clearing the forest, preparing the land, planting young rubber trees, and caring for them during their period of early growth?

The chief problem was finding laborers to do the work. The story of the recruiting of the rubber gatherers is not a pretty one—especially in the eastern parts of Bolivia, Peru, Ecuador, and Colombia, where the arm of the law could scarcely reach across the Andes. The virtual slavery and the almost universal mistreatment of the Indians, many of them recruited from the highland communities of the Andes, makes a sad chapter of human brutality, now long since closed. In the Brazilian Amazon, conditions were scarcely better. Most of the workers who came into the region during the 1870's and 1880's were from the drought-stricken regions of Ceará. People from Ceará poured into the Amazon during part of the rubber period in numbers averaging 20,000 a year, but few of them returned. Today a very large proportion of the Brazilians scattered over this vast territory came originally from the *sertão* of the Brazilian Northeast.

The rubber was gathered by workers who were almost literally buried in the forest. The owner of a tract of land recruited his workers in Belém or Manaus and loaned them the funds with which to buy not only essential items of equipment but also tinned foods. Each family of workers was then transported to a spot on the riverbank accessible to the launch of the owner, and there deposited and left to build a rude shelter for a home. From each isolated camp the gatherer cut for himself a path, or *estrada,* through the forest, leading perhaps to as many as 200 rubber trees. The latex tapped from these trees was brought to the camp and there formed into solid rubber balls by smoking over a slow fire. There could be no supervision of the tapping methods and no care of the trees to insure their continued productivity. At intervals the owner's launch would make its appearance to pick up the product, and to leave supplies, for which the worker was never quite able to pay—thus always remaining in debt.

Pattern of Settlement

Since the only means of transportation was the river boats, and since the rubber was brought down the smaller rivers to the larger ones and finally to the main stream, the chief centers of settlement appeared at such strategic spots as the river junctions or the heads of river navigation. The owner could establish his base at the outlet of the rivers which gave access to his lands, and from that spot control all that passed up or down. The chief concentration of both people and wealth was in the two major cities of Manaus and Belém. In these places money was squandered as it is in a gold-rush town. The Brazilians, lovers of music and the artistic life, built in Manaus that great monument to the Brazilian system—the opera house, whose vast dome with its orange diamonds on a green background (the colors and design of the Brazilian flag) still dominates the city and is visible even over the forest as one approaches from downstream.

There were rich rubber forests beyond the limits of navigation along the southern tributaries of the Amazon. Towns were founded at the heads of navigation, and roads, passable only for oxcarts, were built through the forests to the stretches of water above the rapids which were navigable by canoe. Railroads were projected with unlimited optimism, but only one continued in operation until 1968. In 1878 the construction of a railroad around the great falls of the Madeira was started; but the terrible toll of malaria forced the abandonment of the project. When Brazil succeeded in getting the rich Acre Territory from Bolivia in 1903, part of the agreement included the construction by Brazil of a railroad to give the remainder of eastern Bolivia access to navigable water. The line was to start at Pôrto Velho, to which ocean steamers could come, and was to extend to Riberalta on the Río Beni, above the uppermost rapids. In 1913 the line was completed from Pôrto Velho to the Bolivian border, but a bridge across the Madeira and an extension to Riberalta were left unbuilt—the rubber period was over. The railroad ceased operations in 1968.

Collapse of the Rubber Business

Brazil's system of destructive exploitation of rubber collapsed because someone else planted the trees. In 1876 an Englishman named Henry Wickham collected some Hevea seeds in the Tapajós Valley. These were nurtured in the Kew Gardens at London, and then transplanted in the Botanical Gardens in Colombo, Ceylon. "Wickham's Baby" they call the big rubber tree at Colombo from which came the seeds to start the first rubber plantations of Malaya and Sumatra in 1896. The plantation rubber comes from trees developed by seed selection from the trees that grew wild in the Amazon. But the costs of producing rubber from plantations are only a fraction of the costs of collecting the wild product. The yield per tree per year in the Amazon forest is only about 3 pounds; the Malayan varieties of Hevea yield from 10 to 17 pounds. One man in the Amazon could scarcely attend to more than 200 trees; in a rubber plantation one worker takes care of more than 500 trees. In the Amazon there could be no supervision of the tapping methods and no care of the trees; in a plantation the trees can be given the attention of experts to guarantee maximum yields. In the Amazon the workers were exposed to all the dangers and hardships of life in the forest; on a plantation the workers are carefully housed and are given medical attention and a carefully regulated diet. Close to the rubber-growing region of Malaya and Sumatra are such densely populated lands as Java and India, where large numbers of efficient workers can easily be recruited. No such source of labor is available in the Amazon region.

There could have been but one result. In 1905 the plantations of British Malaya and Dutch Sumatra produced only a small fraction of the world's supply of rubber. In 1910 they produced 9 percent; in 1914 they produced 60 percent; and by 1924 the plantations accounted for about 93 percent. Early in 1909 the increasing demand for rubber for use in the manufacture of automobile tires caused a frenzied boom in the Amazon, even in the face of the growing competition of the plantations. Credits were extended; new laborers were hastily recruited and sent into the forests. But in April, 1910, the whole crazy financial structure of credits collapsed, ruining large numbers of the speculators. Rubber production continued to increase until 1912, and even longer in places where Castilla trees could be cut down. But since 1912 Brazil has had only a very minor share of the world's production.

Decadence

The collapse of the rubber business left many of the rubber workers stranded. Some of them drifted into Manaus, Óbidos, Santarém, or Belém to swell the population of those places. For most of the time, however, there was little economic activity by which these people could gain a living. Many parts of the cities were virtually abandoned in favor of temporary homes scattered in the outskirts. Yet, strange to relate, there was little increase in the amount of land devoted to the production of food crops. It was estimated during the '20's that in the whole Amazon region there were scarcely 100 square miles devoted to any kind of agriculture, let alone the production of local supplies of food. In the interior many of the smaller towns whose names still appear on standard maps are entirely abandoned, engulfed in the rapidly advancing jungle.

It is said in Brazil that if money is to be made from the most poverty-stricken of areas, the Syrian traders will make it. In the Amazon the Syrians have taken over most of the retail trading. By advancing loans to the isolated groups of people outside of the larger urban centers, they have established their control over them. Just as the rubber owners used to do, the traders now control the passage of goods up and down the streams by placing the posts at strategic river junctions. So powerful are some of the larger traders that permission to travel in these remote spots depends on their word. From the pitifully small volume of an enormous variety of forest products contributed by individuals scattered over this vast area, the traders are able to take very considerable profits. The forest products include gums, nuts, roots, cabinet woods, and the skins of rare animals.

One of the valuable products collected in the Amazon forests is an edible nut. The Brazil nut, collected from the forest giant known as *Bertholletia excelsa,* is brought to Belém for shipment. Workers are sent out into the forest, especially along the Rio Tocantins, at the time of the year when the nuts ripen. Again no cultivation is attempted—only the collection of a product which has fallen from the tree. Today Brazil produces the greater part of the world's supply of Brazil nuts; yet already even this supremacy is threatened by plantations of this tree now set out on an experimental basis in Malaya.

The Ford Plantations

In 1927 an event of great importance took place in the North of Brazil. The *Companhia Ford Industrial do Brasil* purchased a tract of land, including some 2,500,000 acres, along the right bank of the Rio Tapajós about 135 miles upstream from the Amazon (Map 119, p. 696). The area was known as Fordlândia. At the nucleus of the settlement a modern town was built. About 8,400 acres of rubber trees were planted before a number of unexpected difficulties began to appear. Diseases attacked the plantations of Hevea trees while the same kinds of trees, widely scattered through the rain forest, seemed to be immune. Also Fordlândia was found to be so hilly that soil erosion became critical and the use of machinery was difficult. In 1934 a part of the original concession was exchanged with the state of Pará for a

THE SANTARÉM AREA

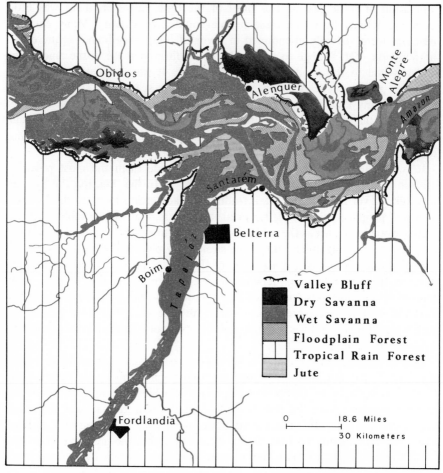

Valley Bluff
Dry Savanna
Wet Savanna
Floodplain Forest
Tropical Rain Forest
Jute

0   18.6 Miles
30 Kilometers

Modified, after J. Zimmerman

Map 136

new tract of land, including 600,000 acres, only 30 miles up the Tapajós from Santarém. This new tract is called Belterra. Before the beginning of World War II about 20,000 acres had been cleared and planted with rubber. The more nearly level land at the new site permitted more efficient use of machinery and better agricultural practices. On the roots of hardy, disease-resistant trees from Marajó Island, trunks from high-yielding Malayan varieties were grafted. Then, when the plume of foliage at the top was found to be subject to insects and leaf diseases, new resistant tops were grafted onto the Malayan trunks. At great expense the Ford Company little by little overcame the technical difficulties involved in raising plantation rubber in the Amazon.

Still the undertaking was not successful from the point of view of the company. In order to supply the needs of the Ford industries for rubber it was

Rubber plantation at Belterra, formerly owned by the Ford Company. *Courtesy of the Companhia Ford Industrial do Brasil.*

estimated that a total of 76,000 acres of rubber trees would be needed. After the work of clearing the forest and planting rubber had been done, to tap and care for the producing trees would require 11,000 tappers. One worker can tap about 300 to 350 trees on alternate days, or a total of 600 to 700 trees, planted on 6 or 7 acres. Each tapper would gather from 14 to 20 pounds of latex per day. At no time was such an acreage of trees, or such a labor force in sight. The 20,000 acres planted before 1941 resulted from 12 years of work at Fordlândia and 7 at Belterra. The largest number of workers gathered together was only 2,723, in March, 1941. In spite of rates of pay some 35 percent higher than the rates prevailing in the Amazon region, and in spite of free hospitalization, free land for subsistence crops, new houses with light and water, and various community services, the fact is that the whole Amazon region, together with the backlands of the Northeast, could supply no more workers. The single great factor which stops the economic development of the Amazon is the scarcity of people. Those who were employed at the Ford plantations proved to be excellent workers, especially after they had been housed, clothed, and fed properly. The plantations ranked among the most healthful places in Brazil, and labor efficiency compared well with other parts of the world. It was not the equatorial climate which made the Ford Company abandon its experiment after World War II and return the plantations to the Brazilian government, which now operates them. It was the scarcity of workers, which meant that there was no hope that the plantations could ever provide more than a fraction of the rubber that was needed.

THE LESSONS OF THE FORD PLANTATIONS

What light does the experiment of the Ford plantations throw on the problem of the empty Amazon? Plainly, the kind of living standards developed at Belterra could not be supported by the traditional exploitive economy. But if a large number of workers are ever to be found willing to enter the Amazon region something spectacular must be done to prove to them the possibility of healthful living in this equatorial country. Can a plantation economy, based on production at costs low enough to provide reasonable profits, ever support such expensive standards of living as those adopted at the Ford plantations? The answer depends on the number of immigrants that might enter the Amazon. An isolated plantation in the midst of empty country might fail where millions of people on many plantations might succeed.

During World War II the United States, with amazing ignorance of real conditions in the Amazon, spent millions of dollars attempting to build up rubber production from wild trees, as in the days before 1912. The almost complete failure of the effort was due to the lack of knowledge of the region on the part of the administrators. The scarcity of workers, the role of the traders, even the conditions of life away from the cities were ignored or overlooked. After World War II, the belief in the inexhaustible productivity of this region again caught the attention of foreign governments, this time through the United Nations. A major survey of the region and its people was launched with the objective of pointing the way to develop the food-producing possibilities of the area. Still the major obstacle to economic development is the lack of workers.

Other Centers of Settlement

Outside of the rubber plantations, which still continue to furnish a small supply of natural rubber for the rubber manufacturers in São Paulo, there are other small spots of settlement and some examples of successful economic growth. Most of the miniature communities along the banks of the great river and its tributaries are occupied by descendants of the people left stranded by the decline of the rubber economy. A small income is made from a great variety of forest products. Around each community are very small areas used for the production of manioc, maize, rice, and beans. The conditions of life in one sample community were vividly presented in a book by the anthro-

A river-front community near Manaus. The only transportation is by canoe or launch along the rivers.

pologist Charles Wagley.[3] Most of these little villages, and the isolated settlers nearby, are tied together by the river which provides the only possible route of travel. But the area of concentrated settlement east of Belém, which first appeared during the late nineteenth century, was developd along the axis of the railroad line from Belém to Bragança. In modern times the highway provides a better means of transportation to the city market. Many decades of land rotation in this district have destroyed the soil and increased the poverty of the farmers. The chief subsistence crops are manioc, maize, rice, and beans. But in modern times the farmers also grow cotton and mallow, a fiber crop.

An important new area of settlement has resulted from the mining of manganese in the Territory of Amapá. The manganese ores were discovered during World War II in the dense forests north of the mouth of the Amazon. Mining rights were assigned to a company of which 51 percent of the capital is owned by Brazilians and the balance by North Americans. A railroad was built, about 120 miles long, to connect the ore body with the port of Macapá. The mines produce some 250,000 tons of ore each year, of which about a third is exported to the United States and the remainder is used in Brazil's steel plants. The sleepy little town of Macapá has come alive.

[3]Charles Wagley, *Amazon Town, A Study of Man in the Tropics*, New York, 1953.

Japanese Producers of Pepper and Jute

The story of Japanese settlement in the Amazon region is important because of the light it throws on the problem of the development of this part of Brazil. Although no large number of colonists from Japan have settled in the Amazon region, their colonies have been successful where settlement by Luso-Brazilians and others have failed, or at least have not provided a permanent and workable economic base.

The first Japanese colonists came to this region in 1925. The state of Pará granted them about 124,000 acres of land along the Rio Acará some 50 miles south of Belém. The colony was reached from Belém by a 12-hour riverboat trip. The Japanese settlers tried to supply Belém with vegetables: they cleared the forest and planted turnips, tomatoes, cabbages, and radishes —all crops with which they were familiar in Japan. But the people of Belém were accustomed to eating rice and beans, with a little manioc flour *(farinha)* and perhaps some dried meat *(carne seca)*. No one would even try these strange products that the Japanese tried to sell—in fact the people of Belém began to call the Japanese *nabos* (the Portuguese word for turnips). The colonists then tried planting cacao, but after a few years they gave this up also because the cacao trees yielded poorly. Epidemics of malaria resulted in the death of about a third of the colonists, and things seemed really bad. Then in 1933 an immigrant from Japan brought with him some twenty sprouts of pepper vines. This plant *(Piper nigrum)* is a woody climber that reaches heights of 30 feet or more and has aerial roots. It requires plenty of rain and high humidity, as well as shade and protection from drying winds. These plants do well where the climatic conditions are favorable, even where the soil is poor. Before World War II this Japanese colony had become a source of black pepper which could be sold throughout Brazil.

During World War II the Japanese were confined to their settlement and deprived of their market. But after the war they were encouraged to return to the production of black pepper. In this effort they were greatly aided by the policies of Sukarno in Indonesia, the world's major source of black pepper. When pepper from Java was no longer available, the Japanese in the Amazon began to expand their plantations and to sell pepper on the world market. In 1947 there were 30,550 pepper vines in Pará; in 1965 the number of plantings had reached nearly 2 million. Not only were the Japanese colonists living well because they had an income with which to purchase the necessities of life, but also the state of Pará had a new source of tax money. Pepper had become the most valuable product of the state.

Another success story has to do with the cultivation of jute, a fiber crop from which burlap bags are made. Brazil had long been a major customer of India for the bags in which coffee was shipped. The jute was grown on the delta of the Ganges-Brahmaputra, and the bags were manufactured in Calcutta. But when India and Pakistan were separated in 1947 the jute farmers in East Pakistan were cut off from the burlap manufacturers in Calcutta, which was in India. In 1950 some Japanese colonists who had settled along the banks of the Amazon in the state of Amazonas decided to try growing jute. The river provides ideal physical conditions for this crop because of the abundance of pure water. Jute grows in flowing water; it is harvested in the water and then left to soak until the stem rots. The fibers can then be extracted, and are hung on wires to dry in the hot sunshine. By 1965 there were some 62,000 acres of jute on the Amazon floodplain. Here again the Japanese made use of a part of the habitat which was favorable for the new product, instead of continuing the traditional use of the deeply leached soils outside of the floodplain. Now the government of Amazonas has distributed jute seeds and a booklet with pictorial instructions on how to grow and harvest the crop to all the scattered settlers along the river banks. Jute has become the most valuable product of the state.

There is also the story of the settlement north of Manaus known as Kilometer 41 (because of its location at this distance along the road from Manaus to Itacoatiara). Here, in 1958, the state of Amazonas established a colony of farmers to grow food crops for the supply of the city. They brought in some people from drought-stricken Ceará. But by the end of the first year most of the settlers had drifted into the *favellas* of Manaus, which consist of houseboats moored along the river bank. At this point the government brought in 25 Japanese families, setting each family on a farm of about 62 acres. The result has been a steady flow of vegetables to the market at Manaus—vegetables that the Brazilians will eat. The Japanese use fertilizer to make the soils productive, and they are not unwilling to put in long hours of hard work on their farms.

These successful developments suggest what must be done to improve the economy of the whole Amazon region. It has been amply demonstrated that shallow-rooted crops cannot be grown in deeply leached soils without the use of fertilizer, insecticides, and other elements of modern farm technology. But the farmer who grows food crops for his own use, and perhaps a little cotton or sugarcane for sale, does not have a large enough income to pay for fertilizer. The subsistence farmer is condemned to poverty. But he is not condemned to poverty because of the land on which he works or because of the climate, or any other elements of the habitat. He is condemned to poverty because of his own attitudes, objectives, and knowledge of technology.

New Programs of Economic Development

In 1966 the federal government of Brazil formulated a program to hasten economic development in the North. A new agency was established similar to SUDENE which was set up to coordinate the development of the Northeast. A new tax program was announced. Any individual or corporation can make use of as much as half of their scheduled income tax payments for investment in the North. There was an immediate flow of new capital, chiefly from São Paulo, into these little-developed parts of the country. For example, a jute textile factory has been built in Santarém. New factories using local raw materials have been built in Belém, which is now stirring with new life and hope.

Between 1956 and 1960 a new all-weather road was built through trackless wilderness from Anápolis in Goiás to Belém. The road is 1,350 miles long. At the southern end, near Brasília, the road connects with paved routes to São Paulo, Rio de Janeiro, and other places in the East. In 1967 some 75 motor trucks per week were making the 4-day trip from Anápolis to Belém, and it was forecast that as soon as the road was completely paved with asphalt the trip would take only 2 days. The trucks going north were loaded with such things as shoes, clothing, barbed wire, canned goods, machinery, foods, and books. Those coming south carried heavy loads of jute, pepper, minerals, fruits, and fish. Fish from the Amazon appeared on the bills of fare of the restaurants in Brasília. Loads of timber from the Amazon forests were sent to factories in São Paulo. All this movement overland did not help the Brazilian-owned coastal shipping, but goods could be exchanged between São Paulo and Belém within a week rather than within 2 months. Belém, which had a population of 230,000 in 1950, by 1967 was rapidly approaching 500,000.

Also by 1967 there were numerous new settlements strung along the road. Just as people from all over the *sertões* are attracted to cities such as Brasília, many are also ready to carve out new clearings in the forest in places made accessible to the outside world by the road. It has been estimated that there are as many as 600,000 new farm settlers. They are still practicing the traditional system of land rotation, but the clearings in the forest are close to the road, and the chance to sell some of their surplus products means that these people can enjoy at least some goods they do not themselves produce.

Another road has been built from Goiânia to the state of Acre to connect with the Bolivian and Peruvian roads. New settlements have appeared also along this road, some as a result of government planning. It is planned to settle at least 40,000 families in western Mato Grosso and Acre by 1970, providing them with access to the national market by motor truck. The road makes use of a part of the old Madeira-Mamoré Railroad from which the tracks have been removed.

New Resources

The whole region is being searched by modern survey methods for new resources to be developed. The new methods include the use of the airborne magnetometer by means of which ore bodies and oil can be identified. They also include the use of infrared photography from the air, which permits a detailed mapping of the distribution of different species of trees. The Brazilians have for a long time been searching for new oilfields to supplement the field in Bahia; but results in the Amazon region have been discouraging.

There can be no doubt that the Amazon forests include a great variety of useful timber. There is wood as light as the balsa used to make rafts, or so dense that the best ax can make little impression on it. There are woods of great strength for beams or bridge timbers, and other woods that are elastic. There are woods that resist marine borers or are immune to the attacks of termites. There are woods with figured grain in different colors that can be used for veneer in furniture or panelling. Every shade of color from the most brilliant to the most delicate can be found, and in São Paulo there are factories that make use of these colored woods to produce inlay pictures that look like paintings. Some are veined or mottled in the most unusual patterns. And also among the plants of the selvas, in addition to rubber, there are others from which a great variety of products can be made: chicle, dyes, tannins, resins, gums, waxes, *guaraná* (a soft drink), edible nuts, vegetable ivory nuts (for buttons), essential oils, ipecac, rotenone, and many others.

But the exploitation of these varied resources has barely started. The river-bank settlers go through the forests gathering such products as grow wild. Lumber is still cut by hand, and hauled to the riverbanks by oxen. Most lumbermen are seeking only one or two species for which there is an immediate market. The real development of the lumber possibilities must await large-scale methods, with machinery, and with a varied list of woods to reach widely diverse markets. This requires capital investment on a large scale; but the economic rewards would be enormous. Furthermore, when the forest is cut, plans for reforestation with useful species must be ready so that the region can continue to provide the economic base for a permanent population.

Tourism

In 1967 the Brazilians were even starting to make use of the backlands for the delight of tourists. People from Rio de Janeiro and São Paulo, as well as foreigners, were being urged to "explore" some of the hitherto inaccessible rivers of the Amazon system. The island of Bananal in northern Goiás is formed where the Araguaia splits into two channels. It is some 200 miles long and mostly less than 35 miles wide. The Brazilian government has made this island into a national park, and it and the land on either side along the Araguaia has been named as a national hunting and fishing preserve. Tourists from the cities are taken by airplane to a place on the Araguaia some 200 miles west of Brasília. Here they find a new kind of riverboat. Accommodations include air-conditioned cabins, an excellent restaurant, and a well-stocked bar. The boat, which the Brazilians call a *boatel,* rides on two pontoons and can glide along the river at high speed. In complete comfort the tourists can visit Bananal Island and its previously isolated Indian tribes— tribes so isolated that the Indians express complete amazement when they first are introduced to an ice cube. The explorers can walk through the forests, observing birds or seeking unfamiliar plants; or they can go hunting or fishing. A big thrill is offered to those who are successful in hooking the world's largest fresh-water fish—the *pirarucú,* which weighs 500 pounds. The river abounds in game fish, many of which are excellent for eating.

The time is almost here when no part of Brazil will remain outside of the effective national territory.

Chapter 32 □ Brazil as a Political Unit

Brazil has been characterized by one of its geographers as a "complex giant."[1] With over 40 percent of the total area of Latin America, and nearly 33 percent of the total population there is no doubt that among the countries of Latin America, Brazil is a giant. And anyone who has visited the various parts of this vast area, and who has met and talked with Brazilians from all the different regions is well aware of the complexity. In spite of the continued efforts of writers about Brazil—including the present one—to identify what may be called "national characteristics," the basic fact remains that all kinds of human attitudes and aptitudes can be found among the people of Brazil. There are dull people who are interested only in their own little problems, and there are notable poets, writers, artists, and composers. There are corrupt and dishonest people who will not hesitate to take personal advantage from any political or business situation, and there are devoted, honest people whose ideal is service to Brazil and to their fellow men. There are fuzzy-minded idealists and hard-headed realists. There are people ready and able to invest their savings in business ventures for the sake of improving their material level of living in the future, as in any modern economic system, and there are people for whom the thought of trusting their savings with some one else, even a bank, is viewed as dangerous nonsense. Furthermore there are regions of Brazil in which economic development and the innovations necessary for such development are accepted as basic objectives, and there are also regions in Brazil in which economic development is viewed as just another scheme for the enrichment of those who are already rich. Yet

[1]Hilgard O'Reilly Sternberg, "Brazil: Complex Giant," *Foreign Affairs,* Vol. 43 (1965): 297–311.

in spite of these many complex diversities, Brazil does hold together as a viable state, and is taking the first uncertain steps toward advancing into the modern world.

Brazil is a country faced with many unsolved economic, social, and political problems. In the background of these problems there are always the increasingly sharp contrasts between urban and rural living, between the cities and the *sertões,* and also the contrasts between the São Paulo region and the other regions of Brazil. The continued movement of rural people into the cities makes the search for solutions all the more difficult.

No wonder most Brazilians dream of living in the cities. The great majority of rural Brazilians can barely support their families, even when they work as hard as their inadequate diet permits. At the first opportunity the rural man moves from his isolated clearing in the woods to a place near a road where there are motor trucks going and coming. Then he moves to the nearest town, and if his good fortune continues he moves to the state capital, and finally to Rio de Janeiro or São Paulo. Some are brave enough to move to the cities without money or even the promise of a job, and these are the people who occupy the *favellas*—the hillside slums of Rio de Janeiro, the *Núcleo Bandeirante* of Brasília, or the houseboats tied to the muddy banks of the Rio Negro at Manaus. In the cities there are other people with whom to share poverty, there are bright lights not far away, and there is always the possibility of finding a job. To be sure, there are new pioneer areas where a farmer can occupy land that he does not own, and there are government-sponsored pioneer colonies. But most of the pioneers in these places are hoping to make enough profit from these new farms in a few years to permit them to move to a city. Even the Germans, the Italians, the Poles, and the Japanese are not so permanently attached to the rural life that some of them are not willing to give up farming for urban pursuits. And the Syrian traders who travel as itinerant merchants to the most remote parts of the *sertões* work gradually up the economic ladder until they occupy the best residential areas, as along the Avenida Paulista in São Paulo.

This internal movement toward the urban places, which causes a local lack of balance between the rural areas and the cities even in remote Manaus, produces a lack of balance also on a national scale. São Paulo was the part of Brazil that first started the process of economic growth, primed by wealth created from the sale of coffee on the world market. Before World War I, when textile factories had been operating in Brazil for more than half a century, there were almost as many workers employed in Recife and Salvador as in São Paulo and Sorocaba. But by 1920, about 29 percent of all the industrial workers in Brazil were in São Paulo State, and by 1950 the proportion had risen to nearly 39 percent. Between 1948 and 1955 the proportion of the total national value of manufactured goods that was produced in São Paulo rose from 39 percent to more than 45 percent; and at the same time the proportion of industrial output in the Northeast dropped from 16 percent to less than 10 percent. In 1955 the state of São Paulo, with a population of some 10 million, had a gross product 2.3 times larger than that of the whole Northeast with a population of 20 million. The income per capita in São Paulo was 4.7 times higher than that of the Northeast.

This rapid forward surge of São Paulo had a number of serious consequences. First of all it attracted a major share of the internal migration within the country. But the increasing number of potential workers in São Paulo had the effect of reducing the rate of gain in industrial wages. Wages failed to keep up with the increasing economic production. This had the further effect of increasing the rate of return on capital investment, and thus attracting an increased flow of domestic savings. Even savings created in the Northeast, or the North, or the Central-West were pulled out of these less developed regions, thereby increasing the contrast between São Paulo and the rest of the country.

To correct this imbalance between São Paulo and the rest of the country has become a major element of government policy. The modernization of the Brazilian economy requires first a nationwide development of the economic underpinnings. These include: (1) health and medical programs, which have already brought spectacular results; (2) a program for increasing the production of basic foods; (3) the construction of an adequate national system of transportation; and (4) the construction of a grid of electric power lines fed from new hydroelectric plants. Actual investment in new manufacturing industries is being spread over all the regions of Brazil, with increased attention to such basic industries as steel and iron, food processing, textiles, automobiles, and shipbuilding, as well as to a large growth of consumer-goods industries. Some parts of this program require the services of trained engineers and scientists; but other parts will require nothing less than a basic change in the attitudes and objectives of more than half of the Brazilian population. More and more people, outside São Paulo, must learn to appreciate the services of scientists and engineers and to accept the innovations they create. More and more people must be ready to do what is needed to seek material improvement in their living conditions, and to provide their families with the larger volume and greater variety of goods and services that a modernized economy can offer them.

Population

The population of Brazil is growing at a faster and faster rate. In 1967 it was estimated that the total population had nearly reached 86 million, and that it would pass 100 million by 1970. The rate of growth during the decade from 1940 to 1950 was 2.5 percent per year; but between 1958 and 1964 the population increased at the rate of 3.1 percent. This is not the highest rate of increase in Latin America, but it is the highest in the world for any similarly large country.

This increasingly rapid rate of population increase is the result of programs for the improvement of health. Even in the 1930's there had been an attack on the spread of yellow fever and malaria, but the new medical procedures developed during World War II have been applied in Brazil mostly since 1950. With insecticides and antibiotics, many killing diseases have been brought under control. Where 4 babies out of 5 used to die in the first month, now 3 or 4 survive. The death rate has been brought down to between 10 and 13 per thousand, yet the birth rate remains at a high 40 to 44 per thousand. Furthermore, since more than half of the total population in 1967 was under fifteen years of age, a continued high rate of births is to be expected as the number of men and women of child-producing age increases.

Immigration is no longer a factor in the growth of the population. The table shows that before World War I, and for a short time between 1920 and 1930, immigration accounted for a substantial part of total growth. But since 1930, although immigrants continue to enter Brazil, the numbers are not great enough to account for the increase in the rate of growth.

IMMIGRATION AND POPULATION INCREASE—1884–1953*

Period	Immigrants	Population Increase	Percentage of Immigrants in Total Increase
1884–93	883,668	2,781,000	31.7
1894–03	862,110	3,964,000	21.7
1904–13	1,006,617	4,480,000	22.5
1914–23	503,981	5,466,000	9.2
1924–33	737,223	6,547,000	11.3
1934–43	197,238	8,420,000	2.3
1944–53	344,851	11,679,000	2.9

Petermann's Mitteilungen, Vol. 100, (1956), p. 154.

Estimates of the ethnic composition of Brazil's population are not at all satisfactory. In few parts of the world is there such a mixture of ethnic types. All kinds of gradations among Indian, Negro, and Caucasian are to be found. Official data on racial proportions, averaged for the country as a whole, are meaningless. Map 4 (p. 13) indicates those regions of Brazil in which there is a relatively large proportion of Africans—especially in the Northeast, the East, and parts of the Central-West. The map also indicates that the population of São Paulo and the South resembles the populations of Uruguay and Argentina in having a very small proportion of Indian or African elements.

The fact is that São Paulo and the South have received a very considerable part of the more than four and a half million foreigners who have come to Brazil since 1822. As we have seen, some of these foreigners have remained in the areas where they first settled, but large numbers have moved into the cities where they have become as thoroughly Brazilianized as the descendants of the *bandeirantes*. An examination of the names listed in the telephone directory of São Paulo City suggests that this metropolis is as cosmopolitan as New York. People have come to Brazil from many parts of Europe, as well as from Japan and from Syria and Lebanon. The largest numbers have come from Italy and Portugal; but over the decades the proportions from different countries have varied. The table shows the proportions by decades.

PROPORTIONS OF IMMIGRANTS FROM VARIOUS SOURCES*

Period	Italian	Portuguese	Spanish	Japanese	German	Russian	Other
1884–1893	57.8	19.3	11.6	—	2.6	4.6	4.1
1894–1903	62.4	18.3	10.9	—	0.8	0.3	7.3
1904–1913	19.5	38.2	22.3	1.2	3.4	4.8	10.6
1914–1923	17.1	39.9	18.8	4.1	5.8	1.6	12.7
1924–1933	9.5	31.7	7.1	14.9	8.4	1.1	27.3
1934–1943	5.8	38.4	2.6	23.4	9.1	0.1	20.6
1944–1953	18.3	41.1	14.4	1.1	4.1	0.5	20.5

*From the *Instituto Brasileiro de Geografia e Estatística*.

The Economy: Agriculture

All these diverse people in different parts of the national territory are, in fact, supported by one of two quite different, but overlapping, economic systems. On the one hand there are those who produce things for sale and who use the money they earn to buy goods and services. On the other hand there are those who produce almost everything they consume and consume very little that they did not themselves produce. In this group are the subsistence farmers—more than half of the Brazilian people. Of course the two economies are not entirely separate. The subsistence farmers sell some surplus farm products in order to buy such things as cotton cloth, needles, matches, machetes, hoes, or kerosene. And the people who produce for sale may cultivate small areas of food crops for their own use. There is, however, a considerable difference in attitude between the two groups.

Crops for Export

For a long time coffee has been Brazil's most valuable export. In the chapter on São Paulo we discussed the spread of coffee in that region, and the subsequent decline. It was in São Paulo that the state government first decided to maintain the price of coffee on the world market by withdrawing some of the supply. Later this became the policy of the federal government. But this effort to defend the coffee producers against declines in price has had the effect of ending Brazil's monopoly position. Before World War I Brazil was producing over 75 percent of the world's coffee. In the 1930's

Brazil's share was still about 60 percent of world production. In 1966 the total world production of coffee amounted to 80,900,000 bags, of which Brazil produced 37,631,000 bags, or 46 percent. As a result of the high market prices, two things took place: (1) the consumption of coffee per capita in the United States, the world's largest coffee market, which was 18.2 pounds in 1947–49, dropped to 14.7 pounds in 1963–65; and (2) many other countries in the world, including chiefly Colombia, Mexico, and the Central American states, increased their production of coffee. But between 1955 and 1965 the coffee production of the African countries doubled. In order to avert a disastrous drop in coffee prices, 36 coffee-producing countries signed the International Coffee Agreement, providing for export quotas to be established each year. In 1966 Brazil's share of the total export market was 17,300,000 bags; yet in that same year the warehouses in Brazil, mostly in São Paulo State, were bulging with 62 million bags, which represented a very considerable investment of government funds. The whole world market per year in the 1960's was only about 50 million bags. It was in 1966 that the Brazilian government began a program of uprooting coffee trees and destroying the poorer quality coffee in storage.

Meanwhile, coffee is still Brazil's most valuable export. The table below gives the proportion of Brazil's total exports accounted for by coffee, cotton, and cacao. Before 1960 coffee usually brought in more than half of Brazil's foreign currency. But in 1965 the share of coffee was down to 44.2 percent, and it is certain to drop still farther as other products increase in value.

EXPORTS OF BRAZIL—VALUE OF COFFEE, COTTON, AND CACAO*

as percentage of the value of all exports in selected years

Years	Coffee	Cotton	Cacao
1901–10	51.3	2.1	2.8
1921–30	69.6	2.4	3.2
1931–40	50.0	14.2	4.2
1947	36.6	14.4	4.9
1949	55.5	9.9	4.7
1953	66.0	7.1	4.9
1965	44.2	6.0	1.7

Annuário Estatistico do Brasil.

Cotton, which for a long time was the second export product of Brazil in terms of value, has never been one of the country's economic "rulers." Cotton, unlike sugar, coffee, and rubber, did not enter the world market as a new product of which Brazil held a virtual monopoly. Cotton-growing in Brazil has brought prosperity only in those years when other sources of supply in the world have failed. Brazil has played the role of a marginal producer whose participation in the world market becomes possible only when areas of cheaper production cannot meet the demand. During the last half of the eighteenth century, Brazilian cotton, coming almost entirely from the Northeast, held a place of importance on the European market, but a decline of cotton prices during the early part of the nineteenth century, resulting from the increasing shipments from regions where the costs of production were lower, forced the Northeast out of the market. Brazilian cotton was again in demand when the Civil War in the United States curtailed production from the "Cotton Belt." The peak of production at this time came in 1871–72, when 362,130 bales were exported from Brazil, with the Northeast accounting for over 350,000 bales, or about 96 percent. This figure was not reached again until 1934. During World War I high prices resulted once more in an increase of cotton growing in Brazil, this time in São Paulo State. In one of the war years São Paulo's share of the Brazilian production was over 50 percent. Since 1930 the share of the total accounted for by São Paulo has varied from about 30 percent to over 80 percent (44 percent in 1961). In the period when Brazil's cotton could not penetrate the international markets, it did find an increasing market in the textile factories of São Paulo. In recent years this has been the chief use of Brazilian cotton. During the 1930's, when the United States had adopted a policy of restricting production to maintain prices, Brazil again entered the world markets; in 1938 cotton made up 18 percent of all exports, and in that year Brazil accounted for 70 percent of the cotton exports of Latin America. During World War II, when shipping space was greatly restricted, there was a large drop in cotton exports, but after the war the exports increased again. The greater part of the annual cotton production is used to supply Brazil's textile factories.

There was a period when cacao was Brazil's third most valuable export product. The cacao district of southern Bahia was rapidly developed out of previously unused tropical forest in the period between World War I and World War II. At that time Brazil pushed ahead of Ecuador and Venezuela in cacao exports. By 1938 Brazil was producing more than half of all the exports of cacao from Latin America. In the 1950's Brazil was producing some 16 percent of the world supply; but in 1965–66 its share of world production was less than 10 percent, and in 1965 cacao exports from Brazil accounted for only 1.7 percent of the value of all exports.

The other agricultural exports which have maintained or increased their importance since 1950 include a variety of products. Sugar from the Northeast and São Paulo again reaches the world market since the decline of exports from Cuba. Fruit exports are chiefly oranges and bananas from São Paulo and the East. From the Northeast come oilseeds, Carnaúba wax, castor oil, oiticica oil, and babaçu oil. Some *maté* comes from Paraná. In the late 1960's jute and pepper were starting to come from the Amazon region. Frozen and canned beef increased in importance.

The Subsistence Farmers

The subsistence farmer is the tenant or sharecropper who occupies a small clearing in the forest (a *roça*) on the large property of the landlord. The landlord wants as many tenants as he can get chiefly because: (1) he will then have a supply of workers nearby when needed; (2) he can secure a larger political patronage if he can guarantee more votes. The *compadre* system ties the farmer to the landlord in the only kind of social security he knows; but he remains always in debt, and his greatest efforts can scarcely provide himself and his family with enough to eat. This is the traditional Brazilian rural system, inherited from the colonial period. In the process of land rotation the farmer's *roça,* after a few years in crops, is turned into pasture for the owner's cattle, then permitted to grow up again in brush. The system is not only an expensive way to produce food, but it is also destructive of the land base.

Commercial agriculture and subsistence agriculture are intermingled in the more densely populated areas, and here, because of the pressure of people on the land, the speed of land destruction is greatest. But the subsistence farmers must of necessity be dispersed rather than concentrated. These farmers occupy isolated clearings in the forest, usually out of sight of neighbors. Over the vast interior of the country, the *sertões* are thinly occupied by a large number of people—people so isolated from each other, so thinly scattered, that they cannot generate the kind of economic production or the kind of market that would lead toward economic development. This is the Brazil which seems to defy the forces of change, yet from which people dream of escaping when opportunity to do so appears.

The Food Supply

What is the Brazilian food supply that needs to be increased, and where does it come from? For a majority of the Brazilians who do not eat imported foods, the need is for rice, beans, *farinha* (manioc flour), and some meat. In São Paulo and Rio de Janeiro there are people who eat fresh vegetables and fruit, such as oranges and bananas. But the typical rural Brazilian never eats fruit, and is not the least interested in vegetables—as the Japanese farmers discovered in Belém. Even the demand for fish is very small. Day after day the diet consists of rice and beans, *farinha,* some *rapadura* (sugar candy), some coffee, and some dried beef. And *caxaça* (brandy made from sugar) can make hunger seem unimportant, at least for a time.

Most of the basic foods are grown by the subsistence farmers for their own use. To be sure, there are a few small areas of commercial rice farming, as in the Jacuí Valley, the middle Paraíba Valley, or along the lower São Francisco; but 75 percent of Brazil's rice is dry-land rice, grown as a part of the typical crop combination of maize, rice, beans, and manioc, perhaps with a little cotton. The rice is harvested first, then the maize, then the beans climb the maize stalks, then the whole *roça* is abandoned to a thicket of manioc bushes.

How is Brazil's food production to be increased? In the days of Malthus the way to increase food production was to clear more land, establish a pioneer colony of farmers. But the enormous technological advances in food production of the modern period require a large investment of capital in agriculture, a concentration of farming on the best suited and most accessible areas, and a decrease in the number of farmers. Which method will be used in Brazil? There is strong pressure for an expansion of the traditional system, for the establishment of new colonies of primarily subsistence farmers in the remote parts of the *sertões*. This is the system familiar to more than half the people of Brazil. But it is a high-cost system. For the purpose of placing excess population in out-of-the-way spots, these new colonies are a solution that remind one of the technique of sweeping a problem under the rug. But a real increase of the food supply, without an increase of food prices, will require a new approach to this kind of farming, a farm system pioneered in São Paulo since 1950. Can this system be applied to the rest of Brazil?

Other Factors in the Economy

The New Roads

The railroads never quite became an integral part of the settlement pattern except in a few places. But away from the railroads the only alternative transportation was by oxcart or mule train over trails impassable for motor vehicles. Where rivers provided water deep enough for boats, transportation was relatively inexpensive.

The construction of all-weather roads for motor trucks and automobiles is a new development in Brazil. The first places where all-weather roads were built were in São Paulo and in the Northeast. The major roads of the Northeast were built during World War II as a defense measure. By 1950 it was possible to travel widely over the backlands of Brazil, but only in dry weather. Now most of the main roads have been paved and are used by large numbers of motor trucks.

The main motor highways are shown on Maps 113 and 118 (pp. 690 and 695). Brasília has been made the hub of a national road system which will soon make the most remote parts of the national territory accessible to the chief urban centers. Road connections have been completed with Uruguay, Argentina, and Paraguay, with new highway bridges over the Paraná and Uruguay Rivers. The road from southern Goiás to Belém has become an important artery of traffic. The road to Cuiabá, Pôrto Velho, and Cruzeiro do Sul will soon be connected with the marginal highway of Peru. A road is being built northward from Manaus to connect, eventually, with the roads of Venezuela and Guyana.

These new roads are of the greatest importance, not only for Brazil, but also for the whole of South America. If there is to be a Latin American Free Trade Association, the geographical separation of the different countries must be overcome. The generalizations presented in Chapter 1, (p. 3) regarding the pattern of population must be basically altered before the plans for international cooperation and economic development could possibly succeed.

Also a part of the transportation development in Brazil is the construction of new ports, or the improvement of older ports. The new iron-ore shipping ports were previously mentioned, and railroads must be built or rebuilt if heavy ores are to be moved at low cost. This work is now being undertaken as a part of Brazil's overall plan for economic development.

Electric Power

Manufacturing industry cannot make a start without some source of cheap power. In the absence of abundant sources of coal, hydroelectric power is the obvious answer—and Brazil has a vast amount of unused water power. We have suggested (p. 796) that the early start of São Paulo City as a manufacturing center was in part a result of the power developments on the Rio Tieté and at Cubatão. Rio de Janeiro was inadequately supplied with electric power from a plant on the Rio Paraíba. The table opposite gives the consumption of electric energy for all purposes by states and regions in 1964. In that year São Paulo State consumed about 44 percent of all the electric energy of Brazil.

By 1967, however, Brazil had started an ambitious program to increase the supply of electric energy. In 1950 the first generator at the Paulo Afonso Falls on the Rio São Francisco started to operate, but by 1971 this plant will have been increased to produce 1,220,000 kilowatts. The Tres Marias plant on the upper Rio São Francisco will supply 520,000 kilowatts. The whole São Francisco, from its headwaters to its mouth, is a huge potential source of untapped power, amounting to an estimated 5 million kilowatts. In Minas Gerais on the Rio Grande, a tributary of the Paraná, the Furnas Dam will soon be generating 1,200,000 kilowatts to feed into the transmission lines over the whole of the East. In 1971 a new plant will be completed on the Rio Doce at Mascarenhas to produce 115,000 kilowatts.

The largest hydroelectric project in all Latin America is the Urubupungá complex on the Paraná River (p. 796). When completed in 1973, the total production of electric energy will amount to almost 5 million kilowatts. And Brazil has reached an agreement with Paraguay to make use of the even greater potential at the *Salto das Sete Quedas*.

Brazil, in 1967, was well started in the construction of the necessary underpinning for a major development of the economy.

CONSUMPTION OF ELECTRIC ENERGY BY STATES AND REGIONS, 1964*

in millions of kilowatt-hours

The Northeast	2,146
Maranhão	20
Piauí	13
Ceará	124
Rio Grande do Norte	36
Paraíba	142
Pernambuco	725
Alagôas	89
Sergipe	58
Bahia	489
The East	7,377
Minas Gerais	2,944
Espírito Santo	105
Rio de Janeiro	1,686
Guanabara	2,642
São Paulo	10,434
The South	2,355
Paraná	932
Santa Catarina	395
Rio Grande do Sul	1,028
The Central-West	295
Mato Grosso	57
Goiás	118
Distrito Federal	120
The North	140
Rondônia	6
Acre	4
Amazonas	37
Roraima	1
Pará	89
Amapá	13
Total	22,747

*Source, *Survey of the Brazilian Economy,* Brazilian Embassy, Washington, D.C., 1965.

Iron Ore, Steel, and Other Manufacturing

After resisting for many years the plans of such foreign businessmen as Percival Farquhar to develop the export of Brazil's iron ore, in 1966 the government finally decreed that privately owned ore-shipping ports could be built. We have described the development at Tubarão in Espírito Santo and also the new port to be built on the Baía de Sepetiba (p. 766). Brazil comes late into the international market for iron ore, after many new sources of high grade ore have been discovered elsewhere in the world. But Brazil's ore is still high in quality and can be mined at relatively low cost. The mining is being developed by joint Brazilian and Japanese firms, and by a Brazilian-North American firm. The largest contract for the export of iron in history was drawn up between Brazil and ten Japanese corporations. The ore will be pelletized at the ore ports in preparation for shipment.

Brazil has had a steel industry since 1817. But the development of large-scale modern steel plants had to await a number of technological developments which did not become available until the 1930's. The lack of coking coal seemed to be an insuperable obstacle because of the high cost of imported coal. The early steel plants all made use of charcoal to produce steel of exceptional quality, and even now many of the Brazilian plants continue to use charcoal. But during the 1930's engineers in India learned how to make use of low-quality coal and how to use less coal in the steel-making process.

The nationally owned steel plant at Volta Redonda in the Paraíba Valley, now known as the Gilherme Guinle Steel Plant, was built during World War II and started production in 1946. This plant makes use of Brazilian coal from Santa Catarina mixed with imported coal from West Virginia. The plant has been enlarged, and further enlargements are planned, so that it retains its position as the leading producer of steel in all Latin America. Other major steel plants built more recently in Brazil include the steel complex at Piaçaguera near Santos, and the plant being built in the Rio Doce Valley (see pp. 762–766).

Manufacturing industries that make use of the steel have been established at an increasing rate since 1960. Brazil has become a major shipbuilding nation, with shipyards on Guanabara Bay that are equipped to manufacture the new 100,000-ton super-tankers. With part Brazilian and part Japanese capital, these shipyards have already produced ships not only for Brazil, but also for Great Britain, Sweden, and Mexico. A new shipyard is planned for Recife.

In 1966 Brazil ranked eighth among the nations of the world in the manufacture of automobiles. In 1956 no automobiles were manufactured in Brazil, although some were assembled from imported parts. But 10 years later, 11 companies were making automobiles. The capital invested in these factories came from Brazil (37 percent), the United States (33 percent), Germany (18 percent), Switzerland (6 percent), and in smaller proportions from France, Japan, Sweden, and Italy. As a result of the completion of the roads, there was a very large domestic market for motor trucks.

Seeking Regional Balance

An important part of the plans for economic development provides for the increase of production in regions outside of São Paulo. Especially in the

Northeast, the North, and the Central-West, the income per capita is dangerously low in comparison with the productivity and the income of São Paulo. In any modern industrial state there is a core area from which a large part of the gross national product comes, and once such a concentration of production appears, there are economies that result from channeling new capital investment into these same areas. The problem in Brazil arises from too great a concentration of production in the one state. It is unlikely that any government could arrange to take away from São Paulo its preeminent position in the national economy; but to build up the other regions of Brazil would, in the long run, benefit not only the less developed regions, but would also benefit São Paulo by increasing the market in these other regions for Paulista products.

The policy of seeking greater regional balance is put into operation by means of tax incentives. Individuals or corporations are relieved of up to half of their total tax obligation if they invest this money in acceptable economic projects in the Northeast or the North. As a result, there has been a substantial flow of new capital into such places as Salvador and Recife, or Belém and Manaus. There are agencies of the government set up for the purpose of planning and coordinating such investment.

Results were already visible in 1967. There was a new shipyard planned for Recife, new sawmill at Belém, a new jute textile factory at Santarém. New factories making a variety of consumer goods have been built in places where previously there were no industries. Between 1964 and 1966 there were 240 new manufacturing plants built in the cities of the Northeast.

Exports

For many years, the leading exports of Brazil have been coffee, cotton, and cacao. During World War II Brazil's manufactured products for the first time appeared in the list of exports. Immediately after the war, manufactured goods were second only to coffee, making up 20 percent of the total value of exports. About 11 percent of the exports were cotton textiles. Brazilian cotton goods were sent in large quantities to South Africa and Argentina, and even appeared in retail stores in the United States. Brazilian rubber overshoes found a substantial market in the United States. By 1956, however, manufactured items had dropped and the three commercial crops had regained their positions. By 1965, manufactured goods were again in second place, and iron ore had climbed to third place. The remainder of the exports included a great variety of items from all over Brazil.

The Political Situation

In 1822, when Brazil became independent from Portugal, it was the son of the Portuguese king who made the declaration. He became Pedro I of

Brazil. In 1831, however, Dom Pedro I abdicated in favor of his five-year-old son, and for nine years Brazil was administered in the name of the Emperor by a regency. From 1840 until the end of the Empire in 1889, Dom Pedro II was the monarch. During the period when most of the other Latin-American countries were torn by internal conflict, Brazilians, for the most part, were ready to give their support to their enlightened and popular ruler. It was the final emancipation of the slaves in 1888 which brought an end to the institution of the monarchy and the landed aristocracy on which the monarchy was based.

In 1894, after a few years of military government, there started a succession of civilian presidents. By this time the modern political alignments had made their appearance. São Paulo State was already the strongest economically, but Minas Gerais had the largest population, and the states of the Northeast, acting as a unit for political purposes, often held the balance of power. For many years the presidency went alternately to a candidate from São Paulo and then to one from Minas Gerais. Some of the presidents turned out to be able and honest administrators, but there were also examples of corruption and confusion.

Always in the background of Brazilian politics were the *sertões,* with their scattered, isolated inhabitants. During the first civilian administration, 1894–98, much money and effort were spent in putting down a revolt in the backlands of Bahia.[2] In the two years between 1925 and 1927 the communist leader, Luiz Carlos Prestes, led a column of rebellious soldiers through the backlands of Brazil, touching at every state and covering a distance of more than two thousand miles. He sought to arouse the spirit of revolt among the people of the back country and among the "serf-like" workers on the coffee plantations and the cattle ranches. He was not successful in gaining many followers; but he gained a mythical reputation as a kind of modern Robin Hood, who had entered the great Brazilian backlands and conquered them.

In 1930, with the collapse of the financial structure that had been erected to maintain the speculative profits in coffee planting, the federal government was attacked and overthrown by army units from Rio Grande do Sul, led by Getúlio Vargas. From 1930 to 1945 Vargas remained in control of Brazil, setting up in 1937 what he called the *Estado Novo,* modeled on Fascist Italy. Although the Brazilian people tolerated their dictator, they would not be regimented on the fascist pattern. In 1945 the army removed Vargas and called for new elections and the end of the New State. Elections were actually held and honestly counted. In fact, after an interval Vargas himself was elected president in 1951, and he held office until his suicide in 1954.

In the period after World War II there were three main political groups. The conservatives were mostly represented by the *União Democrática*

[2]Euclydes da Cunha, *Os Sertões,* translated by Samuel Putnam, *Rebellion in the Backlands,* Chicago, 1944.

Nacional; those who wanted to find political expression for their dissatisfaction with administrative dishonesty and with social and economic inequality either gave their support to Vargas or to the communists under Prestes. In terms of actual numbers the communists reached the peak of their strength in the period between 1945 and 1947. Since then they have declined in number, but are stronger and more tightly disciplined. They have launched verbal attacks on the United States, and have succeeded in blocking the entry of foreign capital in the development of Brazil's presumed oil resources and in the mining and export of iron ore. *"O petróleo é nosso"* is their slogan—"the oil is ours." Supporting the communists in this policy of restricting the investment of foreign capital in resource development were many noncommunist but strongly nationalistic groups, including the politically powerful officers of the army.

Between 1956 and 1964 Brazil had a succession of civilian presidents who continued to resist foreign investments. Juscelino Kubitschek was the president who carried out the project for moving the capital away from Rio de Janeiro and who was chiefly responsible for getting the construction of Brasília under way. He was followed by two presidents whose economic policies have been described as irresponsible. In spite of runaway inflation, the government took no effective steps to bring it under control. The fact is that such steps were highly unpopular, especially among those people who gained from the rapid increase in the value of land. These presidents also brought Brazil closer to the communist orbit, by promoting closer trade relations with the Soviet Union and by awarding medals to the communist leaders of Cuba. There were many people who were certain that president João Goulart was about to follow the lead of Fidel Castro. The fact that Goulart was becoming rich as a result of the increased value of his own large land properties means that he could not, strictly speaking, be described as a communist. But many people considered him one. In 1964 the army intervened, exiled the president, and took control of the government. Thereafter they ruled by decree, or through carefully controlled elections.

The army officers, however, were not seeking personal gain, nor were they seeking political power for its own sake. They were genuinely devoted to returning Brazil to what they considered to be an economically sound program. It has been this government which in 1966 granted permission for a privately owned corporation to build its own ore-shipping port. Foreign investments were again welcomed, but most of the new capital came from Brazilian private investors or from government funds. After 1966 Brazil began to experience a period of notable economic growth.

Forces for Union and Disunion

The political situation, as well as the economic policies of the government, require an examination of the underlying factors in Brazil that lead toward or away from coherence and unity. Can this huge country, with its great diversity of people and of attitudes toward policy questions, and its great contrasts in regional development, continue to form a coherent and viable state? Is it not possible that São Paulo, with its much higher level of living, will grow tired of "pulling the empty cars"?

It is a principle of political geography that if people of strongly different political ideas occupy two clearly separate parts of the national territory, the situation is dangerous. If people of very different political ideas are inter-mingled throughout the different parts of the state, there is much less danger of disintegration. Or if the national territory is marked off into three or more sections in each of which there is a distinctive political stand, again the danger of disintegration is diminished. The greatest danger appears when the national territory is divided into just two parts.

The regional contrasts within Brazil are not simple ones. There is a strong tendency toward state loyalty. The people of Minas Gerais are loyal to their state, as are the Paulistas to theirs. Only in the Northeast is there a sense of regional loyalty, but even here the willingness to cooperate with other states of the Northeast is superimposed on loyalty to the individual states. But in economic terms, the analogy of the locomotive pulling the string of empty cars points to the clear fact that São Paulo enjoys a level of living that is unlike that of any other part of the country, and that the Paulista attitude toward economic development and toward the acceptance of innovation is not like that of other parts of Brazil. There are people in other regions who favor economic development, but there are also many who prefer to maintain the old traditional order. In São Paulo the overwhelming majority support devel-opment and change.

São Paulo, then, does in a sense represent a division of the national terri-tory within which there is a distinctive state-idea. But the geographical position of São Paulo is critical. If São Paulo were located on the periphery of the national territory, as is Rio Grande do Sul, there might be a very real possi-bility that the state would secede from Brazil and declare its independence. There are many Paulistas who resent having to pay taxes to support the poorer parts of the country; but the geographic position of São Paulo in the center of the political unit makes it very unlikely that any serious movement to break away from the rest of the country could be translated into action.

There are many forces leading toward more coherence and unity. Modern transportation, especially the airplane, has come to Brazil in time to permit rapid movement from place to place, and again to minimize the separatist tendencies of some states. The industrial and urban type of economy has come first to São Paulo and Rio de Janeiro; but it has also gained a strong base in Pôrto Alegre and in other parts of the country. The sense of unity is increased, also, by the use of the Portuguese language, which sets off the Brazilians from the other Latin-Americans. Brazil has developed a common heritage and a common tradition which has gone a long way to establish a Brazilian state-idea to which people in all parts of the country remain loyal. And no small part of the modern state-idea is the widespread admiration for Brasília with its ultra-modern but distinctively Brazilian architecture, and especially with its location in the very midst of the *sertões*.

General Conclusion and Appendices

Chapter 33 □ General Conclusion

The economic, social, and political changes which we have examined in specific parts of Latin America are best seen in the perspective of a worldwide process of innovation. Latin America is the culture region in which the transformations of life brought by the industrial and democratic revolutions[1] are currently making the greatest impact on preexisting ways of living. The cultural innovations included in the concept of the twin revolutions have their roots far back in the history of occidental society, but they first appeared in revolutionary form in Western Europe around the shores of the North Sea in the latter half of the eighteenth century. As the innovation waves spread from the place of origin, the content of the industrial and democratic revolutions has been enlarged and further developed, so that the innovations today sweeping over Latin America are not exactly the same as those that appeared around the North Sea two centuries ago. On the other hand, the current changes are derived from the revolutions that started in Europe, and can be traced back to the source region both historically and geographically. From a broad point of view these innovations represent one great worldwide process which is unlike any other process of culture change since the rise of the early city civilizations six thousand years ago.

Both of the world's contemporary revolutions have been given new dimensions in the culture region of Anglo-America. The unprecedented economic growth of the United States and Canada in the twentieth century is due to a number of innovations picked up and developed from European sources, and nurtured in the world's largest common market. Similarly, the ideals of equality of opportunity and social justice were first written down in the Dec-

[1] See pp. 43–51. This worldwide perspective is developed in the author's *One World Divided*, New York, 1964.

laration of Independence and the Constitution of the United States. And in spite of current problems in the application of these ideals, the fact remains that never before in human history, and in no comparable area of the earth, have so many people accepted these ideals as the basis of a way of life. As a result, Anglo-America is today the source of what we have described as a powerful cultural radiation—a major source of innovation in the attitudes, objectives, and technologies of modern life.

This interpretation of the pattern of change currently sweeping over Latin America will not be popular among some Latin-Americans. Heard from the southern part of the American hemisphere is a lot of "noise" carried along with the waves of innovation. "Noise" refers to the fact that the processes of change are not presented clearly, but are accompanied by confusing and conflicting currents of controversy. This confusion is in part the inevitable consequence of policy discussion in an open society; but it is also in part the result of the caricature of the United States commonly accepted by Latin-Americans. When it is discovered that most North Americans accept a similarly blurred caricature of their neighbors to the south the problem of communications becomes all the more difficult.

In this concluding chapter we shall attempt to place the character of culture change in Latin America in perspective. A frequently overlooked result of change is the appearance of the world's largest population explosion. What are the problems and prospects of economic growth, and how can the rate of growth catch up with the expansion of population? There can be no possibility of effective economic growth without a deep-seated change in social attitudes and objectives. And these changes take place in the context of separate states, each struggling to attain coherence and viability. Finally, we shall examine the outlook, and seek some guidelines that might help the United States in its dealings with these other Americans.

Population Problems

The fact that Latin America includes only 7 percent of the world's population on 15 percent of the area of the inhabited continents can be misleading. This does not mean that a vast population increase can be accommodated. We have seen numerous examples of the difficulty in making effective use of these empty areas. We have found that some empty areas have remained empty because of the poverty of the soil, or the lack of water, or the presence of too much water, or the lack of accessibility to markets, or other reasons. But we also know that modern fertilizers and soil conditioners can make a naturally poor soil highly productive. On the other hand, we have seen examples of places where large areas of former agricultural land had to be abandoned when the man with a hoe and machete was replaced by the man with a tractor and plow. The fact is that the relation of settlement to the land base is much too complicated to be summarized by a simple comparison between population and total area.

There are three parts of the population problem in Latin America that should be emphasized. First is the extraordinary rate of increase. Second is the increasing concentration of people in urban areas. And third is the opposite tendency to move out from the areas of concentrated settlement into pioneer zones.

The Rate of Growth

In no other major part of the world is the population increasing so fast as it is in Latin America. In 16 out of the 24 independent countries the rate of increase is 2.4 percent per year or over, and in 13 of these it is 3.0 percent or over. At about 2.5 percent per year, it takes 28 years for the population to double, and at a rate of 3.5 percent it takes only 20 years. Each month in Latin America as a whole there are some 700,000 additional human beings to be fed, clothed, provided with shelter, educated, and eventually employed. The table gives the average annual percentage of growth for certain major world regions between 1900 and 1960, and the forecast for the period 1960 to 2000.

RATES OF POPULATION GROWTH*

	Average annual percent medium estimates	
	1900–1960	1960–2000
The world as a whole	1.0	1.7
China	1.0	1.8
Japan	1.3	0.7
India and Pakistan	1.0	1.9
Europe, excluding USSR	0.6	0.5
USSR	0.8	1.3
United States and Canada	1.5	1.5
Latin America	2.0	2.7

*from United Nations, *Proceedings of the World Population Conference, 1965,* New York, 1967, p. 22.

We have shown that this rapid rate of population growth is a result of a recent unprecedented decline in the death rate and of continued high birth rates. With the exception of a few countries, such as Argentina, Uruguay, Chile, Barbados, Trinidad, and Cuba, the birth rates are between 40 and 50 per thousand. Meanwhile the death rates have been declining since 1920, when the first countrywide programs to eliminate yellow fever and hookworm were started; and since 1950 the continued spread of medical services and of facilities for the control of disease has produced a 50 to 70 percent drop in the death rates. Most death rates in the countries of Latin America are now below 20 per thousand, and several are less than 10. There was a time when 4 out of every 5 babies born would die in the first month; now only 2 or 3 babies die in infancy. As a result, the Latin-American populations all include a high proportion of young people. In Latin America the people less than 15 years of age make up 40 to 50 percent of the total population, compared with 30 percent in the United States and 23 percent in Western Europe. As these young people reach child-producing age they will support a continued high birth rate for the next several decades.

Population Movement to the Cities

All over Latin America the population of the cities is increasing faster than the total population. There is a tendency for people to move away from already thinly peopled areas and to increase the concentration in the already well-populated areas. It is in the cities, and especially in the largest city, the primate city, that one finds the greatest number and variety of economic opportunities. It is to the city, and if possible to the largest city, that the countryman wants to go. And the more the rural farm worker earns, the more he learns, the more he widens the horizons of his knowledge, the more he wants to move into the urban centers. This trend toward increased urbanization, taking people away from the empty areas toward the more densely crowded spots, is a basic fact.

Our study of the population pattern of Latin America has shown that there is an urban core in the midst of each separate cluster of people, and that in most cases there is only one such central city. Because the clusters have generally remained separate, the service areas of the central cities usually do not overlap with those of other cities. Usually, also, each country has a primate city which is many times larger than any other city in the country. Montevideo is seventeen times the size of Uruguay's second city. Buenos Aires is nearly nine times the size of the second city. In only two countries are there two cities of nearly equal size: in Brazil and Ecuador.

The concentration of people in cities is one of the distinguishing traits of the industrial society. The proportion of the people of a country employed in agriculture and the proportion of people in large cities may be used as rough indices of the degree of economic development. In Latin America, however, there are certain peculiarities that ought to be noted. In the urbanized societies of Western Europe, of Anglo-America, and of Australia and New Zealand, employment in manufacturing industry was the first reason for city growth. Capital was invested in factories and machines, and the new jobs that became available as a result of the industrial revolution were in these factories. For each person employed in a "basic industry"—that is, an industry that sends its products outside of the community in which it is located —there are now at least two employed in service occupations: that is, as professional people, teachers, lawyers, police, and many others. The industries appeared first and then led to the multiplication of service employment. But in Latin-American cities the service occupations appeared first, before the rapid increase of jobs in manufacturing. The Economic Commission for Latin America, an agency of the United Nations, concludes that the urban population appears overburdened with services, whose development is apparently out of proportion to existent manufacturing activities. It is for this reason that many of the cities in Latin America seem to be less well served by lines of transportation than cities of comparable size in Western Europe or Anglo-America.

Frontiers of Pioneer Settlement

There is also an opposite, but smaller, tendency. We noted (pp. 4–7) that Latin America has long been characterized by the existence of a clustered pattern of population. There has been little outward movement of new settlement around the margins of the clusters, and as a result the spaces between the clusters remained thinly populated. We have discovered several hollow frontiers, where an outward movement of new settlement is accompanied by a decrease of population in the older settled areas. There were solid frontiers of pioneer settlement in only four parts of mainland Latin America: in highland Costa Rica, in the Antioquia district of Colombia, in southern Chile, and in the three southern states of Brazil.

But in the 1960's a new tendency to develop frontiers of pioneer settlement could be observed. For the first time there were pioneer zones in almost every country where empty spaces were available—such pioneer zones as the Pacific lowland of Central America, the western piedmont of the Andes in Ecuador, the zone along the marginal highway in eastern Peru, or the strings of settlement along the new highways in the Brazilian backlands.

After all these centuries of Spanish and Portuguese settlement in Latin America when pioneer expansion was rare, why did this become important during the 1960's? There seem to have been two chief technological developments that were primarily responsible. One was the new capacity to control disease. Many of the areas that have long remained empty on the population map had the reputation of being death traps because of insect-borne diseases. The medical advances that resulted in the rapid drop of the death rate also made large areas habitable through disease control. And the other technological development was the invention of the huge earth-moving machinery that made it possible to build roads at low enough cost in areas of sparse population. The use of these machines in Latin America was made possible by the financial and technical aid programs of the post-war period. As a result, many miles of new all-weather highways were built, mostly in the 1960's. Motor trucks, operating on these highways, made places accessible to markets that had long suffered from extreme isolation. When the roads were built and the diseases brought under control, pioneers began to move out into these previously empty areas.

Here is a clear illustration of the general principle that changes in the attitudes, objectives, and technical skills of a people require a reappraisal of the resource base on which the people depend for a living.

Economic Development

The idea that economic development is possible and desirable is an innovation in attitudes and objectives introduced by the industrial revolution. Economic development means that there is an increase in the production of goods and services per capita; it suggests that there is an increased return on capital investment; and it also suggests that the purchasing power of the people is gradually enlarged. W. W. Rostow[2] lists the preconditions that make the start of the development process possible, including such changes in the traditional agrarian societies as the willingness to give up land ownership in favor of capital ownership, the willingness to accept innovation and especially to support the findings of scientists and engineers which may run counter to long-established practices. People must want to better their material standard of living by increasing consumption, and they must be willing to accept new kinds of jobs for the purpose of increasing their purchasing power. These represent fundamental changes in the attitudes and objectives of all classes of the traditional Latin-American societies.

These changes are taking place in Latin America, and at an increasing rate. They are associated with the effects of modern medicine and hygiene in reducing the diseases with which the Latin-American population was formerly burdened, and with the widespread attacks on illiteracy which have the effect of increasing the awareness of the possibility of better living. But economic development also becomes more widely desired just at the time when the increased rate of population growth makes gains in the gross national products per capita most difficult.

The Problem of Food

Unfortunately, while the new medical services were saving people from dying, there was no effective program for increasing the supply of food. The United Nations Food and Agriculture Organization (FAO) has estimated that increases in the production of food in Latin America have been less than the increases in population. In 1965–66 an absolute decrease in food production of about 2 percent resulted in a per capita drop of 4 or 5 percent.[3] The amount of food available per capita in Latin America in 1965–66 was less

[2]*Op. Cit.,* see footnote 1, p. 47.

[3]Population Reference Bureau, *Punta del Este, 1961–1967—Early Dawn of a Demographic Awakening.* Population Bulletin, June 1967.

than the amount available in the late 1930's. In 12 countries the average daily per capita supply of calories was well below the 2,550 recommended by FAO for this region. In 13 countries the minimum amount of protein recommended by FAO (71 grams) was not being supplied. Moreover, these are averages: in every country there are large numbers of poor people literally starving, and the situation is getting worse.

On the traditional large, privately owned land property—which is still the chief form of land tenure in most parts of Latin America—the productivity per acre is apt to be low. Of course there are exceptions where the owner is devoted to agriculture as a profession, and where the newest technology is applied. But it is much more common to find the landowner primarily interested in raising cattle, horses, or sheep. He uses the best parts of his property for pasture or feed crops, and permits his tenants to use the more remote, the steeper, or the drier parts of the land for subsistence foods. The crop that occupies a larger acreage than all other crops combined (except in Chile and Panamá) is maize, and this provides a major part of the food supply. Yet the yields per acre are very low.

Furthermore, the rate of land destruction is appalling. Large areas of thinly peopled land have been severely damaged through the practice of slash and burn techniques associated with shifting cultivation. When the forest is removed from watersheds, the rain runs off rapidly, leaving only a small part of the moisture to soak into the ground where it can be used by plants. The soil is carried down into the streams, which turn brown with the load of mud they carry. Then, in the intervals between rains, the land is parched and the streams dry up. The alternation of flood and drought is, in many places, a man-made phenomenon. Under tropical conditions, too, the removal of the shade trees has the effect of killing the soil bacteria which normally perform the function of creating humus from decaying organic matter. When exposed to direct sunlight, the organic matter that falls on the surface is quickly dried before it can be worked into the soil. The progressive impoverishment of the soil over vast areas that look empty on the population map is one of the unexpected discoveries resulting from direct observation in the field in many parts of Latin America.

The result is what we may call the cycle of poverty. The ordinary subsistence farmer, trying to make a bare living on land he does not own, is too poor, and probably also too ignorant, to make use of the modern technology in land use. Since he cannot increase his production of food, or even gain a small surplus for sale, he cannot escape from his condition of poverty. He is forced to accept additional employment for miserable wages on the property of the landowner; but his wages are in many cases not enough to pay off his debts. Even if he knows that he should not try to grow maize on steep slopes, there is nothing else he can do.

To make an effective attack on this cycle of poverty, and to provide adequate food supplies at acceptable prices, will require at least five major changes in the traditional agrarian system. First, if the production of food is to be increased fast enough to take care of the rapidly increasing population, the new farm technology must be accepted. The farmer with a hoe and machete is a high-cost producer. Eventually, farming must be mechanized and modernized with the use of fertilizer, soil conditioners, insecticides, new varieties of plants and animals, and all the other products of scientific research.

Second, if agriculture is to be modernized, something must be done to facilitate the flow of food products to market. Many Latin-American farmers who have had the benefit of technical assistance and have learned how to grow excellent crops have remained thoroughly frustrated by the lack of storage facilities for their harvests, or transportation facilities to markets. The subsistence farmer consumes what he produces; but a farmer who makes use of the modern technology must have money with which to buy what he needs. If he cannot get his crops to market he cannot pay for fertilizer or insecticide. In most parts of Latin America, middlemen purchase the crops at low prices at harvest time. A modern agricultural system will require grain elevators, maize storage silos, and many other facilities that are assumed to be a part of the rural landscape in North America or Europe. Furthermore, these facilities must be accompanied by the institutions to make them work—agricultural credits, technical assistance, experimental farms, and so forth.

Third, these changes in the agricultural system will require a reappraisal of the significance of the resource base—the surface, soil, water, climate, and wild vegetation. Although the new technology will make the natural productivity of the soil less important than before, it will increase the significance of slope. Farming will have to move from the hillsides, where it is now concentrated in most parts of Latin America. It must descend to the flatter places, or ascend to them as in the Planalto Central of Brazil. Hilly lands are suitable for tree crops, and large areas will need to be reforested. The proportion of national territories that can be called arable will decrease, and the pattern of arable land will be redrawn. We may assume that accessibility to a market resulting from location close to a developed transportation facility will become essential.

Fourth, there must be a change in the attitude of the large landowners. The tradition that land ownership gives one status and a position of special privilege cannot be eliminated overnight, except by the kind of violence advocated by some communists. This change has been brought about in Mexico by the confiscation of all properties over a certain size. In other places, taxes have made the holding of land that is not effectively used unprofitable or indeed impossible. But the transition is not easy, and where it is too effectively resisted by the landowners, pressures for change can become explosive.

And fifth, there must be a reduction in the proportion of the total labor force that is employed in farming. One man with a machine can do the work of hundreds of men equipped with hoes and machetes. As long as the men with hoes are not paid very much, they can do the work more cheaply than the tractor. But if they are paid a living wage, the tractor is cheaper.

There are many people in Latin America who contemplate these essential changes with horror. To carry out such a fundamental break with long-established traditions cannot be other than painful, not only for the landowners but also for many of the rural workers. After all, some of the hoes and machetes in use today have been handed down from father to son for generations. In parts of Brazil there is that special relationship of tenant with *fazendeiro* in which both find satisfaction. The question can be honestly raised: should the established way of living of over half of the Brazilians be fundamentally changed in order to provide city people with food? Why did these migrants from rural areas go to the cities in the first place? Why is it that more rural people do not give their support to the *marcha para oeste?* To the landowners, any government program to force them to give up their lands and their positions of privilege looks like a communist plot. There are many Latin-Americans who question sincerely whether the change from a horse-and-wagon economy to an automobile economy, with its accompanying air pollution, and its effect of undermining social and moral values, really represents progress.

The author of this book takes no stand on whether or not economic development leads to a better world for everyone. He only makes the point that the pressure for change is already irresistible. When large numbers of people in a country are both poor and conscious of their poverty, there is an inevitable demand that something be done about it. With a rapidly expanding population, the pressure on government to make a real attack on hunger cannot be avoided. There is no way to produce enough food at acceptable prices without a fundamental revision of the traditional agrarian system.

Manufacturing Industry

The modernization of agriculture cannot be completed without the creation of a large number of new jobs in manufacuring industry or in the service occupations. Manufacturing industry requires the investment of savings either from foreign sources or from well-to-do Latin-Americans. Until recently, however, the wealthy people of Latin America have perferred to spend their money for luxuries, for travel and education, or for investment abroad where conditions were considered more secure. In fact, in many Latin-American countries the landowner who sold his land and entered into business lost his status as a member of the oligarchy. The Chilean landowners for a long time have been unusual because they did not hesitate to invest in manufacturing plants or to become the owners of businesses. In Brazil, although the ownership of unproductive land has never been popular, until recently most of the investment in industry has come from Brazilians of Italian ancestry. In all these countries, on the other hand, the reluctance to invest money in industry is fast disappearing.

Economic development, for the most part, has been dependent on foreign investments, which has come from different sources and has been applied to different parts of Latin America. The period from 1880 to 1914 saw the first important movement of new capital from outside. This was almost exclusively British capital, and a very large proportion of it was invested in Argentina. The British built railroads, packing plants, port facilities, sugar refineries, and a variety of manufacturing plants. By the beginning of World War I, Argentina had become by far the leading country of Latin America in its economic development. It had, by that time, about half of all the production of goods and services in all of Latin America. It was the one important trading country. Its economy was closely tied to that of Great Britain, for Britain absorbed Argentine exports of meat, wheat, maize, and linseed, and supplied the coal on which Argentina was dependent. Most of Argentina's supply of wheat flour was imported from Great Britain, as were also textiles and a variety of other manufactured products. This economic relationship formed almost the perfect example of nineteenth-century ideas of international trade. The industrial development was in Great Britain, and British merchants and manufacturers were the ones who profited most from the import of raw materials and the exports of manufactured goods. British coal provided cargoes for the British ships on the outward voyages, and as Argentina developed it became more and more dependent on the imports of coal. On the return voyage the ships carried wheat and meat. In Argentina the people who gained the most were the large landowners and the political leaders; but the immigrant tenants at that time were better off than they had ever been before. World War I rudely shattered this apparently perfect arrangement, and for the first time the Argentines appreciated the need for developing their own manufacturing industries.

Investments in Latin America from the United States were, at first, exclusively in the mining industries. Chilean copper and nitrate, Peruvian copper, Mexican copper—these were the first raw materials to interest the people of the United States. By the end of the nineteenth century, however, investment of United States capital in such tropical agricultural products as sugar and bananas had started. After World War I, the flow of United States capital into Latin-American economic development increased rapidly. Money was invested in mining, in tropical plantation crops in the Caribbean, in public utilities, and to a certain extent in manufacturing industries. But the largest volume of capital investment from the United States after 1920 went into the oilfields of Venezuela. Just as Argentina rose to preeminence in Latin America in the nineteenth century due to British investment, Venezuela achieved first place in income per capita in the middle of the twentieth century as a result of United States investments. Now, since 1950, United States investments in Mexico and Brazil are producing rapid economic development in those countries—but under very different conditions from those prevailing in either Argentina or Venezuela.

In 1967 the direct investment by private business in Latin America amounted to nearly $12 billion. This represented 20.7 percent of all United States private investments abroad (compared with 30.4 percent invested in European countries and 30.2 percent invested in Canada). The largest investments were in oil, manufacturing industries, and mining. The largest concentration of investment was in Venezuela (23.5 percent of all United States private investments in Latin America), followed by Mexico (11.0 percent), Brazil (10.0 percent), and Argentina (9.2 percent).

In spite of this very considerable flow of North American capital into Latin America, it constituted only a small fraction of the new capital needed to start the process of economic development. The greater part of the capital in any developing country must come from domestic savings, but where the gross national product per capita is less than $250 there is no great reservoir of savings to tap. During the 1950's and 1960's Latin America as a whole was devoting between 15 and 20 percent of the gross national products to new capital formation. Certain countries had already entered the "take-off stage," and although Argentina had reached a period of stagnation, economic development was going forward rapidly in Mexico, Chile, Venezuela, and Puerto Rico. In the state of São Paulo much more development was taking place than in the rest of Brazil. Several other countries seemed about ready to start on the initial phase. The table shows the gross national products per capita of the Latin-American countries.

THE STATES OF LATIN AMERICA RANKED BY GROSS NATIONAL PRODUCT PER CAPITA 1966 (in U.S. dollars)

Puerto Rico	1,120	Guatemala	314
Venezuela	895	Colombia	292
Argentina	700	Guyana	281*
Trinidad	662	El Salvador	279
Uruguay	569	Brazil	271
Cuba	556*	Dominican Republic	264
Panamá	513	Honduras	229
Chile	501	Ecuador	224
Jamaica	500	Paraguay	224
Mexico	470	Bolivia	149
Costa Rica	406	Barbados	140*
Peru	378	Haiti	65*
Nicaragua	365		

*data for 1964
(In 1964 the United States had a gross domestic product per capita of $3,300, and Canada had $2,217.) Revised GNP figures for 1966 and estimates for 1967 are given in the statistical data by countries. See index.

Industrial development is difficult in the absence of a substantial middle class. Before World War II, with certain exceptions, each country had a small number of very wealthy people and large numbers of very poor people, with a large gap between them. In this situation, if the industrial owners subscribe to the principle of large-volume production with low profit per sale, they attempt to enlarge the number of sales by lowering the price of their product. According to Anglo-American economic theory, each drop in the price brings in an increasing number of new customers. But in the Latin America of pre-World War II years, a drop in the price failed to bring in more customers because of the small numbers of people in the middle-income brackets. As a result, the industrial owners attempted to cover the cost of new and more productive machinery by raising prices. The wealthy people could easily afford the higher prices, and the poorer people did not buy in any case.

All this is in process of rapid change, especially since World War II. The development of a middle class results from the attacks on illiteracy, the increased opportunity for employment in retail trade and other service occupations where the need for literate and technically trained people is growing rapidly. Today almost all the political leaders are of middle-class origin. So also are the intellectual leaders: writers, painters, journalists, radio and television performers, professors, school teachers, doctors, lawyers. These are the articulate people who are most open to innovations.[4]

This appearance of a substantial middle class is reflected in the speed of industrial development, and in the diversification of production. There is a decreasing reliance on just one major product. New steel industries are providing materials to be made into a variety of consumer goods not previously marketable in large quantities. The new petrochemical industries are providing the underpinning for continued industrial growth.

Latin-American Exports

This trend toward diversification can be seen in the table of Latin-American exports, showing the percentage of the value of all exports produced by cer-

LATIN AMERICAN EXPORTS—1960 and 1965*

Percent of value of all exports

	1960	1965
oil	29.2	26.4
coffee	18.0	15.0
copper	5.8	5.3
cotton	4.1	5.2
meat	3.5	4.2
wheat	1.8	3.6
iron ore	3.5	3.4
sugar	3.5	2.8
bananas	2.4	2.0
other grains[1]	2.1	1.8
other exports[2]	26.1	30.3

[1]Maize, barley, oats, and rye.
[2]Tobacco, fruits and vegetables, hides and skins, timber, sisal, henequen and Manila hemp, wine, fish, fish meal, shell fish, sorghum, quebracho, oil nuts, oils and fats, nitrate, silver, lead, zinc, and tin.
*Pan American Union, *Latin America's Foreign Trade, Problems and Policies,* 1966.

[4]John P. Gillin, "Some Signposts for Policy," in *Social Change in Latin America Today: Its Implications for United States Policy,* New York, 1960, pp. 14–62.

tain leading commodities. Oil brought the largest returns in both 1960 and 1965, and coffee was second. But both of these commodities produced a smaller proportion of the total value of exports in 1965 than in 1960. The rise in the value of a large number of lesser items is also notable.

It is important, also, that during the period 1961–65 the total value of all Latin America's exports increased more rapidly than it had done for several previous decades. Furthermore, the increase was not due to a larger volume of sales in the largest market—the United States. Rather it was due to increased trade with other countries, notably with the European Economic Community and with Japan.

Changing Social and Political Attitudes

The other great wave of revolutionary change currently sweeping over Latin America is what we have called the democratic revolution. The word "democracy" is used with such different meanings that it is necessary to be very clear about what is intended here. When the communists speak of a "democratic republic" they refer to a strongly centralized, autocratic government which rules in the name of the people. As the term is used here, we refer specifically to those six elements of the democratic revolution listed on page 48.

The Reaction against Autocracy

In Latin America since the early 1950's there has been a strong reaction against autocracy, and against the system of special privilege and social inequity that usually accompanies a strongly centralized autocracy. During the 1930's and 1940's there were numerous dictatorships established, some on the fascist pattern, which is as much a denial of democracy as is the communist pattern. In 1950, 12 of the then 20 Latin-American countries were ruled by army officers who had originally gained the presidency through force. These men were dictators who ruled by decree and who maintained their positions of power with army support. Furthermore, they found the presidency to be highly profitable, making it possible to amass private fortunes and to hide them away in Swiss banks. No deposed dictator has had to apply for a pension.

Between 1955 and 1961, eleven of the twelve dictators were removed from office. Six were removed by revolts of the army, four were assassinated, and one was voted out in an election.[5] This does not mean, however, that in

[5]Removed by revolution: Juan Perón in Argentina, 1955; Paul Magloire in Haiti, 1956; Gustavo Rojas Pinilla in Colombia, 1957; Marco Pérez Jiménez in Venezuela, 1958; Fulgencio Batista in Cuba, 1959; and José María Lemus in El Salvador, 1960. Assassinated: José Antonio Remón in Panamá, 1955; Anastasio Somoza in Nicaragua, 1956; Carlos Castillo Armas in Guatemala, 1957; and Rafael Trujillo in the Dominican Republic, 1961. Manuel Odría of Peru was voted out in 1956. From Edwin Lieuwen, *Generals vs. Presidents,* New York, 1964.

each case a democratic regime replaced the autocracy. In the 1960's the countries farthest toward the autocratic end of the political spectrum were Cuba, Haiti, and Paraguay; the most thoroughly democratic countries were Uruguay, Costa Rica, and Chile.[6] But in all the countries there was a mounting demand that something be done about ending the traditional system of special privilege and social inequity and about relieving the hopeless poverty of large proportions of the populations. In the countries with large proportions of Indians, there was strong popular support for granting them the full rights of citizenship. Especially impatient in calling for immediate action were the students in the universities.

Perhaps the most important reason for this reaction against autocracy and special privilege is the rapid increase in the proportion of middle-class people in the total population. The Latin America of the wealthy aristocratic landowner living in a world apart from the large numbers of hopelessly poor tenant farmers is rapidly disappearing. To be sure, the rise of the middle class is going on faster in some countries than in others. Substantial middle classes were developed in the 1950's in Mexico, Argentina, Uruguay, Chile, and in parts of Brazil. Before 1959 there was a growing middle class in Cuba. On the other hand, the two-class structure is still characteristic of Haiti, Guatemala, Honduras, the Dominican Republic, Nicaragua, El Salvador, Paraguay, and Bolivia.[7]

Attitudes toward Economic Development

As long as the great majority of the ‧people have nothing to say about public policy it makes little or no difference what they think about economic development. Traditionally in Latin America economic development has been for the benefit of a privileged minority—the landowners, the officers of the army, the Church, the political leaders. The concept of a mass market, and of an economy based on high volume–low profit per sale, was something people read about but scarcely understood. Especially in Brazil, the idea was to get quick returns on invested funds: the idea of long-term investments made little sense in the midst of a rapidly shifting speculative economy. In Argentina the people who gained most from the British investments were the landowners. In most countries the man who made the largest income was the president.

In modern Latin America this situation is changing rapidly. The change began with the health programs and with the effort to reduce the proportion of illiterates. As more and more people learned how to read and write, the

---

[6]Russell H. Fitzgibbon, "How Democratic Is Latin America?" *Inter-American Economic Affairs,* Vol. 9 (Spring, 1956): 65–77.

[7]K. H. Silvert, "Leadership Formation and Modernization in Latin America," *Journal of International Affairs,* Vol. 20 (1966): 318–31.

ideas of democracy began to spread. But the centers of change, and the groups most insistent on attacking the traditional system of power and privilege, were the universities and the students. Students have always taken a more active interest in political questions in Latin America than they do in Anglo-America; and students have been accustomed to seek radical solutions, even to the extent of attacking the established order with violence. There was a time when a majority of the people, in a country like Peru, would watch in wonder the student uprisings and strikes; but now, as more people find out what is going on, they are ready to join in the demands for change.

And what do people want to change? Primarily they resent any system in which certain individuals enjoy special treatment before the law or enjoy privileges because of status. Especially do they resent it when foreigners enjoy such privileges. The struggle for independence from Spain derived its support chiefly from people who resented Spanish administrators appointed by the King and sent to govern the colonies. In more recent times, there has been a mounting resentment against foreigners who enjoy a higher standard of living than the Latin-Americans, who receive more pay than the Latin-Americans who work with them, and who live in exclusive "colonies" and patronize exclusive clubs in Latin-American cities. The resentment against the British has been especially strong where the British businessmen were most active—in Argentina; the resentment against North Americans is greatest where there are the most North Americans—in Venezuela and Brazil. As more people find themselves able to express resentment, they cry out as if with one voice against economic colonialism, of the kind developed by the British in Argentina, or by the North Americans in Puerto Rico and Mexico. They are opposed to economic development which involves the production of raw materials by workers who are paid low wages, and which involves the export of raw materials and the import of manufactured articles. Especially are they opposed to systems that reduce the price received for raw materials at the same time that prices of manufactured articles are rising. They want and need investments of foreign capital, but they do not want foreign capital in speculative undertakings. And because public utilities, such as electric power, urban transportation, gas, and water, are so important in the daily affairs of the people, there is an insistent demand that these businesses should be owned by the government, not by private foreign corporations. The strength of this demand bears little relation to the quality of the services rendered. All over Latin America the newly literate people learn of the improved level of living in Venezuela resulting from the profits from oil, and they resent the idea that even half of these profits should be carried away by a foreign-owned corporation. None of the Latin-American countries possesses either the capital or the know-how to explore for oil themselves, yet they are all reluctant to permit exploration and development by the big corporations. The Brazilian slogan *"O petróleo é nosso"* expresses the idea that the Brazilians would prefer to go without oil rather than permit the large oil corporations to develop it.

José Figueres, ex-president of Costa Rica, expressed all this in a commencement address at a North American college.[8]

All this tendency to pay low prices for the work of other countries and then devise means of rendering economic help for their development, we consider undesirable. The healthiest source of income for any nation, as for any man, is the fair compensation for his own efforts.

This fair compensation for the work of our people, represented in our exports, would probably have been obtained long ago if it were not for the short-sightedness of our ruling class, who are often satisfied to make a personal profit in business, basing their calculations on a miserable wage scale. When a sub-human standard of living for the masses is taken for granted by the Latin American employers, it is little wonder that low prices are considered acceptable for our exports, and that no consistent efforts are made to improve such prices.

Since the wealthy class customarily controls our governments, the representatives of our countries to the international organizations care little for the living conditions of the majority of our people, and act as spokesmen of that tiny minority who always live well, whether the national income is low or high. Hence the comparative disregard for the prices of our export products, which constitute an important share of our national income, and the best possible source of savings and development.

The Rise of Nationalism

The spread of democratic ideas has brought fundamental changes in the nature of the state-ideas that bring coherence to national life. There has been a marked rise in the sentiments of nationalism; but there are important differences among the countries. In traditional Latin America, the individual has been brought up to jump from family loyalty and community loyalty to kinds of loyalty formulated by the Church. Most people felt no loyalty to that vague entity called the "state." The new nationalism measures the capacity of the individual to identify himself with his fellow citizens in support of the body of traditions and purposes that distinguish his country from other countries.

The Latin-American countries can be grouped according to the stage in their development of state-ideas.[9] In seven countries a large majority of the people do, in fact, support distinctive state-ideas through which they give expression to the feeling of nationalism. These are Uruguay, Argentina, Chile, Costa Rica, Barbados, Trinidad, and Jamaica. In a second group are countries where a powerful ruling group accepts a unifying state-idea, but where there are large numbers of people who do not. These include Mexico, Colombia, Brazil, Venezuela, and Cuba. In a third group are those countries where

[8]Grinnell College, Grinnell, Iowa.

[9]A. P. Whitaker and D. C. Jordan, *Nationalism in Contemporary Latin America,* New York, 1966. This study omitted the newer Latin American states.

there is a nucleus of citizens who subscribe to the national state-idea, but where the response to this form of nationalism by the great majority of the people is slow. These countries include Peru, Paraguay, Bolivia, Ecuador, Guatemala, El Salvador, and Panamá. The fourth group includes countries in which the feeling of national loyalty has scarcely yet appeared. These are Honduras, Nicaragua, Haiti, the Dominican Republic and Guyana.

Communism

The part played by the communists in Latin America needs to be carefully examined. The communists have had their greatest success in preindustrial countries where there is a small landowning aristocracy and a large majority of peasants. The communists have had much experience in the treatment of problems of land redistribution, and much sympathy for the landless peasant. In Latin America the communists join forces with other groups demanding reform. Wherever there are frustrations and conflicts the communists are on hand to provide expert leadership. Many intelligent Latin-Americans, impatient with the compromises and delays inherent in the democratic processes, support communism as the best way to attack a situation which they consider to be hopeless. The communist movements are strongest in those countries where liberal reform movements are weakest. On the other hand, where successful liberal movements exist, communism has little appeal.

In dealing with the problem of communism, two points should be clearly appreciated. First, it is all too common to label all one's political enemies as communists. The expression of anti-United States feelings is often attributed to communist intrigue. Actually, however, the expression of such feeling is always found to have arisen from purely domestic causes, and the communists have moved in to take advantage of the situation. It is of the utmost importance that we learn to distinguish between communists and liberals. Second, Latin-Americans need to understand that the Communist Party is in reality a group of devoted people, strictly disciplined and totally subservient to the authority of a foreign state. That these groups actually represent an intervention by a foreign power in domestic affairs was not widely recognized until Cuba's subservience to the Soviet Union was clearly demonstrated. When the Communist Party comes to power it does move rapidly to wipe out the privileged class, and also the middle class, only to establish a new privileged class made up of members of the Party. Communism, all over the world, is more than just an economic system—it is also a reaction against the democratic revolution.

Cuba is a base for the spread of communism throughout Latin America. The Soviet Union is not so enthusiastic about fomenting discord as are Cuba and China; but China is in no position to provide real support to Cuba, whereas the Soviet Union must finance Castro's government. Latin-Americans from all the countries have come to Habana to a school for the training of insurgent groups in the tactics of guerrilla warfare. These trained subversives have then been sent to the remote parts of countries such as Venezuela, Colombia, Peru, Bolivia, and Guatemala where they could create dangerous conditions of rural insecurity. But no policy could be more calculated to solidify the opposition to communism than this kind of invasion of national territory.

The Outlook

The worldwide pattern of profound culture change, then, is currently sweeping over Latin America from source regions in Europe and North America. Exposure to the innovations that are brought by cultural radiation is closer where the number of individual contacts with Europe or North America are greater. Accessibility to the sources of innovation can be a matter of distance, but it is also related to the stage of economic development, the percentage of literacy, the volume of international commerce, and many other factors. Generally countries with the higher gross national products per capita are more exposed to innovation than are those with very low gross products. Tourism is an important source of contacts. Furthermore, open societies closer to the democratic end of the political spectrum are more receptive to innovation than are closed societies.

Under certain circumstances, however, close exposure to the source of innovation may set up violent reactions. Reaction is especially likely when the privileged position of an elite is threatened. The strongest reactions against the cultural changes radiating from Anglo-America took place in the two most exposed countries, Mexico and Cuba. Mexico has passed through its phase of reaction and is now eagerly embracing the innovations, but on terms formulated by the Mexicans themselves.

The question is where do we in the United States stand with reference to the revolutionary changes now going on in Latin America? Economic development and social change are so closely interconnected that to look at them as separate problems is really not possible. Economic development and social change are linked in the program of the *Alianza para Progreso* (Alliance for Progress), which the United States has promoted and supported.

The Alliance for Progress

In August, 1961 the representatives of the Latin-American countries, except Cuba, met at Punta del Este, a seaside resort town in Uruguay. With the support of the late President Kennedy, plans were drawn up to promote economic and social change—to adopt a positive program that could replace

A Colombian peasant receives title to land at an INCORA project. *Courtesy of Colombian Information Service.*

the negative one of defense against communism. The Declaration to the Peoples of America included the following objectives of the Alliance:[10]

To improve and strengthen democratic institutions
To accelerate economic and social development
To carry out urban and rural housing programs
To encourage, in accordance with the characteristics of each country, programs of agrarian reform
To assure fair wages and satisfactory working conditions for all workers
To wipe out illiteracy and increase facilities for secondary and higher education
To press forward with programs of health and sanitation
To reform tax laws, demanding more from those who have most
To maintain monetary and fiscal policies which will protect purchasing power
To stimulate private enterprise in order to encourage economic development

[10]J. Warren Nystrom and Nathan A. Haverstock, *The Alliance for Progress,* New York, 1966.

Students in Caracas, Venezuela, demanding the resignation of a dictator. Not everyone knew what the shouting was about. Would the ousting of central authority be followed by the growth of responsible democracy, or only another and more ruthless dictatorship? *Wide World Photo.*

> To solve the problems created by excessive price fluctuations in basic
> commodity exports
> To accelerate the economic integration of Latin America

Each of the participating countries, all members of the Organization of American States, was to draw up its own plan for economic and social development. Between 1961 and 1966 the United States provided six and a half billion dollars to underwrite the cost of various parts of the program. Yet the tangible results in most countries were anything but spectacular. Not enough new capital was drawn from domestic savings to provide jobs for the large numbers of unemployed people in the cities; and the production of basic foods from rural areas lagged behind the population growth. Measures to speed social change were resisted very effectively by the traditional political powers.

In April, 1967, a summit meeting of the presidents of the Latin-American states was called—again at Punta del Este. Bolivia refused to attend because her demand for access to the sea was not placed on the agenda. Ecuador, which was represented, refused to sign the declaration because she considered the document inadequate. Cuba was not invited. Trinidad and Tobago, the newest member of the OAS, was represented.

At this meeting in 1967 the presidents of the attending Latin-American nations, except Ecuador, reaffirmed their support for the Alliance for Progress and adopted specific measures for moving forward more rapidly with the program of development. It was agreed that, starting in 1970, a Latin-American Common Market would be created in progressive steps, so that it would be substantially in operation by 1985. The idea was to build on the already existing Latin-American Free Trade Association and the Central American Common Market. The progressive reduction of artificial barriers to the movements of trade is basic. But it was recognized that without some control there would be a tendency for the more advanced economies to grow faster than the others—for industry to concentrate in São Paulo, Buenos Aires, and Mexico City. Measures will be devised to make certain that some industries will be organized in the less developed parts of the hemisphere, as Brazil is doing with reference to the Northeast, the North, and the Central-West. With access to the whole Latin-American market, industries even in small countries could prosper.

Special efforts are to be made to build the physical facilities essential for economic growth. The development of transportation systems is being pushed rapidly. This includes building highways, railroads, airports, seaports, pipelines, and the physical facilities for handling agriculture products. Transportation systems are being extended to provide access to neighboring countries. Yet only a few years ago, highways were actually built to national borders in only a few places, because of the fear of invasion. Now electric power systems are to be extended across national borders. Systems of telecommunications are to be set up. The effort to provide schools is to be increased, and more money will go to the support of scientific research and development centers. Health programs will be expanded. And the presidents agreed to cut nonessential military expenditures.

Building a New Society

In 1967 the political leaders of the Latin-American countries were ready to agree that any further resistance to the waves of economic, social, and political innovation could bring disaster. The hope was to channel the changes into a controlled evolution rather than to permit the outbreak of violence and destruction. The plan of the Alliance, however, was not imposed from outside: the Alliance was controlled by an executive committee of Latin-Americans, and the distinctive aspirations of each country and each region were to be respected.

There were several new groups in the Latin-American countries that were giving effective support to programs of change. Since the time of Pope John

XXIII, the Catholic Church has been concerned with problems of an economic and social nature. Priests began to take leadership in the establishment of cooperatives among small farmers. The Christian Democratic Party assumed a more active role in the support of liberal leaders, such as Eduardo Frei Montalva of Chile. The party grew in strength in such other countries as Venezuela, Peru, Guatemala, El Salvador, and Panamá. The ideal was to build a new civilization with man himself as the central purpose, rather than a civilization devoted to the pursuit of money profit. The idea was a Catholic society for Catholics.

The Role of the United States

A major problem was presented by the widespread lack of understanding of the United States in Latin America. It was commonly believed that the United States was firmly on the side of autocracy and the maintenance of the traditional system. The United States was charged with preaching the ideals of a free society with social justice, yet acting in the opposite way. When people from the United States talked about the advantages of capitalism and free enterprise they were usually misunderstood. In Latin America, the word "capitalism" is used to describe a system in which the business owners pay wages that permit a bare subsistence and set prices that bring maximum profit per sale; and free enterprise means that no schedule of taxes or other government regulations shall decrease the right of businessmen to exploit customers and workers alike. This may have been a good description of Great Britain in the nineteenth century when Charles Dickens was pointing to the social inequities, or when Karl Marx was developing his ideas about capitalism. It has not been a good description of the United States since 1880. In the modern United States, government regulations forbid the formation of monopolies, and business profits are closely examined by the tax collectors and the officials of the labor unions. Many businessmen have discovered that paying higher wages is one way to build up a market. When the terms "capitalism" and "free enterprise" are used in the United States, they refer to an economic system in which business is regulated and controlled, but in which the market rather than the government controls the distribution of raw materials and finished goods. The words mean something quite different in Latin America.[11]

The situation is ironic. The idealism that leads to an attack on social injustice and poverty is attributed to the communists; the materialism that seeks to solve each problem in its own terms without attempting to formulate any idealistic goals is attributed to the United States. The idealism that prompts business people to assume social responsibilities in the communities of which

---

[11]George C. Lodge, "Revolution in Latin America," *Foreign Affairs,* Vol. 44 (1966): 173–97.

they are parts, or which leads them to join service organizations in which the theme is "service above self," is quite unknown to most Latin-Americans. There is pressing need to communicate a new image of the United States.

But there is also need for a better understanding of Latin America among the people of the United States. Some of the old caricatures, which were not authentic even half a century ago, need to be forgotten. The colorful peon sitting under the cactus, dozing in the sun, was probably sick; the lover strumming his guitar under his lady's balcony really existed only in the opera; the peasant who could not possibly learn any mechanical operations is now operating machines very successfully; the wealthy playboy who was an artist at spending his father's money has not been seen in Paris since 1914, nor in Miami since the 1950's. These are nothing like the new business executives who are starting to appear, or the shifts of workers who stream in and out of the factories of São Paulo or Mexico City.

We in the United States need to understand much more clearly what is happening in Latin America. To see every change as a communist conspiracy is to have only a blurred view of the real world. There can be no holding back the currents of change, for the waves of innovation have already gone too far to be resisted. There are too many people who know that they can expect to achieve a higher level of comfort and security. But the Latin-American ideal does not overlook the central importance of human freedom and dignity —the equal right of every individual to be different, and of each country to develop its own distinctive national character. A society organized to provide for individual differences is the only one that would fit the Latin-American dream. The great question that many Latin-Americans are asking is this: can North American methods of production be adopted to provide for a vast increase in the supply of goods and services without turning Latin-American workers into robots endlessly performing mechanical tasks? Can the ideal of a man-centered society really be achieved?

Appendix A □ Climatic Data

CLIMATIC DATA FOR SELECTED STATIONS* (MEXICO)

T. = Temperature in Degrees Fahrenheit; Rf. = Rainfall in Inches

Station	Altitude (in feet)	Time of Record (temperature)	Time of Record (rainfall)		Jan.	Feb.	Mar.	Apr.	May	June	July	Aug.	Sept.	Oct.	Nov.	Dec.	Year
Tampico	26.3–59.1	1889–1927	1889–1927	T. Rf.	66.0 1.5	68.2 1.2	71.8 1.0	76.5 1.5	80.2 1.9	82.0 8.7	81.9 4.9	82.4 4.8	80.8 10.8	77.2 5.0	72.3 2.0	66.9 1.6	75.5 44.9
Jalapa	4590.4	1894–1927	1894–1927	T. Rf.	57.6 1.9	60.1 2.3	63.5 2.4	66.6 2.9	67.6 4.4	66.6 12.4	66.2 6.8	66.4 6.5	65.8 10.8	63.6 5.7	61.0 3.0	58.8 2.4	63.6 61.5
Veracruz	23–52.5	1878–1927	1878–1927	T. Rf.	70.0 1.0	71.2 0.6	74.1 0.5	77.9 0.6	80.6 1.7	81.3 11.4	80.6 13.0	81.1 10.7	80.1 12.0	78.4 5.7	74.7 3.1	71.2 1.0	76.8 60.3
Mérida	72.2	1894–1927	1894–1927	T. Rf.	72.7 1.1	73.6 0.7	77.9 1.0	80.6 0.9	83.3 2.6	81.7 7.0	81.5 4.5	81.1 5.4	80.6 5.3	78.4 3.3	75.4 1.6	73.2 1.1	78.3 34.6
Saltillo	5278.8–5344.4	1886–1927	1886–1927	T. Rf.	53.1 0.7	55.2 0.6	60.8 0.4	66.2 0.7	71.2 1.0	73.0 2.2	72.3 2.9	71.8 2.9	66.9 2.9	62.6 1.5	56.8 1.2	52.5 0.6	63.5 17.6
Monterrey	1624.0	1886–1927	1896–1927	T. Rf.	57.7 0.6	62.6 0.7	68.0 0.8	73.8 1.3	78.4 1.3	81.5 3.0	81.7 2.3	82.4 2.4	77.9 5.2	71.6 3.0	63.5 1.5	57.6 0.8	71.3 22.9
Galeana	5426.5	1905–1927	1905–1927	T. Rf.	54.5 0.7	57.2 0.7	61.3 0.5	66.7 1.3	70.2 1.5	69.8 2.7	70.0 2.2	68.7 2.6	68.2 3.2	64.6 1.5	60.3 1.0	56.8 1.0	64.0 18.9
San Luis Potosí	6158.1–6223.7	1878–1927	1878–1927	T. Rf.	54.7 0.3	58.1 0.6	62.6 0.5	68.2 0.5	70.9 1.1	69.6 2.8	67.6 1.9	67.6 2.0	65.3 2.0	62.8 1.1	58.1 0.6	54.9 0.5	63.4 13.9
Leon	5902.2–5935.0	1878–1927	1878–1927	T. Rf.	57.2 0.3	60.4 0.3	65.5 0.4	70.5 0.2	73.8 1.1	71.6 4.9	69.3 6.1	69.0 5.1	67.8 4.7	64.8 1.3	61.0 0.5	57.6 0.5	65.7 25.4
Pachuca	7959.3–7992.1	1893–1927	1893–1927	T. Rf.	53.2 0.1	55.4 0.3	58.6 0.5	61.3 1.0	62.8 1.4	63.9 4.1	59.2 2.1	60.4 2.3	58.8 1.9	57.0 1.3	55.2 0.6	53.8 0.2	58.1 14.4
Mexico City	7486.9	1878–1927	1878–1927	T. Rf.	54.3 0.2	57.4 0.3	61.2 0.5	63.3 0.7	65.1 1.9	63.9 4.1	62.1 4.5	62.2 4.3	61.3 4.1	59.2 1.6	57.0 0.5	54.7 0.3	60.1 23.0
Puebla	7053.8–7175.2	1887–1927	1878–1927	T. Rf.	54.3 0.3	57.0 0.4	61.2 0.4	64.6 1.0	67.6 3.3	64.0 6.8	63.0 7.0	63.3 5.6	62.1 6.1	60.4 2.5	57.9 1.0	54.7 0.4	60.8 34.8
Chihuahua	4668.6	1900–1927	1900–1927	T. Rf.	50.0 0.2	53.4 0.4	60.1 0.3	66.4 0.2	73.4 0.2	78.8 1.7	76.6 3.6	75.2 3.7	71.4 3.3	64.8 0.9	55.4 0.5	49.3 0.4	64.6 15.4
Durango	6187.7–6243.4	1878–1903	1878–1927	T. Rf.	54.1 0.3	56.3 0.3	62.2 0.2	65.7 0.2	71.4 0.2	71.1 2.6	69.1 4.1	69.1 3.2	66.2 4.1	63.0 1.1	57.9 0.6	53.8 1.1	63.3 18.0
Zacatecas	8569.6	1878–1927	1878–1927	T. Rf.	50.7 0.5	52.7 0.3	55.6 0.4	61.3 0.2	65.1 0.9	64.2 4.1	60.8 4.1	61.2 3.4	59.4 3.5	57.6 1.6	54.9 0.6	51.1 0.6	57.9 20.2
Ensenada	19.7	1925–1927	1895–1927	T. Rf.	55.0 2.6	57.2 1.9	57.7 1.5	59.5 0.9	62.1 0.2	63.3 0.1	69.6 0.1	69.6 0.1	66.0 0.0	63.0 0.6	60.6 1.1	56.8 1.7	61.7 10.8

*Source: W. Koppen and R. Geiger, *Handbuch der Klimatologie*, Vol. 2, Parts G, H, I, and J. Berlin.

Station	Altitude (in feet)	Time of Record (temperature)	Time of Record (rainfall)		Jan.	Feb.	Mar.	Apr.	May	June	July	Aug.	Sept.	Oct.	Nov.	Dec.	Year
La Paz	32.8-39.4	1906-1927	1907-1927	T. Rf.	63.0 0.2	65.1 0.1	68.4 0.0	70.5 0.0	74.1 0.0	77.9 0.0	82.4 0.4	83.5 1.2	82.2 1.4	78.8 0.6	72.3 0.5	65.7 1.1	73.6 5.7
Ahome	111.6-278.9	1921-1927	1921-1927	T. Rf.	63.1 0.0	64.4 0.2	67.8 0.2	71.8 0.0	77.0 0.0	82.2 0.4	86.7 1.6	86.0 3.2	85.1 3.2	79.7 0.3	71.4 0.5	64.0 2.6	75.0 12.1
Mazatlan	13.1-255.9	1880-1927	1880-1927	T. Rf.	68.4 0.8	67.8 0.5	69.4 0.2	71.8 0.1	76.1 0.1	81.1 1.5	82.6 5.9	82.8 8.3	82.4 8.0	80.4 2.6	75.2 0.9	70.2 1.3	75.7 30.2
Guadalajara	5104.9-5193.5	1878-1927	1878-1927	T. Rf.	59.9 0.4	62.4 0.2	66.0 0.2	70.5 0.2	73.9 1.1	72.1 8.8	69.4 9.4	69.3 8.5	68.4 7.2	67.1 2.2	63.9 0.7	59.9 0.7	66.9 39.6
Manzanillo	9.8-23	1908-1927	1910-1927	T. Rf.	74.7 0.2	73.6 0.2	74.1 0.0	75.2 0.0	78.1 0.0	81.5 4.0	81.7 5.1	82.0 5.7	81.5 13.1	81.9 4.5	77.9 0.5	75.7 3.0	78.2 36.1
Acapulco	9.8	1920-1927	1920-1927	T. Rf.	77.9 0.6	77.7 0.0	78.8 0.0	80.4 0.0	82.6 1.7	82.8 16.5	82.6 6.0	80.8 6.3	81.1 14.7	82.9 5.9	80.2 1.9	78.6 0.7	80.5 54.3
Cuicatlan	1952.1	1906-1925	1906-1925	T. Rf.	71.4 0.0	73.0 0.2	75.7 0.2	80.1 0.5	81.5 0.8	79.2 4.1	77.7 3.0	79.0 2.5	77.5 2.5	76.1 1.3	72.5 0.1	70.9 0.2	76.2 15.4
Oaxaca	5036.1-5164	1878-1927	1878-1927	T. Rf.	62.8 0.1	65.8 0.2	69.4 0.6	72.5 1.5	72.9 3.2	70.7 6.7	69.4 3.5	69.8 4.1	67.1 4.9	65.3 2.0	68.5 0.4	63.0 0.2	68.1 27.4
Salina Cruz	49.2-183.7	1903-1907	1903-1927	T. Rf.	76.3 0.0	77.2 0.4	79.3 0.6	81.3 0.5	82.8 3.3	81.1 11.9	81.9 4.5	82.0 5.5	80.8 7.0	80.2 4.0	79.0 0.9	77.2 0.1	79.9 38.7
Comitan	5364.2	1912-1927	1912-1927	T. Rf.	59.9 0.5	62.2 0.3	64.8 0.3	66.9 1.7	67.5 4.7	66.0 9.1	64.9 4.6	65.3 4.2	65.5 5.9	63.9 4.7	61.3 1.0	61.7 0.4	64.2 37.6

CENTRAL AMERICA

T. = Temperature in Degrees Fahrenheit; Rf. = Rainfall in Inches

Station	Altitude (in feet)	Time of Record (temperature)	Time of Record (rainfall)		Jan.	Feb.	Mar.	Apr.	May	June	July	Aug.	Sept.	Oct.	Nov.	Dec.	Year
Belize	Coast Level	1888-1895	1888-1895	T. Rf.	74.8 5.1	76.8 2.6	79.2 1.6	79.9 1.5	81.9 4.1	82.4 9.1	82.6 9.6	82.6 8.5	82.0 9.4	79.3 11.0	76.1 10.2	73.6 6.3	79.3 79.0
Guatemala City	4888.4	1898-1902	1857-1902	T. Rf.	61.7 0.3	63.2 0.2	65.8 0.5	66.2 1.3	69.4 5.5	67.5 11.7	66.7 7.8	66.7 7.8	66.7 9.3	65.1 6.6	63.5 0.9	61.3 0.2	65.4 52.1
San Salvador	2155.5	1889-1902	1889-1902	T. Rf.	71.8 0.7	72.9 0.2	74.5 0.6	76.3 1.6	75.6 6.6	74.3 11.0	74.1 12.3	74.1 11.5	73.2 11.7	72.7 10.3	72.3 1.9	71.4 0.4	73.6 68.2
San Ubaldo	108.3	1900	1900	T. Rf.	79.5 1.2	80.8 0.2	82.9 0.3	86.4 0.0	85.8 7.4	82.9 9.8	81.3 24.9	82.9 5.3	83.1 14.1	80.6 8.9	80.2 1.4	81.1 0.6	82.3 74.1
Greytown	Coast Level	1898-1900	1890-1900	T. Rf.	77.5 23.3	77.7 11.3	78.8 6.5	80.8 11.4	80.8 20.4	80.1 23.2	79.2 34.4	79.3 27.3	80.4 17.4	80.2 20.0	78.4 36.5	77.5 27.8	79.2 259.4
San José	3723.7	1889-1900	1888-1895	T. Rf.	66.0 0.2	66.7 0.2	67.8 0.5	68.7 1.1	68.9 10.0	68.2 11.0	67.6 8.3	67.5 10.6	67.6 14.2	67.3 13.3	68.7 4.9	65.9 1.7	67.6 76.0

CENTRAL AMERICA—Continued

Station	Altitude	Time of Record (temperature)	Time of Record (rainfall)	T./Rf.	Jan.	Feb.	Mar.	Apr.	May	June	July	Aug.	Sept.	Oct.	Nov.	Dec.	Year
Colon	Coast Level	1907–1926	1907–1926	T.	79.9	79.7	79.7	80.2	80.8	80.4	79.9	79.9	80.8	80.4	79.0	78.6	79.9
				Rf.	3.5	1.7	1.5	4.5	12.2	13.9	15.5	14.8	12.6	15.2	21.7	10.8	127.9
Balboa Heights	98.4	1907–1926	1906–1930	T.	78.3	78.4	79.5	80.1	79.2	78.6	78.6	78.4	78.4	77.7	77.4	78.3	78.4
				Rf.	0.9	0.9	0.6	2.8	7.8	8.2	7.2	7.8	7.9	10.1	10.1	4.2	68.6

THE ANTILLES

T. = Temperature in Degrees Fahrenheit; Rf. = Rainfall in Inches

Station	Altitude (in feet)	Time of Record (temperature)	Time of Record (rainfall)	T./Rf.	Jan.	Feb.	Mar.	Apr.	May	June	July	Aug.	Sept.	Oct.	Nov.	Dec.	Year
Habana	78.7	1899–1927	1899–1927	T.	71.4	71.8	73.7	76.3	78.6	80.4	81.7	81.7	80.8	79.0	75.0	72.7	76.9
				Rf.	3.0	1.5	1.7	1.7	5.1	5.6	4.3	4.3	5.0	7.1	3.2	2.4	44.9
Santiago de Cuba	114.8	1899–1920	1899–1921	T.	75.4	75.0	76.6	78.3	79.7	80.8	81.9	82.2	82.2	80.1	77.7	76.3	78.8
				Rf.	1.4	0.9	1.7	3.3	6.3	5.5	2.2	3.5	6.7	7.3	3.7	1.1	43.6
Kingston	23.0	1908–1927	1899–1927	T.	76.6	76.5	77.4	78.6	80.1	81.3	81.7	81.9	81.3	80.4	79.0	77.5	79.3
				Rf.	0.7	0.5	0.8	1.3	3.1	3.6	1.2	2.7	4.0	6.3	3.5	1.1	28.8
Port-au-Prince	121.4	1906–1927	1899–1927	T.	78.1	78.4	79.2	80.2	81.1	82.8	84.0	83.5	82.2	80.8	79.5	78.4	80.7
				Rf.	1.2	2.7	4.1	6.7	8.0	4.0	2.7	4.8	7.7	7.4	4.2	0.9	54.4
Ciudad Trujillo	59.1	1910–1927	1899–1927	T.	75.7	75.6	75.9	77.4	79.8	79.7	80.2	81.0	81.0	80.0	79.2	77.2	78.5
				Rf.	2.5	1.3	2.4	3.7	5.8	5.9	7.1	6.9	7.1	7.0	5.1	2.0	56.8
Ponce	78.7	1899–1927	1901–1927	T.	75.4	75.4	76.0	77.5	79.5	80.6	81.0	81.5	81.3	80.4	79.0	76.8	78.7
				Rf.	1.1	1.1	1.4	2.2	3.0	3.6	3.0	4.1	4.9	6.4	4.0	1.1	35.9
San Juan	98.4	1899–1927	1899–1927	T.	74.8	74.8	75.2	76.6	78.6	79.5	80.0	80.4	80.4	80.0	78.3	76.3	77.9
				Rf.	4.1	3.0	3.0	4.1	5.2	5.4	5.8	5.9	6.0	5.7	7.0	5.4	60.6
Christiansted	82.0	1899–1927	1899–1927	T.	76.6	76.3	76.8	78.4	80.2	81.1	81.9	82.0	81.9	80.8	79.5	77.7	79.4
				Rf.	2.0	2.1	1.4	3.0	3.4	3.5	3.2	3.7	5.4	5.6	5.1	3.2	41.6
St. John's	78.7	1890–1926	1866–1927	T.	76.1	76.1	76.6	76.0	79.2	80.1	80.4	81.0	81.0	81.7	78.8	77.5	78.7
				Rf.	3.1	2.4	2.2	3.2	4.1	3.9	4.7	4.8	5.8	5.7	5.5	3.7	49.1
St. George's	508.5	1891–1927	1899–1927	T.	76.8	77.2	77.7	78.8	79.7	79.0	79.1	79.9	80.2	80.1	79.3	78.1	78.8
				Rf.	4.4	3.1	2.5	1.8	3.7	8.0	9.4	9.1	7.3	8.1	8.0	6.9	72.3
Bridgetown	180.5	10 years	1899–1927	T.	76.3	76.5	77.0	78.4	80.1	80.2	80.1	80.1	79.9	79.3	78.6	77.2	78.6
				Rf.	2.1	1.7	1.5	1.8	1.7	4.5	4.7	6.0	6.4	6.5	5.0	3.5	45.4
Port of Spain	131.2	1862–1900	1862–1926	T.	75.0	72.2	76.3	77.7	79.0	77.9	77.5	77.5	78.1	77.9	77.2	77.2	77.0
				Rf.	2.6	1.6	1.8	1.9	3.4	7.9	8.6	9.4	7.5	6.6	7.2	4.7	63.2

SOUTH AMERICA

T. = Temperature in Degrees Fahrenheit; Rf. = Rainfall in Inches

Station	Altitude (in feet)	Time of Record (temperature)	Time of Record (rainfall)		Jan.	Feb.	Mar.	Apr.	May	June	July	Aug.	Sept.	Oct.	Nov.	Dec.	Year
Georgetown	6.6	1887–1924	1846–1922	T.	79.3	79.3	79.9	80.6	80.6	80.2	80.6	81.3	82.2	82.0	81.5	79.9	80.6
				Rf.	7.3	5.9	6.1	6.7	11.1	12.1	9.6	6.4	2.8	2.3	5.8	11.3	87.4
Maracaibo	26.3	1918–1925	1920–1925	T.	80.6	81.0	81.1	82.6	83.1	83.5	84.2	84.4	83.5	82.0	81.3	81.0	82.4
				Rf.	0.0	0.0	0.3	0.5	2.4	1.6	1.4	1.3	3.3	4.3	2.5	0.4	18.0
La Guaira	Coast Level	3 years	1920–1925	T.	78.4	78.4	79.3	80.2	81.1	81.7	81.1	82.6	82.9	82.6	81.5	78.8	80.7
				Rf.	0.5	0.2	0.8	0.2	0.6	0.9	1.0	1.1	1.1	1.2	1.6	1.5	10.7
Caracas	3415.4	1895–1925	1891–1925	T.	64.4	64.9	65.8	68.2	69.4	68.7	68.0	68.4	68.5	68.4	67.3	65.3	67.3
				Rf.	0.9	0.4	0.6	1.6	2.8	4.3	4.1	4.3	4.0	3.9	3.4	1.7	32.0
Mérida	5380.6	1918–1925	1918–1925	T.	64.0	65.1	65.5	66.6	66.6	66.0	66.0	66.7	66.4	66.0	65.1	64.2	65.7
				Rf.	2.6	1.5	3.8	6.7	11.2	6.9	4.0	5.7	6.3	9.9	8.0	3.3	69.9
Ciudad Bolivar	124.7	1919–1924	1917–1925	T.	78.8	79.9	81.0	82.2	82.4	80.1	79.7	80.8	81.7	81.7	81.0	78.8	80.7
				Rf.	0.5	0.2	0.2	0.9	2.6	5.6	6.2	6.3	3.1	3.4	3.4	1.9	34.3
Medellin	4950.73	1875–1879	15 years	T.	70.9	71.6	70.9	70.7	70.9	70.7	70.5	70.7	70.5	69.4	69.1	69.8	70.5
				Rf.	2.7	3.5	3.3	6.6	7.7	5.5	4.1	4.6	6.9	6.9	5.2	2.5	58.8
Bogotá	8727	6½ years	{1866–1885 / 1894–1922}	T.	57.9	58.3	59.0	58.8	58.6	58.3	57.2	57.2	57.4	57.9	58.3	57.9	58.1
				Rf.	2.3	2.6	4.0	5.7	4.4	2.4	2.0	2.2	2.4	6.3	4.7	2.6	41.6
Pasto	8510.5	1924–1925	1924–1925	T.	55.9	56.7	57.2	57.7	59.0	57.6	57.7	57.9	57.2	57.7	57.0	57.4	57.4
				Rf.	1.3	1.7	3.4	3.1	0.9	2.6	1.0	0.3	4.6	2.4	7.6	3.4	32.3
Quito	9350.4	1895–1907	16 years	T.	54.7	54.5	54.5	54.5	54.7	54.7	54.5	54.7	54.9	54.7	54.5	54.7	54.6
				Rf.	4.2	4.3	5.2	7.4	5.0	1.5	0.9	1.5	3.0	3.7	3.8	3.8	44.3
Guayaquil	39.4	3 years	3 years	T.	79.3	79.3	79.7	80.4	78.8	77.4	75.4	76.1	77.2	76.6	78.4	80.2	78.2
				Rf.	9.7	10.5	7.4	5.3	2.1	0.7	0.4	0.0	0.1	0.4	0.3	1.9	38.8
Iquitos	347.8	1 year	1 year	T.	77.5	78.3	76.3	77.0	75.6	74.3	74.1	76.3	76.3	77.2	78.4	77.9	76.6
				Rf.	10.0	10.6	12.0	6.6	9.8	7.3	6.5	4.5	8.8	7.1	8.5	11.3	103.0
Chiclayo	Coast Leve	1909–1912	3–4 years	T.	76.1	78.3	77.4	73.2	68.9	63.5	64.0	64.6	65.0	65.6	68.0	72.9	69.8
				Rf.	0.0	0.1	0.5	0.0	0.0	—	0.0	0.0	0.1	0.1	0.0	0.0	0.7
Trujillo	196.9	1896–1915	2–4 years	T.	77.2	77.0	74.3	72.0	68.0	63.0	64.0	64.2	63.7	67.5	68.7	72.0	69.3
				Rf.	0.2	0.5	0.3	0.0	0.0	0.0	0.1	0.0	0.0	0.0	0.1	0.0	1.2
Cerro de Pasco	14,271.6	1909–1912	3–5 years	T.	44.1	43.2	44.1	44.1	42.6	41.0	40.5	40.8	41.0	41.7	42.3	42.4	42.3
				Rf.	4.6	4.5	3.6	3.4	2.3	0.9	1.1	1.2	2.8	3.3	3.4	3.7	34.8
Lima	518.4	{1893–1897 / 1910–1919}	18 years	T.	72.6	74.3	73.6	70.2	66.0	62.6	61.2	61.0	61.3	63.0	65.7	69.6	66.8
				Rf.	0.0	0.0	0.0	0.0	0.0	0.1	0.2	0.4	0.4	0.4	0.2	0.1	1.8

Station				T./Rf.														
Santa Ana	3412.1	1894–1895	1894–1895	T.	71.6	71.1	71.4	71.4	72.1	71.8	71.1	70.2	70.7	72.3	73.9	74.1	73.2	72.0
				Rf.	9.8	6.6	8.1	6.6	3.5	2.8	1.2	0.3	1.1	5.6	4.0	1.5	7.3	51.8
Cuzco	11,089.2	1894–1898	12 years	T.	52.5	52.2	52.0	51.4	51.0	50.5	48.4	46.9	49.4	51.6	52.9	53.8	52.2	51.2
				Rf.	6.4	5.9	4.3	2.0	0.6	0.6	0.2	0.2	0.4	1.0	2.6	3.0	5.4	32.0
Vincocaya	14,370	1896–1900	1 year	T.	38.3	38.7	38.1	38.1	36.3	32.5	29.3	27.9	31.5	34.5	38.7	40.6	38.5	35.4
				Rf.	3.0	4.1	2.6	0.0	0.0	0.0	0.0	0.0	0.2	0.0	0.3	0.0	0.5	10.7
Arequipa	8041.3	1888–1920	1888–1924	T.	57.0	57.0	56.3	57.4	56.8	56.8	55.8	55.6	56.8	57.9	56.5	57.0	57.4	56.8
				Rf.	1.2	1.8	0.6	0.0	0.0	0.0	0.0	0.0	0.0	0.2	0.0	0.0	0.0	4.2
Mollendo	78.7	1889–1895	1888–1900	T.	70.2	70.7	69.6	70.7	67.3	65.3	61.7	59.5	59.4	59.9	62.1	65.8	68.4	64.4
				Rf.	0.0	0.1	0.0	0.1	0.0	0.1	0.0	0.0	0.2	0.2	0.1	0.1	0.0	0.8
La Paz	12,001.3	1918–1925	1898–1902	T.	50.4	50.4	50.0	48.4	47.7	44.8	43.5	46.4	46.2	49.3	50.0	51.8	51.4	48.7
				Rf.	3.8	4.9	2.6	1.5	0.5	0.1	0.2	0.0	1.1	0.8	1.3	1.6	4.2	22.6
Cochabamba	8448.2	3 years	1903–1918	T.	65.8	65.3	63.1	62.4	60.1	59.5	57.2	59.5	61.3	63.9	67.5	68.0	66.2	63.2
				Rf.	4.1	3.8	2.4	0.4	0.4	0.2	0.3	0.0	0.2	0.7	0.6	1.3	3.9	18.3
Arica	16.4	1911–1921	1903–1918	T.	72.3	73.0	71.6	68.4	65.7	63.1	61.3	61.3	61.2	62.4	64.0	66.9	70.0	66.7
				Rf.	0.4	0.0	0.0	0.0	0.0	0.0	0.0	0.0	0.0	0.0	0.0	0.0	0.0	0.4
Iquique	29.5	1911–1924	1886–1925	T.	69.8	69.6	67.6	65.1	63.1	61.3	60.1	60.3	60.3	61.2	63.0	65.7	68.2	64.6
				Rf.	0.0	0.0	0.0	0.0	0.0	0.0	0.0	0.0	0.0	0.0	0.0	0.0	0.0	0.0
Calama	7414.7	1913–1914	1913–1914	T.	62.4	59.7	58.1	54.7	51.8	46.8	46.4	47.5	55.8	54.3	58.3	60.3	61.9	55.9
				Rf.	0.0	0.0	0.0	0.0	0.0	0.0	0.0	0.0	0.0	0.0	0.0	0.0	0.0	0.0
Coquimbo	88.6	1911–1924	1900–1925	T.	64.0	63.7	62.1	58.8	57.0	55.0	54.0	53.6	54.0	55.0	57.0	59.4	61.7	58.4
				Rf.	0.0	0.0	0.0	0.0	0.0	0.2	0.5	1.1	0.2	0.2	0.0	0.0	0.0	4.4
Los Andes	2677.2	1911–1924	1905–1925	T.	71.2	70.2	65.7	59.5	53.1	48.7	47.5	48.7	51.4	54.3	59.9	65.1	69.3	59.7
				Rf.	0.0	0.2	0.1	0.4	2.2	1.3	2.5	1.3	1.0	1.0	0.2	0.2	0.1	8.8
Valparaiso	134.5	1911–1924	1869–1925	T.	63.7	63.1	61.3	58.1	55.6	52.3	52.3	53.1	53.1	54.1	56.7	60.1	62.2	57.7
				Rf.	0.0	0.0	0.4	0.6	3.8	4.0	5.7	2.6	1.3	0.4	0.3	0.3	0.2	19.3
Santiago	1706	1911–1924	1867–1925	T.	68.7	67.1	62.4	56.7	51.1	45.7	45.7	46.2	48.6	51.8	56.8	62.2	66.6	57.0
				Rf.	0.0	0.1	0.2	0.6	2.4	3.3	2.8	2.8	2.1	1.3	0.5	0.2	0.2	13.7
San Fernando	1099	1911–1924	1911–1925	T.	67.8	66.0	61.5	55.2	50.0	44.4	44.4	45.1	48.6	50.4	55.8	62.2	65.5	55.8
				Rf.	0.1	0.0	0.4	5.2	6.1	8.2	4.6	2.8	3.2	2.8	1.0	1.0	0.3	28.8
Contulmo	124.7	1911–1924	1911–1925	T.	62.2	61.0	58.5	54.9	51.8	48.2	48.1	48.2	48.8	49.8	53.6	56.1	59.7	54.4
				Rf.	1.3	1.4	3.3	6.6	12.5	10.9	11.6	8.8	6.5	2.6	4.2	2.3	72.0
Valdivia	19.7	1911–1921	1852–1925	T.	61.9	60.4	57.9	53.1	49.6	45.5	45.9	45.7	49.6	52.0	55.0	57.0	59.0	52.9
				Rf.	2.4	3.0	5.6	9.4	11.3	17.0	16.1	10.8	10.6	5.2	5.0	4.1	101.0
Puerto Montt	32.8	1911–1921	1862–1915	T.	59.5	58.1	55.9	53.6	51.1	47.3	46.0	45.9	49.6	51.1	53.6	57.0	57.0	51.8
				Rf.	4.6	4.4	5.9	6.3	5.5	8.7	10.8	9.3	10.6	5.5	5.0	5.4	5.4	85.7
Evangelistas	180.5	1911–1924	1899–1925	T.	47.5	47.5	47.1	44.4	42.1	40.3	39.6	39.4	40.6	42.3	43.2	45.2	45.5	43.3
				Rf.	11.5	10.4	11.2	11.6	9.6	9.4	9.2	8.5	9.0	8.7	9.9	10.1	10.1	119.1

Punta Arenas	91.9	1888-1925	1911-1924	T. Rf.	52.5 1.1	51.3 1.3	48.7 1.5	43.7 2.1	39.0 2.0	36.5 2.2	35.8 1.7	36.7 2.1	40.6 1.7	45.3 1.1	47.3 1.3	50.9 1.3	44.0 19.4
La Quiaca	11,358.2	1901-1920	1901-1920	T. Rf.	54.5 3.2	54.3 2.6	53.4 2.0	51.4 0.3	42.8 0.0	37.4 0.0	37.4 0.0	42.1 0.0	48.0 0.0	51.4 0.2	54.0 1.1	54.7 2.1	48.5 11.5
Jujuy	4166.7	1901-1920	1901-1920	T. Rf.	70.5 6.5	68.9 5.5	66.2 5.4	62.2 1.3	57.0 0.5	52.2 0.2	54.9 0.1	52.2 0.2	61.5 0.4	65.3 1.5	69.1 2.6	70.2 5.2	62.5 29.4
Salta	3894.9	1901-1920	1901-1920	T. Rf.	72.0 6.7	70.9 6.2	67.6 3.9	63.9 1.2	58.3 0.4	53.1 0.1	56.1 0.2	53.6 0.0	63.3 0.4	67.8 1.2	70.3 2.3	71.2 5.4	64.0 28.0
Tucumán	1476.4	1901-1920	1901-1920	T. Rf.	76.8 6.3	74.7 7.5	71.6 5.5	66.4 3.1	59.9 1.2	53.6 0.6	56.8 0.5	53.6 0.3	64.2 0.6	68.9 2.3	72.7 4.2	75.0 5.9	66.2 38.0
Santiago del Estero	623.4	1901-1920	1901-1920	T. Rf.	83.1 3.3	80.6 3.0	76.6 3.0	70.3 1.3	62.8 0.6	55.9 0.3	60.6 0.5	56.7 0.2	67.5 0.5	72.3 1.4	77.5 2.5	80.6 4.1	70.4 20.4
La Rioja	1673.2	1901-1920	1901-1920	T. Rf.	81.5 2.6	78.1 2.7	74.5 2.2	68.4 0.8	60.1 0.5	51.8 0.2	57.7 0.2	53.1 0.1	63.3 0.2	70.5 0.8	75.9 1.4	79.3 1.8	67.9 13.5
Córdoba	1387.8	1901-1920	1901-1920	T. Rf.	73.9 3.7	72.3 5.0	68.5 3.2	62.1 0.8	55.8 1.1	49.6 0.2	53.4 0.6	50.5 0.6	58.6 0.9	63.3 2.2	68.4 4.0	72.1 4.6	62.4 28.2
San Juan	2178.3	1901-1920	1901-1920	T. Rf.	77.0 0.8	74.7 0.7	69.8 0.4	61.2 0.1	53.2 0.0	47.1 0.0	51.6 0.1	46.9 0.3	58.6 0.1	65.3 0.2	70.3 0.2	75.0 0.4	62.6 3.3
San Luis	2322.9	1901-1920	1901-1920	T. Rf.	75.2 4.2	72.5 4.1	68.5 2.3	61.5 1.5	54.3 0.7	48.0 0.2	51.6 0.4	48.6 0.4	56.1 0.7	63.7 1.3	69.1 2.8	73.4 3.6	61.9 22.2
Buenos Aires	82.0	1856-1924	1901-1920	T. Rf.	73.6 3.1	72.5 2.8	68.7 3.9	61.3 4.8	55.0 2.8	49.6 2.0	51.1 2.2	48.9 2.1	55.0 2.9	59.9 3.3	65.8 4.0	70.9 4.0	61.0 37.9
Mendoza	2477	1901-1920	1901-1920	T. Rf.	74.5 0.9	71.6 1.3	67.5 1.1	59.4 0.5	52.0 0.4	45.5 0.4	50.0 0.3	46.4 0.2	56.1 0.5	61.9 0.7	68.0 0.7	71.6 0.7	60.4 7.7
Mar del Plata	82.0	1901-1920	1901-1920	T. Rf.	66.9 2.1	66.4 3.1	63.9 3.1	59.4 3.1	52.7 1.9	47.3 2.4	46.8 1.8	46.2 2.1	49.6 2.6	53.2 2.4	58.8 2.6	63.7 2.7	56.2 29.9
Bahía Blanca	82.0	1901-1920	1901-1920	T. Rf.	74.5 2.2	71.6 2.4	67.5 2.4	60.1 3.5	53.1 1.1	47.1 0.6	48.9 0.7	46.4 0.9	53.6 0.7	59.2 3.4	66.4 1.9	71.8 2.0	60.0 21.6
Choele Choel	456.0	1901-1920	1901-1920	T. Rf.	75.4 0.7	72.5 0.7	67.3 1.0	58.5 0.9	51.3 1.1	44.8 0.6	47.7 0.3	45.1 0.5	53.1 0.8	59.9 0.9	66.7 0.5	72.1 0.6	59.5 8.6
Col. 16 de Octubre	1837.3	1901-1920	1901-1920	T. Rf.	60.6 0.5	58.8 0.5	54.9 0.8	47.7 2.2	42.3 3.2	37.0 2.8	38.7 2.0	36.7 1.5	42.8 0.8	48.4 0.4	51.8 0.5	55.9 0.6	48.0 15.8
Santa Cruz	39.4	1901-1920	1901-1920	T. Rf.	58.6 0.6	57.6 0.3	54.7 0.4	47.7 0.6	40.8 0.4	35.2 0.5	38.3 0.6	35.2 0.5	43.5 0.3	48.7 0.3	52.9 0.4	56.3 0.7	47.5 5.5
Ushuaia	26.3	1901-1920	1901-1920	T. Rf.	49.6 1.7	49.1 2.1	46.8 1.7	40.5 1.9	36.7 1.5	33.3 1.6	35.2 0.9	33.6 1.2	39.2 1.2	43.0 1.5	44.4 1.9	49.1 1.8	41.7 19.0

Station					Jan	Feb	Mar	Apr	May	June	July	Aug	Sept	Oct	Nov	Dec	Year
Asunción	344.5	1893–1924	1893–1923	T.	80.4	79.9	77.9	72.1	66.6	62.6	64.0	66.0	69.6	72.5	76.1	79.9	72.3
				Rf.	5.4	5.5	4.2	5.3	4.5	2.8	2.2	1.5	3.1	5.4	6.0	6.1	52.0
Montevideo	82.0	1901–1924	1901–1924	T.	72.0	71.8	68.5	63.0	56.7	51.3	50.5	51.3	54.9	58.1	64.6	69.4	61.0
				Rf.	2.6	3.1	3.2	4.6	3.4	3.2	2.4	3.5	3.4	2.5	3.2	3.5	38.6
Belém	32.8	1893–1910	1912–1924	T.	78.6	77.4	77.7	78.1	78.8	78.8	78.6	78.8	78.8	79.5	79.9	79.3	78.7
				Rf.	7.6	13.3	17.0	17.8	11.8	9.1	8.3	2.8	0.6	0.5	0.6	2.6	86.0
São Luiz	65.6	1912–1921	1912–1919	T.	79.7	79.2	79.0	79.0	79.2	79.2	78.8	79.0	79.9	80.4	80.1	80.2	79.5
				Rf.	7.4	10.4	16.6	16.6	12.4	5.8	4.1	1.1	0.5	0.4	0.7	6.5	84.4
Quixeramobim	679.1	1896–1921	1910–1924	T.	82.9	81.9	80.8	80.4	79.5	79.2	79.5	80.8	82.0	82.9	83.3	83.5	81.4
				Rf.	3.7	4.3	5.2	7.0	5.2	2.5	1.3	0.6	0.1	0.1	0.4	1.4	33.6
Natal	9.8	1904–1921	1912–1920	T.	81.0	80.8	81.0	80.9	79.2	77.2	75.9	76.3	78.1	78.3	80.4	80.8	79.1
				Rf.	2.8	5.2	5.9	8.9	7.8	12.3	6.7	3.5	2.4	1.1	0.3	0.7	57.6
Recife	98.4	1911–1921	1875–1922	T.	82.0	82.0	82.2	81.7	79.9	78.3	77.0	77.4	79.0	80.6	81.3	82.0	80.3
				Rf.	2.0	3.5	6.3	8.6	10.8	11.2	10.3	6.3	2.7	1.0	1.1	1.1	64.9
Ondina	154.2	1909–1921	1910–1924	T.	78.3	78.8	78.8	78.1	76.6	75.0	74.1	73.8	74.5	76.1	77.2	78.1	76.6
				Rf.	2.8	5.7	5.9	11.7	10.2	9.5	7.5	4.8	3.8	4.4	4.7	5.9	76.9
Belo Horizonte	2811.7	1910–1912	1910–1919	T.	71.4	72.1	71.1	68.7	65.5	62.6	62.2	64.4	68.4	70.3	70.3	70.2	68.1
				Rf.	12.8	9.5	6.3	2.9	0.6	0.5	0.4	0.9	1.5	4.9	8.3	10.7	59.3
Rezende	1312.3	1913–1921	1912–1924	T.	73.8	74.1	73.2	70.2	66.0	62.6	62.2	63.9	67.5	69.4	71.4	72.5	68.9
				Rf.	10.8	11.2	7.6	4.2	1.4	1.1	0.9	1.0	2.1	4.6	8.0	9.2	62.1
Rio de Janeiro	196.9	1851–1920	1851–1925	T.	78.6	79.0	77.7	75.2	72.0	69.6	68.7	69.6	70.3	71.8	73.9	76.6	73.6
				Rf.	4.9	4.8	5.2	4.3	3.1	2.3	1.7	1.7	2.6	3.2	4.1	5.4	43.3
Ribeirão Preto	1824.2	1901–1917	1910–1922	T.	74.1	75.0	73.9	70.9	65.3	63.3	63.3	62.6	70.5	72.5	74.1	74.3	70.0
				Rf.	11.0	7.9	6.1	3.1	1.4	2.0	0.6	1.2	2.2	4.4	6.8	8.5	55.2
São Paulo	2690.3	1902–1917	1902–1917	T.	68.9	69.1	68.0	64.6	60.4	58.6	57.9	59.0	61.5	63.0	65.5	68.0	63.7
				Rf.	7.7	8.7	5.6	2.2	2.5	2.2	1.7	2.0	3.2	4.7	7.2	8.5	56.2
Santos	9.8	1895–1917	1895–1917	T.	76.3	77.9	75.9	72.7	68.9	66.2	66.4	66.0	66.9	68.9	73.0	75.6	71.2
				Rf.	10.4	9.2	8.1	6.8	6.1	2.4	4.4	4.6	5.6	6.1	7.8	7.0	58.5
Curitiba	2979	1884–1910	1885–1925	T.	68.7	70.0	66.7	62.2	56.7	54.0	54.5	56.3	58.3	61.0	64.4	67.3	61.7
				Rf.	6.6	6.3	4.4	3.1	4.0	4.0	2.5	3.2	4.9	5.5	5.0	5.5	55.0
Paranaguá	13.1	1910–1919	1910–1919	T.	73.6	71.2	69.6	64.9	60.8	59.5	60.1	62.2	64.8	69.1	70.9	73.4	66.7
				Rf.	10.4	10.9	4.8	3.6	3.8	2.3	3.0	5.4	6.3	5.5	8.3	8.9	73.2
Blumenau	49.2	1915–1921	1915–1919	T.	75.9	75.6	72.5	70.5	64.9	59.2	58.3	60.6	63.9	67.3	70.5	73.6	67.7
				Rf.	7.9	11.1	6.5	3.9	3.4	4.1	2.0	3.9	4.7	3.9	3.0	4.8	59.2
Pôrto Alegre	49.2	1909–1922	1909–1922	T.	76.1	76.5	72.9	68.9	63.0	56.3	56.5	58.3	61.7	65.1	70.2	73.8	66.6
				Rf.	4.3	3.7	3.6	4.8	4.1	5.0	4.3	5.1	4.6	3.1	3.3	4.1	50.0

Manaus	147.6	1911–1921	1902–1926	T.	79.9	80.1	79.7	79.9	80.1	80.1	80.6	81.7	82.8	82.8	82.2	80.6	81.0
				Rf.	9.2	9.0	9.6	8.5	7.0	3.6	2.2	1.4	2.0	4.1	5.5	7.7	69.8
Santarém	65.6	1914–1919	1914–1920	T.	77.5	76.6	77.2	77.2	77.0	76.5	77.0	78.3	79.7	80.4	80.4	78.8	78.1
				Rf.	6.2	12.0	10.6	10.9	10.3	6.2	3.0	1.9	1.5	1.1	1.5	5.0	70.2
Corumbá	380.6	1912–1920	1912–1919	T.	80.2	79.5	80.1	78.6	73.9	69.4	70.5	72.7	76.6	78.4	79.9	80.1	76.7
				Rf.	6.4	6.7	4.8	5.0	3.3	1.9	0.3	1.3	2.3	3.9	6.0	7.4	49.2
Tres Lagôas	1148.3	1913–1919	1913–1919	T.	81.0	79.5	79.3	77.7	73.2	69.6	68.4	71.4	75.4	77.9	79.2	79.5	76.0
				Rf.	5.4	4.0	3.0	4.8	4.4	3.2	1.0	1.8	3.9	3.1	5.4	5.0	44.0
Goiás	1706.0	1912–1921	1912–1919	T.	74.3	74.8	75.4	75.9	74.7	72.3	72.3	75.2	78.1	77.7	76.1	74.7	75.1
				Rf.	11.9	11.7	11.4	5.0	0.4	0.5	0.0	0.4	1.8	4.8	8.7	10.2	66.8
Caxambú	2919.2	1914–1922	1912–1924	T.	68.9	69.3	67.6	64.8	59.7	57.4	56.8	59.5	63.9	66.0	67.3	68.0	64.1
				Rf.	12.4	9.8	7.3	2.9	1.0	1.3	0.6	0.9	2.5	5.0	8.1	9.3	71.1

Appendix B □ References

The following selected list of references provides additional material on Latin-American geography. To keep the bibliographies up-to-date, and to provide for additional references, there are several bibliographical sources of importance to students of Latin America. Of major importance is the *Handbook of Latin American Studies*, published annually since 1935, edited at The Hispanic Foundation, Library of Congress (University of Florida Press). This handbook contains a selected and annotated list of publications concerning all aspects of Latin-American studies, not geography only. For geographical writings, the student is referred to the annual *Bibliographie géographique international*, published since 1923 by Armand Colin, Paris. The American Geographical Society of New York publishes its *Current Geographical Publications*, which is the accession list of the Society's library. Among the more important country bibliographies attention is called also to Rubens Borba de Moraes and William Berrien, *Manual Bibliográfico de Estudos Brasileiros*, Rio de Janeiro, 1949. For additional references to bibliographic sources see John Kirtland Wright and Elizabeth T. Platt, *Aids to Geographical Research*, American Geographical Society, (Research Series No. 22) New York, 1947.

For data concerning heights of mountains, elevations, and positions of cities see *The Columbia Lippincott Gazetteer of the World*, New York, 1952. For the most recent statistical data regarding population, production, trade, etc., see the latest Britannica Book of the Year. For a summary of statistical data see Committee on Latin American Studies, University of California at Los Angeles, *Statistical Abstract of Latin America*, published annually since 1955. For concise geographic summaries of selected countries and problem areas see the series of pamphlets—*Focus*—published monthly (except July and August) by the American Geographical Society.

The two most important libraries in the United States containing geographic writings and maps are: The American Geographical Society of New York (Broadway at 156th Street), and the Library of Congress (Washington, D.C.). At the Library of Congress special attention is called to the Hispanic Foundation and the Map Division.

The following selected list of references is arranged by Latin America as a whole and its larger parts, and by countries. References are arranged in order of the dates of publication.

Latin America—General

(Including South America and Middle America)

HUMBOLDT, A. VON. *Essai politique sur le royaume de la Nouvelle Espagne,* 5 volumes, Paris, 1811–12.

HUMBOLDT, A. VON. *Relation . . . du voyage aux régions équinoxiales du nouveau continent,* 3 volumes, Paris, 1814–25.

BRYCE, J. *South America, Observations and Impressions,* New York, 1912.

FRIEDERICI, G. *Der Charakter der Entdeckung und Eroberung Amerikas: Einleitung zur Geschichte der Besiedlung Amerikas durch die Völker der Alten Welt,* 3 volumes, Stuttgart, 1925–36.

DENIS, P. *Amérique du Sud (Géographie universelle,* Vol. 15), Paris, 1927.

SORRE, MAX. *Mexique, Amérique Centrale (Géographie universelle,* Vol. 14), Paris, 1928.

RUHLE, K. "Die Vegetationsformationen Südamerikas in ihrer klimatischen Bedingheit," *Petermanns Mitteilungen,* Vol. 74 (1928): 29–34; 95–100.

SPINDEN, H. J. "The Population of Ancient America," *Geographical Review,* Vol. 18 (1928): 641–60.

KNOCH, K. *Klimakunde von Südamerika* (in W. Köppen and R. Geiger, *Handbuch der Klimatologie,* Vol. 2, Part G), Berlin, 1930.

SAPPER, K. *Klimakunde von Mittelamerika* (in W. Köppen and R. Geiger, *Handbuch der Klimatologie,* Vol. 2, Part H), Berlin, 1932.

SCHUCHERT, C. *Historical Geology of the Antillean-Caribbean Region, or the Lands Bordering the Gulf of Mexico and the Caribbean Sea,* New York, 1935.

IRELAND, G. *Boundaries, Possessions and Conflicts in South America,* Cambridge, Mass., 1938.

KROEBER, A. L. *Cultural and Natural Areas of Native North America,* Berkeley, Cal., 1939.

JAEGER, F. "Die Gewässer Südamerikas," *Petermanns Mitteilungen,* Vol. 86 (1940): 63–69.

IRELAND, G. *Boundaries, Possessions and Conflicts in Central and North America and the Caribbean,* Cambridge, Mass., 1941.

PLATT, R. S. *Latin America, Countrysides and United Regions,* New York, 1942.

RICH, J. L. *The Face of South America; an Aerial Traverse* (American Geographical Society, Special Publication, No. 26), New York, 1942.

SAUER, C. O. The March of Agriculture Across the Western World" (in Eighth American Scientific Congress, *Proceedings,* Vol. V (1942): 63–65.

STEWARD. J. H. (ed.). *Handbook of South American Indians,* 6 vols. (Smithsonian Institution, Bureau of American Ethnology), Washington, D. C., 1946–50.

ZELINSKY, W. "The Historical Geography of the Negro Population of Latin America," *Journal of Negro History*, Vol. 34 (1949): 153–221.

WHITAKER, A. P. *The Western Hemisphere Idea: Its Rise and Decline*, Ithaca, N. Y., 1954.

FIGUERES, J. "Problems of Democracy in Latin America," *Journal of International Affairs*, Vol. 9 (1955): 11–23.

GILLIN, J. "Ethos Components in Modern Latin American Culture," *American Anthropologist*, Vol. 57 (1955): 488–500.

KOHLER, G. "Verkehrsgeographische Ubersicht von Südamerika," *Petermanns Mitteilungen*, Vol. 100 (1956): 115–21.

SCHRODER, R. "Die klimatischen Bedingungen für den Kaffeeanbau auf der Erde, insbesondere in Zentral- und Südamerika," *Petermanns Mitteilungen*, Vol. 100 (1956): 122–36.

WITTHAUER, K. "Zur Bevölkerungsverteilung und -entwicklung in Südamerika," *Petermanns Mitteilungen*, Vol. 100 (1956): 153–60.

ALEXANDER, R. J. *Communism in Latin America*, New Brunswick, N. J., 1957.

PALMER, THOMAS W., JR. *Search for a Latin American Policy*, Gainesville, Fla., 1957.

DAVIS, K. (ed.). "A Crowding Hemisphere: Population Change in the Americas," *The Annals of the American Academy of Political and Social Science*, Vol. 316 (1958): 1–136.

JOHNSON, J. J. *Political Change in Latin America: The Emergence of the Middle Sectors*, Stanford, Cal., 1958.

STEWARD, J. H., and FARON, L. C., *Native Peoples of South America*, New York, 1959.

LIEUWEN, E. *Arms and Politics in Latin America*, New York, 1960.

TEICHERT, P. C. M. "The Main Experiences and Policies of the Industrial Revolution in Latin America," *Weltwirtschaftliches Archiv*, Vol. 85 (1960): 279–302.

SILVERT, K. H. *The Conflict Society, Reaction and Revolution in Latin America*, New York, 1961; revised edition 1966.

BUSEY, J. L. *Latin America, Political Institutions and Processes*, New York, 1964.

JOHNSON, J. J. *The Military and Society in Latin America*, Stanford, Cal., 1964.

MAIER, J., and WEATHERHEAD, R. W. (eds.), *Politics of Change in Latin America*, New York, 1964.

PIKE, F. B. *The Conflict between Church and State in Latin American*, New York, 1964.

TOSI, J. A., and VOERTMAN, R. F. Some Environmental Factors in the Economic Development of the Tropics," *Economic Geography*, Vol. 40 (1964): 189–205.

URQUIDI, V. L. *Free Trade and Economic Integration in Latin America*, Berkeley, Cal., 1964.

DEFFONTAINES, P. "Transhumance et mouvements de bétail en Amérique Latine," *Les Cahiers d'Outre-Mer*, Vol. 19 (1965): 258–94; 321–41.

WIONCZEK, M. S., and ANGULO, E. *Latin American Free Trade Association*, International Conciliation, New York, 1965.

SAUER, C. O. *The Early Spanish Main*, Berkeley, Cal., 1966.

WEST, R. C., and AUGELLI, J. P. *Middle America–Its Lands and Peoples*, New York, 1966.

WHITAKER, A. P., and JORDAN, D. C. *Nationalism in Contemporary Latin America*, New York, 1966.

HUECK, K. *Die Wälder Südamerikas, Okologie, Zusammensetzung und wirtschaftliche Bedeutung*, Stuttgart, 1966.

SMITH, T. L. *The Process of Rural Development in Latin America*, Gainesville, Fla., 1967.

MANGIN, W. "Latin American Squatter Settlements: A Problem and a Solution," *Latin American Research Review*, Vol. 2 (summer, 1967): 65–98.

HANSON, E. P. *South from the Spanish Main*, New York, 1967.

HANKE, L. *Contemporary Latin America*, Princeton, N. J., 1968.

LOUTKA, C. "Ethno-Linguistic Distribution of South American Indians," *Annals of the Association of American Geographers*, Vol. 57, 1967: 437–38.

Mexico

Mexico as a Whole

McBRIDE, G. M. *The Land Systems of Mexico* (American Geographical Society, Research Series No. 12), New York, 1923.

TANNENBAUM, F. *The Mexican Agrarian Revolution*, New York, 1933.

SIMPSON, E. H. *The Ejido, Mexico's Way Out*, Chapel Hill, N. C., 1937.

SAUER, C. O. "The Personality of Mexico," *Geographical Review*, Vol. 31 (1941): 353–64.

WHETTEN, N. L. *Rural Mexico*, Chicago, 1958.

LEOPOLD, A. S. "Zonas de vegetación en México," *Boletín de la Sociedad Méxicana de Geografía y Estadística*, Vol. 73 (1952): 45–93.

CHEVALIER, F. *Land and Society in Colonial Mexico: The Great Hacienda*, trans. by A. Eustis, Berkeley, Cal., 1963.

NELSON, H. J. "Townscapes of Mexico: An Example of the Regional Variation of Townscapes," *Economic Geography*, Vol. 39 (1963): 74–83.

BRAND, D. D. *Mexico: Land of Sunshine and Shadow*, New York, 1966.

SNYDER, D. E. "Urbanization and Population Growth in Mexico," *Revista Geográfica* (Junho 1966): 73–84.

ENJALBERT, H. "L'Elevage au Mexique," *Revista Geográfica* (Junho 1966): 53–72.

Regional Divisions: The North Pacific

SAUER, C. O., and MEIGS, P. "Site and Culture at San Fernando de Velicatá," *University of California Publications in Geography*, Vol. 2 (1927): 271–302.

SCHMIEDER, O. "The Russian Colony of Guadalupe Valley," *University of California Publications in Geography*, Vol. 2 (1928): 409–34.

KNIFFEN, F. B. "The Primitive Cultural Landscape of the Colorado Delta," *University of California Publications in Geography*, Vol. 5 (1931): 43–66.

KNIFFEN, F. B. "The Natural Landscape of the Colorado Delta," *University of California Publications in Geography*, Vol. 5 (1932): 149–244.

SAUER, C. O. *The Road to Cíbola*, Ibero-Americana, 3, Berkeley, Cal., 1932.

MEIGS, P. "The Dominican Mission Frontier of Lower California," *University of California Publications in Geography*, Vol. 7 (1935): 1–232.

SAUER, C. O. *The Aboriginal Population of Northwestern Mexico*, Ibero-Americana, 10, Berkeley, Cal., 1935.

HEWES, L. "Huepac: An Agricultural Village of Sonora, Mexico," *Economic Geography*, Vol. 11 (1935): 284–92.

SYKES, G. *The Colorado Delta* (American Geographical Society, Special Publication No. 19), New York, 1937.

WEST, R. C., and PARSONS, J. J. "The Topia Road: A Trans-Sierran Trail of Colonial Mexico," *Geographical Review*, Vol. 31 (1941): 406–13.

DEASY, G. F., and GERHARD, P. "Settlements in Baja California: 1768–1930," *Geographical Review*, Vol. 34 (1944): 574–86.

HAMMOND, E. H. "A Geomorphic Study of the Cape Region of Baja California," *University of California Publications in Geography*, Vol. 10 (1954): 45–112.

DOZIER, C. L. "Mexico's Transformed Northwest—The Yaqui, Mayo, and Fuerte Examples," *Geographical Review*, Vol. 53 (1963): 548–71.

HENDERSON, D. A. "Arid Lands under Agrarian Reform in Northwest Mexico," *Economic Geography*, Vol. 41 (1965): 300–312.

The North

DICKEN, S. N. "Monterrey and Northeastern Mexico," *Annals of the Association of American Geographers*, Vol. 29 (1939): 127–58.

ALMADA, F. "Geografía humana del Estado de Chihuahua," *Boletín de la Sociedad Mexicana de Geografía y Estadística*, Vol. 57 (1942): 227–300.

HERNANDEZ, T. L. *Geografía del Estado de Nuevo León*, Monterrey, Cal., 1943.

WEST, R. C. *The Mining Community in Northern New Spain: The Parral Mining District*, Ibero-Americana, 30, Berkeley, Cal., 1949.

KENNELLY, R. A. "The Location of the Mexican Steel Industry," *Revista Geográfica*, Vol. 14 (1954): 51–80; Vol. 15 (1954): 105–29; Vol. 16 (1955): 199–213.

The Gulf Coast and Yucatan

SCHMIEDER, O. "The Settlements of the Tzapotec and Mije Indians, State of Oaxaca, Mexico," *University of California Publications in Geography*, Vol. 4 (1930): 1–184.

ZILLI, J. *Geografía del Estado de Veracruz*, Mexico, 1943.

CHAMBERLAIN, R. S. *The Conquest and Colonization of Yucatán* (Carnegie Institution Publication No. 582), Washington, D. C., 1948.

DRAGON, R. G. "Mexican Henequen, The Growth and Decline of a Fiber Monopoly," *Journal of Geography*, Vol. 53 (1954): 49–60.

WINNIE, W. W., JR. "The Papaloapan Project: An Experiment in Tropical Development," *Economic Geography*, Vol. 34 (1958): 227–48.

POLEMAN, T. T. *The Papaloapan Project: Agricultural Development in the Mexican Tropics*, Stanford, Cal., 1964.

The South Pacific

REDFIELD, R. *Tepoztlán: A Mexican Village,* Chicago, 1933.

WAIBEL, L. "Die Sierra Madre de Chiapas," *Mitteilungen der Geographischen Gesellschaft in Hamburg,* Vol. 43 (1933): 12–126.

LEWIS, O. "Social and Economic Changes in a Mexican Village: Tepoztlán, 1926–1944," *América Indígina,* Vol. 4 (1944): 281–314.

CACERES, L. C. *Chiapas: sínteses geográfica e histórica,* Mexico, 1946.

COVARRUBIAS, M. *Mexico South: The Isthmus of Tehuantepec,* New York, 1946.

SAUER, C. O. *Colima of New Spain in the Sixteenth Century,* Ibero-Americana, 29, Berkeley, Cal., 1948.

ALVAREZ del VILLAR, J. "Esquema geobotánico de Chiapas," *Boletín de la Sociedad Méxicana de Geografía y Estadística,* Vol. 73 (1952): 97–124.

WAGNER, P. L. "Natural and Artificial Zonation in a Vegetation Cover: Chiapas, Mexico," *Geographical Review,* Vol. 52 (1962): 253–74.

WAGNER, P. L. "Indian Economic Life in Chiapas," *Economic Geography,* Vol. 39 (1963): 156–64.

GONZALES, A. "Problems of Agricultural Development in a Pioneer Region of Southwestern Mexico," *Revista Geográfica* (Junho 1966): 29–52.

The Central Area

PLATT, R. S. "Magdalena Atlipac—A Study in Terrene Occupancy in Mexico," *Geographical Society of Chicago, Bulletin,* No. 9 (1933): 47–75.

CRIST, R. E. "The Pulque Industry," *Economic Geography,* Vol. 15 (1939): 189-94.

HAYNES, N. S. "Mexico City: Its Growth and Configuration," *American Journal of Sociology,* Vol. 50 (1945): 295–304.

WEST, R. C. *Cultural Geography of the Modern Tarascan Area* (Smithsonian Institution, Institute of Social Anthropology, Publication No. 7), Washington, D. C., 1948.

COOK, S. F., and SIMPSON, L. B. *The Population of Central Mexico in the Sixteenth Century,* Ibero-Americana, 31, Berkeley, Cal., 1948.

COOK, S. F. *Soil Erosion and Population in Central Mexico,* Ibero-Americana, 34, Berkeley, Cal., 1949.

STANISLAWSKI, D. *The Anatomy of Eleven Towns in Michoacán* (Latin-American Studies, No. 10), Austin, Texas, 1950.

FOX, D. J. "Man–Water Relationships in Metropolitan Mexico," *Geographical Review,* Vol. 55 (1965): 523–45.

PFEIFER, G. "The Basin of Puebla—Tlaxcala in Mexico," *Revista Geográfica* (Junho 1966): 85–107.

BATAILLON, C. "L'axe néovolcanique dans la géographie du Mexique Central," *Revista Geográfica* (Junho 1966): 17–28.

Central America

Central America as a Whole

PLATT, R. S. "An Air Traverse of Central America," *Annals of the Association of American Geographers,* Vol. 24 (1934): 29–39.

DOZIER, C. L. *Indigenous Tropical Agriculture in Central America,* National Research Council, Washington, D. C., 1958.

BUSEY, J. L., "Foundations of Political Contrast: Costa Rica and Nicaragua," *The Western Political Quarterly,* Vol. 11 (1958): 627-59.

LAUER, W. "Klimatische und Pflanzengeographische Grundzüge Zentralamerikas," *Erdkunde,* Vol. 13 (1959): 344-54.

PORTIG, W. H. "Central American Rainfall," *Geographical Review,* Vol. 55 (1965): 68-90.

PARSONS, J. J. "Cotton and Cattle in the Pacific Lowlands of Central America," *Journal of Inter-American Studies,* Vol. 7 (1965): 149-59.

MINKEL, C. W. "Programs of Agricultural Colonization and Settlement in Central America," *Revista Geográfica* (Junho, 1967): 19-53.

NUNLEY, R. E. "Population Densities Using a New Approach: A Preliminary Report," *Revista Geográfica,* (Junho, 1967): 55-93.

Guatemala

TERMER, F. "Zur Geographie der Republik Guatemala: Part I, Beiträge zur physischen Geographie . . . ; Part II, Beiträge zur kultur- und wirtschaftsgeographie," *Mitteilungen der geographischen Gesellschaft in Hamburg,* Vol. 44 (1936): 89–257; Vol. 47 (1941): 7–262.

MCBRIDE, G. M., and MCBRIDE, M. A. "Highland Guatemala and its Maya Communities," *Geographical Review,* Vol. 32 (1942): 250–68.

HIGBEE, E. C. "Agricultural Regions of Guatemala," *Geographical Review,* Vol. 37 (1947): 177–201.

MCBRYDE, F. W. *Cultural and Historical Geography of Southwest Guatemala* (Smithsonian Institution, Institute of Social Anthropology, Publication No. 4), Washington, D. C., 1947.

HIGBEE, E. C. "Agriculture in the Maya Homeland," *Geographical Review,* Vol. 38 (1948): 457–64.

WHETTEN, N. *Guatemala: The Land and the People,* New Haven, Conn., 1961.

PEARSON, R. "Zones of Agricultural Development in Guatemala," *Journal of Geography,* Vol. 62 (1963): 11–22.

HORST, O. H. "The Specter of Death in a Guatemalan Highland Community," *Geographical Review,* Vol. 57 (1967): 151–67.

Honduras

VON HAGEN, V. W. "The Mosquito Coast of Honduras and its Inhabitants," *Geographical Review,* Vol. 30 (1940): 238–59.

STOKES, W. S. *Honduras, An Area Study in Government,* Madison, Wis., 1950.

CHECCHI, V., and Associates, *Honduras: A Problem in Economic Development,* New York, 1959.

HELBIG, K. M. "Die Landschaften von Nordost Honduras," *Petermanns Mitteilungen,* Ergänzungsheft 268 (1959): 1–270.

JOHANNESSEN, C. L. *Savannas of Interior Honduras,* Ibero-Americana, 46, Berkeley, Cal., 1963.

El Salvador

BARÓN CASTRO, R. *La población de El Salvador: Estudio acerca de su desenvolvimiento desde la época prehispánica hasta nuestros días,* Madrid, 1942.

LAUER, W. *Vegetation, Landnutzung und Agrarpotential in El Salvador (Zentralamerika),* Schriften des Geographschen Instituts der Universität Kiel, 1956.

Nicaragua

PARSONS, J. J. "Gold Mining in the Nicaragua Rain Forest," *Yearbook of the Association of Pacific Coast Geographers,* Vol. 17 (1955): 49–55.

PARSONS, J. J. "The Miskito Pine Savanna of Nicaragua and Honduras," *Annals of the Association of American Geographers,* Vol. 45 (1955): 36–63.

DENEVAN, W. M. "The Upland Pine Forests of Nicaragua, A study in Cultural Plant Geography," *University of California Publications in Geography,* Vol. 12 (1961): 251–320.

Costa Rica

WAIBEL, L. "White Settlement in Costa Rica," *Geographical Review,* Vol. 29 (1939): 529–60.

BECKER, H. F. "Land Utilization´in Guanacaste Province of Costa Rica," *Geographical Review,* Vol. 33 (1943): 74–85.

LEÓN, J. "Land Utilization in Costa Rica," *Geographical Review,* Vol. 38 (1948): 444–56.

MORRISON, P. C., and LEON, J. "Sequent Occupance, Turrialba Central District, Costa Rica," *Turrialba* (American Institute of Agricultural Sciences), Vol. 1 (1951): 185–98.

JONES, C. F., and MORRISON, P. C. "Evolution of the Banana Industry of Costa Rica," *Economic Geography,* Vol. 28 (1952): 1–19.

MAY, S., and others. *Costa Rica, A Study in Economic Development* (Twentieth Century Fund), New York, 1952.

DIRECCION GENERAL de ESTADISTÍCA y CENSOS. *Atlas estadístico de Costa Rica,* San José, 1953.

LOOMIS, C. P., and others. *Turrialba: Social Systems and the Introduction of Change,* Glencoe, Ill., 1953.

MORRISON, P. C., and NORRIS, T. L. "Coffee Production and Processing on a Large Costa Rican *Finca,*" *Papers of the Michigan Academy of Science, Arts and Letters,* Vol. 39 (1954): 309–22.

MORRISON, P. C. "Land Utilization, Cartago to Turrialba, Costa Rica," *Papers of the Michigan Academy of Science, Arts and Letters,* Vol. 40 (1955): 205–16.

WAGNER, P. L. "Nicoya, a Cultural Geography," *University of California Publications in Geography,* Vol. 12 (1958): 195–250.

SANDNER, G. *Agrarkolonisation in Costa Rica: Siedlung, Wirtschaft, und Sozialgefüge und der Pioniergrenze,* Schriften des Geographischen Instituts der Universität Kiel, 1961.

PARSONS, J. J. "Agricultural Colonization in Costa Rica," *Geographical Review*, Vol. 53 (1963): 451–54.

LASSERE, G. "Le Costa Rica," *Revista Geográfica* (Junho, 1967): 107–33.

Panamá

GUZMÁN, L. E. *Farming and Farmlands in Panamá*, University of Chicago, Department of Geography Research Paper, Chicago, Ill., 1956.

RUBIO, A., and GUZMÁN, L. "Regiones geográficas panameñas," *Revista Geográfica*, (Junho, 1959): 53–66.

FOX, D. "Prospects for the Panama Canal," *Tijdschrift voor economische en sociale geografie*, Vol. 55 (1964): 86–101.

FUSON, R. H. "House Types in Central Panama," *Annals of the Association of American Geographers*, Vol. 54 (1964): 190–208.

The Antilles

The Antilles as a Whole

WARD, R. deC., and BROOKS, C. F. *Climatology of the West Indies* (in W. Köppen and R. Geiger, *Handbuch der Klimatologie*, Part I), Berlin, 1934.

GERLING, W. *Wirtschaftsentwicklung und Landschaftswandel auf den westindischen Inseln Jamaika, Haiti und Puerto Rico: Beiträge zu spanischen, französischen, englischen, und amerikanischen Kolonisationmethoden in Westindien*, Freiburg, 1938.

PARRY, J. H., and SHERLOCK, P. M. *A Short History of the West Indies*, London, 1956.

RUBIN, V. (ed.). *Caribbean Studies: A Symposium*, Institute of Social and Economic Research, University of the West Indies), Kingston, Jamaica, 1957.

DOERR, A. H., and HOY, D. R. "Karst Landscapes of Cuba, Puerto Rico, and Jamaica," *The Scientific Monthly*, Vol. 85 (1957): 178–87.

PARES, R. *Merchants and Planters*, London, 1960.

AUGIER, F. R., GORDON, S. C., HALL, D. G., and RECKORD, M. *The Making of the West Indies*, London, 1960.

CUMPER, C. E. (ed.). *The Economy of the West Indies*, Institute of Social and Economic Research, University of the West Indies, Kingston, Jamaica, 1960.

LOWENTHAL, D. *The West Indies Federation, Perspectives on a New Nation*, American Geographical Society, New York, 1961.

ERICKSEN, E. G. *The West Indies Population Problem, Dimensions for Action*, Lawrence, Kans., 1962.

MACPHERSON, J. *Caribbean Lands: A Geography of the West Indies*, London, 1963.

PEARCY, G. E. *The West Indian Scene*, Princeton, N. J., 1965.

BLUME, H. "Types of Agricultural Regions and Land Tenure in the West Indies," *Revista Geográfica*, No. 67 (1967): 7–20.

Cuba

ORTIZ FERNÁNDEZ, F. *Cuban Counterpoint: Tobacco and Sugar* (translated by Harriet de Onís), New York, 1947.

DYER, D. R. "Sugar Regions of Cuba," *Economic Geography,* Vol. 32 (1956): 177–84.

CRIST, R. E. "Some Notes on Recent Trends in Rice Production in Cuba," *Economic Geography,* Vol. 32 (1956): 126–31.

MACGAFFEY, W. and BARNETT, C. R. *Cuba: Its People, Its Society, Its Culture,* New Haven, Conn., 1962.

GUERRA Y SANCHEZ, R. *Sugar and Society in the Caribbean: An Economic History of Cuban Agriculture,* New Haven, Conn., 1964.

ALVAREZ DIAZ, J. R. (Chairman), *A Study on Cuba,* Cuban Economic Research Project, University of Miami, Miami, Fla., 1965.

JIMENEZ, A. N. *Geografía de Cuba,* Habana, 1965.

SEMEVSKIY, B. N. "Basic National-Economic Problems of the Republic of Cuba," *Soviet Geography,* Vol. 7 (1966): 527–33.

DYER, D. R. "Cuban Sugar Regions," *Revista Geográfica.* No. 67 (1967): 21–30.

Hispaniola

CRIST, R. E. "Cultural Dichotomy in the Island of Hispaniola," *Economic Geography,* Vol. 28 (1952): 105–21.

DYER, D. R. "Distribution of Population on Hispaniola," *Economic Geography,* Vol. 30 (1954): 337–46.

Haiti

HERSKOVITS, M. J. *Life in a Haitian Valley,* New York, 1937.

LEYBURN, J. G. *The Haitian People,* New Haven, Conn., 1941.

MORAL, P. "La Culture du café en Haïti . . . ," *Les Cahiers d'Outre-Mer,* Vol. 8 (1955): 233–56.

HOLLY, M. A. *Agriculture in Haiti,* New York, 1955.

DE YOUNG, M. *Man and Land in the Haitian Economy,* School of Inter-American Studies, University of Florida, Gainesville, Fla., 1958.

MORAL, P. *Le Paysan Haïtien: Etude sur la Vie Rurale en Haïti,* Paris, 1961.

WOOD, H. A. *Northern Haiti: Land, Land Use, and Settlement,* Toronto, 1963.

Dominican Republic

ENJALBERT, H. "La renaissance économique de la République Dominicaine," *Les Cahiers d'Outre-Mer,* Vol. 5 (1952): 330–56; Vol. 6 (1953): 61–87.

AUGELLI, J. P. "Agricultural Colonization in the Dominican Republic," *Economic Geography,* Vol. 38 (1962): 15–27.

Pan American Union. *Reconocimiento y Evaluación de los Recursos Naturales de la República Dominicana,* Washington, D.C., 1967.

Puerto Rico

PICÓ, R. *The Geographic Regions of Puerto Rico,* Río Piedras, P. R., 1950.

PICÓ, R. *Geografía de Puerto Rico, Parte 1, geografía física,* Río Piedras, P. R., 1954.

JONES, C. F., and PICÓ, R. *Symposium on the Geography of Puerto Rico*, Río Piedras, P. R., 1955.

STEAD, W. H. *Fomento—The Economic Development of Puerto Rico* (National Planning Association, Pamphlet No. 103), Washington, D. C., 1958.

HANSON, E. P. *Puerto Rico, Ally for Progress*, New York, 1962.

PICÓ, R. *Puerto Rico, Planificacion y Accion*, San Juan, P. R., 1962.

MACPHAIL, D. D. "Puerto Rican Dairying: A Revolution in Tropical Agriculture," *Geographical Review*, Vol. 53 (1963):224–46.

NIDDRIE, D. L. "The Problems of Population Growth in Puerto Rico," *Journal of Tropical Geography*, Vol. 20 (1965): 26–33.

Jamaica

CUMPER, G. E. "Population Movements in Jamaica," *Social and Economic Studies*, Vol. 5 (1956): 261–80.

PEARSON, R. "The Geography of Recreation on a Tropical Island, Jamaica," *Journal of Geography*, Vol. 56 (1957): 12–22.

PEARSON, R. "The Jamaica Bauxite Industry," *Journal of Geography*, Vol. 56 (1957): 377–85.

ROBERTS, G. W. *The Population of Jamaica: An Analysis of Its Structure and Growth*, Cambridge, England, 1957.

BLAUT, J. M. *et al.* "A Study of Cultural Determinants of Soil Erosion and Conservation in the Blue Mountains of Jamaica," *Social and Economic Studies*, Vol. 8 (1959): 403–20.

Trinidad and Tobago

HERSKOVITS, M. J. *Trinidad Village*, New York, 1947.

JAMES, P. E. "Changes in the Geography of Trinidad," *Scottish Geographical Magazine*, Vol. 73 (1957): 158–66.

KINGSBURY, R. C. *Commercial Geography of Trinidad and Tobago*, Indiana University, Dept. of Geography, Bloomington, Ind., 1960.

AUGELLI, J. P., and TAYLOR, H. W. "Race and Population Patterns in Trinidad," *Annals of the Association of American Geographers*, Vol. 50 (1960): 123–38.

HAREWOOD, J. "Population Growth in Trinidad and Tobago in the Twentieth Century," *Social and Economic Studies*, Vol. 12 (1963): 1–26.

Barbados

STARKEY, O. P. *The Economic Geography of Barbados: A Study of the Relationships between Environmental Variations and Economic Development*, New York, 1939.

LOWENTHAL, D. "The Population of Barbados," *Social and Economic Studies*, Vol. 6 (1957): 445–501.

HENSHALL, J. D., and KING, L. J. "Some Structural Characteristics of Peasant Agriculture in Barbados," *Economic Geography*, Vol. 42 (1966): 74–84.

The Other Lesser Antilles

PLATT, R. R., and others. *The European Possessions in the Caribbean* (American Geographical Society, Map of Hispanic America, Publication No. 4), New York, 1941.

REVERT, E. "L'économie martiniquaise," *Les Cahiers d'Outre-Mer*, Vol. 1 (1948): 28–39.

REVERT, E. *La Martinique: étude géographique et humaine*, Paris, 1949.

ROBEQUAIN, C. "Saint Barthélemy," *Les Cahiers d'Outre-Mer*, Vol. 2 (1949): 14–37.

LASSERRE, G. "Marie Galante," *Les Cahiers d'Outre-Mer*, Vol. 3 (1950): 123–52.

AUGELLI, J. P. "Patterns and Problems of Land Tenure in the Lesser Antilles: Antigua, B.W.I.," *Economic Geography*, Vol. 29 (1953): 362–67.

DORAN, E., JR. *Land Forms of the Southeast Bahamas*, Austin, Tex., 1955.

LOWENTHAL, D. "Economic Tribulations in the Caribbean: A Case Study in the British West Indies," *Inter-American Economic Affairs*, Vol. 9 (1955): 67–81.

AUGELLI, J. P. "The British Virgin Islands: A West Indian Anomaly," *Geographical Review*, Vol. 46 (1956): 43–58.

LOWENTHAL, D. "Two Federations," *Social and Economic Studies*, Vol. 6 (1957): 185–96.

PARSONS, J. J. "San Andrés and Providencia, English-Speaking Islands of the Western Caribbean," *University of California Publications in Geography*, Vol. 12 (1956): 1–84.

NORDLOHNE, E. "The Netherlands Antilles," *Tijdschrift voor Economische en Sociale Geografie*, Vol. 47 (1956): 167–70.

ALEXANDER, C. S. "The Geography of Margarita and Adjacent Islands, Venezuela," *University of California Publications in Geography*, Vol. 12 (1958): 85–192.

FENTEM, A. D. *Commercial Geography of Dominica*, Indiana University, Department of Geography, Bloomington, Ind., 1960.

KINGSBURY, R. C. *Commercial Geography of the British Virgin Islands*, Indiana University, Department of Geography, Bloomington, Ind., 1960.

LASSERRE, G. *La Guadeloupe: Étude géographique*, Bordeaux, 1961.

FENTEM, A. D. *Commercial Geography of Antigua*, Indiana University, Department of Geography, Bloomington, Ind., 1961.

O'LOUGHLIN, C. "Economic Problems of the Smaller West Indies Islands," *Social and Economic Studies*, Vol. 11 (1962): 44–56.

HOY, D. R. "Changing Agricultural Land Use on Guadeloupe, French West Indies," *Annals of the Association of American Geographers*, Vol. 52 (1962): 441–54.

HARRIS, D. R. "Plants, Animals, and Man in the Outer Leeward Islands, West Indies—An Ecological Study of Antigua, Barbuda, and Anguilla," *University of California Publications in Geography*, Vol. 18 (1965): 1–184.

The Guianas

SIR WALTER RALEIGH, *The Discoverie of the Large and Bewtiful Empire of Guiana*, (1596), ed. by V. T. Harlow, London, 1929.

ROTH, V. *Handbook of Natural Resources of British Guiana*, Gerogetown, B. G., 1946.

REVERT, E. *La France Amérique*, Paris, 1949.

INTERNATIONAL BANK FOR RECONSTRUCTION AND DEVELOPMENT, *The Economic Development of British Guiana*, Baltimore, Md., 1954.

PAPY, L. "La Guyane Française," *Les Cahiers d'Outre-Mer*, Vol. 8 (1955): 209–32, 369–400.

HANRATH, J. J. "The Economic-Geographical Structure of Surinam, A Character Sketch," *Tijdschrift voor Economische en Sociale Geografie*, Vol. 47 (1956): 165–67.

LOWENTHAL, D. "Population Contrasts in the Guianas," *Geographical Review*, Vol. 50 (1960): 41–58.

GRITZNER, C. F., JR. "French Guiana Penal Colony: Its Role in Colonial Development," *Journal of Geography*, Vol. 63 (1964): 314–19.

NUNN, A. "Guyana, A New Nation in South America," *The Geographical Magazine*, Vol. 39 (1966): 26–38.

DODGE, P. "Ethnic Fragmentation and Politics: The Case of Surinam," *Political Science Quarterly*, Vol. 81 (1966): 593–601.

Venezuela

CRIST, R. E., and CHARDÓN, C. E. "Changing Patterns of Land Use in the Valencia Lake Basin of Venezuela," *Geographical Review*, Vol. 31 (1941): 430–43.

STERLING, H. S. *et al. Problemas económicos y sociales de Los Andes venezolanos* (Consejo de Bienestar Rural) Caracas, 1955, 1957.

CRIST, R. E. "Along the Llanos-Andes Border in Venezuela: Then and Now," *Geographical Review*, Vol. 46 (1956): 187–208.

SERVICIO DE METEOROLOGÍA, *Atlas Climatológico, provisional: Período 1951–55*, Caracas, 1957

VILA, P. *Geografía de Venezuela; el territorio nacional y su ambiente físico*, Caracas, 1960.

DIRECCIÓN DE PLANIFICACIÓN AGROPECUARIA, *Atlas Agrícola de Venezuela*, Caracas, 1960.

DIRECCIÓN DE RECURSOS NATURALES RENOVABLES, *Atlas Forestal de Venezuela*, Caracas, 1961.

INTERNATIONAL BANK FOR RECONSTRUCTION AND DEVELOPMENT, *The Economic Development of Venezuela*, Baltimore, 1961.

ALEXANDER, R. J. *The Venezuelan Democratic Revolution*, New Brunswick, N. J., 1964.

RODWIN, L. "Ciudad Guayana: A New City," *Scientific American*, Vol. 213 (1965): 122–32.

LOPEZ, J. E. "Tendencias Recientes de la Problación Venezolana," *Revista Geográfica* (Universidad de los Andes, Mérida, Venezuela) Vol. 6 (1965): 5–44.

Colombia

MURPHY, R. C. "Racial Succession in the Colombian Chocó," *Geographical Review*, Vol. 29 (1939): 461–71.

BATES, M. "Climate and Vegetation in the Villavicencio Region of Eastern Colombia," *Geographical Review*, Vol. 38 (1948): 555–74.

PARSONS, J. J. *Antioqueño Colonization in Western Colombia*, Ibero-Americana 32, Berkeley, Cal., 1948.

MURILLO, L. M. "Colombia, un archipiélago biológico," *Revista de la Academía colombiana de ciéncias exactas, físico-químicas, y naturales*, Vol. 8 (1951): 168–220; 409–31.

EIDT, R. C. "La Climatología de Cundinamarca," *Revista de la Academía colombiana de ciéncias exactas, físico-químicas, y naturales*, Vol. 8 (1952): 489–503.

WEST, R. C. *Colonial Placer Mining in Colombia*, Baton Rouge, La., 1952.

GHEERBRANT, A. *Journey to the Far Amazon*, New York, 1954.

WEST, R. C. *The Pacific Lowlands of Colombia, A Negroid Area of the American Tropics*, Baton Rouge, La., 1957.

GORDON, B. LeR. *Human Geography and Ecology of the Sinú Country of Colombia*, Ibero-Americana, 39, Berkeley, Cal., 1957.

EIDT, R. C. "Aboriginal Chibcha Settlement in Colombia," *Annals of the Association of American Geographers*, Vol. 49 (1959): 374–92.

ASCHMANN, H. "Indian Pastoralists of the Goajira Peninsula," *Annals of the Association of American Geographers*, Vol. 50 (1960): 408–18.

PEARSON, R. W. "Trade on the Río Magdalena," *Revista Geográfica*, Vol. 29 (1961): 21–35.

ADAMS, D. W., and MONTERO, L. E. "Land Parcelization in Agrarian Reform: A Colombian Example," *Inter-American Economic Affairs*, Vol. 19 (Autumn, 1965): 67–71.

BLASIER, C. "Power and Social Change in Colombia: The Cauca Valley," *Journal of Inter-American Studies*, Vol. 8 (1966): 386–410.

PARSONS, J. J., and Bowen, W. A. "Ancient Ridged Fields of the San Jorge River Floodplain," *Geographical Review*, Vol. 56 (1966): 317–43.

GADE, D. W. "The Guinea Pig in Andean Culture," *Geographical Review*, Vol. 57 (1967): 213–24.

SMITH, T. L. *Colombia: Social Structure and the Process of Development*, Gainesville, Fla., 1967.

SAFFORD, F. "Significación de los Antioqueños en el Desarrollo Economico Colombiano," *Anuario Colombiano de Historia Social y de la Cultura*, 1967: 49–69.

Ecuador

PARSONS, J. J. "Bananas in Ecuador, A New Chapter in the History of Tropical Agriculture, *Economic Geography*, Vol. 33 (1957): 201–16.

MILLER, E. V. "Agricultural Ecuador," *Geographical Review*, Vol. 49 (1959): 183–207.

SAUNDERS, J. V. D. *La población del Ecuador; un análisis del Censo de 1950*, Quito, 1959.

BURT, A. L., et al. "Santo Domingo de los Colorados—A New Pioneer Zone in Ecuador," *Economic Geography*, Vol. 36 (1960): 221–30.

SICK, W. D. *Wirtschaftsgeographie von Ecuador*, Stuttgarter geographische Studien, Stuttgart, 1963.

BOTTOMLEY, A. "Agricultural Employment Policy in Developing Countries: The Case of Ecuador," *Inter-American Economic Affairs,* Vol. 19 (Spring 1966): 53–79.

BOWMAN, R. I. (ed.). *The Galápagos: Proceedings of the Symposia of the Galápagos International Scientific Project,* Berkeley, Cal., 1966.

Peru

BOWMAN, I. *The Andes of Southern Peru,* New York, 1916.

WEBERBAUER, A. "Die vegetationskarte der peruanischen Anden zwischen 5° und 17°s. Br.," *Petermanns Mitteilungen,* Vol. 68 (1922): 89–91; 120–21.

SCHWALM, H. "Klima, Besiedlung und Landwirtschaft in den peruanisch-nord-bolivianischen Anden," *Ibero-Amerikanisches Archiv,* Vol. 2 (1927): 17–74; 150–96.

BAUDIN, L. *L'Empire socialiste des Inka,* Paris, 1928.

JOHNSON, G. R., and PLATT, R. R. *Peru from the Air* (American Geographical Society, Special Publication, No. 12), New York, 1930.

MEANS, P. A. *The Ancient Civilizations of the Andes,* New York, 1931.

TROLL, C. "Die geographischen Grundlagen der andinen Kulturen und des Incareiches," *Ibero-Amerikanisches Archiv,* Vol. 5 (1931–32): 258–94.

GUNTHER, E. R. "Variations in Behaviour of the Peru Coastal Current, with an Historical Introduction," *Geographical Journal,* Vol. 88 (1936): 37–65.

ROWE, J. R. "The Distribution of Indians and Indian Languages in Peru," *Geographical Review,* Vol. 37 (1947): 202–15.

TSCHOPIK, H. *Highland Communities of Central Peru: A Regional Survey,* Smithsonian Institution, Institute of Social Anthropology, Publication No. 5, Washington, D. C., 1947.

MONGE, C. *Acclimatization in the Andes,* Baltimore, Md., 1948.

KINZL, H., and SCHNEIDER, E. *Cordillera Blanca (Peru),* Innsbruck, 1950.

FORD, T. R. *Man and Land in Peru,* Gainesville, Fla., 1955.

DREWES, W. U. *The Economic Development of the Western Montaña of Central Peru as Related to Transportation,* (Doctoral Dissertation, Syracuse University, 1957); published Peruvian Times, 1958.

SCHWEIGGER, E. "Anomalías en la corriente peruana y sus consecuencias biológicas," *Revista del Instituto Geográfico,* Universidad de San Marcos, No. 5, (1958): 56–64.

TOSSI, J. *Zonas de vida en el Perú, Memoria explicativa sobre el mapa ecológico del Perú,* Boletín Técnico, no. 5, Instituto interamericano de Sciéncias Agrícolas, 1960.

DYER, D. R. "Population of the Quechua Region of Peru," *Geographical Review,* Vol. 52 (1962): 337–45.

HOY, D. R., and TAUBE, S. A. "Power Resources of Peru," *Geographical Review,* Vol. 53 (1963): 580–94.

KELLY, K. "Land-Use Regions in the Central and Northern Portions of the Inca Empire," *Annals of the Association of American Geographers,* Vol. 55 (1965): 327–38.

STEWART, N. R. "Migration and Settlement in the Peruvian Montaña: The Apurimac Valley," *Geographical Review,* Vol. 55 (1965): 143–57.

HOLMBERG, A. R., *et al.* "The Vicos Case; Peasant Society in Transition," *The American Behavioral Scientist,* Vol. 8 (1965): 3–33.

LANNING, E. P. "Early Man in Peru," *Scientific American,* Vol. 213 (1965): 68–76.

ALERS, J. O. "Population and Development in a Peruvian Community (Vicos)," *Journal of Inter-American Studies,* Vol. 7 (1967): 428–48.

SNYDER, D. E. "The 'Carretera Marginal de la Selva,' A Geographical Review and Appraisal," *Revista Geográfica,* No. 67 (1967): 87–100. 1963): 177–212.

Bolivia

SCHMIEDER, O. "The East Bolivian Andes, South of the Río Grande or Guapay," *University of California Publications in Geography,* Vol. 2 (1926): 85–210.

TROLL, C. "Die Cordillera Real," *Zeitschrift der Gesellschaft für Erdkunde zu Berlin* (1929): 279–312.

RUDOLPH, W. E. "The Lakes of Potosí," *Geographical Review,* Vol. 26 (1936): 529–54.

RUDOLPH, W. E. "Bolivia's Water-Power Resources," *Geographical Review,* Vol. 30 (1940): 41–63.

LEONARD, O. E. "La Paz, Bolivia: Its Population and Growth," *American Sociological Review,* Vol. 13 (1948): 448–54.

LABARRE, W. *The Aymara Indians of the Lake Titicaca Plateau, Bolivia* (reprinted from the *American Anthropologist,* Vol. 50 (1948): 1–250, American Anthropological Association, Philadelphia, 1948.

ALEXANDER, R. J. *The Bolivian National Revolution,* New Brunswick, N. J., 1958.

HEATH, D. B. "Bolivian Land Reform," *Inter-American Economic Affairs,* Vol. 12 (Autumn 1959): 3–27.

KLEIN, H. S. "American Oil Companies in Latin America: The Bolivian Experience," *Inter-American Economic Affairs,* Vol. 18 (Spring 1964): 47–72.

KLEIN, H. S. "The Creation of the Patiño Tin Empire," *Inter-American Economic Affairs,* Vol. 19 (Autumn 1965): 3–23.

DENEVAN, W. M. *The Aboriginal Cultural Geography of the Llanos de Mojos of Bolivia,* Ibero-Americana, 48, Berkeley, Cal., 1966.

HEATH, D. B. "The Aymara Indians and Bolivia's Revolutions," *Inter-American Economic Affairs,* Vol. 19 (Spring 1966): 31–40.

EDELMANN, A. T. "Colonization in Bolivia," *Inter-American Economic Affairs,* Vol. 20 (Spring 1967): 39–54.

FIFER, J. V. "Bolivia's Pioneer Fringe," *Geographical Review,* Vol. 57 (1967): 1–23.

Chile

BOWMAN, I. *Desert Trails of Atacama* (American Geographical Society, Special Publication, No. 5), New York, 1924.

RUDOLPH, W. E. "The Río Loa of Northern Chile," *Geographical Review,* Vol. 17 (1927): 553–85.

BERNINGER, O. "Die chilenische Frontera als Landscafts- und Kulturscheide," *Geographische Zeitschrift*, Vol. 39 (1933): 412–20.

LATCHAM, R. E. *La agricultura precolombiana en Chile y los paises vecinos*, Santiago, 1936.

MCBRIDE, G. M. *Chile, Land and Society* (American Geographical Society, Research Series No. 19), New York, 1936.

ALMEYDA ARROYO, E. *Biografía de Chile*, Santiago, 1943.

LIGHT, M. and LIGHT, R. "Atacama Revisited; 'Desert Trails' Seen from the Air," *Geographical Review*, Vol. 36 (1946): 525–45.

BUTLAND, G. *The Human Geography of Southern Chile*, Institute of British Geographers, London, 1957.

MARTIN, G. E. *Land Division in Central Chile*, (Doctoral Dissertation at Syracuse University, 1955) published as *La División de la Tierra en Chile Central*, Santiago, 1960.

WHITE, L. and CHILUTE, R. H. "Chile's New Iron and Steel Industry," *Economic Geography*, Vol. 37 (1961): 258–66.

BECKET, I. "Land Reform in Chile," *Journal of Inter-American Studies*, Vol. 5 (1963): 177–212.

RUDOLPH, W. E. *Vanishing Trails of Atacama*, American Geographical Society, New York, 1963.

CONCHA M., M. "El Uso de la Tierra en el Núcleo Central de Chile," *Revista Geográfica*, Vol. 33 (1964): 5–14.

WINNIE, W. W., JR. "Communal Land Tenure in Chile," *Annals of the Association of American Geographers*, Vol. 55 (1965): 67–86.

THIESENHUSEN, W. C. *Chile's Experiments in Agrarian Reform*, Madison, Wisc., 1966.

PEDERSON, L. R. *The Mining Industry of the Norte Chico, Chile*, Northwestern University Studies in Geography, Evanston, Ill., 1966.

Paraguay

GARSCH, B. *Der Einfluss der Jesuiten-Missionen auf den Wandel der Naturlandschaft zur Kulturlandschaft im Stromgebiet des Paraguay-Paraná während des 17 und 18 Jahrhunderts*, Breslau, 1934.

QUELLE, O. "Das Problem des Jesuitenstaates Paraguay," *Ibero-Amerikanisches Archiv*, Vol. 8 (1934): 260–82.

PENDLE, G. *Paraguay, A Riverside Nation*, New York, 1956.

RAINE, P. *Paraguay*, New Brunswick, N. J., 1956.

MARTINIS, B. "Il Paraguay," *Vie de Mondo*, Vol. 21 (1959): 1181–96.

HACK, H. *Die Kolonisation der Mennoniten im paraguayischen Chaco*, Königliches Tropeninstitut, Amsterdam, 1960.

STEWART, N. R. *Japanese Colonization in Eastern Paraguay*, Publication 1490, National Academy of Sciences–National Research Council, Washington, D. C., 1967.

HOPKINS, E. A., CRIST, R. E., and SNOW, W. P. *Paraguay, 1852 and 1968*, New York (American Geographical Society), 1968.

Argentina

Argentina as a Whole

TAYLOR, C. C. *Rural Life in Argentina*, Baton Rouge, La., 1948.

ARDISSONE, R. "Die Siedlungen am Paraná," *Die Erde*, Vol. 2 (1950–1951): 128–36.

ALEXANDER, R. J. *The Perón Era*, New York, 1951.

DAUS, F. A. *Fisonomía regional de la Repúbica Argentina*, Buenos Aires, 1959.

PEARSON, R. N. "Mapping Population Change in Argentina," *Revista Geografica*, Vol. 33 (1963): 63–77.

FERRER, A. *The Argentine Economy*, (tr. *La Economía Argentina*), Berkeley, Cal., 1967.

GARCIA, C. V. *Análisis de las Clasificaciones Climaticas del Território Argentino*, Buenos Aires (Centro de Estúdios Geográficos), 1967.

LEWIS, C. "Problems of Railway Development in Argentina, 1857–1890," Inter-American Economic Affairs, Vol. 22 (Autumn 1968): 55–75.

WINSBERG, M. D. *Modern Cattle Breeds in Argentina, . . .*, Center for Latin American Studies, University of Kansas, Lawrence, Kas., 1968.

Regional Divisions: The North, The Northwest, Mesopotamia

WRIGLEY, G. M. "Salta, An Early Commercial Center of Argentina," *Geographical Review*, Vol. 2 (1916): 116–33.

SCHMIEDER, O. "The Historic Geography of Tucumán," *University of California Publications in Geography*, Vol. 2 (1928): 359–86.

HUECK, K. *Urlandschaft, Raublandschaft, und Kulturlandschaft in der Provinz Tucumán im nordwestlichen Argentinien* (Bonner geographische Abhandlungen, Heft 10), Bonn, 1953.

CZAJKA, W., and VERVOORST, F. "Die naturräumliche Gliederung Nordwest-Argentiniens," *Petermanns Mitteilungen*, Vol. 100 (1956): 89–102; 196–208.

EIDT, R. C. "Die staatliche und privat Besiedlung von Misiones (Argentinien)," *Geographische Rundschau*, Vol. 17 (1965): 464–70.

Patagonia

WILLIS, B. *Northern Patagonia* (Ministry of Public Works, Argentina) New York, 1914.

CALDENIUS, C. C. "Las glaciaciones cuaternarias en la Patagonia y Tierra del Fuego," *Geografiska Annaler*, Vol. 14 (1932): 1–164.

SIMPSON, G. G. *Attending Marvels, A Patagonian Journal*, New York, 1934.

AUER, V. "Der Kampf zwischen Wald und Steppe auf Feuerland," *Petermanns Mitteilungen*, Vol. 85 (1939): 193–96.

THOMAS, L. "Des peuples en voie de disparition—Les Fuégiens," *Les Cahiers d'Outre-Mer*, Vol. 6 (1953): 379–98.

GAIGNARD, R. "La mise en valeur pionnière de la Terre de Feu (Argentine)," *Les Cahiers d'Outre-Mer*, Vol. 15 (1962): 105–37.

The Humid Pampa

STAPPENBECK, H. *Geologie und Grundwasserkunde der Pampa,* Stuttgart, 1926.

JEFFERSON, M. *Peopling the Argentine Pampa* (American Geographical Society, Research Series No. 16), New York, 1926.

SCHMIEDER, O. "The Pampa—A Natural or Culturally Induced Grassland?" *University of California Publications in Geography,* Vol. 2 (1927): 255–70.

SCHMIEDER, O. "Alteration of the Argentine Pampa in the Colonial Period," *University of California Publications in Geography,* Vol. 2 (1927): 303–21.

HAUTHAL, R. "Untergrund und Grundwasser in der argentinischen Pampa," *Petermanns Mitteilungen,* Vol. 75 (1929): 311–15.

KÜHN, F. "Der Steppencharakter der argentinischen Pampa," *Petermann's Mitteilungen,* Vol. 75 (1929): 57–62.

PLATT, R. S. "Pirovano: Items in the Argentine Pattern of Terrene Occupancy," *Annals of the Association of American Geographers,* Vol. 21 (1931): 215–37.

D'ANGELO, J. V. *La conurbación de Buenos Aires,* Buenos Aires, 1963.

GIBERTI, H. C. E. *El Desarrollo agrário argentino: Estúdio de la region pampeana,* Buenos Aires, 1964.

Uruguay

GIUFFRA, E. S. *La República del Uruguay,* Montevideo, 1935.

CHEBATAROFF, J. "Regiones naturales de Rio Grande del Sur y del Uruguay," *Anais da Associação dos Geógrafos Brasileiros,* Vol. 6 (1951–52): 115–45.

PENDLE, G. *Uruguay, South America's First Welfare State,* London, 1952; third edition, 1963.

SNYDER, D. E. "Commercial Passenger Linkages and the Metropolitan Nodality of Montevideo," *Economic Geography,* Vol. 38 (1962): 95–112.

DALY, H. E. "An Historical Question and three Hypotheses Concerning the Uruguayan Economy," *Inter-American Economic Affairs,* Vol. 20 (Autumn 1966): 87–93.

REDDING, D. C. "The Economic Decline of Uruguay," *Inter-American Economic Affairs,* Vol. 20 (Spring 1967): 55–72.

Brazil

Brazil as a Whole

NASH, R. *The Conquest of Brazil,* New York, 1926.

BUARQUE DE HOLLANDA, S. *Raizes do Brasil,* Rio de Janeiro, 1936.

DEFFONTAINES, P. "The Origin and Growth of the Brazilian Network of Towns," *Geographical Review,* Vol. 28 (1938): 379–99.

JAMES, P. E. "Trends in Brazilian Agricultural Development," *Geographical Review,* Vol. 43 (1953): 301–28.

FREYRE, G. *The Masters and the Slaves* (tr. *Casa Grande e Senzala*), New York, revised edition, 1956.

FRÓES, DE ABREU, S. *Recursos Minerais do Brasil,* Rio de Janeiro, 1960.

BERNARDES, N. "Caracteristicas gerais da agricultura brasileira em meados do século XX," *Revista brasileira de Geografia,* Vol. 23 (1961): 363–420.

FREYRE, G. *The Mansions and the Shanties, The Making of Modern Brazil* (tr. *Sobrados e Mucambos*), New York, 1963.

GEIGER, P. P. "Organização Regional do Brasil," *Revista Geografica,* Vol. 33 (1964): 25–57.

GUIMARÃES, D. *Geologia do Brasil,* Dept. Nacional da Produção Mineral, Rio de Janeiro, 1964.

SMITH, T. L. *Brazil, People and Institutions,* Baton Rouge, La., third edition, 1964.

VIANNA, F. S. "Os diferentes tipos de vegetação do Brasil e sua possibilidade de explotação e utilização," *Revista brasileira de Geografia,* Vol. 26 (1964): 231–44.

FURTADO, C. *The Economic Growth of Brazil, A Survey from Colonial to Modern Times,* (tr. *Formação Econômica do Brasil*), Berkeley, Cal., second edition, 1965.

BAER, W. *Industrialization and Economic Development in Brazil,* Homewood, Ill., 1965.

AZEVEDO, A. DE. "Embriões de cidades Brasileiras," *Comptes rendus du XVIIIᵉ Congrès International de Géographie,* 1956, Vol. 3 (1965): 221–45.

STERNBERG, H. O'R. "Brazil: Complex Giant," *Foreign Affairs,* Vol. 43 (1965): 297–311.

GREENFIELD, S. M., and VASCONCELOS BARROS, E. DE. "Rural Labor and Economic Development in Brazil," *Inter-American Economic Affairs,* Vol. 19 (Summer 1965): 75–81.

DYER, D. R. "Growth of Brazil's Population," *Journal of Geography,* Vol. 65 (1966): 417–28.

Regional Divisions: The Northeast

FREISE, F. W. "The Drought Region of Northeastern Brazil," *Geographical Review,* Vol. 28 (1938): 363–78.

DA CUNHA, E. *Rebellion in the Backlands* (tr. *Os Sertões*), Chicago, 1944.

SERRA, A. "Meteorologia do Nordeste Brasileiro," *Revista Brasileira de Geografia,* Vol. 7 (1945): 358–444.

JAMES, P. E. "Observations on the Physical Geography of Northeast Brazil," *Annals of the Association of American Geographers,* Vol. 42 (1952): 153–76.

JAMES, P. E. "Patterns of Land Use in Northeast Brazil," *Annals of the Association of American Geographers,* Vol. 43 (1953): 98–126.

STEVENS, R. L. and BRANDÃO, P. R. "Diversification of the Economy of the Cacao Coast of Bahia (Brazil), *Economic Geography,* Vol. 37 (1961): 231–53.

LACERDA MELO, M. "Bases Geographicas dos Problemas de Nordeste," *Revista Brasileira de Geografia,* Vol. 24 (1962): 503–38.

ANDRADE, M. C. DE. *A Terra e o Homem no Nordeste,* São Paulo, 1963.

ROBOCK, S. H. *Brazil's Developing Northeast, A Study of Regional Planning and Foreign Aid,* Brookings Institution, Washington, D. C., 1963.

SANTOS, M. "La culture du cacao dans l'état de Bahia," *Les Cahiers d'Outre-Mer,* Vol. 16 (1963): 366–78.

NIMER, E. "Circulação, atmosférica do Nordeste e suas consequencias—o fenômeno, das sêcas," *Revista brasileira de Geografia*, Vol. 26 (1964): 147–57.

GALLOWAY, J. H. "The Sugar Industry of Pernambuco during the Nineteenth Century," *Annals of the Association of American Geographers*, Vol. 58 (1968): 285–303.

The East

SCHMIEDER, O. "The Brazilian Culture Hearth," *University of California Publications in Geography*, Vol. 3 (1929): 159–98.

JAMES, P. E. "Rio de Janeiro and São Paulo," *Geographical Review*, Vol. 23, (1933): 271–98.

LAMEGO, A. R. *O Homen e a Guanabara* (Biblioteca Geográfica Brasileira, Publication No. 5), Rio de Janeiro, 1948.

STERNBERG, H. O'R. "Floods and Landslides in the Paraíba Valley, December 1948: Influence of Destructive Exploitation of the Land," *Comptes Rendus du XVIe Congrès International de Géographie*, Lisbon, 1951.

STRAUCH, N. (ed.). *A Bacia do Rio Doce*, Rio de Janeiro, 1955.

GEIGER, P. P. "Ensaio para a estrutura urbana do Rio de Janeiro," *Revista brasileiro de Geografia*, Vol. 22 (1960): 3–45.

MOMSEN, R. P., JR. "Routes over the Serra do Mar," *Revista Geográfica*, Vol. 32 (1963): 5–167.

BERNARDES, L.M.C. "A Faixa Suburbana do Rio de Janeiro," *Revista Geográfica*, No. 67 (1967): 69–86.

São Paulo

JEFFERSON, M. "An American Colony in Brazil," *Geographical Review*, Vol. 18 (1928): 226–31.

JAMES, P. E. "The Coffee Lands of Southeastern Brazil," *Geographical Review*, Vol. 22 (1932): 225–44.

JAMES, P. E. "The Changing Patterns of Population in São Paulo State," *Geographical Review*, Vol. 28 (1938): 353–62.

MONBEIG, P. *Pionniers et planteurs de São Paulo*, Paris, 1952.

AB'SÁBER, A. N. "A Terra Paulista," *Boletim Paulista de Geografia*, No. 23 (1956): 5–38.

AZEVEDO, A. DE et al. *A cidade de São Paulo, Estudos de Geografía Urbana*, 4 volumes, São Paulo, 1958.

MORSE, R. M. *From Community to Metropolis. A Biography of São Paulo, Brazil*, Gainesville, Fla., 1958.

AUGELLI, J. P. "Latvians of Varpa: A Foreign Colony on the Brazilian Pioneer Fringe," *Geographical Review*, Vol. 48 (1958): 365–87.

SCHATTAN, S. "Algumas funções de produção para a agricultura paulista," *Estadística*, Vol. 23 (1965): 45–60.

DEAN, W. "The Planter as Entrepreneur: The Case of São Paulo," *Hispanic American Historical Review*, Vol. 46 (1966): 138–52.

The South

MAACK, R. "Geographische und geologische Forschungen in Santa Catharina, Brasilien," *Zeitschrift der Gesellschaft für Erdkunde zu Berlin, Ergänzungsheft,* 5 Berlin, 1937.

WAIBEL, L. "European Colonization in Southern Brazil," *Geographical Review,* Vol. 40 (1950): 529–47.

ALMEIDA, F. M. DE. "O Planalto basáltico da Bacia do Paraná," *Boletim Paulista de Geografia,* No. 24 (1956): 3–34.

DOZIER, C. L. "Northern Paraná, Brazil; An Example of Organized Regional Development," *Geographical Review,* Vol. 46 (1956): 318–33.

LEHMANN, E. *Historische Züge der Landesentwicklung im südlichen Brasilien,* Deutschen Instituts für Länderkunde, Leipzig, 1958.

ROCHE, J. *La colonisation allemande et le Rio Grande do Sul,* Institut des Hautes Études de l'Amérique Latine, Paris, 1959.

STOCKMANN, B. "Südbrasilien," *Geographische Rundschau,* Vol. 13 (1961): 482–92.

ROCHE, J. "Les systèmes agraires dans les colonies allemandes du sud du Brésil," *Études Rurales,* No. 10 (1963): 26–36.

CHEBATAROFF, J. "Algunos aspectos de la evolución de la vegetación del Uruguay y de la porción meridional de Rio Grande do Sul," *Comptes Rendus du XVIIIe Congrès International de Géographie, 1956* Vol. 3 (1965): 49–60.

The Central West

ZARUR, J. *A Bacia do Médio Sao Francisco* (Biblioteca Geográfica Brasileira, Publication No. 4), Rio de Janeiro, 1946.

WAIBEL, L. "Vegetation and Land Use in the Planalto Central of Brazil," *Geographical Review,* Vol. 38 (1948): 529–54.

FAISSOL, S. *O Mato Grosso de Goiás* (Biblioteca Geográfica Brasileira, Publication No. 9), Rio de Janeiro, 1952.

PREWETT, V. *Beyond the Great Forest,* New York, 1953.

MOMSEN, R. P. "The Forest–Grassland Boundary between Jaraguá, Anápolis, and Goiânia, on the Central Plateau of Brazil," *Comptes Rendus XVIIIe Congrès International de Géographie, 1956,* Vol. 3 (1965): 82–89.

COLE, M. M. "Cerrado, Caatinga, and Pantanal: The Distribution and Origin of Savanna Vegetation of Brazil," *Geographical Journal,* Vol. 126 (1960): 168–79.

FREITAS, L. M. M. DE. "Possibilidade da Utilizaçao dos Solos de Cerrado na Produçao Brasileira de Alimentos," *Arquivos Brasileiros de Nutriçao,* Vol. 19 (1965): 151–67.

The North

LE COINTE, P. *L'Amazonie brésilienne,* Paris 1922.

HANSON, E. P. "Social Regression in the Orinoco and Amazon Basins: Notes on a Journey in 1931 and 1932," *Geographical Review,* Vol. 23 (1933): 578–98.

HIGBEE, E. C. "Of Man and the Amazon," *Geographical Review,* Vol. 41 (1951): 401–20.

WAGLEY, C. *Amazon Town: A Study of Man in the Tropics,* New York, 1953.

SOARES, L. DE CASTRO, "Limites meridionais e orientais da área de ocorrencia da floresta amazónica em território brasileiro," *Revista Brasileira de Geografia,* Vol. 15 (1953): 3–22.

ZIMMERMANN, J. *Studien zur Anthropogeographie Amazoniens: Die Wirtschafts- raum Santarém* (Bonner geographische Abhandlungen, Heft 21) Bonn, 1958.

OLTMAN, R.E. *et al. Amazon River Investigations, Reconnaissance Measurements of July 1963,* U.S. Geological Survey Circular 486, Washington, D. C., 1964.

STERNBERG, H. O'R. "Land and Man in the Tropics," *American Academy of Polit- ical and Social Science, Annals,* Vol. 27 (1964): 319–29.

Appendix C □ Guides to Pronunciation

SPANISH

Syllabication. A word has as many syllables as it has single vowels (Bu-ca-ra-man'-ga) or vowels and diphthongs, such as *ue* or *ai*, (Bue'-nos Ai'-res). A single consonant between vowels forms a syllable with the following vowel (Li'-ma). Two consonants between vowels are separated (San-tia'-go), except when the second consonant is *l* or *r*, in which case both consonants form a syllable with the following vowel (Chi-cla'-yo, Su'-cre). **ch, ll, and rr** are considered single letters in Spanish and cannot be separated.

Accent or stress. In general, words ending in a consonant, except *n* or *s,* are stressed on the last syllable (La Li-ber-tad'). Words ending in a vowel, or in *n* or *s,* are stressed on the next to the last syllable (Gra-na'-da, Ma-ni-za'-les). Exceptions to this rule are shown by a written accent on the vowel of the stressed syllable (Que-ré-ta-ro, Tu-cu-mán, Bo-lí-var).

Vowels. a is pronounced as in father (Ha-ba'-na). **e** is pronounced as *a* in fate (San Jo-sé). **i** is pronounced as in ma*chi*ne (Ni-ca-ra'-gua). **o** is pronounced as in n*o*te (Co-lón). **u** is pronounced as in fl*u*te (Pe-rú). **u** is silent after **q** (*Q*ue-re-ta-ro); it is also silent in the combinations **gue** and **gui,** in which case it makes the *g* hard, as in go (San Mi-g*u*el'). A diphthong is formed if the *u* in *gue* bears a diaeresis (Ca-ma-g*ü*ey', pronounced Ca-ma-gwāi). **y** is a vowel when standing alone or at the end of a word, and is merely a graphical substitute for *i*. **y** is also a consonant (see under consonants).

Diphthongs consist of a strong vowel (*a, e,* or *o*) and a weak vowel (*i* [*y*] *or u*), or of the two weak vowels, and are stressed on the strong vowel. Common diphthongs are: **ua** and **ue,** the *u* approximating the sound of *u* in quality (G*u*an-to, pronounced Gwan'-to; B*u*e-na-ven-tú-ra, pronounced Bwā-na-ven-tú-ra); **ai** (or **ay**) pronounced like *ai* in a*i*sle (Bue'-nos A*i*'-res); **ei** (or **ey**) pronounced like *ey* in th*ey* (N*ei*'-va; **oi** (or **oy**) pronounced like *oy* in b*oy* (To-ron-t*oy*'); and **ia** in which the two syllables are slightly slurred in pronouncing them (San-t*ia*-go). Two strong vowels do not form a diphthong (Ca-lla'-*o*).

Consonants. d, f, l, m, n, p, and **t** are pronounced as in English. **b** and **v** are similar to a combination of *b* and *v* in English. **c** before *e* or *i* is pronounced as *s* in *s*imilar (Va-len'-cia); otherwise as in *c*actus (Ca-ra'-*c*as). **ch** is pronounced as in *ch*urch (Chia'-pas). **g** is pronounced as in *g*o (Bo-*g*o-tá), but **g,** before *e* or *i,* and **j** are similar to the German *ch* (like English *h* forcibly hissed), as in Car-ta-*g*e'-na, *J*a-lis'-co. (See also the explanation of **gu** under vowels and diphthongs.) **h** is always silent (*H*on-du-ras, pronounced On-du'-ras, and *H*ua-nu-co, pronounced Wa-nu'-co). **k** is not a Spanish letter; it is found only in foreign words, in which it has the same sound as in English. **ll** in Central America and in parts of Mexico is pronounced as *y* in *y*es (Ciu-dad Tru-ji-*ll*o, pronounced Sēudad Truhē-yo); in Spain and in some parts of Spanish America it has the sound of *lli* in mi*lli*on (Vi-*ll*a-ri-ca [Paraguay], pronounced Ve*ly*are'ca); in southern South America and parts of Mexico it has the sound of *zh* in a*z*ure (A-ve-*ll*a-neda, pronounced Avā*zh*anaā'da). **n** is pronounced like *ny* in ca*ny*on (Na-ri-*ñ*o, pronounced Narē'-

*ny*o). **q** is always followed by *u* and is pronounced as in li*qu*or (*Qu*e-ré-ta-ro). **r** is slightly trilled on the tip of the tongue; initial **r** is pronounced with more vibration, and **rr** is pronounced like initial *r*. **s** is pronounced as in *s*imilar. **x,** in Mexico, when between vowels, is pronounced like Spanish *j* (O-a-*x*a'-ca); otherwise like *s* in *s*imilar (Ta*x*-co, pronounced Ta*s*'co); in other parts of Spanish America it is generally pronounced as in ta*x*. **y** as a consonant is pronounced as in *y*et, but with more force (*Y*u-ca-tán). **z** is always pronounced as *s* in *s*imilar.

PORTUGUESE

Syllabication. A word has as many syllables as it has single vowels (Pa-ra-ná) or vowels and diphthongs (São Pau'-lo). A single consonant between vowels forms a syllable with the following vowel (A-ma-zo'-nas). Two consonants between vowels are separated (San'-tos).

Vowels. **a** is pronounced as in f*a*ther (P*a*-rá). **e** is pronounced either as in b*e*t (Per-nam-bu'-co) or as *a* in f*a*te (C*e*-a-rá). **i** varies from m*i*lk (Es-p*i*-ri-to San'-to) to mach*i*ne (San'-ta Ca-ta-ri'na). **o** varies from m*o*ral to c*o*ld, and, when final, is pronounced like *u* in fl*u*te (Cam-p*o* F*o*r-mo-s*o,* pronounced Cam'pu Formõ'su). **u** is pronounced as in fl*u*te (Per-nam-b*u*'-co). It is silent in the combination **gue** and **gui,** in which case it makes the **g** hard as in g*o*; the combination **gua** forms a diphthong as in Spanish (G*u*a-ra-tin-gue-tá, pronounced Gw*a*ratingãtá). For the pronunciation of **u** after **q**, see **q** below.

Diphthongs consist of a strong vowel (*a, e,* or *o*) and a weak vowel (*i* or *u*), as in Mi'-nas Ge-rai*s*', or of the two weak vowels, as in J*ui*z' de Fo'-ra. Exceptions to this rule are shown by a written accent (Pa-ra-í-ba). Two strong vowels do not form a diphthong (A-la-gô'-*a*s).

Nasalization. The tilde always nasalizes the vowel it covers, silencing the following vowel and resulting in a sound approximating a*wng* (São Pau-lo, pronounced, approximately, Sawng Pow'-lo). Final *m* nasalizes the preceding vowel (Be-lém [Bãleng]; Jar-dim [Zharding']), as does final *ns* (To-can-tins [Tocantings']).

Consonants. **b, d, f, k, l, p, t,** and **v** are pronounced as in English. **c,** before the vowels *a* or *o* and before all consonants, is pronounced as in c*a*ctus (Cam'-pos); **c,** before the vowels *e* or *i,* and **ç** are pronounced as in cement (C*e*-a-rá, Al-co-bá'-*ç*a). **ch** is pronounced as *sh* in *sh*awl (C*h*a-pa'da). **g,** before *e* or *i,* is pronounced as *zh* in a*z*ure (Mi'nas Ge-rai*s*'); otherwise it is pronounced as in *g*o (Por'-to A-le'-gre). **h,** following *l* is pronounced as *lli* in mi*lli*on (Il-*h*e-os, pronounced Ilyã'ozh); following *n,* it is pronounced as *ny* in ca*ny*on (U-be-ra-bin-*h*a, pronounced Uberabin'ya); otherwise it is silent. **j** is pronounced as *zh* in a*z*ure (São João, pronounced Sawng Z*h*õawng'). **m** is pronounced as in *m*other (Re-*m*e'-dios), except when it ends a word, in which case it loses its identity, combining with the preceding vowel to form a nasal (Be-lé*m*). **n,** before hard *g,* is pronounced as in si*ng* (Guarati*n*guetá); **n,** before final *s,* nasalizes the preceding vowel (Tocanti*n*s); otherwise it is pronounced as in *n*ame (Dia-ma*n*-ti'na). **q** is always followed by *u; qu* before *e* or *i* is pronounced as in li*qu*or (Pe-*qu*e'-no); before *a* or *o* it forms a diphthong and is pronounced *kw* (Puer-ta Je-ri-co-a-*qu*a-ra, pronounced Pwer'ta Zhericõakwara). **r** is pronounced in the throat and slightly trilled. **s,** between vowels, is pronounced as in ro*s*e (Cam'po Formo'*s*o). When final, or when preceding *b, v, d, g, l, m, n,* or *r,* it is pronounced, in Portugal and in Rio de Janeiro, as *zh* a a*z*ure (Mi-na*s* Ge-rais [Mê'na*zh* Zhari*zh*']); in the outlying districts of Brazil it is pronounced as *s* in *s*imilar in these instances. In all other cases it is pronounced as *s* in *s*imilar. **x,** between vowels, is pronounced as *z* in E*z*ekiel (Fa-*x*i'-ma [Fa*z*ēma]; otherwise, in Portugal and Rio de Janeiro, it is pronounced as *sh* in *sh*awl (Xin-gú [*Sh*ingu']), and in the outlying districts of Brazil as *s* in *s*imilar (Xingú [Singu']). Recent regulations have excluded the use of the letter **y.** **z,** before a vowel, is pronounced as in E*z*ekiel (San'-ta Lu-z*i*'-a); otherwise, in Portugal and Rio de Janeiro, it is pronounced as *sh* in *sh*awl or *zh* in a*z*ure (Santa Cruz [San'ta Cru*sh*']), and in the outlying districts of Brazil it is pronounced as *s* in *s*imilar (Santa Cruz [San'ta Cru*s*']).

Index*

Figures in bold face refer to pages on which there are maps.

935